Economic Development in India

Policies, Reforms and Liberalisation

Third Edition

A V Balakrishnan

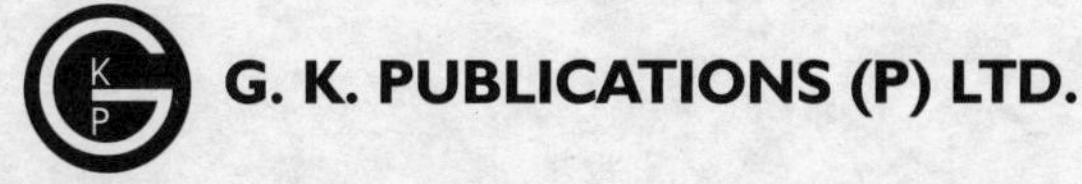

Title : Economic Development in India, 3e

Language : English

Author's Name : A V Balakrishnan

Typeset & Published by :

Career Launcher Infrastructure (P) Ltd.

A-45, Mohan Cooperative Industrial Area, Near Mohan Estate Metro Station, New Delhi - 110044

Marketed by :

G.K. Publications (P) Ltd.

Plot No. 9A, Sector-27A, Mathura Road, Faridabad, Haryana-121003

ISBN : **978-93-92837-51-7**

Printer's Details : Made in India, New Delhi.

For product information :

Visit ***www.gkpublications.com*** or email to ***gkp@gkpublications.com***

Dedicated

to

millions the world over for whom the daily life is a struggle and who deserve a better deal in this inequitable world

"No society can surely be flourishing and happy, of which the far greater part of the members are poor and miserable. It is but equity, besides, that they who feed, clothe and lodge the whole body of the people, should have such a share of the produce of their own labour as to be themselves tolerably well fed, clothed and lodged."

– *Adam Smith in 'An Inquiry into the Nature and Causes of the Wealth of Nations' (1776)*

PREFACE TO THE THIRD EDITION

The last edition was brought out in 2018, and since then the global economy has been buffeted by many fresh challenges. Even as the world was recovering from the impact of the 2007-08 financial crisis, a bruising US-China trade dispute erupted which adversely impacted world trade. The increasing tussle for dominance among world powers, aggressive geopolitical postures such as China's expansionist policies in South China Sea and the Indian Ocean, and its provocative actions against neighbouring countries, especially Taiwan and India, have only compounded the problems.

Above all, the serious, once-in-a-century like health crisis, Covid-19 jolted and turned the world upside down taking its toll on human lives without sparing any nation. Worse still, the impact of the pandemic has been severe on vulnerable sections who were least insulated and equipped to withstand it. Millions of them had to lose jobs, at least in the short run, with loss of incomes pushing many of them back into indigence. The pandemic also undid a great deal of the sustained gains achieved on poverty alleviation in the last two to three decades. It would now require concerted action on the part of countries, and global community as a whole, to bring back economies to pre-pandemic levels and normalcy, even as the pandemic shows no signs of abating. The crisis disrupted supply chains and starkly exposed the risk of over-dependence on any one country (read China) for supply of critical products and brought to the fore the need for building resilient supply chains involving multiple countries.

Yet another major global challenge which is intensifying in its impact, year after year, is global warming and 'Climate Change' with erratic weather patterns, cyclones, floods and earthquakes striking different parts of the world. Some of the States in India, especially those with hilly terrains, have witnessed recurring unseasonal and excessive rains in the last few years causing not only floods and destruction of lives and property, but adversely impacting agriculture which is the main source of sustenance to millions of people. These issues have been highlighted in successive meets of the Conference of the Parties (COP), COP-26 being the latest held in Glasgow in November 2021.

Another perceptible trend is the decline of population in many of the advanced countries. As birth rates fall and population ages, the working-age population is shrinking in Europe, the US, Japan, Russia, China, etc. Fewer workers would mean slower economic growth and adverse consequences for global trading patterns. The trend would necessitate migration of skilled manpower between countries which would result in changes in demographic and societal structures with implications for social stability and racial harmony.

These and other issues of relevance to India and the world economy and their implications are covered in this updated edition. One can only hope that nations would come together to find lasting solutions to these problems and chart a new course for the world in the years ahead.

As with the previous editions, the data presented in this edition are sourced from various national and international publications. These include Reserve Bank of India's *Handbook of Statistics on Indian Economy*, Ministry of Finance's *Economic Surveys*, *Census of India* reports and statistical data put out by NITI Aayog and various Ministries of the Government of India. International sources from which data has been drawn include UNDP's *Human Development Reports*, UN Population Division and The World Bank. The data provided in these publications is gratefully acknowledged.

For enabling access to various libraries where I could source statistical data from publications of both the Government of India and international agencies, thanks are due to authorities of Mumbai University's Jawaharlal Nehru Library at Kalina campus, the Institute for Social and Economic Change at Bengaluru, Connemara Library in Chennai and the National Library in Singapore all of which have extensive collections.

As ever, I am indebted to Ravikumar Mullapudi, who helped me navigate on computer as I worked on the text and tables. I must thank profusely Prakash Kannath of CL Media (P) Ltd., the prime mover behind this work, and the team under him who worked tirelessly and under severe constraints due to the pandemic and accomplished the task, working on WFH mode for the larger part and later in hybrid mode. Further, thanks are due to the Management of CL Media (P) Ltd., without whose active support this publication would not have been possible.

Finally, I must thank my family – Abhinav, Zoya and Ira, in particular – whose sustained interest in the progress of the work and unstinted support have been a source of strength and motivation in undertaking this work.

Needless to say, the views expressed in the book are entirely the author's and the Publishers or those who have rendered help bear no responsibility.

A.V. Balakrishnan
Bengaluru
December 2021

PREFACE TO THE FIRST EDITION

After six decades of planning and development, the Indian economy is presently at a critical stage. The country has passed the take-off stage and is on the cusp of a high trajectory of economic growth. But the economy also faces many daunting challenges both on the developmental and demographic fronts. About a whopping one million youth will be joining the labour force every month for the next one decade and a half or more, and providing jobs for them will be the most challenging task for the government. Lifting millions who are trapped in extreme poverty and deprivation, and removing inequities in society is another important task. All this calls for a joint and concerted effort on the part of all – the legislature and the executive, the political parties and the non-governmental organisations – to pursue the goals whole-heartedly and find solutions. It is imperative that all stakeholders at the central, state and local levels work in unison in a spirit of co-operative federalism to achieve the goals.

Those who are aspiring to join the civil services and various other organs of state, the public and the private sector, and a broad spectrum of the services sector, will have to play their part in this historic task and take the nation to still greater heights. They will, in course of their career, be confronted with many of these issues and be called upon to tackle them. In this context, they should be alive to the various issues involved in the process of development, particularly the process of economic reforms and liberalisation which is being implemented and is an ongoing process. This work is prepared specially keeping their needs in mind while it will also be of use to those interested in the developments in the economy.

The main focus of this work is to expose the reader to the trends in the economy and the reform process in its various ramifications. Issues discussed have been supported by relevant statistical data drawn from various government and non-government sources and international publications. Particular mention must be made of Planning Commission's Five Year Plan documents and Statistical Databook, Reserve Bank of India's Handbook of Statistics on Indian Economy, Ministry of Finance's *Economic Surveys*, Census of India Reports and Statistical data put out by various ministries of the Government of India.

Among the international publications, particular mention must be made of UNDP's Human Development Reports and Statistical publications of UN Population Division,World Trade Organisation, The World Bank and WITS (World Integrated Trade Solution), World Bank's *Ease of Doing Business* reports, Food and Agriculture Organisation and the Asian Development Bank.

The author gratefully acknowledges the data provided in these publications.

This work is divided into **three Parts** : the ***first Part*** *dealing with the colonial legacy and the developments in the economy from Independence and up to 1990.* ***The second Part*** *relates to the period from 1991 when major reforms in the economy were initiated and which can be considered a watershed moment in the* *nation's journey after independence.* For, it gave a new direction and thrust to the development effort quite unlike the path followed in the preceding four decades. *The* ***third Part*** *is concerned with the latest spell of reforms set in motion since May 2014.*

Care has been taken to cover not only national issues but also issues of international import and concern such as Millennium Development Goals and Sustainable Development Goals, regional and international economic co-operation, climate change and environmental degradation – issues which are all of utmost concern not only for the present generation but are portentous for the future of mankind. As a populous and emerging economic power, India, along with other world powers, has a vital role to play in setting the agenda for the future and its effective implementation. In a globalised and highly inter-dependent world that we live in, close co-operation is called among all nations to face these challenges and find workable solutions.

I have received help from many sources in the preparation of this work. Particular mention must be made of the invaluable assistance rendered by Prakash Kannath of Access Publishing who extended cooperation at every stage, Access Publishing India Pvt Ltd, the publishers of this work, and the Editorial, Designing and other staff associated with it, and Uday Balakrishnan, my ex-colleague in the Civil Service and now a Visiting faculty at the Centre for Contemporary Studies, Indian Institute of Science, Bengaluru, who initiated me into this and urged me to take up this work. I express my gratitude to all of them and the press which has undertaken the printing in record time.

While every effort has been made to check the correctness of statistical and other information contained in the book, I may be excused for any inadvertent errors which may have crept in. Any corrections pointed out by readers will be welcome.

The views expressed in the book are solely of the author and are not to be attributed to the publisher or others who have rendered assistance.

A.V. Balakrishnan
Bengaluru

PREFACE TO THE SECOND EDITION

After six decades of planning and development, the Indian economy is presently at a critical stage. The country has passed the take-off stage and is on the cusp of a high trajectory of economic growth. But the economy also faces many daunting challenges both on the developmental and demographic fronts. About a whopping one million youth will be joining the labour force every month for the next one decade and a half or more, and providing jobs for them will be the most challenging task for the government. Lifting millions who are trapped in extreme poverty and deprivation, and removing inequities in society is another important task. All this calls for a joint and concerted effort on the part of all – the legislature and the executive, the political parties and the non-governmental organisations – to pursue the goals whole-heartedly and find solutions. It is imperative that all stakeholders at the central, state and local levels work in unison in a spirit of co-operative federalism to achieve the goals.

Those who are aspiring to join the civil services and various other organs of state, the public and the private sector, and a broad spectrum of the services sector, will have to play their part in this historic task and take the nation to still greater heights. They will, in course of their career, be confronted with many of these issues and be called upon to tackle them. In this context, they should be alive to the various issues involved in the process of development, particularly the process of economic reforms and liberalisation which is being implemented and is an ongoing process. This work is prepared specially keeping their needs in mind while it will also be of use to those interested in the historical developments in the economy.

The main focus of this work is to expose the reader to the trends in the present economy and the reform process in its various ramifications. Issues discussed have been supported by relevant statistical data drawn from various government and non-government sources and international publications. Particular mention must be made of Planning Commission's *Five Year Plan* documents and *Statistical Databook*, Reserve Bank of India's *Handbook of Statistics on Indian Economy*, Ministry of Finance's *Economic Surveys*, *Census of India Reports* and statistical data put out by various ministries of the Government of India.

Among the international publications, particular mention must be made of UNDP's *Human Development Reports* and Statistical publications of UN Population Division, World Trade Organisation, The World Bank and WITS (World Integrated Trade Solution), World Bank's *Ease of Doing Business* reports, Food and Agriculture Organisation and the Asian Development Bank.

The author gratefully acknowledges the data provided in these publications.

This work is divided into **three Parts** : the **first Part** dealing with the colonial legacy and the developments in the economy from Independence and up to 1990. The **second Part** relates to the period from 1991 when major reforms in the economy were initiated and which can be considered a watershed moment in the nation's journey after independence. For, it gave a new direction and thrust to the development effort quite unlike the path followed in the preceding four decades. The **third Part** is concerned with the latest spell of reforms set in motion since May 2014. Issues critical to the economy such as demonetization, fight against black money and the introduction of the historic Goods and Services Tax (GST) have been covered at length. Besides, issues which are in public domain and being widely debated such as Gender bias and Gender inequality, case for Universal Basic Income, Capital account convertibility, etc. also find a place in the work.

Care has been taken to cover not only national issues but also issues of international import and concern such as Millennium Development Goals and Sustainable Development Goals, regional and international economic co-operation, climate change and environmental degradation – issues which are all of utmost concern not only for the present generation but are portentous for the future of mankind. As a populous and emerging economic power, India, along with other world powers, has a vital role to play in setting the agenda for the future and its effective implementation. In a globalised and highly inter-dependent world that we live in, close co-operation is called for among all nations to face these challenges and find workable solutions.

I have received help from many sources in the preparation of this work. I was fortunate to have had access to various libraries where I could mine statistical data from publications of both the Government of India and international agencies. For this, thanks are due to authorities of Mumbai University's Jawaharlal Nehru Library at Kalina campus, the Institute for Social and Economic Change (ISEC) at Bengaluru, Connemara Public Library in Chennai and the National Library in Singapore all of which have extensive collections.

I am grateful to Gautam Bhattacharya who made some useful suggestions on the content of the book and D. Kumaresan with whom I had discussions on parts of the book. I am indebted to Ravikumar Mullapudi, who was always there to help with formatting the initial draft of the work on my computer.

Particular mention must be made of the invaluable assistance rendered at every stage, and sage advice given at various times, by Kannath Prakash of CL Media (P) Ltd . whose editorial expertise and professional competence has been of immense help and lightened my burden to a great extent and I record my gratitude to him. Thanks are also due to the Management and the entire team of Designing, Typesetting and other staff at CL Media (P) Ltd , the publishers of this work. Last but not the least, I am grateful to Uday Balakrishnan, my ex-colleague in the Civil Service and now a Visiting faculty at the *Centre for Contemporary Studies*, Indian Institute of Science, Bengaluru, who initiated me into this and urged me to take up this work. But for his persistent prodding against my initial reluctance, this book would not have been there.

I express my gratitude to all of them and the Press which has undertaken the printing in record time.

And as one who has always stood by me in all ventures in my life and who bore long spells of my absence with utmost patience as I ploughed a lonely furrow working in various libraries, I owe a deep debt to my wife, Sharada.

While every effort has been made to check the correctness of statistical and other information contained in the book, I may be excused for any inadvertent errors which may have crept in. Any corrections pointed out by readers will be welcome.

Finally, the views expressed in the book are solely of the author and are not to be attributed to the publisher or others who have rendered assistance.

A.V. Balakrishnan
Bengaluru

ORIGIN OF ECONOMIC THOUGHT

❑ AN INTRODUCTION

Economic activity in a very crude, rudimentary form existed from the very dawn of human civilization much before any economic theory about them came into vogue. From the dawn of civilization, the primitive man, who initially subsisted by gathering fruits and hunting animals, learnt the art of cultivation. From caves in which he dwelled initially to protect himself from animals, he moved to houses built with mud, clay and stone. Early civilizations formed on river banks, and cultivation of rice and other crops gradually evolved. In course of time, they formed into communities, living together in habitations, settled on river banks and started cultivation and agricultural activity.

The earliest Han Chinese settled in the fertile lands around the Yellow river about 10,000 to 12,000 years ago. The Nile valley had been settled for centuries before the states of Upper and Lower Egypt were united under one king around 3000 BC. The world's first cities were functioning around 3500 BC in Mesopotamia, the land watered by the great rivers, the Tigris and the Euphrates. The Indus Valley or the Harappan civilization had well-organized settlements dating back to 3rd millennium BC. The great city of Babylon flourished astride the Euphrates river around 1800 BC.

In due course, primitive man began to make tools with stone and later metals. Even in the time of the early pastoral civilizations, man had invented the pottery wheel, tools made of iron and stone, plough, wheeled carts and wheelbarrows for carriage of goods. While initially, families lived a self-sufficient existence, gradually they began to exchange items produced by one another leading to a system of barter exchange. It is possible that even in those early days, a kind of division of labour evolved with different groups of people engaged in different activities and occupations leading to a kind of specialization.

People travelled long distances over land by caravans, and later by sea, for trading. Starting with barter system of exchange of goods, gradually the use of coins came into vogue.

Kings and rulers started levying taxes for raising revenues.

❑ ORIGIN OF ECONOMICS

All this while, when material civilization evolved and economic activity was being carried on, there was no systematic body of knowledge or writing on such activities. Production, distribution and consumption were being carried on and trade and commerce flourished even prior to biblical times, but there was no attempt at theorising about them.

It is difficult to say or conclude when the science of Economics or Economic theory had its origin, even in a rudimentary form. In India, a semblance of coherent economic ideas can be found in Kautilya's *Arthaśāstra* (translated as Science of Wealth or Economics), composed in the 4th century BC, which is a treatise on governance, moral conduct and political economy. This work dwells, among other things, on money, use of wealth for the welfare of the masses, etc. *Tirukkural*, an ancient work and one of the great classics in Tamil literature by the savant Tiruvalluvar, believed to have been composed prior to 2nd century AD, deals with themes like agriculture, poverty, labour and prosperity of a nation.

Confucius (551-479 BC), the Chinese philosopher and statesman, who was advisor to various feudal lords had observed that "the petty person is conversant with profit, while the noble person is conversant with righteousness" and warned that "if you are motivated (solely) by profit, you will end up producing much resentment". Confucius laid much stress on the virtues of righteousness and benevolence. The ethical system based on the teachings of Confucius, which came to be known as Confucianism, emphasized personal virtue, devotion to family and justice. In Confucian tradition, if government officials expect the common people to pay homage to the government, it must be evident that they are trustworthy and working for the well-being of society as a whole. The accumulation of wealth, be it at the societal or individual level, must always be subordinated to the pursuit of moral values. Many of the socio-economic policies enunciated and now being followed by the Chinese President, Xi Jinping, have the underpinnings of Confucian thinking and philosophy.

In the west, the writings of Plato (427-347 BC) and Aristotle (384-322 BC) also had a smattering of economic thought. Plato's *Republic* attributes the need for the formation of a state to economic factors, for the fulfilment of needs and wants. It refers to property and agriculture, and different classes of labour such as farmers and artisans. Aristotle, a pupil of Plato, has also written about economy, money, value and exchange, property and finance.

Later, came medieval-age thinkers like St. Thomas Aquinas (1225-74) and Nicholas Oresme (1320-82) who also developed certain economic concepts. They were followed by a group of thinkers known as 'Mercantilists' who argued that a country's economic policies should be directed to enhance its own wealth, power and prosperity. Mercantilism was rooted in the idea of 'protectionism' and amassing wealth in the form of gold and silver and developing industry and mining to attain a favourable balance of trade. Mercantilists advocated regulation and intervention by the state in economic and commercial activities. It was the very anti-thesis of *laissez-faire policy*, the doctrine that governments should not interfere with commerce. The mercantilists came in for severe attack from later thinkers.

The 18th century gave rise to another school of thought in France known as 'Physiocracy'. Physiocrats, as the proponents were known, advocated governance according to 'natural order', gave primacy to agriculture and held that 'soil' alone was the source of all wealth.

François Quesnay (1694-1774) was the foremost among them and had followers like Marquis de Mirabeau (1715-89), Anne Turgot (1727-81) and Pierre de Nemours (1739-1817). They influenced some thinkers in the U.S. and England as well. A major contribution of Quesnay was the formulation of *Tableau Economique* (Economic Table) in 1758 which assessed the wealth of a nation and its circulation on a macro-economic basis and which is considered to be the direct forerunner of circular flow and input-output studies of later times. Over the centuries, Quesnay's *Economic Table* has inspired many scholars including Karl Marx in his studies of capitalism.

The Physiocrats recognized three classes of people in society, viz., proprietors (or, landowners), cultivators and lastly, artificers, manufacturers and merchants. They laid stress on minimum regulatory control and maximum economic freedom and their doctrines were opposed to mercantilism. This group did not survive for long and faced criticism, including from Adam Smith, for their view that agriculture alone was productive and the source of all wealth, and for considering manufacturers and artisans as unproductive. Referring to the Physiocrats, Smith observed, "The capital error of this system, however, seems to lie in its representing the class of artificers, manufacturers and merchants, as altogether barren and unproductive." And Smith went on to argue at length in *The Wealth of Nations* to show how flawed and far from reality their views were.

❑ BEGINNINGS OF ECONOMIC SCIENCE

The beginning of modern economic thought is identified with Adam Smith (1723-90), the Scottish economist and moral philosopher who came into prominence with the publication of *The Theory of Moral Sentiments* in 1759. But he is best known and regarded as the father of economic science for his seminal work on political economy *An Inquiry into the Nature and Causes of the Wealth ofNations.*

It was published in 1776 – incidentally, the very year of American independence–which laid the foundations of classical 'free-market' economic theory. His work covered a whole gamut of economic ideas and concepts upon which later theoreticians built and developed most of the concepts to form the science of economics as we know it today. These included concepts such as division of labour and specialization, theories of value and capital, rent, wages, interest and profits, public finance and international trade.

Smith succinctly developed the concept of '*division of labour*' with the famous example of making a pin or nail. As Smith saw it, the making of a pin or a nail is, by no means, a simple operation. One man, when he solely performs the entire operation, could scarcely make a pin a day and certainly not twenty or thirty. But when the work is divided into distinct operations – one man drawing the wire, another straightening it, a third cutting it, a fourth pointing it, and a fifth person grinding or filing it to enable it to receive the head, each one of them becomes a specialist in his assigned task and he will be able to do the job faster. Underlying this are many of the ideas which led to, and are practised in, the modern factory system – specialization, assembly line of factory operation, increased productivity, and so on. It must be remembered in this context that the Industrial Revolution was just taking shape from the middle of the 18th century and Smith published *The Wealth of Nations* in about two decades of that. In that sense, much of what Smith wrote in his pioneering work on Economics smacked of prescience and foreboding of what was to come. Truly, Smith laid the firm foundations for the science, if one may call it so, upon which later theorists could build the superstructure.

Adam Smith, the philosopher in him, also spoke of the fact that man is motivated by '*self-interest*'. Smith observes that while man constantly needs the help of his brethren, it is vain for him to expect others to be benevolent to him. Smith says, "It is not from the benevolence of the butcher, the brewer, or the baker, that we expect our dinner, but from their regard to their own interest".

Another of his famous idea was that of an *invisible hand* which is always at work, and which will reconcile and harmonize private and public interests and lead to liberalism. If everything is left to free competition, people will use capital to gain the maximum advantage which, in turn, will maximize national wealth.

Adam Smith was followed by many theoreticians who made original contributions to the science, most notably David Ricardo (1772-1823), John Stuart Mill (1806-73), Alfred Marshall (1842-1924), and John Maynard Keynes (1883-1946) and a host of others. Notable among others were Karl Marx (1818-83) and his compatriot Friedrich Engels (1820-95) who worked together and developed different strands of thought leading to socialism and communism.

A major turning point in the development of Economic science were the path-breaking writings of Keynes which came to be called 'Keynesianism'. The revolutionary theories propounded by this Cambridge economist, in the wake of the **Great Depression** of the 1930's, and was vindicated by Franklin D. Roosevelt's 'New Deal' programme which soon followed to fight the recession, stood the test of time, even in the thick of the World War II and its aftermath. The three seminal works of Keynes, viz., *A Tract on Monetary Reform* (1923), *A Treatise on Money* (1930) and *The General Theory of Employment, Interest and Money* (1936) had a revolutionary impact on economic theory and its practical application. Keynes also made a signal contribution with his radical ideas at the Bretton Woods Conference held in the U.S.A. which led to the establishment of two major international institutions in 1945 – the International Monetary Fund (IMF) and the International Bank for Reconstruction and Development (IBRD) which later became The World Bank. Keynesianism had come to stay through a good part of the 20th century and found resonance in the economic policies followed by many governments, though much later it came to be challenged by several economists.

❑ INDIAN ECONOMY AND ECONOMIC THOUGHT

During the colonial era, many of the nationalist leaders wrote copiously on the economic condition and impoverishment of **India**, especially in the context of exploitation of the country and its resources. Prominent among them were Dadabhai Naoroji (1825-1917), Mahadev Govind Ranade (1842-1901), Dinshaw Wacha (1844-1937) and Ramesh Chandra Dutt (1848-1909). Dadabhai Naoroji described the rampant exploitation of the country by the foreign ruler as what he called the 'Drain theory' as they drained away the country's resources to feed the factories in Britain to the utter neglect of India's development. His major work was titled *Poverty and Un-British Rule in India* published in 1901. Naoroji also made an estimation of the 'per capita income' for Bombay Presidency for the years 1867-70 based on official data. Ranade published *Essays on Indian Political Economy* in 1898. And Ramesh Chandra Dutt wrote on *Famines in India* (in 1900) and *Economic History of India* in two volumes (in 1902, 1904) which is an extensive and graphic account of India's economic condition under the British rule.

Once India became independent in 1947 and set herself on the path of planned economic development, it was an exciting period for the economists in the country. There was a flurry of activity with the Planning Commission, set up in 1950, entrusted with the task of drawing up Five-Year Plans. India could already boast of an array of distinguished economists who played key roles in shaping the economic policies. There were already renowned centres of economic studies and research in Delhi, Bombay, Calcutta, Poona, etc. which contributed significantly in the planning exercises. Many foreign economists, renowned for their contributions to academic and applied aspects of the discipline, were also associated with the Planning Commission in evolving strategies to be adopted in the Plans. The 1950s were also a period of intense intellectual debates, especially on the path and the strategies India adopted in the early Plans. It unleashed an orgy of intellectual energy on diverse aspects and approaches to development which India was to adopt. There were copious writings on developmental issues. Many of the Indian economists who were associated with the planning process in the late 1940s and through the 50s went on to occupy distinguished academic positions in India and abroad and earned distinction.

❑ THE COLONIAL ERA AND UNDERDEVELOPMENT

Till about the 17th century, there was not much difference between the stage of development attained by the western nations and the rest of the world. As Keynes observed in his work "*Economic Possibilities for our Grandchildren* (1930)," in "*Essays in Persuasion*": "From the earliest times of which we have record – back, say, to two thousand years before Christ down to the beginning of the eighteenth century, there was no very great change in the standard of life of the average man living in the civilized centres of the earth. Ups and downs certainly. Visitations of plague, famine, and war. Golden intervals. But no progressive, violent change. Some periods, perhaps fifty per cent better than others, at the utmost 100 per cent better – in the four thousand years which ended, say, in A. D. 1700".

Keynes further attributed this stagnation over the millennia to virtual lack of technological progress. He observed: "This slow rate of progress, or lack of progress, was due to two reasons – to the remarkable absence of important technical improvements and to the failure of capital to accumulate. The absence of important technical inventions between the prehistoric age and comparatively modern times is truly remarkable. Almost everything which really matters and which the world possessed at the commencement of the modern age was already known to man at the dawn of history. Language, fire, the same domestic animals which we have today, wheat, barley, the vine and the olive, the plough, the wheel, the oar, the sail, leather, linen and cloth, bricks and pots, gold and silver, copper, tin, and lead – and iron was added to the list before 1000 B.C. – banking, statecraft, mathematics, astronomy, and religion. There is no record of when we first possessed these things".

To put it in perspective, India indeed, was renowned for its capabilities in manufactures and agriculture in the 17th century, even exporting various products to the western nations. But the advent of colonial rule and the onset of Industrial Revolution in the west changed all that. In the face of modern methods of mass production, India, with her traditional manufacturing methods, could not withstand the intense competition from Britain. English shipping opened up new markets, and products manufactured in the factories in Britain were dumped on markets in India and other countries in Asia. While hitherto, India exported many of these products to the West, the trend was drastically reversed. India became the exporter of raw materials to feed the factories in Britain and importer of finished goods. Industries in India were crippled and workers, devoid of skill and expertise and handicapped for want of capital and modern machinery, were thrown out of jobs. Many of these workers had to fall back upon agriculture which was already under much stress. India which was once famous for the manufacture of the most delicate fabrics in the world, became a purely agricultural country exporting raw materials and food items.

❑ END OF COLONIALISM AND AFTER

Colonialism in Asia, Africa and Latin America lasted for over two hundred years. The period was marked by repression, misrule, exploitation and virtual lack of industrialization. During this period, the western nations, spurred by the Industrial Revolution, registered rapid industrial growth. And coupled with advancements in agriculture, those countries were able to make sustained progress and ensure a high standard of living for their people. Whereas, all this while, many countries in Asia, Africa and Latin America languished under their exploitative colonial rule. And by the time these long subjugated countries gained independence, they had inherited a host of problems – overpopulation, stagnant agriculture and little progress in the critical areas of education and health.

Under the weight of this historical burden, sizeable sections of the population in these countries were pushed to appalling levels of poverty. Thus developed a wide chasm between the developed and developing and least developed nations, also referred to as the North–South divide with the former – the developed nations – situated in the northern hemisphere and the latter in the southern hemisphere.

❑ EMERGENCE OF WELFARE ECONOMICS

India's independence in 1947 was followed by a host of nations emerging independent from colonial yoke. These nations brooked no delay in embarking on the path of development and uplifting the masses from poverty and deprivation. It was against this background that the domain of Welfare and Development economics, which had a nascent birth in the 19th century and the first half of the 20th century, began to gain prominence.

Concepts of fairness, equity and justice had their echo even in ancient times in Hebrew thought, Biblical literature and in the writings of thinkers like Confucius (551-479 BC), Plato (428-347 BC), Aristotle (384-322 BC), Kautilya (4th c. BC) and others. Their works laid stress on ethical and moral precepts and cautioned against greed, acquiring wealth by unethical means and amassing excessive wealth. They urged the use of wealth for the welfare of the poor and needy, notions which are analogous to modern concepts of justice and welfare of society at large.

Utilitarianism: The concept of utility and utilitarianism was a dominant theme in the works of early theorists of the 18th century. These concepts, which lie at the root of welfare economics, have been the subject of much debate and given to varied interpretations. In essence, "utility" in economic sense means "the pleasure or satisfaction derived by a person from consuming goods or services". Achieving it is the ultimate goal of all economic activities but its scope goes beyond mere acquisition and use of material goods.

Jeremy Bentham (1748-1832), the English philosopher and economist, who was one of the main proponents of utilitarianism described it as that which augments or diminishes the happiness of a person. It stands for maximisation of the sum of utility, defined in terms of pleasure and pain, in the community as a whole. It applies to a government which aims at ensuring "the greatest happiness of the greatest number" as Bentham put it and strives to maximise the welfare of people.

This concept was further advocated by later scholars in welfare economics like John Stuart Mill (1806-1873), Alfred Marshall (1842-1924), Léon Walras (1834-1910) and A C Pigou (1877-1959).

A.C. Pigou on Welfare: Pigou's *The Economics of Welfare* (1920) was a remarkable treatise on the subject of welfare. He advocated discriminatory taxation involving transfers of purchasing power from the relatively rich to the relatively poor'. He discusses the general relationship between wealth and welfare. Pigou defines economic welfare with reference to social changes which, other things being equal, increase economic welfare. The three social changes that he associates with an increase in economic welfare are 'an increase in the size of the national dividend', 'an increase in the absolute share of the national dividend accruing to the poor' and a 'diminution in the variability of the national income, especially of the part accruing to the poor'.

Pareto Efficiency: Vilfredo Pareto (1848–1923), an Italian engineer-economist, came up with the postulate known as 'Pareto optimal' which indicates the state of an economy in which no one can be made better off without someone being made worse off. In a state of Pareto efficiency, social welfare is maximized when no resources can be reallocated to make one individual better off without making at least one individual worse off. As Amartya Sen observes in his seminal work, ***On Economic Inequality***, "If the lot of the poor cannot be made any better without cutting into the affluence of the rich, the situation would be Pareto optimal despite the disparity between the rich and the poor.......The almost single-minded concern of modern welfare economics with Pareto optimality does not make that engaging branch of study particularly suitable for investigating problems of inequality".

Reforms and Pareto Optimality

But in a society with gross inequalities and concentration of wealth, promoting economic and social welfare, as modern states are attempting, necessarily requires redistribution of wealth, incomes, and resources from one group to another in varying degrees and proportions. Such redistribution may be carried out through fiscal measures – taxation – or through outright legislation as was the case with land reforms in the 1950s, post-independence, when ownership of land, in whole or in part, was transferred from the owners to the tenants and tillers of the soil. Such redistribution does make some groups worse off while trying to make some others better off.

Labour reforms: Similar is the case of labour reforms being implemented which aim to reform the labour markets and improve the lot and working conditions of those in the unorganized and informal sectors by bringing them into the fold of formal economy with working conditions tantamount to those in the organised sector. As part of this, there is a need to privatise or corporatize many of the non-strategic public sector units and expand the role assigned to the private sector in the economy. The State is to only act as a facilitator by improving the climate for investments by the private sector, improving the infrastructure, etc. But such changes are resisted by those working in the organised sector on the specious plea that they stand to lose or that their working conditions would worsen by such a move. But this argument is fallacious considering that the working conditions of labour in the well organised private sector is as good as that of those in the public sector.

And how unjust is the stand of employees in the organised sector can be gauged from the fact that the organised sector labour constitutes a mere 10 to 15 per cent of the total labour force with as much as 80 to 85 per cent being in the unorganised sector. There is also dire need to reduce the workforce in the farm sector by creating more job opportunities in the non-farm sector. By stalling labour and industrial reforms, the miniscule workforce in the organised sector is virtually stalling and shutting the door for the entry of the vast majority of unorganised workers into the organised stream. That apart, the stand that virtually all undertakings should be in the public sector also does not stand to reason when the government's fiscal resources are limited and stretched, and there is greater need for more of the state's resources to be deployed in the social sector – education and health in particular – to improve the facilities in these sectors for the benefit of the vast majority of the poor and vulnerable sections who have been for long denied of facilities comparable to that enjoyed by the well-off sections of society. What is to be ensured is that in the event of privatisation, the working conditions of labour are duly protected.

It is also pertinent to note in this context that Marxian ideas and notions have been largely disproved by the developments in later periods when advancements in technology have not only improved the methods of production and the overall output, but also the working conditions of the labour class itself. This is not to deny the existence of any exploitation of labour which may occur or persist due to other factors. It has been seen that an enlightened and caring industrial system is beneficial not only to the industry and society at large, but to the workers themselves. And due credit has to be given to both industry bodies and workers' organizations for working in a co-operative spirit and their efforts to ameliorate the conditions of workers in regard to wages, housing, health, and education benefits to the workers and their families. This is exemplified by modern concepts such as 'corporate social responsibility' (CSR) under which industries not only take care of their workers but also contribute to society through multifarious social welfare activities.

Agriculture reforms: So is the case with reforms in the agriculture sector where bulk of the farmers – as much as 85 per cent – are small and marginal farmers owning less than 2 hectares and even among them about 65 per cent hold less than just one hectare which make such land holdings quite uneconomic. What is needed are measures to improve the lot of the vast majority of farmers with crop diversification and better marketing facilities to fetch remunerative prices for them. But any attempts to change the status quo are resisted by vested interests who may be well off and benefiting under the present system.

No panacea: It must, however, be conceded that even with redistribution and reform measures, inequalities will tend to persist because when there are additions to wealth and incomes, its distribution would again not be optimal. In reality, perfect equality is an unattainable utopian idea. Inequalities will exist because of differences in endowments, capabilities, social backgrounds, inheritance, etc. of individuals or groups in society. At best, inequality can be minimized but not eliminated.

Income distribution and Inequality

These are concepts which have become an integral part of modern studies on welfare. These received the attention of Max Lorenz (1880-1962), an American economist and Corrado Gini (1884-1965), an Italian statistician. Lorenz devised a graphical representation of variables like incomes, employment and population called Lorenz curve to study the extent of inequality.

Lorenz curve: The data of cumulative percentages of population in a frequency distribution are plotted in a graph against cumulative percentages of incomes or employment. A straight line rising at an angle of 45^0 on the graph indicates perfect equality, say, 10% of the population have 10% share of the income or 10% of the firms employ 10% of the labour force and so on. But if 10% of the population have 60% share of the total income and 90% of the population have a share of only 40%, it is an unequal and skewed distribution. In such cases, the graph will show a curvature below the 45^0 straight line and the degree of curvature will be greater the greater the inequality.

Gini coefficient: A related concept is Gini coefficient which studies the degree of inequality in income levels. If in a frequency distribution, the Lorenz curve coincides with the 45^0 straight line, the Gini coefficient, G = 0 implying perfect equality. And at the maximum value of G =1, it will be complete inequality.

❑ MODERN APPROACHES TO WELFARE

The concept of welfare has since come to acquire a much wider dimension than what it encompassed till 1950s. It is no longer viewed through the narrow prism of monetary terms or wealth. Till some decades back, development was assessed based mainly on growth in gross domestic product (GDP) and per capita income (PCI). But it was seen that even though GDP and PCI showed impressive growth, they were not getting distributed in a fair and equitable manner. Development experience in many countries has shown that even with increase in incomes, large sections of people were left behind in the process and many of them continued to be trapped in poverty and acute deprivation.

This led many economists and international development agencies to redraw the parameters to judge development based on various other social and economic indicators and assess improvement in the "**standards of living**" and '**quality of life**' on a much broader plane. This includes parameters such as literacy and schooling levels, life expectancy, birth and death rates, extent of poverty and deprivation prevailing, access to safe drinking water and sanitation, gender equality, per capita income, etc. in the country.

The Swedish initiative: One of the earliest approaches to assessing development and welfare of the people was made by Sten Johansson of Sweden who conducted Swedish "Level of Living Survey" in 1968. This survey covered aspects such as health and access to health care, diet and nutrition, employment and working conditions, education and skills, housing and family and social integration. This survey was followed by similar surveys in other Nordic countries.

It must be stated that leading modern welfare economists like Gunnar Myrdal, Kenneth Arrow, Amartya Sen, Martha Nussbaum, Jean Drèze, among others, have done commendable work in the domain of welfare economics. Among them, Amartya Sen, who won the Nobel Prize in 1998 for his contributions to welfare economics spanning over three decades stands out. His theory of social choice, work on various dimensions of welfare such as capabilities, functionings and deprivation, and measurement of poverty and empirical studies of famine have expanded the scope of studies on welfare. They are linked closely to distributional issues with special focus on the most impoverished members of society.

❑ ROLE OF INTERNATIONAL AGENCIES

International bodies like The World Bank, UNDP, UNICEF, etc. have also done considerable amount of research and contributed to literature on development and welfare economics. They have also done much practical work on the ground in advancing the cause of welfare and reduction of poverty and inequality in collaboration with member-countries in the United Nations system.

Since 1990, UNDP has been publishing annual *Human Development Report* (HDR) with focus on different developmental themes, with exhaustive statistical data. UNDP collects data on attainments on selected parameters such as literacy, schooling, life expectancy, per capita income, etc. of each country and calculates the Human Development Index (HDI) and ranks countries according to HDI in three groups—High, Medium, and Low Human Development. It also assesses level of poverty and deprivation, gender equality, etc. pertaining to all member countries in the UN system. The initiative for this was taken by Dr. Mahbub ul Haq, a former Finance and Planning Minister of Pakistan, and the first few reports were published by a team under his leadership.

❑ GLOBALISATION AND INTERDEPENDENCE

With globalisation, economies have become more integrated and inter-dependent in many respects. The world has become a 'global village'. It is much like one village with many markets functioning next to one another and what happens in one impacting the others. Examples for this abound – the **south-east and east Asian financial crisis** of 1997 which started in **Thailand** spread to other countries in the region impacting **Indonesia, South Korea**, etc. and the financial crisis which erupted in the US in 2008 following the subprime crisis and the collapse of **Lehman Brothers** led to worldwide recession for many years.

Further, in the recent past there have been ominous signs on the global scene which have put the fragility and failings of globalization into sharp focus. **Britain**'s decision through a referendum to exit from the **European Union**, which is a clear vote against economic integration, the prolonged US – China trade dispute which has impacted production supply chains and international trade and increasing trade restricting measures adopted by various countries are signs of rising anti-free trade sentiments and a pushback against globalization. Disturbing geopolitical developments, instances of armed conflicts and terrorism in some parts of the world leading to mass migration of people from conflict zones to other countries have only compounded the problems.

Against this background, the study of Economics has assumed great relevance and significance. The direction the world economy will take will determine the future of human welfare and well-being. Though the world has seen considerable progress over a century and more, it is still bedevilled with pervasive poverty and gross inequalities affecting a large segment of the population. Added to this are problems like environmental degradation and climate change which, if not tackled with seriousness of purpose by the present generation, hold ominous portents for the future. And serious health crisis like the outbreak of the pandemic, Covid-19 in 2019 which spared no country from its devastating impact and virtually threw global economy out of gear is another cause for concern. The crisis threw millions out of jobs, even if temporarily, and pushed many back into poverty undoing the good work on poverty alleviation done in the last three to four decades.

The present work dwells upon the journey of India and the path she has travelled since independence in her quest for economic and social development, focusing upon the reforms and liberalisation process she has undertaken. For almost three decades, India tread a path of protectionism in the hope of being self-reliant and self-sufficient, largely sheltering the economy from external influences. It was only since the mid-1980s that she began to change the trajectory and introduce some measure of reforms. And as India faced a serious economic crisis in 1991, a tectonic shift in economic policies occurred with the opening up of the economy. The process of further unshackling the economy is still on, and that when the global economic situation is grim. The challenges for the Indian economy have been many, and the task is still, and will remain, unfinished until the nation has been able to lift everyone out of poverty and deprivation.

A.V. Balakrishnan
December 2021

CONTENTS

Preface to Third Edition v
Preface to First Edition vii
Preface to Second Edition ix
Origin of Economic Thought xi
Abbreviations and Acronyms xxix
List of Tables and Boxed Items xxxix

PART-I

1. **The Colonial Legacy** 1.3-1.20
   - Introduction 1.3
   - India's Capabilities in Manufactures 1.3
   - The East India Company 1.4
   - Industrial Revolution and its Impact 1.4
   - Consolidation of British Rule 1.5
   - The Agrarian Scene and Land Tenure 1.5
   - Commercialisation of Agriculture 1.7
   - Industrial Policy 1.8
   - Deindustrialisation of India 1.8
   - Assessment of Colonial Rule 1.10
   - What if India had not been Colonised? 1.12
   - Progress of India on Socio-Economic indicators in Pre-independent and Post-independent period 1.13
2. **India at Independence and After** 2.1-2.17
   - The Beginning and The Early Plans 2.1
   - The Constitutional Rights 2.2
   - The Genesis of Planning 2.2
   - Early Years of Planning: The First Three Plans (1951–66) 2.3
   - Assessment of The Early Plans and Policies 2.6
   - Neglect of School Education 2.7
   - Role of the State 2.8
   - The East Asian Miracle 2.9
3. **Agriculture in India Before and After The Green Revolution** 3.1-3.10
   - Introduction 3.1
   - Land reforms and Changes in the Agrarian Sector 3.2
   - Bhoodan Movement 3.3
   - The Pre-Green Revolution Phase (1951-1968) 3.4
   - Early Green Revolution Phase (1968-1981) 3.6
   - Later Green Revolution Phase (1981-1992) 3.7
   - Agriculture Research and Extension Programmes 3.8
   - Limitations of Technology-driven Approach to Agriculture 3.8
4. **Industrial Policy and Development** 4.1–4.15
   - Industrial Development 1947-1990 4.1
   - Role of Public Sector 4.3

*For more details on the topics, readers can consult the Name and Subject Index given at the end of this book.

- Industrial Licensing, Control Regime, and its Consequences 4.5
- Location and Dispersal of Industries and Regional Balance 4.6
- Large-scale Industries 4.6
- Share of Industrial Sector in GDP and Employment 4.11
- Role of Small-Scale and Village Industries 4.11

5. Banking and Finance 5.1–5.16

- Banking and Finance: 1947 – 1990 5.1
- Reserve Bank of India and its Role 5.2
- Setting up of the State Bank of India 5.5
- Expansion and Penetration of Banks 5.5
- Banks as Agents of Change 5.5
- RBI and Agricultural Credit 5.6
- Nationalisation of Banks 5.7
- Other Financial Institutions 5.9
- Nationalisation of Banks: 5.10

PART-II

6. Economic Reforms of the 1990s 6.3 –6.18

- Background 6.3
- Reforms and Problems During 1985-90 6.3
- The 1991 Economic Crisis 6.4
- The New Reform Measures 6.6
- The New Industrial Policy 6.7
- Impact of the Reforms 6.9
- Conclusion 6.11
- Liberalisation and Inequality 6.12
- Salient Features of 1991 Economic Reforms 6.13

7. Agricultural Development since 1990 7.1–7.50

- Introduction 7.1
- Inter-relationship of Agriculture and Industry 7.1
- Trends in Agriculture: 1950-90 7.2
- Challenges Facing Indian Agriculture 7.4
- Measures Taken to Support Agriculture 7.9
- Food security and Nutrition 7. 10
- The Importance of Agricultural Processing 7.12
- Food Processing Industry in India 7.14
- Agricultural Marketing 7.17
- Farmer Producer Organisations 7.19
- Agricultural Credit and Debt Relief 7.21
- Pradhan Mantri FasalBima Yojana 7.26
- Cooperative Farming 7.26
- Contract Farming 7.29
- Capital Formation and Subsidies 7.31
- Public Distribution System (PDS) 7.32
- Agrarian scene, Farm Reforms and Farm Laws 7.36
- Integrated Farming 7.43

8. Industrial Development since 1990 8.1–8.22

- Introduction 8.1
- Liberalization and Measures to Promote Industry 8.2
- Performance of Industrial Sector: An Overview 8.6
- Fluctuations in Industrial growth 8.8
- Public Sector Enterprises and Disinvestment 8.11
- Constraints Faced by Indian Industry 8.12
- Measures to Boost Manufacturing 8.14
- Ease of Doing Business 8.16
- Promoting Industrial development 8.16
- Privatisation and Disinvestment of Public Sector Enterprises 8.18

9. Small Scale Industry 9.1 – 9.21

- Introduction 9.1
- Small Scale Units Defined 9.2
- MSMEs: Criteria Changed 9.3
- Karve Committee on Village and Small Industries 9.3

- The National Small Industries Corporation (NSIC) 9.3
- Industrial Cooperatives 9.4
- Industrial Estates 9.4
- The Small Industries Development Organization (SIDO) 9.5
- Plan Allocations for SSI Sector 9.5
- Progress of Small Scale Industries sector 9.6
- MSME Sector and Employment 9.7
- MSME Sector and Exports 9.8
- Credit Facilities for the MSME sector 9.8
- The Small Industries Development Bank of India (SIDBI) 9.9
- Marketing Support Needed for Small and Medium Enterprises 9.10
- Tiruppur: An Indian Success Story 9.10
- Expert Committee on Small Enterprises 9.11
- Study Group on Small Scale Enterprises 9.13
- Constraints Faced by the MSME sector 9.13
- Small Scale Sector: The Experience of Other Countries 9.17
- Conclusion: Significance of MSMEs 9.18

10. Infrastructure (Transport and Communications) 10.1–10.37

- Importance of Infrastructure 10.2
- Development of Infrastructure 10.2
- Roadways: Growth 10.3
- Roadways Complementary to Rail 10.7
- Challenges Facing the Road Sector 10.8
- Railways: Growth and Improvements 10.9
- Reforms in Railways 10.12
- Shipping and Ports 10.13
- Inland Water Transport (IWT) 10.14
- Air Transport 10.15
- Modernization and Privatisation of Airports 10.17
- Communications 10.18
- Logistics Industry 10.20
- Telecommunications: 10.21
- National Optical Fibre Network, - BharatNet project 10.24
- Challenges and rise of the Telecom Sector in India 10.25
- Radio, Television and Other Media 10.30
- Infrastructure and Employment 10.30
- Conclusion 10.32
- International North-South Transport Corridor (INSTC) – A Case Study 10.32

11. Energy and Power 11.1–11.23

- Introduction 11.1
- Energy Scenario in India 11.2
- Non-Commercial Primary Energy Resources 11.3
- Electricity: Installed Capacity and Generation 11.5
- Sources of Energy and Power 11.8
- Renewable Energy 11.9
- Power Generation, Distribution and Expansion 11.10
- Rural Electrification 11.13
- Power Sector Reforms 11.16
- Promoting Energy Efficiency 11.17
- Power Sector Reforms 11.19

12. IT Industry 12.1–12.17

- Introduction 12.1
- Computer and Internet Use 12.2
- Genesis of IT Industry in India 12.3
- National Informatics Centre (NIC) 12.3
- Growth of IT Industry 12.4
- National Task Force on IT and Software Development 12.5
- Software Technology Parks 12.7
- Progress of Telecom and IT Sector 12.8
- Export Performance of IT Sector 12.9
- Employment Generation through IT Sector 12.10
- Digital India Programme 12.11
- India's Strategic Advantages in IT Sector 12.12
- Challenges Faced by the Sector 12.13
- Conclusion 12.14

13. Banking and Financial Sector Reforms 13.1–13.28

- Indian Financial System 13.2
- Factors behind Banking Reforms 13.2
- Committee on the Financial System 13.3
- Capital Markets Reform 13.4
- Committee on Banking Sector Reforms 13.5
- Modernisation and Computerisation of Banks 13.6
- Recent Developments in Banking Sectors 13.7
- Insolvency and Bankruptcy Code 13.9
- Regional Rural Banks 13.10
- Non-Banking Financial Companies (NBFCs) 13.11
- Wholesale and Consumer Price Index 13.13
- RBI and Monetary Policy 13.16
- Monetary Policy Transmission in India 13.18
- Transfer of RBI's Reserves to Government 13.22
- Financial Inclusion and Role of Banks 13.23
- Conclusion 13.24

14. Fiscal Policy and Tax Reforms 14.1–14.34

- Introduction 14.2
- Inequalities and Fiscal Policy 14.2
- Fiscal Policy and Inequality 14.3
- Role of Fiscal Policy in an Economy 14.4
- The Tax System and Budget: An Overview 14.4
- Features of a Sound Tax System and Tax Policy 14.5
- Tax Structure and Equity 14.7
- Tax-GDP Ratio 14.8
- Early Tax Reforms 14.9
- The Crisis of 1990-91 14.11
- Chelliah Committee (1991) and Tax Reforms 14.11
- Public Debt 14.14
- Subsidies 14.16
- Fiscal Responsibility and Budget Management (FRBM) Act 14.17
- Centre-State Relations: Fiscal Federalism and Finance Commission 14.20
- 15th Finance Commission 14.23
- Retrospective Taxation and Its Consequences 14.26
- Implications of Taxing Agriculture Sector 14.27

15. Foreign Trade and Commerce 15.1–15.33

- Introduction 15.1
- The Theory of Comparative Advantage 15.2
- Foreign Trade in the 1950s and '60s 15.4
- The 1970s and the Turnaround 15.5
- The 1980s 15.6
- Foreign Trade Ratios 15.6
- 1991 Reforms, Devaluation and After 15.7
- The 2007-08 Financial Crisis 15.9
- Foreign Exchange Reserves 15.11
- Capital Account Convertibility 15.14
- India's Share in World Trade 15.16
- Foreign Trade Policy (FTP) 2015-20 15.22
- India and WTO 15.24
- Multinational Corporations 15.26
- India and Free Trade Agreements 15.28

16. Labour, Employment and Skill Development 16.1-16.41

- Introduction 16.1
- Economists on Labour, Employment and Productivity 16.2
- Labour Data 16.3
- Labour Force and Employment 16.3
- Inflation and Unemployment – Phillip's Curve 16.4
- Measuring Employment/ Unemployment 16.4
- Labourforce and Workforce 16.5
- Features of the Indian Labour Scene 16.7
- Organised and Unorganised Sectors 16.11

- Challenge of Employment Generation 16.13
- Labour Reforms 16.15
- Migrant Labour Issues 16.18
- Child Labour in India 16.24
- Bonded Labour 16.28
- Advent of Computers and Its Aftermath 16.30
- Skill Development 16.31
- Labour Force and Jobs-the Mismatch 16.31
- Highlights of Skill India Mission 16.32
- Technology versus Labour and Employment 16.34
- Automation and Employment 16.34
- Automation in India 16.37

17. Inequality and Poverty Alleviation 17.1-17.58

- Introduction 17.2
- The Constitution of India on Equality and Social Justice 17.2
- Manifestation of Inequality and Poverty 17.3
- Absolute and Relative Poverty 17.3
- Extreme Poverty and Poverty Trap 17.4
- Measuring Poverty, Sen's Poverty Index 17.5
- Development as a Broader Issue 17.5
- Human Development Reports 17.6
- Global Multidimensional Poverty Index (MPI) 17.6
- Five Year Plans and Poverty and Inequality 17.8
- Importance of Social and Political Consciousness 17.12
- Economists and Welfarism 17.12
- Global Poverty Scene 17.14
- Economists on Inequality and Distributive Justice 17.15
- Inequality and Poverty versus Growth: Sen-Bhagwati debate 17.16
- Growth and Inequality-the Asian Experience 17.18
- Estimation of Poverty and Identification of Poverty Line 17.19
- Expert Groups on Methodology for Estimation of Poverty 17.23
- National Rural Employment Guarantee Scheme (NREGS) 17.26
- Rural Housing Programme 17.30
- PM Gram Sadak Yojana 17.30
- Urban Anti-Poverty Measures 17.31
- Panchayati Raj and Rural Rejuvenation 17.33
- Gender Budgeting 17.41
- Universal Basic Income (UBI) 17.43
- Conclusion 17.50
- Growth and Inequality: Kuznet's Hypothesis and a Global Perspective 17.51

18. Demographic Issues and Vital Statistics 18.1 – 18.25

- Introduction 18.1
- Population: The Global Scenario 18.2
- Economists on Population Issue 18.2
- Global Population Growth 18.4
- Food Security and Sustainability Challenges 18.4
- Inefficient Food Supply Chain and Wastages 18.5
- Demographic Transition 18.5
- India's Demographic Scene 18.6
- Performance of States on Population Control 18.8
- Age Structure and Demographic Dividend 18.9
- China's One-child and Three-child Population Policy 18.12
- How India Compares with Other Countries 18.15
- The Global Problem of Declining Population 18.18
- Migration and Demographic Changes 18.20
- Demographic Changes in US and Europe 18.20
- Conclusion 18.23

19. Planning and Developmental Issues 19.1–19.33

- Introduction 19.1
- Economic Growth and Development Process 19.2
- International Comparison 19.3
- A Comparative Profile: Indian States 19.4
- Development Theories 19.4
- Developed and Developing Nations: The Contrast 19.8
- Structural Changes in the Economy 19.9
- Regional Balance in Development 19.11
- Development Goals—MDGs and SDGs 19.13
- Planning Commission and NITI Aayog 19.15
- NITI Aayog's Working: A Critical Assessment 19.19
- India's Growth Pattern 19.21
- Contribution of Dr V.K.R.V. Rao on India's National Income Accounts - an Evaluation 19.22
- Impact of Covid-19 on Indian Economy 19.27

20. International Economic Issues 20.1–20.46

- Introduction 20.2
- Globalisation 20.2
- Free Trade and Crime 20.4
- Globalisation and Inclusivity 20.5
- Is Globalisation in Retreat? Is There a Trend Towards Deglobalisation? 20.6
- Britain's Exit from European Union: Its Causes and Consequences 20.8
- How Globalisation has Impacted Indian Economy 20.11
- Trends in World Trade 20.12
- China's Economic Slowdown and Reforms 20.13
- International Institutions 20.15
- India and International Institutions 20.18
- International Economic Groupings 20.19
- India's Experience with Trade Agreements 20.23
- Note on Trade Agreements 20.27
- WTO Issues and Food Subsidy Regime 20.28
- Geopolitics and Economic Development: The Emerging World Order 20.30
- Transfer of Technology and UNCTAD 20.32
- Europe's Migrants Problem 20.33
- Climate Change 20.35
- 21St Conference of Parties (COP21), Paris 20.36
- The Path Ahead on Climate Change 20.37
- Climate Change Target and India 20.38
- Carbon Sink and Forest Cover 20.40
- El Niño and La Niña and Asian Economies 20.42

PART-III

21. Make in India Programme 21.3–21.17

- Introduction 21.3
- Measures Taken 21.4
- New Labour Laws 21.5
- One District One Product (ODOP) 21.7
- Outcomes of 'Make in India' Initiative 21.9
- Challenges and Limitations to 'Make in India' 21.11
- Production Linked Incentive (PLI) Scheme 21.12
- Conclusion 21.14

22. Ease of Doing Business 22.1–22.13

- Introduction 22.1
- World Bank Rankings on Ease of Doing Business 22.2
- New Generation Reforms 22.2
- WEF Survey 22.3
- Revamp and Simplification of Procedures 22.4
- State Government Initiatives 22.5

- Assessment of State Implementation of Business Reforms 2016 — 22.5
- FDI Policy — 22.7
- Insolvency and Bankruptcy Law — 22.8
- The World Bank to discontinue Doing Business Report — 22.10

23. Start-up Mission and Venture Capital — 23.1–23.13

- Start Up Mission — 23.1
- Steps Taken by the Government to Nurture the Start-Up Ecosystem — 23.2
- India – A Leading Start-Up Nation — 23.5
- Role of Start-Ups — 23.6
- Union Budget 2018-19 and Start-Ups — 23.7
- Changing Manufacturing and Trade Landscape — 23.7
- Funding for Start-Ups — 23.8
- Limitations and Challenges to Start-Ups — 23.9
- Atal Innovation Mission (AIM) — 23.10

24. Infrastructure — 24.1–24.36

- Introduction — 24.1
- Infrastructure in Union Budget — 24.2
- Road Sector - National Highways — 24.2
- National Highway Projects – Funding and Execution — 24.3
- Pradhan Mantri Gram Sadak Yojana (PMGSY) — 24.5
- Electric Vehicles (EVs) — 24.5
- India's Automobile Market – Salient Facts — 24.7
- Promoting Electric Vehicles in India — 24.8
- Setu Bharatam Project — 24.10
- Railways: Growth and Modernisation — 24.11
- Railway Electrification — 24.12
- Aviation Sector — 24.13
- Ports and Shipping — 24.14
- Maritime Summit — 24.15
- Sagarmala Project — 24.16
- Power Sector Reforms — 24.17
- UJALA: Affordable and Health-Safe LED Lighting Scheme — 24.17
- Saubhagya Yojana — 24.19
- Renewable Energy — 24.20
- India's Renewable Energy Scenario — 24.22
- International Solar Alliance — 24.24
- Telecommunications — 24.25
- Digital India: Bharatnet Project — 24.26
- National Investment and Infrastructure Fund (NIIF) — 24.27
- National Monetisation Pipeline (NMP) — 24.28
- Economic Growth and Employment: Role of Infrastructure — 24.31

25. Financial Sector and Tax Reforms — 25.1–25.49

- Introduction — 25.2
- Financial Inclusion (PMJDY) — 25.2
- JAM and Aadhaar — 25.5
- Expansion Of Banking Facilities And Payments Banks And SFBs — 25.5
- Small Finance Banks (SFBs) — 25.6
- Mudra Yojana - Funding the Unfunded — 25.7
- Banks: NPAs and Recapitalisation — 25.8
- Setting up of Bad Bank : The Objectives and Implications — 25.9
- Recapitalisation of Banks — 25.11
- Amalgamation of PSBs — 25.13
- Black Money — 25.14
- Black Money in India — 25.16
- Demonetisation — 25.18
- Pradhan Mantri Garib Kalyan Yojana, 2016 — 25.21
- Assessment of Demonetisation — 25.23
- Towards Digital and Less Cash Economy — 25.24
- Electoral Funding and Electoral Bonds — 25.26
- Black Money Problem in the US and European Countries — 25.29
- Gold Monetisation — 25.30

- Tax Reforms 25.31
- Goods and Services Tax (GST) 25.33

26. Social Sector and CSR 26.1–26.37

- Introduction 26.1
- Education 26.2
- Critical Role of Female Teachers 26.3
- Toilet facility in Schools: Adequacy and Maintenance Issues 26.4
- School Toilets Constructed under Swachh Vidyalaya Abhiyan by CPSEs: An Audit Report 26.5
- Quality and Standards of Education 26.6
- National Education Policy 2020 26.7
- Plan Outlays on Education and Health 26.10
- Health Sector 26.10
- Health Facilities and Outcomes 26.12
- National Rural Health Mission (NRHM) (2005-12) 26.14
- Health Infrastructure and Manpower 26.15
- National Health Policy, 2017 and Ayushman Bharat 26.17
- Challenges for the Health Sector 26.18
- 15th Finance Commission on Health Sector 26.19
- Housing for Weaker Sections 26.20
- Jal Jeevan Mission for Water Supply 26.22
- Swachh Bharat Mission 26.24
- Total Sanitation Campaign (RURAL) 26.24
- Smart Cities Programme 26.26
- Solid Waste Management 26.29
- Corporate Social Responsibility (CSR) 26.30

Glossary G.1 – G.18

Statistical Tables ST.1 – ST.6

Name Index NI.1 – NI.4

Subject Index SI.1 – SI.21

ABBREVIATIONS AND ACRONYMS

ABBREVIATIONS

BCM: billion cubic meter
Bkwh: billion kilowatt hour
Bn : billion
FC : Factor cost
GW : gigawatt
ha : hectare
KgOE : kilogram of oil equivalent
Km : kilometre
kw : kilowatt
KWH: Kilowatt hour
Mn : million
MP: Market price
MT: metric tonne
MtOE: Million tonnes of oil equivalent;
MW : megawatt
na: not available
sq. km. : square kilometre

ACRONYMS

ABD: Area-Based Development
ADB : Asian Development Bank
AIF : ASEAN Infrastructure Fund
AIF : Alternative Investment Fund
AIIB : Asian Infrastructure Investment Bank
AIM : Atal Innovation Mission
ANM : Auxiliary Nurse Midwife
APCTT : Asia and Pacific Centre for Transfer of Technology
APDRP : Accelerated Power Development and Reforms Programme
APEC : Asia-Pacific Economic Cooperation
APL : Above Poverty Line

ARDC : Agricultural Refinance and Development Corporation
ASEAN : Association of South-East Asian Nations
ATL: Atal Tinkering Lab
ATM : Automatic Teller Machine

BBB : Bank Board Bureau
BCA : Business Correspondent Agent
BEPS : Base Erosion and Profit Shifting
BIFR : Board for Industrial and Financial Reconstruction
BIMSTEC : Bengal Initiative for Multi-sectoral Technical and Economic Cooperation
BIS : Bank of International Settlements
BIS : Bureau of Industrial Standards
BNP : Bharat Nirman Programme
BOP : Balance of Payments
BPL : Below Poverty Line
BPM : Business Process Management
BPO : Business Process Outsourcing

CAC : Capital Account Convertibility
CAGR : Compound Annual Growth Rate
CAR : Capital Adequacy Ratio
CBD : Convention on Biological Diversity
CBR : Crude Birth Rate
C-DOT : Centre for Development of Telematics
CDR : Crude Death Rate
CDS : Current Daily Status (of employment/unemployment)
CEA : Central Electricity Authority
CERC : Central Electricity Regulatory Commission
CFL : Compact Fluorescent Lamp
CHC : Community Health Centre
CIL : Coal India Limited
CIS : Commonwealth of Independent States (former States of Soviet Union)
CITES : Convention on International Trade in Endangered Species of Fauna and Flora
COP : Conference of the Parties
CPI : Consumer Price Index
CPR : Couple Protection Rate
CPTPP: Comprehensive and Progressive Agreement for Trans-Pacific Partnership
CRAR : Capital to Risk-weighted Asset Ratio
CRR : Cash Reserve Ratio
CSC : Common Services Centre
CSO : Central Statistical Organization
CSR : Corporate Social Responsibility
CSS : Centrally Sponsored Schemes
CWS : Current Weekly Status (of employment/unemployment)

DAC : Defence Acquisition Council
DBR : Doing Business Report
DBT : Direct Benefit Transfer
DD : Demographic Dividend
DDA : Doha Development Agenda
DDP : Desert Development Programme
DDUGJY : Deen Dayal Upadhyaya Gram Jyoti Yojana
DELP : Domestic Efficient Lighting Programme
DFC : Dedicated Freight Corridor
DICI : Deposit Insurance Corporation of India
DIP : Digital India Project
DIPP : Department of Industrial Policy and Promotion
DISCOM : State (Power) Distribution Company
DNBS : Department of Non-Banking Supervision
DPAP : Drought Prone Areas Programme
DPP : Defence Procurement Procedure
DR : Dependency Ratio
DRT : Debt Recovery Tribunals
DSDE : Department of Skill Development and Entrepreneurship
DTAA : Double Tax Avoidance Agreement
DTC : Direct Tax Code
DWCRA : Development of Women and Children in Rural Areas

EAS : East Asia Summit
EAS : Employment Assurance Scheme
ECM : European Common Market
EEC : European Economic Community
EESL : Energy Efficiency Services Limited
EPS: Employees' Pension Scheme
ERNET : Education and Research Network
ESIC : Employees State Insurance Corporation
EU : European Union
EUAMLFTD : EU Anti-Money Laundering and Financing of Terrorism Directives

FAO : Food and Agriculture Organization
FATCA : Foreign Account Tax Compliance Act
FATF : Financial Action Task Force
FCCB : Foreign Currency Convertible Bond
FCI : Food Corporation of India
FDI : Foreign Direct Investment
FEMA : Foreign Exchange Management Act
FFS : Fund of Funds for Startups
FHTC: Functional Household Tap Connection
FII : Foreign Institutional Investment
FIPB : Foreign Investment Promotion Board

FIU : Financial Intelligence Unit
FLC : Financial Literacy Centre
FPI : Foreign Portfolio Investment
FRBM Act : Fiscal Responsibility and Budget Management Act
FRDI : Financial Resolution and Deposit Insurance
FTA : Free Trade Agreement
FTAAP : Free Trade Area of the Asia-Pacific
FTL : Fluorescent Tube Light
FWP : Food for Work Programme
FWPR : Female Worker Participation Rate

G8/20/77 : Group 8/20/77 Countries
GATT : General Agreement on Tariffs and Trade
GCC : Gulf Cooperation Council
GDP : Gross Domestic Product
GDR : Global Depository Receipts
GEM : Gender Empowerment Measure
GHG : Greenhouse Gas
GIC : General Insurance Corporation
GKY : Ganga KalyanYojana
GNI : Gross National Income
GST : Goods and Services Tax
GTI : Global Terrorism Index

HAM : Hybrid Annuity Model
HDR : Human Development Report
HIC : High Income Country
HRD : Human Resources Development
HSR : High Speed Rail
HUDCO : Housing and Urban Development Corporation
HWC: Health & Wellness Centre
HYV : High Yielding Varieties (of seeds)

IADP : Intensive Agricultural District Programme
IAY : Indira Awas Yojana
IBRD : International Bank for Reconstruction and Development
ICAR : Indian Council for Agricultural Research
ICDS : Integrated Child Development Services
ICDS : Income Computation and Disclosure Standards
ICICI : Industrial Credit and Investment Corporation of India
ICT : Information and Communication Technology
IDA : International Development Association
IDA : Industrial Disputes Act
IDBI : Industrial Development Bank of India
IDRA : Industrial (Development and Regulation) Act

IEP : Institute for Economics and Peace
IFC : Indian Financial Code
IFC : International Finance Corporation
IFCI : Industrial Finance Corporation of ndia
IIBI : Industrial Investment Bank of dia
IIFCL : India Infrastructure Finance Company Ltd
IISCO : Indian Iron and Steel Company
ILCS : Integrated Low Cost Sanitation
ILO : International Labour rganization
IMF : International Monetary Fund
IMR : Infant Mortality Rate
IPCC : Inter-governmental Panel on Climate Change
IPDS : Integrated Power Development Scheme
IPR : Intellectual Property Regime (Right)
IRC : Industrial Relations Code
IRDA : Insurance Regulatory and Development Authority
IRDP : Integrated Rural Development Programme
IRFC : Indian Railway Finance Corporation
ISA : International Solar Alliance
IT : Information Technology
ITeS : Information Technology-enabled Solution
ITI : Industrial Training Institute
ITU : International Telecommunications Union
IWDP : Integrated Watershed Development Programme

JAM : Jan Dhan Yojana, Aadhaar, Mobile
JDY : Jan Dhan Yojana
JJM: Jal Jeevan Mission
JNNURM : Jawaharlal Nehru National Urban Renewal Mission
JRY : Jawahar Rozgar Yojana

KYC : Know Your Customer

LDC: Less (Least) Developed Country
LED : Light-Emitting Diode
LFPR : Labour Force Participation Rate
LIC : Life Insurance Corporation
LPG : Liquefied Petroleum Gas

MAT : Minimum Alternate Tax
MDGs : Millennium Development Goals
MFI : Micro Finance Institution
MMR : Maternal Mortality Rate
MNC : Multi-National Corporation
MNREGS : Mahatma Gandhi National Rural Employment Guarantee Scheme
MPC : Monetary Policy Committee

MRTP Act : Monopolies and Restrictive Trade Practices Act
MSDE : Ministry of Skill Development and Entrepreneurship
MSME : Micro, Small and Medium Enterprise
MSMED Act : Micro, Small and Medium Enterprises Development Act
MSP : Minimum Support Price
MUDRA Bank : Micro Units Development and Refinance Agency Bank
MWS : Million Wells Scheme

NABARD : National Bank for Agriculture and Rural Development
NAS : National Accounts Statistics
NAS : New Agricultural Strategy
NASSCOM : National Association of Software and Services Companies
NBFC : Non-Banking Finance Company
NCAER : National Council of Applied Economic Research
NCEF : National Clean Energy Fund
NCL : National Commission on Labour
NCEUS : National Commission for Employment in the Unorganized Sector
NCVT : National Council for Vocational Training
NCR : National Capital Region
NDB : New Development Bank
NDRC : National Development and Reform Commission (of China)
NEP: National Education Policy (2020)
NGO : Non-Governmental Organization
NGP : Nirmal Gram Puraskar
NHAI : National Highways Authority of India
NHB : National Housing Bank
NHHP : National Housing and Habitat Policy
NIC : National Informatics Centre
NIDHI : National Initiative for Developing and Harnessing Innovations
NIFM : National Institute of Financial Management
NIIF : National Investment and Infrastructure Fund
NIPFP : National Institute of Public Finance and Policy
NITI Aayog : National Institution for Transforming India Aayog
NMCC : National Manufacturing Competitiveness Council
NMS : National Maritime Summit
NOFNP : National Optical Fibre Network Project
NPA : Non Performing Asset
NPCIL : Nuclear Power Corporation of India Ltd.
NPS : National Pension System
NPSDE : National Policy on Skill Development and Entrepreneurship
NRE : Non-Renewable Energy
NREGS : National Rural Employment Guarantee Scheme
NREP : National Rural Employment Programme
NRHM : National Rural Health Mission
NRI : Non Resident Indian

NRLM : National Rural Livelihood Mission
NRRDA : National Rural Road Development Agency
NSDA : National Skill Development Agency
NSDC : National Skill Development Corporation
NSDF : National Skill Development Fund
NSDP : Net State Domestic Product
NSE : National Stock Exchange
NSIC : National Small Industries Corporation
NSS : National Sample Survey
NSSO : National Sample Survey Organization
NTPC : National Thermal Power Corporation

ODF: Open Defecation Free
OECD : Organization for Economic Cooperation and Development
OFC : Optical Fibre Cable
OMO : Open Market Operations (of RBI)
OPEC : Organization for Petroleum Exporting Countries

PACS : Primary Agricultural Credit Society
PCI : Per Capita Income
PDS : Public Distribution System
PFRDA : Pension Fund Regulatory and Development Authority
PHC : Primary Health Centre
PISA : Programme for International Student Assessment (of OECD)
PMAY : Pradhan Mantri Awas Yojana
PMGSY : Prime Minister's Gram Sadak Yojana
PMJAY: PM Jan Arogya Yojana
PMJDY : Pradhan Mantri Jan Dhan Yojana
PMKVY : Pradhan Mantri Kaushal Vikas Yojana
PMMY : Pradhan Mantri Mudra Yojana
PMNCSD : Prime Minister's National Council on Skill Development
PMSBHGY : Pradhan Mantri Sahaj Bijli Har Ghar Yojana (Saubhagya Yojana)
PPP : Public-Private Partnership
PPP : Purchasing Power Parity
PRS : Panchayati Raj System
PSB : Public Sector Bank
PSE (U) : Public Sector Enterprise (Undertaking)

QR : Quantitative Restriction (in foreign trade)

RAY : Rajiv Awas Yojana
RBI : Reserve Bank of India
RCEP : Regional Comprehensive Economic Partnership
REC : Rural Electrification Corporation
RES : Renewable Energy Resources
RGGVY : Rajiv Gandhi Grameen Vidyutikaran Yojana

RGI : Registrar-General of India
RLEGP : Rural Landless Employment Guarantee Programme
RRB : Regional Rural Bank
RSBY : Rashtriya Swasthya Bima Yojana
RTE : Right to Education
RWA : Risk Weighted Asset
RWBS : Rural Wireline Broadband Scheme

SAARC : South Asian Association for Regional Cooperation
SAFTA : South Asia Free Trade Area
SARFAESI Act : Securitisation and Reconstruction of Financial Assets and Enforcement of Security Interest Act
SBI : State Bank of India
SBM : Swachh Bharat Mission
SCB : Scheduled Commercial Bank
SCM : Smart City Mission
SDGs : Sustainable Development Goals
SEB : State Electricity Board
SEBI : Securities and Exchange Board of India
SERC : State Electricity Regulatory Commission
SETU : Self-Employment and Talent Utilization
SFC : State Finance Corporation
SGRY : Sampoorna Gramin Rozgar Yojana
SGSRY : Swarna Jayanti Sahari Rozgar Yojana
SGSY : Swarnajayanti Gram Swarozgar Yojana
SHG : Self-Help Group
SICA : Sick Industrial Companies Act
SIDBI : Small Industries Development Bank of India
SIDC : State Industrial Development Corporation
SIDO : Small Industries Development Organization
SIPP : Startup Intellectual Property Protection (Scheme)
SISFS : Startup India Seed Fund Scheme (SISFS)
SIT : Special Investigation Team
SITRA : Supply of Improved Toolkits to Rural Artisans
SLNP : Street Lighting National Programme
SLR : Statutory Liquidity Ratio
SSA : Sarva Shiksha Abhiyan
SSI : Small Scale Industry
STPI : Software Technology Park of India
STT : Securities Transaction Tax
SVA: Swachh Vidyalaya Abhiyan
SWM : Solid Waste Management
SWM: Swachh Bharat Mission (Abhiyan)
SCM : Swiss Challenge Method

T & D : Transmission and Distribution (of Power)
TBI : Technology Business Incubator
TDS : Tax Deducted at Source
TEA : Tiruppur Exporters' Association
TFA : Trade Facilitation Agreement
TFR :Total Fertlity Rate
TISCO : Tata Iron and Steel Company
TNC : Trans-National Corporation
TPP : Trans-Pacific Partnership
TRAI : Telecom Regulatory Authority of India
TRYSEM : Training of Rural Youth for Self-Employment
TSC : Total Sanitation Campaign
TUFS : Technology Upgradation Fund Scheme

UDA: Urban Development Authority
UDAY : Ujwal Discom Assurance Yojana
UIDAI : Unique Identification Authority of India
UMPP : Ultra Mega Power Project
UN : United Nations
UNCTAD : UN Conference on Trade and Development
UNDP ; United Nations Development Programme
UNFCC : UN Framework Convention on Climate Change
UNICEF : UN International Children's Emergency Fund
UNODOC : UN Office on Drugs and Crime
UNPD : UN Population Division
UPSS : Usual Principal and Subsidiary Status (of employment)
UTI : Unit Trust of India

VAT : Value Added Tax
VDIS : Voluntary Disclosure of Income Scheme
VRC : Village Resource Centre

WB (G) : WorldBank (Group)
WHO : World Health Organization
WITS : World Integrated Trade Solution
WMO : World Meteorological Organization
WPI : Wholesale Price Index
WPR : Worker Population Ratio; Work Participation Rate
WTO : World Trade Organization

LIST OF TABLES AND BOXED ITEMS

List of Table Items

Table 1.1:	Literacy rates	1.14
Table 1.2:	Birth rate and Death rate (per 1,000 population)	1.14
Table 1.3:	Life Expectancy at Birth	1.15
Table 1.4:	Percentage of Rural & Urban Population	1.15
Table 1.5:	Sex Ratio at Birth	1.16
Table 2.1:	Outlay and Investment in First, Second, and Third Plans* (Figures in ₹ crore)	2.6
Table 2.2:	Demographic and Economic Data of Selected Asian Economies	2.11
	(a) Demographic and Literacy data	2.11
	(b) Economic Data	2.11
Table 2.3:	Annual Growth Rates: 1951 to 1985 (in Percentage)	2.13
Table 2.4:	Annual Average Growth in Five Year Plans (at1999-2000 prices)	2.13
Table 3.1 :	Gross Area under Major Crops (Million hectares)	3.4
Table 3.2:	Cropped and Irrigated Area (Million hectares)	3.5
Table 3.3:	Foodgrains Production (Million tonnes)	3.5
Table 3.4:	Area under High-Yielding Varieties (Million hectares)	3.6
Table 3.5:	Foodgrains Production (Million tonnes)	3.6
Table 3.6:	Yields for Major Food Crops (Kgs./hectare)	3.7
Table 3.7:	Foodgrains Production (Million tonnes)	3.7
Table 4.1:	Production in Selected Industries (1950-51 to 1990-91)	4.4
Table 4.2 :	Production of Cotton in Three Largest Producing States in 2013-14 & 2017-18 (In million bales of 170kg. per bale)	4.8
Table 4.3:	Exports of Textile Products (₹ crore)	4.9
Table 4.4 :	Production of Sugarcane in Three Largest Producing States in 2013-14 and 2017-2018 (In Million Tonnes)	4.10

Table 4.5: Sectoral Shares in GDP and Employment 4.11

Table 4.6: Plan Allocation for Village and Small Industries (In ₹ crore) 4.13

Table 5.1: Expansion in Number of Bank Branches 5.8

Table 5.2: Population Group-wise Number of Branches of Scheduled Commercial Banks (Number) 5.8

Table 5.3: Population Covered per Branch of Banks (Number in thousands) 5.8

Table 5.4: Deposits in Scheduled Commercial Banks in India (in ₹ thousand) 5.9

Table 5.5: Non-Performing Assets (NPAs) of Banks Gross and Net NPAs of Scheduled Commercial Banks (Amount in ₹ Crore) 5.14

Table 6.1 : Sector-wise Composition of GDP (at Current prices) (In percentage) 6.10

Table 6.2: The Percentage of Population Below the Poverty Line 6.11

Table 7.1: Production of Major Crops and Foodgrains between 1960–61 and 2019–20 (Million tonnes) 7.2

Table 7.2: All India Area, Production, and Yield of Foodgrains along with Coverage under Irrigation: 1950–51 to 1990–91 7.3

Table 7.3: All India Area, Production, and Yield of Foodgrains along with Coverage under Irrigation: 1992–93––2018-19 7.3

Table 7.4: Growth Rate of Agricultural and Allied Sectors (in percentage) (All Figures based on 2004–05 prices) 7.4

Table 7.5: Yield of Principal Crops in Various Countries during 2016 Yield Kg/Hectare 7.6

Table 7.6: Number and Area of Operational Holdings by Size Group, 2005-06 to 2015-16 7.6

Table 7.7: Average Size of Holdings by Size Group 2015-16 (Provisional) 7.7

Table 7.8: Production of Cereals and Pulses: 1980-81 to 2018-19 (Million Tonnes) 7.11

Table 7.9: Direct Institutional Credit for Agriculture and Allied Activities—Short-Term (In ₹crore) 7.23

Table 7.10: Direct Institutional Credit for Agriculture and Allied Activities—Long-Term (In ₹ crore) 7.23

Table 7.11: Public Sector Capital Formation and Subsidies to Agriculture (Centre and States) (in ⊠ crore and as per cent to GDP from agriculture and allied at current prices) 7.32

Table 8.1: Growth Rate of Industrial Sector—1950 to 2012 8.7

Table 8.2: Annual Rates of Growth of Industry and the Sub-sectors during the Eleventh Plan (2007–12) (In Percentage) 8.8

Table 8.3: Index Numbers of Industrial Production 8.9

Table 8.4: Sectoral Shares of Industry *in GDP at Factor cost 2004–05 prices 8.9

Table 8.5 :(a): Growth Rate & Manufacturing Value added - 2019 8.10

Table 8.5 :(b): Sectoral shares in GDP/Value Added at current prices in 2019 (in Percent) 8.10

Table 8.5 :(c): Manufacturing Output as % of World Total (2010) 8.11

Table 8.6: Contribution of Non-departmental Enterprises to GDP at Factor Cost (Current Price) 8.12
Table 9.1: Distribution of Enterprises (Rural and Urban area wise) (Numbers in lakh) 9.2
Table 9.2: Plan Outlays in 8th, 9th, and 10th Five Year Plans in Village and Small Scale Enterprises Sector (In ₹ Crore) 9.5
Table 9.3: Growth and Contribution of SSI Sector 9.6
Table 9.4: Performance of SSIs, 1981–82–2014–15 9.7
Table 9.5: Distribution of MSMEs – Activity wise and Rural-Urban wise 9.7
Table 9.6: Share of SSI Sector in Exports (in $ Crore) 9.8
Table 9.7 : Scheduled Commercial Banks' Advances to Small-Scale Industries and Allied Services Outstanding (Balance Outstanding) 9.9
Table 10.1: Plan Allocations and Actual Outlay for the Sector (in ₹ crore) 10.3
Table 10.2: Roads and Rail Network: Growth 10.4
Table 10.3: Road Network by Categories (in kilometres) 10.5
Table 10.4: Category-wise Number of Registered Motor Vehicles in India: 1951–2017 (numbers in thousand) 10.5
Table 10.5: Plan Outlays/Expenditure on Railways (In ₹ crore) 10.10
Table 10.6: Civil Aviation: Domestic and International Services 10.16
Table 10.7: Expansion of Postal Network and Telephone Connections 10.19
Table 10.8: Growth and Development of Telecom Facilities since 1991 10.24
Table 10.9: Sectoral Break-up of Employm ent (1993–94, 1999–2000 & 2004–05) 10.31
Table 11.1: Production of Energy in India by Commercial Sources 11.4
Table 11.2: Imports of Petroleum and Other Related Products 11.5
Table 11.3: Electricity: Progress of Installed Capacity (Utilities and Non-utilities) (in Thousand MW) 11.6
Table 11.4: Gross Generation of Electricity from Utilities and Non-Utilities in India (Billion KWh) 11.7
Table 11.5: Installed Capacity of Renewable Energy sources (In Thousand MW) 11.7
Table 11.6: Progress of Rural Electrification: 1950-51 to 2016-17. 11.14
Table 12.1: Number of Internet Users per 1,000 people 12.3
Table 12.2: Performance of IT Industry in the Ninth Plan (1997–2002) (₹ crore) 12.4
Table 12.3: Internet Usage, Broadband Subscribers, and Mobile Subscribers in India 12.9
Table 12.4: IT Software and Services Exports (in US$ Billion) 12.10
Table 12.5: Employment in IT-ITeS Industry (in million) 12.10
Table 13.1: Gross and Net Non-Performing Assets of Scheduled Commercial Banks – Group-wise (Amount in $ Crore) 13.7
Table 13.2: Aggregate Public Deposits of the NBFC Sector (In ₹ Crore) 13.12

Table 13.3:	Position of Households Availing Banking Services	13.24
Table 14.1:	Share of Tax and Non-tax Revenue in Total Revenue of Central Government (in ₹ crore)	14.7
Table 14.2:	Direct and Indirect Tax Revenue of Central Government (in ₹ crore)	14.8
Table 14.3:	Tax–GDP Ratios	14.9
Table 14.4:	India's Internal Debt and Liabilities (in ₹ crore)	14.10
Table 14.5:	Central Government's Gross Fiscal Deficit (in ₹ crore)	14.11
Table 14.6:	Revenue from Service Tax	14.13
Table 14.7:	Fiscal Deficit as Percentage of GDP	14.15
Table 14.8:	Trends in Major Subsidies (in ₹ crore)	14.16
Table 15.1:	India's Foreign Trade: 1950–51 to 1990–91 (in ₹ crore)	15.5
Table 15.2:	India's Foreign Exchange Reserves (in ₹ crore)	15.6
Table 15.3:	Export–Import Ratio and Percentage of Exports/Imports to the GDP	15.7
Table 15.4:	(a):Total Exports and Imports, Trade–GDP Ratio, Export–Import Ratio and Percentage of Exports/Imports to the GDP	15.8
Table 15.4:	(b): Total Exports and Imports, Trade balance	15.8
Table 15.5:	Trade Deficit–GDP Ratio	15.9
Table 15.6:	India's Foreign Exchange Reserves (Figures are in ₹crore)	15.11
Table 15.7:	India's Share in World Exports (US $ million)	15.17
Table 15.8:	Comparative Share of Selected Countries in World Exports (Percentage)	15.17
Table 15.9:	(a) Imports 1951–61 (Annual average in ₹ crore)	15.18
Table 15.9:	(b) Pattern of Exports: 1951–60 (₹ crore)	15.18
Table 15.9:	(c) Pattern of Exports of Principal Items: 1970–91 (Value of exports in ₹ crore)	15.19
Table 15.10:	Direction of India's Trade by Country-Groups (Value in ₹ crore)	15.20
Table 16.1:	Labour Force Participation Rate based on UPS approach for persons aged 15 years and above (per cent per 1000 persons)	16.6
Table 16.2:	LFPR (in per cent) according to Usual status for persons aged 15 years and above during (2017-18 and 2018-19)	16.6
Table 16.3:	Worker Population Ratio based on UPS approach for persons aged 15 years and above (per cent per 1000 persons)	16.7
Table 16.4:	Key Labour Force Estimates according to Usual Principal Status (UPS) Approach based on 2nd, 3rd, 4th and 5th Employment-Unemployment Survey	16.8
Table 16.5:	Organised and Unorganised Sectors and Formal and Informal Employment (million)	16.12
Table 16.6:	India's Population in 2011 (Age-group-wise)	16.31
Table 17.1:	Population below Poverty line in 1972–73 and 1977–78 (in percentage)	17.21

Table 17.2:	(a): Poverty Ratio and Number of Poor: Expert Group (Lakdawala) Method	17.22
Table 17.2:	(b): Poverty Estimates in 2009-10 and 2011-12	17.24
Table 17.3:	(a): Performance under Mahatma Gandhi National Rural	17.28
Table 17.3:	(b): Budget Allocation for MNREG scheme (₹ in crore)	17.29
Table 17.4:	Sex Ratio – India and Selected States	17.36
Table 17.5:	(a): Infant Mortality Rate (By Sex) - 1961 – 2019 (per 1,000 live births)	17.37
Table 17.5:	(b): Under 5 Mortality Rate (By Sex) -1990 – 2019 (per 1,000 live births)	17.37
Table 17.6:	Life Expectancy at Birth (In Years)-Developed & Emerging Countries	17.38
Table 17.7:	Life Expectancy at Birth (In Years) – India	17.39
Table 17.8:	Literacy in India (In Percentage)	17.39
Table 17.9:	Gross Enrolment Ratio in Primary, Upper Primary and Secondary Stages (In Percentage)	17.40
Table 18.1:	Demographic Data of India, 1901–2011	18.7
Table 18.2:	(a) India—Vital Statistics: (1911–1990)	18.7
Table 18.2:	(b): India: Vital Statistics: 2001–2014	18.8
Table 18.3:	Performance of Selected States on Population Control	18.9
Table 18.4:	Demographic Profile of India Age-Specific Population Data (1961–2011) (In Million)	18.11
Table 18.5:	(a): Total population of China & India-1950-2020 (in million)	18.13
Table 18.5:	(b): Average Annual Rate of Population Growth – 1950 – 2020 in China and India (percentage)	18.13
Table 18.6:	Population and Rate of Growth of Population of Selected Countries	18.15
Table 18.7:	Urban Population	18.16
Table 18.8:	Birth Rate, Death Rate, and Infant Mortality Rate (IMR) in Selected Countries	18.16
Table 18.9:	Life Expectancy in Selected Countries	18.17
Table 18.10:	(a): Decadal Population Growth Rate in Advanced Countries: 1950 - 2020	18.18
Table 18.10:	(b): Decadal Population Growth Rate in Emerging Economies: 1950 - 2020	18.18
Table 19.1:	Comparative Performance of Selected Countries	19.3
Table 19.2:	Economic & Social Indicators for Selected States/UTs	19.4
Table 19.3(a):	Developed Countries—Sectoral Share in GDP (Per Cent)	19.9
Table 19.3(b):	Developing Countries—Sectoral Share in GDP (Per Cent)	19.9
Table 19.4:	Developed and Developing Countries: Sectoral Share in Employment (Per Cent)	19.10
Table 19.5:	India—Sectoral Shares in GDP at Factor Cost (per cent)	19.11
Table 19.6:	India—Sectoral Shares in Employment (in per cent)	19.11
Table 20.1:	World Trade—Exports and Imports (in US$ billion)	20.12

Table 20.2:	India's Trade with ASEAN Group (In $ billion)	20.24
Table 20.3:	Electricity: Installed capacity (Percentage share)	20.39
Table 22.1:	Transformation Readiness framework	22.21
Table 22.2:	Time taken for Resolving Insolvency (in years) -Data for 2019	22.26
Table 22.3:	Ease of Doing Business – Ranks in 2020	22.26
Table 24.1:	PMGSY Programme (2000 - 2017)	24.5
Table 24.2:	Sales of Electric Vehicles in FY 2020 and FY 2021	24.7
Table 24.3:	Total Number of Airline Passengers (Domestic & International) (Including Departures and Arrivals)	24.14
Table 24.4:	Shipping Sector – India & China	24.15
Table 24.5:	Installed Generation Capacity (Fuel-wise) As on 31.08.2021	24.21
Table 25.1:	Pradhan Mantri Jan Dhan Yojana (Accounts Opened from 2016 to 2021)	25.3
Table 25.2:	Number and Value of Currencies in Circulation	25.20
Table 26.1:	(a): Number of Female Teachers per 100 Male Teachers (2011-12)	26.3
Table 26.1:	(b): Percentage of Teachers who are Female (%)- India & Selected Countries	26.4
Table 26.2:	Percentage of Schools with Girls' Toilet (2015-16)	26.4
Table 26.3:	Plan Outlays on Education and Health	26.10
Table 26.4:	Infant Mortality Rates and Maternal Mortality Ratios in India and Selected Countries	26.11
Table 26.5:	(a): Three Tier System of Rural Healthcare Infrastructure	26.12
Table 26.5:	(b): Number of PHCs, SCs, and CHCs	26.13
Tables 26.6	(a) and (b) show the position in respect of rural health infrastructure in selected states.	26.14
Table 26.6:	(a): Health Infrastructure in Rural Areas: Group I States	26.14
Table 26.6:	(b): Health facilities in Rural Areas: Group II States	26.14
Table 26.7:	(a): Human Resources for Health	26.15
Table 26.7:	(b): Health Infrastructure	26.15
Table 26.8:	Trends in India's Public Expenditure on Health	26.18
Table 26.9:	Health Expenditure (as % of GDP) and Per capita expenditure on Health - 2017 International comparison	26.19
Table 26. 10:	Progress of Jal Jeevan Mission (as on Oct 13, 2021)	26.24
Table 26.11:	Performance under CSR between 2014-15 and 2019-20 (₹ crore)	26.32
Table 26.12:	Amount Spent under CSR – Development Sector-wise (Figures in ₹ crore)	26.32

List of Box Items

Box 1.1:	Progress of India on Socio-Economic indicators in Pre-independent and Post-independent period	1.13
Box 2.1:	East Asian Recovery	2.10
Box 2.2:	India's growth story prior to, and after, 1991 economic reforms	2.12
Box 3.1:	Bhoodan Movement	3.3
Box 5.1:	Nationalisation of Banks	5.10
Box 6.1:	Liberalisation and Inequality	6.12
Box 6.2:	Salient features of 1991 Economic reforms	6.13
Box 7.1:	Food Processing Industry in India	7.14
Box 7.2:	Farmer Producer Organisations (FPOs)	7.19
Box 7.3:	Agrarian scene, Farm Reforms and Farm Laws	7.36
Box 7.4:	Integrated Farming	7.43
Box 8.1:	Privatisation and Disinvestment of Public Sector Enterprises	8.18
Box 9.1:	Tiruppur: An Indian Success Story	9.10
Box 9.2:	Constraints Faced By The MSME Sector	9.13
Box 9.3:	MSME Sector in Selected Countries	9.18
Box 10.1:	Indian Railways: A Massive Network	10.10
Box 10.2:	Challenges and rise of the telecom sector in India	10.25
Box 10.3:	Open RAN system	10.29
Box 10.4:	International North-South Transport Corridor (INSTC) - A case study	10.32
Box 11.1:	Power Sector Reforms	11.19
Box 12.1:	Evolution of the Computer	12.2
Box 12.2:	Software Technology Parks	12.7
Box 12.3:	Digital India Programme	12.11
Box 13.1:	Wholesale and Consumer Price Index	13.13
Box 13.2:	Monetary Policy Transmission in India	13.18
Box 14.1:	Role of Fiscal Policy in an Economy	14.4
Box 14.2:	Features of a Sound Tax System and Tax Policy	14.5
Box 14.3:	15th Finance Commission	14.23
Box 14.4:	Retrospective Taxation and its Consequences	14.26
Box 14.5:	Implications of Taxing Agriculture Sector	14.27
Box 15.1:	The Theory of Comparative Advantage	15.2
Box 15.2:	Foreign Exchange (forex) Reserves and their Management	15.12
Box 15.3:	Capital Account Convertibility	15.14
Box 15.4:	India and Free Trade Agreements	15.28
Box 16.1:	Economists on Labour, Employment, and Productivity	16.2
Box 16.2:	Inflation and Unemployment–Phillip's Curve	16.4
Box 16.3:	ILO Global Action Programme on Domestic Workers	16.10

Box 16.4:	Labour Reforms	16.15
Box 16.5:	Highlights of Skill India Mission	16.32
Box 16.6:	Automation and Employment	16.34
Box 17.1:	The Constitution of India on Equality and Social Justice	17.2
Box 17.2:	India's Five Year Plans on Inequality, Poverty and Social Justice Social Justice	17.9
Box 17.3:	Economists and Welfarism	17.12
Box 17.4:	Economists on Inequality and Distributive Justice	17.15
Box 17.5:	Growth and Inequality–the Asian Experience	17.18
Box 17.6:	MNREGS – An Assessment of the Programme	17.27
Box 17.7:	Universal Basic Income	17.43
Box 17.8:	Growth and Inequality: Kuznet's Hypothesis and A Global Perspective	17.51
Box 18.1:	Economists on Population Issue	18.2
Box 18.2:	The Global Problem of Declining Population	18.18
Box 18.3:	Demographic Changes in US and Europe	18.20
Box 19.1:	Planning in China	19.2
Box 19.2:	Regional Balance in Development	19.12
Box 19.3:	Brundtland Commission	19.14
Box 19.4:	NITI Aayog's Working: A Critical Assessment	19.19
Box 19.5:	India's Growth Pattern	19.21
Box 19.6:	Contribution of Dr V.K.R.V. Rao on India's National Income Accounts – An Evaluation –	19.22
Box 20.1:	Note on Trade Agreements	20.27
Box 20.2:	Carbon Sink and Forest Cover	20.40
Box 20.3:	El Nino and La Nina and Asian Economies	20.42
Box 21.1:	One District One Product (ODOP)	21.7
Box 22.1:	Ease of Doing Business	22.27
Box 23.1:	Atal Innovation Mission (AIM)	23.10
Box 24.1:	National Highway Projects: Funding and Execution	24.3
Box 24.2:	India's Automobile Market: Salient Facts	24.7
Box 24.3:	Promoting Electric Vehicles in India	24.8
Box 24.4:	India's Renewable Energy Scenario	24.22
Box 24.5:	Status of the Telecommunications Sector (as of May 2021)	24.25
Box 24.6:	National Monetisation Pipeline (NMP)	24.28
Box 24.7:	Economic Growth and Employment: Role of Infrastructure	24.31
Box 25.1:	Setting up of Bad bank: The Objectives and Implications	25.9
Box 25.2:	GST Statistics (as on October 3, 2021)	25.39
Box 25.3:	In what way is the Goods and Taxes (GST) regime more beneficial for the economy than the previous system of indirect taxes? Bring out the relative merits and demerits of the two systems of indirect taxation.	25.40

Box 26.1: School Toilets Constructed under Swachh Vidyalaya Abhiyan by CPSEs: An Audit Report 26.5

Box 26.2: National Education Policy (NEP) 2020 26.7

Box 26.3: Progress of PMAY – Urban and Grameen Housing Scheme 26.21

Box 26.4: Jal Jeevan Mission for Water Supply 26.22

Box 26.5: JJM: Factsheet on the Scheme and Progress (as of October 2021) 26.23

PART-I

1947-1990

Chapter 1 The Colonial Legacy

Chapter 2 India at Independence and After

Chapter 3 Agriculture in India before and after the green revolution

Chapter 4 Industrial Policy and development

Chapter 5 Banking and Finance

CHAPTER

THE COLONIAL LEGACY

- India's position prior to colonial rule
- Industrial Revolution and its impact on India
- Agrarian scene and Land tenure systems
- Commercialisation of agriculture
- Deindustrialisation of India
- Industrial and Trade policy
- Assessment of colonial rule
- India's progress in colonial era and post-independence

❑ INTRODUCTION

The colonial rule in India lasted for over 200 years. After the Portuguese arrived towards the end of 15th century—Vasco da Gama landed in Calicut on the Malabar coast in 1498—came the Dutch, the British, and the French. The western powers initially set up trading posts. The Portuguese established the first European trading centre in Cochin kingdom (now in Kerala) in 1502.

As the Mughal Empire was on the decline and disintegrating in the early 18th century, there was an internecine struggle between the Mughals and the Marathas. Later, as the Maratha Empire also weakened, many relatively weak and unstable Indian states and principalities emerged which were increasingly open to manipulation by the Europeans through dependent Indian rulers.

❑ INDIA'S CAPABILITIES IN MANUFACTURES

Before the advent of the Europeans, though the primary occupation in India was agriculture, she had excellent capabilities and skills in manufacturing. There is record of Chinese merchants calling at Indian ports. In the 17th century, India was a relatively urbanized and commercialized nation with a flourishing export trade consisting of cotton textiles, silk, spices, and rice. As the old caravan route across Asia became unsafe due to lawlessness in Asia Minor, the Red Sea became the route and the Arabs on the west coast of India retained virtual monopoly of sea-borne trade until the advent of the Portuguese. The arrival of the Portuguese in 1498 gave Mohammedan merchants the opportunity to see how much more cheaply and safely goods could be carried to Europe by sea.

India's Trade in the 17th Century

By the end of the 17th century, India was the world's main producer of cotton textiles and had a substantial export trade to Britain as also to other European countries. India was renowned for the finest Dacca muslins, Cashmere shawls, Bengal silks, and Agra marbles which dazzled the eyes of the world. Cotton from Surat and the cloth of Masulipatam were famous. The art of cotton spinning and weaving had attained perfection and Indian handloom had a big market in Europe. India was rich in minerals and manufacture of wrought iron had attained excellence.

Rivalry between European Colonial Powers

Once the western powers came and set up trading establishments, there was intense rivalry between them for economic and political dominance. In 1672, the French established themselves at Pondicherry (now known as Puducherry) and the stage was set for rivalry between the British and the French for control of Indian trade. The British began to compete with the Portuguese, the Dutch, and the French. Through a combination of outright confrontation and deft alliances with local princes, the East India Company gained supremacy and effectively began its rule in India in 1757. Soon the British also gained control of all European trade in India.

❑ THE EAST INDIA COMPANY

It was a private company owned by stockholders and reporting to a board of directors in London. The Company consolidated its hold over large parts of India in the 18th and 19th centuries by fighting against the Sikhs, the Marathas, and the Mysore kings. They also did outright annexation or control of princely states by asserting their power through treaties and alliances.The Indian rulers acknowledged the Company's hegemony in return for limited internal autonomy and on being assured of their defence and protection by the Company.

Steadily Increasing Role

Initially vested with virtual monopoly on trade, the Company steadily took on governmental powers with its own army and judiciary. It seldom generated profit, as employees mismanaged and misappropriated the funds. The British government had little control over it. But the gross abuses committed by the Company officials came to be questioned by the British Government and eventually a Governor-General was appointed in 1773 for administering and overseeing the Company's operations in India. With increased British power in India, the supervision of Indian affairs by the British Crown and Parliament also increased. The company was gradually divested of both commercial and political control. Its commercial monopoly was broken in 1813, and from 1834 it was merely a managing agency for the British government of India. It was deprived of that role also after the Indian Mutiny of 1857. Following the mutiny, the East India Company which had ruled much of India for a century was dissolved, and Britain's possessions and protectorates on the Indian Subcontinent were formally incorporated into the British Empire.

Industrial Revolution and its Impact

A series of inventions which took place in the West, particularly in Britain, between 1740 and 1860 brought about a major transformation in industrial production, especially in the textile industry. During the first phase of the Industrial Revolution, inventions like spinning jenny by James Hargreaves, water frame for spinning by Richard Arkwright, and spinning mule by Samuel Crompton revolutionised the textile industry in Britain. It made production faster and more organised. Many other sectors like metallurgy, machine tools, chemicals, paper, and glass too underwent change and were modernised in their processes. This was followed by a second wave of Industrial Revolution with the invention of steam engine by James Watt and steam locomotive by George Stephenson which ushered in the modern means of transportation by railways.

The Factory System in Production

These transformational developments paved the way for the new factory system where production methods underwent a sea change leading to much higher productivity and lower costs of production. It transformed the industrial conditions not only in Europe but in other parts of the world. These inventions revolutionized the industrial methods of the great powers and brought about perceptible progress and changes in trade and commerce. England's shipping opened up new markets and an unlimited supply of her manufactures found their way to these markets. England's enormous profits, industrial and commercial, made her a financial and economic powerhouse, which further strengthened her position as an imperial power.

How the Factory System Affected India

In the face of these changes and mass production, India, with her traditional manufacturing methods, could not withstand the intense competition from Britain. English shipping opened up new markets and products manufactured in the factories in Britain were dumped on markets in India and other countries in Asia. While hitherto, India exported many of these products to the West, the trend was drastically reversed. India became the exporter of raw materials to feed the factories in Britain and importer of finished goods. Industries in India were crippled and workers devoid of skill and expertise, and handicapped for want of capital and modern machinery, were thrown out of jobs. Many of these workers had to fall back upon agriculture which was already under much stress. India which was once famous for the manufacture of the most delicate fabrics in the world, became a purely agricultural country exporting raw materials and food items.

❑ CONSOLIDATION OF BRITISH RULE

Before examining the economic conditions during the 19th century, it is pertinent to note the steps the British administration in India took to tighten their grip over the native population, which had a deep and enduring impact on Indian society. While the traditional institutions like the village society, the caste system, and joint families remained unaffected, certain other visible changes took place. A significant step was the introduction of English education based on the 'Minute on Indian Education' prepared by **Thomas Macaulay** in 1835. This gradually created a new class of westernized populace which served the British interests in India. The system of District administration also took firm root headed largely by British officials. Indians were appointed to lower posts in civil administration and the judiciary. In due course, the higher posts and the coveted Civil service were also thrown open to Indians. The colonial masters extended their patronage to the Princely states and the rich landholding classes to win over their support and loyalty. The Army manned by British officers and troops formed a deterrent force to keep any resistance from the natives at bay.

❑ THE AGRARIAN SCENE AND LAND TENURE

The East India Company tried to set aside the Zamindari system prevalent during the Mughal period and collect land taxes either directly through company officials, or through revenue-farmers, who collected the rent from peasants and paid a lumpsum to the government. The new system led to widespread corruption and repression at the hands of officials and the peasants suffered much hardship.

❑ THE PERMANENT SETTLEMENT ACT

To reform the system, **Lord Cornwallis** who was appointed as Governor-General in 1786 decided to restore the old system and introduced the 'Permanent Settlement Act' in 1793 in Bengal which included the present states of Bihar and Orissa. Under this system, proprietary and hereditary rights over the land were granted to the zamindars and some dominant families in the villages. In return, they had to pay the government rent which they collected from the tenant-farmers. In many places, lower class families were usually sub-tenants of intermediary owners of land, rather than direct tenants of the zamindars. Often there were multiple layers of tenancy between the zamindars and landlords and the actual tiller. Sub-tenants had no security of tenure and were in many instances exploited by rack-renting by the intermediaries and moneylenders.

The Mahalwari and Ryotwari System

In the northern India, in Punjab, the Gangetic plains of U.P., and parts of Central India, a system called 'Mahalwari' was introduced under which a village or a group of villages was responsible for paying the revenue assessed by the government. While in the western and southern parts of India, viz., Bombay and Madras Presidencies, another system known as 'Ryotwari' came into vogue. Under the ryotwari system, the big zamindars were dispossessed of their lands, and property rights and tax obligations were vested in the peasants. However, these peasants (ryots) were also in many cases the dominant families in the villages who had sub-tenants under them.

These systems of land tenure created vested interests with a class of landed gentry–zamindars, jagirdars, and other dominant groups–with large landholdings who were loyal to the colonial masters. This land tenure system was exploitative in nature and did little good to Indian agriculture. The number of landless labour increased. While incomes in villages increased, the disparities in income also widened. The role of moneylenders became more prononuced. A majority of farmers, and labour who worked for them did not possess the know-how to adopt improved farming methods.

Problems in Agriculture

Agriculture was the only occupation in the villages and three-fourths of the country's population depended on farming. And most parts of the country being dependent on monsoon, which was uncertain and unpredictable even in those days, agriculture was beset with many problems. There were several occurrences of famine in different parts of the country in the 19th century. Though the government made efforts to improve farming practices such as use of hybrid seeds, providing irrigation facilities, etc., these efforts were directed primarily to enhance the production of those items which would serve as raw material for the mills and factories in Britain. By such measures, India's economy was adversely affected leading to discontentment among the people. It was not until the early part of the 20th century that any organized research in agriculture was initiated to improve the farming methods, with the setting up of the Imperial Agriculture Research Institute at Pusa in Bihar in 1905 (which was later shifted to Delhi where it functions now). Due to such neglect, farm productivity and yields remained low and stagnant for long. As the farming was mostly at subsistence level and for self-consumption, there was little scope for ploughing back any capital for investment to improve the systems and increase production.

Irrigation in The Colonial Era

In India, rivers have played an important role in national and local life. Successful agriculture would not have been possible in most parts of the country without utilising the river waters. Evidence exists to the practice of irrigation in India many centuries back. The Grand Anicut is an ancient dam built on the Kaveri river in Tamil Nadu by the Chola king, Karikala Chola in the 2nd century A.D. to divert the waters of the Kaveri across the fertile delta region for irrigation via canals. The large numbers of tanks, which are found in the Deccan, have been in existence for ages. The Yamuna canals were constructed originally around the 14th century.

Tanks and Canals for Irrigation

One redeeming feature of the policy followed by the British to improve agriculture was in regard to irrigation. According to Planning Commission document on the First Five-Year Plan (1951-56), around 1850, about two million acres of land were irrigated by several indigenous irrigation works. These works were in the form of small tanks in southern India, inundation canals in northern India, and reconditioned canals like the Cauvery delta system in Madras (now Tamil Nadu) and the Yamuna canals. About five million acres were under well irrigation at that time, mostly in northern India. The first major irrigation work constructed in India was the Ganga Canal in Uttar Pradesh, opened for irrigation in 1854. This was followed by the Upper Bari Doab canal in the Punjab and the Godavari and Krishna delta systems in Madras Presidency. A number of other large irrigation works were constructed towards the end of the 19th and the beginning of the 20^{th}century. One of the prominent personalities behind some of the major irrigation projects in British India was Sir Arthur Cotton, an engineer who built a dam on Kaveri and the massive dams on Godavari and Krishna rivers in Andhra Pradesh in the middle of the 19th century for which he is still revered by people in those regions. Another great personality was Sir M. Visvesaraya who built the Krishnaraja Sagar dam across Kaveri river in the then Mysore (now Karnataka) state.

Commercialisation of Agriculture

Rice was the staple crop while wheat, millets (mainly jowar and bajra), maize, pulses, and oilseeds were also grown in different parts of India. Rice was the major item among the foodgrains exported from India. A significant aspect of the economic policies followed by the British rulers was the cultivation of a variety of crops of commercial importance and value such as tea, coffee, tobacco, indigo, opium, cotton, jute, and sugarcane. These crops were introduced with different motives. The area under cotton cultivation, including the native states, increased from 14.5 million acres in 1900 to 25 million acres in 1913. Indian opium was exported mainly to China but by 1913, this export was discontinued at the behest of China. Thereafter, opium produced was used for internal consumption and for export to some other countries for medicinal purposes. Indigo was sent to England and used as a dyeing agent for cloth produced in Britain. Unfortunately, cultivation of indigo sapped the fertility of land for some years which acted as a disincentive for the farmers to cultivate it. In the plantations, the ownership changed hands quite often. And many of the plantations were controlled by the British firms who invested capital in them. The workers on these plantations worked under severe hardships.

> The main reasons for the backwardness of agriculture in the pre-Independence period was due to the feudal system of control of land by the zamindars, who did not invest capital for improvements, sub-tenancy of lands with no security of tenure and oppressive rents extracted, and indebtedness of farmers and harassment by moneylenders.

Agricultural Growth in the Colonial Era

Agricultural performance in the colonial era was dismal and the annual growth rate of agricultural output was negligible. Any absolute increase in production was mainly due to increase in acreage under cultivation. Also, farmers holding more fertile and irrigated lands shifted from food crops to non-food, commercial crops which yielded better returns, thus adversely affecting food production. Between

1911 and 1941, the rate of increase of crop yield per acre was almost nil. There were also inter-regional differences in yields. Between 1921 and 1941, while the population increased from 251.3 million to 318.6 million, food output failed to keep pace resulting in acute food shortages and declining availability of food per head. The main reasons for the backwardness of agriculture in the pre-Independence period was due to the feudal system of control of land by the zamindars, who did not invest capital for improvements, sub-tenancy of lands with no security of tenure and oppressive rents extracted, and indebtedness of farmers and harassment by moneylenders.

In times of drought and famines caused mainly by the failure of monsoon, the rural community suffered the most.

❑ INDUSTRIAL POLICY

As stated earlier, while the native industries and manufacturing flourished until the 17-18th centuries, their steady decline started once the British rule started. Only a few cotton textile and jute mills existed in India during the 19th century. Though a steel-making plant, the Bengal Iron Works, was started in 1870, it could not withstand the competition from imported steel and the plant did not survive.With a view to promoting their industries in Britain, there was a deliberate and affirmative policy adopted to discourage industrial development in India. This process got intensified after the Industrial Revolution when British industries needed raw materials for their industries like textiles, iron and steel and metallurgy, and the introduction of railways which facilitated easy movement of goods over long distances. The net result was the draining away of the natural resources of India and impeding the growth of India.

The textile industry of India too had to face stiff competition from items manufactured in Britain. Raw cotton was exported from India and cloth made in British mills were dumped on India crippling the local mills. Though Britain possessed the know-how of steel manufacture, no step was taken to build an iron and steel plant in India, despite India having rich iron ore and coal deposits. Whatever little industrialization had taken place in India during the period was due to the initiative and enterprise of Indians. The Iron and Steel plant pioneered by Jamshedji Tata opened in 1907 at Jamshedpur and the few cotton and jute mills in the country were prime examples of this.

Deindustrialisation of India

That Indian manufacturing suffered serious setback following the Industrial Revolution has been already mentioned. Apart from trying to secure a monopolistic trading position, Britain sought to source raw materials from India and turn India into a free market for her manufactured products. The British companies which invested in banking and shipping services virtually enjoyed monopoly. The Indian handloom industry which had flourished earlier suffered decline as the factory-manufactured textile products imported from Britain were of superior quality and cheaper. It was not until 1850's that textile mills could be set up in India with financial, technical and managerial help from the British. It was around the same time that few jute mills came up in Calcutta.

Before the British arrived, India had seafaring prowess and a thriving shipping and ship-building sector. Till the mid-18th century, Indian ships plied the Arabian sea and the Bay of Bengal carrying sizeable goods and products. After 1757, the East India Company took control over much of these and gave rights to British ships. Duties were imposed on Indian merchant vessels which crippled them and Indian vessels were confined to coastal shipping carrying low-value native products. Even the shipping company pioneered before World War I by V.O. Chidambaram Pillai, a staunch nationalist, in South India was not allowed to succeed. Pillai was jailed for his nationalist activities and the shipping company was eventually liquidated.

The colonial administration persisted with a policy that prevented industrialization of the country, despite the rich natural resources the country had, in order to promote and protect British industry. The natural resources were exploited in a rampant manner and shipped to Britain to feed her domestic industry which leaders like Dadabhai Naoroji condemned. The British also deliberately neglected imparting technical education and managerial training to Indians. Even in the Bombay textile industry, where most of the capital was Indian, a good percentage of the managerial and supervisory staff were British thus keeping a firm control over it. (For more on this, see under 'Assessment of Colonial Rule – The Negative Impact' in a later section in this chapter).

The First Steps of Industrialisation

It was only in the first half on the 20th century that some semblance of industrialization took place. This was due to the growing resentment among the nationalist leaders and the intense pressure brought to bear upon the government by them. A few like-minded and enlightened British administrators in India, who were sympathetic to India's cause, too lent their support to these nationalist sentiments. As a result, came up the second Iron and Steel plant at Burnpur in West Bengal in 1918. A few sugar mills, cement, and paper factories too came up during this period. **The Great Depression** of 1930's which impacted the western nations adversely, and the two World Wars also gave a fillip to these industries due to growing demand and the necessity to look for alternative sources of supply. One positive outcome of these industrial ventures, however limited they were, was that it helped to nurture a breed of promising Indian industrialists and entrepreneurs who laid the foundations upon which India could build further after independence. This positive trend also helped to develop a pool of managerial and technical talent among Indians and also build a base of technically skilled labourforce.

As observed by the Planning Commission, between 1922 when the policy of discriminating protection was adopted and 1939, the production of cotton piece goods, steel ingots, and paper went up substantially. With regard to sugar, in a span of 4 years from 1932 to 1936, the country was able to produce enough to meet its entire requirements. By 1935-36, the cement industry also could meet 95 per cent of the total consumption in the country. The production of matches, glass, vanaspati, soap, and light engineering industries also recorded large increases. Towards the close of the inter-war period, the manufacture of electrical equipment and goods was also initiated. It will thus be seen that prior to independence, there were virtually no capital goods industries and almost all the industries that came up were in the consumer goods sector. Without basic and capital goods sector, India could not have industrialized in any significant manner. No wonder that in 1950, India had to meet 90 per cent of its requirements of machinery and machine tools through imports.

It will thus be seen that prior to independence, there were virtually no capital goods industries and almost all the industries that came up were in the consumer goods sector. Without basic and capital goods sector, India could not have industrialized in any significant manner. No wonder that in 1950, India had to meet 90 per cent of its requirements of machinery and machine tools through imports.

It may be noted that by 1947, industry and manufacturing accounted for minimal share in the national income of the country. According to the Planning Commission, in 1948-49, factory establishments accounted for only 6.6 per cent of the total national income. The backwardness of the Indian economy is also reflected in the skewed occupational pattern. At the beginning of the First Five-Year Plan, about

68 per cent of the working population was engaged in agriculture, about 14 per cent in industry (large and small scale), and about 18 per cent in trade and transport and other professions and services.

Before independence, the services and part of the industrial sector was dominated and controlled by the British who brought in capital and invested in them. Most of the ventures in which they invested catered to British interests and foreign markets. Petroleum and mining companies, tea and coffee plantations, banking, insurance and mercantile firms, and shipping companies were all run by the British with the top management consisting of Englishmen. A good portion of the profits of these companies were repatriated to Britain. Remittances made by the foreign personnel in these companies and by those in the military and civil administration in India and their pensionary liabilities also caused a heavy drain on the wealth of India.

A Trade Policy Against Indian interests

The trade policy adopted by the British administration was weighted against Indian interests. The import of Indian goods to Europe was repressed by prohibitive duties to prevent them from gaining competitive advantage while the export of British goods to India was supported by nominal duties. England herself had followed a policy of 'Protection' until her nascent industries had reached a stage when they no longer needed protection.

During the First World War, lack of British imports strengthened the hold of Indian firms on the home market for textiles and steel. After the war, under nationalist pressure, the colonial government started to favour Indian enterprise in its purchase of stores and it agreed to create a tariff commission in 1921 which started raising tariffs for protective reasons.

The Indian Fiscal Commission, 1921–22 was tasked to study all aspects of the Tariff policy of the Government of India. While five Members of the Commission gave a dissenting note arguing for a policy of 'unqualified protection', the Commission finally recommended the adoption of a policy 'protection with discrimination in the best interests of India'. By 1925, the average tariff level was 14 per cent compared with 5 per cent pre-war. The procedure for fixing tariffs was lengthy and tariff protection was granted more readily to foreign-owned companies than to Indian firms. British imports were accorded a margin of preference.

In spite of its constant favourable balance of trade, India acquired substantial debts. By 1939 foreign assets in India amounted to $2.8 billion, in the form of government debt and foreign direct investment mainly in tea, other plantations and the jute industry. The 'drain' of funds to England continued during the interwar period (1920-40) because of home charges and profit remittances. But during the Second World War, India's financial position was transformed.

Not a Debtor Country at Independence

A significant aspect of Indian economy at the time of Independence was that India was not a debtor country. By the end of the World War II (1939-45), India had liquidated its foreign public debt of ₹ 450 crore and accumulated **Sterling balances** of over ₹ 1,700 crore. This foreign exchange asset was on account of purchases made by Britain in India for her requirements for the war. This asset came quite handy after independence to pay for imports and developmental purposes.

❑ ASSESSMENT OF COLONIAL RULE

Introduction

The advent of the Western powers in the 16th and 17th centuries had a cataclysmic impact on the Indian subcontinent and changed the very course of its history. The existence of disparate kingdoms and many warring princely states, lack of unity and a sense of nationhood among them, and a subservient attitude adopted by them towards the foreign powers, only made it easier for the foreign powers to establish and entrench themselves in the country. Starting with just trading interests, the British, and to a lesser extent the French and the Portuguese, systematically intruded into other areas, set up enclaves, and tightened their control until they gained supremacy.

The Positives and Negatives

The Positive Impact

While the British rule for over 200 years did have some positive impact on India, in retrospect, the negative fall-out far outweighed the positive outcomes. On the positive side, the British introduced a modern administrative, legal, and judicial system, but even in regard to this, these systems were more attuned to serve the interests of colonial rulers and suppress the interests of India. They also introduced English language and western model of education with accent on emerging modern ideas of the 19th and 20th centuries.

After George Stephenson's invention of steam locomotive, railways had become popular in Britain by 1840, Samuel Morse had refined electric telegraph and telegraph codes by 1838, and Graham Bell had invented telephone by 1876. The British promptly introduced railways and telegraphy in India by the 1850's, and the telephone in 1882. While all these, indeed, benefitted India, these were also done partly to serve the interests of colonial rulers. Railways helped various raw materials to be carried faster to the Indian ports from where they were shipped to Britain to feed the home industries. Telegraph and later telephone enabled much faster exchange of communications and this also enabled the British administration to keep a tight grip over the native population, and in putting down any unrest or rebellion against their rule. Needless to say, it helped to prolong the colonial rule.

Though the British introduced modern education, they did not lay adequate emphasis on education in science and technology nor in developing the skills of Indian labour. Also they did not encourage modern industries to come up as that would have pitted their industries at home in direct competition with Indian industries which had the advantage of not only a wealth of natural resources but cheaper labour.

The Negative Impact

The colonial administration exploited the country and its natural resources to serve their economic interests back home. The native manufactures, handicrafts, and cottage industries, which had flourished and were exporting their products until the arrival of foreign powers in the 17th century, gradually declined and were allowed to die. This threw lakhs of workers out of their occupation and impoverished them. It may be argued that with the Industrial Revolution unfolding in the West in the 18-19th centuries leading to modern, faster and cost-effective methods of production, India's native industries would have anyway faced competition and not survived even if India was not under colonial rule. But an independent India would have, with the passage of time, imbibed the technical know-how and these modern means of production and emerged as an industrial power. Though the British introduced modern education, they did not lay adequate emphasis on education in science and technology nor in developing the skills of Indian labour. Also they did not encourage modern industries to come up as that would have pitted their industries at home in direct competition with Indian industries which had the advantage of not only a wealth of natural resources but cheaper labour.

As discussed earlier, during the colonial period, India hardly had any industrial development. The textile industry was largely unable to withstand the competition of modern mills of Manchester.

Dadabhai Naoroji and other leaders raised their voice against the exploitation and misrule of the colonial regime which sapped the nation's energy and vitality and impoverished her. Many of them wrote copiously against the injustices perpetrated by the British in India. Dadabhai Naoroji's monumental work itself was titled '*Poverty and Un-British Rule in India*' wherein he spelt out his economic ideas. And then followed the long-drawn struggle for freedom which culminated in independence in 1947 to make India the most populous democracy.

❑ WHAT IF INDIA HAD *NOT* BEEN COLONISED?

Having studied the positive and negative aspects of the colonial rule, a question that naturally arises is: What would have been the condition of India had she not been colonized at all? This is a question that must be agitating the minds of many.

While no definitive answers are possible, as it is only a matter in the realm of speculation, different scenarios could be thought of. India, towards the close of the 18th century, having been in a state of disunity and disarray, with many centrifugal forces in the form of native rulers fighting among themselves, could have faced instability for an unpredictably long period. The colonial power which appeared on the scene proved to be a uniting force which is reminiscent of what the Mughals did when Babur came in the early part of the 16th century. A house that is divided is an easy prey to an intruder and history is replete with many examples for this dictum.

In such a scenario of disunity and prolonged instability, one possibility was that India would have remained in a state of under-development for long, much like what happened under the British rule. But this was unlikely as, sooner or later, nationalist forces would have emerged to pull the nation out of the quagmire. It may be noted that a galaxy of men, imbued with strong nationalistic and patriotic fervour, appeared on the firmament of India in the 19th century. They included Dadabhai Naoroji (1825-1917), Mahadev Govind Ranade (1842-1901), Dinshaw Edulji Wacha (1844-1937), Ramesh Chandra Dutt (1848-1909), Bal Gangadhar Tilak (1856-1920), Gopal Krishna Gokhale (1866-1915), and Vaman Govind Kale (1876-1946), among others. Above all, Gandhiji (1869-1948) himself belonged to this era. These great men would not have let the nation drift and fall into disarray. They would have mobilized the national sentiments of the masses which, one may visualize, would have been akin to what Gandhiji himself did accomplish under the British rule, though the means adopted may have been different. And the various princely states would have been compelled to fall in line and opt for national unity and integrity as done by Sardar Patel after independence.

If India's history had been destined to take this course, the political and economic history would have been vastly different. An independent India in the 19th century may not have had the benefit of English education or Western liberalism but these great men, along with many others like Rabindranath Tagore (1861-1941), Swami Vivekananda (1863-1902), Bhimrao Ramji Ambedkar (1891-1956), Jawaharlal Nehru (1889-1964), Sardar Vallabhbhai Patel (1875-1950), and Netaji Subhas Chandra Bose (1897-1945) would have guided the destinies of this nation and brought about social and economic progress and transformation much earlier. Of course, there would have been many challenges, the most important of which would have been the lack of a common, unifying language. And without English, India may have struggled to link up and integrate with the international community as she has been able to do now.

On the development front, India would have drawn up plans and schemes as early as from the 19th century, building on her manufacturing capabilities and handicrafts, and further modernized them with the onset of the Industrial Revolution. Technology transfer may have taken time to reach India but surely India would have taken full advantage of the railways, telegraphy, telephony, and other inventions to build a modern, vibrant economy.

It can also be conjectured that India may not have had the baggage of a colonial administration with which we are beset even now, but would have evolved one according to her own capabilities and suited to her own conditions. It is also to difficult to say whether her administration and legal system would have been as tardy as it has been as these deficiencies are, in great part, due to colonial legacy and mindset. So also it is difficult to conceive whether the scourge of corruption which has eaten into the vitals of India would have been there to the same degree. These are all imponderables for which there are no easy answers.

❑ CONCLUSION

To sum up, the colonization of India has cost the nation dear and for which the nation has had to pay a heavy price, notwithstanding some of the beneficial effects it had. But, on balance, perhaps the incalculable harm it did far outweighed the benefits it brought.

This will be evident from a comparative study of the progress attained by India on various socio-economic parameters during the 200 years of colonial rule (1757-1947) and 70 years after Independence as brought out in Box 1.1 below.

Box 1.1 Progress of India on Socio-Economic indicators in Pre-independent and Post-independent period

The statistical presentation below will amply bear out the extent to which the British colonial administration neglected the basic and genuine needs of Indian population during the rule spanning 200 years. It held back India's progress in the fields of literacy, education, health and social awareness and upliftment of people resulting in mass illiteracy, ill-health and widespread poverty. It was a deliberate policy to keep the native population in check and deprive them of substantial progress.

Whatever little improvements that may have been achieved during this period of darkness were marred by the gross neglect and indifference shown by the colonial rulers. The contrast in progress before and after independence, as seen from the data below, proves that an independent India would have recorded much more progress during these "lost years".

Apart from these data, it must be kept in mind that India faced several famines and epidemics prior to independence. It points to the state of neglect and indifference shown by the colonial administration in regard to the availability of food and its proper distribution to the masses, and in providing public health facilities (**see Section VI below**).

These and other aspects are analysed with relevant data below.

I. Literacy rates

Literacy rates were appallingly low in the case of both males and females prior to independence. Also, the rates were much worse in the case of females which would have affected their status both within home and outside. This is also a reflection on the importance attached to "literacy and education" by the colonial government in the scheme of things.

Table 1.1: Literacy rates

Year	Male	Female	Total	Year	Male	Female	Total
1901	9.8	0.7	5.4	1951	25.0	7.9	16.7
1911	10.6	1.0	5.9	1961	34.4	13.0	24.0
1921	12.2	1.8	7.2	1971	39.4	18.7	29.5
1931	15.6	2.9	9.5	1981	56.4	29.8	43.6
				1991	64.1	39.3	52.2
				2001	75.3	53.7	64.8
				2011	82.1	65.5	74.0

Source; Census of India, Registrar General of India.

After independence, India took sustained effort to improve the literacy rates. But admittedly, there have been significant gaps between the literacy rates of males and females even since 1981 (Sixth Plan period) though the gap is being somewhat reduced. **(On literacy and education, also see chapter 17, p.17.39-40).**

II. Birth rate and Death rates

Before independence, both the birth and death rates were more or less at the same level though death rate had shown decline after 1911-20 period. Birth rate declined after 1931-40. But barring for the period 1941-50, birth rate prior to independence was higher than that after independence. Besides, the death rate during the colonial period was much higher than what was achieved post-independence.

From 1951, death rate steadily came down indicating better health and medical facilities. While the birth rate held stable till 1970, it started declining after that due to intensive family planning programmes implemented.

Table 1.2: Birth rate and Death rate (per 1,000 population)

Year	Birth rate	Death rate	Year	Birth rate	Death rate
1901-10	49.2	42.6	1951-60	41.7	22.8
1911-20	48.1	47.6	1961-70	41.2	19.0
1921-30	46.4	36.3	1971-80	37.2	15.0
1931-40	45.2	31.2	1981-86	33.2	12.2
1941-50	39.9	27.4	1990-91	30.2	9.7
			2010-15	20.4	7.4

And total fertility rate (TFR), an important indicator of population control, has significantly come down since independence, and for the country as a whole, it stood at 2.2 in 2018, as against the Replacement rate of 2.1 which is the target. It is also noteworthy that many states have attained TFR below even 2.2, with rates around 1.5 to 1.7. This again is the result of sustained family planning programmes implemented from the First Plan (1951-56) to restrict family size.

III. Life Expectancy at Birth

Life expectancy was very low for both males and females prior to independence, again a reflection of the state of health and healthcare facilities. Since independence, it has shown steady improvement though it is still low compared to the rates in the advanced countries where it ranges between 75 and 80 years. Significantly, life expectancy of females is higher than that of males from 1980's.

Table 1.3: Life Expectancy at Birth

Year	Male	Female	Total	Year	Male	Female	Total
1901-10	22.6	23.3	23.0	1951-60	41.9	40.6	41.3
1911-20	19.4	20.9	20.2	1970-75	50.5	49.0	49.7
1921-30	26.9	26.6	26.8	1990-94	59.4	60.4	60.0
1931-40	32.1	31.4	31.8	2000-04	62.8	65.2	63.9
1941-50	32.4	31.7	32.1	2012-16	67.4	70.2	68.7
				2019	68.4	70.9	69.6

Source: Data from 1970-75 is from National Health Profile, 2019, Central Bureau of Health Intelligence, DGHS, Ministry of Health & Family Welfare.

IV: Percentage of Rural & Urban Population

Urbanisation is a sign of economic progress. Historically, the economic development of western Europe and north America was accomplished with continuous transfer of economic activity and people from rural to urban areas, both within and between countries. As urban industries expanded, new employment opportunities were created and, over the same period, rural manpower requirements were reduced due to labour-saving technological progress in agriculture. Although urban slums and unemployment existed in the 19th century Europe, the combination of the above two phenomena – industrialization and increased employment opportunities – enabled Western nations to undergo a major transformation through systematic rural-to-urban transfer of their human resources.

In India that did not happen during the colonial period as there was no industrialisation to the extent required to withdraw the surplus labour from agriculture to industries and services. It will be seen from data below that the percentage of rural population continued to be well over80 per cent till independence. In fact, even after independence, the percentage of rural population continued to be little above 80 percent till the middle of the Fourth Plan (1969-73).

Table 1.4: Percentage of Rural & Urban Population

Year	Rural	Urban	Total	Year	Rural	Urban	Total
1901	89.2	10.8	100.0	1951	82.7	17.3	100.0
1911	89.7	10.3	100.0	1961	82.0	18.0	100.0
1921	88.8	11.2	100.0	1971	80.1	19.9	100.0
1931	88.0	12.0	100.0	1981	76.7	23.3	100.0
1941	86.1	13.9	100.0	1991	74.3	25.7	100.0
				2001	72.2	27.8	100.0
				2011	68.2	31.8	100.0

Growth in urban population: It was only following the impact of large-scale industrialisation implemented from the Second (1956-61) and Third (1961-66) Plans that the urban population started showing increase and rural population has been declining. With expansion of Indian economy, the share of urban population is expected to rise to 39 per cent by 2036 and, according to UN projections, 50 per cent of India's population will be living in urban areas by 2050. India will need to ensure that the growth of urban population takes place in the smaller towns and newly developed townships without burdening the existing metros and large cities, and has to provide civic amenities on adequate scale for this growing urban population.

As for the percentage of people employed in the agriculture sector, it was 69.1 per cent in 1951 and even by 1983, it came down to only 65.42 per cent apparently due to the steady increase in population. But during the next three decades, it has shown substantial decline to 50.2 per cent in 2006-07 and 48.9 per cent in 2011-12. With this, the percentage of urban population has been going up though at a rather moderate pace. There is need to withdraw more workers from agriculture and employ them in industries and service sectors in a more productive way.

At the same time, India has to tackle the problem of migrant labour due to regional imbalances in development. It is ironic that the migration of labour is taking place from the mineral-rich states in eastern and central Indian states to the western and southern states. It points to lack of industrial growth in states from where there is out-migration of people on large scale in search of employment and better job opportunities. This issue came to the fore during the Covid-19 pandemic in 2020. **(For more on regional imbalances in development see Chapters 4.6, 8.4-5 and 19.11-2).**

V: Female-Male (Sex) Ratio (No. of Females per 1,000 Males)

The number of females per 1,000 males in the population, termed as "**Female-Male** (Sex) ratio" is one of the indicators of the status of women and the extent of gender equality prevailing. Advanced countries in Europe, the US, etc. have healthy sex ratio in which females outnumber males. Whereas, the Third World and developing countries in Asia and Africa have skewed sex ratio with males outnumbering females.

Sex ratio in India as per data shown below has been in favour of males both in pre- and post-independence era. In fact, the sex ratio was comparatively better before independence.

There have been very few exceptions among states with females being more than males. Kerala and Pondicherry (now called Puducherry) both had more females than males as per 2001 and 2011 census. Kerala had 1,058 females in 2001 census and 1,084 females in 2011 census to 1,000 males. And Puducherry had 1,001 females in 2001 census and 1,037 females in 2011 census to 1,000 males. Other states have all had more males than females.

The main cause for the decline in sex ratio in India is low level of literacy and education and an overtly biased attitude towards women in society including cases like female infanticide.

Table 1.5: Sex Ratio at Birth

Year	No. of Females to 1,000 Males	Year	No. of Females to 1,000 Males	Year	No. of Females to 1,000 Males
1901	972	1951	946	2001	933
1911	963	1961	941	2011	940
1921	955	1971	930	2013-15	900
1931	950	1981	934	2020	924
1941	945	1991	927		

Source: Data for years 1901 to 2011 from Census of India, Registrar General of India.
Data for 2013-15 is from Sample Registration System cited by NITI Aayog. Data for 2020 is from UN Population Division Statistics.

VI: Famines and Epidemics

Another stark contrast between the period before and after independence has been the periodic occurrence of severe famines in the pre-independence era which caused untold hardship to, and took a toll of, millions of lives. That such famines have not been seen since independence can be attributed to the political consciousness of the people and political parties in a democratic setup, and the presence of an alert free press all of which makes the government more accountable. There was hardly any such accountability during the colonial rule with the ruling dispensation riding rough shod over the natives.

A series of horrific and grisly famines occurred at regular intervals and devastated the lives of people in different parts of colonial India. These included the Great Bengal Famine (1770), Madras famine (1782-83), Chalisa famine (1783-84) in Delhi and adjoining areas, Dojibara famine (1791-92) around Hyderabad, Agra famine (1837-38), Upper Doab famine of 1860-61 in Agra, Delhi region, famine in Orissa (1866-67), Rajaputana (Rajasthan) Famine of 1869-70, Bihar famine (1873-74), famine in Southern India (1876-78); India famine (1896-1900) and Bombay famine (1905-06).

And the most devastating **Great Bengal famine** occurred in 1943-44 in the midst of the Second World War (1939-45) which took the lives of an estimated 1.5 million though, according to the state appointed Famine Commission's own method of calculation, the death toll was close to three million.

Famines and starvation are not always or only caused by shortages of food. Even when enough food supply is available, many may go without it due to sheer poverty and lack of income, earnings and purchasing power. Which is why India still have people even now without getting food despite overflowing granaries with excess buffer stocks of foodgrains, and an extensive public food distribution system (PDS) and the "right to food" guaranteed under the National Food Security Act.

Many are deprived of their entitlement of ration just due to not having the Family (Ration) card or due to exclusion and maldistribution of rations or sheer lack of wherewithal to buy food. That apart, merely the items supplied through PDS may not be sufficient to provide adequate nutrition which is why malnourishment continues to be a chronic problem in India. Food and nutrition are complex issues and grinding poverty lies at the root of these problems. That even after independence and sustained efforts of successive governments, it has not been possible to completely eradicate hunger and malnutrition reinforces such conclusions.

It is pertinent to note that the colonial regime did not introduce a public distribution system (PDS) for food as was done after independence, except the rationing introduced during the Second World War. Had it been done during the early days of colonisation or even later, much of the misery and hardship which the poor had to endure, not only in times of famine but even in normal times, could have been averted to a great extent. This is yet another instance of the callousness and indifference shown by the British administration in India towards the people. **(For more on poverty in India and its alleviation, see Chapter 17: Inequality and Poverty Alleviation).**

Epidemics: Apart from all these, several instances of epidemics such as plague, cholera, smallpox, malaria, etc. struck different parts of India during the colonial era. The lack of sanitation and proper public health facilities and consequent unhygienic conditions of living aggravated the problems for the people. It is, of course, to be conceded that medical science has also advanced considerably since the colonial era which has made much difference to health conditions.

But though health facilities have vastly improved since independence, they still fall far short of the needs of the people as was starkly proved during the deadly pandemic Covid-19 which erupted in 2020.

VII: Economic impact of colonial rule

To sum up, the British rule held back India's progress in manifold ways.

- On the agricultural front, the colonial administration expanded irrigation facilities leading to reasonable increases in output. But with the highly skewed pattern of land ownership and vested interests involved, there was little incentive to plough back capital to improve farm practices. Little was done to promote agricultural technology, use of fertilizers or better farm equipments. There was no system of extension service to impart training to farmers who were mostly illiterate and lacked skills.

- From being an exporter of cotton textiles and various other items in pre-colonial period, during the colonial era, India became a net importer of textiles and other manufactured goods following the Industrial Revolution. Mineral resources and items like raw cotton were shipped to Britain and finished goods were dumped on Indian markets resulting in virtual deindustrialization of India.
- India became dependent on British commercial capital and many sectors of industry and services such as coal, jute, tea and coffee, shipping, banking and insurance were dominated and controlled by British firms and expatriates. This virtually impeded the initiative and entrepreneurship of natives in industry for long.
- India's industrial efficiency was also hampered by the colonial administration's neglect of technical education, and the reluctance of British firms and managing agencies to provide training in managerial expertise to Indians.
- During the period from 1858 to 1947, there were official transfers of funds by the colonial government to UK, called the 'Home Charges', towards pensions and savings of expat officials, India Office expenses in the UK, purchases of military items and railway equipment. Government procurement of civilian goods, armaments and shipping were carried out almost exclusively in the UK. By the 1930s, these home charges were in the range of £40 to £50 million a year. Dadabhai Naoroji termed these transfers substantial "drain" of India's resources.

In this Chapter we discussed.....

- India's capabilities in manufactures in the 17th century.
- The advent of East India Company.
- Industrial Revolution; Evolution of new factory system.
- Impact of these changes on India.
- Steps taken by the British to consolidate their rule in India.
- The agrarian scene and land tenure; Permanent Settlement Act of 1793; Zamindari, Mahalwari, and Ryotwari systems.
- Problems faced by Indian agriculture; Inadequate steps to improve farming.
- Irrigation in India in early times and in the colonial era.
- Commercialisation of agriculture; Cultivation of crops of commercial value.
- Industrial policy; Deindustrialisation of India.
- A Trade Policy against Indian Interests.
- Assessment of colonial rule; Positive and negative aspects; Exploitation of India; Voices against colonial rule.
- What if India had not been colonised ? Likely outcomes.
- Conclusion
- Progress of India on Socio-Economic indicators in Pre-independent and Post-independent period.

Important Terms to Note in this Chapter

Indian Mutiny; Industrial Revolution; Permanent Settlement Act; Land tenure; Zamindari, Mahalwari, and Ryotwari systems; Protection (of industries); Deindustrialisation; Home charges; The Great Depression; Capital goods industries; Sterling balances

Practice Questions

1. India's economy was a flourishing one before the advent of the colonial powers and the decline started after that. Do you agree? Substantiate your answer.
2. What were the steps taken by the British to consolidate colonial rule in India?
3. What was the condition of agriculture in India during the colonial period?
4. Discuss the industrial policy followed by the British during the colonial period. Would it be correct to say that their policy led to de-industrialisation of India?
5. What impact did the Industrial Revolution have on Indian industry during the colonial era?
6. The British took prompt measures like the introduction of railways, telegraph and telephone in India but these were done to serve the British interests to tighten their grip over India. Do you agree with this view? Justify your answer.
7. The trade policy adopted by the British in India was mainly to serve the British interests. Do you agree? Justify your views.
8. Explain why nationalist leaders like Dadabhai Naoroji and others criticised British rule in India as one of exploitation and draining of the country's resources?
9. The colonial administration had both positive and negative impact on India. Do you agree with this view? Explain with cogent reasons.
10. What, in your view, would have been the state of India had she not been colonised by foreign powers? Would India have been a more developed country than it is today? Explain with reasons.
11. Land system during the British period was responsible for sustained poverty in India and stagnant growth of Indian economy. Discuss. *[UPSC Main 2014 (Economics Optional Paper)]*
12. Assess the impact of land tenure system adopted by the British on the peasants and productivity of Indian agriculture. *[UPSC Main 2020 (Economics Optional Paper)]*
13. Critically examine condition of agriculture and rural economy during the pre-independence era. *[UPSC Main 2016 (Economics Optional Paper)]*
14. Account for the commercialisation of Indian agriculture during the second half of the 19th century and analyse its effects. *[UPSC Main 2019 (Economics Optional Paper)]*
15. Write about the policy of discriminating protection during the British rule and, its impact on industrial development in India. *[UPSC Main 2014 (Economics Optional Paper)]*

16. What were the economic consequences of discriminating protection in the trade policy during British regime? *[UPSC Main 2016 (Economics Optional Paper)]*

17. What specific trade policies during the British period led to the decline of Indian industry? Explain. *[UPSC Main 2015 (Economics Optional Paper)]*

18. During the British Rule, India was rooted with seeds of modernisation, but the country remained underdeveloped. Discuss. *[UPSC Main 2015 (Economics Optional Paper)]*

19. Explain the underlying causes and effects of deindustrialisation in India during the 19th century. *[UPSC Main 2019 (Economics Optional Paper)]*

20. Do you agree that the development of Indian railways during the British Rule helped facilitate the process of industrialisation? Give reasons.

    [UPSC Main 2019 (Economics Optional Paper)]

21. How did railways contribute to India's economic development in the pre-independence era?

    [UPSC Main 2015 (Economics Optional Paper)]

22. Evaluate the development of the transport system in India during 1857 to 1947.

    [UPSC Main 2020 (Economics Optional Paper)]

23. Examine critically the various facets of economic policies of the British in India from the mid-18th century till independence. *[UPSC Main 2014 (Economics Optional Paper)]*

24. Examine how the currency policy of the British affected the growth of monetisation in the Indian economy during the 19th century. *[UPSC Main 2020 (Economics Optional Paper)]*

25. Examine the theory of "Economic Drain" in the second half of the 19th century in India and discuss its economic effects. *[UPSC Main 2019 (Economics Optional Paper)]*

26. Examine the comparative progress of India on socio-economic indicators prior to independence and after independence. Would it be correct to say that India suffered neglect on these parameters due to colonial rule? Justify your answer with supporting data.

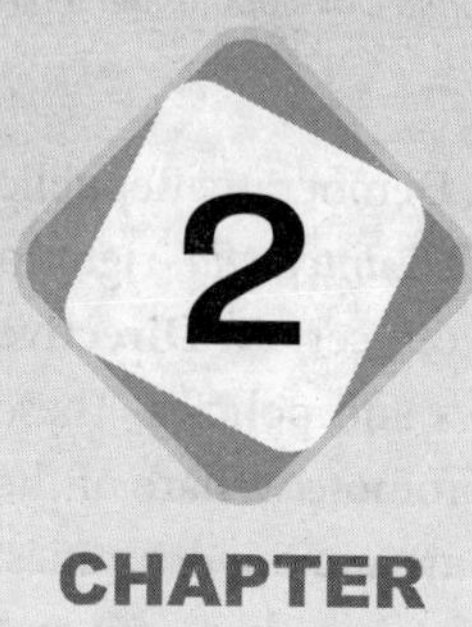

CHAPTER

INDIA AT INDEPENDENCE AND AFTER

- India's condition at Independence
- The Constitutional Rights
- The Genesis of Planning: The Bombay Plan
- Towards a Socialistic Model
- The Planning Commission
- Early Plans: First Three Plans (1951 – 1966)
- Socialist Pattern of Society
- The Second Plan & Mahalanobis Model
- Divergent views: Vakil-Brahmananda Model
- Assessment of Early Plans: Growth vs Poverty
- Neglect of School Education
- An Inward-looking Approach
- The East Asian Miracle
- India's Growth before and after 1991 Reforms

❑ THE BEGINNING AND THE EARLY PLANS

Introduction

After over two centuries of colonial rule and a prolonged struggle, India gained Independence in 1947. With a population of about 35 crores, India's socioeconomic condition at that time was dismal. There was widespread and appalling poverty, acute shortage of food and famines, low life expectancy, and abysmally low level of literacy. Literacy percentage was a mere 17 per cent, male literacy was 25 per cent, and female literacy just 8 per cent.

Agriculture which was the preponderant occupation was in dire straits with heavy pressure of population on land, low yields, and high level of indebtedness of farmers. Due to decades of exploitation by the colonial administration, there was virtually no industrial development barring a few industries in steel and textile sectors. There was acute shortage of skilled manpower and a high rate of unemployment. The Second World War which lasted from 1939 to 1945 and the painful Partition of the country following independence which caused a large influx of refugees accentuated the problems.

India also faced many other societal challenges. A vast country with diverse cultures and languages, a hierarchical social structure with rigid caste system, and wide disparities in the distribution of wealth and incomes, it was an uphill task that India faced after independence. The government had to accommodate these diversities while formulating policies and evolve an integrated perspective for the country as a whole.

The Constitutional Rights

The framers of the Constitution declared India to be a Sovereign, Socialist, Secular, Democratic Republic which guaranteed certain Fundamental Rights to the citizens. These rights included, *inter alia*, right to freedom and equality and right against exploitation. The Constitution also spelt out certain **Directive Principles of State Policy** which serve as guiding principles in formulating laws and policies. These directives, which are not enforceable in courts of law, enjoin upon the State to promote welfare of the people, ensure a just social and economic order, and minimize inequalities in income and opportunities. It also sought to ensure adequate means of livelihood to all people, equal pay for equal work to men and women, and prevent concentration of wealth and resources.

❑ THE GENESIS OF PLANNING

The Bombay Plan

Thus the nascent nation-state had to grapple with a host of socio-economic problems. It placed a heavy strain on the scarce resources. But even during the pre-Independence days, the Indian National Congress was seized of the question of the path India should take for economic and social development once she attained freedom. Even as early as 1938, Congress had appointed a National Planning Committee headed by Pandit Nehru. The Committee explored several aspects of planned economic development and social transformation to be initiated and brought out its views in a '**Handbook of National Committee**'. Later, during the Second War period, prominent industrialists including Sir Purushothamdas Thakurdas, J.R.D. Tata, G.D. Birla, and others studied the problems confronting the nation and came out with a detailed report titled '*A Plan for Economic Development of India*' which came to be known as the 'Bombay Plan'. Their report stressed the importance of developing basic industries, enlarging the role of the State as a facilitator and regulator, and taking steps to reduce inequalities in society.

These deliberations led to the acceptance of 'planned economic development' as the primary goal to overcome the damages inflicted on the country by centuries of economic exploitation. The urgent need to make optimum use of the vast untapped natural and human resources of the country and harnessing the benefits of modern science and technology for building a strong industrial base was emphasized. After years of stagnation and stupor, the nation was reawakened to take the path of rapid progress and catch up with the industrialized nations.

> The two concurrent developments – capitalism in crisis and the success of socialism – had a profound influence on the nascent, under-developed countries aiming to industrialize at a rapid pace, reduce inequalities and establish an egalitarian society.

Toward a Socialistic Model

After the Great Depression of 1930's and the ravages caused by an excruciating war, the capitalist societies of the West were also then in dire straits. Many of them were in shambles and struggling to recover and rebuild their economies. Meanwhile, during this period–in the first half of the 20th century–Soviet Union was economically taking rapid strides following the Bolshevik Revolution in 1917. Vladimir Lenin had initiated a New Economic Policy (NEP), nationalized all landed properties and introduced

'Collectivization' of agriculture. Adopting the socialist path of Planning, she had built a large industrial network of basic and heavy industries, constructed large dams and power plants, and rebuilt the economy on an unprecedented scale while at the same time taking steps to reduce inequalities in the society under a Communist regime. Thus at a time when the world was facing grave economic crises brought about by capitalism, socialist ideals held out great appeal to many young nations which were under colonial rule and had gained independence. The so–called success of the Soviet Union through planning had shown a new way – planned socialist development as an alternative to crises-ridden capitalism to bring about rapid economic and social transformation. The two concurrent developments – capitalism in crisis and the success of socialism – had a profound influence on the nascent, under-developed countries aiming to industrialize at a rapid pace, reduce inequalities and establish an egalitarian society.

The primary goal was to reduce inequalities in the distribution of income and wealth and prevent concentration of economic power. This system adopted by the Soviet Union held great appeal to many leaders in India, particularly Pandit Nehru, and under his leadership, the Government decided to adopt planning as the mode of development. And soon after, India was to adopt formally the establishment of 'Socialist Pattern of Society' as its goal.

The Planning Commission

The Planning Commission was set up in March 1950 by a Resolution of the Government of India with the objective of promoting rapid rise in the standard of living of the people by efficient exploitation of the resources of the country, increasing production, and providing opportunities for employment to all sections of people. The Commission was entrusted with the task of determining the priorities for development, assessing the resources available, and formulating plans for their effective and optimum utilization to achieve the set objectives. Prime Minister was the Chairman of the Commission.

The First Five-year Plan was launched in 1951 and ended in 1956. The next two Plans were from 1956–61 and 1961–66. Thereafter, there was a break because of the Indo-Pakistan conflict in 1965. Two successive years of drought in 1965 and 1966, devaluation of the Rupee in 1966, a general rise in prices, and erosion of resources also caused disruption in the planning process. Hence, there were three Annual Plans between 1966 and 1969, and then the Fourth Five-year plan was started in 1969.

At the time of independence, the share of agriculture in national income was 49 per cent, that of industry and mining only 17 per cent, and of services and construction sector 34 per cent. As for employment, agriculture accounted for 71.8 per cent of the total workforce, industry for 9.5 per cent, and services for 18.7 per cent.

❑ EARLY YEARS OF PLANNING: THE FIRST THREE PLANS (1951–66)

First Five-Year Plan (1951–56)

Drafted under the guidance of Dr. K.N. Raj, then a young economist who later rose to fame, the Plan aimed to pull India out of the vicious cycle of poverty. The primary objective of the early plans was to achieve growth with equity and social justice. The First Plan placed stress on agriculture, irrigation, power, and transport with the aim of creating the base for more rapid economic and industrial advance in the future. An important feature of the early Plans was the primacy accorded to the role of the State in development. This was considered necessary then because soon after independence, India was facing basic problems–deficiency of capital and low level of savings. It was recognized that the State would be in a better position to mobilize resources, raise the level of domestic savings, put it to more productive use, and prevent concentration of wealth.

The First Plan was constrained by lack of financial resources as the nation was burdened with problems arising out of the Second World War and the Partition. It had a modest total investment of ₹ 3,360 crore in the public and private sectors. The outlay in the public sector was ₹ 1,960 crore. *See Table 2.1* for outlays and investments in the first three Plans.

The estimated national income in 1950–51 (at 1952–53 prices) was ₹ 9,110 crore. While the targeted growth rate was 2.1per cent, growth rate of 3.6 per cent was achieved. Another target was to raise the rate of investment from 4.9 per cent of the national income in 1950–51 to 7 per cent by the end of the Plan period and it rose to 7.3 per cent by 1955–56. Foodgrains production rose from 51 million tonnes (MT) in 1950–51 to 66 MT in 1955–56.

The First Plan thus laid the ground for more ambitious plans in future.

Socialist Pattern of Society

Meanwhile in 1954, Parliament had adopted evolving a 'socialist pattern of society' as the broad objective of economic development. In 1955, at the Avadi (Madras) session of the Indian National Congress, a resolution was passed for attaining the goal of 'Socialist pattern of society'. This further reinforced the overarching role of the State in development. In such a polity, development not only aims at increasing national income and employment opportunities, but also ensuring equitable and fair distribution of wealth and incomes to bring down inequalities. Although India opted for a 'Mixed Economy' with roles for both the public and the private sectors, in the initial stages the private sector was given a relatively minor role. It was against this background that the Second Plan was framed and implemented. . (For more on this, see 'Role of the state – The Socialist pattern and its Aftermath' on pp. 2.8)

Second Five-Year Plan (1956–61) and the Mahalanobis Model

The Second Plan was conceptualized by Prof. P.C. Mahalanobis, a renowned statistician, and prepared, after wide consultations, by a group of planners under his guidance. The thrust of the strategy in this Plan was rapid industrialisation and sustaining an accelerated rate of growth in the long-term. Mahalananobis presented a two-sector and four-sector model focussing on rapid development of the Capital-goods sector and enhancing the output of Consumption-goods sector at a subsequent stage. Current demand for consumption goods was to be met by utilizing labour-intensive means of production It was recognized that during the transitional period, employment may not keep pace with the growth of the labourforce. The interests of employment in the medium term was to be balanced with the long-term objectives by encouraging small and village industries which are labour-intensive to produce mass consumption goods. However, while the allocation for large and medium industries was ₹ 617 crore (12.9% of the total provision), allocation for small and village industries was rather modest at ₹ 200 crore (4.1%). With a total investment of ₹ 6,750 crore, it was an ambitious plan to develop basic and capital goods industries which would provide a strong base for building a self-reliant economy. Of the total investment of ₹ 6,750 crore, ₹ 3,650 crore was in the public sector and ₹ 3,100 crore in the private sector (***see Table 2.1***).

The Industrial Policy Resolution of 1956 reiterated the idea of establishing a 'socialist pattern of society' and assigned an important role for the State to develop industries of basic and strategic nature in the public sector. Many key industries like steel, fertilizers, heavy engineering, chemicals, and machine-building were set up to energize and modernize the economy. These large-scale industries were set up in the public sector as private sector would not have ventured to invest in these areas as they required heavy investment and had rather long gestation period. Small-scale and cottage industries were also to be encouraged as they were labour-intensive in nature and would provide greater employment.

The broad-based industrialization which was initiated in the Second Plan was carried forward in subsequent Plans. While the First Plan was about making a beginning and laying the foundation, the Second Plan sought to bring about structural transformation in the economy.

An Alternate Model and Divergent Views

It may be noted in this context that when the Second Plan was being formulated, two Bombay economists—Professors C.N. Vakil and P.R. Brahmananda—came out with an alternate model in their book, *'Planning for an Expanding Economy: Accumulation, Employment and Technical Progress in Underdeveloped Countries'*. They argued against all-out expansion of heavy industry and laid greater stress on agriculture and employment. The Indian economy was characterized by surplus labour and disguised unemployment in agriculture. According to them, the task was to transfer the disguised unemployed to more productive work in rural infrastructural schemes and small agro-industrial enterprises with focus on wage goods -food and industrial consumer goods. In the industrial sector, the need was for manufacture of consumer goods both for domestic consumption and for exports. More production of consumer goods would have resulted in more employment and exports which would pay for import of capital goods needed by the consumer goods industries. It would have meant giving lower priority for machine goods industry. This model, however, was not accepted. (See also chapter 19 pp. 19.7 for more on this)

Criticism of the Second Plan

The Second Plan was not without its critics and there were many divergent views put forth by prominent economists from the academia and within the government. It was argued by some that issues like inflation, availability of resources, and unemployment did not receive adequate attention in the Plan. The Plan's neglect of agriculture became a major problem leading to food shortages till the Green Revolution turned the tide in 1970's. The Plan also faced serious foreign exchange crisis in 1956-58 when India had also exhausted the Sterling balances accumulated during Second World War. A policy of liberalization of imports and heavy import requirements of the Second Plan led to the exchange crisis. This necessitated the imposition of exchange controls which became endemic and developed their own vested interests.

There were other discordant voices too which viewed the Plan to be protectionist and capital-intensive that bred proliferating controls. The size of the Plan and resort to deficit financing which would lead to inflation was also criticized.

However, a comparison between the allocations for agriculture and industry in the first two Plans would show that the planners did try to do a balancing act with the resource constraints they faced. The allocation for agriculture and community development in the First Plan was ₹ 357 crore which was 15.1 per cent of total investment. Besides, ₹ 384 crore (16.3%) was allocated for irrigation. And the allocation for industry and mining was ₹ 179 crore (7.6%). While in the Second Plan, out of the total investment, the allocation for agriculture and community development was ₹ 568 crore (11.8%), for irrigation ₹ 381 crore (7.9%), and industry and mining ₹ 890 crore (18.5%). The moot question which arises then about the Second Plan is the extent to which it gave priority to heavy industries and if it should have given more allocation for consumer goods industries to meet both domestic needs and encourage exports as well as boost employment, as some had contended.

Third Five-Year Plan (1961–66)

The broad objectives in the Third Plan were in line with what was envisaged in the earlier two Plans:

- Increase national income by over 5 per cent per annum and sustain this rate of growth during subsequent Plan periods ;

- Achieve self-sufficiency in food grains and increase agricultural production to meet the requirements of industry and exports;
- Expand basic industries like steel, chemicals, fuel, and power and establish machine-building capacity so as to achieve further industrialization mainly from the country's own resources;
- Utilize the manpower resources of the country to the fullest possible extent and ensure further expansion in employment opportunities; and
- Ensure greater equality of opportunity and reduce disparities in income and wealth.

The total investment planned was ₹ 10,400 crore of which ₹ 6,300 crore was in the public sector and ₹ 4,100 crore in the private sector. The allocation for agriculture and community development was ₹ 1,068 crore (14%), ₹ 650 crore (9%) for irrigation, and ₹ 1,520 crore (20%) for industry and mining.

The Third Plan also faced many challenges. The war with China in 1962 and the Indo-Pak war in 1965 caused much disruption in the implementation of the plan. The back-to-back droughts in 1965 and 1966 also added to the problems. However, due to the accelerated efforts at development from 1950's–the start of the First Plan–by improvements in farming, irrigation, and power supply, food grains production had risen steadily from 51 million tonnes (MT) in 1950-51 to 82 MT in 1960-61 and 89 MT by 1965-66. However, the production was insufficient to meet demands which had to be covered by food imports under PL 480 programme from the United States. The shortages of food also led to food-price inflation.

Table 2.1: Outlay and Investment in First, Second, and Third Plans*
(Figures in ₹ crore)

Plan	Public Sector Outlay	Investment (Public Sector)	Investment (Private Sector)	Total Investment
First Plan (1951–56)	1,960	1,560	1,800	3,360
Second Plan (1956–61)	4,600	3,650	3,100	6,750
Third Plan (1961–66)	8,577	6,300	4,100	10,400

* **Source**: *Planning Commission, Five-Year Plan documents.*

Annual Plans (1966–69)

Period of Instability

As a result of various disruptions referred to earlier, the next (Fourth) Five-Year Plan could commence only in 1969 leaving a gap of three years when only Annual Plans could be implemented. These three years also witnessed political instability due to intra-party conflicts within the Congress Party between Prime Minister Indira Gandhi and the older leaders who were dubbed the 'Syndicate' which was centred around Morarji Desai who was then the Finance Minister and had to resign. During this period, in July 1969, the PM took a major decision of nationalizing 14 of the largest private commercial banks ostensibly to bring them under the State control but also to strengthen the Government and her hold over the party.

❑ ASSESSMENT OF THE EARLY PLANS AND POLICIES

Introduction

While India made much progress since the initiation of the planning process in 1951, the achievements fell short of the pressing needs and demands of an ever-increasing population. The population which stood at 361 million in 1951 rose to 439 million by 1961 and 548 million by 1971. Due to improvements in health standards, increasing birth rates, and falling death rates, population was rising at a steady annual rate of 2.1 per cent which partly neutralized the fruits of development. But it can be said that within the various financial and other constraints, the nation could make modest, though insufficient, progress in the first two decades of planned development. And more was to come in the next two decades primarily in the agricultural sector through the Green Revolution which was a significant breakthrough.

Much debate has since taken place among economists and others on as to whether the policies pursued by India in the early phase of planning, viz., the dominant role assigned to the State and the public sector in development process and relegation of private enterprise, the socialist stance adopted, 'importsubstitution' policy adopted instead of an open 'export oriented' economy have hampered and slowed down the growth process and failed to realize the full potential of the country. It would be pertinent to look into these issues.

Growth vs Poverty

Did India go wrong ?

Some have argued that by the over-emphasis on industrialization, the Second Plan neglected investment in areas more critical to the economy which would have benefitted the poorer and lower-rung sections more. The early Plans also failed to recognize the crucial importance of social sectors–education, especially at the primary level, and public health. But the answer to this was that, within the limited resources available then, the Plan attempted to bring about rapid industrial development and growth which would create the much needed jobs, raise income levels, and standards of living. Creation of jobs would draw the unemployed into gainful employment. Also, the poverty prevalent was so immense and pervasive that any redistributive policy or schemes to help the poor would have had minimal and no perceptible effect. A positive approach of ensuring development and growth is considered to be the best antidote to overcome the debilitating poverty and deprivation. This debate is still relevant in the present context of anti-poverty employment schemes and such other measures being operated where it is argued that the benefits do not reach the intended beneficiaries due to leakages in the system, that the works undertaken are not adequately productive and commensurate with the huge expenditure involved, and that these measures are at best temporary palliatives. The counter argument to this is that in the Indian context of appalling poverty, which refuses to go away and persists partly due to the ever-increasing population, these schemes serve as a safety or social security net for the poor. (*For more on this, see Chapter 17 on Inequality and Poverty Alleviation*).

Neglect of School Education

Yet another criticism of India's early planning is that while India did place considerable emphasis on higher education with its string of Universities, IIT's, IIM's, etc., the neglect of education at primary and secondary levels in the initial years has inhibited her developmental efforts. A strong literate and educated population with sufficient skills is considered to be an important prerequisite for development. The neglect of education at school level has been endemic with lack of trained teachers affecting the quality of teaching and standards attained in education, absence of teachers in schools, lack of infrastructure (labs, libraries, toilets, etc.), high drop-out of students at various stages–all these have compounded the problem. So much so the industry is complaining that even the educated workforce coming out of schools, technical institutions, and even colleges are not readily employable due to lack of specific skills required for the jobs and the recruits have to be intensively trained which involves considerable time and expenditure. The bare fact is that while in the field of school education there has been improvement after 1980's due to state intervention and many Plan schemes to train teachers, opening more schools, arresting drop-out at various levels, etc., the improvement has been more quantitative rather than qualitative as numerous surveys have shown. Thus, the returns on investment made in school education have not been commensurate with the money spent. The adverse impact of all this has been mostly on the lower strata of society who cannot afford to send children to private institutions which are better run and better equipped, and have to depend on Government-run schools which are found wanting in many respects.

> The path India took around this time of self-reliant economic development, of an inward-looking development strategy disassociated with global markets, has also been questioned later by economists. India adopted an 'Import-substitution' policy instead of an 'Export-promotion' strategy, one which kept the Indian economy closed to external forces and influences.

An Inward-looking Approach

The path India took around this time of self-reliant economic development, of an inward-looking development strategy disassociated with global markets, has also been questioned later by economists. India adopted an 'Import-substitution' policy instead of an 'Export-promotion' strategy, one which kept the Indian economy closed to external forces and influences.

Added to this were the policies of licensing and controls which bred corruption and inefficiency and stifled the industry and industrial growth. Lack of exposure to latest technologies also held industry back. India's growth story in 1960's and 1970's has been compared with the growth registered by the East Asian economies during the same period. This is discussed later in this chapter.

❑ ROLE OF THE STATE

The Socialist Pattern and its Aftermath

In the state of gross inequalities and mass poverty that prevailed when India gained independence, assigning a major role to the State, with a view to establish an egalitarian society, appeared quite justified and inevitable. However, as things turned out, the system became highly centralized and interventionist with rigid bureaucratic control, and for nearly the next two decades, free and private enterprise, which could have side-by-side played a dynamic and complementary role, was virtually relegated to the background and not allowed to play its legitimate role. Added to this, as time passed, there was a steady decline in the authority of the Central Government, the rise of regionalism and parochialism, friction between the Centre and the States leading to conflicting agendas, deterioration and corruption in public services resulting in delays and cost overruns in projects, and perceptible fall in the delivery standards of developmental and welfare schemes which impacted mostly the poor and the deprived sections of society. These deficiencies became more pronounced with each passing decade. These were consequences which perhaps the framers of the policies did not visualize and for which the nation has had to pay a heavy price as evidenced by the persistence of poverty and deprivation amongst a still large segment of the population.

Divergent Views, Dissenting Voices

Even as India set herself firmly on path of Socialist mode of development, there was a chorus of dissenting voices from a section of the intelligentsia, led by C. Rajagopalachari (Rajaji), a former Governor-General of independent India, a freedom fighter, veteran statesman and close associate of Mahatma Gandhi who considered Rajaji to be his 'conscience-keeper'. He, along with Prof. N.G. Ranga, formed the 'Swatantra Party' in 1959 which attracted many eminent persons into its fold. This included K.M. Munshi, a former Congress leader, Minoo Masani, a former socialist, civil servants H.M. Patel and Lobo Prabhu, A.D. Shroff, who co-founded the Forum of Free Enterprise, a think-tank advocating the role of private enterprise and B.R. Shenoy, a noted monetary economist.

They spoke vociferously against the socialist stance of the government and the policy which placed the State at 'commanding heights' of the economy and the dominant role assigned to the public sector thereby denying the private sector its due place in the scheme of things. They were for effecting economic reforms and for relying on market forces instead of leaving all decisions to bureaucracy. But the government paid no heed to these views and successive administrations continued on the socialist path. This, as already pointed out earlier, led to excessive state intervention in various spheres leading to red-tapism and spawning the notorious 'licence-permit-raj' which bred widespread corruption and stifled industrial development for decades as events proved later. How prophetic their words were as India had to make a radical shift in her economic policy on the very same lines almost three decades later! In the process, India lost precious time in opening up the economy and hastening the process of development.

❑ THE EAST ASIAN MIRACLE

Introduction

Most of the East Asian countries were in the same—some even in worse—position as India was at Independence and in the following decade. In 1945 Japan, then the most advanced country in Asia, lay in shambles, ravaged by the Second World War. About 20 million Chinese had died in the 1937–45 war with Japan and in civil wars before and after Japanese occupation. China lost another 40 million due to starvation during Mao Zedong's 'Great Leap Forward' programme during 1958–61, and later millions during the Cultural Revolution of 1966–76. The Korean war (1950–53) took a heavy toll of millions of lives and ruined the economy of the divided Koreas. The prolonged Indo-China wars between Communists and non-Communists in Vietnam between 1946 and 1975 which affected Laos and Cambodia too, the brutal regime of Khmers Rouges in Cambodia between 1975 and 1979 that slaughtered one million people, and a failed coup by communists in Indonesia during 1965–66 which resulted in mass killings–all inflicted heavy costs and much instability on those countries.

The Rise of Japan

In early 1950s, all these countries which had very low per capita income were struggling to recover and rebuild their economies anew. From then on, Japan had a meteoric rise, expanding its manufacturing base. Japan was on the cusp of a technological revolution, fast developing its automobile, electronics, and heavy engineering industries which would capture world markets for the next few decades with its unmatched quality products. Between 1960 and 1985, the real per capita income of Japanese grew four-fold to make Japan one of the richest countries in the world.

Box 2.1 East Asian Recovery

There was considerable increase in population in the East Asian countries in 1960s and 1970s leading to growth in the labour force. But as the population stabilized and economic growth gained momentum, household savings increased which, in turn, helped to augment investments. Education and health conditions also steadily improved. Higher literacy and education helped to improve the productivity of the workforce and make quality products at competitive rates. While these countries too had a policy of state intervention to direct the course of the economy and protect larger social good, they encouraged the private sector to flourish and play a positive role in the development process.

South Korea, Taiwan Singapore and Hong Kong

South Korea and Taiwan began to develop their economies backed by technology and research. Even the small economies of Hong Kong and Singapore with limited land, and no natural resources, lost no time to take to their heels, opened up their economies, invited foreign capital and technical know-how, imported new-generation machinery and equipments, and developed a robust industrial base. They also developed strong banking and financial sectors and built modern ports and world class infrastructure. These economies, particularly South Korea, Taiwan, Hong Kong and Singapore, adopted 'Export Promotion' strategy, in contrast to India's 'Inward-looking, import substitution policy', and developed manufacturing capacity which they effectively used to cater to the world markets. It is no wonder these countries have all been aptly dubbed 'Asian tigers'.

Malaysia and Thailand

Other countries like Malaysia and Thailand too followed suit and modernized their economies. By 1980's, they had all been successful in raising the real incomes and join the group of developed and high-income countries. Now economies of Indonesia and Vietnam too are trying to catch up and are strong competitors to India in the global markets.

Data given in Table 2.2 (a and b) will show how far the East Asian countries have forged ahead of India on demographic, literacy, and economic parameters in the last three to four decades. True, India is burdened by an ever-burgeoning population which partly neutralizes the developmental efforts. But China, which is placed in a comparable position, is also far ahead of India. It only underlines the need for India to make quick amends on social parameters like literacy and education, health and population control, and ensure greater productivity by its workforce, and improve the competitive strength of its economy. With a large population in working age-group, India is at an advantage and should harness this potential to the fullest extent.

Table 2.2 Demographic and Economic Data of Selected Asian Economies

Table 2.2 (a) Demographic and Literacy data

Country	Population (in millions)				Life Expectancy (in years)				Adult Literacy Rate (% ages 15 and older)			
Years	1960	1985	2000	2019	1970	1990	2000	2018	1980	1990	2000	2018
Japan	94.1	120.0	125.7	126.9	73.3	79.0	81.2	84.2	-	-	-	-
S Korea	25.0	40.5	45.9	51.2	60.1	71.7	76.1	82.6	-	97.9	-	-
Taiwan	-	20.4(1990)	22.3	23.6	-	74.0	76.5	80.7	-	-	-	98.4
H Kong	-	5.4	6.8	7.4	72.0	77.5	80.4	84.9	-	73,6	-	-
Singapore	1.6	2.7	3.9	5.8	68.8	76.0	78.3	83.1	82.9	89.1	92.5	96.8
Malaysia	8.1	15.8	23.4	31.9	61.3	70.7	72.8	76.0	69.5	82.9	88.7	94.9
Thailand	26.4	52.0	62.3		58.3	70.4	70.9	76.9	87.9	-	92.6	92.8
Indonesia	96.2	162.5	208.9	270.6	47.6	63.5	67.3	71.5	67.3	81.5	90.4	95.1
Philippines	27.6	54.3	77.7	108.1	56.9	65.2	66.8	71.1	83.3	93.5	92.6	98.2
China	657.5	1062.3	1280	1486	62.0	69.5	72.1	76.7	65.5	77.8	90.9	96.8
India	442.3	781.7	1042	1342	49.1	58.5	62.1	69.4	40.7	48.2	61.0	74.3

Note & Source: 1. *Above data are from UNDP Human Development Reports and UN Population Division Statistics and World Bank data site. LifeExpectancy data shown for 2018 is for most recent year available.*

2. *Adult literacy rate: Percentage of the population of ages 15 and older that can, with understanding, both read and write a short simple statement on everyday life(UNDP HDR, 2018).Data are for years shown or for the most recent year for which data is available.*

3. *Data for Taiwan is from Key Indicators for Asia and the Pacific, 2020, Asian Development Bank.*

Table 2.2 (b) Economic Data

Country	GDP (PPP US $Billions)			GDP Per Capita (PPP US $)		
Year	2001	2013	2019	2001	2013	2019
Japan	3,193.0	4,535.1	5,456.9	25,130	35,614	43,218
S Korea	714.2	1,642.6	2,224.9	15,090	32,708	43,029
Taiwan#	478.6	1,066.1	1,256.5	21,574	45,553	53,251
Hong Kong	167.1	370.2	467.8	24.074	51,509	62,321
Singapore	93.7	411.6	578.2	22,680	76,237	101,376
Malaysia	208.3	671.3	943.3	8,750	22,589	28,953
Thailand	391.7	933.6	1,338.7	6,400	13,932	19,314
Indonesia	615.2	2,312.4	3,329.1	2,940	9,254	12,418
Philippines	301.1	622.5	1,003.0	3,840	6,326	9,348
China	5,111.2	15,643.2	23,460	4,020	11,525	16,757
India	2,930.0	6,558.7	9,590	2,840	5,238	7,143

Note: 1. *Gross domestic product (GDP): Sum of gross value added by all resident producers in the economy plus any product taxes and minus any subsidies not included in the value of the products, expressed in international dollars using purchasing power parity (PPP) rates*

2. *The term PPP stands for 'Purchasing Power Parity' and indicates a rate of exchange that accounts for price differences across countries, allowing international comparisons of real output and incomes. At the PPP US$ rate, a PPP US$1 has the same purchasing power in the respective domestic economy as $1 has in the United States.*
3. *GDP per capita: GDP in a particular period divided by the total population for the same period.*

Source: *2001 and 2013 data from Human Development Reports, UNDP, 2003 and 2015 respectively.*

Data for 2019, and all data for Taiwan from Key Indicators for Asia and the Pacific, 2020, Asian Development Bank. # Data for Taiwan given under 2001 and 2013 are for 2000 and 2014.

Box 2.2 India's growth story prior to, and after, 1991 economic reforms

India's growth after independence and during the decades prior to the launch of 1991 reforms was laggard. Do you agree with this statement? Justify the answer with cogent reasons and supporting data.

On attaining Independence, India chose to adopt "Socialistic Pattern of Society" and follow the path of "planned development". The primary objective was to reduce inequalities in the distribution of income and wealth and prevent concentration of economic power. Also, India aimed to achieve rapid industrialisation and sustain an accelerated rate of growth in the long-term. In the initial years of planning, India laid emphasis on setting up basic and heavy industries. These had to be in the Public sector as they had long gestation periods and the Private sector did not have the wherewithal to make heavy capital investments. This emphasis on heavy industries was justified since prior to independence, there were virtually no capital goods industries and almost all the industries that came up were in the consumer goods sector. Without a strong basic and capital goods sector, India could not have industrialized in any significant manner.

Though India achieved much during the first three Five Year Plans (1951-66), the path India took in the three decades from 1950, which retarded her progress has been later faulted by economists on several grounds as discussed below.

- **Inward-looking policy:** The path of self-reliant development, of an "inward-looking"strategy disassociated with global markets, has been questioned by economists. India adopted an 'Import-substitution' policy instead of an 'Export-promotion' strategy, which kept the Indian economy closed to external forces and influences. This was in stark contrast to the policy adopted by other nations in south-east Asia, which also emerged independent around the same time, which laid emphasis on inviting foreign capital and technology, building modern infrastructure and aimed at export-driven growth. Those nations registered high levels of growth in contrast to India's tardy progress.
- **Lop-sided priorities:** While the emphasis placed on heavy industries in the first three Plans to make India self-reliant and put the country on a path of "take-off" into self-sustained growth was justifiable, India could have shifted gear in the mid-1960s. India should then have laid more stress on light engineering and consumer goods industries which were labour-intensive and offered greater scope to boost employment. This was imperative considering that India was burdened by a rapidly growing population and high levels of unemployment and needed to create jobs on a massive scale.

  Conventional wisdom suggests that a country would be better suited to produce goods that require inputs which are locally available in abundance than to produce goods that require inputs that are scarce and dear. It would have been advantageous for India which lacked capital but had abundance of labour to specialize in labour-intensive industries. That apart, many of the heavy industries set up in the public sector later needed subsidies and protection which made them inefficient and globally less competitive. In this context, it is pertinent to note that prominent economists had put forth alternate plan but their views went unheeded. (See Vakil-Brahmananda Plan discussed earlier in this chapter).

- **Relegation of Private sector:** Though India adopted a "Mixed economy" approach of development with roles for both the Public and Private sectors, during these early decades, India assigned a dominant role to the Public sector relegating the Private sector which could have side-by-side played a legitimate, dynamic and complementary role. The government even stepped into areas of production of light engineering and consumer goods such as electronics, cables, telephones, photo films, watches and even bread where the private sector could have made significant contribution. And the government has been faced with the onerous task of disinvesting from these sectors and privatising many of those loss-making enterprises.
- **Restrictive policies:** Faced with heavy import requirements needed for the heavy industries, the country ran into serious foreign exchange crisis in 1950s leading to the imposition of exchange controls which became endemic and developed vested interests. Extensive restrictions and government controls in issuing licences and permits for industries resulted in a regime that came to be termed the notorious "licence-permit raj". The administrative system became highly centralized and interventionist with rigid bureaucratic control that stifled private enterprise.
- Data given in Tables 2.3 and 2.4 show the relative performance of Indian economy before and after the 1991 economic reforms.

Table 2.3: Annual Growth Rates: 1951 to 1985
(in Percentage)

Period	National Income	Per capita income
1951-60	3.0	1.1
1961-70	2.9	0.9
1971-80	2.5	0.5
1981-85	4.5	2.3
1951-85	3.5	1.4

Note: National income and Per capita income data are at 1970-71 prices.

Source: National Income Statistics, Govt. of India.

Table 2.4: Annual Average Growth in Five Year Plans
(at1999-2000 prices)

Plan	National income at Factor cost	Per capita National income at Factor cost
First Plan (1951-56)	4.4	2.6
Second Plan (1956-61)	3.8	1.7
Third Plan (1961-66)	2.6	0.4
Annual Plans (1966-69)	3.9	1.6
Fourth Plan (1969-74)	3.1	0.8
Fifth Plan (1974-79)	4.9	2.6

Annual Plan (1979-80)	–6.0	– 8.2
Sixth Plan (1980-85)	5.4	3.1
Seventh Plan (1985-90)	5.5	3.3
Annual Plans (1990-92)	5.5	3.3
Eighth Plan (1992-97)	6.7	4.5
Ninth Plan (1997-2002)	5.3	3.3
Tenth Plan (2002-07)	7.8	6.1
Eleventh Plan (2007-12)	7.6	6.2

Source: National Accounts Statistics, CSO and Economic Surveys.

- **Declining share of India:** In the four decades from 1950, India had become marginalized in the world economy. India's share in world trade which was nearly 2 per cent in 1950 shrunk to a mere 0.5 per cent by 1980. And the low growth rate of the country's GDP meant that her share in global GDP declined from 2 per cent in 1950 to 1.4 per cent in 1980. Also, India's share in the combined GDP of Third World countries fell from 10 per cent to 5 per cent during the same period.
- **Governance issues:** As years passed, India was beset with many political and governance issues which further impeded her progress. With the rise of regionalism and parochialism over the years, there was steady decline in the authority of the Central Government and friction between the Centre and the States leading to conflicting agendas, deterioration and corruption in public services. This led to delays in implementation and cost overruns in projects, and perceptible fall in the delivery standards of developmental and welfare schemes which adversely impacted the poor and the deprived sections of society. Many prominent leaders had drawn the attention of the government to these nagging issues but it took the country over three decades to change course.
- **Low growth rates and breakthrough in agriculture:** Due to diverse factors mentioned above, India recorded very low growth rates between 1950 and 1980. The annual (compound) growth rates of national income which averaged 3 per cent in 1951– 60, 2.9 per cent in 1961– 70, and 2.5 per cent in 1971– 80 period was termed 'Hindu rate of growth' by Prof. Raj Krishna, an eminent economist.

  However, a major achievement during these years was the remarkable breakthrough in agriculture following the Green Revolution which helped India to not only become self-sufficient in food but later even to become an exporter of foodgrains.

➢ Reforms and After

- Though macro-economic stabilisation and major structural reforms were initiated only in 1991-92, liberalisation on a limited scale was carried out in 1980s. But the growth of public spending through the 1980s, and the high fiscal deficit, which rose to 8 per cent of GDP by 1990-91 compared to 6 per cent at the beginning of 1980s and 4 per cent in mid-1970s, led to steep rise in public debt which stood at 55 per cent of the GDP by 1990. Added to that, persistent current account deficit caused serious balance of payments crisis. It was against this background that India embarked on major economic reforms in the1991-92.

  The reform agenda comprised reforms in trade and industrial policy, removal of import restrictions, liberalised exchange rate policy and major tax reforms. The opening up of the economy helped to integrate India to the global economy, attract foreign investments and technology and give fillip to economic growth. However, reform is a continuous process and India has been carrying out further measures like 'Ease of Doing Business', Insolvency and Bankruptcy resolution code, further easing of foreign investments and the introduction of Goods and Services Tax (GST). These measures need to be further refined and taken forward to help the economy fare even better. It is to be noted in this context that India still has substantial section of population below poverty level and also ranks low on global indices on education, health, nutrition and malnourishment. This points to the need for greater thrust and investments in the Social sector, especially education, skill development and health. (For more on 1991 Economic Reforms, see Chapter 6.)

In this Chapter we discussed.....

- Rights under the Constitution.
- The genesis of Planning.
- Planning Commission and its functions.
- The first three five-year plans. First Plan (1951–56)
- Socialist pattern of society. India adopts 'Mixed economy' pattern.
- The Second Plan (1956–61) —the Industrial Policy Resolution, 1956.
- Foreign exchange crisis (1956–58).
- An alternate Plan and divergent views on the Second Plan.
- Vakil-Brahmananda model of development.
- Allocations for agriculture and industry in the First and Second Plans.
- The Third Plan (1961–66). Challenges faced during the Third Plan.
- Annual plans (1966–69). A period of instability.
- Assessment of the early Plans and policies.
- Growth vs. Poverty: Did India go wrong ?
- Neglect of school education.
- India's 'Inward looking approach' and its ill effects.
- Role of the State: Socialist pattern and its aftermath.
- Divergent Views, Dissenting Voices: the Swatantra Party.
- Relegation of the private sector.
- The East Asian miracle: How the East Asian countries developed and forged ahead.
- India's economic growth before and after the 1991 economic reforms.

Important Terms to Note in this Chapter

Socialist pattern of society; Public sector; Private sector; Mixed economy; Great Depression (of 1930's); Wage goods; Capital goods; Consumer goods; Disguised unemployment; Green revolution; Foreign exchange; Exchange control; Devaluation; Deficit financing; Inflation; Labour-intensive and capital-intensive industry; Import substitution; Labourforce; Workforce; Gross Domestic Product; National income; Per capita income; Purchasing power parity; Demography; Birth rate; Death rate; Life expectancy at birth; Human development

Practice Questions

1. Describe briefly the socio-economic condition of India at the time of independence in 1947.

2. In the initial stages of planning, India adopted 'Socialist pattern of society' as the objective of development. Do you think this was the correct approach? Give your views with arguments for and against it.

3. Discuss the role played by the Public and Private sector in India's economic development. Do you think the Private sector could have been assigned a greater role? Give reasons for your views.

4. There is a view held that the path and strategy adopted by India in the initial stages of planning for socio-economic development were flawed. Do you agree? Discuss bringing out the pros and cons of it.

5. India did not assign adequate priority to, and invest in, the social sector, viz., education and health, in the initial years of planning which retarded her overall progress in later years. Do you agree with this view? Justify your answer with cogent reasons.

6. In spite of intensive family planning measures adopted by India, there has been significant increase in India's population since independence. Do you think this has hampered economic progress and neutralised the developmental efforts? Discuss with cogent reasons.

7. Unlike the East Asian economies which adopted 'Export Promotion' strategy and forged ahead achieving remarkable socio-economic progress, India followed a policy of 'Import Substitution' which held back her progress. Do you agree with this view? Analyze the implications of the two approaches.

8. What were the major hurdles to development as experienced in India during first decade after independence? Discuss them and what steps were taken to remove them?

[UPSC Main 2016 (Economics Optional Paper)]

9. During post-independence era India assigned the role of 'Commanding Heights' to the public under-takings. Was this policy right and should it be continued? Give reasons for your answer.

[UPSC Main 2016 (Economics Optional Paper)]

10. Describe India's development strategy of Selective Inter-dependence after attaining Independence.

[Indiani Economic Science/Indian Statitical Science 2014 Paper]

11. What were the economic and non-economic rationale for adopting mixed-economy model in India?

[UPSC Main 2016 (Economics Optional Paper)]

12. Discuss the basic features of the Second Five-Year Plan in India.

[UPSC Main 2016 (Economics Optional Paper)]

13. Discuss the Wage-Goods model of development as given by C.N. Vakil and P.R. Bramhananda.

[UPSC Main 2016 (Economics Optional Paper)]

14. Highlight the main contributions of C.N. Vakil to Indian planning as opposed to that of Mahalanobis model at the time of formulation of the second five year plan for India.

[UPSC Main 2019 (Economics Optional Paper)]

15. Do you think that pursuit of wage-goods model could have been more appropriate for post-independence strategy of development? Give reasons.

[UPSC Main 2016 (Economics Optional Paper)]

CHAPTER

AGRICULTURE IN INDIA BEFORE AND AFTER THE GREEN REVOLUTION

- Land reforms and changes in agrarian structure
- Bhoodan Movement
- Pre-Green Revolution Phase (1951-1968)
- Early Green Revolution Phase (1968-1981)
- Later Green Revolution Phase (1981-1992)
- Agriculture Research and Extension Programmes & Role of Scientists and Farmers
- Limitations of Technology-driven Approach to Agriculture

(For later developments in the Agriculture sector, see Chapter 7)

❑ INTRODUCTION

At the time of independence in 1947, India was predominantly an agrarian economy with over 80 per cent of the population living in rural areas and about 70 per cent of the workforce engaged in agriculture. In 1950-51, the share of agriculture in national income was 56.5 per cent. Yet, productivity and yields were very low. It was realized that rapid progress in the agricultural sector was imperative for eradication of widespread poverty and malnutrition prevalent in the country, and for ameliorating the living standards of the people.

***The developments in Indian agriculture from the beginning of the First Five-Year Plan (1951) to the early 1990s can be studied in three distinct phases*:**

1. Pre-Green Revolution phase (1951–68)
2. Early Green Revolution phase (1968–81)
3. Later Green Revolution phase (1981–92)

In the initial phase from 1950 to '67, firm foundations were laid through various steps initiated in the first three Five-Year Plans (1951–1966) which enabled kickstarting the agricultural sector in subsequent decades. This was attempted mainly through institutional changes by way of land reforms and various strategies to boost production.

❑ LAND REFORMS AND CHANGES IN THE AGRARIAN SECTOR

Introduction

In 1947, India inherited a highly inequitous system of land tenure with bulk of the cultivable land held by a relatively small section of the population and the rest forming a large segment of small peasants and landless labour. One of the first tasks undertaken by the government after independence was to implement land reforms. Considering the highly skewed and unequal distribution of agricultural land perpetuated over centuries, effecting land reforms was the urgent need of the hour.

As discussed in Chapter 1, this lop-sided system was perpetuated by the colonial rulers. It had adverse consequences on agriculture in colonial India. Insecurity of tenure and indeterminable rights over land impacted on agricultural operations and output. Land records were not maintained systematically which made mortgaging of land to raise funds difficult for the farmer who had to depend on usurious moneylenders. All these placed crushing burdens on the peasantry and sporadic riots and peasant uprisings broke out in different parts of India, particularly Bengal, Andhra, and Malabar.

Key Features of Land Reforms

The land reform was to be achieved by eliminating or reducing exploitation of small and marginal farmers, affording security of tenure to sharecroppers and tenants, and providing land to the landless through redistribution of land. It involved abolition of intermediaries like zamindars and jagirdars, imposition of ceilings on landholdings, and allotting surplus land among the tillers and the landless. *The Indian government was committed to land reforms and consequently laws were passed by all the State Governments in 1950's touching upon the following aspects*:

(i) Abolition of intermediaries;

(ii) Tenancy reforms to regulate fair rent and provide security of tenure to cultivators;

(iii) Ceilings on holdings and distribution of surplus land among the landless;

(iv) Consolidation of fragmented landholdings and prevention of their further fragmentation, and

(v) Development of co-operative farming.

The land reforms had to be implemented by the states. The legislative initiatives for land reforms met with resistance from vested interests in many states. It was argued that tenancy changes and putting ceilings on landholdings would come in conflict with constitutional guarantees. Another argument was that reducing the size of holdings and distributing land among many small cultivators would affect the efficiency of operations and adversely impact agricultural output. It would also prevent the adoption of modern methods of farming and mechanization of agriculture.

The fact that redistribution of land resulting in smaller holdings would affect productivity has been contested and some studies have shown that even if such redistribution does not increase the gross produce, it does not result in a decrease in the produce. It is further argued that redistribution of land cannot be seen merely from the economic benefits it may confer, but also on considerations of social justice in view of the wide disparities and inequities prevalent in the rural sector.

Abolition of Intermediaries

Abolition of intermediaries was one significant step. The intermediaries were abolished within a few years after the independence covering about 40 per cent of the cultivated area. About 20 million, who were hitherto tenants, became owners of the land and were brought in direct relationship with the State. This acted as an incentive for investment and progress of agriculture. Also, considerable areas of cultivable wasteland and private forests came under the management of government.

As to the other major objective of imposing ceilings on landholdings and distributing the surplus land among the landless, there were two rounds of legislation, one in 1950's and another in the early 70's. The state legislatures passed the radical laws imposing ceilings on landholdings.

However, the land reforms were implemented in a half-hearted manner and due to various factors such as pressure exerted by vested interests, exemptions granted in many cases, and division of large holdings by families into smaller holdings among the family members to circumvent land ceiling laws, the reform measures fell short of the avowed objectives. Especially, it did not meet with much success in certain parts of Bihar and former Andhra state where erstwhile landlords continued to hold on to large holdings.

Payment of Compensation

While abolishing the intermediaries, the government decided to pay them compensation but as the basis and rate of compensation was not clearly spelt out, the Zamindari Abolition Acts were contested by the landowners in High Courts and finally in the Supreme Court. The Court, while upholding the rights of the State to acquire lands for public purpose, ruled that just and reasonable compensation be paid to those divested of their lands. As a result, the rates and ceilings of compensation and methods of determining them were revised, and landlords greatly benefitted by the higher compensation paid. The compensation was paid in cash to small landowners while big landowners were paid in bonds.

Also, as a result of the tenancy reforms, tenant-farmers were able to get security of tenure, have their rents reduced, or buy up the land from the landlords at less than the market price. If they did not buy the land, they could continue perpetually as tenants on that land without being evicted and their children too could enjoy that property. Thus, security of tenure was guaranteed. However, this was also not achieved uniformly all over the country and absentee ownership of land and insecure tenancy continued to persist in many parts of the country. The benefits of tenancy reform were mainly achieved in Kerala, West Bengal, Maharashtra, Karnataka, Himachal Pradesh, Gujarat, and Assam.

Box 3.1 Bhoodan Movement

While on the subject of land reforms and landless labour, mention must be made of the Bhoodan Movement, a voluntary effort started in 1951 by Acharya Vinobha Bhave (1895–1982), a Gandhian and a social reformer. Visiting naxal-affected areas in Telengana part of the erstwhile Andhra Pradesh state, and after meeting landless people, the idea of gifting land to the landless by those holding surplus land was mooted by Bhave. Getting instant response from a landlord to his clarion call to gift land, Bhave caught on the idea, took it forward, and made it into a national movement which also attracted international attention. Bhave carried on the movement by going from village to village across the length and breadth of India on foot, over a span of thirteen years, and was able to collect about 4 million acres of land. But only about 1.2 million acres could be distributed among the landless people. The rest was either unfit for distribution and use, or was involved in legal issues. Yet, as a movement spreading the message of peace and social harmony between different strata of society on the lines of Gandhiji's peaceful, non-violent struggle, Bhave's unique effort inspired and awakened the nation on the lot of the poor and the suffering masses in the villages, and it struck a chord in the hearts of the people.

❑ THE PRE-GREEN REVOLUTION PHASE (1951–1968)

Introduction

One of the major objectives in the initial years of planning was to augment agricultural production, more specifically the output of foodgrains, to meet the needs of the growing population. A major challenge to this was the existence of a large number of small and uneconomic holdings. Though some farm studies had shown an inverse relationship between the size of the holding and the yields under traditional agriculture, this could not be generalized, as yield of crops depended on a variety of factors other than the size of the farm. A contrary view held by some economists in the context of land reforms was that reducing large holdings into smaller units would hamper production and yields which again was open to debate.

In the light of these different perspectives, the government conceived a policy of consolidation of holdings by trying to group small farms and promoting co-operative farming. Though government attempted this in all earnestness backed by an intensive Community Development programme in the first three Plans, the idea of co-operative farming was not a success and did not take off. One of the main reasons for this was the reluctance of farmers to give up the rights to land which they got following the land reforms.

Steps to Boost Output

Nonetheless, the Government accorded priority to agriculture and undertook several other measures in the first three Plans (1951-66) to enhance production. These included implementing large and small irrigation projects, steps for soil conservation, dry farming and land reclamation, supply of fertilisers and manures, distribution of improved seeds, measures for plant protection, use of improved ploughs and agricultural implements, and adoption of scientific agricultural practices. Besides the resources provided under the Plans, finance—short and medium-term loans—from co-operative agencies were also arranged for the farm sector to boost production.

The gross area *under foodgrain crops (cereals and pulses) increased from 101.19 million (mn.) hectares (ha) in 1950-51 to 124.91mn. ha. in 1970-71 (see Table 3.1).

Table 3.1 Gross Area under Major Crops (Million hectares)

Crop	1950–51	1960–61	1970–71	1980–81	1990–91
Rice	NA*	NA	37.59	40.15	42.69
Wheat	NA	NA	18.24	22.28	24.17
Coarse Cereals	NA	NA	45.95	41.78	36.32
Cereals (Total)	80.64	91.90	101.78	104.21	103.18
Pulses	20.55	23.66	23.13	22.80	24.70
Total Foodgrains (Cereals +Pulses)	**101.19**	**115.56**	**124.91**	**127.01**	**127.88**

Source: *Ministry of Agriculture, Govt. of India*

NA: Not Available

Note: **Net area represents the actual area cropped while gross area considers intensity/multiple cropping.*

The net irrigated area which was 20.85 mn. ha. in 1950–51 rose to 31.10 mn. ha. by 1970–71 (see Table 3.2).

Table 3.2 Cropped and Irrigated Area (Million hectares)

Year	Total Cropped area	Net irrigated area	Gross irrigated area	Total irrigated area	Total irrigated area as %age of total cropped area
1950–51	131.89	20.85	1.71	22.56	17.11
1960–61	152.77	24.66	3.32	27.48	17.99
1970–71	165.77	31.10	7.09	38.19	23.04
1975–76	171.30	34.59	8.77	43.36	25.31
1980–81	173.32	38.80	10.78	49.58	28.61

Source: *Indian Agriculture in Brief, Ministry of Agriculture.*

These steps did yield results and foodgrains output increased steadily during the first two decades of planning (see Table 3.3).

Despite all these favourable trends, the years through 1950's and the '60s were very challenging for Indian agriculture. Due to acute shortage of food in some years, India had to depend on food imports from other countries including the U.S. under the PL 480 programme. These imports helped to meet the shortages and prevent the incidence of runaway food-price inflation. Two back-to-back droughts in 1965-66 and 1966-67 made matters even more difficult. Foodgrains output dipped to 72.3 mn. tonnes in 1965-66 and 74.2 mn. tonnes in 1966-67 but again recovered to 95.1 mn. tonnes in 1967-68 It further rose to 108.42 mn tonnes by 1970-71.

Table 3.3 Foodgrains Production (Million tonnes)

Crop	1950–51	1955–56	1960–61	1967–68	1970–71
1. Rice	20.58	27.1	34.58	37.7	42.22
2.Wheat	6.46	8.6	11.00	16.5	23.83
3.Coarse Cereals	15.38	19.2	23.74	28.8	30.55
4.Pulses	8.41	10.9	12.70	12.1	11.82
5.Total Foodgrains	**50.83**	**65.8**	**82.02**	**95.1**	**108.42**

Source: *Agricultural Statistics, 2013: Ministry of Agriculture, and Planning Commission, Plan documents.*

During this period, there was considerable pressure from the U.S. government on India, during the Presidency of Lyndon B. Johnson, by discouraging dependence on the U.S. for food aid, and goading India to take effective steps to adopt scientific measures to boost food production and strive towards self-sufficiency. As mentioned earlier, India had already been taking various steps under the three Plans to increase food output. A new strategy was initiated from the Third Plan beginning in 1961, and an Intensive Agricultural District Programme (IADP) was put into operation in selected districts. The farmers responded favourably to a combination of high-yielding seeds, adequate fertilisers and water supply, and institutional credit. They took to the improved farm practices readily and positively, and these initiatives were gradually expanded to cover more parts of the country. In fact, it may be said that the seeds for the Green Revolution, which was to occur in the coming years, were sown in the early sixties.

❑ EARLY GREEN REVOLUTION PHASE (1968–1981)

The breakthrough came in the mid-sixties with the adoption of New Agricultural Strategy (NAS). The main elements of this strategy were the adoption of new technology in the form of high yielding variety (HYV) seeds for wheat, rice, and coarse cereals, better application of fertlizers, and increased use of modern inputs such as pumpsets and tractors. Public and private investment in agriculture was stepped up resulting in higher capital formation. The irrigation facilties were augmented and the net and gross area under irrigation expanded significantly between 1960-61 and 1980-81(see Table 3.2). The area under high-yielding varieties for rice and wheat cultivation also increased steadily from the mid-sixties until the end of the nineties (see Table 3.4). Area under high-yielding varieties for maize, jowar, and bajra also went up considerably during this period.

Table 3.4 Area under High-Yielding Varieties (Million hectares)

Crop	1966–67	1970–71	1975–76	1980–81	1984–85	1990–91	1996–97	1998–99
Rice	0.89	5.59	12.44	18.23	23.44	27.4	33.4	33.0
Wheat	0.54	6.48	13.46	16.10	19.58	21.0	23.7	24.0

Source: *Ministry of Agriculture, Govt. of India.*

Use of hybrid seeds, which had been initiated as early as 1960, began to be widely adopted by 1963. For wheat and rice cultivation, HYV seeds were tried experimentally to begin with and were introduced over fairly large areas as a full-fledged programme from 1966 onwards. It may be noted that the yields per hectare did increase between 1950-51 and 1960-61 which covered the period of the first two Plans (1951-1961).

The overall growth rate of crop output of 2.3 per cent, between 1967-68 and 1980-81, which covers the first phase of the Green Revolution, fell short of the growth rate of 3.1 per cent recorded during the pre-Green Revolution period. However, this shortfall was made up by a strong recovery during the later phase of the Green Revolution in the eighties. It is also to be noted that the increase in output was more marked and substantial in regard to wheat than rice. As these new varieties matured quicker and could be harvested at shorter interval, farmers could do double cropping in a year and thus put the land to more intensive use. With higher yields per hectare and more output, there was greater incentive and profitability for the farmers (see Tables 3.5 and 3.6).

Table 3.5 Foodgrains Production (Million tonnes)

Crop	1967–68	1971–72	1975–76	1981–82
1. Rice	37.7	43.07	48.74	53.25
2. Wheat	16.5	26.41	28.85	37.45
3. Coarse cereals	28.8	24.60	30.40	31.08
4. Pulses	12.1	11.09	13.04	11.51
5. Total Foodgrains	**95.1**	**105.17**	**121.03**	**133.29**

Source: *Economic Survey, Ministry of Finance.*

Table 3.6 Yields for Major Food Crops (Kgs./hectare)

Crop	1950–51	1960–61	1970–71	1980–81	1990–91
Rice	668	1013	1123	1336	1740
Wheat	663	851	1307	1630	2281
Coarse Cereals	408	528	665	695	900
Pulses	441	539	524	473	578
Total Foodgrains	**522**	**710**	**872**	**1023**	**1380**

Source: *Agricultural Statistics at a Glance, Ministry of Agriculture & Planning Commission. Plan documents.*

❑ LATER GREEN REVOLUTION PHASE (1981–1992)

In the second phase of the Green Revolution, the focus shifted from intensification of Green Revolution in the best areas to its spread to new areas. Foodgrains production continued to rise during this phase (see Table 3.7).

Table 3.7 Foodgrains Production (Million tonnes)

Crop	1981–82	1984–85	1988–89	1991–92
1. Rice	53.25	58.64	70.50	74.70
2. Wheat	37.45	44.23	54.10	55.70
3. Coarse Cereals	31.08	31.15	31.50	26.00
4. Pulses	11.51	12.20	13.80	12.00
5. Total Foodgrains	**133.29**	**146.22**	**169.90**	**168.40**

Source: *Economic Survey, Ministry of Finance & Planning Commission, Plan documents.*

As stated earlier, the growth rate of output at 3.4 per cent during the second phase of the Green Revolution was higher than the rate of 2.3 per cent recorded in the earlier phase. During the earlier phase, breakthrough in crop production was achieved in the north-west India and parts of the southern region. However, the eastern region, comprising Madhya Pradesh, Bihar, Orissa, West Bengal, and Assam, were not impacted much during this phase. But during the second phase, i.e., the eighties, the eastern and western regions showed greater progress than the north and the south.

It must be recognized that the Green Revolution, which spanned from the mid-sixties to the early nineties of the last century in two phases, was the result of sustained and tenacious efforts of India's agricultural research community and the positive response from the farmers. The role played by Norman Borlaug, a U.S. biologist who had successfully worked on high-yielding, disease-resistant varieties of seeds for wheat production in Mexico, and who assisted India in this pursuit is noteworthy.

❑ AGRICULTURAL RESEARCH AND EXTENSION PROGRAMMES

Role of Scientists and Farmers

It must be recognized that the Green Revolution, which spanned from the mid-sixties to the early nineties of the last century in two phases, was the result of sustained and tenacious efforts of India's agricultural research community led by the renowned Indian agricultural scientist, Dr. M. S. Swaminathan, and the positive response from the farmers. The role played by Norman Borlaug, a U.S. biologist who had successfully worked on high-yielding, disease-resistant varieties of seeds for wheat production in Mexico, and who assisted India in this pursuit is noteworthy.

Agricultural research was given a boost in the Five-Year Plans and the scientists at the Indian Council of Agricultural Research (ICAR) and other centres played a stellar role in accomplishing this. Through experimentation, demonstrations involving farmers, and intensive extension schemes executed under the Plans, the results of research were taken from the Lab-to-Land and farmers were actively involved and assisted in the process with dramatic results. It helped India to augment the output of cereals, especially wheat and rice, cut down imports, build up buffer stocks, and attain self-sufficiency. It was, indeed, a transformational change in independent India's growth story.

Limitations of Technology–driven Approach to Agriculture

It must, however, be noted that there are certain limitations in the technology-driven approach to agriculture. The cultivation of HYV seeds requires intensive use of fertilizers and assured water supply. Only about 45 per cent of crop area is covered by irrigation. About two-thirds of the cultivated area is dependent on monsoon and is subject to its vagaries. Thus, in the absence of irrigation facilities and with the possibility of deficient monsoon, farmers run greater risk in adopting practices with the new technologies. As the wheat growing areas had assured irrigation facilities, the new technology had the maximum impact on production of wheat. The same impact was not found in respect of rice, pulses, and oilseeds. The new seed-technology based intensive farming is neutral as far as the size of the farm is concerned but it requires more inputs such as optimum dosage of fertilizers and pesticides. Where small and marginal farmers have been able to provide these, they have achieved the same results as those holding larger tracts of land. These factors explain the uneven growth in output as also the inter-regional variations observed following the adoption of new technology in agriculture.

Other issues in Agriculture sector

After the spectacular performance in agriculture following the Green Revolution, the farm sector has been facing various other issues of concern. There was deceleration in output in the 1990s and though it has gone up since then, the scope for further increases in output may be constrained. Scope for more cultivatable land being limited, marginal increases in output in future has to come through higher cropping intensity or development of cultivable wasteland and mainly from yield improvement. The per unit area productivity of our crops is much lower as compared to that of the other major crop producing countries.

Agricultural research in the past focussed mostly on increasing yields by more intensive use of water and biochemical inputs, paying less attention to the long-term environmental impact of this approach or more efficient use of inputs and natural resources. As this approach has proved its limitations, research institutes have to focus on problems of rain-fed agriculture, conserving water resources by diversification of crops, depending less on high water-guzzling crops and choosing those that are suited to varied agro-climatic conditions in different regions. There is imperative need to reduce post-harvest crop losses and carry out reforms in marketing and ensure that farmers get remunerative prices for the produce. (For more on these, see Chapter 7).

In this Chapter we discussed.....

- At independence, India was a predominantly agricultural country. 80 per cent of population lived in rural areas and about 70 per cent of the workforce was engaged in agriculture.
- In 1950-51, the share of agriculture in national income was 56.5 per cent. But productivity and yields were low.
- There were three distinct phases in Indian agriculture between 1951 and 1991: Pre-Green Revolution phase (1951-52–1967-68); Early Green Revolution phase (1968-69–1980-81); Later Green Revolution phase (1981-82 – 1991-92)
- Land reforms implemented; Intermediaries abolished; Resistance from vested interests; Litigation in courts and payment of compensation; Security of tenure for tenant-farmers.
- Bhoodan Movement launched by Acharya Vinobha Bhave.
- Pre-Green Revolution phase (1951-52 - 1967-68); Steps taken to boost output; Increase in area cultivated and irrigated; Shortages of food and need for imports; Pressure on the government to adopt scientific practices to attain self-sufficiency.
- Early Green Revolution phase (1968-69 - 1980-81); New Agricultural Strategy (NAS); Adoption of high-yielding variety of seeds; Increase in yields per hectare.
- Later Green Revolution phase (1981-82 – 1991-92); Higher growth rate of output in the second phase.
- Role of agricultural research, scientists, and farmers in Green Revolution.
- Limitations of technology and other issues; Need for irrigation and assured water supply; Need for optimum use of fertilizers and pesticides for intensive cultivation; Inter-regional variations in output; limits to arable land and need to increase yields, optimize use of water and effect reforms in marketing.

Important Terms to Note in this Chapter

National income; Green Revolution; Land reforms; Co-operative farming; Land ceilings; Bhoodan movement; Community Development Programme; Gross area and Net area; PL 480 Programme; Intensive Agricultural District Programme (IADP); New Agricultural Strategy (NAS); High Yielding Variety (HYV) seeds; Extension programmes; Indian Council of Agricultural Research (ICAR).

Practice Questions

1. What was the state of Indian agriculture before the Green Revolution and what impact this transformational development had on Indian economy? Elucidate with supporting data.
2. What were the factors which led to the Green Revolution in India?
3. Discuss the role played by the agricultural scientific community and farmers in bringing about the Green Revolution.
4. What are the limitations of technology-driven approach to agriculture in India?
5. Discuss the role of land reforms in agricultural development. Identity the factors that were responsible for the success of land reforms in India.
   [UPSC Main 2016 (Economics Optional Paper)]
6. Why are land reforms still not complete in India? What are the obstacles in its way? Elaborate.
   [UPSC Main 2014 (Economics Optional Paper)]
7. Establish the relationship between land reform, agricultural productivity and elimination of poverty in Indian economy. Discuss the difficulties in designing and implementation of agriculture friendly land reforms in India. *[UPSC Main 2013 (Economics Optional Paper)]*
8. "The progress in the implementation of tenancy and revenue reforms during the first three decades after independence in India was not satisfactory." Do you agree with this view? Do you think that the advent of the Green Revolution made such land reforms policy redundant?
   [UPSC 2019 Main (Economics Optional Paper)]
9. Critically discuss the objectives of Bhoodan and Gramdan movements initiated by Acharya Vinoba Bhave and their success. *[UPSC 2013 Main (Economics Optional Paper)]*
10. Discuss the technological factors relating to the Green Revolution in India.
    [UPSC Main 2019 (Economics Optional Paper)]

CHAPTER

INDUSTRIAL POLICY AND DEVELOPMENT

- Industrial development: 1947-1990
- Industrial Policy Resolutions, 1956, 1977 and 1980
- Role of Public Sector
- Industrial Licensing, Control Regime, and its Consequences
- Location and Dispersal of Industries and Regional Balance
- Large-scale industries: Iron & Steel, Textiles and Sugar industry
- Share of Industrial Sector in GDP and Employment
- Role of Small-Scale and Village Industries

❑ INDUSTRIAL DEVELOPMENT: 1947–1990

After being under the British rule for over 200 years and having suffered utter neglect in regard to industrial development, India, on attainment of independence in 1947, could not brook any delay in embarking on industrialization. Even prior to independence, India had planned and initiated steps for developing industries. The Statement of Industrial Policy issued in 1945 had stressed the need to set up basic and heavy industries such as iron and steel, heavy engineering, machine tools, and chemical industries. The idea of industrial licensing and establishing key industries under government control found mention in the statement. After independence, further thrust was given when the Industrial Policy Resolution was issued in 1948 followed by the passing of the Industrial (Development and Regulation) Act of 1951. The 1948 Resolution emphasized the responsibility of Government in promoting, assisting, and regulating the development of industry in the national interest and it envisaged an increasingly active role for the public sector. It stressed the need for continuous increase in production and its equitable distribution and laid down a certain demarcation of fields for the public and private sectors in the industrial sphere.

Industrial Policy Resolution, 1956

The 1948 Resolution was further reviewed with the experience gained during the First Plan (1951–56) and a new Industrial Policy Resolution was issued in 1956. The 1956 Resolution was an important statement of industrial policy to be followed. While the State would play a dominant role in industrialization, the resolution recognized the importance of the private sector and outlined steps to facilitate their healthy development. Financial institutions would provide the necessary resources to the private sector. It also laid stress on promoting small-scale and cottage industries and on ensuring balanced development of all regions to reduce regional disparities and imbalances. While welcoming foreign capital and collaboration for industrialization, it enjoined that ownership and control of industries would rest with Indian hands.

Industrial Policy Statement, 1977

When the Janata Government came to power, it issued an Industrial Policy Statement in 1977 which emphasized the development of the small-scale sector which had potential for creating employment opportunities on a large scale. It also assigned a wider role for the public sector not only as a producer of strategic items, but also as a facilitator for developing ancillary industries by making available its technological expertise to the small-scale and cottage industries. It also sought to encourage medium-size enterprises even in capital-intensive sectors with a view to ensure that there would be no concentration of economic power in the hands of large, dominant business houses. Large business houses were required to raise resources internally, and not depend on banks or financial institutions, for starting new units or expanding their existing units.

Some of the provisions of this statement like priority for the small-scale sector and measures for its growth, an expanded role for the public sector, participation of workers in the management and ownership of enterprises, and steps to check the dominance of large business houses were considered as redeeming features of this policy.

Industrial Policy, 1980

This policy, framed by the newly elected Congress government, was primarily based on the 1956 Resolution with suitable modifications to suit the changed circumstances. It sought to remove a misconception and an artificial barrier seen to have been created between large enterprises and the small-scale sector by the 1977 Policy. It recognized the vital role played by both these sectors and emphasized the need for integrated industrial development to achieve the maximum potential. To promote small-scale units, the permissible maximum limits of investment in these units were raised. It regularized the excess capacity created over and above what was licensed and also permitted automatic expansion of capacity. This was done with a view to make full use of the existing and potential capacity and maximize industrial production.

In this context, the observations of the Planning Commission while preparing the strategy for the Sixth Plan (1980–85) are relevant. **The Commission observed** :

In addition to the conventional strategies of aiming at optimum utilization of existing capacities and improvement of productivity, certain other elements of policy would be necessary in the medium term perspective. These would encompass the following:—

(a) Substantial enhancement of manufacturing capacities in public/private sector covering a wide range of industries for providing not only consumer goods and consumer durables, but also for supporting agricultural and industrial growth through supply of intermediate and capital goods. The pace of industrial investment will need to be speeded up so that manufacturing capacities are in position well ahead of demand to permit competitive market forces to operate and to avoid possibilities of shortages with attendant adverse effects on the economy.

(b) The capital goods industry in general, and the electronics industry in particular, will need special attention as they support the growth of a wide range of economic activity. The proper development of these industries in terms of competitive costs and high quality would be essential to ensure that the projects based on domestic capital goods do not become very costly. Similarly, other selected industries would need to be identified (such as machine tools and commercial vehicles) for accelerated development for supporting not only the domestic requirements but also for exploiting the export potential in a larger measure than hitherto." (Sixth Plan document).

Role of Public Sector

The adoption of the socialist pattern of society in 1954 as the national objective, as well as the need for planned and rapid development, also required that all industries of basic and strategic importance, or in the nature of public utility services, should be in the public sector. Thus many important industries like Hindustan Aircraft, Sindri Fertilizers, a unit at Chittaranjan for manufacture of locomotives, the Integral Coach Factory for manufacture of rail coaches, Hindustan Machine Tools, Indian Telephone Industries, Hindustan Cables, and a Penicillin manufacturing unit came to be set up in the public sector. By the end of the First Plan, firm foundation had been laid for future industrial growth.

The state was to extend financial aid to private sector and for this purpose set up financial institutions such as the Industrial Finance Corporation (IFC), the National Industrial Development Corporation (NIDC), and the Industrial Credit and Investment Corporation (ICIC). Industries like textiles, rayon and staple fibre, chemicals, pharmaceuticals, dyestuffs and plastics, cement, paper and paper board, sugar, jute textiles, etc. were those in which private sector mostly set up units.

As already mentioned in Chapter 2, the Second Five-Year Plan (1956–61) was drafted with a view to give major thrust to industrialization. Three major steel plants were set up during this Plan–at Bhilai in Madhya Pradesh (now in Chhattisgarh) with Russian collaboration, at Rourkela in Orissa (Odisha) with German co-operation, and at Durgapur in West Bengal with the aid from United Kingdom. The expansion of the iron and steel industry received the highest priority as the levels of production of steel and allied items determine the tempo of progress of the economy as a whole, and it would accelerate the development of many other intermediate and consumer goods industries.

As the private sector would be guided largely by considerations of locational advantages such as proximity to raw material sources, the public sector had to play a greater role in ensuring that development extended to other regions which were in a less advantageous position. This is even more so in regard to basic and heavy industries like steel, heavy engineering and heavy electricals, oil, and power generation which involved heavy investments with long gestation periods, and which the private sector may have not been able to undertake. These factors explain the dominant role given to the public sector in the initial years of planning and the 'commanding heights' of the economy which it came to occupy. However, with the passage of time, this policy was overstretched and the public sector intruded into many areas like light goods and consumer goods industries which could have been left for the private sector. This approach has come to be questioned later, especially because many of the public sector undertakings (PSUs) did not function optimally and efficiently, went into losses, and have turned sick. This has led to a rethink of the policy and forced the government to go in for disinvestment of such loss-making and unproductive units.

Due to the thrust given to the industrial sector from the Second Plan onwards, there was perceptible progress in the field of industry and manufacturing. Production in mining, metallurgy, and other industrial products witnessed considerable increase. (*See Table 4.1 for more details*). Also, the share of industry in GDP increased substantially between 1950–51 and 1990–91. (*See Table 4.5, p. 4.11 for more details*).

Table 4.1 Production in Selected Industries (1950-51 to 1990-91)

Industry	Unit	1950-51	1960-61	1970-71	1980-81	1990-91
I. Mining						
1. Coal and lignite	Mn.Tns	32.3	55.2	76.3	119.0	225.5
2. Petroleum (Crude)	Mn.Tns	0.3#	0.5#	6.8#	10.5	33.0
3. Iron Ore	Mn.Tns	3.0	10.9	32.5	42.2	53.7
II. Metallurgical Industries						
4. Crude Steel	Mn.Tns	1.5	3.5	6.1	10.3	12.6
5. Finished Steel	Mn.Tns	1.0	2.4	4.6	6.8	13.5
III. Mechanical Engineering Industries						
6. Machine Tools	million	3	8	430	1692	7731
7. Railway wagons	Thousand	NA	9.0#	11.1	13.6	25.3
IV. Chemical & Allied Industries						
8. Cement	Mn. Tns	2.7	8.0	14.3	18.6	48.8
V. Textile Industries						
9. Jute Textiles	'000 tonnes	837	1071	1060	1392	1430
10. Cotton Cloth.	Mn.Sq. mtrs	4215	6738	7602	8368	15431
i. Mill Sector	Mn.Sq. mtrs	3401	4649	4055	3434	1859
ii. Decentralized Sector	Mn.Sq. mtrs	814	2089	3547	4934	13572

On a calendar year basis; Mn. = Million; Tns: Tonnes; NA: Not available.

Source: *Five-Year Plans, Planning Commission & Economic Surveys, Ministry of Finance.*

The public sector was, however, beset with several constraints. As observed by the Planning Commission, "the internal resources generated by the public sector undertakings for financing the Plan have been comparatively meagre. The major factors responsible for these are :

(a) low return on investment on account of price constraints imposed on some public sector undertakings;

(b) considerable number of private sector sick units (particularly in the textile and engineering industries) which the Central Government had to take over in the interest of maintaining employment and production; and

(c) the technological complexity of the industries which had to be promoted in the public sector where a longer gestation period and slower learning curve are inevitable." (Sixth Plan document).

Despite the industrial growth and building a robust industrial base, the industrial policy followed by India in the initial decades came in for critical scrutiny as discussed in this section.

> That the system of licensing and controls acted as an inhibiting force in industrial growth became evident even during the 1960s and the '70s. It did not result in proper regional dispersal of indus¬tries or wider distribution of entrepreneurship for preventing the concen-tration of economic power.

Industrial Licensing, Control Regime, and its Consequences

India adopted a system of industrial licensing from the beginning. The primary and ostensible purpose of control and licensing was to ensure proper allocation and utilization of scarce resources. The Industries (Development and Regulation) Act, 1951 stipulated licensing of industries and setting up of Development Councils for individual industries to ensure industrial development in conformity with the objectives set out in the Plans. The Act was amended in 1953 with a view to bringing additional industries within the schedule. The Licensing Committee set up in accordance with the provisions of the Act functioned as an advisory body to the Ministry of Commerce and Industry for the scrutiny of applications for new units and expansion of capacity in the scheduled industries.

Under this system, an entrepreneur required approval from the Industry Ministry at every stage. Apart from licence to start an industry, approvals were required for import of any capital goods, components, or raw materials required for the unit or for any foreign collaboration or foreign technology. If funds had to be raised from the capital market, it required separate sanction from the Finance Ministry.

Many sectors were reserved exclusively for the public sector and a large number of items were reserved for the small-scale industries to promote that sector. All these inhibited the growth of private enterprise. That the system of licensing and controls acted as an inhibiting force in industrial growth became evident even during the 1960s and the '70s. It did not result in proper regional dispersal of industries or wider distribution of entrepreneurship for preventing the concentration of economic power.

There were periods of stagnation and slowdown in industrial activity caused by low productivity, rising costs, and lack of technological upgradation. Vested political interests, rigid bureaucratic control, and the influence of multinationals that supplied technology and capital all added to the impediments. This phase of Indian economy is referred to as the 'License-Permit Raj' which acted as a major stumbling block in industrial growth. Various Committees–the Swaminathan Committee (1964), the Hazari Committee (1967), and the Dutt Committee (1969)–were appointed to study these problems. The reports of all these Committees pointed to the deficiencies of the 'licence and control' regime which were hampering industrial growth and recommended the need to bring about radical changes. Despite all these, the government took no worthwhile steps to change the course, and it took nearly a decade more to do some serious thinking on the issue.

Stagnation in industry persisted from the mid-1960s and through 1970s. It was realized that Indian industry was handicapped by technological, qualitative, and cost disadvantages compared to foreign competitors. Against this background, the government set up, during the eighties, more expert committies to examine the problems plaguing the industrial sector. These were the Arjun Sengupta Committee on Public Enterprises (1984), the Abid Hussain Committee on Trade policy (1984), and the Narasimhan Committee on the shift from physical to fiscal control measures (1985). These committees recommended liberalising the regime in their respective area of study, i.e., trade policy, substitution of physical and quantitative controls by fiscal and other means of macro-economic management, and providing greater autonomy to the public sector in taking managerial and business decisions, and to enhance their productive efficiency and modernization process.

As a result of these measures, there was some progress in the process of deregulation during the 1980s. Thirty-two groups of industries were delicensed without any investment limit. And in 1988, all industries were exempted from licensing except for a specified negative list of twenty-six industries. But this exemption was subject to investment and location conditions and thus again became rather restrictive. In regard to trade policy, a major change was that exporters were given greater access to inputs at international prices. But tariff protection to industries increased substantially in 1980's as compared to previous decades. Thus the policy needed further reform measures which came to be taken from 1991. (See Chapter 8 for more details).

Location and Dispersal of Industries and Regional Balance

Location of industries tend to be near areas where raw materials are available. This is done to minimize the need for their transportation over long distances and thus keep down production costs. Availability of good infrastructure such as roads, railheads, proximity to ports, water, and power are other critical factors which industries consider while deciding on their location. Besides, availability of skilled manpower needed for a particular type of industry could also influence location of industries.

Keeping the above aspects in view, the 1956 Industrial Resolution recognized the need to ensure the balanced growth of all regions to avert disparities between various regions. A fair and even spread of industries was essential to provide employment in a satisfactory manner and bring about all-round improvement in the standards of living in all regions. As stated earlier, since the private sector would be largely guided by considerations of locational advantages in setting up industries, the public sector had to step in to ensure balanced development of all regions. Also, one of the objectives of national planning was to ensure that the various infrastructural facilities were steadily made available in areas which were lagging behind industrially.

During the formulation of the Fourth Plan (1969–74), the Planning Commission observed thus: *"Measures are proposed to be taken for the development of industries in the backward areas. The normal economic forces governing the location of industries are at present so overwhelmingly in favour of the developed areas that the problem of dispersal of industries to backward regions would require co-ordinated action at the Central, State, and local levels. The problem is so widespread that during the Fourth Plan it would be possible to make only a beginning. It is through a continuing programme of economic development supported by measures to attract industries to backward regions that the present imbalance can be rectified over a period of time."*

In pursuance of such a policy, the government set up more steel plants at locations away from the sources of main raw materials. Three more steel plants were set up in south India. These were the Salem Steel Plant in Tamil Nadu, the Vizag Steel Plant at Visakhapatnam (Andhra Pradesh), and the Vijayanagar Steel Plant at Hospet (Karnataka). Apart from these major plants, there are many smaller units located in different parts of the country. The Central Government also extended subsidy for the establishment of industrial units in backward areas.

The issue of the need for more balanced development of all regions, particularly of states in central and eastern India, has come to the fore due to the serious crisis faced by migrant labour which was witnessed when the pandemic, Covid-19, broke out in all virulence during 2020-2022. Such migration takes place mostly from these states, which are otherwise well endowed with rich mineral resources but remain industrially backward, forcing people to migrate to other states in the west and the south in search of employment. (For more on the problems of migrant labour and regional balance in development, (see Chapters 16, p. 16. 19-22 and 19, p. 19.11-2).

A look at some of the large-scale industries such as iron and steel, textiles, and sugar, discussed here, would reveal the pattern and rationale of location and dispersal of industries, see also page 19.11.

❑ LARGE-SCALE INDUSTRIES

Iron and steel industry

This is one of the most strategic and basic industries upon which depends the development of most other sectors. It was for this very reason that the Second Five-year Plan laid utmost stress on it as mentioned earlier. This is a highly capital-intensive industry requiring large investment and hence under the Plans, they have been set up in the public sector. The two notable exceptions were the Tata Iron and Steel

Company (TISCO) set up by Jamshedji Tata at Jamshepur (now in Jharkhand) and the Indian Iron and Steel Company (IISCO) set up at Burnpur in West Bengal, both set up as private enterprises much before independence. While the former continues to be in the private sector, IISCO was taken over by the government after independence and now functions under the Steel Authority of India Limited (SAIL).

The steel plants at Rourkela (Odisha), Bhilai (now in Chhattisgarh), Durgapur (West Bengal) and Bokaro (in Jharkahand) were all set up in the public sector. As stated earlier, there are other steel plants at Salem, Hospet, Visakhapatnam, and other places.

The major integrated steel plants, which come under SAIL, are located principally in the eastern and central regions of India and are situated close to the sources of raw materials, viz., iron ore and coking coal which are both weight-losing materials. As transportation costs of these raw materials over long distances would not only be prohibitive but would also pose logistical problems, steel plants had to be located as close to the sources of raw materials as possible. Most of the mines for these raw materials are located in Jharkand, Chhattisgarh, Odisha, and West Bengal. These are also available, to a lesser extent, in the south in Karnataka, Goa, and Tamil Nadu.

It may be noted that India is endowed with fairly abundant supply of iron ore, estimated to be about 20 billion tonnes. The iron mines are located mainly in Mayurbhanj and Sundergarh in Odisha, Singhbhum in Jharkhand, and Durg and Bailadila in Chhattisgarh. There are also iron ore deposits in Bellari, Chikkamangaluru, Chitradurga and Tumkur districts in Karnataka, Salem and Nilgiris in Tamil Nadu, and in parts of Telengana and Andhra Pradesh.

Coal, which is used for smelting of iron ore, is mainly available at Jharia, Raniganj, Giridih, and Bokaro in the Jharkhand-Bengal coal belt, Singrauli in Madhya Pradesh, Korba in Chhattisgarh, Talcher and Rampur in Odisha, and Singareni in Telengana.

With the advent of the Industrial revolution and modernisation of mills in Britain, the British government began to export raw cotton from India to feed the mills in Britain and import finished goods made in Britain into India. This caused much setback to the growth of this industry before independence .

Textile industry

Cotton textile industry is one of the oldest and traditional industries in India. Indian cotton and cloth products have been renowned since the medieval times and it used to be exported to the markets in western countries. It was essentially a cottage industry in which the artisans and weavers perfected their skills and passed them on from one generation to another. It was only in the middle of the 19th century that the first modern cotton mill came to be established in Mumbai (then Bombay). Though more textile mills were established in course of time, during the colonial era, the British discouraged the development of this industry as it posed a competition with the textile industry in Britain. With the advent of the Industrial revolution and modernisation of mills in Britain, the British government began to export raw cotton from India to feed the mills in Britain and import finished goods made in Britain into India. This caused much setback to the growth of this industry before independence.

However, some of the Indian entrepreneurs took initiative and started mills in India and the Swadeshi movement also gave impetus to the industry as it called for boycott of English-made fabrics. The mills were located primarily in Mumbai, Ahmedabad, Surat, Coimbatore, etc. By 1947, India had over 400 textile mills.

India being a tropical country with a hot and humid climate, fabrics made of cotton are ideally suited for Indian conditions. India is one of the largest cotton producing countries in the world, though a good part of the cotton producing area went to West Pakistan after the Partition. In 2013–14, India's cotton output was 36.7 million bales (each bale is of 170 kgs.). Largely a rainfed crop, India produces both the short staple and the long staple variety of cotton. The main cotton growing areas are Gujarat and Maharashtra in the west, Telangana, Tamil Nadu and Karnataka in the south, and Punjab, Haryana, and Rajasthan in the north. (See Table 4.2 for more details). The total gross area on which cotton was cultivated increased from 7.6 million hectares in 1970–71 to 11.7 million hectares in 2013-14.

Table 4.2 Production of Cotton in Three Largest Producing States in 2013-14 & 2017-18 (In million bales of 170kg. per bale)

2013-14			2017-18		
State	Production	Share in All India Production (%)	State	Production	Share in All India Production (%)
Gujarat	11.0	29.9	Gujarat	12.64	36.23
Maharashtra	8.5	23.3	Maharashtra	6.55	18.77
Andhra Pradesh	7.1	19.5	Telangana	4.75	13.61

Source: *Directorate of Economics & Statistics, Ministry of Agriculture, Cooperation and Farmers Welfare, Govt. of India.*

Bt cotton: The Planning Commission has observed that "with more than 90 per cent of cotton area now under Bt hybrids, and cotton yields more than doubling over the last decade, there is no doubt either about general farmer acceptance or its being a clear case of technological transformation unlike other rainfed crops. But disagreements continue about the extent to which Bt contributed to this yield increase and on wisdom of India's total dependence on Bt hybrids rather than the Bt varieties used in the rest of the world. There are also legitimate complaints of non-availability of non-Bt seeds. Genetically modified organisms (GMOs), therefore, remain controversial, as was evident in case of Bt Brinjal. Nonetheless, since significant breakthroughs in production technologies are required to cope with increasing stress, particularly for rainfed crops, it is necessary to remain abreast with latest advances in biotechnology." (*Twelfth Plan document, Vol. II*).

The cotton textile industry is spread over almost every state in India. Apart from the proximity of the source of raw materials, other factors like availability of cheaper labour, land, power supply, etc. have also influenced the growth and spread of this industry. Bhiwandi, Ahmedabad, Solapur, Kolhapur, Nagpur, and Indore are important centres of textile industry. Kanpur, Saharanpur, Modinagar in Uttar Pradesh, Kolkata, Hugli and Howrah in West Bengal, and Karnataka are important centres for cotton textiles. Tamil Nadu has the largest number of mills producing mostly yarn. While Coimbatore is the most important centre in Tamil Nadu with most of the mills located there, Chennai, Madurai, and Salem also are important centres. Ludhiana in Punjab is an important for the woollen textiles and Mysore in Karnataka is noted for the silk industry.

The textile industry can be classified into two broad categories, viz., the organized sector and the unorganized sector. The former consists of the modern, mechanised mills while the latter comprises the handlooms and the powerlooms. The production in the mill sector has declined drastically over the years due to intense competition from the powerloom sector. The textile industry plays a pivotal role in the economy being the second largest provider of employment after agriculture. It makes a major contribution to the national economy in terms of generation of direct and indirect employment and net foreign exchange earnings.

> The textile industry plays a pivotal role in the economy being the second largest provider of employment after agriculture. It makes a major contribution to the national economy in terms of genera¬tion of direct and indirect employment and net foreign exchange earnings.

It contributes about 12 per cent of the manufacturing output, 11 per cent of merchandise exports, and employs about 45 million people. It has a major presence in the unorganized sector as compared to the organized sector, both in terms of the workforce and the number of enterprises. Thus, the growth and all-round development of this industry has a direct bearing on the improvement of India's economy.

Table 4.3 Exports of Textile Products
(₹ crore)

Commodity/ Year	2009-10	2011-12	2014-15	2017-18	2018-19	2019-20
Cotton yarn, Fabs/ Made-ups, Handloom products, etc.	25227	43073	65911	66141	78374	71042

Source: *Reserve Bank of India, Handbook of Statistics on Indian Economy, 2014– 15 and 2020.*

Textiles exports have risen substantially over the years as will be seen from Table 4.3. It is expected to go up further given adequate support from the government.

The Indian textile industry has many positive features–a strong raw-material base, indigenous design capabilities, an entire value chain, large and growing domestic demand, and the availability of trained manpower at internationally competitive rates. Yet, it is handicapped by the fact that technologically it is still not adequately developed though the government has taken up various schemes to strengthen the sector. A Technology Upgradation Fund Scheme (TUFS) was set up to modernize the sector and a Scheme for Integrated Textile Parks (SITP) was launched in 2005 to neutralise the weakness of fragmentation in the various sub-sectors of textiles value chain, and the non-availability of quality infrastructure. An Apparel Parks for Exports Scheme (APES) has been started to promote setting up modern apparel units at major growth centres. The modernization process that began during the Ninth Five-Year Plan (1997–2002), though accelerated through the Tenth (2002–07) and Eleventh (2007–12) Five-Year Plans, has not made adequate progress. The modernization process is to be pursued on a continual basis to upgrade systems, especially because India faces stiff competition in this industry in the international markets.

Sugar industry

Next to textiles, sugar industry is the largest agro-based industry in India. India is one of the largest producer—consumer of sugar in the world. Sugar, a crop grown in tropical areas, is mainly an irrigated crop in India. The main sugarcane producing states are Uttar Pradesh which is the largest producer, Maharashtra, Karnataka, Gujarat, Karnataka, Tamil Nadu, Andhra Pradesh and Telangana. (*See Table 4.4 for details*). Gross area under sugarcane cultivation has gone up from 2.6 million hectares (mn. ha.) in 1970–71 to 4.3 mn. ha. in 2000–01 and 5.0 mn. ha. in 2012–13. But by 2017-18, it has come down to 4.73 mn. ha. With over 45 million persons engaged in sugarcane farming in the country, a sizeable chunk of the rural population is dependent on this crop.

About five lakh workers are directly employed in the sugar industry, besides many more in industries, which utilize by-products of sugar industry as raw material. Sugarcane is a weight-losing crop and as sugar is recovered better when crushing is done within 24 hours of harvesting, sugar factories are located in areas cultivating sugarcane. In 2011–12, there were 529 sugar factories in operation which crushed 257 million tons of sugarcane, producing 26.34 million tons of sugar.

Table 4.4 Production of Sugarcane in Three Largest Producing States in 2013-14 and 2017-2018

(In Million Tonnes)

2013-14			2017-18		
State	Production	Share in All India Production (%)	State	Production	Share in All India Production (%)
Uttar Pradesh	135.2	38.6	Uttar Pradesh	177.06	46.9
Maharashtra	76.6	21.9	Maharashtra	83.13	22.1
Karnataka	35.9	10.3	Karnataka	28.26	7.5

Source: *Directorate of Economics & Statistics, Ministry of Agriculture, Cooperation and Farmers Welfare, Govt. of India.*

Uttar Pradesh is the leading producer of sugar, followed by Maharashtra. While Sangli, Kolhapur, Latur, Amaravati, and Aurangabad have sugar factories in Maharashtra, in U.P., the factories are mainly in Saharanpur, Meerut, Ghaziabad, Gorakhpur, Gonda, and Bahraich. Some of the other districts having sugar mills are Coimbatore, Tiruchirappalli and Vellore in Tamil Nadu, Bellari, Shivamogga and Chitradurg in Karnataka, Visakhapatnam, East and West Godavari in Andhra Pradesh, Patiala and Amritsar in Punjab and Saran, Muzaffarnagar, and Gaya in Bihar. There are also sugar factories in Gujarat, Haryana, and Madhya Pradesh.

Indian sugar industry is amongst the most diversified industry in the world. It has an installed capacity to produce 1000 MW co-generated power against a potential of 7500 MW. In India, alcohol, which is used as a raw material for industrial uses, is produced from molasses. The economics of sugar production is also crucially dependent on the production of ethanol as by-product. Fuel ethanol can be used as a substitute for gasoline. The programme of ethanol-doping has been extended to the country as a whole. Considering the heavy consumption of petrol and the bulk import of oil involving valuable foreign exchange, a long-term policy needs to be devised on the mixing of petroleum fuel with ethanol.

The sugar industry is also facing many challenges. State Governments keep advising sugar factories to pay cane price at a higher level than the statutory minimum price (SMP). The sugar industry thus faces a predicament in which it is asked to pay more for the raw materials even as it gets less for its produce in the market. Delays in the offtake of sugarcane by mills and delays in farmers getting remuneration for their produce are some of the problems plaguing this sector.

The industry also faces problems in exports due to wide fluctuations of international prices from year to year. While exports are restricted in the years when international prices are high, they need to be subsidized in years in which such prices are low. Export subsidies have become inconsistent with India's obligations under the WTO Agreement.

Share of Industrial Sector in GDP and Employment

An important indicator of economic progress is the relative share of the three sectors–primary, secondary, and tertiary–in both the GDP and employment. As the economy grows and becomes more diversified, the share of agriculture and allied activities becomes less and less while that of industry and manufacturing and the services sector goes up. In the Indian context too, this trend is visible in the first four decades of planned development. (See Table 4.5 for details).

Table 4.5 Sectoral Shares in GDP and Employment

Sector	GDP (At Factor Cost)				Employment (In Percentage)			
	1950–51	1960–61	1980–81	1990–91	1951	1961	1971	1987–88
Primary	55.8	45.8	38.1	34.0	69.1	68.0	70.4	63.90
Secondary	15.2	20.7	25.9	24.9	12.6	12.7	11.2	11.90
Tertiary	29.0	33.5	36.0	41.1	18.3	19.3	18.3	24.01

Source: *Sectoral shares in GDP from Statistical Outline of India, 2003–04, Tata Services Ltd.; Shares in Employment based on Changing Structure of the Economy, Paper by V.K.R.V. Rao, and NSS Rounds.*

From the above, it will be seen that over the years, between 1950–51 and 1990–91, the share of agriculture and allied activities in GDP has gone down while that of both industry and services sectors have gone up. However, the changes in occupational structure, i.e., the share of these sectors in employment have not changed to the same degree and extent. The percentage of people employed in agriculture has come down only marginally indicating the continued pressure of population on land. Also, the percentage increase in employment in industry has been fluctuating though, in absolute terms, the number of persons engaged in the sector may have shown increase due to increase in the labour force. On the other hand, the growth of employment in the services sector has been more significant.

Role of Small-Scale and Village Industries

Small and village industries have played a vital role in India's industrial development, especially because of its labour-intensive nature of production, lower capital base requirement, and employment generating potential. Right from the First Five Year Plan, this sector has been accorded due priority. The 1948 Industrial Resolution had indicated Government's approach to the problems faced by the cottage and small-scale industries. These industries suffered from a variety of handicaps such as lack of access to quality raw materials at the right price, lack of adequate finance resulting in unsatisfactory state of equipment and machinery, inadequate marketing arrangements, and lack of exposure to new techniques of production to keep pace with the changing demands of the market. Considering that the small industries provide large-scale employment, offer means of ensuring a more equitable distribution of the national income, and facilitate effective mobilization of resources of capital and skill which might otherwise remain unutilized, the new Resolution also reiterated the importance of, and the need for strengthening this sector.

The Karve Committee which was appointed by the Planning Commission in 1955 to study the working of this sector recommended that :

(i) as far as possible, technological unemployment which occurs specially in the traditional village industries should be avoided ;
(ii) to provide for as large a measure of increased employment as possible during the Second Plan period through different village and small industries; and,
(iii) to provide the basis for the structure of an essentially decentralized society for progressive economic development at a fairly rapid rate.

The Committee, however, envisaged that even in the traditional village industries, to the extent possible, technical improvements should be adopted, and for the future, there should be a regular programme of gradual transition to better techniques.

> Village and small industries have been an integral part of the economic structure and the scheme of national planning. The primary object of developing small industries in rural areas was to extend work opportunities, raise incomes and standard of living, and to bring about a more balanced and integrated rural economy.

Special institutions were considered necessary for providing assistance to, and for promotion of small businesses. With this in view, the government established State Finance Corporations and the Central Small Industries Corporation. Community workshops were organized in rural areas where workers in different types of cottage industries could come together and carry on production activities in an enabling environment. Also, small and medium-scale enterprise were supported through establishment of industrial estates with common facilities for transport, power, etc. provided by public authorities. Village and small industries have been an integral part of the economic structure and the scheme of national planning. The primary object of developing small industries in rural areas was to extend work opportunities, raise incomes and standard of living, and to bring about a more balanced and integrated rural economy.

It was recognized that as the rural economy developed, technical changes would take place in different fields, and correspondingly, the pattern of rural industrialization would also change from cottage industry employing simple crafts and rudimentary techniques to small and medium enterprises based on steadily improving and more advanced techniques. These developments were supported through legislation and various affirmative actions aimed at strengthening the village economy. The small and village industries were to be developed as a progressive, efficient, and decentralized sector closely integrated, on the one hand, with agriculture and, on the other, with the large-scale industry. It could play a vital complementary role as ancillary to the large-scale sector.

With the above considerations in view, successive Five-Year Plans made increased allocations for this sector as shown below. (*See Table 4.6 for details*). Various measures like reservation of production of items exclusively by the small-scale sector, preference in government's procurement for items made by the SSI sector, and special financial assistance to the small enterprises helped this sector to register robust growth.

Table 4.6 Plan Allocation for Village and Small Industries (In ₹ crore)

Plan	Plan Provision	Actual Outlay	% of col. 3 to col. 2
First Plan (1951–56)	50	42	84
Second Plan (1956–61)	160	187	117
Third Plan (1961–66)	264	241	91
Annual Plans (1966–69)	132	126	95
Fourth Plan (1969–74)	293	243	83
Fifth Plan (1974–79)	510	592	116
Sixth Plan (1980–85)	1,781	1,980	111

Source: Five Year Plan Document: Planning Commission

The small-scale industries in India have grown significantly since 1960, when there were only 12,376 enterprises providing employment to 10 lakh people, of which direct employment was 1.85 lakh, and with annual production of ₹ 875 crore. By 1980–81, there were 8.7 lakh small scale enterprises which produced output worth ₹ 281 billion (at current prices) and employing 7.1 million persons. SSI units exported goods valued ₹16 billion which worked out to 23 per cent of India's total exports. By 1990–91, there were 6.79 million SSI units producing goods worth ₹ 788.02 billion and employing 15.83 million persons. Exports by SSI units had risen to ₹ 96.64 billion which was 29.79 per cent of total exports. *(For more on Micro, Small and Medium Enterprises (MSMEs), see Chapter 9).*

In this Chapter we discussed.....

- Statement of Industrial Policy, 1945
- Industrial (Development and Regulation) Act of 1951
- Industrial Policy Resolution, 1956; dominant role for State in industrialization; role for private sector too; balanced development of all regions; ownership and control of industries to be in Indian hands.
- Industrial Policy Statement, 1977: stress on development of small-scale sector; technological support to the small-scale and cottage industries; restraint on large business houses.
- Industrial Policy, 1980: role for both large and small enterprises for balanced and integrated industrial development; regularization of excess capacity in industries; automatic expansion of capacity allowed.
- Role of public sector; setting up of major basic industries; setting up of financial institutions; major thrust to industrialization in Second Plan; setting up of large steel plants; constraints on private sector in setting up heavy, capital-intensive industries; role of public sector overstretched and its consequences; increase in industrial production.

- Industrial licensing, control regime, and its consequences : industrial growth stifled; various Committee reports on the 'permit-licence raj' and the need to liberalize; limited deregulation in 1980's.
- Location and dispersal of industries and regional balance: factors behind location of industries; Planning Commission on the need for balanced development of all regions; steel plants at new centres.
- Large-scale industries: iron and steel industry; location near sources of raw materials; various steel plants set up.
- Textile industry: decline before independence and revival since 1947; Planning Commission on hybrid Bt cotton; spread of cotton industry; importance of textile industry in the economy; positive features of Indian textile industry and challenges; need for modernization.
- Sugar industry: sugarcane cultivation and sugar mills; production and diverse use of by-products; challenges faced by the industry.
- Share of industrial sector in GDP and employment; structural changes in the economy.
- Role of small-scale and village industries; handicaps of small-scale sector; Karve Committee on the sector; need for technical upgradation; role of small-scale sector in the economy and measures to support it; share of the sector in industrial output, employment, and exports.

Important Terms to Note in this Chapter

Industrial policy; Basic and heavy industries; Public and Private sector; Capital-intensive industry; Capital goods; Consumer goods (durables); Hybrid Bt seeds; Small-scale, cottage, and village industries; Small-scale sector; Sectors in economy: Primary, secondary, and tertiary.

Practice Questions

1. What was India's position in regard to industrial development at the time of independence? What steps were taken in the first two Five Year Plans to speed up industrialisation?
2. Outline the Industrial Policies enunciated from time to time after independence by the Central government to promote industrial development.
3. Why are the initial decades, from 1950 to about 1980 in India dubbed 'the Permit-Licence Raj'? What steps were taken by the government to bring about changes from this policy?
4. In what way the policy of licensing and controls hindered industrial progress of India in the initial decades?
5. Describe the relative roles assigned to the Public and Private sectors in India's industrial development. Do you think the overarching role assigned to the Public sector was justified? Did it impede the role of the Private sector and consequently industrial progress?
6. What steps have been taken by the government on location and dispersal of industries to ensure regional balance in development?
7. Which are some of the large-scale industries developed in India and explain the role played by them in the economy.
8. Discuss the critical role played by small-scale and village industries in Indian economy. What steps have been taken by the government to promote them?
9. Account for the change in the spatial pattern of the Iron and Steel industry in the world. *[UPSC Main 2014 (General Studies Paper)]*
10. Can the strategy of regional resource-based manufacturing help in promoting employment in India? *[UPSC Main 2019 (General Studies Paper)]*
11. Account for the present location of iron and steel industries away from the source of raw material, by giving examples. *[UPSC Main 2020 (General Studies Paper)]*

Practice Questions

1. What was India's position in regard to industrial development at the time of independence? What steps were taken in the first two Five Year Plans to speed up industrialisation?

2. Outline the Industrial Policies enunciated from time to time after independence by the Central government to promote industrial development.

3. Why are the initial decades, from 1950 to about 1980 in India dubbed the 'Permit Licence Raj'? What steps were taken by the government to bring about changes from this policy?

4. What was the policy of licensing and controls hindered industrial progress of India in the initial decades?

5. Describe the relative roles assigned to the Public and Private sector in India's industrial development. Do you think the overarching role assigned to the Public sector was justified? Did it impede the role of the Private sector and consequently industrial progress?

6. What steps have been taken by the government on location and dispersal of industries to ensure regional balance in development?

7. Which are some of the large scale industries developed in India and explain the role played by them in the economy.

8. Discuss the critical role played by small scale and village industries in Indian economy. What steps have been taken by the government to promote them?

9. Account for the change in the spatial pattern of the Iron and Steel Industry in the world.

[UPSC Main 2014 (General Studies Paper)]

10. Can the strategy of regional resource-based manufacturing help in promoting employment in India? [UPSC Main 2019 (General Studies Paper)]

11. Account for the present location of iron and steel industries away from the source of raw material, by giving examples. [UPSC Main 2020 (General Studies Paper)]

CHAPTER 5 BANKING AND FINANCE

- Banking Scenario at Independence
- Amalgamation and Consolidation
- Reserve Bank of India and its Role
- Planning Commission on the role of RBI
- Functions of the Reserve Bank of India
- Setting up of the State Bank of India
- Expansion and Penetration of Banks
- Banks as Agents of Change
- RBI and Agricultural Credit
- Regional Rural Banks and NABARD
- Nationalisation of Banks
- Factors behind Nationalisation of Banks
- Impact of Bank Nationalization
- Limitations of Bank Nationalisation
- Other Financial Institutions
- Conclusion
- Nationalisation of banks: its pros and cons

❑ BANKING AND FINANCE: 1947–1990

The banking sector has played an important role in the economic development of India since independence. The sector, as with all other sectors, not having been developed to the full potential during the Colonial era, and with bulk of the population not exposed to banking facilities, the Government had to take a series of measures to expand and strengthen it after independence.

Banking Scenario at Independence

The early years of independence posed several challenges for the banking sector in India. On the eve of independence, the banking system was concentrated primarily in the urban and metropolitan areas. It was entirely in the private sector, largely controlled by business families and other groups who held considerable volume of deposits. Being dominated by business groups, the lending policy was also lopsided. In the process, agriculture, which was the most critical sector in the economy, suffered neglect so far as bank credit was concerned.

Even the Reserve Bank of India was not completely State-owned until it was nationalized under the Reserve Bank of India (Public Ownership) Act, 1948. The Imperial Bank (which was later to become the State Bank of India) and other major banks such as the Central Bank of India Ltd., Punjab National Bank Ltd., Bank of India Ltd., Bank of Baroda Ltd., and United Commercial Bank Ltd., each holding public deposits of ₹ 100 Crore and more, and other scheduled commercial banks were all in the private sector and had a regional character. Most of the scheduled commercial banks were located in West Bengal, followed by Madras and Bombay states. Though there were numerous non-scheduled banks, they had only a relatively small share in the banking sector.

Yet another problem was the series of bank failures which continued to occur after independence. In 1948 itself, several banks had to be closed down as they had over-stretched themselves by opening more branches than they could sustain on the strength of their resources, and by advancing large loans against property or inadequate security. Repeated bank failures caused great hardships to the savers and eroded the faith of public in the banking system. Many non-scheduled banks, especially in West Bengal became untraceable. Of the 165 non-scheduled banks reported to exist in June 1954, the whereabouts of 107 banks were not known. The licence of all these and the remaining non-scheduled banks, barring six, was cancelled.

Amalgamation and Consolidation

In view of the bank failures and weakness and unviability of several banks, and in order to protect the savings of depositors, it was felt that it would be prudent to wind up insolvent banks or amalgamate them with stronger banks. Accordingly, in the 1950s, efforts were directed at formulating legislation for consolidation, compulsory amalgamation, and liquidation of banks. Thus, the Banking Regulation Act, 1949 was passed which provided for the supervision and regulation of banking and had provisions for amalgamation of banks. The Reserve Bank of India (Transfer to Public Ownership) Act, 1948 was also passed bringing the Central Bank under full State control in order to regulate and streamline the working of the banking system. Between 1954 and 1966, some 300 banks which were unviable were either amalgamated or otherwise ceased to function, or their liabilities and assets were transferred to other banks.

The process of bank consolidation was accompanied by a vigorous bank licensing policy. A number of banks that did not comply with the requisite norms were also delicensed.

Consequently, the incidence of bank failures came down considerably.

The bank failures and the hardship caused to the depositors led the Reserve Bank to provide safety nets to depositors. The Banking Companies (Second Amendment) Act, 1960, which came into force in September, 1960 sought to facilitate expeditious payments to the depositors of banks in case of liquidation and also vested the Government and the Reserve Bank with additional powers to rehabilitate banks in difficulties. Further, to ensure the safety of deposits of small depositors in banks, the Deposit Insurance Corporation Act, 1961 was enacted and the Deposit Insurance Corporation of India was established in January 1962. India was then one of the few countries to introduce such a deposit insurance scheme. These measures were expected to boost depositors' confidence in the banking system and thereby, facilitate mobilization of deposits and promote the spread and growth of the banking sector.

❑ RESERVE BANK OF INDIA AND ITS ROLE

Background

Various committees that went into the causes of bank failures during the colonial period had recommended the setting up of a central bank for the country. Accordingly, the Reserve Bank of India Act, 1934 was enacted paving the way for the establishment of the Reserve Bank of India (RBI). The twin issues of bank failures and the need for catering to the requirements of agriculture were the two prime reasons for setting up RBI.

As stated earlier, it was brought under full state ownership only when it was nationalized under the Reserve Bank of India (Transfer to Public Ownership) Act, 1948.

It was felt that the establishment of a central bank would provide for proper regulation, better governance, and greater cohesion in the banking sector of the country.

> The twin issues of bank failures and the need for catering to the requirements of agriculture were the two prime reasons for setting up RBI.

The first task before the Reserve Bank after independence was to develop a sound architecture alongside modern banking practices. It was recognized that banks had a crucial role to play in promoting economic prosperity and stability. Through expansion and better penetration, banks could deepen financial inclusion, popularize banking, and encourage saving habits. This was essential, formalizing the much-needed resources for investment and rapid development. This was especially necessary in the context of the initiation of planned socio-economic development with ambitious schemes and targets involving heavy outlays.

As a regulator of the banking system, the Reserve Bank was empowered by the Banking Companies Act to inspect banks. The instances of failures of banks that occurred due to misappropriation of depositors' funds underscored the need to strengthen the mechanism of inspection. In 1949, the Reserve Bank decided to organise an efficient machinery for the systematic and periodical inspection of all banking institutions in the country, irrespective of their size and standing.

The Reserve Bank assumed a unique role in this context that was occasioned by the predominantly agricultural base of the Indian economy and the urgent need to expand and co-ordinate the institutional credit structure for agriculture and rural development. The policy initiative by the Reserve Bank and the Government on rural finance had three-fold objectives. First, to understand the dimension of the problem, a committee was set up to make comprehensive study. Second, the Imperial Bank of India was nationalized. Third, for training bank officials in the area of agricultural banking, an institution was set up.

Planning Commission on the role of RBI

While drafting the First Five Year Plan, the Planning Commission observed as follows on the role of the RBI in the economy:

"There is no doubt that the Reserve Bank of India, which is a nationalized institution, will play its appropriate part in furthering economic development along agreed lines. The Bank has succeeded in bringing the organised sector of the money market well under its control. It has recently initiated measures for the development of a bill market in India which will impart greater elasticity to the credit system. The Bank is also playing a more active role in the provision of rural finance and is devoting special attention to the problem of promoting banking development in parts of the country in which it has hitherto been lacking. These developments will strengthen the credit system materially. Under the Banking Companies Act, the Reserve Bank has wide powers for regulation and supervision of the credit policy of banks. More than these legal powers, it is, we feel, the moral prestige of the Reserve Bank and the close understanding between its management and the management of private banks that is of special importance in the alignment of the banking system to the needs of a planned economy".

"Central banking in a planned economy can hardly be confined to the regulation of the overall supply of credit or to a somewhat negative regulation of the flow of bank credit. It would have to take on a direct and active role, firstly, in creating or helping to create the machinery needed for financing developmental activities all over the country and, secondly, in ensuring that the finance available flows in the directions intended. For the successful fulfilment of the Plan it may become necessary to direct special credit facilities to certain lines of high priority; banking development, through the normal incentives of private banking, is apt to be a slow process, particularly in a country in which deposit banking and the use of cheques is likely to take root only slowly among the masses of the people." (First Five Year Plan, Planning Commission).

Functions of the Reserve Bank of India

The Reserve Bank of India not only discharges its regulatory functions in the sphere of banking, but also plays an active and supporting role in the process of socio-economic development of the country. *Its main functions are*:

- Formulating and implementing monetary policy with the objective of maintaining price stability and ensuring adequate flow of credit to productive sectors. It periodically reviews the policy and fixes the Bank rate through which it regulates the general level of interest rates in the banking system. When the RBI changes the bank rate, commercial banks are expected to change their deposit and lending rates in tandem. Monetary policy has as its objectives controlling price levels, stimulating growth, and ensuring financial stability in the economy.
- For implementing the monetary policy, the RBI has the instruments of Repo rate and Reverse Repo rate. Repo (Repurchase) rate is the rate at which the Reserve Bank of India lends short-term money to commercial banks against securities. When the repo rate increases, borrowing from RBI becomes more expensive for banks (implying tighter money policy) and when the RBI reduces the repo rate, it becomes cheaper for banks to borrow money (cheaper or easy money policy). Reverse Repo rate is the rate which the RBI pays banks when they park their short-term excess liquidity with the RBI; it signifies the rate at which the central bank absorbs surplus liquidity from the banks.
- As banker to banks, RBI regulates and varies the cash reserves of the commercial banks through the mechanism of Statutory Liquidity Ratio (SLR) and Cash Reserve Ratio (CRR). The RBI holds part of the cash reserves of banks and also lends funds to banks. CRR is the proportion of the deposits which the commercial banks are required to keep with the RBI. SLR is the fraction of their total demand and time deposits which the commercial banks are required by RBI to invest in specified liquid assets—gold, cash, or other approved securities. RBI acts as the lender of last resort.
- As banker to government, it undertakes the banking business of the Union and State governments. It accepts money and makes payments on behalf of these governments and provides loans and advances. RBI also manages both the internal and external public debt of the country.
- RBI has the sole authority for issuing currency notes except the one-Rupee note/coin and coins of smaller denominations which are issued by the Central Government. It has to ensure adequate supply of currency in the economy.
- RBI is the custodian of foreign exchange reserves of the country and manages the utilization of the reserves. With the introduction of floating exchange rate and convertibility of the Rupee following reforms, RBI intervenes in the foreign exchange market only to keep the value of the Rupee stable within reasonable limits. RBI also helps to facilitate external trade.
- As regulator and supervisor of the financial system, RBI lays down the broad parameters within which the country's banking and financial system functions with a view to maintain public confidence in the system, protect depositors' interests and provide cost-effective banking services to the public.

The role and autonomy of Reserve Bank of India, and the relationship between RBI and the Government has, of late, been the subject-matter of much discussion. (See also chapter 13, pp. 13.16-7).

❑ SETTING UP OF THE STATE BANK OF INDIA

One of the important steps the government took as part of its policy of extending banking facilities on a substantial scale was the conversion of the Imperial Bank into the State Bank of India (SBI) by enacting the State Bank of India Act, 1955. Though nationalized, the government took care to provide autonomy to State Bank to keep it free from governmental and political interference, and to maintain high professional standards of banking practices. Even while orienting its policies towards developmental goals, the government took care to maintain the corporate character of the SBI.

The State Bank was not only expected to embark on a major branch expansion strategy, but also play an important role in mobilizing deposits and help in the implementation of development schemes under the Five Year Plans. As against a target of opening 400 branches in unbanked centres within 5 years, it could open 416 branches.

The State Bank of India was required to act as the principal agent of the Reserve Bank to handle banking transactions of the Union and the State Governments throughout the country. This was in furtherance of the objective of promoting a robust rural credit movement to strengthen the agrarian sector. The establishment of SBI led to a major transformation in the banking scenario in the country.

The nationalization of Imperial Bank and the formation of SBI was a landmark event in the banking sphere and was a precursor to the nationalization of banks which was to come later.

❑ EXPANSION AND PENETRATION OF BANKS

At the time of independence, banking had not penetrated into semi-urban and rural areas. Against this background, proactive steps were taken to extend banking facilities through branch expansion. The number of bank branches rose from 4151 in 1951 to 7025 in 1967. This increase was mainly on account of rise in the number of branches of scheduled commercial banks that rose from 2647 offices in 1951 to 6816 offices in 1967.

Extending the banking facilities to the rural areas was a major objective at the time of independence. It was proposed that the Imperial Bank of India (which was later to become State Bank of India) should extend its branches to taluk or tehsil towns where the volume of government transactions and business potential justified opening of branches. Though the Imperial Bank of India was given a target of opening 114 offices within a period of 5 years commencing from July 1951, it could open only 63 branches till June 1955. Other commercial banks and co-operative banks were advised to open branches in smaller towns and semi-urban areas. It was felt that postal savings banks and cooperative banks could be expanded to cater to villages.

But banking had still not penetrated sufficiently into the rural and semi-urban centres and usurious moneylenders played a dominant role in the rural sector. An exploitative nature of linkage existed between agricultural output and credit, with the moneylenders and landlords giving advances to the cultivator and purchasing his produce at less than the market price. It resulted in high interest rates and low price for the produce which harmed the interests of not only the farmers, but artisans, self-employed entrepreneurs, and small-time traders in villages who also needed loans and advances. This was on account of institutional bank credit not being available to agriculture, small industries, and small traders in the rural sector. Since the rural credit markets were isolated, the moneylenders and landlords could act as monopolists and charge exorbitant interest rates.

❑ BANKS AS AGENTS OF CHANGE

The primary objective of the Government's policy after independence was to make banks important agents of change by enhancing the outreach of institutional credit. Banks were considered to be unique among financial institutions and were assigned an important role in development from the very beginning of the planned era. Resources mobilized through deposits were required to be channelled to productive uses, and the banking system was expected to function as an effective conduit to spread institutional credit to various sectors across the country.

❑ RBI AND AGRICULTURAL CREDIT

As stated earlier, lack of institutional finance to agriculturists posed a major problem. For banks, lack of knowledge of the local area and conditions was a handicap in extending agricultural loans. Besides, granting small agricultural loans required the banks to maintain a large number of small accounts which was both time-consuming and less profitable. Also, banks' lending operations were largely based on security, and the small borrowers had little security apart from their land, which was often not unencumbered. Most banks in the organized sector extended loans primarily to traders dealing in agricultural produce.

The government and the Reserve Bank were seized of the problem of rural finance soon after independence. A major initiative was taken in 1951 with the appointment of a Committee headed by A.D. Gorwala, known as the All India Rural Credit Survey Committee. The Committee studied various issues related to rural finance and submitted its report in 1954. It observed that large parts of the country were not covered by co-operatives and even in areas which had been covered, a large segment of the agricultural population remained outside its membership. Also, even where membership did exist, the bulk of the credit requirement was met from other sources. The Committee recommended introducing an integrated system of rural credit, partnership of the government in the share capital of the cooperatives, and also appointment of government nominees on their boards, thus participating in their management. The Committee emphasized the importance of training of personnel on all related aspects.

According to the Committee, the total borrowing of the farmers was estimated at ₹750 crore in 1951–52. Of this, commercial banks provided only 0.9 per cent, co-operatives 3.3 per cent, while the rest was provided by moneylenders, landlords, and traders at much higher interest rates. The recommendations of this Committee laid the foundation for furthering the role of institutional credit to the rural sector through formal channel of cooperatives and commercial banks. Primary Agricultural Credit Societies (PACS) and District and State Co-operative Banks and Land Mortgage Banks were set up to lend finances to the rural sector. Agricultural Refinance Corporation of India was also set up in 1963, which was to provide funds by way of refinance to central land mortgage banks, State cooperative banks, and scheduled commercial banks.

Though these measures made some headway in improving the position of finances for agriculture, the system had many shortcomings such as inadequacy of funds with co-operative credit societies, inability to provide timely credit, or fully meet the credit requirements of agriculturists, especially the small and marginal farmers. Existence of multiple agencies which followed different policies and procedures in regard to extending credit facilities and lack of co-ordination among them also compounded the problem. Besides, inability of borrowers to repay loans on time and accumulation of overdues and debts weakened the functioning of credit societies and co-operative banks.

Later, in 1966, RBI set up another All India Rural Credit Survey Committee to look into the progress in the area of agricultural credit since 1954. This Committee observed that the requirements of rural credit could not be met fully by the co-operative societies and recommended that commercial banks too should play an active role in financing the rural sector. The concept of 'priority sector' consisting of agriculture, small, and village industries, etc., for lending by banks was formalized in the 1972, although initially there were no specific targets for priority sector lending. However, in November 1974, public sector banks were advised that their priority sector lending should reach a level of not less than one-third of the outstanding credit by March 1979.

Primary Agricultural Credit Societies (PACS) and District and State Co-operative Banks and Land Mortgage Banks were set up to lend finances to the rural sector. Agricultural Refinance Corporation of India was also set up in 1963, which was to provide funds by way of refinance to central land mortgage banks, State cooperative banks, and scheduled commercial banks.

Regional Rural Banks and NABARD

It was against this background that the government nationalized 14 leading banks in 1969 to exercise social control and reorient their working to better serve the needs of the economy. Later, Regional Rural Banks (RRBs) were established in 1975 under the provisions of an Ordinance promulgated in September 1975 and followed by Regional Rural Banks Act, 1976 to develop the rural economy and provide institutional credit for the rural and agriculture sector. In 1982, the National Bank for Agriculture and Rural Development (NABARD) was set up and the agricultural credit functions of RBI and refinance functions of the then Agricultural Refinance and Development Corporation (ARDC) were transferred to NABARD. NABARD serves as a refinancing institution and extends credit for agriculture, small, village and cottage industries and rural artisans to foster integrated rural development. It also provides short, medium, and long-term credit to Co-operative banks, RRBs and other agencies as authorized by the Reserve Bank. It has played a significant role in strengthening the co-operative credit institutions in the country and rejuvenating the rural sector.

❑ NATIONALIZATION OF BANKS

Nationalization of banks in 1969 was a watershed movement in the history of banking in India. The Government of India issued the 'Banking Companies (Acquisition and Transfer of Undertakings) Ordinance, 1969' under which 14 major commercial banks with deposits of ₹ 50 crore and more were nationalized in July 1969. Later in 1980, 6 more commercial banks were nationalized, thus bringing bulk of the banking sector under the control of Government of India.

Factors Behind Nationalization of Banks

Even two decades after independence, banks in India, except for the State Bank of India, were in private hands, controlled and operated by large business houses and big industrialists. It was seen that they failed to cater to the credit needs of a large segment of the economy which comprised the smaller business and industrial units, small-scale, cottage and village industries, farmers, rural artisans, etc. Bank branches were being opened mostly in major cities and bigger towns leaving many areas without banking facilities. There was imperative need for expansion and penetration of banks into the vast stretches of semi-urban and rural areas to reduce regional imbalances and the rural-urban divide. Also banks had to play a constructive and proactive role in unison with the various developmental programmes under the Five Year Plans.The objective was to make the banking sector better serve the needs of development of the economy in conformity with national policy objectives.

Impact of Bank Nationalisation

Nationalisation of banks had a salutary effect by giving the much needed fillip to the economy. During the two decades after nationalisation, i.e., between 1969 and 1991, the year when India effected major economic reforms, there was considerable expansion in the banking sector, both geographically and functionally. The number of branches of commercial banks increased from 8,262 in 1969 to 60,190 in 1991 and further to 149,775 by 2020. (See Table 5.1 for details). Likewise, there was significant increase in the number of branches in the rural and semi-urban areas as will be seen from Table 5.2. The number of rural branches increased from 1,833 in 1969 to 35,187 in 1991 which works out to 58.4 per cent of the total number of branches in 1991 as against just 22.2 per cent in 1969. The number of rural branches has further risen to 52,320.

The Lead Bank scheme, launched by the Reserve Bank with a view to mobilizing deposits on a massive scale throughout the country and also for stepping up lending to weaker sections of the economy, became the principal mode for branch expansion. The 'lead bank' designated for the district was responsible for taking lead role in surveying the credit needs of the population and development of banking and credit facilities in the district allotted to it.

Table 5.1 Expansion in Number of Bank Branches

Year	No. of Bank Branches	Year	No. of Bank Branches
1951	4151	1991	60220
1967	7025	2001	65919
1969	8262	2020	149775

Table 5.2: Population Group-wise Number of Branches of Scheduled Commercial Banks (Number)

Year	Rural	Semi-urban	Urban	Metropolitan	Total
1975	6807	5598	3489	2836	18730
1980	15105	8122	5178	4014	32419
1985	30185	9816	6578	4806	51385
1990	34791	11324	8042	5595	59752
2000	32734	14407	10052	8219	65412
2010	32430	20788	16684	15254	85156
2015	48557	33766	23036	20498	125857
2020	52320	42249	27182	28024	149775

Source: Reserve Bank of India: Handbook of Statistics on Indian Economy, 2015 & 2019-20.

Following the rapid expansion in branches of banks, the average population served per office also came down significantly implying better coverage of population for banking. (*See Table 5.3 for details*).

Table 5.3 Population Covered per Branch of Banks (Number in thousands)

	June 1969	March 1991	March 2000	March 2006	March 2010	March 2014
Population per office (in ₹ thousands)	64.0	14	15	16.0	13.8	10.8

Source: Reserve Bank of India, Basic Statistical Returns of Scheduled Commercial Banks in India, 1996–2014.

There was also manifold increase in deposits in the scheduled banks over the years as will be seen from Table 5.4. As a ratio of GDP at current prices, bank deposits increased from 13 per cent in 1969–70 to about 38 per cent in 1990–91 which points to the important role of banks in the mobilization of savings. Advances made by banks during this period also showed significant increase from 10 per cent to about 25 per cent of GDP which shows the increased support by banks to agriculture, industry, and the services sector.

The ratio of advances by banks to the priority sector—agriculture, small-scale industries, and small borrowers—to net bank credit increased from 15 per cent in 1969 to 41 per cent in 1991. This helped to minimize the role of moneylenders and indigenous bankers over the years. Dependence of rural households for loans from non-institutional agencies declined significantly from 93 per cent in 1950–51 to39 per cent in 1981. Thus, the benefits of banking facilities reached a much wider section of the population and served as an important agency of socio-economic change.

Table 5.4 Deposits in Scheduled Commercial Banks in India (in ₹ thousand)

	June 1969	March 1991	March 1995	March 2000	March 2010	March 2014
Deposits In ₹ thousand	4646	210199	386859	851593*	4492826	7913443

* March 2000 figure includes Resurgent India Bonds (RIB) of ₹17945 Crore.

Source: *Reserve Bank of India, Basic Statistical Returns of Scheduled Commercial Banks in India, 1996–2014.*

❑ LIMITATIONS OF BANK NATIONALISATION

Though the banking sector registered significant progress since nationalisation, in due course, it led to many limitations and shortcomings in its working. Though justified on socio-economic considerations, the dominance of banks in the public sector led to a high degree of regulation and rigidity. Entry and expansion was subjected to control. Despite the quantitative expansion, many areas especially in the backward and hilly regions did not have banking facility. Besides, there was growing concern about operational efficiency. Lack of accountability, political interference, and declining productivity affected the performance and profitability of banks. Mandatory allocation of credit for specific sectors, concessional and differential interest rates, and a system of administered interest rates all told upon the financial results of banks.

With decline in the quality of assets and rise in sticky advances, banks had to make adequate provision for the bad assets and this caused much stress on their financial position. The Regional Rural Banks were in even more difficult position with accumulated losses. (For more on nationalization of banks, see Box 5.1 at the end of this Chapter).

❑ OTHER FINANCIAL INSTITUTIONS

While commercial and co-operative banks primarily cater to short-term credit needs, there are other major development banks and state financial institutions which provide medium and long-term finance. The Industrial Finance Corporation (IFC), the Industrial Development Bank of India (IDBI), Small Industries Development Bank of India (SIDBI), Industrial Credit and Investment Corporation of India (ICICI), Industrial Investment Bank of India (IIBI), India Infrastructure Finance Company Ltd (IIFCL), Export-Import Bank, National Housing Bank, etc. provide long-term finance to industry and other areas on which they focus. These institutions have all played an important role in extending financial assistance to new ventures and thus helped to foster industrial development.

❑ CONCLUSION

The developments in the Indian financial system during the four decades from 1950 to 1990 presents a mixed picture. While in regard to realizing the socio-economic goals set forth in the development plans, the outcome has been noteworthy, over-regulation, a certain degree of lack of accountability, and political compulsions have impinged upon, and retarded, the performance of the sector. This has affected the standing and viability of some of the institutions necessitating major reforms which have been initiated after 1991. These are discussed in Chapter 13.

Box 5.1 Nationalisation of Banks

Examine the factors which led to nationalisation of banks in 1969 and 1980, and analyse its pros and cons. What measures can be taken to improve the working of Public Sector Banks (PSBs)?

The Indian financial sector underwent a major change in July 1969 when the government nationalized the 14 biggest commercial banks with deposits of over ₹ 50 crore. The Supreme Court held the step void on the ground that it was discriminatory against the 14 banks and that the compensation proposed to be paid by Govt was not fair compensation. But government passed the Banking Companies (Acquisition and Transfer of Undertakings) Act, 1970 which ratified the action.

Later in 1980, 6 more commercial banks were nationalized, thus bringing bulk of the banking sector under the control of Government of India.

The prelude to this major step was taken in Dec.1967 with the "Introduction of Social Controls" over banks to ensure better alignment of the banking system to the needs of economic policy. Soon after, a National Credit Council was set up to assist RBI and government to assess credit priorities on an all-India basis.

➢ **The backdrop of the Economy**

The landmark step came at the end of a troubled decade for India and was necessitated by various factors:

- The country had been buffeted by economic as well as political shocks. There were two wars – with China in 1962 and Pakistan in 1965 – which put immense pressure on public finances.
- Two back-to-back droughts during 1965-67 not only led to food shortages, but also compromised national security because India had to depend on American food aid.
- The three-year plan holiday from 1966-69 was a period of instability which disrupted aggregate demand as public investment was cut.

➢ **Factors behind Nationalisation**

- ♦ The need for the nationalisation was felt mainly because private commercial banks were not fulfilling the social and developmental goals of banking which were essential for speedy industrialisation.
- ♦ The developmental goals of financial intermediation were not being achieved other than for large industries and established business houses.
- ♦ While the industry's share in credit disbursed by commercial banks almost doubled between 1951 and 1968, from 34 per cent to 68 per cent, agriculture received less than 2 per cent of total credit. Other key areas such as credit to small-scale industries and for exports were also neglected.

- Despite the enactment of the Banking Regulation Act in 1949 and the nationalisation of the largest bank, the State Bank of India in 1955, the expansion of commercial banking had largely excluded rural areas, agriculture sector and small borrowers.

Benefits of nationalisation

- **Aligning with State policy:** The main objective of bank nationalisation was to serve better the needs of development of the economy and to promote the welfare of the people in conformity with the State policy.
- **Expansion of the sector:** After nationalisation, there was steady expansion of banks both geographically and functionally. The number of branches of banks rose from 8,262 in 1969 to 65,898 in 2001 and 149,775 by 2020.
- **Expansion to rural areas:** The expansion of rural branches was especially noteworthy. It rose from 6,807 in 1975 to 48,557 by 2015 and stood at 52,320 in 2020.
- **Better coverage:** The expansion resulted in better coverage of population. The average population served by a branch declined from 65,000 in 1969 to 15,000 in 2001.
- **Increase in savings:** A positive impact was that financial savings rose as banks opened new branches in areas that were unbanked. Deposits in Scheduled Commercial banks rose from ₹ 4,646 crore in 1969 to ₹ 79,13,443 crore in 2014 and to ₹ 126,39,009 crore in 2019. Bank deposits expanded as a ratio of GDP (at current prices) from 13 per cent in 1969-70 to around 38 per cent in 1990-91 which highlights the role of banks in mobilising savings.
- **Increase in domestic savings:** Gross domestic savings almost doubled as a percentage of national income in the 1970s. A growing part of this was absorbed by the government itself through increases in the statutory liquidity ratio (SLR). (SLR is the fraction of the total demand and time deposits, with the commercial banks, which they are required by the RBI to invest in specified liquid assets – gold, cash or other approved securities.) Thus, resources available for developmental and welfare expenditure kept increasing.
- **Catering to Priority sectors:** The purpose of nationalization was to promote rapid growth in agriculture, small industries and small borrowers. The ratio of priority sector advances to net bank credit increased from 15 per cent in June 1969 to about 41 per cent by June 1991.
- **Reduction of role of middlemen:** Increased lending by banks helped to bring down the role of middlemen such as moneylenders and indigenous bankers. Dependence of rural households for loans from non-institutional agencies also came down.
- **Support for Small industries and Exports:** Financial support by banks for exports and small industries encouraged new entrepreneurs and helped to develop the hinterland and backward areas. Banks had to reserve as much as 40 percent of credit to the priority sectors – agriculture and small and medium industries. Banks directing more funds towards these sectors gave fillip to development.

➤ The downside of nationalisation

While nationalisation of banks did bring about many benefits for the economy, it also led to certain undesirable consequences and unhealthy practices.

- **Political influence:** Bank nationalisation had political undertones. As an overall political strategy to squeeze big business houses that owned and controlled banks and was unfriendly to the government, it was a good step. But it was also done to help the then ruling party build a new and wider political base.
- **Impact on autonomy of banks:** The government had assured that there will be autonomy for banks and that Bank boards would have well-defined powers. The government was to only issue broad directions on policy and would guard against interference in the working of banks on political or other considerations. But as things turned out, over time banks came under political pressure, and successive governments continued to maintain tight grip on the banking sector.
- **Loan "melas" and bad debts:** The political control and influence which promoted indiscriminate "loan melas" is one of the factors which led to bad loans and non-performing assets (NPAs) that has weighed down on the banking sector.
- **Efficiency and productivity:** There has been growing concern over the operational efficiency of public sector banks (PSBs) and perceptible decline in the productivity and profitability of commercial banks.
- **Rising NPAs:** The growing volume of non-performing assets (NPAs) of banks has been a matter of concern. While NPAs have gone up over the years in all categories of banks (see Table 5.5 at the end of this Box), the Public sector banks (PSBs) account for a substantial part of it. While NPAs remained largely unchanged during the period immediately following the global financial crisis, it started rising from 2011 onwards, and increased sharply after 2015. This may have been because in 2015, the Reserve Bank began to carry out Asset Quality Review (AQR) to encourage banks to proactively recognise such bad assets.
- **Need for provisioning and write-offs:** With the decline in the quality of loans and NPAs, banks are constrained to set apart funds for provisioning towards doubtful debts or write-off unrecoverable debts which impairs their financial health. Further it is a matter of concern that debts of large borrowers (with exposure of ₹ 5 crore and above) constituted 79.8 per cent of NPAs and 53.7 per cent of total loans in 2020. Efforts are being made by banks to recover as much of debt as possible.
- **Incidence of frauds:** Frauds have emerged as a major source of operational risk in PSBs. While there have been such instances in private banks too, the vulnerability of PSBs to frauds is greater due to its vast network and coverage. Several factors account for frauds. These include lack of due diligence in granting loans, unsecured loans, loans to unscrupulous borrowers, collusion with parties seeking loans, slack administration, loopholes in procedures and systems and flaws in technology adopted.

According to RBI report, 98 per cent of frauds in terms of value were related to loans granted. Besides, there has been concentration of large value frauds, with top fifty credit-related frauds constituting 76 per cent of the total amount reported as frauds during 2019-20.

- **Delayed detection of frauds:** Of greater concern is that the incidence of frauds was spread over several previous years indicating that detection of frauds has taken long time which makes their resolution even more difficult. The average lag between the date of occurrence of frauds and their detection by banks was 24 months during 2019-20. In large frauds, those involving ₹ 100 crore and above, the average lag was 63 months and the dates of occurrence of these frauds were spread over several previous years.

  The RBI has taken several measures to plug loopholes in they system, tightened reporting systems by banks and increased supervision and oversight.

➤ **Way forward for Banking Reforms: P J Nayak Committee report**

It is worth noting in this context that a committee to "Review Governance of Boards of Banks in India", headed by P.J. Nayak, a former Chairman and CEO, Axis Bank, and Former Country Head, Morgan Stanley India was appointed by the Governor of RBI in 2014 with broad terms of reference. The Committee had observed the following aspects relating to PSBs:

- The financial position of public sector banks (PSBs) is fragile, partly masked by regulatory forbearance. Forbearance delays, but does not extinguish, the recognition of this fragility.
- Capital is significantly eroded with the proportion of stressed assets rising rapidly.
- Governance difficulties in PSBs arise from several externally imposed constraints which include dual regulation, by the Finance Ministry in addition to RBI.
- Differences in compensation compared to private sector banks, leading to the erosion of specialist skills. External vigilance enforcement though the CVC and CBI.
- Limited applicability of RTI Act.

➤ **The Committee recommended as follows:**

- The Government distances itself from several bank governance functions which it presently discharges.
- For this purpose, the Bank Nationalisation Acts of 1970 and 1980, together with the SBI Act and the SBI (Subsidiary Banks) Act, be repealed and all banks be incorporated under the Companies Act.
- A Bank Investment Company (BIC) be constituted to which the Government transfers its holdings in banks. The Government's powers in relation to the governance of banks should also be transferred to BIC.
- This would be a beneficial trade-off for the Government because it would continue to be the dominant shareholder and, without its control in banks diminishing, it would create the conditions for its banks to compete more successfully.
- It is a fundamental irony that presently the Government disadvantages the very banks it has invested in.

- If the Government stake in these banks were to reduce to less than 50%, together with certain other executive measures taken, the external constraints mentioned above would disappear.

Table 5.5: Non-Performing Assets (NPAs) of Banks

Gross and Net NPAs of Scheduled Commercial Banks

(Amount in ₹ Crore)

Non-Performing Assets (NPAs)						
	Gross			Net		
Year	Amount	As %-age of Gross Advances	As %-age of Total Assets	Amount	As %-age of Gross Advances	As %-age of Total Assets
Scheduled Commercial Banks						
2007-08	56309	2.2	1.3	24730	1.0	0.6
2014-15	323335	4.3	2.7	175841	2.4	1.5
2018-19	936474	9.1	5.6	355076	3.7	2.1
Public Sector banks						
2007-08	40452	2.2	1.3	17836	1.0	0.6
2014-15	278468	5.0	3.2	159951	2.9	1.8
2018-19	739541	11.6	7.3	285123	4.8	2.8
New Private Sector banks						
2007-08	12997	2.5	1.4	5647	1.1	0.6
2014-15	34106	2.1	1.3	14128	0.9	0.5
2018-19	183604	5.3	3.5	67309	2.0	1.3
Foreign Banks in India						
2007-08	2859	1.8	0.8	1247	0.8	0.3
2014-15	10761	3.2	1.4	1762	0.5	0.2
2018-19	12242	3.0	1.2	2050	0.5	0.2

Source: *Reserve Bank of India, Handbook of Statistics on Indian Economy, 2019-20, Table 58.*

In this Chapter we discussed.....

- Banking scenario at Independence.
- Bank failures and amalgamation and consolidation of banks.
- Passage of the Banking Companies (Second Amendment) Act, 1960 and Deposit Insurance Corporation Act, 1961; Deposit Insurance Corporation of India set up in 1962.
- Reserve Bank of India Act, 1934 was enacted and Reserve Bank of India (RBI) established; it was nationalized under the Reserve Bank of India (Transfer to Public Ownership) Act, 1948; role of RBI; Planning Commission on the role of RBI; functions of RBI.
- Nationalization of the Imperial Bank and formation of State Bank of India (SBI) under the State Bank of India Act, 1955; State Bank of
- India, as the principal agent of the Reserve Bank.
- Expansion and penetration of banks into semi-urban and rural areas; increase in the number of bank branches between 1951 and 1967; agricultural sector dominated by moneylenders and landlords for financing; lack of institutional bank credit to agriculture, small industries, and small traders in the rural sector; banks as agents of change, to mobilize resources and provide institutional credit to various sectors.
- RBI and agricultural credit; All India Rural Credit Survey Committee studies rural credit problem (1951–54); recommends rural credit to be provided through cooperatives and commercial banks; Primary
- Agricultural Credit Societies (PACS) and District and State Co-operative
- Banks and Land Mortgage Banks set up; Agricultural Refinance
- Corporation of India set up in 1963; problems persist in regard to rural credit; All India Rural Credit Survey Committee, 1966 reviews the position of rural credit; concept of 'priority sector', consisting of agriculture, small, and village industries, etc., for lending by banks was formalized in the 1972; Regional Rural Banks set up in 1976 and NABARD in 1982.
- Nationalization of banks and factors leading to it; impact of bank nationalization; increase in bank branches and branches in rural and semi-urban areas between 1969 and 1990; the Lead Bank scheme launched; manifold increase in deposits; limitations of bank nationalization.
- Other financial institutions providing medium and long-term credit to industry and services: IFC, IDBI, ICICI, SIDBI, IIFCL, EXIM Bank, NHB.
- Benefits and Drawbacks of Bank nationalization.

Important Terms to Note in this Chapter

Monetary policy; Bank rate; Repo (Repurchase) Rate and Reverse Repo Rate; Statutory Liquidity Ratio (SLR); Cash Reserve Ratio (CRR); Floating Exchange rate; Convertibility of rupee; Priority sector ; Lead Banks; Bank nationalisation

Practice Questions

1. Describe the state of banking sector soon after independence. What measures were taken by the government to improve it?
2. What is the role of the Reserve Bank of India in the economy and what are its functions?
3. What were the factors which led to nationalisation of banks? How far it benefited the economy and what were its shortcomings?
4. Describe the steps taken by the government to expand India's banking sector after independence. How far it helped the urban and rural sectors of the economy?
5. What measures were taken by the government and the Reserve Bank of India to promote agricultural credit after independence?
6. Describe the role played by Regional Rural Banks and the National Bank for Agriculture and Rural Development (NABARD) in helping the rural sector.
7. Mention some of the development banks and financial institutions which provide medium and long term finance and the role played by them in Indian economy.

PART-II

1991 Reforms and After

Chapter 6 Economic Reforms of the 1990s

Chapter 7 Agricultural Development since 1990

Chapter 8 Industrial Development since 1990

Chapter 9 Small Scale Industry

Chapter 10 Infrastructure (Transport and Communications)

Chapter 11 Energy and Power

Chapter 12 IT Industry

Chapter 13 Banking and Financial Sector Reforms

Chapter 14 Fiscal Policy and Tax Reforms

Chapter 15 Foreign Trade and Commerce

Chapter 16 Labour, Employment, and Skill Development

Chapter 17 Inequality and Poverty Alleviation

Chapter 18 Demographic Issues and Vital Statistics

Chapter 19 Planning and Developmental Issues

Chapter 20 International Economic Issues

CHAPTER

ECONOMIC REFORMS OF THE 1990s

- Reforms and problems during 1985-90
- 1991 Economic crisis: The Background
- Reforms and the Turnaround
- New Trade policy
- Measures to Promote Exports
- New Industrial Policy
- Delicensing and other steps
- Impact of the Reforms
    - Sectoral Share in GDP
    - Employment Pattern in Sectors
- Impact of Reforms on Poverty
- Liberalisation and Inequality
- Salient Features of 1991 Reforms

❑ BACKGROUND

From all accounts, 1991 was one of the most significant turning points for the Indian economy. The nation charted a new path moving towards a liberalized and market-driven economy and greater integration with the global economy. The country was then on the brink of a deep crisis on many fronts. The balance of payments position was precarious and international confidence in our economy had eroded considerably. Despite large external borrowings, there was sharp reduction in foreign exchange reserves and there were strong inflationary pressures. Before examining the various aspects of the critical position in which the country found itself and the measures taken to tackle them, it is necessary to look at its genesis and the factors which led to the crisis.

❑ REFORMS AND PROBLEMS DURING 1985–90

The decade starting from 1980 was relatively better for the economy. While the annual rate of growth of GDP for the preceding 30 years (1950 to 1980) was only 3.52 per cent, which is cynically referred to as the 'Hindu rate of growth', during the decade 1980–81 to 1989–90, the annual rate of growth was 5.13 per cent. Also, while the per capita GDP increased at an annual rate of 1.37 per cent during 1950–51 to 1980–81, the same increased during the period 1980–81 to 1989–90 at an annual rate of 3.09 per cent.

Foodgrains production which stood at 50.8 million tonnes (MT) in 1950–51 had reached 129.5 MT by 1980–81 and 145.5 MT by 1984–85. In the 1980's, the industrial sector too fared impressively compared to the 70's. The annual growth rate of manufacturing sector was 7 per cent and of registerd manufacturing 8.1 per cent. Against such benign growth environment, the Seventh Plan (1985–90) started on an optimistic note.

The Government under Rajiv Gandhi (1984–89) initiated several reform measures. These included reducing state control and regulation of the private sector, greater freedom to import even capital goods, liberalization in the application of FERA, and the operation of companies under MRTP Act. In short, it aimed at replacing government control by market forces.

But there were also many ominous signs on the fiscal front which became visible during this period. Prudent fiscal management requires that revenue receipts not only meet revenue expenditures, but also generate surplus to finance the Plan and other capital and development outlays. But all through the 1980's, the government revenues fell short of expenditure. The gross fiscal deficit as a proportion of GDP increased from 5.4 per cent in 1981–82 to 8.0 per cent in 1989–90. The fiscal imbalance persisted and worsened during the 1980's, as the gross fiscal deficit, on an average, rose from 6.3 per cent in the Sixth Plan period (1980–85) to 8.2 per cent in the Seventh Plan period (1985–90).

Another disturbing trend was that almost throughout the 1980s, non-development expenditure increased faster than development outlays. While the non-developmental expenditure in 1990–91 was about 5.5 times the 1980–81 level, developmental outlays increased only 4.4 times. It indicates that long-term development of the country received less priority.

Another adverse factor was that the relative share of direct taxes in the total tax revenue continued to decline while the share of indirect taxes, the burden of which falls mostly on the masses, showed increase.

❑ THE 1991 ECONOMIC CRISIS

Background to the Crisis

The process to reform the economy had begun from the mid-eighties under the Rajiv Gandhi government (1984–89) whose vision was to take India to the 21st century. With a view to modernize the economy, boost investment, and achieve rapid industrial growth, many controls and restrictions were removed, industrial licensing policy was revamped, and greater role was accorded to the private corporate sector. Import controls were relaxed to upgrade industrial technology and improve capacity utilization and productivity.

However, towards the late 1980s, macroeconomic imbalances began to emerge. The fiscal deficit of the Central Government, which is a measure of the difference between revenue receipts and total expenditure, was over 8 per cent of the GDP in 1990–91 as compared with 6 per cent at the beginning of 1980s and 4 per cent in mid-1970s. This deficit had to be met by borrowing at home. The internal public debt had accumulated to about 55 per cent of GDP. By 1990, the deficit of the Central Government had mounted to ₹ 13,000 crore as a result of revenue shortfalls and expenditure overruns. Productivity of investment was low and there were poor rates of return on past investments.

On the foreign exchange front, the balance of payments position came under severe stress. During the eighties, India's imports were more than what could be covered by the exports and normal aid on concessional terms. The current account deficits had to be financed by borrowing from abroad on commercial terms both from the capital market and Non-resident Indians (NRI's). The external debt which was $22.8 billion in 1983–84 had risen to $69.3 billion in 1990-91. The burden of servicing the accumulated internal and external debt became onerous. This was further exacerbated by the steep increase in oil prices and disruptions caused by the Iraqi invasion of Kuwait in August 1990. With the disintegration of Soviet Union in December 1991, India lost a major trading partner.

The persistent fiscal imbalances accentuated inflationary pressures. That inflation was concentrated in essential commodities, despite good monsoons and good harvests in the three preceding years, was of greater concern as it hurt the poorer sections the most. Besides all these, there was political instability at home–there were two changes in the Government at the Centre between December 1989 and June 1991.

All these led to considerable erosion of international confidence in our economy. Despite large borrowings from the International Monetary Fund (IMF) in July 1990 and January 1991, the foreign exchange reserves had touched rock bottom, and it was barely enough to meet the needs of two weeks of imports. Foreign commercial banks had stopped lending to India and NRI's were withdrawing their deposits. Shortage of foreign exchange forced massive import squeeze which further impeded the industrial growth.

Due to the combined effect of all these, the nation was on the brink of a major crisis which called for drastic remedial measures.

The Turnaround–The Reforms of 1991

It was against this grim background that a newly elected Government headed by P.V. Narasimha Rao took over in June 1991. He at once set about the task of pulling the economy back from the brink, and appointed Manmohan Singh as the Finance Minister. The new Government initiated a number of radical measures to bring about macroeconomic stability and address the balance of payments crisis through fiscal consolidation and tax reforms. Urgent steps were taken to avert default in international debt obligations and to control inflation. A decision taken earlier to use part of the gold held by the Reserve Bank of India to mobilize temporary liquidity abroad was implemented, but as planned the gold was redeemed as soon as the foreign exchange position stabilized. The situation also called for credible fiscal adjustment followed by fiscal consolidation.

This involved progressively reducing the fiscal and revenue deficits of the Central Government and reduction of current account deficit in the balance of payments. The aim was to contain the unfettered rise in internal and external debt and thus limit the burden of debt servicing. Efforts were made to raise more resources internally without burdening the poor.

The steps taken by the new government to tackle the balance of payments crisis involved both short-term and long-term measures. Devaluation of the Rupee by about 18 per cent was effected in two steps on July 1 and 3, 1991. International Monetary Fund (IMF) and the World Bank which had to be approached for a major loan had stipulated that economic reforms be undertaken to revive the economy. As a result of short-term measures proposed to be put in place, the country was able to raise funds from the IMF and other aid agencies. It helped to to tide over the crisis and restore international confidence in the country's economic management.

Urgent steps were taken to avert default in international debt obligations and to control inflation. A decision taken earlier to use part of the gold held by the Reserve Bank of India to mobilize temporary liquidity abroad was implemented, but as planned the gold was redeemed as soon as the foreign exchange position stabilized. The situation also called for credible fiscal adjustment followed by fiscal consolidation.

At this juncture, concerns had been expressed whether the country implemented these reform measures at the dictates of IMF and the World Bank who were approached for financial assistance to tide over the crisis. The Government had clarified that the discussions held with the lending institutions were only on the amount and type of assistance and the viability of the programmes for which assistance was sought. The conditions laid down and accepted for the assistance were only in consonance with the reform programme already envisaged and drawn up by the Government, and which formed part of the party's election manifesto. Thus, it was contended that the country's national interests or sovereignty had in no way been compromised.

❑ THE NEW REFORM MEASURES

New Trade Policy

As part of the reform measures, a new Trade policy was drawn up in 1991. It marked a radical shift from the Import Substitution policy which India had relied on for the last four decades. While it may have been necessary in the very early stages of development to protect our nascent industries from foreign competition, in the long-term it proved to be neither efficient nor one that helped the industry for its robust growth. In fact, in contrast, the East Asian economies which took to the path of 'Export Promotion' strategy in 1970's forged far ahead of India in development.

It was, therefore, realized rather quite belatedly, that the time had come to open up the economy and expose Indian industry to competition from abroad in a phased manner. With this in view, the Government introduced changes in the Import-Export policy, liberalized import licensing, optimally reduced imports, and aimed at vigorous export promotion. The two-step devaluation of the Rupee effected in July 1991, referred to above, and easing of the replenishment licence system were two major steps in Trade Policy reform. It involved a transition from a regime of Quantitative Restrictions (QR's) to one of price-based mechanism.

Measures to Promote Exports

The trade policy was further revamped in 1992. A system of partial convertibility of the Rupee on the Current Account was introduced. Under this system, all foreign exchange earned through exports of goods or services, or remittances, could be converted into rupees. 40 per cent of the foreign exchange could be converted at the official exchange rate while the remaining 60 per cent was to be converted at a market-determined rate. The foreign exchange surrendered at official exchange rate could be used to meet the foreign exchange requirements of essential imports like petroleum, oil products, fertilisers, defence, and life-saving drugs. Imports of raw materials and capital goods were made freely importable on Open General Licence (OGL) but the foreign exchange required for these had to be obtained from the market. There was only a specified 'negative list of raw materials and capital goods which continued to be importable only against licences. The benefit of dual exchange rate of 40 per cent-60 per cent, extended to exporters, was made available also to Indian workers working abroad who were making considerable amount of remittances and thus making valuable contribution to India's foreign exchange earnings.

Earlier, to provide incentive for exports, a complex scheme of import replenishment was in vogue under which an exporter was allowed to import certain raw materials and components equal to the actual import content of exports. Also, there was a compensatory cash support scheme to compensate for taxes not refunded under a duty drawback scheme (i.e., refunds of indirect taxes including import duties on inputs used in exports) and losses incurred on exports when domestic demand was inadequate to use installed capacity fully. By eliminating import licensing and introducing partial convertibility of the Rupee, the reforms got rid of these complex web of incentives with varying rates for different commodities which prevailed under the import replenishment and compensatory cash support schemes.

Removal of Import Controls

These reforms removed import controls which had earlier resulted in inefficiency, bureaucratic delays, and left scope for corrupt practices. Trade policies were further modified and refined in subsequent years. Import licences were eliminated on most items of capital goods, raw materials, and components. These items became freely importable against foreign exchange purchased in the market. The system had worked fairly well and the market exchange rate had remained remarkably stable. It created an environment in which Indian entrepreneurs had the flexibility needed to compete with other developing countries in the world markets.

However, the existence of a dual rate hurt exporters and other foreign exchange earners who had to surrender 40 per cent of their earnings at the official rate and getting the benefit of higher market rate on only 60 per cent. Exporters represented that this amounted to a tax on exporters at a time when they needed full support. The Government considered this and finding that the balance of payments could be reasonably managed with a unified exchange rate, the dual rate arrangement was dispensed with. All exporters as well as foreign exchange earners like Indian expat workers abroad were allowed to convert 100 per cent of their earnings at the market rate. All imports were also liable to be paid for at the market rate.

Other Important Measures

Several other steps were also taken in 1993–94 to promote exports. Various restrictions on items of export were removed. Reserve Bank of India took steps to ensure availability of adequate credit for export. Banks were asked to see that credits given for exports amounted to at least 10 per cent of their total advances. The interest rate on rupee export credit was reduced by one percentage point. Further, banks were exempted from levying interest tax on export credit provided by them.

In order to promote new investment in industry, the customs duty levied on capital goods and import items for projects such as general machinery was progressively reduced from 1993–94. These duties were quite high compared to what was prevailing in competitive countries. This was to benefit critical sectors like power, coal mining, and petroleum refining. At the same time, to ensure that the lower duties on imported machinery did not hurt the domestic capital goods industry, import duty on components were also lowered to enable our domestic manufacturers to compete effectively. Duties on many other capital goods, metals, and chemicals were also reduced and rationalized to help domestic industries.

To promote the electronics industry which was a major provider of employment and with much potential for export, and to make it world class, rates of duty for project imports, raw materials, and components were brought down.

The New Industrial Policy

Introduction

Another major plank of the structural reform was opening up the industrial sector to infuse new dynamism into the economy. It was felt that the industrial sector faced many constraints and there was much scope for upgradation of technology, improving quality standards, and reduction in costs which would increase the efficiency and competitiveness of the Indian industry and benefit both the producers and the consumers. Restrictive policies like barriers to entry and limits on the size of firms had shackled industry and led to a degree of monopoly in the sector. The time was also ripe to improve the performance of the public sector by facilitating foreign investment and infusing foreign technology to increase productivity.

With these objectives in view, a New Industrial Policy was unveiled in 1991. The salient features of the new policy were:

Delicensing

Industrial licensing was abolished for all industries except for a short list of 18 industries involving security and strategic factors, social considerations, hazardous and environmental aspects, and those producing items of elitist consumption (white goods such as refrigerators, domestic washing machines, microwave ovens, and airconditioners). Later, more industries were delicensed and presently compulsory licensing applies only to six industries. Coal and lignite have also been removed from the list of industries reserved for the public sector.

Industries reserved for the small scale sector continued to be so reserved. The removal of licensing was to benefit particularly the many dynamic small and medium entrepreneurs who had been hampered by the licensing system. Also, this was to make industry more competitive, more efficient and modern, and take its rightful place in the world of industrial progress.

The compulsory licensing provisions were not to apply to the small-scale units taking up the manufacture of any of the items reserved for exclusive manufacture in the small scale sector.

Promotion of foreign investment

For promoting foreign investments in high priority industries, requiring large investments and advanced technology, direct foreign investment up to 51 per cent foreign equity in such industries was allowed. Also, foreign equity up to 51 per cent was allowed for trading companies primarily engaged in export activities. Foreign investment would facilitate technology transfer, help to enhance productivity, nurture better management practices, and provide greater access to world markets. High priority industries could get automatic approval for entering into technology agreements and were allowed to negotiate the terms of technology transfer directly with their foreign counterparts according to their own commercial judgement.

Promotion of exports

For promoting exports of Indian products, which required interaction with some of the world's largest international manufacturing and marketing firms, services of foreign trading companies were to be availed to assist us in the export activities.

MRTP Act

The Monopolies and Restrictive Trade Practices Act (MRTP Act) which came into force in 1970 had over the years hampered industrial growth and expansion. To foster healthy competition, achieve economies of scale, and enhance productivity, it was imperative to remove interference by the Government, through the provisions of this Act, in decisions of large companies regarding investment, capacity addition, etc. The legal provision for getting prior government approval for expansion of existing undertakings and setting up new ones was removed. The accent was to be only on controlling unfair and restrictive business practices and the MRTP Commission was empowered to investigate and act on such practices.

The MRTP Act was later repealed and replaced by the Competition Act, 2002.

Strengthening the Public Sector

The Industrial Policy Resolution of 1956 had given the public sector a strategic role in the economy. Public sector enterprises have been set up in key sectors such as steel, power, heavy engineering and heavy electricals, telecom, defence, aircraft manufacture, etc. Massive investments were made over the past four decades to expand the public sector which has come to occupy a commanding role in the economy. However, while some of the public sector units have played a notable role in the country's development process, many of them face a plethora of problems such as lagging productivity, lack of R & D and technological upgradation, low returns on capital invested, and HR and labour issues which have retarded their progress. Many of them were also considered sick units which called for some drastic measures. The government considered the need to reinvigorate them and hence took certain steps under the Industrial Policy of 1991.

Specified sectors of the economy were reserved for the public sector. These were:

(i) Essential infrastructure goods and services;

(ii) Exploration and exploitation of oil and mineral resources;

(iii) Technology development and building of manufacturing capabilities in areas crucial for the long-term development of the economy and where private sector investment is inadequate; and,

(iv) Manufacture of products where strategic considerations predominate such as defence equipment.

Government would strengthen those public enterprises which fall in the reserved or high priority areas that have successfully expanded production, built up technical competence, or are generating profits. Such enterprises would be given much greater degree of autonomy. Competition will also be induced in these areas by allowing private sector to participate. And in the case of enterprises which have been chronically sick and incurring heavy losses, part of Government holdings in their equity share capital would be disinvested in order to provide market discipline to their performance.

❑ IMPACT OF THE REFORMS

Broad Indicators

Some of the indicators of the progress of the economy are the growth rate of Gross Domestic Product (GDP), the changing sectoral composition of the GDP, and the standards of living of the people as reflected in the quality of life. The growth rate of the economy had fallen to less than one per cent in the crisis year 1991–92 but rebounded to 5 per cent per annum in 1992–93 and 1993–94. It further accelerated to 6.3 per cent in 1994–95.

While the annual average growth rate during the decade 1980–81 to 1989–90, the pre-reform period, was 5.18 per cent, the average rate for the period 1993–94 to 1998–99 was 6.8 per cent based on the new series of GDP.

Sectoral Share in GDP

The sectoral share in GDP of the three sectors — primary which includes agriculture, fisheries, and forestry, secondary which includes industry, manufacturing, and mining, and tertiary which includes all services such as banking, insurance, transport and communications, construction and real estate, hotels, trade, etc.— is an indication of the progress of the economy. Table 6.1 shows that between 1980–81 and 1990–91 (pre-reform period), share of primary sector declined from 38.1 per cent to 34.0 per cent, that of secondary declined marginally from 25.9 per cent to 24.9 per cent, while the tertiary sector showed perceptible increase.

While the share of agriculture has been steadily declining and that of services rising consistently, the share of industry had been sluggish and fluctuating even during the post-reform period (1991–92 to 2000–01). Industrial growth which had fallen below one per cent in 1991–92, showed broad-based recovery by 1994 and rose to 8.7 per cent. Manufacturing sector grew even faster at 9.2 per cent in 1991–92 and at 10.6 per cent in 1996–97.

The growth rate of agriculture and allied sector was 3.6 per cent in the Eleventh Plan (2007–12) as against 2.5 per cent and 2.4 per cent respectively in the Ninth Plan (1997–2002) and Tenth Plan (2002–07). As for the industrial growth rate, after a decline of 0.8 per cent in 1991–92, it rose to 2.2 per cent in 1992–93, 8.6 per cent in 1994–95, and 10.6 per cent in 1996–97. During the Ninth Plan, industrial growth declined to 4.3 per cent but recovered to touch 9.4 per cent in the Tenth Plan. And again it recorded only 7.9 per cent in the Eleventh Plan. The deceleration and fluctuation in industry is due to structural and cyclical factors affecting business, lack of domestic demand in case of failure of monsoon which adversely affects the rural sector, which is a major source of demand for manufactured items, and lack of demand for items of exports. But it can be said that the New Industrial Policy has helped to reinvigorate and energize the industrial sector.

The services sector has shown steady growth both in regard to its share in GDP as well as rate of growth. Its share in GDP which was 48.5 per cent in 2000–01 has risen to an estimated 59 per cent in 2013–14. It recorded a growth rate of 7.9 per cent in the Ninth Plan, 9.3 per cent in the Tenth Plan, and 10.1 per cent in the Eleventh Plan.

Table 6.1 Sector-wise Composition of GDP (at Current prices) (In percentage)

Year	Primary	Secondary	Tertiary
1980–81	38.1	25.9	36.0
1990–91	34.0	24.9	41.1
2000–01	27.3	24.2	48.5

Employment Pattern in Sectors

From the above account, it will be seen that there have been significant changes in the sectoral composition of GDP which is a positive indication of economic development. Though a vital sector in the economy, the share of agriculture has steadily come down and the contribution of industry and services to GDP has been going up. However, the declining share of agriculture in the national income has not been accompanied by corresponding decline in the workforce employed in the sector as has been the case in all the developed countries. This shows that a significant portion of the workforce has still not moved to non-agricultural occupations and the pressure of population on land continues. It also indicates that there is disguised and under-employment in the sector resulting in low productivity per person engaged.

The percentage share of agriculture in total workforce declined only marginally from 72 per cent in 1951 to 69.8 per cent in 1971, 66.7 per cent in 1981, and 64.75 in 1993–94. Though it has further declined, it still provides employment to about 55 per cent of the workforce in the country. Employment in industry (excluding construction) has also been hovering from 12.43 per cent in 1993–94 to 12.1 per cent in 1999–2000. In 2012–13, it stood at 11.9 per cent. Whereas it is the services sector which has provided more additional employment—the shares of the services (including construction sector) in employment increased from 22.82 per cent in 1993–94 to 34.90 per cent in 2009–10.

Though employment levels have gone up, it has not kept pace with the increase in the labour force resulting in creeping unemployment. Also, the qualitative nature of jobs generated has been a matter of concern as bulk of it is informal jobs in the unorganized sector where labour laws and working conditions may be lax.

All this apart, a major challenge confronting the country is the huge number of youth entering the labour force. An estimated 12 million persons will be entering the job market each year—an average of one million every month—for the next ten years who have to be provided employment. This is a major challenge for the present and future governments.

(For more on this, see Chapter 16, Labour, Employment and Skill Development).

Impact of Reforms on Poverty

One of the primary aims of India's economic policy right after independence has been to achieve growth with equity and social justice. This was natural considering the all-pervasive poverty and widespread inequality which persisted in the country. Though several measures such as rural development and anti-poverty schemes have been implemented to remedy this, both poverty and inequality continue to be a challenge. There have been different studies and surveys on ascertaining number of people who live below the 'poverty line'. According to data released by National Sample Survey Organization (NSSO) and erstwhile Planning Commission, the percentage of population below the poverty line was as shown in Table 6.2 (the figures are combined for both rural and urban areas).

Table 6.2 The Percentage of Population Below the Poverty Line

Year	Percentage Below Poverty Line	Year	Percentage Below Poverty Line
1983	44.48	1999–2000	26.10
1987–88	38.86	2004–05	27.50
1993–94	35.97	2009-10	29.8

Source: Planning Commission data, 2012 & Databook 2014.

Economic reform measures coupled with poverty alleviation programmes like Mahatma Gandhi Rural Employment Guarantee Scheme (MNREGS) have helped to lift a significant section of the population above the poverty line. The extent and spread of it, however, has not been uniform. As a result of much of the reform measures being directed at the organized sector, its effects are felt first on the urban organized sector, next on the urban informal sector, and then on the rural sector. The rural sector is influenced more by the anti-poverty schemes which make a direct impact on the income and living conditions of the rural poor. Another significant factor impacting the rural population is the state of agriculture which again is largely dependent on the monsoon and various other factors.

There is also concern that following the implementation of reforms, inequality between different segments of society has widened. (See Box 6.1 at the end of this chapter on this). This can be remedied only through a vigorous process of growth with equity, more investments in the social sector—education, public health, and housing—directed to benefit particularly the lower sections of the population, and redistributive measures through fiscal policies. **(See chapter 17, 'Inequality and Poverty Alleviation' and chapter 26 'Social Sector and CSR' for more on this).**

❑ CONCLUSION

To sum up, the result of 1991 reforms has been a mixed one. While it has certainly opened up the economy after decades of keeping India as a 'protected and virtually closed economy' on the plank of Import Substitution policy, and has helped to integrate it with the global economy, India has not been able to realize the full potential. This is despite having a large technically skilled workforce and opportunities of building a robust manufacturing base as China did over the last two decades. In hindsight, much precious time and ground has been lost and now India has to compete with other developing countries in East Asia and Latin America. There is urgent need to push for another round of major reforms which the present government has embarked upon. But in the democratic framework in which the country is placed, there are many legislative and political roadblocks which are already playing out and due to delays caused by them, the country may be forced to pay a heavy price.

Box 6.1: Liberalisation and Inequality

Has liberalization in India led to lower income growth for the poor and increased inequality?

Since liberalization of the economy from the mid-eighties and more so after 1991, economy has registered faster growth than the previous decades. But distribution of income following the faster growth has also been more unequal. This fits in with Kuznet's theory that inequality will increase in the initial stages as an economy grows but will decline in later phases (see chapter 17, p. 17.51 for more on this). Yet another concern is that even job creation has not been commensurate with the rate of growth, the impact of which will be mostly on the lower and middle classes. And even the jobs created have been mostly in the informal sector where those employed enjoy lesser benefits as compared to those in the formal sector.

A study, "Indian Income Inequality 1922-2014" by two economists, Thomas Piketty and Lucas Chancel, has highlighted that income inequality in India has increased during the post-1991 liberalization period as compared to the previous three decades. The bottom half of the population saw higher income growth in the decades before liberalization than in the decades after that. Of the total income growth between 1951 and 1980, the bottom 50 per cent of the total population captured 28 per cent, the middle 40 per cent got 49 per cent while the top 10 per cent got only 24 per cent of the increase. But this proportion changed dramatically after liberalization started in the 1980s when the bottom half got only 11 per cent, the middle 40 per cent got 23 per cent while the top 10 per cent captured two-thirds of the income growth.

It is not only Piketty-Chancel study that has pointed to such gross inequalities in income. The IMF has estimated that the Gini coefficient, a popular measure of inequality, rose from 45 to 51 between 1990 and 2013. Two other studies, LIS Data Centre In Luxembourg and the World Inequality Lab in its 'World Inequality Report 2018' have also pointed to rising inequality. The National Sample Survey (NSS) data had found that in 2004-05 income inequality had increased sharply.

However, economists opine that it is very difficult to find income inequality data for India. The NSS measures consumption which underestimates the degree of inequality. Income tax data, which is one of the measures used by Piketty, is not a reliable basis for measuring income inequality in India.

India and China: the Difference

In this context, a comparison with China which too undertook liberalization after 1980 is revealing. The share of bottom half of population in national income in both India and China after 1980 was broadly similar. But a significant difference between the two countries is in that while the middle 40 per cent in India got 23 per cent of the increase in national income since 1980, the middle section in China got 43 per cent -- a gap of 20 per cent. The enormous success of labour-intensive manufacturing and expansion of large enterprises, both of which helped to absorb millions of people from farming, account for the headway that China was able to make. It lifted sizable sections out of poverty and enabled those in lower income sections to move up to middle income group. India could not bring about such a major structural transformation.

Conclusion

In conclusion, it must be said that while India's economic growth helped to bring down the extent of absolute poverty and lifted millions above poverty line, relative inequality between various sections of the population has widened following liberalization.

Box 6.2: Salient features of 1991 Economic reforms

The economic reforms of 1991 marked a watershed moment. The thrust was on reforming the industrial and trade policies which was being discussed even in the 1980s when some tentative steps were initiated. But that was not a full-fledged blueprint for systemic reform which the reforms of 1991 accomplished.

➢ **The background**

When a new government, headed by P.V. Narasimha Rao, took office in June 1991, the nation was on the brink of a serious economic crisis due to a combination of several factors which had been building up. A brief look at the serious problems the nation faced in 1991 would highlight the significance of the reform measures undertaken.

- **Balance of payments:** The nation faced a massive balance of payments crisis, with foreign exchange reserves down and sufficient to meet just two months of imports. There was much talk of the possibility of a default in payments by the government of India, which, if it happened, would have been a very serious situation affecting the credibility of the country.
- **Fiscal deficit:** The fiscal deficit had touched nearly 8 percent of GDP by 1990-91 which had to be met by borrowing.
- **Public debt:** The internal public debt of the Central Government had accumulated to about 55 per cent of GDP. With interest payments on debt at about 4 per cent of GDP and almost 20 per cent of the total expenditure of the government, the position was unsustainable.
- **Tax system:** The tax system lacked transparency and had many loopholes. As a result, it was not easy to assess the social and economic impact of various concessions built into the tax structure.
- **Industrial scene:** Despite the heavy investments made, the public sector was unable to generate large investible resources. The excessive and indiscriminate protection provided to industry had weakened the incentive to develop a vibrant export sector. It also accentuated the disparities in income and wealth.

➢ **Rationale for the Reforms**

The government felt the need for structural reforms as the economy had failed to generate adequate rates of growth of income and per capita income. Despite the ambitious steps taken in successive Five-Year Plans, India was constrained by a maze of bureaucratic controls on investment and production. As a result, India's growth lagged far behind that achieved by the economies in south-east Asia. India had also become marginalised in the world economy.

Faced with a major macro-economic crisis, the government lost no time in setting in motion a series of steps to tide over the critical situation as detailed below. The reform measures were further refined and continued over the next few years.

➢ Devaluation of Rupee

Less than a fortnight after the government's formation, Finance Minister, Manmohan Singh,effected devaluation of the Indian currency against the US dollar by 9.5 per cent on July 2, 1991 and followed it up with another depreciation by 12 per cent a day later. The two-stage downward adjustment in the value of the rupee was not a step taken in isolation but was to be part of a series of reform measures.

➢ **Trade policy:** The Commerce Ministry unveiled a package of trade policy reforms. These included:

- Export subsidies like providing cash compensatory support to exporters were abolished.
- The facility of supplementary licences which used to help exporters with import facilities was removed.
- State Trading Corporations (STCs) were divested of their monopoly over import of a range of goods
- Replenishment licences issued to exporters, with which they could undertake duty-free imports, were scrapped. In its place, "Exim scrips" were introduced to be issued to exporters which were tradeable in the market.
- Raw materials and capital goods were made freely importable on Open General Licence (OGL) but the foreign exchange required for these had to be obtained from the market. There was only a specified 'negative list' of raw materials and capital goods which continued to be importable only against licences.

➢ **Foreign Exchange and Export promotion**

- Import licences were eliminated on most items of capital goods, raw materials, and components and these items became freely importable against foreign exchange purchased in the market.
- The system worked fairly well and the market exchange rate remained remarkably stable. It helped Indian entrepreneurs who had the flexibility needed to compete with other developing countries in the world markets.
- A system of partial convertibility of the Rupee on the Current Account was introduced. Under this system, all foreign exchange earned through exports of goods or services, or remittances, could be converted into rupees. 40 per cent of the foreign exchange could be converted at the official exchange rate while the remaining 60 per cent was to be converted at a market-determined rate.
- The foreign exchange surrendered at official exchange rate could be used to meet the foreign exchange requirements of essential imports like petroleum, oil products, fertilisers, defence, and life-saving drugs.

- The benefit of dual exchange rate of was made available also to Indian workers serving abroad who were making substantial remittances and thus making valuable contribution to India's foreign exchange earnings.
- But the existence of a 'dual exchange rate' hurt exporters and other foreign exchange earners. Hence, considering that the balance of payments could be reasonably managed with a unified exchange rate, the dual rate arrangement was dispensed with. All exporters as well as foreign exchange earners like Indian expat workers abroad were allowed to convert 100 per cent of their earnings at the market rate.

➢ **Industrial policy**

Due to a long-standing rigid policy of licensing and controls, known infamously as the"Licence Permit Raj", Indian industry had been rendered uncompetitive in world markets. The industrial sector had all along only stunted growth and the full potential for employment in manufacturing was not realized. A succession of committees, headed by noted technocrats and civil servants, had recommended on overall deregulation, trade reform and public enterprise reform. It was against this background that the New Industrial Policy of 1990-91 was drawn up.

The New Industrial Policy was a comprehensive statement that looked at issues ranging fromremoving unnecessary bureaucratic shackles, the promotion of small and medium enterprises and easing raw material import restrictions to de-licensing, deregulation and welcoming foreign investment. Its main thrust was as follows:

- **Delicensing:** Industrial Licensing was abolished for all industries, except for a specified list and irrespective of the levels of investment. Some industries were to continue to be subjected to compulsory licensing, for reasons of security and strategic concerns, social and safety factors such as manufacture of hazardous products and environmental issues.
- **Locational restrictions:** The previous stringent restrictions on location of industries in large towns were also abolished, save in respect of cities with population of over 1 million.
- **Foreign Investment:** To attract foreign investment in high priority industries, which require large investments and advanced technology, it was decided to give approval for direct foreign investment up to 51 per cent foreign equity in a specified list of industries. This was expected to fetch attendant advantages of technology transfer, marketing expertise, modern managerial techniques and new avenues for exports. This was particularly necessary in the changing global scenario of industrial and economic cooperation marked by mobility of capital.
- **Foreign Technology:** Contrary to the previous practice of the need to obtain specific approvals for every technology agreement, automatic approvals for foreign technology agreements within specified parameters was allowed. Indian companies were free to negotiate the terms of technology transfer with their foreign counterparts, according to their own commercial judgements.

- **MRTP Act:** The Monopolies and Restrictive Trade Practices Act (MRTP Act) of 1970 had stifled industrial growth and expansion. There was need tofoster healthy competition and enable companies tomake investments,add capacity, achieve economies of scale and enhance productivity. To achieve these objectives, the legal provisions for getting prior government approval for these were removed.The MRTP Commission was only to control unfair and restrictive business practices. Still later, the MRTP Act was repealed and replaced by the Competition Act, 2002.
- **Public-sector policy:** Eighteen industries wereearlier reserved for investment by publicsector enterprises only. This list was pruned down to only eight industries which covered minerals, atomic energy, defence equipment and railways. This was a significant departure from the position of 'commanding heights' in the economy provided to the public sector since the 1950s. The policy also paved the way for disinvestment in publicsector companies through the public floatation of shares.

It was also stated that sick public sector enterprises could be closed down after due process. A National Renewal Fund (NRF) was proposed to provide for rehabilitation packages, as a social security measure, to protect the interests of workers who would be affected by such closures. It would also provide retraining facilities to affected workers so that they remain active productive partners in the process of modernization of industries.

These reforms paved the way for a policy framework that encouraged new entry, enabled new competition, from both domestic and foreign firms, and thereby induced the attainment of much greater efficiency in industry over a period of time.

➢ Conclusion

Although the 1991 Industrial Policy Statement was comprehensive and self-contained, there were some important elements of industrial policy that were not addressed, due to perceived political difficulties, viz., labour reforms and the abolition of reservations for small-scale industry. If these areas had also been addressed in the first flush of enthusiasm for reforms during the 1991–96 period, the progress of Indian industry could have been such that a higher level of growth as achieved by the East Asian economies might have been possible.

It must, however, be stated that successive governments have later built on these reforms and brought about significant changes in investment, trade, industry and infrastructure policies to boost India's economic growth. The latest in these are the much needed reforms in the agriculture sector which are under consideration but being contested by certain sections of farmers.

In this Chapter we discussed.....

- 1991 was a major turning point for Indian economy; precarious balance of payments position and inflationary pressures.
- 1980s started on a good note – higher GDP growth rate, comfortable food position and industrial sector looking up; liberalisation measures undertaken by Rajiv Gandhi government.
- But problems were building up; considerable increase in gross fiscal deficit and worsening fiscal imbalance persisted; increase in non-developmental expenditure added to the problems.

- Factors which led to the 1991 economic crisis -- high fiscal deficit and unsustainable internal public debt; foreign exchange position became critical resulting in erosion of international confidence; inflation was hurting the poorer sections.
- Radical reforms were initiated in 1991 by the government under Narasimha Rao to achieve macroeconomic stability; measures included containing fiscal deficit, improving balance of payments position; rupee was devalued in two steps and funds raised from the IMF and other sources.
- New trade policy drawn up replacing the' import substitution' policy followed hitherto; imports were liberalised and several measures were taken to vigorously promote exports; the economy was steadily opened up.
- New Industrial Policy was introduced which included industrial delicensing, except in strategic sectors;foreign investment was promoted to help industries upgrade technology and enhance their competitiveness; the MRTP Act was repealed and Competition Act of 2002 enacted; public sector units performing well were to be strengthened while sick units were to be subjected to disinvestment.
- Growth rate of the economy improved by 1992-93 and again in 1994-95; there were fluctuations in industrial growth due to cyclical factors, but overall, industry benefited from the new policy; services sector also made steady advances with its share in GDP touching 48.5 per cent in 2000-01.
- Significant changes were taking place in sectoral shares in GDP; share of agriculture was declining and that of industry and services were going up; but these changes wrere not reflected in a commensurate way in their shares in employment; agriculture continued to support 55 per cent of the worlkforce while employment in the services sector showed substantial increase; that in industry was rather stagnant.
- Providing employment to the huge numbers of youth joining the labourforce, a major challenge.
- Impact of reforms on poverty; despite many rural development and anti-poverty programmes launched, poverty continues to persist though the number of those below the poverty line has been coming down; there is also concern about widening inequities in society following the reform measures.
- While India did integrate with the global economy, she has not been able to realize the full potential from it unlike China could do over the last two decades; India lost precious time in the process and has now to compete with other emerging nations; India's legislative and political roadblocks also hamper rapid development.
- The impact of liberalization on inequality in India.
- The salient features of 1991 Economic reforms.

Important Terms to Note in this Chapter

Fiscal deficit; Public debt; Balance of payments; Capital market; Devaluation; Quantitative restrictions; Exchange rate; Currency convertibility; Disinvestment; Poverty line.

Practice Questions

1. Explain the salient features of the economic reforms implemented in Indian economy in 1991.
2. What were the factors and circumstances which led to an economic crisis due to which India was constrained to carry out major reforms in 1991?
3. What were the measures taken in 1991 by India to promote exports?
4. Explain the main features of the New Industrial Policy India introduced as part of the 1991 economic reforms and explain how it helped to improve the economy.
5. What were the main features of liberalized trade policy India adopted in 1991?
6. What impact did the economic reforms adopted in 1991 and thereafter have on poverty in India?
7. Has liberalization in India led to lower income growth for the poor and increased inequality among various sections? Explain with cogent reasoning.
8. Second generation economic reforms are crucial for raising the growth rate of economy. Throw light on these dimensions.

   [UPSC Main 2014 (Economics Optional Paper)]
9. How was the economic crisis faced by India in the early nineties related to her internal fiscal imbalance?

   [UPSC Main 2017 (Economics Optional Paper)]
10. Economic growth in India in the post-liberalisation period is service-led. Is this growth sustainable ?

    [Indian Economic Service/Indian Statistical Service 2017]
11. Critically examine the new manufacturing policy, 2011 for fostering industrial growth in India.

    [UPSC Main 2020 (Economics Optional Paper)]
12. How does the strategy of industrialisation under the New Economic Policy promote productivity growth in manufacturing industries in India? Explain.

    [UPSC Main 2019 (Economics Optional Paper)]
13. Analyse the trends in GDP growth and inequality during the first three decades of planning in India. Has the distribution of income in India become more equal during the post reform period? Suggest some policy measures that could help reduce income inequalities.

    [UPSC Main 2020 (Economics Optional Paper)]

CHAPTER

AGRICULTURAL DEVELOPMENT SINCE 1990

Food Security and Nutrition

- Inter-relationship of Agriculture and Industry
- Trends in Agriculture: 1950-90
- Recent trends
- Challenges facing Indian agriculture
- Measures taken to support agriculture
- Food security and Nutrition
- The Importance of agricultural Processing
- Food Processing Industry in India
- Agricultural Marketing
- Farmer Producer Organisations (FPOs)
- Agricultural Credit and Debt relief
- Pradhan Mantri FasalBima Yojana (PMFBY)
- Cooperative Farming
- Contract Farming
- Capital Formation and Subsidies
- Public Distribution System (PDS)
- Agrarian scene, Farm reforms and Farm laws
- Integrated Farming

❑ INTRODUCTION

Even with all the positive developments that has taken place in the last six decades, agriculture still remains the most critical sector in the economy. Though agriculture now accounts for only 14 per cent of Gross Domestic Product (GDP), it is still the predominant sector in terms of employment with more than half of India's workforce—263 million persons out of a labour force of 477.9 million, constituting 53 per cent as per 2011 census—engaged in it as the principal occupation. It is still the main source of livelihood for the majority of the rural population, which as per 2011 Census was 83.4 crore, and formed 68.9 per cent of the total population of the country.

❑ INTER-RELATIONSHIP OF AGRICULTURE AND INDUSTRY

There is close inter-relationship between the agricultural and industrial sectors. The performance of agriculture and the overall prosperity of the rural sector is vital as the rural sector is a major source of demand for goods, particularly fast-moving consumer goods (FMCGs) and consumer durables, manufactured by the industry. Thus, any setback to agriculture due to drought, poor rainfall, etc. causing rural distress, adversely impacts the industrial sector and the overall performance of the economy. Agriculture is also an important source of raw materials for the agro-based industries such as sugar, textiles, and jute besides tea and coffee, and also contributes significantly to export earnings.

❑ TRENDS IN AGRICULTURE: 1950–90

As seen in chapter 3, starting in the late-1960's and ending by early 1990's, the Green Revolution had run its full course in two phases. It had a dramatic impact on the Indian economy, particularly on the agricultural sector. Foodgrains output which stood at 82.02 million tonnes (MT) in 1960–61 rose to 129.59 MT in 1980–81 and 176.39 MT by 1990–91. (See Table 7.1).

Table 7.1: Production of Major Crops and Foodgrains between 1960–61 and 2019–20 (Million tonnes)

Crop	1960-61	1970-71	1980-81	1990-91	2000-01	2010-11	2019-20
Rice	34.57	42.22	53.63	74.29	84.98	95.98	118.43
Wheat	11.01	23.83	36.31	55.14	69.68	86.87	107.59
Coarse Cereals	23.74	30.55	29.02	32.70	31.08	43.4	47.48
Pulses	12.70	11.82	10.63	14.26	11.07	18.24	23.15
Total Foodgrains	**82.02**	**108.42**	**129.59**	**176.39**	**196.81**	**244.49**	**296.65**

Source: *Ministry of Agriculture & Farmers Welfare, Government of India, cited in Reserve Bank of India, Handbook of Statistics on Indian Economy, 2014–15.*

A number of factors contributed to the all-round success of agriculture between 1950 and 1990. These include land reforms and consolidation of holdings, increase in net sown area, expansion of irrigation facilities, intensive and multiple cropping, development and introduction of high yielding varieties (HYVs) of seeds, increased use of fertilizers, improved implements and farm machines, technology for pest management, price policy based on Minimum Support Price (MSP) and procurement operations, infrastructure for storage/cold storage, improvements in trade system, and increase in both public and private investments in agriculture.

The increase in output between 1950 and 1970 came mainly from increase in the area cultivated—from 97.32 million hectares (mn. ha.) in 1950-51 to 123.57 mn. ha. in 1970 and increase in the area under irrigation. There was high complementarity between public and private investment in agriculture during the early decades. This is reflected in the accelerated increase in the gross irrigated area from 22.56 mn. ha. in 1950-51 to 38.19 mn. ha. in 1970-71 and 49.58 mn. ha. in 1980-81. Percentage of irrigated area rose from 18.1 in 1950-51 to 30.3 in 1979-80.

However, the increase in output after 1980 was mainly attributable to increase in yields per hectare when there was only marginal increase in the area cultivated under foodgrains. The introduction of High Yielding Varieties (HYV) of seeds for wheat and rice from the mid-sixties coupled with increase in irrigated area greatly aided in boosting output. (See Table 7.2)

Table 7.2: All India Area, Production, and Yield of Foodgrains along with Coverage under Irrigation: 1950–51 to 1990–91

(Area—in Million Hectares; Production—in Million Tonnes; Yield—Kg/Hectare)

Year	Area	Production	Yield	Area Under irrigation (%)
1950–51	97.32	50.82	522	18.1
1960–61	115.58	82.02	710	19.1
1969–70	123.57	99.50	805	23.7
1974–75	121.08	99.83	824	26.5
1979–80	125.21	109.70	876	30.3
1985–86	128.02	150.44	1175	31.4
1990–91	127.84	176.39	1380	35.1

Source: *Directorate of Economics and Statistics, Department of Agriculture and Cooperation, Agricultural Statistics at a Glance 2014.*

Recent Trends

Since the mid-1990s, agriculture and allied sectors have not shown the dynamism seen in the preceding decades. There has been deceleration in growth and stagnation and volatility in year-to-year output in some years, though there is some recovery from 2007-08, as will be seen from Table 7.3. During the last decade, Indian agriculture has faced a number of severe challenges, compounded by demographic pressure, giving rise to serious concern regarding the prospects for food security, income of farmers, and alleviation of poverty in the years ahead.

Table 7.3: All India Area, Production, and Yield of Foodgrains along with Coverage under Irrigation: 1992–93—2018-19

(Area—in Million Hectares; Production—in Million Tonnes; Yield—Kg/Hectare)

Year	Area	Production	Yield	Area Under Irrigation (%)
1992-93	123.15	179.48	1457	37.4
1996-97	123.58	199.34	1614	40.0
2001-02	122.78	212.85	1734	43.0
2006-07	123.71	217.28	1756	46.3
2010-11	126.67	244.49	1930	47.8
2013-14	126.04	265.04	2120	–
2017-18	129.23	275.11	2129	–
2018-19	127.56	284.83	2233	–

Source: *Directorate of Economics and Statistics, Department of Agriculture and Cooperation, Agricultural Statistics at a Glance 2014 & 2018.*

The problems confronting the rural sector are mentioned below. These are discussed in more detail later in this chapter.

- Slowdown in growth.
- Widening economic disparities between irrigated and rain-fed areas.
- Decline and changing pattern of rainfall adversely affecting crops and cropping pattern.
- Rising input costs and vulnerability in output resulting in income losses and financial stress to farmers and consequent indebtedness.
- Uneven and slow development of new technologies to boost output; inefficient use of available technology and inputs.
- Degradation of natural resource base and soil fertility.
- Rampant exploitation of water and rapid and widespread decline in groundwater table, which impacts small and marginal farmers the most.
- Increased vulnerability to world commodity price volatility following trade liberalization. This had an adverse effect on agricultural economies of regions growing crops such as cotton and oilseeds.
- Lack of adequate incentives and appropriate institutional support.

Table 7.4: Growth Rate of Agricultural and Allied Sectors (in percentage) (All Figures based on 2004–05 prices)

Plan	Share of Agriculture in the Economy	Growth Rate of Agriculture and Allied Sectors	Growth Rate of Total Economy
Ninth Five Year Plan (1997–2002)	23.4	2.5	5.7
Tenth Five Year Plan (2002–07)	19.0	2.4	7.6
Eleventh Plan (2007–12)	15.2	3.7	8.0

Source: *Central Statistical Office, New Delhi, cited in Twelfth Five-Year Plan document, Planning Commission.*

❑ CHALLENGES FACING INDIAN AGRICULTURE

The problems confronting Indian agriculture vary based on geographical, agro-climatic, hydrological, and ecological factors in different regions. While there are region-specific problems, there are many issues common to all regions.

Climatic factors

With assured irrigation covering only about 40 per cent of arable land, monsoon is critical for India as the rest of the area depends entirely on rain. India receives 70 per cent of the annual rainfall during the south-west monsoon in June-September period, which is the 'kharif' crop season, and it is crucial for the country's rural economy. The timing, pattern, and spread of this monsoon have become increasingly unpredictable due to 'climate change' factors. There is considerable spatial and temporal variation in rainfall in India.

Temperature and climatic conditions have been deteriorating and warming has increased at an accelerating pace. Adverse monsoon, unseasonal showers, and deficit in rainfall result in crop losses, lower output, and financial distress to farmers—phenomena which have become more pronounced in recent years, leading to even unfortunate incidents of farmers committing suicide.

Natural calamities caused by floods, cyclones, etc. have also devastating consequences due to damage to crops worth crores of rupees. For instance, in 2013, crops worth of ₹3214.99 crore grown on 31.58 million hectares were damaged affecting an estimated 21.13 million peoples due to such calamities.

Irrigation

With erratic and insufficient rainfall, irrigation is a critical factor. Though the government has been giving priority to extend irrigation facilities, lack of adequate irrigation is still a major constraint in many parts. Net irrigated area in India has increased from nearly 14 per cent in 1950-51 to 48 per cent in recent times due to government initiatives.

The excessive exploitation of groundwater resources following adoption of technology and shift in cropping pattern towards paddy has been a source of concern. Agricultural advancement in Punjab was achieved at the cost of over-exploitation of groundwater. Introduction of policy of free electricity for irrigation in 1997 has been one major cause for depleting ground water table in Punjab.

The Government of India has accorded high priority to water conservation and its management. The Pradhan Mantri Krishi Sinchayee Yojana (PMKSY) has been approved in 2015 to extend the coverage of irrigation and improve water use efficiency through 'More crop per drop'campaign to ensure optimum utilization of water. The scheme envisages total outlay of ₹ 50,000 crore over five years. In 2015-16, an outlay of ₹ 5300 crore was approved. NABARD has also made a provision of ₹ 5,000 crore in 2019-20 to extend micro-irrigation. State governments are also expected to mobilise additional funds.

Problems of soil fertility

There are indications of technology fatigue in Indian agriculture. Various factors such as intensive farming resulting in nutrient imbalance, greater mining of soil nutrients depleting soil fertility, deficiencies of micro-nutrients, falling ground water levels, and erosion and degradation of soil are leading to overall deterioration of soil fertility and health. Extensive use of urea and imbalanced use of fertilizers have been leading to receding soil fertility. India is one of the largest consumers of nitrogenous and phosphatic fertilizers in the world. Experts have urged that nitrogen (N), phosphorus (P), and potash (K) are to be applied in a certain proportion to get optimum results in the output of various crops.

The rate of growth of foodgrains production has slowed in spite of increase in fertilizer consumption which points to imbalanced use of fertilizers. ICAR studies have shown that use of chemical fertilizers in combination with organic manures has helped to increase crop yields. Thus, there is imperative need to maintain soil fertility and arrest further degradation. This calls for greater co-ordination between agricultural research centres and institutions and the farming community and constant monitoring and guidance to the latter.

Low Productivity

Though India has had the Green Revolution and seen dramatic increase in yields and output, the per unit area productivity of our crops is much lower as compared to that of the other major crop producing countries. (See Table 7.5). There is also a wide gap in the yield levels among and within the states in India. Though land, climatic, and ecological conditions may vary vastly from country to country, India should be able to increase the yields to the fullest potential and must pursue this objective vigorously.

Dr. M.S. Swaminathan, the renowned agricultural scientist, has opined that it is unrealistic to draw comparisons of yield of various crops in different countries, as cropping systems and cropping patterns may vary from country to country. Hence, it would be more prudent to compare cropping system as a whole.

While the problems India faces may be due to some of the factors explained above, the wide disparities in yields points to the need to study the problems in depth and infuse new technologies and innovative methods of farming which could enhance the yields.

Table 7.5: Yield of Principal Crops in Various Countries during 2016
Yield Kg/Hectare

Paddy		Wheat		Maize		Sugarcane	
Country	Yield	Country	Yield	Country	Yield	Country	Yield
World	4577	World	3401	World	5632	World	70134
China	6866	Germany	7641	USA	10960	Guatemala	129049
Vietnam	5574	China	5396	Canada	10540	Colombia	86399
Brazil	5464	France	5304	Argentina	7443	USA	80033
Indonesia	5236	Ukraine	4206	Ukraine	6602	Australia	76929
Bangladesh	4586	USA	3541	China	5967	Brazil	75180
Philippines	3869	Canada	3470	Russia	5513	China	73620
Myanmar	3818	India	3034	Indonesia	5306	Mexico	72270
India	3790	Pakistan	2779	Brazil	4288	India	70394
Thailand	2854	Russia	2684	Mexico	3718	Thailand	63948
Nigeria	2823	Australia	1974	India	2616		

Source: *Agricultural Statistics at a Glance 2014, Ministry of Agriculture and Co-operation.*

Size of farms

Another factor hampering the adoption and spread of modern technology in general, and high-yielding varieties of seeds in particular, is the small size of farms in India. Due to sub-division and fragmentation of landholdings over many decades, by 2015-16, as much as 68 per cent of ownership farms have size less than one hectare. (See Table 7.6). And of them, about 40 per cent of farmers hold land smaller than 0.5 hectare.

Table 7.6: Number and Area of Operational Holdings by Size Group, 2005-06 to 2015-16

	No. Holdings ('000 Number)			Area Operated: ('000 Hectares)			Average size:(Hectares) 2000–01* 2005–06* 2010–11		
	2005-06*	2010-11	2015-16	2005-06*	2010-11	2015-16	2005-06*	2010-11	2015-16
Marginal	83694	92826	99858	32026	35908	37960	0.38	0.39	0.38
	(64.8)	(67.1)	(68.52)	(20.2)	(22.5)	24.16			
Small	23930	24779	25777	33101	35244	36435	1.38	1.42	1.41
	(18.5)	(17.9)	(17.69)	(20.9)	(22.1)	23.19			
Semi – Medium	14127	13896	13776	37898	37705	37168	2.68	2.71	2.70
	(10.9)	(10.0)	(9.45)	(23.9)	(23.6)	23.65			
Medium	6375	5875	5485	36583	33828	31367	5.74	5.76	5.72
	(4.9)	(4.2)	(3.76)	(23.1)	(21.2)	19.96			
Large	1096	973	831	18715	16907	14212	17.08	17.38	17.1
	(0.8)	(0.7)	(0.57)	(11.8)	(10.6)	(9.04)			
All Holdings	129222	138348	145727	158323	159592	157142	1.23	1.15	1.08
	(100.0)	(100.0)	(100.0)	(100.0)	(100.0)	(100.0)			

Source: Department of Agriculture and Cooperation, Agriculture Census 2015-16 (Phase-1). Agricultural Statistics at a Glance 2018. 2015-16 figures are Provisional.

Note: Marginal: (Less than 1 hectare); Small: (1.0 to 2.0 hectares); Semi-medium: (2.0 to 4.0 hectares); Medium; (4.0 to 10.0 hectares); Large: (10.0 hectares and above); *Excludes Jharkhand;

Figures in brackets are percentages tototal.

As per agricultural census data, in 1990-91, the average size was less than one hectare in States like Bihar (0.83 ha.), Goa (0.93 ha.), Jammu & Kashmir (0.83 ha.), Kerala (0.33 ha.), Tamil Nadu (0.93 ha.), Tripura (0.97 ha.), Uttar Pradesh (0.90 ha.) and West Bengal (0.90 ha.). This has come down further by 2015-16 in all these states as will be seen from Table 7.7. In Bihar the average size per holding is 0.39 ha., 0.73 ha. in UP, 0.76 ha. in West Bengal, 0.75 ha. in Tamil Nadu and 0.94 ha. in Andhra Pradesh. It may also be seen that the lowest size of holding is in Kerala (0.18 ha.) which indicates the maximum pressure on land in this State.

There is wide variation in average farm size between states ranging from 3.62 ha. in Punjab to 2.73 ha. in Rajasthan, 2.22 ha. in Haryana, i.57 ha. in Madhya Pradesh and 1.00 ha. in Telangana.

Table 7.7: Average Size of Holdings by Size Group 2015-16 (Provisional)

State	Marginal	Small	Semi-Medium	Medium	Large	All Holdings
Andhra Pr.	0.40	1.42	2.62	5.49	18.71	0.94
Bihar	0.25	1.25	2.60	5.29	14.48	0.39
Haryana	0.49	1.46	2.89	6.07	19.04	2.22
Kerala	0.12	1.34	2.54	5.32	51.04	0.18
Madhya Pr.	0.49	1.41	2.70	5.67	14.83	1.57
Maharashtra	0.46	1.41	2.65	5.55	17.05	1.35
Punjab	0.60	1.40	2.67	5.67	14.85	3.62
Rajasthan	0.48	1.42	2.82	6.10	17.04	2.73
Tamil Nadu	0.35	1.39	2.69	5.59	21.84	0.75
Telangana	0.44	1.40	2.60	5.48	14.22	1.00
Uttar Pr.	0.38	1.39	2.71	5.51	14.98	0.73
West Bengal	0.49	1.60	2.74	4.81	361.08	0.76
All India	0.38	1.41	2.70	5.72	17.10	1.08

Source: *Agricultural Statistics at a Glance 2018, Ministry of Agriculture & Farmers Welfare, Govt. of India.*

Between 1985-86 and 1990-91, the averagesize of holding in the country as a whole decreased by 8.3percent i.e., from 1.69 ha. to 1.55 ha. It has further come down to 1.08 ha. In 2015-16.

It is said that the new technology is neutral to the size of the farm, implying that a 0.5 hectare farm is as good as 5 or 10 hectare farm in terms of yield per hectare if adequate inputs are applied. However,a large farmer has an edge over a small farmer in as much as the latter may be handicapped for lack of irrigation support, proper drainage, proper pest control programme, etc. Considering the cost of inputs and the likely returns from a small farm which lacks the economies of scale, the small farmer may need greater support and technical guidance to have access to, and reap full advantage of, the aforementioned facilities.

Limits to technology

The adoption of improved technological practices, including use of High Yielding Varieties (HYV) seeds helped to transform Indian agriculture in the 1970s and the 1980s. In the absence of proper irrigation facilities, the cultivation of HYV seeds involves greater risk of variations in yields, as compared to the traditional varieties of seeds. The new technology and cultivation of HYV seeds needs intensive use of fertilizers and pesticides with adequate and assured water supply. A significant factor limiting the adoption of the new technology is that about 60 per cent of country's cultivated land is rain-fed and lacks irrigation, and a substantial portion of the country is drought prone. While Rajasthan, Gujarat, Telangana, and parts of Maharashtra (Marathawada and Vidarbha areas) have higher probability of incidence of drought, even the agriculturally crucial states of Punjab, Haryana, Uttar Pradesh, and Karnataka have probability of droughts occurring.

Labour Issues

Shortages of labour and rise in wages in rural areas have also been posing problems to farmers in different parts of the country. Various factors such as shift of rural workers from farm to non-farm jobs, migration of labour from rural areas to urban centres in search of better employment prospects, and higher wages given to rural workers under the Mahatma Gandhi Rural Employment Guarantee (MNREG) program have led to shortages of labour to undertake farm jobs and also resulted in farmers having to pay higher wages causing production costs to rise. Shift of rural workers from farm to non-farm jobs though is a positive sign as it reduces the pressure of population on land and reduces under- or disguised unemployment in the farm sector.

Financial Constraints

While greater private investment in farming is desirable where a farmer is able to invest with a view to increase productivity and output, it can become a source of distress if he does not get adequate returns for the investment. Most of the farmers, particularly the small and marginal farmers, who do not have the wherewithal to carry out farming operations, borrow funds from banks or from other local sources at exorbitant rates. They run the risk of crop failures in case of monsoon failure, unseasonal showers, or pest attacks leaving them in dire financial straits. Such instances have been on the rise in the recent past where farmers have faced untold hardship.

The government does take certain measures to mitigate the hardships to farmers. One important step is to increase public investment to lessen the private burden through supply of inputs like quality seeds, fertilizers, and pest control items at reasonable and subsidized rates. Help is also rendered through extension services, technical advice and support for marketing the produce.

However, despite two key government interventions viz., Minimum Support Price (MSP) and procurement by government agencies, farmers are often compelled to sell their produce below the support price, either due to exploitation by middlemen or large market players or due to bumper harvest resulting in glut in the market and depressed prices.

To alleviate such problems, the government has introduced income support scheme, "PM Kisan Samman Nidhi", under which ₹6,000 per year is given to eligible farmers in three instalments. The amount granted, however, is modest compared to income support under "RythuBandhu" scheme of Telangana and the "KALIA" scheme of Odisha which provide higher amounts. The government could consider enhancing the amount by rationalising the subsidies given for inputs to farmers. Some studies have shown that farmers prefer direct income support to their bank accounts in lieu of input subsidies.

❑ MEASURES TAKEN TO SUPPORT AGRICULTURE

Agriculture being the most critical sector in the economy, successive governments have paid special attention to the problems facing this sector and tried to frame policies to mitigate the constraints faced by it. The rural population depending on this sector also being huge, the farm lobby, with its political connections, has been a strong force in the polity and is a significant vote bank whose interests cannot be ignored by any political regime. With its contribution to the economy in regard to share in GDP, employment, exports, and as a source of raw materials to industry, the sector justifiably merits utmost attention of the government. The various steps taken by the government to support this sector are discussed below.

Price Policy

The government over the years has taken steps to frame agriculture price policy keeping in view the interests of all stakeholders—producers, consumers, and agro-based industries. Pricing is a critical factor to encourage private investment in irrigation, tubewells, farm machinery, etc. to boost production. In 1965, the government set up a permanent body, the Agricultural Price Commission (APC), to evolve a balanced price structure keeping in view the overall interests of the economy and all sections concerned. The Commission looks into the need to provide price incentives to promote agricultural growth and ensure optimum utilization of land and other resources. The APC was only an advisory body and had no decision-making powers.

The Commission consists of prominent economists and civil servants who have specialized in the domain of agriculture and representative(s) of farmers. In 1980, the mandate of the APC was widened to fix pricestaking into account changes in the terms of trade between agricultural and non-agricultural sectors.

In 1985, the APC was renamed as the Commission for Agricultural Costs and Prices (CACP). The It has the task of reconciling the conflicting interests of producers and consumers and between buyers and sellers of produce. Foodgrainshave to be channelled into the Public Distribution System (PDS) at subsidized rates. At the same time, it has to be procured from farmers at prices remunerative to them.

The agricultural price policy takes into account the prices of inputs for agriculture and the final product prices. The price policy can also be used to effect changes in the cropping patterns. Thus, price advantage could be provided to a nutritionally superior food crop or one in which the country has a comparative advantage vis-a-vis other countries to boost exports. It can also be used to encourage farmers to take to producing crops using new technology as was done during the Green Revolution.

Minimum Support Price

The prices of agricultural commodities are inherently unstable mainly due to variations in their supply, lack of market integration and information asymmetry. In a year of very good harvest of a crop, its price would fall sharply causing an adverse impact on the future supply of that commodity as farmers tend to withdraw from sowing that crop in the next / following years. This then causes paucity of supply next year and hence would result in price increase for consumers. To counter this trend, Minimum Support Price (MSP) is fixed by the Government each year for major agricultural products. The Central Government considers the report and views of the State Governments while taking the decision on MSP.

MSP ensures guaranteed price to the farmers, fixed prior to the sowing season, that afair amount of to incentivise higher investment and output. The MSP is in the nature of an assured market at a minimum guaranteed price offered by the Government.

While the MSP fixed has to be such as to provide incentives to farmers to boost and maximize production, it must also protect consumers from excessive price levels, especially in the open market. As extending MSP to a wide range of commodities will require vast administrative machinery, it is now confined to 24 crops.

Procurement Price

The government also has a policy of 'Procurement price', i.e., the price at which it buys from farmers which is higher than the MSP. Determining the procurement price is more complex as it involves determining the quantity and categories of items to be procured, sources from where, and rates at which they are to be procured.

Food Security and Nutrition

The National Development Council (NDC) adopted a resolution in 2007 to launch a National Food Security Mission to increase the production of rice, wheat, and pulses during the Eleventh Plan (2007–12). Accordingly, a Centrally Sponsored Scheme, 'National Food Security Mission' (NFSM), was launched in October 2007. The Mission was continued during 12th Five Year Plan (2012–17) with new targets of additional production of food grains.

In 2013, the government took a further step in this direction by passing the National Food Security Act (NFSA), 2013 which is a major intervention to ensure food security in the country. It will provide assured quantum of foodgrains – 5 kg. per person—to all priority and Antyodaya households, covering 75 per cent of the rural population and 50 per cent of the urban population at subsidized rates of ₹ 3/2/1 per kg. of rice/ wheat/millets. It also provides for free mid-day meal for children aged 6–14 years in government and government-aided schools up to grade VII and free meal for pregnant and lactating women from Anganwadis. This mission has resulted in increased production of cereals and pulses though there have been some fluctuations in output.

- **National Nutrition Mission:** The National Nutrition Mission (NNM), also known as RashtriyaPoshan Mission was launched by the Government of India, commencing from 2017-18, with a three-year budget of ₹9046.17 crore. The Mission, under the Ministry of Women and Child Development, fixes targets, monitors and guides nutrition-related interventions including schemes which address malnutrition.

  The programme in particular strives to reduce the level of stunting, under-nutrition, anemia and low birth weight babies and assess the height of children at Anganwadi Centres. Nutrition Resource Centres will involve masses through 'Jan Andolan' for participation on nutrition issues. Social Audits are to be conducted to evaluate the impact of the mission.

- **Food consumption pattern:** The pattern of consumption of food and dietary habits has significant impact on nutrition intake, health and overall welfare of the population. Various studies conducted in India have shown shift in dietary habits of people both in urban and rural areas. There has been shift in consumption away from cereals to high calorie commodities such as meat, milk, fish, etc, in other words, a shift from low value to high value commodities.While the traditional food basket was dominated by cereals, there is higher expenditure on beverages and milk & milk products.

  The trend of decline in the expenditure on cereals, and correspondingly a substantial rise in the expenditure on milk & milk products, fruits &nuts and beverages, has been seen in both urban and rural areas.

- **Need for further changes:** While the above developments augur well, experts have pointed out the need for further changes in the fight against hunger and malnutrition.

Dr. M.S. Swaminathan, the well-known agricultural scientist and father of the Green Revolution, has urged for moving from the notion of "food security" to "nutritional security" through steps such as getting nutrient-rich minor millets like ragi, and introducing bio-fortified varieties of crops into the food basket. He has pointed to nutritional problems such a protein hunger and hidden hunger caused by the deficiency of micro-nutrients such as iron, zinc, iodine and Vitamin-A. According to him, nutritional security involves both food and non-food factors, such as attention to balanced diet and ensuring clean drinking water, as well as sanitation. He has stressed the need for promoting bio-fortified nutritional gardens having nutrient-rich vegetables and crops.

The international rice research body, ICRISAT, opines that "pearl millet" is a nutritious dryland cereal, rich in protein, fibre and essential micronutrients like iron, zinc and folate. Nutrition studies have shown its potential to fight iron deficiency, the most widespread micronutrient deficiency and major cause of, affecting the health and development of a third of the global population. Pearl millet is grown on about 27 million hectares worldwide and is a daily food for more than 90 million people, among the most vulnerable in arid and semi-arid Africa and Asia. It is also an important source of fodder for millions of farms.

Dr. M S Swaminathan has been a strong advocate of nutritious pearl millet, which is now included in the food basket of the public distribution system in some Indian states, including Karnataka.

The focussed implementation of the mission has resulted in increased production of cereals and pulses in the last few years though there have been some fluctuations and decline in 2014–15 as per the advanced estimates. (See Table 7.8).

Table 7.8: Production of Cereals and Pulses: 1980-81 to 2018-19 (Million Tonnes)

Year	Rice	Wheat	Coarse Cereals	Total 2 to 4	Pulses	Total 5 + 6
1	2	3	4	5	6	7
1980-81	53.63	36.31	29.02	118.96	10.63	129.59
1990-91	74.29	55.14	32.70	162.13	14.26	176.39
2000-01	84.98	69.68	31.08	185.74	11.07	196.81
2010-11	95.98	86.87	43.40	226.25	18.24	244.49
2014-15	105.48	86.53	42.86	234.87	17.15	252.02
2018-19	116.48	103.60	43.06	263.14	22.08	285.21

Source: Ministry of Agriculture & Farmers Welfare, Government of India, Handbook of Statistics on Indian Economy, 2015 & 2020, Reserve Bank of India.

Note: Data for 2014–15 are based on Fourth Advance Estimates.

Agricultural production needs to be diversified to satisfy both tastes and nutrition. In particular, MSP policy should be more restrained for rice and wheat and made more effective in respect of pulses and oilseeds, production of which is to be increased, as India is a net importer of these items.

Diversification of Crops and Nutrition

In this context, it may be emphasized that there is need for diversification of crops both from the viewpoint of promoting nutrition and conserving water resources. The government is now promoting cultivation of water-efficient and climate-resilient summer sown crops like millets – bajra, hybrid jowar and ragi – which consume less water, unlike water guzzling paddy, and also have high nutritional value. The Minimum Support Price (MSP) for these cereals is getting bigger hike than paddy. This may spur farmers to switch over to these crops and optimise the use of water in cultivation. Some of the States have started supplying these cereals in PDS along with rice and wheat.

Thus, while the output of major crops, rice and wheat, has shown only marginal increase year-on-year, the overall foodgrains output, including output of maize and nutri-cereals, has been showing good increase. For instance, the total foodgrains output which stood at 257.13 million (mn.) tonnes (tns.) in 2012-13 rose to 275.11 mn. tns. in 2016-17 and 284.83 mn. tns. in 2017-18. Of this, the share of maize and nutri-cereals which together was 62.3 mn. tns. in 2012-13 has gone up to 75.71 mn. tns. in 2017-18

There is thus need for India to go in for crop diversification, cropping pattern in tune with climate changes, reduce dependence on water-guzzling crops and ensure efficient water management to remedy the situation as has been stressed by expert bodies.

Depletion of water resources:

The impact of growing water-guzzling crops like paddy and wheat is starkly observed in Punjab. Rice cultivation in Punjab, which thrived in the past due to the easy availability of water resources and free supply of electricity to farmers, is under considerable strain now. Farmers in Punjab who were mainly cultivating crops like pulses, maize, vegetables and cotton shifted to cultivation of rice and wheat during the Green Revolution. This led to proliferation of tube wells, unchecked use of groundwater for irrigation, drinking and other domestic purposes and depletion of groundwater at alarming rates. As a result, the state is facing a looming water crisis.

India's Status on Global Hunger Index

Suitable changes in India's cropping pattern and food basket are especially critical because of India's position on Global Hunger Index (GHI). According to rankings in GHI 2020 report, India ranked 94th out of the 107 countries. The index is based on four indicators mentioned below:

- **Undernourishment:** The share of the population that is undernourished (that is whose caloric intake is insufficient).
- **Child wasting:** The share of children under the age of five who are wasted (that is, who have low weight for their height, reflecting acute undernutrition).
- **Child stunting:** The share of children under the age of five who are stunted (that is, who have low height for their age, reflecting chronic undernutrition), and
- **Child mortality:** The mortality rate of children under the age of five (in part, a reflection of the fatal mix of inadequate nutrition and unhealthy environment).

However, some experts have questioned the validity of this study and its findings because, according to them, there will be wide variations in biological factors of people in different countries and such comparisons may not lead to proper conclusions.But factors like child mortality – of under one and under 5 years -- are actual recorded events and are reliable indicators of status of health in the country.

Conclusion

There is need fora farm-based approach to development and tackling malnutrition. According to experts, biofortification, a process of breeding crops to increase their nutritional value, which is relatively simple and economical, and cultivation of micro-nutrient rich crops would help to mitigate hidden hunger and malnutrition.

Simultaneously, food items provided under the PDS and other schemes need to be suitably altered, in consultation with health experts, keeping in view local and regional conditions and bring about changes in people's dietary habits through sustained education and informed campaigns.

The success of this scheme depends on proper identification of beneficiaries, including all eligible families, ensuring adequate supplies of quality foodgrains and further improving the PDS machinery. Some of the states like Tamil Nadu, Chhattisgarh, and Rajasthan have taken steps to improve the PDS.

The Importance of Agricultural Processing

The imperative need for agricultural processing (agro-processing) cannot be over-emphasized, especially in view of the importance of agriculture in the economy, the plight of farmers who toil and raise crops against heavy odds. There are different agricultural seasons when a wide range of crops are raised which are exposed to unpredictable climatic conditions resulting in uncertainties in the final output and widely fluctuating price levels impacting the returns to farmers. In case of a bumper crop, the prices crash and farmers suffer. In case of drought, crops fail and farmers who borrow money and invest in inputs run into debts unable to repay loans apart from suffering income losses.

Apart from all these vagaries, on the one hand, there are unacceptable levels of spoilage and wastage of valuable produce post-harvest while, on the other hand, even with bumper harvest and mounting stock of foodgrains, the very poor struggle to have a square meal. Although India ranks second in world production of fruits and vegetables, only 6-7 per cent of this is processed, compared to 70 per cent in Brazil, 65 per cent in US and 23 per cent in China. According to estimates, India's agri-wastage – of foodgrains, vegetables and fruits – is of the order of a whopping ₹92,000 crore. A significant part of this is perishables. The ever-increasing demand for vegetables and fruits could benefit farmers given the higher prices for such items. A major thrust on agro- processing and a well-developed food processing industry could increase farm-gate prices, reduce wastage, ensure value addition, promote crop diversification, generate employment opportunities and boost exports.

Lessons from the Dairy sector: Due to lack of proper storage, about 18 per cent of vegetables and fruits produced perish every year in India. While only 2 per cent of vegetables and fruits are processed, in milk 37 percent are processed resulting in wastage of only 1 per cent. The model followed in the dairy sector holds many lessons for the agri-sector. The daily milk collection of Amul is 180 lakh litres which benefits about 36 lakh farmers. India, the largest producer of milk in the world, processes milk as curd, ghee, cheese, etc. which are marketed in India and abroad.

Agro-processing in India: India has taken some steps in this direction. Under the 'Contract Farming Initiatives', some of the corporates have tied up with farmers in different States to procure agri products in bulk on a regular basis and process them further and market the products. Banks have also financed such schemes. Items covered include tomato, chilly, soyabean, barley, wheat, maize, basmati and non-basmati rice, cotton, sugarcane, fruits and vegetables and flowers. Such an approach confers many benefits to the farmers, the processing company and the final consumer as stated below:

- Adoption of modern mechanized agro technology;
- Provision of quality inputs to farmers;
- Uninterrupted and regular flow of raw material;
- Investment in infrastructure like warehouses, silos, cold storage units, etc.;
- Technical, financial, extension, transportation and marketing support;
- Enhanced productivity;
- Superior quality produce;
- Protection from fluctuations in market pricing; and
- Long term planning made possible.

Steps to give fillip to agro-processing

The effort should be to extend the scheme of agro-processing to more commodities and over a wider area to reap the full benefits of economies of scale for the entire production-supply value chain. In the Union Budget for 2017-18, the Finance Minister has emphasized on this and stated that it is proposed "to integrate farmers who grow fruits and vegetables with agro-processing units for better price realisation and reduction of post-harvest losses. (See Box 7.1 on Food Processing Industry in India for more on this).

Box 7.1: Food Processing Industry in India

Food Processing Industry in India

The food processing industry (FPI) is crucial for Indian economy, inter alia, on account of the following factors:

(i) The employment and income generation potential it has for boosting the non-farm sector if a greater proportion of the agricultural produce is processed.

(ii) The relatively low skilled labour gets employment due to the significant role played by the unregistered or informal sector in food processing, though this may not provide high wage levels, and

(iii) Increasing Total Factor Productivity (TFP) in the FPI indicates sustainable linkage between agriculture and industry, and a sustained growth of the former would further enhance the prospects of raising non-farm income.

Main features of FPI in India

Some of the main features of the Indian food processing industry are:

i) **Low level of processing:** The processing of perishable agricultural produce is low, except in some cases such as milk and fish. Studies of the "Extent of Processing of Agricultural Products" (EPA) have shown that the share of foodgrains alone in EPA is 70 per cent while the extent to which other food items are processed is quite low in India. It is only in the fisheries (26 per cent) and milk (35 per cent) sectors that the processing level is more than one-fifth of the net value produced. It is followed by the processing of buffalo meat at 20 per cent, and of poultry at 6 per cent. Significantly, the processing of fruits and vegetables is very low at 2.2 per cent.

For all the major crops grown in India, the average weighted processing in organised manufacturing turns out to be 11.01 per cent, which is quite low as compared to that in other countries.

ii) **Unsold stocks and post-harvest losses (PHL):**

At the all-India level, the proportions of the production of fruits, vegetables, and fruits and vegetables combined, that farmers are not able to sell, are 34 per cent, 44.6 per cent, and 40 per cent, respectively. Assuming that 3 to 4 per cent of the production is retained by the farmer for seed and self-consumption, the unsold production would be around 36 per cent for fruits and vegetables.

In the case of sensitive commodities, potato and onion, the losses indicated at the national level are of the order of 39 per cent and 14.4 per cent, respectively.

iii) **Potential for horticulture products:** Since fruits and vegetables (horticulture), which are highly perishable, offer much scope to directly raise the income of farmers through the sale of fresh produce, it would be ideally suited useful for value addition through processing and thereby enhance the incomes of their growers and reduce their wastage. It is, however, to be noted that not all of horticulture produce may be available for processing if the demand for fresh produce is on the rise.

iv) The overall growth of the food processing sector is constrained by the nature of the fragmented market leading to lower level of processing and value addition. But the sector also offers opportunities to tap the growth potential since it provides an alternate market for the farmers if they are suitably linked.

Role of Formal and Informal sectors in FPI

- In general, the food processing sector has a dualistic structure. The unorganised segment dominates in the numbers of small enterprises and workers, while the organised segment dominates in terms of the value of output and investment.
- Though the share of informal sector in the FPI segment is much smaller than the formal sector, the informal sector still plays an important role by contributing about 29 per cent of the Gross Value Added (GVA) in FPI. The formal sector plays a larger role than the informal MSME sector in the manufacturing of dairy products, wherein it accounts for 63.3 per cent of the total produce. This could be attributed to the significant role of well-knit Cooperatives in the dairy sector.
- The informal sector, on the other hand, contributes a large percentage (42.3 per cent) of the GVA of FPI in the processing and manufacture of grain mill products, starch products and processed animal feeds.

Linkage between the Formal sector and SMEs

While there islinkage between large enterprises in the formal sector of FPI and small and medium enterprises (SMEs), the latter face challenges in the following areas:

(i) Lack of adequate infrastructure.

(ii) Inadequate provision for skilled manpower, and

(iii) Lack of financial resources needed for holding inventory due to the seasonal nature of agriculture and for sourcing raw materials for processing.

Measures taken to Promote FPI

There is scope for exponential growth of the food processing sector which will help to commercialise the farm sector, increase farmers' incomes, generate more non-farm jobs in rural India and create export market for agro-foods. With this in view, a number of initiatives have been taken by the Government to strengthen the industry, ranging from speedy approvals for foreign collaborations and industrial licenses, to permitting 100 per cent FDI through the automatic route.

The Pradhan Mantri Kisan SAMPADA Yojana (PMKSY) has been launched with an intent to create modern infrastructure, with an efficient supply chain management system from the gate to the retail outlet. A special focus has been placed on developing integrated cold chain and preservation facilities at the grassroots level.

It is expected to leverage investment of ₹31,400 crore for handling an estimated 334 lakh MT agro-produce valued at ₹1,04,125 crore, benefiting 20 lakh farmers and generating 5,30,500 direct/indirect employment in the country by the year 2019-20.

The growth of food processing needs to be accelerated to:

(i) match with the rising demand;

(ii) boost agri-diversification; and

(iii) create more jobs in the rural economy.

For this, processors need raw material of desired quality and at the desired time. Buying so many small lots of different quality in scattered markets adds to the cost of raw materials. This requires new arrangement and partnership between processors and producers.

The scheme will not only provide a big boost to the growth of food processing sector in the country but also help in providing better returns to farmers and is a major step towards doubling farmers' income, creating non-farm employment opportunities on large scale, especially in the rural areas, reducing wastage of agricultural produce, increasing the processing level and enhancing the export of the processed foods.

A dedicated investor portal, ***NiveshBandhu***, has been set up as a resource base for detailing land availability, fiscal incentives and state policies and to disseminate information about agricultural reforms.

Under the aegis of the Ministry of Agriculture and Farmers' Welfare and led by the Small Farmers Agribusiness Consortium (SFAC), a **National Agriculture Market (e-NAM)** has been created as a unified electronic trading portal for agricultural commodities.

Cold chain and Mega Food Parks

- **Cold chain facility:** A scheme of setting up Cold Chain, Value Addition and Preservation Infrastructure is under implementation to provide integrated preservation facilities, without any break, from the farm gate to the consumer. It involves creation of infrastructure along the entire supply chain viz. pre-cooling, weighing, sorting, grading, waxing facilities at farm level, multi product/ multi temperature cold storage. It will facilitate distribution of horticulture, organic produce, marine, dairy, meat and poultry etc.

The integrated cold chain project is being set up by Companies, Corporations, Cooperatives, Self Help Groups (SHGs), Farmer Producer Organizations (FPOs), NGOs, Central / State PSUs, etc. subject to fulfilment of eligibility conditions of scheme guidelines.

- **Mega Food Park:** The scheme of Mega Food Parks aims at providing a mechanism to link agricultural production to the market by bringing together farmers, processors and retailers to ensure maximizing value addition, minimizing wastage, increasing farmers' income and creating employment opportunities particularly in the rural sector.

The scheme is based on "Cluster" approach and envisages creation of state-of-the-art support infrastructure in a well-defined agri / horticultural zone and will set up of modern food processing units in the industrial plots provided in the park. Mega food park typically consists of supply chain infrastructure including collection centres, primary processing centres, central processing centres, cold chain and around 25 to 30 fully developed plots for entrepreneurs to set up food processing units.

The project is being implemented by a Special Purpose Vehicle (SPV) which is a corporate entity registered under the Companies Act. State Governments and Cooperatives are not required to form separate SPV for implementing this project. Subject to fulfillment of the conditions of the Scheme, funds are released to the SPVs.

41 Mega Food Park Projects have been approved under the scheme to be set up across the country the country along with their sand are under various stages of implementation.

AGRICULTURAL MARKETING

Agricultural markets are crucial for supporting farmers' incomes as they link farmers with consumers, agrarian sector with industrial sectors and villages with towns and cities. Farmers dispose their surplus produce through village markets, mandis or wholesale markets and agents. If they sell through cooperative marketing societies, they could get better price for the produce.

The wholesale agriculture markets are governed by various Agricultural Produce Marketing Committees (APMCs) which are tasked with operating these markets under the state APMC Acts. While the intention of the Acts was to ensure that farmers get fair prices in a transparent manner, it has led to the creation of local monopsonies, with just a single or few buyers controlling the market. Mandi functionaries often do not allow new entrants in the market further reducing competition. This has resulted in fragmented and inefficient markets making the farmers the ultimate losers.

Drawbacks in the system

- **Excessive regulation:** Agriculture markets are subject to rigorous regulatory regime creating barriers in trading which adversely impact farmers. The regulations include controls on storage, transport, processing, exports, imports, credit access and market infrastructure development. Once an area is brought under the jurisdiction of a Market Committee, no person or agency is allowed to carry on wholesale marketing activities elsewhere.
- **Lack of competition:** Mandi functionaries often do not allow new entrants in the market reducing competition. The stranglehold of intermediaries in rural markets deprives the farmers the option of choosing between multiple market sites and options to sell their produce at most competitive rates. They are also deprived of other benefits of commodity exchange, such as accurate weighing, reduction in marketing costs and timely payments.
- **Multiple levies:** Farmers needed multiple licenses for trading in different APMCs.It has resulted in multiple levies like mandi fees at various levels, charges for entry, registration etc.
- **Role of middlemen:**The agriculture markets are dominated by middlemen such asarhatiyasor commission agents, local traders and regional processors who exercise considerable clout and prevent reforms to open up the markets to competition. They also influence public procurement of commodities due to which farmers are unable to get remunerative prices for their produce.
- **Infrastructural and logistics issues:** Lack of grading and auction facilities, drying yards and cold storage arrangements add to the problems faced by farmers. It is estimated that as much as 40 per cent of all fruits and vegetables are lost annually in India between the grower and the consumer mainly due to lack of proper warehousing facilities, weak transportation system and bad roads.
- **Information gaps:** Two key government interventions that affect agriculture markets and commodity prices are the policy of Minimum Support Price (MSP) and procurement by government agencies. The rationale of the MSP is to ensure that farmers are not forced to sell their produce below the support price either due to exploitation by large market players or due to bumper harvest. But most farmers are not even aware of the existence of MSPs.

These deficiencies have resulted in fragmented and inefficient markets which makes it imperative to reform the current APMC mandi system, open it to competition and give farmers the freedom to sell through multiple channels and points of exchange to realize better prices for the produce.

Reforms initiated

e-NAM: A major reform initiated was setting up the e-National Agricultural Market (e-NAM), launched in 2016, and designed to serve as a pan-India electronic trading portal which networks the existing APMC mandis to create a unified national market for agricultural commodities. This can be accessed online enabling buyers situated even outside the State to participate in trading at the local level. The e-NAM would network 585 APMC mandis across 18 states.

Salient features of e-NAM

- Facilitates transparent sale and price discovery in regulated markets, kisan mandis, warehouses and private markets.
- Helps farmers to get remunerative prices for their produce.
- Enables liberal licensing of traders/buyers and commission agents by State authorities without any pre-condition of physical presence or possession of shop / premises in the market yard.
- One license for a trader valid across all markets in the State.
- Harmonization of quality standards of agricultural produce and provisions of quality testing infrastructure in every market to enable informed bidding by buyers.
- Single point levy of market fees, i.e., on the first wholesale purchase from the farmer.
- **Challenges in Registration:** One of the major challenges in the system is to get farmers registered on the portal. According to data furnished in Parliament, e-NAM has not reached majority of farmers. By June 2019, out of almost 12 crore cultivators in the country, just over 1.64 crore cultivators and over 1.24 lakhs traders had been registered on e-NAM platform. While trade transactions having total volume of 2.59 crore tonnes valued at ₹71,069 crore, had been recorded on e-NAM platform till June 2019.
- **Role for CSCs:** It shows that there is a long way to go in getting farmers on the portal. One factor may be that most of them are not tech-savvy and also may not have easy access to the portal facility in their villages. To popularise the scheme, the State governments could utilise the Common Service Centres (CSCs), being set up under the Digital India programme which covers 2.5 lakh Gram Panchayats as Facilitation Centres to serve e-NAM scheme and help farmers get registered and also do transactions through these centres.
- Further steps required: Alongside these, other measures also need to be taken to improve the plight of farmers, reduce the risk of loss of crops and incomes. These are:
- A critical part of the relationship between production and markets is the farmer's capacity to respond to markets by changing production decisions and diversifying cropping systems in line with changing climate patterns.
- Agricultural institutes and scientists will have to work closely with farmers in diversifying production and educating farmers on optimising the use of fertilisers and water.
- Research has shown that cereals like rice and wheat may not be constant source of nutrition. There is need to bring about changes in dietary habits of the population, in consultation with experts in health domain, and promoting items like millets and other nutritious cereals, vegetables, fruits, etc. These will have to be chosen suited to local conditions like climate and nutri-items grown locally.
- Such nutritious cereals will have to be brought into the Public Distribution System to cater to local population.

- These changes are crucial because, as pointed out earlier, the Global Hunger Index Report of 2020 has ranked India a low 94th among 107 countries. Various studies have highlighted persistence of high levels of malnutrition, especially among children and women.(See under earlier section 'Food security and Nutrition').
- Warehousing and cold storage infrastructure need to be improved. This could be done enlisting agro-business firms in the private sector. (For more on reforms, see Box 7.3Agrarian scene, Farm Reforms and Farm Laws).

Box 7.2: Farmer Producer Organisations (FPOs)

An important step taken to revitalize agriculture sector and ameliorate the condition of farmers is the formation of Farmer Producer Organisations (FPOs). The concept, its objectives, the structure and progress of the scheme are discussed below.

The genesis

The Companies Act 1956 was amended in 2002 to enable registration of producer companies (PCs) and the provision was retained when the Act was modified in 2013. The Small Farmers Agri-business Consortium (SFAC) was tasked with the formation of Farmer Producer Companies (FPCs) in 2010-11 under various schemes of Ministry of Agriculture. NABARD was tasked with the formation of 2,000 Farmer Produce Organisations (FPOs) in 2014-15 with a budgetary support of ₹ 200 crore. This gave fillip to the scheme which is expected to transform agri-economy on the lines of successful farmer-owned milk co-operatives and enterprises like Amul.

The government plans to add 10,000 FPOs (most of them FPCs), with financial and technical support amounting to ₹ 4,496 crore during 2021-24 and with a possible addition of another ₹ 2,369 crore during 2025-28.

Concept and Rationale for Formation of FPOs/FPCs

- The concept behind FPOs is that farmers, who are the producers of agricultural products, can form groups and register themselves under the Companies Act. To facilitate this process, SFAC was mandated by the Ministry of Agriculture, to support State Governments in the formation of (FPOs).
- The aim is to enhance farmers' competitiveness and increase their advantage in emerging market opportunities.
- There is a need for aggregation of farmers in order to benefit from economies of scale.
- Producers' organizations help in reducing the transaction costs and provide a forum for members to share information, coordinate activities and make collective decisions.
- FPOs (cooperatives/ SHGs/FIGs/Producer Companies), have the potential to bring about vertical integration in the traditional fragmented supply chains with need-based long term business plans.
- They also create opportunities for producers to get involved in value all supply chain activities such as input supply, credit, processing, marketing and distribution.

Objectives and Role of FPOs

- The FPO's major operations include the supply of seed, fertilizer, market linkages, training and networking and financial and technical advice.

- Production, harvesting, procurement, grading, pooling, handling, marketing, selling, export of primary produce of members or import of goods or services for their benefit.
- Processing including preserving, drying, distilling, brewing, venting, canning and packaging of produce of its members.
- Rendering technical services, consultancy services, training, education, research and development and all other activities for the promotion of the interests of its members.
- Generation, transmission and distribution of power, revitalization of land and water resources, their use, conservation and communications relatable to primary produce.
- Manufacture, sale or supply of machinery, equipment or consumables mainly to its members.
- Promoting mutual assistance, welfare measures, financial services, insurance of producers or their primary produce.

The scheme

- There are three implementation agencies: SFAC, National Cooperative Development Corporation (NCDC) and NABARD. SFAC is for FPCs, NCDC for co-operatives and NABARD for both.
- There will be two expert support organisations, viz. a National Project Management Agency (NPMA) to be set up in SFAC and a number of cluster-based business organisations (CBBOs) under this to support FPOs who may serve as consultants.
- The scheme's central theme is a 'production-cluster based approach', but has multiple objectives including 'One District, One Product' (ODOP) with 15 per cent of FPOs in aspirational districts.
- Identification of the 'produce-cluster area' is to be done with 'inputs' from agencies at the district level to the national level and approved at fairly high levels in the government.
- National-level Project Management Advisory & Fund Sanctioning Committee (N-PMAFSC), state level consultative committee (SLCC) and district level monitoring committee (D-MC) serve as empowered committees to approve projects and sanction money.

Organisation and Coverage

- An FPO may cover farmers having their lands in contiguous micro-watersheds to address the issues relating to sustainability.
- The number of farmer producers that need to be covered may be around 700 to 1000.
- The productive land under an FPO may be around 4000 hectares.
- The FPO may cover generally one or two contiguous Gram Panchayats for ease of management.
- The cost of managing a FPO of the above nature may be around ₹ 2 lakh per month
- The total value of the produce of the farmers/non-farmers handled by the FPO may be around ₹ 2.5 crore, assuming that approximately 10 per cent of the total turnover of the PO may be reasonably spent towards cost of management.
- The markets selected for the Producer Organisation for selling their produce may be within 200 KM to make their marketing activities viable.

Role of States

- Government of India had issued guidelines to encourage states to directly support FPO promotion as a regular activity under various Schemes during the Twelfth Plan (2012-17).
- These guidelines are meant to help the states follow a standard methodology for FPO promotion and to provide indicative costs and a monitoring framework.
- States may directly engage promoters (such as NGOs, private companies, research bodies, cooperatives, farmers' groups) to mobilize the small farmers.
- Alternatively, SFAC is empanelling suitable Resource Institutions (RIs) on their behalf.
- Another option for the States would be to award the work directly to SFAC, to undertake FPO promotion by providing the necessary budget to SFAC from the RKVY head.

Progress

- NABARD was tasked with formation of 2,000 FPOs in 2014-15 and by 2020 about 7,000 active FPOs have come into being and they are getting financial support.
- 7,374 FPCs have been registered till 2019, of which 6,926 are active (average number of members is 582). While 445 FPCs were registered till 2013, 6,000 were registered during 2016-19.As of January 2021, about 8,500 FPOs have been promoted in the country by various agencies with 4,868 of them by NABARD alone.
- As usual, some regions grew faster. Four states, Maharashtra, Madhya Pradesh, Karnataka and Tamil Nadu, account for about 50% of FPCs.
- The top 20 companies account for more than half of the paid-up capital are primarily in dairy and coconut, the largest being Visakha Dairy, transformed from a co-operative. The second, Sahyadri, is primarily in fruits.
- NABARD has to ensure that they get working capital at reasonable rate of interest.

Conclusion

The strategy of achieving higher growth in agriculture needs to be based on forming new farmer producer organisations (FPOs) and nurturing the existing ones. To be successful, the FPOs must be based on local community interests, attain scale and be managed by farmers themselves with sufficient autonomy on an entrepreneurial mode, without any political or bureaucratic interference. With large membership of farmers, they must get linked to nearest markets, develop bargaining power to deal with large buyers. They may be guided by some experts or NGOs working in the domain of agriculture who will serve as Consultants

Agricultural Credit and Debt Relief

Credit for the agricultural sector is a critical element in agricultural operations. Farmers, especially the small and marginal farmers, need timely credit for carrying on farming—buying inputs, payment of wages, transportation of produce, etc. Rural credit has been a major problem with farmers if they do not get institutional credit from banks, co-operative societies, etc. at affordable interest rates and, instead, had to depend on moneylenders, traders, etc. who charged exorbitant interest on borrowings. Ever since independence, successive governments have addressed this problem and taken several steps to mitigate it.

Some of the important steps taken were (Refer to Chapter 5, pp. 5.6–9 ....for more details on this):

- Making commercial banks accord priority in lending to sectors identified as priority sectors, viz., agriculture, small-scale industries, and small borrowers. In 1974, public sector banks were advised that their priority sector lending should reach a level of not less than one-third of the outstanding credit by March 1979.
- In November 1978, private sector banks were also advised to maintain one-third of their total advances to the priority sectors by the end of March 1980. Subsequently, the target was enhanced to 40 per cent of aggregate advances.
- Various measures initiated had a positive impact on lending to agriculture as the share of agricultural credit in total bank credit increased from 2.2 per cent in 1967 to 8.0 per cent in 1970–71 and further to 9.1 per cent in 1974–75. The ratio of advances by banks to the priority sector to net bank credit increased from 15 per cent in 1969 to 41 per cent in 1991.
- Co-operative banks, Primary Agricultural Credit Societies, Land Mortgage banks, etc. were also set up for lending to rural sector but their functioning was found to be weak.
- A major thrust was given to agricultural credit policy with the nationalization of banks in 1969 and 1980. It led to significant expansion of bank branches in urban, semi-urban, and rural areas which greatly helped in extending credit to needy sectors.
- While the idea of starting rural banks was first suggested by the Banking Commission (1972), action along these lines was initiated after the 'Twenty Point Programme' or the 'New Economic Programme' of the Government of India launched in the mid-1970s. The Regional Rural Banks Ordinance was promulgated on September 26, 1975, which was subsequently replaced by the Regional Rural Banks Act on February 9, 1976. Regional Rural Banks (RRBs) were set up with a view to developing the rural economy by providing credit for the purpose of development of agriculture, trade, commerce, industry, and other facilities, particularly to the small and marginal farmers, agricultural labourers, artisans, and small entrepreneurs.
- Another significant step was the establishment of National Bank for Agriculture and Rural Development (NABARD) which functions as the apex organization in regard to rural credit for agriculture, small, cottage and village industries, handicrafts, and other rural crafts. NABARD provides refinance to State Co-operative banks and RRB's.

Direct Institutional Credit for Agriculture and Allied Activities

Loans—short-term and long-term—are advanced to the agriculture sector by institutions such as co-operatives, scheduled commercial banks, regional rural banks, and State Governments. These loans are issued directly to the beneficiary/ borrower by the concerned institutions. Data for selected years given in Tables 7.9 and 7.10 show the loans issued and outstanding. The quantum of loans advanced has increased considerably over the years indicating the increased support given to this priority sector. It will be seen that short-term loans to this sector have increased from about ₹ 1,500 crore in 1977–78 to over ₹ 3,400 billion in 2011–12 and long-term loans from over ₹ 668 crore to over ₹11,07,162 crore during the same period. Also, loans issued to cooperatives and RRBs have risen considerably by 2015-16.

Table 7.9: Direct Institutional Credit for Agriculture and Allied Activities—Short-Term(In ₹ crore)

Year	Loans issued				Loans Outstanding			
	Co-operatives (In billion)	SCBs	RRBs	Total	Co-operatives	SCBs	RRBs	Total
1977-78	1058	288	44	1488	1348	547	-	1894
1990-91	3448	2048	125	5979	5178	4235	590	10002
2011-12	81829	217897	47011	346737	44517	269030	460580	360127
2014-15	199872	-	84686	-	189399	464920	82620	736939
2015-16	227571	-	98150	-	203190	520395	96702	820287

Table 7.10: Direct Institutional Credit for Agriculture and Allied Activities—Long-Term (In ₹ crore)

Year	Loans issued				Loans Outstanding			
	Co-operatives (In billion)	SCBs	RRBs	Total	Co-operatives	SCBs	RRBs	Total
1977-78	387	281	44	668	1727	793	-	2520
1990-91	1372	2628	210	4209	5353	12797	1163	19313
2011-12	6134	94980	6048	107162	28028	174268	17244	219540
2014-15	8119	-	13151	-	32763	219049	27742	225957
2015-16	9492	-	20384	-	26587	294446	36110	279554

SCBs: Scheduled Commercial Banks RRBs: Regional Rural Banks

Notes:
1. Data up to 1990-91 pertain to the period July-June and April-March thereafter. In case of SCBs, data for all the years pertain to July-June period.
2. RRBs came into existence in 1975-76
3. Data on total loans issued includes loans issued by the State Governments.
4. Data on cooperatives and RRBs is not available after 2015-16 as classification of priority sector lending into direct and indirect financing has been stopped.

Sources: 1. Reserve Bank of India. 2. National Bank for Agriculture and Rural Development..

According to the RBI, in its Annual Report 2014–15, "Priority sector refers to those sectors of the economy which, though viable and creditworthy, may not get timely and adequate credit in the absence of a special dispensation. Typically, priority sector loans are small value loans to farmers for agriculture and allied activities, micro and small enterprises, poor people for housing, students for education, other low income groups, and weaker sections. Such sectors are spread across the length and breadth of the country and especially prevalent in the hilly and coastal regions."

"In pursuance of its developmental role, the Reserve Bank accords priority to efficient and comprehensive credit delivery, particularly to priority sectors comprising primarily of the agricultural and MSME sectors, and the weaker sections of society. The guidelines on priority sector lending were revised during the year with a view to widening the scope of the sector and improving the flow of credit. Financial inclusion efforts received a big fillip with the launch of the Pradhan Mantri Jan Dhan Yojana (PMJDY) coupled with synchronized efforts by the Reserve Bank."

Debt Relief for Farmers

As stated earlier, in India, agricultural risks are aggravated by a variety of factors, ranging from erratic weather, recurring natural disasters, uncertainties in yields and prices, weak rural infrastructure, imperfect markets and inadequate and sub-optimal financial services. These factors not only endanger the livelihoods and incomes of small farmers but also undermine the viability of the agriculture sector and its potential tosolve the problem of the endemic poverty of farmers. The question of farm loan waivers, an issue around which there is often much debate, is to be viewed against this background and the challenges confronting the farming community, especially the small and marginal farmers.

From time to time the government has had to waive thousands of crores of farm loans given to farmers. This has been mostly in years following severe drought causing massive crop failures, loss of income of farmers leaving them in acute distress and even leading to suicides by some farmers. According to the National Crime Records Bureau's estimate, the number of farmer suicides between 1995 and 2015 added up to over 3,18,000. Even granting that not all of them may be due to failure of crops and losses incurred by farmers, it points to a serious crisis in the critical agriculture sector.

A major instance of such loan waiver was the one provided by the UPA government in the Union budget for 2008–09. As per this waiver, all agricultural loans disbursed by scheduled commercial banks, RRBs, and co-operative credit institutions up to March 31, 2007 and overdue as on December 31, 2007 were waived. It had special dispensation for small and marginal farmers. The government estimated that this scheme of waiver would benefit three crore small and marginal farmers and about one crore other farmers. The total value of overdue loans waived was about ₹60,000 crore. In 2017, farm loans waived by four states – UP (₹36,400 crore), Maharashtra (₹32,000 crore), Punjab (₹10,000 crore) and Rajasthan (₹20,000 crore) amounted to about ₹98,000 crore.

❑ THE PROS AND CONS OF FARM LOAN WAIVERS

There has been much debate over the issue of waiver of farm loans. The arguments advanced in favour and against it are given below:

Arguments against farm loan waivers

- Loans waived are those given to farmers by public sector banks and cooperative credit societies and when they are written off, the latter have to bear the loss which affects their balance sheets.
- Loan waivers also hurts State finances breaching fiscal deficit threshold of States.
- Waiving loans undermines honest credit culture, impacts credit discipline and may induce borrowers not to repay loans in future.
- Rule, loan waivers apply only to those who borrow from banks and cooperatives. A survey done in 2013 showed that small farmers account for 82 per cent of all indebted farm households in India. The small farmers borrow mostly from private moneylenders or local traders as banks are unwilling to lend without collateral like jewellery, tractors, etc. which the small and marginal farmers may not have. Thus, majority of indebted farmers do not benefit from loan waivers.

Arguments in favour of loan waivers

- Waiving farm loans is not just an ethical or moral issue but has vital social and economic implications. Though the share of agriculture (including fisheries and forestry) in GDP was only 17.4 per cent in 2015-16, 263 million persons, constituting 53 per cent of labour force as per 2011 census, were engaged in agriculture. It is the lifeline for bulk of the rural population who depend on it for their livelihood and survival. Any serious crisis, as happened again due to two back-to-back droughts in 2014-16, causes much distress to farmers and rural population at large.

- In the years following grant of loan waivers, there has been no evidence of slackening in farm loan repayments or of repeated demands being made for loan waivers.
- As for credit culture and moral hazard, these are attributes of individual behaviour. The banks and RBI have, over the years, shown greater forbearance towards large loans given to the corporate sector many of which remain unpaid and have become stressed assets as evidenced by the mounting NPAs in the loan books of banks.
- Agricultural loans by banks are mandatorily insured by the Agriculture Insurance Company of India (AIC) Limited whose liabilities are covered by the Central government through budgetary support. Hence, even if loans are not waived, there is no loss to banks. In situations of severe and widespread distress to farmers resulting in substantial loan defaults, the Centre will step in and provide funds. The difference is that while loan waivers are borne by the States, defaults are borne by the Centre.

  As farming has become more technology driven and commercial, farmers have to incur higher costs towards inputs which entail greater risks, especially in case of crop failure due to various factors. Where farmers, especially the small and marginal ones, depend on moneylenders for loans, the risks become even greater.
- Despite subsidies on power, fertilizers, etc., input costs have been rising faster than prices realised thus squeezing the meagre income of small farmers and driving them into debt. Over 50 per cent of farming households are estimated to be debt-ridden. In case of crop failure or price shocks, farmers are driven to extreme despair and distress leading even to suicides.
- Average household size of farmers is 5.5 at the all-India level. In the low-income groups, the average size goes up to 6.9. According to NSSO-59th round, the average monthly per capita consumption expenditure of farm households across India was ₹503 in 2003. The all India average monthly income per farmer household during the same period was ₹2115. Endemic hunger (i.e., chronic undernutrition), is high both in families without assets like land or livestock, as well as in families with small land holdings without access to irrigation. Hence, there is need to support especially such families in times of crisis.

Remedial Measures

- Under the Pradhan Mantri FasalBima Yojana, a crop insurance scheme introduced by the government, the farmers get monetary support to cover losses incurred due to crop failures. The scheme assists farmers in getting the policy claims settled quickly and without much bureaucratic hassles. (For more details on this scheme, see the section on Pradhan Mantri FasalBima Yojana in this chapter).
- The National Commission on Farmers, headed by Dr. M.S. Swaminathan, has recommended as follows "The Government of India may step in to create an Agriculture-Risk Fund to provide relief [waiver in full/part of loan and interest] to the farmers in the case of successive droughts, etc. and also waiver of interest on loans in areas hit by droughts, floods, heavy pest infestation etc. This Fund should have contributions from the Central Government, State Governments and Banks in a predetermined fashion."
- Strengthening post-harvest operations like agro-processing will enable farmers to get better prices for their produce in the markets. (See section on 'Importance of Agro-processing' in this chapter). The government has decided to expand the coverage of National Agricultural Market (e-NAM) from

the current 250 markets to 585 APMCs. Every e-NAM market would get assistance up to a ceiling of ₹75 lakhs for establishment of cleaning, grading and packaging facilities. This will lead to value addition of farmers' produce.

- Farmers who grow fruits and vegetables, which are highly perishable, would be integrated with agro-processing units for better price realisation and reduction of post-harvest losses. As part of market reforms, States would be urged to denotify perishables from APMC.
- Contract farming is in vogue in certain States. To streamline the system, a model law on contract farming would be prepared and circulated among the States for adoption.

Pradhan Mantri FasalBima Yojana (PMFBY)

An important step to mitigate the problems faced by farmers following crop losses due to erratic weather, monsoon failure, droughts, etc. has been crop insurance. Earlier, National Agricultural Insurance Scheme (NAIS) and Modified NAIS were in operation but it has since been replaced by the **Pradhan Mantri FasalBima Yojana (PMFBY)**, which was introduced in January 2016. The new scheme helps in decreasing the burden of premiums on farmers who take loans for their cultivation and will also safeguard them against the inclement weather. It aims to make the settlement process of the insurance claim, fast and easy so that the farmers do not face any trouble regarding the crop insurance plan.

PMFBY is being implemented under the guidance of the Ministry of Agriculture & Farmers Welfare of the Central Government in co-ordination with all the States and other agencies like financial institutions, commercial and co-operative banks and Regional Rural Banks. Agriculture Insurance Company of India (AIC) and some private insurance companies are participating in the agriculture /crop insurance schemes.

The main objectives of PMFBY are as follows:

- Provide insurance coverage and financial support to the farmers in the event of failure of any of the notified crop as a result of natural calamities, pests and diseases.
- Stabilise the income of farmers to ensure their continuance in farming.
- Encourage farmers to adopt innovative and modern agricultural practices.
- Ensure flow of credit to the agriculture sector.

Cooperative Farming

The role of cooperative farming in the reconstruction of the rural economy was stressed both in the First and in the Second Five Year Plans. Cooperative farming where rural households pool their land holdings and jointly undertake cultivation would have resulted in economies of scale in farming operations, acquiring and use of inputs, joint water management, availing credit and marketing of produce. However, the idea did not gain acceptance save in regard to setting up cooperatives for credit, processing and marketing for which societies were set up. Cooperatives took initiative for providing agricultural inputs by setting up fertiliser mixing units, production and processing of improved seeds, formulations of pesticides and manufacture of small agricultural implements.

Co-operatives in Sugar and Dairy Sectors

Two sectors in which cooperative movement achieved major success were sugar and dairy. By 1968-69, nearly 1,600 cooperative processing units had been organised which included cooperative sugar factories, cotton ginning and pressing units, cotton spinning mills, paddy pressing units, oil mills, and fruit and vegetable units.

In the context of poverty and malnutrition, milk has played a special role due to its many nutritional advantages and the potential of dairy industry to provide supplementary income to some 70 million farmers in over 5,00,000 remote villages. Milk contributes more to the national economy than any other farm commodity. Operation Flood, launched in 1970, introduced co-operatives into the dairy sector with the objectives of increasing milk production, augmenting rural income, and providing fair prices for consumers.

India is the world's largest dairy producer. Annual milk production in India more than tripled from 21 million tonnes in 1968 to 80 million tonnes in 2001 and 140 million tonnes in 2013-14. This rapid growth and modernization is largely credited to the contribution of dairy co-operatives under the Operation Flood (OF) Project, assisted by many multi-lateral agencies including the European Union, the World Bank, Food and Agriculture Organization (FAO). Through an investment of ₹1700 crore spread over 25 years, Operation Flood helped to raise India's milk production in value terms to ₹55000 crore per annum, an output ratio unmatched by any other development programme in the world. Operation Flood has emerged as India's largest rural employment programme and unleashed the larger dimension of dairy development – institutional, techno-economic, industrial and social.

Group Farming and Collective Action

Despite lack of progress in cooperative farming in the early years of planning, a new variant of voluntary cooperation in the form of 'group farming' has taken shape in the last two decades. Planning Commission's Working Group on Disadvantaged Farmers, including women, has observed that insecurities of tenure from urbanisation and industrialisation are impacting small farms which are efficient but lack adequate access. It had recommended that a collective approach should be promoted in agriculture for small and women farmers at all points of the value chain. How such a collective approach could bring about remarkable transformation in the lives of women and whole families among the most disadvantaged groups can be seen from some of the successful and shining examples discussed below.

Deccan Development Society

In former Andhra Pradesh (now in Telangana), beginning in 1989 with the support of the Deccan Development Society (DDS), poor, low-caste women have been leasing-in or purchasing land in groups, through various government credit schemes, and practising group farming for subsistence. A grassroot organization working across 75 villages with some 5,000 members, it involves poorest of poor women, cultivating in groups which are financially viable. The harvest is shared equally by the members. Many landlords now want to lease their land to these groups, confident that they, unlike individual leasers, will not default. Each woman owns a certain share of land but pools the land for farming with other women, in groups of 8 to 10. Poor women's groups are cultivating several hundred acres of purchased land. On both leased and purchased land, women practice organic rain-fed farming and multi-cropping to reduce the risk of crop failure and provide a balanced diet. Collective cultivation allows women flexible work time, cost sharing, and the pooling of differential skills. Both the labour and the produce is shared. The women buy inputs and market the produce. As a result, farm productivity and family food security have increased.

The group runs a Krishi Vigyan Kendra and community gene banks and lays emphasis on factors like organic farming, environmental care, biodiversity and water conservation. Its activities are not confined to just farming but extends to diverse areas critical to women and their families like education through night schools, child care with balwadies, affirmative action for women's all-round empowerment and against domestic violence. It has infused among its members confidence to stand on their own legs and a sense of dignity and self-respect. Truly, it has broken new grounds as a movement for the social and economic upliftment of women belonging to very vulnerable groups.

Kudumbasree

Launched by the Government of Kerala in 1998 for eradicating absolute poverty from the State through concerted community action under the leadership of Local Self Governments, Kudumbashree has evolved into one of the largest women-empowering projects in the country. The term 'Kudumbashree' in Malayalam means 'prosperity of the family'.

It was founded in the context of the devolution of powers to the Panchayat Raj Institutions (PRIs) in Kerala, and the 'People's Plan' concept, which attempted to draw up the Ninth Plan of the local governments from below through the PRIs. In 2011, the Ministry of Rural Development (MoRD), the Union Government recognisedKudumbashree as a Rural Livelihoods Mission under the National Rural Livelihoods Mission (NRLM).

Kudumbashree has a three-tier structure for its women community network, with Neighbourhood Groups (NHGs) at the lowest level, Area Development Societies (ADS) at the middle level, and Community Development Societies (CDS) at the local government level. The community network was extended to cover the entire State in three phases during 2000-2002. By 2017 it had a network of over 2,77,000 NHGs affiliated to 19,854 ADSs and 1073 CDSs with a total membership of over 43,000 lakh women. The membership is open to all adult women but limited to one member per family.

Its main focus is local economic and social development and empowerment of women and many centrally-sponsored rural programmes are undertaken by it. The projects taken up include construction and cement brick units, plastic recycling, apparel collectives, coir defibering units, vector control, organizing fairs and fests and training of personnel. Dairy, fisheries, production of baby food supplements, banana and vegetable cultivation, bee-farming (apiculture) are projects taken up by members which has helped to generate employment and income to thousands of women in various districts.

Joint Liability Group (JLG) of women farmers are formed under the collective farming initiative to help women cultivators access agricultural credit from the banking system. About 36,000 JLGs have been formed. The JLGs avail loans for cultivating items like paddy, bananas and vegetables and area cultivated by them covered 27,270 hectares.

A NHG consists of about 20-40 women members selected from poor families One volunteer bears the responsibility for the collection, consolidation and maintenance of accounts and records of NHG. She also receives training imparted by NABARD for increasing their capability. The thrift and credit activities of the NHGs are monitored at the panchayat or municipal level.

Kudumbashree has gone a long way in the process of empowerment of poor women in Kerala.

Gambhira Cooperative Farming Society, Gujarat

This Society, functioning for over five decades in Gujarat, has scripted a success story in group farming. It has been able to rehabilitate destitute small and marginal farmers and landless labourers. As early as 1951, the government gave away 246 acres of fertile land to about 170 farmers from four villages. Initially the farmers took to cultivating on individual basis. Which led to problems of scarce resources and consequent ineffective cultivation. Then under the guidance of some visionary leaders, they surrendered their land ownership titles and pooled the common land resources, formed into groups and started joint cultivation. The society started distributing inputs such as crop seeds, fertilisers and pesticides and provided irrigation, tractor services etc.

The remuneration model was unique. Instead of daily wage, the society distributed 50 per cent of the foodgrains produced among the farmer members through the group leaders and the remaining 50 per cent was retained by the co-operative. The incentive-oriented group farming method has helped in enlisting the active participation of the members and resulted in steady increase in net income per acre per member from collective cultivation. The society's policies have proved to be a successful experiment in ensuring the viability of agriculture on cooperative lines.

Group Management of Forests

The forest dwelling tribal people and the forests are inseparable and forestry plays a crucial role in their lives as a primary source of livelihood. The very ethos of tribal life ensures conservation of ecological resources stemming from forests. India's Joint Forestry Management program, initiated in 1990, was designed to give communities a financial stake in forests so that they have an incentive to preserve them. The Forest Rights Act which came into operation in 2008 has further recognized and given momentum to Community Forest Rights. The Act empowers the forest rights holders, Gram Sabhas and local level institutions to protect, regenerate, conserve and manage any community forest resource.

The community forestry groups (CFGs) involving millions of rural families protect government forests in a co-management arrangement under which village communities and the government share the responsibilities and benefits of regenerating degraded local forests. In terms of forest regeneration, many CFGs have had notable success. Within five to seven years of protection, many of the severely degraded tracts in semi-arid India have been covered with trees and vegetation showing encouraging signs of regeneration.

Experience has shown that wherever forest lands are handed over to user groups, the vegetative cover has improved dramatically which again points to the inherent strengths of collective, cooperative working. Yet there are certain limitations noticed in their working, viz., due to traditional hierarchies, social norms that exclude women from public decision-making, women's lack of bargaining power, and men's entrenched claims and control over natural resources, women are generally under-represented in forest user groups, such as village forest committees.

Self Help Groups

Apart from the above examples of cooperative working are lakhs of women's 'Self Help Groups' (SHGs) successfully operating across India. They are engaged in diverse income-generating activities, pro-actively supported under government's rural development programmes and financed by from banks and micro-financing institutions (MFIs). These self-employment ventures have not only resulted in financial security for millions of women from poor and disadvantaged sections but infused a sense of self-confidence and empowerment.

❑ CONTRACT FARMING

Introduction

Under 'Contract farming', the farmer is contracted to plant the crop on his land, harvest and deliver a quantum of produce, based upon anticipated yield and contracted acreage. This is delivered at a pre-agreed price. The contracting party will provide key equipment and inputs to the farmer.

Contract farming arrangements of different types have existed in various parts of the country for both subsistence crops and commercial crops like sugarcane, cotton, tea, coffee etc. Even in the case of some fruit crops and fisheries, contract farming arrangements, involving mainly the forward trading of commodities, have been prevalent. In the wake of economic liberalization, the concept of contract farming under which national or multinational companies enter into contracts for marketing of the horticultural produce and also provide technologies and capital to contract farmers has gained importance.

Main Features of Contract Farming

- Bipartite agreements are made between the farmer and the company and the latter contributes directly to the management of the farm through input supply as well as technical guidance and also markets the produce.

- Selected crops are grown by farmers under a buy back agreement with an agency engaged in trading or processing.
- The centralized processing and marketing agencies supply technology and resources, including planting materials and, if need be, crop supervision.
- The inputs and services supplied by firms may include seeds, fertilizers, pesticides, credit, farm machinery, technical advice, extension etc., or may involve only the supply of hybrid seeds and marketing of produce.
- The company and the farmers enter into contracts to supply or purchase a specified quantum of the commodity at agreed prices.
- The farmer assumes the production-related risks, while the price risk is transferred to the company.
- The contracting company may also bear the production risk, depending on the stage of crop growth at which the contract is made. If the contract is made at flowering or fruiting stage, the company bears the production risks also.
- The company bears the entire costs of transaction and marketing.

Benefits of Contract Farming

- Farmers in India mostly lack capital and other resources and are unable to make major investment in land improvement and quality inputs.
- Contract farming fills this gap by providing the farmers with quality inputs, equipments needed, technical guidance and management skills.
- The corporate entity undertakes to do collection, transportation, processing and marketing of the produce.
- Although the company may deal only with the contracted crop, the arrangement helps to improve the farmer's overall management skill, thereby helping him to raise the yields of both contracted and non-contracted crops, if any.
- From the standpoint of contacting companies or bodies, this system reduces the supply risk and risk of non-availability of raw material, while the farmer benefits by being insulated from price risks.
- Where the farms are too small, a group of small farmers may have to join together to provide a certain minimum acreage to make the contract viable.

Need for and Importance of Contract Farming in India

- The farm-firm linkages of contract farming model integrates production and marketing which is critical for high value agricultural commodities.
- Agriculture sector is handicapped by the presence of small and fragmented land holdings, and contract farming helps to consolidate their operations and undertake group farming with various benefits for the small farmers as outlined earlier.
- It also helps to tackle issues of lack of capital, poor rural infrastructure, inadequate dissemination of information to farmers, etc.
- Corporates can be involved in providing warehousing and cold storage facilities to minimise and prevent loss and wastage of large quantities of fruits, vegetables and other perishables value of which runs into thousands of crores. The system also helps agro-based and food industry to acquire timely and adequate supply of good quality agricultural produce.

- The system can better respond to changing consumption patterns and the needs of the fast-food sector and supermarkets.

In the Union budget for 2017-18, the Finance Minister stated that the government "propose to integrate farmers who grow fruits and vegetables with agro processing units for better price realisation and reduction of post-harvest losses. A model law on contract farming would therefore be prepared and circulated among the States for adoption."(See also Box 7.1 on Food Processing Industry in this chapter).

Issues with Contract Farming

Studies of the system of contract farming have highlighted following problems which may arise.

- Either the contracting firms or the farmers breach contracts when market conditions change and provide arbitrage opportunities, i.e., switching to more favourabledeals;
- Firms reject more of the contracted produce citing quality grounds when market prices fall below contracted prices;
- Farmers resort to side-selling in open markets when market prices rise higher than the contract prices.
- Restrictive and regulated agricultural marketing system and presence of middlemen act as disincentives.
- Companies prefer medium and large farmers because of economies of scale and to optimise transaction costs. They may want farmers to dedicate a certain minimum acreage, say, five to ten acres of land, to the contract crop. In India, 85 per cent of the farmers are marginal or small, operating less than two acres and will be outside the scope of contract farming. In this, collectivisation of farms of say, 10 to 15 farmers could help;
- It will also help to bring down the operational and transaction costs, the farmers will be better protected; it will be a win-win situation for both the farmer and the corporate entity.

Contract Farming in India: Private Sector Involvement

A number of companies in India have entered the field of contract farming. Among them are Pepsi Foods, Hindustan Unilever, Cargill, Nestle, Rallis India, ITC-International, Mahindra Shubhlabh, Escorts, Himalaya Drugs, United Breweries, Marico, NijjerAgro Foods, Venkateshwara Hatcheries, Global Green Company, DD International, Appachi Cotton Company, AVT Natural Products and Gherkin Exporters.

Farm produce covered under contract farming in India include wheat, basmati rice, maize, pulses, spices, fruits and vegetables, soyabean, flowers, cotton, poultry and milk.

States that Provide favourable conditions for contract farming are Andhra Pradesh, Chhattisgarh, Haryana, Karnataka, Madhya Pradesh, Maharashtra, Punjab, Rajasthan, Tamil Nadu, Uttarakhand, and Uttar Pradesh. The success of contract farming in these States owes to availability of land under marginal fields, better irrigation facilities, soil productivity and yield per hectare.

❑ CAPITAL FORMATION AND SUBSIDIES

Capital formation in agriculture is vital as it helps to build assets and accelerate growth. Public investment in critical areas like irrigation facilities, power supply for drawing groundwater, improving drainage and flood control systems, intensifying soil and moisture conservation measures, building storage and warehousing facilities, providing all-weather roads, integrated marketing facilities, etc. is essential. Public investment in these areas will also stimulate private investment.

Table 7.11: Public Sector Capital Formation and Subsidies to Agriculture (Centre and States)
(in ₹ crore and as per cent to GDP from agriculture and allied at current prices)

Plan Period	Year	Public GCF Agriculture and Allied (CSO)		Budgetary Subsidies		Food Subsidy		Total Fertilizer Subsidy		Subsidy on indigenous Urea		All other Agriculture Subsidies	
		₹	%	₹	%	₹	%	₹	%	₹	%	₹	%
Tenth Plan(2002-07)													
	2002–03	9,563	2.0	43,597	9.0	24,176	5.0	11,015	2.3	7,790	1.6	16,196	3.3
	2006–07	25,606	3.5	59,510	8.2	24,014	3.3	26,222	3.6	12,650	1.7	21,924	3.0
Eleventh Plan(2007-12)													
	2007–08	27,638	3.3	85,698	10.2	31,328	3.7	32,490	3.9	12,950	1.5	34,830	4.2
	2010–11	34,548	2.7	1,50,170	11.8	63,844	5.0	62,301	4.9	15,081	1.2	39,106	3.1

Source: *Twelfth Plan document, Planning Commission.*

Note: Public sector agricultural GCF and GDP are from CSO, National Accounts Division; budgetary subsidies, are also from CSO and are based on the economic and purpose classification of Government expenditure. Food and Fertilizer subsidies are from budget documents of the Central Government. 'All other agriculture subsidies' in the table are defined as budgetary subsidies (CSO) plus subsidy on indigenous urea minus food subsidy. This is because CSO classifies food subsidy as subsidy to agriculture but classifies subsidies on indigenous urea as subsidy to industry.

Public investment in agriculture as percentage of agricultural GDP had halved between the 1980s and the end of the Ninth Plan (1997–2002), while simultaneously budgetary subsidies to agriculture had doubled as proportion of agricultural GDP. The tendency for subsidies to increase much faster than public investment was arrested to some extent during the Tenth Plan (2002–07), but it reappeared again during the Eleventh Plan (2007–12). (See Table 7.11).

There is need to contain subsidies and boost public investment aimed at increasing land productivity as that would produce better agricultural outcomes and would also be more inclusive. This is particularly important in the context of strategies for combating the effect of climate change where public investment in conservation and management of water resources will be crucial. Besides, fertilizer subsidy payment system should be revamped to make direct payment to farmers through Direct Benefit Transfer (DBT) method so that it goes to actual beneficiaries. **(For more on Subsidies, see chapter 14, pp.14.16-7).**

Investment and capital formation in agriculture, which is so essential for the progress and growth of any sector, has seen an unhealthy trend in recent years – the growth rate fell from close to 10 per cent per year during 2002-03 to 2011-12 to 2 per cent in the following decade. The private corporate sector has almost avoided the sector and constitutes less than 2 per cent of the total investments in agriculture and less than 0.5 per cent of the total annual investments of the corporate sector in the Indian economy. There is a pressing need to revive investments in agriculture to modernize the sector.

❑ PUBLIC DISTRIBUTION SYSTEM (PDS)

The Public Distribution System (PDS) for supply of essential food items, operated jointly by the Central and State governments, is the largest such operation in the world. Rice, wheat, sugar, kerosene, etc. are distributed to about 16 crore families through a network of over 4.5 lakh Fair Price Shops (FPS).

Identification of families entitled for items under the PDS and overseeing the functioning of FPS, etc. is the responsibility of State governments. The PDS which has been the subject of criticism for various malpractices like leakages of items into the open market and black marketing by FP shops, the existence of bogus ration cards, etc. has been revamped from time to time to make it more foolproof.

In 1997, a Targeted PDS was introduced under which families were classified as Below Poverty Line (BPL) and Above Poverty Line (APL) and they were entitled for items under a 2-tier subsidized rates. Further in 2000, another scheme, Antyodaya Anna Yojana, was started to cater to the poorest among the BPL families by providing them 25 kg. of cereals per family per month at a low price of ₹2 per kg. of wheat and ₹ 3 per kg. of rice.

The functioning of the Food Corporation of India (FCI), which is one of the main agencies involved in the PDS, is beset with many problems. Higher procurements have led to overstocking by the FCI, with stocks exceeding the buffer norms, and FCI is forced to carry them over to subsequent years, resulting in heavy storage and carrying costs, deterioration and wastage of stocks, etc.

❑ PROS AND CONS OF PDS

While the scheme confers many benefits, especially the poor and vulnerable sections, it suffers from many infirmities too as discussed below.

Merits of the scheme

- PDS meets the requirements of the demand for major food items, mainly rice and wheat among cereals, and sugar.
- Items are supplied at highly subsidised rates and in regular manner.
- As open market prices are quite high and subject to fluctuations, the PDS provides protection against price fluctuations and ensure availability of items at fixed rates.
- PDS which is still very popular especially among the poor households. has had a positive impact on household welfare due to regular supply at affordable prices.
- State governments have put in place various monitoring mechanisms to prevent malpractices. These include grievance redressal mechanism, vigilance committee to monitor functioning of PDS and involving Gram Sabhas in rural areas and Ward Committees in urban areas to oversee its working.

Deficiencies of the scheme

- Beneficiaries are sometimes charged higher prices by the Fair Price Shops (FPS) than the price fixed., though it will still be lower than the market prices.
- FPS dealers justify this on the ground that they are not always reimbursed for the transportation cost incurred to ferry the grain from the nearest FCI warehouse to the ration shop. This is adjusted by charging a higher price for grain from the beneficiaries.
- Appropriate identification of target households is a serious deficiency. There are both "exclusion" and "inclusion" errors due to which eligible households do not get the benefit while many ineligible households are covered under the scheme. This is a serious administrative lapse affecting the efficacy of the scheme.
- Often Duplicate or dubious and fake ration cards are found who get the benefit.
- Lack of awareness about their entitlement and the issue price among beneficiaries is another challenge. Display boards containing the correct information about entitlement, availability of food grain and the issue price are not maintained at all FPSs.
- Leakages and black-marketing occur whereby items under the PDS do not reach the beneficiary households but find their way to open markets where they are sold at higher prices. FPS entities are responsible for such malpractices which result in wasteful expenditure for the government.
- Inspection of FPSs is not done regular basis or in an unbiased manner Often, inspectors visit FPSs only occasionally and they do not always check all the records in the FPS.

Reform of the scheme

A high-level Committee on restructuring the FCI and PDS set up by the government in 2014 had suggested various measures to further streamline the structure and working of the FCI and the PDS. Central and State govts have also initiated several steps over the years, some of which are still under execution, to plug loopholes in the system. These include:

- Proper identification of eligible households through biometrics and linking of Aadhaar card to Ration card.
- Digitisation of Ration cards and records at FPS outlets though this is still not completed in all states.
- Introduction of an SMS alert to beneficiaries is an important measure to increase awareness. All states should adopt a scheme to send an SMS to beneficiaries at the beginning of the month regarding their entitlement and the exact price to be paid at the FPS.
- State departments at district and lower levels should tighten the inspection of FPS outlets through surprise checks by Vigilance Committee, Gram Sabhas and Ward Committees.
- **One Nation, One Card:** This is a major step to make Ration Cards inter-operable anywhere to eligible persons. Due to lack of such a facility, migrant persons and labour who live away from their homes where family cards are registered were not able to draw their entitlements. This problem came to the fore during the Covid-19 pandemic in 2020-21 due to which migrants had to leave their place of work. Now many States have put in place the "One Nation, One Card: scheme which, if implemented efficiently, should go a long way in resolving this issue.

PDS and WTO

A related issue is the objection India and other developing countries are facing in World Trade Organization (WTO) over the public procurement of food and subsidies involved in it. The agricultural trade rules in the WTO's 'Agreement on Agriculture' do not bar public procurement and stockholding for food security. However, if food for such programmes is acquired at administered prices and not market prices, then it is deemed to be support to farmers.

WTO rules: As per WTO rules negotiated in the Uruguay Round, all such support has to be kept within a limit of 10 per cent of the value of production of the product in question. This cap can constrain procurement and food aid programmes in developing countries. The WTO rules are made apparently keeping the interests of the developed countries uppermost, overlooking the interests of the developing countries.

These are issues of utmost concern to India which has a food procurement programme, minimum support price (MSP) policy in the interests of farmers, and the extensive Public Distribution System (PDS) to help especially the poor and vulnerable sections of the population. India has been working closely with her coalition partners in developing country groupings such as the G-20 and the G-33 in order to achieve an outcome in the agricultural negotiations that would safeguard the interests of developing countries.

Ahead of the WTO's Ministerial meeting in Buenos Aires, Argentina in December 2017, India and China had jointly proposed to the WTO against trade distorting farm subsidies by developed countries. Developed countries like US and those in Europe extend agricultural subsidies to their farmers which depresses world food prices. And they are also insisting on freer access to the markets of developing countries with a view to export their subsidized farm products. These measures will result not only in dumping of farm products in the markets of less developed nations, but also restrict the scope for developing countries to export their farm products, thus posing a direct threat to farmers and food and livelihood security in developing countries.

Intransigence of developed nations

The developed countries led by the US have been intransigent in following through their commitment in Bali to negotiate a permanent settlement on India's programme of administered prices and stockholding for food security. The stratagem and insincerity of US is exposed by the US Farm Bill of 2014 under which the government provides indirect support to producers and compensates them for low prices for farm produce. Besides, they get subsidized crop insurance coverage from the federal government. It is patently unfair on the part of developed nations to extend support to their farming community which is relatively much better off while objecting to any support to the much poorer and indigent farmers in countries like India. And this is when negligible portion of the farm produce of less developed countries gets exported whereas countries like US export sizeable portion of their production.

The 'Peace clause': When the issue came up in the 11th Ministerial conference of WTO held in Buenos Aires in December2017, India aggressively pursued solving the question of public procurement and stockholding offood grains and ensuring food security for the vulnerable sections and farmers. But the US refused toagree to a permanent solution to the issue, as committed at the Nairobi ministerial meet in 2015. Thishas cast a pall over the sanctity of pledges made at WTO and the very functioning of the world body.

However, India is protected by a 'peace clause' secured in 2013 in Bali meet and which receivedpermanent status in 2014. The peace clause implies that even if a developing country gave subsidy forfood procurement exceeding 10 percent of the value of production, which is the provision under WTO'sAgreement on Agriculture (AOA), no other country could challenge it at WTO till 2017. In 2014, theWTO General Council approved extension of peace clause till such time a permanent solution is agreedto by the members. Thus, India has protection but yet it is seeking a permanent solution over and abovethe existing 'peace clause' to give stronger legal basis to its programme to procure, stock and distributefood.

India's current subsidy regime includes permissible subsidies such as PM-KISAN and payments for relief for natural disasters (both being forms of income support) which should not be included in subsidy calculations. The truce, struck essentially between the US and India after the Bali meet, was that India's food subsidy would not be questioned before the WTO arrived at a permanent solution to the vexed issue of calculating this figure.

A country's farm subsidies are calculated as a sum of product-specific and non-product specific support. Product-specific support is the difference between domestic and international prices for all products, while non-product support includes credit and input subsidies (on fertilizer, irrigation and electricity). If some product-specific subsidies have turned positive in recent years, it is not merely on account of an increase in procurement but more so because of the underestimated international price.

Another bone of contention is that the difference between the procurement and PDS price should also be included in the subsidy calculations. However, Article 6 of the 'Agreement on Agriculture' allows a developed country to protect livelihoods of the poor, as a result of which many of these subsidies can be struck off in the calculations — more so in times of crisis such as these.

Need to Reform Food Subsidy Regime

Public procurement of foodgrains at remunerative prices is needed to protect the farmers and, equally, food security through the Public Distribution System (PDS) is vital for a country like India with a sizeable poor population. But there is no reason why India should persist with the expensive manner in which it pursues food security and there is imperative need to reform them. Foodgrains are procured far in excess of requirements and the buffer stocking norms under the PDS. This takes away grains from themarket pushing up prices and adds to the government's costs of procurement, storage and carryover.

The inability and inefficiency of the public sector agency, viz., the Food Corporation of India (FCI), which has a monopoly, results, year after year, in spoilage and pilferage of millions of tonnes of food grains meant for public distribution. There is scope to decentralize the stockholding by involving private trade, limit the role of FCI to holding minimum physical stocks and play an active role in the forward markets in grains to stabilize prices. The use of cash subsidies in urban areas through the Direct Benefit Transfer(DBT) scheme could also help to streamline the PDS by preventing leakages and save valuable public funds.

Box 7.3: Agrarian scene, Farm Reforms and Farm Laws

The agricultural sector has seen impressive growth since 1947 due to technological changes in farming methods and farmers' resilience to multiple challenges and determination to serve and secure the nation's requirements of food and raw material for the agro-industries. It is a paradox that despite all these, the farmer is caught in the vortex of serious challenges mentioned below:

- **Income factor:** The average income of an agricultural household during 2012-13 was as low as ₹6,426, as against its average monthly consumption expenditure of ₹6,223.
- **Subsistence living:** As many as 22.50 per cent of the farmers live below official poverty line.
- **Soil condition:** Large tracts of arable land have turned problem soils, becoming acidic, alkaline & saline physico-chemically.
- **Water stress:** Another primary factor of production, namely, water is also under stress with fast depleting levels of underground water in many parts of the country and lack of adequate irrigation.
- **Climate change:** Climate change is beginning to challenge the farmer's ability to adopt coping and adaptation measures that are warranted.
- **Technology fatigue:** After the Green Revolution, technology fatigue is manifesting in the form of plateauing yield. India's yield averages for most crops at global level do not compare favourably.
- **Input costs:** The costs of cultivation are rising which makes farming unremunerative resulting in income losses and debts for farmers.
- **Post-harvest factors:** The magnitude of food loss and food waste is alarming. The markets do not assure the farmer of remunerative returns on his produce. In short, sustainability of agricultural growth faces serious doubt, and agrarian challenge even in the midst of surpluses has emerged as a core concern.
- **Supply-Demand mismatch:** There is mismatch between supply and demand. India's population growth rate is decelerating whereas production of main cereals is at record levels even as domestic demand is shifting from cereals to other high nutrient value items like milk, fruits, vegetables, etc. Hence India will need to step up imports of surplus food crops like grains and sugar for which these items have to be competitive in world markets. This is not possible in the present setting of complex supply chain with intermediaries, small markets, and high transaction costs.

India needs to reform the farm sector to achieve these goals.

The government has set in motion reform measures to achieve the goal of taking Indian agriculture to new heights and ushering in the transformation of the rural economy.

❑ FARM SECTOR REFORMS

In September 2020, the Union government introduced three bills in Parliament aimed at transformation of agriculture sector in the country and raising farmers' income. They became Acts after approval by both the Houses of Parliament.

- The Farmers' Produce Trade and Commerce (Promotion and Facilitation) Act 2020 (FPTC Act).
- The Farmers (Empowerment and Protection) Agreement on Price Assurance and Farm Services Act 2020 (FAPAFS Act); and
- The Essential Commodities (Amendment) Act 2020 (ECA Act 2020).

Thegovernment enacted two new laws for agriculture and modified the Essential Commodities Act 1951 for agricultural commodities. The new acts have been widely acclaimed as historic and path-breaking, akin to the 1991 economic reforms which propelled the industrial and foreign trade sectors. But some sections of farmers, traders and experts have expressed apprehensions about the adverse effects these acts would have on farmers and the agriculture sector. The gist of the farm laws passed areas follows.

The Farmers' Produce Trade and Commerce (FPTC) Act 2020:

- ♦ This Act permits intra-state and inter-state trade of farmers' produce beyond the premises of Agriculture Produce Market Committee (APMC) markets. Trade could be conducted in any place of production and collection of farmers' produce such as farm gates, silos, factory premises, warehouses and cold storages. Thus, it provides greater flexibility to farmers and buyers resulting in more competition and realization of better prices for farmers.
- ♦ State governments are prohibited from levying any market fee, cess or levy on farmers, traders, and electronic trading platforms for trade of farmers' produce conducted outside APMC areas.
- ♦ An electronic trading and transaction platform may be set up to facilitate the direct and online buying and selling of produce through electronic devices and internet.
- ♦ The Standing Committee of Parliament on Agriculture (2018-19) had also observed that availability of a transparent, easily accessible, and efficient marketing platform is a pre-requisite to ensure remunerative prices for farmers.
- ♦ The Standing Committee also recommended that the Gramin Agricultural Markets scheme (which aims to improve infrastructure and civic facilities in 22,000 GraminHaats across the country) should be made a fully funded central scheme and scaled to ensure presence of a Haat in each panchayat of the country.

The Farmer Agreement on Price Assurance and Farm Services (FAPAFS) Act 2020

- ▪ This Actcreates a framework for "Contract farming" through an agreement between a farmer and a buyer prior to the production or growing of any farm produce.
- ▪ The minimum period of an agreement will be one crop season, or one production cycle of livestock.
- ▪ The price of farm produce should be mentioned in the agreement. For prices which are subject to variation, a guaranteed price for the produce and a clear reference for any additional amount, above the guaranteed price, must be specified in the agreement.
- ▪ For settling disputes, there will be a Conciliation Board as well as a conciliation process. The Board will have a fair and balanced representation of parties to the agreement. If the dispute remains unresolved by the Board after thirty days, parties may approach the Sub-divisional Magistrate for

resolution. Parties will have a right to appeal to an Appellate Authority (presided by Collector or Additional Collector) against decision(s) of the Magistrate.

The Essential Commodities Act (ECA)2020

This Act was passed in 1955 when the country was facing acute shortage of food and hence distribution needed to be regulated. It has lost its relevance in the original form now that the country has adequate food supply and even surplus in cereals, viz., wheat and rice. Hence the amendment.

The Act now amended allows the central government to regulate the supply of certain food items only under extraordinary circumstances (such as war and famine).

Limits on stocking on agricultural produce may be imposed only if there is a steep price rise – if there is 100 per cent increase in the retail price of horticultural produce or 50 per cent increase in the retail price of non-perishable agricultural foodstuffs over the price prevailing immediately preceding 12 months, or average retail price of last 5 years, whichever is lower" subject to certain other conditions.

The Rationale for Reforms

There are several significant factors behind stagnation in the farm sector after the spectacular growth during the Green Revolution of 1970-1990 period. This situation in agriculture and the plight of farmers called for some radical reforms. The rationale for major reforms in the sector are:-

1991 reforms and Farm sector: The major policy reforms of 1991pushed up India's growth rate, helped India step out of the Third world group and enter the league of modern, emerging economies. But these reforms did not cover the agricultural sector.

Negative income growth: But agricultural growth remained stuck at the earlier level, with negative growth in farm income in five out of 12 years following 1990-91. The gap in the income of a farmer and that of a non-agriculture worker widened from ₹ 25,398 in 1993-94 to ₹ 54,377 by 1999-2000. In the next decade, the income of a non-agriculture worker exceeded that of a farmer by a still wider margin of ₹ 1.42 lakh.

Supply-Demand mismatch: There is mismatch between supply and demand. India's population growth rate is decelerating whereas production of main cereals is at record levels even as domestic demand is shifting from cereals to other high nutrient value items like milk, fruits, vegetables, etc. Hence India will need to step up exports of surplus food crops like grains and sugar for which these items have to be competitive in world markets. India needs to improve export competitiveness of Indian agriculture which is not possible in the present setting of complex supply chain of many intermediaries, small markets and high transaction costs.

Wide disparities in prices: Data collected on wholesale prices across 122 centres by the Ministry of Consumer Affairs, Food and Public Distribution has shown wide disparity in prices across regions. Prior to these reforms, farmers were required to sell their produce via auctions to licensed traders at the APMC mandis (markets) in the specified geographical jurisdictions.

Most major states had implemented the APMC Act, Kerala and Bihar being notable exceptions. There were considerable differences in the scope and stringency with which APMC Act was implemented. This resulted in fragmented markets and hampered the emergence of a single national market.

Inter-state barriers: There were inter-state barriers in moving produce which also worked to the disadvantage of farmers. The restrictions on inter-state trade due to the APMC law undermined market power and it adversely affected prices accruing to farmers. Studies have shown that removal of inter-state barriers could significantly increase prices accruing to farmers. The barriers have been removed. India is now one common market for agri-produce.

Stocking: While the passing of EC Act removing restrictions on stock limits is an important step, the Act provides for "regulating stock limit of any agricultural produce" subject to certain conditions mentioned earlier. The restrictions on stocking discouraged private sector investments in storage facilities as under the earlier Act, stock limits could be imposed on a trader, processor or exporter at will. Due to this there was lack of storage facility. So when farmers bring their produce to the market after harvest, there is a glut and prices tend to fall steeply, while in the lean season prices shoot up hurting the consumers. So both are adversely affected by the lack of storage facilities.

But on the conditions laid down in the Act for intervention in the event of price changes (mentioned earlier), experts have reservations. They say, for instance, if the price of a vegetable, say potato which is at ₹ 20/kg rises to ₹40/kg, it would be absurd to impose restrictions under the Act (condition of 100 per cent increase in price). Hence, the provisions of the Act have to be applied only under exceptional circumstances when the burden of price rise inflicts unusually heavy burden on the food budget of households. In short, the Act has to be applied with utmost discretion or else, its very purpose would be defeated.

Marketing: According to experts on agriculture, these reforms have been under consideration for a long time and were long overdue and are far-reaching. The major problem in agriculture was not production but was on the marketing front. The APMC markets function as monopolistic and exploitative entities and charge high rates of commission.

Agricultural segments such as horticulture, milk and fishery – where market intervention by the government is either nil or very little – show 4-10 per cent annual growth. Compared to this, the growth rate in cereals – where MSP and other interventions are quite high – remained 1.1 per cent after 2011–12. This clearly indicates that in recent times liberalized markets are more favourable to agricultural growth than government support and intervention in markets.

The changes introduced create alternative channels for farmers to sell their produce. Farmers will have the freedom not just in production of commodities but also to directly join hands with processors, exporters or retailers to sell the produce. These measures would unshackle commodities like onion, potatoes, oilseeds, etc. from the clutches of regulation.

As bulk of the farms are small holdings, farmers typically have only small marketable surpluses. These farmers lack scale, resources, and the ability to take price-risk to go for high-value crops. It is not economically viable for them to take small quantities of produce to mandies which may be located far away. This is especially true in the case of fruit and vegetables which are highly perishable. If such farmers get markets close to production, as in the case of milk collection centres, and have price assurance, they will be encouraged to diversify towards diverse crops, get better prices and earn more income.

Farmer Produce Organisations (FPOs): Another major step the government has taken is to create 10,000 FPOs to transform agri-economy on the lines of successful farmer-owned milk co-operatives and enterprises like Amul. NABARD was tasked with formation of 2,000 FPOs in 2014-15. 7,374 FPCs have been registered till 2019, of which 6,926 are active (average number of members is 582). As of January 2021, about 8,500 FPOs have been promoted in the country by various agencies with 4,868 of them by NABARD alone. As of January 2021, about 8,500 FPOs have been promoted in the country by various agencies with 4,868 of them by NABAR Dalone. NABARD will ensure that they get working capital at reasonable rate of interest.(For more on FPOs, see Box 7.2 in this chapter).

Opposition to Reforms

- **Vested interests:** There has been strident opposition to, and protests against, these reforms from some States and certain groups of farmers, especially from Punjab and Haryana, whose vested interests would be adversely impacted. However, the dire need for reforms in agricultural marketing which has been a major weak link in the chain of agricultural operations in India and causing problems to farmers has been emphasized by many Committees, experts and even previous governments.

It may be mentioned that nearly 85 per cent of farmers in India are small and marginal farmers who hold less than 2 hectares (and of them about 65 per cent hold less than just one hectare). These small farmers are unable to go to mandies which may be located far away while the large farmers are able to go to wholesale markets. The small farmers are in a vulnerable position as they face difficulties in storage and transportation of produce and have little bargaining power which the buyers, who are mostly moneylenders, traders, or commission agents, exploit.

- **Fears unfounded:** The fears that deregulation of APMCs would lead to farmers switching *en masse* to private markets are misplaced. The experience of Bihar, Kerala and Maharashtra do not indicate such a trend. Bihar annulled the APMC Act in 2006 and Kerala never had an APMC Act. Still there have been no private investments in these states. Most big corporate retail firms purchase their food items directly from APMC markets, and not directly from farmers.
- **Revenue loss:** States where state-run procurement is wholly routed through APMC mandies levy high taxes on agricultural trade which inflates Centre's food procurement expenditure. Punjab and Haryana are two such states. Punjab levies an aggregate tax of 8.5 per cent of MSP (price) at which FCI and other agencies buy grains. This levy includes market fee, rural development cess and 'arhtiyas' commission. Both these states collect substantial sums as mandi fees. With the reforms introduced, FCI and other agencies could start procuring grains at market rates bypassing the mandies. These states and middlemen in the trade stand to lose revenue which is why there is vociferous protest from states like Punjab and Haryana.
- **MSP:** One of the main contentions against the reforms is that it does not assure continuance of the policy of minimum support price (MSP) and APMC markets, and it would leave the farmers at the mercy of big companies and corporate entities. Though the government has assured that the MSP regime would continue, it has not assuaged the fears of farmers. Nor are the APMC markets going to be abolished. Only that, farmers are given the freedom to sell produce not only in a specific APMC market or location but anywhere and to anyone as per their choice with a view to get the best return.

Furthermore, a National Sample Survey on key indicators of agricultural households showed that only 19 per cent of households were aware of MSP and 15 per cent of procurement agency. Only 7 per cent of households sell crops to procurement agency and only 10 per cent of total crops are sold at MSP. This indicates that almost 93 per cent of households sell produce in open market and face market imperfections, according to the study.

It is also pertinent to note that the mere existence of APMC markets does not ensure MSP, as seen in the case of many crops in Punjab and Haryana and with wheat and paddy in several states. There are also cases of sizable procurement at MSP in states without the APMC Act (20 lakh tons of paddy procured in Bihar and 7 lakh tons in Kerala in 2019-20).

Implementation and continuation of MSP is an administrative decision and in the case of rice and wheat it is part of the four pillars of food security, that include procurement, buffer stock and PDS in addition to MSP. The system will be disrupted if one pillar is done away with. No responsible government would do damage to the system that has served the purpose of food security, price stability, food self-sufficiency so well. During the ongoing agitation, the government has assured farmers, and even given written assurance, that the MSP system will continue after implementation of the new farm laws.

Farmers are insisting on providing legal guarantees for continuance of both MSP and APMC Markets.

- **State laws:** Some States who are opposed to the reforms have enacted laws undoing the reforms enunciated in the Central laws. Agriculture is a Concurrent subject under the Constitution, with both the Centre and the States having powers to legislate. It remains to be seen if the laws enacted by the States would come into effect as they require the assent of the President of India. States could possibly circumvent the problem by issuing executive orders.

- **Scrutiny of the Laws**

  Apart from the objections raised by farmers to the new laws, another objection is that these laws were passed without adequate scrutiny or detailed discussion in the Parliament. However, the issue of reforms in the agriculture sector has been examined at length by various Committees appointed by successive governments, State Ministers and Parliamentary Committees as detailed below. A way out of the impasse has to be found if the farm sector is to overcome stagnation and progress further.

Detailed Studies by Expert Groups and Legislators

The growing disparity between agriculture and non-agriculture incomes drew the attention of experts who stressed the need for reforms in the sector. It was also examined by some high-powered Committees set up by the government and the Parliament. These included:

The National Commission on Farmers (NCF) set up in 2004 headed by Dr. M.S. Swaminathan, the eminent agricultural expert and father of the Green Revolution. This Committee submitted four reports between 2004 and 2006 and made wide-ranging recommendations to achieve the goal of "faster and more inclusive growth" as envisaged in the Eleventh Five Year Plan (2007-12).

In 2013, a Committee of State Ministers on Agricultural Marketing and Reforms had studied the issues involved in marketing and suggested remedial measures.

The Standing Committee on Agriculture of 2018-2019 and 2019-20 (of the 16th and 17th Lok Sabha) had looked into "Agriculture Marketing and Role of Weekly GraminHaats". The Parliamentary Committee which consisted of 32 MPs drawn from across the political spectrum in the Lok Sabha and Rajya Sabha.

A broad-based Expert Committee on "Doubling Farmers' Income" was set up by the government under the Chairmanship of Ashok Dalwai, CEO, National Rainfed Area Authority in 2016 consisting of experts drawn from the field of research, academics, non-government organizations, farmers' organizations, professional associations, trade, industry, commerce, consultancy bodies and policy makers at Central and State levels. The Committee held detailed discussions with various stakeholders in the domain of agriculture and made field visits to study relevant issues including marketing and pricing of produce, production and its sustainability and post-production strategies to enhance farmers' incomes.

Parliament Committee's observations

- While the Agriculture Produce Marketing Committees Act (APMC Act) was enacted by various State Governments to ensure an environment of fair play for an effective price discovery for farm produce, regulate market practices and attain transparency in transactions, they have been riddled with politics, monopoly of traders and middleman and abuse of the system.
- It is found that the APMC markets across the country are not working in the interest of farmers due to reasons such as limited numbers of traders thereby reducing competition, cartelization of traders, undue levies in the form of market fee, commission charges etc.
- Though the market fee and commission charges are legally to be levied on traders the same are collected from farmers by deductions from farmers' net proceeds. The system is highly restrictive and prevents promotion of multiple channels of marketing and competition.
- The Committee opined that "Gramin Haats", being ingrained in the cultural ethos of rural India and their proximity to the farmers, may emerge as alternative agriculture marketing platform and can help in ensuring remunerative prices for agriculture produces due to direct access to the consumers and less transportation cost.
- The Committee recommended for the creation and upgradation of infrastructure such as sheds, storage facilities for produce, connectivity through roads, civic facilities such as toilet, drinking water, etc.in 22,000 GraminHaats across the country. Such steps will help to make them viable and vibrant marketing platforms for agriculture produce and help in doubling the income of farmers.
- The Committee observed that there is urgent need for radical reform in the APMC Act to do justice to the farmers.

Planning Commission on Reforms

It is also worth recalling that while preparing the Twelfth Plan (2012-17), the erstwhile Planning Commission had observed: "Reforming the Agricultural Produce Marketing Committee (APMC) Acts should, therefore, have priority as emphasized in the Eleventh Plan and the Mid-term Appraisal. The introduction of the **Model Act in 2003** was directed towards allowing private market yards, **direct buying and selling**, and also to **promote and regulate contract farming** in high-value agriculture with a view to **boost private sector investment** in developing new regularised markets, logistics and warehouse receipt systems, and in infrastructure (such as cold storage facilities)." (Twelfth Plan, Vol. II, Chapter 12, Agriculture).

Conclusion

To sum up, these long overdue and far-reaching reforms in the crucial agriculture sector are positive steps in the right direction and have the following implications:

- **More choice and freedom:** The economic rationale of all these bills is to provide greater choice and freedom to farmers to sell their produce and buyers to buy and store, thereby creating competition in agricultural marketing. In effect, they unshackle farmers from archaic restrictions which fettered them and kept them subjugated to intermediaries and middlemen who thrived at the expense of farmers.
- **Benefit of competition:** This competition is expected to help build more efficient value chains in agriculture by reducing marketing costs, enabling better price discovery, improving price realizationfor farmers and yet reducing the price paid by consumers.
- **Price and market trends:** In the absence of regulation, market forces may induce buyers to move to regions where prices are low. In that case, farmers in regions that have a relative cost disadvantage might lose out. On the flip side, barrier-free trade and more supply chain investments can increase earnings for farmers.
- **Storage facilities:**It calls for creating more silos and warehouses for storage and cold storage facilities for perishables closer to villages for easy access. India processes less than 10 per cent of its food production and loses about ₹900 billion ($12.3 billion) a year due to wastage from inadequate cold storage.
- **Cold storage facilities:** The government has been promoting private investment in storage facilities to reduce wastages and help contain the seasonal price volatility. Private sector has been showing interest in expanding facilities like cold storage chains.

The Ministry of Food Processing Industries has been having a scheme, since 2008, of building "Cold Chain, Value Addition and Preservation Infrastructure" to provide integrated cold chain and preservation facilities, without any break, from the farm gate to the consumer.

The integrated cold chain projects are set up by Companies, Corporations, Cooperatives, Self Help Groups (SHGs), Farmer Producer Organizations, NGOs and Central and State PSUs.

There are 308 approved Cold Chain Projects across India as of October 2020 with total project cost of ₹ 8,358 crore against which ₹ 2,314 crore have been approved as grant-in-aid. Of this grant, ₹ 1,675 had been released.

- **Improved transportation:**Further improving transport facilities from villages to nearby towns, on which – village all-weather road connectivity – much work has been already done through PM's Gram Sadak Yojana. There is need to connect remaining villages and hamlets too to nearby towns. Private sector could be enlisted in providing better transport facilities.
- **Objectives of the Farm laws:** The overall objectiveof the three Acts is to ensure that there are more buyers for farmers' produce, allow them to trade freely without any license or stock limit, so that increase in competition among them results in better prices for farmers.

Essentially, the FPTC breaks the monopolistic powers of Agriculture Produce Market Committee (APMC) markets, while FAPAFS allows contract farming, and ECA removes stocking limits on traders for a large number of commodities, with some caveats in place.

Repeal of new Farm Laws

Though the Government tried to convince the section of farmers who were agitating against the three farm laws discussed above, the government eventually decided in November 2021 to repeal these laws. The Government also decided to set up a committee consisting of Central and State Government representatives, farmers, scientists and economists to study and promote zero-budget farming, make Minimum Support Price (MSP) for farm produce effective and transparent and look into crop diversification issues.

Zero-budget natural farming refers to a method of chemical-free agriculture and farming in which natural resources are used to ensure soil nutrition, fertility, pests and weeds based on traditional practices in the country.

Box 7.4: Integrated Farming

The concept

- Integrated farming refers to a "biologically integrated system" which integrates natural resources in a regulated manner into farming activities to achieve maximum benefits from off-farm inputs and boost and sustain farm income. A diversified cropping system has the potential to enhance productivity when it is integrated with dairy, poultry or fishery components.
- Integrated fish farming systems refer to the production, integrated management and wide adoption of aquaculture, agriculture and livestock, with emphasis on aquaculture.
- Integrated farming system (IFS) helps farmers, especially the small and marginal farmers, to achieve maximum returns and income from different integrated components, thereby improving their standard of living.
- The IFS approach provides scope for changes in farming techniques for maximum output from the cropping pattern and ensures optimal utilization of resources.
- Integration of various agricultural enterprises viz., cropping, animal husbandry, fishery, forestry etc. have great potentialities in the agricultural economy

The benefits

- The IFS helps to provide nutritional security to a farmer's family as the farmer is able to provide various IFS components such as vegetables, fruits, egg, milk, fish, etc. to his family.
- The farmer is able to get income from the sale of surplus yield of these components.
- The higher returns with the farming system are not only due to higher productivity of the system but also due to lower cost of production and recycling of by-products of crop components. There is increase in the value for labour in IFS farms due to additional components brought into integration within the farm.
- Where farmers concentrate mainly on crop production, which is susceptible to a high degree of uncertainty in income, IFS provides alternatives for insulating against crop losses and ensuring source of income.
- It helps not only supplement the income of the farmers but also in increasing the family labour employment.
- The farm wastes are better recycled for productive purposes in the integrated system.
- A judicious mix of agricultural enterprises like dairy, poultry, piggery, duck farming, fishery, sericulture, bee-keeping, etc. suited to the given agro-climatic conditions and socio-economic status of the farmers would bring prosperity in the farm sector.

Secondary Agriculture

A related concept is secondary agriculture" which adds value to primary agriculture and helps to build agricultural enterprises. It implies diversification of farm-linked activities and production activity at enterprise/farm level.

It creates facilities for primary processing in agriculture adding value to the basic agro commodities to allow farmers to get better returns from their harvest. It also creates new job avenues in the rural sector which helps in the growth of rural economy which is dependent on agriculture.

Examples of secondary agriculture are oil from rice bran, starched sugar from corn, milk and protein from soybean, vitamins from grains, industrial chemicals and biofuel from sugarcane, fibre board from rice straw, high value animal by-products, and medicinal plants and herbal products.

Dalwai Committee on Secondary Agriculture

Ashok Dalwai Committee on "Doubling Farmers Income" (DFI) in its report had stressed the importance of Secondary Agriculture in enhancing farmers' income and alleviating rural poverty. According to DFI Committee, secondary agriculture could build agricultural enterprises in rural India through "farm-linked activities" with a four-fold strategy:

- Sustainability of production;
- Monetisation of farmers' produce;
- Strengthening of extension services; and
- Recognising agriculture as an enterprise, and enabling it to operate as such, by addressing various structuralweaknesses.
- The system encompasses the following initiatives:
- Utilize as raw material the primary product and by-products of agriculture and other biological resources available locally in its rural agrarian neighbourhood.
- Deploy locally available skills of rural manpower to operate/manage/ maintain the production of goods and services; and
- Such enterprises can be categorised appropriately under the Micro, Small or Medium Enterprises Development (MSMED) Act 2006 and under the Khadi and Village Industries Act.
- There is need to promote secondary agriculture activities whose outputs can be in the nature of either value added goods or services, that help the primary sector actors to capture more value from its primary produce (grain, fruit, vegetable, milk, fish, fibre, etc.) and from the by-products (straw, stalk, biomass), etc. Production of bio-fertilisers and bio-pesticides, value addition on wastes and residues from coconut and banana are additional avenues for income generation.
- Secondary agricultural micro-enterprises are a window for women to develop income opportunities. Women rural entrepreneurs should be provided special support to organise their existing activities into micro-enterprises, through special capacity building, training and access to credit.
- Household level cottage industry and village producer organisations can be linked to large-scale industries by providing primary processing services. Industry can deploy vendor development budgets to train the village community for taking up such activities.
- The agricultural and allied industries (food and non-food processing, medicinal), should be encouragedto procureprimary processed material from secondary agricultural units at village level.

- Collective or cooperative integrated farming could be promoted through a nodal entity such asNational Cooperative Development Corporation (NCDC) to encourage the formation of model cooperatives across the country.
- There is need to promote agricultural entrepreneurship and agricultural enterprises, skilling and knowledge-based exposure of farm communities and specialised extension services for enterprises owned by females.Agriculture having recognition for "priority sector" status for institutional credit could help in this process.
- It may be noted that in 2017-18, the Indian Council of Agricultural Research (ICAR), in association with the World Bank, had instituted the National Agricultural Higher Education Project, with $165 million funding support over five-year period to promote skill development and agri-entrepreneurship amongst graduates of agricultural colleges, apart from institutional development and innovation funding to education. Agribusiness incubation can help farm communities, and appropriate market linkages can improve farmers' realisations through cooperatives. This calls for concerted effort by the Centre and States to achieve the goals set.

The Dalwai Committee has pointed out that considering farm income on an average is 60 per cent of the total farmers' income, and that the farm families are engaged in agriculture operations for about 185 days in a year, there is scope and need to develop opportunities for additional productive activities using the farm resources that are now not used for value creation.

The Committee highlighted the importance of such farm-linked activities in the context of the dire need for income generation in the rural areas, and the various options that are available to increase the efficiency of factors of production (land, labour and capital) that are available in the agriculture sector.

The provision of alternative means of livelihoods in rural areas, especially when these are directly linked to the core activity of agriculture, will not only supplement the existing income of farming households, but also enhance the value captured from agriculture itself.

In this Chapter we discussed.....

- Share of Agriculture in GDP only 14 per cent but the sector is vital as it employs more than half of India's labour force; It is the main source of livelihood for majority of the rural population.
- Close inter-relationship between agricultural and industrial sectors.
- Trends in foodgrains output between 1950 and 1990; Green Revolution and dramatic increase in output;
- Factors which contributed to this increase; Increase in output up to 1980 mainly due to increase in area cultivated and area under irrigation; Whereas after 1980, increase was mainly due to adoption of HYV seeds.
- Since mid-1990's, deceleration in growth of output and stagnation; But some recovery seen since 2007-08; Problems confronting the rural sector; Instability and sluggishness in foodgrains output a cause for concern.
- Challenges facing Indian agriculture—climatic factors; limits to technology; lack of irrigation; problems of soil fertility and health; low productivity; size of farms; labour issues and financial constraints.
- Measures taken to support agricultural sector—price policy; minimum support price (MSP); procurement price.

- Food security and Nutrition; National Food Security Mission and National Nutrition Mission; India's Status on Global Hunger Index.
- The Importance of Agricultural Processing; Food Processing Industry in India.
- Agricultural marketing and problems faced by farmers; steps taken by the government to mitigate the problems;e-National Agricultural Market (e-NAM.
- Farmer Producer Organisations (FPOs).
- Agricultural credit and its importance; agriculture as Priority sector.
- Debt relief for farmers; The Pros and Cons of Farm Loan Waivers.
- Pradhan Mantri FasalBima Yojana (PMFBY) coverage and premium; deficiencies of the scheme and need for improvement.
- Cooperative Farming; Group Farming and Collective Action; Case study of Group Farming.
- Contract farming: main features and benefits; need for and importance of contract farming in India; issues with contract farming; private sector involvement in contract farming in India.
- Capital formation and Subsidies; Public investment in agriculture.
- Public Distribution System (PDS); Reform of the scheme; PDS and WTO.
- Agrarian scene, Farm Reforms and Farm Laws; Reforms in marketing; Rationale for reforms; Opposition to reforms; Detailed Studies by Expert Groups and Legislators; Parliament Committee's observations; Planning Commission on Reforms.
- Integrated Farming: The Concept and its benefits; Secondary agriculture; Dalwai Committee on Secondary Agriculture

Important Terms to Note in this Chapter

Green Revolution; Intensive and multiple cropping; Demographic pressure; Kharif crop; Nutrient imbalance; Cropping system; Cropping pattern; Gender equity; Eco-farming; Sub-division and fragmentation of landholdings; Economies of scale; Terms of trade; Minimum support price (MSP); Procurement price; Food security and Nutrition;Farmer Producer Organisation; Food Processing; Public distribution system (PDS); Poverty line and BPL and APL; Antyodaya scheme; Direct benefit transfer (DBT); Debt relief and debt waiver; FasalBima Yojana; Priority sector; Micro, small, and medium enterprises (MSME) sector; Jan Dhan Yojana; Food security; Cooperative farming; Contract farming; Self-help groups; Capital formation; Subsidies; Integrated Farming; Secondary Agriculture; Zero-budget farming;.

Practice Questions

1. What are the problems and challenges faced by Indian farmers and what steps have been taken by the government to mitigate them?
2. After the Green Revolution had run its course, there has been deceleration in the growth of farm output. What are the reasons for this and how India can overcome the problem?
3. The rural sector and farmers have been facing much distress in recent years. What are the reasons for this and what remedial measures can be taken to mitigate it?
4. Bring out the inter-relationship between agriculture and industrial sectors. How crucial is the prosperity of the agriculture for the industrial sector?
5. Discuss the various steps taken by the government and the Reserve Bank of India over the years to improve the facility of agricultural credit.
6. What are the causes for farmers' inability to repay loans and consequent debt? What steps have been taken by the government to help farmers on this issue?
7. Explain the pros and cons of writing off farmers' loans? How does it impact the finances of the Centre and the States?
8. Describe the role of National Bank for Agriculture and Rural Development (NABARD) in promoting agriculture and rural sector.
9. What are the deficiencies in the agriculture marketing system in India? What steps need to be taken to reform and improve it?
10. What are the main features of the National Food Security Act introduced by the government? How far do you think it will be beneficial to the people?
11. What is meant by co-operative farming? What are its advantages for farming community?
12. Explain the main features and advantages of Contract farming. Give some instances of contract farming adopted in India.
13. "Green Revolution in India has improved Indian farming but has failed to address challenges." Do you agree? Give reasons in support of your answer.

    [Indian Economic Service/Indian Statistical Service 2016]
14. Do you agree with the view that an increase in the productivity of agriculture as a result of Green Revolution was only short-term? Give reasons.

    [UPSC Main 2016 (Economics Optional Paper)]
15. Why Green Revolution lost its steam and India needs yet another Green Revolution or Evergreen Revolution? Discuss. *[UPSC Main 2014 (Economics Optional Paper)]*
16. What are the factors responsible for large number of farmers' suicides in relatively richer Indian States? Examine. *[UPSC Main 2014 (Economics Optional Paper)]*
17. What is your opinion on the view that the economic reform process has largely bypassed agriculture?

    [UPSC Main 2015 (Economics Optional Paper)]
18. Discuss the trends of agricultural growth rates in India during the post-reform period. What are the factors responsible for the decline in growth rates? Evaluate the measures taken by the Government to revive this sector. *[Indian Economic Service/Indian Statistical Service 2020]*

19. What are the major factors responsible for making rice-wheat system a success? In spite of this success how has this system become bane in India? *[UPSC Main 2020 (General Studies Paper)]*

20. How has the emphasis on certain crops brought about changes in cropping pattern in recent past? Elaborate the emphasis on millets production and consumption.

[UPSC Main 2018 (General Studies Paper)]

21. How far is Integrated Farming System (IFS) helpful in sustaining agricultural production?

[UPSC Main 2019 (General Studies Paper)]

22. How can biotechnology help to improve the living standards of farmers?

[UPSC Main 2019 (General Studies Paper)]

23. What are the salient features of the Jal Shakti Abhiyan launched by the Government of India for water conservation and water security? *[UPSC Main 2020 (General Studies Paper)]*

24. Suggest measures to improve water storage and irrigation system to make its judicious use under depleting scenario. *[UPSC Main 2020 (General Studies Paper)]*

25. Elaborate the impact of National Watershed Project in increasing agricultural production from water-stressed areas. *[UPSC Main 2019 (General Studies Paper)]*

26. "The ideal solution of depleting ground water resources in India is water harvesting system." How can it be made effective in urban areas? *[UPSC Main 2020 (General Studies Paper)]*

27. Assess the role of National Horticulture Mission (NHM) in boosting the production, productivity and income of horticulture farms. How far has it succeeded in increasing the income of farmers?

[UPSC Main 2018 (General Studies Paper)]

28. Given the vulnerability of Indian agriculture to the vagaries of nature, discuss the need for crop insurance and bring out the silent features of the Pradhan Mantri FasalBima Yojana (PMFBY).

[UPSC Main 2016 (General Studies Paper)]

29. What constraints and challenges do financial institutions supplying agricultural finance face? How can technology be used to better reach and serve rural clients?

[UPSC Main 2014 (General Studies Paper)]

30. Explain the trend in gross capital formation in agriculture in India during the post liberalisation period. Do you think that private investment has been crowded out by the public investment during this period?

[UPSC Main 2020 (Economics Optional Paper)]

31. Do you think that the fall in public investment in agriculture adversely affects the productivity growth of this sector in India? Give reasons. *[UPSC Main 2019 (Economics Optional Paper)]*

32. High Minimum Support Prices (MSP) induce distortions, some of which ultimately hurt the poor. Examine its merits and demerits. *[UPSC Main 2015 (Economics Optional Paper)]*

33. How has the movement of agricultural prices during the post-liberalisation period been responsible for farmers' distress in India? *[UPSC Main 2019 (Economics Optional Paper)]*

34. What do you mean by Minimum Support Price (MSP)? How will MSP rescue the farmers from the Sow income trap? *[UPSC Main 2018 (General Studies Paper)]*

35. There is also a point of view that Agricultural Produce Market Committees (APMCs) set up under the State Acts have not only impeded the development of agriculture but also have been the cause of food inflation in India. Critically examine. *[UPSC Main 2014 (General Studies Paper)]*

36. Briefly discuss the salient features of the National Agriculture Market (NAM) in India.

[Indian Economic Service /Indian Statistical Service 2020]

37. Livestock rearing has a big potential for providing non-farm employment and income in rural areas. Discuss suggesting suitable measures to promote this sector in India.

[UPSC Main 2015 (General Studies Paper)]

38. What are the impediments in marketing and supply chain management in developing the food processing industry in India? Can e-commerce help in overcoming these bottlenecks?

[UPSC Main 2015 (General Studies Paper)]

39. What are the main constraints in transport and marketing of agricultural produce in India?

[UPSC Main 2020 (General Studies Paper)]

40. Agro-based industries, especially food-processing units, can alter the fate of rural India. Discuss.

[UPSC Main 2015 (Economics Optional Paper)]

41. What are the challenges and opportunities of food processing sector in the country? How can income of the farmers be substantially increased byencouraging food processing?

[UPSC Main 2020 (General Studies Paper)]

42. Do you think the food processing sector as the sunrise sector in India during the post-reform period? Justify your answer. [UPSC Main 2020 (Economics Optional Paper)]

43. Discuss the factors for localisation of agro-based food processing industries of North-West India.

[UPSC Main 2019 (General Studies Paper)]

44. Elaborate the policy taken by the Government of India to meet the challenges of the food processing sector. *[UPSC Main 2019 (General Studies Paper)]*

45. In view of the declining average size of land holdings in India which has made agriculture non-viable for a majority of farmers, should contract farming and land leasing be promoted in agriculture? Critically evaluate the pros and cons. *[UPSC Main 2015 (General Studies Paper)]*

46. How can the 'Digital India' programme help farmers to improve farm productivity and income? What steps has the Government taken in this regard? *[UPSC Main 2015 (General Studies Paper)]*

47. In what way could replacement of price subsidy with Direct Benefit Transfer (DBT) change the scenario of subsidies in India? Discuss. *[UPSC Main 2015 (General Studies Paper)]*

48. What are the different types of agricultural subsidies that are given to the farmers in India? How can these be rationalised? *[UPSC Main 2015 (Economics Optional Paper)]*

49. What are the different types of agricultural subsidies that are given to the farmers at the national and state levels? Critically analyse the agricultural subsidy regime with reference to the distortions created by it. *[UPSC Main 2013 (General Studies Paper)]*

50. "Agriculture Subsidy is both an Economic as well as Social issue, hence the Government finds it difficult to take a decisive decision". Comment on the above statement.

[UPSC Main 2016 (Economics Optional Paper)]

51. Analyse the impact of fertilizer subsidy on agricultural productivity growth during the post reform period. *[UPSC Main 2020 (Economics Optional Paper)]*

52. "Subsidies may be a hidden culprit in India's farm crisis." Critically examine the statement. *[Indian Economic Service/Indian Statistical Service 2020]*

53. Examine the efficacy and resilience of the Public Distribution System in India for providing food security. *[UPSC Main 2020 (Economics Optional Paper)]*

54. What reforms would you advocate to make the public distribution system (PDS) in India more effective? *[UPSC Main 2019 (Economics Optional Paper)]*

55. What are the reformative steps taken by the Government to make food grain distribution system more effective? *[UPSC Main 2020 (General Studies Paper)]*

56. Discuss the salient features of the National Food Security Act (2013) in India. Give a critical assessment of it. *[Indian Economic Service/Indian Statistical Service 2020]*

CHAPTER 8: INDUSTRIAL DEVELOPMENT SINCE 1990

- Liberalization and Measures to promote Industry
- New Industrial Policy, 1991
- Export Processing Zones and Special Economic Zones
- Industrial Regions
- Industrial and Rail Freight Corridors
- National Manufacturing Policy
- eBiz Mission Mode Project
- Performance of Industrial Sector: An Overview
- Industrial development in Eighth to Eleventh Plans
- Fluctuations in Industrial growth
- Growth of GDP, Manufacturing and Sectoral Share in GDP:
- A Comparative position of select countries
- Public Sector Enterprises and Disinvestment
- Constraints faced by Indian Industry
- Industry and Employment
- Measures to Boost Manufacturing:
- Make in India programme,
- Productivity-linked Incentive (PLI) scheme, and
- Ease of Doing Business process
- Promoting Industrial development: Agenda for the Future
- Privatisation and Disinvestment of PSEs

❑ INTRODUCTION

As seen in Chapter 4, after gaining independence, India hastened to industrialize and diversify the economy. Though the process was initiated in the First Five Year Plan (1951-56), it gained momentum during the Second and subsequent Plans. The share of the industrial sector in National Product and employment which was low in 1951 showed increase over the years. But between 1950 and 1980, as India followed a policy of self-reliance with little exposure to world markets and a highly regulated industrial structure, the sector registered only halting and stunted growth and did not achieve its full potential. There were periods of growth interrupted by years of stagnation. There was virtually no effort to enforce competition among the industries or upgrade technology. The only redeeming feature was that while at the time of independence, consumer goods industries dominated the sector with almost 50 per cent share, in the first four decades from 1950, the share of capital goods industries went up from 4 per cent to 24 per cent. India had built up a strong industrial base with many basic and heavy industries.

❑ LIBERALIZATION AND MEASURES TO PROMOTE INDUSTRY

Though full-fledged reforms were initiated only in 1991, the process of liberalization of policy measures in the industrial sector was started even in 1985, at the beginning of the Seventh Plan (1985-90).

The major steps taken were: delicensing of non-MRTP (Monopolies and Restrictive Trade Practices) and non-FERA (Foreign Exchange Regulations Act) companies for 31 industry groups and MRTP/FERA companies in backward areas for 72 industry groups; raising the assets limit for exemption of companies from the purview of the MRTP Act; exempting 83 industries under the MRTP Act for entry of dominant industries, etc. Some other changes were also made in the areas of licensing and procedures, import of technology, import of capital goods, allowing broad banding of products in a number of industries, etc. The Government also took some major decisions regarding the public sector reforms, e.g., limiting the role of the public sector to strategic, hi-tech, and essential infrastructure areas and gradually withdrawing from other areas.

Other measures taken to give impetus to industrial development were:

- Foreign direct investment policy was liberalized.
- Disinvestment Commission was constituted for preparing an overall long-term disinvestment programme for public sector enterprises (PSEs) referred to it and to work out the modalities for disinvestment.
- Sick Industrial Companies Act (SICA), 1985 amended to bring PSEs within the ambit of SICA,1985 and Bureau of Industrial and Financial Reconstruction (BIFR).
- National Renewal Fund was set up to protect the interests of workers likely to be affected due to restructuring or closure of industrial units.
- Growth Centres Scheme taken up to develop infrastructure in backward areas to promote industrialization.
- New National Minerals Policy announced opening mining industry to private sector, including 50 per cent foreign equity in 13 minerals.
- Technology Development Board set up to facilitate development of new technologies and assimilation of imported technologies.

New Industrial Policy, 1991

The New Industrial Policy announced in July 1991, was comprehensive in scope and provided greater stimulus to the domestic industry. This was followed by a series of reforms introduced in the fiscal, trade, and foreign investment policies. These reforms freed the Indian economy in general, and industry in particular, from controls and opened them up to international competition and led to integration of Indian economy with the world economy. The policy reforms continued through the Eighth Plan (1992-97) period and during the subsequent Plans. (For more details on the 1991 Industrial Policy, see Chapter 6 pp. 6.7–8).

Further, reform measures taken included reduction of areas reserved exclusively for the public sector, disinvestment of equity of selected public sector enterprises (PSEs), and enhancing the limits of foreign equity participation in domestic industrial undertakings. Customs and excise duties, and personal and corporate income taxes were rationalized and reduced with a view to promote growth, efficiency, and international competitiveness of the Indian industry. Trade liberalization reduced protection to import substitution activities and encouraged export-oriented industries based on the comparative advantage that India had. These policy measures were meant to change the basic orientation of industry from an inward-looking one to one with closer linkage with the global economy.

Under the National Mineral Policy of 1993, mining industry was opened to private sector for 13 minerals, and allowed direct foreign investment up to 50 per cent equity participation. Beyond this limit, approvals were to be given on case-by-case basis. The other important objective of the new mineral policy was to give more powers to the States for mineral development.

Ninth Plan (1997–2002)

During the Ninth Plan, further structural changes and modifications in sectoral policies were effected to liberalize and simplify the processes. These were:

- Delicensing of coal, lignite, and petroleum (other than crude oil).
- Amendment of Mines and Minerals (Regulation and Development) Act, 1957.
- Allowing buy-back of shares.
- Liberalization of technology imports.
- Foreign equity up to 100 per cent was allowed under the automatic route for major infrastructure sectors and the time-frame for consideration of FDI proposals was reduced from six weeks to 30 days.
- A Foreign Investment Implementation Authority was set up in the Department of Industrial Policy and Promotion (DIPP) to provide a single-point interface between foreign investors and the Government.
- FDI up to 26 per cent under the automatic route was permitted in the insurance sector, subject to a licence from the Insurance Regulatory and Development Authority (IRDA).

Tenth Plan (2002–07)

The Tenth Plan focussed on creating a favourable industrial climate in which private sector companies, including erstwhile public sector companies, could become efficient and competitive. While industrial liberalization had been extensively implemented at the Central level, it had not percolated to the State level. Industry circles often complained that regulatory measures at the state level were extremely cumbersome and entrepreneurs faced much harassment. The transaction costs and delays caused by such a system, including costs on account of corruption spawned by excessive regulation, were burdensome, more so for the small-scale units.

It was recognized that India had inherent strength and comparative advantage of having entrepreneurial acumen of a high calibre, an established scientific and industrial base, skilled and relatively cheap English-speaking workforce, and a large domestic market. The relocation by some of the large transnational companies of their manufacturing base to India and sourcing of products from here by other Fortune 500 companies are evidence of the potential and bright prospects for the Indian industry.

Participation in world trade was essential for India as it could fetch multiple advantages. Rising exports help to pay for the much needed imports while also bridging the trade deficit. Also, enhanced productivity and quality of goods manufactured for export would help to raise our own standard of living through improved availability of diverse high quality products. Globally, trade was emerging as a powerful engine of economic growth and development. Raising India's share in the world exports of manufactured products was an important objective for the industrial sector in the Tenth Plan.

Export Processing Zones and Special Economic Zones

India was one of the first in Asia to recognize the effectiveness of the concept of Export Processing Zone (EPZ) in promoting exports and set up the first EPZ in Kandla in 1965. Later, EPZs were started at Kochi, Vishakhapatnam, Mumbai, Chennai, Falta, and Noida. Among these, the major ones are Mumbai, Noida, and Kandla.

With a view to overcome the shortcomings experienced on account of the multiplicity of controls and clearances, absence of world-class infrastructure, an unstable fiscal regime, and with a view to attract larger foreign investments in India, the Special Economic Zones (SEZs) Policy was announced in April 2000. The EPZs were converted into Special Economic Zones (SEZs) in two phases in 2000 and 2003. The SEZs benefit from various tax incentives such as exemption from excise and customs duty.

To instill confidence in investors, signal the Government's commitment to a stable SEZ policy regime, and give fillip to the SEZ scheme which helps in generating economic activity and employment, the Special Economic Zones Act, 2005 was passed which came into effect in 2006. It provided for drastic simplification of procedures and for single window clearance on matters relating to central as well as state governments. *The main objectives of the SEZ Act are*:

(a) generation of additional economic activity;
(b) promotion of exports of goods and services;
(c) promotion of investment from domestic and foreign sources;
(d) creation of employment opportunities, and
(e) development of infrastructure facilities.

Industrial Regions

There are certain regions in the country where there is heavy concentration of industries and which have developed over the years due to locational and logistical advantages. Such regions are in Mumbai-Pune, Chennai-Bengaluru, Delhi-Gurgaon industrial belts, and certain areas in Gujarat, Kolkata-Hugli, and near Kochi and Visakhapatnam. These areas have large number of industrial units, employing large workforce and producing sizeable quantum of industrial output.

The government has been taking steps to lessen such concentration of industries and ensure more balanced industrial development in different regions and reduce inter-regional disparities.Thus, for promoting industrialization of backward areas in an effective manner by developing the infrastructure, a centrally-sponsored scheme of Growth Centres was taken up during the Eighth Plan (1992-97). And to promote industrialization of specific hilly, remote, and inaccessible areas such as Jammu and Kashmir, Himachal Pradesh, Sikkim, North-Eastern States, Andaman and Nicobar Islands, Lakshadweep, eight hill districts of Uttar Pradesh, and Darjeeling district of West Bengal, the Government of India has extended a Transport Subsidy Scheme.

Industrial and Rail Freight Corridors

Delhi-Mumbai Project

One major scheme now being undertaken is the development of industrial corridors. Setting up industrial corridors between major cities and passing through the hinterland has been mooted to develop industries in areas along the route. One mega industrial corridor is being developed on PPP mode between Delhi and Mumbai – Delhi-Mumbai Industrial Corridor (DMIC)– with financial and technical aid from Japan. It will have an overall length of 1483 kms. and will have a dedicated, multi-modal freight corridor. It will pass through six states, viz., Delhi NCR, U.P., Haryana, Rajasthan, Gujarat, and Maharashtra and will help to develop specified areas on either side of the route. Several large hubs/nodes have been identified for development as large industrial regions in consultation with the government of the six States. In the first phase (2008-09 to 2012-13), it was proposed to have six investment regions and six industrial areas (about 100 sq km each).

This project was approved by Union Cabinet of India in 2007. Later, the institutional and financial structure of the project was approved by the Government of India. Further, NICDIT (National Industrial Corridor Development and Implementation Trust) was approved in 2016 for the expansion of the scope of DMIC-Project.

Other Industrial Corridors

Other Industrial Corridor projects being implemented are:

- Chennai Bengaluru Industrial Corridor (CBIC) and its extension to Kochi via Coimbatore
- Amritsar Kolkata Industrial Corridor (AKIC)
- Vizag- Chennai Industrial Corridor
- Bengaluru Mumbai Industrial Corridor (BMIC)
- Hyderabad Warangal and Hyderabad Nagpur Industrial Corridor
- Hyderabad Bengaluru Industrial Corridor (HBIC)
- Odisha Economic Corridor (OEC) Project

Besides the Industrial Corridors, Dedicated Rail Freight Corridors are also being built as mentioned below.

Rail Freight Corridors

The growth of Indian economy has created demand for additional capacity of rail freight transportation, and this is likely to grow further in the future. This burgeoning demand led to the conception of the dedicated rail freight corridors along the Eastern and Western rail routes.

Ministry of Railways initiated action to establish a Special Purpose Vehicle (SPV) for construction, operation and maintenance of the dedicated freight corridors. This led to the establishment of "Dedicated Freight Corridor Corporation of India Limited (DFCC)", to undertake planning & development, mobilization of financial resources and construction, maintenance and operation of the dedicated freight corridors. DFCC was incorporated as a company under the Companies Act 1956 in October 2006.

Rail-Road-Port synergy

The Industrial Corridors can leverage the Dedicated Rail Freight Corridors (DFCs) being implemented and the rail-road linkage can boost industrial expansion and economic activity in the hinterland all along their routes. This will also give fillip to the expansion of ports on the west and east coast of India and promote India's foreign trade.

National Manufacturing Policy

It was recognized that a cluster approach for industries would help in enhancing their manufacturing and technological capabilities. With this in view, a National Manufacturing Policy was approved in November 2011 which outlines the creation of National Investment and Manufacturing Zones (NIMZs) to provide businesses with the ecosystem required for growth, not only in manufacturing, but also for investments in research and development. The usefulness of NIMZs will be even more for new high-tech industries, which will benefit from the localized presence of the entire value chain of participants. Also, the concept of industrial clusters would be specially beneficial for Micro, Small, and Medium Enterprises (MSMEs) and the ministry for MSME is using the cluster approach to drive the growth and depth of those industries.

The objectives of the National Manufacturing Policy are:

- Increase manufacturing sector growth to 12–14 percent over the medium-term to make it the engine of growth for the economy.
- Increase the rate of job creation in manufacturing to create 100 million additional jobs by 2025. Emphasis would be on creation of appropriate skill sets among the rural migrants and urban poor to make growth inclusive.
- Increase 'depth' in manufacturing, with focus on the level of domestic value addition, to address the national strategic requirements.
- Enhance global competitiveness of Indian manufacturing through appropriate policy support.
- Ensure sustainability of growth, particularly with regard to the environment.

eBiz Mission Mode Project

An eBiz Mission Mode Project has been initiated under the National e-Governance Plan which aims to create a business and investor-friendly ecosystem in India by making all business and investment related regulatory services across Central, State, and Local governments available on a single portal, obviating the need for the investors or the business to visit multiple offices or a plethora of websites. It is envisaged that the services offered on eBiz will eventually cover the entire life cycle of a business–right from its establishment, through its ongoing operations, and to even its possible closure. Once operational, this project will also create a platform for multiple government agencies to cross check and validate their information.

The project is being implemented on a10-year PPP mode with an IT company. The initial pilot phase was to cover eight Central Departments and the states of Andhra Pradesh, Haryana, Maharashtra, Tamil Nadu, and Delhi and would cover 29 core services. Five more states–Punjab, Uttar Pradesh, Odisha, West Bengal, and Rajasthan–and 21 more services would be added during the next pilot phase. An end-to-end solution providing the services, along with a payment solution gateway, under the Andhra Pradesh Single Window Act on the eBiz platform has also been envisaged.

❑ PERFORMANCE OF INDUSTRIAL SECTOR: AN OVERVIEW

Introduction

The industrial sector has witnessed much fluctuation in growth rates over the last six decades. This sector comprises Manufacturing, Mining and Quarrying, Electricity and Gas and Water supply. The Index of Industrial Production (IIP), a series published monthly, measures the trends in industrial production. The composition of IIP, industries, and items covered by it, are revised periodically to reflect the structural changes in the sector.

Due to varied reasons, the sector has shown robust growth in some periods while it has been sluggish at other times. The performance of the agricultural sector which affects rural demand for industrial products, demand from the urban sector, exports, availability of credit, etc. all have a significant bearing on the industry's performance. The recent example of persisting and continuing recession in the major economies like the U.S., European countries, and Japan have taken a toll on industries in India as exports have been adversely impacted.

Initially, India had rapid industrial growth of 7.7 per cent per annum from 1950 to 1966 covering the period of the first three Plans. Then there was deceleration between 1966 and 1979 which covers the period of three Annual Plans (1966-69) and the Fourth and Fifth Plans with an annual growth rate of about 4.0 per cent. In the third phase, 1981-89, there was recovery with growth rate at about 7.7 per cent per annum.

Table 8.1 shows the growth rates of the sector from the First Plan to the Eleventh Plan.

Table 8.1: Growth Rate of Industrial Sector—1950 to 2012

First Plan to Third Plan	1950–66	7.7 per cent
Fourth & Fifth Plans	1969–79	4.6 per cent
Sixth Plan	1980–85	5.5 per cent
Seventh Plan	1985–90	8.5 per cent
Eighth Plan	1992–97	7.3 per cent
Ninth Plan	1997–02	4.5 per cent
Tenth Plan	2002–07	8.0 per cent
Eleventh Plan	2007–12	6.7 per cent

Source: *Central Statistical Organisation and Five Year Plan documents, Planning Commission.*

Note: Growth rates are based on IIP Base revised periodically. Hence data between these periods are not comparable.

The industrial sector recorded an average annual compound growth rate of 4.6 per cent from 1970-71 to 1979-80 and it rose to 5.5 per cent in the Sixth Plan (1980-85) and 8.5 per cent in the Seventh Plan (1985-90). The liberalization process initiated and the various policy measures taken during the Seventh Plan period regarding import of technology and capital goods, coupled with a reasonable rate of public investment helped to boost growth.

Eighth (1992-97) and Ninth (1997-2002) Plans

The period immediately following 1991 reforms showed low growth rate during 1991-93 but recovered between 1993 and 1996. There was again deceleration from 1996-97. In 1996-97, all the sub-sectors of industry registered lower growth as compared to previous years. On the whole, the annual growth rate in the Eighth Plan was lower than in the Seventh Plan.

Though further measures involving structural changes were taken during the Ninth Plan (1997-2002) such as delicensing of coal, lignite, and petroleum (other than crude oil), amendment of Mines and Minerals (Regulation and Development) Act, 1957, special package for revival of exports and liberalization of technology imports, the actual growth rate (value added actual at factor cost) achieved in the Plan was only 4.5 per cent.

Tenth Plan (2002-07)

After a tepid performance in the Ninth Plan, the industrial sector bounced back to register a growth rate of 8 per cent in the Tenth Plan. The share of manufacturing maintained a rising trend after falling in the first year. Though the overall industrial growth rate of 8 per cent fell short of the Plan target of 10 per cent, there was acceleration during the Plan and the target was exceeded in the terminal year with 11 per cent growth. Also, the manufacturing sub-sector rose consistently during the period, registering 12.3 per cent in 2006-07. For the first time in many years, the industrial growth at 11 per cent in 2006-07 equalled the growth rate in the Services sector while the manufacturing growth rate of 12.3 per cent surpassed both agriculture and services.

The increased demand in both domestic and foreign markets was a major contributory factor but the impressive performance of manufacturing was attributable to the cumulative effect of the industrial and fiscal policy changes carried out since the economic reforms of 1991-92. The competitive environment created by the reduction of external barriers to trade had also started to bear fruit. Against a Compound Annual Growth Rate (CAGR) of 6.3 per cent in the Ninth Plan, exports of manufactures recorded a CAGR of more than 19 per cent during the Tenth Plan.

Eleventh Plan (2007-12)

In about two decades from the mid-eighties, India had emerged as one of the fastest growing economies in the world, aided by a slew of economic reforms she had launched. The striking aspect of this growth has been the dynamism of the Service sector. The share of Services sector in GDP which was 27.5 per cent in 1950–51 rose to 32.1 per cent in 1970–71, 40.6 per cent in 1990–91 and 59.6 per cent in 2012–13.

In contrast, however, while the share of industry in GDP was 21.6 per cent in 1970-71 and rose to 27.2 per cent in 1990-91 and 24.8 per cent in 2012-13, the contribution of manufacturing sub-sector to GDP has been much less robust, stagnating at around 15 per cent. This is in contrast to the trend in other emerging economies, where manufacturing has grown much faster than GDP. This has raised questions about India's development strategy as manufacturing is one of the prime sources for employment generation.

It must, however, be borne in mind that the Eleventh Plan period was impacted by unfavourable economic headwinds brought on by the global financial crisis of 2007-09, persisting recessionary trends, and fragile economic recovery in the developed countries. While this has led to slump in demand and fall in exports, other factors like exchange-rate volatility, economic uncertainty, and domestic problems causing delays in implementation of further reforms have also led to slowdown in the Indian manufacturing sector.

❑ FLUCTUATIONS IN INDUSTRIAL GROWTH

But even after 1990, with the reforms and liberalization of the sector and the New Industrial Policy, 1991 unveiled, (as discussed in detail in chapter 6 (see pp. 6.5–6), the growth trends in the industrial sector, during the period from the Eighth Plan (1992-97) to the Eleventh Plan (2007-12), had been fluctuating. For instance, the annual rate of growth of industry, and the sub-sectors under it, during the Eleventh Plan, given below (Table 8.2), shows the uneven trends in their year-to-year performance.

Table 8.2: Annual Rates of Growth of Industry and the Sub-sectors during the Eleventh Plan (2007–12)

(In Percentage)

	2007–08	2008–09	2009–10 PE	2010–11 QE	2011–12 AE
Industry	9.7	4.4	8.4	7.2	3.9
(i) Mining and Quarrying	3.7	2.1	6.3	5	–2.2
(ii) Manufacturing	10.3	4.3	9.7	7.6	3.9
(iii) Electricity, Gas and Water Supply	8.3	4.6	6.3	3	8.3

Source: *Twelfth Five Year Plan (20012-17), Planning Commission.*

The manufacturing sector averaged a growth of 7.7 per cent till 2009-10 during the Eleventh Plan (2007-12). Growth peaked at 10.3 per cent in 2007-08 and then started decelerating. The decline in manufacturing growth was primarily responsible for the slowdown in GDP in 2011-12.

According to the Planning Commission, "Initial deceleration in industrial growth was largely on account of the global economic meltdown. Fragile economic recovery in the U.S. and European countries, and subdued business sentiments affected the growth of the manufacturing sector. Rising interest rates and appreciation of the rupee during the Eleventh Plan period also contributed to this slowdown. It is significant to note though, that volatility of manufacturing growth has become more pronounced over the last five years. An important implication of this is the need for greater flexibility both in policy and non-policy factors which have a bearing on the manufacturing sector." (Twelfth Plan document).

Table 8.3: Index Numbers of Industrial Production

Base: 1980 – 81 = 100		Base: 1993 – 94 = 100		Base: 2011 – 12 = 100	
Year	**Index**	**Year**	**Index**	**Year**	**Index**
1985-86	142.1	1999-00	154.9	2012-13	103.3
1990-91	212.6	2000-01	162.5	2014-15	111.0
1993-94	232.0	2004-05	211.1	2019-20	129.0

Source: *Handbook of Statistics on Indian Economy, 2015, Reserve Bank of India.*

Share of Industry in GDP

The share of Industrial sector in the GDP has been going up since the 1990's. (See Table 8.4). (The data are not comparable with the data used in the Ninth Five Year Plan as the base year has been changed by CSO.)

Table 8.4: Sectoral Shares of Industry *in GDP at Factor cost 2004–05 prices

1990–91	27.6	2005–06	27.9
1995–96	28.4	2010–11	27.9
2000–01	27.2	2012–13	27.3

Source: *Central Statistical Organisation (CSO), Databook for PC and Plan documents, Planning Commission.*

Note: *The term Industry includes Manufacturing, Mining and Quarrying, Electricity, Gas, and Water supply.

Growth of GDP, Manufacturing as per cent of GDP and Sectoral Share in GDP

A Comparative position of select countries

Tables 8.5 (a) shows GDP growth and the share of Manufacturing value added as percentage of GDP in 2019 for select countries. It will be seen that China, Thailand and Malaysia have a high share of Manufacturing Value added in GDP while other countries have share ranging between 13.3 per cent in India and 17.7 per cent in Hungary.

Table 8.5 (a): Growth Rate & Manufacturing Value added - 2019

Country	Manufacturing Value added as Percentage of GDP (2019)	GDP Growth (annual %)
China	26.8 %	5.95 %
India	13.3 %	4.04 %
Poland	16.6 %	4.54 %
Malaysia	21.4 %	4.30%
Russia	13.0 %	2.03 %
Thailand	25.6 %	2.26 %
Egypt	15.9 %	5.56 %
Hungary	17.7 %	4.64 %

Source: *World Bank data: https://data.worldbank.org/*

Table 8.5 (b): Sectoral shares in GDP/Value Added at current prices in 2019 (in Percent)

	Agriculture & Allied activities	Manufacturing, Mining & Utilities	Manufacturing,
South Korea	1.8	29.9	27.7
China	7.4	32.0	27.9
Italy	2.1	19.6	16.6
Thailand	8.3	32.9	27.3
Russia	3.9	26.5	13.5
Argentina	8.6	23.0	15.3
Malaysia	7.3	33.1	21.7
India	17.7	21.4	16.4
Hungary	4.0	24.0	21.0
Germany	0.8	24.2	21.2
Japan	1.2	23.3	20.7
Switzerland	0.7	20.7	18.7
Finland	2.7	20.5	17.0

Source: *United Nations, Statistics Division.*

Table 8.5 (b) shows the share of Agriculture & Allied activities, Manufacturing, and Manufacturing, Mining & Utilities in GDP for some of the advanced countries and countries with medium development. It shows that the advanced industrial nations like Japan, South Korea, Germany, Switzerland, Finland and Italy have minimal share of agriculture and allied activities (such as fisheries, forestry and hunting) in GDP and have a highshare of manufacturing alone. Among countries with medium development, China, Malaysia and Thailand have a high share of manufacturing, mining &utilities in GDP and among them China and Thailand have a high share for manufacturing alone. Russia and Argentina have rather low share of manufacturing alone (13.5 % and 15.3 % respectively) in GDP while the combined share of manufacturing, mining &utilities in their GDP is 26.5 and 23.0 per cent.

The share of agriculture and allied activities in India's GDP is 17.7 per cent and the share of manufacturing alone is only 16.4 per cent. It points to the need for India to step up manufacturing activity and enhance its share in GDP if India is to have higher growth and create jobs on a substantial scale.

Table 8.5 (c): Manufacturing Output as % of World Total (2010)

China	18.9%	Germany	6.0%	France	2.6%
USA	8.2%	Italy	3.0%	UK	2.3%
				India	2.2%

Source: *Table 8.5 (c): Twelfth Plan, Vol. II, Planning Commission.*

❑ PUBLIC SECTOR ENTERPRISES AND DISINVESTMENT

Introduction

Public Sector Enterprises (PSEs) have played a notable role and made significant contribution to the economic development of the country. Many large basic and heavy industries–iron and steel, oil and petrochemicals, heavy engineering, heavy electricals, machine tools, rail coach and locomotive units, and aeronautical industries–have been set up in the public sector. It has helped to create a vast and diversified industrial base, create a strong technical workforce, and save valuable foreign exchange.

The top ten Central PSEs made a net profit of ₹ 47,371 crore in 2005–06 while top ten loss-making CPSEs accounted for a net loss of ₹ 4,552 crore. While the top ten profit-making enterprises are diversified, the top ten loss-making enterprises are largely engaged in manufacturing.

Based on various criteria relating to their status and performance such as capital employed, productivity, returns, and profits earned, the PSEs have been classified as Maharatnas, Navaratnas, and Miniratnas.

Disinvestment

Further, considering the performance of some of the PSEs, the Industrial Policy Statement, 1991 envisaged disinvestment of a part of the Government holding in the share capital of selected PSE's. This was a major step towards revamping the functioning of PSEs, enforcing their accountability, and broad-basing their management and ownership. A Disinvestment Commission was constituted in August, 1996 to suggest the modalities of disinvestment. The Government had referred 43 PSEs to the Commission up to March 1998 and the Commission recommended varying levels of disinvestment in some of the PSEs and strategic sale or closure and sale of assets in some of the PSEs.

The recommendations also relate to ensuring corporate governance in PSEs, professionalizing the management, setting up a Disinvestment Fund, providing them greater autonomy, reduction of Government equity, Voluntary Retirement Scheme, etc. The two main elements of the policy have been devolution of full managerial and commercial autonomy to successful, profit-making companies, modernization and restructuring of sick PSEs, and also sale or closure of chronically sick PSEs. Later, an ad hoc group of experts, under the chairmanship of Arjun Sengupta, also recommended a series of measures for enhanced financial delegation to Navratnas, Miniratnas, and other profit-making Central PSEs which the government has implemented.

According to the erstwhile Planning Commission, "After the introduction of economic reforms in 1991-92, a policy of disinvestments and privatization was adopted and upto 2001-02, equity had been sold in 123 enterprises and receipt of ₹26,012 crore realized. During the first two years of the Tenth Five Year Plan, the process intensified and a sum of ₹18,895 crore was realized from disinvestments. In 2004-

05, there was a policy shift and the United Progressive Alliance (UPA) government, while expressing a commitment toward a strong and effective public sector, decided that 'generally profit making companies will not be privatized'. Residual disinvestments made in the last three years of the Plan brought in receipts of ₹4,335 crore." (Eleventh Five Year Plan, 2007-12).

Impact of disinvestment

But even after the privatization of PSEs accomplished upto the middle of the Tenth Five Year Plan (2002-07), when the policy changed, the role of PSEs and their contribution to the GDP has not diminished. In fact, the GDP from non-departmental enterprises (NDEs) registered an increase during the first two years of the Tenth Five Year Plan. The contribution of NDEs to GDP at Factor Cost (Current Price) during 2003-04 and 2004-05 was as follows (Table 8.6):

Table 8.6: Contribution of Non-departmental Enterprises to GDP at Factor Cost (Current Price)

Year	GDP from NDEs (₹ Crore)	GDP at Factor Cost (₹ Crore)	Share in GDP (%)
2003–04	312364	2549418	12.25
2004–05	338352	2855933	11.85

Source: *National Accounts Statistics 2007, CSO cited in Eleventh Five Year Plan document, Planning Commission.*

In 2004-05, the share of central PSEs in the GDP was 6.82 per cent out of 11.85 per cent for NDEs. The number of operational central PSEs has decreased marginally from 231 in 2001-02, the end of the Ninth Five Year Plan, to 225 in 2005-06. But significantly, the number of profit-making central PSEs rose from 120 to 157 and the number of loss-making central PSEs has come down substantially from 109 to 58. The profits of profit-making central PSEs also increased from ₹ 36,432 crore to ₹ 76,240 crore, and the losses of loss-making ones has come down from ₹ 10,454 crore to ₹ 5,752 crore during the same period which are positive trends.

The net profits made by the central PSEs has led to the accumulation of large reserves which totalled ₹ 3,53,641.62 crore for 157 profit-making enterprises at the end of 2006-07. Also, between 2002-03 and 2005-06, the balances held by all the central PSEs rose from ₹ 53,453 crore to ₹ 1,50,680 crore which could be put to productive use. **(See Box 8.1 at the end of this chapter for more on this)**.

❑ CONSTRAINTS FACED BY INDIAN INDUSTRY

When compared to industries in many other developing and emerging economies like China, Brazil, South Africa, and Indonesia, industries in India face a plethora of problems. Limited land availability, a burgeoning population, migration from rural to urban areas, and overburdened urban centres all pose severe challenges in development.

Major Challenges

Infrastructure

One of the major constraints faced by the industrial sector is inadequate and poor quality infrastructure. Interruptions in power supply, transportation bottlenecks, communication problems, delays in handling cargo at ports, etc. are adding to the real costs of manufacture and thus affecting the competitiveness of domestic manufacturers and providers of services. These are also affecting exports adversely.

Unless the existing infrastructural capabilities—roads, rail, ports, power supply, etc.— are upgraded and strengthened substantially, it would be difficult to achieve high targets of industrial growth. With the opening up of the economy and globalization, the importance of competitiveness and the need for quality of infrastructure cannot be overemphasized.

The land issue

Availability of land for industrialization has been another vexatious issue. There are many legal and administrative impediments in acquiring land for industry due to opposition from the owners of land, much of which lie in the hinterland and agricultural belts. While conversion of cultivable and fertile land for non-agricultural purposes should be guarded against, especially in view of the imperative need to augment food production, a way out has to be found to release non-arable land for industrial purposes. It is to be emphasized here that to reduce the pressure of population on land and bring down disguised unemployment in the farm sector, jobs have to be created in the industrial sector which, given the necessary facilities and support, has great potential to generate employment.

Trade barriers

Tariffs and non-tariff barriers imposed by the industrialized countries are much loaded against manufactured imports from developing countries, making it more difficult for them to penetrate those markets. Resort to non-tariff measures like anti-dumping measures, social safeguards and standards, imposing rigid technical standards, and subsidies provided by those countries while, at the same time, contesting subsidies given by developing countries, have limited the opportunities for developing countries. A re-balancing of the international trading system to the mutual benefit of all countries would entail freer access to developed markets and transfer of technology to developing countries for modernization leading to enhanced productivity and international competitiveness.

India's exports

India's export basket now consists more of raw materials and low technology products which account for over 80 per cent of the total manufactured exports. Against this, the world average ranged between 43 per cent and 35 per cent between 1985 and 1996. India's high technology exports have performed rather poorly and their share has risen by only 1.4 points compared to 7.6 points for the world as a whole during the 1986 to 1996 period, though the automobile sector has been able to export lately to developed markets. The ratio of high technology products to total manufactured exports in the case of India is only one-fifth of that of China and one-tenth of South Korea and Taiwan.

Low share of manufactures in GDP

The consumption of manufactured consumer goods is recognized as one of the most widely accepted indices of standard of living and quality of life. Manufacturing industry provides the driving force for stimulating rapid economic growth. The growth rate of the manufacturing industry normally surpasses that of the agriculture and the service sectors. It is for this reason that industry is considered the backbone of an economy. From this point of view, special emphasis should be placed on raising industry's share in GDP. The comparatively low share of India in the world export of manufacturers is reflected in its low share of manufacturing value added in GDP as compared to some of the other countries in Asia, as per 2013 data shown in Table 8.5 (b):12.9 per cent of India compared to South Korea (31.1%), China (29.9%), Thailand (25.7%), and Malaysia (24.2%).

Need for suitable Trade Agreements

India has not fully benefited from Free Trade Agreements (FTAs)entered into with other countries or regional groups and this impacts the ability of Indian industry in boosting exports and having larger share in world trade. For instance, India's garment exporters face stiff competition from Bangladesh, Vietnam and Thailand in exporting textiles and apparels because these countries have FTAs with European countries which make their products competitive. And textile and apparel industry is one of India's strengths and second largest employer providing direct and indirect employment to about 105 million people.

Other measures like reform of the labour laws, legal and judicial processes, bankruptcy laws, and seamless exit provisions are also needed to give a boost to industry.

A positive aspect is that the Indian industry has responded reasonably well to the challenge of liberalization and opening up of the economy. There is good awareness and the urge to act on upgrading processes and technologies, modernizing plant and equipment, achieving economies of scale, improving product quality, and paying greater attention to research and development. Such positive responses to the challenges of market forces are resulting in improved competitiveness as well as increased exports.

Industry and Employment

The occupational structure in India is skewed in favour of the agriculture sector which accounts for about 60 per cent of total employment. As a consequence, there is widespread unemployment especially among skilled workers and educated youth, both in urban and rural areas. Demographic projections suggest that about 60 per cent of the population would soon be in the 15-59 year age–the working age group–leading to a substantial increase in the labour force. Unless jobs are created in the more productive manufacturing sector, the unemployment situation could become quite alarming. Also, most of the jobs created in the Services sector, which has rapidly expanded in the last two decades, were low quality jobs of informal nature. There is also need to pull workers out of the agricultural sector where there is rampant under- and disguised unemployment by creating non-farm jobs. All this can be achieved only by rapid expansion of the industrial sector with stress on manufacturing.

While employment in manufacturing increased from 44 million to nearly 56 million between 2000-01 and 2004-05, it declined by 5 million between 2004-05 and 2009-10. The net increase in employment over the decade 2000-01 to 2009-10 was around 6 million, a 13 per cent increase over 10 years. Share of manufacturing in India in total employment is only 11 per cent. This compares adversely with other emerging economies where employment in manufacturing ranges from 15 per cent to 30 per cent.

Measures to Boost Manufacturing

The government has been taking several measures to revitalize the Manufacturing sector in India. These include the Make in India programme, the Productivity-linked Incentive (PLI) scheme and Ease of Doing Business process. These are discussed below.

Make in India

Launched in September 2014 as part of a wide range of nation building initiatives, it is one of the government's main plans for re-energising the economy, give fillip to the industrial and manufacturing sector and transform India into a global design and manufacturing hub.

The salient features of this programme, piloted by the Department of Industrial Policy and Promotion (DIPP, are as follows:)

- To raise the share of the manufacturing sector, which is now around 16 per cent to 25 per cent of the GDP.
- The programme is a collaborative effort involving the Central and State governments, industry leaders, chambers and associations and various knowledge partners.
- It seeks to leverage the transformational power of public-private partnership (PPP), including India's global partners, as evidenced by the in-depth interactions between India and various other countries and transnational corporations at the highest levels.

This initiative is crucial from the viewpoint of economic growth, modernising and diversifying the economy, and the imperative need to create jobs for the millions of youth who are joining the labour force each year. The current environment for international trade presents India an unprecedented opportunity to chart a China-like, labour-intensive, export-driven growth and thereby create job opportunities on a large-scale for our burgeoning youth.

India is already doing well in the automotive and pharmaceutical sectors as supplier to global markets. India is also a manufacturer for aircraft components and undertaking production of defenceequipments besides shipbuilding.

But India has a long wayto go as the Make in India scheme has not made much headway so far. To give fillip to it, it the government has initiated steps like indigenising production of more high-tech defence items which will help India, the world's second-largest arms importer of arms, to become more self-reliant, reduce imports and save valuable foreign exchange.

To promotedomestic manufacture of electronics products, mobile phones, solar equipments, medical devices, etc., India has initiated the Productivity-linked Incentive (PLI) scheme.**(For more on Make in India scheme, see Chapter 21)**.

Productivity-linked Incentive (PLI) scheme

The PLI Scheme was notified by the Govt. of India in April 2020 to provide financial incentives to boost domestic mobile and electronics manufacturing and attract large scale investments. Later the scheme was expanded, and it now covers diverse sectors such as pharma for bulk drugs and Active Pharmaceutical Ingredients (API) and medical devices, automotive and auto components, textiles, air conditioners, batteries, LED lights, solar PV modules, battery storage, food processing and specialty steel.

The main features of the scheme are:

- The scheme is open to companies registered in India and involved in manufacturing of goods covered under the target segments.
- The government will pay a certain percentage of the value of additional production that companies make after fulfilling incremental investment and production criteria.
- The companies could earn as direct payments, on an average, 4 to 6 per cent more than what they would otherwise get.

Objectives of the scheme

- It would significantly boost investment, production and creation of jobs. For instance, the electronics sector could create 2 lakh direct and 6 lakh indirect jobs over five years.

- It would offset higher costs incurred by industry due to high taxes, power tariffs, logistics costs, land prices, etc. and thus help manufacturing sector achieve scale and become globally competitive.
- This is especially opportune when MNCs are planning to relocate from China to other countries due to cost considerations and many geopolitical factors and security issues.
- To promote exports and reduce dependence on imports for many critical items. Of an estimated production of ₹ 10.5 lakh crore, around 60 per cent would be exported.(See Chapter 21 also on this).

Ease of Doing Business

To speed up development of industry and services sector, the process of starting industries and business has to be made smooth and hassle-free. One of the main constraints of industrial development in India has been the complex procedures of 'red tape' hampering growth.

Regulatory environment is an important factor impacting business development. Low regulatory burden enables entrepreneurs to concentrate on productive activities. It also leads to lower costs as the requirement of engaging regulatory experts is reduced.

Since 2014, India has been striving to create a more conducive environment by simplifying regulations and eliminating unnecessary procedures. A detailed plan of regulatory reforms is being implemented both at the Central and State levels in response to the "Ease of Doing Business" (EODB) framework drawn up by the World Bank which reviews the systems in 190 countries and rank them in a DoingBusiness Report (DBR).

As per DBR 2019, India was ranked 77 among 190 countries assessed by the World Bank Team, which was improvement by 23 places over India's rank of 100 in the DBR 2018.

The DBR covers 10 indicators which span the lifecycle of a business. The indicators covered in the review and India's rank in each of them are as follows:

(a) Protecting Minority Investors (rank 7), Getting Credit (22), Getting Electricity (24) and Dealing with Construction Permits (52).

(b) Trading Across Borders (80), Resolving Insolvency (108), Paying Taxes (121), Starting a Business (137), Enforcing Contracts (163) and Registering Property (166).

Thus, it will be seen that while India ranked high on the indicators listed at (a) above, India ranks low on other crucial parameters at (b), which points to the need for further reform and simplification on those items. Though the World Bank survey covers only the two cities, Mumbai and Delhi, the Department for Promotion of Industry & Internal Trade (DPIIT) has initiated similar reform exercise in all States and UTs since setting up businesses concerns them also. States and UTs are being ranked based on implementation of reforms by them to create a conducive business environment by streamlining regulatory structures and creating an investor-friendly business climate. **(For more on this, see Chapter 22)**

❑ PROMOTING INDUSTRIAL DEVELOPMENT

The Agenda for The Future

Countries that managed to forge ahead and catch up with the earlier industrialized, high-income countries were the ones whose governments proactively promoted structural changes in the economy. In Japan and many of the East Asian countries, there was close and harmonious relationship between the government and the private sector in promoting industrial development. Industrial policy, with special focus on manufacturing, is back on the national agendas of many countries.

The government has to act more as a facilitator than a regulator for industry. This is even more necessary as modern technologies deployed in industry are fast-changing and dynamic in nature and government policies have to be in tune with them. Processes like 3D printing, robotics, etc. which are now being tried and used in industry are disruptive and will bring about transformational changes in the way industries operate.

The industrial development strategy needs a paradigm shift and is to be reoriented to enable the private sector to play a greater role and make it vibrant and attain its full entrepreneurial potential to contribute towards production, employment, and income generation. Unless the economic environment is made conducive for active participation of the private sector, there can be little progress in accelerating industrial development and growth. Government should dismantle existing barriers to industrial growth and act as a facilitator to create an enabling environment.

The government has to act more as a facilitator than a regulator for industry. This is even more necessary as modern technologies deployed in industry are fast-changing and dynamic in nature and government policies have to be in tune with them. Processes like 3D printing, robotics, etc. which are now being tried and used in industry are disruptive and will bring about transformational changes in the way industries operate. **(For more on this see Box 16.6, pp. 16.34-7)**

Conclusion

A conducive investment climate requires a considerable widening and deepening of economic reforms cutting across the Centre and States and local bodies, including Panchayati Raj Institutions (PRIs). These reforms must be aimed at ending or easing the rigidities in labour policies, reforming real estate laws, updating of land records digitally, ensuring security, transferability and enforceability of property rights, and bankruptcy, and exit and foreclosure laws. Restrictions on the inter-State movement of goods, octroi checkposts, and other local levies/regulations also needed to be removed to make the functioning of markets seamless. This is being achieved under the new Goods and Services Tax (GST) regime. Creating an efficient and world-class physical, financial, and social infrastructure is a *sine qua non* for industrial growth.

Developments in the social sectors, viz., education, health, and housing, has a great bearing on the capabilities to enhance the overall economic growth. India has been lagging behind many other countries on these parameters as reflected in Human Development Index and various other indices, such as Transparency and Ease of Doing Business, brought out by international agencies. Skilling the labour force, enforcing transparency and openness in all governmental procedures and dealings, and making the bureaucracy accountable for time-bound decisions and action should all be an integral part of the government's agenda and urgent action is called for on these fronts. Though India has taken several steps on these, it still has a long way to go to catch up with many other countries. Some of these measures being taken by the government now are discussed in later chapters.

Box 8.1: Privatisation and Disinvestment of Public Sector Enterprises

Privatisation means transfer of ownership, management and control of public assets, such as public sector enterprises (PSEs), from the public sector to the private Sector. Disinvestment, or divestment, refers to the act of government selling or liquidating an asset or subsidiary, or the process of dilution of a government's stake in a PSE. Disinvestment may be only a partial dilution of control with the government still retaining overall ownership of a particular enterprise, whereas privatisation, for all purposes, signify relinquishing the entire ownership in favour of private parties.

- **The Rationale:** Disinvestments and privatisation are primarily motivated by the optimization of resources to deliver maximum returns or as a way to pare losses from a non-performing asset. They are also aimed at improving the inflow of Foreign Direct Investment (FDI) or investment in sectors that require technological advancements, thereby directly providing a boost to Economy.

One reason advanced for privatisation of public sector units is that a government has no "business to be in business" save in the case of strategic sectors like defence, atomic energy and basic industries of vital importance to, and security of, the nation.

The Union Budget for 2021-22 reiterated the government's decision on disinvestment in non-strategic and strategic sectors keeping only four strategic areas where bare minimum of Central public sector enterprises (CPSEs) will be maintained and the rest privatized.

Presenting the Union Budget for 2020-21, the FinanceMinister had observed that listing of companies on stock exchanges disciplines the company and provides access to financial markets and unlocks its value. It also gives an opportunity for retail investors to participate in the wealth so created. The government now proposes to sell a part of its holding in LIC by way of Initial Public Offer (IPO).

A number of PSUs, set up many years back, are not able to maintain a steady business due to competition, disruption, management issues, financial constraints, face lack of product demand or are not able to update obsolete technology. The government wants to exit such loss-making enterprises.

The government has permitted 100 per cent foreign investment, under the automatic route, in oil and gas PSUs which have received in-principle approval for strategic disinvestment.

It may be recalled that the Expert Committee appointed by the Governor of RBI in 2014 to "Review Governance of Boards of Banks in India", headed by P.J. Nayak, a former Chairman and CEO, Axis Bank, had recommended to reduce to less than 50 per cent the Government stake in Public Sector Banks (PSBs) which is needed to reform these banks which are saddled with high volume of bad debts and non-performing assets.

- **The progress:** India's attempt at dismantling the PSEs over the years has seen only limited success, with the last big-ticket privatization taking place between 1999 and 2004. Since then, attempts to disinvest and privatize has led only to incremental progress, with no major privatization having taken place. A prime example is Air India, the national carrier, the privatisation of which has not fructified despite repeated attempts due to various reasons.

The government has approved disinvestment of LIC of India and will go for the Initial Public Offer (IPO) of LIC. But the government will retain the ownership and control over this institution and hence there would not be much change in its functioning and performance of LIC due to the IPO. This offers a great opportunity for retail investors and employees to invest in the company for the long term.

In the financial year 2021-22 till July, the government has raised ₹ 7646 crore by disinvestment.The LIC share sale will help the government move closer to its disinvestment target of ₹ 1.5 lakh crore for FY 2021- 22.

Before LIC's mega IPO, the government plans to disinvest its stake in 3 PSEs. The three PSEs are National Fertilisers Limited NFL), Mishra Dhatu Nigam Limited (MDNL), and Rashtriya Chemical & Fertilizers Limited (RCFL). The government propose to sell 20 per cent of its 74 per cent stake in NFL and 10 per cent each of its stake of 74 per cent in MDNL and 75 per cent stake in RCFL.

- **Reasons for slow progress:** Criticism of the sale of "family silver", of valuable public assets, concerns of possible allegations of graft in the sale process and stiff opposition from labour unions act as major obstacles to the drive for privatization. Subdued market conditions, lower valuations and potential lesser realisations in the backdrop of an overall slowdown and global recessionary trends also hinder the process of disinvestment.
- **Corporatisation of OFB:** Another major development is the corporatisation of Ordnance Factory Board (OFB). 41 factories under OFB would be converted into 7 Government-owned corporate entities. This is being done to improve productivity and create specialisation in weapons manufacturing. It will also lead to greater accountability and efficiency. The Parliamentary Standing Committee on Defence had also observed that corporatisation will improve the quality of its products and expand its market.

The government has assured to safeguard the interests and service conditions of the employees of OFB including their pay scales, allowances, leave, medical facilities, career progression as are applicable to the Central Government servants.

This step is especially significant as India is going to step up domestic manufacture of defence items, reduce their imports and expand exports.

In this Chapter we discussed.....

- Liberalization and measures to promote industry from 1985 and 1991.
- New Industrial Policy, 1991 and industrial policy under Five Year Plans.
- Export Processing Zones and Special Economic Zones; Special Economic Zones Act, 2005.
- Industrial regions and policy of balanced development of various regions.
- Industrial Corridors: Delhi-Mumbai Industrial Corridor and Multi- modal Freight Corridor Project covering six states.
- National Manufacturing Policy, 2011; creation of National Investment and Manufacturing Zone (NIMZs).
- eBiz Mission Mode Project under the National e-Governance Plan.
- Performance of industrial sector: An overview.
- Fluctuations in industrial growth.
- Index numbers of industrial production and sectoral shares of industry in GDP.

- India's manufacturing: A comparative view; Manufacturing and GDP growth rates and share of manufacturing in GDP in various countries and comparison with India.
- Manufacturing output as percentage of world total output: comparison of various countries' share with India's.
- Public sector enterprises: important role played by them in economic development; disinvestment policy; impact of disinvestment; Navaratna enterprises among PSE's.
- Constraints faced by Indian industry; infrastructure; land issue; trade barriers.
- India's export basket consist of mostly raw materials and low technology products.
- Low share of manufactures in GDP in comparison to some of the other Asian countries.
- Positive aspects of the Indian industry.
- Industry and employment; occupational structure in India skewed in favour of agriculture; substantial increase in the labour force and need to create jobs in the more productive manufacturing sector.
- Other measures toboost manufacturing: Make in India programme, Productivity Linked Incentive (PLI) scheme and Ease of Doing Business process.
- Promoting industrial development: agenda for future; need for close and harmonious relationship between the government and the private sector in promoting industrial development and creating conducive investment climate.
- Government to act more as a facilitator than a regulator for industry; government policies to be in tune with changes in the industrial sphere; enforce transparency and openness in all governmental procedures.
- Need for further reforms and progress in the social sectors, viz., education, health, and housing and to speed up skilling the labour force.
- Privatisation and Disinvestment of PSUs

Important Terms to Note in this Chapter

Monopolies and Restrictive Trade Practices (MRTP); Foreign Exchange Regulations Act (FERA); Foreign Direct Investment (FDI); Fiscal policy; Insurance Regulatory and Development Authority (IRDA); Transaction costs; Comparative advantage; Transnational companies; Fortune 500 companies; Trade deficit; Export Processing Zone; Special Economic Zone; Industrial Corridor; Cluster approach for industries; Ecosystem; e-Biz; e-Governance; Index of Industrial Production (IIP); Economic recession; Exchange rate; Globalization; Public Sector Enterprises; Disinvestment; Tariff and non-tariff barriers; Occupational structure of economy; Bankruptcy law; Octroi; 3D Printing; Robotics

Practice Questions

1. What are the salient features of the New Industrial Policy enunciated in 1991 as part of the economic reforms? How far it helped to promote Indian industries?
2. Enumerate the features of Special Economic Zones and Export Processing Zones set up in India.
3. Despite heavy investments made in industrial sector over the years, the share of industry and manufacturing in both Gross Domestic Product (GDP) and employment has been relatively low in India. Identify the reasons for this and this deficiency can be overcome.
4. What are the constraints and challenges faced by industries in India? How can they be resolved?
5. There is a clear acknowledgement that Special Economic Zones (SEZs) are a tool of industrial development,manufacturing and exports. Recognizing this potential, the whole instrumentality of SEZs requires augmentation. Discuss the issues plaguing the success of SEZs.

   [UPSC Main 2015 (General Studies Paper)]
6. What are the main components of the National Manufacturing Policy, 2014? Discuss.

   [UPSC (Main 2020 Economics) Optional Paper]
7. Explain the principal causes of deceleration in industrial growth during the mid-1960's to mid- 1970's in India. Do you think that the reasons for the slowdown in industrial growth since the late 1990s are basically different from those of the earlier deceleration? Answer with proper arguments.

   [UPSC Main 2019 (Economics Optional Paper)]
8. Discuss recent initiatives undertaken by the Government to boost industrial growth in India.

   (Indian Economic Service/Indian Statistical Service 2016)
9. How far is the restructuring of PSUs to make them more competitive a better strategy to enhance theirrelevance, rather than the tacit policy of privatizing them? Discuss in the light of practical evidence and recommendations. *(Indian Economic Service/Indian Statistical Service 2014)*

10. Industrial development and agricultural development are the two sides of the same coin. What Policyprescriptions would you advocate in the context of the Indian economy?

(Indian Economic Service/Indian Statistical Service 2015)

11. Disinvestment policy of the Government has failed to deliver desired results. Do you agree?

(Indian Economic Service/ Indian Statistical Service 2016)

12. Critically examine the strategy of disinvestment in improving the growth of the manufacturing sector.

[UPSC Main 2020 (Economics Optional Paper)]

13. Discuss the disinvestment policy adopted by the Government of India as a part of structural adjustment programme of the IMF and the World Bank. Examine the impact of such a policy on industrial growth in India. *[UPSC Main 2019 (Economics Optional Paper)]*

14. Discuss the rationale and objectives of Disinvestment Policy in India. Assess its performance.

[Indian Economic Service/Indian Statistical Service 2020]

15. Critically evaluate the government policies towards the public sector enterprises since 1991. Do you think these enterprises are still relevant for industrial development in India?

(Indian Economic Service/Indian Statistical Service 2017)

16. What is the significance of Industrial Corridors in India? Identifying industrial corridors, explain their main characteristics. *[UPSC Main 2018 (General Studies Paper)]*

17. Evaluate the Competition Act, 2002, relative to the Monopolies and Restrictive Trade Practices Act.

[UPSC Main 2019 (Economics Optional Paper)]

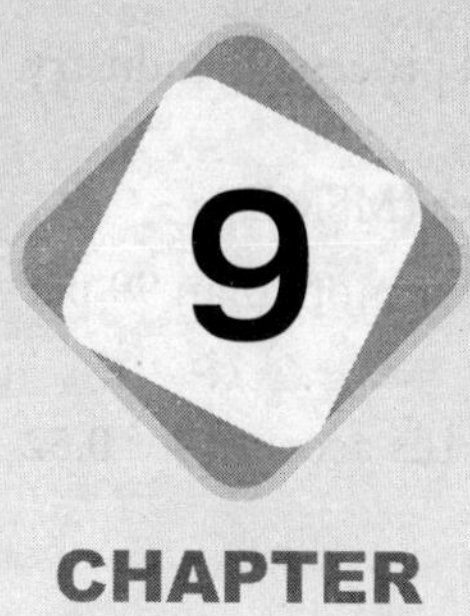

CHAPTER

SMALL SCALE INDUSTRY

- Small Scale Industry defined
- MSMEs: Criteria changed
- Karve Committee on Village and Small industries
- National Small Industries Corporation (NSIC)
- Industrial Cooperatives
- Industrial Estates
- Small Industries Development Organization (SIDO
- Plan Allocations for Small Scale sector
- Progress of Small Scale Industries sector
- Credit facilities for the MSME sector
- Small Industries Development Bank of India (SIDBI)
- Tiruppur: A success story
- Expert Committee on Small Enterprises (1995)
- Study Group on Small Scale Enterprises (1999)
- Constraints faced by the MSME sector
- Measures taken by the Government to support MSMEs
- Small Scale sector: Experience of Other countries
- Conclusion: Significance of MSMEs

❑ INTRODUCTION

Small scale industry has played a very significant role in India's economic progress during the post-independence era. From the very First Five Year Plan, its importance for generating employment and income and broadening the industrial base has been recognized. Its importance for the economy can be gauged from the fact that in 2006-07 there were 12.84 million units in this sector employing 31.25 million people. The sector accounted for 39 per cent of the country's manufacturing output and 33 per cent of its exports in 2004-05.

The small scale sector has diverse segments such as khadi, village and small industries, handlooms, powerlooms, handicrafts, coir industry, and sericulture. They can be grouped into 'traditional' small industries which relied more on human skill, primitive tools, and manual power, and 'modern' small industries which use mechanical power and higher skills and better tools. Now food processing industry (FPI) is also included in this sector.

The units in the sector are now classified as Micro, Small and Medium enterprises (MSMEs).

- As in 2020- 21, Micro sector with 630.52 lakh estimated enterprises accounts for more than 99 per cent of totalestimated number of MSMEs.
- Small sector with 3.31 lakh and Medium sector with 0.05 lakh estimated MSMEs account for 0.52 per cent and 0.01 per cent respectively of total estimated MSMEs.
- About 51 per cent of total MSMEs operate in rural areas

Table 9.1 shows the number of enterprises category-wise and their distribution in rural and urban areas.

The government has in 2020-21 taken a major decision to include Retail and Wholesale trade, which consist of about 2.5 crore establishments, under MSMEs. Thismakes them to be eligible to get the benefit of priority sector lending under the Reserve Bank of India guidelines.Besides, now the traders can avail the benefits of several other government schemes meant for MSMEs.

Table 9.1 Distribution of Enterprises (Rural and Urban area wise)

(Numbers in lakh)

Sector	Micro	Small	Medium	Total	Share (%)
1	2	3	4	5	6
Rural	324.09	0.78	0.01	324.88	51
Urban	306.43	2.53	0.04	309.00	49
Total	630.52	3.31	0.05	633.88	100

❑ SMALL SCALE UNITS DEFINED

In 1950, units or establishments using power, having a capital investment of less than ₹ 5 lakh, and employing less than 50 persons were categorized as 'small scale industries'. In 1966, this was revised and units with investment not exceeding ₹ 7.5 lakh in plant and machinery alone and ₹ 10 lakh in the case of ancillary units were deemed to be small scale enterprises. In 1975, these limits were raised to ₹10 lakh and ₹20 lakh for small scale units and ancillary units, and in 1980 to ₹20 lakh and ₹25 lakh respectively.

As per the 1977 Industrial Policy, within the small scale sector, a category called 'tiny sector' was introduced which consisted of units with investment in machinery and equipment upto ₹1 lakh and which were located in villages and in towns, with a population of less than 50,000 as per 1971 census.

The investment limits were further raised in 1980, 1990, and in 1997 based on the Abid Hussain Committee Report.

Since 2006-07, the Ministry dealing with the small scale sector has been renamed as Ministry of Micro, Small and Medium Enterprises (MSME). As recommended by Abid Hussain Committee, the sector now includes small enterprises in the Service sector also. Under the Micro, Small and Medium Enterprises Development Act, 2006, MSMEs have been classified as follows:

Manufacturing Sector Investment in plant and machinery:

- Micro enterprises: Not exceeding ₹25 lakh.
- Small enterprises: More than ₹25 lakh and less than ₹5 crore.
- Medium enterprises : More than ₹5 crore and less than ₹10 crore.

Service Sector: Investment in equipments

- Micro enterprises: Not exceeding ₹10 lakh.
- Small enterprises: More than ₹10 lakh and less than ₹2 crore.
- Medium enterprises: More than ₹2 crore and less than ₹5 crore.

Source: Micro, Small and Medium Enterprises Development Act, 2006, Eleventh Five Year Plan, Planning Commission.

MSMEs: Criteria changed

The above criteria for MSMEs laid down under the MSME Development (MSED) Act, 2006 based on investment in plant and machinery in the case of enterprises engaged in Manufacturing, and investment in equipment for enterprises providing Services has since been revised.

In May 2020, the government changed the criteria to recognizeMSMEs based not only on their investments but also on their turnover. Also, the distinction that existed earlier between manufacturing and services units has been removed.

The revised norms are as follows.

(i) A unit with investment up to ₹ 1 crore and turnover up to ₹ 5 crore will qualify as a Micro enterprise.

(ii) A unit with investment up to ₹ 10 crore and turnover up to ₹ 50 crore will qualify as a Small enterprise.

(iii) A unit with investment up to ₹ 50 crore and turnover up to ₹ 250 crore will be a Medium enterprise.

The revised criteria came into effect from July 1, 2020.

The changes in the definition of MSMEs may result in many enterprises which were earlier classified as Small enterprises being reclassified as Micro, and those classified as Medium enterprises being reclassified as Small. Further, there may be many enterprises which were not hitherto classified as MSMEs, which may now fall under the MSME classification as per the new definition. Such enterprises will also now benefit from the various schemes related to MSMEs mentioned earlier.

❑ KARVE COMMITTEE ON VILLAGE AND SMALL INDUSTRIES

As mentioned in Chapter 4 (pp. 4. 11-3), the government had recognized the vital role this sector could play and referred to it in the 1948 Industrial Resolution. And in 1955, the Planning Commission appointed a Committee headed by D.G. Karve, a well-known economist, to study the issues connected with the implementation of programmes for the 'Village and Small Industries' during the Second Plan (1956-61). The Committee had urged the need for constantly upgrading the skills and improving production techniques to avert technological unemployment and obsolescence, and for strengthening the decentralized nature of the sector.

The process initiated in the First Plan was continued in the Second and Third Plans (1956-1966). Following the issue of the Industrial Policy Resolution, 1956, there was greater stress on the broader objectives of the small scale sector creating employment on a large scale with relatively low capital investment, meeting a substantial part of the increased demand for consumer and simple producer goods, facilitating mobilization of resources of capital, tapping unutilized skills, and bringing about synergy between these industries in the rural sector and the large-scale industry.

❑ THE NATIONAL SMALL INDUSTRIES CORPORATION

Steps were taken during the First Plan (1951-56) itself to promote village and small industries. The National Small Industries Corporation (NSIC) was established in 1955 to promote and foster the growth of small industries and enterprises in the country. The Corporation provides machinery on hire purchase, equipment on lease, raw material assistance, marketing inputs for exports, single point registration, technical and managerial assistance, etc. The NSIC also helps SSI units in marketing, with exhibitions, enterprise building, software technology, training to promote viable small industries all over the country, particularly in backward areas, and in selected lines of production identified as priority areas for exports. It is now a fully government-owned enterprise under the Ministry of Micro, Small and Medium Enterprises (MSME). NSIC has a countrywide network of offices and operates Technical Centres serving the small scale sector. It has established technical service centres to provide technical and consultancy services to SSI units.With the passing of the Micro, Small and Medium Enterprises Development (MSMED) Act, 2006, NSIC has also included medium enterprises in its ambit for providing assistance under some of its schemes.

Technological obsolescence is high in small industries. To improve marketability, there was need to induct better and appropriate technology. Need was felt for an agency to take up the functions of conducting studies and preparing technology guidelines, assessing the need for establishment of tool rooms, testing centres, provision of technology inputs, assimilation of technology, assisting entrepreneurs in obtaining suitable know- how from indigenous sources, and coordination with organizations engaged in technology development and its transfer.

It was felt the NSIC could handle these functions for small industries. As a result, the role of NSIC has expanded over the years. The Corporation helps in material testing, product design, acts as an incubator for prospective entrepreneurs and start-ups in small enterprises sector, and provides Information Technology support. It also organises Tech Marts in collaboration with the Asia and Pacific Centre for Transfer of Technology and also helps SSI units in technology transfer from abroad through the Technology Transfer Centre. An Internet portal has been set up for sourcing technologies from international partner institutions.

❑ INDUSTRIAL CO-OPERATIVES

The importance of setting up industrial co-operatives both as an agency for developing village industries and as an essential channel for extending financial assistance to village artisans was emphasised even in the First Five Year Plan. The rationale for this was that a common forum or organization would be beneficial for purchase of raw materials or for sale of finished products or both. And, in due course, members of such associations, especially the small entrepreneurs, could work together for specific purposes and form themselves into co-operatives. But the progress on this turned out to be uneven both between different industries and between different regions and States. However, the experience in the handloom industry was encouraging as it had conditions conducive for the growth of co-operation. The number of handloom units included in the co-operative fold increased from 6.26 lakhs in 1950-51 to 7.88 lakhs in 1953-54 and to 8.79 lakhs by 1954-55.

❑ INDUSTRIAL ESTATES

The concept of industrial estates was mooted considering its benefits for the small enterprises in as much as they provide all common infrastructural and logistical facilities like buildings, power, water, transportation facilities, etc. which they would find difficult to provide on their own due to the capital expenditure involved. It also helps to bring in economies of scale, as far as these facilities are concerned, thereby optimizing production costs, and in modernizing and upgrading the facilities.

Even in the initial Plans, the importance of industrial estates had been recognized. About 346 industrial estates were set up by the end of March 1969 as compared to 66 estates in 1960-61. Of about 8670 sheds provided, about 6600 sheds had been occupied. The small units set up in these estates provided employment to about 82,700 persons. Their annual production then amounted to ₹99.25 crore. The programme generally was a success in urban areas. But industrial estates started in rural and semi-urban areas languished owing mainly to unsuitable location, lack of integrated planning, marketing facilities, and shortage of raw materials. By the end of 1969, 125 co-operative societies had been registered for establishment of co-operative industrial estates.

❑ THE SMALL INDUSTRIES DEVELOPMENT ORGANIZATION (SIDO)

The Small Industries Development Organization (SIDO), now known as Micro, Small and Medium Enterprises Development Organization, is the nodal agency for assisting small scale industries (SSIs) on technology, marketing, infrastructure, and training support. It has a network of over 3000 technically qualified personnel working through its Small Industries Service Institutes (SISIs) and branch SISIs, testing centres, and autonomous organizations such as the Tool Room, Product and Process Development Centres, etc. It works with the Reserve Bank of India, Small Industries Development Bank of India (SIDBI), and commercial banks in making credit available to SSI units.

❑ PLAN ALLOCATIONS FOR THE SSI SECTOR

In the initial years, the plan allocations for this sector were nominal as the the size of the plans itself was relatively small and resources were scarce with many competing demands. The public sector outlay under the first three Plans for this sector ranged between 2.1 per cent to 4 per cent in the First Three Plans. Thereafter, till the Sixth Plan (1980-85), the percentage of allocation was only around 1.5 to 2 per cent, though in absolute terms the allocations went up except during the Annual Plans in 1966-69. (See Table 4.6 on p. 4.13, Chapter 4).

The provision in the Seventh Plan (1985-90) for Village and Small Industries was ₹2,753 Crore. The outlays in the Eighth to Tenth Plans are given in Table 9.2.

Table 9.2 Plan Outlays in 8th, 9th, and 10th Five Year Plans in Village and Small Scale Enterprises Sector

(In ₹ Crore)

Sector	Eighth Plan	Ninth Plan	Tenth Plan
MSME*	1629.55	4303.85	5534.00
Textiles	1157.00	1270.00	1600.00
FPI#	146.00	235.04	650.00
Total	**2932.55**	**5,808.89**	**7784.00**

Source: *Ninth and Tenth Plan documents, Planning Commission.*

Note: *MSME: Micro, Small and Medium Enterprises; # FPI: Food Processing Industry.

To boost the development of the MSME sector, the government has allocated ₹ 24,124 Crore in the Twelfth Five Year Plan (2012-17), as against the allocation of ₹ 10,330 Crore in the Eleventh Plan (2007-12), an increase of 133.53 per cent.

❑ PROGRESS OF SMALL SCALE INDUSTRIES SECTOR

With various promotional measures taken in the first two decades, by the Fourth Plan (1969-74), the small scale sector had registered perceptible progress. The growth of modern small scale industries got impetus during the sixties. According to the Planning Commission, by "the end of 1968-69, about 140,000 small scale units had been registered with the States Industries Directorates, as compared to about 36,000 units at the beginning of 1962. Machines worth ₹4.5 Crore were supplied on hire-purchase terms to these industries in 1968-69, as compared to about ₹1.8 Crore in 1960-61. The value of purchases by the Central Government departments from small industries increased from ₹6.5 Crore in 1960-61 to about ₹28.6 Crore in 1968-69."

Apart from quantitative growth, there was significant improvement in the quality of the products of many small scale industries. This was reflected in the increased variety of items produced conforming to the standards and specifications prescribed by the defence services, railways, and several large scale industries. A number of small scale units became suppliers of parts and components to large industries engaged in the manufacture of machine tools, bicycles, automobiles, coach building and other railway equipment, electronics and electrical appliances, and machinery. Products of some of these industries were exported. Production of a number of new items, parts, and components requiring high technology and precision, some of which were being imported till then, were successfully undertaken in the small scale sector.

According to data from the National Accounts Statistics and CSO, in 1979-80, the share of Village and Small Industries (VSI) sector in the contribution made by the Manufacturing sector was around 49 per cent in terms of gross value of output and 51 per cent in terms of value added. And this sector provided employment to about 23.58 million persons (both part-time and full-time) as against around 4.5 million persons engaged on full-time basis in the large and medium industries sector. In exports, this sector accounted for more than one-third of the total exports of the country.

Table 9.3 shows the impressive growth of the small scale sector and its valuable contribution to the economy in terms of output, employment, and exports.

Table 9.3 Growth and Contribution of SSI Sector

Year	No. of Units (In Lakhs)	Output (₹ Crore)	Employment (In Lakhs)	Exports (₹ Crore)
(At Current Prices)				
1980–81	8.70	28,100	71.00	1,600
1985–86	13.50	61,200	96.00	2,800
1990–91	67.90	78,802	158.30	9,664
1995–96	82.80	147,712	197.90	36,470

Source: *Data 1980-81 to 1995-96 from Handbook of Statistics on Indian Economy, RBI Publication.*

There was further spurt in output, employment, and exports generated by the SSI sector during the Tenth Plan (2002-07) period as will be seen from Table 9.4.

Table 9.4 Performance of SSIs, 1981–82–2014–15

Year	SSI Units (Million)	Production* (₹ Crore) (At Constant prices)	Employment (In Million Persons)	SSI Exports (₹ Crore)
1981–82	0.96	78300	7.50	2100
1990–91	6.79	84728	15.83	9664
2000–01	10.11	184401	24.09	15278
2006–07	36.18	1198818	80.52	182538
2010–11	42.87	1653622	96.52	507739
2012–13	46.75	1809976	106.14	698166
2014–15# (Prov.)	51.06	–	117.13	849248

Note: *Production figures from 2001-02 are at 2001-02 prices and from 2006-2007 are at 2004-05 prices. #Data for 2006-07 includes activities of wholesale/retail trade, legal, education & social services, hotel & restaurants, transports and storage & warehousing. Data for the period upto 2005-06 is of Small Scale Industries (SSI) and after 2005-06 refer to Micro, Small and Medium Enterprises MSMEs. # indicates projected figures of units and employment.

Source: *Ministry of Micro, Small & Medium Enterprises, Government of India, cited in Handbook of Statistics on Indian Economy, 2017, Reserve Bank of India.*

MSME sector & Employment

After agriculture, the small scale sector is one of the largest provider of employment. As per the National Sample Survey (NSS) 73rd round conducted during the period 2015-16, MSME sector employs 110.99 million persons.And, the employment is across diverse sectors like Manufacturing, Non-captive Electricity Generation and Transmission, Trade and various other Services. Importantly, the enterprises are spread both in the rural and the urban areas and providing crucial non-farm jobs in rural areas thus lessening the pressure of population on the agriculture sector.Table 9.5 shows the distribution of MSMEs activity wise and rural-urban wise.

Table 9.5: Distribution of MSMEs – Activity wise and Rural-Urban wise

Activity	Employment (in Lakh)			Share (%)
	Rural	Urban	Total	
1	2	3	4	5
Manufacturing	186.56	173.86	360.41	32
Electricity*	0.06	0.02	0.07	0
Trade	160.64	226.54	387.18	35
Other Services	150.53	211.69	362.22	33
All	**497.78**	**612.10**	**1109.89**	**100**

MSME Sector & and Exports

Exports of this sector, as percentage of total exports, has also risen from about 24 per cent in 1980-81 to about 34 per cent 2004-05 and further to nearly 50 per cent by 2015-16.(See Table 9.6). This signifies that

Table 9.6: Share of SSI Sector in Exports (in ₹ Crore)

Year	Exports by SSI Sector	Total Exports	Percentage of Col. 2 to Col. 3
1980-81	1,600	6,710	23.84
1985-86	2,800	10,894	25.70
1990-91	9,664	32,557	29.68
1995-96	36,470	106,353	34.29
2000-01	69,797	203,571	34.29
2004-05	124,417	375,340	33.15
2010-11	507,739	1,14,2922	44.42
2015-16	855,352	1,71,6378	49.83

Source: *Handbook of Statistics on Indian Economy, Reserve Bank of India.*

Indian MSMEs are becoming globally competitive and their products/services are being accepted overseas.In view of this, special attention needs to be given to improve the competitiveness and technology up-gradation endeavours of MSM enterprises. Various schemes of the Government in this regard should be continued and effectively implemented.

❑ CREDIT FACILITIES FOR THE MSME SECTOR

One of the critical problems faced by the MSM enterprises is the inadequacy of credit facilities. In 1991, the Reserve Bank of India constituted a Committee headed by P.R. Nayak, Deputy Governor, to examine the difficulties confronting the small industries in securing finance. The committee made a number of recommendations to ease the problems of finance for the sector. Most of its recommendations have been accepted by the RBI. Banks were required to adhere to the guidelines issued by the RBI in regard to extending credit to the sector, particularly the tiny and small enterprises. Bank branches were to give priority to those village and tiny industries which, having established production successfully, could use working capital efficiently, but were unable to make progress for lack of working capital. The amounts of Scheduled commercial banks' advances to the small scale sector which were outstanding in different years, shown in Table 9.7, is an indication of the extent of financing done and priority accorded to this sector. The non-banking financial companies (NBFCs) were encouraged through suitable financial incentives to provide enhanced loans and increase lending to the SSI units.

Table 9.7 Scheduled Commercial Banks' Advances to Small-Scale Industries and Allied Services Outstanding

(Balance Outstanding)

Year	Small Enterprises (in ₹ Billion)	Small Road and Water Transport Operators (in ₹ Billion)	For Setting Up Industrial Estate (in ₹ Billion)
1	2	3	4
		(Figures in Colns. 2 to 4 in ₹ Billion)	
1976–77	14.03	2.91	0.21
1990–91	179.38	26.79	0.60
2000–01	601.41	49.73	1.67
2006–07	1273.23	264.16	3.24
2014–15	9664.78	–	–

Source: *Handbook of Statistics on Indian Economy, 2015, Reserve Bank of India.*

Notes: 1. Data for 2014-15 are provisional.

2. The data for the period up to 2006-07 are of Small Scale Industries (SSI). Subsequent to 2006-07, data with reference to Micro and Small Enterprises (MSEs) are being compiled.

Credit plays a vital role in development of MSME sector as funds at a reasonable cost can increase their competitiveness. Credit disbursal to this sector has, however, remained sluggish in recent periods. At an aggregate level, the total credit outstanding from banks and NBFCs to the MSME sector was approximately ₹16.6 lakh crore as at end of September 2019. Scheduled commercial banks accounted for 90 per cent of the share of total credit outstanding.

Promoters of small scale and micro units, particularly the first generation entrepreneurs, faced difficulties in accessing bank credit because of their inability to provide adequate collateral security for loans. Considering this, the Government launched the 'Credit Guarantee Fund Scheme for Small Industries' in 2000 with a view to alleviating the problem of collateral security and removing impediments in the flow of credit to the SSI sector. The scheme is being operated by the Credit Guarantee Trust Fund for Small Industries set up by the Government of India and SIDBI.

(On credit for MSMEs, see also the Section 'Measures taken by the Government and RBI to support MSMEs' later in this chapter).

❑ THE SMALL INDUSTRIES DEVELOPMENT BANK OF INDIA

The Small Industries Development Bank of India (SIDBI), set up in 1990 under an Act of the Parliament, is the principal financial institution for the promotion, financing, and development of the MSME sector. It also co-ordinates with institutions engaged in similar activities.

Apart from extending direct assistance to MSMEs in niche areas, viz., energy efficiency, cleaner environment, etc., SIDBI also extends Direct Risk Capital assistance to MSMEs and provides equity assistance to units, including start-ups, through Venture Capital funds.

Marketing Support Needed for Small and Medium Enterprises

Marketing is another area in which the sector needs support and hand-holding. Marketing is a crucial factor in business development, and is vital for the growth and survival of micro, small, and medium enterprises. They need to adopt better methods and higher levels of technology in production to remain competitive in a rapidly globalizing environment.

There is vast potential to increase the exports of the products of sectors like handlooms, handicrafts, khadi, village industries, silk, woollen, and coir industry. Enhancement of design inputs, adoption of new production techniques, and information about trends in export markets regarding products, utility aspects, prices, demand, etc., would help these sub-sectors to improve their performance and to achieve higher export targets.

A 'consortium' approach for consumer items with approved quality standards is considered to be helpful to SSI units in marketing their consumer products. The National Small Industries Corporation provides marketing support to these enterprises under a Marketing Assistance Scheme and facilitates the formation of consortia of MSMEs for marketing their products and services. The Corporation updates MSMEs on the prevalent market scenario and its impact on their activities, and provides a platform to MSMEs for interaction with large institutional buyers. While the medium enterprises are also target beneficiaries under the scheme, special attention is given to marketing of products and services of micro and small enterprises, in rural as well as urban areas.

Likewise, Small Industries Development Organization (SIDO) also helps in collecting and disseminating information related to marketing, identifies new markets and new technologies for the products, supports in networking with other organizations in India and abroad, and organises trade fairs and exhibitions. See Box 9.1 for Tiruppur's remarkable success story.

Box 9.1 Tiruppur: An Indian Success Story

Tiruppur, a major textile and knitwear hub near Coimbatore in Tamil Nadu, provides an example of flourishing small scale sector specializing in the manufacture of garments and apparels, much of which is exported to the developed countries. Tiruppur had been an industrial cluster for a long time before it embarked on its recent dynamic phase and is a dominant player in the international market. Its proximity to Coimbatore, which itself is a major centre of textile industry, has helped in its organic growth.

Over the years, it has become a major centre of cotton knitwear for both the export and home markets. Despite severe competition among the large number of small and medium firms, there were proper linkages in production and collective efforts on sharing of information about markets and design development which helped to sustain its development.

The industry works through a web of small to mid-sized units which separately undertake processing, fabrication, and stitching. These networks of firms operate through jobworking, contracting, and sourcing arrangements. The business families set up small 'sister concerns' rather than go in for large fully integrated factories. Despite the difficulties faced by this textile hub, such as intense competition in the international apparel market and challenges in export prospects due to slowdown in the U.S. and Europe which are its major export markets, the business culture in Tiruppur has been flourishing. The exports from Tiruppur have grown by leaps and bounds, from less than ₹ 10 crore in 1984 to about ₹ 20,730 crore in 2014–15. The Tiruppur Exporters' Association (TEA) has been playing a very significant and proactive role in Tiruppur's remarkable success story. In the 2019-2020 fiscal, the exports figure stood at ₹ 27,280 crore, a slight dip from ₹ 27,650 crore in 2018-2019 fiscal. Tiruppur accounts for about 50 percent share of India's total exports in the apparel sector. Besides the anti-Chinese sentiments, new orders from several key players in the US and EU markets to update their portfolios has helped early recovery of the industry.

Considering the importance of the sector for the economy, the government had set up committees to study the problems faced by this sector and suggest measures to resolve them and improve the performance of the sector. The Expert Committee on Small Enterprises, headed by Abid Hussain, and an Expert Group, headed by S. P. Gupta, have studied the working of the sector and come up with several steps to revitalize it. Many of these suggestions have been acted upon by the government as will be seen from the foregoing account on the small scale sector.

❑ EXPERT COMMITTEE ON SMALL ENTERPRISES

The government had appointed an Expert Committee on Small Enterprises in 1995, headed by Abid Hussain, to study the various issues confronting the small scale sector. The Committee submitted its report in 1997. After carrying out a detailed study of the sector, the Committee made several recommendations for revitalizing the sector. *Some of the major recommendations are given below.*

- Evidence exists of the capacity of SSEs to survive competition from large companies in India.
- The principle of protection of fledgling enterprises at the stage of their formation is to remain valid in the future as well.
- Beyond their initial state of development, the policy of protection be replaced by a policy of promotion as the cornerstone of future policy.
- Adequate supply of credit, services, technology assistance, infrastructure, and low transaction costs are the hallmarks of the proposed strategy for promotion of SSEs. This can be achieved by developing a variety of linkages between enterprises and their support institutions, partnerships between the private sector and the government, greater information flows, and by streamlining the legal and institutional framework.
- The centre piece of the new approach should be increasing public private partnership (PPP) in setting up support systems for small scale enterprises. Such public private partnership would thrive

particularly in clusters of small scale enterprises. Agglomeration of SSE's facilitates accretion of skills and economies in infrastructure development. Spontaneous growth of over 300 clusters has already taken place in the country mostly unaided by the state. This growth has been fuelled by access to domestic and international markets and cheap labour. However, further progress in clusters is hamstrung by decrepit infrastructure, environmental degradation, technological obsolescence, and meagre skills of the workforce. World wide experience confirms that growth in clusters can be buttressed by institutional development, and aided by the abundant provision of services and infrastructure development.

- *Infrastructure Development in Clusters*: The private sector be encouraged to develop industrial estates as infrastructure projects. The State should form State Industrial Park Authorities to facilitate the entry of the private sector.
- *The definition of SSEs and Raising Investment Limits*:
  The concept of the SSE sector, should include all business enterprises in the Service sector which provide services to industrial enterprises. Incentives, credit facilities, and promotional facilities should then be available to all small scale enterprises. Taking into account all these factors, an investment limit of ₹ 25 lakh for tiny units is adjudged to be most appropriate. For small scale enterprises, the level should be immediately raised to ₹ 3 crore for the same reasons.
- *Revitalizing District Industry Centres (DIC's)*: District Industry Centres will play a pivotal role on account of the regional focus in small enterprises development.
- *Abolish Reservations*: One of the most important planks of the policy for the development of small scale enterprises has been the reservation of products which can be manufactured only by them. The existence of reservation policy has also provided an illusion to the government and the country at large that adequate protection/promotion was being provided to small scale industries. Past experience leads to the conclusion that reservation does little for the promotion of small enterprises and play only a negative role of keeping out large enterprises. This policy is now inconsistent with the current trade reform which allows the free import of the large majority of goods and most of the remaining consumer goods.
- Excise incentives for graduating Tiny and Small Scale units.
- *Restructuring of Financial Support*: The financial system also need to be reformed to increase access of small scale units to term loans and working capital and to lower the costs of credit. Available evidence suggests that the access of small scale enterprises to credit is generally inadequate. The existing institutional structure for delivering credit to SSEs needs a thorough overhaul. State Finance Corporations (SFCs) and State Industrial Development Corporations (SIDCs) have suffered from very poor recovery rates. Moreover, they have also been characterized by heavy political and bureaucratic interference in their functioning.
- *Support for Technology Development in SSEs*: The Expert Group recommended that the government should provide funds to the Bureau of Industrial Standards (BIS) in the Ninth Plan to fund a special exercise for providing technology support to SSEs to achieve prescribed technical standards.
- *Marketing Assistance*: The Expert Group suggested that on the lines of Marketing Development Assistance Fund set up earlier in EXIM Bank with World Bank assistance, a fund be created and operated through SIDBI for assisting targeted SSE exporting units numbering around 5000 in the Ninth Plan period. The Expert Group also recommends that a suitable mechanism be evolved to promote marketing outlets specializing in marketing the products manufactured by the tiny sector.

❑ STUDY GROUP ON SMALL SCALE ENTERPRISES

In 1999, the government appointed a Study Group on Development of Small Scale Enterprises which submitted its report in 2001. Highlighting the importance of the sector, the Group observed that small enterprises accounted for about 95 per cent of industrial units, contributed 40 per cent of value addition in the manufacturing sector, had 80 per cent share in manufacturing employment, and 35 per cent in exports. Over 32 lakh small units were operating, spread all over the country employing 178 lakh persons. Hence, its utmost significance for the economy.

Some of the important recommendations made by the Group were:

- To have three a 3-tier structure of tiny, small, and medium sector;
- To continue reservation of production by SSE sector but non-SSI units could take up production of such items with 30 per cent export obligation to be complied over three years;
- Need to have a single comprehensive law for the SSI sector;
- To make SSI units aware of the obligations under WTO regime and its impact on the sector;
- To raise the investment ceiling from ₹ 1 crore to ₹ 5 crore for plant and machinery in certain export-oriented industries like leather products, garments, hosiery, etc.;
- To reduce the cost of credit for SSI units.
- To encourage technocrat entrepreneurs in hi-tech industries like IT, Bio-tech, etc.

The government accepted many of these suggestions and implemented them in phases.

Box 9.2 Constraints Faced By The MSME Sector

The Economic Survey for 2018-19 has done a detailed study of the MSME sector, its progress over the years and constraints which shackle them. It also makes a comparative study of firms that are small and large, and those that are young and aged (in existence for long). The following are the main findings of this study.

- **Small versus Large firms:** Firms that have continued to remain small and not grown are at a disadvantage compared to firms that are large or have grown in size over the years.
- MSMEs that grow over time not only create greater profits for their promoters but also contribute to job creation and productivity in the economy. The policies must, therefore, focus on enabling MSMEs to grow by unshackling them.
- Job creation in India, however, suffers from policies that foster small firms that never grow, because it is the infant firms (those newly set up and young and not old in age) that have the potential to grow and become giants rapidly.
- Even among the small firms, firms with less than 50 employees dominate in number but create the least jobs and remain the most unproductive. Thus, the contribution of small firms to output and employment in the manufacturing sector is insignificant though they constitute nearly 85 per cent of all firms.
- Firms that did not grow and remained small in size, dominates the Indian economy and holds back job creation and productivity.
- **Old and large firms:** Old, but large, firms (firms that have more than 100 employees and are more than 10 years old) account for only 10.2 per cent of firms by number, but contribute half of the employment as well as the value added. Thus, firms that are able to grow over

time and become large are the biggest contributors to employment and productivity in the economy. In contrast, units that remain small, despite being older, contribute the least to employment and productivity in the economy.

- **Impact of SSI Reservation policy:** The Small-Scale Industries (SSI) reservation policy was introduced in 1967 to promote employment growth and income re-distribution. From 1997 to 2007, reservation for small-scale firms in respect of several product categories was eliminated

  After the elimination of reservations, large firms – be it new entrants or incumbents – have created more employment than small firms. Among both new entrants and incumbents, the small firms destroyed jobs while the large firms created jobs.
- **Priority Sector Lending:** The guidelines under Priority Sector Lending (PSL) may be re-calibrated to direct credit flow to young firms in sectors, with high employment elasticity, which will help to accelerate employment generation. Focus must be on service sectors such as tourism, which has high spill-over effects on other sectors such as hotel & catering, transport, real estate, entertainment, etc. Identifying and promoting tourist spots for development will also help create jobs.
- **Adverse impact of labour laws:** India has a plethora of labour laws, regulations and rules, both at the centre and the state levels, that govern the employer-employee relationship. These rigid labour laws create perverse incentives for firms to remain small.
- Each of these legislations exempt smaller firms from complying with these laws.
- For instance, the Industrial Disputes Act (IDA), 1947 requires companies to get permission from the Government before retrenching employees but this stipulation is applicable only to firms with more than 100 employees. Thus, firms with less than 100 employees are exempt from the need to get permission from the Government before retrenching their employees.
- As complying with such regulations entail transaction costs, naturally a large majority of firms would prefer to remain below the threshold of 100 employees and thus will continue to remain small.
- Deregulating labour law restrictions can create significantly more jobs, as seen by the recent changes in Rajasthan, when compared to the rest of the States. Rajasthan took steps to reform labour laws.

  There is, therefore, need to put in place various policies that incentivise firms to grow in size over time, leverage economies of scale, become more productive and competitive and are able to create more jobs.
- **Delayed Payments:** A large number of MSMEs are ancillary units catering to the needs of large industries, both in the public and private sector. They often face the problem of delayed payments, affecting their cash flow and working capital availability. Most of the time, delay in realisation of such receivables increases their operating cycle and reduces their ability to procure new orders or fulfil the existing ones. A primary survey conducted by Reserve Bank in December 2019 showed that 44 per cent of MSMEs engaged in manufacturing activities faced delay in payments.

  Although MSME Development Act, 2006 contains provisions related to penalty in case of delayed payments by the buyers, weak bargaining power and the fear of losing the business prevents MSMEs to invoke this provision.

- **Challenges on the Export front:** Some of the challenges faced by this sector in exports are:
- Limitation of information about products and services in demand in various countries.
- Working of the foreign markets, and in particular difficulties in accessing export distribution channels and in connecting with overseas customers.
- Lack of awareness on export promotion and assistance programmes offered by the government.
- Unfamiliarity with legal and regulatory frameworks of the exporting and importing countries. Lack of awareness on Intellectual Property Rights (IPR) issues and various International Trade Agreements (ITAs).

Measures taken by the Government and RBI to support MSMEs

The Small Scale industry is the second largest employer after agriculture. The sector accounts for 45 per cent of total industrial production, over 45 per cent of total exports and contributes 30 per cent of the country's GDP.

Recognizingsignificant role played by MSMEs, successive Governments have put in place several measures to support MSMEs including boosting of exports by MSMEs. Apart from the support extended by National Small Industries Corporation (NSIC) and Small Industries Development Organization (SIDO) and various other steps discussed earlier, the government has initiated the following measures to promote MSMEs.

- **U K Sinha Committee (2019):**To understand the structural bottlenecks and factors affecting the performance of the MSMEs, RBI had set up an Expert Committee on MSMEs under the Chairmanship of U.K Sinha in January 2019. The Committee undertook comprehensive review of the sector and gave several wide-ranging recommendations for the economic and financial sustainability of the MSME sector. These recommendations broadly relate to legislative changes, infrastructure development, capacity building, technological upgradation, improving backward and forward linkages, improving financial support from formal sources, newer technological interventions for robust underwriting practices and credit delivery, among others. While some of the recommendations of the Committee have already been implemented, others are under consideration by the authorities concerned.
- ***Factoring facility:***As pointed out above, delayed receipt of payments is a major issue faced by MSME units. To overcome this problem, the government has passed the Factoring*Regulation (Amendment) Bill 2021*which expands the credit facilities for small businesses and aid them in accessing funds from 9,000 Non-Banking Financial Companies. It will also give a boost to the economy by providing effective working capital cycle for MSMEs.

  Factoring is a monetary transaction in which a firm sells its "receivables" from a customer to banks or a third party called a "factoring firm" at a discount so that it gets money immediately to carry on its business. The bank or factoring firm pays a percentage of the invoices quickly. As per the original Act of 2011, only specialized NBFCs and banks were allowed to engage in factoring but the amendment allows all NBFCs interested to engage in such business.

  This, of course, entails the associated risk of bad debts for NBFCs and banks as more bills come from various firms for discounting. But it may be noted that most of the "receivables" are against government work and while the government does not default, it is slow to clear the bills. Corporate receivables have shorter payment delays against their bills but they are susceptible to potential defaults. But large NBFCS and banks have better means to recover the dues than the MSMEs.

The bill also seeks to provide strong oversight mechanism for the factoring ecosystemand it empowers the RBI to make regulations with respect to factoring business.

- **Pre-packaged Insolvency Resolution:**The Insolvency and Bankruptcy Code (Amendment) Bill, 2021 passed by the Parliament enables an efficient alternative insolvency resolution framework for MSMEs.

  Salient features of the Bill include:

- Pre-pack for MSMEs combines the benefits of informal settlement with the legal certainty of formal insolvency proceedings. It is a hybrid mode of out-of-court resolution to be recognized under insolvency law.
- It provides for the guidance and oversight of Resolution Professional.
- Finality of the process, with judicial approval.
- The process offers flexibility – quicker, cost-effective, and value-maximizing outcomes for all stakeholders.
- **Role for MSMEs in Supply chains:**The capability and viability of the defence and aerospace industry is built on the strength of supply chains, in which the MSMES are intricately intertwined. There are substantially large number of MSMES across the country supplying components and sub-assemblies and systems to the Defence Public Sector Undertakings, Ordnance Factories, Defence Research and Development Organization and private industries.

  Government has been focussing on providing special incentives to MSMES in the policies – be it Offsets, Make in India scheme or reservation in procurements. Interaction with vendors and concerned stakeholders are organized regularly at various levels to understand their issues and decisions are taken to address their concerns.
- **Measures to boost Exports:** With MSMEs accounting for over 45 per cent of total exports of India, providing adequate support to them is of critical importance. Besides the schemes and programmes launched by the Ministry of MSME mentioned earlier, the government has announced Nirvik (Niryat Rin Vikas Yojana) scheme to provide enhanced insurance cover and reduce premium for small exporters. The scheme will expand the scope of export credit and it will offer high insurance cover. This will enable reduction in overall cost of export credit, including interest rates concessions to the MSMEs.
- **Measures by RBI to Improve Liquidity and Credit Flow:** Apart from the steps taken by the government, the RBI has also taken several measures to ease the liquidity and credit position of the MSME sector. This was imperative as a large number of MSMEs were seriouslyimpacted by the Covid-19 pandemic. These measures included:
- **TReDSand Priority lending:**To tackle delays in getting payments faced by MSMEs. the RBI introduced the Trade Receivables Discounting System (TReDS) in 2014. TReDS is an electronic platform where receivables of MSMEs drawn against buyers (large corporates, PSUs, Government departments) are financed through multiple financiers at competitive rates. This is done through an auction-based mechanism. To widen the scope of TReDS and to incentivise more players to be part of this platform, banks' exposure through this platform were brought under priority sector lending in 2016.
- TReDS platform has registered 1,592 companies with turnover of more than ₹ 500 crore by the end of May 2021, to facilitate credit to MSMEs. Besides, the Department of Public

Enterprises – the nodal department for all central public sector enterprises (CPSEs) – has asked all CPSEs to onboard on TReDS platform and 170 CPSEs have already complied.

- **Priority lending through NBFCs:** Banks form the predominant source of formal credit to MSMEs with all such loans by banks qualifying for Priority Sector Lending classification. In August 2019, RBI further incentivised banks to lend to MSMEs through the NBFC sector. Consequently, bank credit to registered NBFCs (other than Micro Finance Institutions) for on-lending to micro and small enterprises up to ₹20 lakh per borrower are eligible for classification as priority sector lending.
- **Restructuring debt:** A scheme of one-time restructuring, without an asset classification downgrade, was permitted to GST registered MSME accounts that were in default as in January 2019. As the process of formalisation of the MSME sector has a positive impact on financial stability, the scheme was extended to accounts that are standard but in default as in January 2020 and restructuring, wherever eligible, had to be implemented latest by the end of December 2020. This benefited the eligible MSME entities including MSME entities which became stressed thereafter. By March 2020, banks had restructured 6 lakh accounts out of 15 lakh eligible accounts under the scheme.

❑ SMALL SCALE SECTOR: THE EXPERIENCE OF OTHER COUNTRIES

Hong Kong

Manufacturing is the largest sub-sector of industry in Hong Kong. In the late 1990's, there were about 23,500 manufacturing establishments in Hong Kong and most of them were very small. The average number of employees per establishment was ten. After it became a part of China, many labour-intensive and sophisticated industries were moved to China resulting in the loss of several thousand industrial jobs in the nineties. Scarcity of land in the island and mainland China's ability to undertake mass production at more competitive rates led to the migration of industries from Hong Kong. The existing small industries which are export-oriented produce textiles, electronic and telecom items, and a variety of other products.

Taiwan

Taiwan is another country where SME's have played an important role. Like Hong Kong, the adaptability of relatively small units seems to have been an important factor behind Taiwan's overall success in exports. The role of financial institutions in helping the SME sector is also an important element. Taiwan developed a widely distributed structure of manufacturing enterprises, many of which had low start-up capital like in Hong Kong. The importance of government supported financial institutions specializing in 'Venture capital' lending has also helped the growth of SME's.

Japan

Japan presents the example of promoting small industries through 'subcontracting' mode. Even with a substantial presence of large industries, Japan could successfully develop a small scale sector with large industries subcontracting production of items. The small industrial units provide a large share of employment and value added in manufacturing.

While subcontracting is an efficient way of promoting the small enterprises, as it provides greater labour market flexibility, its successful development is critically dependent on large firms being able to transfer the know-how and technology to the ancillary units to ensure quality production. There should be a healthy relationship of co-operation between the large and small industry rather than dominance of one over the other.

South Korea

South Korea is another country where small establishments have played an important part through 'subcontracting' mode. In the 1990's, about half of the output of small establishments was subcontracted. It was as a result of the changing composition of industrial output and also due to a policy aimed at spreading the fruits of industrial growth more widely. For more information about the MSME sector in selected countries, see Box 9.3.

Box 9.3 MSME Sector in Selected Countries

Following data on MSE's in some other countries reveal the crucial role played by them in the economy:

- In Brazil, MSEs represent 20% of the total GDP. Of the country's 4.7 million registered businesses, 96.8% are MSEs and along with the other 9.5 million informal enterprises—they employ 59% of the economically active population.
- Similarly, informal and micro enterprises accounted for 39% of labour force and contribute to 24% of the GDP in South Africa; SMEs employ 27% of the labour force and contribute 32% to the GDP; while large enterprises employ 34% people and account for 44% of the GDP.
- SMEs comprise over 90% of all industrial units in Bangladesh contributing between 80% and 85% of the industrial employment and 23% of the total civilian employment. They contribute three-quarters of the household income in both the urban and the rural areas.
- In Japan, SMEs employ more than 70% of the wage earners, contributing over 55% of value added in the manufacturing sector.
- In Thailand in 2003, there were 2006528 enterprises of which 99.5% were SMEs. These SMEs generated products worth 38.1% of GDP, and in 2003 they employed 60.7% of Thailand's working population.
- The real importance of the SMEs, however, can be seen in China where over 68% of the exports come from the SMEs. China has created more SMEs in the last 20 years than the total number of SMEs in Europe and the US combined. Their numbers have increased from about 1 million private sector SMEs in the 1990s to 40 million in 2004. In China, an industrial SME is defined as having up to 2000 employees, while a small business has less than 300 employees and a medium-size business has employees between 301 and 2000.

Source: *Eleventh Five Year Plan (2007–12), Vol. III, Planning Commission.*

❑ CONCLUSION

Significance of MSMEs

The Micro, Small and Medium Enterprises (MSMEs) sector has emerged as a highly vibrant and dynamic sector of the Indian economy over the last six decades. It is not only a significant contributor to the

GDP but a major provider of employment in both urban and rural areas, and thus ensures inclusive growth touching upon the lives of the most vulnerable and the marginalized sections—women, SCs, and STs. The sector enables millions in small towns, remote villages, and isolated hamlets to use indigenous knowledge, dextrous hands, and entrepreneurial skills for the sustenance of their lives and livelihoods. It also promotes and nurtures entrepreneurial spirit.

In a country like India with a population size of about 1.3 billion, the Micro, Small and Medium Enterprises (MSME) sector has a vital role in the economy. It fosters entrepreneurship and generates large employment opportunities. As MSMEs absorb the surplus agricultural labour, they help reduce the problem of disguised unemployment in rural areas. MSMEs are also complementary to large industries as ancillary units and also play an important role in the whole eco-system of the secondary and tertiary sector.

The decision taken by the government, referred to earlier, to include Retail and Wholesale trade, which include about 2.5 crore establishments, under MSME category would give a boost to the MSME sector. Thismakes these units to be eligible to get the benefit of priority sector lending under the RBI guidelines.Besides, the traders can also avail the benefits of several other government schemes meant for MSMEs.

The role of this sector is bound to grow with the new emphasis on the Manufacturing sector with the 'Make in India' programme in which the MSME's can play the role of ancillary industries to the large industries in the private and public sector which are pitching for production of major items, in collaboration with transnational companies, for the defence sector, aerospace industry, expanding infrastructure sectors such as roads, railway, ports, shipping, etc. and Smart Cities project which will create much demand for industrial goods.

A part of the MSME sector also represents India's rich cultural diversity and heritage with many creative entities like the handicrafts, artefacts, and handlooms which, with aggressive promotion and exposure, are capable of giving the country a stronger presence in the global market than it does now.

In this Chapter we discussed.....

- Small scale industry has played a very significant role in India's economic progress.
- The sector accounted for 39 per cent of the country's manufacturing output and 33 per cent of its exports in 2004-05.
- The sector has diverse segments such as khadi, village and small industries, handlooms, powerlooms, handicrafts, wool, coir industry, sericulture, and food processing industry. The sector now includes small enterprises in the Service sector also.
- The investment limits for being considered as a small scale unit have been revised from time to time.
- The 1955 Karve Committee on Village and Small Industries had suggested measures for strengthening the sector.
- The National Small Industries Corporation (NSIC) was established in 1955 to promote and foster the growth of small industries. The Corporation is tasked with many functions to help micro, small, and medium (MSM) industries.

- Industrial Co-operatives and Industrial Estates set up to strengthen the sector.
- The Small Industries Development Organization (SIDO), now known as Micro, Small and Medium Enterprises Development Organization, is the nodal agency for assisting small scale industries (SSIs) on technology, marketing, infrastructure, and training support.
- Plan allocations for this sector has been raised significantly from Plan to Plan. The allocation for the Twelfth Five Year Plan (2012-17) is ₹ 24,124 crore as against the allocation of ₹ 10,330 crore in the Eleventh Plan (2007-12).
- The sector has made steady progress in terms of output, employment, and exports over the last six decades and made valuable contribution to the economy. In 2006–07, there were 361.80 lakh MSM units employing 805.20 lakh persons and exporting items worth ₹ 182538 crore.
- Constraints faced by the sector are problems relating to production methods, adapting to new technologies, technological upgradation, and inadequacy of credit. Task forces and Committees have studied the problems of the sector and the Government and various institutions like NSIC, SIDO, SIDBI, and RBI have taken several steps to alleviate the problems. Commercial banks have also been doing priority lending of credit to this sector, especially the micro and small units.
- Marketing has been a critical element in the performance of the sector. It has been helped in this by NSIC, SIDO, and SIDBI. Tiruppur apparel and knitwear industry, consisting of large number of small units, has blazed a new trail with creditable performance both in production and exports. It is a remarkable success story.
- The Expert Committee on Small Enterprises, headed by Abid Hussain, set up in 1995 and the Expert Group on Small Enterprises under S.P. Gupta set up in 1999 had studied the various issues confronting the small scale sector. They had made several suggestions to revitalize the sector and many of them have since been implemented.
- Small scale sector has played an important role in other countries like China, Hong Kong, South Korea, Japan, Brazil, and South Africa in industrial development.
- India should continue to support this sector which has much potential to contribute to the economy in terms of output, employment, and exports. The role of this sector is bound to grow with the new emphasis on the Manufacturing sector with the 'Make in India' programme in which the MSME's can play the role of ancillary industries to the large industries in the private and public sector in the context of large Indian companies collaborating with transnational companies for production of major items for defence, aerospace, railways, and other sectors.

- Constraints faced by the MSME sector.
- Measures taken by the Government and RBI to support MSMEs

Important Terms to Note in this Chapter

Technological unemployment; Technological obsolescence; Industrial co-operatives; Industrial estates; National Accounts Statistics; Non-banking financial companies (NBFCs); Collateral security; Venture capital; Protection policy; Transaction costs; Public Private Partnership (PPP) Factoring facility; Pre-packaged Insolvency resolution.

Practice Questions

1. Explain the role played by the Small Scale sector since independence and its contribution to Indian economy.
2. Describe the role of National Small Industries Corporation in promoting the small scale industries.
3. What are the features of 'Industrial Estates' and what are its advantages for the small and medium industries?
4. The importance of small and medium industries lies in providing employment on a substantial scale and its share in exports of the country. Do you agree with this statement? Justify your answer.
5. What are the challenges faced by Micro, Small and Medium Enterprises (MSMEs)? What were the recommendations of the Expert Committee on Small Enterprises headed by Abid Hussain on revitalizing the sector?
6. Small and medium industries could play an important role as ancillaries to large-scale industries. Do you agree with this view? Justify your answer with cogent reasoning.
7. What was the impact of policy reservation in favour of small scale industries in India during the post-independence but pre-liberalisation era? *[UPSC Main 2015 (Economics Optional Paper)]*
8. Bring out the importance of micro, small and medium enterprises in the context of the Indian economy. *[UPSC 2015 - Indian Economic Source/Indian Statistical Service Paper)*
9. What are the major problems faced by the Small Scale Industries (SSIs)? Examine the role of the MSMED Act, 2006, in enhancing productivity of Small Scale Industries in India.

   [UPSC Main 2020 (Economics Optional Paper)]

CHAPTER

INFRASTRUCTURE (TRANSPORT AND COMMUNICATIONS)

- Importance of Infrastructure
- Development of Infrastructure
- Roadways: Growth and Overburdened Roads
- Major Developments: PMGSY & Golden Quadrilateral
- Problems in Highway Projects Construction
- Roadways Complementary to Rail
- Challenges Facing the Road Sector
- PMGSY and Golden Quadrilateral
- Railways: Growth and Improvements
- Reforms in Railways
- Shipping, Ports and Inland Waterways
- Air Transport and Open Skies Policy
- Modernisation and Privatisation of Airports
- Post, Courier and Logistics industry
- Telecommunications: Telecom policies
- BharatNet project
- Challenges and Rise of Telecom sector
- Financial state of Telecom sector
- Spectrum Allocation and Pricing
- Open Radio Access Networks (RAN)
- Radio, Television and Satellite Communication
- Infrastructure and Employment
- International North-South Transport Corridor (INSTC)
- Multi-modal transport network

❑ INTRODUCTION

An efficient and well-developed system of transport and communications is vital for the success of plans for economic development which lays stress on rapid industrialization. While agriculture, industry and services are important and integral parts of an economy, infrastructure is another important cog in the wheels on which any economy moves. No other sector can develop and contribute to their fullest potential unless infrastructure is well developed. Physical infrastucture includes a whole gamut of facilities– roads, rail, air transport, shipping and ports and inland waterways. Apart from these transport facilities, communication modes–telecom, information technology (IT), satellite services, postal and courier sectors–and power sector also form part of infrastructure which are essential for enabling various activities.

Importance of Infrastructure

Needless to say, poor roads, a decrepit transport system, malfunctioning electricity grids, outdated and inefficient telecom networks, and above all, a cumbersome red tape will have a crippling effect on productivity and competitiveness of various sectors. One of the major drawbacks and hindrances in India's developmental efforts has been the poor state of her infrastructure. India's roadways–both in cities, towns, and villages as well as the highways–have been notorious for their poor standards and maintenance, though the highways are being built to international standards in the last fifteen years which is a major step forward. The railways, though one of the largest networks in the world and has expanded and progressed a great deal over the years, still suffers from many infirmities. Air transport–including both airline operations and airport facilities–until recently under-developed, has since been opened up and begun to show signs of its potential. So also, the telecommunications sector has expanded exponentially ever since it was opened to the private sector. While shipping has been performing relatively well, port facilities are still far below par when compared to international standards. And power output and supply, though augmented over time, is still far short of the demand, and due to shortages and erratic supply, even in the present times, has been a drag on the economy.

Development of Infrastructure

Among all the modes of transport, railways and roads are the dominant means of transport carrying more than 95 per cent of total traffic generated in the country. Although other modes such as coastal shipping and inland water transport could play a greater role, the railways and roads would continue to dominate the transport landscape in the foreseeable future.

Infrastructure provides the basic support system for all other sectors and is the backbone of an economy. Agricultural commodities, raw materials for the industry, and maufactured goods have to be moved all over the country. Items being imported have to be moved from ports and airports to the destinations. Likewise, items to be exported have to be moved from the originating points to the ports and airports. Just like goods, people also depend on various modes of transport for movement. Tardy movement, bottlenecks along the routes, congestion of traffic, etc. adversely impact industry and service sectors the most, while lack of road connectivity to villages affects the agricultural sector. Indian economy has had to suffer from all these handicaps and deficiencies ever since independence, and again due to lack of adequate attention and affirmative action to develop the infrastructure during the colonial era.

Beginning with the planning era in 1951, India faced the Herculean task of developing the road and rail network even as the country had scarce financial resources with many competing demands. This was all the more difficult as India, being a large sub-continent, about 3,000 kms. long from the north to the south and equally wide from the west to the east, with difficult terrain and widely varying climatic conditions, needed high quality, all-weather road and rail network for transportation. Though there has been significant quantitative expansion in the network (see Table 10.2), it has fallen far short of the needs of the economy and the quality and condition of the network also leave much to be desired. Various types of problems in the implementation of projects have been plaguing the sector as will be seen from discussions later in this chapter.

The Plan allocations for infrastructure in the initial decades was understandably low as the overall plan size (total outlay) itself was rather modest. But from the Sixth Plan onwards, the allocations and expenditure incurred were substantial and in keeping with the real needs of the two sectors–Transport and Communications. (See Table 10.1). As the outlays in the early plans were relatively less, the outcomes and results achieved were also far below what the country needed to lift the economy.

Table 10.1: Plan Allocations and Actual Outlay for the Sector (in ₹ crore)

Plan	Transport & Communications	
	Allocation	Actual Outlay
First Plan (1951–56)	570	518
Second Plan (1956–61)	1340	1261
Third Plan (1961–66)	1486	2112
Annual Plans (1966–69)	1273	1222
Fourth Plan (1969–74)	3237	3080
Fifth Plan (1974–79)	6917	6870

	Transport		Communications	
	Allocation	Actual Outlay	Allocation	Actual Outlay
Sixth Plan (1980–85)	12412	14208	3134	3470
Seventh Plan (1985–90)	22645	29548	4474	8425
Annual Plans (1991–92)	9916	9314	3385	3614
Eighth Plan (1992–97)	55925.6	65173	25110	36374.9
Ninth Plan (1997–2002)	119373	117562.8	47280	85509.6
Tenth Plan (2002–07)	225977	200569	98968	36456
Eleventh Plan (2007–12)	572443	612058	95380	53108
Twelfth Plan (2012–17)	1204172	–	80984	–

Source: Five Year Plan documents, Planning Commission and Economic Surveys, Ministry of Finance.

❑ ROADWAYS : GROWTH

While, as stated earlier, the transport demand for freight and passenger movement is met mainly by road transport and railways, between these two modes, the share of road transport has steadily grown. According to the Planning Commission, the roadways' "intermodal share in carrying freight, which was around 14% in 1950–51, had increased to around 61% in 2004–05. The share of road transport in passenger movement has also witnessed a quantum jump from 15% in 1950–51 to an estimated 87% of the total traffic by the end of the Tenth Plan." (Eleventh Plan, 2007–12)

Table 10.2: Roads and Rail Network: Growth

Item	1950–51	1970–71	1990–91	2000–01	2011–12	2019-20
Roads	399	918	1998	3374	4690	5898
Total Length ('000kms)						
National Highways (kms)	19700	24000	34000	57700	76818	114158
Rail						
Route kms.	53600	59790	62367	63028	64600	67956
Running kms.	59315	71669	78607	81865	89801	99235

Source: Roads: Five Year Plans, Planning Commission; Ministry of Road Transport Highways, Govt. of India; Rail: Statistical Summary, Indian Railways, Ministry of Railways (Railway Board).

The total road length in India increased more than 11 times during the six decades between 1951 and 2011. From 3.99 lakh kilometres (kms.) in March 1951, the road length increased to 46.90 lakh kilometres by March 2011 and to 58.98 lakh kms. by 2019-20. Concomitantly, the surfaced road length increased both in absolute and relative terms. The length of surfaced roads which was 1.57 lakh kilometres (39.35 per cent of total road length) in 1951 increased to 25.25 lakh kilometres (53.83 per cent of total road length) in March 2011 and further to 37.30 lakh kms. (63.24 per cent) by 2019-20. Though India has one of the largest road networks in the world, the quality and standard of construction and upkeep of the road system, especially on state highways and in cities and towns, have been grossly neglected and are matters of great concern which need lot of attention. These have to receive the same kind of attention and rigor in standards that the National Highway network has been getting since 2000. It must be conceded that even the Rural roads under the PMGSY scheme, which carry much less traffic and vehicle loads, have been receiving better attention and quality control in their construction than what the state highways and city roads have been getting.

There are six categories of roads and their growth was as shown in Table 10.3. It shows that there has been significant increase in National highways, Rural, and Urban roads in the two decades from 1991. The National Highway network, however, has come under considerable pressure as large segments of State Highways were upgraded to National Highways.

Some of the constraints of the road sector can be gauged from the following facts:

- While the aggregate length of roads increased 8-fold from 0.4 million kms in 1950-51 to 3.32 million kms in 1995-96 and 5.89 million kms. in 2019-20. The number of passenger buses went up 13-fold from 0.34 lakh to 4.5 lakh and goods vehicle fleet 22-fold from 0.82 lakh to 17.85 lakh in the same period. The number of passenger buses has further gone up phenomenally to 18.64 lakh and goods vehicle fleet to 122.56 lakh during the same period.

- The number of two-wheelers and cars, jeeps, and taxis has increased by leaps and bounds between 1951 and 2017 placing a heavy burden on roads, especially in cities and towns, apart from the problems due to pollution. (See Table 10.4).

- Despite its importance to the national economy, the road network is grossly inadequate in various respects. It is unable to handle high traffic density and high speeds at many places and has poor riding quality.
- Out of the total road length constructed during the Eighth Plan (1992–97), 66 per cent were constructed under the Jawahar Rozgar Yojana (JRY). These roads were not of much use for the movement of heavy traffic.
- Out of the surfaced roads, only about 20 per cent are considered to be in good condition, which compares adversely with other countries.
- The national highway network, which carries about 40 per cent of the road traffic, forms only 1.93 per cent of the total road network.

Table 10.3: Road Network by Categories (in kilometres)

Item	1951	1991	2001	2011	2017
1. National Highways	19,811 (4.95)	33.650 (1.45)	57,737 (1.71)	70,934 (1.51)	1,14,158 (1.93)
2. State Highways	1,73,723 (43.44)	1,27,311 (5.47)	1.32,100 (3.99)	1,63,898 (3.49)	1,75,036 (2.96)
3. District/PWD Roads	–	5,09,435 (21.89)	7,36,001 (21.82)	10,05,327 (21.43)	5,86,181 (9.94)
4. Rural Roads	2.06,408 (51.61)	12,60,430 (54.16)	19,72,016 (58.46)	27,49,805 (58.63)	41,66,916 (70.65)
5. Urban Roads	–	186,799 (8.03)	252,001 (7.12)	411,840 (8.78)	5,26,483 (8.93)
6. Project Roads	–	2,09,737 (9.01)	2,23,665 (6.32)	2,88,539 (6.15)	3,28,897 (5.58)
Total	**3,99,942**	**23,27,362**	**33,73,520**	**46,90,342**	**58,97,671**

Note: Figures in brackets are percentages to total road network.

Source: Basic Road Statistics of India, Ministry of Road Transport Highways, Govt. of India.

Table 10.4: Category-wise Number of Registered Motor Vehicles in India: 1951–2017 (numbers in thousand)

Year	All Vehicles	Two Wheelers	Cars, Jeeps & Taxis	Buses	Goods Vehicles	Others
1951	306	27	159	34	82	4
Per cent	100	8.82	51.96	11.1	26.80	1.31
2001	54991	38556	7058	634	2948	5795
Per cent	100	70.1	12.8	1.2	5.4	10.5
2006	89618	64743	11526	992	4436	7921
Per cent	100	72.2	12.9	1.1	4.9	8.8
2017	253311	187091	33688	1864	12256	18411
Per cent	100	73.86	13.30	0.74	4.84	7.27

Source: Ministry of Surface Transport and Shipping, Five Year Plans, Planning Commission.

Overburdened Roads

In India, about 57 per cent of the total goods is transported by road, as compared to 22 per cent in China and 37 per cent in the US. And the share of rail is only 36 per cent compared to 48 per cent in the US and 47 per cent in China. Though a large part of India's freight traffic comprises bulk materials which can be moved conveniently over long distances by rail and waterways, the share of coastal shipping and inland waterways is just 6 per cent as compared to 14 per cent in US and 30 per cent in China. This implies greater dependence on fossil fuels and high level of greenhouse gas emissions.

Two Major Developments

Two major, game-changing developments took place in India's road sector towards the end of 1990's and the early part of 2000's. Firstly, the decision taken in 1999 to launch a **Golden Quadrilateral project** to establish high-class transportation link between the four Metros, covering many other cities of India and to develop the National Highways to international standards, and secondly, the decision in December 2000 to launch the **PM's Gram Sadak Yojana (PMGSY)** to link rural habitations with a certain population with the nearby town through all-weather roads.

A Task Force on Infrastructure, headed by the Deputy Chairman of the Planning Commission, proposed in 1999 building a six-lane expressway of 7,000 km. length, having North-South and East-West corridors, four-laning of National Highways, and upgrading five airports to world-class standards.

The Golden Quadrilateral is a network of highways connecting India's four major metropolitan cities, viz., Delhi, Mumbai, Chennai, and Kolkata thereby forming a quadrilateral link. The largest highway project in India, it was started in 2001 as part of National Highways Development Project (NHDP).The overall length of the quadrilateral is 5,846 km consisting of four/six lane express highways. It was built to international standards and paved the way for public-private partnerships (PPPs) mode in infrastructure building.

The Golden Quadrilateral, work on which has been completed, had four sections:

- 1,454 km stretch of National Highway from Delhi to Kolkata. It runs through Delhi, Haryana, Uttar Pradesh, Bihar, Jharkhand, and West Bengal connecting major cities, viz., Delhi, Agra, Kanpur, Allahabad, and Varanasi.
- 1,684 km stretch from Kolkata to Chennai passing through the states of West Bengal, Orissa, Andhra Pradesh, and Tamil Nadu connecting Kolkata, Kharagpur, Bhubaneswar, Visakhapatanam, and Chennai.
- 1,290 km stretch from Chennai to Mumbai passing through Maharashtra, Karnataka, Andhra Pradesh, and Tamil Nadu connecting Chennai, Krishnagiri, Bengaluru, Hubbali, Pune, and Mumbai.
- 1,419 km stretch between Delhi and Mumbai passing through Maharashtra, Gujarat, Rajasthan, and Haryana connecting Delhi, Gurgaon, Jaipur, Ajmer, Udaipur, Ahmedabad, Vadodara, Surat, and Mumbai.

Besides, North-South and East-West corridors link Kashmir to Kanyakumari and Silchar to Porbandar. The project envisages four/six-laning of the existing network. The National highway projects initially made considerable progress but later ran into problems.

Problems in Highway Projects Construction

The financial package for the Golden Quadrilateral was met through cess on petrol and diesel, multilateral funding, normal budgetary allocations, and market borrowing. But many other highway projects got stalled due to issues associated with land acquisition, shifting of utilities, obtaining environment and forest clearance, approval for road over bridges, poor performance of some contractors due to cash flow constraints, and law and order problems in some cases. The Build-Operate-Transfer (BOT) model has not received the expected response from the private sector in road construction, due to concerns and uncertainties about future toll receipts. The relatively better response of the private sector to BOT Annuity scheme, which involves a guaranteed annuity payment by the National Highway Authority of India (NHAI) to the investor, is a pointer to this fact. The stalled projects have resulted in stressed assets for banks which had lent funds for such projects. (For more on this, see Ch. 24, pp.24.1-4)

Hybrid Annuity Model

The government has approved the hybrid annuity model (HAM) for building National Highways (NH) to speed up the construction of roads in the country by renewing interest of private developers in highway projects. 40 per cent the Project Cost is to be provided by the Government as Construction Support during the construction period and the balance 60 per cent as annuity payments over the operations period along with interest thereon to the concessionaire.

National Highway projects worth about ₹ 10,000 crore were approved during 2018-19 under the hybrid annuity mode. The objective was to maximize the quantum of implemented projects within the available financial resources of the Government and to revive private sector participation in the sector. Toll fee collection from the highways projects developed under the HAM is the responsibility of the Government/Authority.

In order to tap the benefit of long-term funds like pension fund, insurance fund, wealth fund etc. into road construction sector, Ministry for Road Transport and Highways introduced models like HAM and TOT (Toll-Operate-Transfer) for execution of highway projects.

PM's Gram Sadak Yojana (PMGSY)

A major rural roads programme, transformational in nature, called the Pradhan Mantri Gram Sadak Yojana (PMGSY), was launched in October 2000 to provide connectivity to villages with nearby towns. The primary objective was to link unconnected habitations in rural areas, with a population of 1,000 and above, with all-weather roads by 2003, and those with a population of 500 and above by the end of the Tenth Plan Period, i.e., 2007. In respect of the hill states in the North-East, Sikkim, Himachal Pradesh, Jammu and Kashmir, Uttaranchal, and the desert areas, habitations with a population of 250 persons and above were to be covered under the scheme. The programme was meant to ensure equitable development of the rural roads network in different states and districts to fully tap the latent potential for growth in rural areas. The PMGSY is being implemented as a 100 per cent centrally sponsored scheme.

Following the 73rd Constitution Amendment Act, the upkeep of rural roads has become the responsibility of the Panchayati Raj Institutions (PRIs). All the rural roads constructed or upgraded are transferred to the concerned PRIs and are to be maintained by them. The state authorities would remit the required funds from the State Government funds for maintenance to the PRI.

Under the PMGSY, a total of 6,26,497 kilometres (kms.) of all-weather rural roads have been so far sanctioned for construction out of which 5,19,847 kms. had been constructed till October 2017 and construction of 1,06,650 kms. was in progress. (See also Chapter 17 on PMGSY).

Roadways Complementary to Rail

Road transport has steadily expanded its scope of operation and now, not merely carries freight over long distances but also acts as a mode for the last mile for goods carried, and for passengers who travel by rail, since in the interior parts and hinterlands, railway does not operate and have access. It thus not only plays a complementary role to railways in moving freight and passengers, but even has a dominant share. In fact, there is need for railways to assume a bigger role than it does at present, but due to various limitations such as track capacity, problems in building more tracks in urban areas, funds crunch, etc., this is not happening. The limitations in expanding the suburban train service in Mumbai due to heavily populated areas and lack of space for laying additional tracks is a case in point.

Impact of Liberalization and Growth

The process of liberalization and opening up of the economy since the mid-1980's, and even more so from 1991, has resulted in much faster economic growth than the preceding decades. This has led to an ever increasing demand for an efficient transportation system to meet the needs of industry and trade. A reliable and modern transport infrastructure and services are important factors that enable the country to become competitive in international trade and attract foreign direct investment. That China was able to attract foreign investment on a massive scale and become a manufacturing powerhouse in the last two decades was, in no small measure, due to the massive expansion of infrastructural facilities. It must, however, be conceded that China has about three times land area than India, and even with a larger population, China's density of population is far less—142 per sq. km. compared to India's 382 per sq. km. And China's political system is vastly different from India's which makes a big difference when it comes to policy making and implementation.

The structural changes in the economy, the increasing share of industry and services in country's GDP, large-scale migration from rural to urban areas, and steep increase in vehicular traffic, year after year, all place a heavy burden on the transport system. There are limits to public investments and unless more private investment is forthcoming, the task of augmenting facilities in the sector will continue to pose problems. That more foreign investment and foreign aid are becoming available is a positive sign but this is dependent on the country's policies becoming more attractive, transparent, and business-friendly.

Challenges Facing the Road Sector

Maintenance of Roadways

The road network built at a huge cost needs to be maintained properly to prevent deterioration, ensure its continuous use in an optimum manner, and ensure safety of road users. But maintenance of roads, being a non-plan activity, has tended to be neglected due to lack of finances. Even as new assets are created to meet the increasing demands, it is equally important to ensure that the assets already created are in good shape. While the maintenance of the National Highways which bear high density traffic is undertaken by NHAI, the State, district roads and roads in cities and towns are poorly maintained. State governments and municipal corporations have to pay greater attention on this aspect.

Safety on Roads

This is an area of great concern in the road sector as accident rates are quite high in India. Over 1.3 lakh people are reported to die annually in road accidents alone and their number is rising. This is about 10 per cent of the world figure, though India's share in number of vehicles in the world is only 1 per cent. Accidents are due to a variety of reasons such as bad condition of roads, congestion, speeding and rash driving of vehicles, non-observance of traffic rules, poor street lighting causing difficulties at night, etc. Much of these is due to inadequacy of the road system and apathy on the part of authorities responsible for construction and maintenance of roads and for provision of various other facilities–lighting, signages, speed barriers, enforcement of traffic regulations, etc. Some efforts have been taken in educating and training drivers, especially truck drivers who operate on the highways, at Motor Driving Schools, but this effort has been on a very limited scale compared to the magnitude of task involved.

Traffic and Pollution

There has been a phenomenal growth in the number of personal vehicles in recent years, especially in the metros and larger cities, as will be seen from Table 10.4. This is a major problem in cities and towns which have not been able to provide adequate and reliable mass public transport facility. It is only, of late, that some of the cities are having, or in the process of providing, rapid transit system like Metro rail. And special funds have been allotted to cities and towns under the Jawaharlal Nehru National Urban Renewal Mission (JNNURM) for modernizing transport systems with new-age vehicles. But even these measures may not be enough to solve the problem, as is now being experienced in New Delhi where there is a raging debate on solutions to be adopted to contain vehicular pollution. Despite having an excellent metro network which carries sizeable section of commuters, the problems of pollution on the roads in Delhi continue unabated and is even getting worse with massive addition of vehicles everyday.

The problem lies elsewhere as much of the pollution is caused by motor vehicles which ply on petrol and diesel. That pollution is a source of health hazard is by now a well established fact. Unless solutions can be found in the form of pollution-free bus systems on adequate scale to carry the mass of commuters and thus reducing the use of personalized means of transport, the problem will persist. Technological solutions like electric vehicles operting on batteries and minimizing, if not eliminating, the use of vehicles dependent on fossil fuels are imperative steps needed. In some cities in other countries, restrictions of various types are imposed—limiting the ownership of vehicles, prohibitive parking or congestion fees in busy areas, restrictions on entry of motor vehicles into busy areas, etc. But these are just palliative measures and not long-term and enduring solutions.

User-pay Concept

Provision of infrastructural facilities calls for heavy investments. Apart from private investment which may be forthcoming, at least a portion of this will have to be borne by the users also. This is done through cess levied on petrol and diesel and/or toll collected from vehicles using the roads after construction. However, sometimes such measures are met with resistance from public, political parties, etc. who expect such facilities to be provided free. There have even been violent protests and attacks on toll booths at some places which is detrimental to public interests. While such facilities are primarily the responsibility of the State, the industry, trade and corporate bodies, and public at large too have to share the burden to an extent. This is especially justified considering that in India, fuel for vehicles is supplied at subsidized rates. An exemption may be provided for public transport such as buses which carry bulk of the common people.

❑ RAILWAYS GROWTH AND IMPROVEMENTS

Indian Railways is a behemoth organization employing over 13 lakh staff, operating over 13,000 trains carrying about 23 million passengers daily, and connecting over 7,000 stations spread across the country. It is one of the largest railway systems in the world in terms of route kilometers. (See Box 10.1). Considering the size of the country and the requirements of the economy, the expansion of the railway network has been inadequate. Indian Railways have added 11,864 km of new lines since independence. The length of broad gauge route has doubled from 25,258 km to 55,188 km through new lines as well as gauge conversion of 21,658 km from meter and narrow gauges to broad gauge.

Box 10.1: Indian Railways: A Massive Network

(Data as on 2019-20)

Route Length: 67,956 km.

Route Length Electrified: 20,275 (31.45 % of total route length)

Running Track Length: 99,235 km.

Route Km. Electrified: 39,329 km. (57.87% of Route km.)

Total Track Length: 1,26,360 km.

Originating Passengers: 8086 million

8,479 freight trains carry about 3.32 million tonnes of freight every day.

The allocations and investments in railways under the Plans have shown steady increase though up to the Fifth Plan, the allocations were modest. (See Table 10.5).

Table 10.5: Plan Outlays/Expenditure on Railways (In ₹ crore)

First Plan (1951–56):	267	Seventh Plan (1985–90):	12334
Second Plan (1956–61):	900	Eighth Plan (1992–97):	27202
Third Plan (1961–66):	1326	Ninth Plan (1997–2002):	49590
Fourth Plan (1969–74):	1050	Tenth Plan (2002–07):	84708
Fifth Plan (1974–79):	2202	Eleventh Plan (2007–12):	219717
Sixth Plan (1980–85):	5100	Twelfth Plan (2012–17):	519221

Improvements and Upgradation of Systems and Facilities

With increased outlays from the Seventh Plan onwards, the railways could take up measures to improve and upgrade various facilities and modernize the system. These included improvements, renewal and doubling of tracks, electrification of routes, improvements in signalling and communication systems, improved railway coaches and locomotives, better facilities at stations and railway booking centres, and putting more safety and security measures in place. Adoption of information technology in various activities, particularly the computerization of railway seat booking system was one of the most important changes from the viewpoint of rail users. All this helped to improve the image of the railways though much more has to be done to further modernize and perfect the systems. A proposal to modernize about 400 railway stations with private partnership and investment is also being actively pursued.

Focus Areas and Reform Measures

The areas on which the railways have to focus further and some of the reform measures required are discussed below:

Overburdened routes

The railways' Golden Quadrilateral linking the North-South and East-West arterial routes with extended corridors, referred to earlier, make up only about 15 per cent of the total route length of the railways but it transports 52 per cent of passenger traffic and 58 per cent of total freight load. This highlights the high saturation and over-utilized capacity on popular trunk routes. Since passenger and freight traffic move on the same tracks in India, it has not been able to increase speed or capacity in a significant manner relative to global benchmarks.

With the Indian Railways building two world-class dedicated freight corridors (see below on this), it will not only transform the way goods are transported along India's busiest routes but also release more space for carrying passenger traffic on the trunk routes.

While at present, railways operate 13,000 passenger trains on its network, it is estimated that it would require more additional 20,000 trains to meet the rising demand by 2024. The railways have invited request for qualification (RFQ) from private players to operate passenger trains, a project that entails huge investment. It would also require additional coaches to be built which would give boost to Make in India programme.

Freight Movement

Railways play a major role in transporting bulk freight and long-distance passenger traffic. While freight has been the key earner for railways, one of the reasons for the decline in the financial fortunes of the railways was due to losing out on the freight market share to roadways. The railways cannot afford to continue with the historical growth rate of 3 to 4 per cent in freight traffic and need to pursue a higher growth rate. In view of the massive investment taking place in the highway and pipeline sectors, the railways must reorient its strategy to cope with the competitive market. Or else, railways would get marginalized and this would also lead to a slowdown in the economy due to infrastructural bottlenecks.

It is a positive sign that freight loading has lately shown much improvement with railways adopting a market-focused strategy aimed at capturing large volumes of traffic using efficiently the assets and resources. The improved performance was achieved by optimally increasing the carrying capacity and loading of wagons on critical routes. A realignment of tariffs in response to the competitive conditions in the market and tapping the potential during the lean season also helped to achieve this.

While the Indian Railways carry more passengers than the Chinese Railways, the latter carries 4.5 times more freight than the Indian Railways, due to the larger investments made in expanding the railway infrastructure which also helped to improve productivity.

Dedicated Freight Corridors (DFCs)

The Dedicated Railway Freight Corridor (DFC) projects initiated on the Western and the Eastern routes to create capacity and improve quality of services is a significant step. The 1469 km Western corridor is to connect Jawaharlal Nehru Port to Dadri and Tughlakabad in the North while the 1232 km Eastern corridor will connect Ludhiana to Sonnagar via Dadri and Khurja, which will facilitate transfer from one corridor to another. The Eastern corridor is to be extended to the Kolkata region to connect the proposed deep-sea port. For increased throughput and to reduce the cost of operations, DFCs are designed to run double stack container trains with 25 tonne axle load running at higher speed.

Safety and Security

Safety should be the paramount concern of railways. Even occasional occurrences of train accidents resulting in the loss of precious human lives dents the image of the organization. The accidents occur due to faults in the systems-signalling, defects in track or coaches, unmanned level crossings, human errors, etc. Many committees, including the High-level Safety Review Committee headed by Anil Kakodkar, former Chairman of the Atomic Energy Commission, which submitted its report in 2012, have gone into the issue of safety and made several recommendations. Apart from pointing out deficiencies in performance due to poor infrastructure and insufficient resources, the Committee pointed out the need for greater empowerment at the functional level, elimination of all manned and unmanned level crossings, inducting coaches with higher safety features-fire-proof and crash-resistant coaches to reduce fatalities in the event of accidents-and adoption of anti-collision devices and advanced signalling system for the entire trunk route length of 19,000 km within 5 years. The Committee suggested setting up a Special Purpose Vehicle for implementing some of the measures and raising funds through a cess on passengers, deferring dividend and grant from the Central government. The Railway Board is looking into the implementation of the recommendations.

Railways have also taken additional measures to strengthen security of passengers on board the trains and at stations. Security of railway passengers is a shared responsibility of the Railway Protection Force (RPF) and the Government Reserve Police (GRP). More powers are given to the RPF in ensuring security of passengers on trains and within railway premises. Deployment of women police force has been made for security and assistance of women passengers.

REFORMS IN RAILWAYS

Rationalization of Rail Tariff

An important distortion in policy is the skewed tariff policy which overcharges freight movement in order to subsidize ordinary passenger traffic which also affects the competitiveness of the freight segment. At present, there is excessive cross-subsidization from freight to passenger services which needs to be corrected gradually. This will provide scope for greater resource mobilization.

Accounting System Reform

The system of accounting followed by Indian Railways is not transparent. While this system has worked well for the internal management of the railways, it is not well understood in the business world outside the railways. The Expert Group on Railways has suggested that the accounts of the railways should be in accordance with the standard business procedures.

The Union Budget Speech of 2016-17 had referred to reforming railway accounting system. The Railways initiated "Accounting Reforms Project' which envisaged the introduction of "Accrual Accounting" which would give a true and fair picture of railways' financial position and bring about transparency. A further step to achieve real transformation was to adopt "Outcome Budgeting" which would track and link expenditures to desired outcomes. Railways introduced Accrual Accounting in Zonal Railways and Production Units in a phased manner. This was to be followed by introduction of Performance Costing and Outcome Budgeting in all the units.

Managerial Reform

An Expert Group on Railways had considered the issue of restructuring the organization. The Group recommended that the Indian Railways should function on commercial lines and its management may be given a certain degree of autonomy as available to any other commercial organization. It suggested that the railways should be compensated for meeting obligations that are purely social and developmental in nature. The Group felt that the railways may be corporatized, to enable it to work as an independent commercial organization.

Corporatization and Outsourcing

Indian Railways have initiated the process of the corporatization of its production units such as Chittaranjan Locomotive Works, Integral Coach Factory, etc. The Railways have seven production units which are to be corporatized in a phased manner. Once corporatized, these units will be autonomous and will be able to take independent decisions and upgrade their technology without waiting for the approval of the Railway Ministry.

Further, in order to provide fast and high-quality services comparable to that of the developed countries, enhance efficiency and competitiveness, the Railways have begun to outsource many of its non-core activities/works including maintenance and management of stations, railway colonies and hospitals, as well as management of schools through contracting agencies. Outsourcing by railways would create lakhs of jobs while the strength of staff in railways may be gradually brought down making the railways leaner and more productive.

New Generation Locomotives

Ministry of Railways is setting up a factory at Madhepura in Bihar with a foreign partner for supply of advanced electric locomotives. During the period of supply programme, the factory at Madhepura will supply 800 electric locomotives with performance guarantees based on best international practices. This locomotive will have very high energy efficiency and will help in mitigating the emission of greenhouse gases. This is an initiative on the lines envisaged under the 'Make in India' programme and successful execution of this project by the joint venture (JV) route will usher Indian Railways into a new era of reforms and will provide impetus to PPP funding of railway projects. Another factory planned at Marowhra, also in Bihar, will manufacture diesel locomotives with higher capacity.

High Speed Train

As part of the railway modernization programme, India is to build a High-speed rail link between Mumbai and Ahmedabad with technical and financial aid from Japan which had undertaken the feasibility study. The agreement signed with Japan includes long-term financial aid at a nominal rate of interest.

The work being executed by National High Speed Rail Corporation Limited (NHSRCL) is in progress. Though it has faced hurdles due to land acquisition issues, the authorities are hopeful of completing it as planned.

❑ SHIPPING AND PORTS

Shipping

India has a vast coastline of about 7,517 km. including islands. There are 12 major ports and 187 minor ports along the coast providing infrastructural facilities for shipping. The spurt in the growth of the economy and foreign trade in the last two decades has underlined the importance and criticality of the shipping sector for India. Bulk of the country's Export-Import trade takes place through the maritime route. One of the objectives of the Foreign Trade Policy 2004-09 was to double the percentage of India's share of global merchandize trade within the next five years taking it to 1.5 per cent. With 8.42 million gross tonnages (GT), India stands at 20th rank among the maritime nations, in terms of fleet size, with a share of 1.19 per cent of the world fleet.

Share of Indian Ships

The share of Indian ships in the carriage of India's overseas trade declined consistently from 31.5 per cent in 1999-2000 to 13.7 per cent in 2004-05 and further to 7 per cent in 2015-16. There is a need for policy intervention to arrest this declining trend. Indian shipping fleet is characterized by the predominance of oil tankers and bulk carriers. While at the end of March 2012, oil tankers accounted for 63.76 per cent of the Deadweight Tonnage (DWT) and bulk carriers for 28.77 per cent, all other vessel types such as liner vessels, offshore supply vessels, etc. accounted for a mere 7.47 per cent.

During the Twelfth Plan (2012-17), it is planned to increase Indian tonnage from 11.03 million Gross tonne (GT) to 12.4 million GT.

Coastal Shipping

Coastal shipping serves as an integral part of the domestic and overseas trade of merchandize. It is a viable, eco-friendly alternative to the stretched rail and road infrastructure with low socio-economic cost. Apart from their substantial contribution to the nation's trade and economy, shipping services play a crucial role as the major source of income for the population in many of the coastal states and act as the lifeline, especially for places such as Andaman & Nicobar Islands and Lakshadweep Islands. During 2004-05, the coastal traffic at major ports was 109.80 mt, accounting for 28.6 per cent of the total major ports traffic and growing at 5.81per cent CAGR.

During the last decade, coastal shipping has exhibited significant growth in smaller size vessels such as Liners passenger-cum-cargo launches, tugs, dredgers, pilot/survey launches, etc. Now, coastal shipping also includes activities like offshore supply and multi-purpose support for the oil and gas exploration and production, port and harbour services, and dredging.

Ports

Ports constitute the inter-modal interface between maritime and road and rail transport. India has 12 major ports and 187 notified non-major (minor or intermediate) ports along the coastline and sea islands. Almost 95 per cent by volume and 70 per cent by value of India's global merchandize trade is carried through the sea route. Overseas cargo accounts for about 77 per cent of the total cargo handled at Indian ports. Of the 12 major ports, 11 are administered by the respective Port Trusts and Ennore Port at Chennai, the 12th major port, which started functioning in February 2001, is corporatized.

Some of the problems and deficiencies at Indian ports contributing to longer turnaround time and detentions of ships are:

- The average turnaround time for ships berthed at the port improved from 4.24 days during the last year of the Ninth Plan (1997-2002) to 2.58 days during the last year of the Tenth Plan, viz., 2006-07.
- Most of the ports are not equipped with latest navigational aides and facilities such as Vessel Traffic Management System, sophisticated marine crafts, etc.
- There are channel restrictions in width leading to unidirectional movements of ships.
- Also, the number of dedicated berths available is limited leading to bunching of vessels.
- Inadequate cargo handling equipments to handle larger vessels combined.

The government has drawn up a scheme for private participation in major ports mainly in container terminals, specialized cargo berths, warehousing /storage facilities, etc. on BOT basis with a concession period not exceeding 30 years. The scheme also includes formation of joint venture by the ports with private operators selected on the basis of competitive bidding.The Indian ports need further modernization and expansion to meet the growing needs of the economy and also to play a larger role in international shipping.The bulk of capacity augmentation would have to be undertaken through the PPPs and with investment by captive users. New berths at major ports may have to be constructed through the PPP mode.

❑ INLAND WATER TRANSPORT (IWT)

India has about 14,500 km of navigable waterways which comprise rivers, canals, backwaters, creeks, etc. About 45 million tons of cargo is being moved annually by IWT. The Inland Waterways Authority of India (IWAI) was constituted in 1986 for the development and regulation of inland waterways for shipping and navigation. However, most waterways suffer from navigational inadequacies such as shallow waters, narrow width, siltation, and bank erosion. Consequently, its operations are currently restricted to about

5,200 km of major rivers and 485 km of canals suitable for mechanized craft operations. (See Box 10.4 on p.10.32 on International Multi-Modal Transport)

National Waterways

Initially, three waterways were declared as National Waterways (NWs). These are:

NW 1: Ganga from Haldia to Allahabad (1620 km);

NW 2: Brahmaputra from Dhubri to Dadiya (891 km); and

NW3: West Coast Canal from Kottapuram to Kollam, including Champakara and Udyogamandal canals (205 km).

The first one covers the states of Uttar Pradesh, Bihar, Jharkhand, and West Bengal. The second covers Assam, and the third Kerala. A number of private operators provide their services in all the three waterways while the public sector unit, the Central Inland Water Transport Corporation operates on the first and the second waterway.

Later in November 2008, two more waterways, NW 4 and NW 5, were declared as National Waterways.

NW 4: Canal system from Kakinada to Puducherry (Pondicherry) integrated with Godavari and Krishna rivers (1095 km).

NW 5: East Coast Canal integrated with Brahmani river and delta of Mahanadi river (623 km), and Barak river in Assam (152 km).

When these two waterways are added to the existing three, the total coverage will be 4,500 km.

Steps to Promote Waterways

During the Tenth Plan (2002–07), action was taken on various fronts to promote this segment. These included maintenance of fairway including procurement of vessels for channel development (dredgers, survey launches, etc.), setting up terminals, provision of navigational aids, procurement of cargo vessels for demonstration purpose, techno-economic feasibility studies on other waterways, assistance to States under Centrally Sponsored Schemes (CSS), and Inland Vessel Building Subsidy Scheme to entrepreneurs for procurement of IWT vessels.

❑ AIR TRANSPORT

Air transport, which is the fastest means of travel, is critical for a country of sub-continental size like India. Civil aviation is one of the fastest growing sectors in India since it was thrown open to the private sector.

The beginning of aviation in India dates back to 1911 when an airmail flight was operated over a short distance between Allahabad and Naini by a French pilot, Henri Piquet, with a load of mail on a two-seater bi-plane. In 1912, a domestic air service was started between Karachi and Delhi by Indian Air Services in collaboration with the UK-based Imperial Airways, as an extension of the latter's London-Karachi flight. In 1932, J.R.D. Tata flew a single-engine Puss Moth plane from Karachi to Bombay with a load of mail. And thus, India's first airline—Tata Airlines—was born.

In 1948, J.R.D. Tata went on to start Air India International which helped to place the Indian aviation industry on a firm footing. Though the airline was nationalized in 1953, Tata, a visionary leader, remained at the helm of Air India till 1978, making it one of the most efficient airlines in the world.

Indian Airlines was another entity which focused primarily on the domestic routes, along with some international services to neighbouring countries in Asia. It was state-owned, and administered by the Ministry of Civil Aviation. Along with Air India, it was one of the two flag carriers of India. The two airlines were merged in 2007. The airline industry grew rapidly both in terms of passengers and cargo carried as the data in Table 10.6 show, but at the same time, it was constrained by lack of resources for expansion and upgradation, and was burdened by bureaucratic control until reform measures were taken in the 1990's. As a result, the sector, till it was opened up and private entities were allowed to enter, could not meet customers' demands and expectations through the 1970's and '80's when the economy was expanding. There were not enough flights to accommodate the rising traffic and there were other operational problems as airports had not been modernized to cope with the growing volume of traffic.

As will be seen from Table 10.6, there has been phenomenal growth in both passengers cargo, carried by airlines and handled by airports in India, driven by the surge in economic growth in the last three decades. In the recent past, the opening of more airports in smaller towns and underserved areas under the UDAN Regional Connectivity Scheme (RCS) has helped in this growth. During 2019, 136 RCS routes were started under UDAN and over 25 lakh passengers were flown under this scheme. 44 RCS airports have been operationalized for flights by January 2020 and 248 routes had commenced functioning.

Table 10.6: Civil Aviation: Domestic and International Services

	2002-03	2010-11	2013-14	2019
Passengers (in Million)				
International	16.65	34.37	46.63	69.36
Domestic	**32.04**	**89.38**	**122.42**	**277.57**
Total	48.69	123.75	169.05	346.93
Cargo (in '000 tons)	6	19	74	90
International	693.36	1270.71	1442.51	2079.02
Domestic	375.08	690.90	835.40	1362.98
Total	1068.44	1961.61	2277.91	3442.00

Source: Ministry of Civil Aviation, Annual Reports.

Open Skies policy: Till 1990, government-owned airlines dominated the Indian aviation industry. A policy of "open skies" for air cargo was adopted in 1990 whereby Indian or foreign carriers were allowed to operate scheduled and non-scheduled cargo services to/from any airports in India. The Government followed it up with a policy of allowing private carriers to operate passenger flights. The period since the adoption of an open skies policy has seen a strong growth in international air cargo traffic and the Indian aviation sector was set for rapid and dramatic transformation. Many private Indian carriers entered the scene and started services. Besides, many foreign airlines also were given greater access to the Indian aviation market. Foreign airlines have partnered with Indian private carriers to boost capacity and expand the services. All these had a salutary effect on the aviation industry which has seen rapid, healthy growth in both passenger and cargo traffic.

Meanwhile, the government merged Air India and Indian Airlines in 2007. By merging the two national carriers, the government hoped to trim the set-up and eliminate duplication and overlap of services and optimize their potential strengths. This was considered necessary in view of the losses incurred by the airlines. The integration, however, has proved to be a challenge as it gave rise to various organizational and managerial issues.

Airports in India

Airports in India are managed by the Airports Authority of India (AAI) under the Ministry of Civil Aviation. The Government of India constituted the International Airports Authority of India (IAAI) in

1972 to manage the nation's international airports while the National Airports Authority (NAA) was constituted in 1986 to look after domestic airports. The organizations were merged in April 1995 by an Act of Parliament and was named as Airports Authority of India (AAI). AAI provides Air Traffic Management Services (ATMS) over the entire Indian air space and adjoining oceanic areas with ground installations at all airports. It is responsible for creating, upgrading, maintaining, and managing civil aviation infrastructure in India.

Modernization and Privatisation of Airports

With the phenomenal growth in air traffic, the importance of air transport in the whole economy has increased considerably and the need for modernizing airports and other related facilities arose. Accordingly, the government took steps to modernize airports–both major ones and those in smaller cities. The major airports have been upgraded to international standards. Aviation infrastructure, especially airport facilities and air navigation services, have also been significantly expanded and improved to meet the increasing needs of both operational requirements and facilities for travellers.

Alongside, the government has drawn up a policy of privatizing airports and has privatized some of the major and medium-size airports. This involves handing over the airport to private companies on lease for a specific period of time. The private entity would not only manage the airports but also carry out expansion and modernization. The government had handed over the Mumbai airport by a transaction governed by Operations Management and Development Agreement (OMDA), which was a 30-years' concessions agreement with a further 30-year optional scope of renewal. Delhi airport was also privatized. After the lease period is over, the privatized airports will once again be back under the control of Airports Authority of India (AAI).

In the Union Budget for 2021-22, Finance Minister referred to "monetizing operating public infrastructure assets a very important financing option for new infrastructure construction" and stated that more airports in Tier II and III towns will be monetized for operations and management concession.

* There has been a lot of debate over the rationale of privatization of airports with arguments for and against the move. Some of the implications of airport privatization are mentioned below.
* Proponents of privatization argue that since public airports were being poorly managed, it was time that India modernised its airports to improve their functioning and service standards and this requires management by private entities.
* The modernization and expansion of airports to serve the expanding needs of the growing economy calls for substantial capital expenditure which the government would not be able to meet considering the scarce resources and other competing needs especially in the Social sector.
* Efficiency might improve substantially, including passenger experience but might not result in profitability. A case study found out that the efficiency of Mumbai airport improved substantially post privatisation but profitability and performance improvement of employees is a long way ahead.
* Experience of airports initially privatized showed that services like managing the terminals and operations improved substantially in comparison to the past and it had a positive impact on the passenger experience and perceptions.
* With privatization, a large proportion of the AAI employees, technical and non-technical including all the contract staff and labour transitioned to the private entity. Those who thus moved over to the private operator have been able to continue operations and merge well by coordinating with the new management including foreign consultants and expatriates working with the private operator in ensuring smooth operations on the technical front.

* **The process of privatization was, however, not without challenges. These include:**
* With the government keen on pursuing privatisation of airports, it is essential to fix socio-economic and legal issues and finetune the policy framework.
* Any prospective government hiring, training and retention of staff at other airports which may come up for privatization in future has to be consistent to blend well with the privatization process.
* It is argued by the critics of privatization that given the importance and potential of airport infrastructure, private players would tend to overcharge for the facilities hurting the users of airports. For this the government would have oversight with some government nominees on the Management Boards of such airports.
* The private operator has to manage two set of employees – those who were transferred from Airport Authority's rolls and others freshly recruited by the private operator who has to. Develop HR policies and practices to enhance inclusivity and blend the disparate cultures into one post privatisation.
* Mechanisation, automation and digitisation of activities at airports are essential for reducing manual operations and people interfaces and interventions to enhance productivity, efficiency and service standards. Use of Artificial intelligence, machine learning, robotics etc., will be the way forward in many terminal and cargo operations thereby reducing the dependence on manpower with increased application of technology in a distributed and dispersed employee work scenario. This calls for upskilling and huge investments in equipments and on employee training and development.

❑ COMMUNICATIONS

Along with transport, communications is the most important part of infrastructure. Communications comprises a broad spectrum of services–the Post and Courier services, Telecommunications, Information Technology (IT), and Satellite services. Print and electronic media, including television and broadcasting, which come under the Information and Broadcasting Ministry also form part of this sector. For long, the post, telephone, telegraph and wireless services, radio, and the print media constituted the mode of communications.

The Communication Revolution

With the advent of television, electronics, and computer technology, the whole scene underwent a sea change. It has virtually wrought a communications revolution. This was further fuelled by innovations in telephony such as Mobile phone and the launching of satellites which are used both in telephone and television.

These developments have made communications faster than ever before, bringing people and places much closer. It has had a massive impact on the traditional modes like the post and even the old telephone system. It has helped not only to make messaging faster, but also in transmitting massive amounts of data, transfer of funds, etc. instantaneously. It has also deeply impacted sectors like industry, trade, transport, banking, insurance, hotel, tourism, and a host of other activities. Besides saving on travel and time, these innovations and new technologies have brought down the cost of various services.

Post and Courier Services

While the system of exchange of letters in various forms existed since time immemorial, formal organization of post offices and postal network came into vogue only in the 18th century. A rudimentary runner and courier system did evolve during the Middle Ages. In India, the medieval era saw the building of Grand Trunk road and *sarais* and rest-houses which facilitated exchange of messages. Later, the East India Company improved the system and formal postal system gradually took shape.

The Postal system

Even after the invention of telegraphy and telephone, the postal system thrived as it was the only means of conveying physical mail, documents and parcels, and remitting money. Telegraph and telephone served the purpose of conveying brief messages in quicker time but its use was rather limited as technology had not developed and the services were not on an extensive scale. Table 10.7 shows the relative growth and expansion of the traditional post and telecom services after independence.

Table 10.7: Expansion of Postal Network and Telephone Connections

	1960-61	1968-69	1980-81	1990-91	2002	2010	2020
Post offices	77, 000	102, 000	139, 000	150, 000	155, 000	154, 970	156.600
No. of Phones (in million)	0.46	1.12	2.79	6.02	38.60	787.29	1175.22

Source: Annual Reports of Dept. of Post and Dept. of Telecommunications.

The Rural Postal Network and Services

- India Post has a vast network of 1,41,000 post offices (i.e., 90 percent of total post offices in the country) located in rural areas.
- The Post Office is executing Rural ICT project – Digital Advancement of Rural Post Office for A New India (DARPAN). DARPAN envisages computerizing about 1,30,000 rural post offices and equipping them with computer hardware and software, other peripherals, solar charging devices and providing network connectivity.
- Postal Department has equipped 1,29,688 Branch Post offices in rural areas with SIM-based handheld devices for carrying out online Postal and Financial transactions.
- With the vast network of offices in rural areas, the Post Office carries out a wide range of services for the rural population. These include Financial Inclusion through Postal Savings Bank (POSB) which operates Savings Bank, Recurring and Time Deposit accounts, Sukanya Samridhi Yojana and Rural Postal Life Insurance (RPLI) Scheme among others.
- Other services include Online deposit and withdrawal of money on Core Banking System (CBS), disbursement of benefits under MGNREGS and other Social Sector payments, booking of Registered & Speed Post articles and Money Orders and deposit of Rural Postal Life Insurance (RPLI) premium. These are being done through DARPAN devices giving a boost to digital transactions in the remote rural areas.
- So far, 26 crore digital transactions through DARPAN amounting to ₹ 30,473 crore have taken place.

In the initial years after the independence, the postal department functioned with great efficiency ensuring speedy and timely delivery of mail and other postal items. Even an All-Up scheme was introduced in 1949 by which first-class mails between the four Metro cities were carried by a night airmail service, with no surcharge, with Nagpur as the focal point where bags between the metros were exchanged. This ensured overnight delivery of such mail which was greatly appreciated and was popular.

Genesis and Rise of Courier Industry

But with rapid expansion of the economy and trade and industry, and phenomenal increase in commercial and business mails by the 1980's, the volume of mail to be handled increased by leaps and bounds and it became difficult for the postal service to cope with the mails. This led to frequent delays to mails and delivery and as a response to this situation, the Courier industry (also known as Express industry) took shape. Soon the courier industry expanded rapidly and several courier firms started operations carrying documents and merchandize which posed competition to the postal service. The rise of the courier industry happened not only in India but the world over, and firms like DHL, Blue Dart, Fedex, and UPS operated internationally carrying large volumes of mail. In India several private courier companies operate delivering documents and merchandize parcels.

Logistics Industry

Logistics is about moving materials, information, and funds from one business to another business or from a business to the consumer. Logistics is an important part of the business ecosystem and is a major global economic activity. The three major cost components of logistics operations are inventory carrying, transportation, and administration. It encompasses activities like freight transportation, warehousing, material handling, protective packaging, inventory control, order processing, marketing, forecasting, and customer service.

Intense competition in today's global market, the introduction of products with short life cycles, the heightened expectations of customers, and the cost cutting measures have forced business enterprises to focus attention on the logistics industry. Recent years have been witnessing continuous growth in the logistics area. Globalization and developments in the IT sector, coupled with the need for supply chain optimization are reshaping the physical trade flow.

The European and US markets for logistics industry are mature and crowded with several global giants of logistics players. Logistics industry in India is still in its infancy and is highly fragmented. There are scores of logistics companies, ranging from the international giants to the highly localized, small players in the country. As the logistics industry in India is in a nascent stage, there are several issues to be resolved and improved.

The trend of deregulation in the economy since the 1990s, which resulted in the opening up of sectors to foreign MNC's and investments, liberalization of current and capital account, have given a fillip to the logistics industry. The Indian logistics industry has come a long way from being a labour intensive structure during the 1960's and the 70's to the present technology-oriented set-up that provides wide range of logistics services.

India being a globally acknowledged IT powerhouse, this strength could be leveraged by Indian companies to develop specific capabilities in IT-enabled logistics such as the development and management of logistics planning and coordination systems. Leading IT companies can complement their expertise with logistics domain knowledge to develop logistics capabilities and solutions for different industries and sectors.

As an emerging economy with a high growth rate and a large market, India has all the potential to develop the logistics industry in a more organized and professional manner. The rapid growth of E-commerce companies, which are facing last-mile problems in time-bound delivery, offers an ideal platform for the growth of this sector. India should recognize the extraordinary role logistics could play in development and in enhancing the competitiveness of various sectors of the economy. As such, India should move forward for an integrated strategy towards developing a world-class logistics industry.

Commenting on 'Logistic solutions', the Planning Commission had observed thus: "Railways have to play an increasing role in the integrated multi-modal transport system to capture the new traffic thrown up by the growing Indian economy. To realize this, Railways needs to seriously consider provision of complete logistic solutions to freight customers, in addition to decreasing unit costs and providing superior services. It is proposed to develop logistic parks integrating bonded warehousing, logistic processing, commodity exposition, and logistic distribution. The key development is targeted at import/export logistic distribution facilitating international purchasers, third-party and fourth-party logistic companies, and logistic agencies.

"Further, logistic hubs can be developed along or near important railheads through joint ventures between State Governments and Railways, through PPPs, and direct private sector participation. These hubs will be strategically located to capture agro industrial produce in the hinterland and to provide competitive transport to expand access to markets for industries in the covered areas. These hubs could be developed as mini-freight villages or as logistics parks." (Eleventh Five Year Plan, Vol. III).

The roadways can play a complementary role to the railways to serve areas where the latter does not have reach. Such an integrated approach could serve the best interests of the economy.

(On Logistics sector, see also Box 25.3 on p.25.42 on GST in Chapter 25)

❑ TELECOMMUNICATIONS

Advances in Telecommunications

Another major development in this sector was the rapid technological advances in the field of telecommunications. Telephone services in the western and other developed countries, particularly Japan, underwent great changes. Whereas earlier users had to depend on telephone exchanges to make long distance calls, advances in technology enabled subscribers to make trunk calls directly. Not only that, the services became more reliable and fault-free, ensuring greater customer satisfaction.

Further advances like the computer and the laptop, which is portable, and which enabled instant transmission of mail, data, voice, etc. through Internet changed the whole scenario like never before. This greatly impacted traditional mail and even the telephone services. In fact, the telegraph services have been discontinued. The advent of Mobile telephony further revolutionized the sector. As charges for mobile came down drastically, it became the common man's handy tool for instant communication.

Telecom Scenario in India

For over four decades since independence, the telecom sector was a monopoly under the government, the Telephone Department. Due to this and the lack of finances to develop to the extent required, the demand for telephones far outstripped supply and there was a huge waiting list for phone connections. That apart, despite the best efforts of the department to upgrade the systems, the quality and standard of service was much below par with calls not going through, delays in getting through on trunk calls, frequent disruptions in the lines, etc. All this led to much dissatisfaction and criticism amongst the users and the general public and there was pressing demand to open up the sector to private operators and liberalize it with a view to allow competition and improve the services.

The first breakthrough in the telephone sector in India happened when the government invited the India-born US telecom innovator and entrepreneur, Sam Pitroda, to improve and enhance the standards in the telecom sector. One of the concepts he relied upon was that telephone accessibility was as crucial as phone density. Based on this approach, the government opened Public Call Office (PCO) outlets throughout the length and breadth of the country where people could make local and long-distance phone calls at nominal rates. This enabled people who did not have phones to access the facility and it proved to be very popular. He also worked on upgrading rural telephone exchanges to suit Indian conditions with a band of Indian engineers at a centre called 'Centre for Development of Telematics' (C-DOT).

Contribution of Telecom Sector to the Economy

- Direct contribution includes capital investment, production of goods and services, generation of employment and international trade, among others.
- Indirect ways include an increase in business efficiency, enhanced speed and quality of information flows, better access to markets and diffusion of innovation.
- Its role in linking rural, remote and inaccessible areas with the rest of the country gives considerable boost to economic activity. For a vast country like India with about 70 per cent of population living in rural and far-flung areas, this is of crucial importance.
- The role it plays in the education and health sectors through on-line education and spread of knowledge through fixed-line telephony, mobile phones, wireline and wireless Internet, telemedicine, etc. makes significant impact on the society.
- Employment generation: The sector generates employment in diverse ways: jobs for engineers, infrastructure and cyber security experts, application developers, sales executives, in manufacturing of phone equipments, service and repair technicians, call centre executives among others. In addition, it creates employment in various dependent and allied sectors such as e-commerce, online content industry, etc. In 2015, the mobile industry in India provided direct and indirect employment to 4 million people.

Telecommunications is a prime infrastructure service needed for rapid growth and modernization of the economy. It had the potential to be one of the fastest growing sectors in India and had immense potential for growth. The telecommunication activity being commercial in nature, people were willing to pay for it. Of all the infrastructure sectors, it was perhaps ideally suited for private sector participation which would help to create a competitive environment and improve the quality of services. Deregulation and competition were the key elements in telecommunications reforms the world over and such an approach held much promise for this sector in India. Following the liberalization policies initiated in 1991, the telecom sector too was opened up to the private sector.

National Telecom Policy 1994

When the National Telecom Policy, 1994 was announced, there were about 8 million lines working with a waiting list of about 2.5 million. Only 1.4 lakh villages, out of a total of 5.76 lakh villages in the country, were covered by telephone services. But there were more than 1 lakh public call offices (PCOs) in the urban areas. The policy envisaged companies registered in India to participate in the expansion of the telecom network in the area of basic telephone services. These companies were required to maintain a balance in their coverage between urban and rural areas. Their conditions of operation also included agreed tariff and revenue sharing arrangements.

In 1997, the **Telecom Regulatory Authority of India (TRAI)** was set up to regulate the industry and tariffs, ensure fair competition among the service providers, and protect consumer interest.

National Telecom Policy 1999

As it was found that there was more potential to develop the sector and that policies needed to be reoriented further, the government reviewed the earlier policy and came up with a new National Telecom Policy in 1999. Its objectives included:

- To transform the competitive telecom network in both rural and urban areas in a time bound manner.
- To achieve efficiency and transparency in spectrum management.
- To protect the defence and security interests of the country.
- To enable Indian Telecom Companies to become truly global players.
- To encourage research and development efforts in the country.

To meet the needs of changing times, the government came out with new telecom policies in 2012 and 2018. These had the following objectives:

- **NTP 2012:** Keeping in view the modern technological advancements in the telecom sector such as 5G, Internet of Things (IoT), Machine to Machine (M2M) interface, etc., need was felt to introduce a 'customer focused' and 'application driven' policy for the Indian telecom sector.

Hence the government came out with National Telecom Policy-2012 (NTP-2012) to maximize public good by providing affordable and reliable and broadband services across the entire country. Its main thrust was to reap the multiplier effect and transformational impact of these services to advance the national development agenda while enhancing equity and inclusiveness.

- **NTP 2018:** As India was moving towards greater 'digitisation' in diverse sectors, the NTP-2012 was re-christened as National Digital Communications Policy-2018 (NDCP-2018) and launched in 2018 after detailed consultations with all stakeholders.

The key objectives of the policy, to be achieved by 2022, are:

- Providing Broadband for all.
- Creating 4 Million additional jobs in the Digital Communications sector.
- Enhancing the contribution of the Digital Communications sector to 8% of India's GDP from ~ 6% in 2017.
- Propelling India to the top 50 Nations in the ICT Development Index of ITU from 134 in 2017.
- Enhancing India's contribution to Global Value Chains and ensuring Digital Sovereignty.

For accomplishing these objectives by year 2022, the NDCP-2018 envisages three missions, viz., Connect, Propel and Secure India.

These measures gave further impetus to the Telecom sector. The impressive growth in telephone facilities in India since the 1990's can be seen from Table 10.8.

Table 10.8: Growth and Development of Telecom Facilities since 1991

Year	No. of Phones (In million)	Year	Teledensity (per 100 population)
1991	6.02	1988	0.52
2001	36.28	1999	2.9
2007	206.83	2002	4.9
2011	846.33	2007	18.2
2015	1002.05	2011	76.86
2016	1059.33	2014	77.12
2020	1175.22	2020	86.55

Source: Five Year Plans, Planning Commission and Department of Telecommunications.

India being a vast country and with a large population, once these policies were set in motion, changes in the communication sector have taken place on a much larger scale. With a booming and thriving middle class, India offered a large market for all the new devices and services. In fact, as subsequent developments have shown, the mobile or cellular phone has helped even the very common people at the 'bottom of the pyramid' and virtually every individual, in the urban and rural areas, who could not have dreamt of having a phone just a decade ago, to possess a mobile phone. A ‘mobile in everyone’s hand’ has become a catchy slogan and it has transformed not only the daily lives of the people, but has had a multiplier effect on diverse sectors like transport and travel, banking, education, and health giving all-round boost to the economy. The tariffs also steadily came down as the volumes of connections and traffic increased enormously.

Broadband Policy 2004

Demand for Broadband is primarily conditioned and driven by Internet and computer penetration. When India initiated this policy in 2004, the level of Internet and Broadband access in the country was low as compared to many Asian countries. Penetration of Broadband, Internet, and Personal Computer (PC) in the country was 0.02 per cent, 0.4 per cent, and 0.8 per cent respectively in December, 2003. There were no uniform standards for Broadband connectivity and countries followed different standards. Government envisioned an accelerated growth in Internet and PC penetration as the success of Broadband would largely be dependent on their spread.

Though the Internet penetration in India is only about 16 per cent of the population, in absolute numbers it works out to nearly ten times the population of Australia. According to one estimate, India was to have 243 million Internet users by June 2014, overtaking the US as the world's second largest Internet base after China. The US has an estimated 207 million Internet users, while China has 300 million. Though all the Internet users in India were not active, it is expected that they would turn into active users. In India, the Internet is used primarily for communication, mostly in the form of email, but social media is also an important driver of Internet use in India. India had about 82 million monthly active users in 2013 and is the second largest geographical region for Facebook after the US and Canada. Facebook does not operate in China.

National Optical Fibre Network, BharatNet Project

This is another ambitious project connected with the Digital India programme. In order to ensure equity in access and to accelerate socio-economic growth in rural areas, the Department of Telecommunications

(DoT) has planned to connect all 2,50,000 Gram Panchayats in the country with minimum 100 Mbps bandwidth under the National Optical Fibre Network Project (NOFN). The work of cable laying is in progress.

According to the Annual Report of the Dept. of Telecom for 2020-21, under the BharatNet project, the progress is as under:

- Around 1.5 lakh Gram Panchayats (GPs) have already been connected with high speed broadband connectivity which will help in providing various services in the rural areas.
- By the end of December 2020, Wi-Fi hotspots have been installed in 1 lakh GPs and about 5.0 lakh Fibre to the Home (FTTH) broadband connections have been provided.
- In addition to Wi-Fi hotspots, the number of GPs taken on SWAN (State Wide Area Network) stands at 5,330.
- The scope of BharatNet has now been enhanced to connect all 6 lakh inhabited villages in the country as announced by the Prime Minister in his 2020 Independence Day address.
- To leverage the potential and entrepreneurship of private sector, a major part of the roll out is being done through Public Private Partnership in 16 States covering about 3.5 lakh villages.

When completed, it will help educational and health institutions in villages and promote private sector investment in rural areas. It will also help to bridge the existing 'digital divide' due to which large segments of the population have no access to computer facility. The increased demand for telecom equipments and electronic hardware due to this project will give a fillip to the manufacture of those items.

5G services in Rural India

Providing 5G services, as and when it is rolled out, in rural areas also is crucial as broadband services are being provided under the BharatNet project. A positive development in this context is that the Telecom Standards Development Society, India (TSDSI), a national body responsible for the development of Indian telecom standards, has successfully introduced an indigenously developed 5G candidate standard. The TSDSI 5G technology could deliver, mobile internet and next-generation IoT services. This will ensure that nearly all of India's villages can be covered from towers located at gram panchayats, whereas nearly a third of such villages would be out of coverage otherwise.

Expert groups at International Telecommunication Union (ITU) meetings which evaluated the TSDSI technology have ratified that the technology meets ITU requirements.

Adoption of TSDSI's 5G standard in India by the government will enable India to leap-frog in the 5G space, with key innovations introduced by Indian entities accepted as part of global wireless standards for the first time. The nation stands to gain enormously both in achieving the required 5G penetration in rural and urban areas as well as in nurturing the nascent Indian R&D ecosystem to make global impact.

This innovation suited for rural coverage and connectivity will be useful for the 5G eco-system that will be deployed in India and in other countries similarly placed.

Box 10.2: Challenges and rise of the telecom sector in India

- The challenges which India's telecom sector faced in the mid-1980's can be gauged from the fact that by the end of 1988, India was among the large number of Afro-Asian countries which had a telephone density of less than 1.0 per 100 persons, when in the advanced countries of North Americia and West Europe, the telephone density was 45 to 50 per 100 persons. While comparisons with developed countries may not be proper, but even by the standard of many developing countries, India was then far behind in providing telephone facility to the population. India's telephone density, then at 0.52 per 100 persons, was less than that in China (0.78), Iran (3.43), Brazil (5.5), Egypt (5.1), Philippines (1.01), Malaysia (7.37), Pakistan (0.7), Singapore (35.42), and Thailand (1.84).

- Large population and the huge size of the country adversely affected the telephone density in India in spite of the considerable growth in the telephone network. In 1988, the total number of local calls recorded was 19,334 million. It was way ahead of the traffic density registered in Australia, Germany, Denmark, Netherlands, Israel, Saudi Arabia, and several other developed and developing countries.
- In 1989, India ranked 19th among the 66 nations in terms of the size of the network. Countries like the USA, Japan, Germany, United Kingdom, and Italy were ahead of India, but other advanced countries like Switzerland, Denmark, Norway, New Zealand, and Belgium had smaller telecommunication networks than India.
- The number of Mobile phone subscribers which was 700 million in October 2012 rose to 975.78 million in May 2015.
- Indian telecom operators added a staggering 227.27 million wireless subscribers in the 12 months between March 2010 and March 2011, averaging 18.94 million subscribers every month. To put this into perspective, China which had the world's largest telecom network added 119.2 million wireless subscribers during the same period—averaging 9.93 million subscribers every month—a little over half the number India was adding every month. So, while India may have been second to China in the total number of mobile subscribers, India has been adding nearly twice as many subscribers every month until March 2011.
- During the Eleventh Plan (2007–12), total telephone connections increased four-fold from 205.86 million in March 2007 to 951.34 million in March 2012. The overall teledensity also increased from 18.31 per cent to 78.66 per cent during that Plan period. But the subscriber base for telecom services is skewed in favour of urban areas. Urban teledensity is around 4.4 times that of rural teledensity. Also, the sector is dominated by wireless phones which increased from 165.09 million (80.19 per cent) in March 2007 to 919.17 million (96.62 per cent) in March 2012. And, there had been continuous

decline in the number of wireline telephones in the country from 40.77 million in March 2007 to 32.17 million in March 2012. The service providers have to leverage the wireline infrastructure, and incentivize this segment with innovative facilities, to reverse this trend and salvage the investments made.

- The telecom sector continued to grow rapidly. During April–November 2014–15, 31.2 million new telephone connections were added, way ahead of the 12.13 million new connections in the corresponding period of 2013–14. Overall teledensity has increased from 75.23 per cent at the beginning of April 2014 to 77.12 per cent at the end of November 2014, while total broadband connections have touched 82.22 million.
- Mobile Number Portability is a user-friendly facility introduced which enables mobile telephone users to retain their mobile telephone numbers when changing from one mobile network operator to another. Till the end of January, 2014, about 111.94 million subscribers had submitted requests to different service providers for porting their mobile number.

Financial state of Telecom sector

A major issue facing the Telecom sector in India is its perilous financial state caused by a variety of factors such as high Spectrum prices, fierce competition among the service providers, the accumulated Adjusted Gross Revenue (AGR) charges the companies are obliged to pay on which they did not get relief even from the Supreme Court on appeals they filed.

However, it must be emphasized that despite all this, the Telecom industry has contributed immensely to the country's overall growth and has been the backbone of the nation's economy. Factors such as India's large population, steady economic growth, intense competition in the sector, low tariffs, infrastructure sharing and the introduction of enabling regulatory reforms, all have helped the telecom industry in India grow at a rapid pace.

- **Revenue:** In the decade from 2006 - 2016, the sector's revenues increased from ₹ 873.12 billion to ₹ 2,453.51 billion, at a CAGR of more than 10 percent.
- **Capital investment:** And capital investment in gross fixed assets has risen continuously since 2001. During 2001-2016 period, it increased by more than seven times, from ₹ 1,031 billion to ₹ 7,605 billion.
- **Financial stress and AGR:** But the industry is reeling under a daunting debt burden of about ₹ 4 lakh crore and is in dire financial straits. The problem is compounded by the dispute regarding Adjusted Gross Revenue (AGR) dues under which telecom companies together are asked to pay a huge sum of ₹ 1.47 lakh crore to the Department of Telecom (DoT). Of this, ₹ 92,000 crore is towards licence fee and ₹ 55,100 crore as spectrum usage charges.

The genesis of the issue is that in 1999 the government gave an option to telecom licensees to migrate from "fixed license fee" regime to the "revenue sharing fee" model. Under the latter, mobile telephone operators were required to share a percentage of their AGR with the government as annual license fee and spectrum usage charges.

The dispute between DoT and the mobile operators was mainly on what constitutes AGR. The DoT argued that AGR includes all revenues from both telecom and non-telecom services. Whereas the companies claimed that AGR should comprise just the revenue accrued from core (telecom) services and not revenue from dividend, interest or profit on sale of any investment or fixed assets. The matter went to courts and eventually the Supreme Court upheld the contention of DoT. This has added to the financial woes of telecom companies.

Following this the companies have made part payments and sought time to pay the balance over a long-term settlement.

Spectrum Allocation and Pricing

This is another vexatious issue and subject of debate between the Telecom service provider and the Government. The main issues involved in this are mentioned below.

- **Spectrum pricing:** Pricing of spectrum sold in auctions has been a major issue between the service providers, on the following grounds.
- **Reserve price:** Telecom companies fault the government for fixing the base reserve price for different spectrum bands unreasonably high. High reserve prices and/or unrealistic pre-determined spectrum value have resulted in poor response from potential bidders and led to valuable spectrum being left unsold and unused.
- **5G spectrum:** The base price of 5G spectrum in 3400 to 3800 megahertz (MHz)z band is highest in India. The base price per MHz for spectrum in this band is $65 million (mn.) in India as compared to $26 mn. in Italy, $18 mn. in South Korea, $10 mn. in the UK and $5 mn. in Australia. Though various industry bodies and Broadband India Forum (BIF) have taken up the issue of exorbitant spectrum price with the government, their plea has not been acceded to.
- **Financial woes:** There is also the prospect of demand for 5G spectrum being low as the sector is highly concentrated with very few service providers, and the major players like Airtel and Vodafone virtually crippled by debt and financial woes arising out of Supreme Court orders to pay huge amount to the government on account of Adjusted Gross Revenue arrears.
- **Impact of high prices:** The high prices might also undermine the country's National Digital Communications Policy (NDCP) goals, making the provision of inclusive and affordable high-speed 5G services to all sections of the population, notably users in rural areas, uneconomic.
- **Impact on investments:** The undue financial burden due to high spectrum prices will also have impact on the capacity of service providers to make investments in infrastructure required to ensure quality service to customers, meet demand in highly populated urban areas and expand networks to provide coverage to people in rural areas.
- **Timing of auctions:** The timing of auction of spectrum also plays a major role. The opportunity cost of unused spectrum is enormous and far outweighs any short-term gains in auction revenue by postponing the auction process. For instance, the sale of 5G spectrum bands has been put off

repeatedly which delayed its roll-out with consequences for the efficiency of not only the telecom sector but a host of other entities in the industrial and services sectors who would benefit from this vastly upgraded technology. It is to be noted that quite a few other countries have already gone ahead and started roll-out of 5G service.

These issues are of vital concern in the context of India launching 5G technology and services on which India is already lagging behind other countries. The introduction of the highly advanced 5G network will make communications manifold faster and efficient and will have a transformational impact on all sectors of the economy.

Box 10.3: Open RAN system

A system known as Open Radio Access Network (RAN) that will help telecom companies with cost-effective options and generate more revenue is in the offing. It will help them to reduce both capital expenditure (Capex) and operating expenditure (Opex) and offer innovative digital solutions. Open RAN has much commercial potential as it will fetch substantial savings for telecom operators.

RAN was based on proprietary technologies of global telecom equipment manufacturers and telecom service providers had to procure an entire system of software and hardware from one vendor. Once Open RAN comes into vogue, telcos will have the option to deploy and use systems from multiple vendors. Open RAN, which is still being developed, is the way forward and it will transform the future landscape of mobile networks.

For Indian telecom firms which are reeling under acute financial stress, Open RAN will offer much scope to cut network costs even as they upgrade their networks to 5G technology. Indian telcos are focusing on Open RAN for 5G networks. While the cost of 5G system will come down, it is to be seen to what extent the telcos would be able to pass on cost benefits to subscribers.

Leading software equipment manufacturers are working with Indian system integrators to build and operate Open RAN-based networks. It will not only give a fillip to the induction of 5G technology but provide opportunity for Indian software equipment makers to manufacture Open RAN products under the 'Make in India' scheme for the domestic and global markets.

Indian smartphone users are one of the highest consumers of data globally. It is estimated that the data consumption which averaged about 14 GB per month in 2020 will increase to 40 GB per month by 2024. The introduction of 5G system will boost data consumption exponentially. Hence systems which will bring down capital expenditure and operating costs through automation and innovative solutions are the need of the times.

❑ RADIO, TELEVISION, AND OTHER MEDIA

Entertainment and Media Services is a major sector in the economy considering its reach among the population and its profound influence in forming public opinion. All segments of this sector have consistently outperformed the GDP growth year after year. This sector comprises television with compound annual growth rate (CAGR) of 22 per cent, films (16%), radio (28%), music (4%), print media (13%), live entertainment (16%), out-of-home advertisement (17%), and Internet advertising (43%).

Radio and television are two of the most important segments in this sector. Though with the advent of television, the role of radio has been eclipsed, radio still has considerable reach in towns and villages. Particularly, the FM radio is a very popular medium in cities and towns. Television had its beginnings in India in the mid-1960's, but it gained momentum in the early 1980's when national telecasting and colour TV was introduced. Television is today a dominant medium and is almost ubiquitous.

As per 2001 census, out of 210 million houses, television had reached 108 million homes, and now over 161 million households possess a TV set. In 2001, the number of radio sets was 132 million. Total radio coverage had reached 99.13 per cent of population. There are in all 229 AIR channels and 42 private FM stations.

The television broadcasting has a vast set-up consisting of 1,398 analogue terrestrial transmitters and 4 digital transmitters in the public sector, 6,000 Multi-System Operators, 65,000 Local Cable Operators in the private sector, and 3 digital DTH satellite television operators in the public and the private sector.

Growth in infrastructure, technology, and institutional support in the information and broadcasting (I&B) sector has been in consonance with the overall national development perspective. Film, information, and broadcasting sectors have acquired formidable strength. With rapid expansion, the share of I&B sector in total employment, income, and investment has also gone up significantly.

❑ SATELLITES AND COMMUNICATION

The role played by satellites launched by the Indian Space Research Organization (ISRO) in supporting telecommunications and TV transmission in India must be recognized. The INSAT system ushered in a revolution in India's television and radio broadcasting, telecommunications, and meteorological sectors. It enabled the rapid expansion of TV and modern telecommunication facilities to even the remote areas and off-shore islands. Together, the system provides transponders in various bands for a variety of communication services.

❑ INFRASTRUCTURE AND EMPLOYMENT

Infrastructure is a critical sector from the viewpoint of employment generation. With diverse sub-sectors that it encompasses, it has significant potential to create jobs as many of the activities are of labour intensive nature. Transport, communications, construction, etc. need considerable labour force. Besides, infrastructure required in other sectors like education and health also can give a boost to employment.

The data given in Table 10.9 shows the employment generated in this sector during the post-1991 reform and liberalization era. There has been considerable increase in absorption of labour between 1993–94 and 2004–05. As the data reveal, most of the job creation has taken place in the hospitality, transport, communications, and construction segments. One major drawback of this trend has been that bulk of the jobs created have been in the unorganized sector and the jobs created have been of informal nature and low quality jobs.

Table 10.9: Sectoral Break-up of Employment (1993–94, 1999–2000 & 2004–05)

Total Employment UPS * (millions)				Organised			Unorganised		
	1993–94	1999–2000	2004–05	1993–94	1999–2000	2004–05	1993–94	1999–2000	2004–05
1. Electricity, water	1.4	1.0	1.2	1.4	1.0	1.2	0.0	0.0	0.0
2. Construction	12.0	17.2	25.7	1.2	1.2	1.0	10.7	16.0	24.7
3. Trade, Hotel, Restaurants	27.1	39.5	48.4	0.4	0.5	0.6	26.6	39.0	47.8
4. Transport, Storage, Communications	10.5	14.4	18.5	3.1	3.2	3.2	7.4	11.2	15.4
5. Finance, Insurance, Real estate etc.	2.8	4.7	7.7	1.5	1.7	1.9	1.3	3.0	5.8
Total	**53.8**	**76.8**	**101.5**	**7.6**	**7.6**	**7.9**	**36.0**	**69.2**	**93.7**

*The term UPS stands for **Usual Principal Status** of employment. The figures shown here are in **millions** and are only for the Infrastructure sector and does not include other sectors.

Source: Planning Commission, Databook, December 2014.

Commenting on the issue of 'Informalization of Employment', the Planning Commission has observed thus: "A critical issue in assessing employment behaviour of the economy is the growth of employment in the organized sector vis-à-vis the unorganized sector. Public debate on this issue is usually conducted on the basis that unorganized sector employment is generally of low quality while organized sector employment is of high quality, and the focus of attention is on whether employment has increased in the organized sector. Concerns about the quality of employment appear valid although different sources of data are not easily reconciled. However, it does appear that total employment provided by the organized sector has expanded in the period 1999-2000 to 2004-05 and this is entirely because of the growth of informal employment in the organized sector." (Eleventh Five Year Plan, Vol. I, Planning Commission). The concern is because casual and informal jobs do not ensure job security or carry much of the social security benefits like retirement benefits, healthcare, insurance, etc.

Potential for job creation

Developing proper infrastructure in the less developed states and smaller towns, as mentioned earlier, and encouraging industries to gravitate towards them could trigger exponential growth, create jobs locally and keep people aspiring for work nearer their homes and stem migration. These states could offer special incentives like land allotment, assured power and water supply and arrange industrial housing. The government has already planned housing for workers near industrial clusters but this should now be directed more towards the backward regions in a phased manner.

Construction and housing, improving health and education facilities in rural and semi-urban areas are potential areas for job creation. The 'Housing for All' scheme, promoting agro-based industries and building silos and cold storage chains and promoting small industries and artisans in rural areas will rejuvenate rural economy.

Conclusion

Infrastructure investment has a significant impact on economic growth, employment generation and quality of life. It serves the twin benefits of improving productivity and generating employment. It is, therefore, imperative that governments get their investment priorities right and direct them to areas which deserve greater attention. Besides improving infrastructure, imparting necessary skills to workers required for industries to be set up in such areas will go a long way in attracting investment.

(For more on this, see Box 24.7 in chapter 24, pp. 24.31-3)

❑ CONCLUSION

India's transport system comprises a number of distinct modes and services. As stated earlier, these include railways, roads, ports, inland water transport, coastal shipping, airports, and airlines. The sector has expanded manifold in the six decades of planned development, both in terms of spread and capacity. Along with the increase in quantity, there have been several developments of qualitative nature, such as emergence of a multi-modal system in the form of container transport, reduction in obsolete assets, and improvements in financing.

Going forward, there is need to take a more integrated approach while planning and developing transport, communications, and other related facilities. The vision for transport should be guided by a modal mix that will lead to an efficient, sustainable, economical, safe, reliable, environment friendly, and regionally balanced transportation system. This is particularly relevant as the country is embarking on mega projects involving heavy investments like Metro rail system in more cities, High-speed rail, Dedicated freight corridors, Smart cities, etc. Utilizing inland waterways and coastal shipping must be taken holistically so that the objective of speed and efficient energy usage is achieved. Saving on energy and averting environmental pollution will be of paramount importance.

Box 10.4 : International North-South Transport Corridor (INSTC) - A case study

The International North-South Transport Corridor (INSTC) is a 7,200-km long, multi-modal transport network involving sea, rail, and road route linking India, Iran, Central Asia, Russia and Europe for moving freight. The INSTC project was initiated by Russia, India and Iran in September 2000 and an agreement was signed in May 2002. Given India's strategic interests in the West and the Central Asian region, and the need for greater economic and energy cooperation, India has stepped up efforts to re-connect with countries in this region. Iran and Russia are taking initiative in activating this route since 2000, through existing land route and developing the gaps existing in rail links in this multi-mode network.

The INST corridor passes through Indian Ocean and Persian Gulf to the Caspian Sea via Iran, and onward to northern Europe via St. Petersburg in Russia. It will facilitate movement of goods from Mumbai to Bandar Abbas (Iran) by sea, from Bandar Abbas to an Iranian port on the Caspian Sea by road, and then from there to Astrakhan, a Caspian port in Russia by ship and onwards to other parts of Russia and Europe by rail.

To study the full potential of the route and issues which may arise in the implementation of the project, a dry run was conducted on the Mumbai Nhava Sheva port-Bandar Abbas (Iran)-Azerbaijan and the Nhava Sheva-Bandar Abbas-Russia route via Caspian Sea in 2014 by the Federation of Freight Forwarders' Associations in India (FFFAI). The dry run showed that the route via Bandar Abbas in Iran to Russia and transiting through CIS (former Russian states), could be the best route with optimal transit/cost for the Indian exporters/importers.

India reaches out to Iran & Afghanistan

India has been developing Chabahar port in cooperation with Iran and there is a transit trade agreement on this port between Iran, India and Afghanistan Besides the port, India is building the 650-km rail link from Chabahar to Zahedan and into Afghanistan. India also built the 215-km long strategic Delaram-Zaranj highway providing a shorter alternative route connecting Kabul to Iran. This would not only help India bypass Pakistan and reach out to Afghanistan, Central Asia and Russia but gives Indian exports competitive advantage due to lower cost and less delivery time. It would contribute to bilateral and regional trade and economic development and also provide alternate access to landlocked Afghanistan to regional and global markets.

Benefits from INSTC Corridor

- The route offers many opportunities to enhance India's connectivity with Iran, Afghanistan and the vast Eurasian region and vice versa. Compared to the present route through the Suez Canal and the Mediterranean Sea, the INSTC is much shorter and cost effective. While the Suez Canal route takes 45-60 days, the INSTC would take 25-30 days. The INSTC is 40 per cent shorter in transit time and 30 per cent cheaper in terms of cost.
- Presently, India has to depend on the sea route via Rotterdam to St. Petersburg (Russia) or through China and then by land route to transport goods to Russia.
- To access Central Asia, goods have to be routed through China, Europe or Iran. The routes through China and Europe are long, expensive and time consuming.
- The benefit for India from this corridor will be manifold if it is linked with the Southeast Asian countries. This will boost trade between Europe and Southeast Asia as well.
- The route through Chabahar port gives India access to crisis-ridden Afghanistan, where India is carrying out many developmental works. It is of much strategic advantage as it also helps India to sends goods and render humanitarian assistance to Afghanistan.

- The INSTC could also serve as an alternative to China's ambitious One Belt, One Road (OBOR) initiative involving a large number of nations and which India has shunned as it violates India's sovereign rights. (See chapter 20. p.20.14-5 for more on OBOR initiative).

Importance of link with Europe, Central Asia

With the US exerting pressure on its allies and partners, including India, to look at alternatives for their geo-political and economic interests, Europe with its technological strengths and economic prowess, holds much promise in meeting India's needs. India, which is a member of G-20 has, of late, intensified relations with countries in the European Union and Russia. While China has been courting Europe with its ambitious Belt and Road Initiative (BM), there is increasing concern in European capitals over the way it is being implemented. While Europe needs Chinese funds, it is wary about China's designs in furthering its strategic interests across the globe.

Close cooperation with countries in the Central Asian region, which has vast energy resources, is also in India's interests considering India's ever-increasing energy requirements.

In the context of all this, the INSTC project could play a vital role for India.

Need to Review Position

This scheme will need to be reworked in the context of political changes which have taken place in Afghanistan with the return of Taliban regime and India's changing relations with Iran on which depends the successful operation of Chabahar port which is the gateway for India to Afghanistan. The Afghanistan regime under Taliban has stated that they want good diplomatic and trade ties with India. Besides, they will support the role of Chabahar port, built by India in cooperation with Iran, in facilitating regional and global trade. Already the port has seen increase in traffic with cargo from Russia, Qatar, Romania and Australia, and exports to Kuwait, UAE and Bangladesh being handled by it in the last few months. Afghanistan is facing a dire situation and a looming humanitarian crisis, and the United Nations and countries like India have expressed willingness to provide essential food items which can go through this port. The successful operation of Chabahar port is a positive sign and augurs well for India and other countries in the Middle East, Central Asia and Eurasia.

In this Chapter we discussed.....

- Importance of infrastructure to economy.
- Development of infrastructure; share of rail and roads in traffic.
- India's challenges in building infrastructure after independence.
- Allocations in Plans (from First Plan to Twelfth Plan) for infrastructure; transport and communications sectors.
- Increase in share of roads in passenger traffic and cargo.
- Growth of roads and rail network; quality and standards of roads a matter of great concern.
- Six categories of roads; constraints faced by the road sector.
- Number of motorized vehicles in India and overburdened roads.
- Two major developments; construction of Golden Quadrilateral and other National Highways as per international standards; construction of Rural roads under PMGSY for rural road connectivity.
- Problems in implementation of highway projects; Hybrid Annuity PPP model for projects.
- Maintenance of PMGSY roads responsibility of Panchayati Raj institutions.
- Roadways play a complementary role to railways.
- Impact of liberalization and growth on transport system.
- Challenges facing the Road sector—maintenance of roads; safety on roads; traffic and pollution; user-pay concept.
- Railways, a behemoth organization; Plan outlays/expenditure on railways.
- Improvements and upgradation of systems and facilities in railways— safety and security; freight movement; dedicated freight corridors; rationalization of rail tariff; change in accounting system; managerial reform; new generation locomotives; high speed rail link.
- India's vast coastline and criticality of the shipping sector for India. India stands at 20th rank among the maritime nations, in terms of fleet size, with a share of 1.19 per cent of theworld fleet.
- The share of Indian ships in the carriage of India's overseas trade declined consistently, it needs corrective steps. Indian shipping fleet characterized by the predominance of oil tankers and bulk carriers.
- Coastal shipping serves as an integral part of the domestic and overseas trade of merchandize; coastal shipping a major source of income for the population in many of the coastal states.

- Ports constitute the inter-modal interface between maritime and road and rail transport; India has 12 major ports and 187 notified non-major ports.
- Problems and deficiencies at Indian ports contributing to longer turnaround time and detentions of ships.
- Scheme for private participation in major ports development.
- India has about 14,500 km of navigable inland waterways. Five national waterways; steps to promote waterways.
- Air transport is critical for a country of sub-continental size like India. Civil aviation is one of the fastest growing sectors in India since liberalization.
- J.R.D. Tata and Indian aviation; founding of Air India International in 1948 and its nationalization in 1953; starting of Indian Airlines.
- Steady increase in passenger and cargo traffic in both domestic and international sectors. Rapid growth after liberalization and the sector was opened to private operators.
- Merger of Indian Airlines and Air India.
- Airports in India managed by the Airports Authority of India (AAI); modernization of airports.
- Communications is the most important part of infrastructure along with transport.
- Advent of television, electronics, and computer technology and the communications revolution.
- Post and courier services; growth and expansion of post and telecom services between 1960 and 1994; decline of post and telegraph services; genesis and rise of courier industry.
- There is considerable scope to develop the Logistics sector and make it more organized and professional. This is necessary as the economy is growing fast and various sectors need logistic support in reaching out to their customers.
- Advances in telecommunications and major technological changes; advent of mobile telephony.
- Telecom scenario in India; for over four decades since independence, the telecom sector was a monopoly; problems with the sector and the first breakthrough with setting up of large number of PCO's.
- Deregulation and competition were the key elements in telecom sector reforms.
- National Telecom Policy, 1994, and 1999; Telecom Regulatory Authority of India (TRAI) was set up in 1997.

Important Terms to Note in this Chapter

Golden Quadrilateral; Public-Private Partnerships (PPP); Build-Operate-Transfer (BOT); BOT Annuity scheme; User-pay concept; Dedicated Freight Corridor; Deadweight Tonnage ; Broadband; Optical fibre network; Digital India; Wi-Fi hotspots; Tele-density; Mobile Number Portability; Adjusted Gross Revenue (AGR); Spectrum; 5G Technology; Radio Access Network (RAN); Informal employment; Un-organized sector; Multi-modal Transport.

Practice Questions

1. Explain the role and importance of infrastructure in economy. Do you think inadequacies and deficiencies in infrastructure has hampered India's development? Explain with cogent reasons.
2. What steps the government has taken in recent years to improve and upgrade infrastructural sectors such as roads, rail, ports, aviation and telecommunications?
3. Describe the steps taken to develop and modernise India's national highways. What are the obstacles faced in executing highway projects and mention the steps taken by the government to overcome them.
4. Describe the salient features and progress of Prime Minister's Gram Sadak Yojana (PMGSY) programme. Discuss its impact and role in uplifting the rural economy.
5. Compare the position of India's telecommunication sector before and after its liberalisation in 1980's and 1990's. How far the liberalisation has helped to reform and expand the sector?
6. Discuss the role which inland waterways and coastal shipping can play in Indian economy. What steps have been taken by the government to develop them?
7. Examine the role of Logistics industry and the steps needed to modernize it to serve better the fast expanding Indian economy.
8. Critically examine the potential of infrastructure sector in creating employment opportunities. Identify those areas in this sector where there is greater scope for job creation.
9. Explain how Private Public Partnership arrangements, in long gestation infrastructure projects, can transfer unsustainable liabilities to the future. What arrangements need to be put in place to ensure that successive generations' capacities are not compromised?

   [UPSC Main 2014 (General Studies Paper)]
10. National Urban Transport Policy emphasises on 'moving people' instead of 'moving vehicles'. Discuss critically the success of the various strategies of the Government in this regard.

    [UPSC Main 2014 (General Studies Paper)]

CHAPTER 11 ENERGY AND POWER

- Energy scenario in India
- Non-commercial Primary Energy sources
- Importance of LPG Supply
- Commercial Energy Resources and Production
- Primary Commercial Energy Supply
- Electricity: Installed Capacity and Generation
- Sources of Energy and Power:
- Hydro, Nuclear, Thermal, Oil and Natural Gas
- Renewable Energy: Solar Power
- Power Generation, Distribution and Expansion
- Transmission and Distribution
- Losses to Discoms
- Expansion of Transmission System and Capacity
- Rural Electrification
- Benefits and Limitations of Rural Electrification
- Power Sector Reforms
- Resolving SEBs' Problems
- New Rural Electrification scheme
- Promoting Energy Efficiency
- Legislative Reforms in Power sector

❑ INTRODUCTION

Energy and power (electricity) are two essential requirements for any economy. They are required for a variety of purposes–in agriculture, industry, transport, and above all, in day to day lives of people. Energy is a critical input for economic development and the development experience the world over is associated with a massive increase in energy requirement. Traditional, non-commercial sources of energy are firewood, dried cowdung, agricultural waste, etc. which are obtained from nature and are generally renewable. Commercial sources of energy include coal, oil (petroleum), and natural gas which are called mineral fuels or fossil fuels which are exhaustible. Power includes various types of electricity generated from different sources–hydro-electric, thermal, nuclear, and renewable sources of energy such as solar and wind energy, tidal power, and biogas. Each of them has its advantages and disadvantages from the viewpoint of cost, pollution, impact on environment, climate, etc.

Both commercial and non-commercial energy sources are known as 'conventional' sources of energy. The renewables, which are known as non-conventional sources of energy, include solar and wind energy and tidal power. India being in the tropical zone and with a long coastline has immense potential to generate power from these sources and in a commercially viable manner by adopting and improving the technologies. The government has been pursuing these possibilities.

❑ ENERGY SCENARIO IN INDIA

Economic growth cannot be realized without ensuring availability of adequate energy. In India, about half of the country's population does not have access to electricity or other forms of commercial energy. Providing access to clean energy to all is essential for empowering individuals, especially women and girls, who are forced to depend on non- commercial fuels such as firewood, crop residues, and dung cakes. These constitute the primary energy source for cooking in over two-thirds of the households, especially in rural areas, where women have to trudge miles to fetch these items. Provision of clean fuels or sources for wood near their habitation and educating and encouraging them on the use of clean fuels is vital for good health and making growth inclusive.

India is both a major energy producer and a consumer. India currently ranks high among the world's energy producers, accounting for about 2.49 per cent of the world's total annual energy production and for about 3.45 per cent of the world's annual energy consumption. It must, however, be noted that India's per capita energy consumption is one of the lowest in the world.

Share of Commercial and Non-commercial Energy

Since independence, the country has registered significant increase in the energy consumption with a shift from non-commercial to commercial sources. The share of commercial energy in total primary energy supply has increased substantially from 29 per cent in 1950–51 to 68 per cent in 2001–02. Whereas the share of non-commercial fuels–fuelwood, cowdung, and agricultural waste–has declined from 71 per cent to about 32 per cent during the same period.

Though the share of the non-commercial sources has been coming down, in absolute terms, their consumption is still high. Traditional sources like fuelwood and dung cake account for nearly 65 per cent of the total non-commercial energy consumed in the country as households, mostly in the rural areas, use them for cooking and heating purposes. These renewable, non-commercial sources have been used extensively for hundreds of years but in an unchecked and inefficient manner. The indiscriminate use of non-commercial energy sources is leading to an energy crisis in the rural areas. This needs to be tackled with a sense of urgency. Development and accelerated utilization of renewable energy sources such as solar and wind energy needs to be pursued on a large scale, both in the rural and urban areas, wherever these are found to be technically feasible and economically viable.

Even though there has been considerable increase in the availability of the two petroleum based domestic fuels–liquefied petroleum gas (LPG) and kerosene–they are yet to make any significant impact on the pattern of fuel consumption in the rural areas. To some extent, the biogas programme has made progress in rural areas and it was estimated that about 3.2 million plants had been installed by 2001.

❑ NON-COMMERCIAL PRIMARY ENERGY RESOURCES

Fuelwood, Dung and Crop Residues

As stated earlier, fuelwood is a major source of energy for cooking and heating in the rural and, to some extent, in the urban households. Out of India's total geographic area of 3.286 million (mn.) sq. km., the total forest cover was 0.637 mn. sq. km. in 1999 which works out to 19.36 per cent of forest cover. The forest cover in 1987 was 0.6408 mn. sq. km. which was 19.49 per cent of the total area. Thus there has been a decline in the forest cover despite various measures taken by the government to preserve and augment the forest area, including social forestry. Various factors such as use of wood for industry, construction, cooking, etc. has resulted in gradual denudation of forests with consequent adverse impact on the environment and climate.

Fuelwood is supplemented by animal dung and crop residues in meeting the domestic energy needs in the rural areas. Greater use of dung cake as a source of energy reduces the availability of dung as a valuable organic manure. The draught animal population in the country has been estimated at 70 million and animal energy continues to be used in agricultural operations and for rural transportation.

Importance of LPG Supply in this context

The demand for non-commercial energy is expected to decline with increasing supply of commercial energy, expansion of the network, and providing better access to commercial energy. In this context, it may be mentioned that one of the main factors which will help to reduce the use of non-commercial energy is the spread of Liquefied Petroleum Gas (LPG) cooking fuel network and its supply, especially in the rural areas. The government has been working in this direction for quite sometime. The percentage of households using LPG as cooking fuel increased from 57 per cent in 2004–05 to around 66 per cent in 2009–10. Access to LPG supplies in rural areas increased from 8.6 per cent in 2004–05 to around 15.5 per cent in 2009–10. However, the per capita consumption reported in rural areas was 0.3 kg per month as compared to 1.8 kg in urban areas. The disparity in per capita consumption between urban and rural areas being not very significant, it may be presumed that there is much potential for the spread of LPG in rural areas, and the demand remains unfulfilled due to insufficient outlets for supply and difficulty of access. Women being the main users and beneficiaries of this facility, they are the worst affected by limitations in LPG supply.

The government decided to cut LPG subsidy to those in the higher income brackets and utilize the savings to supply LPG at subsidized rates to the vulnerable sections of the society. This should help to further popularize the use of this energy among the deprived sections. It is worth noting here that as on August 2021, 8.03 crore households have been provided with LPG connections under the PM UjjwalaYojana. This was a major step towards the empowerment of women.

❑ COMMERCIAL ENERGY RESOURCES AND PRODUCTION

Introduction

The country has seen an expansion in total energy use during the last five decades, with a shift from non-commercial to commercial sources. While total *primary energy* needs registered an average annual growth rate of 3.67 per cent between 1990–91 and 2006–07, the *primary commercial energy* needs registered an average annual growth rate of 4.93 per cent during the same period. The production of commercial sources of energy has also increased significantly. Table 11.1 indicates the trends in production of various primary commercial energy resources. It may be noted that the share of, and dependence on, Coal has gone up considerably from 55.67 mn. tonnes in 1960-61 to 728.72 mn. tonnes in 2018-19. This has serious implications for India complying with the emission targets laid down under 2015 Paris Climate Change Conference. India has to take twin-pronged approach to reduce production of coal-based thermal energy and also increase the use of clean coal technology in energy production. (For more on this, see Chapter 20, pp. 20.38-9)

Table 11.1: Production of Energy in India by Commercial Sources

Year		Coal	Lignite	Crude oil	Natural Gas
	Unit	Mn. tns.	Mn. tns.	Mn. tns.	Bn. Cu. mtrs
1960-61		55.67	0.05	0.45	--
1980-81		114.01	4.80	10.51	2.35
1990-91		211.73	14.07	33.02	1.79
2010-11		532.69	37.73	37.68	52.22
2014-15		612.44	48.27	37.46	33.66
2018-19 (P)		728.72	44.28	34.20	32.87

Source: Tenth Five Year Plan, Planning Commission & Energy Statistics, 2020, Central Statistical Office, Ministry of Statistics and Programme Implementation.

Note: Mn. tns.: Million tonnes; Bn. Cu. Mtrs: Billion cubic metres.

India's energy use is mostly based on fossil fuels. While the country has significant coal and hydro potential, it is relatively deficient in oil and gas resources and hence it has to depend on imports to meet its energy needs. The geographical distribution of primary commercial energy sources in the country is also lopsided, with 77 per cent of the hydro potential located in the northern and north-eastern region of the country. Similarly, about 70 per cent of the total coal reserves are located in the eastern region while most of the hydrocarbon reserves lie in the west, and to an extent, in the south.

Primary Commercial Energy Supply

While the share of coal and lignite in total primary commercial energy supply has been declining progressively over the years, the share of oil and natural gas in the total primary commercial energy supply has been rising. The share of oil and natural gas rose from 37.89 per cent in 1980–81 to 42.93 per cent in 2006–07, while the share of coal and lignite declined from 56.83 per cent in 1980–81 to 53.11 per cent in 2006–07.

India has had to meet its oil (petroleum, etc.) requirements mostly from imports though the domestic production of oil has been ramped up over the years. Data on the value of petroleum imports for selected are given in Table 11.2 reflects the extent of dependence on imports.

Table 11.2: Imports of Petroleum and Other Related Products

Year	Value in US $ (In *Million*)	Value in Indian ₹ (In *Billion*)
1994–95	5,927.8	186.13
2000–01	15,650.1	714.97
2009–10	87,136.9	4,116.49
2013-14	164,770.3	9,978.85
2016-17	86963.8	5832.17
2019-20	130531.9	9250.31

Source: Handbook of Statistics on Indian Economy, Reserve Bank of India.

Trends In Commercial Energy Consumption

Out of total energy consumed in India, the share of commercial energy consumed is about 70 per cent. The sectors of industry and transport had the highest share of commercial energy consumed in 1953–54 with 40 and 44 per cent respectively. But this trend has changed by 2009–10 when the share of industry was 45 per cent and the share of transport came down drastically to 2 per cent. The share of both household sector and agriculture in commercial energy consumption registered increase during the same period–that of the household sector from 10 per cent in 1953–54 to 22 per cent in 2009–10, and that of agriculture from 1 per cent to 18 per cent.

The growth in population and number of households using power, rapid industrialization, expansion of rural electrification, and increased use of power for pumpsets for irrigation, etc. have led to the changed scenario and the pattern of consumption.

❑ ELECTRICITY: INSTALLED CAPACITY AND GENERATION

India is the fourth largest consumer of energy in the world after USA, China, and Russia but it is not endowed with sufficient energy resources. It must, therefore, meet its development needs by accessing all available domestic resources of coal, oil, uranium, hydro, and renewable resources such as solar and wind energy, and meet the shortfall through imports.

Per capita energy consumption:India's per capita electricity consumption in 2014 was 804.52 kilowatt-hours (kWh) as against 2619.96 kWh in Brazil, 3297.04 kWh in China and 2538.80 kWh in Thailand when the world average was 3131.68 kWh. Likewise, energy use (kg of oil equivalent per capita) in 2014 in India was 636.57 kilogram of oil equivalent (kgoe) per person while it was 1495.54 kgoe in Brazil, 2236.73 kgoe in China and 1969.00 kgoe in Thailand when the world average was 1922.13 kgoe.

As will be seen from Table 11.3, the total installed capacity for electricity generation has gone up from 2,500 MW in 1950–51 to 3,70,400 MW in 2019-20. And electricity generated has gone up from 6.6 billion KW hours to 1166 billion KW hours during the same period. (See Table 11.4). Despite this massive increase during the six decades, there is acute shortfall in power. Power cuts, interruptions in power supply, and load shedding are endemic, due to which industries suffer a great deal impacting industrial production and their overall performance. Though high targets were fixed under each Five

Year Plan for capacity addition, they were seldom fully met resulting in shortfalls. While the Eleventh Plan (2007–12) aimed at a substantial increase in the installed capacity with a target of 78,700 MW, the target was reduced to 62,374 MW during the Mid-term Appraisal of the Plan and the actual achievement was 54,964 MW.

Table 11.3: Electricity: Progress of Installed Capacity (Utilities and Non-utilities)

(in Thousand MW)

Year	Utilities				Total	Non- Utilities	Grand Total
	Hydel	Thermal	Nuclear	RES*			
1950 – 51	0.6	1.3	Nil	Nil	1.9	0.6	2.5
	(31.6)	(68.4)			(100)		
1960 - 61	1.9	2.8	Nil	Nil	4.7	1	5.67
	(40.4)	(59.6)			(100)		
1980-81	11.8	17.6	0.9	Nil	30.3	3.1	33.4
	(38.9)	(58.1)	(3.0)		(100)		
2000-01	25.1	73.6	2.8	Nil	101.5	16.2	117.7
	(24.7)	(72.5)	(2.8)		(100)		
2009-10	36.9	102.4	4.5	15.5	159.3	31.5	190.8
	(23.2)	(64.3)	(2.8)	(9.7)	(100)		
2015-16	42.8	210.6	5.8	42.8	302	48.3	350.3
	(14.2)	(69.7)	(1.9)	(14.2)	(100)		
2019 – 20	42.3	143.7	6.8	4.0	196.8	173.6	370.4
	(21.5)	(73.0)	(3.5)	(2.0)	(100)		

Source: Installed capacity and capacity utilization: Ministry of Statistics and Programme Implementation. The figures in brackets indicate percentages.

Table 11.4: Gross Generation of Electricity from Utilities and Non-Utilities in India

(Billion KWh)

Year	Utilities				Non-Utilities	Total [5]+[6]
	Thermal+ RES*	Hydro	Nuclear	Total		
1950-51	2.6	2.5	--	5.1	1.5	6.6
1960-61	9.1	7.8	--	16.9	3.2	20.1
1970-71	28.2	25.2	2.4	55.8	5.4	61.2
1980-81	61.3	56.5	3.0	120.8	8.4	129.2
1990-91	186.5	71.7	6.1	264.3	25.1	289.4
2000-01	408.1	74.5	16.9	499.5	55.0	554.5
2010-11	704.1	114.4	26.3	844.8	120.9	965.7
2014-15	951.5	129.2	36.1	1116.8	162.1	1278.9
2018-19 (P)	1199.1	134.9	37.8	1371.8	175.0	1546.8

Note: * RES stands for Renewable energy sources; KWh: Kilowatt hours.

Source: Economic Survey, Ministry of Finance & Energy Statistics, 2020, Central Statistical Office, Ministry of Statistics and Programme Implementation.

Table 11.5: Installed Capacity of Renewable Energy sources

(In Thousand MW)

Break-up of Renewables as on 30 – 04 – 2020 (Both Utilities & Private)					
Small Hydro Power/ Cogen.	Wind Power Energy	Bio-Power BM Power	Waste to Energy	Solar Power	Total Capacity
4.7	37.7	9.9	0.1	34.8	87.3

Source: Ministry of New and Renewable Energy, Govt. of India, Annual Report, 2019-20.

Relative shares: For long, thermal power has been having a dominant share in India's electricity matrix as can been from Table 11.3. Its share has risen over the years while the share of hydel power has declined. Thermal power meets over 70 per cent of India's electricity needs while the share of nuclear energy is very low. As stated earlier, this has serious implications for India complying with the emission targets laid down under 2015 Paris Climate Change Conference. India is trying to increase the share of Renewable energy and reduce dependence on coal-based thermal energy to the extent feasible keeping in view her developmental imperatives. The installed capacity of various Renewable sources as in April 2020 is given in Table 11.5.Further, India has achieved a cumulative installed renewable energy capacity (excluding large hydro) of 92.54 by January 2021.

❑ SOURCES OF ENERGY AND POWER

As on March 2011, India's estimated coal reserves were about 286 billion tonnes, lignite 41 billion tonnes, crude oil 757 MT, and natural gas 1241 billion cubic metres (BCM). Estimated hydro potential (above 25 MW) is about 145 gigawatts (GW). The total potential for renewable power generation from various sources, other than large hydro projects was 89,760 MW.

Hydroelectric Potential

Hydroelectric power has the advantage of being stored and used flexibly to meet the peak period demand. India is well endowed with economically viable hydro potential. However, hydro energy generation is adversely affected in years when the monsoon is weak and deficient, as it happened in 2014–15 when its growth was negative.

Studies have been conducted on the hydo power potential of the east and west flowing rivers in the South, the rivers of Central India, and the Himalayan and other river systems in Northern India. According to the Central Electricity Authority (CEA), India's hydro potential is estimated to be 148,700 MW of installed capacity, while the capacity installed up to 2019–20 is 42,300 MW (See Table 11.3 coln. 2). The CEA has plans for pumped storage schemes and to add more capacity from small, mini, and micro hydel schemes.

Nuclear Resources

India has uranium resources adequate to meet the requirement of the first stage of nuclear power development of 10,000 MW. Apart from this, there are also vast deposits of thorium available in the country. Nuclear energy has the potential to meet the future needs of electricity demand in the country.The country has developed the capability to build and operate nuclear power plants as per the international safety standards. The share of nuclear power in commercial energy production in 2006–07 was 1.86 per cent while its share in total commercial energy supply was 1.24 per cent.

The installed capacity of nuclear power plants in 2013–14 was 4,800 MW accounting for 1.96 per cent of the total installed capacity of the country. The Nuclear Power Corporation of India Ltd. (NPCIL) plans to increase the installed capacity for power generation using indigenous natural uranium resources and the vast thorium resources available in the country.

Thermal Power

Coal continues to be the major energy resource of the country. As per 2007 estimates, India's coal reserves were 253.3 billion tonnes (bt), out of which 97.92 bt are in the proved category. The lignite reserves in 2006 were estimated at 38.27 bt, out of which 4.5 bt are in the proved category.

Coal-based thermal power stations are important sources of electrical energy in India. With the known reserves of coal and lignite, there should be no difficulty in meeting the coal requirements for power generation in the foreseeable future. Only about 10 per cent of the coal raised is being used for power generation at present.

Thermal Power and Pollution

Coal-fired thermal power is one of the major contributors to greenhouse gas emissions and at present, bulk of power generation in India, over 60 per cent, is by thermal plants which are high polluting agents. Old, inefficient, and polluting thermal plants are mostly in the public sector which should adopt better technologies to lower the emissions. Adoption of clean coal technologies such as ultra-super critical thermal power technology could help reduce emissions which cause both environmental pollution and adversely impact public health. This is an issue debated at International Climate Change conferences as discussed under 'India and Climate Change' in a later chapter. (See pp.20.38-9)

Coal Production and Coal Sector Reforms

There has been acute shortage of coal which is required for power plants and, despite having large reserves, India has had to import coal for meeting the gap. The government has lately taken several measures to boost coal production. The mode of allocation of coal mines has been a vexatious issue as actions taken in the last few years came to be questioned for their probity and had come under the scanner. Hence, the government has been at pains to adopt a more transparent and unimpeachable process.

In order to reform the process of allocation, it was initially proposed to allot coal blocks through a reverse-auction process under which the Central government awards the coal block to the company that quotes the lowest mining charge. Power producers could add this mining cost to the price at which they sell power to the distributors. But under a new proposal, the States can select the companies that offer the lowest price tariff based on coal from the blocks, which is similar to the model followed in the Ultra Mega Power Projects (UMPP). But unlike in the UMPP scheme, companies do not have an obligation to build new plants and could use the coal mined to operate units that are lying idle for want of fuel. Coal supplies from Coal India will also be awarded in the same manner. This scheme would help State distribution companies (Discoms) procure power cheaper while the power producers would get coal and are also assured of power purchase. Thus, it serves the purpose of ensuring fuel supply as well as assured power purchase.

♦ Oil and Natural Gas

India has about 0.04 per cent of the world's proven reserves of hydrocarbons. The balance of recoverable reserves as estimated in 2001 was placed at 733.70 million tonnes (mt) of crude oil and 749.65 billion cubic meters (BCM) of natural gas.

The share of hydrocarbons in the primary commercial energy consumption of the country has been increasing over the years and is now estimated at 44.9 per cent (36.0 per cent for oil and 8.9 per cent for natural gas). The demand for oil is bound to increase further during the next two decades. The transportation sector will be the main cause of increase in oil demand. Though India is making concerted efforts at exploration and increased extraction of oil, the dependence for imported oil, which is presently about 70 per cent, is bound to continue and even increase further.

Meanwhile, several steps have been initiated to increase the domestic production of oil and natural gas. The new gas pricing formula provides for incentives to investors in the sector and also protects the consumer interests. Various issues plaguing production-sharing contracts have been ironed out to restart production which was held up. Elaborate plans have been drawn up to reassess the hydrocarbon potential in the country. Incentives have been provided for exploration and production of gas in the North-east and gas pipeline network is also being extended.

❑ RENEWABLE ENERGY

As mentioned earlier, renewable energy, also known as non-conventional energy, consist of solar energy, wind energy, tidal power, and biogas. Unlike the traditional and conventional energy, except hydropower, they are inexhaustible sources and hence called renewable. They are also much cleaner than the conventional energy based on fossil fuels. Because of their non-polluting property and the worsening environmental situation arising out of energy sources like coal, there is great stress being laid on tapping renewables and increasing their share in energy produced and consumed the world over.

Among the non-fossil energy sources are hydropower, wind, and solar power, small hydro, and biomass. India is endowed with abundant natural and renewable resources of energy viz., sun, wind, and biomass. The share of power based on non-fossil fuel plants is presently very low and should be increased over time to promote low carbon growth strategy. Though India would continue to rely increasingly on imported oil, gas, and coal in the foreseeable future, the importance and role of new and renewable energy in replacing coal or oil assumes great significance. Promoting new and renewable energy is in the country's long-term interest, even if it might be costlier and place a burden in the medium term. Thus, energy planning for the future should take into account the need to develop rapidly renewable sources of energy.

The share of renewables in total commercial energy used will remain small. It was expected to rise from about 1 per cent in 2011–12 to 1.43 per cent in 2016–17 and just under 2 per cent in 2021–22. Though small, the share of renewable energy in India is comparable with that in many other countries: USA (1.7 per cent), Indonesia (1.4 per cent), Thailand (1.0 per cent), and China (0.5 per cent). Brazil at (3.1 per cent) has a significantly higher figure.

♦ Solar Power

Among the renewables, solar power could be critical for attaining energy independence as well as ensuring an energy system free of greenhouse gas emissions in the long run. The cost of generating solar power has been coming down and in the next couple of years, it could even be lower than the cost of conventional power due to dramatic improvements in storage technology. One challenge is to expand transmission networks rapidly enough to absorb the capacity of solar power being built.

India has ambitious plans to tap solar energy. To give a major thrust to it, two new schemes, viz., 'Scheme for Development of Solar Parks and Ultra Mega Solar Power Projects' and a 'Pilot-cum-Demonstration Project for Development of Grid Connected Solar PV Power Plants on Canal Banks and Canal Tops' were rolled out in December, 2014. Guidelines were issued under the 'Solar Pumping Programme for Irrigation and Drinking Water' scheme to use solar power for one lakh pumps throughout the country during 2014–15.

It would require concerted efforts to increase the share of renewables in primary energy to 5 to 6 per cent in the next decade or more. Though even this share of renewable sources may appear insignificant, it would confer many socio-economic benefits and lay the ground for their future growth even as advances in technology make them commercially and economically more viable.

India is the world's third largest polluter after the US and China, and its drive towards increasing the share of renewable energy is to be seen in the context of the pledges India has given at the 21st Conference of Parties (COP21) in Paris to reduce the emissions intensity of its GDP by 33–35 per cent by 2030 and achieve 40 per cent cumulative electric power installed capacity from non-fossil fuel-based resources by 2030. (For more on this and Renewable energy, see chapter 20 pp. 38-40 and chapter 24, pp. 24.20-24).

❑ POWER GENERATION, DISTRIBUTION AND EXPANSION

Share and Limitations of Modes of Power Generation

Data in Tables 11.4 and 11.5 show that power generated by thermal mode has grown rapidly over the years as compared to hydro and nuclear which are relatively cleaner sources of energy. Ambitious plans to develop large-scale hydro electric projects are stymied by environmental and land acquisition issues, and problems of displacement and rehabilitation of people affected. Hydro energy is also impacted by the vagaries of monsoon.

As regards nuclear plants, though it is a cleaner source, there is some public resistance and opposition to building nuclear plants due to safety concerns arising out of nuclear disasters which have occurred at plants in Russia and Japan, and the likely impact of radiation on health of people living in proximity to nuclear plants. There is also resistance from people living close to areas from where uranium, etc. is extracted. However, experts aver that there is no ground for such apprehensions.

The raging debate which has been hogging the headlines of the world for the past several years has been about the greenhouse gas emissions and its impact on climatic conditions. This is bound to have a major impact on the pattern of India's energy mix and generation plans in the coming decades.

Transmission and Distribution

Transmission and Distribution (T&D) are two of the weakest links in the power supply system in India leading to leakages and substantial revenue losses to the State distribution companies (Discoms). T&D losses in India are one of the highest in the world and form an impediment in the development of the power sector. The reported all-India average T&D losses increased from 19.8 per cent in 1992–93, the beginning of the Eighth Plan, to 33.98 per cent in 2002–03, the beginning of the Tenth Plan. While T&D losses for the country as a whole which stood at 31.25 per cent in 2004-05 was brought down to 22.77 per cent in 2014-15. But there is wide variation in the losses reported by different States and among the distribution companies within the States. The technical losses are due to energy dissipation in the transmission and distribution lines, transformers, and other equipment used in the system. The other losses are caused by meter-reading errors, defective meters, unmetered supplies, and pilferage of energy. A major portion of the losses is due to theft and pilferage, which is estimated to be about ₹20,000 crore annually. More than 75 to 80 per cent of the total technical loss and almost the entire commercial loss occur at the distribution stage.

As the T&D loss figures did not capture the discrepancies occurring between billing and the collection, the concept of Aggregate Technical and Commercial (AT& C) loss was introduced in 2001–02 to ascertain the total performance of the utility. The AT&C losses range between 18 per cent and 62 per cent in different States. The average AT&C loss in the country which was 34.33 per cent in 2004-05 was brought down to 24.62 per cent in 2014-15.

Losses to State Discoms

A major problem in the power sector are the heavy financial losses sustained by the State utilities which has led to them being in heavy debt. The cash losses of utilities selling power directly to consumers, after accounting for subsidy from the State Governments, increased from ₹17,620 crore in 2007–08 to ₹ 42,415 crore in 2009–10. The cumulative losses (on accrual basis) of State Discoms have increased from ₹ 79,339 crore in March 2009 to ₹ 1,06,247 crore at the end of 2009–10. While some of the States have taken remedial measures and shown improvements in the financial health of their utilities, others are yet to demonstrate the impact of the policy and reform initiatives.

The losses of state-run power distribution companies (discoms) are estimated to have surged to ₹90,000 crore in FY 2021, according to a report by NITI Aayog.Part of the reason for these losses is the conflict between two different approaches:

(a) Electricity is an essential public service whose provision at low rates is necessary for citizen welfare, and

(b) It should be a service to be bought and sold at market rates like any other service.

Due to these accumulated losses, Discoms are unable to pay for generators on time – as of March 2021 an amount of ₹67,917 crore was overdue to generators (Gencos).Discoms are also unable to make the investments necessary for ensuring continuous high quality power, or build the infrastructure required to facilitate the transition to the required extent from fossil fuel to renewable energy sources, such as solar or wind which is essential to fulfil climate change targets.

Reforms in Distribution Network

To encourage reforms in the distribution system, the Accelerated Power Development and Reforms Programme (APDRP) was launched in March 2003 consisting of an investment financing component and an incentive component for improved performance. This scheme needs restructuring using technological and managerial tools such as smart metering and GIS mapping for real time monitoring and accountability at each distribution transformer with a target set for the State Governments to bring down AT&C losses.

A new scheme, the 'Integrated Power Development Scheme' (IPDS), which subsumes the Restructured Accelerated Power Development and Reforms Programme (R-APDRP), has been launched. It aims to reduce the AT&C losses, establish IT-enabled energy accounting and auditing, and improve collective efficiency. Its key features include strengthening of the sub-transmission and distribution network in urban areas, metering of distribution feeders/transformers and consumers in urban areas, and fixing roof top solar panels. An outlay of ₹ 32,612crore has been envisaged for the IPDS.

Various steps were initiated during the Seventh Plan (1985–90) to reduce T&D losses. Theft of energy was made a cognizable offence under the Indian Electricity Act which provided for stringent punishment of all offenders. The Department of Power had introduced in 1989 an incentive scheme for the reduction of T&D losses. Upgradation and revamping of urban distribution systems and system improvement schemes in the rural areas had been undertaken for major urban centres with financial support of Power Finance Corporation and Rural Electrification Corporation.

Since the '90s, most state electricity boards have been unbundled into separate entities for generation, transmission, and distribution. The Electricity Act (EA), 2003, brought about major changes in the power sector, including delicensing of generation, open access in distribution, and independent regulators at the state and central levels. A series of schemes was launched, by central and state governments, to upgrade the distribution infrastructure and help the Discoms improve their finances.However, the schemes implemented so far have not been able to ensure a sustainable turnaround of the Discoms. A turnaround, in terms of both finances and operations, remains urgent.

Further Measures needed

The solution lies in significant policy, organisational, managerial, and technological changes. Different states have followed different pathways of reforms, providingvaluable set of policy options to choose from.

- The Union Budget for 2021-22 has observed that Discoms across the country are monopolies, either State-owned or private and there is a need to provide choice to consumers by promoting competition.
- The Budget has paved the way for delicensing distribution and to allow Discomsnon-discriminatory access to the distribution system. Delicensing distribution can introduce competition and enable retail choice for customers.
- A public-private partnership (PPP) model can be especially useful in loss-making areas, where commercial operation might not be feasible without support in the form of viability gap funding (VGF) by the government.
- The state governments should promote autonomy, competence, and transparency of the State Electricity Regulatory Commission (SERC).
- Tariffs should be regularly revised to ensure that they fairly reflect the actual fixed and variable costs.
- The overall AT&C loss figure in India being as high as 24.54 percent, many Discoms need to improve their billing efficiency through better metering. They should fully utilize the revamped central government reform scheme to achieve 100 percent metering using prepaid or smart meters while being cognizant of cybersecurity threats.
- Thefts can be reduced through concerted action by the Discoms and states. Prepaid metering can help reduce thefts and increase collection, as in the case of Manipur, according to NITI Aayog study.

- Another frequent reason for low collection is default in payment by state government departments and municipal bodies. These entities should be mandated to pay bills on time.

(See also Box 11.1 on Power Sector Reforms at the end of this Chapter)

Expansion of Transmission System and Capacity

One of the main reasons for power shortages in different parts of the country has been the lack of transmission capacity to evacuate power and supply to areas needing power. For instance, the recent power shortages in south India were attributed to this factor as the southern grid was not connected to other grids in the country. Electricity transmission capacity to southern states has been increased by 71 per cent in 2014–15 period by commissioning new lines.

The large increases in production and consumption of electricity has to be supported by a significant expansion and strengthening of the transmission network. Technological advances are important in the case of transmission lines to reduce land requirement and transmission losses. It would be prudent to opt for gas insulated substations which need only about 20 per cent of the space required for conventional stations.

Transmission expansion is an area where public investment can be supplemented by private investment and a beginning was made in the Eleventh Plan (2007–12). The power transmission sector in India, which has for long been the preserve of the state-owned transmission company, Power Grid Corporation, was opened up to the private sector. As the segment loosens its rigidity, even foreign companies are showing interest. The Western Region System Strengthening Scheme was the acid test for the private sector companies, and the prospect of strengthening transmission lines in western India has seen many private firms/consortia joining the fray. A policy framework for public–private partnership (PPP) and a standardized documentation was under preparation for use by the States.

During the Eleventh Plan, it was targeted to build 88,515 ckm transmission lines for evacuation of power from generating stations. But as the capacity target was scaled down to 62,374 MW at the time of the Mid-Term Appraisal (MTA), the target for transmission lines was scaled down to 68,673 ckm. But 69,926 ckm was achieved during the Eleventh Plan which was greater than the scaled-down target.

The Centre is proposing to provide electricity transmission connectivity to 20 power plants with a generation capacity of 11,000 MW and has initiated steps to expedite forest clearances and other regulatory approvals to transmission projects.

Creation of National Grid

The power system in the country is demarcated into five regions. They have been integrated and operate as a single synchronized national grid. This is one of the largest such single systems in the world, both in terms of the grid size and system capacity of around 2,00,000 MW, though, at a given point of time, actual power flow may be lower than this level.

❑ RURAL ELECTRIFICATION

As electricity is vital for agriculture, industry, and all other activities, it is a key catalyst for economic development and raising the living standards of people. With India having over 6,40,000 villages, and nearly 70 per cent of the population living in rural areas, the government realized the imperative need for providing electricity in villages in the early years of planning. Rural Electrification Corporation (REC), a public sector enterprise under the Ministry of Power, was set up in July 1969, with the objective of financing and promoting rural electrification projects all over the country in a planned and speedy manner. REC provides financial assistance to State Electricity Boards, State Government Departments, and Rural Electric Cooperatives for rural electrification projects sponsored by them.

There was significant progress in providing electricity to villages after the formation of REC in 1969 and more funds being allocated under the various Plans. (See Table 11.6). Electrification of villages was also important as it helped to energize pumpsets used in agriculture. By March 1985, the end of the Sixth Plan (1980–85), out of a total of 12 million pumpsets, 5.7 million had been energized.

Table 11.6: Progress of Rural Electrification: 1950-51 to 2016-17.

Year	Total No. of Villages	No. of Villages Electrified	Percentage of Villages Electrified
1950–51	6,12,200	3,061	0.5
1960–61	5,61,076	21,750	3.8
1973–74	5,76,210	1,56,729	27.2
1980–81	5,76,374	2,72,625	47.3
1984–85	5,76,126	3,70,322	64.3
1995-96	5,87,288	4,99,195	85.0
2007-08	5,93,732	4,97,236	83.7
2012-13	5,97,464	5,61,613	93.9
2016-17	5,97,464	5,97,464	100.0

Note: Number of villages for 1950–51, 60–61, and 73–74 estimated based on data in columns 3 and 4. Data for different years obtained from Five Year Plan documents and Ministry of Power.

Rural Electrification was being implemented under the 'Rajiv Gandhi Grameen Vidyutikaran Yojana (RGGVY)' which was launched in April 2005. According to the Planning Commission, this programme planned "to provide electricity access to all rural households and extend free connections to all BPL households (estimated at 2.3 crore) by 2009. RGGVY subsidizes the capital cost by 90% through GoI grants. The approved capital cost estimate for RGGVY is ₹ 16,000 crore with a subsidy component of ₹ 14,750 crore. The physical targets included electrification of 1,25,000 un-electrified villages by creating rural electricity distribution backbone and village electrification infrastructure and last mile service connectivity to 10% households in the village at a rate of ₹ 6.50 lakh per village. The Rural Electrification component under the Bharat Nirman Programme envisages electrification of all 1,25,000 un-electrified villages and 2.3 crore households (out of total 7.8 crore un-electrified households in the country) by 2009. Thus the Rural Electrification component under Bharat Nirman Programme is the sub-set of RGGVY." (Eleventh Plan).

By 2016-17, electrification of 100 per cent villages had been achieved as shown in Table 11.6.

Major Benefits of Rural Electrification

Rural electrification has brought about a perceptible change in the living conditions of the rural households. These benefits include:

- It has altered the household energy mix by replacing traditional kerosene-based lighting with electric light. This has helped rural households to save on energy and expenses as families would no longer be subject to problems like shortages of kerosene, its excessive price, etc.

- More security within the villages as well as improved quality of life.
- More mobility and comfort, especially for women, and less drudgery in performing household chores.
- Electrification helps to energize pumpsets used in agriculture; it also helps village and cottage industries, shopkeepers, and other entrepreneurial activities in villages.
- Availability of electricity during night helps students by facilitating extended hours of study.

Limitations of Rural Electrification Programme

On a review of the Rural Electrification Programme during the Seventh Plan (1985–90), the Planning Commission had observed that "the low tariff charged on the sale of electricity to agriculture sector has not only resulted in heavy financial losses to State Electricity Boards but also led to the wasteful use of electricity and also of water. There is also no incentive for energy conservation."

Power used for irrigation pumping in farms is touted as one of the principle causes of poor cost recovery of SEBs and a prime cause of the poor financial health of the SEBs. While these negative aspects of rural electrification programme may be valid and need to be rectified, they have to be weighed against the overall benefits the scheme confers on the economy. Farming is the primary occupation on which a large majority of the rural population depends for livelihood. The pivotal role played by agriculture in the scheme of things and the importance of rural prosperity, which creates crucial demand for the products of industry and the manufacturing sector, cannot be denied. Any slack in rural demand, as happens during poor monsoon or drought years, adversely impacts the industrial sector and results in a slowdown in the economy's growth. Irrigation helps to mitigate rural poverty and stress by increasing employment, incomes, and real wages and by reducing food prices for rural and urban poor. Hence, any step taken to curtail facilities to rural areas or to correct the pricing of electricity for agriculture should take into account the above factors and should not jeopardize the interests of farmers, particularly the vast majority of small and marginal farmers.

Further, assessing the progress of the scheme during the Ninth Plan (1997–2002), the Commission observed : "As per the 1991 census, there are 5,87,288 villages in the country of which about 85% have been electrified by the end of March, 1996. As many as 13 States in the country have completed 100% village electrification. However, this achievement is to be viewed with the existing definition which declares 'a village as electrified if electricity is used for any purpose within the revenue boundary of that village'. Thus, even in all these electrified villages, power connection may or may not be available on demand. A large number of hamlets and harijan bastis adjoining the villages are yet to be electrified. In this context, the Government of India has notified a change in the definition of village electrification as follows:

"A village will be deemed to be electrified if electricity is used in the inhabited locality, within the revenue boundary of the village for any purpose whatsoever" against the old definition "a village should be classified as electrified if electricity is being used within its revenue area for any purpose whatsoever".

Another lacuna in the programme was that though considerable amounts were invested and the percentage of villages provided with electricity showed impressive growth, with attendant benefits to agriculture, its actual benefit to the village population in the form of electric connection to households was not commensurate. States which had raced ahead in rural electrification have not seen significant change in per capita power consumption.

However, this has been rectified from the Tenth Plan (2002–07) onwards. Below poverty line (BPL) households are provided connections free of cost. The Government of India provided 90 per cent capital subsidy for projects under the scheme. By November 2012, electrification works in 1,06,116 un-electrified villages and intensive electrification in 2,73,328 partially electrified villages have been completed.

❑ POWER SECTOR REFORMS

New Rural Electrification Scheme

A new scheme, the 'Deen Dayal Upadhyaya Gram Jyoti Yojana' (DDUGJY), has been launched in 2014–15 and the RGGVY programme is subsumed under the new programme. The DD Gram Jyoti Yojana has the following objectives:

- Separating agriculture and non-agriculture feeder lines to facilitate distribution companies (Discoms) in the judicious fostering of supply to agricultural and non-agricultural consumers;
- Strengthening and augmentation of sub-transmission and distribution infrastructure in rural areas; and
- metering in rural areas.

Under the new scheme, all distribution companies (Discoms), including private sector Discoms, are eligible for availing of financial support.

The separate, dedicated feeder lines for agriculture and non-agricultural purposes in rural areas will help the distribution company (Discom) to regulate power supply to agricultural consumers as and when needed to meet effective demand. It also helps in balancing the load by shifting the agricultural load to off-peak hours and facilitate peak load management. The primary objective and advantage of this arrangement is regulated supply to agricultural consumers and continuous power supply to non-agricultural consumers in rural areas.

The poor financial health of the distribution utilities has prevented distribution networks from making adequate investments in infrastructure and led to poor upkeep and maintenance of assets, especially in rural areas. Strengthening and augmentation of sub-transmission and distribution network is essential to ensure reliable and quality power supply in rural areas. Metering for all categories of consumers, at distribution transformers and feeders would ensure proper accounting and billing, plug leakages in the system, and improve collection of charges. This will reduce losses incurred by Discoms and make their operations commercially viable and efficient. (For more on Electrification of rural and urban low-income households, see Saubhagya scheme in chapter 24, p.24.19-20).

KUSUM scheme: De-dieselising Agriculture

- **The scheme:** The PM-KUSUM) scheme (PM Kisan Urja SurakshaevamUtthaanMahabhiyan) was announced in 2018 which was to bring relief to farmers. The goal of this scheme, reiterated in Union Budget for 2018-19, is to de-dieselise the farm sector by replacing diesel pumps with solar-powered pump sets. It would benefit farmers who could earn money from farming and also by selling the extra solar power generated at their farms.

The Union Budget for 2020-21 also referred to this scheme to reduce farmers' dependence on diesel and kerosene by linking pumpsets to solar energy. The budget stated that the scheme would be expanded to cover 20 lakh farmers for setting up stand-alone solar pumps and that another 15 lakh farmers would be helped to solarize their grid-connected pumpsets. It would enable farmers to set up solar power generation capacity on their fallow/barren lands and to sell surplus power to the grid.

- **The benefits:** The scheme would help achieve multiple benefits.

- Discoms would buy the surplus solar power generated from the farmers providing them extra source of income.
- It would reduce the burden on state owned Discoms that supply subsidized electricity to agriculture sector.

- It would also aid India in honouringthe commitment made on Climate Change to increase the share of installed capacity of electric power from non-fossil-fuel sources to 40 per cent by 2030 as part of Intended Nationally Determined Contributions (INDCs).
- The size of solar plant has been reduced to enable participation of small farmers.
- The scheme provides to pay 10 per cent of the amount to install solar power equipment. The central government will transfer the subsidy amount to the bank account of the farmers.
- Central Financial Assistance (CFA) allowed for solar pumps to be set up and used by Water User Associations (WUAs)/Farmer Producer Organisations (FPOs)/Primary Agriculture Credit Societies (PACSs) or for cluster-based irrigation system.
- The scheme has the potential to generate about 6 lakh direct and indirect employment – non-farm jobs – in the rural sector.
- The scheme will have substantial environmental impact in terms of savings of CO2 emissions. It is expected to result in saving of about 32 million tonnes of CO2 emission per annum.
- Implementation: The success of the scheme depends on proper implementation by the Centre and the States. and financial support provided. The scheme is now part of the new reform programme for State-owned Discoms.

Subsidised electricity in the farm sector results in wastage of both electricity and precious water resources. Once the feeder separation for agriculture is done, farmers would effectively get free power from solar powered irrigation systems and depend less on diesel generators. Discoms would also be able to redirect the surplus electricity to other consumers.

Promoting Energy Efficiency

With a view to promoting efficient lighting, the government has initiated a programme to popularize the use of LED bulbs. LED (light-emitting diode) lamps have a lifespan and electrical efficiency that is several times better than incandescent lamps, and significantly better than most fluorescent lamps. LED bulbs have a very long life, almost 50 times more than ordinary bulbs.

The 'Unnat Jyoti by Affordable LEDs for All' (UJALA) scheme was launched in 2015 to become the largest LED distribution program in the world. It has targeted to distribute 770 million LEDs by March 2019 across 100 cities in the country. As of August 2021, 36.74 crore LEDs have been distributed. The program aims to rectify India's high cost of electrification, electricity consumption and charges and increased emissions caused by inefficient lighting, even as electricity demand is expected to increase five-fold over the coming years.

The scheme is managed by Energy Efficiency Services Limited (EESL) – a joint venture, set up by the Ministry of Power, Government of India, comprising four National Public Sector Enterprises – National Thermal Power Corporation Limited, Power Finance Corporation Limited, Rural Electrification Corporation Limited and POWERGRID Corporation of India Limited, It is implementing one of the largest energy efficiency programmes in the world and through energy-efficient appliances and technologies has helped India to save over 35 billion kWh energy annually.

Under the scheme, the state makes available 20W LED tube lights and BEE 5-star rated energy efficient fans at reduced rates to the consumers. 20W LED tube lights are 50 per cent more energy efficient than conventional 40W tube lights. It has transformed the market for fans by providing energy efficient fans under the UJALA scheme that come with higher quality rating. These ceiling fans are rated 30 per cent more energy efficient than conventional fans.

By 2017, 270 million LED bulbs have been distributed which is estimated to save 35,043 million KWh of energy in a year. It will also save the consumers ₹14,017 crore by way of reduction in electricity bills. Besides, these measures are estimated to reduce greenhouse gas (CO_2) emissions to the tune of 28 million tonnes in a year. This programme, which has been appreciated by the World Bank, is crucial against the backdrop of India's commitments made at the Paris Climate Change Conference (COP 21) (see chapter 20, p.20.38-9).

The use of LED bulbs is expected to grow manifold in the coming decade. And if through technological advance, its cost can be brought down, it will be readily accepted by consumers because of its longer life and energy efficiency.

Progress made and Challenges ahead

India has accomplished much in increasing generation and providing power to large sections of the population. All sectors of the economy have benefitted from the various positive measures and reforms undertaken by the government. Yet, much remains to be done as there are still frequent incidents of power shortage, and power outages affecting particularly the industrial sector. With increasing population and economic growth, the demand for energy is bound to go up substantially.

Progress made

- Delicensing power supply, allowing multiple distributors in the same area, promoting competition and giving consumers the option to choose the supplier. This reform is being implemented after consultation with States.
- Integration of regional power system in the country into a single synchronized national grid which is one of the largest single systems in the world.
- As of August 2021, 2.81 crore households in rural and urban areas have got electric connection under Saubhagya scheme since October 2017.
- A multi-pronged action has improved power supply in rural areas from 12 hours in 2015 to over 22 hours in 2021 and in urban areas to 23.5 hours.
- The Power Ministry has come up with a scheme to ensure Discoms improve their billing efficiency with cent per cent metering by installing prepaid and smart meters.
- The government has approved in June 2021 a major power Discom reform scheme entailing an outlay of ₹3.03 lakh crore in which the Centre's share will be ₹97,631 crore.

◆ Challenges ahead

- Disruptions occur due to glitches in the distribution system or because Discoms do not have money to buy power.
- There is need to ensure better grid integration of renewable energy and based on time-of-day tariffs.
- State governments have to overcome the tendency to provide free electricity or unbudgeted subsidies driven by political considerations which adversely impact the financial health of the power sector and the very efficiency of the sector.
- To see that generation and supply of power is conducted as per commercial principles by having competitive tariffs and see that the resources are utilized optimally.
- As part of India's commitments to reduce greenhouse gas emission levels, India will have to develop large amounts of clean fuel like hydrogen and promote electric vehicles (EVs) in a big way. The government has already announced a National Hydrogen Mission and the automotive sector has initiated production

of EVs starting with 2- and 3-wheelers. Even as it offers new opportunities, these measures will place considerable burden on the economy in the coming years. Hopefully, technology in regard to solar and wind power, new forms of lighting such as LED bulbs and electric vehicles and batteries will change dramatically to make them commercially more viable and bring their costs within the reach of the common man.

(For more on Electric vehicles, see Chapter 24).

Box 11.1: Power Sector Reforms

Over the last two decades, the government has tried to chart a new course and bring about crucial reforms in the power sector. New initiatives were taken to ensure that the government's efforts to speed up the development of the sector, which involves heavy capital outlays, were supplemented by private investment. The Government has been endeavouring to provide a conducive policy environment that encourages free and fair competition in each element of the energy value chain and attract capital from all sources, including domestic and foreign.

Central Electricity Act 2003

The passing of a new Act known as the Central Electricity Act 2003, replacing the old legislation of 1948, was a major step towards reforming and revamping the power sector. While promoting competition to ensure healthy development of the sector, it also seeks to protect the interests of consumers.

The objectives of the Act are to consolidate the laws relating to generation, transmission, distribution, trading, and use of electricity and taking measures conducive for the development of electrical industry, supply of electricity to all areas, rationalization of electricity tariffs, ensuring transparent policies regarding subsidies, and promotion of efficient and environmentally benign policies. The Act has provided a regulatory framework for the sector and prescribed the functions of the Central Electricity Authority and the Central Electricity Regulatory Commission. Setting up of State Electricity Regulatory Commission (SERC) in states was made mandatory.

Central Electricity Authority (CEA)

Under the new Act, the Central Electricity Authority (CEA) has been entrusted, *inter alia*, with the following functions :

- Advise the Central Government on matters relating to the national electricity policy, formulate short-term and perspective plans for development of the electricity system, and coordinate the activities of the planning agencies for the optimal utilization of resources and provide reliable and affordable electricity for all consumers;

- Specify the technical standards for construction of electrical plants and lines and connectivity to the grid;
- Specify the safety requirements for construction, operation, and maintenance of electrical plants and lines;
- Specify the Grid Standards for operation and maintenance of transmission lines and conditions for installation of meters for transmission and supply of electricity;
- Promote and assist in the timely completion of schemes and projects for improving and augmenting the electricity system.

Central Electricity Regulatory Commission

The 2003 Act has also laid down the functions of Central Electricity Regulatory Commission (CERC) established under the Electricity Regulatory Commissions Act, 1998. The Commission's functions include:

- Regulate the tariff of generating companies owned or controlled by the Central Government;
- Regulate the tariff of generating companies other than those owned or controlled by the Central Government specified in clause (a), if such generating companies enter into or otherwise have a composite scheme for generation and sale of electricity in more than one State;
- Regulate the inter-State transmission of electricity and determine tariff for inter-State transmission of electricity;
- Issue licenses to persons to function as transmission licensee and electricity trader with respect to their inter-State operations;
- Adjudicate on disputes involving generating companies or transmission licensee and refer any dispute for arbitration.

Other Important Reform Measures

Other measures taken to reform the sector are:

- States have restructured or corporatized their power sector and unbundled their boards into separate entities for transmission, distribution, and generation.
- Setting up of State Electricity Regulatory Commissions (SERCs) made mandatory. States have constituted or notified the constitution of SERC and SERCs have issued tariff orders.
- In compliance with Section 3 of the Electricity Act 2003, the Central Government notified the National Electricity Policy in 2005. Similarly, National Tariff Policy was also notified in 2006.

- In compliance with Sections 4 and 5 of the Electricity Act 2003, the Central Government notified the Rural Electrification Policy in August 2006.
- The Central Government constituted the Appellate Tribunal for Electricity and the same became operational in July 2005. The Tribunal hears appeals against orders of the Regulatory Commissions/ Adjudicating Officers.

In this Chapter we discussed.....

- Importance of energy and power for the economy.
- Energy scenario in India.
- Share of commercial and non-commercial energy; shift from non-commercial to commercial sources and increase in share of commercial energy in total primary energy.
- Traditional sources like fuelwood and dung cake account for nearly 65 per cent of the total non-commercial energy consumed; households, mostly in the rural areas, use them for cooking and heating purposes.
- Trends in commercial energy consumption; share of industry and transport has come down while share of both household sector and agriculture in commercial energy consumption registered increase.
- Non-commercial primary energy resources: fuelwood, animal dung, and agricultural waste; fuelwood is a major source of energy for cooking and heating in the rural and, to some extent, in the urban households; this has led to decline in the forest cover.
- With increase in LPG supply especially in rural areas, demand for non- commercial energy will decline; cut in LPG subsidy for those in higher income brackets and the savings to be utilized to supply LPG at subsidized rates to the vulnerable sections.
- Increase in primary commercial energy needs and its production; India's energy use is mostly based on fossil fuels; geographical distribution of primary commercial energy sources in the country is also lopsided.
- Share of coal and lignite in total primary commercial energy supply declining progressively over the years, while the share of oil and natural gas in the total primary commercial energy supply has been rising.
- India meets its oil (petroleum,etc.) requirements mostly from imports; there has been steep increase in oil imports.

- India is the fourth largest consumer of energy in the world; increase in installed capacity and generation of electricity.
- Various sources of power and their potential: hydro, nuclear, thermal, oil and natural gas; thermal power and pollution.
- Coal production and coal sector reforms.
- Renewable energy, also known as non-conventional energy, consists of solar energy, wind energy, tidal power, and biogas; their advantage, potential, and need to tap; importance of solar power.
- Share and limitations of various modes of power generation; need to contain greenhouse gas emissions.
- Transmission and distribution (T&D) system and losses to State Discoms; Reforms in distribution network and steps to contain losses of SEB's.
- Expansion of transmission system and capacity; Creation of National Grid.
- Rural Electrification, a major scheme which has benefited villages; role of REC in the scheme; about 84 per cent villages covered by 2007–08; benefits of the scheme to rural areas and rural households; limitations of the programme; free electricity connections have been released to BPL households.
- Power sector reforms; Central Electricity Act 2003; Central Electricity Authority (CEA) and Central Electricity Regulatory Commission and their functions; Other reform measures.
- Resolving SEBs' problems; steps to bring down their losses and debts; Ujwal Discom Assurance Yojana (UDAY).
- New rural electrification scheme: 'Deen Dayal Upadhyaya Gram Jyoti Yojana' (DDUGJY).
- Promoting energy efficiency; LED lighting and its benefits; scheme to popularize it.
- Demand for power bound to grow; India to rely more on renewable energy.
- KUSUM scheme: De-dieselising Agriculture.
- Promoting Energy Efficiency.
- Progress and Challenges ahead.
- Legislative Reforms in Power sector

Important Terms to Note in this Chapter

Commercial and non-commercial energy; Conventional and non-conventional energy; Renewable energy; Fossil fuels; Hydrocarbons; Transmission and Distribution (T & D); Environmental pollution; Climate change; Energy Efficiency; LED lighting; Hydrogen fuel; Electric vehicles..

Practice Questions

1. What are the issues ailing the power sector in India? What steps have been taken to improve the position?
2. Mention the relative share of Hydel, Thermal and Nuclear power in India's overall power production. In what way the commitments given by India at International Climate Change conferences (Conference of Parties-COP) will impact the relative shares of different sources of power?
3. Discuss the role which can be played by Solar and Wind power in India. How far, do you think, it can improve the power position and what steps are being taken by the government to promote them?
4. What are the problems faced by State Electricity Boards (Discoms)? Mention the steps taken to solve them and improve their position.
5. Mention the main features of the Ujwal Discom Assurance Yojana (UDAY) scheme. Explain how it has helped State Electricity Distribution companies (DISCOMS) to bring down the financial losses.
6. Describe the main features of India's Rural Electrification programme. How far it has progressed and helped the rural areas?
7. Explain the energy efficient LED lighting scheme being implemented by India and the benefits accruing from it both for the nation and the consumers.
8. Should the pursuit of carbon-credits and clean development mechanisms set up under UNFCCC be maintained even though there has been a massive slide in the value of a carbon credit? Discuss with respect to India's energy needs for economic growth.

   [UPSC Main 2014 (General Studies Paper)]
9. To what factors can the recent dramatic fall in equipment costs and tariff of solar energy be attributed? What implications does the trend have for the thermal power producers and the related industry? *[UPSC Main 2015 (General Studies Paper)]*
10. Discuss the recent initiatives for augmenting power generation in India.

    [UPSC Main 2015 (Economics Optional Paper)]

CHAPTER

IT INDUSTRY

- Evolution of the Computer
- Computer and Internet use
- Genesis of IT Industry in India
- National Informatics Centre (NIC)
- Growth of IT Industry
- National Task Force on IT and Software Development
- Steps to Rejuvenate IT Sector
- Software Technology Parks
- Growth of Telecom and IT Sector
- Export Performance of IT Sector
- Employment Generation through IT Sector
- Digital India (BharatNet)Programme
- India's Strategic Advantages in IT Sector
- Challenges faced by the IT Sector

❑ INTRODUCTION

The advent of modern computers has had a revolutionary impact on human civilization comparable to the invention of the wheel, the steam engine, the airplane, and the transistor. It has brought about transformational change in virtually all spheres of human activity. It is difficult to even imagine how mankind would have managed to handle the mounting volume of information, data, and various other activities in contemporary times which the exponentially growing population demands in the absence of computer facility, and that too at the speed at which computer is able to do. Also, the various scientific and technological advances in domains like medicine, aviation, space exploration, education, etc. would not have been possible without the aid of computers. While computer has brought about these changes, it has created a great divide between the 'haves' and the 'have-nots', as bulk of the world population has no access to this facility. It is akin to the 'urban–rural divide' where the rural population is deprived of many facilities which their urban counterparts enjoy. Unlike the ubiquitous mobile phone, which even those at 'the bottom of the pyramid' are able to access and use, the computer facility is beyond the reach of large sections of the population. Box 12.1 describes the evolution of the computer.

Box 12.1: Evolution of the Computer

Man had been fascinated with mathematical numbers and computing for centuries, and had been toying with various crude computing devices long before the modern day computers came into being. It went through many evolutionary stages—the Abacus, mechanical devices, the punch card, and electro-mechanical contrivances—until the digital computers and electronic, programmable computers were developed.

Researches during the Second World War and in the late 1940's and the 1950's resulted in major breakthroughs. The advent of transistors and integrated circuits led to further advancements in computing technology. This was followed by developing programming and languages suited to computers. With miniaturization, large main-frame computers gave way to small-size table top personal computers (PC's) and still later to portable laptops, tablets, etc. The start of the Internet facilitated instantaneous exchange of written communication. These developments have impacted modern day living like never before. While the indirect benefits of what has come to be called Information Technology (IT) has benefitted bulk of the world's population, large sections of it have no direct access to it, resulting in a wide chasm called 'Digital divide'.

❑ COMPUTER AND INTERNET USE

Though the early models of Personal Computers (PC's) had been produced towards the end of 1970's and further perfected by mid-1980's, it took more time for PC's to come into use on a large scale. The U.S. Census Bureau carried out a survey in 2011, as part of the Current Population Survey (CPS), and asked households questions about computer use since 1984 and Internet use since 1997. The questions covered computer ownership and Internet use both inside and outside the home. According to the survey done in the US, only 8.2 per cent of households reported having a computer in 1984 and this percentage rose to 36.6 per cent households in 1997, 61.8 per cent in 2003, and 75.6 per cent in 2011.

As for Internet penetration, only 18.0 per cent households in the US reported accessing the Internet in 1997 but this rose to 41.5 per cent in 2000, 54.7 per cent in 2003, and 71.7 per cent by 2011.

The data on Internet users in the UNDP's *Human Development Report*, 2006 also indicate a similar position as shown in Table 12.1. In 1990, Internet penetration was very low even in developed countries, not to speak of the less developed countries (LDC's). But in the next decade and more, access to Internet showed dramatic increase in developed nations while it was still very low in LDC's.

The position regarding possession of PC also may have been similar as those having a PC must have had access to Internet, at least in the developed nations, though in LDC's there may have been limitations due to inadequate telecom and Internet expansion—in other words, in LDC's, people may have possessed PC but without access to Internet connection for some years.

As per data from International Telecommunications Union (ITU), by 2019, the number of Internet users has gone up considerably in the advanced countries and in some of the medium-stage developed countries like Malaysia and Brazil and, to a lesser extent, in South Africa, Thailand and China as seen from Table 12.1. India lags behind these countries though it leads among South Asian countries. India's position should improve significantly with the completion of Digital India (BharatNet) programmes (discussed later in this chapter) when 2.5 lakh Gram Panchayats and many more villages would get Broadband facility.

Table 12.1: Number of Internet Users per 1,000 people

Country	1990	2004	2019	Country	1990	2004	2019
USA	8	630	894	China	0	73	645
UK	1	628	925	Brazil	0	120	739
Australia	6	646	865	Malaysia	0	397	842
Switzerland	6	474	931	Thailand	0	109	666
Germany	1	500	881	Philppines	0	54	469
Japan	n.a.	587	927	Sri Lanka	0	14	290
Norway	7	390	980	South Africa	0	78	682
South Korea	n.a.	657	961	India	0	32	410
France	1	414	833	Pakistan	0	13	170
Russia	0	111	826	Bangladesh	0	2	129

Source: UNDP, Human Development Report, 2006 Data for 2019 from International Telecommunications Union (ITU) Statistics.

❑ GENESIS OF IT INDUSTRY IN INDIA

Introduction

The genesis of Information Technology (IT) industry in India can be traced back to the mid-1950s when the Indian Statistical Institute (ISI) under Prof. P.C. Mahalanobis, the architect of planning in India, inducted computers in ISI. India's first two computers, the HEC-2M from the UK in 1955, and the Ural from the Soviet Union in 1958, were imported and set up in ISI. Later, the development of the IT sector began to take more concrete shape in India towards the late 1960's. Tata Consultancy Services (TCS) was set up in 1968 and during the 1970's and the '80's, more IT companies came to be established. With the establishment of the IIT's and a large number of engineering institutions through the 1950's and the '60's, India had built up a large pool of technical talent and this came handy for the growth of the IT industry. The top IT consultancies like TCS, Infosys, Wipro, and HCL were able to garner considerable business both at home and overseas, and grew fast into major, internationally known companies. Bengaluru, Hyderabad, Chennai, New Delhi, and Pune became major growth centres in this sector.

India took to the Internet in the 1980's and the increasing use of personal computers in the 1990s saw rapid rate of adoption of the Internet. The Internet came to be widely used for personal, official, and business communication.

National Informatics Centre

The establishment of National Informatics Centre (NIC) in 1976, under the aegis of the Government of India, was an important step in introducing IT applications in governance. NIC, whose crucial role has been recognized and functioning supported by successive governments, has helped to modernize administration both at the Centre and the States. It created an ICT Network, "NICNET", with linkages with all the Ministries and Departments of the Central Government, State Governments and Union Territories, and District administrations. It has helped to promote decentralized planning and management, and improve government services by bringing about transparency, accountability, and efficiency in administration and in delivery of services to the people.

The NIC serves as consultant to, and aids in capacity building in IT in Central and State governments, develops systems and services, and takes up research and development activities. The initiatives of the NIC have been supplemented by many private IT companies who took up and implemented many government projects.

NIC developed expertise in the design, development, and operationalization of various e-Government projects in areas as wide and varied as Agriculture & Food, Animal Husbandry, Fisheries, Forestry and Environment, Industry, Health, Education, Budget and Treasury, Fiscal Resources, Transport, Water Resources, Court Management, Rural Development, Land Records and Property registration, Culture and Tourism, Import and Exports facilitation, Social Welfare Services, Micro-level Planning, etc.

❑ GROWTH OF IT INDUSTRY

Introduction

The Indian IT and IT-enabled Services (IT-ITeS) industry has been one of the most dynamic and rapidly growing sectors in the Indian economy and has won for India global recognition as a 'soft' power. The consistent growth of the sector has created enormous wealth, created employment on a large scale, earned valuable foreign exchange through exports, and created a large pool of entrpreneurial talent, innovators, and highly competent technical workforce.

Majority of the Fortune 500 and Global 2000 corporations are sourcing IT-ITeS from India. Indian IT companies have set up hundreds of delivery centres across the world which are engaged in providing services in over 200 cities spread across many countries. The revenues of the sector have risen from 1.2 per cent of the GDP in 1997–98 to nearly 9.5 per cent in 2014–15. India continues to maintain leadership position in the global sourcing arena, accounting for almost 55 per cent of the global sourcing market in 2014 as compared to 52 per cent in 2012.

Over two decades of outsourcing experience has helped the Indian IT industry move from the position of being a vendor to a partner, with expertise in designing best practices across services, helping clients in achieving significant top line growth, business, and operational improvements. The industry has been constantly expanding its service offerings and capabilities, evolving its business models, and exerting tight control over operational parameters to ensure high customer satisfaction.

India has become the hub of Information Technology and developed into a destination for IT outsourcing business. The industry has grown from ₹ 13,200 crore in 1992–93 to ₹ 80,884 crore in 2001–02. The growth during the Ninth Plan (1997–2002) period is given in Table 12.2.

Table 12.2: Performance of IT Industry in the Ninth Plan (1997–2002) (₹ crore)

Item	1997–98	1998–99	1999–2000	2000–01	2001–02
1. IT Hardware	22,100	25,250	28,100	30,700	32,750
2. Software Exports	6,500	10,940	17,150	28,350	36,500
3. Domestic Software	3,470	4,950	7,200	9,400	11,634
Total	**32,070**	**41,140**	**52,450**	**68,450**	**80,884**

Source: Tenth Five Year Plan, Planning Commission.

The government has taken several measures to promote the IT industry in successive Plans to ensure the sustained growth of software and IT-enabled services and increase India's share in the global IT market, as also to expand the domestic market. It has put in place a policy framework to make India a major force in the hardware manufacturing sector, make greater use of IT in governance, develop software in Indian languages, and bridge the digital divide. The government also took steps to expand education in computer technology at different levels to improve the quality of manpower and enhance skills, and to promote research and development in the sector.

In 2011–12, i.e., by the end of the Eleventh Plan (2007–12), Electronics hardware production touched an estimated US$ 33 billion and hardware exports US$ 7 billion. While in Software services, the IT-ITeS exports, employing 2.8 million persons, touched US$ 69 billion.

The Indian IT industry which comprises IT services and products, business process management (BPM), engineering, and R&D, was estimated to be US$ 132 billion in 2014-15 andatUS $194 billion in 2020-21.During 2020-21 the Indian tech sector contributed 8 per cent share to the national GDP, with 52 per cent share in services exports, and 50 per cent share in total Foreign Direct Investment (FDI). It is expected to expand exponentially to touch US$ 225 billion by 2020 and US$ 350 billion by 2025 as digital opportunities grow in the years to come.

National Task Force on IT and Software Development

Recognizing the potential of the IT sector to develop and be a catalyst for the growth of many other sectors in the economy, and to enable India to emerge as an IT Superpower within a decade, the government set up a National Task Force on IT and Software Development in 1998 with Jaswant Singh, Deputy Chairman of the Planning Commission as chairperson. The Task Force had a mandate to formulate the draft of a National Informatics Policy and it submitted reports covering three areas:

- IT Action Plan on development and export of Software and Data Communication;
- Development, manufacture, and export of IT Hardware; and
- Citizens IT interface, content industry, IT R&D, IT HRD, and strategic policies.

The report of the Task Force covered a wide spectrum of issues relating to Telecom, Finance, Banking, Revenue, Commerce, Electronics, HRD, Defence, and Rural Development. *The major recommendations of the group were:*

- Make conscious efforts to spread the IT culture to all walks of economic and social life of the country. An 'Operation Knowledge' campaign was launched for universalizing IT and IT-based education in the country in a phased manner.
- A policy framework and industrial strategy was designed for making the Indian IT industry strong enough to meet the demands of a zero duty regime under the WTO-ITA by the year 2003.
- A Soft-Bonded IT units (S-BIT) scheme planned to seamlessly integrate the local and export production for maximizing the economies of scale and substitute a-posteriori controls for the existing a-priori controls so as to maximize the velocity of business.
- Plan to give every Secondary school, Polytechnic, College, and University library computer and Internet access by 2003.

Following the recommendations of the Task Force, 1.3 per cent of the budget of all Ministries/ Departments was earmarked for expenditure on IT applications. It was expected to generate about one million additional jobs every year. It would also lead to increased productivity in various sectors, timeliness of implementation of projects leading to the minimization of time and cost overruns, as well as creation of new units for Software Export and Electronic Commerce, Internet-based enterprises, etc. Action taken on the report set the pace for major advances in the IT sector in the country and it impacted, and led to a paradigm shift in, virtually every sector, particularly, industry, business and trade, banking and insurance, travel and tourism, health, and education. These developments combined with India's strength in software skills placed India in the forefront of global leaders in the IT sector.

Steps to Rejuvenate IT Sector

In late 1990's and the early part of 2000, the government took further steps to give fillip to the IT sector. These were:

- The Ministry of Information Technology was combined with the Ministry of Communication in 2001 and rechristened as the Ministry of Communication and IT for better coordination, given the increasing synergy between the two domains.
- A National Task Force on Human Resources Development in IT was set up in July 2000.
- Education and Research Network (ERNET) was upgraded to link various Universities and Regional Engineering Colleges (RECs) through a high speed network. REC's were upgraded as National Institutes of Technology (NIT's).
- HR development (HRD) for the IT sector was promoted through a multi-pronged approach to IT education which aimed to increase the availability and improve the quality of education. For this, many states set up Indian Institutes of Information Technology (IIITs) as centres of excellence.
- R&D in the frontier areas of technology and supercomputing were to be pursued.
- An IT Venture Capital Fund of ₹100 crore proposed in 1999.
- A comprehensive law 'Information Technology (IT) Act, 2000' was enacted which provided legal sanction for transactions through electronic data interchange.
- Custom duties on IT products were lowered and 100 per cent foreign direct investment (FDI) was allowed in the sector, and raised the limit on the issue of American Depository Receipts (ADR's)/ Global Depository receipts (GDR's) subject to certain conditions.
- Computerization of government departments was taken up by spending up to 3 per cent of the budget on IT and many e-governance applications were initiated. A number of government portals were hosted and technology development and content creation in Indian languages was promoted.
- The Government decided to set up 487 Community Information Centres at the block headquarters in the North-eastern states and Sikkim for bridging the digital divide.
- The Media Lab Asia project was initiated in 2001 for taking IT to the masses.

Box 12.2 Software Technology Parks

Software Technology Parks of India (STPI), set up in 1991, is a premier S&T organization under the Ministry of Electronics and Information Technology (MeitY). It is engaged in promoting IT/ITES Industry, innovation, R&D, Start-ups, Product creation in the field of emerging technologies like Internet of Things (IOT), Blockchain, Artificial Intelligence (AI), Machine Learning (ML), Robotics Process Automation (RPA), Animation, Data Science and Analytics, Fintech, Drone technology and Cyber security among others. The main objectives of STPI are:

Objectives

- To promote the development and export of software and software services including Information Technology (I.T.) Enabled Services / Bio-IT.
- To provide statutory and other promotional services to the exporters by implementing Software Technology Park/ Electronics and Hardware Technology Park Schemes and other such schemes which may be formulated and entrusted by the Government from time to time.
- To provide data communication services including value added services to IT / IT Enabled Services related industries.
- To promote micro, small and medium entrepreneurs by creating conducive environment for entrepreneurship in the field of IT / IT Enabled Services.

Functions of STPI

- Establish and manage the infrastructural resources such as integrated infrastructure including International communication / Data center / Incubating facilities etc. for 100% export-oriented units and to render similar services to the users other than exporters.
- Undertake other export promotional activities such as technology assessments, market analysis, market segmentation as also to organize workshops/exhibitions/seminars/conferences etc.
- Facilitate specialized training in the niche areas to meet the above objectives.
- Work closely with State Governments and act as interface between Industry and Government.
- Establish STPI's presence in secondary and tertiary locations to promote Software Technology Park / Electronics

Hardware Technology Park Scheme, and other promotional schemes.

- Promote entrepreneurship through incubation programmes and seed funds.
- Assist State Governments in formulating IT policies and liaison for promoting IT industries states to achieve an exponential growth of exports.
- Promote quality and security standards in the IT industries.
- Work jointly with venture capitalists for providing financial assistance to IT industries.
- Provide Project Management and Consultancy services both at national and international level in the areas of expertise of Software Technology Parks of India.

Growth & Expansion

STPI has expanded its presence across India since its inception and has 60 centres, of which 52 centres are in Tier-II and Tier III cities, to promote tech-driven entrepreneurship. These centres have been playing a pivotal role in boosting IT and IT enabled services and exports from the respective regions, generating employment and fostering Startups to develop software products.

STPI has also embarked on launching "Next Generation Incubation", a futuristic incubation scheme to offer comprehensive support and services and extend seed funding to startups from 12 STPI incubation facilities pan-India located at Agartala, Guwahati,Dehradun,Bhilai, Jaipur, Lucknow,Prayagraj, Mohali,Bhubaneswar, Bhopal, Patna and Vijayawada.

STPI has played a key role in transforming the country as the preferred IT destination, which is amply proven by the spectacular growth in exports by STPI-registered units from `52 crore in 1992-93 to `5,08,438 crore in 2020-21, which is about 50 per cent of the national software exports and 2.3 per cent of India's GDP.

❑ PROGRESS OF TELECOM AND IT SECTOR

The various steps taken by the government over the years and the positive role played by the Telecom and IT industry and the industry association NASSCOM, led to significant accomplishments in the IT sector. The software industry forged ahead, large-scale computerization took place in various sectors of the economy, computer education expanded, and there was greater Internet usage. It led to rapid development of the software industry, IT-based automation in various industries, development of supercomputer technology, etc. The expansion of telecom sector played a crucial part in this regard.

The Internet, which is another growing mode of communication, is a worldwide system of computer networks. Broadband is called 'high-speed' Internet, because it usually has a high rate of data transmission.

There was exponential increase in the percentage of persons using Internet and the number of Fixed Broadband and Mobile-cellular Subscriptions between 2001 and 2014 as shown in Table 12.3. Though the percentage of Internet users in India in 2014 was only 18.0, but in absolute numbers this percentage works out to nearly ten times Australia's population which is about 24 million. It is estimated that the number of Internet users in India at 250 million would have exceeded that in USA and India would be behind only China.

Table 12.3: Internet Usage, Broadband Subscribers, and Mobile Subscribers in India

Year	2001	2003	2005	2008	2010	2012	2015	2019
1. Individuals using Internet (Percentage)	0.66	1.69	2.39	4.38	7.50	11.10	14.90	41.0
2. Fixed-Broadband Subscriptions (Lakhs)	0.50	1.40	13.48	52.80	109.90	149.82	169.43	191.57
3. Mobile-cellular Telephone Subscriptions (Millions)	6.54	33.69	90.14	346.89	752.19	864.72	1001.06	1151.48

Source: International Telecommunications Union (ITU) Statistics.

The massive expansion of telecom networks—both Fixed line and Mobile phone, and Broadband connectivity—following the liberalization of the telecom sector, and with private sector investment on a large scale, has driven the IT sector also in a big way. This helped the IT sector to increase its turnover, absorb large volume of workforce, and boost exports in a relatively short period.

❑ EXPORT PERFORMANCE OF IT SECTOR

The IT sector is the single largest contributor to Services exports. India's performance in the export of IT Software and related Services over the past decade and a half has been impressive. Net exports of software services rose from US $ 87.3 billion in 2013-14 to US $ 126 billion in 2017-18(See Table 12.4).

In 2014, India ranked first and remains the pre-eminent destination for offshore services, with excellence in IT, BPO, and voice services. The sector continues to be one of the largest employers in the country, directly employing nearly 3.5 million people.

Table 12.4: IT Software and Services Exports

(in US$ Billion)

Exports	Year				
	2013- 14	2014- 15	2015-16	2016-17	17-18 (E)
	87.3	97.8	107.8	117.0	126.0

Source: Ministry of Electronics & Information Technology, Govt. of India.

❑ EMPLOYMENT GENERATION THROUGH IT SECTOR

The IT-ITeS sector is a large employment generator and has triggered the growth of several ancillary industries such as transportation, infrastructure, real estate, travel and tourism, security, hospitality, etc. The total IT Software and Services employment is estimated to be 3.51 million in 2014–15. The indirect employment attributed by the sector is estimated at about 10 million in 2014–15.

The IT-ITeS exports constitute the major source of employment and its share has increased over the years. The details of direct employment by the sector for both, the Exports segment and domestic market segment, from 2010–11 to 2017–18 are given in Table 12.5.

Table 12.5: Employment in IT-ITeS Industry (in million)

Year/Segment	2010-11	2012-13	2013-14	2014-15	2015-16	2016-17	2017-18
IT Services & Exports	1.0	1.29	1.60	1.74	1.85	1.92	1.98
BPO Exports	0.77	0.88	0.99	1.03	1.09	1.15	1.19
Domestic Market	0.53	0.60	0.70	0.74	0.75	0.79	0.79
Total Employment	2.30	2.77	3.29	3.51	3.69	3.86	3.96

Source: Ministry of Electronics & Information Technology, Govt. of India.

With expansion of opportunities in the digital field, India would require more professionals in the IT and IT-enabled services to get ahead. The country needs to ensure the right mix of technical, business, and functional skills in the workforce to meet the needs of individual business segments and customer markets. Educational and training institutions need to keep in view the changing environment and reorient their programmes to match the demands of the industry.

Box 12.3 Digital India Programme

Bharat Broadband Network Limited (BBNL)was set up as a Special Purpose Vehicle (SPV) in 2012 for establishing and managing BharatNet in 2.5 Lakh Gram Panchayats (GPs) in the country.

❖ Project

The project earlier known as National Optical Fibre Network (NOFN) and now called BharatNet is being implemented in a phased manner.

Phase -I was to cover 1 lakh GPs by tapping BSNL's existing Fibre and laying incremental cable upto GPs. Each GP is to be provided with at least 100 Mbps bandwidth on sharing basis. The government has since adopted a modified strategy for implementing the project in collaboration with States, Private sector and CPSUs. Under Ph- II, Fibres are to be laid from Block to GP. Technology offered is linear with GPON and 1 Gbps bandwidth has been planned at each GP.

❖ Progress

- The Phase -I target of covering 1 lakh GPs under Phase-1 was completed by Dec 2017. Additional 25,000 GPs was covered under Phase-1. More than 1,21,000 GPs have been made service ready.
- Phase- II would connect remaining 1,25,000 GPs by a mix of different modes like underground optical fibre cable(OFC), Aerial OFC, Radio and Satellite. It would be implemented through three models:
- States and state agencies: AP, Telangana, Chhattisgarh, Tamil Nadu, Jharkhand, Gujarat, Odisha, Maharashtra and Uttarakhand are being covered under the State Model.
- BBNL-led private Model: Two States namely Punjab and Bihar have been implemented through private sector model directly by BBNL and work has been completed in both the States.
- CPSU Model: BSNL is executing under CPSU model in Madhya Pradesh, Uttar Pradesh, Sikkim and Jammu & Kashmir.
- Satellite: The satellite component of the Phase- II is being implemented by BBNL and BSNL.

Public Private Partnership (PPP): PPP based model has been adopted for network upgradation and meeting future requirement and village connectivity through broadband. This will provide connectivity between the Block headquarters (BHQs) and the GPs. Assam, Haryana, Kerala, MP, Punjab, Rajasthan, UP, West Bengal, Himachal Pradesh, Arunachal Pradesh, Manipur, Mizoram, Meghalaya, Nagaland and Tripura are to be covered in PPP mode.

NITI Aayog which has been reviewing the progress of BharatNet has recommended to utilize capacity of private sector partners in creation, upgradation, operations, maintenance and utilization of the project.

❖ Common Services Centers

- A major objective and focus of BharatNet project is to provide Common Services Centers (CSCs) in rural India internet enabled access points for delivery of various Digital Services (e-Services) to the citizens.
- Setting up 3.7 lakh CSCs across India has not only encouraged digital entrepreneurship in rural areas butalso improved access to digital services for common man.
- The CSCs will enable citizens to avail Government and other services closer to their locality in a transparent and timely manner. The e-Governance services will be a single-point facility within easy reach of the citizens and eliminate the need for citizens having to go to various Government offices.
- Digital services like eHospital, BHIM-UPI, online scholarships, DigiLocker, Umangapp, eCourts, Tele Law, eWay Bills etc. have improved ease of living for citizens. The Government eMarketplace (GeM) has not only made government procurement transparent but has also enabled small businesses and even Start-Ups to sell their products and services to governmentorganisations.
- The CSCs are run by Village Level Entrepreneurs (VLEs), who are co-opted into the ecosystem from the local community they serve. To ensure sustainability of the CSC, the capabilities of the VLEs are nurtured through entrepreneurship development programs and training workshops.
- The personnel manning CSCs will serve as change agents, promoting rural entrepreneurship and building rural capacities and livelihoods. They will enable community participation and collective action for engendering social change through a bottom-up approach with key focus on the rural citizens.

❖ Services

To begin with 28 Central Government services are offered to the citizens through the CSC network using the centralized Digital Seva Portal. State services, ranging from 10 to 400 in various States are also being delivered through the CSCs in collaboration with various State Governments and their Departments. By partnering with Government and private service providers, CSCs are able to deliver a wide range of services.

❑ INDIA'S STRATEGIC ADVANTAGES IN IT SECTOR

India had several strategic advantages which helped her to secure a premier position in the global IT industry. India was an early entrant in this domain and has continued to maintain its first mover advantage and retained its leadership position in the global sourcing arena with a share of 55 per cent. India developed and honed the IT skills and formed many start-ups, which with their technical expertise, innovative, and entrepreneurial capabilities, captured much of the overseas business. These companies steadily grew into large enterprises and earned global fame for their impeccable performance and excellence in service delivery.

India's skilled, English-speaking technical personnel, and relatively low-cost operations, helped to attract much of the outsourced business from abroad. India also showed prowess in technology development and innovation as a result of which some of the major MNCs set up not only their offices in India, but even R&D centres in Bengaluru, Hyderabad, etc.

India also remains a high potential market worldwide, offering multiple opportunities. With the world's second largest population, India offers a large, burgeoning end-user market. With 1150 million mobile subscribers, 760 million Internet users, a US$ 84 billion e-Commerce marketin 2021 and a growth rate that is surpassing that of China, India has virtually leapfrogged into the digital world. The Government's Digital India and Make in India initiatives would help India to reinforce the ecosystem already built up and further consolidate her position in the global IT arena.

India's IT industry is mostly concentrated in the large Metro cities, viz., Bengaluru, Hyderabad, Chennai, New Delhi, and Mumbai which have matured and are almost saturated. As these cities are bursting at the seams, with consequent problems of land availability, overcrowding, transportation bottlenecks, housing shortages, and rising costs both for the employers and employees, the IT companies have been trying to gravitate towards Tier-II and Tier-III cities and towns which could mitigate some of these problems. Already cities like Coimbatore, Kochi, Thiruvananthapuram, Mysuru, Nagpur, Visakhapatanam, Bhubaneswar, etc. have IT campuses from where IT companies operate. As India implements the planned Smart Cities programme, facilities for IT companies could be provided there, thus relieving the Metros of congestion and attendant problems.

❑ CHALLENGES FACED BY THE SECTOR

Offshoring conundrum

The Indian software industry has, of late, been facing many challenges. The major threat is from the US which provides sizeable chunk of the outsourced business to Indian IT companies. The transfer of work and jobs to India and other countries, causing loss of job opportunities to their citizens, has been the subject of much debate in the US legislatures and some of their legislators have moved resolutions blocking shipping of jobs offshore. Consequently, many of the major Indian IT firms have set up offices in the US and Europe to undertake the jobs onshore and, to the extent possible, employing locals.

Visa restrictions and fees

The US has also been placing quantitative restrictions on the number of visas issued to personnel from different countries to be stationed in the US by overseas IT firms, and this has impacted India which has a major share of business in the US. US has also raised the Visa charges exorbitantly, as a restrictive measure, to discourage IT firms from engaging foreign personnel for jobs in the US.

However, as getting jobs done in the US and engaging local US personnel, who have to be paid higher salaries and perks, would lead to increased operational costs for the US companies, the industry there has been lobbying with the US government against the above restrictions and to permit work to be done offshore. This, however, will be an ongoing issue as the US economy continues to face economic slowdown and unemployment persists there.

Competition

India is also under threat of competition from other emerging countries like China, Philippines, Vietnam, countries of the Commonwealth of Independent States (CIS), South Korea, etc. who are also trying to grab the global IT business. Many of those countries which were not proficient in English have taken steps to overcome this deficiency and are trying to catch up with other countries which have bulk of this business. India would, therefore, have to plan strategies for retaining competitive advantage in terms of pricing, skills, and efficiency in service delivery.

Insourcing

This is a new, emerging issue confronting Indian IT companies. After nearly two decades of outsourcing back-office operations and software projects to Indian IT firms, some of the transnational companies plan to shift the work—software development, programming, maintenance, etc. —back to their own offices to get the jobs done inhouse. This will put an end to assigning jobs to third party vendors as the hiring companies try to tap their inhouse potential and core capabilities which will mean more productive use of their own personnel. While the threat is not imminent, if this trend happens on a large scale, it is bound to impact the revenues of Indian companies which have been earning millions of dollars from outsourcing mode.

Global Slowdown

Amidst the current global economic slowdown, hiring companies are also forced to cut their IT spending which will affect outsourcing deals. Also, there is more competition among IT companies in India vying for business which will put pressure on prices quoted for deals and margins. Some hiring companies also ask for more work to be turned out even as they bargain for lesser rates. These are bound to impact the profit margins of IT companies.

❑ CONCLUSION

The phenomenal success achieved by the IT sector in the last three decades brought not only economic dividends for India, but also had far-reaching socio-political undercurrents. India's reputation both as a source and a destination for skilled and highly prized workforce helped the nation to improve its image and relations with a number of countries. In fact, the migration of thousands of highly qualified technocrats from India to the US in the 1960's and '70's, who went on to make immense contribution to diverse technology-based industries in the US, is well documented, and has won for India global recognition and acclaim. Many of these professionals turned entrepreneurs and set up successful start-ups and ventures, giving a boost to the US economy.

At home, the rapid growth of the IT sector created employment opportunities on an unprecedented scale, at a critical period, to absorb the thousands of engineering and technically qualified students being turned out by educational institutions. If this sector continues to grow, along with the manufacturing and industrial sectors, as the digital economy expands, it would create more job opportunities. This is crucial for India as an estimated one million youth are now joining the labour force every month—which makes for a whopping 12 million in a year—and this trend is expected to continue for the next decade and more.

India's growing stature in the IT sector has enabled it to redefine and leverage its ties with the developed countries, particularly the US and the European Union countries. Just as many of their outsourced business has come to IT and ITeS firms in India, Indian companies have also set up on-shore enterprises in those countries thereby benefitting their economies. Likewise, many MNCs in the IT and other domains have set up large units in India taking advantage of the local talent and lower operating costs which has given fillip to the Indian economy. However, lately the persisting global financial crises and economic meltdown and consequent scaling down of projects by large multinationals have created headwinds which may impact the Indian IT companies as also other global companies. Hopefully, the global economy will, sooner or later, make a turnaround.

In this Chapter we discussed.....

- The advent of modern computers and its revolutionary impact.
- Evolution of the computer.
- Computer and Internet use; comparative position in various countries.
- Genesis of IT industry in India; top Indian IT companies; India's large pool of technical talent came handy for the growth of the IT industry.
- National Informatics Centre established in 1976; its significant role in computerization and modernization of administration both at the Centre and the States.
- Rapid growth of IT industry; Indian IT companies serving many global MNCs; many top foreign IT companies have also set up units in India to utilize Indian talent.
- India, an important destination for IT outsourcing business; the industry has grown from ₹ 13,200 crore in 1992–93 to ₹ 80,884 crore in 2001–02.
- The government took many steps to promote the industry; by 2011–12, the end of the Eleventh Plan, Electronics hardware production touched US$ 33 billion and hardware exports US$ 7 billion; in Software services, the IT-ITeS exports, employing 2.8 million persons, touched US$ 69 billion.
- The Indian IT industry was estimated at US$ 132 billion in 2014-15, and stands at US $194 billion in 2020-21.
- National Task Force on IT and Software Development set up in 1998, made several recommendation for the development of the IT sector.
- The government took further steps in late 1990's and the early part of 2000, to give fillip to the IT sector.
- Software Technology Parks of India (STPI) was set up by the Ministry of Communications and IT in 1991; STP's were set up in many cities and smaller towns; they have made significant contributions to software exports.
- Positive role played by the Telecom and IT industry and the industry association NASSCOM, led to significant accomplishments in the IT sector.
- Expansion of telecom networks—both Fixed line and Mobile phone, and Broadband connectivity has driven IT sector growth.

- Impressive growth in IT exports, particularly Software exports; In 2017-18, the net earnings from Softwareand Services services exports was US$ 126 billion.
- The sector continues to be one of the largest employers in the country, directly employing nearly 3.5 million people.
- Digital India (BharatNet) programme to transform India into a digitally empowered society and knowledge economy; Common Services Centres (CSCs), with Broadband facilities,being set up in 2.5 lakh Gram Panchayats to render various services to the people.
- India has several strategic advantages which helped her to secure a premier position in the global IT industry—skilled, English-speaking workforce, low cost operations, efficient delivery, etc.
- Challenges faced by the sector—restrictions by the US on offshoring and outsourcing of work; visa restrictions and high visa fees; competition from other emerging countries; insourcing of work by hiring companies; global economic meltdown and reduction in work.
- Benefits to India from phenomenal success in IT sector; contribution of Indian technocrats and entrepreneurs to US economy; rise in country's prestige and leverage with developed countries.

Important Terms to Note in this Chapter

Abacus; Digital divide; IT-enabled services (ITeS); SoftwareTechnology Park(STP); Broadband; e-Governance; Digital India (BhataNet) project; Optical FibreCable (OFC) network; Outsourcing; Insourcing; Global slowdown/meltdown.

Practice Questions

1. Give an account of the contribution of Information Technology (IT) industry to Indian economy.
2. What were the factors which helped India to become a major player in the Information Technology (IT) sector at the global level.
3. What are the challenges confronting Information Technology (IT) companies in India and what steps need to be taken to overcome them?
4. Describe the changes and benefits brought about by the introduction of Computers in various sectors in the economy. Mention some specific instances.
5. In what way computerisation has helped to improve governance at the Central and State levels. Mention some specific examples.

6. Describe the role played by National Informatics Centre (NIC) in promoting computerization in administration at Central and State government levels. In what way it has helped to improve administration and services to public at large.

7. Mention the features of the 'Digital India' programme under implementation. How far do you think it will help to improve governance and provision of services to the people in rural areas?

8. In the context of the information technology revolution, Digital India Programme, is a significant instrument of administrative reforms. Do you agree?

   [UPSC Main 2015 (Economics Optional Paper)]

9. Discuss in brief the salient features of the Digital India Programme.

   [UPSC 2020-Indian Economic Service/Indian Statical Service Paper]

BANKING AND FINANCIAL SECTOR REFORMS

- Indian Financial System
- Factors behind Banking Reforms
- Committee on the Financial System
- Narasimham-I Committee, 1991
- Capital Markets Reform
- Narasimham-II Committee, 1998
- Basel Committee Norms
- Modernisation and Computerisation of Banks
- Problem of Debt and Stressed Assets
- SARFAESI Act, Debt Recovery Tribunals
- Relieving SEBs of Debt
- Insolvency and Bankruptcy Code
- Regional Rural Banks
- Non-Banking Financial Companies (NBFCs)
- Shah Committee on NBFCs
- Wholesale Price Index and Consumer Price Index
- Monetary Policy and Autonomy of RBI
- Efficacy of Monetary Policy
- Monetary policy transmission
- Transfer of RBI's Reserves to Government
- Fiscal Policy and Growth
- Financial Inclusion and Role of Banks

(See also Chapter 25 for more on Banking)

❑ INTRODUCTION

As seen in Chapter 5, the banking sector in India had made substantial progress during the four decades since Independence. To recapitulate, the State Bank of India was formed in 1955 under the State Bank of India Act, 1955 by taking over the Imperial Bank of India. 14 of the large commercial banks were nationalized in 1969 and six more private banks were nationalized in 1980. The number of bank branches which stood at 4,151 in 1951 rose to 60,190 by 1991. The deposits in Scheduled Commercial banks increased from ₹ 4,646 crore in June 1969 to ₹ 79,13,443 crore in March 2014 and ₹135,67,492 crore in March 2020.

❑ INDIAN FINANCIAL SYSTEM

Indian financial system has an impressive array of banks and financial institutions which are at the very core of the financial architecture of the economy. While commercial and co-operative banks provided short-term credit, all India development banks and state-level financial institutions catered to medium-term and long-term finance. The co-operative banking sector consist of a large number of co-operative banks and co-operative land development banks at state, district, and taluk levels.

The financial sector can also be classified into the Money Market and the Capital Market—the former dealing with short-term funds while the latter with medium-term and long-term funds. The money market consists of the organized and the unorganized sectors—the former comprising the commercial banks—public sector banks, private, and foreign banks—and co-operative and regional rural banks while the unorganized sector consists of indigenous bankers, commission and trading agents, and money lenders.

There are investment institutions such as Life Insurance Corporation (LIC), General Insurance Corporation (GIC), and Unit Trust of India (UTI). Banks and financial institutions have also set up Mutual Funds which undertakes financing activities. And several Non-banking financial companies (NBFCs) and Micro-finance institutions are also part of the system.

As stated in Chapter 5 (pp. 5.7, 5.9), there is a wide spectrum of development banks to provide long-term finance. These include IFCI, IDBI, ICICI, SIDBI, IIFCl, NHB, EXIM Bank, etc. and NABARD for agricultural finance.

❑ FACTORS BEHIND BANKING REFORMS

The widening and deepening of the financial system helped the spread of institutional finance over a vast area and significantly contributed to augment financial savings and providing the much needed resources for economic development. While this was a laudable achievement, when the major economic reforms were being initiated in 1991, it was observed that the financial system had developed certain weaknesses and rigidities.

There was deterioration in the financial health of the banks. Liberal, unchecked grant of loans through 'loan melas' during the 1970's and the '80's, and grant of loans of dubious nature to industry and agriculture, often under political patronage, resulted in growing volume of non-performing assets (NPAs). This led to poor portfolio quality and there was inadequate provisioning by banks for bad debts.

Indiscriminate opening of bank branches had resulted in many of them becoming uneconomic and unsustainable. While there was large scale recruitment of staff, the productivity of banks declined. The increasing level of cash reserve ratio (CRR) —the fraction of the deposits which the commercial banks have to keep with RBI—and statutory liquidity ratio (SLR) —the fraction of their total demand and time deposits which the commercial banks are required by RBI to invest in specified liquid assets—also adversely affected the income of the banks.

Due to all these factors, the banking system was not performing at its full potential and the government felt the need to bring about reforms and overhaul the sector. While the basic role of the banking system in promoting growth and competitive efficiency would be preserved, the objective of the reforms was to strengthen the institutions by ensuring their capital adequacy and profitability and laying down appropriate operational norms to be followed. With this in view, the government set up a high-level committee to look into the structure, organization, functioning, and procedures of the financial system.

Banking Sector Reforms

The government set up a 'Committee on the Financial System' in 1991 headed by M. Narasimham, a former Governor of the Reserve Bank of India (RBI) which came to be referred to as Narasimham-I Committee (1991). Later, another 'Committee on Banking Sector Reforms', also headed by Narasimham, which was referred to as Narasimham-II Committee (1998), further reviewed the system and the progress of reforms effected. The two committees made several important recommendations, as discussed in this section, which were implemented by the government in a phased manner, bringing about far-reaching changes in the working of the sector. It must be mentioned that there was resistance from various quarters, including the bank employees' unions, to the Committee's reports on liberalizing and opening up the banking sector, but the government was determined to reform and bring about changes.

Committee on the Financial System (Narasimham-I Committee, 1991)

While acknowledging the positive contributions made by the banking sector after nationalization, the Committee identified the problems posed by the deterioration in the financial health of the system. It put forth comprehensive recommendations for reform of all aspects of banking such as better provisioning for bad debts, rationalization of the conditions for directed lending and interest rate structure, better capital adequacy norms, and giving a wide role for the private sector in banking. The thrust of the Committee's recommendations, discussed below, was to make the banking system more efficient, resilient, and competitive.

1991 Committee's Recommendations and Action Taken:

- The level of CRR had over the years had been increased to 15 per cent and that of SLR to 38.5 per cent. Thus, banks had to statutorily keep 53.5 per cent of their aggregate deposits with RBI or in securities of government or public sector financial institutions. The Committee suggested that the SLR be brought down to 25 per cent over a period of five years and the CRR be reduced to 3 to 5 per cent.

  The CRR was brought down in a phased manner from 15 per cent to 5.5 per cent by 2001 while the SLR was reduced from 38.5 per cent to 25 per cent by 1997. These measures helped to increase the liquidity in the system and making available more bank credit for industry, agriculture, etc.

- The 'Priority sector' would include only the weakest sections of the rural community such as marginal farmers, village and cottage industries, rural artisans, etc. and lending to this sector be limited to 10 per cent of aggregate bank credit.

- Interest rates should be determined by market forces and all controls on interest rates should be dispensed with. Accordingly, lending rate structure was rationalized and interest rate on term deposits was decontrolled.

- Regarding capital adequacy requirements, banks and financial institutions were required to achieve a certain risk assets ratio. In April 1992, the RBI introduced a risk assets ratio under which banks, including foreign banks in India, had to achieve a capital to risk weighted asset ratio (CRAR) of 8 per cent. By March 1996, public sector banks and foreign banks attained the 8 per cent norm.

- Towards recapitalization of public sector banks and help banks to make provision against bad loans, the government provided a total sum of ₹ 11,840 crore over a period of three years starting from 1993–94. Some of the banks were in a position to return part of the capital indicating an improvement in their performance.
- Nationalized banks were to be allowed to access capital markets to raise fresh capital. Accordingly, legislative amendments were made and banks were allowed to access capital markets to mobilize the capital they needed. In 1993–94, the State Bank of India was able to raise over ₹ 2,200 crore from the public through issue of equity and another ₹ 1,000 crore through a bond issue.
- To tackle the problem of bad debts, the government passed the 'Recovery of Debt due to Banks and Financial Institutions Act, 1993' which provided for setting up Special Debt Recovery Tribunals. The Tribunals were expected to improve the recovery of banks' dues.
- The system of licensing of opening and closing branches was to be discontinued and banks would have the freedom to decide it on the basis of economic and profitability factors.
- There would be no further nationalization of banks. Also, setting up of private banks was to be allowed. Banking Regulation Act was amended in 1993 and private sector banks were allowed to be set up subject to certain conditions. Apart from competition, the presence of new private sector banks helped to infuse an element of dynamism and fillip to modernization of the sector. Foreign banks were also allowed to open offices in India and do banking operations.
- Supervision of banks was tightened by RBI, which was also recommended by a Working Group under S. Padmanabhan.

❑ CAPITAL MARKETS REFORM

Alongside the banking sector reforms, the government also took steps to reform and strengthen the capital markets. A securities scam which was uncovered in April 1992 had revealed weaknesses which necessitated reform of this sector. The objective of the reform was to create an efficient and competitive capital market which was subject to regulation by the Securities and Exchange Board of India (SEBI). SEBI was created in 1992 to ensure investor protection and develop the capital market.

After a temporary setback in 1992 following the securities scam, the capital market rebounded quickly. The reforms resulted in increased mobilization of investible funds through primary issues from about ₹ 6,000 crore in 1991–92 to over ₹ 27,500 crore in 1994–95. A number of Indian companies raised funds through Euro-equity issues and Foreign Currency Convertible Bond issues. Most importantly, the reform process strengthened the supervision and regulation of capital markets and greatly helped to enhance the integrity, transparency, and efficiency of the Stock Exchanges. Concerted efforts were made to modernize the operations and infrastructure of the capital markets. Steps were also taken to set up a system of depositories to improve the settlement systems. While the National Stock Exchange did not exist in 1992, by 1995 this modern, computerized, and screen-based exchange, which set new standards of transparency in trading, handled more trading than any other stock exchange in the country.

❑ RESULT OF THE REFORMS

As a result of these sweeping measures taken to revamp both the banking and the capital market sectors, the number of public sector banks reporting losses fell dramatically from eight in 1992–93 to just one in 1994–95. The average ratio of NPAs to total advances of public sector banks declined considerably from 26 per cent in 1992–93 to 20 per cent in 1994–95.

The first phase of banking sector reforms, based on the Narasimham committee's recommendations, aimed at improving performance of banks through prudential norms and regulations, in contrast to the earlier system of quantitative controls. The policy shift witnessed in the wake of these reforms also facilitated entry of private sector banks, thereby creating an environment conducive to market-based banking capable of fostering economic development.

❑ COMMITTEE ON BANKING SECTOR REFORMS

Narasimham-II Committee, 1998

Though the Indian banking system registered commendable progress in terms of geographical and functional coverage, its performance in terms of operational efficiency and viability still left considerable room for improvement. Despite branch expansion, significant increase in deposits, etc., several distortions such as increasing NPAs and obsolete technology had crept into the system, mainly due to the failure to adapt to the changes occurring at the global level.

To assess the progress of reforms implemented till then and examine further measures required to strengthen the banking sector and make it internationally competitive, the Government of India set up 'Committee on Banking Sector Reforms', again headed by M. Narasimham. The Narasimham-II Committee submitted its report in April 1998. This report covered issues relating to capital adequacy, bank mergers, the condition of global sized banks, recasting of banks boards, etc.

Strengthening banking system

A 1997 Committee on Capital Account Convertibility, headed by S.S. Tarapore, had studied the question of India's move towards full capital account liberalization. While the opening up of capital account could make available more capital at lower cost and help to foster growth, it would require conditions such as fiscal consolidation, control of inflation, and a robust financial system. Capital account convertibility would involve large sums of capital flows, both inward and outward, and could lead to complications in exchange rate management and domestic liquidity. Hence, the Tarapore Committee had suggested caution in giving effect to it. Also, to handle this, India would need a strong and resilient banking and financial system. Against this background, the Narasimham Committee emphasized the need to further strengthen the banking system. It suggested merger of strong banks which could also have a salutary effect on the industrial sector. It cautioned against the merger of weak banks with strong banks as it might adversely affect the asset quality of the latter. (On 'Capital account convertibility', see Box 15.3, chapter 15, pp.15.14–6)

Concept of narrow banking

The Committee observed that some of the weak PSBs had high level of NPAs and needed to be rehabilitated. Such banks may be allowed to invest their funds only in risk-free and safe assets. If this also does not help, closure of such entities should be considered.

Large and small banks

Two or three large banks should develop to the level of international banks. Other large banks could cater to the large and medium industries in the corporate sector while the small banks could serve at State and District levels and cater to small industries, local trade, and the agricultural sector.

Capital adequacy ratio

The government to consider raising the prescribed capital adequacy ratio to improve the inherent strength of banks and to improve their risk taking ability.

Autonomy of banks and review of bank legislations

The Committee observed that government's ownership and involvement in the management of public sector banks curtailed their autonomy in functioning. It suggested to review the functioning of banks' management boards and enable them to adopt professional corporate strategy. So also, the Committee opined that RBI's regulatory and supervisory functions over banks must be separated, and RBI is not to be involved in day-to-day functioning of banks. It further pointed out the need for review and amendment of various Acts concerning the banking sector such as the RBI Act, Banking Regulation Act, Bank Nationalisation Act, and the State Bank of India Act.

Basel Norms

A group of Central Banks known as the 'Basel Committee on Banking Supervision', under the aegis of the Bank of International Settlements (BIS), formulated an accord in 1988 called Basel I to ensure that financial institutions had adequate capital to meet obligations and unforeseen losses. It fixed minimum capital requirement at 8 per cent of risk weighted assets (RWA). The Narasimham Committee also suggested this norm to be followed by banks in India and, as stated earlier, the public sector banks and foreign banks in India had attained this norm. The government aided in this process by infusing fresh capital in banks.

The Basel I accord was further reviewed and refined by adopting Basel II and Basel III norms. Under Basel II, while ensuring capital adequacy, banks have to develop and use better risk management techniques in monitoring and managing risks and mandatorily disclose their risk exposure, etc. to the central bank.

Basel III norms aim to promote a more resilient banking system by focusing on vital banking parameters. These include better quality capital for higher loss absorbing capacity, leverage ratio which is the relative amount of capital to total assets (not risk-weighted), minimum requirement for common equity, the highest form of loss-absorbing capital, which has been raised from 2 per cent to 4.5 per cent of total risk-weighted assets, and a framework for liquidity risk management. RBI has issued guidelines in 2013 for implementation of Base III Capital Regulations by banks in a phased manner. (On 'Recapitalisation of Banks', see chapter 25, pp. 25.8-9 and 25.11-2)

❑ MODERNIZATION AND COMPUTERIZATION OF BANKS

The Narasimham Committee had also urged that functioning of banks was to be made more professional, staffing and training of personnel was to be reviewed, and computerization of banks taken up. During 1994–95 and the following years, the newly licenced private banks had leveraged technology in a big way, differentiating themselves from state-run banks. The securities scam of 1992 exposed the chinks in the system and it added urgency to the process of computerization. Public sector and other banks too started computerizing their operations though it was a rather gradual process. This helped speed up clearing, payments, settlements, funds transfer, etc. There was further upgradation of systems enabling customers to do diverse transactions through Netbanking and, still later, mobile banking was introduced which has radically changed the way banking is done. The introduction of Credit and Debit Cards drastically reduced the use and handling of cash and obviated the need for cash for a diverse range of purposes. The government is keen to popularize 'cashless transactions' through wider use of these cards among larger sections of the population so as to reduce use of cash to the minimum. This could be achieved to a great extent if the new scheme of financial inclusion, 'Jan Dhan Yojana' is taken to its logical end. Installation of ATMs across the country has also enabled customers to do withdrawals, ascertain bank balance, etc. in a seamless manner. However, some of these facilities have also created security issues both for banks and customers, and various counter measures have been devised to minimize and overcome the problem. (For more on 'computerisation, see chapter 16, p. 16.30).

❑ RECENT DEVELOPMENTS IN BANKING SECTOR

Problem of Debt and Stressed Assets

Even with all the reform measures initiated in the 1990's and early 2000's, the problem of non-performing assets (NPAs) and bad debts not only persists but has even increased manifold. As will be seen from Table 13.1, the total Gross NPAs and Net NPAs of Scheduled Commercial banks which stood at ₹97,973 crore in 2010-11 rose to ₹9,36,474 crore by 2018-19. The NPAs of Public Sector Banks were the highest while that of Private Sector Banks and Foreign Banks were comparatively less.

Bad loans in the banking system have mounted as many projects, for which advances were given, have got stalled due to delays in land acquisition, getting statutory approvals, etc. Aluminium, steel, textiles, and infrastructure are some of the sectors facing stress and loan defaults. The government and the banks have been deeply concerned about the stressed assets and their non-recovery. Of late, RBI has placed much emphasis on recovery of loans by banks as the bad debts have impacted the performance and profitability of banks. These measures are discussed in this section. (On NPAs of Banks, see also section 'RBI and Debt Resolution' later in this chapter and chapter 25, pp. 25.8-9)

Table 13.1 Gross and Net Non-Performing Assets of Scheduled Commercial Banks – Group-wise

(Amount in ₹ Crore)

Bank Group	Gross		Net	
	2010-11	2018-19	2010-11	2018-19
Scheduled Commercial Banks	97973	936474	41799	355076
Public Sector Banks	74664	739541	36055	285123
Private Sector Banks	18241	183604	4432	67309
Foreign Banks	5069	12242	1312	2050

Source: Statistical Tables relating to Banks in India, Reserve Bank of India.

Note: Scheduled Commercial Banks includes data relating to scheduled small finance banks.

Data on Private Sector Banks relate to New Private Sector Banks.

SARFAESI Act

The government had passed the Securitisation and Reconstruction of Financial Assets and Enforcement of Security Interest Act, 2002 under which banks and financial institutions can auction residential and commercial properties of borrowers who fail to repay their loans. This will help to clear or bring down NPAs. The government is working on strengthening the debt recovery laws to give more powers to lenders to deal with debts and recover loans.

Debt Recovery Tribunals

The government has set up Debt Recovery Tribunals (DRTs) which function as quasi-judicial forums to handle cases of debt recovery by banks. While a DRT is to dispose of a case within 180 days of the receipt of an application, cases get delayed due to repeated appeals. Administrative factors like too many cases for a tribunal to handle and unfilled vacanies in posts, etc. also cause delays. The government is planning to set up more tribunals to bring down pendency. There is also need to enforce transparency and accountability in the functioning of the tribunals for effective outcomes.

Strategic Debt Restructuring

One of the important steps taken in the context of loan recovery is the Strategic Debt Restructuring (SDR) scheme that RBI introduced in June 2015. The scheme allows lenders to take majority control of a defaulting company by converting debt into equity. Besides, consortium of banks which have advanced funds form joint lenders' forums to make co-ordinated efforts to make recoveries. A central database of big-ticket loans known as the Central Repository of Information on Large Credits has been set up to collate information about borrowings from different banks and other financial institutions to prevent companies from taking advantage of asymmetry of information.

While most of the stressed accounts are on the verge of being declared NPAs, lenders are invoking the SDR provisions to defer classifying the asset as NPA by 18 months. Invocation of SDR provision allows a lender, the bank, to take over the management of a firm after converting the debt into equity in cases where debt restructuring has failed or is unlikely to succeed. It helps the bank to hold the equity for 18 months, and during this period sell assets, or look for a new management to take over the firm.

Stressed assets in banks' credit portfolio restrain further credit delivery to the defaulter. Once a loan is classified as NPA, bank has to set aside money to cover the risk of default which will affect its profitability. But once the bank takes control of the company, it may have to give out further loans to keep the company going and to run the operations till they find a buyer. These additional loans will add to the debt of the company. After the SDR scheme was notified, some banks have taken charge of some companies.

Relieving SEBs of Debt

State Electricity Boards (SEBs) owe substantial sums to banks. As most of the SEBs are in heavy losses, they have been unable to repay, due to which banks are also not lending further to SEBs. The Central government has come up with 'Ujjwal Discom Assurance Yojna' (UDAY) scheme under which the Union government will allow State governments, which own the power distribution companies, Discoms, to take over 75 per cent of the debt and pay back lenders by selling bonds. For the remaining 25 per cent dues, Discoms have been allowed to issue bonds. Many states have come on board the scheme and this process is expected to clear the debt in a few years and thus improve the health of Discoms. (On Relieving SEBs' Debt problems, see chapter 11, p. 11.11-3).

RBI and Debt Resolution

RBI has taken a serious view of the sharp increase in the NPAs of banks, particularly those owed by large borrowers. The RBI in the Financial Stability Report has observed that nearly a fifth of all listed companies have high levels of debt which poses high risk to the banking system. RBI Governor has stressed that corporate sector vulnerability and the impact of weak balance sheets on the financial system need closer monitoring. It is further stressed that the richer and well-to-do debtors, who owe substantial sums, have a greater obligation to clear the debts and banks cannot deal with them with any leniency. While pushing debt-laden banks to clean up their books, RBI has also been scathing on the promoters of companies and other borrowers who are betraying a sense of impunity with regard to their obligation to clear the debts.

Insolvency and Bankruptcy Code

India did not have an effective bankruptcy code and there was no single law dealing with insolvency and bankruptcy. The framework that exited for insolvency and bankruptcy was inadequate, ineffective, and resulted in undue delays in resolution. While India is a uniquely attractive destination for investments, promoters and lenders—both domestic and foreign—are deterred by its archaic laws to deal with insolvency. Laws which deal with the issue included SICA (Sick Industrial Companies Act), 1985, Recovery of Debt Due to Banks and Financial Institutions Act, 1993, SARFAESI Act, 2002, and the Companies Act, 2013.

As a result, multiple agencies, viz., the High Courts, the Company Law Board, the Board for Industrial and Financial Reconstruction (BIFR), and the Debt Recovery Tribunals (DRTs) had overlapping jurisdiction, giving rise to the systemic delays and complexities in the process. A strong bankruptcy law can help overcome these challenges.

The World Bank's 'Ease of Doing Business Index 2016' ranked India 136 out of 189 countries on the ease of resolving insolvencies based on various parameters such as time, costs, recovery rate for creditors, the management of a debtor's assets during the insolvency proceedings, creditor participation, and the strength of the insolvency law framework. As per World Bank's DoingBusiness Report (DBR), 2019, India's rank improved to 77 among 190 countries. (For more details on this, see Chapter 22).

New legal framework

The government prepared the bill on 'Insolvency and Bankruptcy Code, 2015' that provides for resolution of insolvency in a speedier and time-bound manner. The bill aims at promoting investments, freeing up banks' resources for other productive uses, boosting credit markets, and improving ease of doing business in India. The law passed by the Parliament, would help in the development of credit markets and encourage entrepreneurship.

Regulatory mechanism

The bill provides for setting up of a regulatory board, 'Insolvency and Bankruptcy Board of India', to regulate professionals, agencies, and information utilities engaged in resolution of insolvencies of companies, partnership firms, and individuals. It will improve the ease of doing business and ensure better debt recovery for creditors. An 'Insolvency and Bankruptcy Fund' will also be created.

❖ **Benefits and Shortcomings of IBC:** The Insolvency and Bankruptcy Code (IBC) has brought in many benefits and improvements but has also faced challenges and fallen short of expectations in some respects. These are discussed below.

- **Advantages and Benefits of Insolvency and Bankruptcy Code:** The IBC mechanism has proved to be a game changer in many respects.
- The new regime protects the interests of lenders and creditors to the company in default.
- It enables failed businesses to wind up in a time-bound manner and helps entrepreneurs exit business quickly.
- The code aims at early identification of incipient stress in banks' assets and creates an environment in which maximum value can be realised from troubled assets.
- The RBI is also now empowered to issue directions to any bank to initiate action for insolvency in respect of a default under the IBC.
- The IBC represents a paradigm shift in which creditors take control of the assets of the defaulting debtors, in contrast to the earlier system in which assets remained in possession of debtors till resolution or liquidation.

- It has changed the equation between banks and defaulting debtors. The banks are in a stronger position than they were under SARFAESI. And Debt Recovery Tribunals (DRTs).
- **Challenges faced**
- One of the major problems is the huge caseload in National Company Law Tribunals (NCLTs) and Appellate Tribunalsresulting in delays in settlement of cases. Delay tactics by debtors and litigation in courts also add to the delays.
- Inadequacy ofmanpower, shortage of judgesin relation to cases to be handled has added to the problems.
- Under IBC, loan recoveries have been very low and banks have had to take large amounts of "haircuts", i.e., amount of loans which have to be forgone. Recoveries critically hinges on at what stage of stress a company enters insolvency proceedings.
- **Changes inInsolvency and Bankruptcy Code:** Considering the shortcomings found in the operation of IBC, the government amended certain provisions in it in 2019 to make it more effective. These include:
- Lenders are to recognise incipient stress in loan accounts, immediately on default, by classifying such assets as special mention accounts.
- Defaults are to be recognized within 30 days. During this review period of 30 days, lenders may decide on the strategy for its resolution, including the nature of the resolution plan (RP) and how the plan will be implemented.
- The amended IBC Bill of 2019 gives the Committee of Creditors of a loan defaulting company explicit authority over the distribution of proceeds in the resolution process, and fixes a firm timeline of 330 days for resolving cases referred to the IBC.
- Reserve Bank's resolution framework on recognising bad loans and the IBC have paved the way for attracting investors into the stressed-assets space and helped speed up resolution. Of this, the corporate sector has seen active interest from most investors.
- The Parliamentary Committee on Finance has suggested that the "pre-pack scheme" – an informal alternative bankruptcy resolution scheme offered to small businesses (which has been approved by the Parliament in 2021) may be extended to bigger companies. This will require further examination.
- **Amalgamation and Merger of Banks:** Another major step taken to resolve issues faced by the public sector banks (PSBs) is consolidation of some of these banks through amalgamation and merger.(On this, see chapter 25, pp. 25.13-4).

Regional Rural Banks

Regional rural banks (RRBs) had been set up to provide institutional credit for the rural and agriculture sectors. Over a period of time, the condition of RRBs had become weak causing concern in the area of rural credit. By 1994-95, of the 196 RRBs, as many as 150 reported losses in each of the preceding five years. Many had completely wiped out their equity and reserves, and, in some of them, the losses were eating into the deposits. It was an unsustainable situation and called for structural measures to rehabilitate them.

Reforming the RRBs

The RBI had taken steps to give the RRB's flexibility in their lending operations to make them viable.

The government took up in 1994–95, 50 of these banks for restructuring, cleaning up their balance sheets, and infusing fresh capital into them. The objective was to transform the ailing RRBs into effective agencies for decentralized rural banking and ensure free flow of credit to the rural sector. Based on the experience of this measure, later more RRBs were taken up for restoring their health. With these efforts, by 2000, 158 RRBs were posting operating profits. About 48 of them were also able to wipe out their accumulated losses.

Vyas Committee

In 2001, the RBI set up a committee headed by Dr V. S. Vyas on 'Flow of Credit to Agriculture and Related Activities from the Banking System' which examined the relevance of RRBs in the rural credit system and the steps to make them viable. Following the recommendations of the committee, a process of consolidation of RRBs was initiated in 2005 to improve customer service by having better infrastructure, computerized operations, more experienced workforce, common publicity and marketing efforts, etc. The amalgamation process would also enable RRBs to have larger area of operation and enhanced credit exposure limits for high value and diverse banking activities.

As a result of amalgamation, number of RRBs has been reduced from 196 to 64 as on March 31, 2013. The number of branches of RRBs stood at 17,856 as on March 31, 2013 covering 635 districts across the country. Deposits of RRBs increased from ₹1,86,336 crore to ₹ 2,11,458 crore during 2012–13, a growth rate of 13.48 per cent. 33 RRBs had deposits of more than ₹ 3,000 crore each.

With a view to enable RRBs to minimize their overhead expenses, optimize the use of technology, enhance the capital base and area of operation and increase their exposure, Government of India carried out further the amalgamation process of RRBs in 2017-18 on the basis of their location within a State. As a part of this process, during 2019-20 16 RRBs were amalgamated into 8 RRBs in seven States of Assam, Gujarat, Jharkhand, Karnataka, Madhya Pradesh, Tamil Nadu and Uttar Pradesh, thereby bringing down the number of RRBs to 45 by March, 2020. The deposits of RRBs stood at ₹4,78,737 crore in March 2020.

Recapitalization of RRBs

Considering the vital role played by the RRBs in providing rural credit, the process of recapitalizing them was continued. In March 2013, an amount of ₹ 2,015.86 crore was released to 37 RRBs in twenty States.

Non-Banking Financial Companies (NBFCs)

Non-banking financial companies (NBFCs) are fast emerging as an important segment of the Indian financial system. It is a heterogeneous group of institutions performing financial intermediation in a variety of ways like accepting deposits, making loans and advances, leasing, hire purchase, etc.

The working and operations of NBFCs are regulated by the Reserve Bank of India (RBI) within the framework of the Reserve Bank of India Act, 1934 and as per the directions issued by RBI. Under the Act, it is mandatory for a NBFC to get itself registered with the RBI as a deposit taking company. This registration authorizes it to conduct its business as an NBFC.

The NBFCs raise funds from the public, directly or indirectly, and lend them to ultimate users. They advance loans to various wholesale and retail traders, small-scale industries, and self-employed persons. Over time, they have broadened and diversified the range of products and services offered. Gradually, they are being recognized as complementary to the banking sector due to their customer-oriented services, simplified procedures, attractive rates of return on deposits, flexibility, and timeliness in meeting the credit needs of specified sectors, etc. Table 13.2 shows the aggregate of Public deposits held by the NBFC sector is substantial – from ₹14,390 crore in 2013-14 it has gone up to ₹49,719 crore in 2019-20.

Table 13.2: Aggregate Public Deposits of the NBFC Sector

(In ₹ Crore)

Year	Total Public Deposits	Year	Total Public Deposits
1997 - 98	23820	2013 – 14	14390
2000 - 01	18085	2016 - 17	32176
2009 – 10	17352	2019-20 (P)	49719

Note: NBFCs here include Deposit taking NBFCs (NBFCs-D), Mutual Benefit Financial Companies (MBFCs)/ Notified Nidhis, Mutual Benefit Companies (MBCs)/ Potential Nidhis, etc. till 2004-05 and only NBFCs-D thereafter.

Source: Handbook of Statistics on Indian Economy, 2020, Reserve Bank of India.

Shah Committee on NBFCs

In keeping with the spirit of financial sector liberalization, efforts were made to integrate NBFCs into the mainstream of the overall financial sector. The first phase of this process was initiated on the basis of the recommendations of the Shah Committee. The Reserve Bank of India (Amendment) Act, 1997 conferred wide ranging powers on the RBI for registration, regulation, and supervision, issue of guidelines, and even winding up of these companies. Under the amendment, compulsory registration, a minimum net owned fund (NOF) of Rs. 25 lakh, maintenance of certain percentage of liquid assets, creation of reserve fund, etc. were prescribed for the NBFC's.

The Department of Non-Banking Supervision (DNBS) of RBI is entrusted with the responsibility of regulation and supervision of NBFCs under the regulatory provisions contained in the Reserve Bank of India Act, 1934. The focus of regulation and supervision is three fold, viz., depositor protection, consumer protection, and financial stability.

The Reserve Bank of India (RBI), in September, 2013 had set up a 'Committee on Comprehensive Financial Services for Small Businesses and Low-Income Households', headed by Dr Nachiket Mor, Member on RBI's Central Board of Directors. The main objective of the Committee was to prepare a detailed report on India's vision for financial inclusion and financial deepening and to review the existing strategies and develop new ones to achieve the objective of financial inclusion and financial deepening. The Committee advocated convergence of certain regulatory aspects between banks and non-banking financial companies (NBFCs) based on the principle of neutrality.

After certain malpractices pertaining to NBFCs came to light in May 1997, the RBI took prompt corrective steps. The financial sector was also resilient enough to withstand this shock. The percentage of liquid assets to be maintained by NBFCs was revised upward uniformly for all NBFCs to 12.5 per cent and 15 per cent of their 'public deposits' with effect from 1.4.1998 and 1.4.1999 respectively. The process of registration of 37,478 NBFCs, over 9000 of which have Net Owned Funds (NOF) of ₹ 25 lakh and above, was also taken up on priority. The RBI supervises NBFCs accepting public deposits as such companies are subjected to deposit regulations and prudential norms in their entirety. In respect of NBFCs not accepting public deposits, auditors are entrusted with the task of ensuring compliance with regulations and any non-compliance has to be reported to the Bank.

Box 13.1: Wholesale and Consumer Price Index

- **Price levels:** Price of commodities and price levels in an economy are of vital concern not only to households and individual consumers but are significant aspects in the formulation of policies by the government and the central bank. Inflation which implies a sustained increase in the general price level of goods and services over a period of time, and deflation which is sustained reduction in the general price level, are the two important aspects of price movements. In view of their importance, the government and the Central bank (Reserve Bank in India) constantly monitor the price movements.

Price movements are studied closely by the RBI while formulating the monetary policy. (See section in page 13.16 on Monetary Policy).

- **Price index:** The price index is an indicator of the average price movement over time of a fixed basket of goods and services. It allows comparison of the prices of commodities over different years. The choice of the basket of goods and services is done keeping into the consideration, whether the changes are to be measured in retail, wholesale or producer prices.

In India, separate series of index numbers are compiled to capture the price movements at retail and wholesale level. The two indicators are the Wholesale Price Index (WPI) and the Consumer Price Index (CPI). These are explained below.

❖ **Wholesale price index (WPI):** WPI captures prices of bulk transactions of goods in the domestic market. The universe of WPI comprises all possible transactions at first point of bulk sale in the domestic market. WPI is compiled and released on monthly basis by the Office of Economic Adviser, Department of Industrial Policy and Promotion (DIPP), Ministry of Commerce & Industry.

The prices for compiling WPI are collected at ex-factory level for manufactured products, at ex-mine level for mineral products and mandi level for agricultural products.

WPI is an important measure to monitor the dynamic movement of prices at the wholesale level. In a dynamic world, prices keep on changing. WPI is used as a deflator of various nominal macroeconomic variables including Gross Domestic Product (GDP). The WPI-based inflation estimates also serve as an important input in the formulation of trade, fiscal and other economic policies by the Government.

❖ **Consumer Price Index (CPI):** CPI reflects the average change in prices of goods and services at retail level paid by the consumer. It is a measure that examines the weighted average of prices of a basket of consumer goods and services such as transportation, food, education and medical care. Changes in CPI are used to assess price changes associated with the cost of living.

The CPI comprised CPI for Industrial Workers (IW), CPI for Agricultural Labourers (AL), CPI for Rural Labourers (RL) for which price data are collected. These capture the heterogeneity of the economic structure and the differences in the consumption basket across different population segments.

The National Statistical Commission (NSC), headed by Dr. C. Rangarajan, in its report in 2001 had observed that CPI numbers catering to specific segments of the population can be considered as partial indices only. These indices are not oriented to reflect a true picture of the price behaviour and effect of price fluctuations of various goods and services consumed by the general population in the country over a period of time. The Commission recommended for compilation of CPI for rural and urban areas catering to all segments of the population.

The introduction of new CPIs in 2011, viz, All India CPI-Combined, CPI-Rural and CPI-Urban provided a nationwide retail price index that captures the inflation faced by households, i.e., cost of living inflation. The new CPIs have a comprehensive coverage across regions as well as commodity groups including services.

- **Price forecasts:** Since October 2013, the Reserve Bank of India has started providing indicative projections of inflation in terms of the broader CPI-Combined.

To make price forecasting more robust, the RBI also conducts 'Inflation Expectations Survey of Households' (IESH) with wide coverage and methodological improvements, including in sampling design, The survey elicits qualitative and quantitative responses from households regarding their expectations on changes in price levels and inflation three months ahead as well as a year ahead.

- **Concept of Base Year:** For examining the performance of the economy in real terms, estimates of the macro-economic aggregates like Gross Domestic Product (GDP), National Income, consumption expenditure of Government and individuals, capital formation, etc. are prepared at the prices of selected year known as 'base year'.
- **Current and Constant prices:** Estimates of these macro-economic aggregates calculated at the prevailing prices of the current year are termed "atcurrent prices", while estimates prepared at "base year" prices are termed "at constant prices". The comparison of the estimates at constant prices, which means 'in real terms', over the years gives the measure of real growth.

The Base year for calculating the price indexes is changed and updated periodically to reflect changes over a period of time and give a more realistic picture of changes in the economy.

❖ **Headline inflation and Core inflation:** Two related concepts are Headline inflation and Core inflation.

- **Headline inflation:** This is a measure of overall inflation in the economy including commodities such as food and energy prices. Whereas core inflation measure excludes the prices of highly volatile items like food and fuel (energy, gas).

There has also been debate among experts as to whether the RBI's Monetary Policy Committee (MPC) should focus on headline inflation or core inflation while deciding on the policy and fixing the Bank rate, as sometimes these two measures send different signals.

Both headline inflation and core inflation seem to be important determinants in formulating monetary policy.

- **Core inflation:** Core inflation which excludes the highly volatile food and fuel components, is often termed as 'underlying trend inflation'. It is critical for guiding the future trend of inflation in the economy. Sometimes the headline retail inflation could be low almost entirely because of falling food prices. But if the volatile food and fuel prices are taken out, inflation levels may present a different picture.

The trend inflation is an indicator of the future path of overall inflation. Hence, even when food and fuel inflation moderates over time, if there is high inflation in non-food, non-fuel components, it would pose an upward risk to overall future inflation, creating challenges to monetary policy.

❖ **India switches from WPI to CPI:**

Although India had traditionally used the WPI for assessing inflationary pressures, an RBI Expert Committee, headed by Urjit Patel, had studied in 2013 the issue of choosing an appropriate metric for gauging inflation. Based on the recommendations of the Committee, India switched from WPI to CPI to assess inflation and for inflation-targeting as part of monetary policy of the RBI. The reasons for this were:

- The average Indian household's major chunk of expenses is food related, on food and beverages, which is the most important category in the CPI.
- Inflation expectations surveys show that changes in food and fuel prices drive inflation expectations. With food and fuel inflation constituting 57.1 per cent of the CPI basket, targeting headline CPI and not core CPI (which excludes food and fuel) is a critical pre-requisite to anchor inflation expectations.
- WPI measuresprice changes of commodities in the wholesale market charged by manufacturers and wholesalers. It does not reflect the price position at retail level to which the consumer is exposed.
- CPI is the metric familiar to large segments of the population and used in both public and private sectors for provision of government benefits or for wage contracts and negotiations.
- The CPI is a widely used in most countries as an economic indicator to measure the rate of inflation and deflation.

❑ RBI AND MONETARY POLICY

Monetary policy is the macroeconomic policy laid down by the central bank. It involves management of money supply and interest rate and is used by the government to achieve macroeconomic objectives like inflation control, consumption, growth, and availability of credit.

One of the primary functions of the RBI is the conduct of monetary policy. RBI lays down the monetary policy and monitors its implementation to ensure price stability and adequate flow of credit to productive sectors of the economy.

The RBI has different instruments like regulating the Cash Reserve Ratio (CRR), Statutory Liquidity Ratio (SLR), the Bank Rate, and Open Market Operations, which involves purchase and sale of Government securities for implementing monetary policy and thereby, guide the course of the economy.

Repos and Reverse Repos

The RBI has two tools—Repos and Reverse Repos—to regulate liquidity in the economy. If the banking system experiences liquidity shortage and interest rate is rising, RBI repurchases government securities from the market by RBI paying commercial banks and thus adding to their liquidity. This repurchase auctions, known as Repos in brief, was introduced in 1992. Under Reverse Repos, introduced in 1996, RBI sells government securities at fixed rate of interest and by this process it sucks out excess liquidity in the money market.

Monetary Policy and Autonomy of RBI

A related issue is the autonomy of the RBI, which is considered as sacrosanct and inviolable, in formulating monetary policy and carrying out its other functions. From time to time, there has been divergence between the government and the RBI on the objectives of monetary policy. This becomes more pronounced in times of economic slowdown when the government is trying to stimulate the economy which is in a sluggish mode. While the government bats for easy money policy with easing of interest rate to ensure greater flow of credit to various sectors, the primary concern of the RBI is to maintain stable price levels. By tradition, the government pushes for rate cuts for short-term growth while the central bank's primary mandate is curbing inflation, and, in the long run, only low inflation and price stability can fuel sustainable economic growth.

In the past few years, there have been rather conflicting views between the RBI and the government on the role of interest rates. While the RBI argued for using it to rein in inflation and maintain stable price levels, the government was of the view that a high interest rate impeded growth and egged on for lowering the rate to foster growth. This divergence of views sometimes tends to lead to a rather tenuous relationship between the government and the RBI, though both try to dispel the notion and express that they remain on the same page as far as the broad goals of the economy are concerned.

Autonomy of Central Bank: This debate on differing perspectives that the RBI and the government may have on the economy and monetary policy to be followed raises the delicate issue of the autonomy of the Bank. Experts are of the view that the autonomy of Central bank is not to be impaired by any governmental pressure on it. There could be purposeful discussions between the top echelons of the RBI and the Finance Ministry on the state of the economy keeping in view the broader objectives of the nation's economic policy. In the ultimate analysis, a fine balance has to be struck between the Bank's independence and the imperative needs and goals of the economy in the larger national interest.

These issues led to the setting up of a Monetary Policy Committee to formulate monetary policy.

Monetary Policy Committee

Earlier, RBI had a Technical Advisory Committee (TAC) to advise the RBI on the monetary policy to be adopted and setting the interest rate. The TAC consisted of top officials of the Bank and experts in the domains of monetary economics, central banking, financial markets and public finance. The recommendations of the Committee were only advisory and not binding, and the Governor of RBI had veto power and final say in fixing the interest rate. But as per an amendment of the RBI Act, the Central Government has set up an empowered six-member Monetary Policy Committee (MPC) in September 2016. The MPC consists of the Governor of RBI as Chairperson, the Deputy Governor of RBI in charge of monetary policy, one officer of RBI and three experts nominated by the government. The government nominees will have a four-year term or until further orders, whichever is earlier. With the formation of MPC, the TAC on monetary policy has ceased to exist.

The members from the RBI in the Committee are the Governor, Deputy Governor in charge of monetary policy and Executive Director in the Bank. Those nominated by the government are three academics who are domain experts.

Monetary Policy

The RBI and the government had signed a Monetary Policy Framework Agreement on February 20, 2015 under which the RBI is tasked with the responsibility for ensuring price stability and inflation targeting. Under the new arrangement, the RBI is to contain consumer inflation at 4 per cent, within a band of 6 per cent as the upper limit and 2 per cent as the lower limit. The MPC is to meet at least four times a year and will publish its decisions after each meeting. Each member of the MPC has one vote, and in the event of an equality of votes, the Governor has a second or casting vote. Though the Governor has the power of casting vote in case of divergent views among the members, it takes away the sole discretion which was vested in him under the previous system and this is considered to be a more judicious approach in setting the policy.

Efficacy of Monetary Policy

The efficacy of monetary policy and changes in interest rates as tools to combat inflation or to promote growth has been questioned by economists. In the past few years, there have been rather conflicting views between the RBI and the government on the role of interest rates. While the RBI argued for using it to rein in inflation and maintain stable price levels, the government was of the view that a high interest rate impeded growth and egged on for lowering the rate to foster growth. But there are multiple factors which influence price levels and economic growth and setting the benchmark rate, i.e., the rate fixed by the Central Bank alone may not produce, or serve as trigger for, the desired impact. There have been occasions when, despite demands and expectations from various quarters, the RBI declined to lower the rate keeping in view the imperative need to maintain price stability. The RBI also takes into account various other favourable or adverse factors such as volatility in the international oil and commodity prices, recessionary trends and slump in demand in the domestic and international markets while deciding on monetary policy.

Another aspect is that a change in the interest rate, say a lowering of rate by the RBI, is not invariably or fully transmitted by corresponding lowering of the lending rates by the banks. As lowering of interest rate may have a dampening effect on bank deposits, banks may be reluctant to fully implement the cut and thus the purpose of the cut may not be fully achieved. (On this see Box 13.2:Monetary Policy Transmission in India below).

Raising interest rates impacts prices primarily by increase in the cost of bank lending and reining in demand. Also, in cases where inflation is of the 'cost-push' kind and rising costs are leading to price rise, raising interest rate may not help.

The arguments advanced for lowering the interest rate is to boost investment and stimulate consumption in the face of slackening demand. The economy had lost momentum in growth in the last few years, This was accentuated by the global slowdown and consequent slump in exports which impacted not only India but most of the developing countries. Hence there was a need to counter the recessionary trend and revive the economy through an 'easy money' policy. It was also argued that high interest rate discourage investment, results in excess capacity in industry and holds back growth below the full potential.

Box 13.2: Monetary Policy Transmission in India

Monetary policy transmission is a process through which changes in the central bank's (in India, the Reserve Bank's) policy rate are transmitted to the real economy in pursuit of its ultimate objectives of price stability and growth. Being the sole supplier of currency and reserves, when the RBI changes the rate at which these reserves are borrowed or lent by the commercial banks, that influence other market interest rates.

❖ Significance of Monetary transmission

A smooth transmission of monetary impulses to the long-term interest rate is essential to influence the aggregate demand – consumption and investment – and pursue the ultimate goals of monetary policy. Though interest rate is not the only channel through which monetary policy works, in a country like India where the banking system constitutes a predominant segment of the financial system and plays a leading role in financial intermediation, efficient transmission to banks' deposit and lending interest rates assumes* significance.

Recognizing the important role played by banks in the financial system in India, the RBI has consistently made efforts to address the impediments in the transmission to banks' lending rates and to improve it.

❖ The Mechanism of Monetary transmission

The monetary transmission takes place to various segments of the financial system mentioned below.

- Transmission to the Money and Bond Market.
- Transmission to Deposit and Lending Rates of Banks.
- Transmission across sectors.

❖ Benchmark for pricing of loans. This is done in two ways:

- **Internal benchmarking of loans**

When a bank lends money, say for purchasing a house, car or for business purposes, interest is levied based on certain methodologies approved by the RBI. Earlier, banks used Marginal Cost-based Lending Rate (MCLR), and the Benchmark Prime Lending Rate (BPLR) to arrive at their lending rate. These were called "internal benchmarks". All loans such as for car and home disbursed from April 2016 were linked to MCLR.

The MCLR-based method replaced the earlier base rate method to provide transparency in the transmission of monetary policy decisions. This caused impediments in monetary transmission.

- The problem with this system was the lack of required transmission of policy rates. When the RBI cuts repo rate there was no guarantee that a borrower would get the benefit of the rate cut or that the rate cut will be transmitted down to him. Due to internal benchmarking of loan price, policy rate cuts often don't reach the borrowers.
- Further, the MCLR system is opaque since it is an internal benchmark that depends on the way a bank does its business. MCLR rate depends on various factors such as fixed deposit rates, source of funds and savings rate and the bank's profit margin.
- The problem with the MCLR regime was that when RBI cut the repo and reverse repo rates, banks did not pass the full benefits to borrowers. It is not that banks did not cut their MCLR. They did but by a much lower percentage.
- *The Study Group report:* The Reserve Bank had set up an Internal Study Group (ISG) to examine various aspects of the marginal cost of funds-based lending rate (MCLR) system. The ISG observed that internal benchmarks such as the Base rate/MCLR have not delivered effective transmission of monetary policy. The Study Group had, therefore, recommended a switchover to an external benchmark in a time-bound manner. The ISG's report was published in 2017 for public feedback and was later accepted by RBI.

The switchover to an external benchmark found favour with borrowers who had grievance that the banks were not cutting loan rates in tandem with the RBI cut in policy rates

- **External benchmarking of loans**

In 2019, theRBI announced a major change in the way interest rates on loans are calculated and directed that interest rate on all new floating loans has to be linked to any of the four "external benchmarks" instead of the marginal cost-based lending rate (MCLR). This was done to ensure that the RBI's action on key policy rates is transmitted in a timely and transparent manner to the ender user, i.e., the borrower.

Banks are free to offer such external benchmark linked loans to other types of borrowers as well. In order to ensure transparency, standardisation, and ease of understanding of loan products by borrowers, a bank must adopt a uniform external benchmark within a loan category; in other words, the adoption of multiple benchmarks by the same bank is not allowed within a loan category.

The four external benchmarks are:

- Reserve Bank of India policy repo rate.
- Government of India 3-Months Treasury Bill yield published by the Financial Benchmarks India PrivateLtd (FBIL).
- Government of India 6-Months Treasury Bill yield published by the FBIL
- Any other benchmark market interest rate published by the FBIL

The adoption of external benchmark-based pricing of loans has strengthened market impulses for quicker adjustments in deposit rates.

❖ Impediments to Transmission

There are several factors which impede monetary transmission to deposit and lending rates of banks.

- **A larger share of fixed deposit rates**

The banks lend based on the deposits they get from the market. There is a mismatch between the banks' assets (loans) and the liabilities (deposits). The term deposit rates are generally locked in for a longer period of, say, 3 to 5 years and these rates do not change with the repo rate changes that are reviewed bi-monthly basis by the RBI. Whereas the banks' loans are linked to the floating rates and changes based on the repo rate changes. This creates a mismatchbetween banks' assets and liabilities and often delays the transmission of a policy rate cut to the borrowers.

- **Past loans priced under the older schemes**

  Banks' loans like home loans are for a longer period of 15 to 20 years. In the past two decades, there were many benchmark interest rates prevalent like the benchmark prime lending rate (BPLR), base rate and MCLR. These three schemes together account for 71.5 percent of outstanding floating rate rupee loans. The share of loans linked to MCLR stood at 62.9 percent in March 2021. The method of setting interest rates in the older schemes was quite opaque. The opacity in interest rate-setting processes under the internal benchmark regime hindered transmission to lending rates.

- **Higher Government Savings rates**

  The interest rates on small saving schemes are administered and set by the Government of India.The higher interest rates offered by postal savings also force the bankers to go slow on cutting deposits rates. The interest rates on the various small savings instruments, after being lowered sometime remain unchanged later, and thus remain higher than the interest rates offered by banks, and this leads to reluctance on the part of bankers to change their deposit and lending rates.

- **Higher default rates**

  The bank loans are priced based on the likely default rates in the loan segments. For instance, the default rate is higher in unsecured personal or credit cards but lower in home loans. In the event of slowdown in the economy, as has happened during 2018-21 period, the risk perception of bankers has increased. This results in banks keeping a higher margin for risk, which impacts the transmission of rates as people do not see any substantial reduction in the lending rates despite RBI's policy rate cuts.

- **Different interest rates charged by NBFCs**

  The non-banking finance company (NBFC) sector, which has total assets of close to ₹30 lakh crore, follows a different loan pricing strategy. This is because they are catering to a different segment of customers which are mostly not served by the bank. While some NBFCs use their own prime lending rates as interest rate benchmark, others use base rates or MCLR of banks as external benchmarks and a few do not even have an interest rate benchmark for their loan pricing.

❖ Conclusion

Over the years, the Reserve Bank's efforts in improving transmission of its rate changes to deposit and lending rates of banks have started to bear some fruits, particularly with the introduction of the external benchmark system.For instance, the transmission of policy repo rate changes to deposit and lending rates of banks has witnessed significant improvement during the liquidity easing cycle following the Covid-19 pandemic. Further, the combination of surplus liquidity conditions amidst weak credit demand has enabled banks to lower their deposit rates and hence the lending rates.

❖ Transfer of RBI's reserves to Government

Another issue which has cropped up between the Central Government and the RBI pertains to transfer of RBI's reserves to Government. Under Section 47 of the RBI Act, surplus profits of RBI can be transferred to the Central government after making allocations to its statutory reserve funds and after providing for other requirements of RBI. The RBI maintains part of it as risk capital for absorbing the losses in its various money and forex market operations and to meet any financial contingency due to liquidity crisis or other eventualities.

RBI has been transferring funds out of its surplus income/reserves to the government. Between 2013-14 and 2017-18, out of its income of ₹3.3 lakh crore, RBI had transferred ₹2.48 lakh crore to the government. In 2018-19, ₹68,000 crore was transferred to the government.

The Central government's stand: The Central government has been suggesting that the RBI should transfer to it a much larger share of its surplus reserves contending that there is no need for the RBI to hold a large reserve amount with it. The transfer of a higher surplus could help the government tide over any potential shortfall in tax revenue and contain fiscal deficit. It would also help to meet requirement of funds for welfare schemes like PM Kisan Samman Nidhi, the ambitious Jal Jeevan Mission, PM Kisan Pension scheme, etc. even as tax collection, especially under the GST, has fallen short of targets.

This triggered a debate, both within the RBI and among experts, on the justification for the government's demand and on how the largesse would be used. As a sequel to this, the RBI set up a panel on Economic Capital Framework (ECF), headed by Bimal Jalan, a former Governor of RBI, to study the issue and recommend guidelines on the transfer of surplus reserves from the Bank to the government.

The Bimal Jalan panel, in its report submitted to the RBI in August 2019, recommended as follows:

- The RBI's surplus, or the contingency risk buffer for meeting monetary and financial risks, may be kept at 4.5 – 5.5 per cent of its balance sheet. The buffer helps RBI to maintain India's monetary and financial stability.
- It will further keep 1 per cent buffer to meet credit and operational risks.
- The RBI would transfer ₹1.76 trillion to the government in 2019-20 fiscal. This includes ₹1.23 trillion of surplus for 2018-19 ₹52,637 crore of excess provisions identified as per the revised ECF. Thus the government would receive ₹86,000 crore over and above ₹90,000 crore budgeted.
- The RBI will pay interim dividend to the government, a practice started in 2016-17, only under exceptional circumstances.
- The RBI's capital framework be reviewed every five years and its accounting year which is now July – June be aligned with the fiscal year April – March.

The Central Board of RBI accepted the recommendations of the panel. These measures will not require RBI to sell assets nor it would shrink the size of its balance sheet. This largesse from the RBI would help the government to reduce off-balance sheet borrowings, meet shortfall in revenue collections or to provide fiscal stimulus to a sagging economy.

Fiscal Policy and Growth

Another view is that lowering of interest rate may not necessarily lead to growth. In a period when the economy is in a sluggish mode and demand is not picking up, business expectations tend to be bleak and investment may not go up. In such a scenario, it is contended that fiscal policy has to play a greater role in reviving economic sentiment and driving growth. When private investment is slack, public investment needs to be stepped up with appropriate fiscal measures. While fiscal deficit needs to be contained, the accent has to be on mobilising domestic savings, raising revenues through direct taxation and curtailing wasteful and unproductive expenditure.

Computing Interest Rates

The Reserve Bank of India has laid down guidelines on computing interest rates on advances based on the marginal cost of funds. The new guidelines came into effect from April 1, 2016. Apart from helping to improve the transmission of policy rates into the lending rates of banks, it is expected to improve transparency in the methodology followed by banks for determining interest rates on advances. The guidelines are also expected to ensure availability of bank credit at interest rates which are fair to the borrowers as well as the banks. Further, marginal cost pricing of loans will help the banks to become more competitive and contribute to economic growth.

❑ FINANCIAL INCLUSION AND ROLE OF BANKS

Financial Inclusion is an important policy and priority of the Government. Even after six decades of development, large sections of the population, mostly those in the lower strata of society, have been left out of the banking system. The objective of 'Financial Inclusion' is to bring them into the mainstream and extend financial services to the unbanked and unserved population, ameliorate their condition, and unlock the latent growth potential. It will lead to a more inclusive society by making financing facilities available to these sections and the most vulnerable among them in particular.

Table 13.3 shows the percentage of households availing banking services as per 2001 and 2011 Census data. While the percentage has increased between the two census, both in rural and urban areas, still a sizeable percentage of households—45.6 per cent in rural and 32.2 per cent in urban—were left out of the system even in 2011. The government has been taking various steps to reach out to more sections of the population in this regard by opening more branches of banks, expanding the scope and coverage of Rural and Co-operative banks, and through post office savings banks in rural and urban areas, thereby reducing the population covered per bank or per branch and increasing accessibility.

Table 13.3: Position of Households Availing Banking Services

	As per 2001 Census			As per 2011 Census		
	No. of ouse holds	Total No. of Households availing banking services	%	Total No. of Households	No. of House holds availing banking services	%
Rural	138,271,559	41,639,949	30.1	167,826,730	91,369,805	54.4
Urban	53,692,376	26,590,693	49.5	78,865,937	53,444,983	67.8
Total	191,963,935	68,230,642	35.5	246,692,667	144,814,788	58.7

Source: Department of Financial Services, Government of India.

Earlier, under the Swabhimaan campaign, the banks were advised to provide appropriate banking facilities to habitations having a population in excess of 2,000 (as per 2001 census) by March 2012. The banks identified approximately 74,000 habitations across the country having a population of over 2,000 for providing banking facilities. As per reports from banks, 74,351 villages with population of above 2,000 have been covered with banking facilities by branches, Business Correspondents, mobile banking, etc. by March 31, 2012.

Recently, more steps have been taken for financial inclusion under the 'Jan Dhan Yojana' scheme. Financial inclusion confers many benefits to those brought into its fold such as encouraging saving habits, direct transfer of social security and welfare benefits into the beneficiary's account, thus plugging any scope for leakeages or abuse of the system and, above all, it empowers people, especially the womenfolk. (These aspects are discussed in greater detail in Chapter 25, pp.25.2-4).

Payments Banks

Starting of a new category of banks called Payment Banks is another important development in the banking sector. This again is part of the financial inclusion agenda and will help to bring more people into banking fold. (These are discussed in detail in Chapter 25, pp. 25.5-6).

❑ CONCLUSION

The Indian banking scene is undergoing a major transformation and evidently changing for the better. The increasing adoption of technology with Netbanking, Mobile banking, ATMs, etc. helps to render personalized delivery of services to customers. It enables more effective and lower cost delivery of financial services to corporates and institutional customers and facilitate seamless transactions enhancing customer satisfaction. Customers are also becoming more tech-savvy and adapting fast to modern means of availing facilities which reduces personal, direct interface at banking counters, thus helping to economize on staff, time, etc.

Indian banks have to scale up and keep abreast of latest trends in technology and best global banking practices to face up to global competition in this increasingly interdependent world. Further, banks have to strictly adhere to stringent regulatory norms and overcome issues like stressed assets, NPAs, etc.

As a step towards restructuring and strengthening Public Sector Banks, the government has taken steps to amalgamate and merge some of them.(For details on this, see Chapter 25, pp. 25.13-4).

In this Chapter we discussed.....

- Banking sector in India had made substantial progress during the four decades since Independence.
- Indian financial system has a wide array of banks and financial institutions.
- The financial sector can be classified into the Money Market and the Capital Market—the former dealing with short-term funds while the latter with medium-term and long-term funds; the money market consists of the organized and the unorganized sectors.
- There are investment institutions and development banks.
- Factors behind banking reforms; financial system had developed weaknesses and rigidities; deterioration in the financial health of the banks; liberal, unchecked grant of loans; growing volume of non-performing assets (NPAs); uneconomic branches and less productivity; increasing level of CRR and SLR.
- 'Committee on the Financial System' (Narasimham-I Committee, 1991) and another 'Committee on Banking Sector Reforms', known as Narasimham-II Committee (1998) reviewed the system and made many recommendations; recommendations included lowering CRR and SLR, restricting priority sector, to achieve capital to risk weighted asset ratio (CRAR) of 8 per cent, recapitalization of banks, access for banks to Capital markets, resolving bad debts, and NPAs.
- Capital markets reform; SEBI, the regulator, set up in 1992; securities scam in 1992; increased mobilization of investible funds; modernized National Stock Exchange set up.
- Public sector banks reporting losses fell dramatically.
- 1998 Narasimham Committee recommended Narrow banking, on role of large and small banks, on capital adequacy ratio, autonomy of banks, and review of bank legislations.
- Basel norms: Basel I, II, and III.
- Modernization and computerization of banks.
- Recent developments in banking sector; problem of debt and stressed assets; SARFAESI Act; debt recovery tribunals; strategic debt restructuring.

- Relieving debt of State electricity boards.
- RBI and debt resolution.
- Insolvency and bankruptcy code; bill on 'Insolvency and Bankruptcy Code, 2015'; Insolvency and Bankruptcy Fund proposed.
- Regional rural banks (RRBs); reforms and recapitalization; Vyas Committee.
- Non-banking financial companies (NBFCs); regulated by RBI; Shah Committee on NBFCs; Nachiket Mor Committee on Comprehensive Financial Services for Small Businesses and Low-Income Households.
- Price levels: Wholesale Price Index and Consumer Price Index.
- RBI and Monetary Policy; price stability, primary goal of monetary policy for RBI; for government growth is paramount; tools of monetary policy; repos and reverse repos.
- Monetary Policy and Autonomy of RBI.
- Monetary policy committee set up.
- Monetary policy transmission: Computing and transmission of interest rates by banks to customers.
- Transfer of RBI's Reserves to Government.
- Fiscal policy and growth .
- Transfer of RBI's Reserves to Government.
- Position of households availing banking services; Swabhimaan campaign and Jan Dhan Yojana.
- Payments banks.
- Banks to further modernize and adopt best global banking practices.

Important Terms to Note in this Chapter

Money market; Capital market; Non-performing assets (NPAs); Cash reserve ratio (CRR); Statutory liquidity ratio (SLR); Priority sector; Capital adequacy ratio; Capital to risk weighted asset ratio (CRAR); Recapitalization of banks; Debt Recovery Tribunals; Account Convertibility; Basel norms—Basel I, II , III; SARFAESI Act; Strategic Debt Restructuring; Insolvency and Bankruptcy Code; Non-banking financial companies (NBFCs); Monetary policy; Repos; Reverse Repos; Monetary policytransmission; Fiscal policy; Financial Inclusion; Payments Bank.

Practice Questions

1. What were the major reforms effected in the banking sector following the recommendations of the two Committees of 1991 and 1998 headed by M. Narasimham?
2. What is meant by Repo rate and Reverse Repo rate? When does the Reserve Bank of India resort to these measures and what are its implications?
3. What are the objectives of monetary policy of the Reserve Bank of India? Is there any conflict between the views of the Central government and the Reserve Bank on the monetary policy? What in your view should be the primary objective of the policy? Substantiate your views.
4. What are the new trends in banking and the steps taken to modernise banking in India? How have these measures benefited the customers and the economy?
5. The banking sector has, of late, come under severe stress due to bad loans and non-performing assets. Discuss the reasons which led to this and the steps taken by the government and the Reserve Bank of India to contain the problem.
6. Explain how the Insolvency and Bankruptcy Code will help to resolve the issue of bad debts incurred by banks.
7. Explain the role of Regional Rural Banks, problems faced by them and steps taken to solve them.
8. Non-banking financial companies (NBFCs) have an important role to play in the economy but they need to be regulated properly. Critically analyse this statement. Mention the steps taken to regulate them.
9. What is meant by 'Financial inclusion' and what is its significance in the Indian context? What steps have been taken by successive governments to promote it and how effective they have been?
10. What is meant by "Payments banks' and what is their role in the economy? How far do you think they will be beneficial to the economy and the people at large?
11. What are the major factors behind accumulation of non-performing assets in the Indian banking sector in recent years? Discuss. *[UPSC Main 2015 (Economics Optional Paper)]*
12. What are the factors responsible for deterioration in the asset quality of banks in India?

    [UPSC 2016-Indian Economic Service/Indian Statistical Service Paper]
13. Monetary Policy in India is often criticised as ineffective because large part of the country is not yet monetised. Do you agree with the view? Give reasons.

    [UPSC Main 2016 (Economics Optional Paper)]
14. Examine the extent to which RBI's monetary policy stance on achieving twin objectives of containing inflation and facilitating growth has been successful.

    [UPSC 2014-Indian Economic Service/Indian Statistical Service Paper]

15. Trace the development of Non-Banking Financial Companies in India since the liberalisation era and comment on their impact on the effectiveness of the interest rate policies of the RBI.

[UPSC Main 2016 (Economics Optional Paper)]

16. Non-banking financial institutions need to be effectively regulated and monitored in India. Can you suggest some measures in this direction?

[UPSC Main 2015 (Economics Optional Paper)]

17. Why is monetary transmission not effective in India? In the context of the recent announcement by the RBI, compare the efficacy of external benchmarks in bank loans with internal benchmarks for improving monetary transmissions through the banking channel.

[UPSC Main 2019 (Economics Optional Paper)]

18. Distinguish between Wholesale Price Index' and 'Consumer Price Index' in India.

[UPSC 2020-Indian Economic Service/Indian Statistical Service Paper]

19. What are the causes and consequences of inflation in India? What are the initiatives and measures taken by the RBI to contain it? In this context, discuss the relevance of inflation targeting in India.

[UPSC 2020-Indian Economic Service/Indian Statistical Service Paper]

20. Discuss the Capital Market Reforms in India. What is the role of capital market in India's industrial growth? Highlight the measures taken by the Securities and Exchange Board of India (SEBI) in the development of capital market in India.

[UPSC 2020-Indian Economic Service/Indian Statistical Service Paper]

FISCAL POLICY AND TAX REFORMS

- Fiscal Policy and Distributive Justice
- Committee on Distribution of Income and Levels of Living
- Fiscal Policy and Inequality
- Distortions in subsidies
- Role ofFiscal policy in an Economy
- The Tax System and Budget: An overview
- Features of a sound Tax System and Tax Policy
- Receipts of the Government
- Tax Structure and Equity
- Regressive Tax regime
- Tax-GDP Ratio
- Early Direct and Indirect Tax Reforms
- The Crisis f 1990-91
- Chelliah Committee (1991) and Tax Reforms
- Central VAT and Service Tax
- Public Debt, Fiscal Deficit
- Subsidies and PDS
- Fiscal Responsibility and Budget Management Act, 2003
- Fiscal federalism and Finance Commissions
- 15th Finance Commission
- Retrospective Taxation and its Consequences
- Implications of Taxing Agriculture Sector

(See also Chapter 25 for more on Tax reforms)

❑ INTRODUCTION

Fiscal policy refers to the budgetary stance of the central government and involves decisions regarding changes in taxes and expenditure. Through these changes, the government is able to increase output and income and thereby stabilize the economy. The budget may be balanced when total expenditure equals total receipts or may have surplus or deficit depending on whether the total receipts exceed or fall short of the total expenditure. (See Box 14.1).

❑ INEQUALITIES AND FISCAL POLICY

Fiscal Policy and Distributive Justice

The effectiveness of taxation in regard to redistribution of income, property, and wealth, and reducing disparities between various sections of society has been a subject of debate. The experience of many other countries has also shown that economic growth, more often than not, leads to growing inequalities of income and wealth. Though the tax system attempts to bring about institutional changes to place increasing proportion of productive re- sources and the community's surpluses in the hands of the vulnerable sections and thereby reduce the concentration of wealth in the hands of a small section, it has not been found to be effective.

India has been concerned with inequality of income and wealth from the beginning of planning process. The Second Plan emphasized that the productive resources and class relationships should be so aligned as to bring about reduction in economic and social inequality together with growth of income. It recognized that planned development on these lines had so far not been attempted on any significant scale under democratic conditions. The Plan suggested measures like changes in income tax, taxation of wealth, enhanced yields from estate duty, ceilings on incomes and removal of regional disparities.

Committee on Distribution of Income and Levels of Living

The seriousness with which the government viewed the issue can be gauged from the fact that the then Prime Minister, Jawaharlal Nehru, was keen to know how the increase in national income and per capita income, which resulted from the first two Plans, got distributed. The government set up a Committee of experts on "Distribution of Income and Levels of Living" in 1960, i.e., towards the end of the Second Plan (1956–61), headed by Prof. P. C. Mahalanobis and with prominent economists, Prof. V. K.. R. .V. Rao, Dr. P.S. Lokanathan, Prof. B.N. Madan and P.C. Mathew as Members. As the names of members suggest, it was a very high-level Committee, representing a wide range of views. The Committee was tasked with the following terms:

- To review changes in levels of living during the First and Second Five Year Plans;
- To study the recent trends in the distribution of income and wealth; and
- To ascertain the extent to which the operation of the economic system has resulted in concentration of wealth and means of production.

Though the Committee examined wide spectrum of evidence and submitted two reports in 1964 and 1969 and observed that it was handicapped by the non-availability of voluminous data required to study the problem in depth. While it could not come to any definitive conclusion on inequality resulting from development, it came to the unanimous conclusion that the working of planned economy has helped concentration of economic power and aided the growth of big business in India.

Some 20 years later, the Draft Five Year Plan for 1978-83, brought out in 1979, admitted the ineffectiveness of taxation alone to bring down disparities in income and property. It emphasized the need for a strategy with "distributive bias" to effect changes in the pattern of ownership of agricultural land, urban real estate and corporate property. But not much could be achieved on these lines.

Fiscal Policy and Inequality

Many advanced and developing economies are facing the challenge of rising inequality. And it is seen that wealth is more unequally distributed than income. While fiscal policy has played a more significant role reducing inequality in the advanced economies, its role has been much more modest in developing countries where poverty is much more pronounced. Not only are the tax levels and tax revenue much lower in developing economies, it is also lop-sided with indirect taxes, which are regressive and hurt the poor most, outweigh direct taxes.

The evolution of India's tax system has been different from the experience of other developing economies. It has been beset with distortions and inequity. Even with increase in incomes, the share of direct taxes steadily fell from about 30 per cent in 1960's to as low as 16 per cent in 1990. The share of indirect taxes remained disproportionately high though this been corrected since 2000 (see Tables 14.2 (a) and 14.2 (b).

Also, with a very low tax base with a very low percentage of individuals and companies paying personal income tax and corporate tax respectively (see tax compliance data given in chapter 25, p.25.18), using taxes to promote equity will not be purposeful. Rather, productive public expenditure which will raise consumption of the poor will be far more effective in promoting equity.

Distortions in Subsidies

The problems faced with fiscal policy is compounded by distortions arising from subsidies extended by the State. As pointed out in the Economic Survey for 2015-16, "Subsidies for the poor tends to attract policy attention. But a number of policies provide benefits to the well-off. We estimate these benefits for the small savings schemes and the tax/subsidy policies on cooking gas, railways, power, aviation turbine fuel, gold and kerosene.............together provide a bounty to the well-off of about ₹1 lakh crore."

Thus a fair amount of government interventions, in the form of explicit subsidisation, meant for the poorer sections help the relatively better-off in society and, in many cases, this help is substantial in magnitude. For instance, electricity subsidy benefits 67.2 per cent households which are electrified and even among them, the affluent households who consume more power stand to benefit more. So also, LPG subsidy is enjoyed by relatively well-to-do sections while the poor who do not use LPG are deprived of the benefit.

On the other hand, subsidising social sectors like education and public health specially targeted to improve these services for the poor and uplift them will produce better results in the long run. Here again, the focus must be on primary and secondary education and skill-oriented vocational and technical education which will benefit the lower sections. And in public health, the focus must be on improving rural health and government hospitals. The State should have an affirmative policy to direct subsidies towards 'merit goods' and to benefit the most deserving sections.

Box 14.1 Role of Fiscal Policy in an Economy

Fiscal policy is a crucial macroeconomic tool governments use to alter the levels of taxation, public debt, levels of economic activity, stabilize output and employment, and redistribute income and wealth. Its main objectives are to maintain stable economic growth, counter the cycles of economic boom and depression, stimulate growth during recession, contain inflationary trends, and ensure that the vulnerable sections are adequately protected with some basic income.

Before the high levels of unemployment in the 1920's and the Great Depression of the 1930's, maintaining balanced budgets was considered as the primary aim of fiscal policy. However, following these major crises, John Maynard Keynes, the British economist, argued that governments should use taxes and expenditure policies to influence output and income and thereby counter the cyclical trends—the ups and downs—in the economy. Keynes argued that in a period of recession, public spending would stimulate aggregate demand for goods and services and counter unemployment and deflation. It is argued that the government spending or 'pump-priming', as it is referred to, will stimulate private spending, which in turn would lead to economic expansion. This approach was adopted by Franklin Roosevelt, the US President through his 'New Deal' programme with some effect to overcome the debilitating effects of the 'Great Depression' of 1930's.

❑ THE TAX SYSTEM AND BUDGET: AN OVERVIEW

Under Article 112 of the Constitution, the Central Government is required to present before the Parliament an Annual Financial Statement of estimated receipts and expenditure of the government which is the Budget document. The government also presents an 'Economic Survey' prepared by the Ministry of Finance which reviews the developments in the Indian economy over the previous 12 months, summarizes the performance on major development programmes, and highlights the policy initiatives of the government and the prospects of the economy in the short to medium term. This document is presented to both Houses of Parliament during the Budget Session prior to Budget presentation. See Box 14.2 for the features of a sound tax system.

Till 2016-17, the budget was being presented towards the end of February for the next financial year running from April 1 to March 31. This document, presented by the Finance Minister, spells out the general state of the economy, proposals for development of various sectors and programmes, and allocations for them. Importantly, the budget will contain the Annual Financial statement, Demand for Grants, receipt and expenditure budget, fiscal policy strategy, etc.

But beginning with the budget for 2017-18, the Government decided to present the budget in Parliament on February 1. The rationale for this change is that by advancing the date of budget presentation, the Parliament can pass it earlier so that authorization for incurring expenditure is in place by April 1 when the new financial year begins. Whereas in the earlier budget calendar, the authorization of expenditure came with the onset of monsoon and this resulted in government programmes being relatively inactive during the productive pre-monsoon months. Advancing the date of budget presentation thus helps to speed up investment expenditure in the productive pre-monsoon months.

Box 14.2 Features of a Sound Tax System and Tax Policy

While discussing about Indian tax system, it is pertinent to know what constitutes a sound taxation or fiscal policy. Economists and public policy makers have pointed out some essential features that go to make a sound tax system. These features include the following:

Simplicity

A good tax system should be simple and easily comprehensible to all, especially the assessees who are to comply with the tax rules. Though governments try to make tax regime simple, often the individual assessees have to seek the help of some experts. A complex tax regime provides room for deviant persons to look for loopholes and evade paying taxes. Proper compliance by all also helps to maximize the tax collections.

Transparency

The features of the tax rules should be widely made known to all and not be shrouded in secrecy or wrapped in complexities. Educating the public on taxes levied is important and people have a right to know how the State utilizes and expends the funds collected, to what uses they are put, and how far it benefits the public and their welfare. Often, it is at the lower levels of government, i.e., the municipal corporations and panchayats, which are the closest to the general public and which undertake public works of critical importance to the citizens, such as upkeep of roads, water supply, drainage, electricity, etc., that there is lack of transparency, misallocation and misuse of funds. Also, the budgets of these bodies—receipts and expenditures—are not so well publicized as that of Central and State budgets. This points to the imperative need for tax regime and budgets to be transparent and made widely known and publicized.

Equity

While the direct taxes are levied on the affluent and the well-to-do sections of society, the burden of indirect taxes falls on everyone irrespective of income earned. Hence, on considerations of equity, the burden due to indirect taxes should be kept as low as possible.

Moderation

Tax rates should be moderate so as to optimize collections. Exorbitant and extortionist tax rates will induce people to not disclose income and wealth, and stash them away or make stealthy investments to evade paying taxes. Also such undisclosed, illicit funds may be used for anti-social activities like smuggling, drug trafficking, etc. which ultimately harms not only the economy, but society at large. Apart from this, the taxes on corporates, firms, etc. should be reasonable as not to discourage entrepreneurship and industry which will hurt the economy. Simply put, as the old adage goes, 'don't kill the goose that lays golden eggs'. (See note below on 'Laffer curve').

Stability

The tax regime should, as far as possible, be stable and not subjected to frequent changes. While the rates may be changed depending on the state of the economy and developmental needs, the broad regime should remain the same so that it becomes easy to comply with. In view of this, any retrospective changes in taxation are to be avoided as they upset the calculations of the assessees, and may lead to disputes and litigations. (In this context, see Box 14.4 on Retrospective Taxation at the end of this chapter).

Non-adversarial

A good tax regime should not be adversarial towards the tax payers. The tax authorities should not give the impression of harassing in any manner. If some of the principles mentioned above are followed, the tax regime will be friendly which will encourage people to comply. Conversely, the tax payers too should view paying taxes as a duty and obligation towards society, as a good part of the collections is used by the State towards the welfare of the less privileged sections of society. The concept of CSR—Corporate Social Responsibility—imposed on the corporates to use a small part of their profits to undertake tasks to promote welfare of the society exemplifies this aspect.

Economical

The costs incurred in collection of taxes should be kept to a minimum and redundancy avoided. For it is ultimately the public who bears the burden of not only the taxes but the administrative costs involved.

A Note on Laffer Curve: The Laffer curve principle is based on the relationship that exists between the tax rates and the total revenue collected. Tax collection will be maximum at a certain level of tax rates which are neither too low nor too high. Raising tax rates beyond a point may prove counterproductive. The postulate is attributed to Arthur Laffer, an American economist who was in Ronald Reagan's Economic Policy Advisory Board, as he put forth this argument during an official meeting. Though named after Laffer, this view has been stated by a few others also before him.

This principle is contested by many on the ground that there is no simple, direct correlation between tax rates and total tax collection as the latter is influenced by many other factors in the economy such as production and income levels, savings and investment, aggregate demand, labour market conditions, etc.

Receipts of the Government

The total receipts of the Central government consist of **Revenue receipts** and **Capital receipts.** Revenue receipts consist of Tax revenue and Non-tax revenue. Tax revenue consists of Direct taxes which include mainly personal income tax on individuals and corporate tax on firms (companies), and taxes on property or capital assets which is not very significant from the point of view of revenue earned. Indirect taxes consist of excise duties levied on goods produced in the country, customs duties on items imported or exported, and service tax on a range of services availed by the people. Excise and other duties have now been replaced by Goods and Services Tax (GST). (See chapter 25 on this).

Non-tax revenue consists of interest earned on loans given by the Central government, dividends and profits of government enterprises, fees for services rendered by the government, etc.

Table 14.1 shows the share of tax and non-tax revenue in total revenue of the Central Government. It will be seen that tax revenue forms the bulk of total revenue receipts. Capital receipts of the Central government consist of market borrowings which are loans raised by the government from public, borrowing by the government from the Reserve Bank of India, commercial banks, and other financial institutions through sale of treasury bills, recoveries of loans and advances given to State governments, loans from foreign governments and international organizations, Union territories, and public sector enterprises, small savings collections, and receipts from disinvestment of public sector enterprises.

Table 14.1 Share of Tax and Non-tax Revenue in Total Revenue of Central Government
(in ₹ crore)

Year	Tax Revenue	Non-tax Revenue	Total Revenue Receipts
1972-73	3443 (76.12)	1080 (23.88)	4523 (100)
1980-81	9358 (75.63)	3015 (24.37)	12373 (100)
1990-91	43042 (78.27)	11948 (21.73)	54990 (100)
2000-01	136659 (70.90)	56083 (29.10)	192742 (100)
2010-11	569869 (72.70)	213941 (27.30)	783810 (100)
2014-15	903615 (82.72)	188747 (17.28)	1092362 (100)
2017-18	1227014 (81.45)	279388 (18.55)	1506402 (100)

Source: Indian Public Finance Statistics, Dept. of Economic Affairs, Ministry of Finance.
Note: Figures in brackets represent percentages.

Tax Structure and Equity

One of the cardinal principles of taxation is that it should be equitable in its impact on various sections of society so that the vulnerable groups are not made to bear a heavy burden. While the impact of direct taxes is felt by the affluent and well-to-do persons in the higher income brackets, the effect of indirect taxes, other than the service tax, will affect everyone across the board as the burden of these is passed on by the manufacturers to consumers of products and goods. Indirect taxes, by their very nature, are regressive in their effect as their burden is shared by citizens irrespective of income. Hence while levying indirect taxes, conspicuous consumption must be curbed and the burden of taxing such items should be borne by the affluent sections. Care has to be taken to ensure that prices of essential commodities and products used by the common people are kept in check. Excessive reliance on indirect taxes to garner more resources escalates the costs of items, feeds inflation, and is regressive in its impact.

Regressive tax regime

A review of the share of direct and indirect taxes in total revenue collections in India shows that, over the years, indirect taxes accounted for a major share in total tax collections. It can be partly explained by the fact the tax base for direct taxes has been rather narrow. As the Finance Minister observed in 1992-93, even with a population of over 800 million, hardly about 7 million people paid income and corporate tax. And, as per the budget presented in 1997-98, only about 12 million people, out of 900 million, were assessed to income tax, and worse still, only about 12,000 assessees were in the tax bracket of income above ₹ 10 lakh. Also, as the economy expanded and production and range of goods increased, with the levy of excise duties and custom duties, the collection and share of indirect taxes was bound to go up. Yet, there was a need to rectify this distortion in the tax system to ensure the principle of equity. (For more recent data on those under Direct tax coverage, see chapter 25, p. 25.22-3).

Table 14.2: Direct and Indirect Tax Revenue of Central Government (in ₹ crore)

Year	Direct Tax	Indirect Tax	Total Tax Revenue
1980-81	2907 (22.11)	10242 (77.89)	13149 (100)
1990-91	11024 (19.15)	46552 (80.85)	57576 (100)
1995-96	33563 (30.18)	77661(69.82)	111224 (100)
2000-01	68306 (36.27)	120040 (63.73)	188346 (100)
2010-11	445994 (56.51)	343178 (43.49)	789172 (100)
2015-16	741945 (51.17)	708013 (48.83)	1449958 (100)
2019-20	1335000 (54.24)	1126195 (45.76)	2461195 (100)

Source: Handbook of Statistics on Indian Economy, Reserve Bank of India.
Note: Figures in bracketsrepresent percentages to Total Tax Revenue.

As Table 14.2 shows, prior to the economic reforms in 1991, 'socialist' India had one of the most regressive tax regimes. It was only after the reforms were initiated in 1991 that a course correction took place, and from 1992-93 onwards the share of direct taxes went up, touching almost 55 per cent by 2014-15, and the share of indirect taxes was progressively brought down.

Tax-GDP Ratio

India has one of the lowest Tax-GDP ratios, lower than that of countries with similar sovereign ratings. Central taxes (gross) was 9.82 in 1990-91, the declined to 8.66 by 2000-01 but regained from 2010-11. (See Table 14.3).

The reasons for the low tax-GDP ratio are factors such as low per capita income, less number of assessees paying direct taxes, and various exemptions granted which result in lower collections. The share of indirect taxes in total tax collection has been coming down since the mid-1990's. And, while the share of Services sector in GDP is about 55 per cent, its share in indirect tax collection is not commensurate to its share in the GDP. Also, when the tax revenues grow at a slower rate than the GDP, the tax-to-GDP ratio declines.

Table 14.3 Tax–GDP Ratios

Year	Central Taxes (Gross)*	Central Taxes (Net)*	Year	Central Taxes (Gross)*	Central Taxes (Net)*
1950-51	3.89	3.43	2000-01	8.66	6.28
1970-71	6.73	5.15	2010-11	10.19	7.32
1990-91	9.82	7.34	2017-18	11.18	7,18

Source: Indian Public Finance Statistics, Dept. of Economic Affairs, Ministry of Finance.

Note: 1. The ratios to GDP at market prices are based on CSO's National Accounts 2004-05 series/2011-12 onwards National Accounts 2011-12 series.

2. *Central taxes (gross) include States' share in Central taxes while Central Taxes (net) excludes States' share in Central taxes.

The tax-GDP ratio in the OECD (Organisation for Economic Co-operation and Development) countries and other developed nations is far higher, ranging between 25 to 50 per cent. In the US, it was 26 per cent in 2014 while the percentage in France was 45.2, Germany 36.1, U.K. 32.6, and S. Korea 24.6. Taxes paid by individuals and corporations often account for majority of the tax receipts in the developed countries.

One view is that that higher tax-GDP ratio would translate into better infrastructure, public goods, etc. by taxing the affluent through direct taxes, provided the revenue is put to productive use and wastages are avoided. In the present context of the globalized world, things have become more complex. For instance, increasing corporate taxes could have repercussions of business moving elsewhere. Also, excise and customs levies have to be calibrated in a manner that indigenous industries are encouraged, and at the same time, imports of items required for production of items for exports are not unduly burdened.

Early Tax Reforms

The Indian tax system, as it evolved in the 1950's, was aligned to a planned economy with the State and the public sector playing a dominant role. Raising maximum revenue and achieving redistribution became the avowed objectives and the tax structure became one of discretionary nature and with confiscatory rates and distortions. The resultant disincentives led to a high degree of tax evasion, both in regard to income and wealth, with little possibility of detection and ineffective penal measures. Over time, this spawned a vast underground, parallel economy which has had deleterious effects on the economy. The tax system had many loopholes and lacked transparency, so much so, it was difficult to assess the social and economic impact of various concessions built into it.

Direct tax reform

A Direct Taxes Enquiry Committee was set up in 1971, headed by Justice K.N. Wanchoo, the retired Chief Justice of the Supreme Court of India. This Committee looked into various aspects of the tax system and tax evasion. As per this Committee, factors like high tax rates, controls, licenses, and ineffective information system were major problems in Indian direct tax system. The Committee recommended significant reduction in marginal tax rates. Personal income tax rates in India were quite high in earlier times. At its peak in 1973-74, the maximum marginal rate of tax (with surcharge) was as high as 97.75 per cent. Following the recommendations of the Wanchoo Committee, marginal tax rates were reduced gradually to 50 per cent in 1985-86.

Indirect tax reform

Recognizing the need for reform of the indirect tax system, the Central Government appointed an Indirect Taxation Enquiry Committee in 1976 under the chairmanship of L.K. Jha for an overhaul of the system of indirect taxes. A major recommendation the Committee submitted in 1978 was that the Central Excise be gradually transformed into a Value Added Tax (VAT) at the manufacturing stage (MANVAT). However, it was only in the budget for 1986-87 that, as a step towards the VAT scheme, Modified VAT (MODVAT) was introduced to minimize the incidence of taxation on inputs.

MODVAT

Under the MODVAT scheme, a manufacturer can take credit of excise duty paid on raw materials and components used by him in his manufacture. It amounts to excise duty being levied only on additions in value by each manufacturer at each stage. MODVAT scheme reduces distortions in the production structure, mitigates the cascading effect of taxes on inputs, makes the system more transparent, and helps to reduce costs and prices.

Fiscal Imbalance

The fiscal imbalance persisted and worsened during the 1980's, as the gross fiscal deficit, on average, rose from 4 per cent in the 1970's to 6.3 per cent of GDP in the Sixth Plan (1980-85) period and to 8.2 per cent of GDP in the Seventh Plan (1985-90) period. Excessive fiscal deficit becomes unsustainable as it has to be covered by printing money or by borrowing from domestic and foreign sources. Printing money has the potential to fuel inflation and borrowing will be unsustainable if the interest rate exceeds the growth rate of GDP. The total internal liabilities of the Central Government rose inordinately between 1980 and 2014-15 and but has come down to 45.8 per cent in 2018-19. (See Table 14.4).

Table 14.4: India's Internal Debt and Liabilities (in ₹ crore)

Year	Internal Debt	Total Internal Liabilities	GDP at FC (at current prices)	Percentage of column	
				2 to 4	3 to 4
1980–81	30864	48451	136838	22.6	37.2
1990–91	154004	283033	531813	29.0	53.2
1995–96	307869	554983	1118586	27.5	49.6
2000–01	803698	1102596	2000743	40.1	55.1
2010–11	2667115	3781135	7248860	36.8	52.2
2014–15	4775900	6084568	11550240	41.3	52.7
2018-19	--	8703357	18971237	--	45.8

Source: Handbook of Statistics on Indian Economy, Reserve Bank of India, 2006 for data for 1980-81 and 1985-86, and ibid 2015 for data from 1990-91 to 2014-15.

Note: 1. Internal Debt Data from 2004-05 to 2012-13 include liabilities on account of Market Stabilization Scheme (MSS).

2. GDP at FC: GDP at Factor Cost at current prices for years 1980–81 to 2010–11 are on Base year 2004–05 and for 2014–15 is on Base year 2011–12.

❑ THE CRISIS OF 1990-91

The persistent macroeconomic instability and fiscal imbalances towards the late 1980s led to the grave economic crisis which the country faced in 1990-91. The fiscal deficit was well above 8 per cent (see Table 14.5) and internal liabilities stood at 53.2 per cent of the GDP. Interest payments amounted to 4 per cent of the GDP and accounted for about 20 per cent of the total expenditure of the Central Government. Servicing the debt placed a heavy burden on the government finances. The balance of payments position was precarious. The persisting current account deficits had to be financed by borrowing from abroad which led to continuous increase in external debt. The problem of servicing the external debt added to the problems and this was further compounded by the Gulf War of 1990. The foreign exchange reserves had reached a low of ₹ 2,500 crore which was barely sufficient to finance imports for a fortnight. The situation was grim and it called for drastic corrective action. And the far-reaching economic reforms initiated by Manmohan Singh, Finance Minister in the Narasimha Rao government, ensued.

Table 14.5: Central Government's Gross Fiscal Deficit (in ₹ crore)

Year	Gross Fiscal Deficit	GDP at FC (at Current prices)	Percentage of coln. 2 to 3
1980–81	8299	136838	6.06
1985–86	21858	262717	8.32
1990–91	44632	531813	8.39
1995–96	60243	1118586	5.39
2000–01	118816	2000743	5.94
2005–06	146435	3390503	4.32
2010–11	373592	7248860	5.15
2014–15	512628	11550240	4.44

Source: Handbook of Statistics on Indian Economy, 2015, Reserve Bank of India.

Note: GDP at FC; GDP at Factor Cost at current prices for years 1980–81 to 2010–11 are on Base year 2004–05 and for 2014–15 is on Base year 2011–12.

Chelliah Committee (1991) and Tax Reforms

When the market-based economic reforms and liberalization measures were initiated in 1991, simultaneously, a Tax Reforms Committee (TRC) was set up under the chairmanship of Prof. Raja

J. Chelliah, a renowned expert on India's public finance. The Committee's recommendations led to systematic and comprehensive reforms in the tax system at the central level. The TRC laid out a framework and a roadmap for reform of direct and indirect taxes as a part of the structural reform process.

The TRC's recommendations included:

- simplification and rationalization of the rate structure;
- reduction in the rates of all major taxes, i.e., customs, individual and corporate income taxes, and excises to reasonable levels;
- the taxes on domestic production be fully converted into a Value Added Tax (VAT), and it should be extended to the wholesale level in agreement with the States, with additional revenues beyond post-manufacturing stage passed on to the State governments;
- introduction of Service tax;
- rationalize the structure and scope of tax incentives;
- broadening the tax base;
- improving the tax administration;
- promoting fairness in the tax system to check adverse effects on efficiency and neutrality;
- building a proper information system and computerization of tax returns, revamping, and modernization of administrative and enforcement machinery.

The paradigm of reform adopted by the TRC was in keeping with the best fiscal practices such as broadening the base, lowering marginal tax rates, reducing rate differentiation, minimizing exemptions and concessions, simplifying the tax structure, and making the tax administration more effective. The reforms were to bring about revenue neutrality in the short term and enhance revenue productivity in the medium and long term. The overall thrust of TRC was to increase the relative contribution of direct taxes, decrease the share of trade taxes in the total tax revenue, and increase the share of domestic consumption taxes by transforming the domestic excises into VAT.

A wide range of reform measures were undertaken on the basis of the report of the Committee. It set the stage for achieving a higher Tax-GDP ratio which has helped the country achieve a higher level of growth. Both personal income tax and corporate tax rates were rationalized and brought down. On the indirect taxes front, there was gradual unification of rates, and later, a single rate of CENVAT came to be introduced along with three additional excise rates for some commodities.

Central VAT (CENVAT)

MODVAT was changed and came to be known as Central VAT (CENVAT) in the 2000-01 budget. The change was effected as MODVAT gave rise to many issues and disputes in assessment and there was need to simplify the system. Under the CENVAT scheme, a manufacturer of final product or provider of taxable service was allowed to take credit of duty of excise as well as of service tax paid on any input received in the factory or any input service received. All inputs and capital goods, save a few items, were made eligible for credit. The special excise duty was rationalized to only three, viz., 8 per cent, 16 per cent, and 24 per cent and the CENVAT rate was fixed at 16 per cent. The single rate of CENVAT contributed about 68 per cent of total excise revenue.

Value Added Tax (VAT)

Meanwhile, the government was working on major reform of indirect taxes at State level by replacing the Sales tax with a unified Value Added Tax (VAT). Though States had agreed to it in principle as early as 2001, the issue got delayed due to various reasons and prolonged discussions in the meetings of the

Empowered Committee of State Finance Ministers. The States expressed fear of loss of revenue in the initial years of the new system. In view of this, the Central Government agreed to compensate States for any revenue loss to the extent of 100 per cent in the first year, 75 per cent in the second year, and 50 per cent in the third year. With the introduction of VAT, the Central sales tax was to be phased out.

While presenting the 2005-06 budget, the Finance Minister, P. Chidambaram, stated that in a remarkable display of the spirit of co-operative federalism, the States were poised to undertake the most important tax reform ever attempted in the country. All States, barring a few, agreed to introduce the VAT with effect from April 1, 2005. In due course, all the States came on board and adopted the VAT which was a landmark development.

The Finance Minister then further expressed the hope that the eventual goal was to cover the entire production-distribution chain by a national VAT, or still better, a Goods and Services Tax (GST) encompassing both the Centre and the States. As is well-known, this is an issue which has been in the works for quite a while and after much debate in the Parliament and in public domain was finally approved by the Parliament. This historic measure, which is touted as one of the biggest reforms on taxation, is expected to give immense boost to the economy, apart from simplifying the indirect tax system. The issue of GST is discussed in detail in Chapter 25 (See pp. 25.33-40 and Box 25.3 on pp. 25.40-4).

Service Tax

Among the many recommendations made by the Chelliah Committee, an important one was the levy of tax on services which was introduced in 1994. The Committee was of the view that indirect taxes at the Central level should be broadly neutral in relation to production and consumption of goods, and should, in course of time, cover services too. The tax on services is relatively non-regressive as the items coming under it could be selective and related to the type of clientele of the services. And, services being one of the fastest growing sectors accounting for over 50 per cent of the GDP, there was much potential for levying the tax and extending its scope and coverage. Service tax has a very large base of taxpayers.

Revenue collected from service tax has shown considerable increase. (See Table 14.6). Service tax also is now part of the GST regime.

Table 14.6 Revenue from Service Tax

	1994–95	2002–03	2005–06	2008–09	2011–12	2012–13
Revenue (in ₹ crore)	407	4122	23055	60941	97509	132498
No. of Assessees (in lakhs)	0.034	2.32	8.46	12.04	15.36	17.13

Minimum Alternate Tax (MAT)

The concept of MAT was introduced in India in the Income Tax Act, 1961, in 1987 to facilitate the taxation of "zero tax companies". By introducing this, the government wanted to fill the lacuna of avoidance of tax by many companies, who despite showing high profits in their books and paying substantial dividends, were paying marginal or no tax, by taking advantage of various tax concessions and other incentives. MAT was thus introduced to levy a minimum tax on such companies deeming a certain percentage of their book profits, computed under the Companies Act, as taxable income. For a few years, the MAT was made inoperative. In 1996, it was reintroduced.

In 2015, the Income Tax department had issued notices to some foreign investors. Responding to objections from foreign investors, the government appointed a committee under Justice A.P. Shah to study the various legal positions and give its recommendations. The Committee pointed out that the provisions of MAT were never intended to tax Foreign Portfolio Investors (FPI's) and Foreign Institutional Investors (FII's) who have no place of business in India. Accordingly, the government had exempted these categories from MAT from April 1, 2015. The government has further considered the issue and decided to amend this provision in the IT Act ret-respectively from April 1, 2001 so that past cases are also not opened giving much relief to the FPI's and FII's.

❑ PUBLIC DEBT

The term public debt of India would mean both the internal and external debt. Internal debt and liabilities of the Government of India consist of market loans, treasury bills which represent borrowing from the Reserve Bank of India, small savings deposits and provident funds, reserve funds and deposits, and other accounts. This has been rising steeply over the years as will be seen from Table 14.4.

India's debt level went up consistently during 1980's and 1990's and the combined debt-GDP ratio of the Centre and the States reached a peak of 83.3 per cent by the end of 2003-04. Thereafter, debt-GDP ratio has shown a secular decline. There was marginal increase during 2008-09 and 2009-10 mainly on account of global factors. General government debt-GDP ratio stood at 65.2 per cent at the end of March 2013.

India recorded a government debt equivalent to 69.62 percent of the country's Gross Domestic Product in the 2019-20 fiscal year.

Role of Debt Finance

Increase in debt finance is a matter of concern because the money may be put to unproductive use with no direct or indirect returns. Also, it would result in crowding out private investment. Deficit financing to counter recession and unemployment–the Keynesian prescription–is not found successful even in developed countries and, therefore, has no role in fiscal policy. All current expenditures of the government have to be met out of revenue collections. Any borrowings by the State should be for remunerative, physical, or social capital formation or increasing productivity in the economy.

Interest Payments

While the key aspect of fiscal policy is the fiscal deficit expressed as a proportion of GDP, the absolute level of fiscal deficit is also important as it indicates the interest payment obligations. The interest payment will be based on the cumulative debt of the previous year and the incremental debt incurred in the current year. After the Fiscal Responsibility and Budget Management (FRBM) Act came into force in 2003, interest payments on debt, as a proportion of GDP, have been falling. However, due to the expansionary fiscal policy followed to avert the adverse impact of the global financial crisis of 2008-09, interest payments as a proportion of GDP increased somewhat in the post-crisis period.

External Debt

According to RBI data, India's external liabilities in 2015-16 was ₹ 4,119.07 billion out of the total liabilities of ₹ 71,014.39 billion which works out to 5.8 per cent. Since the Indian government's borrowing is mostly internal and it owes a very small portion of its debt in foreign currency compared to its peers, currency depreciation and changes in global financial conditions would impact India's borrowing costs less than in countries where the proportion of foreign currency and international borrowing was higher. The financial system's ability to absorb rising government debt could weaken if economic growth is slow, inflation persists, and fiscal deficit is not contained.

Fiscal Deficit

Fiscal deficit is the difference between the government's total expenditure and its total receipts excluding borrowing. As stated earlier, the fiscal deficit worsened during the 1980's and stood over 8 per cent in 1990-91. India has been making concerted efforts to bring down the fiscal deficit and it was well under control, particularly in the post-FRBM period. But due to the stress following the global financial crisis, there was some increase during 2008-10 period. (See Table 14.7).

Table 14.7 Fiscal Deficit as Percentage of GDP

Year	FD (per cent of GDP)	Year	FD (per cent of GDP)	Year	FD (per cent of GDP)
2003–04	4.3	2007–08	2.5	2011–12	5.7
2004–05	3.9	2008–09	6.0	2012–13	4.8
2005–06	4.0	2009–10	6.5	2013–14	* 4.5
2006–07	3.3	2010–11	4.8	2014–15	# 4.1

Source: Economic Survey, 20013-14 & 2014-15, Ministry of Finance.

Note: FD: Fiscal deficit; * Provisional Actuals; # Target; The ratios to GDP at current market prices are based on the Central Statistics Office's (CSO) National Accounts 2004-05 Series.

The expansionary policy following the global financial crisis well into 2010-11 had macroeconomic implications of higher inflation, which necessitated a tightening of monetary policy and gradually led to a slowdown in investments and growth. This was reflected in lower revenues making the process of fiscal consolidation arduous and had to be effected through curbs on expenditure. Correcting the fiscal imbalance depends on reduction of expenditure and increasing the income of the government so as to reduce the fiscal deficit. Outlining the roadmap for fiscal consolidation, the Budget for 2014-15 envisaged a fiscal deficit target at 4.1 per cent of GDP and sought to reduce it further to 3 per cent of GDP by 2016-17. Achieving this target was found to be daunting due to only a moderate increase in indirect taxes and a large subsidy bill, despite significant decline in the subsidies burden in 2014-15, mainly due to lower prices of crude oil in the international market.

However, in the budget for 2015-16, the Finance Minister stated that as the economy was improving, the need for accelerated fiscal consolidation has receded, and in view of this, the target time for bringing down the fiscal deficit to 3 per cent would be three years instead of two years as announced earlier. Thus, the target set was to achieve 3.9 per cent in 2015-16, 3.5 per cent in 2016-17, and 3 per cent in 2017-18. It was further mentioned that the additional fiscal space available due to this would be utilized towards funding investment in infrastructure which had shown tepid growth due to various problems. Factors like implementation of the Pay Commission recommendations on revision of pay scales and pensions of Central government staff impact the financial position of the government. (On fiscal deficit, see further under Fiscal Responsibility and Budget Management Act later in this chapter).

❑ SUBSIDIES

One of the major reasons for the increase in the centre's fiscal deficit after 2008-09 has been the build-up in subsidies. The three major subsidy items are food, fertiliser, and petroleum. There was sharp increase in total subsidies from 1.42 per cent of GDP in 2007-08 to 2.26 per cent in 2013-14 (RE). (See Table 14.8). Food subsidy has been increasing owing to the widening gap between the economic cost of procurement by the Food Corporation of India (FCI) and the central issue prices fixed for cereals under the public distribution system (PDS). The oil subsidy has eased in the recent past due to depressed oil prices in the international market which has aided the government's efforts on the fiscal front.

Table 14.8 Trends in Major Subsidies

(in ₹ crore)

Subsidy heads	2009–10	2010–11	2011–12	2012–13	2013–14 (RE)
Food	58443	63844	72822	85000	92000
Fertilizer	61264	62301	70013	65613	67971
Petroleum	14951	38371	68484	96880	85480
Major subsidy	134658	164516	211319	247493	245451
Total subsidies	141351	173420	217941	257079	255516
As % of GDP	2.18	2.22	2.42	2.56	2.26

Source: Union Budget Document, Economic Survey, 2013-14, Ministry of Finance.

Rationalizing Subsidies

The government has taken some major initiatives to rationalize the budgetary subsidies such as targeted approach to food subsidy (for BPL families) under the PDS, allowing FCI to access market loans carrying lower interest rates, encouraging private trade in foodgrains, liquidating excess foodgrain stocks, replacing unit-based retention price scheme with a group-based scheme in the case of fertiliser subsidies, and gradually phasing out subsidies on PDS kerosene and LPG to ineligible categories. The administered price mechanism for petroleum products was dismantled from April 1, 2002.

Leakages in the System

Unmerited subsidies and leakages from the system also contribute substantially to the overall increase in subsidy liabilities. Fuel subsidies are not properly targeted, with the upper section of households benefitting more than the poorer households. Similarly, in the case of food, the '*Performance Evaluation Report of the Planning Commission on Targeted PDS (2005)*', which was a detailed study, states that for every kilogram of grains delivered to the poor, the Government of India released 2.4 kg from the central pool. This has grave implications for the cost of delivery of subsidized items through the existing mechanism. The benefits of subsidy regime can be maximized only when it is transparent, well targeted, and suitably designed for effective implementation.

❑ PUBLIC DISTRIBUTION SYSTEM (PDS)

Though a laudable programme considering its critical benefits to the poor and the needy, it is well known that the PDS is grossly maladministered and mismanaged. Errors in identifying eligible families–BPL and APL, the existence of bogus Family/Ration cards, diversion of stocks to the open market, and black-marketing results in gross wastages in the system. The Planning Commission study, referred to above found that about 58 per cent of the subsidized food grains issued from the Central Pool do not reach the BPL families because of identification errors, non-transparent operation, and unethical practices in implementation. The cost of handling food grains by public agencies is also very high. According to the study, for one rupee worth of income transfer to the poor, the government spends ₹ 3.65, indicating that one rupee of budgetary consumer subsidy is worth only 27 paise to the poor.

Remedial Measures

Though many State governments have taken measures to reform the PDS with some encouraging results, the system still needs total revamp. One effective way would be putting in place the Direct Benefit Transfer (DBT) mechanism for the PDS, as done in the case of LPG distribution, but this can be done only when PDS retail outlets are upgraded and computerized.

Containing Subsidies

Containing and proper targeting of subsidies form an important part of fiscal reforms strategy and can serve the following objectives:

- remove economic distortions, thereby improving economic efficiency and growth;
- achieve redistributive objective;
- reduce budgetary burden and release precious resources for other productive purposes.

Apart from the above, there are many other poverty alleviation schemes funded by the Centre but administered through lower level governments–districts and panchayats. These are Centrally Sponsored Schemes (CSS). Some of the schemes are somewhere between a pure transfer and a more complex subsidy. The Central government has since transferred some of the CSS programmes to the States.

❑ FISCAL RESPONSIBILITY AND BUDGET MANAGEMENT (FRBM) ACT

The Fiscal Responsibility and Budget Management Act, 2003, or the FRBM Act, mandates the Central Government to ensure equity in fiscal management and long term macro-economic stability. The Act also aims at prudential debt management consistent with fiscal sustainability through:

- Limits on the Central Government borrowings, debt and revenue, and fiscal deficits;
- Greater transparency in fiscal operations of the Central Government; and
- Conducting fiscal policy in a medium term framework.

The Act also enjoins upon the Central government:

- not to borrow from the Reserve Bank to India except under exceptional circumstances when there is temporary shortage of cash;
- to place, in each financial year, in both Houses of Parliament, a Medium-term Fiscal Policy Statement, Fiscal Policy Strategy Statement, and Macro-economic Framework Statement along with the Annual Financial Statement and Demands for Grants.

❑ N K SINGH COMMITTEE ON FRBM ACT AND FISCAL POLICY

As announced by the Finance Minister in the 2016-17 budget, the government set up a committee to review the implementation of the FRBM Act and give recommendations on the course to be adopted in future. The FRBM Act has been under implementation for over a decade. Both Central and State Governments have benefited from the implementation of the Act.

There is a view that instead of fixed fiscal deficit targets, it may be better to have a fiscal deficit range as the target which would give necessary policy space to the government to deal with dynamic situations.

While remaining committed to fiscal prudence, the government felt that a time had come to review the working of the FRBM Act especially in the context of volatile global economic conditions. Hence as announced in 2016-17 budget, a committee headed by N. K. Singh, a former Secretary in the Ministry of Finance and a former Rajya Sabah member was set up to review the Act. The Committee included Governor of Reserve Bank of India, Chief Economic Advisor to the Union government and two other experts.

The terms of reference of the committee included:

- To review the working of the FRBM Act since it was introduced and to suggest the way forward keeping in view the broad objective of fiscal consolidation and prudence and the changes required in the context of the uncertainty and volatility in the global economy".
- The committee was to make its assessment and provide its views on the expected impact of its recommendations on the general government deficit and other FRBM parameters.
- It was also to examine and give recommendations on any other aspect considered relevant in relation to the determination and implementation of the FRBM road map,

  The Committee which examined various aspects of the Act and its working made several recommendations as mentioned below:
- A sustainable debt path must be the principal macroeconomic anchor of the fiscal policy. The Committee favoured a prudent medium-term ceiling for general government debt of 60 per cent of GDP, to be achieved by no later than FY23. consisting of 38.7 per cent for Central government and 20 per cent for the State governments. Within the above overall ceiling, adopt a ceiling of 40 per cent for the Centre, and the balance 20 per cent for the States.
- Within this framework, it recommended fiscal deficit of 3 per cent of GDP for 3 years from 2017-18 to 2019-20.
- Fiscal deficit to be brought down to 2.5 per cent of GDP by 2022-23.
- The Committee also provided for 'escape clauses' for deviations from the stipulated fiscal deficit target up to 0.5 per cent of GDP.
- For taking recourse to the 'escape clauses', the Committee has suggested "far-reaching structural reforms in the economy or unforeseen events such as war, calamities of national proportion, setbacks in agriculture and sharp decline in real output growth with unanticipated fiscal implications" as some of the factors.
- The panel has recommended enacting a new Debt and Fiscal Responsibility Act after repealing the existing FRBM Act.
- The administration of the FRBM Act was entirely in the domain of the government and did not have the benefit of analytical inputs of a robust independent organization like many countries have. Hence the Committee has proposed setting up a Fiscal Council which will do fiscal analysis round the year and advise the government on any corrective action to be taken. It will also advise on whether conditions are appropriate for triggering the 'escape clauses'.

  Fiscal Council: The Committee has suggested the following functions for the Fiscal Council:

(a) Prepare multi-year fiscal forecasts for Central and General Government;

(b) Prepare a debt and fiscal sustainability analysis that makes projections on key fiscal indicators;

(c) Provide an independent assessment of the Central Government's fiscal performance and compliance with targets set under the proposed Debt and Fiscal Responsibility Act;

(d) Prepare the Macroeconomic Framework Statement;

(e) Recommend suitable changes to fiscal strategy to ensure consistency of the annual financial statement with targets set under this Act;

(f) Take steps to improve quality of fiscal data;

(g) Prepare a comprehensive statement of liabilities;

(h) Produce an annual fiscal strategy report relating to clauses (a) to (g) as may be prescribed;

(i) Provide policy guidance to Central Government on any matter relating to fiscal policy where advice is sought;

(j) Advise the Central Government on whether conditions exist to permit a deviation for invocation in the escape or buoyancy clause;

(k) Make recommendations to the Central Government on the action plan for returning to the stipulated fiscal targets from which the deviations have taken place.

The FRBM Act, 2003 has streamlined the Budget presentation process and helped to enforce fiscal discipline. By bringing in the Act, the government has demonstrated its commitment to prudent fiscal and financial policies. The implementation of the Act at the Centre and corresponding Acts at the State level helped in the consolidation of fiscal balance prior to the global financial crisis of 2008. However, as the outbreak of the financial crisis coincided with the year when the mandated targets of 3 per cent fiscal deficit and elimination of revenue deficit were to be achieved, the Government had to postpone these targets due to fiscal stimulus injected into the economy.

While the revenue deficit was to be wiped out by March 2008, this was not achieved and in the budget for 2013-14, it was mentioned that revenue deficit would be brought down to 1.5 per cent by 2016-17. The target time for bringing down the fiscal deficit to 3 per cent also had to be postponed and the target was to achieve 3.9 per cent fiscal deficit in 2015-16, 3.5 per cent in 2016-17, and 3 per cent in 2017-18.

Slowdown and the Pandemic: The above calculations have been upset by subsequent developments. Since 2017-18, the economy was in a sluggish mode when there was perceptible decline in economic activity. The government has had to ease liquidity conditions and as private investment was slack, public expenditure had to be stepped up substantially, to spur consumption and employment. Even as the economy was showing signs of recovery, the pandemic Covid-19, which broke out in February 2020, struck a devastating blow to global and Indian economy. The containment measures such as total and partial lockdowns imposed to combat the pandemic posed more challenges to the economy. All this placed severe financial strain and has disrupted the fiscal position.

As per the Union budget for FY 2021-22 presented in February 2021, the fiscal deficit for 2020-21 is pegged at 9.5 per cent of the GDP. The fiscal deficit in 2021-22 (BE) is estimated to be 6.8 per cent of GDP. The government propose to continue on the path of fiscal consolidation and reach a fiscal deficit level below 4.5 per cent of GDP by 2025-26 with a fairly steady decline over the period.

❑ DIRECT TAX CODE BILL, 2010

The direct taxation of the income of individuals, companies, and other entities is governed by the Income Tax Act, 1961. The Direct Taxes Code (DTC) Bill, which was introduced in Parliament in 2010, was to replace the Income Tax Act, 1961 and the Wealth Tax Act, 1957 and consolidate the law relating to direct taxes. The Bill aimed to widen tax slabs, and lower corporate tax rates. It sought to do away with tax deductions currently allowed for companies, but retaining some of the deductions available to individuals. The distinction between short term and long term capital gains for all assets except securities listed on stock exchanges was to be removed.

Referring to the DTC Bill, Kelkar Committee, set up to suggest a 'Roadmap for Fiscal Consolidation', had stated in its report in 2012 that the DTC which intends "to revamp the law relating to direct taxes is likely to result in considerable unacceptable losses on a continuing basis. Given the low tax-GDP ratio and the existing fiscal crisis, there is absolutely no fiscal space for such large revenue loss. Therefore, the Direct Taxes Code Bill, 2010 should be comprehensively reviewed before it is enacted into law for implementation."

Presenting the Budget for 2015-16, Finance Minister, Arun Jaitley, informed the Parliament that most of the provisions of the DTC have already been incorporated in the Income Tax Act and that among the very few aspects of DTC which were left out, some have been addressed in the 2015-16 budget. He added that the jurisprudence under the IT Act is well evolved and in view of all this, there is no great merit in going ahead with the DTC as it exists today.

❑ CENTRE-STATE RELATIONS: FISCAL FEDERALISM AND FINANCE COMMISSION

Introduction

India's political and financial landscape has undergone vast changes since independence and this has impacted the Centre-State relations in a perceptible manner. From centralized planning to greater decentralisation of power structures and market-oriented economic policies, India has seen dramatic, even if gradual and slow, transformation spanning over seven decades. This trend critically helped to strengthen the federal characteristics of Indian Union giving greater voice to States and local bodies in the polity.

• Planning and Centralisation

In the initial three decades from 1950 to 1980, centralized economic planning, with pronounced socialist bias, resulted in concentration of powers in the Centre. Planning covered a wide gamut of sectors, and lopsided allocation of financial resources between the Centre and the States negated the principle of true federalism. The Centre had not only exclusive powers over many activities of national and strategic importance but also shared concurrent powers with States over certain other domains while states were left with exclusive powers over the remaining domains.

• Trend towards decentralization

As time passed, with the rise of many regional parties which came to power in the States and at times even at the Centre, the clamour for more powers for the states arose and this led to greater decentralization. The passage of the 72nd and 73rd Amendments to the Constitution in 1992 vested greater powers in the Panchayats and Municipal bodies strengthening local governance from district level to the villages.

• Division of Financial Powers

Under the division of financial powers in the Indian state, there is sharp imbalance between the powers of the Centre and the States and local bodies to tax and raise revenues, and the responsibilities and resultant financial liabilities devolving on them. As the more potential revenue sources lie with the Centre, viz., the income tax, excise, and customs duties, there is a high degree of concentration of revenues in favour of the Centre. The assignment of a large share of responsibilities involving expenditure to lower governmental levels has resulted in a vertical fiscal imbalance necessitating transfer of resources from the Centre to the States.

While the arrangement worked rather smoothly in the first two decades, problems emerged in the 1980's with rising deficits both at the Centre and the States. Successive Finance Commissions have been recommending increasing sums of grants-in-aid and transfer of tax revenues to the States.

♦ Finance Commission and its Role

Under Article 280 of the Constitution of India, the President is to appoint a Finance Commission, once in every five years, to look into the financial relations between the Union and the States. The Commission will recommend:

- as to the allocation of the net proceeds of taxes between the Union and the States which are to be divided between them and the allocation between the States of the respective shares of such proceeds;
- the principles which should govern the grants-in-aid of the revenues of the States out of the Consolidated Fund of India;
- the measures needed to augment the Consolidated Fund of a State to supplement the resources of the Panchayats in the State on the basis of the recommendations made by the Finance Commission of the State;
- the measures needed to augment the Consolidated Fund of a State to supplement the resources of Municipalities in the State on the basis of the recommendations made by the Finance Commission of the State;
- any other matter referred to the Commission by the President in the interests of sound finance.

♦ Composition of the Finance Commission

The Finance Commission which will be headed by a Chairperson will have four other Members who are selected from amongst:

(i) those who are, have been, or are qualified to be Judges of a High Court; or,
(ii) have knowledge of Government finances or accounts, or,
(iii) have had experience in administration and financial expertise; or,
(iv) have special knowledge of Economics.

The report of the Finance Commission is to be laid in both Houses of Parliament.

♦ Task of the Finance Commission

While making the recommendations, Finance Commission has to take into account the following factors:

- the resources of the Central and State Governments for the five year period under reference;
- the levels of tax and non-tax revenues likely to be reached by the Centre and the States;
- the demands on the resources of the Central Government on account of the expenditure on civil administration, defence, internal and border security, debt-servicing, and other expenditure and liabilities;
- the resources of the State Governments and the demands on such resources under different heads such as administration, law and order, welfare and development, and the impact of debt levels on resource availability, particularly in states stressed by debt;
- level of subsidies required, having regard to the need for sustainable and inclusive growth, and equitable sharing of subsidies between the Central Government and State Governments;

- balancing the receipts and expenditure on revenue account of all the States and the Union, and generating surpluses for capital investment;
- the taxation efforts of the Central Government and each State Government and the potential for additional resource mobilization to improve the tax-Gross Domestic Product ratio in the case of the Union and tax-Gross State Domestic Product ratio in the case of the States.

♦ Competing claims

- **The Centre:** Apart from rising commitments on defence, national security, etc., the increasing integration of India with the global economy requires the Union Government to be empowered to manage global shocks, reassure financial markets and adopt counter-cyclical policies as and when the need arises. Also, global opinion makers and credit rating agencies give over-riding importance to the Union Government's fiscal position in their assessment of the national economy.
- **The States:** At the same time, the Union government is increasingly aware of the need to provide greater flexibility and funds to the States for implementing socio-economic policies at state level, including large number of Centrally Sponsored Schemes (CSS). The share of state spending on rural and urban development, and on capital expenditure, primarily to fund sanitation and housing, has seen sharp spurt in recent years.
- **Local bodies:** The local governments, both rural and urban, are constrained not only by the lack of resources, but also by the inadequate administrative infrastructure, as well as the lack of discretion available to them in providing basic services. They contend that they are the most appropriate level of government for the provision of most of the local-level public goods. And they face constraints in raising resources locally and look for higher allocations.

♦ Changed scenario

In the changed and fast evolving scenario, impacted by domestic and external factors, the Finance Commission has to look at a wider canvas while giving its recommendations. The balance between the public and private sectors, the government and the public enterprises, and the fiscal and non-fiscal elements have dramatically changed over the years, and this has had a significant impact on the Centre-State fiscal relations. Several fundamental issues relating to the economy such as those in the financial and banking sector, fiscal deficit, public debt levels, subsidies, disinvestment, environmental concerns, regulatory policies, etc. have also to be taken into account. In short, the Commission has to take cognisance of the new realities of macro-economic management.

The work and recommendations of the Commission plays a vital role in ensuring just, equitable and healthy financial relations between the Centre and the States. It has helped to promote co-operative federalism, improve the quality of public spending and ensure fiscal and financial stability.

♦ Finance Commissions from 1952

So far, starting from 1952, there have been 14 Finance Commissions. The work and reports of the first twelve Commissions covered the period from 1952 to 2010. The 13th Commission, headed by Dr. Vijay Kelkar, was constituted in 2007 and it made recommendations for the period 2010 to 2015. The Fourteenth Finance Commission, headed by Dr. Y. V. Reddy, was constituted in 2013 to make recommendations for the period 2015-20.

The recommendations of the 12th Finance Commission, headed by Dr. C. Rangarajan, for the period 2005-10 covered tax devolution, grants to States, debt relief, financing of relief expenditure, and related matters. The Commission recommended that the share of the States in the net proceeds of shareable central taxes would be 30.5 per cent during 2005-10 as against 29.5 per cent fixed by the Eleventh

Commission for the period 2000-05. For this purpose, additional excise duties in lieu of sales tax on textiles, tobacco, and sugar are treated as part of the general pool of central taxes. The 12th Commission recommended that indicative amount of overall transfer to States may be fixed at 38 per cent of the central gross revenue receipts, as against 37.5% of the gross revenue receipts of the Central Government recommended by the Eleventh Commission for 2000-05.

The 13th Commission recommended that share of the States in net proceeds of shareable central taxes shall be 32 per cent during the financial years from 2010-11 to 2014-15. The 14th Commission (covering the period 2015-20) has recommended that States' share in net proceeds of tax revenues be 42 per cent, a huge jump from the 32 per cent recommended by the 13th Commission. This is the largest change ever in the percentage of devolution, an unprecedented increase which would endow and empower States with more resources. This devolution would be of the order of ₹ 5.24 lakh crore in 2015-16. Another ₹ 3.04 lakh crore would be transferred by way of grants and Plan transfers.

♦ Transfer of Central Schemes to States

Against the background of larger devolution of funds to States after accepting the 14th Finance Commission recommendations, the Centre has decided, in consultation with States, to transfer many of the centrally sponsored schemes (CSS) to be undertaken by the States within their resources. The amount of funds in each CSS which States can spend on their discretion within the overall parameters of the main scheme, known as 'flexi-funds', has also been proposed to be raised to 25 per cent from 10 per cent. However, some States still want the Centre to share a greater burden of the these schemes.

Box 14.3: 15th Finance Commission

The government set up the 15th Finance Commission. Discuss the main tasks before, andrecommendations of, the 15th Commission.

The government appointed 15th Finance Commission in December 2017, headed by N.K. Singh, a former Finance Secretary,and with four other members. It was to make recommendations on tax devolution and grants for the period 2020-25.

♦ Core tasks for the Commission

Apart from the core tasks listed as per Constitutional mandate, viz., devolution of taxes, grants in aid to be given to states and measures to supplement the consolidated funds of states to supplement the resources of urban and rural local bodies, the Commission was asked to make recommendations on other crucial issues.

• Population Criteria

An important difference from the earlier Commissions is that while the past Commissions were asked to take into account 1971 population figures while deciding the devolution formula, the 15th Commission was asked to use the 2011 population data. The 14th Commission was asked to take into account 1971 population and subsequent demographic changes. The shift to latest demographics could be justified since expenditure by states on public goods has to be linked to number of citizens. But this was a sore point for the southern states which have been more successful in reducing their rate of population growth.

• Fiscal Targets

The Commission had to recommend new fiscal targets for the Union and State governments. While the states have, by and large, complied with the targets, the Centre has not been able to stick to them. After the 14th Finance Commission proposed a fiscal roadmap, the Fiscal Review Committee, headed by N K Singh, was asked to revisit it for the period up to 2023. The Commission had to keep in view the recommendations of the Committee on Fiscal Responsibility and Budget Management (FRBM) Act, 2003. (See pp.14.18-9 on FRBM Act).

• Review of funds devolution

Another task was to review the impact of the liberal increase in the devolution of funds to the States/UTs from 32 per cent to 42 per cent as recommended by the 14th Commission. This was relevant in the context of the imperative of national development programme including New India 2022. While the fiscal health of the Union government is important for overall macro performance of Indian economy, close look is also needed on State finances given the tight fiscal position of the states.

♦ Goods and Services Tax (GST)

The task before this Commission was unique since the rules and position of fiscal federalism has undergone a profound change with the introduction of GST. The Commission had to assess the impact of GST on the Centre and the States, including payment of compensation by the Centre to the States for possible loss of revenue for five years and on abolition of cesses. This new tax being a destination levy, shifts the incidence of tax from production to consumption and hence the distribution of indirect taxes between different states would undergo significant change. As the power to levy GST rests with the GST Council, states have limited maneuverability.

♦ Performance-based transfer of funds to States

An important task under the Terms of Reference of the Commission was to examine linking transfer of funds to a range of parameters, such as efforts made by States to deepen GST, how quickly a state moves towards the replacement level of fertility (i.e., Total Fertility Rate - TFR - of 2.1), eliminate power sector losses, improve the ease of doing business, adoption of direct benefit transfer (DBT) and progress in sanitation. These parameters clearly reflect the policy preferences of the Union government.

To sum up, the major focus of the Finance Commission was to strengthen cooperative federalism, frame the parameters needed to shift public spending in the desired direction and, at the same time, to ensure that fiscal discipline and stability is maintained.

- Changes in Terms of Reference (TOR): A controversy erupted with the Centre, while extending the tenure of the 15th Commission, amended the TOR to examine whether "....a separate mechanism for funding of defence and internal security ought to be set up and, if so, how such a mechanism could be operationalized". This was criticized by some as an attempt by the Centre to nudge the Commission to apportion larger share of taxes to it before devolution.

► Recommendations of the 15th Commission: The 15th Finance Commission submitted its Report to the President of India in November 2020. Its recommendations lay down the blueprint for devolution of Centre's tax revenue to States for the five-year period 2020-21 to 2025-26. Its main recommendations are:

- For the year 2020-21, the Commission had recommended that States be given 41 per cent of the divisible tax pool of the Centre. The same will hold good for the full five-year period. The 14th Finance Commission had recommended 42 per cent tax devolution to states including the then J & K state for the period 2015-20.
- The 1 per cent decrease is to provide for the newly formed Union Territories of Jammu and Kashmir, and Ladakh from the resources of the Central government.
- Further, out of all revenues received by the Centre, including the divisible taxes and borrowed funds, a tidy sum will be earmarked each year during the five-year period for a dedicated special fund for modernisation of defence/internal security forces. This will effectively reduce the states' tax receipt from the Centre.

- Efforts to be made to raise the public outlay in the health sector to 2.5 per cent of GDP as envisaged in the National Health Policy, 2017. The Commission observed that the allocation for the health sector is woefully inadequate as was evidenced during the pandemic, Covid-19. It is also deficient due to the skewed geographical spread of the health infrastructure.
- The report also took into account the concerns of southern states on population criteria adopted.

Box 14.4: Retrospective Taxation and its Consequences

A basic tenet of sound tax and legal system is that laws should have only prospective effect and must not be made retrospective jeopardizing old deals that were finalized in consonance with laws extant earlier. Contrary to this, in 2012 the UPA government amended the tax law enabling it to levy capital gains tax with retrospective effect from 1962.

- The genesis: The above amendment enabled the government to renew the tax demand on the telecom firm, Vodafone with tax claim plus interest and penalties finally amounting to a whopping $ 3.7 billion. The deal had its origin when a Hutchison unit in Hong Kong sold its telecom interests in India to Vodafone at substantial profit. Indian tax authorities claimed that capital gains should be paid even though the deal was done abroad between two foreign entities, as the concerned assets were in India. When the case went to Supreme Court, the Court gave verdict in favour of Vodafone. Instead of accepting the verdict, the government amended the tax law with retrospective effect from 1962.
- Other cases: This retrospective change in law impacted 17 cases in all. Another major claim which came under dispute was that of Cairn Energy, the Scottish firm which sold its India unit to Vedanta in 2011. The tax claim in this case amounted to $ 2.7 billion and the government recovered ₹ 7,600 crore by seizing shares of Cairn in its former India arm, dividend and withholding tax refunds. When Cairn took the matter to arbitration, the Hague tribunal ruled against India's claim. Following this, Cairn took steps to enforce the arbitration award by attaching Indian assets overseas such as airplanes, ships and financial assets.
- The Retreat: As negotiations with disputing parties failed to resolve the issue, the NDA government had no other go but to amend the controversial law. The government brought the "Taxation Laws (Amendment) Bill, 2021 to the Parliament in August 2021 which provides for the withdrawal of tax demand made on "indirect transfer of Indian assets if the transaction was undertaken before May 28, 2012", the day the retrospective tax law came into being. It also proposed to refund the amount paid in such cases without any interest on them.

For amicable settlement of the case, the government deem that the disputing parties would withdraw

Pending litigation and not claim cost, damages, interest, etc. The government, on its part, would refund amount paid in these cases without interest.

- Implications of the case: The discredited tax claims and resultant disputes damaged India's image on the international font which would dent the country's prospects for attracting foreign investment. The modest gains on the revenue side by collecting taxes retrospectively was more than offset by the loss of India's reputation as a benign and predictable tax destination. This amendment, which was long overdue, should make India an attractive destination for both domestic and foreign investment as India has a relatively low- rate tax regime for Corporates.

Box 14.5: Implications of Taxing Agriculture Sector

India does not tax income from agriculture. Should India levy tax on income from agriculture? Give arguments for and against it.

India does not tax income derived from agriculture by farmers. This issue has been debated by some economists and examined by expert committees and there have been arguments for and against it. Some states -- Tamil Nadu, Kerala, Bihar and West Bengal - had levied tax on income from agriculture. While some of them levied tax on income from plantations. Some other states did introduce agricultural tax only to roll it back.

Historically speaking, there have been studies and reports of Expert Committees on this sensitive issue - sensitive because agriculture is the main lifeline of the nation with bulk of the population in rural areas dependent on it and its vulnerabilities due to recurring vagaries of nature and consequent distress to farming community.

- An early attempt on this issue dates back to 1947 when an expert committee on financial provisions to the Constituent Assembly suggested consulting States on it.
- The 1972 Committee on Taxation of Agricultural Wealth and Income, headed by the noted economist K N Raj, had comprehensively examined the issue. Raj committee had recommended imposing a progressive 'Agricultural Holdings Tax' on agriculturists, taxing income from livestock, poultry, dairy farming etc., including income from agriculture in respect of assessees paying non-agricultural tax and levying a wealth tax on agricultural property.
- The Task Force on Direct and Indirect Taxes under Dr. Vijay Kelkar had also examined the issue in 2002, and observed that States should be persuaded to pass a resolution authorizing the Centre to pass a tax on agricultural income that would then be assigned to the respective states.
- Bibek Debroy, economist and Member, NITI Aayog has suggested that agricultural income above a certain threshold may be taxed.

Arguments for taxing income from agriculture

- Agricultural income above a certain threshold should be taxed. There are large landholdings which fetch substantial income and equity demands that they should be liable to pay tax.
- There is an anomaly in exempting agricultural income from being taxed, especially where such income is substantial, when income tax is levied on non-agricultural incomes.
- A study of cooperative farms by the erstwhile Planning Commission showed incidence of tax avoidance as mechanized farms with hired labour took advantage of the exemptions provided to cooperative farms. That evasion grew over the decades. In assessment year 2014-15, for instance, nine of the top ten claimants for tax exemption of agricultural income were corporations and the tenth was a state government department.
- The Tax Administration Reform Commission report of 2014 observed that agricultural income of non-agriculturists is being increasingly used as a conduit to avoid tax and for laundering funds, resulting in leakage to the tune of crores in revenue annually.
- According to the 70th round of National Sample Survey, over 86 per cent of agricultural households have land holdings of less than 2 hectares. Low-income farmers would obviously fall outside the ambit of an equitable tax regime. But there is no justification to exempt those who derive substantial income from agricultural sources. It is due to the pressure brought to bear on governments by the political class and the rural elite, many of whom are large landowners, command substantial income and can fetch votes in large chunks in elections and have vested interests, that they remain outside the tax net.
- A crop-specific levy on landholdings above a threshold, assessed and implemented at the panchayat level for accuracy and flexibility, could be considered with the added incentive of tax yields being ploughed back into agricultural sector infrastructure - for facilities like irrigation, water conservation, soil rejuvenation, etc.
- Where 'contract farming' is being done by farmers, in group or otherwise, and in collaboration with corpoates and multi-nationals, appropriate levy could be collected keeping in view cost- income considerations.

Arguments against taxing income from agriculture

- Given the extent of the informality that still exists in the agricultural sector, implementation of an agricultural tax would admittedly not be easy. Evolving crop-specific norms of returns to land poses problems.

- Taxing agriculture pose a problem everywhere and more so in developing countries like India.. Records of inputs, yields, costs incurred, etc. are not maintained except in the plantation sector or where contract farming is done. Transactions by farmers are done in cash and not through banking channels making verification and assessment of income difficult.
- Agriculture in India being largely dependent on monsoon which is quite unpredictable, it is highly subject to the vagaries of nature. In years of erratic monsoon or drought, farmers incur heavy losses.
- Apart from the periodic adverse impact of nature, volatility in prices of agricultural commodities, due to both domestic and international factors, farmers incur losses. In fact, the government has to subsidise and support major crops through a policy of 'Minimum Support Price' (MSP). In these circumstances, it becomes unjust to tax farmers.
- Farming has increasingly become unremunerative and unprofitable due to rising costs, declining soil fertility, lack of water and irrigation facility, heavy debts incurred and inability of farmers to repay loans, etc. The country has been witnessing acute distress in large parts of rural areas resulting in even farmer suicides on a substantial scale. In the above scenario, there is not much scope to introduce taxes on agriculture.

Conclusion

To sum up, taxing agricultural income in India poses many problems, save in the case of organized plantations and on contract farming. Also, the prosperity of the rural population and rural sector is critical for the performance of the industrial and tertiary sectors and has an overall impact on the performance of the economy. Any taxes, if at all, levied on agriculture has to be done prudently and with caution since, as already pointed out, this sector is vital lifeline of the nation on which a large section of the population is dependent and any adverse impact on it will set off a chain reaction in the economy.

❑ CONCLUSION

Sound fiscal policy and macroeconomic stabilization measures should be accompanied by economic reforms to increase productivity and international competitiveness of the industry. Increased savings and investment, reduction of public debt, and avoiding unproductive expenditure are prerequisites for rapid growth. While growth is necessary, there is a compelling moral case for progress with equity and inclusiveness for without them, large sections of the people will be left behind in the process.

In this Chapter we discussed.....

- Role of fiscal policy in an economy; its role in removing inequalities.
- Study of inequalities following the first two Five Year Plans; problem of concentration of wealth.
- India's tax system and budget: an overview.
- Features of a sound tax system and tax policy: simplicity, transparency, equity, moderation, stability, non-adversarial and administrative economy; Laffer curve principle.
- Receipts of the Government: revenue receipts and capital receipts; tax revenue and non-tax revenue; direct and indirect taxes.
- Tax structure and equity; tax system to be just and fair towards vulnerable sections; burden of indirect taxes and regressive tax regime to be avoided.
- Prior to 1991 reforms, India had a regressive tax regime with indirect taxes having a major share.
- India has one of the lowest tax-GDP ratios due to low per capita income, less number of assessees paying direct taxes, and various exemptions granted; higher tax-GDP ratio with more direct tax collection would help in building better infrastructure and providing public goods; indirect taxes to be properly calibrated so as not to hurt industry.
- Early tax reforms; Direct Taxes Enquiry Committee of 1971; recommends direct taxes to be moderated; Indirect Tax Reform Committee of 1976; recommends central excise to be changed to value added tax (VAT); modified VAT (MODVAT) introduced in 1986-87 to minimize the incidence and cascading effect of taxation on inputs.
- Fiscal imbalance persists and worsens in 1980's and fiscal deficit rose; internal liabilities of the Central Government rose inordinately between 1980 and 2015 but came down to 52.7 per cent in 2014-15.
- Persistent macroeconomic instability and fiscal imbalances towards the late 1980's lead to serious crisis in 1990-91; fiscal deficit above 8 per cent; major economic reforms initiated.
- Chelliah Committee set up in 1991 to look into tax reforms; committee recommends, *inter alia*, introduction of full-fledged VAT and Service tax.
- MODVAT was changed and came to be known as Central VAT (CENVAT) in 2000-01 budget; VAT introduced by States with effect from April 1, 2005.

- Eventual goal was to cover the entire production-distribution chain by a national VAT, or a Goods and Service Tax (GST) encompassing both the Centre and the States.
- Service tax introduced in 1994.
- Minimum Alternate tax (MAT) was introduced in the Income Tax Act, 1961, in 1987 to facilitate taxing "zero tax companies"; following disputes and recommendation of Justice Shah Committee, FPI's and FII's were exempted from MAT from April 1, 2015.
- Combined debt-GDP ratio of the Centre and the States reached a peak by the end of 2003-04. Thereafter, it has shown decline; increase in debt finance a matter of concern as it may be put to unproductive use.
- Fiscal Responsibility and Budget Management (FRBM) Act came into force in 2003; interest payments on debt, as a proportion of GDP, have been falling as fiscal deficit was contained; but due to the expansionary fiscal policy followed to avert the impact of global financial crisis of 2008-09, interest payments as a proportion of GDP increased.
- Review of FRBM Act – Report of N K Singh Committee.
- Targets set to bring down fiscal deficit; rationalization of subsidies and steps to plug leakages; public distribution system (PDS), its deficiencies and steps to remedy them; need for direct benefit transfer (DBT) system.
- FRBM Act, 2003 has streamlined the budget presentation process and helped to enforce fiscal discipline.
- Direct Tax Code Bill, 2010; its provisions incorporated in annual budgets and hence no need for the Bill.
- Centre-State relations and the role of Finance Commission; composition and task of Finance Commission.
- Division of financial powers in the Indian state; sharp imbalance between the powers of the Centre and the States and local bodies to tax and raise revenues, and the responsibilities and resultant financial liabilities devolving on them.
- Recommendations of the 12th, 13th, and 14th Finance Commissions.
- Against the background of larger devolution of funds to States, Centre decides to transfer implementation of some of the centrally sponsored schemes to States.
- The 15th Finance Commission and tasks before it. Recommendations of the 15th Commission.

- Retrospective Taxation and its Consequences.
- Levying taxes on agriculture: case for and against it.
- Need for sound fiscal policy and macroeconomic stabilization measures to increase productivity and international competitiveness of industry; growth and progress should ensure equity and be inclusive.

Important Terms to Note in this Chapter

Fiscal policy; Aggregate demand; Poverty line; Laffer curve; Revenue receipts; Capital receipts; Tax revenue; Non-tax revenue; Direct tax; Indirect tax; Regressive tax; Tax–GDP ratio; Fiscal deficit; VAT; GST; Public debt; External debt; Subsidy; Direct Benefit Transfer (DBT)

Practice Questions

1. What are the salient features of a sound taxation policy? How far the Indian taxation system meets those features?
2. Compare and contrast direct and indirect taxes and their impact on the people. What should be their relative share in the overall tax structure?
3. It is said that excessive reliance on indirect taxes make the tax system regressive. Do you agree with this statement? Explain with reasons.
4. India's tax structure is considered to be regressive. Do you agree? If so, what measures have been, or need to be, taken to make it less regressive?
5. India's direct tax base is considered to be very narrow and need to widened. Do you agree with this view? Mention relevant data to justify your view. Suggest measures to make the direct tax system more broad-based.
6. Briefly discuss the various tax reforms implemented in India post- independence.
7. What were the tax reform measures recommended by the Committee on Tax Reforms headed by Prof. Raja Chelliah? How far it has helped to improve the tax system?
8. What are the major subsidies provided in Indian economy? What are their financial implications and how far, in your view, these subsidies are justified?
9. Mention the salient features of the Goods and Services Tax. In what ways is it an improvement over the previous tax system it replaces and what are the benefits to the economy due to its adoption?

10. A Committee headed by N K Singh has reviewed the Fiscal Responsibility and Budget Management (FRBM) Act, 2003. What are the main recommendations of this Committee?

11. It is argued by some experts that rigidly adhering to fiscal discipline hurts economic growth and hence the government need not adhere to it always. Do you agree? What are the views of FRBM Committee headed by NK Singh in this regard?

12. The government has set up the 15th Finance Commission. What are its Terms of Reference and the main tasks before the Commission?

13. India does not tax income from agriculture. Should India levy tax on income from agriculture? Give arguments for and against it.

14. Despite increased collections from taxes, tax-GDP ratio in the case of Central Government continues to be stagnant. Give reasons.

[UPSC 2016-Indian Economic Service/Indian Statistical Service Paper]

15. What are the salient features of FRBM Act? Examine the criticisms labelled against it.

[UPSC Main 2014 (Economics Optional Paper)]

16. What are the major recommendations of the Fourteenth Finance Commission?

[UPSC Main 20215(Economics Optional Paper)]

17. Critically examine the salient features of Fiscal Responsibility Act.

[UPSC Main 2016 (Economics Optional Paper)]

18. Do you think that Fiscal Responsibility and Budget Management Act, 2003 should be modified? Give reasons. *[UPSC 2015-Indian Economic Service/Indian Statistical Service Paper]*

19. Comment on the major federal fiscal problems between the Centre and States in India.

[UPSC 2015-Indian Economic Service/Indian Statistical Service Paper]

20. Do you think that fiscal reforms should supplement financial sector reforms to achieve the objective of stabilization and employment generation in the Indian economy? Explain.

[UPSC 2015-Indian Economic Service/Indian Statistical Service Paper]

21. Do you think that the recommendations of Finance Commissions help in promoting cooperative federalism in the country.

[UPSC 2016-Indian Economic Service/Indian Statistical Service Paper]

22. Do you think that the Union Budget (2016-17) is pro-poor? Give reasons in support of your answer. *[UPSC 2016-Indian Economic Service/Indian Statistical Service Paper]*

23. Describe briefly how resources are transferred from the Centre to the States in India.

[UPSC 2017-Indian Economic Service/Indian Statistical Service Paper]

24. Do you think that the agricultural income in India should be taxed? Give reasons for your answer.

[UPSC 2017-Indian Economic Service/Indian Statistical Service Paper]

25. The public expenditure management is a challenge to the Government of India in the context of budget making during the post-liberalization period. Clarify it.

[UPSC Main 2019 (General Studies Paper)]

26. Under what circumstances can the Financial Emergency be proclaimed by the President of India? What consequences follow when such declaration remains in force?

[UPSC Main 2018 (General Studies Paper)]

27. Discuss the role of the Fiscal Responsibility and Budget Management Act, 2003, in improving the fiscal health of the State finances in India.

[UPSC Main 2020 (Economics Optional Paper)]

28. Explain the concept, features and recent changes of the Fiscal Responsibility and Budget Management (FRBM) Act (2003) in the context of limiting India's fiscal deficit and debt deficit.

[UPSC Main 2020 (General Studies Paper)]

29. How is the Finance Commission of India constituted? What do you know about the terms of reference of the recently constituted Finance Commission? Discuss.

[UPSC Main 2018 (General Studies Paper)]

30. Distinguish between Fiscal Federalism and Fiscal Consolidation. Discuss the fundamental changes in Indian fiscal federalism after introducing GST.

[UPSC Main 2020 (Economics Optional Paper)]

31. What is fiscal federalism? Examine the role of the various Finance Commissions since 2001 in reducing horizontal and vertical fiscal imbalances.

[UPSC (Main) Optional 2019]

32. Discuss the criteria, weightage assigned for determining the sharing of Union Tax proceeds and recommendations of the 14th Finance Commission in India.

[UPSC 2020-Indian Economic Service/Indian Statistical Service Paper]

CHAPTER

FOREIGN TRADE AND COMMERCE

- International trade: Theory of Comparative advantage
- Foreign trade in the 1950s and 1960s
- Devaluation of the Rupee (1966)
- The 1970s and the Turnaround
- The 1980s
- Foreign trade ratios
- 1991 Reforms, Devaluation and After
- The East Asian crisis of 1997-98
- Trade-GDP and Trade Deficit-GDP Ratios
- The 2007-08 Financial Crisis
- Pandemic- Covid-19
- Foreign Exchange Reserves and their Management
- Capital Account Convertibility
- India's share in World trade
- Composition and Direction of India's trade
- India's Leading sectors in Foreign Trade
- Foreign Trade Policy (FTP) 2015-20
- India and WTO
- Multinational corporations (MNCs)
- India and Free Trade Agreements

❑ INTRODUCTION

Foreign trade plays an important part in the process of development of any economy. Just as no man can live in isolation, no country can either. This is even more so in the present-day context of globalization which has brought about greater integration of nations than ever before. Nations are ever more dependent on one another and, in this respect, trade between nations has assumed much importance. The rationale for trade between nations has found resonance in Adam Smith's classical work, *An Inquiry Into the Nature and Causes of the Wealth of Nations (1776)* where he says. "What is prudence in the conduct of every private family, can scarce be folly in that of a great kingdom. If a foreign country can supply us with a commodity cheaper than we ourselves can make it, better buy it of them with some part of the produce of our own industry, employed in a way in which we have some advantage. It is as foolish for a nation as for an individual to make what can be bought cheaper." This is the very concept underlying the 'Theory of Comparative Advantage' (see Box 15.1) in international trade which was refined and developed later by other economists.

For nearly three decades from 1950, India traversed on this path of 'import substitution' (IS) and discarding the approach of 'export strategy' (ES) which, in hindsight, proved to be much to her disadvantage.

That being so, it would be pertinent to see how and why India, in the initial years of planning and development, opted for a policy of self-reliance and self-sufficiency, virtually shutting herself out from the world markets. For nearly three decades from 1950, India traversed on this path of 'import substitution' (IS) and discarding the approach of 'export strategy' (ES) which, in hindsight, proved to be much to her disadvantage. At the same time, many other nations in Asia followed an 'open economy' approach, forged ahead, and developed native industries with an eye on exports, which catapulted them on to a high growth trajectory, which came to be called the 'East Asian miracle'.

Box 15.1 The Theory of Comparative Advantage

Although the concept is attributed to the English economist, David Ricardo (1772–1823), the idea of territorial division of labour, the original description of the concept, finds mention in the 1815 work, 'An Essay on the External Corn Trade' by Col. Robert Torrens (1780–1864). It was, however, left to Ricardo to formalize and provide a theoretical basis for the idea using a simple numerical example in his 1817 classic titled, 'The Principles of Political Economy and Taxation'. The idea was further developed by James Mill (1773–1836) in his work, 'Elements of Political Economy' in 1821. Finally, the concept became a central theme of international trade theory.

Simply stated, the theory is that if country A can produce some goods at lower cost than country B, and if country B can produce some other goods at lower cost than country A, then it would be advantageous for country A to trade its cheaper goods for the relatively cheaper goods of country B. In this way, both the countries stand to gain from trade and exchange of these goods.

And with both countries specializing in the production of goods in which they had comparative advantage, the total output of both goods could rise. If an appropriate terms of trade (i.e., amount of one good traded for another) were chosen, then both countries could end up with more of both goods after specialization and free trade than what they would have had in the absence of trade. Trade based on comparative advantage will lead to an increase in the real incomes of both the countries.

To identify a country's comparative advantage in goods it produces, it is necessary to make a comparison of production costs between the countries. However, it is not enough to compare only the monetary costs of production or the resource costs (labour needed per unit of output) of production. Instead, one must compare the 'opportunity costs' of producing goods across countries. (Opportunity cost is the value of an item which must be given up to acquire another item). Another way to find comparative advantage is by comparing productivities across industries and countries.

However, the application of this concept becomes more complex when the study and comparison involves not just two countries and few goods, as in the example discussed earlier, but involves multiple countries and production and exchange of a wide range of goods.

Eli Heckscher (1879–1952) and Bertil Ohlin (1899–1979) of the Stockholm School of Economics further developed Ricardo's theory of comparative advantage with a mathematical model of international trade known as Heckscher–Ohlin model (H–O model). According to it, the relative endowments of the factors of production (land, labour, and capital) will determine a country's comparative advantage. As the profitability of goods is dependent on input costs, countries will have comparative advantage in producing those goods for which the required factors of production are locally available in relative abundance. This is because it will be cheaper to produce goods that require inputs which are available in abundance than to produce goods that require inputs that are locally scarce and dear. For instance, a country having labour and natural resources in abundance but little capital will find it advantageous to specialize in labour-intensive industries as the price of labour and natural resources will be cheap while the cost of capital will be high. Ohlin was awarded a Nobel prize for his work in international trade theory.

However, the development process in many countries have shown that they adopted a strategy counter to the above concept, and despite having abundant skilled and unskilled labour and natural resources but scarce capital, went in for developing heavy industries requiring large capital investment, mainly with a view to become self-reliant and develop rapidly. But many of such industries later needed subsidies and protection which made them inefficient and less competitive. India's experience in the first three decades after independence is an example of this approach.

The path India chose in the early years is an issue which has baffled many in later years. This was despite India having had an array of distinguished economists, apart from many foreign experts, to advise the Government and the Planning Commission in the early 1950's. While the attempts at industrialization in the first three Plans (1951-66) cannot be faulted, the relative neglect of agriculture, constraints placed on private sector investment, and isolation from the world markets hampered growth. The annual (compound) growth rates of national income which was 3 per cent in 1951-60, 2.9 per cent in 1961-70, and 2.5 per cent in 1971-80 period was termed 'Hindu rate of growth' by Prof. Raj Krishna.

The path India chose in the early years is an issue which has baffled many in later years. This was despite India having had an array of distinguished economists, apart from many foreign experts, to advise the Government and the Planning Commission in the early 1950's.

In defence of the policy adopted in the early years, it is said that given the stage of development at which India was at that time, it seemed to be the right course of action, that India was trying to 'take-off' into self-sustained growth, and that the country could afford to have a large deficit which would be covered with external borrowings and foreign aid. From the mid-1950's, India started to face serious foreign exchange crisis which made India look inward. India could have changed course in the mid-1960's by when she had laid the foundation and created the basic infrastructure for further development. But it took another two decades to change the path.

❑ FOREIGN TRADE IN 1950s AND '60s

With the growth of industrial production and the development of the economy as a whole during the first two Five Year Plans (1951-61), the level of imports rose sharply during this decade. In the Second Plan (1956-61), there was a substantial increase in the level of imports on account of the larger requirements of capital goods, raw materials, intermediate products, components, etc. During the First Plan (1951-56) itself, India imposed strict control and regulation of imports and exports, and state trading in respect of certain essential commodities, in order to conserve scarce foreign exchange resources. The system of industrial licensing and exchange controls stifled private initiative and the private sector. Total imports declined in the last two years—1959-61—of the Second Plan. This decline in imports resulted from the tightening up of import licensing which the country had to follow in face of severe foreign exchange difficulties.

In view of the critical balance of payments position and the severe foreign exchange shortage, the government imposed tight import controls through a regime of quantitative restrictions (QR's), apart from industrial licensing. As the QR's were imposed, the Open General Licence (OGL) was discontinued in 1957. The imports of consumer goods were drastically curtailed and import of capital goods was confined to those which were needed for the highest priority programmes. The QR's were imposed in a selective manner to provide protection to industries which helped to achieve substitution of imports.

The 1960s continued to be testing times for the economy. The 1962 war with China, the 1965 war with Pakistan, and the 1971 Bangladesh liberation war all placed a heavy strain on the economy. Added to these was a back-to-back drought in the two years, 1965-67, which adversely impacted agricultural exports and food production necessitating food imports.

Devaluation of the Rupee (1966)

India had been in desperate need of foreign currency, and the World Bank and the IMF had made granting aid subject to the condition of a substantial devaluation of the Rupee which would be a step towards liberalization. The Rupee was devalued in June 1966 by a massive 57 percent, from ₹ 4.76 to ₹ 7.50 to a dollar, inviting bitter criticism from various quarters due to the perception that it was done at the behest of the international agencies. After the devaluation, exports rose faster than before, imports declined, and with the narrowing trade deficit, the balance of payments and the exchange reserves position improved by 1968-69. Though the devaluation was to be followed by liberalization measures, it did not happen. The regime of industrial licensing, import controls, and export subsidies was continued. It may also be recalled, in this context, that the nationalization of banks was also to follow soon in 1969.

Table 15.1 India's Foreign Trade: 1950–51 to 1990–91

(in ₹ crore)

Year	Exports	Imports	Balance of Trade	Year	Exports	Imports	Balance of Trade
1950–51	601	650	–49	1975–76	4036	5265	–1229
1956–57	635	1096	–461	1978–79	5726	6811	–1085
1960–61	642	1122	–480	1980–81	6711	12549	–5838
1965–66	806	1409	–603	1985–86	10895	19658	–8763
1970–71	1535	1634	–99	1990–91	32558	43193	–10635

Source: Economic Surveys, Ministry of Finance; Handbook of Statistics on Indian Economy, Reserve Bank of India.

India's foreign trade data from 1950-51 to 1990-91 (See Table 15.1) show varying trends and consistent negative trade balance with imports outstripping exports. Trade deficit steadily increased over the years. The total value of exports and imports which was ₹1,251 Crore in 1950-51 increased manifold to ₹3,169 Crore in 1970-71, ₹19,260 Crore in 1980-81, and ₹75,751 Crore in 1990-91.

❑ THE 1970s AND THE TURNAROUND

The initial years of the 1970s again proved to be trying times on the foreign exchange front. The food position was critical in 1973 necessitating food imports on a large scale at exorbitant international prices. The huge import bill due to food imports and oil price hike resulted in heavy trade deficit in spite of good export performance.

But there was a dramatic turnaround from the mid-1970's when the foreign exchange position eased and the reserves went up substantially. (See Table 15.2). There was increase in external aid and a spurt in remittances by Indians overseas, particularly those in the Persian Gulf. The Indian Rupee was delinked from the Pound sterling in September 1975 and was linked to a basket of currencies of India's major trading partners in order to impart stability to the exchange rate of the Rupee. The period also saw significant increases in the food output due to the early Green Revolution which helped to not only meet the current demands for foodgrains, but to build up buffer stock of grains and avoid food imports. This rebound of the economy helped to ease import controls to give a boost to industrial production and accelerate growth.

Table 15.2 India's Foreign Exchange Reserves

(in ₹ crore)

Year	Foreign Exchange Reserves	Year	Foreign Exchange Reserves
1970–71	733	1980–81	5545
1973–74	994	1982–83	4782
1975–76	1886	1984–85	7243
1976–77	3243	1986–87	8151
1977–78	4863	1988–89	7040
1979–80	5164	1989–90	6252

Source: Handbook of Statistics on Indian Economy, Reserve Bank of India, 2015.

❑ THE 1980s

The import policy of 1978-79 liberalized the regime and allowed import of all items, other than those restricted, under the Open General Licence (OGL). Following this and the second 'oil shock' of 1979, the trade deficit rose from ₹ 1,085 crore in 1978-79 ₹ 5,838 crore in 1980-81, by 1990-91, trade deficit touched ₹ 10,635 crore (see Table 15.1). As the economy was expanding during the Sixth (1980-85) and the Seventh (1985-90) Plans, imports increased substantially while exports lagged behind.

Even as the trade deficit increased through the 1980's, there was also decline in the net invisibles—receipts from services such as consulting services, shipping services, tourism, and other items — which could have covered the deficit. At the same time, India had to resort to external borrowings on commercial terms from the capital market and NRI's. The proportion of concessional funds on soft terms from multilateral sources declined from about 90 per cent in 1980 to about 30 per cent in 1990.

Following a liberal import and industrial policy, the second half of the 1980s saw an acceleration in economic growth. But the flip side was that India was importing more than what could be sustained by her exports leading to a widening trade deficit which had to be covered by commercial borrowings on hard terms. The expansionary policy followed during this period also led to high fiscal deficits. The fiscal deficit which was 6 per cent at the beginning of 1980s rose to over 8 per cent by 1990-91.

❑ FOREIGN TRADE RATIOS

A study of foreign trade data for selected years from 1950-51 to 1989-90 (Table 15.3) shows that as the economy expanded, both exports and imports rose steadily and rather steeply in later years. Exports as a percentage to the GDP (at market prices) declined between 1950 and 1971 and then showed increase. Exports as a percentage to imports, which indicates the extent to which exports covered the import liabilities, declined between 1951 and 1961, then showed improvement in 1970-71, but again declined till 1985-86. Some of these trends changed significantly after the 1991 reforms as will be seen in the next section.

Table 15.3 Export–Import Ratio and Percentage of Exports/Imports to the GDP

Year	Total Exports (in ₹ crore)	Total Imports (in ₹ crore)	GDP at MP (Current Prices) (in ₹ crore)	Export %age to GDP–MP	Import %age to GDP–MP	Export–Import Ratio
1	2	3	4	5	6	7
1950–51	601	650	10721	5.61	6.06	92.46
1960–61	642	1122	17407	3.69	6.45	54.55
1970–71	1535	1634	46249	3.32	3.53	93.94
1975–76	4036	5265	84221	4.79	6.25	76.66
1980–81	6711	12549	145370	4.62	8.63	53.48
1985–86	10895	19658	281330	3.87	6.99	55.42
1989–90	27658	35328	487684	5.67	7.24	78.29

Source: GDP data for 1950-51 & 1960-61 from National Accounts Statistics/Plan documents. GDP data for other years and foreign trade data from Handbook of Statistics on Indian Economy, Reserve Bank of India, 2010, 2012 and 2015.
Note: GDP at Market Prices (at Current prices) from 1950-51 to 2000-01 is on Base year 1999-2000, GDP at MP for 2004-05 to 2012-13 is on Base year 2004-05, and for 2014-15 on Base year 2011-12.

❑ 1991 REFORMS, DEVALUATION AND AFTER

The Beginning of the Crisis

The decade of the nineties began on a precipitous note when the economy was on the verge of collapse. The balance of payments was in deep crisis, foreign exchange reserves had touched rock bottom, and payments towards external debt were in danger of default. The Gulf War accentuated the problems and the government had to pledge a part of the gold held by the Reserve Bank of India to garner temporary resources from abroad. The Rupee was devalued in July 1991. The government effected structural changes in trade and industrial policies. Import tariffs were reduced, particularly for capital goods required for domestic industries.

It became evident that unless local entrepreneurship and industry were encouraged and enabled to improve production standards to face up to international competition, the country would become dependent on imports in perpetuity. This difference in attitude and approach gradually brought about perceptible change in India's position and growing stature in world economy. (For more on these aspects and reform measures initiated, see Chapter 6).

Robust Growth in Trade Due to Reforms

Following the reforms initiated in 1991, India's trade growth has been buoyant. (See Table 15.4). While India's trade growth has a strong correlation with world trade growth, it was significantly higher than world trade growth, particularly in two phases—first just after the 1991 reforms and again after 2003. Exports responded well to the major reform initiatives and the ratio of export earnings to import liabilities improved considerably from 75 per cent in 1990-91 to 2000-01. But as imports increased substantially after 2000-01, the trade deficit began to rise and export-import ratio declined. (See Table 15.4 (a).

Table 15.4 (a):Total Exports and Imports, Trade–GDP Ratio, Export–Import Ratio and Percentage of Exports/Imports to the GDP

Year	Total Exports (in ₹ crore)	Total Imports (in ₹ crore)	GDP at MP (Current Prices) (in ₹ crore)	Trade–GDP–MP Ratio	Export %age to GDP–MP	Import %age to GDP–MP	Export–Import Ratio
1990-91	32558	43193	569624	13.30	5.72	7.58	75.38
1992-93	53688	63375	752591	15.55	7.13	8.42	84.71
1995-96	106353	122678	1191813	19.22	8.92	10.29	86.69
2000-01	203571	230873	2102314	20.67	9.68	10.98	88.17
2004-05	375340	501065	3242209	27.03	11.58	15.45	74.91
2008-09	840755	1374436	5630063	39.35	14.93	24.41	61.17
2010-11	1142922	1683467	7674148	36.83	14.89	21.94	67.89
2013-14	1905011	2715434	11345056	40.73	16.79	23.93	70.15

Source: Handbook of Statistics on Indian Economy, 2010, 2012, and 2015, Reserve Bank of India.

Note: GDP at Market Prices (at Current prices) from 1990-91 to 2002-03 is on Base year 1999-2000, GDP at MP for 2004-05 to 2012-13 is on Base year 2004-05, and for 2013-14 on Base year 2011-12.

As per the World Bank-UNCTAD's World Integrated Trade Solution (WITS) data, India's trade as percentage of GDP was 40.08 % in 2016, 40.72 % in 2017, 43.40 % in 2018 and 39.55 % in 2019. After maintaining the momentum between 2016 and 2018, there has been sharp fall in 2019 which was the period when the economy was also in slowdown.

The export – import position and trade balance between 2015-16 and 2019-20 was as shown below. The trade deficit increased substantially between 2015-16 and 2018-19 and then reduced slightly in 2019-20.

Table 15.4 (b): Total Exports and Imports, Trade balance

Year	Exports	Imports	Trade balance
2015-16	1716384	2490306	– 773921
2018-19	2307726	3594675	– 1286948
2019-20	2218233	3355762	– 1137530

Source: Handbook of Statistics on Indian Economy, 2020, Reserve Bank of India.

The East Asian crisis of 1997-98

Global financial markets experienced turmoil as a fall-out of the crisis that erupted in East Asia in July 1997, and which worsened in 1998. The turbulence spread rapidly and exposed the fragility of emerging markets as investment destinations. The economies of Thailand, South Korea, and Indonesia were most impacted by the crisis and experienced currency depreciation, and decline in domestic demand and growth. Flow of international capital to these countries dwindled. Japan, which was an important market for the exports of East Asian countries, was already in recession. The crisis had a profound impact on world economy, demonstrating how the adverse trends in one region could spread and affect other regions.

Though India could withstand the East Asian crisis to a fair extent, with foreign exchange reserves at a comfortable level (see Table 15.6), export growth had slowed down and the current account deficit rose to 1.58 per cent of GDP in 1997-98.

Trade-GDP and Trade Deficit-GDP Ratios

As Table 15.4 (column 5) shows, the trade-GDP ratio, which is a measure of the extent to which the economy is linked to the world economy, has been on the rise since 1991 but more robustly after 2003. The world economy, led by the US, Japan, and the Euro zone, was on an upswing in 2004 and there was robust growth both in the developed and emerging economies. Development in Asia was driven by China with sharp increase in investment and output while India also recorded impressive growth. As the trade-GDP ratio rose in the post-1991 period, the trade deficit-GDP ratio fell till 2000-01 which reflects a healthy trend. But the trade deficit-GDP ratio started rising from 2004-05 even as the trade-GDP ratio was rising. (See Table 15.5).

Table 15.5: Trade Deficit–GDP Ratio

Year	Trade Deficit in ₹ crore	GDP at MP (Current prices) in ₹ crore	Trade Deficit GDP-MP ratio	Year	Trade Deficit in ₹ crore	GDP at MP (Current prices)	Trade Deficit GDP-MP ratio in ₹ crore
1980-81	– 5,838	1,45,370	4.02	2004-05	– 1,25,725	32,42,209	3.88
1985-86	– 8,763	2,81,330	3.11	2006-07	–2,68,727	42,94,706	6.26
1990-91	–10,635	5,69,624	1.87	2008-09	–5,33,680	56,30,063	9.48
1993-94	– 3,350	8,65,805	0.38	2010-11	– 5,95,600	76,74,148	7.76
1997-98	– 24,076	15,27,158	1.58	2012-13	– 10,37,850	101,13,281	10.26
2000-01	– 27,302	21,02,314	1.30	2013-14	– 8,20,000	113,45,056	7.23

Source: GDP data for 1950-51 & 1960-61 from National Accounts Statistics/Plan documents. GDP data for other years and foreign trade data from Handbook of Statistics on Indian Economy, Reserve Bank of India, 2012 and 2015.

Note: GDP at Market Prices (at Current prices) from 1980-81 to 2000-01 is on Base year 1999-2000, GDP-MP for 2004-05 to 2012-13 is on Base year 2004-05, and for 2013-14 and 2014-15 on Base year 2011-12.

❑ THE 2007–08 FINANCIAL CRISIS

Background of the Crisis

During 2007-08, a major financial crisis erupted in the US, considered to be the worst since the Great Depression of 1930's. There occurred a chain of events throwing the world's largest economy into turmoil. Reckless mortgage lending to 'sub-prime' borrowers in the US housing sector led to mortgage defaults and foreclosures. The crisis affected financial institutions like investment banks, hedge funds, and private equity in the US and Europe and disrupted the stability of the financial system. During 2007-08, American investors lost more than a quarter of their net worth. Lehman Brothers, one of the largest investment banks in the US, went bankrupt while two others, Bear Stearns and Merrill Lynch, were sold at heavily discounted rates. The full-blown crisis impacted many other developed and emerging economies which had to take interventionist measures like financial stimulus to combat recession and bailout packages for businesses in trouble.

Impact on India

No country, including India, could remain immune to the grave economic crisis for long. Initially, the impact on India was positive as it led to increased Foreign Institutional Investments (FII's) in India during 2007-08. But as the financial meltdown and consequent economic recession deepened in developed economies, there was economic slowdown and outflow of FII's from India. There was decline in consumer demand and exports while higher expenditure to stimulate the economy resulted in widening of fiscal deficit. India's fiscal deficit increased from 2.54 per cent of GDP in 2007-08 to 5.99 per cent in 2008-09 and 6.46 per cent in 2009-10.

With the post-financial crisis stimulus, Indian economy posted robust growth of 8.6 per cent and 9.3 per cent in 2009-10 and 2010-11 respectively. But with rising consumption, coupled with supply-side constraints, inflation set in prompting Reserve Bank of India to adopt tight monetary policy and raise interest rates. This impacted investments and led to slowdown in the economy, and growth rate slumped to 6.2 per cent in 2011-12, 4.5 per cent in 2012-13, and 4.7 per cent in 2013-14.

Impact on Foreign Trade

Following the financial crisis of 2007-08, growth in volume of world trade of both goods and services declined to 2.8 per cent in 2008 compared to 7.3 per cent in 2007. There was steep fall in foreign trade growth in different countries during the crisis-ridden years of 2008 and 2009. The fall in trade, which was more pronounced than the decline in real GDP, was arrested in 2010, and trade growth recovered faster than real GDP growth. The recovery in trade growth was partly due to the fiscal stimulus effected by the governments.

The global recession also impacted the consistent growth in India's export sector. During the five years between 2008 and 2103, India's export growth faced many ups and downs. It was in negative territory twice—in 2009-10 due to the 2008 crisis and again in 2012-13 as a result of the Euro zone crisis and global slowdown. However, the economy showed resilience during these critical years and it recovered by 2012-13. The trade-GDP ratio which was 39.35 per cent in 2008-09 rose to 42.55 per cent in 2012-13 and 40.73 per cent in 2013-14 (see Table 15.4). And the export-import ratio also rose from 61.17 per cent to 70.15 per cent in 2013-14. Trade deficit on BOP basis, as a proportion of GDP, was 7.23 per cent of GDP in 2013-14 as against 10.26 per cent in 2012-13 (See Table 15.5).

> The current account deficit would have been unmanageable but for software exports bringing in more than $ 70 billion per annum and remittances from Indians overseas in the range of $ 70 billion. The steep fall in the world prices of crude oil from about $ 110 per barrel in 2014 to less than $ 50 in 2015 also helped to ease the situation.

As already stated, India's foreign trade has been under great stress in the last few years, especially due to the global economic slowdown, with exports being able to cover just two-thirds of the imports.

Though not out of the woods yet, the world economy is gradually recovering from the crisis, led by the buoyant economic activity in emerging economies. However, the risks remain, as the developed economies face large fiscal deficit, tepid demand, unemployment, high public debt, and have shown only subdued and fragile growth. The sovereign debt crisis in the peripheral Euro-zone countries, the slowdown in China's economy resulting in falling demand for commodities, and fall in oil prices have all added to the uncertainty which may affect the nascent global recovery.

Pandemic Covid-19

Even as the global economy was facing the above challenges, the pandemic, Covid-19 has struck a devastating blow to global economy. It has not spared any country from is virulent attack. As India imposed stringent and nationwide lockdown in the initial phase to contain its spread and further lockdowns had to be imposed in phases, the impact was severe, both on lives and livelihood of people. All sectors had to bear the brunt due to virtual cessation of all economic activity for nearly a year and millions of people sustained not only loss of incomes but even their jobs. The impact of this health crisis was compounded by the fact that even prior to its outbreak, the Indian economy was on a downward trend since 2016-17 and the annual GDP growth had declined to 4.2 per cent in 2019-20. As the Covid-19 virus persists even in 2021, the recovery process may be prolonged. (For more on the pandemic Covid-19 and its impact, see Chapter 10).

❑ FOREIGN EXCHANGE RESERVES

India continues to be one of the countries that have sizeable foreign exchange reserves, particularly considering that some of the other major reserve holders are nations with large current account surpluses. Intervention in the foreign exchange markets by the RBI to stabilize the exchange rate of the Rupee and watch kept over volatility has helped the accumulation of reserves.

India's foreign exchange (forex) reserves have risen steadily from ₹733 crore in 1970-71 to ₹36,02,155 crore in 2019-20. (See Table 15.6). As will be seen from Table 15.6, foreign currency assets form the largest share in India's foreign exchange (forex) reserves. It has risen from ₹438 crore (59.8 per cent of total reserves) in 1970-71 to ₹3,33,3815 crore (92.5 per cent of total reserves) in 2019-20.

Remittances from Abroad

India is one of the largest remittance receiving countries in the world. According to the *World Bank's Migration and Remittances Factbook, 2016*, Indians living abroad sent home an estimated $72 billion (₹ 4.75 lakh crore) in 2015, making India the largest remittance receiving country, surpassing China ($64 billion), and the Philippines ($30 billion).

Table 15.6 India's Foreign Exchange Reserves
(Figures are in `crore)

End of Financial Year	SDRs	Gold	Foreign Currency Assets	Reserve Tranche Position	Total
1	2	3	4	5	6
1970-71	112 (15.2)	183 (24.9)	438 (59.8)	--	733
1980-81	497 (8.9)	226 (4-1)	4822 (86.9)	--	5545
1990-91	200 (1.7)	6828 (59.8)	4388 (38.4)	--	11416
1992-93	55 (0.18)	10549 (34.3)	20140 (65.5)	--	30744
2000-01	11 (0.005)	12711 (6.4)	184482 (93.5)	--	197204
2010-11	20401 (1.5)	102572 (7.5)	1224883 (89.9)	13158	1361013
2014-15	24940 (1.16)	119160 (5.5)	1985460 (92.8)	8080	2137640
2016-17	9380 (0.39)	128830 (5.37)	2244940 (93.6)	15050	2398200
2019-20	10800 (0.3)	230527 (6.4)	3333815 (92.5)	27013	3602155

Note: Figures in brackets are percentages to total in column 6. Percentages may not add up to exactly 100 due to rounding off.; - denotes Negligible.

Source: Handbook of Statistics on Indian Economy, 2019-20, Reserve Bank of India.

Remittances from Abroad

India is also one of the largest remittance receiving countries in the world. According to the World Bank's Migration and Remittances Fact book, 2016, Indians living abroad sent home an estimated $72 billion (₹4.75 lakh crore) in 2015, making India the largest remittance receiving country, surpassing China ($64 billion), and the Philippines ($30 billion). According to World Bank data, personal remittances received by India from abroad stood at US$ 83.15 billion in 2020 which formed 3.17 per cent of GDP.

Box 15.2: Foreign Exchange (forex) Reserves and their Management

The Reserve Bank of India (RBI) is vested with the responsibility of managing the country's foreign exchange reserves and their utilization within the overall policy framework agreed upon with the government. The RBI oversees and regulates the foreign exchange market in India under the provisions of the Foreign Exchange Management Act, 1999.

♦ **Managing Foreign exchange (forex) reserves**

The foreign exchange reserves include Foreign Currency Assets (FCA), Special Drawing Rights (SDRs) with the International Monetary Fund (IMF) and Gold. SDRs held by the Govt. of India refer to an international reserve currency created by IMF in 1969 that serves as a supplement to the money reserves of member countries.

♦ **Importance of Forex Reserves**

- Foreign exchange reserves play an important role in an economy.
- A strong reserve of foreign exchange gives fillip to the Government and the Central bank (RBI) to implement fiscal and monetary policies and manage liquidity and cash flows in the domestic markets.
- This reserve helps to meet any contingency in case of an abrupt interruption in capital flows from external sources, which could occur during an emergency.
- Holding fluid forex provides cushion against such impacts and gives the certainty that there would be sufficient reserve to meet the nation's critical imports.
- This rise in reserve will also strengthen currency, Indian rupee, against the dollar.

♦ **Deployment of Reserves**

♦ In deploying reserves, RBI pays attention to currency composition, interest rate risks and liquidity needs. All foreign currency assets (FCA) are invested in assets of top quality and a good proportion can be converted into cash at short notice.

♦ A crucial concern in investing foreign currency assets in the overseas markets relates to the risks involved. The counterparties with whom deals are conducted are subject to a rigorous selection process. While there is no set formula to meet all situations, the RBI follows the accepted portfolio management criteria of identifying and studying the risks, developing responses and monitoring to contain the risks.

♦ In assessing the returns from deployment, the total return (both interest and capital gains) is taken into consideration.

♦ Objectives of Foreign exchange reserves management

- The basic parameters of the RBI's policies for managing foreign exchange reserves are safety, liquidity and optimising returns. Within this framework, the Reserve Bank focuses on:
- Maintaining market's confidence in monetary and exchange rate policies.
- Enhancing the Reserve Bank's intervention capacity to stabilise foreign exchange markets.
- Limiting external vulnerability by maintaining foreign currency liquidity to absorb shocks during times of crisis, including national disasters or emergencies.
- Providing confidence to the markets that external obligations can always be met, thus reducing the costs at which foreign exchange resources are available to market participants.
- Adding to the comfort of market participants by demonstrating the backing of domestic currency by external assets.

♦ Utilization of Forex reserves

With the exception of a small proportion of gold, the forex reserves are invested in liquid assets like U.S. treasuries and Euro-denominated bonds of other advanced economies. Most of these economies have seen interest rates fall to near zero, with some securities even trading at negative yields.

According to the RBI data, as much as 64 per cent of the foreign currency reserves are held in securities like Treasury bills of foreign countries, mainly the US, 28 per cent is deposited in foreign central banks and 7.4 per cent is also deposited in commercial banks abroad.

One common view is that India's foreign exchange reserves may be used to finance infrastructure development in the country. Yet another view is that RBI could deploy excess forex reserves for commercial returns which would mean the central bank shifting from the conventional role and turning partly commercial.

In the last few years, RBI has become a critical part of the Union Budget as the surpluses in its earnings are being transferred to the Centre, and these transfers go up to nearly ₹one lakh crore which adds to the non-tax revenue of the government.

♦ Paradigm shift in Exchange rate policy

The Reserve Bank's approach to foreign exchange reserves management has undergone significant change over the years. Until the balance of payments crisis of 1991, India's approach to forex reserves was essentially aimed at maintaining reserves at appropriate levels to cover imports.

The approach underwent a paradigm shift following the recommendations of the 1991 Rangarajan Committee. The Committee stressed the need to maintain sufficient reserves to meet all external payment obligations, ensure a reasonable level of confidence in the international community about India's capacity to honour its obligations, and counter the speculative tendencies in the market.

After the introduction of the system of market-determined exchange rates in 1993, the objective of smoothening the volatility in the exchange rates assumed importance.

♦ Conclusion

The RBI's function of managing foreign exchange reserves has in recent years grown, both in terms of importance and sophistication, for two main reasons.

First, the share of foreign currency assets in the balance sheet of the Reserve Bank has substantially increased.

Second, with the increased volatility in exchange and interest rates in the global market, the task of preserving the value of reserves and obtaining a reasonable return on them has become challenging.

Box 15.3: Capital Account Convertibility

The concept – Its benefits and drawbacks – India and capital account convertibility

Capital account of the balance of payments refers to cross border transactions in assets such as equity, debt, immovable property or any combination of these. It includes inward and outward flow of money for investment and international grants and loans.

Capital account convertibility implies that a country's currency is freely convertible with foreign currencies. In other words, there is no restriction on conversion of the domestic currency into a foreign currency or on conversion of a foreign currency to the domestic currency. The former process enables a resident of the country to acquire foreign assets while the latter enables a non-resident to acquire a domestic asset. It enables unrestricted mobility of capital.

In the earlier decades under the IMF regime, 'fixed exchange rate' was the norm and the idea of 'full capital account convertibility' had not received much attention. Liberalisation of capital account transactions as a policy objective gained prominence in the 1990's. The 1990's saw significant increase in global capital flows, following the triumph of market capitalism and increasing trend towards globalisation, and advocacy of capital account convertibility as a policy goal, particularly for the developing countries, started gaining momentum.

Benefits of Capital Account Convertibility

(i) Free global capital flows result in more efficient allocation of the global pool of savings to the more productive uses. Developing countries benefit from free access to global capital markets as they get more investible resources which augments domestic savings, reduces marginal cost of capital, accelerates investment and growth.

(ii) Open capital accounts widens the channels through which countries can finance trade and investment and thus support the multilateral trading systems.

(iii) It will deepen capital markets and will help India to play a more meaningful role in the global economy.

(iv) It provides greater scope for investors in both developed and developing countries to invest in diverse portfolios.

(v) Since capital account convertibility calls for sound macroeconomic policy, it induces the countries concerned to commit themselves to healthy macroeconomic management.

(vi) Currencies of all developed countries are fully capital account convertible; by striving to make their currencies fully convertible, developing countries progress on the path towards development

Drawbacks and pitfalls of Capital Account Convertibility

(i) Capital flows are sensitive to macroeconomic conditions. Any deterioration in fiscal conditions, inflation management, balance of payments, or any other macroeconomic shock may cause a disruption, stoppage or reversal of capital flows.

(ii) Capital flows which result mainly from trade in financial assets are prone to volatilities caused by information asymmetries, herd behaviour, panic reaction, etc.

(iii) An open and unfettered capital account calls for complete abandonment of the exchange rate management and can lead to extreme volatility in the exchange rate and large fluctuations from its equilibrium value.

(iv) It is recognized that capital flows carry risks, and that liberalisation of capital flows before nations reach a certain level of financial and institutional development can accentuate those risks. Under certain circumstances, cross-border capital flows need to be regulated to avoid the worst effects of capital flow surges and sudden cessation.

(v)The practice of capital controls in times of currency and banking crisis is now part of the accepted wisdom. Capital controls are used by the state to protect the economy from potential shocks from unpredictable capital flows. It may be noted that India has been using capital controls to effectively manage the flows.

Reforms implemented

After economic liberalisation process set in motion in 1990s, following measures were taken to unshackle India's external sector.

- A significant step was to move to a flexible exchange rate regime to allow the overvalued Rupee to float. However, down the years the exchange rate was sometimes 'managed' in response to prevailing conditions.
- Another important step India took was to comply with the obligations under Article VIII of the Articles of Agreement of the International Monetary Fund (IMF) that there will not be any unreasonable restriction on current account transactions. (Current account in 'Balance of Payments' refers to trade in goods – also called merchandise or 'visible trade' – and to services and profits and interest from assets overseas – which are called 'invisibles').

- Finally, India put in place a new statute – the Foreign Exchange Management Act (FEMA), 1999 that recognised and discriminated between current and capital account transactions – the former was unrestricted while the latter was subject to regulations. Capital account transactions have been further progressively liberalised.
- While India has not opted for full capital account convertibility, the government has taken steps to ease access to foreign capital, be it Foreign Direct Investment (FDI) or Foreign Portfolio Investment (FPI) which includes equity and debt. There is virtually no restriction on FDI. Any foreign individual or firm or any other association of people can invest in any Indian company or set up an Indian company through FDI which essentially means long term engagement with influence on management. There are some restrictions on the extent of entry into select sectors on account of security or strategic interests like in defence sector.
- New instruments have been made available for foreign investors such as rupee-dominated offshore bonds (called 'masala bonds') and alternate investment funds.

Conclusion

Considering that India is still an emerging economy and not matured and fully developed economy, India needs to move towards full capital account convertibility in a calibrated manner. This is especially pertinent as changes in US fiscal and monetary policy will impact on India's capital flows and exchange rates. Markets are factoring in a regime change in advanced countries, especially US macroeconomic policy, with expectations of changes in interest rates, fiscal stimulus and monetary policies which would impact emerging nations. Yet the fact remains that foreign capital brings in modern technology and management practices and aids in promoting growth and welfare which is at the root of programmes like 'Make in India'.

❑ INDIA'S SHARE IN WORLD TRADE

India's imports have always outstripped exports resulting in trade deficit and India has had to face balance of payments problems and foreign exchange crisis from time to time. This was inevitable considering that India started from a low base of economic development after independence and had ambitious plans to develop the industrial and infrastructure sectors which required heavy capital equipment, much of which had to be imported. However, over time, India developed heavy industries with a view not only to reduce dependence on imports, but to be in a position to export industrial and engineering goods. India has succeeded in this effort as her export basket contains significant share of engineering and electronic goods, petroleum products, chemicals and pharmaceuticals, etc. (See 'Composition of India's Foreign Trade' section below).

Table 15.7: India's Share in World Exports (US $ million)

Year	World	India	India's Share (%)	Year	World	India	India's Share (%)
1950	NA	NA	2.1	1990	3303563	18143	0.5
1960	NA	NA	1.1	2000	6254511	41543	0.7
1970	313804	2031	0.6	2010	15102605	226334	1.5
1980	1997686	8486	0.4	2015	16361680	264381	1.6
				2018	19132268	322492	1.7

Source: United Nations' International Trade Statistics Year Book, cited in Handbook of Statistics on Indian Economy, RBI and Economic Survey, Ministry of Finance, Govt. of India.

As will be seen from Tables 15.7, India's share in world exports which was 2.1 per cent in 1950 declined to 1.1 per cent by 1960 and it fell further till it showed some recovery from 2000. India's share improved after the economic reforms of 1991 when proactive steps were taken to promote exports. Table 15.8 shows that while China and the high income countries of south-east Asia, viz., South Korea, Hong Kong, Singapore, and Taiwan have a higher share in world exports, India's share has gone up from 2010 and compares favourably with those of some other countries like Malaysia, Thailand, Indonesia, and Brazil. India has to improve her manufacturing capabilities by improving the range and quality of products to compete with other nations and increase the share in world exports.

Table 15.8: Comparative Share of Selected Countries in World Exports (Percentage)

	2000	2009	2010		2000	2009	2010
China	3.9	9.7	10.5	Malaysia	1.5	1.3	1.3
South Korea	2.7	2.9	3.1	Taiwan	2.3	1.6	1.8
Hong Kong	3.2	2.6	2.6	Thailand	1.1	1.2	1.3
Singapore	2.2	2.2	2.3	Indonesia	1.0	1.0	1.0
Russia	1.7	2.5	2.7	Brazil	0.9	1.2	1.3
Mexico	2.6	1.9	2.0	South Africa	0.5	0.5	0.5
India	0.7	1.3	1.5				

Source: Economic Survey, 2011-12, Ministry of Finance.

Composition of India's Trade

The composition of imports and exports of a country is reflective of the state of its economy and economic strength. Thus, in the initial stages covering the first two Plans (1951-61), India had to import more of consumer goods, raw materials, and intermediate and capital goods {see Table 15.9(a)}. Also, exports consisted mostly of agricultural commodities and manufactures related to them {Table 15.9(b)}. But after India built a strong industrial base and both the public sector and the private sector industries developed, India began to export many industrial goods and manufactured items {see Table 15.9(c)}.

In the early stages of planning in the 1950's, the scope for exports was under-estimated due to the belief that the size of foreign markets was limited, that developed countries may not accept consumer goods produced by under-developed countries, and that the 'terms of trade' would be unfavourable to developing nations. All this resulted in production for the domestic market with little or no effort at promoting exports. But the trends of the 1950's and the '60's belied these calculations as world trade expanded rapidly, and many of the developing countries such as those in south-east Asia (dubbed the 'Asian Tigers') ramped up production for exports and forged ahead even as India was left behind.

Table 15.9 (a) Imports 1951–61
(Annual average in ₹ crore)

	Category	1951–56	1956–61
1.	Consumer goods	235 (32.46)	247 (23.04)
2.	Raw materials and Intermediate goods	364 (50.28)	502 (46.83)
3.	Capital goods	125 (17.27)	323 (30.13)
	Total Imports	724	1072

Table 15.9 (b) Pattern of Exports: 1951–60
(₹ crore)

	Category	1950–51	1955–56	1959–60
1.	Agricultural items	496.5 (85.86)	489.3 (83.68)	473.6 (74.98)
2.	Manufactures	58.4 (10.10)	61.0 (10.43)	105.0 (16.62)
3.	Minerals	23.4 (4.05)	34.4 (5.88)	53.0 (8.39)
	Total Exports	578.3	584.7	631.6

Source: Five Year Plans, Planning Commission, Economic Surveys, Ministry of Finance.

Note: Figures in brackets indicate percentage share of items in total imports/exports.

The process of reform and liberalization initiated in 1991 placed special emphasis on foreign trade and boosting exports. The composition of Indian exports had undergone much change from the 1970's and the '80's. There was significant shift from primary products to manufactured items, particularly engineering goods, petroleum products, chemicals, gems and jewellery, and textile apparels. The increase in the share of these items in total exports is even more visible from the 1990's. {(Table 15.9 (c)}. The import policy after 1991 facilitated the import of those items required for the industry and which would stimulate the economy. This approach has helped India to increase her share in world exports.

Table 15.9 (c) Pattern of Exports of Principal Items: 1970–91

(Value of exports in ₹ crore)

	Category	1970–71	1980–81		Category	1990–91	2000–01	2019-20
1.	Agriculture and allied items and Tobacco	445.25 (29.00)	1846.49 (27.52)	1.	Agriculture, allied items	6018.70 (1.90)	27288.19 (13.40)	248385 (11.1)
2.	Crude, Petroleum products	264.24 (17.21)	842.33 (12.55)	2.	Ores & Minerals	1739.72 (5.34)	5267.36 (2.59)	48308 (2.18)
3.	Chemicals, Plastics, etc.	36.37 (2.37)	235.42 (3.51)	3.	Manufactured goods	23319.10 (71.62)	156858.42 (77.05)	1582387 (71.28)
4.	Manufactured goods	615.96 (40.11)	2320.32 (34.58)	4.	Petroleum products	937.80 (2.88)	8541.67 (4.20)	na
5.	Machinery, Transport equipment	83.29 (5.43)	525.86 (7.84)					
6.	Miscellaneous manufactures	76.24 (4.97)	870.58 (12.97)					
	Total Exports	1535.25	6710.71		Total Exports	32557.63	203571.01	2219854

Source: Handbook of Statistics on Indian Economy, Reserve Bank of India.

Note: Figures in brackets indicate percentage share of items in total exports.

Direction of India's Trade

In the 1960's, a major part of India's trade – both imports and exports – was with UK, USA, Japan, and some of the European countries and to a lesser extent with Australia, Canada, and some of the Arab nations. During the 1970's and the '80's, this underwent change and India came to have trading relations with more diverse group of countries as will be seen from Table 15.10.

Imports

Though the share of USA rose due to large scale imports of food and fertilizers, its share in India's total imports declined steeply during the 1970s due to the phasing out of food imports from the US. Also, the share of East European countries in India's imports too declined while the share of USSR increased during the same period. Of the imports from the Asia-Pacific region which increased during the 1970s, Japan accounted for over 50 per cent.

India, the world's third-biggest oil consumer after US, China and Japan and meets more than 80 per cent of its crude oil requirements and around 40 per cent of its natural gas needs through imports. Domestic oil and natural gas production have been declining for the last few years, even as the energy needs of the economy have grown. India's oil import bill in 2019-20 was $101.4 billion. India aims to reduce oil imports to 67 per cent by 2022 by exploring local production options, green energy.

Traditionally, Opec+ and Saudi Arabia have been India's mainstay suppliers, accounting for 86 per cent of Indian oil imports. But India has been diversifying its sources of crude oil imports to reduce dependence on any one region. India has been sourcing oil from the US, Iran and Nigeria.

Table 15.10 Direction of India's Trade by Country-Groups (Value in ₹ crore)

Country-Group		1970-71		1980-81		1990-91		2000-01		2019-20	
		Value	%-age	Value	%-age	Value	%-age	Value	%-age	Value	%-age
OECD Countries*	Exports	769.1	50.1	3126.2	46.6	18389.3	56.48	107237.8	52.68	878953	39.6
	Imports	1042.2	63.8	5739.5	45.7	24712.6	55.97	92090.3	39.89	941581	28.1
OPEC #	Exports	98.5	6.5	744.6	11.1	1830.9	5.63	22156.9	10.88	341229	15.38
	Imports	125.5	7.7	3487.5	27.8	7040.7	16.52	12283.6	5.32	877719	26.16
East Europe	Exports	323.1	21.0	1486.3	22.1	5819.2	17.87	6020.4	2.96	30029	1.35
	Imports	220.0	13.5	1296.3	10.3	3377.2	7.84	3884.2	1.68	84865	2.53
Developing countries	Exports	304.7	19.8	1285.8	19.2	5560.0	17.08	59447.1	29.20	949695	42.8
	Imports	238.8	14.6	1966.4	15.7	8057.1	18.66	50966.4	22.08	1450156	43.2
Others	Exports	39.8	2.6	67.7	1.0	958.2	2.94	8708.7	4.28	944	0.04
	Imports	7.7	0.4	59.5	0.5	5.3	0.01	71648.3	31.03	756	0.02
Total	Exports	1535.2	100	6710.7	100	32557.6	100	203571.0	100	2218233	100
	Imports	1634.2	100	12549.2	100	43192.9	100	230872.8	100	3355762	100

Source: Economic Surveys, Ministry of Finance; Handbook of Statistics on Indian Economy, Reserve Bank of India.
Note: *OECD group includes European Union, North America, and advanced countries in Asia and Oceania.
OPEC includes major oil exporting countries. Developing countries include all such countries in Asia, Africa, and Latin America.

Exports

Exports to OPEC countries increased during the 1970s. The market share of this group in India's total exports also doubled in the same period. Exports to European Common Market countries and US also increased in the 1970s.

The decade of 1980s showed much diversification in India's exports. By late 1980s, the share of exports going to industrial market economies of OECD group was 58.2 per cent which is reflective of India's growing stature in world trade. The bulk of these exports to OECD went to European Economic Community, USA, and Japan.

There was high growth in exports to, and imports from, south-east and east Asian countries such as Korea, Singapore, Hong Kong, Malaysia, and Taiwan which had liberalized and deregulated trade regimes. Trade with the ASEAN has also been buoyant with exports and imports growing, mainly because of higher trade with Indonesia, Malaysia, Thailand, and Singapore. With the potential to expand trade with China, Japan, and South Korea, India's stakes with ASEAN+3 (China, Japan, and Korea) group has been on the rise. In fact, these countries have emerged as India's dominant trading partners.

The market diversification in India's trade has been a continuous process that has helped India in her developmental journey. It has also helped in coping with any sluggish demand in one region or group of countries by increasing exports to other regions. For instance, due to problems in the Euro zone and the US, India's export shares to Europe and America declined by 2004-05 and in 2013-14. Exports to OECD group declined from 52.68 per cent in 2000-01 to 39.6 per cent in 2019-20. (Table 15.10).

India's exports to, and imports from, developing countries have steadily been rising between 1990-91 and 2019-20 as Table 15.10 shows. The shares of India's exports to Asia and Africa have been on the rise. So also, there has been significant increase in the share of West Asia-GCC (Gulf Cooperation Council) countries, particularly U.A.E., in India's exports.

Services exports

Services sector business is extremely important for the Indian economy as it contributes more than 40 per cent to India's total global exports. India is the 8th largest trader of services in the world with around USD 85 billion of trade surplus and is ranked 2nd in Asia-Pacific region. In 2019, India's services exports was around US$ 213 billion and imports US$ 128 billion.

India's rising services trade surplus has helped reduce country's trade deficit for the year 2019-20 creating a net positive buffer of US$ 85 billion to adjust the negative trade balance on the merchandise trade. The service trade surplus is largely driven by Computer and ICT services, and to some extent, travel and financial services. India runs a very small trade surplus in construction services & pensions and faces trade deficit in services such as intellectual property rights and business services.

According to WTO data, India's share in world's commercial services exports has risen steadily over the past decade to reach 4 per cent in 2019 more than twice the share in world's merchandise exports at 1.3 per cent. India continues to register strong growth performance relative to the other major services-exporting countries as well as world services export growth.

India's Leading sectors in Foreign Trade

- **Gem and Jewellery: This** is an employment oriented sector with a major share in merchandise exports and **one of** India's leading foreign exchange earners. It. Exports from this sector suffered significantly during 2020-21 on account of the global economic slowdown due to the pandemic Covid 19. Exports during 2020-21 (up to September 2020) realized US$ 8690.32 million which was less than that in the previous year due to the pandemic.
- **Textiles:** The Indian textile industry is one of the largest in the world with an unmatched raw material base and manufacturing strength across the value chain. Textile industry contributes to 7 per cent of industry output in value terms, 5 per cent of India's GDP and 15 per cent of the country's export earnings. It also provides direct employment to 45 million people. Textiles exports which stood at US$ 36,727.51 million in 2015-16 rose to US$ 37,497.77 million in 208-19. The major export destinations of Indian textiles export include USA, United Arab Emirates, European Union, etc.

- **Leather Industry**: Leather industry holds a prominent place in the Indian economy being fourth largest exporter of leather goods in the world. The sector provides employment to about 4.42 million people, mostly from the weaker sections of the society. Women employment is predominant in this sector with about 40 per cent share. India has an abundance of raw material and skilled manpower for this industry. Its strength lies in innovative technology, improved compliance to international environmental standards and dedicated support of allied industries. India is the second largest producer of footwear, second largest exporter of leather garments and third largest exporter of saddlery and harness. The value of export of leather and leather products during 2019-20 was US$ 5070.55 million.
- **Indian Pharma industry:** Indian pharma is a highly knowledge-based industry which plays an important role in the economy. The sector has shown positive and consistent growth over the last few years. Through robust quality management and as a sensitive provider of standard, safe and efficacious medicines at affordable prices across the globe, it has acquired the reputation as the "Pharmacy of the World". Other salient features of this sector are:
  - 8 out of top 20 global generic companies are from India.
  - Over 55% of India's exports are to the highly regulated markets like North America, Europe and Japan.
  - USA is the largest exporting destination for India.
  - India contributes about 50 per cent of Africa's generic market of US$ 6 billion.
  - There is still huge market opportunity for Indian manufacturers in the untapped but potential markets of Latin America, Africa and Asia.
- **Engineering Exports:** Engineering exports account for nearly a quarter of India's total merchandise exports and around 3 per cent of GDP and achieved a Compound Annual Growth Rate (CAGR) of 5.1 per cent over the period 2010-11 to 2019-20. After a record performance of US$ 81.02 billion in 2018-19 with 6.32 per cent growth over the previous fiscal 2017-18, the sector faces uncertain global trade outlook due to US-China trade war, protectionism by leading nations, withdrawal of US GSP regime for Indian imports and geopolitical crises in some regions.

An allied sector is that of Telecom equipments which has lately shown much potential. It consists of the complete telecom ecosystem including hardware manufactures, telecom service providers and software vendors. Many domestic and multinational companies have started manufacture of high-end mobile and other telecom devices for domestic and global markets. The new Productivity-linked incentive (PLI) scheme launched has also given a boost to this sector. The Telecom Equipment and Services Export Promotion Council (TEPC), set up by the Government of India, helps in the promotion of export of telecom equipment and services, and assists the member companies in easy facilitation of exports.

Foreign Trade Policy (FTP) 2015-20

The Govt. of India has released the five-year Foreign Trade Policy (FTP) 2015-20 in April 2015 which lays down the vision, goals and objectives underpinning the trade policy for the five-year period. It describes the market and product strategy envisaged and the measures required not just for export promotion but also for the enhancement of the entire trade ecosystem. It is a comprehensive statement on the priorities in the foreign trade sector for improving foreign trade performance.

FTP 2015-20 has the following objectives:

- Have a framework for increasing exports of goods and services.
- Provide a stable and sustainable policy environment for foreign trade in merchandise and services.

- Link rules, procedures and incentives for exports and imports with other initiatives such as "Make in India",
- "Digital India" and "Skills India" to create an "Export Promotion Mission".
- Promote the diversification of India's exports basket by helping various sectors of the Indian economy to gain global competitiveness.
- Create an architecture for India's global trade engagement with a view to expanding its markets and better integrating with major regions, thereby increasing the demand for India's products and contributing to the "Make in India" initiative.
- Provide a mechanism for regular appraisal in order to rationalize imports and reduce the trade imbalance.
- It also brings into the fold States, Union Territories and various departments of the government to play a proactive role in promoting foreign trade.

Initiatives as part of FTP 2015-20

- The Government has launched several schemes and measures to increase India's share in global trade, which are as follows:
- The "Merchandise Exports from India Scheme" (MEIS) was introduced in April 2015 with 4,914 tariff lines. The Government has extended market coverage to all countries in respect of 7,914 tariff lines. The revenue forgone under the scheme (MEIS) is V23,500 crore per annum.
- Remission of Duties and Taxes on Exported Products (RoDTEP): Under this scheme, a mechanism to digitally refund to exporters, duties and taxes levied at the Central, State and local levels, such as electricity duties and VAT on fuel used for transportation, which are not getting exempted or refunded under any other existing mechanism is available.
- A "Services Exports from India Scheme" (SEIS) has been launched. The Scheme provided rewards to service providers of notified services who are providing service from India.
- The "Niryat Bandhu" Scheme seeks to reach out to new and potential exporters including exporters from Micro, Small & Medium Enterprises (MSMEs) and mentor them through orientation programmes, counseling sessions, individual facilitation, etc., on various aspects of foreign trade to have better access to international trade and thereby boost exports.
- To enhance the ease of doing business, the number of mandatory documents required for exports and imports has been reduced to three each, which is comparable with international benchmarks.
- The trade community can file applications online for various trade related schemes. Online payment of application fees through Credit/Debit cards and electronic funds transfer from 53 Banks has been put in place.
- Interest Equalization Scheme on pre- and post-shipment credit launched to provide cheaper credit to exporters.
- Government continues to provide the facility of access to duty free raw materials and capital goods for exports through schemes like Advance Authorization, Duty Free Import Authorization (DFIA), Export Promotion Capital Goods (EPCG) and drawback / refund of duties.

❑ INDIA AND WTO

Introduction

The World Trade Organization (WTO) is the international organization dealing with the rules of trade between nations and helps producers of goods and services, exporters, and importers conduct their business.The WTO was created after negotiations during 1986–94 known as the Uruguay Round and earlier negotiations under the General Agreement on Tariffs and Trade (GATT).

India, as a Member, has been actively engaged in WTO negotiations that impacts the external sector as well as overall economy. The fourth WTO Ministerial Conference was held at Doha, Qatar in November, 2001 where India played a proactive role in the deliberations. India, along with like-minded countries, was able to ensure the adoption of an agenda that focussed not only trade, but also on larger developmental goals and priorities of developing countries. Of particular concern was increased market access in agriculture and sufficient clarity on public health policies. India was strongly opposed to introduction of non-trade issues like labour in the agenda.

India has submitted its comprehensive proposals on issues like Domestic Support, Market Access, Export Competition, and Food Security. India has urged the imperative need for protecting India's food and livelihood security concerns by having freedom to take necessary domestic policy measures for poverty alleviation, rural development and rural employment, and also to create opportunities for expansion of agricultural exports by securing due access to markets in developed countries.

The Ninth Ministerial Conference of the WTO held in Bali in December 2013 issued a Declaration and decisions on various issues including Trade Facilitation, issues relating to agricultural trade rules, and others relating to development and Least Developed Countries (LDCs). Of these, the important ones from India's standpoint are the Ministerial Decisions for an 'Agreement on Trade Facilitation' and on 'Public Stockholding for Food Security Purposes'.

Trade Facilitation Agreement

An important area of the Doha round is the negotiations on Trade Facilitation Agreement (TFA). Simplificationof trade procedures by reducing trading costs is in the interest of all WTO members. It involves the lowering of tariffs and the removal of quantitative restrictions, and the focus in international trade has shifted to the simplification of trade procedures in general and customs procedures in particular. The TFA which was also endorsed by India at the Bali Conference (2013) was basically aimed at greater transparency, simplification of customs procedures, and use of electronic payments.

Agricultural Trade Rules

The agricultural trade rules in the WTO's 'Agreement on Agriculture' do not bar public procurement and stockholding for food security. However, if food for such programmes is acquired at administered prices and not market prices, then it is deemed to be support to farmers. As per WTO rules negotiated in the Uruguay Round, all such support has to be kept within a limit of 10 per cent of the value of production of the product in question. This cap can constrain procurement and food aid programmes in developing countries. The WTO rules, made apparently keeping the interests of the developed countries uppermost, have overlooked the interests of the developing countries. These are issues of utmost concern to India which has a food procurement programme, minimum support price (MSP) policy in the interests of farmers, and an extensive Public Distribution System (PDS) to help especially the vulnerable sections of the population.

India has been working closely with her coalition partners in developing country groupings such as the G-20 and the G-33 in order to achieve an outcome in the agricultural negotiations that would reflect the Doha mandate and safeguard the interests of developing countries. Ahead of the WTO's Ministerial meeting in Buenos Aires, Argentina in December 2017, India and China have jointly proposed to the WTO against trade distorting farm subsidies by developed countries.

Developed countries like US and those in Europe extend agricultural subsidies to their farmers which depresses world food prices. And they are also insisting on freer access to the markets of developing countries with a view to export their subsidized farm products. These measures will result not only in dumping of farm products in the markets of less developed nations, but also restrict the scope for developing countries to export their farm products, thus posing a direct threat to farmers and food and livelihood security in developing countries.

Intransigence of developed nations

The developed countries led by the US have been intransigent in following through their commitment in Bali to negotiate a permanent settlement on India's programme of administered prices and stockholding for food security. The stratagem and insincerity of US is exposed by the US Farm Bill of 2014 under which the government provides indirect support to producers and compensates them for low prices for farm produce. Besides, they get subsidized crop insurance coverage from the federal government. It is patently unfair on the part of developed nations to extend support to their farming community which is relatively much better off while objecting to any support to the much poorer and indigent farmers in countries like India. And this is when negligible portion of the farm produce of less developed countries gets exported whereas countries like US export sizeable portion of their production.

Nairobi meet

At the latest round of WTO Ministerial meet held in Nairobi in December 2015, trade ministers of India, China, Venezuela, Ecuador, and the African group of countries took a stand against the US and a few advanced countries and called for the continuation of the Doha Development Agenda (DDA) negotiations till they are concluded in all areas. The US representative wanted Doha agenda to be terminated as there was no agreement on it even after 14 years. While the Doha round made some progress in some areas, it hit a major roadblock on the crucial question of reduction of trade-distorting farm subsidies. Whereas the developing countries wanted a permanent outcome on special safeguard mechanism and public stockholding for food security, the advanced countries were not prepared to make any commitments as it would have jeopardized their farm subsidy regime.

The Nairobi meet outcome is perceived to have gone against the interests of developing and least developed countries. On public stockholding for food security, no permanent solution was arrived at. While India cannot be dragged to the Dispute Settlement Body in case of breach of subsidy limit, a permanent solution would have bound the US and EU from not going back on their commitment. And there is no guarantee that the US and EU will lower subsidies on agriculture or allow easier visa rules for Indian IT professionals going to US. It remains to be seen how things will pan out in future negotiations.

The fundamental problem in these negotiations has been that developed countries do not want to change their trade or subsidy regimes while they expect others to do so. Developing countries, by and large, adopt a very defensive and chauvinistic approach to negotiations. Least developed countries (LDC's), in general, do not want to make any binding commitment due to their capacity constraints and lack of resources, both of which are of vital and genuine concern to them. In the ultimate analysis, every country tries to safeguard its supreme national interests which may not align with considerations of equity and justice in the international framework.

The negotiations were continued during 2016 also and several sessions were held on public stockholding for food security purposes. Proponents of this scheme contend that stockpiles procured at administered prices are needed to ensure food security while others fear that, without appropriate safeguards, such schemes lead to over production and high stockpiles that could depress prices and affect farm incomes and food security in other countries.

One proposal mooted is to have a Special Safeguard Mechanism (SSM) which will allow developing countries to raise tariffs temporarily to deal with import surges or when price falls. Members, however, differ on whether the decision on SSM can be taken independently and irrespective of progress in discussions on agricultural market access, which the developed countries are pressing for, as well as other outstanding issues in the negotiations.

Major exporting countries of agriculture products (including some of the developing countries) remain concerned that an SSM could limit their exports. They argue that trade offs in market access will be necessary to compensate.

Thus, while WTO members consider food security a legitimate policy objective, they continue to disagree on how to forge a permanent solution. Members are also keen to resolve the issue at the 11th Ministerial Conference (MC11) in Buenos Aires, Argentina in December 2017. (On WTO issues, see also Chapter 20).

❑ MULTINATIONAL CORPORATIONS

A multinational corporation (MNC) is a company or enterprise operating in a number of countries and having production or service facilities outside the country of its origin. MNCs have headquarters in a single country but their activities take place in several countries. Whereas transnational corporations (TNCs), while operating and controlling assets in two or more countries, do not have a centralized office in a certain country. Both types of corporations operate beyond the national borders. Many of the large MNCs have finances and budgets larger than that of countries in which they operate and thus have both economic and political clout and are able to influence host governments.

These corporations set up offices and factories for production in regions where they can get cheap labour and other resources. They bring in capital, technology and management skills from the developed economies and set up plants in emerging economies. The products that are made in the host country are transported to developed countries and global markets and sold there with a certain added value. The sectors where most multinational corporations operate in are manufacturing and finance.

Automobile majors like Ford Motors, Toyota, Hyundai and Renault, oil conglomerates like like Royal Dutch Shell, BP (British Petroleum), Exxon Mobil, Total, engineering giant General Electric, food and beverage giants like Coca Cola, Pepsi and Nestlé have production units all over the world.

Many MNCs have set up units for manufacturing diverse products in China to take advantage of cheap factors of production like land and labour and subsidized facilities like water and power. Similarly, many major automobile companies have set up manufacturing plants in India considering cheaper production costs and availability of skilled manpower. So is the case with services where major IT companies have set up their offices and R&D centres in India in view of engineering talents and lesser operating costs to provide services across the globe.

Business Models

Production by these corporations is organized in complex ways. The production process may be divided into small segments and spread across different countries. In another production model, MNCs also enter into production contracts with other business entities in various countries. For instance, major aircraft manufacturers like Boeing and Airbus source many components used in aircrafts from other countries including India. In sectors like apparel, sports items and footwear, large MNCs source products made by smaller units in developing countries which helps in economising production costs.

A common model for MNC operations is to invest and buy local companies and then expand and modernise production.

Many MNCs by moving their production processes to developing countries helps the latter in their quest for economic development. Thus, many MNCs who shifted production to China over the last three decades have helped China to become a manufacturing powerhouse, propel her economic growth, move millions from the farms to factories and lift them out of poverty.

The operation of multinationals have both positive and negative effects on the economies of host countries which they enter. These are enumerated below:

Positive aspects of MNCs

- MNCs and TNCs bring in capital and modern technology to host countries. This helps to upgrade technological process in those countries and in upgrading skills of the local workforce. Thus they act as a modernising force.
- Improved technology helps to increase productivity and quality of products which could be exported to global markets. The MNCs in automobile sector in India like Hyundai and Toyota are examples of this.
- Industries set up by multinationals create employment opportunities and with new technologies also improve and upgrade the skills of local workforce.
- Investments and innovations brought by multinationals not only provides better quality products but helps to raise the standard of living of the local populace.
- They help to integrate the national economy with the global economy, and by optimising production costs helps in strengthening global economy.

Negative aspects of MNCs

- MNCs take advantage of cheap labour and exploit raw materials and other resources of the host country.
- They compete with local rival concerns and with more capital and better technology at their command, they tend to weaken local companies which may not be able to survive and are forced to wind up or get merged with the former.
- They take advantage of weak law enforcement and tax legislations in developing countries and try to evade taxes by various means. In fact, some of the MNCs in the US are alleged to park their profits in countries where taxes are low, not repatriate earnings to the US thus evading US taxes.
- The MNCs may set unfair conditions while investing in less developed countries (LDCs), exploit by dictating on pricing of products. This has happened in pharmaceutical industry where medicine prices are fixed at higher levels.
- Multinationals often are unwilling to part with and transfer high-end technologies due to strategic and commercial considerations in sectors like defence and aerospace and they prefer only to source some components from other countries. The developing countries are thus denied the benefit of such technologies.

MNCs and India

In the early 1990s, MNCs catered to the basic needs of the Indian consumer in fast-moving consumer goods (FMCG) and automobiles sectors. With India's economic liberalization, the demographics of successful MNCs shifted to new and diverse sectors such as technology and consumer durables which gained prominence. Moreover, firms from many more countries came to the field, with South Korea establishing a significant presence alongside the US and Japan, while the dominance of UK significantly diminished.

Though MNCs face many challenges in doing business in India, many of them have been quite successful in the Indian market over the past 25 years. A key factor for the success of multinationals has been the ability to adapt global business models to support local conditions in the host country. Between

1991 and 2012, the number of MNCs in India more than quadrupled. And over 20 years, total MNC revenue grew at a compound annual rate of 18 per cent faster than the overall economy.

By 2010, Maruti Suzuki, Hyundai, Samsung and LG Electronics have become top MNCs in India.

Over the years, the factors attracting multinationals to India have evolved depending on domestic market scenario and global economic conditions. MNCs in India can be broadly grouped into three categories. Those who view India:

- As an end market;
- As a centre for back-office operations; or
- As a global business hub (including for exports).

Not all MNCs have been successful though in their attempts. In 2005, South Korean steel producer Posco entered India after signing an agreement to build a $12 billion steel plant in Odisha, then billed as the largest foreign direct investment in India. However, due to delays in land clearances, environmental concerns and objections raised by the locals, the project got mired in controversies and could not take off. Posco later proposed to set up a plant in Maharashtra.

A number of companies, including IBM and Coca-Cola, entered but had to exit due to changed policies but re-entered India later and have since been doing successful business.

It is not only foreign companies who are multinationals. India, as an emerging power, has homegrown industrial houses which have become multinationals. Tatas who acquired Corus Steel and Jaguar-Land Rover in UK, M &M (Mahindras) which has a group automobile unit in South Korea, pharma firms like Dr. Reddy's Lab and major Indian IT companies which acquired many foreign entities and have units abroad have all become MNCs.

Box 15.4: India and Free Trade Agreements

Free Trade Agreements (FTAs) are arrangements between two or more countries or trading blocs that mainly agree to mutually reduce or eliminate customs tariff and non-tariff barriers on substantial trade between them. FTAs normally cover trade in goods such as agricultural or industrial products, or trade in services such as banking, construction, trading etc. FTAs can also cover other areas such as intellectual property rights (IPRs), investment, government procurement, competition policy, etc.

♦ **Benefits of Free Trade Agreement (FTA)**

Countries entering into FTAs could derive many benefits from them as stated below.

- By eliminating tariffs and some non-tariff barriers, FTA partners get easier market access into one another's markets.
- FTA contributes to greater economic activity and job creation in the economy and deliver opportunities for big and small businesses to benefit from greater trade and investment.
- FTA not just reduce and eliminate tariffs, but also helps address behind-the-border barriers that would otherwise impede the flow of goods and services.
- Encourages investment; and improve the rules affecting such issues as intellectual property, e-commerce and government procurement.
- Gives businesses and consumers improved access to a wider range of competitively priced goods and services and new technologies.
- Helps to obtain more benefits from foreign investment.

- Promotes regional economic integration and builds shared approaches to trade and investment between the free trade partners.
- It can deliver enhanced trade and investment opportunities that contribute to the economic growth of less-developed economies.
- Supports stronger people-to-people and business-to-business links that enhance bilateral relationships with FTA partners.
- It can continue to provide additional benefits to the trading partners over time, including via in-built agendas that encourage ongoing domestic reform and trade liberalisation.
- Exporters prefer FTAs to multilateral trade liberalization because they get preferential treatment over non-FTA member country competitors.

♦ **Pitfalls in Free Trade Agreement (FTA)**

While FTA could provide various benefits mentioned above, it also has pitfalls and downsides to it if all aspects are not considered carefully while entering into the agreement as explained below.

♦ **Divergences:** If the parties entering into the pact are not at the same level of economic development and strength, it could turn out to be a lop-sided deal. Often, while requiring a developing country to dismantle barriers, a developed country may raise significant tariff and non-tariff barriers as it negotiates on trade deals from a position of strength. Such a trend has been seen in many instances between developed and developing countries in multilateral and regional trade negotiations.

♦ **Unfair practices:** In the negotiations in agriculture and food under the aegis of the WTO, advanced countries like USA and those in European Union, have been adopting a hard stance wherein they object to subsidies given to farmers in developing countries like India and Brazil while they themselves provide subsidies on a much larger scale to farmers in their countries who are much better off. Such patently unfair negotiations and deals are inimical to the less developed countries.

♦ **Market access:** Further, developed countries are pressing developing nations to provide unfettered access to their markets for agricultural products while they themselves restrict entry for the products of developing nations. One of the sticking points in the negotiations under the Regional Comprehensive Economic Partnership (RCEP), one of the most ambitious trade pacts, was the fate of India's robust and growing dairy industry. India joining the pact under the terms being negotiated would have thrown open its dairy market to New Zealand, one of the largest exporters of milk and dairy products accounting for nearly 20 per cent of world exports worth $ 5.4 billion in 2018. Once RCEP comes into force with India in it, New Zealand could dump its surplus milk and milk products in Indian market with severe consequences for India which is the largest producer of milk globally. It would hurt the livelihood of millions of small and marginal dairy farmers.

- **Trade imbalances:** If a country which is a major industrial power is negotiating a deal with a country which is industrially less competitive, there is likelihood of the latter being flooded with industrial products resulting in trade imbalance and trade deficit issues. India has faced such a situation in free trade agreement with Japan and South Korea. Having free trade between a country with a per capita income of, say $4,000 per year, and one with $50,000 per year, has its own pitfalls. As stated earlier, free trade between trading partners poses a challenge if their level of development is vastly different.
- **Misuse FTA:** A third country, outside the trade pact, could take advantage of tariff concessions provided in the FTA by routing its products through one of the partners in the pact. Such misuse of the concessions has been observed in India's FTA with Asean nations where products from China have been routed to India through some of the Asean countries thereby Chinese exporters getting the benefit of tariff concessions. It is not only a violation of the agreement but also places the domestic producers in India, whose products may be less competitive, at a disadvantage. It will also distort India's trade balance.

Conclusion

Free trade agreements are useful for expanding a country's trade basket. But if it results in a surge in imports without corresponding expansion of exports, it would hurt domestic industry. The success of an FTA is to be judged on the criterion of enhancing trade and fairness of the deal. If the proportion of both imports and exports between the countries have grown, then the FTA is successful for both parties. **(For more on FTAs, see Chapter 20 also).**

In this Chapter we discussed.....

- Importance of foreign trade in economic development.
- Need for, and advantage of, foreign trade; theory of Comparative Advantage.
- Import substitution policy India adopted versus export strategy.
- Trends in India's foreign trade in the 1950s and 1960s; control of imports and exports; regime of quantitative restrictions (QR's) and industrial licensing.
- Devaluation of the Rupee in 1966 and its consequences.
- The turnaround from mid-1970s; foreign exchange position eases and the reserves go up.
- The 1980s: import policy of 1978-79 liberalized; while growth accelerates, trade deficit widens and reaches a peak by 1990-91.
- Exports as a percentage to the GDP (at market prices) declined between 1950 and 1971 and then increased; percentage of imports to GDP tapered in 1970-71 and then rose again from the mid-seventies.

- Export-import ratio declined between 1951 and 1961, showed improvement in 1970-71 but again declined till 1985-86.
- 1990-91 crisis; balance of payments and external debt problems; initiation of reforms and devaluation of Rupee; relaxation of import controls and steps to boost exports; robust growth in trade.
- East Asia crisis of 1997-98 and its impact on India and world economy.
- Changes in India's trade-GDP and trade deficit-GDP ratios.
- 2007-08 financial crisis and its impact on world economy and India's economy and foreign trade.
- India's foreign exchange reserves and record remittances from abroad.
- Capital account convertibility. India's stance on capital account convertibility
- India's share in world trade and structural changes; increasing share in world exports.
- Changing composition of India's trade and pattern of imports and exports.
- Direction of India's trade; diversification of markets; rising share of Services exports.
- India and WTO; negotiations on Trade Facilitation Agreement (TFA) and Agricultural Trade rules; intransigent attitude of developed nations; the 2015 Nairobi meet; conflict between national and international interests.
- Multinationals- India and multinationals.

Important Terms to Note in this Chapter

Comparative advantage; Opportunity cost; Terms of trade; 'Hindu rate of growth'; Quantitative restrictions; Devaluation; Trade deficit; Current account; Capital account; Invisibles (in foreign trade) ; Sub-prime lending; Foreign exchange (Forex) reserves; Multinational C.orporation; Free trade.

Practice Questions

1. What is meant by theory of 'comparative advantage' in international trade? How does it benefit world economy and the countries trading?
2. What is meant by an 'Open economy' and a 'Closed economy'? What has been India's position in this regard over the years?
3. What is meant by 'Protectionist policy' in the context of foreign trade? When and why do countries resort to it? What are the pros and cons of such a policy?
4. What is India's position in world trade? What steps need to be taken to improve her position?
5. Describe the new Trade policy adopted following the economic reforms of 1991. How far it benefited in promoting India's foreign trade?
6. What is India's share in world trade? What are the major items of India's imports and exports?
7. What is the position and major sources of India's foreign exchange reserves? What role does it play in the country's development process?
8. Discuss the role played by foreign aid in India's development since independence.
9. What steps have been taken and policies put in place recently by the government to attract foreign investment and foreign technology to boost manufacturing in India?
10. What is India's position in WTO on public stockholding of foodgrains? Why does the issue remain unresolved despite India pursuing it steadfastly and what are the implications of this impasse?
11. What is meant by Capital Account Convertibility? What are its benefits and drawbacks? Is India ready for full Capital Account Convertibility? Give your views for and against it.
12. Critically examine the role of Multinational Corporations in economic development. What are the positives and negatives in their role?
13. Are the operations of Multinational Corporations beneficial for developing countries like India? Justify your answer.
14. Critically examine the major changes in FDI policies of the Govt. of India since 1991.

    [UPSC Main 2016 (Economics Optional Paper)]
15. Why is it crucial to bring about a shift in India's direction of foreign trade towards trading blocs such as SAARC and ASEAN, and economic grouping like BRICS? Discuss the expected benefits and pitfalls in the light of the evidence since the last decade.

    [Indian Economic Service/Indian Statistical Service 2014]
16. Enumerate reasons for decline in growth rate of India's exports.

    [Indian Economic Service/Indian Statistical Service 2016]
17. Analyse the extent to which the composition and direction of India's foreign trade have undergone changes during last ten years.

    [Indian Economic Service/Indian Statistical Service 2016]

18. Mention the major trade policy reforms in India since 1991. How has it affected the structure of India's foreign trade?

[Indian Economic Service/Indian Statistical Service 2017]

19. Critically evaluate the issue of capital account convertibility in the context of the Indian economy.

[Indian Economic Service/Indian Statistical Service 2017]

20. Discuss the issues involved in Capital Account Convertibility. In the light of this, explain India's important Capital Account Liberalization measures.

[UPSC Main 2014 (Economics Optional Paper)]

21. "Partial Capital Account Convertibility cannot serve the purpose of integrating Indian Economy with World Economy". Critically examine.

[UPSC Main 2016 (Economics Optional Paper)]

22. How would the recent phenomena of protectionism and currency manipulations in world trade affect macro-economic Stability of India?

[UPSC Main 2018 (General Studies Paper)

23. Evaluate the role of FDI in contributing economic growth of India.

[UPSC Main 2020 (Economics Optional Paper)]

24. Do you think that Indian currency is fully convertible? Explain.

[UPSC Main 2020 (Economics Optional Paper)]

25. Examine the role of capital account convertibility in controlling deficit in the current account of India's Balance of Payments (BOPs).

[UPSC Main 2019 (Economics Optional Paper)]

26. Describe the salient features of New Foreign Trade Policy (2015-20) in India. Examine its role in improving the current account balance.

[UPSC Main 2020 (Economics Optional Paper)]

27. Examine the Foreign Trade Policy in India (2015-2020) in the context of its Vision', 'mission' and 'objectives'.

[Indian Economic Service/Indian Statistical Service 2020]

28. Has India been able to exploit the potential of foreign direct investment (FDI) for export-oriented production? Give reasons for your answer.

[UPSC Main 2019 (Economics Optional Paper)]

CHAPTER

LABOUR, EMPLOYMENT, AND SKILL DEVELOPMENT

- Economists on Labour, Employment and Productivity
- Labour data: Labour Force and Employment
- Inflation and Unemployment – Phillip's Curve
- Measuring Employment/Unemployment
- Labourforce and Workforce
- Employment and Unemployment Trends
- Organised and Unorganised Sectors
- Challenge of Employment Generation
- Problem of Jobless Growth & Employability
- Labour Reforms
- Migrant Labour issues
- Child Labour in India
- Bonded Labour
- Advent of Computers and its Aftermath
- Skill Development: the Challenge
- Labour Force and Jobs-the Mismatch
- Skill India Mission and its Highlights
- Technology versus Labour and Employment
- Automation and Employment
- ILO on Automation
- Automation in India

❑ INTRODUCTION

The ultimate aim of economic growth is the well-being of the people. But to ensure that, growth must be accompanied by job opportunities for all those who need and seek work, income generation, and equitable distribution of the incomes. Jobless growth and inequitable distribution of incomes have been some of the major factors responsible for the persistence of poverty and inequality (see Box 16.1).

While successive Five Year Plans, which aimed at rapid economic development, had creation of jobs, reduction, if not elimination of unemployment, and removal of poverty as their primary objectives, these could not be fulfilled, to a large extent, due to a variety of factors and circumstances such as ever increasing population, inadequacy of financial and physical resources compared to the magnitude of the tasks involved, resulting in inadequate job creation and perpetuation of poverty. With the bulk of the rural population engaged in agriculture, the pressure of population on land continued to be severe which caused both under-employment and disguised unemployment in the farm sector.

Box 16.1: Economists on Labour, Employment, and Productivity

From the very early times, economists have been engaged in the study of various aspects of labour, employment, and wages and there have been copious writings on these issues. Physiocrats, the 18th century French group of thinkers, laid great stress on agriculture and argued, apparently unjustifiably, that agriculture alone created wealth and value, and that all other economic activities were appendages to agriculture. According to them, agricultural labour alone was the source of all wealth. They also proposed that wages should be paid to workers at the subsistence level, an idea further developed by Ricardo.

Adam Smith's *Wealth of Nations* dwells on division of labour and productivity, productive and unproductive labour, economic growth and higher wages, etc. While accepting the subsistence theory of wages, Smith pointed out that there would be inequalities in wages and profit "arising from the nature of the employments themselves" and identified the reasons for this. Ricardo who developed the 'Iron law of wages' spoke of the demand for, and supply of labour as capital and investment increased, and how the excess or shortage of labour influenced the wage levels.

Thorstein Veblen, the American economist, identified two classes in society—the productive class who laboured and created value and the acquisitive or the leisure class who were parasitic and indulged in conspicuous consumption. Veblen was critical of the Classical economists as, according to him, their ideas were more rooted in hedonism.

Karl Marx who developed his radical socialist ideas in the 'Manifesto of the Communist Party' and 'Das Capital' overturned much of the views of classical economists. He spoke of society having two classes—the bourgeoisie and the proletariat or the working class—and how the capitalist system of production was exploitative of labour who create surplus value which is appropriated by the capitalist class. Also, technological advancement reduces demand for labour which, as a consequence, is rendered surplus. Marx's clarion call to 'workers of the world to unite' aroused the consciousness of the labouring class, gave rise to the formation of trade unions, and led to many working class struggles.

However, these Marxian ideas and notions have been largely disproved by the developments in later periods when advancements in technology have not only improved the methods of production and the overall output, but also the working conditions of the labour class itself. This is not to deny the existence of any exploitation of labour which may occur or persist due to other factors. It has been seen that an enlightened and caring industrial system is beneficial not only to the industry and society at large, but to the workers themselves. And due credit has to be given to both industry bodies and workers' organizations for working in a co-operative spirit and their efforts to ameliorate the conditions of workers in regard to wages, housing, health, and education benefits to the workers and their families. This is exemplified by modern concepts such as 'corporate social responsibility' (CSR) devolving upon industries. (For more on CSR, see chapter 26, pp. 26.30-3)

❑ LABOUR DATA

In regard to labour studies, important sets of data are 'labour force participation rate' (LFPR), 'worker population ratio' (WPR), and 'proportion unemployed' (PU). The data can be presented according to gender and different age-groups also. Collection of labour data is essential for formulating relevant policies and assessing the extent of human resources available, unemployment, etc.

Labour force, workforce, employment, and unemployment data are collected by different agencies in India, viz., the Registrar-General of India which collects Census and Economic census, the National Sample Survey (NSS), and the Labour Bureau of the Ministry of Labour and Employment, Government of India.

LFPR is the the proportion of a country's working-age population in the labour market, and includes all those who are employed and those who are not working but seeking, or are available for, work. It is the number of persons in the labour force per 1,000 persons. It indicates the labour force available in the economy for production of goods and services.

Worker population ratio (WPR) is the number of persons employed per 1,000 persons. It is the total number of workers as percentage of the total population.

Proportion unemployed (PU) or unemployment rate is the number of persons unemployed per 1,000 persons in the labour force.

❑ LABOUR FORCE AND EMPLOYMENT

The growth rate of the labour force is determined partly by the age structure of the population and the age and sex specific labour force participation rates. The age structure of the population changes in response to fertility trends experienced in the past, and projected for the future. Moderation in the growth of population brought about by a decline in birth rate will, over a period of time, result in decline in the labour force growth. Whereas, an acceleration in the growth rate of population and consequent increase in the labour force will pose a challenge in providing more employment opportunities.

Certain other factors could also impact LFPR. For instance, there could be a decline in labour force participation in the age group 15–19 years, if a thrust on literacy and education impels more people in this age group to continue with education and not enter the labour market.

The employment intensity of the growth process will determine the extent of challenge of job creation. Economic growth without commensurate expansion of employment opportunities, in other words, a trend of jobless growth will exert pressure and will be retrograde. According to some economists, there exists an inverse relationship between inflation and unemployment (See Box 16.2).

Box 16.2 Inflation and Unemployment–Phillip's Curve

The proposition that there exists an inverse relationship and trade-off between inflation and unemployment is represented by 'Phillip's Curve'. Known after William Phillips (1914–75), an economist who studied the relation between unemployment and changes in money wages in the United Kingdom covering the period 1861–1957, the work titled 'The Relationship between Unemployment and the Rate of Change of Money Wage Rates in the United Kingdom, 1861–1957' was published in Economica in 1958. The study deduced that the lower the unemployment, the higher the rate of change of wages and implied that low level of unemployment would be inconsistent with a low rate of inflation. The government has to choose between possible levels of inflation and unemployment—for instance, 4 per cent unemployment and no inflation, or 1 per cent unemployment and 7 per cent inflation. Phillip's curve provided empirical basis for Keynesian argument that there is a permanent trade-off between inflation and unemployment. However, this proposition came under severe attack from economists like Milton Friedman of the Chicago School who argued that the phenomenon depicted by Phillip's curve could, at best, hold good only in the short term. Moreover, in the 1970's, many of the industrialized countries, viz., the US, Canada, UK, and France, experienced high levels of unemployment and high inflation which disproved the contention.

Following these trends and thinking, there was renewed interest among economists on the relation and linkage between price stability and growth, particularly in the context of developing countries. High inflation imposes both economic and social costs on a country and the people, and would adversely impact savings, investment, and output, and also employment potential. The uncertainty arising from acute inflationary trends could affect investment decisions of firms, build-up inventories, and result in excess capacity in industry. Central banks increasingly use monetary policy instruments to contain inflation and maintain macroeconomic stability. The East Asian economies of S. Korea, Taiwan, Singapore, Thailand, and Malaysia which had high growth rates in the range of 8 to 9 per cent in the 1990's had reasonable rates of inflation.

Measuring Employment/Unemployment

In measuring employment/unemployment in a country like India, certain specific features of the workforce need to be kept in mind. The composition of workforce, engaged predominantly in self-employment and the primary sector, where work-sharing is common, tends to depress unemployment rates in general, and chronic, long-period unemployment rates in particular. Inadequacies in assessing open, visible unemployment have been a problem in the measurement and analysis of unemployment in India.

The National Sample Survey Organisation (NSSO), which provides estimates of the rates of unemployment on the basis of its quinquennial surveys uses three different concepts.

(a) number of persons usually unemployed based on 'usual status' approach;

(b) number of persons unemployed on an average in a week based or the 'weekly status' approach, and

(c) number of person-days unemployed on an average during the reference period of seven days preceding the survey.

Usual Status

A person is considered unemployed on Usual Status (US) basis, if he or she was not working, but was either seeking or was available for work, for the major part of the reference year. The US unemployment rate is generally regarded as the measure of chronic, open unemployment during the reference year. The Usual Principal and Subsidiary Status (UPSS) approach takes into account the principal activity and the subsidiary economic activity of a person during the reference period of twelve months preceding the survey. A person who has worked for 30 days or more in any economic activity during the reference period of last twelve months is considered as employed under this approach.

Current Weekly Status

On the basis of a week as the reference period, a person is considered unemployed by Current Weekly Status (CWS), if he or she had not worked even for one hour during the week, but was seeking or was available for work. Conversely, a person is considered working (or employed) if he or she, while pursuing any economic activity, had worked for at least one hour on at least one day during the 7 days preceding the date of survey.

Current Daily Status

The third concept of unemployment is the Current Daily Status (CDS), which is in terms of total person-days of unemployment, and is the aggregate of all the unemployment days of all persons in the labour force during the reference week. The CWS unemployment rates also measure chronic unemployment, but with the reduced reference period of a week. This method records every day's, and even half day's, work of the person over a week. The CDS is considered to be a comprehensive measure of unemployment, including both chronic and invisible unemployment.

❑ LABOUR FORCE AND WORKFORCE

The gender-wise labour force participation rate (LFPR), based on UPS approach for persons aged 15 years and above, with rural–urban break-up, for 2011-12, 2013-14 and 2015-16 is given in Table 16.1.

Table 16.1 Labour Force Participation Rate based on UPS approach for persons aged 15 years and above (per cent per 1000 persons)

	2011-12		2013-14		2015-16	
Rural	78.8	28.0	74.7	29.1	77.3	26.7
Urban	73.3	17.9	73.8	18.5	69.1	16.2
Rural + Urban	77.4	25.4	74.4	25.8	75.0	23.7

Source: Labour Statistics, 2017, Labour Bureau, Ministry of Labour & Employment, Govt. of India.

It shows that males far outnumber females in the labourforce, both in the rural and the urban areas. The percentage of males and females in labourforce has shown some decline by 2015-16 both in rural and urban areas. However, LFPR (in per cent) according to Usual status (Principal status + Subsidiary status) during 2017-18 and 2018-19 shows more or less stable position though there is some marginal increase in 2018-19 in the case of females in rural areas and of persons (males and females combined) in rural and urban areas combined. (See Table 16.2).

Table 16.2 LFPR (in per cent) according to Usual status for persons aged 15 years and above during (2017-18 and 2018-19)

	2017-18			2018-19		
	Male	Female	Total	Male	Female	Total
1	2	3	4	5	6	7
Rural	76.4	24.6	50.7	76.4	26.4	51.5
Urban	74.5	20.4	47.6	73.7	20.4	47.5
Rural + Urban	75.8	23.3	49.8	75.5	24.5	50.2

Source: Periodic Labour Force Survey (PLFS), July 2018-June 2019, National Statistical Office (NSO), Ministry of Statistics and Programme Implementation.

A similar trend is seen in the case of Worker Population Ratio (WPR) also. (Table 16.3). Males far outnumber females in the workforce and there is decline in WPR of both males and females by 2015-16.

Table 16.3 Worker Population Ratio based on UPS approach for persons aged 15 years and above

(per cent per 1000 persons)

	2011-12		2013-14		2015-16	
	Male	Female	Male	Female	Male	Female
Rural	76.6	26.5	71.6	27.2	74.1	24.6
Urban	70.9	15.7	70.9	16.2	66.8	14.3
Rural + Urban	75.1	23.6	71.4	23.8	72.1	21.7

Source: Labour Statistics, 2017, Labour Bureau, Ministry of Labour & Employment, Govt. of India.

❑ FEATURES OF THE INDIAN LABOUR SCENE

Some of the salient features of, and trends in, the Indian scene are mentioned below.

Declining Female Labour Participation Rate (FLPR)

A rather disquieting feature in the Indian labour market is the declining rate of female participation in labourforce. In spite of high economic growth, decline in fertility, and rise in schooling of girls, the Female Labourforce Participation Rate (FLPR) has declined in rural areas and stagnated in urban areas since the late 1980s. Unlike in India, the global experience has been one of substantial increase in the FLPR as a result of similar factors.

The conventional definition of labour force participation excludes unpaid domestic work and the free collection of goods such as firewood and water, mostly done by women. These activities produce essential goods and services that are used by the household members, and should, therefore, be recognized in the definition of work. Lately, there is a view among experts that the household work performed by women should be reckoned while assessing the national income of an economy. ILO, the international body on labour affairs, is of the view that not giving due credit for the work performed by domestic workers, 80 per cent of whom are women, is unfair and reflects gender bias. (See Box 16.3 at the end of this section).

Trend based on Employment-Unemployment Survey

Table 16.4 which shows Labour Force Participation Rate (LFPR), Worker Population Ratio (WPR) and Unemployment Rates (UR) for persons aged 15 years and above, gender-wise, for the years 2011-12 and 2015-16 based on Employment-Unemployment Survey which is the most comprehensive survey. It will be seen that both LFPR and WPR are considerably lower in the case of women than men. And both LFPR and WPR have declined by 2015-16 in respect of both men and women.

Table 16.4 Key Labour Force Estimates according to Usual Principal Status (UPS) Approach based on 2nd, 3rd, 4th and 5th Employment-Unemployment Survey

Parameter	2011-12		2012-13		2013-14		2015-16	
	Male	Female	Male	Female	Male	Female	Male	Female
LFPR	77.4	25.4	76.6	22.6	74.4	25.8	75.0	23.7
WPR	75.1	23.6	73.5	20.9	71.4	23.8	72.1	21.7
UR	2.9	6.9	4.0	7.2	4.1	7.7	4.0	8.7

Source: Ministry of Labour, Govt. of India, Annual Report, 2018-19.

Note: LFPR: Labour Force Participation Rate; WPR: Worker Population Ratio; UR: Unemployment rate (UR) is defined as the percentage of unemployed persons in the labourforce.

Another trend seen from Table 16.4 is that while the unemployment rate has been steadily going up in the case of both men and women over the period 2011-12 and 2015-16, the rate is much higher in the case of women. Unemployment rate for men has gone up from 2.9 per cent in 2011-12 to 4.0 per cent in 2015-16 in the case of men while it has gone up from 6.9 per cent in 2011-12 to 8.7 per cent in 2015-16 for women. This is even when the educational levels of women are comparable to that of men.

Trend between 2004-05 and 2011-12

According to a NITI Aayog study, "*Changing Structure of Rural Economy of India Implications for Employment and Growth*", the declining trend in FLPR was observed even prior to 2011-12 in India's rural economy. During the period of high output growth and falling employment (2004-05 to 2011-12), rural population increased by 62 million, distributed almost equally between male and female. As indicated by labour-force participation rate (LFPR), the proportion of male population joining labour force remained almost unchanged (55 per cent) and 16 million out of 31 million incremental male population joined labour-force between 2004-05 and 2011-12. But female labour-force participation declined significantly from 33 per cent in 2004-05 to 25 per cent in 2011-12, resulting in decline in the female labour-force by 22 million.

It was also seen that female withdrawal from labour-force happened across all types of households in the rural areas. Withdrawal of female from labourforce was highest among agricultural labour households followed by cultivators and non-farm households, both in percentage and absolute terms. In the case of male, withdrawal from workforce was found only among the agricultural labour households.

Factors behind Decline in FLPR

Some recent studies have shown that India's low and falling female labour participation rate is not just because they are continuing their education or that their families are now better off such that they do not have to work. Women are even keen to get back to work after quitting due to domestic factors and compulsions like marriage, childbirth, rearing children, etc. Women have had to shift jobs due to interruptions in career which shows how keen they are to find jobs. This declining trend is also not explained by factors like conservative social norms, patriarchal attitudes, harassment at workplace, discrimination, etc. which are the conventional narratives put forward.

A factor that facilitates entry of female youth in labourforce is the declining fertility rate. The total fertility rate (TFR) in rural India has declined from 3.7 in 1993–1994 to 2.6 in 2011–2012 and to 2.4 in 2018. The TFR in urban India is even less at 1.7 in 2018. But even with the decline in the TFR, females are seen withdrawing from the labourforce.

The Impact of Pandemic Covid-19

The FLPR has declined further during the pandemic, Covid-19. The percentage of women in the labour force had fallen to a record low of 15.5 per cent during the April-June 2020 quarter, when India imposed strict lockdown to curb the spread of COVID-19 virus. It stood at 16.1 per cent during the July-September 2020 quarter, the lowest among the major economies, according to government report, reflecting the impact of pandemic and a widening job crisis.

According to World Bank estimates, the FLPR in India had fallen from more than 26 per cent in 2005 to 20.3 per cent in 2019, compared with 30.5 per cent in Bangladesh and 33.7 per cent in Sri Lanka.

Conclusion

If household income and educational factors and falling fertility rates do not explain the phenomenon of declining FLPR, the reason could be due to various other underlying factors. It may be due to structural transformation of the economy and its resultant impact on the female labour market in the whole process. Plausibly, with fewer job avenues, women no longer prefer working in underpaid jobs, as domestic helper or as a casual worker like informal jobs in gig economy (like in transport sector, food and courier delivery) which are on the increase.

That women could make significant contribution to economic and social progress is evidenced by the role they play not only as teachers, nurses, in professions like doctors and lawyers, banking and insurance, and even in higher echelons in the corporate sector where many have excelled. Given the opportunity, women could contribute as much to society as men.

With structural changes in the economy and more and more high skilled jobs coming up due to automation and technology, women have to catch up on education and skilling to become more adaptable to the fast-changing scenario. Skilling under the Digital India programme and better telecom and power facilities being developed in rural India, there is scope for more women joining the labourforce in years to come. Many IT companies are moving to Tier-2 and Tier-3 towns where the cost of operations would be less than in large cities and Metros. Likewise, more industries could also be set up in Tier-2 and Tier-3 towns which will provide opportunities for more congenial jobs for women closer to their home.

(For more on this, see Section "Gender Bias and Gender Inequality" in Chapter 17).

Box 16.3 ILO Global Action Programme on Domestic Workers

Domestic work is defined as "work performed in or for a household or households" (ILO Convention 189). Domestic work is therefore defined according to the workplace, which is the private household. Broadly speaking, domestic workers provide personal and household care. Occupations and tasks considered to be domestic work vary across countries: ; they may cook, clean, take care of children, the elderly and the disabled, attend to the garden or pets, or drive the family car. They may work part-time, full-time or on an hourly basis, and may live in the home of the employer or not.

According to this definition, the ILO estimates there are at least 67 million domestic workers over

the age of 15 worldwide, 80% of which are women. About 17% of domestic workers are migrant workers. Historically and across a diverse range of countries, domestic workers from disadvantaged racial and ethnic groups have tended to provide care services to meet the needs of wealthier households.

To a large extent, it is thanks to the labour of domestic workers that other women have succeeded in entering the paid labour market in increasingly larger proportions and in breaking the glass ceiling. When women engage in paid work outside the home, they either have to reduce their rest and leisure time, enlist the help of partners or other family members or – if the family or woman can afford it – pay someone else to do the care work that they would normally do. Thus domestic workers' contribution to economic growth is substantial, enabling an increase in dual-income families.

Domestic work is also an important source of income for women – as much as 14 per cent of female wage employment in Latin America and 11 per cent in Asia. By all estimates, the sector is poised to grow: according to UN estimates, The proportion of people aged 60 or above will multiply by 1.8 by 2050 and by 2.3 by 2100, as compared to 2015 (UN DESA, 2015). At the same time, multigenerational households are becoming less common, meaning more and more of the elderly live alone, or in institutions, where these are available and affordable. Studies have also found that people prefer home-based care over institutional care.

Despite their contributions to households and national economies, domestic work is situated at the low end of the care economy, working some of the longest hours, for very low wages. These conditions result in part from exclusion of domestic workers from labour and social rights in many countries, which effectively legitimizes discrimination of a female-dominated class of workers. Even when they are covered by the law, domestic workers suffer severe decent work deficits due to high levels of non-compliance, fostered in part by bigh levels of informality, status in migration, and low level of collective organization. Long term caregivers in particular work extremely long hours for very low pay. The toll on their health and well-being is clear, but often unrecognized in law and policy. This unequal situation reflects and perpetuates a deep-seated social perception that the unpaid care work that women do for their families, has little value to economies and societies.

In homes, workers, employers, and care-recipients all face challenges due to the lack of integrated policies and clear guidelines. Employers hire long-term caregivers for a variety of needs, from light support and companionship, to regular medical oversight. While these needs are sometimes met by publicly funded home health aides, in the absence of such policies, many households turn to workers in the informal economy because it is easier and more affordable. As a result, the ILO estimates some 50 million domestic workers are working in the informal economy, in which there is a concentration of decent work deficits.

Delivering quality care goes hand in hand with ensuring decent working conditions. Assuring decent work for domestic workers establishes the principle that domestic workers, like any other workers, are entitled to a minimum set of protections under labour law. The mere fact of regulating domestic work is an acknowledgement of the crucial social and economic contribution of care work. In turn, ensuring decent working conditions for domestic workers will contribute to reducing gender inequalities in the world of work while improving the quality of care received by households.

❑ ORGANISED AND UNORGANISED SECTORS

One of the disquieting features of employment in India is that bulk of the people are employed in the unorganized sector. Thus, in 2004–05, 394.9 million workers out of 457.46 million were engaged in the unorganized sector which works out to 86.32 per cent, with only 13.68% working in the organized sector (See Table 16.5). Employment in the unorganized sector has increased from 342.64 million in 1999–2000 to 394.9 million in 2004–05. Again, in both the organized and unorganized sectors, there were two categories employed–those in formal employment and those in informal employment. In the unorganized sector, those in informal employment far outnumber those in formal employment whereas in the organized sector, formal workers are more than informal workers.

Table 16.5 Organised and Unorganised Sectors and Formal and Informal Employment (million)

Sector	1999–2000			2004–2005		
	Informal	Formal	Total	Informal	Formal	Total
Unorganized Sector	341.28 (99.60)	1.36 (0.40)	342.64 (100)	393.47 (99.64)	1.43 (0.36)	394.90 (100)
Organized Sector	20.46 (37.80)	33.67 (62.20)	54.12 (100)	29.14 (46.58)	33.42 (53.42)	62.57 (100)
Total	361.74 (91.17)	35.02 (8.83)	396.76 (100)	422.61 (92.38)	34.85 (7.46)	457.46 (100)

Source: Estimates by National Commission for Employment in the Unorganized Sector (NCEUS), Eleventh Plan (2007–12), Planning Commission.

Notes: 1. Usual Principal and Subsidiary Status (UPSS) basis.

2. Figures in bracket indicate percentages.

As per a survey carried out by the NSSO in 2011-12, the total employment in both organized and unorganized sector in the country was of the order of 47 crores. Out of this, about 8 crore (17.1 per cent) were in the organized sector and the balance of 39 crore (82.9 per cent) in the unorganized sector. According to some other estimates, about 93 per cent of workers are in the unorganized sector.

The general concern is that employment in the unorganized sector is generally of low quality while organized sector employment is of high quality. There has been decline in employment in the organized sector primarily on account of decline in employment in the public sector units. Though employment in the private sector units has accelerated, it has not been adequate to offset the decline in public sector employment. Compared to regular employees in the organized sector, the casual, informal employees in the unorganized sector do not have social security benefits like Provident Fund, gratuity, medical and house allowances, etc. which place them at a disadvantage.

Commission on the Unorganised Sector

The National Commission for Employment in the Unorganized Sector (NCEUS), headed by Arjun Sengupta, was set up by the government in September 2004. The Commission studied in depth various problems confronting the Unorganized sector and suggested a series of measures to ameliorate their conditions and also on the need to augment employment generation. The Commission identified unorganized sector and unorganized or informal employment as follows:

- The unorganized sector consists of all unincorporated private enterprises owned by individuals or households engaged in the sale and production of goods and services and with less than ten total workers.
- Unorganized workers consist of those working in the unorganized enterprises or households, excluding regular workers with social security benefits, and the workers in the formal sector without any employment/social security.

Steps taken to Improve Conditions of Unorganized Workers

To ensure welfare of workers in the unorganized sector, the Ministry of Labour & Employment enacted the 'Unorganised Workers' Social Security Act, 2008' which came into force in May.2009. The Unorganised Workers' Social Security Rules, 2009 was framed under the Act.

The Act provided for formulation of schemes relating to provident fund, employment injury benefits, housing, educational schemes f or children, skill upgradation and setting up old age homes by the State Governments.

A National Social Security Board was constituted under the chairmanship of Union Minister for Labour & Employment with wide representation from all stakeholders.

Various welfare schemes as mentioned below are being operated by Central and State governments.

- A pension scheme for Unorganized Workers •National Old Age Pension Scheme •National Family Benefit Scheme • Janani Suraksha Yojana • Handloom Weavers' Comprehensive Welfare Scheme • Handicraft Artisans' Comprehensive Welfare Scheme • Pension to Master Craft Persons • National Scheme for Welfare of Fishermen and Training and Extension • Rashtriya Swasthya Bima Yojana (now Ayushman Bharat-Pradhan Mantri Jan Arogya Yojana) • Pradhan Mantri Shram Yogi Maandhan.

  Construction workers numbering about 5.02 crore constitute one of the largest categories in the unorganized sector. Various laws have been passed to safeguard their interests by regulating their employment and service conditions, safety and health measures through State Welfare Boards. The welfare measures are financed by levy of a cess on all construction works at a percentage of the construction cost incurred by an employer.

  To protect the rights and safeguard the interests of migrant workers, the Inter-State Migrant Workmen (Regulation of Employment and Conditions of Service) Act, 1979 was enacted. While various provisions have been made under tis, migrant workers face many problems as evidenced by their plight when the pandemic Covid-19 broke out in early 2020. (For more on Migrant worker issues, see a later section in this chapter).

Challenge of Employment Generation

One of the major challenges facing the Indian economy is the creation of adequate number of jobs, and that too of sufficiently good quality, to absorb the burgeoning labour force. A whopping 12 million people are being added to the labour force every year. As per the 2011 Census, 730.07 million people, out of the total population of 1210.84 million, were within the age-group of 15 and 59, which works out to 60.29 per cent of the total population. And, according to Labour Bureau data, only about 50 per cent of those aged 15 years and above is employed, leaving a huge gap between those employed and those seeking jobs.

There is also need to shift the surplus labour from the agriculture sector by creating non-farm jobs in the rural areas itself to prevent migration of people to urban areas in search of jobs and adding to problems in urban areas.

In short, growth has to be inclusive and with adequate job potential to provide productive and gainful employment to those in both rural and urban areas. The crux lies in India creating jobs on a large scale in both the manufacturing and the services sectors. Besides manufacturing, sectors like infrastructure, real estate, tourism and hospitality, etc. are those with maximum potential for generating employment. Government has recently proposed that every government funded scheme, including public-private partnership (PPP) projects, may be assessed, along with techno-economic appraisal, for employment generation potential. The process may entail delay but it will be in sync with the government's commitment to create more jobs in the country.

Guaranteed Employment Scheme

The government enacted the National Rural Employment Guarantee Act (NREGA) in 2005 and introduced the scheme to provide at least 100 days of wage employment to one adult member of every rural household who volunteers to do unskilled manual labour. The scheme was renamed as Mahatma Gandhi NREG Act (MNREGA) in 2009. The scheme was devised to combat rural distress, especially in drought years, and to provide employment to rural families in the off season when there is no work on the farms, and thus supplement their income. (For more on the working of this scheme, see Chapter 17, p. 17.26–30).

Problem of Jobless Growth & Employability

The issue of jobless growth has been a nagging issue for over a decade. Whereas about 46 million jobs were created between 1999-2000 and 2004-05, While the economy grew at an average rate of 8.43 per cent annually between 2004-05 and 2009-10, only one million jobs could be added per year. Thus of the 55 million who joined the labourforce, only 5 million could join the workforce. This trend of inadequate job creation has been persisting from 2010 also despite strenuous efforts by the government to step up investment and create jobs.

Infrastructure and construction are two major sectors with much potential for job creation. Other sectors with potential are education and health. India's public investment in education is about 3 per cent of GDP while that in health is a low 1 per cent of GDP. Both these need to be stepped up. Apart from these, the Digital India Programme which is to cover 2,50,000 Panchayats across India has much potential to create both direct and indirect jobs. Apart from manpower required to man these rural digital centres, it will create jobs for skilling and maintenance in villages. If the health centres in rural areas -- PHCs, Sub-Centres and CHCs -- are expanded and manned adequately with trained medical and paramedical staff, it will create large number of jobs. So too with expansion of education sector which needs to be expanded and upgraded both in rural and semi-urban areas. With digital technology reaching villages, rural schools could also be provided IT education and trained computer hands will be needed to impart training.

For all these measures to materialise, both the Central and State governments have to direct more investment in these directions with the active participation of the private corporate sector who will also stand to benefit from such expansion in the economy. Side by side, the manufacturing sector will also get a fillip as demand for capital and consumer goods will go up. India's expertise in science and technology has to be fully harnessed in realizing this potential.

Box 16.4 LBOUR REFORMS

Economists and industry bodies have for long argued that India's labour laws are stringent and rigid and create perverse incentives in the industrial sector hampering its growth. This is especially so in respect of units with over 100 employees. They acted as incentives for small firms to remain small in size, so they are not subject to these rules. This held back investments, growth of industries, job creation and productivity.

Successive governments have been trying to reform the labour laws to remove these drawbacks. The main objective and challenge in reforming these laws has been to reduce compliance burden, facilitate ease of doing business and generate more formal jobs while protecting workers' rights. The process of enacting these laws, initiated in 2003, was finally approved by the Parliament in September 2020.

The laws passed include three labour codes. A code on minimum wages was already passed in 2019. A total of 44 extant labour laws have now been subsumed into four codes. The laws merged with these codes include the Factories Act, the Trade Union Act, the Mining Act, the Industrial Disputes Act, the ESI Act, the EPF Act and the Maternity Benefit Act. The four codes approved are:

- Industrial Relations Code Bill, 2020.
- Code on Social Security Bill, 2020.
- Occupational Safety, Health and Working Conditions Code Bill, 2020.
- Minimum wages code (passed in 2019).

Role of States: As labour is a concurrent subject under the Constitution, the 100-odd State level acts that exist will need to be rationalized in line with the codes passed by the Union government. Sixteen states have already effected many of the changes which have been newly incorporated under these four labour codes.

Salient features: The salient features and implications of these codes are mentioned below.

Industrial Relations Code

This Code deals with recognition of trade unions, conditions on strikes and lockouts, standing orders and resolution of industrial disputes. It subsumes the Industrial Disputes Act, 1947, the Trade Unions Act, 1926, and the Industrial Employment (Standing Orders) Act, 1946.

- **Standing orders:** Standing orders on matters related to workers' classification, holidays, paydays, and wage rates, termination of employment and grievance redressal mechanisms is mandated for establishments with at least 300 workers, instead of 100 workers. This raises concern that units with less than 300 workers not being covered by such a mandate could make the terms of employment of workers in such units ambiguous and less secure.

- **Layoffs and Retrenchment:** The threshold for layoffs and retrenchment has been raised from 100 workers or more to 300 workers. Experts opine that this would enable industrial establishments with less than 300 workers to introduce arbitrary service conditions for workers. A worker could be dismissed for alleged misconduct or retrenched on economic grounds jeopardizing employee's security. As about 90 per cent of India's workforce work in small-size firms, they may be adversely affected by this provision.
- **Striking work:** This code introduces new conditions for resorting to strike. Flash strikes will be illegal.

  Earlier, workers could go on strike by giving between two weeks and six weeks of notice. Henceforth, Unions have to give 60 days' strike notice.

  Further, if proceedings are pending before a labour tribunal or the National Industrial Tribunal, workers cannot go on a strike for 60 days after they are concluded. These conditions apply to all industries and could significantly limit the scope for striking work.
- **Trade unions:** It lays down new provisions for recognition of unions. Trade unions that have a membership of at least 10per cent of the workers or 100 workers will be registered. The union with 51 per cent of workers in an establishment will be the sole negotiating union.
- **Dispute Resolution:** Establishments with 100 or more workers will have a Works Committee which will help resolve conflicts between workers and employers. The central or state governments may appoint Conciliation Officers to mediate and promote settlement of industrial disputes. Industrial Tribunals consisting of a Judicial Member and an Administrative Member may be set up for settling industrial disputes. The Code allows for industrial disputes to be referred to arbitration by the employer and workers if both parties agree to do so.

Social Security Code

This Code on social security brings together laws relating to Employees' Provident Fund, (EPF) Employees' State Insurance (ESI), Maternity Benefit, Gratuity and other entitlements and the Unorganised Workers' Social Security under a single law.

- **Social security benefits:** It provides for universal social security for both organised and informal workers as well as gig and platform workers. The government shall formulate and notify, from time to time, suitable welfare schemes, including schemes relating to provident fund, employment injury benefit, housing, skill upgradation of workers and educational schemes for children.

- **Social Security Fund:** Provision has been made for creation of a Social Security Fund to fund schemes for extending benefits like death and accident insurance, maternity benefit and pension to cover 80 per cent of the county's workforce who do not now come under any kind of social security cover.
- **Social Security Board:** A National Social Security Board will be set up for formulating suitable schemes for unorganized workers, gig workers and platform workers. It also brings these sections of workers under the ambit of social security schemes that include life and disability insurance, PF, health and maternity benefits and skill upgradation.
- **Gender equality:** To promote gender equality, employment of women has been allowed in all establishments for all types of works and in the night shift, subject to their consent and subject to provisions of safety, holidays, working hours or any other condition being in place. The Codes also ensure their pay parity with their male counterparts.
- **Formalisation of jobs:** All employees will get appointment letter, a step to promote formalisation of workforce. Contractors have to pay wages electronically. They will be issued pan-India licence for five years as against work order-based licensing at present.

Occupational Safety, Health and Working Conditions Code

This Code brings together all laws relating to health and hazardous working conditions.

- **Safety and health:** The Central Government shall declare, by notification, standards on occupational safety and health for work places relating to factories, mines, dock work, building and other construction work and other establishments.
- **Working environment:** The employer shall ensure cleanliness and hygiene, proper ventilation, temperature and humidity, environment free from dust, noxious gas, fumes and other impurities, cooling in work rooms, potable drinking water and hygienic sanitation facilities.
- **Migrant worker:** The Code defines inter-state migrant workers to be those not only engaged by an establishment through a contractor but also those workers who have come on their own from one state and obtained employment in another state and earning up to ₹18,000 a month. They will be duly protected as an unorganized workers.
- **Housing for Migrant workers:** To ensure ease of living at affordable rent, the Central Government has announced a scheme of housing for migrant workers, as being done for urban poor. This will be done by converting government funded houses in the cities into Affordable Rental Housing Complexes (ARHC) under PPP mode through concessionaire. State and Central Govt. agencies, industries and other institutions will be incentivized to develop ARH complexes for migrant workers which will help industries to improve productivity.

- **Ration card portability:** It is also proposed to make the Ration (Family) Card portable so that any member of a family included in a card could draw ration anywhere in the country. This will particularly help migrant workers and others who move places due to job requirements or other reasons. The government is working on the technology platform to put this decision into practice.
- **Conclusion:** The new labour laws remove the rigidities which persisted and which was one of the reasons impeding India's industrial growth, especially in the manufacturing sector. While the reforms should aim at faster development and growth in employment, it must also protect workers' incomes and jobs when they get disrupted when technology and modes of production change. When employers have to change the production processes, they must provide workers opportunities to learn the new skills required and arrange to provide in-house training as off-line training institutions may not be able to respond properly.

  Understandably the unions have expressed concern about radical reforms which may hurt their interests. The unions demand fair treatment, decent working conditions and adequate social security to take care of their families when employers retrench them because of economic exigencies.
- **Role of Tripartism:** The reforms need to be implemented taking the workers and their unions into confidence. It has to be executed without disrupting the harmonious relations between the employers and workers. Even the ILO has urged the aspect of protecting the genuine rights of workers in the course of reforms.

A tripartite approach involving the government, the workers and the employers is needed in resolving labour issues smoothly. A via media has to be found and a middle ground struck with all the parties adopting a conciliatory approach.

It must be impressed upon workers' representatives that advancements in technology have not only improved the methods of production and the overall output, but also the working conditions of the labour class itself. It has been seen that an enlightened and caring industrial system is beneficial not only to the industry and society at large, but to the workers themselves.

For such a milieu to prevail, both the industry bodies and workers' organizations have to work in a co-operative spirit and focus efforts to ameliorate the conditions of workers in regard to wages, housing, health and education benefits to the workers and their families. This can be realized by adopting modern concepts such as 'corporate social responsibility' (CSR) devolving upon industries.

❑ MIGRANT LABOUR ISSUES

Migration of labour has emerged as a central issue in contemporary times which throws up many economic and social issues. The problem assumed serious proportions when a total lockdown was imposed in the country when the pandemic Covid-19 broke out in early 2020.

Each year, men and women in large numbers leave their homes and cross district, state and even national borders in search of livelihood and financial security for themselves and their families. While many move after marriage, many others are motivated by desire to seek better work opportunities and earn higher incomes.

India has been witnessing high levels of work-related migration within the country (internal migration) and across the borders (international migration). While the phenomenon has been there been there since decades, it has accelerated following the spurt in economic growth after the 1980s.

- **Migrant worker:** According to Census, a migrant within India is one who is enumerated in census at a place other than his or her place of birth. External migrants are those who go out of India and work and live in a foreign country but remain to be citizens of India.
- **Inter-State migrant worker:** The Code on Social Security, 2020 enacted by the Parliament in September 2020, as part of the labour reforms, defines an "inter-State migrant worker" as a person who is employed in an establishment and
  - (i) has been recruited directly by the employer or indirectly through contractor in one State for employment in an establishment in another State, or
  - (ii) has come on his own from one State and obtained employment in an establishment of another State (called destination State), and
  - (iii) drawing wages not exceeding ₹18,000 per month or a higher amount notified by the Central Government from time to time.

Internal migration

To understand the magnitude of the problem, it is necessary to have an idea of the scale of migration taking place within India and from India to other countries. Despite wide divergences and heterogeneity among the peoples in different states in the country, language, social or cultural diversities have not been a barrier in inter-state migration. The same holds good for international migration out of India.

Level of Internal Migration

- **Census estimates**

- According to 2011 Census estimates, during the decade 2001-11, the annual rate of growth of labour migrants nearly doubled compared to the previous decade, increasing from 2.4 per cent in 1991-2001 to 4.5 per cent per annum in 2001-11.
- Successive Censuses have estimated annual average number of migrants to be about 3.3 million.
- **Intra-state migration:** Between 2001 and 2011, there was an increase in the growth rate of migrants moving to places within their own states (intra-state) as compared to those leaving for other states (inter-state). As per census, the rate of growth of inter-district migrants (within the same state) increased from 30 per cent between the 1991 and 2001 to 58 per cent between 2001 and 2011.

- **Other estimates**

However, other studies have found that migration within India is at a much higher level than estimated in the Census. Ministry of Finance's *Economic Survey of 2016-17* has confirmed this and observes as follows.

- Annually, inter-state labour mobility averaged 5-6 million people between 2001 and 2011, yielding an inter-state migrant population of about 60 million and inter-district migration as high as 80 million during the decade.
- The first-ever estimates of internal work-related migration using railways' passenger data for the period 2011-2016 indicate an annual average flow of close to 9 million people between the states.
- In 2007-08, the NSSO estimated the size of India's migrant labour to be seven crore which was 17 per cent of the total workforce of the survey year.

- The above estimates are significantly higher than the Census estimates.

Pattern of Internal migration

The pattern of movement of people is broadly in line with popular conception, i.e., more people migrating out of less affluent states, while the most affluent states are the largest recipients of migrants. The cost of moving for people is about twice as much as it is for goods.

- **Skewed pattern:** India's migration patterns are skewed on more than one count. Uttar Pradesh and Bihar have a disproportionately high number of out-migrants. According to the 2011 Census, 20.9 million people migrated outside the state from these two states which was 37 per cent of the total number of inter-state migrants.
- **Hindi belt, the main source:** The Hindi belt is the main source of migrants. According to the census, four states of Uttar Pradesh, Bihar, Rajasthan and Madhya Pradesh accounted for 50 per cent of India's total inter-state migrants.
- **UP has both Outward and Inward migrants:** Paradoxically, Uttar Pradesh has both outward and inward migrants. While people leave UP in search of livelihoods, there are also people who head to UP in search of livelihoods.
- **Major recipient states:** On the other hand, Maharashtra, Delhi, Gujarat, Uttar Pradesh and Haryana are recipient states for 50 per cent of the country's inter-state migrants. Migrants constitute more than one-third of the population in metros like Delhi and Mumbai.

Factors behind Internal Migration

- One of the major reasons for migration is the lop-sided industrial development. Paradoxically, it is some of the states in eastern and central India, which are richly endowed with mineral resources and have much potential for industrial development, that witness large scale migration. Lack of educated and skilled labour in those states has also been a contributory factor for this. In fact, the Planning Commission had emphasized the need for balanced regional development from as early as 1950s in the Second Plan (1956-61) and even in the Third (1961-66) and Fourth (1969-74) Plans. **(Pages 4.6, 8.4-5 and 19.11-2 for more on this).**
- In the initial stages of development, when a country transforms itself from an agrarian economy to more an industrialized economy, there will be more migration from rural areas to urban centres. Such movement of people paves the way for the release of "surplus labour" from relatively low-productive agricultural activities (primary sector) to higher productivity sectors, viz., industry (secondary) and service (tertiary) sectors.
- Migration of people for work and education has been a phenomenon that happens with structural transformation of economies.
- A primary reason for migration within a country and across the national borders is livelihood and in search of jobs with better prospects and higher emoluments.
- Marriage and moving with households are also major factors for migration. An important feature is the growing share of female migrants. Until the 2000s, migration was largely a male dominated phenomenon.

Problems faced by migrants

It is well known that migrants face a host of problems which are deep-rooted and existing for long. Only that, as stated earlier, this was exposed, in a stark and visible manner, before the whole nation during the stringent lockdown impose in March-April 2020 due to the widespread Covid-19 pandemic.

- **Housing:** A major issue migrant workers face is proper housing and accommodation. Living away from one's family and mostly living in unsatisfactory and unhygienic conditions, lacking in basic amenities, this has a deep impact on the psyche and productivity of the workers.
- **Lack of access to PDS:** Lack of access to benefits like food under the public distribution system (PDS) at the place of work where they reside (away from home) as their entitlement for this will be where their family resides. This is due to the Family Ration Card being not portable across states.
- **Lack of welfare benefits:** Migrant workers are not covered under the Employees State Insurance (ESI) and Employees Provident Fund (EPF) benefits due to non-fulfilment of criteria on certain minimum number of employees and wages prescribed for extending these benefits.
- **Lack of job security:** Majority of the migrant workers are employed in informal jobs and in the informal sector which does not ensure job security. Due to this, they could be retrenched anytime causing undue hardship to them.
- **Worker safety:** A sizeable section of migrant labour is engaged in construction and other work which are of hazardous nature prone to accidents and they are not covered by medical benefits or insurance.

Remedial measures

Part of the problems faced by migrants has been addressed in the new Labour reforms introduced by the government. **(See section 'Occupational Safety, Health and Working Conditions Code' in Box 16.4 above).** The under-mentioned measures need to be pursued to ameliorate the condition of migrant workers.

- ♦ **Housing:** Solving the housing issue faced by migrant workers should be a priority as the problem got magnified during the Covid-19 pandemic in 2020. For lack of proper housing and unable to pay rental following the outbreak, lakhs of migrant workers who lost their livelihoods had to trudge back hundreds of miles to their home towns and villages facing undue hardship.

The Central government has since announced a scheme for building "Affordable Rental Housing Complexes (ARHCs) for Migrant Workers/ Urban Poor" which is being pursued by the Ministry of Housing. It aims ensure ease of living to urban migrants in Industrial Sector as well as in non-formal urban economy to get decent, affordable rental housing close to their workplace. The ARHC scheme will be implemented through two models:

- Utilizing existing Government funded vacant houses to convert into ARHCs through Public Private Partnership or by Public Agencies.
- Construction, Operation and Maintenance of ARHCs by Public/ Private Entities on their own vacant land.

Considering the magnitude of the task involved, this scheme calls for close co-operation between the Central and State governments, Industry bodies and Building and Construction agencies. A medium-term plan has to be drawn up to achieve set targets.

- **Welfare provisions:** While the following welfare provisions have been made in the Occupational Safety, Health and Working Conditions Code, 2020, a condition is put that it would apply to establishments in which ten or more inter-State migrant workers are employed. This may leave out many small units where less than ten workers are engaged.
- **ESI and EPF benefits:** Under the above Code, inter-State migrant workers are to be provided the benefits of Employees' State Insurance (ESI), Employees' Provident Fund (EPF), facility of medical check and other benefits which are available to workers in the establishment.
- **Portability of PDS facility:** The new labour code approved has laid down that the concerned Government shall provide the option to inter-State migrant workers to avail the benefits of public distribution system (PDS) either in his native State or the destination State where he is employed. For this purpose, technology is being developed to have "One Nation one Ration Card" which will to enable migrant workers to access ration under PDS from any Fair Price Shop, either at their native place or their place of work.
- **Travel fare:** The employer will pay every inter-State migrant worker in his establishment an annual lump sum to cover the fare for to-and-fro journey from the place of his employment to his native place.
- **Registration:** The Act provides for registration of inter-state migrant workers on a portal that the Central government and the state governments are required to set up which is a positive step as it will help in data collection, access to, and provision, of welfare benefits, etc.
- **Contract workers:** In the case of contract workers, the welfare provisions in the Safety and Health code apply to establishments with fifty or more contract labour. This condition again may leave out many units where less number of labour is employed.
- **Database of workers:** One lacuna observed when Covid-19 pandemic broke out was that there was no proper data of migrant labour working in various cities and towns and the State to which they belonged. The government is creating a national database of the unorganized workforce, including migrant labourers, and will seed their profiles with the 12-digit Aadhaar number to provide them social security coverage, as announced by the labour ministry in Parliament. As part of this exercise, the skills of the workers could also be mapped which will help to provide them suitable employment nearer home to the extent feasible.

In this task, the next Census as well as NSS surveys could also be utilized to collect reliable data of both inter-state and intra-state migrant workers.

Deficiencies in the new laws

While the new labour laws do address many of the issues faced by the working class, experts point out some deficiencies in them particularly in regard to migrant workers.

- **No separate law for Migrants:** By subsuming the Inter-State Migrant Workmen Act, 1979 into the Occupational Safety Code 2020, the new Code gloss over certain special needs of migrant labour. Having a separate legislation addressing the complex issues faced by the vulnerable migrant workers would have been ideal.
- **Intra-state migrants:** While Part I of the Code deals with Contract workers, Part II relates to Inter-state migrant workers. Thus, the Code makes no mention of intra-state migrants, i.e., those who migrate *within* a state and so do not cover intra-state migrants.

However, under the Social Security Code passed by the Parliament, it is laid down that "The State Government shall frame and notify, from time to time, suitable welfare schemes for unorganised workers, including schemes relating to (i) provident fund; (ii) employment injury benefit; (iii) housing; (iv) educational schemes for children; (v) skill upgradation of workers; (vi) funeral assistance; and (vii) old age homes."

It is to be seen if all States will enact laws to protect the interests of migrants within their borders also, apart from inter-state migrants, with measures such as housing, PDS portability, medical assistance, etc. as per the above provision.

As per the 2011 Census, out of a total of 45 crore migrants, 39.57 crore people (i.e., 88 per cent) moved only within the state borders while inter-state migrants constituted just 5.43 crore (12 per cent). Hence the importance of intra-state migrants too.

- **Threshold limitations:** Certain thresholds of number of workers employed have been prescribed to be covered under the new Codes.
- In the case of Contract labour, the establishment in which fifty or more contract labour are employed or were employed on any day of the preceding twelve months.
- Under the Code on Social Security 2020 approved by the Parliament, its stated: A "factory" is defined as: i) Premises where ten or more employees are working and where manufacturing process is carried on using power.

  ii) Premises where twenty or more employees are working and where manufacturing process is carried without the aid of power.

Such conditions would mean that a large number of very small units, with lesser number of workers (which form a large percentage), would get excluded from the social security benefits which will be a major setback in achieving the laudable objectives of the labour codes.

International migration

India is a major country for workers migrating across national borders and is also a destination for emigrants from other countries. As per official data, there are over 30 million Indians overseas, with about nine million of the Indian diaspora concentrated in the GCC (Gulf Cooperation Council for the Arab States) region. Over 90 per cent of Indian migrant workers, most of whom are low- and semi-skilled workers, work in the Gulf region and South-East Asia.

Migration has both positive and negative aspects. It helps those migrating to earn better salaries, support families better and improve their lives. In fact, huge remittances from migrants to India has helped the economies of some of the states like Kerala, UP, Tamil Nadu and Andhra Pradesh. But migration throws up various problems also, both for the migrants and families back home in the case of those who go abroad for leaving family behind.

- Migrants' issues

- ♦ International migrants also face problems similar to what migrants within India confront.

  Besides – both white and blue collar migrants – face other problems like culture shock, living and working in a totally alien environment and getting assimilated into, and accepted by, the local society, all of which take time.
- ♦ While their salaries are usually better than what they earn in their home countries, those who take up less skilled jobs abroad, in particular, face problems pertaining to proper living accommodation, long working hours, job security, etc. despite the standards laid down by ILO.

- ♦ There have also been many instances of exploitation due to improper and unauthorized job contracts and dubious sponsors, at home and abroad, taking innocent job seekers for a ride. Those who go as domestic help may face various other forms of exploitation if their employers are not compassionate and unscrupulous.
- ♦ In the case of white collar migrants who are skilled take up certain professional jobs at higher levels, they could face some resistance from the local community abroad as they may be depriving the native people of their job prospects. Sometimes this leads to tensions and even racial feelings disturbing social harmony, though such cases may be isolated.

Mandatory checks

To prevent exploitation and abuse of migrant workers and protect them, the government has taken various measures over the years.

- Under the Ministry of External Affairs, there is the Protector General of Emigrants who is responsible for protecting the interest of Indian workers going abroad.
- Besides, the International Labour Organization (ILO) has also laid down various standards on working conditions and humane treatment of migrants, especially the labour class. ILO also works closely with all governments to ensure compliance of the standards.
- From 2016, recruitment of Indian nurses and domestic workers to be done only through authorized state-run recruitment agencies was made mandatory. There are such agencies in Kerala, UP, Andhra Pradesh, Telengana and Tamil Nadu.
- Also, a minimum age criterion of 30 years was prescribed for all women (except nurses) emigrating on ECR (Emigration Check Required) passports to ECR countries, irrespective of the nature of employment.

Reverse trends

Since the last few years, Indian migrants, particularly semi-skilled and unskilled workers, have lost jobs and have had to return home in large numbers. This has been due to a variety of reasons such as global recession, slowdown in many economies, "localisation" policy by which native workers are given preference in jobs, etc. This has been compounded by the pandemic, Covid-19, which has caused serious health issues placing undue burdens on economies the world over. This has raised the issue of rehabilitating returning migrants for many states.

❑ CHILD LABOUR IN INDIA

ILO observes that "child labour" is defined as work that deprives children of their childhood, their potential and their dignity, and that is harmful to physical and mental development. The term work implies what:

- is mentally, physically, socially or morally dangerous and harmful to children; and/or
- interferes with a child's ability to attend and participate in school fully by obliging them to leave school prematurely; or requiring them to attempt to combine school attendance with excessively long and heavy work.

Factors behind Child labour and Consequences

There are many inter-linked factors contributing to the prevalence of child labour. Child labour is both a cause and consequence of poverty. Household poverty, irregular income streams for the family, economic shocks, ignorance, lack of access to social security, education, health facilities, food security etc. force children into the labour market to earn money and support their family. While some perform child labour to supplement family income, many are in it for sheer survival. They miss out on an opportunity to gain education, further perpetuating household poverty across generations, slowing the economic growth and social development.

Child labour impedes children from gaining the skills and education they need to have opportunities of decent work as an adult. Inequality, lack of educational opportunities, slow demographic transition, traditions and cultural expectations all contribute to the persistence of child labour in India. Age, sex, ethnicity, caste and deprivation affect the type and intensity of work that children perform. Agriculture and informal sector employment continue to be sectors where children end up working.

The 2013 World Report on Child Labour prepared by the ILO has observed that child labour can compromise the productive capacity of workers during adulthood and thereby constrain both national economic growth and efforts to reduce poverty.

Child labour in India

As per Census 2011, the total child population in India in the age group (5-14) years was 259.6 million. Of these, 10.1 million (3.9 per cent of total child population) were reported to be working, either as 'main worker' or as 'marginal worker'. According to another estimate, 12.9 million children aged between 7 and 17 years are engaged in work. And about 42.7 million children in India are out of school.

The states in India where child labour is largely present are Bihar, Uttar Pradesh, Rajasthan, Madhya Pradesh and Maharashtra. This is where over half of the country's total child labour population works. Uttar Pradesh has the highest number of child laborers, with over 20 per cent of India's child workers being present in that state alone.

It is noteworthy that the incidence of child labour had decreased in India by 2.6 million between 2001 and 2011. But the decline was more visible in rural areas, while the number of child workers in urban areas increased, indicating the growing demand for child workers in menial jobs. Child labour has different ramifications in both rural and urban India.

Sectors employing Child labour

In India, child labour persists in agriculture sector, including plantations as domestic workers or in hotels and restaurants. Other major sectors are small and cottage industries engaged in apparels and carpet making, gem polishing, back-breaking work in brick kilns, quarrying and 'beedi' making. Children are used as cheap labour in these sectors.

Worse still, a large number of girls are victims of child trafficking, whether through traditional bondage or through organized crime or are used for begging on streets and even sexually exploited.

Countries like USA, Canada and European Union impose trade restrictions – non-tariff barriers – on products which use child labour in their manufacture with a view to end this practice.

Remedial Measures

The government in India has been making consistent efforts with the cooperation of social organizations and the civil society to tackle the issue. The ILO and UNICEF have also been collaborating with the Indian government in various ways to address the issue.

- ♦ The Government enacted the Child Labour (Prohibition & Regulation) Act, 1986 which prohibited the engagement of children in certain employments and to regulate the conditions of work of children in certain other employments. It barred employment of children below the age of 14 years in 18 occupations and 65 processes.

- ♦ National Child Labour Project Scheme (NCLPS) was started in 1988 to rehabilitate child labour. The Scheme aimed to adopt a sequential approach with focus on rehabilitation of children working in hazardous occupations and processes. Under the Scheme, a survey is conducted of children engaged in hazardous occupations and processes in a district or a specified area; then children in the age group of 9-14 years are withdrawn from these occupations and processes, and put into NCLP Special Training Centres. In the NCLP Special Training Centres, these children are provided bridge education, vocational training, mid-day meal, stipend, health care and recreation etc. with the ultimate objective of preparing them to be mainstreamed into the formal system of education.
- ♦ The Action Plan for tackling the problem of Child Labour enjoined the following measures:
  - State Governments were made responsible for enforcing the provisions under the Act.
  - Focusing and convergence of general development programmes to benefit children.
  - A Core Group on convergence of various welfare schemes of the Government was constituted in the Ministry of Labour and Employment to ensure that, the families of the Child Labour are given priority for their upliftment.
  - Project-based plan of action for launching projects for the welfare of working children in areas of high concentration of Child Labour.
  - Rescue & Repatriation: During inspections and raids conducted under CLPRA, Child Labour instances are identified, rescued and rehabilitative measures are taken.
  - Migrant children engaged in labour are provided "bridge education" with the objective of mainstreaming them into the formal system of education. Besides, pre-vocational training is also provided to the rescued children to make them skilled which would help them in career later in life.
  - Measures like Sarva Shiksha Abhiyan and Mid-day meal scheme in schools have gone a long way to induce very poor families to send children to school and continue education.
  - Considering that poverty and illiteracy of the family are the root cause for Child Labour, the government ensures that educational rehabilitation of the children is supplemented with economic rehabilitation of the families, so that they are not compelled by economic circumstances to send their children back to work.
  - The Union government monitors and special drives on enforcement and creating awareness are launched from time to time.

Other Institutional Mechanisms

Various other Ministries are also collaborating on ending the practice of child labour.

- Ministry of Women and Child Development has scheme of Shelter Homes to provide food and shelter to the children withdrawn from work.
- Ministry of Education provides Mid-day meal to the NCLP school children, teachers training, supply of books, etc under Sarva Shiksha Abhiyan and mainstreaming of NCLP children into the formal education system
- Convergence of schemes of Ministries of Rural Development and Panchyati Raj, Urban Housing and Poverty Alleviation cover these children under their various income and employment generation schemes for their families.

- In every State, one officer from the State Department of Labour is nominated to man Anti-Human Trafficking Unit (AHTU) and act as link officer for coordinating with the State Ministry of Education for prevention of trafficking of children.
- Convergence with Ministry of Railways for generating awareness and restricting trafficking of children in trains and railway premises..
- Further, the Ministry of Labour is implementing a pilot project "Converging Against Child Labour" in collaboration with ILO, funded by US Dept. of Labour, with the objective of prevention and elimination of hazardous child labour, including trafficking and migration of children. The Project is covering two districts each in Bihar, Jharkhand, Gujarat, Madhya Pradesh and Orissa for duration of 42 months.

India Ratifies ILO Conventions

In June 2017, the Government of India took a major step by depositing with the International Labour Office the instruments of ratification of the two fundamental ILO Conventions concerning the elimination of child labour, the Minimum Age Convention, 1973 (No. 138) and the Worst Forms of Child Labour Convention, 1999 (No. 182). This should spur India to further fight the problem of child labour and save the children.

The Pandemic and Child Labour

- The COVID-19 pandemic has undone a lot of gains achieved over the years. The crisis has aggravated poverty among the already vulnerable population and may reverse years of progress in the fight against child labour.
- A report by the ILO and UNICEF warns that 9 million additional children are at the risk of being pushed into child labour by the end of 2022 globally, as a result of the pandemic.
- In India, the closure of schools and the economic crisis faced by the vulnerable families, triggered by the pandemic, are likely drivers pushing children into poverty and thus into child labour and unsafe migration.
- There has been a significant increase in the proportion of working children mainly because of the COVID-19 pandemic and closure of schools. It has forced out-of-school children into farms and factories to work, worsening a child-labour problem that was already a challenge.
- Orphaned children are particularly vulnerable to trafficking and other exploitation like forced begging, or child labour. In such families, there is also the likelihood of older children dropping out of school to support their younger siblings.

Conclusion

The ultimate solution for the problem lies in stable economic growth, rooting out poverty, respect for labour standards, universal education, social protection, recognizing the needs and rights of the children. These together would help root out child labour.

❑ BONDED LABOUR

Bonded labour and its Ramifications

- The term "bonded labour" refers to a long-term relationship between employee and employer which is cemented through a loan, by custom or by force. It denies the employee various freedoms including to choose his or her employer, to enter into a fresh contract with the same employer or to negotiate the terms and condition of her/his contract.
- The Bonded Labour System Abolition Act (1976) of India defines 'bonded labour' as a service rendered under the 'bonded labour system'. This is a system of forced, or partly forced, labour under which the debtor enters into an agreement, oral or written, with the creditor which has the following wide ramifications for the debtor (borrower).
- For an 'advance' obtained by the debtor or for any customary obligation or by reason of his birth in a particular caste or community, the debtor agrees to render, by himself or through any member of his family, labour for the creditor.
- Such labour may be for a specified or unspecified period of time either without wages or for nominal wages. He forfeits the freedom of employment or other means of livelihood and forfeits the right to move freely in India.
- Also forfeits the right to appropriate or sell at market value any of his property or the produce of his own labour or that of any of his family members.

Bonded or Forced Labour in India

The phenomenon of bonded labour is a historical legacy dating back to the distant past when the caste system took root in India. The system continued to thrive during the medieval era and later the colonial period especially in agriculture sector. It was underpinned by a relationship of dominance and dependence between the rich landed aristocracy and the dependent serfs. These traditional or customary relationships gave rise to a form of debt-bondage and forced labour. Studies of labour relations have highlighted the link between caste and social structure and bondage, on the one hand, and traditional feudal social relations and bonded labour, on the other. Colonialism heightened the dimension of debt bondage, both within and outside agriculture

The incidence of bonded labour is now mostly in the unorganised and informal sector in India. And among the unorganised sectors, the incidence of bondage is high in quarries and open mines. These industries are mainly characterised by the predominance of manual processes, seasonality, remoteness and contract migrant labour. Brick kilns is another industry which has sizeable incidence of bonded labour. Other industries include power looms, handlooms, rice mills, sericulture and silk weaving, woollen carpets, fish processing, and construction.

India, with abject levels of poverty among the very poor and downtrodden, and diversity of labour arrangements, presents a complex picture of bonded labour incidence with varying characteristics. India was the first country in the South Asian region to enact legislation against bonded labour in 1976. Since then, many important measures have been taken to eradicate forced and bonded labour.

Measures taken on Bonded Labour

The issue of 'bonded labour' came to the fore as a national priority when it was included in the 20-Point Programme of the Government of India in 1975 aimed at eradicating poverty, raising productivity, reducing income inequalities and removing social and economic disparities. Bonded labour was outlawed in India through an ordinance in 1975 and then through legislation, the Bonded Labour System Abolition Act in 1976.

The first systematic survey of bonded labour was carried out by the Gandhi Peace Foundation and the National Labour Institute in1978 which placed the total number of bonded labourers at 2.62 million. The majority of employers were agriculturalists. The 32nd Round of the National Sample Survey Organisation (NSSO) estimated bonded labourers to be of the order of 3,43,000 spread across 16 major states.

The National Commission on Rural Labour (NCRL), 1991, had also made a comprehensive study of the nature, incidence and causes of bonded labour and suggested amendments to the 1976 legislation. The Government of India ratified the ILO Forced Labour Convention of 1930 (Co29) in 1954 which, *inter alia*, defines forced labour as "all work or service which is exacted from any person under the menace of penalty and for which the said person has not offered himself voluntarily".

The Ministry of Labour & Employment has conducted an in-depth study of scheme on Bonded labour, in consultation with important stakeholders such as National Human Rights Commission, ILO, NGOs and activists working for bonded labours and others and revised the scheme which came into effect in 2016. The revised scheme improved various steps relating to rescue and rehabilitation of those subjected to forced, bonded labour.

Constitutional and Legal implications

Forced and bonded labour violates the fundamental rights guaranteed to all citizens by the Indian Constitution. Article 23(1) in Part III of the Constitution, relating to Fundamental Rights, states that "Traffic in human beings and *begar* and other forms of forced labour are prohibited and any contravention of the provision shall be an offence, punishable by law."

The law dealing with bonded and forced labour was legislated by the Indian Parliament in 1976. The Bonded Labour System Abolition Act (1976) of India recognises and makes the following illegal:

- The overlap between forced labour and bonded labour in customary relationships.
- The manifestation of these relationships in contract labour and inter-state migration, and
- Considers the nature of restraints suffered by the labourer as a result of the bonded/forced labour relationship.

The Supreme Court has ruled in various decisions that bonded labour is a form of forced labour and hence is unconstitutional under Article 23 of the Constitution.

International Conventions

The ILO Conventions on Forced Labour and relevant UN Conventions define and prohibit various types of forced labour, slavery and servitude, and debt bondage. Many international Conventions have prohibited any kind of forced or bonded labour, practice of slavery, etc. These include:

- The League of Nations adopted the Slavery Convention in 1926, which was followed by the first ILO Forced Labour Convention, 1930 (No. 29), ratified by India in 1951. Article 2(1) of the Convention defines forced labour as "all work or service which is exacted from any person under the menace of any penalty and for which the said person has not offered himself voluntarily".
- The UN Supplementary Convention on the Abolition of Slavery, the Slave Trade and Institutions and Practices Similar to Slavery (1956) defines debt bondage as "the status or condition arising

from a pledge by a debtor of his personal services or those of a person under his control as security for a debt, if the value of those services as reasonably assessed is not applied towards the liquidation of the debt or the length and nature of those services are not respectively limited or defined." ILO's Committee of Experts has emphasized that 'debt bondage' is one form of 'forced labour' and is covered by the Convention.

- The ILO's Worst Forms of Child Labour Convention, 1999 (No.182) specifically includes forced labour, debt bondage and serfdom of children in its purview.
- The United Nations' Universal Declaration of Human Rights (UDHR) of 1948 has also reaffirmed these principles. Article 4 this Declaration states: "No one shall be held in slavery or servitude; slavery and the slave trade shall be prohibited in all their forms." And Article 23 (1) states "Everyone has the right to work, to free choice of employment, to just and favourable conditions of work and to protection against unemployment."
- In June 1998, the International Labour Conference, under the aegis of ILO, adopted a Declaration on "Fundamental Principles and Rights at Work and its Follow-up" that obligates member States to respect, promote and realize freedom of association and the right to collective bargaining, the elimination of all forms of forced or compulsory labour, the effective abolition of child labour, and the elimination of discrimination in respect of employment and occupation.

Conclusion

Emerging forms of forced labour and traffic in human beings, especially of children and other disadvantaged sections of society, require a holistic approach for law enforcement as well as comprehensive rehabilitation mechanism for social, psychological, educational and economic rehabilitation.

Advent of Computers and its Aftermath

In this context, it is worth recalling that unions in some States and some sectors like banking were vehemently opposed to the introduction of computers, when they first appeared, fearing it would displace labour in a massive way. However, after much persuasion and with a bit of compulsion, the Government went ahead, despite the stiff resistance, and introduced computers in the whole gamut of governmental machinery. And lo, how it has benefitted the people–the consumers who avail the services–and those who serve–the working class! How easy it has become for the workers and staff to perform their duties, and that too in a much better ambience than before, and how pleasurable it has become for customers to avail the services.

One shudders to think how banks, railways, airlines, factories, industries, and the whole range of administration at all levels could have managed to cope with the ever mounting volume of work, in the face of increasing population and demands on the services, without the veritable computer revolution. Staff got trained in the use of computers, their skills were upgraded, and better working conditions were provided. And the IT industry has turned out to be one of the largest employment generating sectors and bringing in valuable foreign exchange.

It only proves that all arms of the society have to work in harmony and unison and adapt themselves to the fast changing environment or else they will be left behind on the path of progress. A glaring example is how China and Russia, both of which were citadels of communism, opened themselves up, reformed their laws and regulations, and marched ahead, and, despite some pockets of deprivation, are far ahead of India on the path of progress. And within India too, those states, which are rigid and resistant to change, are lagging behind in industrialization, compared to other states which are more forward-looking. And ultimately who, but the workers, are the losers in the bargain.

❑ SKILL DEVELOPMENT

Introduction

India has a large young population, both below 15 years and between 15 and 59 years (See Table 16.6). As already stated earlier, about one million people each month–a massive 12 million a year–will be entering the labour market for the next decade and more for whom jobs are to be provided which is, by any standards, a formidable task. The problem is compounded by the fact that bulk of this labour force will be unskilled or less skilled and hence not readily employable. According to industry associations, even a good part of the educated youth coming out of schools, colleges, and technical institutions do not possess the specific skills needed in the industry and for jobs.

Table 16.6 India's Population in 2011 (Age-group-wise)

Age Group (years)	Total Population in the Group (in million.)	Percentage of Total Population
0 – 14	372.44	30.76
15 – 59	730.07	60.29
60 – 80 and above	108.33	8.95
Total	1210.84 million	100.00

Source: Census of India, 2011, Registrar General of India.

Challenge of Skill Development

Based on data from the 68th Round of NSSO, it is estimated that only 4.69 percent of India's total workforce has undergone formal skill training, compared with 52 percent in the USA, 68 percent in the UK, 75 percent in Germany, 80 percent in Japan, and 96 percent in South Korea. Thus, the task ahead is of mammoth proportions.

Recognizing the scale of the task involved, the Government created a dedicated Department of Skill Development and Entrepreneurship in July, 2014. It became a full-fledged Ministry in November, 2014 with all the implementing agencies, viz., National Skill Development Agency (NSDA), National Skill Development Corporation (NSDC), and National Skill Development Fund (NSDF) brought under its purview. Further, for effective implementation, the Training and Apprenticeship verticals, comprising of the entire network of Industrial Training Institutes (ITIs) and Apprenticeship Training schemes, were transferred from the Ministry of Labour and Employment to Ministry of Skill Development and Entrepreneurship (MSDE) in April, 2015. These changes have paved the way for a new skilling ecosystem, with closer coordination across the public and private sectors.

Labour Force and Jobs–the Mismatch

The mismatch between labour force and jobs has meant that recruits have to be specially trained for the jobs which entails considerable time and costs. Imparting skills to the youth has assumed great importance in view of the rapid advances and changes in technology in the present-day globalized world. Unless manufacturing industries keep themselves abreast of these changes and have an efficient, skilled workforce, India will not be able to succeed in her ambitious 'Make in India' programme or compete with other nations in the international markets for exports.

The Government has already embarked on a massive programme of 'Skill Development' especially for jobs involving technical skills. At the start of the Eleventh Plan (2007–12), various Central ministries and departments were imparting vocational training to some 3.1 million persons every year in varied fields like health, education, handlooms, tourism, child development, etc. But this was a disjointed effort resulting in redundancy. Besides, India had 1,244 polytechnics with a capacity of 2.95 lakh students, 5,114 ITI's training 7.42 lakh students, and other institutions to train for nursing, paramedical staff, teaching, etc. But the inadequacy of the facilities can be gauged from the fact that against 12 million new entrants to the workforce per year, the available training capacity was just 3.1 million per year.

A report by a leading chamber of commerce has stated that the employability of Indian workforce has gone up from 34 per cent to 40 per cent which implies that the remaining 60 per cent are not readily employable. The skill development programme has also not attained the required pace. In a report submitted to a Parliamentary Committee on the Pradhan Mantri Kaushal Vikas Yojana, the flagship skill development programme, the government has stated that of the 1.76 million people trained under the programme till April 2016, only 5,60,000 could be certified as having successfully completed the training and only 82,000 were actually placed in jobs. This points to the serious challenges that lie ahead on skilling people on a massive scale and even more to ensure that the trained hands have actually imbibed the skills and could be placed in jobs.

Demographic Dividend

The decline in the growth of population in the past few decades means that fewer people will join the labour force in coming years and a working person would have fewer dependents. Also, if more women enter the workforce, it would further lowering the dependency ratio. This decline in the dependency ratio contrasts with the demographic trend in the industrialized countries and in China, where the dependency ratio is rising. Low dependency ratio gives India a comparative cost advantage and a progressively lowering dependency ratio will result in improving our competitiveness.

Skill India Mission

The programme involves the Central Government, State Governments, and the private sector. The government has set up Prime Minister's National Council on Skill Development, to co-ordinate and give a thrust to the programme which is being executed on PPP mode.

As part of the Skill India mission, the NDA government has drawn up a 'National Policy on Skill Development and Entrepreneurship, 2015' which supercedes the 2009 policy. It aims to to cope with the challenge of skilling at scale with speed and quality and provide an umbrella framework to all skilling activities within the country and align them to common standards. The policy will link skills development practices to improved standards of employability and productivity.

Box 16.5: Highlights of Skill India Mission

- The National Skill Development Agency set up in 2013 has been working with State governments to synergize skilling efforts in states.
- The Pradhan Mantri Kaushal Vikas Yojana (PMKVY) is a unique initiative by the government that aims to offer 24 lakh Indian youth meaningful, industry-relevant, skill-based training. Under this scheme, the trainees are given a financial reward and a government certification on successful completion of training and assessment, which will help them in securing a job for a better future.

- The number of ITI's has reached 14,779 by 2021, affiliated to the National Council for Vocational Training, which collectively train 1.86 million students in skills related to fabrication, electronics, and automobile industry, among other trades.
- The government has planned to set up within one year 7,000 more ITI's, or nearly half the number of existing ITI's opened in six decades.
- As government alone cannot set up so many ITI's, it is exploring the possibility of offering soft loans to private players to open ITI's.
- Expanding the capacity of these institutes is to create trained manpower for the manufacturing sector to boost manufacturing and provide jobs to millions of youth joining the labour force each year.
- The number of polytechnics has also increased from 1,244 to about 3,200.
- The NSDC has developed capacity to train 82 million with 159 training partners having 1,408 centres in 356 districts in 27 states and 5 Union Territories.
- NSDC has established a framework for short-term skilling VET in India Through a network of more than 11,000 centres and 37 Sector Skill Councils. It has trained about 2.53 crore individuals across its grant-based and fee-based trainings.
- Deen Dayal Upadyaya Grameen Kaushalya Yojana (DDU-GKY) is a placement-linked skill development scheme for poor rural youth under the Ministry of Rural Development. Department of Rural development has 577 functional rural self-employment training institutes spread over 556 districts.
- Ministries of Textiles and Micro, Small and Medium Enterprises are also running pan-India training centres.
- The government is also contemplating to frame a new law to grant the youth the 'Right to Skill' and impose a cess to fund the ambitious Skill India mission.
- A high-level sub-group headed by Punjab Chief Minister has recommended using the funds from the Education cess and half of corporate funds under the CSR to create a non-lapsable pool of funds to be used to provide vocational training to millions of youth.
- The government has set a target to skill 119 million persons in 24 sectors.

Thus, a massive and widespread skill development programme is under implementation which, if effectively executed, should go a long way in absorbing the large inflow of youth into the labour force in the coming years.

❑ TECHNOLOGY VERSUS LABOUR AND EMPLOYMENT

Fast-changing modern technology will also pose a major challenge in the coming years. With all the relentless advancements in technology–3-D printing, robotics, artificial intelligence, and automation–the question will arise if there would still be need for people to spend most of their lives on the daily drudgery of work. Or would the new, emerging social and economic systems make work less stressful and more pleasurable? Instead of working daily, could work be managed to be done at intervals interspersed with spells of leisure and recreation? There are already visible signs of changes to come with flexitimings at work, videoconferences, conference calls, people working from home, etc. which avert transportation and physical movements of people and thus, saves fuel and reduces environmental pollution. And on-line repair of gadgets, machines, etc. could also help factories a great deal in saving time, effort, and costs. In the health field too, measures like telemedicine help in on-line patient treatment thus averting physical movements.

If the emerging, disruptive technologies result in less workforce being needed to perform tasks, it would pose yet another challenge in the future.

Box 16.6 Automation and Employment

Automation is an emerging trend which will have a perceptible impact on the way industry operates in the years to come. Advances in robotics, artificial intelligence, and machine learning are ushering in a new age of automation, as machines match or outperform human performance in a range of work activities, including those which require cognitive capabilities. Technological advances are creating ever smarter and more flexible machines that will be deployed on an ever larger scale at the workplace.

Significant efforts are underway in Japan and the western world on various modes of automation – robotics, 3D printing, artificial intelligence and advancements in digital technology–that will change the way industry and the corporate world function. Disruptive technologies are creating new industries and business models and making old ones redundant and irrelevant. New systems like data analytics, internet-of-things, cloud computing and social networks are having a huge impact on the way people communicate, handle data, collaborate and work.

Japanese are ahead of the curve in robotics technology which finds application in domains like assembly line in manufacturing, energy efficiency, climate change, nursing and elder care and boosting productivity in a tight labour market. Researchers in Italy have been able to train a robot to imitate natural human actions. It has been found tha humans and robots can effectively co-ordinate their actions during high-stakes surgeries. This may improve safety during surgeries because unlike their human counterparts, robots do not tire and can carry out endless series of precise movements.

❑ Impact on Employment and Jobs

There are divergent views on the impact automation will have on employment. One view is that it would help to improve product quality and living standards while another view is it would result in massive dislocation of jobs. However, the advances in technology are not likely to impact all sectors to the same extent.

While automation is desirable or even expedient for many of the advanced nations which are faced with the problem of declining and ageing population, it will pose a real threat to most of the developing countries where ever increasing population makes creation of jobs a dire necessity.

The pace and degree at which automation will take place depends on various factors – technical, economic and social. Technical feasibility, the relative cost of technology vis-à-vis labour, supply and demand factors and social acceptance will determine the extent of automation. Also despite automation, humans will be needed to work alongside machines. Labour displaced by automation could find alternate modes of employment as happened with computer revolution.

Commenting on the trend towards automation, the International Labour Organization (ILO) has observed: "The world is experiencing an unprecedented acceleration in technological advancement and implementation. Indeed, profound shifts are taking place – entire sectors are accommodating these innovations, rendering several human-performed occupations redundant. In the near future, these positions may be eliminated entirely. At the same time, other jobs are experiencing a rapid increase in demand, and some occupations are revising the skill sets they traditionally require." (ILO: ASEAN in Transformation: The Future of Jobs at Risk of Automation)

In traditional economic theory, capital (meaning machinery and tools) combine with labour to produce output and are complementary to each other. Whereas robots and other new technologies can displace human labour and could thus have significant impact on employment potential.

❑ Advent of Computers and its Aftermath

Against this background, a look at the advent of computers and the impact it had on employment would not be out of place. As computers were being introduced in various sectors like banking, railways, government administration, etc., it was thought that it would result in massive displacement of labour. There was vehement opposition from labour unions to these moves. But later experience has shown that not only no such thing happened, at least to the extent feared, but computers have enabled labour to upgrade its skills, improve productivity, and render work more efficiently and in much better ambience. To the extent some displacement of labour may have taken place, it has also created new avenues for job creation by way of manufacture and maintenance of computers, training and skill development. It has also opened up new ways of performing jobs, reducing physical movements through online operations, video-conferencing, tele-conferences, etc.

❑ ILO Study on Automation

Based on extensive interviews with stakeholders and case studies, the ILO carried out a detailed study of various sectors in countries in ASEAN region and came out with the report, **'ASEAN in Transformation : The Future of Jobs at Risk of Automation'**. The study covered the technological trends in the ASEAN region and how they impact enterprises and workers within five major sectors: automotive and auto parts; electrical and electronic parts; business process outsourcing; textile, clothing and footwear; and retail.

Some of the key findings of ILO study are:

- Nearly three in five jobs face a high risk of automation;
- Technology will shape the future of manufacturing and services; and
- Women, workers with less education and workers in lower-wage occupations are more likely to be impacted.

❑ Robotics in Automation

A study carried out for the International Federation of Robots (IFR), an association formed by robotics organisations across the world, predicts that industrial robots will create more than two million jobs over the next eight years. The study predicted that the use of robots in product development and the possibilities created by the current industry expansion will produce jobs downstream.

IFR opines that productivity and competiveness are indispensable for a manufacturing enterprise to be successful on the global market. Robotics and automation provide the solution. Many innovative American companies have already invested in an automated system which allows them to reallocate job roles while improving productivity and gaining in quality control.

Growth with robots has gained momentum in recent years. In 2011 and 2012, 1.66 lakh and 160 lakh industrial robots respectively were sold in the North American robotics market, in spite of the weak global economy. The technology has the potential to benefit manufacturers across the board. Investments in robots always generate sound practical returns both at economic and technical levels. Robotized automation is a key strategic factor to enhance competitiveness both for the big, medium and small enterprises. It is estimated that 3 to 5 roles will be created for every robot in service.

❑ Automation in India

India needs to carve out its own path towards adoption of automation to improve productivity and competitiveness and meet her growth aspirations. While India may borrow the best practices and policies from other nations, she has to choose the path best suited to her demographic and social conditions and capabilities. Automation could create the kind of jobs required by an aspirational India.

While globally robotics and automation has seen an upward trend in the last decade with rapid increase in volumes, their adoption in India lags way behind that in industrialized countries. China has embraced it about seven years back and is emerging as a global hub for automation and robotics. India needs to catch up to remain competitive.

Industrial sector has a high employment multiplier effect – for each direct job it creates, 2 to 3 other indirect jobs are created in the Manufacturing or Services sectors. The multiplier effect could be even higher for smart manufacturing. Automation will also drive competitiveness, improve quality of products and services and enhance safety in industry. The various 'Skill India' programmes that India has initiated must also be attuned to suit changes in work environment that may result from automation in the days to come.

❑ Challenge for Policymakers

While for industry and businesses, the benefits of automation are evident, it poses a major challenge for policy-makers. Policymakers should seize the opportunities to harness the potential for greater efficiency and improved productivity that automation offers. This will call for reworking educational systems and curricula, reskilling the workforce to keep pace with changing technology and promoting innovation and R & D.

Resource scarcity, climate change, demographic shifts and rapid urbanisation and technological breakthroughs will all exert pressure in transforming the way people work over the next decade. And all countries will have to be prepared for such eventual changes comparable to what happened following the Industrial Revolution in the 18th and 19th centuries.

In this Chapter we discussed.....

- Creation of jobs, reduction of unemployment, and removal of poverty are the primary objectives of development. Growth must be accompanied by job opportunities for all those who need and seek work.
- Despite impressive growth, unemployment and poverty could not be eradicated due to a variety of factors such as ever increasing population, inadequacy of financial and physical resources.
- Views of economists and thinkers on labour, employment and productivity.
- Types and sources of labour data—labour force participation rate (LFPR) worker population ratio (WPR), and proportion unemployed (PU).
- Factors impacting labour force and employment.

- Measuring employment / unemployment—NSSO methods: usual status, current weekly status, and current daily status.
- India's labour force and workforce—their growth and gender-wise composition.
- Salient features of the Indian labour scene.
- Employment and unemployment trends: Position in 1999–2000 to 2004–05 period better than the earlier period—1993–94 to 1999–2000.
- Organized and unorganized sectors: bulk of the people in India are employed in the unorganized sector. There are also those in formal and informal employment. In the unorganized sector, those in informal employment far outnumber those in formal employment whereas in the organized sector, formal workers are more than informal workers.
- Compared to regular employees in the organized sector, the casual, informal employees in the unorganized sector do not have social security benefits like Provident Fund, gratuity, medical and house allowances, etc. which place them at a disadvantage.
- The National Commission for Employment in the Unorganized Sector (NCEUS), set up in September 2004, studied various problems confronting the unorganized sector and suggested measures to ameliorate their conditions.
- NCEUS observed that the growth rate of employment was much less among the poor and vulnerable groups compared to the middle and higher income groups. Between 1993 and 2004, while there was impressive growth of the manufacturing sector, there was little growth of formal employment.
- Employment generation is one of the major challenges facing the Indian economy. 60.29 per cent of the population in 2011 aged between 15 and 59, the working age-group. 12 million people are being added to the labour force every year. Only about 50 per cent of those aged 15 years and above is employed, leaving a huge gap between those employed and those seeking jobs.
- National Rural Employment Guarantee scheme (NREGS) started in 2005 to provide at least 100 days of wage employment to one adult member of every rural household to combat rural distress, especially in drought years, and to provide employment in the off season of farming.
- Inverse relationship between inflation and unemployment and 'Phillip's Curve'. The proposition not found valid.
- Labour reforms: need for reform. National Labour Commissions and Working Group on Labour Laws. The reforms and tripartite consultation process. Resistance to reforms.
- Child labour and Bonded labour issues.

- Advent of computers and its aftermath. Its positive impact on services and working conditions.
- Skill development: India's large, young population and their skills and employability issues. Ambitious programmes for improving skills of the youth. Highlights of 'Skill India mission'. Challenges in skill development.
- Automation and employment; Emerging, disruptive technologies and their likely impact on versus labour and employment in future.

Important Terms to Note in this Chapter

Labour Force Participation rate; Worker Population ratio; Employment on Usual Status, Current Weekly Status, and Current Daily Status; Organized sector; Unorganized sector; Formal employment; Informal employment; Child labour; Bonded and Forced labour; Skill development; Demographic dividend; 3-D printing; Robotics; Artificial intelligence; Automation

Practice Questions

1. A large proportion of India's population is dependent on the agriculture sector. What are the problems faced by this sector due to this and how can they be remedied?
2. It is estimated that about ten million people are due to join India's labourforce each year for the next several years and creating jobs for them will be a major challenge for the economy. Suggest ways in which India can create employment opportunities for them.
3. Identify the sectors in the economy which have relatively greater scope and potential to create jobs.
4. According to industry bodies and associations, a large proportion of India's youth entering the labour market are not readily employable. What are the reasons for this and what steps need to be taken to remedy them?
5. Analyse the factors behind migration of labour in India and mention the problems faced by migrant labour. Suggest remedies to improve their condition.
6. Examine the new Labour reforms introduced and their implications for economic development of the country.
7. The nature of economic growth in India in recent times is often described as jobless growth. Do you agree with this view? Give arguments in favour of your answer.

[UPSC Main 2015 (General Studies Paper)]

8. How globalization has led to the reduction of employment in the formal sector of the Indian economy? Is informalization detrimental to the development of the country?

[UPSC Main 2016 (General Studies Paper)]

9. Comment on the challenges for inclusive growth which include careless and useless manpower in the Indian context. Suggest measures to be taken for facing these challenges.

[UPSC Main 2016 (General Studies Paper)]

10. Examine the Labour Policy of India and its impact on employment (labour) market in Indian economy.

[UPSC Main 2014 (Economics Optional Paper)]

11. Discuss the recent reforms in labour market in India.

[Indian Economic Service/Indian Statistical Service 2020]

12. Has New Economic Policy promoted jobless growth in India? Comment with evidence.

[Indian Economic Service/Indian Statistical Service 2014]

13. Do you think that the employment generation strategy adopted by the Government of India since 1991 can reduce unemployment significantly?

[Indian Economic Service/Indian Statistical Service 2017]

14. How is unemployment measured in India? Discuss giving estimates of various forms of Unemployment in the Indian economy.

[Indian Economic Service/Indian Statistical Service 2014]

15. What are the causes and extent of unemployment in India? What do you understand by the term 'Jobless Growth*? Explain this in the light of recent experience.

[Indian Economic Service/Indian Statistical Service 2020]

16. Employment pattern in India in post-reform period has moved in favour of contractual, casual and self-employment. How public sector employment deceleration would impact the future of labour (employment) market in India? Elaborate.

[UPSC Main 2014 (Economics Optional Paper)]

17. Skill development and thereby raising labour productivity like that in China would be the only panacea for long-term growth in Indian economy. Discuss.

[UPSC Main 2014 (Economics Optional Paper)]

18. Skill development and increase in labour productivity will impact India's growth rate. In this context, would you suggest changes in India's education policy?

[Indian Economic Service/Indian Statistical Service 2015]

19. India is presently facing dual challenges of developing skills and using skills. Discuss.

    [Indian Economic Service/Indian Statistical Service 2016]

20. What provisions have been enshrined in the National Social Security Act, 2008 for Unorganized Sector Workers? Discuss critically giving evidence on its progress and achievements so far.

    [Indian Economic Service/Indian Statistical Service 2014]

21. Child labour continues to be a permanent problem in India. Suggest pragmatic ways to control it

    [Indian Economic Service/Indian Statistical Service 2014]

22. 'Bonded labour continues to exist in India despite Government's efforts to regulate it.' Comment.

    [Indian Economic Service/Indian Statistical Service 2016]

CHAPTER

INEQUALITY AND POVERTY ALLEVIATION

- The Constitution of India on Equality and Social Justice
- Manifestation of Inequality and Poverty
- Absolute and Relative Poverty
- Extreme Poverty and Poverty Trap
- Measuring Poverty, Sen's Poverty Index
- Development as a Broader Issue
- Human Development Reports
- Five Year Plans and Poverty and Inequality
- Importance of Social and Political Consciousness
- Economists and Welfarism
- Global Poverty Scene
- Economists on Inequality and Distributive Justice
- Inequality and Poverty versus Growth: Sen-Bhagawati debate
- Growth and Inequality-the Asian Experience
- Estimation of Poverty and Identification of Poverty Line
- Angus Deaton on India's Poverty
- Expert Groups on Methodology for Estimation of Poverty
- Poverty Alleviation Measures: Rural and Urban
- Integrated Child Development Services
- National Rural Employment Guarantee Scheme (NREGS)
- Rural Housing Programme and PM Gram Sadak Yojana
- Panchayati Raj and Rural Rejuvenation
- Gender Bias and Gender Inequality: Various Dimensions
- Gender Budgeting and Its Impact
- Universal Basic Income (UBI)
- Growth and Inequality: Kuznet's Hypothesis and a Global Perspective

❑ INTRODUCTION

While the Constitution of India proclaims laudable objectives of equality and social justice (See Box 17.1), the fact remains that even after six decades of strenuous efforts at economic and social development through planning, there is pervasive poverty and inequality persisting in the country. While India had prospered till the 17th century (as seen in Chapter 1), the decline started with the arrival of the colonial powers who sought to exploit the country for their own selfish ends. This was further accentuated by the Industrial Revolution, when the western powers forged ahead industrially, leaving India in the lurch. While colonialism may have had some positive impact, the fact remains that the widespread poverty and backwardness India has had to suffer is the legacy and baggage of two centuries that the colonialists left behind.

Box 17.1: The Constitution of India on Equality and Social Justice

The Constitution of India, in its Preamble, resolves, inter alia, " to secure to all its citizens: JUSTICE, social, economic and political;................. EQUALITY of status and of opportunity and to promote among them all FRATERNITY assuring the dignity of the individual......"

Further, Article 16 of the Constitution stipulates that "There shall be equality of opportunity for all citizens in matters relating to employment or appointment to any office under the State", subject to certain conditions as may be laid down by the Parliament.

Further, the 'Directive Principles of State Policy', enunciated in the Constitution, state that the State shall strive to promote the welfare of the people by securing and protecting as effectively as it may a social order in which justice, social, economic, and political, shall inform all the institutions of the national life. The State shall, in particular, strive to minimize the inequalities in income, and endeavour to eliminate inequalities in status, facilities, and opportunities, not only amongst individuals, but also amongst groups of people residing in different areas or engaged in different vocations.

The State shall, in particular, direct its policy towards securing

(i) that the citizens, men and women equally, have the right to an adequate means of livelihood;

(ii) that the ownership and control of the material resources of the community are so distributed as best to subserve the common good;

(iii) that the operation of the economic system does not result in the concentration of wealth and means of production to the common detriment; and

(iv) that there is equal pay for equal work for both men and women.

❑ MANIFESTATION OF INEQUALITY AND POVERTY

Poverty and inequality are interrelated and they act upon one another like cause and effect. Since everyone in a group or society cannot be equally well off, some are bound to be poorer or richer than others, and it is the question of degree of inequality or poverty that matters. There is inequality and poverty even in developed countries but not so widespread, severe, or abject as in developing nations.

Poverty and inequality manifests in different forms. Misallocation of resources and lack of opportunities or access to basic facilities and necessities result in deprivation. Lack of income, food, nutrition, and decent housing, and lack of access to water and sanitation, not to speak of proper educational and health facilities, are all manifestations of poverty. Unemployment is another major factor causing poverty. People having to live in overcrowded slums amidst squalor, ill-fed, ill-clothed, and malnourished children, under-nourished women who have to toil at home and trudge miles in rural areas to fetch a pail of water, weak lactating mothers—these are all common sights and visible signs of grinding poverty. Besides, other social indicators such as morbidity, high infant and maternal mortality, and high birth and death rates in the population are also indications of poverty and poor standard of living.

In rural India, where agriculture is the mainstay of the people, vagaries of monsoon, large tracts of unirrigated land, drought, crop losses, rising debts, etc. cause acute distress to farming community and their families.

Absolute and Relative poverty

Absolute Poverty refers to a state in which people do not have enough money or income to meet the basic, minimum needs that are required for survival. People who fall below this level do not have enough money to buy food, shelter, clothing, etc. that are essential for survival and are classified as poor. In other words, absolute poverty indicates the lack of biological necessities such as food, water, clothing, housing, and sanitation. This concept is directly related to the minimum level of consumption.

Absolute poverty is more prevalent in the poorer and developing (what are also called 'third world') countries, where more people are living below a certain threshold of income required for bare necessities.

Relative Poverty is a condition in which people have enough money or income to meet the basic needs required to survive but are still relatively poor when compared to others. It is not based merely on a basic amount necessary for survival but takes into account the 'standard or quality of life' a person enjoys. Thus, a person may live in an affluent neighbourhood and have everything needed for survival but does not have the comforts or luxuries which others may have.

Absolute poverty refers to a set condition, which is the same in every country, and does not change over a period of time. Relative poverty, on the other hand, refers to conditions which are subjective to the society in which the person lives, and, therefore, vary between regions and countries, and may change over a period of time. For example, countries which are more urbanised and advanced will have higher costs for food, housing, education, energy, and transportation, etc. and so the poverty line will be higher in those countries, compared to that in poorer countries. Again, within a country, the urban areas will have more facilities than rural areas and this will be reflected in the standard and costs of living and in the relative poverty level. Relative poverty is based on the socio-cultural environment around, not on a basic amount necessary for people to subsist. Relative poverty changes more often and adjusts to the changes in society – say, food and housing becoming more expensive in certain areas or over a period of time.

In basic terms, absolute poverty is having a lack of basic resources while relative poverty is more to do with income inequality. People in relative poverty do have an income, but it is lower than the set income level. They are seen as poor because they do not have the capabilities to meet certain standard set by, or prevailing in, the community.

Extreme poverty

The World Bank is the main source for global information on extreme poverty and it sets the International Poverty Line (IPL). The poverty line has been revised from time to time and since 2015, a person having an income less than $1.90 per day, based on 2011 PPP conversion rates, is considered to be in extreme poverty. (PPP or Purchasing Power Parity conversion rate takes into account differences in prices levels across countries as well as inflation). People living in extreme poverty suffer from marginalization, malnutrition, vulnerability to diseases and various other deprivations.

It is important to note that the International Poverty Line fixed is extremely low and those living below this low threshold are considered to be in 'extreme poverty'. Focusing on extreme poverty is important precisely because it captures those utmost in need of attention and support. However, it is also important to note that the living conditions of those just above the International Poverty Line can still be characterized by poverty and hardship. The World Bank also reports poverty headcount ratios using a higher line at $3.10 per day on 2011 PPP prices.

Extreme poverty was prevalent even in today's advanced countries until fairly recently. In fact, in most of these countries, sizeable sections of the population lived in extreme deprivation only a few generations ago. But socio-economic progress took place at a fast pace following the Industrial Revolution and scientific advancement which helped to wipe out poverty. It points to the fact that sustained economic progress in the less developed countries of today could definitely bring down, and eventually end, extreme poverty.

Poverty trap

Economists use the term 'poverty trap' to denote a situation in which individuals are stuck in deprivation over long periods of time, and there is nothing they can do by themselves to escape their situation. Simply stated, it means that poverty perpetuates poverty in a vicious cycle, so households that start poor continue to remain poor and are unable to break out of it. This is true of those who remain extremely poor and are farthest below from the poverty line.

Insufficient nutrition, which again is due to lack of income, and consequent extreme poverty can be the cause of poverty trap, both of an individual and a household. Low intake of food and malnutrition impairs the capacity to work; poor nutrition then becomes both the cause and consequence of poor incomes.

Poverty traps can also occur at a collective, 'macro' level. For example, low-income countries might lack the requisite growth fundamentals – technology, education, infrastructure, etc. – that are necessary for the high saving rates which lead to productivity gains and rising national incomes. Such low-income countries have to resort to 'big push' macro policies like expansion of micro-finance or public investments which will have permanent positive effects and trigger a virtuous cycle of more savings, more investment, and economic growth to break out of the poverty trap. Governments could also launch programs to reduce poverty through short-term interventions that have lasting effects. While this is not an easy task, there is evidence to suggest that in different countries, multifaceted programs offering short and medium-term support to households have produced lasting progress for the very poor. They produce significant impact on consumption, food security, productive and household assets, financial inclusion, income generation, physical and mental health and women's empowerment.

Measuring Poverty

There is need for a measure of poverty to evaluate how the economy is performing in terms of providing a certain minimum standard of living to all its citizens. Measurement of Poverty has important policy implications.

Income and consumption expenditure are two significant parameters for gauging poverty and fixing poverty line in an economy. According to this, the income required by an individual or a household for consumption expenditure to maintain a desirable minimum level of living is assessed. It may include food and non-food items and will take into account minimum calorie requirements to ensure healthy living.

India has been adopting income and consumption expenditure (related to calorie intake) criteria for fixing the poverty line. (For detailed discussion on this, see from section 'Estimation of Poverty and Identification of Poverty Line' later in this chapter).

Sen's poverty index

The conventional approach to identify the poor and measure poverty is to count the number of people who are below a certain level of income defined as 'poverty line'. This is called 'head count' method and the index of poverty is the proportion of the total population that happens to be below the poverty line -- the head count ratio.

Prof. Amartya Sen, who has made signal contribution to the study of poverty issues, has pointed out certain inadequacies of this approach. The head count ratio, which only takes note of the number of people below the poverty line, does not examine and bring out the inequality existing among those who are below the poverty line.

The method suggested by Sen measures not only the proportion of poor people, but looks into the depth of their poverty, inequality among them and the distribution of welfare among the poor. This measure allows one to decompose poverty into three components and asks:

- Are there more poor?
- Are some of the poor poorer?
- Is there higher inequality among the poor?

The headcount index does not indicate how poor the poor are, and hence does not change if people below the poverty line become poorer.

The easiest way to reduce the headcount index, i.e., number of those below the poverty line is to target benefits to people who are just below the poverty line, because they are the ones who will cost the least to be lifted above the poverty threshold. But by most normative standards, people just below the poverty line are the least deserving among the poor but lifting them up will require more concerted efforts involving more expenditure. Those who are far below the poverty line deserve priority in targeted poverty alleviation measures. This approach has important policy implications.

Development As a Broader Issue

Till about two decades back, economic development was assessed based mainly on growth in GDP and per capita income (PCI). But even though GDP and PCI may show impressive growth, they may not get distributed in a fair and equitable manner. Development experience in many countries has shown that even with increase in incomes, large sections of people were left behind in the process and many of them continued to be trapped in poverty and acute deprivation. This led many economists and international development agencies to redraw the parameters to judge development based on various other social and economic indicators and assess improvement in the 'quality of life' on a much broader plane. Many writings began to appear focussing on human welfare based on a broad spectrum as mentioned above. It was emphasized that growth has to be judged on inclusivity and on more broad-based criteria such as educational attainments, longevity (life expectancy), gender equity, access to public health facilities, good housing, safe drinking water, sanitation, mortality rates, etc.

Human Development Studies

The genesis of research on human development and studies on poverty and inequality got impetus, and was considerably enriched by the pioneering work of welfare economists like Amartya Sen, Atkinson, Ravallion and others who had done considerable study in these domains from the 1970s. By 1980s, James Foster, Joel Greer and Erik Thorbecke had developed, at Cornell University in the US, a method of decomposable poverty measures which came to be known as Foster-Greer-Thorbecke measure of poverty. Their work was substantively influenced by methods drawn from social choice theory and welfare economics and motivated by applied research undertaken in Kenya.

In time, these empirical studies and measures became the standard for international evaluations of poverty, and were reported regularly by the World Bank's PovcalNet, UN agencies, and by individual countries. (PovcalNet is an online analysis tool for global poverty monitoring, developed by the World Bank's Development Economics Division and is the source of the World Bank's official poverty estimates).

Human Development Reports

Since 1990, UNDP has been publishing annual *Human Development Report* (HDR) based on the aforementioned approach, with focus on different developmental themes, with exhaustive statistical data pertaining to all member countries in the UN system. The initiative for this was taken by Dr. Mahbub ul Haq, a former Finance and Planning Minister of Pakistan, and the first few reports were published by a team under his leadership. UNDP collects data on attainments on selected parameters such as literacy, schooling, life expectancy, per capita income, etc. of each country and calculates the Human Development Index (HDI) and ranks countries according to HDI in three groups—High, Medium, and Low Human Development. It also assesses level of poverty and deprivation, gender equality, etc.

In 2020 HDR which covers a total of 189 countries, India with HDI value of 0.645 is placed at rank 131 (among the group of Medium Human Development countries) while Bangladesh is ranked 133 and Pakistan at 154. It may be noted that Bhutan ranks higher than India at 129 with HDI value of 0.654. Sri Lanka ranks much higher at 72 with HDI value of 0.782 and is placed among High Human Development group of countries.

Other Human Development Studies

There have been other studies also on global and country-wise poverty levels and human development. Two such studies are: Global Multidimensional Poverty Index (MPI) and Alkire-Foster Multidimensional Index of Poverty (MPI). Their methodologies are summarised below.

➤ **Global Multidimensional Poverty Index (MPI)**

The Global MPI stands for Multidimensional Poverty Index that is released by Oxford Poverty and Human Development Initiative (OPHI). It was developed by OPHI with the UN Development Programme (UNDP) for inclusion in UNDP's Human Development Report (HDR) in 2010 and it is now part of UNDP's HDRs released annually.

This index measures acute multidimensional poverty across developing countries using various indicators. This study covers over 100 developing countries and complements traditional monetary poverty measures by capturing the acute deprivations in health, education and living standards that a person faces simultaneously.

The MPI assesses poverty at the individual level. If a person is deprived of one-third or more of ten indicators, the global MPI identifies them as 'MPI poor'. The extent or intensity of their poverty is also measured through the percentage of deprivations they are experiencing.

❖ **MPI value:** The incidence of poverty is the proportion of people (within a given population) who are identified as poor on the basis of the multiple deprivations they experience. It is denoted H for headcount ratio.

The intensity of poverty is the average proportion of (weighted) deprivations poor people experience – how poor people are, on average. It is denoted A for average deprivation share.

The MPI value is the product of both these two measures: the multidimensional headcount ratio (H) and the intensity (A), i.e., MPI = H x A.

❖ **Acute poverty:** The global MPI is an adjusted headcount ratio measure designed to measure acute poverty. Acute poverty has two main characteristics:

♦ Firstly, it includes people living under conditions where they do not reach the minimum internationally agreed standards in indicators of basic functionings such as being well-nourished, being able to attend school, or using clean fuel for cooking. In Amartya Sen's "capability approach", functionings are the valuable beings and doings that a person can achieve.

♦ Second, it refers to people living under conditions where they do not reach the minimum standards in several aspects of poverty at the same time.

In other words, the global MPI measures those experiencing multiple joint deprivations – people who, for example, are undernourished, have a school-aged child out of school, do not have safe drinking water, have inadequate sanitation, and lack clean cooking fuel – all at the same time.

❖ **Dimensions and Indicators**

The three dimensions are Health, Education and Living standards. On these, the ten indicators and deprivations in household used in MPI to measure a country's performance are as follows.

- **Health:** Nutrition: An undernourished person under the age 70.

  Child mortality: A child under the age18 has died in five-years preceding the survey for MPI.

- **Education:** Years of Schooling: No eligible household member has completed six years of schooling.

  School Attendance: Any school-aged child is not attending school up to the age at which he/she would complete class 8.

- **Living Standards:** Access to cooking oil, safe drinking water, electricity, proper housing, improved sanitation and the household does not own more than one of these assets: Radio, TV, Telephone, Computer, Animal cart, Bicycle, Motorbike, Refrigerator.

❖ **Salient features of Global MPI:**

♦ The global MPI shows who is poor and how they are considered poor and this helps to create a comprehensive picture of people living in deprivation and poverty.

♦ It permits comparisons both across countries and different regions.

♦ It can also be used to compare position within a country by ethnic group, urban/rural area, sub-national region, and age group, as well as other key household and community characteristics.

♦ For each group and for countries as a whole, the composition of MPI by each of the 10 indicators shows how people are poor.

India ranked 62 among 107 countries in the Global MPI 2020

> *Alkire-Foster (AF) method*

The Alkire-Foster (AF) method adopts multi-dimensional approach which involves counting deprivations that individuals experience at the same time. Building on the Foster-Greer-Thorbecke poverty measures, referred to earlier, this method, developed by Sabina Alkire and James Foster at Oxford University, is a way of measuring multidimensional poverty. It reckons different types of deprivation such as a lack of education or employment, poor health and living standards. These deprivation profiles are analyzed to identify who is poor, and then used to construct a multidimensional index of poverty (MPI).

To identify the poor, the AF method counts the overlapping or simultaneous deprivations that a person or household experiences in different indicators of poverty. The indicators may be equally weighted or take different weights. This method is used to construct the multidimensional index of poverty (MPI) of Oxford Poverty and Human Development Initiative (OPHI).

Bhutan's Gross National Happiness (GNH) Index is a single number index developed from 33 indicators under nine domains based on the Alkire-Foster multi-dimensional methodology. It includes both traditional areas of socio-economic concern such as living standards, health and education and less traditional aspects of culture and psychological well-being.

> **HDR Surveys in India**

India has also issued a National HDR in 2001 and States and Union Territories (UTs) in India have also been bringing out HDRs pertaining to them. This has led to awareness among the States and UTs of the need for development on various socio-economic parameters and has also created a healthy competition among them to perform better.

The National Council of Applied Economic Research (NCAER) had brought out Indian Human Development Survey (IHDS) covering a wide range of indicators in a single survey. The first round (IHDS-1) of the survey was completed in 2004-5 covering 41,554 urban and rural households in all states and union territories of India (except Andaman/Nicobar and Lakshadweep). During 2011-12, the second round (IHDS-II) re-interviewed the same households, creating one of the largest surveys providing a measure of India's economic progress over seven years. The data gathered is made widely available to researchers and wider public.

Besides, Union Ministries of Health and Family Welfare, Education and Census Office put out detailed State-wise data on health, vital statistics, education, etc. which help to assess the progress of States and UTs on these parameters.

❑ FIVE YEAR PLANS AND POVERTY AND INEQUALITY

Before looking into the concept of Poverty Line, its determinants, implications, etc., it would be pertinent to see how the Five Year Plans have viewed the problem. Indian planners cannot be faulted for losing sight of, or for not striving to tackle poverty and inequality. Successive plans have stressed the avowed objective of eradicating poverty, removing inequality, and ensuring equity and social justice (See Box 17.2). If anything, the fault for not having been able to accomplish these objectives to the fullest potential can be ascribed to not having resources commensurate with the magnitude of tasks involved and, to a great extent, to ineffective implementation of well-intentioned policies and gaping loopholes in the delivery mechanism.

Box 17.2 India's Five Year Plans on Inequality, Poverty and Social Justice

First Plan (1951–56): It is no longer possible to think of development as a process merely of increasing the available supplies of material goods; it is necessary to ensure that simultaneously a steady advance is made towards the realization of wider objectives such as full employment and the removal of economic inequalities. Maximum production, full employment, the attainment of economic equality, and social justice which constitute the accepted objectives of planning under present-day conditions are not really so many different ideas but a series of related aims which the country must work for.

Second Plan (1956–61): Our Second Five Year Plan seeks to rebuild rural India, to lay the foundations of industrial progress, to secure to the greatest extent feasible opportunities for weaker and under-privilteged sections of our people, and the balanced development of all parts of the country. For a country whose economic development was long retarded these are difficult tasks but, given the effort and the sacrifice, they are well within our capacity to achieve.

Third Plan (1961–66): The basic objective of India's development must necessarily be to provide the masses of the Indian people the opportunity to lead a good life. That indeed is the objective of all countries for their peoples, even though the good life may be defined in many ways. The more immediate problem is to combat the curse of poverty, with all the ills that it produces, and it is recognized that this can only be done by social and economic advancement, so as to build up a technologically mature society and a social order which offers equal opportunities to all citizens.

Fourth Plan (1969–74): The basic aim is to raise the standard of living of the people, especially of the less privileged sections of the society. Our planning should result not only in an integrated process of increased production, but rational distribution of the added wealth. The overriding inspiration must be a burning sense of social justice. While increased production is of the utmost importance, it is equally important to remove or reduce and prevent the concentration of wealth and economic power. The benefits of development should accrue in increasing measure to the common man and the weaker sections of the society, so that the forces of production can be fully unleashed. A sense of involvement, of participation by the people as a whole, is vital for the success of any plan of rapid economic growth. This can only be evoked by securing social justice, by reducing disparities of income and wealth, and by redressing regional imbalances.

Fifth Plan (1974–79): The objectives in view are removal of poverty and achievement of self-reliance. The strategies relate to growth in the three leading sectors, viz., agriculture, energy and critical intermediates, and the creation of additional employment opportunities.

Sixth Plan (1980–85): While the precise formulation of Plan objectives adopted in successive plans has varied, the essential goals of Indian Planning have been growth, removal of poverty, and achievement of self-reliance.

Seventh Plan (1985–90): Removal of poverty, the building of a modern society making maximum possible use of science and technology, and attainment of self-reliance are the basic objectives of planning in India. The previous Plans have made valuable contribution to the achievement of these national goals.

Eighth Plan (1992–97): The launching of the First Five Year Plan in April 1951 initiated a process of development aimed not only at raising the standard of living of the people, but also opening out to them new opportunities for a richer and more varied life. This was sought to be achieved by planning for growth, modernization, self-reliance, and social justice. We have come a long way over the past forty years. A largely agrarian feudal economy at the time of independence has been transformed into one based on a well developed and a highly diversified infrastructure with immense potential for industrialization. Income and consumption levels have significantly risen. Consumption basket has diversified. Incidence of poverty has visibly declined. The average life expectancy has gone up. The death and the birth rates have declined. Literacy has improved and the educational base has widened.

Ninth Plan (1997–2002): As the millennium draws to a close, the time has come to redouble our efforts at development, especially in the social and economic spheres, so that the country will realize its full economic potential and the poorest and the weakest will be able to shape their destiny in an unfettered manner. This will require not only higher rates of growth of output and employment, but also a special emphasis on all-round human development, with stress on social sectors and a thrust on eradication of poverty.

Tenth Plan (2002–07): The last decade of the 20th century has seen a visible shift in the focus of development planning from the mere expansion of production of goods and services, and the consequent growth of per capita income, to planning for enhancement of human well-being. The notion of human well-being itself is to ensure that the basic material requirements of all sections of the population, especially those below the poverty line, are met and that they have access to basic social services such as health and education. An equitable development process must provide expanding opportunities for advancement to all sections of the population. Equality of outcomes may not be a feasible goal of social justice but equality of opportunity is a goal for which we must all strive.

While in the two decades after the First Plan, India attained self-sufficiency in food production, and despite having one of the largest, subsidized food distribution programme targeted mainly at the vulnerable sections, sizeable sections of the population in the lower rungs, particularly women and children, suffer from malnutrition. While educational facilities did expand, somewhat gradually in the earlier years but at a much faster pace in the last three decades, the expansion, according to many credible surveys, has been more quantitative than qualitative, which again has impacted the poorer sections the most. Inadequacy and frequent absence of teachers, lack of trained teachers, poor buildings, lack of facilities like libraries, labs, and toilets are endemic to schools catering to the poorer sections, both in the urban and rural areas. The same is the case with the domain of public health where the well-equipped hospitals are beyond the reach of the disadvantaged sections who have to depend on ill-equipped and overcrowded government hospitals and community and primary health centres.

Importance of Social and Political Consciousness

That a literate, well-educated, politically conscious, and alert people could exert pressure on the State and its agencies to provide improved delivery of public services is amply proved by the examples of states like Kerala and West Bengal and many Union Territories which have registered progress on social indicators comparable to many developed countries. Sadly, this has been lacking in a majority of other states which are large and much more populous. Illiteracy and incapacity of large sections of people to exert any pressure and assert themselves is exploited by the people's representatives as well as an inefficient and tainted bureaucracy. The net result is that much of the precious, heavy public investments made in the infrastructure and social sectors go down the drain, do not give proper returns, or commensurate benefits to people.

A silver lining in all this dismal picture is that some of the hitherto laggard states have belatedly woken up and are striving to improve services, thanks to some enlightened political and executive leadership. As democracy has matured in India, people even in the urban and rural areas have learnt to assert and overthrow ineffective governments and slothful elected representatives.

With the introduction of technology and computerization in the government at Central, State, and District levels and schemes like Aadhaar, there will be greater transparency in governance and better services to the public. The Digital India programme now under execution, which will connect 250,000 Gram Panchayats electronically, combined with the ubiquitous mobile phones, should help to improve services and bring about a sea change in rural India. See Box 17.3 to know how economists have viewed social welfare over the years.

Box 17.3 Economists and Welfarism

Many of the Classical and latter-day economists have been besieged by issues of poverty, unemployment, and welfare, both individual and social. In his work, 'The Wealth of Nations' (1776), Adam Smith (1723–1790) has spoken of declining economy, unemployment, low standard of living, and the labouring poor. His earlier work, 'The Theory of Moral Sentiments' (1759) provided the ethical and moral foundation for the ideas developed in the more famous 1776 magnum opus. Smith was a precursor of Bentham and John Rawls when he expresses, most emotively, in the 'The Wealth of Nations': "No society can surely be flourishing and happy, of which the far greater part of the members are poor and miserable. It is but equity, besides, that they who feed, clothe and lodge the whole body of the people, should have such a share of the produce of their own labour as to be themselves tolerably well fed, clothed and lodged."

Jeremy Bentham (1748–1832), one of the earliest proponents of 'Utilitarianism' (those who advocated that the aim of the government was the maximization of 'utility' of the community as a whole), came up with the axiom of "the greatest happiness of the greatest number that is the measure of right and wrong". Leon Walras (1834–1910), the French mathematical economist, wrote about distributional justice when he referred to equality of conditions and inequality of position. He distinguished between general social conditions and individual interests. He also emphasized the need for the State to intervene and bring into equilibrium and harmony the rights of the individual and those of the State.

Vilfredo Pareto (1848–1923), an Italian engineer-economist, is famously known for the postulate known as 'Pareto optimal' which indicates the state of an economy in which no one can be made better off without someone being made worse off.

As Amartya Sen explains it in his seminal work, *On Economic Inequality*: "A change implies Pareto-improvement if it makes no one worse off and someone better off. A situation is Pareto optimal if there is no other attainable situation such that a move to it would be Pareto-improvement. That is, Pareto optimality only guarantees that no change is possible such that someone would become better off without making anyone worse off. If the lot of the poor cannot be made any better without cutting into the affluence of the rich, the situation would be Pareto optimal despite the disparity between the rich and the poor."

Sen goes on to illustrate it with a lucid example: "Suppose we are considering the division of a cake. Assuming that each person prefers to have more of the cake rather than less of it, every possible distribution will be Pareto optimal, because any change that makes someone better off is going to make someone else worse off. Since the only issue in this problem is that of distribution, Pareto optimality has no cutting power at all. The almost single-minded concern of modern welfare economics with Pareto optimality does not make that engaging branch of study particularly suitable for investigating problems of inequality."

In a society with gross inequalities and concentration of wealth, promoting economic and social welfare, as modern states are attempting, necessarily requires redistribution of wealth, incomes, and resources from one group to another in varying degrees and proportions. Such redistribution may be effected through fiscal measures—taxation—or through outright legislation as was the case with land reforms when ownership of land, in whole or in part, was transferred from the owners to the tenants. Such redistribution does make some groups worse off while trying to make some others better off. But even with such redistribution, inequalities will tend to persist because when there are additions to wealth and incomes, its distribution would again not be optimal. In reality, perfect equality is an unattainable utopian idea. Inequalities will exist because of differences in endowments, capabilities, social backgrounds, inheritance, etc. of individuals or groups in society. At best, inequality can be minimized but not eliminated.

Pareto's writings gave impetus to many others to focus on welfare economics who came up with divergent views on the subject. Among them were John Hobson (1858–1940), Wesley Mitchell (1874–1948), A.C. Pigou (1877–1959), and other modern economists like John Hicks, Nicholas Kaldor, Paul Samuelson, Amartya Sen, and American philosopher John Rawls (1921–2002).

❑ GLOBAL POVERTY SCENE

Poverty is a worldwide phenomenon cutting across continents. The World Bank has been tracking population living below poverty line fixed on certain criteria. The Bank has reviewed its poverty line threshold and calculation methodologies and revised periodically over the last two decades. In early 1990s, the World Bank had fixed 'absolute poverty line' at $1 per day. This was revised in 1993, to $1.08 a day for all countries on a purchasing power parity (PPP) basis, after adjusting for inflation. In 2005, after studies of cost of living across the world, the World Bank raised it to US$ 1.25 per day on 2005 PPP basis and to $1.90 per day on 2011 PPP basis.

At $1.90 per day on 2011 PPP basis, India had 21.3 per cent of the population below the poverty line.

♦ Decline in Poverty

There has been significant progress on reducing poverty over the past few decades. The world attained the first Millennium Development Goal (MDG) target-to reduce the 1990 poverty rate by half by 2015 five years ahead of schedule, in 2010. Despite this progress, the number of people living in extreme poverty globally remains unacceptably high.

According to the World Bank:

- Less than a tenth of the world's population lives on less than $1.90 a day.
- Close to a quarter of the world's population lives below the $3.20 line; and
- More than 40 per cent of the world's population – almost 3.3 billion people – live below the $5.50 line.

♦ Uneven progress

While poverty rates have declined in all regions, the progress has been uneven. East Asia saw the most dramatic reduction in extreme poverty, from 80 per cent in 1981 to 7.2 per cent in 2012. China accounted for most of the decline in extreme poverty over the past three decades. Between 1981 and 2011, 753 million people moved above the $1.90 a day threshold.

♦ Multidimensional Poverty

As per the Global Multidimensional Poverty Index (MPI), across 107 developing countries, 1.3 billion people – 22 percent – live in multidimensional poverty based on various parameters like education and health standards, proper housing and access to other basic requirements such as nutrition, safe drinking water, sanitation, etc.

About 84.3 per cent of multidimensionally poor people live in Sub-Saharan Africa (558 million) and South Asia (530 million). And 67 per cent of multidimensionally poor people are in middle-income countries.

Every multidimensionally poor person is being left behind in access to basic needs. For example, 803 million multidimensionally poor people live in a household where someone is undernourished, 476 million have an out-of-school child at home, 1.2 billion lack access to clean cooking fuel, 687 million lack electricity and 1.03 billion have substandard housing materials. (See an earlier Section on **Global Multidimensional Poverty Index (MPI)** in this chapter).

♦ COVID-19 pandemic and Poverty

The World Bank has observed that global extreme poverty has risen since 2020, for the first time in over 20 years, as the disruption of the COVID-19 pandemic is compounded by factors like displacement of people due to armed conflicts, climate change and adverse weather events like cyclones, floods, excessive heat, forest fires, etc. which were already slowing the process of poverty reduction.

The COVID-19 pandemic is estimated to push an additional 88 million to 115 million people into extreme poverty, with the total rising to as many as 150 million by 2021, depending on the severity of the pandemic and economic contraction. Extreme poverty, defined as living on less than $1.90 a day, is likely to affect between 9 per cent of the world's population in 2020. Had the pandemic not convulsed the world, the poverty rate was expected to drop to 7.9 per cent in 2020. **(For more on the impact of Covid-19 on India and world at large, see Chapter 19).**

Box 17.4 Economists on Inequality and Distributive Justice

Inequality in society has existed all through the ages and many social thinkers and economists have been troubled by it. Among the economists, David Ricardo (1772–1823), who has made a major contribution to the theory of distribution, in his 1817 work,'The Principles of Political Economy and Taxation' had brought out that the interests of capitalists, landlords, and labour invariably come into conflict. The produce of the earth which is the result of the contribution of land, labour, machinery, and capital is divided among three groups of people, viz., landowners, the labour class, and owners of machinery or capital. But the proportion in which the produce is shared between them as rent, wages, and profits would be different at different stages of the society, as it depended on many variable factors like fertility of the soil, population, skill and productivity of labour, and capital accumulation. Ricardo's writings placed him in the mould of a socialist and his views came to be known as Ricardian socialism.

Many other thinkers like Jean Sismondi (1773–1842), the French economist-philosopher, Saint Simon (1760–1825), Charles Hall (1740–1820), a socialist in Ricardian tradition, and Pierre Proudhon (1809–1865), the French thinker, were all deeply concerned with issues of inequality and fair distribution of wealth. Robert Owen (1771–1858) propagated the concept of 'Co-operation' aimed at fair and just distribution of wealth in a voluntary manner, and William Thompson (1775–1833), an ardent follower of Bentham's utilitarian and welfarist philosophy, also advanced socialist thinking.

It was an era when Europe was in ferment and many thinkers were assailed by the exploitative streaks in society. The writings of Rousseau (1712–1778) and Voltaire (1694–1778) had aroused the consciousness of the vast masses leading to the French Revolution. Many of these thinkers and their egalitarian views were harbingers of Marxism and benign socialism of later years. These ideas have further got crystallized in contemporary times as economic progress throws up troubling issues of gross inequalities, and nations and international agencies are grappling with, and groping to, overcome them.

❑ INEQUALITY AND POVERTY VERSUS GROWTH

Sen-Bhagawati debate on development and poverty alleviation

There is an inherent relationship, or call it conflict or contradiction, between economic growth and equality. While growth can pull people at the bottom of the pyramid out of poverty, it is also bound to lead to inequality in varying degrees depending on endogenous and exogenous factors. For growth results from the contributions of the four basic factors of production–land, labour, capital, and organization–and these are possessed by different sections which may keep changing with time and progress. The resultant fruits of growth get distributed in varying degrees according to the interplay of the control of these factors as Ricardo had forcefully put forth in his writings (See Box 17.4). This inherent conflict is also at the root of the engaging debate between the two eminent Indian economists, Jagdish Bhagwati and Amartya Sen. To root out poverty and lessen inequality, growth is essential, for without growth, the cake to be distributed will not grow. As someone famously said, 'development is not about distribution or division of poverty'. But as with growth inequality may rise, and not all would benefit from it in equal or proportionate or fair measure, some safety nets to protect those left behind in the growth process becomes inevitable.

While Sen believes that India should invest more in its social infrastructure to boost the productivity of its people and thereby raise growth, Bhagwati argues that only a focus on growth can yield enough resources for investing in social sector schemes. Investing in health and education to improve human capabilities is central to Sen's scheme of things. Without such investments, inequality will widen and the growth process itself will falter, Sen believes. Bhagwati argues that growth may raise inequality initially but sustained growth will eventually raise enough resources for the state to redistribute and mitigate the effects of the initial inequality.

In their work '*Why Growth Matters*: *How Economic Growth in India Reduced Poverty and the Lessons for Other Developing Countries*', Bhagwati and Panagariya hold up growth as the panacea for all of India's ills. Whereas Sen and Drèze prescribe state-led redistributive efforts as the solution to India's problems in their '*An Uncertain Glory: India and its Contradictions*'.

According to Bhagawati, India had too few rich and too many poor. Redistribution, in effect, taking money from the rich and distributing it among the poor would have increased their well-being only marginally. Growth had to come first, then "redistribution" from the enhanced revenues. Bhagwati argues that by providing the intellectual foundations for populist excesses and fiscal profligacy that stoke inflation, Sen is actually hurting the life chances of the poor. By arguing for redistribution to precede growth, Sen is putting the cart before the horse.

Sen argues that both growth and welfare programs are needed, and not at the cost of each other. Subsidies that don't aid the poor must go, says Sen. According to Sen, in a developing country like India burdened with poverty, malnutrition, ill-health, etc., focussing obsessively on growth, without making a direct assault on poverty, is not a rational approach.

Bhagwati argued that it is the reforms of 1991 that have made even the lowest social classes greatly more prosperous today. Hence, those reforms must be strengthened. Critiquing the critics of India's growth experience, Bhagwati argued that a low rank on the human development index (HDI) did not mean much.

Commenting on the debate between these two eminent economists, some experts have pointed out that inclusive growth aimed at job creation and measures to lessen inequalities resulting from development would be a balanced approach. There is consensus among economists that while growth is essential, whether the process of growth benefits, or even enriches, some sections leaving out the masses is as crucial as the rate of growth itself. It is also seen that welfare schemes, rather than just growth, have helped to pull people out of poverty in India.

Yet some question whether redistributive welfare schemes work best in alleviating poverty. According to them, the faster rise in farm wages in the past few years, compared to earlier years, was primarily due to the 'pull' effect of growth. The agricultural sector as well as the overall economy grew much faster in the second half of the decade 2000-10 than in the first. The higher growth and consequent increases in construction wages had a greater role in driving up farm wages in recent years than MNREGS, the government-sponsored right to employment scheme operational in rural areas.

Also, the Bhagawati-Sen debate has not paid attention to critical factors like high population growth and fast depleting natural resources and its impact on current and future generations which portend to have serious consequences on development.

In a sense, both Bhagwati and Sen are saying much the same and striving for the same end, except that there may be slight difference in emphasis.

The Asian Development Bank study of 2012, '*Confronting Rising Inequality in Asia*', has drawn attention to this conflict between growth and inequality (See Box 17.5).

Box 17.5 Growth and Inequality–the Asian Experience

The economic growth experience of many countries over time has shown that the fruits of development get distributed inequitably. But that is no reason to sacrifice growth at the altar of equality and fairness because a nation seeking equity to the neglect of growth is bound to stagnate and lag behind, which will only hurt those at the bottom of the pyramid the most. The only pragmatic approach would be to foster growth and work for a skewed distribution of the fruits of development in favour of those who need them the most.

An insightful study by the Asian Development Bank (ADB) carried out in 2012, '*Asian Development Outlook 2012—Confronting Rising Inequality in Asia*', has graphically brought out the gains and challenges of development seen in the Asian economies. While there has been significant growth and achievements in many economies, inequality has also widened. Some of the highlights from the ADB report are cited below.

- Developing Asia had moderate growth of 7.2 per cent in 2011 due to weak global demand. And growth in the region was to ease further before picking up. Asia with 45 countries in Asia-Pacific region grew at 6.2 per cent in 2014 and is expected to grow at 5.8 per cent and 6.0 per cent in 2015 and 2016. One of the reasons for the moderation in growth is the slowdown in China's economy which adversely impacts demand.
- While highlighting the great strides the region has taken in raising living standards and reducing poverty, it has also drawn attention to the surge in income disparities which threaten to undermine that success, and stressed the need to ensure that the benefits of growth are widely shared.
- The region is likely to eradicate absolute poverty by the mid-2020s—i.e., the number of people living on less than $1.25 a day. However, this poverty threshold is insufficient for poor populations in developing member countries to even subsist. More than 1.6 billion people continue to live on less than $2 a day and remain highly vulnerable to frequent economic and environmental shocks and natural hazards. They also confront non-income aspects of poverty, including those related to nutrition, maternal and child health, and gender equality.
- The Gini coefficient for per capita expenditure (with zero indicating absolute equality and 100 absolute inequality on the percentile scale) in India deteriorated from 32.5 in 1993 to 37 in 2010, in China from 32.4 in 1990 to 43.4 in 2008, and in Indonesia from 29 in 1990 to 39 in 2011.
- In India, the urban Gini coefficient grew from 34.4 in 1993 to 39.3 in 2010, much faster than the growth of the rural Gini during the same period, from 28.6 to 30.0. India's urban inequality is higher than rural inequality which is the pattern seen in most developing countries.

- In keeping with the changes in the Gini coefficient, the expenditure shares of the top 1 per cent and 5 per cent of the population in total expenditure increased during the periods under review. In India, the share of the top 1 per cent in total expenditure increased from 6.5 per cent in 1993 to 9 per cent in 2010 and that of the top 5 per cent from 17.7 per cent in 1993 to 21 per cent in 2010. Similar data for China for the period 1995–2008 show that the share of the top 1 per cent of the population rose from 4.6 per cent to 6.4 per cent and that of the top 5 per cent from 17 per cent to 20.5 per cent. Thus, the share of India's top 1 per cent is more than that of China's. These results show that rising inequality is closely associated with very rapid increases in the very top income groups—that is, the rich are getting richer much faster.
- It is also to be noted that income-based inequality measures tend to run higher than expenditure-based ones.
- A 2011 study by the Organization for Economic Co-operation and Development (OECD) reports that in many OECD countries, household incomes increased much faster at the top income ranges from the mid-1990s to the late 2000s, similar to the experiences of many developing Asian countries.
- Yet another disquieting feature is that inequality in the distribution of wealth and assets is much higher than income or expenditure inequality. India's Gini coefficient for wealth distribution is about 65 which is higher than that of China.
- And inequalities, including gender inequalities, of opportunities and access to many basic facilities—education, health, housing, jobs, etc. in developing countries are even more glaring and they tend to aggravate further income and wealth inequalities over time. Asia and the Pacific region faces widening inequalities in income and access to economic and social opportunities.

❑ ESTIMATION OF POVERTY AND IDENTIFICATION OF POVERTY LINE

Several Indian economists have carried out studies of poverty levels in India and arrived at some estimation. Prior to independence, Dadabhai Naoroji, who was a bitter critic of Britain for draining away India's wealth, had made pioneering studies about poverty in India and made some estimations of per capita income (PCI). Naoroji calculated PCI in Bombay Presidency for 1867–70 to be ₹ 20 whereas the income needed for bare subsistence then was ₹ 34. He observed that while the upper classes had much higher income, the poor masses could barely make both ends meet and were poverty-stricken. Though Naoroji's study lacked some details and had flaws in the methodology, Dr. V.K.R.V. Rao who had examined the study later defended him and stated that the results obtained by Naoroji were based on data used by a government commission and hence it was to be accepted as authoritative.

Soon after independence, India passed the Minimum Wages Act, 1948 which laid down that minimum wages must be paid to skilled and unskilled labour that would be sufficient not only for the bare sustenance of life, but for the preservation of the efficiency of the worker and be adequate for some measure of education, medical requirements, and amenities. Thus, India was conscious, even in the early days, of the need to protect the interests of the working classes.

Working Group on Minimum Standard of Living

Debate had begun from the late 1950's as to who constituted the 'poor' in India and on how to identify them. The Indian Labour Conference 1957 brought the issue to the fore in connection with principles of wage fixation. The question of defining the poverty threshold was raised. The task of identifying a poverty threshold was entrusted in 1962 to a Working Group consisting of eminent economists and social scientists. The Working Group comprised Prof. D.R. Gadgil, Dr. B.N. Ganguli, Dr. P.S. Lokanathan, M.R. Masani, Ashok Mehta, Pitambar Pant, and Dr. V.K.R.V. Rao, among others. Taking into consideration the recommendations of a Nutrition Advisory Committee of the Indian Council of Medical Research (ICMR) on balanced diet, and after much deliberations on a minimum standard of living, the Group recommended as follows:

(i) The national minimum for each household of 5 persons (4 adult consumption units) should be not less than ₹ 100 per month at 1960–61 prices or ₹ 20 per capita. For urban areas, this figure will have to be raised to
₹ 125 per month per household or ₹ 25 per capita to cover the higher prices of the physical volume of commodities on which the national minimum is calculated.

(ii) This national minimum excludes expenditure on health and education, both of which are expected to be provided by the State according to the Constitution and in the light of its other commitments.

(iii) An element of subsidy in urban housing will have to be included after taking ₹ 10 per month, or 10 per cent as the rent element payable from the proposed national minimum of ₹ 100 per month.

Early Studies on Poverty

Economists V.M. Dandekar and N. Rath who carried out a study on poverty argued for defining the poverty line based on minimum income required for nutritional diet and other essential needs. They suggested an average of 2,250 calories per capita daily as a minimum nutitional norm for both rural and urban areas. While the Planning Commission had adopted ₹ 240 per capita at 1960–61 prices as the minimum for annual household expenditure, Dandekar and Rath recommended a minimum of ₹ 180 per capita per annum for rural population and ₹ 270 per head per annum for urban population.

The early 1970s generated much interest in studies on poverty. By then, more data and sophisticated methodology had become available. P.K. Bardhan, B.S. Minhas, and Montek S. Ahluwalia undertook studies on rural poverty which brought out the close linkage between agricultural performance and rural incomes and rural distress.

Development economists in India and abroad and the World Bank and other aid agencies began to take interest in the issue. It was also felt that besides developmental agenda, considering the deep and pervasive nature of poverty, there was need to take up programmes for direct assault on poverty.

Task Force Report

A 1979 Task Force of the Perspective Planning Division prepared a report on 'Projections of Minimum Needs and Effective Consumption Demand' bringing together the results of some of the earlier studies and attempted to redefine the poverty line. The methodology as formulated by the Task Force has since then been used by the Planning Commission in estimating the incidence of poverty. The Task Force identified the poverty line as the per capita expenditure at which the average daily per capita calorie intake was 2,435 in rural areas and 2,095 calories in urban areas. Based on the consumption pattern prevalent in 1973–74, the group recommended monthly per capita expenditure of ₹ 49.09 for daily intake of 2,400 calories in rural areas and monthly per capita expenditure of ₹ 56.64 for daily intake of 2,100 calories in urban areas.

Deficiencies in the approach

The above approach based on calorie consumption and nutritional requirement had certain deficiencies:

- Poverty line derived from personal consumption patterns and levels does not take into account inter-personal differences of consumption behaviour.
- It does not cover other social needs such as basic education and health, drinking water supply, sanitation, environmental standards, etc.
- As the poverty line is based on consumption, and not income, it does not reflect dependence on debt, use of common property resources, and informal social security.
- The head-count ratio based on the poverty line does not capture the severity of poverty and differences among groups below the poverty line–between those just below the poverty line and those further down who will be far worse off.
- While adopting a common commodity basket can be justified, ignoring differences in price levels between states and between urban and rural areas and price fluctuations is not in order, since the income required to meet consumption expenditure is a function of the price levels.

NSS Surveys

Successive rounds of National Sample Surveys (NSS) of household consumer expenditure in the 1970's have shown that nearly 50 per cent of the Indian population has been living below the poverty line over a long period. Table 17.1 gives the figures of two successive rounds of National Sample Survey.

Table 17.1 Population below Poverty line in 1972–73 and 1977–78 (in percentage)

Area	1972–73	1977–78
Rural	54.09	50.82
Urban	41.22	38.19
All India	51.49	48.13

Source: Sixth Five Year Plan (1980–85), Planning Commission.

Thus, the percentage of rural population below the poverty line came down from 54 in 1972–73 to 51 in 1977–78–not a very significant change. The total percentage was also hovering around 50. On the basis of the revised population estimates according to 1981 census, the figures of population below poverty line in 1979–80 were revised and worked out to 51.1 per cent (nearly 339 million persons in absolute terms). These figures were unacceptably high. During the 1970's, the share of the bottom 30 per cent of the population in consumer expenditure showed a slight deterioration.

Angus Deaton on India's Poverty

Prof. Angus Deaton, who was awarded Nobel Prize in Economics for his contribution to analytical study of consumption, poverty, and welfare, has been a keen observer of India's poverty scene and a prolific scholar on consumption, healthcare, and welfare of the poor in India. He had pointed out how a price index dominated by cereals understated poverty when demand has shifted to non-cereals whose prices rose faster than that of cereals. Cereals' prices have increased much less than non-cereals' prices between

1973–74 and 2004–05 which justifies Deaton's observation about underestimation in the inflation rate of food, particularly in the rural poverty line calculations, compared to inflation rates obtained from the NSSO consumption expenditure surveys.

According to Deaton, poverty rate has declined whatever measure we may use but much more slowly than growth in GDP or aggregate consumption seem to warrant. Also, there is conflict between consumption figures of National Accounts Statistics (NAS) and those from household surveys by National Sample Surveys (NSS). In spite of increase in real income and consumption growth even among the poor, health issues like malnutrition, stunted growth of children, etc. persist though some economists have questioned the validity of these observations. Deaton argues that schemes like employment guarantee are needed even as rapid growth transforms society.

1989 Expert Group

An Expert Group on 'Estimation of Proportion and Number of Poor' was constituted in September 1989 under the Chairmanship of Prof. D.T. Lakdawala which submitted its report in 1993 (See Table 17.2). The Group recommended as follows:

1. The Poverty Line recommended by the Task Force on projection of minimum needs and effective consumption demand, namely a monthly per capita total expenditure of ₹ 49.09 (rural) and ₹ 56.64 (urban) rounded off to ₹ 49 and ₹ 57 at all India level at 1973–74 prices be adopted as the base line. This was anchored in the recommended per capita daily intake of 2,400 calories in rural areas and 2,100 calories in urban areas with reference to the consumption pattern as obtained in 1973–74. The Group recommended that these norms may be adopted uniformly for all States.
2. Poverty estimates will vary according to the base year chosen for defining the Poverty line. Since much systematic work had already been done with the base 1973–74, the Group proposed to continue with the same base year for estimating the poverty line.
3. State-specific poverty line was to be estimated. The standardized commodity basket corresponding to the poverty line at the national level would be valued at the prices prevailing in each State in the base year, i.e., 1973–74. For updating poverty line to the current prices in a given year, State-specific consumer price-index would be worked out.

Table 17.2 (a): Poverty Ratio and Number of Poor: Expert Group (Lakdawala) Method

Year	No. of Poor (in millions)			Percentage of Total Population		
	Rural	Urban	Total	Rural	Urban	Total
1973–74	261.3	60.0	321.3	56.4	49.0	54.9
1977–78	264.3	64.6	328.9	53.1	45.2	51.3
1983	252.0	70.9	322.9	45.7	40.8	44.5
1987–88	231.9	75.2	307.1	39.1	38.2	38.9
1993–94	244.0	76.3	320.3	37.3	32.4	36.0
2004–05	220.9	80.8	301.7	28.3	25.7	27.5

Source: Report of the Expert Group (Dr. C. Rangarajan) to Review the Methodology for Measurement of Poverty, June 2014.

The percentage of population below poverty line has steadily come down from 54.9 per cent to 38.9 per cent between 1973–74 and 1987–88. The number of poor, in absolute terms, has shown increase, apparently due to the growing population. The increase in urban poor would also have been due to migration from rural to urban areas. For detailed state-wise data on population below Poverty line, see Table 4 on pp. ST. 4.5 in statistical tables.

❑ EXPERT GROUPS ON METHODOLOGY FOR ESTIMATION OF POVERTY

There was growing concern on the accuracy of official estimates of poverty released by the Planning Commission. The official poverty estimates have been severely criticized on various counts, particularly that the poverty lines (threshold) fixed were unrealistic and thus the poverty ratios were much understated. In view of this, Planning Commission set up an expert group under the chairmanship of Professor Suresh Tendulkar in 2005 to examine the issue and suggest a new poverty line and estimate. Another Expert Group was set up in 2014, headed by Dr. C. Rangarajan, to review the methodology adopted by the Expert Group under Tendulkar. The methodology adopted by these two Groups for estimation of poverty are discussed in this section. The two Groups are referred as Expert Group (T) for Tendulkar Group and Expert Group (R) for the Rangarajan Group.

The poverty lines defined by the Tendulkar Committee did not reflect the changing times and aspirations of the people. The high rate of increase in per capita income and consumption in the first decade of this century and the consequential changes in the structure of the economy as well as in people's perspectives on poverty warranted a fresh look at the poverty line and its composition. This was the backdrop to the setting up of the Expert Group (Rangarajan).

1. The Expert Group (T) used all-India urban poverty line basket as the reference to derive state-level rural and urban poverty. This was a departure from the earlier practice of using two separate poverty line baskets for rural and urban areas. The Expert Group (R) reverted to the practice of having separate all-India rural and urban poverty basket lines and deriving state-level rural and urban estimates from these.
2. The Expert Group (T) had decided not to anchor the poverty line to the then available official calorie norms used in all poverty estimations since 1979 as it found a poor correlation between food consumed and nutrition outcomes. On a review of subsequent research, the Expert Group (R) was of the view that deriving the food component of the poverty line basket by reference to the simultaneous satisfaction of all nutrient norms would be appropriate considering the full range of policies and programmes for child-nutrition support and on public provisioning of a range of public goods and services for the amelioration of the environmental diseases facing the population.
3. Estimates of consumption expenditure seen in the National Accounts Statistics (NAS) and as inferred from the sample surveys of the National Sample Survey Organisation (NSSO) show a large and growing variance. The Expert Group (R) preferred NSSO's estimates and decided not to use the NAS estimates. This is in line with the approach adopted by Expert Group (Lakdawala) and Expert Group (T).
4. The capture of spatial and temporal variation in prices in estimating the State-level and rural-urban poverty levels (given all-India rural and urban estimates) has undergone substantial refinement since 1979. The Expert Group (R) agreed with the methodology adopted by the Expert Group (T) on this.

The New Poverty Line and Estimate

The new poverty line worked out by the Expert Group (R) came to monthly per capita consumption expenditure of ₹ 972 in rural areas and ₹ 1,407 in urban areas in 2011–12. For a family of five, this translates into a monthly consumption expenditure of ₹ 4,860 in rural areas and ₹ 7,035 in urban areas. Compared to the poverty lines based on the methodology of the Expert Group (T), the poverty lines estimated by the Expert Group (R) are 19 per cent and 41 per cent higher in rural and urban areas, respectively.

The Expert Group (R) estimated that the 30.9 per cent of the rural population and 26.4 per cent of the urban population was below the poverty line in 2011–12. The all-India ratio was 29.5 per cent. In rural India, 260.5 million individuals were below poverty line and in urban India 102.5 million were under poverty line. Totally, 363 million were below poverty in 2011–12. (See Table 17.2 (b).

Table 17.2 (b): Poverty Estimates in 2009-10 and 2011-12

Year	Poverty Ratio			No. of Poor (Million)		
	Rural	Urban	Total	Rural	Urban	Total
Expert Group (Tendulkar)						
2009-10	33.8	20.9	29.8	278.2	76.5	354.7
2011-12	25.7	13.7	21.9	216.7	53.1	269.8
Reduction (% Points)	252.0	70.9	322.9	45.7	40.8	44.5
Expert Group (Rangarajan)						
2009-10	39.6	35.1	38.2	325.9	128.7	454.6
2011-12	30.9	26.4	29.5	260.5	102.5	363.0
Reduction (% Points)	8.7	8.7	8.7	65.4	26.2	91.6

Source: Report of the Rangarajan Expert Group to review the Methodology for Measurement of poverty, Planning Commission, Government of India (2014).

According to Rangarajan Group, the poverty ratio has declined from 39.6 per cent in 2009–10 to 30.9 per cent in 2011–12 in rural India and from 35.1 per cent to 26.4 per cent in urban India. The decline was thus a uniform 8.7 percentage points over the two years. The all-India poverty ratio fell from 38.2 per cent to 29.5 per cent. Totally, 91.6 million individuals were lifted out of poverty during this period. NITI Aayog proposes to have a fresh look at the poverty line and assess the results of poverty alleviation measures.

❑ POVERTY ALLEVIATION MEASURES

The high incidence of poverty, both in rural and urban India, has been a matter of grave concern. As shown in Box 17.2, successive Five Year Plans had emphasized eradication of poverty as one of the primary goals of development. From time to time, India has drawn up and implemented many poverty alleviation and employment schemes to help the vulnerable sections. Besides, Central and State governments have been running large scale subsidized schemes like Public Distribution System (PDS), free mid-day meals to school children, etc. Some of these schemes are discussed here. (See also Box 17.7 Universal Basic Income).

Integrated Rural Development Programme (IRDP)

The bulk of the 'Below Poverty Line' (BPL) population are in rural areas—they are agricultural labour, small and marginal farmers, and casual workers engaged in non-agricultural activities. Small land holdings, low productivity, poor educational base, and lack of other vocational skills perpetuate poverty. Due to the poor physical and social capital base, most of them are forced to seek employment in vocations with extremely low levels of productivity and wages. The creation of employment opportunities for the unskilled workforce has been a major challenge.

Against this background, anti-poverty programmes that seek to transfer assets and skills to people for self-employment, combined with public works programmes to enable people to cope with transient poverty, has been an important plank in anti-poverty strategy. As part of rural poverty alleviation programmes, schemes were drawn up directly targeted at the poor rural households. The major programmes of this Ministry that directly targeted poor families for creation of assets, skill development, and self-employment started with Integrated Rural Development Programme (IRDP) in the year 1980. It included several other programmes like the Training of Rural Youth for Self Employment (TRYSEM), Development of Women and Children in Rural Areas (DWCRA), Supply of Improved Toolkits to Rural Artisans (SITRA), Ganga KalyanYojana (GKY), and the Million Wells Scheme (MWS). Due to multiplicity of programmes, which operated more as separate, stand-alone schemes, the desired linkages could not be established among them effectively. They functioned more with individual programme targets in view, rather than focusing on the more critical issue of sustainable income generation.

Wage Employment Programmes

Wage employment programmes have been an important component of the anti-poverty strategy. In rural areas, they not only provide employment opportunities during lean agricultural seasons but also in times of floods, droughts, and other natural calamities. These schemes create rural infrastructure which supports further economic activity. The National Rural Employment Programme (NREP) and Rural Landless Employment Guarantee Programme (RLEGP) were started in the Sixth (1980-85) and Seventh (1985-90) Plans.

Later, based on the recommendations of the Planning Commission, in April 1999, the various schemes were merged into a single self-employment programme called the "Swarnajayanti Gram Swarozgar Yojana" (SGSY), to be implemented by the States. SGSY had the objective of improving the family incomes of the rural poor and it proved to be more effective. Several Self-Help Groups (SHGs), particularly run by women, were formed all over India and it helped these groups to take up income generating activities. Necessary financial aid was extended through bank credits.

Between 1999 and 2010, about 3.68 million SHGs were formed and 8.74 million SHG Swarozgaris and 4.09 million individual Swarozgaris were given financial assistance under the programme. A major spin-off of the programme was that it helped to create a sense of economic independence among the women thus benefitting their families, and further the cause of women's empowerment. An example of this can be seen in the 'Kudumbasree' (which translates into 'family welfare') programme being successfully run in Kerala for several years. Similar programmes have been run in other states too.

In 2001, another programme called the "Sampoorna Gramin Rozgar Yojana" (SGRY) was introduced with the aim of generating wage employment, creation of durable economic infrastructure in rural areas, and provision of food and nutrition security to the poor.

National Rural Livelihoods Mission (NRLM)

The NRLM mission, later known as "Aajeevika" was launched in 2011 and is implemented by the Union Ministry of Rural Development (MoRD) in partnership with the State governments. The scheme has since been renamed as 'Deendayal Antyodaya Yojana'- National Rural Livelihoods Mission (DAY-NRLM).

Objectives of the scheme:

- Reducing poverty through promotion of diversified and gainful self-employment.
- Providing skilled wage employment opportunities resulting in appreciable increase in incomes of the rural poor on sustainable basis.
- To strengthen community institutions which are in turn expected to promote the livelihoods of the rural poor.
- It seeks to reach out to all rural poor households in a phased manner and impact their livelihoods significantly by 2024-25.
- To impact 9 to 10 crore rural poor households spread across over 646 districts, 2.38 lakh gram panchayats covering about 6.4 lakh villages across 28 states and 6 Union Territories.

♦ **Financial assistance:** NRLM has made a major departure from the erstwhile SGSY scheme by abolishing "capital subsidy". To strengthen the financial base of the community institutions engaged in NRLM and enable them to undertake livelihood activities, capital support is provided so that the fund remains with them in perpetuity from which the members could borrow for their consumption and investment requirements and repay at convenient rate of interest in easy instalments. This motivates them to build their institutional and financial management capacity and prove their track record to attract mainstream bank finance.

♦ **Farm Livelihoods and Role of Women SHGs:** The "Farm Livelihoods" interventions under NRLM are designed to diversify income sources, mitigate fluctuations in income and assure sustainable income along with food and nutritional security at the household level. These interventions touch women in SHGs through one or more of its programmatic pillars, viz. -Mahila Kisan Sashaktikaran Pariyojana (MKSP).

♦ **Role during Pandemic:** Since inception, women SHGs are playing an important role in the mission. These SHGs and their federations have initiated numerous activities to support the poor and needy members and the rural community at large. This was evident from the role they played in the aftermath of COVID-19 pandemic and the lockdowns. Based on advisories issued by the Ministries of Health and Family Welfare, Consumers Affairs and State Health Departments women SHG members took the initiative to mass produce masks, sanitizers, hand wash, protective gears, etc., run community kitchen with supplies of ration, fruits and vegetables and provide them to the poor and needy. The sum of ₹30,956 crore transferred under the PM Garib Kalyan Yojana (PMGKY) to Jan Dhan Yojana accounts benefited 20.65 crore women. In these efforts, the Banking Correspondence Sakhis (BC Sakhi) supported under NRLM have played a significant role.

♦ **Credit for SHGs:** The credit accessed by SHGs increased from ₹22,238 crore in 2013-14 to ₹70,789 crore by March 2020. Cumulatively, ₹3.47 lakh crore worth of bank credit has been leveraged by the SHGs since FY 2013-14.

National Rural Employment Guarantee Scheme (NREGS)

A landmark development in the plan for poverty alleviation was the enactment of the National Rural Employment Guarantee (NREG) Act in 2005 by merging then ongoing schemes of Jawahar Gram Samridhi Yojana (JGSY), Employment Assurance Scheme (EAS), and Sampoorna Grameen Rojgar Yojana (SGRY). NREG (later renamed as Mahatma Gandhi NREG) programme aims at enhancing the livelihood security of the people in rural areas by guaranteeing one hundred days of wage employment in a financial year to every rural household whose members volunteer to do unskilled manual work. The second objective of the Act is to create durable assets in rural areas and strengthen the livelihood resource base of the rural poor.

The private sector has also been involved in designing special projects for capacity building of the poor for wage employment. The convergence of SGSY and other development programmes with MNREGS would strengthen the self-employment initiatives through value addition. Graduation of unskilled MNREGS workers into skilled labour force is an integral part of the strategy for poverty eradication on a sustainable basis.

Box 17.6 MNREGS – An Assessment of the Programme

♦ **Primary objective**

A primary objective of Mahatma Gandhi National Rural Employment Guarantee Scheme (MNREGS) being to provide livelihood security to poor households in rural India, the thrust is on ensuring that agricultural labourers earn higher wages and improve their well-being during the lean agricultural season. Its main focus is to create durable assets such as farm ponds, dug wells, goat shed, poultry shed, support for dairy shed and water conservation. The scheme has been a major source of strengthening livelihood security of rural population in a transparent manner with people's participation.

Various field studies have shown the sheer transformation and positive impact that the scheme has had on rural incomes – especially of small/marginal farmers and also agricultural families having only homesteads through creation of assets at the individual household level.

♦ **Transformation of rural economy**

The rural economy has also been undergoing a major transformation and is now very different from what it was many years ago. Data from CSO and NITI Aayog research has shown that half of manufacturing and construction and one fourth of services sector income are now part of the rural economy. This shows rising scope and vast opportunities for raising income of farmers through farm and non-farm linkages.

♦ **Increasing acreage and Crop diversification**

The most tangible effect of individual asset creation through MNREGS was increased crop acreages. This involves land levelling and fallow/wasteland development, with the higher planted area being mostly in traditional food grains. The average dug well, farm pond or mud/field bund have helped boost crop acreage. Irrigation assets have also resulted in augmenting yields and aiding crop diversification, particularly cultivation of vegetables, oilseeds and cotton. Beneficiary households have reported substantial increases in gross incomes from fish ponds and animal sheds.

This suggests that creation of assets under MNREGS, through a decentralised production-centric approach, helps in raising farmers' income. Land development and irrigation assets created on the lands of small and marginal farmers can, indeed, confer the triple benefits of increased acreages, higher yields and crop diversification.

♦ **Natural Resource Management and its Benefits**

Natural Resource Management (NRM) has become an important component of MNREGS to promote sustainable livelihoods for the poor. It focusses on the creation of natural resource assets (both community and individual assets). The beneficiary households have reported several types of benefits being derived from the NRM assets created in NREGS.

- Increase in irrigation potential was reported as the prime benefit from the creation of community assets. Beneficiaries experienced increase in ground water table.
- NRM assets have helped small and marginal farmers to improve livelihood opportunities.
- Significant proportion of household beneficiaries found that access to water for livestock has increased. These are important factors contributing to sustainability of rural livelihood of small and marginal farmers.

♦ Performance and Funding: Considering the manifold benefits of MNREGS for rural households, successive governments have been committed to ensure effective implementation of the scheme. Over the years from its inception in 2005, the scheme has seen many refinements to remove deficiencies and plug loopholes in it.

This commitment is reflected in substantial allocation in budget and number of households which have been benefited and person-days of employment generated over the years under the scheme. (See Tables 17.3 (a) and 17.3 (b). The allocation in 2020-21 was much higher due to the Covid-19 pandemic which forced many migrant labour to return to their villages and needed employment support as they had lost their jobs in cities. The MNREGS came handy to provide them work in the villages and hence the higher allocation.

(See also section on **MNREGS and Rural wages** below)

Table 17.3 (a): Performance under Mahatma Gandhi National Rural Employment Guarantee Scheme (MNREGS)

Year	2006–07	2007–08	2008–09	2009–10	2010–11	2011–12
Households Provided Employment (no. in crore)	2.10	4.51	5.49	3.63	5.12	6.9
Person-days of Employment Generated (in crore)	90.5	216.32	257.15	235.14	235.6	305.71

Source: Ministry of Rural Development, Annual Reports.

Table 17.3 (b): Budget Allocation for MNREG scheme (₹ in crore)

2011-12	31,000	2017-18	55,167
2014-15	33,000	2018-19	61,084
2015-16	37,346	2020-21	1,10,000
2016-17	48,220	2021-22	73,000

Source: Report of the Sub-Group of Chief Ministers on Co-ordination of Agriculture and MNREGS and Ministry of Rural development, Annual Reports.

MNREGS and Rural wages

The impact of MNREG scheme on rural wages and farmers' income has engaged the attention of policy makers as well as experts and researchers. The primary objective of MNREGS is to provide livelihood security to poor rural households and ensuring that agricultural labourers earn higher wages to secure their well-being during the lean agricultural season.

While farmers' income needs to be protected, the rights of labourers cannot also be compromised. While examining the issue of wages of agricultural labour, it has been found that farmers are having to pay higher wages on account of rising wages under MNREG scheme. The seasonality in demand for work under MGNREGA indicates that during peak agricultural season wage rates are already high.

MNREGS and Labour supply: One of the criticisms of MNREGS is the negative impact it has on agriculture in terms of creating labor scarcity during peak season, leading to higher wage rates and non-availability of hired labor to perform critical farm operations. This is because of diversion of rural farm labor to MGNREGA works as wage rates for MGNREGA are higher than the prevailing farm wages.

MNREGS may not be the sole reason for labour shortage. Rural workers are engaged in multiple occupations. Most of the small and marginal farmers participate in both farm and non-farm activities. As pointed out earlier (in Box 17.6), the rural economy today is very different from what it was many years ago. Studies by NITI Aayog and data from CSO have shown that half of manufacturing and construction and one fourth of services sector income now comes from the rural economy. This shows rising scope and vast opportunities for raising income of farmers through farm and non-farm linkages.

As the shortage of male labour for farm work increased, there was greater participation of female labor in some states and in major crop cultivation which shows trend towards feminization of labour. At the same time, the proportion of hired labour has reduced much faster rate than the family labor with the adoption of farm mechanization. There has been drop in the area under cultivation of crops like paddy, rabi sorghum, maize and cotton which are highly labor intensive.

Rural wages and Farmers' income: The share of value of output that is to be paid as wages to labour is a matter of concern to farmers. Tight labor supply along with the higher MGNREGA wages would cause farm wages to rise significantly leading to increased cost of production and squeezing net returns to the famers.

CSO data at national level has shown that wage bill paid to hired labour in agriculture increased in tandem with the increase in the cost of other inputs used in agriculture. Wages paid by farmers as a proportion of the total cost of inputs, including wages for hired labour, started showing increase with the implementation of MGNREGS in 2005.

Share of wage bill in cost increased from 32 per cent during 2004-05 to 36.8 per cent during 2011-12 and stagnated at this level. This change is consistent with the trend in real wage rate. But what matters more for the farmers is what share of value of output is to be paid as wage bill to labour. This share shows a small increase from 13.0 per cent during 2004-05 to 13.8 per cent during 2010-11, and thereafter returned to same level by 2016-17 as prevailed during 2004-05. This indicates that MGNREG did not cause adverse effect on farmers' income in medium to long term despite rise in real wages in rural India though there may be variations in states in respect of this trend. The reason for this is that the period of high increase in wages also experienced high increase in prices of agricultural commodities which benefited farmers and cushioned the impact of rise in wages.

Nominal and Real wages: As nominal wages increased faster than Consumer Price Index (AL-for agricultural labour) for a couple of years after implementation of MNREGS, the real wages in rural India increased during the period 2008-9 to 2014-15 and stabilized thereafter. After the MNREGS lifted low wage rate to a reasonably higher level, there was near stagnation in real rural wages over the last few years.

The rise in nominal wages of agriculture labour is very strongly linked to food inflation. Since food inflation has been low in the last few years, the increase in nominal wages has also been modest.

(Nominal wage is the wage measured in money (say, rupees) while real wage is the wage in terms of goods and services that a worker could purchase from the nominal wage. The real wage is the nominal wage in an economy adjusted for changes in purchasing power. If the wages of workers remain the same as the prices go up, the real wages come down).

Rural Housing Programme

Initiated in 1985–86, the Indira Awas Yojana (IAY) is the core programme for providing free housing to BPL families in rural areas and targets SC/STs households and freed bonded labourers. It was first merged with the JRY in 1989 and then converted into a separate housing scheme for the rural poor in 1996. The Ninth Plan (1997–2002) Housing Programme under IAY was recast in the light of the National Housing and Habitat Policy 1998, which set an ambitious target of providing shelter for all in the rural areas by the end of the Plan period. The IAY helps BPL households to build their houses and upgrade old houses. The scheme has been continued through subsequent Plans. Since inception, about 252.4 lakh houses were either constructed or upgraded as on March 2012.

- **Pradhan Mantri Awaas Yojana – Gramin (PMAY-G):** In 2016, the Government re-structured IAY and launched the scheme PMAY-G to provide "Housing for All" by 2022. The scheme aims at providing a pucca house, with basic amenities, to all houseless householders and those households living in kutcha and dilapidated house by 2022. The immediate the objective was to cover one crore households living in kutcha house/dilapidated house in three years from 2016-17 to 2018- 19.

The minimum size of the house has been increased to 25 sq.mt (from 20 sq.mt) with a hygienic cooking space. The unit assistance has been increased from ₹70,000 to ₹1.20 lakh in plain and from ₹75,000 to ₹1.30 lakh in hilly states, difficult areas. The beneficiary is entitled to 90.95 person-day of unskilled labour from MGNREGS. The assistance for construction of toilet shall be leveraged though convergence with SBM-G, MNREGS or any other dedicated the source of funding. Convergence of other government programmers like piped drinking water, electricity connection, LPG gas connection, etc. is also being attempted.

Pradhan Mantri Awas Yojana (Urban): A similar scheme has been launched to address 'Housing for All' in urban areas also. About 4,331 cities/towns have been included under PMAY (U). (On this, see under section "Urban Anti-Poverty Measures" further down in this chapter).

By June September 2021, a total of 2.05 crore houses have been provided under these schemes.

Prime Minister's Gram Sadak Yojana (PMGSY)

This is an important rural infrastructure–village road connectivity–programme for linking villages with the nearest town. Over the last decade and a half, the PMGSY has carved out a place for itself as a programme characterized by creation of good quality assets, effective management, and technical proficiency by the National Rural Road Development Agency (NRRDA), along with capable state road agencies.

Under the PMGSY, more than 4.50 lakh kilometres of all-weather rural roads have been constructed, targeting more than 1.67 lakh unconnected habitations with a population of more than 500 persons in plain areas and 250 persons in hilly areas, deserts, and tribal areas. To sustain the benefits arising from this improved connectivity, NRRDA with funding support from respective states, has also introduced a mechanism of integrated five-year maintenance of the roads constructed or upgraded under PMGSY. This programme has helped to rejuvenate not only agriculture, but all other economic and social activities in rural areas by enabling convenient and efficient transportation of people and goods.

According to Ministry of Rural Development Annual Report for 2020-21, against 1,78,184 eligible habitations of 250+ and 500+ population criteria identified for coverage under the scheme, 16,086 habitations have been provided connectivity by the States out of their own resources and 4,655 habitations have either been dropped or have not been found feasible. Out of the balance 1,57,443 habitations sanctioned for providing connectivity under the PMGSY, 1,53,918 have already been covered. Further construction and upgradation of existing village roads is in progress. Special focus is given on consolidation of existing Through Routes and Major Rural Links that connect habitations to Gramin Agricultural Markets (GrAMs), Higher Secondary Schools and Hospitals.

This is significant considering that contrary to the common perception about predominance of agriculture in rural economy, about two-third of rural income is now generated in non-agricultural activities and more than half of the value added in manufacturing sector in India is contributed by rural areas as observed in a NITI Aayog paper on "Changing Structure of Rural Economy of India: Implications for Employment and Growth".

Other Rural Programmes

Other rural development programmes such as Integrated Watershed Development Programme (IWDP), Drought Prone Areas Programme (DPAP), and Desert Development Programme (DDP) have also been helpful in improving conditions in rural areas and alleviating rural distress.

Urban Anti-Poverty Measures

As with rural poverty, poverty in urban areas has also been a challenging problem. There is a concentration of the urban population in large cities and existing urban agglomerations. As per census 2011, there are 53 million-plus cities accounting for about 43 per cent of India's urban population. Providing proper housing and sanitation facilities, apart from suitable job opportunities for the urban poor are the biggest challenges. People living in overcrowded slums in unhygienic and unhealthy environment face health hazards. Their social conditions, like quality education for children and access to good health facilities, are anything but satisfactory.

According to NSSO report (2004-05), the number of urban poor has increased by 34.4 per cent between 1973 and 2004. As unemployment rates are high, there is imperative need to create adequate jobs in the urban sector. The Jawaharlal Nehru National Urban Renewal Mission (JNNURM) was launched in 2005 for a period of seven years with an outlay of ₹66,085 crore and with an overall commitment of '₹1.23 lakh crore. The scheme aimed at empowering Urban Local Bodies, planned and holistic development of cities, and making them inclusive. City development plans and urban reforms at State and Municipal levels were also envisaged under the programme.

Swarna Jayanti Sahari Rozgar Yojana (SJSRY) was designed to help urban poor to get gainful employment. The scheme covered 3,941 towns and assistance of ₹3,360 crore was released. Since inception, 12.3 lakh persons have been imparted training under the scheme. For making India free of slums, a pilot phase of Rajiv Awas Yojana was launched in 2011 for in-situ rehabilitation of slums and give legal property rights to slum dwellers. Construction of toilets in place of dry latrines to end scavenging was also taken up. Under the Integrated Low Cost Sanitation (ILCS) scheme, 2.5 lakh dry latrines were converted into the sanitary type and about 1.55 new toilets have been sanctioned.

A major thrust was given to improving transport network in urban centres. Improvements in public transport, including building of freeways, flyovers for easing traffic congestion, and Metro rail system in large cities, have brought about a major transformation in the urban landscape.

Pradhan Mantri Awas Yojana – Urban (PMAY-U)

This is a flagship Mission of being implemented by the Ministry of Housing and Urban Affairs and launched in 2015. The scheme addresses urban housing shortage among the economically weaker sections (EWS) and Low Income and Middle Income Groups (LIG/MIG) including the slum dwellers, by ensuring a pucca house to all eligible urban households by 2022, when the nation completes 75 years of its Independence. 113 lakh houses have been sanctioned and ₹1.82 lakh crore has been committed for the scheme, out of which ₹1.08 lakh crore has been released by the government till 2021. By 2021, 50.21 lakh houses have been constructed.

Besides, Ministry of Housing & Urban Affairs has initiated "Affordable Rental Housing Complexes" (ARHCs), a sub-scheme under Pradhan Mantri Awas Yojana - Urban (PMAY-U). This will provide ease of living to urban migrants/ poor in Industrial Sector as well as in non-formal urban economy to get access to dignified affordable rental housing close to their workplace.

Integrated Child Development Services

Integrated Child Development Services (ICDS) in India is the world's largest integrated early childhood programme, with over 40,000 centres nationwide. Since its inception in 1975, the programme has matured and expanded, despite difficulties in adapting to the vastly different local circumstances prevalent in the country. UNICEF had helped launch the ICDS programme and continued to provide financial and technical assistance along with the World Bank.

The programme has covered millions of expectant and nursing mothers and children under the age of six. Of these children, more than half participate in early learning activities. The purpose of ICDS is to improve the health, nutrition, and development of children. The programme offers health, nutrition, and hygiene education to mothers, non-formal pre-school education to children aged three to six, supplementary feeding for all children and pregnant and nursing mothers, growth monitoring and promotion, and links to primary healthcare services such as immunization and vitamin A supplements.

These services are delivered in an integrated manner at the anganwadi or childcare centre. Each centre is run by an anganwadi worker and one helper, who undergo three months of institutional training and four months of community-based training.

Although the programme's spread and growth was greater in underserved than well-served areas during the 1990s, the poorest states and those with the highest levels of undernutrition had the lowest levels of programme funding and coverage by ICDS activities.

The Union Ministry of Women and Child Development is implementing various schemes for promoting welfare of women in co-ordination with State Governments. These include:

- Pan-India PM Matru Vandana Yojana (PMMVY) effective from 2017. The Scheme envisages providing cash incentive amounting to ₹5,000 in three installments directly to the Bank/Post Office account of Pregnant Women and Lactating Mother (PW&LM) in DBT Mode during pregnancy and lactation.
- Beti Bachao Beti Padhao programme focusses on promoting girls' education for which funds are allocated.
- Mahila Sakthi Kendras (MSKs) facilitates training and economic activities to be undertaken by women. These kendras also create awareness among women at Block/village levels about various schemes for welfare, including health and hygiene with the help of NGOs and volunteers.

- State Resource Centres for Women are also functioning to provide technical assistance to the State Governments and UT Administrations and ensure effective coordination at the State/Union Territory level.
- Schemes also aim at women's empowerment in regard to issues like prevention of dowry, domestic violence, crime, trafficking, etc.

Midday Meal Scheme

The Midday Meal Scheme was introduced as an innovative programme in schools to improve the nutritional status of school-age children. It was pioneered on a limited scale in Tamil Nadu and later extended to cover the whole state. Seeing its beneficial impact, later it was introduced in other states and Central government has also been providing funds for the programme. The programme supplies free lunches on working days for children in primary and upper primary classes in government, government aided, and local body schools. The scheme has induced families to send children to schools and helped in bringing down drop-out rates at primary and upper primary levels.

❑ PANCHAYATI RAJ AND RURAL REJUVENATION

Introduction

In Indian polity, the Local governments under the Panchayats in the villages and Municipalities in towns occupy an important place. Article 243 under Parts IX and IXA of the Constitution of India deals respectively with Panchayats and Municipalities. Local governments are significant as they are grassroot organizations working at the local level and are closest to the people they serve. Their governance and activities touches upon the day to day lives of the people and their efficient functioning and accountability is of critical importance. They are democratic in their set-up, and function with active participation of the local citizenry. However, despite the role assigned to them in the Constitution, for nearly four decades, they were in a moribund state with no effective role for, or participation of, the people who had little voice in their functioning or decision-making.

Efforts had been made even in the early years after independence to develop and empower local bodies. The Community Development Programme initiated in 1952 which sought to promote people's participation in local development in diverse activities was the first such attempt. Later many expert committees examined the issue of village governance and development and proposed many measures. Balwant Rai Committee in 1957 recommended a three tier system – Village level, Block level and Zilla (District) level and giving statutory status to these institutions. In 1960, some states adopted the system of elected local bodies. But these bodies did not have adequate powers and functions to promote development. In 1989, P K Thungon Committee recommended granting constitutional recognition to local bodies.

In a historic development during 1992-93, these institutions underwent a major transformation. The 73rd and 74th Amendment Acts of 1992 under the Constitution have given primacy to the local bodies in villages and towns and this was a major step towards democratic decentralization of administrative authority. The 73rd Amendment Act, 1992, commonly referred to as the Panchayati Raj Act, came into force on April 24, 1993, and the 74th Amendment Act known as the Nagarpalika Act came into effect on June 1, 1993.

Reservation for Women: A significant feature of the Constitution amendments was that as a measure of empowerment of women, it provided for reservation of seats for women. Under the Constitution, not less than one-third of the total number of seats to be filled by direct election in the local bodies – Panchayats and Municipalities – (including the seats reserved for women belonging to the SC/ST) would be reserved for women and such seats are to be allotted by rotation to different constituencies in the local bodies.

It is heartening to note that Bihar was the first state to increase the representation of women in Panchayats from one-third to 50 per cent and that some other states have also taken steps to increase their representation.

Panchayati Raj

The primary objective of Panchayati Raj (PR) is to strengthen the base of democracy at the grass roots and enable the people to actively participate, on a continual basis, in the inclusive development of the entire population in the village, irrespective of the caste, class or religion.

The important features of Panchayati Raj Institution (PRI) are:

- There will be three-tier structure of self-governing bodies, viz., the Village Panchayat, Taluk Panchayat and District (Zilla) Panchayat;
- There will be direct elections to all seats in the panchayats at all levels;
- Mandatory reservation of seats in panchayats at all levels for SC, ST and women in proportion to their share of the population in the panchayat;
- There should be genuine transfer of power and responsibility to these bodies;
- Adequate financial resources should be transferred to those bodies to enable to them to effectively discharge their responsibility;
- All decisions regarding identifying and prioritising development programs of the village and their execution will be taken at appropriate levels of the three tiers and with the active involvement of the Gram Sabha;
- The local area plans drawn up at lower tiers will be consolidated by a District Planning Committee (DPC).

Features of Gram Sabha

A Gram Sabha is established for a village or a group of villages and serves as an assembly of villagers. The size of the Gram Sabha differs from State to State. Gram Sabha (GS) is the core of the Panchayati Raj system where residents of the village can directly participate and exercise their rights, obligations and concerns about their own development process.

Gram Sabhas are mandated to perform the following functions:

- Discuss the report on socio-economic development programmes implemented by the Gram Panchayat (GP) in the previous financial year;
- Examine the annual statement of the accounts and audit report as well as annual report of administration of the GP in the last financial year;
- Examine the budget of the GP for the next financial year;
- Identification of the beneficiaries of various anti-poverty and rural development programmes;
- Scrutinize on-going and completed schemes and works of the GP;
- Undertake programmes of adult education and family welfare in the village;
- Mobilisation of voluntary labour and contributions in kind or cash or both for community welfare programmes and promotion and unity and harmony among all sections of society in the village.

The extent of devolution of powers and funds to panchayats has differed from state to state. Also, the degree of efficiency with which they function has not been uniform even within states. However, it is an evolutionary process and has given voice to local people, especially women, in playing their part in the process of development of villages.

❑ GENDER BIAS AND GENDER INEQUALITY : VARIOUS DIMENSIONS

Gender bias and gender inequality are important aspects to be considered in the context of social and economic development. Gender bias adversely impacts women and girls in manifold ways which leads to inequality in society, particularly in less developed countries. Speaking on "Women's Empowerment: An Economic Game Changer", International Monetary Fund Chief, Christine Lagarde had observed that "pay parity and equal opportunities to women in the workplace will boost economic growth and create a bigger piece for everyone to share." She added that "India's national income will rise by 27 per cent if women contribute to the workforce as much as men."

The Constitution and Gender Equality

Gender equality is recognized as part of fundamental rights enshrined in the Constitution of India. The Constitution guarantees the following:

- The Preamble says: "**EQUALITY** of status and of opportunity; and to promote among them all.
- Further, **Article 14** says, "The State shall not deny to any person equality before the law or the equal protection of the laws within the territory of India."
- **Article 15 (1)** lays down that: "The State shall not discriminate against any citizen on grounds only of religion, race, caste, sex, place of birth or any of them. "(2) No citizen shall, on grounds only of religion, race, caste, **sex**, place of birth or any of them, be subject to any disability, liability, restriction or condition" with regard to various facilities.
- **Article 15 (3)** even reinforces the position of women and children stating that "Nothing in this article shall prevent the State from making any special provision for women and children."
- **Article 16 (2)** states: "No citizen shall, on grounds only of religion, race, caste, sex, descent, place of birth, residence or any of them, be ineligible for, or discriminated against in respect of any employment or office under the State".
- And under the **Directive Principles of State Policy**, it is provided that the State shall, in particular, direct its policy towards securing for the citizens, men and women equally, the right to an adequate means of livelihood.
- **Article 39(a)** - The State shall direct its policy towards securing all citizens men and women, equally, the right to means of livelihood.
- **Article 39(d)** - Equal pay for equal work for both men and women. **Article 42** - The State to make provision for ensuring just and humane conditions of work and maternity relief.
- **Article 51 (A)(e)** - To renounce the practices derogatory to the dignity of women.
- And under the **Directive Principles of State Policy**, it is provided that the State shall, in particular, direct its policy towards securing for the citizens, men and women equally, the right to an adequate means of livelihood.

Adverse effects of Gender Bias and Gender Inequality

Gender bias and inequality manifests itself in adverse sex (female-male) ratio in population, higher mortality rates among girl children and women, less literacy and educational attainments, less access to jobs, lower representation in electoral politics and in administration at national, state and local (municipal and village) levels, apart from their primary responsibility to look after home and family and, worse still, bias against girl child and women in intra-family matters.

Though the government has endeavoured to pay special attention to these aspects and devised various schemes to ensure justice for women over the years, a sizeable section of women and girl children have had to endure various kinds of disabilities and discrimination both at home and outside. This has had a debilitating effect on the social and economic progress of Indian society.

It is pertinent to note that as much as 48.4 per cent of India's population (as per 2011 census) consist of women. The extent and degree of gender bias and gender inequality in India, the various forms in which it manifests, its adverse effects on women and progress made to redress them are discussed below.

Sex Ratio and Missing Women

While sex ratio is in favour of female in western and advanced countries – Europe, US, etc. – it is quite skewed against females in most of the Third world, countries, especially in Asia and N Africa. India is no exception. There are only two states, Kerala and Puducherry, where the number of women outnumber men. As per 2011 census, Kerala had 1,084 females to 1,000 males and Puducherry had 1,037 females to 1,000 males. While some states like Karnataka, Andhra Pradesh, Madhya Pradesh and Maharashtra have shown signs of improvement in the sex ratio, many other states including economically progressive states like Haryana, Gujarat and Punjab have low sex ratio. Haryana, which has the lowest rate of sex ratio among the major states with 879 females to 1000 males, is showing a decreasing trend in the population of women which is a cause for concern. While overall India has for decades seen decrease in sex ratio, there has been slight increase during the last two decades – from 927 in 1991 to 933 in 2001 and to 940 in 2011. The main cause for the decline in sex ratio in India is lack of literacy and education and an overtly biased attitude towards women.

Table 17.4 shows sex ratio and child sex ratio figures of some of the well-performing states and weaker states as per 2001 and 2011 census. It shows a mixed picture. Child sex ratio is lower than overall sex ratio in many of the states with UP in 2011 and Bihar in both census being rather unlikely exceptions. For India too, child sex ratio is higher than overall sex ratio in 2011. Child sex ratio being less than overall sex ratio is not an encouraging sign as it may indicate higher female infant mortality or sex-selective abortion and increase in male births to female births.

Table 17.4 Sex Ratio – India and Selected States

State	2001 Sex Ratio	Census Child Sex Ratio	2011 Sex Ratio	Census Child Sex Ratio
1	2	3	4	5
India	**927**	**933**	**943**	**919**
Kerala	1058	960	1084	964
Puducherry	1001	967	1037	967
Tamil Nadu	987	942	996	943
Andhra Pradesh	978	961	993	939
Chhattisgarh	989	975	991	969

	2001 Sex Ratio	Census Child Sex ratio	2011 Sex Ratio	Census Child Sex ratio
6	7	8	9	10
Rajasthan	921	909	928	888
Gujarat	920	833	919	890
Bihar	919	942	918	935
UP	898	916	912	902
Punjab	876	798	895	846
Haryana	861	819	879	834

Mortality Rates

Infant mortality rate (IMR) and Under 5 years mortality rate (U5MR) has been coming down steadily in the case of both females and males which is a positive sign. {See Table 17.5 (a) and (b)}. According to World Bank data, the overall IMR (which refers to the number of deaths per 1,000 live births in the first year of a child's life) has come down from 161 in 1960 to 28 in 2019. Significantly, the IMR for female children was less than that for male children till 1990 but thereafter it was slightly more until it has equalled by 2019. In the case of Under 5 mortality rate (the probability of a child dying before attaining 5 years of age), the rate for female children has always been more than that for male children which shows that the survival rate of female children was less than that of male children.

Table 17.5 (a): Infant Mortality Rate (By Sex) - 1961 – 2019

(per 1,000 live births)

Year	Female	Male	Total
1960	156	165	161
1970	138	146	142
1980	111	117	114
1990	86	90	88
2000	67	66	66
2010	46	44	45
2019	28	28	28

Table 17.5 (b): Under 5 Mortality Rate (By Sex) -1990 – 2019

(per 1,000 live births)

Year	Female	Male	Total
1960	248	234	241
1970	218	207	213
1980	173	163	168
1990	130	122	126
2000	96	87	92
2010	61	55	58
2019	35	34	34

Source: Tables 17.5 (a) & (b): World Bank Data.

The present level of IMR (28 infant deaths per 1,000 live births, for the year 2019) is about one-fourth as compared to 1980 (114 infant deaths per 1,000 births). According to Census of India, despite the decline in IMR over the last decades, one in every 31 infants die within first year of their life at overall National level, while one in every 28 infants in rural areas and one in every 43 infants in urban areas still die within one year of life.

It is important to note that unlike the indicators on life expectancy (discussed in the next section) that are relatively stable and slow to change, infant and child mortality indicators are likely to be more sensitive to changes that have bearing on the quality of life, particularly to the health and longevity. These could be due to sudden adversities or non-availability of critical public health and life support services. The health of infants and small children is also dependent on factors like the health and nutrition intake of mothers during pregnancy, extent of breast feeding by mothers in the early stages of the child's life and overall sanitary conditions to which children are exposed.

Life Expectancy

Life expectancy is an important indicator of health attainments of a country and is related to nutrition and relative lack of morbidity.

A significant feature seen from Table 17.6 is that both in the developed and emerging countries and for India in Table 17.7, women have higher longevity and survival rate than men. It will be noticed that in 2019, females in all advanced countries represented here have overall life expectancy of over 80 years, save Russia where it is 78 years. And in the case of males, except US, UK, Germany and Russia, all have life expectancy of 80 years or more.

And among the emerging countries, females in Brazil and Thailand have life expectancy at birth of 80 and more, while in other countries both females and males have life expectancy of less than 80 years.

Table 17.6 Life Expectancy at Birth (In Years)-Developed & Emerging Countries

Country	Female	Male	Female	Male	Female	Male
	1998		2004		2019	
(A) Developed Countries						
USA	80.2	73.5	80.2	74.8	81	76
Canada	81.9	76.2	82.6	77.6	84	80
Japan	83.0	76.9	85.6	78.6	87	81
Australia	81.2	75.6	83.0	77.9	85	81
UK	80.0	74.7	80.8	76.2	83	79
France	82.1	74.4	83.1	76.0	86	80
Germany	80.3	74.1	81.7	75.9	83	79
Russia	72.9	60.7	72.0	58.9	78	68
(B) Emerging Countries						
India	63.3	62.5	65.3	62.1	71	68
China	72.3	68.1	73.7	70.2	79	75
Brazil	71.2	63.3	74.8	67	80	72
South Africa	56.2	50.3	48.2	45.7	68	61
Malaysia	74.5	70.1	75.8	71.1	78	74
Thailand	72.1	65.9	74	66.7	81	73
Indonesia	67.5	63.7	69.2	65.3	74	70

According to Census of India, the life expectancy at birth for the country has undergone a significant change from 49.7 in 1971-75 to 69.4 in 2014-18, registering an increase of 19.7 years in the last four decade. It is noteworthy that in 1971-75, the life expectancy at birth for male (50.5) was more than that of female (49.0). But the trend has been reversed since 1981-85. In 2014-18, the female life expectancy (70.7) is higher than that of male (68.2) by more than two years.

The gap between the rural and urban life expectancy has also narrowed down significantly from 1970-75 to 2014-18. In case of life expectancy at birth, most of the states in India have reported higher life expectancy in urban areas than in rural areas, except Kerala. There is a difference of about 4.6 years in urban-rural life expectancy at birth and about 1.3 years in urban-rural life expectancy at age 70, for the country. The position on mortality and general health status would have been impacted by Covid-19 pandemic. (For more on the impact of Covid-19, see Chapter 19).

Table 17.7 Life Expectancy at Birth (In Years) – India

Year	Female	Male	Total
1971-75	49.0	50.5	49.7
1981-85	55.7	55.4	55.5
1991-95	60.9	59.7	60.3
2001-05	66.1	63.8	63.5
2011-15	70.0	66.9	68.3
2014-18	70.7	68.2	69.4

Source: Census of India and UN Population Division.

Literacy and Educational Attainments

Literacy

Literacy and education of females are two of the critical factors that help to reduce gender inequality, bridge the gap between the two sexes and empower women. But both in respect of literacy and educational attainments, though there have been exceptions, women, in general, have traditionally lagged behind men in India. (See Tables 17.8 and 17.9). Literacy rate of females has been all through far less than that of males.

Table 17.8 Literacy in India (In Percentage)

	1951	1961	1971	1981	1991	2001	2011
Female	7.9	13	18.7	24.8	39.3	53.6	65.46
Male	25	34.4	39.5	46.9	64.1	75.2	82.14
Total	16.7	24	29.5	36.2	52.2	64.8	74.04

Source: Tenth Plan, Vol. III, Planning Commission & Registrar General of India, Census of India.

A positive sign: But a redeeming feature of 2011 census is that out of total of 21.77 crore literates added during the decade (2001-2011), female literates (11.00 crore) outnumber male literates (10.76 crore). A reverse trend was noticed during 1991-2001. The decadal increase in number of literates among males is of 31.98 percentage points while the corresponding increase in case of females is of 49.10 percentage points. A notable feature is that out of the total decrease of 3.11 crore in the number of illiterates, the females (1.71 crore) outnumber males (1.41 crore). The above two trends are a clear indication that the gender gap in literacy is shrinking in the country. This trend of rising female literates will have far reaching consequences for the overall development of society.

Where women are more literate and better educated, there is better record on parameters like birth rate and total fertility rate (TFR) as evidenced by the performance of states like Kerala, Tamil Nadu and some of the North-eastern states.

Education

Trends in Gross Enrolment Ratios (GERs)

Between 2000-2001 and 2013-14, the GERs in primary, upper primary and elementary education has increased substantially, especially in upper primary education. But gross enrolment ratio of girls at primary and secondary level is less than that of boys. (Table 17.9)

Table 17.9 Gross Enrolment Ratio in Primary, Upper Primary and Secondary Stages

(In Percentage)

	Primary Stage (Classes I-V)			Upper Primary Stage (Classes VI-VIII)			Secondary Education (Classes IX-X)		
	Boys	**Girls**	**Total**	**Boys**	**Girls**	**Total**	**Boys**	**Girls**	**Total**
1950-51	60.6	24.8	43.1	20.6	4.6	12.9	--	--	--
1980-81	95.8	64.1	80.5	54.3	28.6	41.9	--	--	--
2000-01	104.9	85.9	95.7	66.7	49.9	58.6	--	--	--
2005-06	112.8	105.8	109.4	75.2	66.4	71	57.6	46.2	52.2
2010-11	115.4	116.7	116	87.7	83.1	85.5	69	60.8	65
2013-14	100.2	102.7	101.4	86.3	92.8	89.3	76.8	76.5	76.6

Source: Data for 1950-51 & 1980-81 from Ministry of Education cited in 'Selected Socio-Economic Statistics, India 2000' and for 2000-01 to 2013-14 from 'India: Education for All – Towards Quality with Equity', Ministry of Human Resources Development, 2014.

While there was considerable gap between enrollment of boys and girls in the initial three decades -- 1950-80 -- the gap has been considerably reduced in subsequent two decades. There have been considerable efforts and affirmative action on the part of the governments, at both central and state levels, to promote education of girls and retain them in schools by reducing dropouts. Increasing the proportion of female teachers, exemption from payment or incentives on fees, midday meals scheme and provision of separate toilets for girls in schools, etc. have helped to bolster attendance of girls in schools. However, issues like dropout and discontinuance of education, though this trend has come down, standard and quality of education, etc. are issues still plaguing the system.

Also compared to boys, girls suffer from various handicaps in education. Girls are either not sent to schools, more so in rural areas, or if they do attend school, discontinue midway due to a number of factors -- school being far from home and safety concerns, lack of toilet in school or need to attend to household chores in the absence of both father and mother who may be at work. However, there are some encouraging trends of parents paying as much attention to education of girl child as to that of boys.

Gender issues in Labour and Wages

In labour participation rate and employment, women lag behind men. Early marriages and multiple child-bearing in working age are major handicaps for women in India which result in lower female participation rate in the labour force. In most households, both in urban and rural areas, women are constrained to tend to domestic chores and are unable to take up employment. Not only that, the services rendered by women at home are invisible, are not given due credit and is not reckoned at all or not reckoned properly in the National accounts.

That women are paid less than men for similar work in many sectors and jobs in the informal sector is known. This is widely prevalent in jobs on farms which is a major source of employment of women in rural areas, though a 2011-12 NSSO survey has shown some decline in gender wage gap due to MG National Rural Employment Guarantee Scheme (MNREGS). The decline in wage gap is partly due to supply crunch on account of declining female participation rate in labourforce.

The gender pay gap issue is relevant in the formal sector too. It exists in the case of teachers, in jobs in banking, insurance, financial and information technology sectors where informal employment is widely prevalent. Women are also at a disadvantage when it comes to education, skills and experience. As family incomes rise, the trend is for women to cease working and attend to family and domestic chores which highlights the patriarchal attitude of Indian society. Even as they are employed, women bear the additional burden of caring for children and household duties making it stressful for them. This also places them at a disadvantage when seeking jobs as employers may reckon them to be less dependable due to likely interruptions in service. This affects them in their career progression, economic security, etc. It is heartening to note that lately the private sector and even the government have recognized these issues and introduced facilities like extended maternity leave, paternity leave when a child is born, re-employing women who had to break service due to pregnancy and childbirth, etc.

Discrimination, sexual harassment and safety at work are other issues confronting women at work. Construction sector, the largest source of employment in the urban informal sector, is notoriously prone to discrimination and sexual harassment of women workforce.

Social Disparities and Intra-family Bias

Compared to men, women are placed at a disadvantage in many respects in both urban and rural areas in India. They bear the brunt of taking care of the family, rearing children due to which they have to forsake and sacrifice their interests. The plight of women in rural areas is, in most cases, still worse than that of their urban counterparts. They are denied of many of the urban conveniences like electricity and cooking gas, have to trudge long distances for fetching firewood for cooking, lack piped water supply, a problem faced by lower sections in urban areas too.

In intra-family divisions and sharing of income and food, on healthcare, education, etc., women come behind men, particularly among families in the lower income strata.

❑ GENDER BUDGETING

The concept of gender budgeting does not imply a separate budget for either women nor increase in overall public expenditure but prioritising programmes within specific sectors to meet the special needs of women. The rationale for it is that macroeconomic policies or a gender-neutral budget may not solve the problem of gender inequality. As already pointed out above, gender inequality hampers socio-economic progress, that it inhibits women from playing their rightful role, not only in respect of themselves but for the family as a whole, and realizing their full potential. By targeting public spending towards sectors and programmes which will make a direct impact on women and children, gender equity can be ensured to a greater extent.

Five Year Plans on Gender issues

The genesis of the idea of gender budgeting in India can be traced back to the early Five Year Plans. Gender-mainstreaming and development has been a priority goal in the country's development efforts since the starting of the first Five Year Plan.

- While the First to Fifth Five Year Plans treated development of women as a subject of 'welfare', there was a paradigm shift from 'women's welfare' to 'women's development' during the Sixth Plan (1980-85). Sixth Plan also had special thrust for women in three core sectors viz., health, education and employment.
- The Seventh Plan (1985-90), continued the developmental approach. The major objective was of raising economic and social status of women and bringing them into the mainstream of national

development. Subsequent plans also had special programmes for women to complement the efforts of the general development programmes.

- National Commission for Women (NCW) was set up in 1992 to work towards safeguarding the rights and interest of women and many policies and programmes like Rashtriya Mahila Kosh to meet the microcredit needs of poor and women without assets, Mahila Samridhi Yojana to promote thrift activities amongst women, National Nutrition Policy to ensure adequate nutritional standard of the people, National Crèche Fund to provide crèche services to the children of working mothers and Indira Mahila Yojana for economic empowerment through women Self Help Groups were launched.
- 'Empowerment of Women' to be agents of socio-economic change and development became one of the nine specific objectives of the Ninth Plan (1997- 2002).
- Since 2005-06, the Ministry of Finance has been issuing a note on Gender Budgeting which is incorporated in the Expenditure Budget Document. It comprises two parts – one on 'Women Specific Schemes' having 100 per cent allocation for women and another on 'Pro Women Schemes' which have at least 30 per cent of the allocation for women.
- In 2010, it was decided to adopt 'Gender Responsive Budget' with sub-targets covering women and SC/ST beneficiaries under various developmental schemes and schemes for the benefit of North Eastern Region.
- Gender Budgeting Cells were set up by the Union Government to serve as focal points for coordinating gender budgeting initiatives within their Ministries and across Departments.

Impact of Gender Budgeting

Specific programmes and targets designed to improve the welfare of, and empower, women and girl children can bring about transformational changes in their lives. Given below are some of the areas and instances where gender budgeting could bring about beneficial changes in their lives.

- Incidence and severity of poverty is greater among women than among men. Empirical evidence has shown that promoting and funding women's Self-help groups (SHGs) to undertake income-generating activities helps to augment family incomes. It also enhances the freedom, self-confidence and self-esteem of women which has a beneficial impact on the family as a whole.
- Funding programmes like Integrated Child Development Scheme (ICDS) meant for both women and children has helped to improve nutrition of children in Anganwadis, of pregnant and lactating women. It also creates greater awareness among women about health and nutrition.
- Outlays on augmenting supply of safe drinking water, especially in rural areas, benefits women more than men by reducing the time required to fetch water for which they have to trudge long distances to rivers and ponds. Such outlays will be equally beneficial to women of low income households in urban areas who do not have water supply at home and have to depend on common pipe connection provided in streets which, apart from the time consumed, causes much inconvenience to them.
- Schemes to extend supply of cooking gas to rural areas will go a long way to help rural women who have to depend on firewood for cooking which they have to fetch from distant places from their homes.
- Funding to incentivise and promote education of girl children and retaining them in schools will help the whole family in the long run. An educated girl will have greater awareness about the value of hygiene, health, nutrition, etc. which will have salutary effect when she grows up, assumes motherhood and brings up a family. As the saying goes, educating a boy helps one person whereas educating a girl helps an entire family. The drawbacks of lack of literacy and education among large sections of women in India and how it has held back the country's progress have been only too starkly visible.

Conclusion

Gender equity has significant implications for issues like economic participation and opportunity, educational attainment, health and survival, and political empowerment. Gender inequality has multiple deleterious effects on the economy and retards growth. India is ranked 108 out of a total of 144 countries on the World Economic Forum's "*Global Gender Gap Report 2017*" which looks at a number of dimensions from economic opportunities to political empowerment and healthcare. India has to adopt a multi-pronged approach and tackle gender issues with sensitivity and empathy while changing labour laws and effecting labour reforms.

Box 17.7 Universal Basic Income

The Concept and its Implications

The concept of Universal Basic Income (or UBI, in brief) has been a subject of debate in various parts of the world for quite a while. This idea has lately been put forth by some Indian economists and been part of public discourse in India. The concept of UBI implies the State or a public institution granting unconditionally a 'basic guaranteed sum of money' on regular basis to every citizen in a country, including children, irrespective of their economic status or occupation. This will be in addition to any other source of income or earnings of the citizens. It is a social security measure, the primary objective being to combat poverty, assist those who are unemployed and enable every citizen to meet the basic needs and maintain a decent standard of life.

Though the issue has been debated in the US, Canada and some European countries, it has not been implemented in those countries. Polls held on the issue in some of those countries have shown that a majority of the general population do not favour the idea of UBI. But many countries in the west have robust social welfare schemes, apart from much better educational and health facilities than available in India. Some social scientists in the West and a few Indian economists have been advocating adoption of this measure in India.

Rationale for Universal Basic Income

Distortions in Subsidy Schemes

One of the main arguments for implementing the scheme of UBI is that a good portion of the subsidies doled out by governments, which are primarily meant for the poorer sections, are being enjoyed by the well-to-do and affluent sections of the population who do not merit such assistance. In the Indian context, there are 'explicit' subsidies like those under the Public Distribution System (PDS), fertilizers, railways, electricity, sugar, LPG, kerosene and water and 'hidden' subsidies in the provision of social and economic services. Subsidies are also categorised as 'merit' and 'non-merit' subsidies. Merit subsidy is for sectors like education, primary healthcare, nutrition, forestry, ecology, environment, rural development programmes, village and small industries, etc. where the benefits are reaped by the society as a whole. Non-merit subsidy is directed towards specific groups of population, such as subsidy on food, fertilizer, petroleum, electricity, etc.

It is well known that while dispensing subsidies in India, there is considerable amount of leakage and distortions, especially in the case of subsidies meant for specific target groups. Instances of exclusion also are rampant due to which many in the target groups get excluded from receiving benefits defeating the very purpose of such social assistance schemes. This is one of the reasons put forth for introducing a social assistance scheme which will be 'universal' covering every citizen so that none gets excluded. Such a scheme may be in replacement of all or some of the existing schemes involving subsidies so that the amounts saved could be channelled into the universal scheme. The financial implications of such a UBI scheme are discussed later in this section.

Loss of Jobs and Unemployment

The scheme will also serve as a prop to those who are seeking jobs but can't get employment. The concept of UBI has got traction as automation with increasingly efficient computer systems, robotics and artificial intelligence is causing loss of jobs in various countries. In India, in the Information Technology (IT) sector which has been one with high potential for job creation, IT companies are embracing automation and artificial intelligence in complex areas of business which is resulting in improved productivity and helps to keep down costs. This is taking a toll on jobs in this sector.

With changing demographic landscape and rising number of aged people, there is need to provide adequate assured income to the aged in societies which do not have proper welfare schemes like 'Old age pension' covering all such persons.

Poverty and Gross Inequalities

Rising inequalities in societies, even as development takes place, is a matter of serious concern. Globalisation, while improving overall well-being, also dislocates workers and disrupts industries, and results in greater income and wealth disparity. An alternative view is that technological advances, more than globalisation, have exacerbated economic inequalities, setting the stage for political disruptions in developed countries.

Policymakers in emerging countries have identified inequality as a major problem and are seeking to improve social mobility, lest globalisation and new technologies displace and leave behind the middle and working classes. For Asian countries, the future path is clear : take care of the disadvantaged sections and provide retraining, skills and new employment opportunities for displaced and unemployed workers.

Policies that focus on the poor and the middle class can mitigate inequality. Irrespective of the level of economic development, better access to education and health care and well-targeted social policies, while ensuring that labour market policies do not excessively burden the poor, can help raise the income share for the poor and the middle class.

Not only inequality within a country but growing and glaring inequalities between countries are also of great concern. Organizations like The World Bank, IMF, Asian Development Bank and UNICEF have drawn attention to this issue. *Global Wealth Report 2016* brought out by Credit Suisse also highlights growing disparities in income and wealth within and among nations.

The following facts are quite revealing.

Estimates suggest that just 1 per cent of the population owns almost half of the world's wealth amounting to $110 trillion – 65 times the total wealth of the bottom half of the world's population.

There are large disparities across Emerging and Developing Countries (EDC's) with Asia and Eastern Europe experiencing marked increases in inequality, and countries in Latin America exhibiting notable declines.

Rising income inequality in most advanced and many emerging market economies has been driven primarily by the growing income share of the top 10 per cent. The top 10 per cent now has an income close to nine times that of the bottom 10 per cent.

While poverty has declined in many countries, it is on the rise in advanced economies. The top 1 per cent now account for around 10 per cent of total income in advanced economies.

In many EDCs, poverty – measured in terms of the share of population living below a pre-defined poverty line – has declined, while income inequality has been on the rise in some countries.

Some measures of global inequality exhibit a declining trend in the last few decades in response to rising incomes for those living in China and India, where hundreds of millions of people have been lifted out of poverty.

The US with 5.1 per cent of adults accounts for 33.2 per cent of global wealth. Whereas India with 16.7 per cent of adult population has just 1.2 per cent of the world's wealth.

The richest 1 per cent of people in the world now account for 50.8 per cent of global wealth (up from 43.6 per cent in 2010) while the share of the bottom half of the global population which was 1.6 per cent in 2010 has come down to a mere 0.2 per cent of the world's wealth.

According to a Sample Household Survey (ICE3600) carried out in India in 2016, the richest 20 per cent account for 44.9 per cent share in total national household disposable income while the poorest 20 per cent has just 7 per cent share.

Universal Basic Income may simply be the fastest way of reducing poverty. In the Indian context, a relatively low level of assured regular income to every individual could serve as a prop and enhance family's welfare. Unlike the present system of subsidies, UBI may empower families at the bottom rung of the ladder and help them to become more self-reliant and take economic decisions relevant to their lives.

The Indian Scene : Case for a Universal Basic Income

In the Indian context, many anti-poverty welfare schemes have been implemented from time to time. Besides, Central and State governments have been subsidising many commodities and services such as food, fertiliser, petorl, kerosene, water, electricity, transport by rail and road. While these steps have helped to mitigate hardships of the poor to some extent, poverty still afflicts a sizeable section of the population – due to droughts, distress in the agricultural sector, unemployment, malnutrition, disease, etc.

As observed in *Economic Survey 2015-16*, "Prima facie, price subsidies do not appear to have had a transformative effect on the living standards of the poor, though they have helped poor households weather inflation and price volatility. A closer look at the price subsidy landscape reveals why they may not be the government's best weapon of choice in the fight against poverty" for the following reasons.

Many of these subsidies are regressive in as much as they benefit the rich more than the deserving poorer sections.

For instance, as Economic Survey points out, the elctricity subsidy benefits only the 67.2 per cent households which are electrified and even among them, the richer households who consume more power stand to benefit more. So also, the LPG subsidy is enjoyed by the relatively better off sections while the poorer sections who may not even use LPG for cooking are deprived of the benefit. This holds true for petrol, diesel and fertilizer where the affluent sections get the benefits.

As mentioned earlier, there is considerable leakage in many of the programmes like Public Distribution Scheme (PDS) for food, distribution of LPG, MaNREGA, ICDS, etc. where the benefits do not reach all the targeted beneficiaries, especially the very poor and vulnerable sections.

Against this background, some economists have suggested that a scheme of 'universal basic income' (UBI) may be introduced replacing various existing subsidies and other welfare hand-outs. Under the UBI, the government provides every citizen, on a regular basis, a pre-determined amount sufficient to meet the basic and essential requirements to maintain a reasonably good standard of life. While the better off and affluent sections may not need this prop, it will assuredly help the poor and destitute, who are at the very bottom of the pyramid, to lead a better life and be rid of abject poverty and starvation. Such a hand-out will be in addition to any income or earnings of the people.

The money saved by the abolition of subsidies and welfare schemes like MaNREGA, and even tax exemptions enjoyed by tax payers, would be utilized to fund the UBI scheme. And as it a scheme of universal coverage, there will be no scope for exclusion of any beneficiary which has been the case with the extant welfare schemes and which results in leakages and siphoning off funds.

Some of the eminent economists like Pranab Bardhan of the University of California, Debraj Ray of New York University, Vijay Joshi of University of Oxford and Maitreesh Ghatak of London School of Economics have all put forth the idea of UBI. They have outlined the savings and expenditure involved in its introduction and shown that such a scheme is affordable and fiscally manageable in India. Guy Standing, Research Associate at the School of Oriental and African Studies (SOAS), University of London and a founder member and honorary co-president of the Basic Income Earth Network (BIEN), a non-governmental organisation that promotes a basic income for all, has been an ardent advocate of UBI scheme.

The scheme could use the Aadhaar for identity of beneficiaries and with the financial inclusion drives and Digital India programme covering rural areas, roll-out of a UBI scheme can be worked out.

Fiscal and Financial Implications of UBI

A crucial question in regard to UBI is if it is affordable considering that a fixed sum will have to be paid to every person – adults and children – on a continuing basis which becomes a permanent commitment on the part of the government. The sum fixed may also have to be revised periodically if it is to cover inflation since, over a period of time, a constant amount of 'cash transfer' may not buy the same amount of goods. According to one estimate, the total amount of 'non-merit' Central and State subsidies which are accruing to the well-off sections of society and are of regressive nature account for abor 9 per cent of the GDP. This is excluding 'merit' subsidies in education, health, transportation, enviroment, etc. part of which may also be going to well-off sections. Apart from these, 'revenue forgone' through tax concessions and exemptions in budget, which mainly benefit the rich and Corporates, may amount to about 6 per cent of the GDP.

As stated in *Economic Survey 2016-17*, "In 1998-99, aggregate budgetary subsidies of the central and state governments are estimated to be 13.54 per cent of GDP at market prices, and 85.8 per cent of the combined revenue receipts of the centre and states. After adjustment done for salary arrears paid in 1998-99, the aggregate all India subsidies are estimated to be about 13 per cent of GDP."

The 2014-15 Economic Survey observed that it is not only commodity subsidies that are regressive, there are subsidies even in services like rail passenger tariffs which are artificially low. The Survey states, "Controlled rail prices actually provide more benefits for wealthy households than poor households, since the bottom 80 per cent of households constitute only 28.1 per cent of total originating passengers on non-suburban rail routes."

The 2014-15 Economic Survey further goes on to show how the expenditure incurred on some of these regressive subsidies compares with the expenditure that may be involved in raising the income of the poorest sections, the very objective of UBI policy. "Rice, wheat, pulses, sugar, kerosene, LPG, naphtha, water, electricity, diesel, fertiliser, iron ore, railways – these are just a few of the commodities and services that the government subsidises. The estimated direct fiscal cost of this illustrative subset of subsidies is about ₹ 3,78,000 crore or about 4.24 per cent of GDP. Just to give a sense of how large this amount is: ₹ 3,94,000 is roughly how much it would cost to raise the expenditure of every household to that of a household at the 35th percentile of the income distribution (which is well above the poverty line of 21.9 percent)."

Economic Survey 2016-17 on UBI

The *Economic Survey 2016-17* has taken the debate on UBI forward and observed "that the Indian state's generosity is not restricted to its poorest citizens. In fact, in many cases, the beneficiaries are disproportionately the well-off. In at least one area – corporate taxes – the government has recently taken decisive action, by identifying and quantifying exemptions amounting to about ₹ 62,000 crore and announcing a clear path for phasing them out. A move to GST would also eliminate leakages due to rationalisation of indirect tax exemptions estimated to cost ₹ 3.3 lakh crore."

The Survey assesses UBI for poverty reduction at ₹ 600 per capita per year and for vulnerability at ₹ 3,000 per capita per year in 2011-12. The inflation adjusted figures for 2016-17 are ₹ 840 and ₹ 4,200. Taking an average of the two estimates implies a UBI of ₹ 2,520. This will translate to only about 2.2 per cent of the GDP. Assuming that it excludes the top 25 percent of the population, it will cost 1.6 per cent of the GDP. This level of UBI reduces poverty rate to 9 percent and vulnerability to 7.5 percent.

If the UBI would become an add-on to, rather than a replacement of, existing anti-poverty and social programs, it would become more burdensome and fiscally unaffordable and unsustainable. One option, as Economic Survey suggests, is that even under the UBI scheme, efforts could be made to make the 'non-deserving' groups forgo the benefits of the scheme by various means as stated below:

- Based on ownership of assets like automobiles, airconditioners, bank balances above a certain level, etc.
- A voluntary scheme of 'giving up' as done in the case of LPG and giving due credit and recognition for the same.
- In addition, those who are paying income tax, property tax above a certain threshold could be excluded from the UBI scheme.

Case Against UBI

Apart from financial implications and affordability, certain other arguments have also been made out against UBI. These are:

Being an 'unearned income', it may lead to conspicuous and wasteful spending by households, especially the male members, on items like alcohol and tobacco.

A minimum guaranteed income may tend to make people lazy and opt out of the labour market. However, some studies by economists of welfare programmes in Inonesia, Honduras, Moroco, etc. have found no systematic evidence that cash transfer programs discourage work. According to them, "Attacking welfare recipients as lazy is easy rhetoric, but when you actually test the proposition scientifically, it doesn't hold up". (On this, see also section on pilot project in Madhya Pradesh below).

Gender factors may influence the control and sharing of UBI within a household, with men exercising control over spending of the UBI, especially in the lower rungs of society who need it the most. This does not happen with other in-kind transfer schemes like PDS, LPG, etc.

Given the extent of financial inclusion of the poor and their access to banking, UBI scheme may face implementation issues and cause stress on the banking system. This can, however, be overcome with schemes like Banking Correspondents in rural and semi-urban areas, opening of Payments Banks, Common Service Centres envisaged under the Digital India project, etc.

As pointed out earlier, the sum fixed may also have to be revised periodically if it is to cover inflation since, over a period of time, a constant amount of 'cash transfer' may not buy the same amount of goods.

Once introduced, it may become difficult for the government to wind up a UBI in case of failure. Also, due to opposition from pressure groups, it may be difficult to roll back existing subsidies under PDS, LPG, electricity, water, etc. and schemes like MaNREGA. Introducing UBI over and above this will be financially unsustainable.

UBI in India: Pilot Projects

Scheme in Madhya Pradesh

India Network for Basic Income, the Indian chapter of the Basic Income Earth Network, an international advocacy group, along with SEWA Bharat, a voluntary group, implemented two pilot projects in Madhya Pradesh. The first was for 18 months in eight villages juxtaposed with eight other villages, where the handout was not given, to study the results in contrast, and the second for a year in one tribal village with one other tribal village where no handout was given. The projects were launched in 2011, funded by UNICEF. The monthly handouts per individual were small, Rs 300 per adult, and Rs 150 for every child, the money for children being deposited into the mother's account.

The pilot showed some dramatic and encouraging results. Guy Standing, who had worked on the pilot cash transfer projects in Madhya Pradesh, said the scheme improved nutrition among the children, healthcare, sanitation, and school attendance and performance.

First, there was change in the employment pattern. Sixty per cent of the population in the village was engaged in wage-labour, working on odd jobs not related to farming and mostly in nearby towns or villages. The rest were engaged in agricultural work. With the infusion of money, there was a complete transformation and the sixty per cent of the people took to cultivate their own lands. As most of the villagers owned small plots of farmland of one or two bighas, they took to buying seeds and other inputs and worked their own fields rather than go in search of other jobs. And those who did not have land of their own found agricultural work in their own village.

Another major finding was the avoidance of debt. Earlier, they had to borrow funds at high rates of interest to buy seeds and fertiliser. But with money coming in, they not only stopped borrowing from usurious lenders, they were even able to repay loans given under the pilot scheme.

There were overall health benefits reported from the village. Spending on food, too, had improved and around the time the project came to an end, children were found to have made weight gains.

Villagers also improvised on ways to use the money to take small steps towards self-sufficiency. Some of them saved money to buy livestock to supplement their income. The animal chosen was usually a goat, because it could be bought with no more than two months' earnings.

A monthly unconditional income that was predictable gave the villagers a sense of security, when their other sources of earning, such as wage labour or farming, were uncertain.

Scheme in Jammu and Kashmir

Jammu and Kashmir (J&K) has become the first State to propose a variant scheme of targeted 'Direct Cash Transfer' to citizens living below poverty line. The scheme, announced in the budget for 2017-18 by J&K Finance Minister, will help to eliminate leakages occurring in a plethora of social sector schemes and also significantly reduce the cost of delivery. Till such time that the State is able to provide a safety net for all the people living "below the poverty line", it will be a social security system for all the construction workers in the state. The measure is in keeping with the State's plans to recast the State budget with focus on outcomes. The actual rollout of the scheme is subject to procedural clearances. According to the Finance Minister, it is a first step in transition from running social welfare schemes to a well laid out social security system which will need assistance from the central government as well.

Under the scheme, the Jammu & Kashmir Bank will link the bank accounts of construction workers registered with the J&K Building and Other Construction Workers Welfare Board. The construction workers will be able to avail of cash credit facility up to Rs10,000 in one year along with inbuilt life, health and accident insurance.

(For a detailed discussion and analysis of, UBI concept, see Chapter 9 of Economic Survey 2016-17, Dept. of Economic Affairs, Ministry of Finance, Govt. of India.)

❑ CONCLUSION

Rapid and inclusive growth has been one of the avowed goals of planning and development. The various anti-poverty schemes have been instrumental in mitigating hardships of the poor, both in rural and urban areas, by providing opportunities for economic activity and improving their living conditions. However, such programmes are at best transient palliatives and the ultimate objective should be to not only lift the poor out of the poverty trap, but enable them to become self-reliant and empowered to lead a dignified life on their own merit. For this to happen, the public services they use like schools to which they send their children, the government hospitals and village health centres they depend on, etc. should be raised to the same standards that the upper classes in the society enjoy. In this noble endeavour, the private, corporate sector too could play a part and lend a helping hand to the State by channelizing the CSR funds towards this.

And above all, our elected reprsentatives at all levels—Parliament, State legislatures, town, and village levels must render unblemished services and be made more accountable to deliver on the promises they make to the electorate during elections as they have a critical role to play in the success of these efforts. It should be mandated by legislation that they meet people in their constituencies in small groups at periodic intervals, say every six moths, to listen to the people's grievances and needs, and review the progress of delivery of various socio-economic programmes and on the promises they themselves have made. The concerned government functionaries should also be present at such reviews. At present, there is no such mandated, institutional arrangement to make people's reprsentatives accountable directly to the people at the ground level—a weakness in the system fully exploited by many of them to get away with no accountability. Their indirect accountability in Parliament, or state legislatures, or municipal councils has not been effective in this regard. At least in the villages, under the Panchayati Raj system, the Gram Sabhas function as an open forum and meet at intervals where people in a group can confront their representatives and government functionaries on various issues and development programmes.

Box 17.8 Growth and Inequality: Kuznet's Hypothesis and A Global Perspective

Kuznets Hypothesis

A hypothesis formulated in 1950s by Simon Kuznets, a Nobel Prize-winning economist who did pioneering studies on economic growth and National Income of the US, is the centrepiece of `inequality economics'. According to it, as countries industrialize and average incomes grow, inequality will at first increase and then begin to decline, resulting in an inverted U-shaped curve when one plots inequality level against income.

East Asian Experience

But the experience during the East Asian miracle has been used to question the validity of the Kuznets curve theory. Kuznets' theory stated that rapid capital accumulation would lead to an initial increase in inequality. The eight East Asian countries - Japan, South Korea, Hong Kong, Taiwan, Singapore (four Asian Tigers), Indonesia, Thailand, and Malaysia - witnessed rapid economic growth between 1965 and 1990 coupled with decrease in inequality. Sustained long-term growth in these economies helped to expand employment, reduce unemployment and raise productivity and wages and this in turn reduced inequality and poverty. This was due to immediate re-investment of initial benefits into agrarian reforms such as increasing rural productivity, income, and savings, spread of universal education, and industrial policies that distributed income more equally through high and rising wages. These factors increased the average citizen's ability to consume and invest within the economy, further contributing to economic growth. The high rates of growth provided the resources to promote equality which, in turn, helped to support the high rates of growth.

Trend in Advanced Economies

Again, Kuznet's hypothesis does not explain the phenomenon in the US and other rich countries where income inequality, which had been decreasing through much of the 20th century, has again been on an upswing. While the trend of declining inequality held good until the 1980s, since then there has been increase in inequality in the US, UK and even in some of the fairly egalitarian countries like Sweden and Germany which is incompatible with Kuznets hypothesis.

Inequality is on the rise in most of the OECD countries where the average income of the richest 10 per cent of the population is about nine times that of the poorest 10 per cent - a ratio of 9 to 1. Over the two decades prior to the onset of the global economic crisis (2007-08), real disposable household incomes increased by an average 1.7 per cent a year in OECD countries. But in a large majority of them, the household incomes of the richest 10 per cent grew faster than those of the poorest 10 per cent, thus widening income inequality. Differences in the pace of income growth across household groups were particularly pronounced in some of the English-speaking countries, some Nordic countries, and Israel. In Japan, the real incomes of those at the bottom of the income ladder fell compared with the mid-1980s.

It is the interplay of economic, social and political factors that influence the trends in growth and income equality and not economic factors alone. Political forces, the power of trade unions, globalisation and technological changes which impact the skills of labour all combine to influence growth and income distribution. The mismatch between rapid technological changes and availability of skilled labour has led to wage inequalities both within countries and between countries.

There have been some significant trends in income distribution following the technological advances, globalisation and economic growth in the last two decades:

- Increasing disparities between the very rich and the very poor - the upper most and the lower most segments of society; and
- The rise of a vast middle class, especially in the emerging and developing countries such as China, India, Brazil, Indonesia and Vietnam.
- Uplift of large segments of the poor out of poverty.

In this Chapter we discussed.....

- Decline of India with colonization and following the Industrial Revolution.
- The Constitution of India and Directive Principles of State policy on equality and social justice.
- Absolute, Relative and Extreme poverty; Poverty trap; Measuring poverty.
- Manifestation of inequality and poverty; factors behind poverty.
- Development not only a matter of GDP and per capita income; need to assess other social and economic indicators and parameters to judge 'quality of life' of people.
- UNDP's Human Development Reports and human development index.

- India's Five Year Plans have spoken eloquently on poverty and inequality and imperative need to remedy them and ensure social justice. If these aims have not been achieved largely, the fault lies in implementation and delivery of services.
- Despite impressive progress, the poor do not have access to good education, health facilities, and suffer from hunger and malnutrition.
- Importance of social and political consciousness; examples of Kerala, West Bengal, and some of the UTs; some hitherto laggard states are also waking up now.
- Importance of technology, Aadhaar, Digital India, etc. in improving services.
- Economics and welfarism—views of various economists.
- Global poverty scenario; poverty assessments by the World Bank.
- Economists on inequality and distributive justice.
- Inequality and poverty versus growth: Sen-Bhagawati debate on development and poverty alleviation
- Growth and inequality—the Asian experience; study by Asian Development Bank on growth and confronting rising inequality in Asia; inequalities in India, China, etc.
- Estimation of poverty and identification of poverty line; studies by Indian economists; 1962 Working Group on Minimum Standard of Living; 1979 Task Force report and deficiencies in its approach; NSS surveys; Nobel laureate Angus Deaton on India's poverty.
- 1989 Expert Group under Prof. D.T. Lakdawala; poverty ratio and number of poor (Lakdawala method).
- Expert Groups on methodology for estimation of poverty headed by S. Tendulkar (2005) and C. Rangarajan (2014) and their findings.
- NITI Aayog propse ot have a fresh look at the poverty line and assess the results of poverty alleviation measures.
- Poverty alleviation measures —Integrated Rural Development Programme (IRDP); Self-employment scheme (SGSY); wage employment programmes; Sampoorna Gramin Rozgar Yojana (SGRY); National Rural Livelihood Mission; Mahatma Gandhi National Rural Employment Guarantee Scheme (MNREGS); Rural housing programme—Indira Awas Yojana (IAY); Prime Minister's Gram Sadak Yojana (PMGSY); Other rural programmes—IWDP, DPAP, and DDP.
- Panchayati Raj and Rural rejuvenation
- Urban anti-poverty measures; JNNURM; Swarna Jayanti Sahari Rozgar Yojana (SJSRY).
- Integrated Child Development Services (ICDS); Midday meal scheme.

- Gender bias and Gender inequality; Its implications; Gender budgeting.
- Universal Basic Income (UBI): the concept and its implications.
- Need for poor to have access to better facilities in education, health; greater accountability of elected representatives and bureaucracy on implementation of various schemes; need for mandated and institutionalized framework for periodical meetings between public and political representatives to review progress of schemes as with Gram sabhas in villages.

Important Terms to Note in this Chapter

Quality of life; Life expectancy; Human development index; Absolute and Relative poverty; Poverty trap; Poverty line; Poverty ratio; Head count ratio; Purchasing power parity; Factors of production; Gini coefficient; Public goods; Self-help groups; Wage employment; Panchayati Raj; Gram sabhas; Literacy rate; Gross enrolment ratio; Gender equity; Gender budgeting

Practice Questions

1. What are the manifestations of poverty? What is meant by 'poverty trap'?
2. Distinguish between Absolute and Relative poverty? What are the attributes of Extreme poverty?
3. What are the methods adopted for measuring poverty? In what respects does the method suggested by Prof. Amartya Sen differ from them?
4. What is meant by 'poverty line' and how is it gauged in India? What methodologies are adopted to determine the extent of population below the poverty line in India?
5. Discuss the deficiencies in the methodologies adopted by India to assess the population below poverty line. Why have they led to controversies among experts?
6. What are the major poverty alleviation measures taken by the Central and State governments? How far they have been effective in tackling poverty?
7. The deficiencies in anti-poverty measures adopted in India do not lie in the policies per se but in their implementation. Critically analyse this statement.
8. Mention some of the poverty alleviation programmes adopted in India. How far they have helped to bring down the poverty in the country?
9. Despite six decades of intensive efforts at promoting socio-economic development through Five Year Plans, sizeable section of India's population remains trapped in poverty. Analyse the reasons for this and put forth your views on eradicating poverty more effectively.

10. Successive Five Year Plans of India did have as their objectives reduction of inequalities and wiping out poverty. If so, why poverty still persists in India?
11. What is meant by 'gender bias' and 'gender inequality'? What are its manifestations? What steps need to be taken to overcome them?
12. Explain the concept and purpose of 'gender budgeting'. How has India implemented this policy and how far it has helped to mitigate gender discrimination?
13. Enumerate the various Rural Development schemes executed by the government. How well they are being implemented?
14. How far do you think the Rural Development schemes have benefited the rural population? Identify the deficiencies, if any, in their execution.
15. Explain the features of the programme under Mahatma Gandhi National Rural Employment Guarantee Act (MaNREGA). Critically evaluate its implementation.
16. What are the main features and positive aspects of the 'Mahatma Gandhi National Rural Employment Guarantee Scheme' (MNREGS)? Has it had any adverse impact on rural economy, particularly agriculture, if so, what? Explain.
17. Outline the features of 'Panchayati Raj' scheme. How far do you think it has benefited the rural economy of India?
18. Explain, in brief, the concept of 'Universal Basic Income' (UBI) mooted by some economists and its implications. Do you think it is advisable and practicable to be adopted in India? Give reasons for your views.
19. Migration of people from the rural areas to the urban areas is a major problem in India. What are the reasons for such migration and what steps can be taken to prevent it?
20. Is there any inherent conflict between economic growth and ensuring equality in society? Does growth result in widening inequalities? Discuss this in the light of India's experience since independence.
21. Economic growth and development are not the same thing, or to put it differently, growth per se does not lead to development in the real sense. Do you agree with this? Elaborate your views on this.
22. What is meant by the term 'quality of life' which is widely used in development discourse. How has India fared on the parameters which go to make quality of life?
23. Specify the main factors which hindered trickle-down in Indian economy and agenda of 'inclusive growth' is being pressed into for economic justice.

    [UPSC Main 2014 (Economics Optional Paper)]
24. What are the consequences of deviation from socialistic pattern of society and 1 mixed economy particularly for the persons below the poverty line? Explain.

    [UPSC Main 2014 (Economics Optional Paper)]
25. Elaborate growth-mediated security and support-led security strategies of poverty alleviation given by Jean Dreze and Amartya Sen. *[UPSC Main 2014 (Economics Optional Paper)]*

26. National Rural Employment Guarantee Scheme should be reoriented to create productive permanent assets to promote employment and generate income in the rural sector. Critically evaluate. *[UPSC Main 2014 (Economics Optional Paper)]*

27. Highlight the issues of Bhagwati-Sen controversy over tackling poverty and slow growth rate. *[UPSC Main 2014 (Economics Optional Paper)]*

28. Highlight the basic features of National Food Security Act (NFSA), 2013.Can it solve the problem of malnutrition in the country? Discuss.

[UPSC Main 2015 (Economics Optional Paper)]

29. Rural poverty continues to be a chronic problem in India, which cannot be taken care of by anti-poverty programmes but by creation of permanent productive assets. Discuss.

[UPSC Main 2015 (Economics Optional Paper)]

30. Explain the salient features of 73rd and 74th Constitutional Amendments in India and elaborate the impact of its implementation.

[UPSC Main 2016 (Economics Optional Paper)]

31. Critically examine the difference between absolute poverty and relative poverty. Between the two which is more appropriate? Give reasons.

[UPSC Main 2016 (Economics Optional Paper)]

32. Explain the major tools for measuring inequality. Highlight the more appropriate method of measuring inequality. *[UPSC Main 2016 (Economics Optional Paper)]*

33. Examine the basic features of the National Food Security Act 2013.

[UPSC Main 2016 (Economics Optional Paper)]

34. What are the basic features of the new national rural employment scheme? What are the impediments in their implementation? *[UPSC Main 2016 (Economics Optional Paper)]*

35. Comment on the plausibility of the current poverty estimates in the context of the controversy surrounding the procedures for poverty estimation.

[Indian Economic Service/Indian Statistical Service 2014]

36. Do you agree that urban inequalities have grown with the passage of time in India? Give reasons in support of your answer.

[Indian Economic Service/Indian Statistical Service 2014]

37. Antipoverty programmes need to be reoriented for assets creation rather than providing employment in rural areas. Comment

[Indian Economic Service/Indian Statistical Service 2015]

38. Subsidies are a source of inefficiency and corruption. They should be rationalized and ultimately phased out. Illustrate your answer in the Indian context.

[Indian Economic Service/Indian Statistical Service 2015]

39. Comment on the present poverty line and poverty ratio debate in India.

[Indian Economic Service/Indian Statistical Service 2016]

40. What are the various dimensions of poverty? Has the economic reform package ultimately reduced the incidence of poverty in India?

[Indian Economic Service/Indian Statistical Service 2017]

41. What are the flaws in the Public Distribution System (PDS) in India? Do you think Targeted Public Distribution System (TPDS) can remove these flaws? Explain.

[Indian Economic Service/Indian Statistical Service 2017]

42. COVID-19 pandemic accelerated class inequalities and poverty in India. Comment.

[UPSC Main 2020 (General Studies Paper)]

43. Examine the relation between casualisation of employment and poverty in India.

[UPSC Main 2019 (Economics Optional Paper)]

44. There is a growing divergence in the relationship between poverty and hunger in India. The shrinking of social expenditure by the government is forcing the poor to spend more on non-food essential items squeezing their food-budget. — Elucidate.

[UPSC Main 2019 (General Studies Paper)]

45. Performance of welfare schemes that are implemented for vulnerable sections is not so effective due to absence of their awareness and active involvement at all stages of policy process. — Discuss.

[UPSC Main 2019 (Economics Optional Paper)]

46. Despite implementation of various programmes for eradication of poverty by the government in India, poverty is still existing/ Explain by giving reasons.

[UPSC Main 2018 (General Studies Paper)]

47. How far do you agree with the view that the focus on lack of availability of food as the main cause of hunger takes the attention away from ineffective human development policies in India?

[UPSC Main 2018 (General Studies Paper)]

48. Assess the importance of the Panchayat bodies in India as a part of local government. Apart from governmental grants, what other sources the Panchayats can look for financing developmental projects.

[UPSC Main 2018 (General Studies Paper)]

49. Analyse the validity of the inverted 'U'-shaped hypothesis of Kuznets in the context of changes in inequality in India.

[UPSC Main 2020 (Economics Optional Paper)]

50. "While absolute poverty declines over the decades, the poverty gap between different social groups shows rising trend in India". Discuss.

[UPSC Main 2020 (Economics Optional Paper)]

51. Comment on poverty alleviation schemes undertaken by the Government of India for urban poor.

[UPSC Main 2020 (Economics Optional Paper)]

52. What are the core objectives of the Mahatma Gandhi National Rural Employment Guarantee Scheme (MGNREGS)? In what ways has a paradigm shift taken place with the implementation of MGNREGA?

[UPSC Main 2019 (Economics Optional Paper)]

53. Give an account of MGNREGA in India. Explain the extent to which it has been successful in combating rural unemployment and poverty. What are your suggestions to make it more effective?

[Indian Economic Service/Indian Statistical Service 2020]

54. Examine the recent trend in rural wages in India. Discuss the role of MGNREGA in determining this trend. *[UPSC Main 2020 (Economics Optional Paper)]*

55. Would you advocate a programme of Universal Basic Income (UBI) to reduce extreme poverty in India? Discuss in detail.

[UPSC Main 2019 (Economics Optional Paper)]

56. How is the methodology followed by the Rangarajan Committee different from that of the Tendulkar Committee in measuring poverty in India?

[UPSC Main 2019 (Economics Optional Paper)]

57. Write a note on Human Development Report (HDR), 2019 with reference to India.

[Indian Economic Service/Indian Statistical Service 2020]

CHAPTER

DEMOGRAPHIC ISSUES AND VITAL STATISTICS

- Population: The Global scenario
- Economists on Population issue
- Global Population Growth
- Food Security and Sustainability Challenges
- Inefficient Food Supply Chain and Wastages
- Environmental Concerns
- Demographic Transition
- India's Demographic Scene
- Performance of States on Population Control
- Age Structure and Demographic Dividend
- India's Demographic Dividend
- Divergence in Democratic Dividend
- China's One-child and Three-child Population Policy
- How India Compares with Other Countries
- The Global Problem of Declining Population
- Migration and Demographic Changes
- Demographic Changes in US and Europe

❑ INTRODUCTION

The population of a country, or the human capital or human resources, along with the physical capital (plant, machinery, equipment, etc.), is an important factor and determinant in the socio-economic development of the nation. The successful transition from a traditional economy dominated by agriculture to a modern, growing, industrialized economy depends on both the accumulation, and the quality, of its human capital. Development of human capital by means of education and hands-on experience is a long-drawn process with a considerable gestation period.

A developing economy needs to invest in human capital well ahead, and alongside the growth process, to prepare the people and enable them to acquire the skill sets required to cope with and manage the industries and technologies which will be the engines of growth. Unless the investment in physical capital is accompanied by commensurate accretion of human capital, the development process will be tardy. India's own experience is a case in point. While after independence India developed higher education in a big way–Universities, Engineering colleges, IIMs, and IITs–she lagged behind in the progress, both in quality and quantity, of primary and secondary education in the first three decades, and in encouraging mid-level technical institutions, like polytechnics and upgraded Industrial Training Institutes (ITIs), which could have built an army of technically skilled workforce needed for faster industrial development.

❑ POPULATION: THE GLOBAL SCENARIO

From a global perspective, the population issue is a multi-dimensional challenge (See Box 18.1). While many of the poorer nations are facing increasing population, much of the developed world, consisting of the economically advanced nations, face the problem of declining and ageing population. Though the global poverty rate–the share of the population living on less than US$1.25 per day–has been cut by half between 1990 and 2010, still about 1.2 billion people continue to live in extreme poverty, and more than 75 per cent of them reside in rural areas which are primarily dependent on agricultural production. **Also, though the number of those living below the poverty line has been brought down, it can by no means be said that the living conditions, or the quality of life, of those brought above the poverty threshold has been substantially improved from the point of view of housing, education, health, sanitation, etc. Apart from being rid of the lack of food and some very basic necessities, their daily existence continues to be far from satisfactory, much less what can be considered ideal.**

While the global production of food is enough to feed everyone in the world, yet about 840 million people suffer from food insecurity and malnourishment. A high proportion of these food insecure and poor rural people are subsistence farmers, herders, and fishers, living in South Asia and Africa who, while themselves struggling to survive, have the onerous task of not only maintaining the existing levels of food output but augmenting it to meet the needs of the growing population. And they are pitted against serious challenges posed by climate change, declining soil fertility, and other adverse environmental factors, all of which will have a significant bearing on agricultural productivity in the years to come.

Box 18.1 Economists on Population Issue

A moot question that arises with burgeoning population and longer life expectancy is, would not higher survival rates result in increasing pressure on the requirements of food and, in the event of inadequate supplies of food, would not hunger and malnutrition continue to haunt humanity? It was these questions that troubled Thomas Robert Malthus (1766–1834) to no end, and led him to enunciate his pessimistic views on unchecked population growth. Malthus in his famous work, '*An Essay on Population*', published in 1798, was concerned with the effects and pressure of population growth on scarce land. According to him, when natural resources are limited, human fecundity makes population pressure inevitable. He presaged that the geometrical rise in population would eventually outstrip the arithmetical rise in available resources—and a thesis that population, when unchecked, goes on doubling itself every twenty-five years or increases in a geometrical ratio, which came to be known as 'Malthusian crisis' and also dubbed as Malthusian pessimism. Rational individuals may adopt some 'preventive' measures to restrict procreation, such as delay of marriage, which was Malthus' preferred solution, to contraception as suggested by neo-Malthusians like John Stuart Mill (1806–1873). If these measures fail, real incomes will fall so low that some 'positive' natural checks will come into play and the population growth will be arrested by famine, starvation and disease, high incidence of mortality, and shorter adult lifespan.

Though the name of Malthus is synonymous with problems posed by population growth, he was not the first to recognize and red-flag the issue. Malthus recognized this as much when he disputed the views of some of his predecessors in his works. François Quesnay (1694–1774), the French economist of the Physiocratic school, Richard Cantillon (circa 1680–1734), an Irish-French economist, Marquis de Condorcet (1743–1794), the French philosopher-mathematician, and Adam Smith (1723–1790), all of whom preceded Malthus, had dwelt on population issues in their writings.

William Godwin (1756–1836), an English political philosopher, well known for his work, *An Enquiry Concerning the Principles of Political Justice and its Influence on General Virtue and Happiness*, had written an essay titled '*Of Avarice and Profusion*' which is considered to have prompted Malthus to write his famous '*Essay on the Principle of Population*'. Malthus refuted Godwin's and Condorcet's belief in 'human perfectability'. Godwin also authored another work 'Of Population. An Enquiry Concerning the Power of Increase in the Numbers of Mankind' being an answer to Mr. Malthus's Essay on that Subject', which was a riposte to Malthus. Godwin viewed humans as naturally benevolent and believed in a 'beautiful system of equality' which, if fully realized, would remove the economic and social constraints on procreation and population could grow exponentially. But as fertile land becomes scarce, food needed to support more people cannot be produced at the same rate, and imbalance between population growth and food sets in.

While Malthus argued that sustained economic growth is impossible, Condorcet was much more optimistic about the prospects of sustained economic growth and "the perfectibility of man". A strong advocate of women's rights in the Age of Enlightenment, he advocated birth control, woman's right to plan her pregnancy sensibly, and for a man's obligations to his child's welfare after birth.

Cantillon provided a rather coherent theory on population growth. Unlike William Petty (1623–1687), the English economist-statistician, who believed that there always existed a considerable amount of unused land and economic opportunity to support economic growth, Cantillon propounded that population would grow only to the extent economic opportunities permit. Cantillon also identified three variables which determined the size of population and its growth, viz., natural resources, technology, and culture. Cantillon's population theory was more comprehensive than that of Malthus in as much as Cantillon recognized a much wider spectrum of factors which affect population growth, including the tendency for population growth to fall to zero as a society becomes more industrialized and developed.

❑ GLOBAL POPULATION GROWTH

Before examining India's population issues, it would be relevant to place them in the global context as India, along with China and a few other countries, is going to be a critical factor in the population dynamics of the future as will be seen from the following facts. According to UN population data, the following facts emerge:

- The world's population, which was 1.6 billion in 1901, rose to 3 billion by 1960, crossed the 6 billion mark in 1999, and touched 7 billion in 2011. According to projections, it is expected to reach 8.5 billion by 2030, 9.7 billion by 2050, and exceed 11 billion in 2100.
- About 78 million people are added to the world's population every year. This means that, by 2050, the global economy should be able to provide a decent living for more than 9 billion people, of which 85 per cent will be living in what are now the developing countries.
- China and India remain the two most populous countries in the world, each with more than 1 billion people, presently accounting for about 19 and 18 per cent of the world population, respectively.
- India is expected to surpass China as the most populous nation around 2022.
- Nigeria will overtake the United States to become the world's third most populous country 35 years from now, i.e., around 2050.
- Most of the projected increase in the world's population can be attributed to a short list of high-fertility countries, mainly in Africa, or countries with already large populations.
- During the period 2015–2050, half of the world's population growth is expected to take place in nine countries: India, Nigeria, Pakistan, Democratic Republic of Congo, Ethiopia, United Republic of Tanzania, USA, Indonesia, and Uganda, in that order, according to the size of their contribution to the total population growth.

But global population is on a downward slope with population declining in many countries with serious ramifications for future, requiring hard choices and difficulty adjustments on a global level. (On this, see Box 18.2: The Global Problem of Declining Population" at the end of this chapter).

Food Security and Sustainability Challenges

Apart from containing the ever growing population, the world community will be confronted with the problems of providing adequate food, housing and health facilities, and employment opportunities.

Increasing urbanization will mean overcrowded cities and towns, congested housing, more slums, shanties and ghettos, traffic snarls, and excessive pollution levels giving rise to health and hygiene problems. Due to paucity of jobs, if unemployment levels remain high among the youth in urban areas, and more people are caught in the poverty trap, the resulting inequity among the urban inhabitants could lead to social disharmony and political instability.

Growing urban populations will also place pressure on municipalities to improve their resilience to natural and human disasters. Disasters can be a source of increased migration towards cities, but can also be a consequence of densely populated areas that lack access to food and water. Larger urban populations will also change food and land-use patterns—a factor with potentially vast implications. Changes in production methods and land-use patterns due to higher demand, deforestation, higher energy use, rising food prices, and regional food shortages, etc. will exacerbate the problems.

Inefficient Food Supply Chain and Wastages

The food supply chain in many countries is highly inefficient resulting in wastages of food. While there are no precise estimates of food wastages, as per rough estimates, worldwide losses or waste of food amount to between 30 and 50 per cent of all food produced. Food losses occur mainly after the harvest which is more often a problem in developing countries, due to lack of storage facilities, exposure to weather, and inefficient transportation and marketing arrangements. Though the world produces enough food, it is confronted with the twin issues of under- and over-nutrition. Food waste in usage and consumption is primarily a problem in the rich countries, where around 220 million tons of food is estimated to be wasted every year.

It would, however, be overly simplistic to suggest that eliminating food losses and wastages will solve the problem of hunger and malnutrition. For that, a multi-pronged approach is required, including increasing productivity in farming and overall food output, making distribution and marketing of food more efficient, ensuring access of poorer sections to food through proper interventionist policies, and rationalising the use of food for non-human consumption.

Environmental Concerns

Agricultural operations, which is crucially dependent on climatic factors, water resources, and energy, have major environmental implications. The process of both production and consumption of food involve the use of energy and is estimated to account for about 30 per cent of the total energy consumption of the world. Food production, supply, and consumption chain also give rise to greenhouse gas emissions. With depleting fossil fuel sources, the cost of increasing food output will also rise, which may adversely impact food security in the years to come. Unchecked tapping of groundwater sources for both farming and non-agricultural purposes is also a matter for concern.

❑ DEMOGRAPHIC TRANSITION

Historically, it is seen that nations undergo changes in their demographic patterns, in three or four stages, depending on the stage of their socio-economic development. In the initial stages, when an economy is traditional and agrarian in structure, it will have high levels of death rates and less longevity of life due to poor health and sanitation facilities, diseases, and epidemics. Birth rate will also be high as, due to the high mortality rate and the economic benefits of having a large family, people are inclined to have more children. Further, due to low levels of literacy and education and rigid modes of customs and beliefs, people tend to have more children. But the growth in population in this stage is somewhat balanced by the high death rates.

As development takes place and living conditions improve with more food intake and better health facilities, the longevity of life improves and the death rate tends to decline, but it is not followed by commensurate decline in fertility. Thus, in this second stage, the population will rise with increase in the average family size also. In the third phase, with industrial development and modernization of the economy, expanding educational and public health facilities, and greater participation of women in economic activities outside their homes, there will be more awareness of the benefits of small family size. As the replacement rate is attained, the fertility rate will decline in this stage, and with death rate already falling, the population will stabilize at a lower level. There could be a fourth stage, where, with the reduction in the proportion of population in the reproductive age group and the birth rate falling below the replacement level, there will be negative growth in the population. Many of the advanced economies in western Europe are presently going through this phase of declining population with the total fertlity rates (TFR) less than the replacement level of 2.1.

India's Demographic Scene

The history of the Census began in 1800 when England had its Census. The population of England's dependencies was not known at that time. In India, the first formal Census was undertaken 1866-67 by the actual counting of heads in most of the part of the country, which is known as the Census of 1872. This Census did not cover all territories possessed or controlled by the British. In this Census, the information gathered pertained to name, age, religion, caste or class, race or nationality, attendance at school/college, and ability to read and write. While these common questions were asked separately for males and females, information on occupation was collected in respect of males only.

The 1881 Census which was undertaken by the Census Commissioner of India was a great step towards the modern synchronous Census. Since then, Censuses have been undertaken uninterruptedly once every ten years.

India, the second most populous country in the world and home to one-sixth of the world's population, has barely 2.5 per cent of the world's land area. The prevalence of high maternal and infant mortality, childhood morbidity, low life expectancy, and high fertility has been a source of concern to planners and public health professionals ever since independence.

Prior to independence, India experienced low growth in population–less than two-thirds of one per cent between 1901 and 1911 and even negative growth between 1911 and 1921. It was a period of stagnant phase in India's population growth. Birth rate continued to remain high declining only marginally, while death rate declined between 1911 and 1940. Yet, the increase in population was rather subdued due to recurrence of epidemics like cholera, plague, malaria, etc., and famines. (See Tables 18.1 and 18.2 (a) and 18.2 (b)).

Death rate kept declining because of more effective control of epidemics, better sanitation, and improvements in distribution system due to better transport facilities and this is reflected in moderate growth rate in population between 1921 and 1941. This trend in stable growth rate continued between 1941 and 1951 due to the Great Bengal famine of 1943 in which an estimated 3 million people are reported to have died, though the official Commission put the death toll at 1.5 million. The large-scale migration, with influx of refugees from Pakistan following the partition of India, added to the problems. With modest growth in population between 1921 and 1951, India can be considered to have been in the second stage of demographic transition during this period.

During the four decades from 1951 till 1991, there has been steady and significant growth in population with the growth rate ranging around 2.5 per cent. The population increased from 361.1 million in 1951 to 846.3 million in 1991.

Table 18.1 Demographic Data of India, 1901–2011

Census year	Total population (million)	Average annual growth rate (%)	Density (persons per sq km)	Sex ratio (females per 1000 males)	Literacy rate (%)	Urban population (%)
1901	238.4	0.3	77	972	–	10.8
1911	252.1	0.6	82	963	–	10.3
1921	251.3	–ve	81	955	–	11.2
1931	278.9	1.1	90	950	–	12.0
1941	318.6	1.3	103	945	–	13.9
1951	361.1	1.3	117	946	18.3	17.3
1961	439.2	2.2	142	941	28.3	18.0
1971	548.2	2.5	177	930	34.4	19.9
1981	683.3	2.5	216	934	43.6	23.4
1991	846.3	2.4	267	927	52.2	25.7
2001	1028.7	2.1	325	933	64.8	27.8
2011	1210.2	1.8	382	940	74.0	31.2

Source: Census of India, Registrar General of India.

Table 18.2 (a) India—Vital Statistics: (1911–1990)

Year	Birth Rate (per 1,000)	Death Rate (per 1,000)	Life Expectancy # (Years at birth)	
			Male	Female
1911–20	48.1	48.6	19.4	20.9
1921–30	46.4	36.3	26.9	26.6
1931–40	45.2	31.2	32.1	31.4
1941–50	39.9	27.4	32.4	31.7
1951–60	41.7	22.8	41.9	40.6
1961–70	41.2	19.0	46.4	44.7
1971–80	37.2	15.0	50.9	50.0
1981–90	32.5	11.4	57.7	58.7

Source: Sample Registration System (SRS) Bulletin, Registrar General of India; Plan documents, Planning Commission.

Note:# Life expectancy is the average number of years a person is expected to live at the time of birth if current mortality rates were to continue.

Despite concerted and sustained efforts at family planning and birth control measures under the Five Year Plans starting with the very First Plan (see next section), with a *slogan* to restrict the number of children per family to two, the growth in population continued apace. This was because of persisting high fertility rates while the mortality rate came down as a result of improved living conditions and better healthcare facilities in urban and rural areas. However, there has been much variation between the performances of states in regard to birth control as discussed in the next section. That the growth rate has shown slight decline in 2001 and 2011 (see column 3 in Table 18.1) is a positive sign which, if sustained, augurs well.

Table 18.2 (b): India: Vital Statistics: 2001–2014 (with Total and Rural–Urban break-up)

Year	Birth Rate			Death Rate			IMR #		
	T	R	U	T	R	U	T	R	U
2001	26.1	27.6	20.8	8.7	9.4	6.3	70	75	44
2005	24.8	26.4	19.8	8.0	8.7	6.0	60	66	38
2011	22.5	24.1	18.3	7.3	7.8	5.8	50	55	34
2014	21.4	22.9	17.3	7.0	7.5	5.6	40	44	27

Source: Sample Registration System (SRS) Bulletin, Registrar General of India; Plan documents, Planning Commission.

Note: T – Total; R – Rural; U – Urban. # : IMR: Infant Mortality Rate. IMR refers to the measurement of mortality in the first year of life and is computed by relating the number of deaths under one year of age to the annual number of live births.

Both the birth and death rates have been brought down significantly–birth rate from 41.7 per 1,000 in 1951 to 21.4 in 2014 and death rate from 22.8 per 1,000 to 7.0 in 2014.

Performance of States on Population Control

India has had an intensive family planning programme to contain population from the very early days of planning. The First Five Year Plan (1951-56) document had referred to the importance of population control and stated thus:

"The recent increase in the population of India and the pressure exercised on the limited resources of the country have brought to the forefront the urgency of the problem of family planning and population control. The application of medical knowledge and social care has lowered the death rate, while the birth rate remains fairly constant. This has led to the rapid increase in the growth of population. While a lowering of the birth rate may occur as a result of improvements in the standards of living, such improvements are not likely to materialize if there is a concurrent increase of population. It is, therefore, apparent that population control can be achieved only by the reduction of the birth rate to the extent necessary to stabilize the population at a level consistent with the requirements of the national economy. This can be secured only by the realization of the need for family limitation on a wide scale by the people. The main appeal for family planning is based on considerations of the health and welfare of the family. Family limitation or spacing of the children is necessary and desirable in order to secure better health for the mother and better care and upbringing of children. Measures directed to this end should, therefore, form part of the public health programme."

Subsequent Plans have also made sustained efforts to control the population growth rate. It may be mentioned that literacy and education levels, besides improvement in the standard of living, have a profound influence on population control and family welfare. There has been considerable progress over the years in all States and Union territories in regard to population control by bringing down both the birth rates and the total fertility rates (TFR), though there are variations in performance, as can be seen from Table 18.3. By 2010, while TFR for the country as a whole stood at 2.5, many States have attained the targeted 'Replacement level TFR' of 2.1 and quite a few have even surpassed it. Some states like UP, Bihar, MP, and Rajasthan, which are all states with a high population, still have a higher level of TFR above 3.0. They need to bring it down so that TFR for the country as a whole also comes down and it will have a significant impact on the country's population growth.

Table 18.3 Performance of Selected States on Population Control

State	Literacy Rate			Birth Rate			TFR			CPR	
	1951	1971	2011	1960	1999	2010	1980–82	1990–92	2010	1992–93	1998–99
Kerala	40.7	60.4	93.9	22.6	18.0	16.4	2.9	1.8	1.8	63.3	63.7
Mahar	20.9	39.2	82.9	29.5	21.1	15.6	3.7	3.0	1.9	53.7	60.9
TN	20.8	39.5	80.3	28.0	19.3	14.8	3.4	2.2	1.7	49.8	52.1
AP	13.1	24.6	67.6	21.2	21.7	16.7	3.9	3.0	1.8	47.0	59.6
WB	24.0	33.2	77.1	19.2	20.7	11.5	4.1	3.2	1.8	57.4	66.6
HP	7.7	32.0	83.8	17.1	23.8	19.3	na	3.0	1.8	58.4	67.7
Karnataka	19.3	31.5	75.6	27.9	22.3	20.5	3.6	3.1	2.0	49.1	58.3
Odisha	15.8	26.2	73.45	24.6	24.1	14.6	4.2	3.3	2.3	36.3	46.8
Goa	na	44.8	87.4	na	14.3	19.4	na	1.6	na	47.8	47.5
	1951	1971	2011	1960	1999	2010	1980–82	1990–92	2010	1992–93	1998–99
UP	10.8	21.7	69.72	15.9	32.8	16.0	5.8	5.2	3.5	19.8	28.1
Bihar	12.2	19.9	63.82	11.4	31.5	18.6	5.6	4.6	3.7	23.1	24.5
MP	9.8	22.1	70.63	18.1	31.1	15.2	5.2	4.7	3.1	36.5	44.3
Rajas	8.9	19.1	67.06	36.4	31.1	11.5	5.5	4.5	3.1	31.8	40.3

Source: Literacy data from Statistical Abstract, India, CSO and Census of India; Birth Rate from Sample Registration System, Registrar General of India; TFR data from National Human Development Report, 2001 and Tenth Five Year Plan, Vol. III; CPR data from National Family Health Survey and National Human Development Report, 2001.

Note: **Literacy data** in percentage; **Birth rate** is number of live births per 1,000 population in a given year; **TFR: Total Fertility Rate** measures average number of children born to a woman during her entire productive period; **CPR: Couple Protection Rate** is the percentage of currently married women aged 15-49 using family planning methods at the time of survey; na: not available

❑ AGE-STRUCTURE AND DEMOGRAPHIC DIVIDEND

During demographic transition, along with the growth in population, changes also take place in the population age-structure. While the importance of population growth as a determinant of the quality of life is generally understood, the profound and far-reaching consequences of changing age- structure, especially if it occurs too rapidly, is not grasped by many. Demographic dividend is when a country has a large labour force or working population which outgrows the number of people who are dependents–children and/or elderly people–who do not contribute to the country's productive activities and economic growth.

In many of the developed countries, the population in the reproductive age group is relatively small and their fertility rate is low while the life expectancy–longevity of life–is high. These countries have the advantage of having achieved a stable population but face the problems of having a relatively small productive workforce which has to support the large aged population with a substantial burden of health problems. Such countries with relatively large numbers of those who are of non-working age relative to those who are of working age have a high 'dependency ratio' indicating pressure on the productive population. Currently, many of the west European nations, especially those hit hard by the Eurozone debt crisis, are witnessing drops in birth rates that will speed up decline in, and ageing of, the population. They are struggling with low economic growth and high public spending. Lately, Europe is also faced with a massive migration crisis with huge inflow of immigrants from west Asian and north African countries which will place enormous burden on their economies. Though this migration will partly make up for the shortage of young labour force, it may not help if the migrants are mostly unskilled or not suited for jobs which are on offer. (See Table 18.6 on p. 18.15, Box 18.2 and Box 18.3 at the end of this chapter and chapter 20, pp. 20.33-5).

In contrast, the population in many of the developing countries, including India, consist of a large proportion of children and persons in the reproductive age group because of which the population will continue to grow even when replacement level of fertility is reached–with couples having only two children. While this young population is a dividend and a positive factor, it also poses many challenges. It is imperative that these countries should generate enough employment opportunities for this workforce and utilize the human resources for accelerating economic growth.

India's Demographic Dividend

India's demographic profile reveals certain distinct features that have key implications for the growth of India and the Indian states. India's demographic cycle is such that the next few decades present an opportunity for India to catch up to the per capita income levels attained by China, South Korea and Brazil. India will remain close to its peak for a much longer period than other countries. China and Korea had very high Total Fertility or Replacement Rates (TFR) i.e., well above 2.1 like India, but then it declined rapidly in those countries whereas in India the decline in TFR has been more gradual.

India may not see surges or decelerations of growth on account of the demographic dividend but might be able to sustain high levels of growth due to it for a longer time.

India is now having one of the largest young population in the world, aged between 15 and 59 (the working age group). (See Table 18.4). If relevant policies are drawn up to capitalize on this advantage, it would greatly benefit the economy. In the absence of such policies and lag in economic growth and creation of jobs, this may turn into a formidable problem. The magnitude of the problem can be gauged from the fact that about one million youth are joining India's labour force every month and this trend is expected to continue for the next decade and half or even longer. That many jobs have to be created to absorb this relentless surge in the labour force. Employment opportunities have to be created at a fast pace in the manufacturing sector, infrastructure areas, and sectors such as education and health, tourism, hospitality, etc. which have employment generation potential.

Table 18.4 Demographic Profile of India Age-Specific Population Data (1961–2011) (In Million)

Age-Group	1961	1971	1981	1991	2001	2011
0–4	66.10	79.56	83.51	102.38	110.45	112.80
5–14	113.98	150.78	179.60	209.98	253.17	259.64
15–59	233.95	285.01	358.68	464.81	585.63	730.07
60 & above	24.73	32.69	43.50	56.70	76.62	108.33
Total	438.76	548.04	664.96	833.87	1025.87	1206.35

(Total excludes 'Age Not Stated' category)

Source: Census of India, Registrar-General of India.

Divergence in Democratic Dividend

However, an important feature of this trend is that this demographic dividend window will be available at different points of time in different states because of varying behaviour of the population dynamics. They fall into three categories:

- In Kerala, Tamil Nadu, Andhra Pradesh, Telangana, Gujarat, Punjab and West Bengal, this window of dividend opportunity may close in about five years.
- Then there are states which include Karnataka, Odisha, Himachal Pradesh, Maharashtra, Jammu and Kashmir, Assam, Uttarakhand and Haryana where the window will remain open for another 10-15 years.
- The window of dividend opportunity is yet to open in the high-fertility states in the hinterland which includes Chhattisgarh, Jharkhand, Madhya Pradesh, Rajasthan, Uttar Pradesh and Bihar. These states will have the window of opportunity even in the 2050s and 2060s.
- As India's fertility transition will be staggered, with the window of demographic advantage open in different regions during different time-periods, India will not draw a high dividend at any time but will have a moderate dividend over a longer time span.

Need for nuanced policies

India will enjoy a longer span of demographic dividend because, as the window closes in some states, it will open in other states. This has important implications for planning socio-economic development policies based on the age and sex structures in states or a set of states. It calls for a differential and forward-looking approach in policy making and programme planning to harness maximum potential of the demographic dividend.

For example, the focus in the states where the window is closing soon will have to be on ageing and migrant-friendly policies and programmes, while the focus in the states where the window is open and will close in the next 10-15 years will have to be on empowering girls and women, provisioning of health, education and skill development for young people, and employment generation.

The focus in the states where the window is yet to open will have to be threefold:

- Addressing harmful practices such as child marriage.
- Access to quality sexual and reproductive health services and family planning services to all, and

- Providing for health and education facilities, life and vocational skills to all the young people.
- The window of dividend opportunity is yet to open in the high-fertility states in the hinterland which includes Chhattisgarh, Jharkhand, Madhya Pradesh, Rajasthan, Uttar Pradesh and Bihar. These states will have the window of opportunity even in the 2050s and 2060s.
- As India's fertility transition will be staggered, with the window of demographic advantage open in different regions during different time-periods, India will not draw a high dividend at any time but will have a moderate dividend over a longer time span.

Challenges

- This varying population dynamics and the surge in the population of working age population also throws up challenges and opportunities for the economy as discussed below:
- Creation of jobs to absorb the burgeoning young population is a major challenge. This will require India to expand its manufacturing and industrial base. It is estimated that India need to sustain 8 to 8.5 per cent growth to gainfully employ 60 million new workers expected to join the labour force by 2030. The enormity of the task can be gauged from the fact that India is presently creating only about 4 million jobs per year against the 10 to 12 million persons joining the labour force each year.
- Construction and manufacturing sectors have the maximum potential to create jobs. The government has initiated steps to expand domestic manufacturing of defence, energy, telecom, and electronic items, pharmaceuticals and a range of other products, both for domestic consumption and exports.
- More speedy expansion of infrastructure projects and rural and urban housing, travel and tourism industry offer much scope for employment.
- Expansion of education and health sectors will be crucial not only from the point of view of job creation, for which they have great potential, but also to cater to the educational and skilling needs of the youth and health needs of an expanding and ageing population.
- Skilling the labour force to meet the increasing needs of industry, and continually upgrading skills to cope with the rapid technological changes is to be carefully planned. Suitable changes in educational curriculum have to be carried out, on a continuing basis, in consultation with domain experts and industry to ensure employability of labour.
- As there is bound to be increasing inter-state migration owing to shortage and surplus of labour in different states due to differing population trends, planning for jobs and housing and other infrastructure facilities have to be aligned with the demographic changes. Regional balance in development in line with changing demographic patterns is crucial. The lop-sided development India has had is evident from the fact that while Eastern and Central India are rich in minerals, much of the industrial development has taken place in Western and Southern India. This has led to large-scale migration of labour with consequent problems faced by the migrants as witnessed when the pandemic broke out in early 2020.

China's One-child and Three-child Population Policy

China and India have the rather unsavoury distinction of being the two most populous countries in the world. Out of the total world population of 7,794 million (or, 7.79 billion) in 2020, China (including Hong Kong which had 7.5 million) accounted for 1,446.5 million (i.e., 18.5 per cent) and India had

1,380 million (i.e., 17.7 per cent). Together, the two countries had 2,826.5 million which works out to a whopping 36.26 per cent of the world population.

The increase in the population and the average annual rate of population change in the two countries between 1950 and 2020 are given in Tables 18.5 (a) and 18.5 (b). It will be seen from it that India's population has been rising at a faster rate than China's from the 1970s and the difference has been more pronounced from the 1995-2000 period.

It may be noted here that China introduced 'One-child' policy in 1979 and its official implementation began in 1980. The policy took shape when the late Deng Xiaoping, architect of China's radical and far-reaching market economy reforms, and other leaders concluded that China's growing population and high birth rate of almost three children per woman would jeopardize economic growth.

Table 18.5 (a): Total population of China & India-1950-2020 (in million)

	1950	1960	1980	1990	2000	2010	2020
China	554	660	1000	1176	1290	1368	1439
India	376	450	698	873	1056	1234	1380

Source: United Nations, Department of Economic and Social Affairs, Population Division (2019). World Population Prospects 2019, Online Edition. Rev. 1.

Table 18.5 (b): Average Annual Rate of Population Growth – 1950 – 2020 in China and India (percentage)

	1950–55	1960–65	1965–70	1970–75	1975–80	1980–85	1985–90	1995–2000	2010–15	2010–15
China	1.98	1.85	2.67	2.25	1.53	1.46	1.80	0.78	0.55	0.46
India	1.71	2.05	2.13	2.31	2.30	2.31	2.15	1.84	1.19	1.04

Source: United Nations, Department of Economic and Social Affairs, Population Division (2019). World Population Prospects 2019, Online Edition. Rev. 1.

While the restriction was adhered to in cities, in the countryside many families continued having two or more children. Ethnic minorities were also exempted from the provision. As years passed, harsh official campaigns to fine and punish couples who violated the rules, including forcing women to have abortions, were carried out. This bred much public discontent and a number of scholars urged the government to relax the rules. Sometimes, Chinese families preferring to have boys also resorted to aborting female foetuses which affected the sex (female-male) ratio.

From the mid-1980s, the policy was gradually relaxed by permitting families in rural areas and households where parents were the only child to have two children. But the relaxation, which aimed at augmenting population, failed to achieve the goal of boosting births by 2 million a year.

But amid concerns over China's ageing population, gender imbalance, and shrinking labour force, the government announced in October 2015 to end the policy which took effect from January 1, 2016. Though it was a major liberalization, many couples and scholars felt that the measure has come too late and would not have the effect to the desired extent because the economic pressure of raising children is very high in China. Many families do not have the wherewithal to raise more children.

The government credits the one-child policy with preventing some 400 million births and helping to lift countless families out of poverty by easing the pressure on the country's limited resources. But this has been contested by Prof. Amartya Sen according to whom China's population growth rate had been showing decline even prior to the adoption of the one-child policy. As seen from Table 18.5(b), the average annual rate of population change had come down between 1950-55 and 1960-65, and again between 1965-70 and 1975-80 while the policy was introduced in 1979. As Prof. Sen puts it, "the two most potent factors that induce fertility reduction globally are women's schooling and women's paid employment." While the lifting of one-child policy is a historic development, Prof. Sen attributes the fall in China's fertility rate more to women's progress and "reasoned family decisions in favour of a new norm of smaller families". It may also be mentioned that a 50-50 gender parity in the workforce can boost a country's GDP.

China's new Three-Child Policy

Table 18.5 (b) shows China's population growth between 1985-90 and 2015-20 slipping to its slowest rate since the 1950s. China has been concerned over this declining trend and its implications for China's growth in the years to come. Hence in a major policy shift aimed at reversing the trend and boosting the country's declining birth rate, the National People's Congress (NPC), China's supreme body, relaxed the two-child norm and endorsed a three-child policy in August 2021.

However, experts are of the view that relaxing limits on reproductive rights alone cannot do much in averting an adverse demographic trend. There are many factors behind people in China choosing to have fewer children. These include:

- Rising costs of living and costs of raising children. From the time of birth to the time children start working, healthcare, housing, education and other costs are all problems which China's millennials find they cannot afford.
- Many of China's young couples are facing mounting debt due to exorbitant living costs and they have been putting off having children to avoid the financial burden that comes with reproducing.
- The issue is not just about giving birth to a child, but the real problem parents confront for the next 21 years after the child is born – having to sacrifice time, money, and energy into child-rearing.
- People need substantial subsidies not just encouragement. The subsidies offered by the State would be meagre and too insufficient to convince most women to have more children.
- The norm of "9-9-6", a term used to describe prevailing work culture in China, where people are made to work 12 hours a day, from 9 am to 9 pm, 6 days a week. Such punishing working hours have become not only common in most companies but is routinely expected of staff.
- The desire of the young people to pursue education and career and, in addition, the problem of supporting ageing parents. The problem is made worse by the pervasive culture of long working hours.
- There has also been an attitudinal and cultural shift during the decades in which the one-child policy remained in force, when many couples believed that one child is enough, and many even expressing no interest in having children.

The Chinese government, however, has said that the new policy will be accompanied by supportive measures, which will be conducive to improving the population structure, fulfilling the country's strategy of actively coping with an ageing population and maintaining the advantage of being endowed with adequate human resources to meet development imperatives. It remains to be seen how far the new policy will deliver the desired results.

How India Compares with Other Countries

In the early years (1960-65), many developing countries had a higher population growth rate than India's, but over a period, their rates have become less than that of India. Though India's population growth rate has come down, it is now somewhat higher than that of most other countries as will be seen from Table 18.6.

Table 18.6 Population and Rate of Growth of Population of Selected Countries

Country	Population (in Mn.)				Annual Growth Rate of Population (%)		
	1960	1975	1998	2012	1960–65	1990–95	2000–05
Developed Nations							
U.S.A.	186.2	220.2	274.0	315.8	1.37	1.2	1.0
Canada	17.91	23.2	30.6	34.7	1.90	1.1	1.0
Australia	10.30	13.9	18.5	22.9	1.99	1.2	1.3
Japan	92.5	111.5	126.3	126.4	1.02	0.4	0.1
France	45.7	52.7	58.7	63.5	1.30	0.4	0.6
Germany	72.7	78.7	82.1	82.0	0.75	0.5	0.0
U.K	52.3	56.2	58.6	62.8	0.70	0.3	0.4
Emerging Nations							
China	657.5	927.8	1255.7	1353.6	1.84	1.2	0.6
India	449.7	620.7	982.2	1258.4	2.04	2.0	1.6
Brazil	72.5	108.2	165.9	198.4	2.98	1.6	1.3
S. Africa	17.4	24.7	39.4	50.7	2.60	1.3	1.3
Malaysia	8.2	12.3	21.4	29.3	3.19	2.6	2.2
Thailand	27.4	41.4	60.3	69.9	3.00	1.2	1.1
Indonesia	87.8	135.7	206.3	244.8	2.67	1.5	1.3

Source: United Nations, Population Division, Population Statistics.

India's density of population which was 382 per sq. km. as per 2011 Census is one of the highest, surpassing Japan's 347 per sq. km. and China's 146 per sq. km. (excluding Hong Kong which is now part of China and has a very high density).

Table 18.7 shows the extent of urbanisation which has taken place over the years. Most of the advanced economies have a high percentage of urban population ranging between 70 and 85 per cent. Among the developing, emerging nations, while India's urban population is only 32.4 per cent in 2014, other nations which are relatively more developed, such as Brazil, S. Africa, and Malaysia have a much higher percentage of urban population. China and Indonesia too have over 50 per cent urban population.

Table 18.7 Urban Population

Country	Urban Populations #			Country	Urban Population #		
	1975	1990	2014		1975	1990	2014
Developed Nations				**Emerging Nations**			
U.S.A.	73.7	75.3	83.1	China	17.4	27.4	54.4
Canada	75.6	76.6	81.0	India	21.3	25.5	32.4
Australia	85.9	85.4	89.6	Brazil	61.2	74.8	85.4
Japan	56.8	63.1	93.0	S. Africa	48.0	52.0	63.3
France	72.9	74.1	87.4	Malaysia	37.7	49.8	74.8
Germany	81.2	73.1	74.3	Thailand	23.8	29.4	35.2
U.K.	82.7	88.7	80.0	Indonesia	19.3	30.6	53.0

Source: United Nations Development Programme, Human Development Reports. *Note:* # Urban population as percentage of total population.

Table 18.8 shows the comparative position of Crude Birth rate (CBR), Crude Death rate (CDR), and Infant Mortality rate (IMR) while Table 18.9 shows Life Expectancy at birth in different countries. These are all important vital statistics and social indicators of the health of the population and the stage of development of a country. These indicators are profoundly influenced by factors such as literacy and education levels, state of poverty, and affluence of the people which again depends on the income and standards of living of the people. In short, while developed countries show much progress on these parameters, developing and least developed countries, barring a few, show higher percentages indicating that they have a long way to go.

Among the developing, emerging nations, Brazil, Mexico, Malaysia, Thailand, and Sri Lanka have a better record than others. While on death rate India has made much progress by bringing down the rate, both on birth rate and IMR, India has to make considerable progress. A revealing feature is that on birth rate during the 2010-15 period, Bangladesh stands on par with India with a rate of 20.4, while both on death rate and IMR, Bangladesh has outdone India clocking lower rates. Bangladesh's death rate of 5.5 is on par with S. Korea's which is a commendable achievement. Another startling fact is that the death rate for the 2010-15 period in most of the advanced countries is higher than that of many developing countries.

Table 18.8 Birth Rate, Death Rate, and Infant Mortality Rate (IMR) in Selected Countries

Country	Birth Rate			Death Rate			IMR		
	1950–55	1980–85	2010–15	1950–55	1980–85	2010–15	1950–55	1980–85	2010–15
Developed Nations									
U.S.A.	24.4	15.4	12.6	9.6	8.8	8.2	30	12	6
Canada	27.4	14.6	10.9	8.6	7.0	7.3	39	9	5
France	19.1	14.1	12.4	12.8	10.2	8.9	46	9	3
Germany	15.6	10.7	8.3	11.1	12.2	10.8	46	11	3
U.K.	15.1	12.8	12.6	11.8	11.8	9.2	29	11	4
Norway	18.7	12.3	11.7	8.6	10.3	8.4	22	7	3

Japan	23.8	12.8	8.3	9.4	6.3	10.0	50	7	2
Australia	23.0	15.5	13.5	9.3	7.3	6.7	24	10	4
S. Korea	35.8	20.4	9.2	16.4	6.4	5.5	138	25	3
Emerging Nations									
China	42.2	21.4	12.4	23.1	6.6	7.0	129	45	12
India	43.6	35.5	20.4	26.8	12.7	7.4	186	106	41
Mexico	48.3	32.3	19.3	16.7	6.3	4.8	121	47	19
Brazil	44.2	30.9	15.1	15.6	8.3	6.1	137	72	20
S. Africa	43.7	33.9	21.0	20.2	9.9	12.5	110	61	38
Thailand	42.5	24.2	11.2	15.5	6.8	7.7	128	42	11
Malaysia	42.7	29.5	16.9	14.4	5.5	4.8	102	21	7
Indonesia	42.7	31.7	20.5	21.4	9.2	7.2	193	80	25
Sri Lanka	37.2	25.8	16.4	18.9	6.1	6.7	89	29	8
Bangla-desh	46.2	42.2	20.4	24.8	13.5	5.5	221	126	33

Source: United Nations, Population Division: Population Statistics.

On life expectancy, which is the average number of years a person is expected to live at the time of birth if current mortality rates were to continue, some of the developing countries have made remarkable progress, having achieved over 70 years, as Table 18.9 shows, while some have achieved between 60 and 70 years. People in most of the advanced, high income countries have life expectancy of over 80 years.

Table 18.9 Life Expectancy in Selected Countries

Developed Nations				Emerging Nations			
Country	**Life Expectancy**			**Country**	**Life Expectancy**		
	1970	1997	2007		1970	1997	2007
U.S.A.	70.7	76.7	79.1	China	62.0	69.8	72.9
Canada	72.6	79.0	80.6	India	49.1	62.6	63.4
France	71.9	78.1	81.0	S. Korea	60.1	72.4	79.2
Germany	70.8	77.2	79.8	Thailand	58.3	68.8	68.7
U.K.	71.7	77.2	79.3	Malaysia	61.3	72.0	74.1
Norway	74.1	78.1	80.5	Brazil	58.7	66.8	72.2
Japan	72.2	80.0	82.7	S. Africa	52.8	54.7	51.5
Australia	71.1	78.2	81.4	Indonesia	47.6	65.1	70.5
				Sri Lanka	64.5	73.1	74.0
				Mexico	61.1	72.2	76.0
				Bangla-desh	44.2	58.1	65.7

Source: United Nations Development Programme, Human Development Reports.
Note: On Life Expectancy, see Note under Table 18.2(a).

Box 18.2 The Global Problem of Declining Population

All over the world, countries are confronting population stagnation and fertility decline, a phenomenal reversal unmatched in recorded history. According to United Nations, since 2010, 27 countries or areas have seen a drop of at least one per cent, because of persistently low fertility rates. Between now and 2050, that is expected to expand to 55 countries which will see a population decrease of one per cent or more, and almost half of these will experience a drop of at least 10 per cent.

Table 18.10 (a): Decadal Population Growth Rate in Advanced Countries: 1950 - 2020

	1950-55	1960-65	1970-75	1980-85	1990-95	1995-2000	2010-15	2015-20
USA	1.56	1.35	0.89	0.94	1.01	1.21	0.70	0.62
Canada	2.64	1.90	1.52	1.06	1.15	0.95	1.07	0.93
Japan	1.45	0.99	1.38	0.68	0.30	0.18	-- 0.09	-- 0.24
France	0.74	1.30	0.74	0.51	0.40	0.42	0.49	0.25
UK	0.18	0.70	0.21	0.07	0.28	0.34	0.74	0.61
Germany	0.44	0.76	0.07	-- 0.15	0.52	0.07	0.24	0.48
Australia	2.28	1.99	1.48	1.42	1.18	1.08	1.54	1.27
Australia	2.28	1.99	1.48	1.42	1.18	1.08	1.54	1.27
S Korea	2.27	2.63	1.89	1.40	1.08	0.90	0.51	0.18

Table 18.10 (b): Decadal Population Growth Rate in Emerging Economies: 1950 - 2020

	1950-55	1960-65	1970-75	1980-85	1990-95	1995-2000	2010-15	2015-20
Bangladesh	2.10	2.86	1.74	2.62	2.20	2.06	1.14	1.05
Sri Lanka	1.93	2.36	1.94	1.45	1.03	0.58	0.63	0.48
Malaysia	2.83	3.11	2.37	2.45	2.56	2.48	1.41	1.34
Indonesia	2.11	2.67	2.59	2.25	1.64	1.43	1.32	1.14
Thailand	2.71	3.00	2.75	1.87	1.00	1.14	0.45	0.31
Viet Nam	2.52	2.95	2.31	2.30	1.94	1.29	1.04	0.98
Brazil	2.94	2.88	2.40	2.28	1.68	1.52	0.88	0.78
S. Africa	2.19	2.51	2.65	2.70	2.37	1.64	1.57	1.37

Source for Tables 18.10 (a) and 18.10 (b): United Nations, Department of Economic and Social Affairs, Population Division (2019). World Population Prospects 2019, Online Edition. Rev. 1.

As Table 18.10 (a) shows, population growth rate has been consistently declining in many of the Advanced countries, with rates far below the Replacement level of 2.1. Japan is even facing negative growth while South Korea, among the advanced countries, is having the lowest growth rate.

The position is not much different in the Emerging economies. The trend of population growth in China and India has been already shown in Table 18.5 (b). The position in some of the other Emerging economies is presented in Table 18.10 (b). It will be seen from it that after rise in population growth rates during the initial years of development, i.e., from the 1950s to 1980s, growth rate has been declining and by the 1990s, it is well below 2.1, the Replacement level. It is particularly low and below 1.0 in in Sri Lanka from 1995-2000 period, in Thailand and Brazil from 2010-15 period and in Viet Nam during 2015-20.

A Striking Contrast

This trend is in contrast to the 20th century which presented a very different challenge. Then the global population saw its greatest increase in known history, from 1.6 billion in 1900 to 6 billion in 2000, when health conditions improved, life spans increased and mortality rates declined.

Those growth dynamics are still in play in some countries representing about a third of the world's population. By the end of the century, Nigeria could surpass China in population and across sub-Saharan Africa, families are still having four to five children. Though some countries continue to see their populations grow, especially in Africa, fertility rates are falling nearly everywhere else.

Like an avalanche, the demographic forces, which cause more deaths than births, seem to be expanding and accelerating. Demographers now predict that by the latter half of this century or possibly earlier, the global population will enter a sustained decline for the first time.

Ramification of Declining Population

The consistent decline in population has several ramifications to contend with as explained below.

- Containing unchecked population growth is good, and even an imperative, from the viewpoint of ensuring economic progress and raising living standards.
- But these census trends which show the slowest rates of population growth in decades for a host of countries, point to the dire need for making difficult choices and social and economic adjustments. A paradigm shift is necessary and countries need to learn to live with and adapt to decline.
- The ramifications and responses have already begun to appear, especially in Europe, Americas and Asia. From USA, UK and France to Japan, China and South Korea, governments are grappling with having to balance the demands of a swelling aged population with the needs of young people.
- The strain of increasing longevity and low fertility, leading to fewer workers and more retirees, threatens the population pyramid in many countries resulting in high "dependency ratios". (Dependency ratio is the total number of children (0-14 years of age) and/or retirees and non-working people to the working population).
- As women gain more access to education and birth control measures, the anxieties associated with having children continue to intensify. As a result, more parents are delaying pregnancy and fewer babies are being born.
- The decisions of the young people about childbearing are being shaped by both positive factors like more work opportunities for women and negative factors such as persistent gender inequality (with greater burden falling on women) and rising costs of living.
- In some cases, the falling population size is reinforced by high rates of emigration, and migration flows have become a major reason for population change in certain regions. For those countries where population is falling, immigration is expected to plug the gaps, particularly in the Americas and Europe. (See section on "Migration and Demographic Changes" below).

- ♦ Declining birthrate, coupled with rapid industrialization, would push people from rural towns to big cities. Major metropolises and cities continue to grow, putting intense pressure on infrastructure, housing, transport and other facilities.
- ♦ A positive aspect is that the planet with fewer people could ease pressure on resources, slow the destructive impact of climate change and environmental degradation and reduce household burdens for women.

Migration and Demographic Changes

Immigration plays a significant role in the annual population growth of many of the advanced countries where foreign-born population is growing and diversifying. Migration is a multi-faceted and multi-dimensional phenomenon which impacts profoundly the demographic structure and features of the recipient countries. Countries, like USA, Australia and Canada where fertility rates hover between 1 and 2 are blunting the impact of population decline with immigration. On the other hand, for countries in Eastern Europe, migration out of the region has compounded the problem of depopulation,

Factors behind International Migration

Diverse factors account for migration of people between countries. The major facs behind migration are:

- **Family-linked immigration:** Family-linked immigration for accompanying families and family reunion which has been predominant in Australia, United States, France, Sweden, etc.
- **Employment related:** One of the salient features of recent years has been the rise in migration for employment purposes, both permanent and temporary. Employment-related immigration has been on the rise in USA, Canada, United Kingdom and Australia. Many of the advanced nations are facing labour shortages, especially of skilled workforce in domains like Information Technology and professions like doctors and nurses.

  According to some estimates, there is a shortfall of some 850 000 IT technicians in the United States and nearly 2 million in Europe. Due to this, those countries are competing to attract the human resources and talent they lack and have adjusted their rules in order to allow intake of skilled foreign workers.
- **Refugees and Asylum seekers:** There is the inflow of refugees and asylum seekers. Refugees generally arrive within in the framework of programmes negotiated either between governments or through specialised international organisations. Countries authorise migrants on humanitarian grounds and allow them to remain temporarily or on more permanent basis. Armed conflict and economic crisis are important drivers of migration.

Box 18.3 Demographic Changes in US and Europe

The population trends in the US and Europe present a clear picture on the demographic changes taking place and the impact which migration would have on the population make up. Due to low fertility and declining population and inflow of migrants, the demographic make-up of the US and European countries is bound to change over the coming decades. There are already visible signs of such changes taking place.

Position in the US and Europe

United States: According to U.S. Census data for 2020, the United States has experienced sweeping changes in America's racial and ethnic makeup in the decade from 2010. Some of the major changes are:

- There has been an unprecedented growth in multiracial population and decline in the white population for the first time in the nation's history.
- The changes reveal that the US population is becoming less White, much more multiracial, and more racially and ethnically diverse, than in the past. The U.S. is now 57.8% white, 18.7% Hispanic, 12.4% Black and 6% Asian. The share of White in the country's adult population shrank by six percentage points.
- The non-Hispanic White share of the US population fell to 57 per cent in 2020, shrinking by six percentage points since 2010, the largest decrease of any race or ethnic group. Still, the white, non-Hispanic population is the largest racial group in the U.S.
- The share of those who identified as Hispanic or Latino, Asian or as multiracial grew the most.
- The population younger than 18 has become more diverse. While the under-18 population decreased during the last decade, non-White US residents, less than 18 years, now make up 53 per cent of the population among minors, as compared to 47 per cent in 2010.
- The US population has aged overall since 2010. The share of the adult-aged population has increased slightly, from 76% in 2010 to 78% in 2020.

Europe:

- Due to low fertility, increasing longevity and restricted immigration policies, Europe's demographic composition is undergoing dramatic changes.
- Population trends in EU countries are, however, not all consistent. Countries in Western Europe, which have previously opened their doors to immigrants, have seen their populations grow steadily in recent years, but those in Eastern Europe, which have shut their doors, are seeing their populations decline.
- Some of the countries with the fastest shrinking populations in the world are in Eastern Europe. In some of these countries, the decline in population is unprecedented in peace times.

Impact and Implications of Migration

The US, European countries and others with declining population would face significant challenges. They would need migrants to make up for the shrinking population.

But immigration can only partially and temporarily compensate for the population decline. It is not by itself sufficient to counter the decline and ageing of the population. It calls for additional measures like changes in working age and better utilisation of the domestic workforce to compensate for the effects of low birth rates and ageing. This will entail significant challenges in terms of competitiveness of these countries on the global market and the viability of their existing social security systems.

In order for migration to be an effective solution to population ageing, these countries will need to do more to attract migrants with required skills to meet short term and long term needs of labour market. At the same time, they have to prevent the undesired flows of migrants and human trafficking.

The assimilation and integration of migrants will continue to be a major challenge. On a long term, these states have to adopt a set of policy measures to tackle low fertility, ageing and migration management. They need to adopt a comprehensive approach to be able to adapt to the new demographic realities.

Britain and Immigration

The experience of Britain on immigration, when it was part of the European Union (EU) holds a lesson. Till the late 1990s, the EU did not face the issue of migration when migrants came from countries with more or less similar standards of living. But between 2004 and 2007, expansion of EU happened due to the entry of the former communist countries of Central and Eastern Europe which brought into the bloc 12 new nations, most of them far poorer than the West European nations.

Britain chose to open its borders to newcomers from Eastern Europe. The ostensible reason for this generosity was to show up Britain as a more enlightened country than Germany or France, which kept their immigration controls on East Europeans.

Britain was already home to a large chunk of immigrants, including from outside the EU as over the past two decades, Britain has admitted more than five million foreigners as permanent residents. One of the reasons for opening the doors was that East European migrants were found to be 10 per cent more productive to the British economy than local citizens. Besides, the arrival of migrants boosted prosperity – it improved services, increased consumption and sustained rising property prices.

> But this totally ignored the broader social cost imposed by immigration. For the millions of Britons, immigration proved an economic disaster as they had to compete with the immigrants for jobs. Migrants – both white collar and blue collar – take away jobs from native citizens which lead to tensions, often taking on racial tones. They also put pressure on housing, civic amenities causing prices to rise and with adverse impact on living standards. If the migrants are not fully integrated with local culture, it may even lead to social tensions and disturb social harmony.

Conclusion

In conclusion, it may be said that economic growth and social development are closely interlinked and have to go hand in hand. For, it is the poor and vulnerable sections of the population who are most adversely affected by lack of progress on social indicators like birth and death rates, IMR, and life expectancy due to their acute deprivation and lack of access to proper healthcare. They also suffer from low incomes and poor quality of life due to poor housing facilities and lack of proper sanitation and safe drinking water, especially in the rural areas and remote and far-flung places.

International agencies like the United Nations, Unicef, the UNDP, the World Bank, and the Asian Development Bank have played an important role and have been working closely with all member countries and funding many specific projects to bring about substantial improvement in these fields.

In this Chapter we discussed.....

- Importance of developing human resources or human capital in the development process.
- While India developed higher education in the initial stages, progress in education at primary and secondary levels lagged behind.
- Global population scenario: ageing population in the advanced economies and 'Below poverty line' population in the developing and least developed countries.
- Problem of food insecurity and malnourishment; the onerous task and challenges faced by the farming community in augmenting food output.
- Global population growth: some salient facts.
- Economists on the population issue: views of Malthus, Quesnay, Cantillon, Condorcet, Adam Smith. Problem of increase in population as against scarcity of land and other resources.
- Food security and sustainability challenges; problems due to increasing urbanization and changes in land-use patterns.
- Inefficient food supply chain and wastages; food losses after harvest in developing countries and in consumption and usage in the developed world; rationalizing the use of food for non-human consumption.
- Environmental concerns in agricultural operations; energy consumption, depleting fossil fuel, and groundwater resources.

- Demographic transition and its various stages with changes in birth and death rates and total fertility rates (TFR).
- India's demographic scene; the early Census; variations in India's population growth over the years and problems due to over population; persisting increase in birth rates but decline in death rates; family planning programme.
- Family planning programme given priority from the very First Five Year Plan and in subsequent Plans.
- Performance of States on population control; States which have performed well on birth control and lowering TFR and those who have lagged behind.
- Demographic transition, changes in the age-structure and demographic dividend; contrasting situation on population in developed and developing countries.
- India's demographic dividend, demographic profile of India and changing age-structure; its impact on the labour force and imperative need to create jobs.
- China's One-child and three-child population policy and the benefits it conferred and adverse consequences; policy since abandoned; population decline more due to women's progress and empowerment; India predicted to surpass China in population in a few years.
- How India compares with other countries on demography and vital statistics parameters–population growth rate, birth and death rates, infant mortality rate, urban population, and life expectancy.
- Economic growth and social development closely interlinked; vulnerable sections of population most adversely affected by lack of progress on social indicators.
- Global problem of declining population migration and demographic changes.
- Demographic changes in US

Important Terms to Note in this Chapter

Physical capital; Human capital; Malthusian crisis; Demographic transition; Demographic dividend; Dependency ratio; Crude Birth rate; Crude Death rate; Infant mortality rate (IMR); Total fertility rate (TFR); Life expectancy

Practice Questions

1. India's rapid population growth has hampered economic progress. Do you agree with this and, if so, in what way it has affected the country's progress?
2. Discuss the trends in India's birth and death rates since independence. How have they impacted India's demographic structure and socio-economic development?
3. What are the reasons for the high infant and maternal mortality rates in India as compared to many of the middle and high income countries? What steps need to be taken to bring down these rates?
4. What is meant by 'demographic dividend'? Is India now having the benefit of this phenomenon and, if so, in what way it could be beneficial to India? Explain with relevant data.
5. India is expected to overtake China as the most populous nation in the world. What are its implications for India and how do you think India will face and tackle this challenge.
6. "While we flaunt India's demographic dividend, we ignore the dropping rates of employability." What are we missing while doing so? Where will the jobs that India desperately needs come from? Explain. *[UPSC Main 2014 (Economic Optional Paper]*
7. How does population growth affect economic development of a country? Can the age structure of population alter the pattern of development in a country? Examine in the light of the Indian experience. *[UPSC Main 2015 (Economic Optional Paper]*
8. Is increasing urbanization in India the result of push factors rather than pull factors? Discuss.

   [Indian Economic Service/Indian Statistical Service 2016]
9. Empowering women is the key to control population growth. Discuss.

   [UPSC Main 2019 (General Studies Paper]
10. Population in many of the advanced countries is declining and ageing. Examine the impact it will have on the global economy and the developing countries in the years to come.

CHAPTER

PLANNING AND DEVELOPMENTAL ISSUES

- Planning in China
- Economic Growth and Development Process
- International Comparison
- A Comparative Profile: Indian States
- Development Theories
- Vakil-Brahmananda Model
- Developed and Developing Nations: the Contrast
- Structural Changes in the Economy
- Regional Balance in Development
- Development Goals: MDGs and SDGs
- MDGs and SDGs: Steps Taken by India
- Planning Commission and NITI Aayog
- NITI Aayog's Working: A Critical Assessment
- India' Growth Pattern
- Ensuring Inclusive Growth
- Contribution of Dr V.K.R.V. Rao on India's National Income Accounts
- Impact of Covid-19 on Indian Economy

❑ INTRODUCTION

The primary objective of every nation is to develop the country to its maximum potential and ensure a decent standard of living for all its people. The pace and stage of socio-economic development of a country is conditioned by several factors: geographic, historical, political, societal, resource endowments, etc. The climate, natural and human resources, political maturity, social awareness, literacy, education, and health, all play a critical role in the growth process. A nation well endowed with natural resources but burdened with low levels of literacy, education, and health standards is bound to be handicapped and would register low growth. China and India, with a huge population and heavy historical baggage, have been at a disadvantage from the development point of view. Yet, China's spectacular rise, within a span of three decades, shows that given the necessary policies conducive to growth and incentives for development, a nation can get out of 'low-income and poverty trap' and catch up with developed nations.

Box 19.1: Planning in China

China which set up a State Planning Commission in 1952, around the same time as India, has recast the body as National Development and Reform Commission (NDRC) and its role has undergone change since the country transformed from a planned economy to a socialist market economy.

The NDRC's functions include formulating policies for economic and social development, guiding restructuring of China's economic system, monitoring performance of the national economy, correlating industrial development with development of agriculture and rural economy, promoting growth in backward regions, and approving major projects. The NDRC submits the Plans to the supreme body, the National People's Congress for approval. China's 13th Five Year Plan will run during 2016–20, following the 12th Plan (2011–15).

Till about the 17th century, there was not much difference between the stage of development attained by the western nations and the rest of the world. To put it in perspective, as mentioned in Chapter 1, India was renowned for its capabilities in manufactures and agriculture in the 17th century, even exporting various products to the western nations.

And then came the Industrial Revolution in the 18th and the 19th centuries in the west European countries, particularly England, which they took full advantage of and forged ahead. With rapid industrial growth, coupled with advancements in agriculture, those countries were able to make sustained progress and ensure a high standard of living for their people. Whereas, all the while, many countries in Asia, Africa, and Latin America, which had been colonized by the developed western nations for nearly two centuries, languished under their exploitative colonial rule. And by the time these long subjugated countries gained independence, they had inherited a host of problems–overpopulation, stagnant agriculture, hardly any industrial development, and little progress in the critical areas of education and health. Under the weight of this historical burden, sizeable sections of the population in these countries were pushed to appalling levels of poverty. Thus developed a wide chasm between the developed and developing and least developed nations, also referred to as the North-South divide with the former–the developed nations–situated in the northern hemisphere and the latter in the southern hemisphere.

❑ ECONOMIC GROWTH AND DEVELOPMENT PROCESS

Economic development is a gradual and evolutionary process which unfolds in stages. Modern development economists have drawn attention to the distinction between 'growth' and 'development'– to the fact that growth and development are not one and the same thing. Economic growth is not an end in itself but only a 'means' to an 'end', one part of the development process. Nations may register impressive growth in terms of increase in national or per capita income or even capital accumulation, but unless it translates into positive outcomes by improving the 'quality of life' of the people–say, improved literacy, high level of education and health, reduction in infant and maternal mortality, and higher life expectancy–it does not amount to development in the real sense. Some countries may score high on economic parameters like per capita income but may not necessarily be high on social parameters cited above.

Many classical and neo-classical economists were also concerned with, and have written on economic growth and development. But traditional development economists seem to have laid less stress on human development aspects. Development economics, in the modern sense, and as a distinct branch of serious study, took shape in the post-World War II era. And as many of the colonized nations, which emerged independent in the 1950's and set out on the path of development, experienced glaring deficiencies in the growth process such as widening and gross inequalities, appalling and persisting poverty, and lack of access for large sections of their population to quality educational and health facilities, these issues became eye-openers for them. Though international aid agencies did recognize this and were helping various countries to tackle these problems, it was in 1990 when the UN Development Programme (UNDP) began to highlight them through its annual Human Development Reports, covering a wide range of socio-economic parameters and measuring the progress attained by member countries, that these issues took centrestage and began to receive world's focussed attention. This has helped to sensitize governments, aid agencies, NGOs, etc. on the criticality of issues like inequality, poverty, illiteracy, malnourishment, health issues, etc. (See Tables 19.1 and 19.2).

❑ INTERNATIONAL COMPARISON

A comparative study of the record of some of the countries in the high- and middle-income group, on selected economic and social indicators in the recent past will throw more light on this (See Table 19.1). Though some of the countries have performed well both on economic and social indicators, there are some variations. It may be seen that while S. Africa has a fairly high per capita (p.c.) Gross National Income (GNI), it has a low life expectancy of 53.4 years and a high infant mortality rate (IMR) of 41. S. Korea, Malaysia, Mexico, Brazil, Thailand, and Sri Lanka have good record on both the p.c. GNI and the social indices and China is close on the heels of these countries. It may be noted that though S. Africa and India have a higher p.c. GNI than Bangladesh, the latter has outperformed both these countries on life expectancy and IMR. A detailed analysis of data in respect of more countries could bring to light more such inconsistencies.

Table 19.1: Comparative Performance of Selected Countries

Country	GNI per capita in 2005 PPP $	Life Expectancy at birth (years)	IMR #	Population (%) below Income Poverty line 2012 PPP $1.25 a day	HDI Value 2012	Rank 2012
S. Korea	28231	80.7	4	–	0.909	12
Malaysia	13676	74.5	5	–	0.769	64
Mexico	12947	77.1	14	1.2	0.775	61
Brazil	10152	73.8	17	6.1	0.730	85
S. Africa	9594	53.4	41	13.8	0.629	121
China	7945	73.7	16	13.1	0.699	101
Thailand	7722	74.3	11	0.4	0.690	103
Sri Lanka	5170	75.1	14	7.0	0.715	92
Bangladesh	1785	69.2	38	43.3	0.515	146
Myanmar	1817	65.7	50	–	0.498	149
India	3285	65.8	48	32.7	0.554	136

Source: Human Development Reports, UNDP.

Note: #IMR (Infant Mortality Rate) indicates the probability of dying between birth and exactly age 1, expressed per 1,000 live births.

❑ A COMPARATIVE PROFILE: INDIAN STATES

A similar picture can be seen in respect of some of the Indian states (See Table 19.2). It presents a mixed picture where some states which have high per capita (p.c.) Net State Domestic Product (NSDP) have shown lower results on social indicators than states with lower p.c. NSDP. On the other hand, some states have done well on both p.c. NSDP as well as social indicators.

Table 19.2: Economic & Social Indicators for Selected States/UTs

State/UT	Per capita NSDP (₹)		Literacy Rate (%)		Sex Ratio #		IMR	
	2012–13	2013–14	2001	2011	2001	2011	1999	2013
Andhra Pr.*	78958	88876	60.47	67.66	978	992	66	39
Gujarat	96976	na	69.14	79.31	920	918	63	36
Haryana	119158	132089	67.91	76.64	861	877	68	41
Karnataka	76578	84709	66.64	75.60	965	968	58	31
Kerala	88527	na	90.86	93.91	1058	1084	14	12
Maharashtra	103991	114392	76.88	82.91	922	925	48	24
Punjab	84526	92638	69.65	76.88	876	893	53	26
Tamil Nadu	98628	112664	73.45	80.33	987	995	52	21
Bihar	27202	31229	47.00	63.82	919	916	63	42
UP	33616	37630	56.27	69.72	898	908	84	50
Chandigarh	141926	156951	81.94	86.43	777	818	28	21
Delhi	192587	219979	81.67	86.34	821	866	31	24
Puducherry	114034	148784	81.24	86.55	1001	1038	22	17
Sikkim	151395	176491	68.81	82.20	875	889	49	22
India	67839	74380	64.83	74.04	940	947	70	40

Source: Per capita NSDP at Current prices—2004–05 series from Economic Survey, 2015–16, Ministry of Finance; Literacy Rate and Sex Ratio from Census of India, Registrar General of India; IMR from SRS, Registrar General of India.

Note: #No of females per 1,000 males; * Data is for undivided Andhra Pradesh.

Haryana has high per capita (p.c.) NSDP but on literacy rate, sex ratio, and IMR, it lags behind many other states which have lower p.c. NSDP. Kerala and Puducherry have very good record on all social indices and has fairly high p.c. NSDP. Among the larger States, Maharashtra, and Tamil Nadu have good record on social indices and quite high p.c. NSDP. Former undivided Andhra Pradesh, Karnataka, Gujarat, and Punjab can be grouped together though AP and Karnataka have better record on sex ratio while Punjab and Gujarat have higher literacy rate. Also, Punjab's sex ratio is quite low like that of Haryana, Chandigarh, Delhi, and Sikkim. Bihar and UP come at the bottom on all counts, except sex ratio, which is better than that of Punjab, Haryana, Chandigarh, and even Delhi. Bihar and UP have a long way to go to catch up with other progressive States.

❑ DEVELOPMENT THEORIES

As stated earlier, a number of economists have devoted attention to this domain since the 1940's and various coherent theories of development and growth models have been developed. These include Walt Rostow's '*Stages of Economic Growth*' (1960), Arthur Lewis' seminal work on '*Development with unlimited supplies of labour* (1954), Ragnar Nurkse's 1953 celebrated work on '*Capital formation in Underdeveloped*

Countries and 'Balanced growth' theory, Paul Rosenstein-Rodan's classic 'Big push' theory (1943), Harrod-Domar model, and Albert Hirschman's 'Unbalanced growth' approach. These theories cover a wide range of variables which influence and determine growth–capital formation and accumulation, savings and investment, disguised unemployment and utilization of surplus labour, technological changes, agricultural and industrial sector development, etc.

Rostow's 'Stages of Economic Growth'

According to Walt Rostow (1916-2003), an American economist, who also served the US government, economic growth takes place in five stages as detailed below:

The five stages of economic growth:

(i) *Traditional society:* In the initial stage, an economy will be agrarian and at subsistence level with intensive labour, low levels of productivity, and lacking in scientific and technical skills.

(ii) *Preconditions for take-off:* In the next stage, the society is in a transitional phase when it develops capacity to absorb and apply the benefits of modern science, and improve agriculture and industry. It develops banking, financial and political institutions, entrepreneurs emerge, and investments take place. Transport, communications, and trading improve and industry gets modernized. In the social sphere, educational facilities are widened and people have higher standards of living. Pre-conditions for the next stage of 'take-off' are in place.

(iii) *Take-off:* In this phase, the economy goes through perceptible change and society becomes more modern and urbanized. Science and technology is harnessed, and industry, manufacturing, and agriculture sectors are further modernized. Entrepreneurship becomes more savvy and investments increase. Social and political structures are transformed and the economy registers steady growth. England was in this stage with the advent of Industrial Revolution.

(iv) *Drive to maturity:* After take-off, the economy enters a phase when there is spurt in economic activity, industrialization gets accelerated, production becomes more efficient and, with international trade, imports and exports increase. According to Rostow, it takes about four decades from the end of take-off stage for an economy to attain maturity when the industrial sector will be transformed and more hi-tech industries will emerge. Technological and entrepreneurial skills of people will be of a high order.

(v) *Age of high mass consumption:* In this stage of mass consumption, real incomes of people go up, and consumption levels rise dramatically giving a boost to consumer goods industries. Labour force also undergoes change with more people engaged in white collar and high skill jobs. Domestic savings rate would be adequate to meet the investment rate. In this post-maturity phase, the economy may allocate more resources towards welfare measures and social security, as some of the advanced Western societies like the Scandinavian countries have done. The emergence of the welfare state is a manifestation of the society moving beyond technical maturity.

Critical assessment of Rostow's model

Rostow's model of development, published in 1960, which is based on the experience of societies adhering to the capitalist system has come to be questioned by many. While it may hold good in the case of some countries placed in identical situations and with similar resource endowments, it may not hold good for many other countries. Economic development may not take place in a linear pattern as Rostow envisages. Development is conditioned by many variable factors and imponderables such as geographical situation, resources, population dynamics, societal structure and customs, progress in education, health, etc. This model is also considered to have a 'top-down' approach with development policies and programmes imposed from above leading to 'trickle-down' effect, whereas in many countries a 'bottom-up' approach, relying on a more decentralized system providing space for localized initiatives with active participation of the people, may lead to better and self-sustaining growth.

Lewis' and Nurkse's Theories

Arthur Lewis (1915-91) published in 1954 a paper, '*Economic Development with Unlimited Supplies of Labour*' and '*The Theory of Economic Growth*' in 1955. Lewis proposes a simple dual sector model consisting of agriculture and non-agriculture, in which agriculture is the dominant, subsistence sector, with only two factors at play, landlords and workers. Lewis, like Nurkse (1907-59),was optimistic about the ability to mobilize the hidden rural savings once the surplus farm labour is withdrawn. His work was considered a classic contribution in development economics and won for him the Nobel Prize.

The Lewis model

Lewis combined an analysis of the historical experience of developed countries with the central ideas of the classical economists to produce a broad picture of the development process. According to Lewis, the 'capitalist' industrial sector develops by taking labour from a non-capitalist backward 'subsistence' sector. In the early stages of development, the 'unlimited' supply of labour from the subsistence economy enables the capitalist sector to expand for some time without having to raise wages. This results in higher returns to capital, which results in capital accumulation and could be reinvested. In turn, the increase in the capital stock leads the capitalist sector to expand employment by drawing further labour from the subsistence sector. As the cycle of capital accumulation and reinvestment continues, the process becomes self-sustaining and leads to modernization and economic development.

The point at which the surplus labour in the subsistence sector is fully absorbed into the modern sector, and where further demand for labour results in increase in wages, is called the '**Lewisian turning point**'. This aspect has been widely discussed in the context of economic development in China where the rural surplus labour has been absorbed in the expanding industrial sector. Rapid industrial growth in China over the past three decades has led to large-scale migration of countryside's huge surplus labour to urban centres.

China has reached a stage in its development at which demand for labour has outstripped supply, creating labour shortages and pushing up the cost of labour, a sign of 'Lewis turning point'. The fundamental reason for the acceleration in wages is that China is ceasing to be a labour surplus country and also increase in rural wages. This is potentially eroding the country's low-cost manufacturing advantage.

Nurkse and Balanced growth theory

Ragnar Nurkse refers to the vicious cycle of poverty in underdeveloped countries and the problem posed by low savings and capital formation. Lack of investment, low productivity, low incomes, low aggregate demand, and small size of markets create the cycle of poverty. Inadequate savings and limited size of markets hampers investment. Both Lewis and Nurkse pointed out the existence of disguised unemployment, i.e., surplus or redundant labour in agriculture in these countries and the need to shift them to work on investment projects. It was contended that since the contribution of the 'disguised unemployed' or surplus labour would be marginal and negligible, withdrawal of such labour would not affect the farm output. And the earnings and wage goods of such workers would form a pool of savings which could be utilized for investment in productive ventures like road construction, irrigation projects, setting up small enterprises, factories, etc. to which the surplus labour will be redeployed. But it is possible that part of their consumption will be used up by those left behind on the farms. Even after allowing for this, the surplus accruing from the farm sector will could be mobilized by means of taxation or increase in land revenue and used for providing consumption goods and necessary tools and capital equipment for use in the investment sector.

Nurkse and Lewis presuppose that the capital required for such a pattern of growth, which is referred to as 'balanced growth', would be forthcoming from the 'hidden resources' in the underdeveloped country. The theory of balanced growth has come in for criticism on the ground that underdeveloped countries suffer from acute scarcity of capital and cannot afford to embark on simultaneous development of various sectors which would require massive investments. The extent of savings in consumption due to withdrawal of suplus labour is also open to question as people who stay back in the farms may use up such surplus. Also, a part of the surplus consumption items–wage goods–may have to be provided to the labour shifted to the investment sector which will further eat into the surplus resources available for investment.

Vakil-Brahmananda Model

The alternative to Mahalanobis' Second Plan model, suggested by Professors C.N. Vakil and P.R. Brahmananda, referred to in Chapter 2 (See p. 2.5), is analogous to the Lewis-Nurkse model based on utilizing the surplus labour in the investment sector. The Vakil-Brahmananda plan also envisaged shifting the redundant farm labour to more productive occupations such as rural infrastructural works and industries producing wage goods (wage goods include food items, clothing, and other basic items of daily consumption). They argued against the strategy of developing heavy, capital goods industries on a massive scale as proposed by Mahalanobis. But the Vakil-Brahmananda view was also somewhat flawed as neglecting capital goods sector at that stage of development would have held back India, which was already industrially weak and way behind other major countries having suffered centuries of neglect and deindustrialization. India then opted for a 'pull up' strategy in the hope that rapid and sustained growth would uplift large sections of people from the vicious grip of poverty and that it would make a substantial dent on poverty. But as things turned out, though there was economic progress through successive Plans, disparities in income and wealth widened, large sections were still trapped in poverty, partly because of the increasing population which neutralized the fruits of development, and India had to resort to direct anti-poverty programmes like MNREGS even after some five decades of development. (See chapter 2 also on this).

The 'Big Push' Theory

Rosenstein-Rodan advanced a variation of balanced growth theory known as the 'Big push' theory in 1943. According to him, considering the backwardness of underdeveloped countries, there is need for large investments of a critical mass for achieving rapid growth. Private entrepreneurs cannot be expected to make such investments in the absence of assurance of investments by others which would create demand for their products. Hence, it calls for co-ordinated plan of State intervention and public investment to ensure 'balanced growth'. This view provided the intellectual basis and rationale for 'planned economic development' steered by the State which countries like India adopted.

The Harrod-Domar Model

The Harrod-Domar model of growth was developed independently by Sir Roy Harrod (1900-78) in 1939 and Evsey Domar (1914-97) in 1946. According to it, the growth rate of an economy depends on the level of savings and the capital- output ratio which is a measure of the productivity of capital. If there is a high level of savings in the country, it provides funds for firms to borrow and invest. Investment can increase the capital stock of the economy and generate economic growth through increase in production of goods and services.

The thrust of this model is to augment the resources required for investment. Such resources could come from domestic savimgs and foreign aid. If an economy targets to achieve growth rate of 4 per cent and if the capital-output ratio was 4:1, the net investment rate targeted would be 16 per cent. And if the undeveloped country had a low savings rate of, say 6 per cent, it cannot hope to achieve the desired investment target of 16 per cent with the current savings rate and hence the gap will have to be covered by foreign aid. And as the economy develops and the savings rate go up, the need for, and dependence on, foreign aid would come down. The Harrod-Domar model postulates that other things being equal, the economic growth rate will increase or decline proportionally to the national savings rate.

Unbalanced Growth Approach

As against the planned, balanced growth approach proposed by Lewis and Nurkse, Albert Hirschman (1915–2012) advocated an unbalanced and uncoordinated growth approach as suitable for underdeveloped economies. More than the shortage of capital, these economies lack entrepreneurial skills. Under this approach, imbalances and disequilibria will be generated which will pose challenges and exert pressure on various sectors and bring out latent entrepreneurship and new technologies. As there is complementarity between sectors, development in one sector will impact and lead to growth in other sectors, thus producing a chain reaction in the economy. There will be forward and backward linkages between various sectors which will stimulate growth. Hirschman urges investment on a large scale in 'social overhead capital' which include items like roads, schools, hospitals, and public parks, transport, power supply, irrigation, etc. This will spur investment in 'directly productive activities'. For instance, irrigation will aid agriculture, power supply will help develop industries, hospitals, and so on. Investment in intermediate manufacturing industries which have linkage to many other industries will promote all round industrial development.

❑ DEVELOPED AND DEVELOPING NATIONS: THE CONTRAST

The pattern of development in the industrialized and developing economies is a study in contrast. Historically, the economic development of western Europe and north America was accomplished with continuous transfer of economic activity and people from rural to urban areas, both within and between countries. As urban industries expanded, new employment opportunities were created and, over the same period, rural manpower requirements were reduced due to labour-saving technological progress in agriculture. Although urban slums and unemployment existed in the 19th century Europe, the combination of the above two phenomena enabled Western nations to undergo a major transformation through systematic rural-to-urban transfer of their human resources.

Another contrast between the present urban situation in developing countries and the historical situation in the now developed economies is worth noting. In 19th-century western Europe, the pace of industrialization was much faster than that of urbanization. As noted by Michel Todaro the percentage of workforce in industry was always higher than that of the population in cities. For example, in France in 1856, only 10 per cent of the population lived in cities of 20,000 inhabitants and more, while 20 per cent of the workforce was engaged in manufacturing. In Germany in 1870, the corresponding figures were 12 and 30 per cent respectively. As the labour forces of both France and Germany were growing at no more than 1 per cent per annum over this period, the manufacturing sector needed to grow at a rate of only 3.3 per cent to absorb the total yearly labour increases. Above all, the now developing economies are burdened with much greater population pressure than the developed countries had to face in the initial years of their industrialization.

On the basis of this experience, many economists were led to believe that economic development in the Third World, too, called for a sustained effort to promote rapid industrial growth. They were inclined to view cities as 'Growth Centres' and focal points of industrialization and development. Unfortunately, this strategy of rapid industrialization has, in many instances, failed to achieve the desired results predicted by historical experience.

Today, many developing countries are beset by a historically unique combination of stagnant agriculture, large-scale shifts of population from rural to urban areas, and growing rural and urban unemployment and under-employment. The incidence of unemployment is much higher among the young and educated in the 15–30 age-group. Large segments of both rural and urban labour force are under-employed with no alternative avenues to augment their meagre incomes. The unemployment crisis in developing countries was the result of inadequate job creation commensurate with the growth of industrial output and it was further accentuated by external factors such as worsening balance of payments and debt problems. Large-scale migration of population to urban areas has also caused enormous problems in regard to housing, urban slums, sanitation, health, and education.

❑ STRUCTURAL CHANGES IN THE ECONOMY

One of the indices of development is the relative shares of Agriculture, Industry, and Services—the Primary, Secondary, and Tertiary—sectors in the output and employment in the economy. The more developed a nation is, the lesser will be the share of agricultural sector and greater the share of industry and services sectors, both in GDP and employment of the labour force, i.e., the occupational pattern. Tables 19.3 (a) and (b) give the comparative position of sectoral shares in GDP while Table 19.4 gives the share of agriculture and services sectors in employment in selected developed and developing countries.

Table 19.3(a): Developed Countries—Sectoral Share in GDP (Per Cent)

	Agriculture			Industry			Services		
	1980	1995	2013	1980	1995	2013	1980	1995	2013
USA	2.3	1.4	1.4	26.5	20.8	16.4	71.1	77.8	82.2
Japan	3.4	1.8	1.2	29.8	25.0	20.8	66.8	73.3	78.0
Australia	5.9	3.7	2.4	29.1	22.0	19.8	64.9	74.2	77.8
France	4.1	2.7	1.7	23.2	19.2	13.8	72.7	78.1	84.5
UK	1.7	1.5	0.7	31.6	24.2	14.1	66.9	74.3	85.2
Finland	9.6	4.3	2.7	30.7	28.8	20.4	59.7	66.9	76.9
Russia	–	7.7	3.9	–	30.1	29.0	–	62.3	66.9

Table 19.3(b): Developing Countries—Sectoral Share in GDP (Per Cent)

	Agriculture			Industry			Services		
	1980	1995	2013	1980	1995	2013	1980	1995	2013
China	43.9	20.0	10.0	30.2	41.2	37.0	25.9	38.8	53.0
Brazil	10.2	5.8	5.7	33.9	22.0	19.5	55.9	72.2	74.8
Mexico	7.6	5.0	3.3	34.2	31.5	30.3	58.1	63.4	66.5
Indonesia	23.5	15.4	14.4	37.1	34.8	35.7	39.5	49.8	49.8
Egypt	21.0	16.8	13.9	30.3	27.7	32.9	48.7	55.9	53.2
Philippines	22.0	18.8	11.2	32.3	28.9	24.9	45.6	52.4	64.0

Source: Data in Tables 19.3 (a) and (b) from UN Population Division statistics. *Note:* Figures in both the Tables are percentages. In some cases, the percentage total may not add up to exactly 100.

It may be noted that the percentage share of agriculture in the GDP in developed countries is very small and is much less than that in the case of developing economies, though in both developed and developing countries, the share has come down over the years. So also, the share of industry in the GDP, which is more than that of agriculture, has also shown decline in the advanced economies. The decline in the share of industry in the developing economies is less sharp except in Brazil where the share of services has gone up significantly. As the economies progressed, the share of the services sector has gone up substantially in both groups of countries.

Likewise, the sectoral share in employment also shows similar trends with share of agriculture coming down and that of services going up.

Table 19.4: Developed and Developing Countries: Sectoral Share in Employment (Per Cent)

	Agriculture		Services			Agriculture		Services	
	1990	2012	1990	2012		1990	2012	1990	2012
Developed Countries					**Developing Countries**				
USA	2.9	1.6	70.7	81.2	China	60.1	34.8	18.5	35.7
Japan	7.2	3.7	58.2	69.7	Brazil	22.8	15.3	54.5	62.7
France	5.6	2.9	64.8	74.9	Indonesia	55.9	35.9	30.2	43.5
UK	2.1	1.2	64.9	78.9	Mexico	22.6	13.4	46.1	61.9
Australia	5.6	3.3	69.3	75.5	Philippines	45.2	32.2	39.7	52.5
Russia	13.9	9.7	45.6	62.3	Egypt	39.0	29.2	40.1	47.1
Germany	–	1.5	–	70.2					
S. Korea	17.9	6.6	46.7	76.4					

Source: Human Development Report, UNDP, New York.

Data given in Tables 19.5 and 19.6 also show similar trends in India. The share of Primary sector, i.e., agriculture and allied activities in GDP as well as employment has been going down while that of industry and services has been increasing. The share of services in GDP is substantial now, being nearly 60 per cent, but it is still far less than the share of services sector in the advanced economies where it ranges between 70 and 80 per cent, as will be seen from Table 19.3 (a). The share of persons employed in agriculture in India has come down to 48.9 per cent by 2011–12 and that in industry and services has shown increase. But the extent of decline of workforce in the agriculture sector is not commensurate with its decline in the GDP share. So also, the employment in the services sector is not commensurate with this sector's substantial share in GDP. There is, therefore, need to step up the share of industry and manufacturing in employment in India as in China where it has touched 35.7 per cent in 2012 as will be seen from Table 19.4. It will also help to shift more labour from agriculture to other sectors. (See Box 19.5 at the end of this chapter for more on this).

Table 19.5: India—Sectoral Shares in GDP at Factor Cost (per cent)

Year	Primary	Secondary	Tertiary
1950–51	55.8	15.2	29.0
1960–61	45.8	20.7	33.5
1970–71	45.2	21.9	32.9
1980–81	38.1	25.9	36.0
1990–91	34.0	24.9	41.1
2000–01	27.3	24.2	48.5
2004–05	20.2	26.1	53.7
2012–13	15.6	24.8	59.6

Source: Economic Surveys, Ministry of Finance and Plan documents, Planning Commission.
Note: Data upto 1990–91 are those prior to revision of GDP.

Table 19.6: India—Sectoral Shares in Employment (in per cent)

Sector	1972–73	1983	1993–94	1999–2000	2006–07	2011–12
Agriculture & Allied Activities	74.0	65.42	61.03	56.64	50.19	48.9
Industry	11.2	14.83	15.92	17.58	20.37	24.3
Services	14.6	19.74	23.06	25.78	29.43	26.9

Source: Planning Commission Data book and Plan documents; Economic Survey, Ministry of Finance.

❑ REGIONAL BALANCE IN DEVELOPMENT

Balanced growth of various regions and States is an important aspect of development which was referred to in Chapter 4 (See pp. 4.6). While formulating Five Year Plans, the Planning Commission has also been keeping this aspect in view to ensure development is spread evenly between regions. Endowments of natural resources being skewed and unequal, and due to heavy costs involved in their transportation over long distances, there is bound to be unevenness in development. But through affirmative action and ensuring growth of other sectors which do not require mineral resources, the government has been able to ensure development of other regions. Such alternative sectors promoted to develop regions less well-endowed include small scale and village industries, ancillary industries, agro-based industries, consumer goods industries, pharmaceuticals and chemical industries, Information Technology, etc.

In the last few years, many States have also taken initiatives to attract investments on a large scale to set up various industries and develop infrastructure such as roads, ports, Metro rail, waterways, etc. In fact, there has been healthy competition called 'competitive federalism' among the States in attracting both foreign and domestic investment by holding 'Global Investor Meets'. And as the global economy is going through recession and slowdown for the past few years and India being one of the few bright spots for investment, many States have been able to attract investment in varied sectors. India has to capitalize and grab this opportunity by improving her business practices and regulatory regime with policies like 'Ease of Doing Business', 'Make in India' initiative, etc. These are discussed further in Part III.

Box 19.2: Regional Balance in Development

As already pointed out in Chapters 4 and 16, the Five Year Plans of India had taken cognizance of the need for balanced development of all regions to avert lopsided development and stem the migration of labour.

One of the major reasons for migration is the lack of development in the states from where the exodus of workers take place in search of jobs. Paradoxically, it is some of the states in eastern and central India, which are richly endowed with mineral resources and have much potential for industrial development, that witness large scale migration. In fact, as early as 1950s, the Planning Commission had observed in the Second Plan (1956-61) document thus:

"This brings us to the question of regional disparities. In any comprehensive plan of development, it is axiomatic that the special needs of the less developed areas should receive due attention. The pattern of investment must be so devised as to lead to balanced regional development..............

"The question was discussed recently by the National Development Council and it has been agreed in principle that within the resources available, every effort must be made to provide for balanced development in different parts of the country. The problem has to be approached in a variety of ways. In the first place, the National Development Council has recommended programmes for setting up decentralised industrial production. Secondly, it has been suggested that in the location of new enterprises, whether public or private, consideration should be given to the need for developing a balanced economy for different parts of the country."

The Commission even recognized that "Some industries have to be located in particular areas in view of the availability of the necessary raw materials or other natural resources." (Second Plan, Chapter 2, Approach to Second Five Year Plan).

This was emphasized in subsequent Plans too. The Third Plan (1961-66) stated: "......Such a plan should be conceived not merely in broad national terms but should take into account the possibilities of development of resources in different regions of the country so as to spread the benefits of development as widely as possible without slowing down growth itself." (Third Plan, Chapter 2, Long-term Economic Development).

And the Fourth Plan (1969-74) observed: "In terms of regional development, there has been a natural tendency for new enterprises and investments to gravitate towards the already overcrowded metropolitan areas because they are better endowed with economic and social infrastructure. Not enough has been done to restrain this process. While a certain measure of dispersal has been achieved, a much larger effort is necessary to bring about greater dispersal of industrial activity." (Fourth Plan, Chapter 1, Approach and Policy).

Again, the Fourth Plan emphasized: "Second important consideration in industrial planning is the desirability of dispersed industrial development. The requirement of non-farm employment is so large and so widely spread throughout the country that a greater dispersal of industrial development is a matter of necessity." (Fourth Plan, Chapter 14, Industry and Minerals).

❑ DEVELOPMENT GOALS—MDGs AND SDGs

The United Nations had adopted two development paths to be followed by the member countries, viz., Millennium Development Goals (MDGs) and Sustainable Development Goals (SDGs). The MDGs consisted of eight international development goals adopted by the UN following the Millennium Summit in 2000. These were:

- Eradicate extreme poverty and hunger;
- Achieve universal primary education;
- Promote gender equality and empower women;
- Reduce child mortality;
- Improve maternal health;
- Combat HIV/AIDS, malaria, and other diseases;
- Ensure environmental sustainability; and
- Develop a global partnership for development.

The member countries of the UN and various international organizations had committed to help attain these goals by 2015. The G-8 countries, a group of advanced nations, had committed to provide adequate funds to the World Bank and the IMF to accelerate progress on these goals to help improve health and education and alleviate poverty in the poor and heavily indebted countries. Official development assistance (ODA) flows reflected the continued international commitment of developed countries to provide concessional financial and technical resources to support the development efforts of developing countries, including achieving the MDGs.

A UN MDG Task Force, which included many organizations with specialized competence, has taken stock of the achievements and shortfalls in the implementation of the 8 Millennium Development Goals (MDG 8) in various identified domains.

India and MDGs

The UN which has taken stock of the implementation of MDG programme has observed that while India made notable progress towards reaching the Goals, the achievements across the Goals have shown varied progress. India can improve performance by helping the weaker States emulate the good performers. There is need for accelerated and broad-based economic growth creating employment which will alleviate poverty.

India has channeled resources into human development areas and States spending more on health and education in per capita terms have seen their human development surpass others. Also, the importance of good governance and effective delivery of public services can be gauged from the fact that States with better, more accountable, and responsive service delivery have performed better on the MDGs. For example, States that provided more work to the poor under the MGNREGS rural jobs programme and provided more food grains for poor households under the Public Distribution System (PDS) achieved better overall MDG performance scores.

The UN review has also stressed the criticality of promoting gender equality and empowerment of women. It helps to achieve the MDGs by reducing fertility, population growth and child mortality, improve nutrition, hygiene and health of households, and children's performance in schools. States that have empowered women more than others, measured by the Gender Empowerment Measure (GEM), also performed better on the MDGs.

Sustainable Development and SDGs

Economic and social development has significant bearing on nature, the bio-physical environment around us, as well as the natural resources consumed in the process of development. It also has a perceptible impact on climatic conditions as the world has been witnessing in the last few decades. The unchecked exploitation of natural resources by every generation will have lasting, adverse impact on the future generations.

Any development that ignores or neglects the ecological and environmental impact on our fragile planet poses a serious threat to the already deteriorating ecosystem. There are already visible signs of it which the world is experiencing in the form of unpredictable and unprecedented climate change, natural disasters like floods, deforestation, melting of glaciers, rising sea level, depletion of the ozone layer, contamination of freshwater, depleting groundwater levels, global warming, etc.

Recognizing the dangers posed by these disturbing trends, much of which is caused by reckless human actions, the world organizations like the United Nations (UN), UN Development Programme (UNDP), the World Bank, and other inter-governmental bodies have been urging all countries to ensure that the development pursued has to be '*sustainable*' over a long period and without causing harm to future generations.

Box 19.3: Brundtland Commission

To spur all nations to work together to combat deterioration of the human environment and natural resources and to jointly pursue the path of sustainable development, the UN established in 1983 the World Commission on Environment and Development (WCED), also known as the Brundtland Commission after Gro Harlem Brundtland, a former Prime Minister of Norway who headed it. The Brundtland Commission which submitted its report in 1987 defined sustainable development as "*development which meets the needs of current generations without compromising the ability of future generations to meet their own needs*".

Moving ahead from the Millennium Development Goals (MDGs), SDGs have been evolved through a long inclusive process to be accomplished during the period 2016–2030. It aims at 'Transforming our world: the 2030 Agenda for Sustainable Development' (called as SDGs). The SDGs cover 17 goals and 169 related targets resolved in the UN Summit held in September 2015, in which India was represented at the level of the Prime Minister. The SDGs will stimulate, align, and accomplish action over the 15-year period in areas of critical importance for the humanity and the planet.

India has been actively involved in international fora relating to environmental protection, and has been part of many 'Multilateral Environmental Agreements' such as the Ramsar Convention on Wetlands, Convention on International Trade in Endangered Species of Fauna and Flora (CITES), Convention on Biological Diversity (CBD), and on Climate Change, among many others. India is a signatory to the UN Framework Convention on Climate Change (UNFCCC), and has acceded to the Kyoto Protocol in 2002. (On 'Climate Change' agreements, see Chapter 20).

Steps Taken By India

Both industrial and agricultural development, which play a major part in boosting the GDP, can cause some environmental damage. Manufacturing sector may lead to environmental degradation during the production cycle and disposal of industrial waste, effluents, etc. Agricultural sector also has certain practices which harm the environment like excessive use of fertilizers and pesticides, soil degradation, and pollution and wastage of water.

Some of the remedial steps initiated by India to promote sustainable developemnt are mentioned here:

- Developing green technology to replace obsolete and inefficient systems with more energy-efficient and clean technologies.
- A National Clean Energy Fund (NCEF) was created in 2010 by imposing a cess on coal. The NCEF will support projects that promote clean energy technologies. This fund can be used by companies investing in green technology, and environment-friendly ventures such as renewable energy, green transport, and water and waste management, among others.
- Industries are urged to adopt sound technologies and management techniques, which are a key element of any sustainable development strategy.
- The thrust of agricultural development programmes is to ensure efficient use of scarce natural resources, viz., land, water, and energy. By improving productivity, welfare of farmers and agricultural labour can be promoted, and thereby eradicate rural poverty. Conservation of land resources by optimum land use, controlled use of fertlizers, and appropriate pricing of water and electricity will help recharge the depleting aquifers and energy conservation.
- Greater recourse to clean energy sources such as Solar and Wind power will help reduce pollution. India has been trying to tap increasingly these sources.
- Compensatory Afforestation Fund is an innovative Mechanism set up for mobilizing additional resources to the forestry sector. Money is collected for compensatory afforestation from user agencies in lieu of the land granted for non-forestry purpose.
- A major environmental concern and health hazard is the rapid urbanization which results in water and air pollution on account of motor vehicles, poor waste disposal, inadequate sanitation, sewerage, and drainage facilities. The dumping of solid waste, including medical and industrial waste, contributes to both land and groundwater pollution. The government has allotted funds to State governments under the Jawaharlal Nehru National Urban Renewal Mission (JNNURM) to improve the urban environment.

❑ PLANNING COMMISSION AND NITI AAYOG

Genesis of Planning in India

India set up the erstwhile Planning Commission in 1950 in the heyday of centralized planning in Soviet Union and many east European countries. But the genesis of the idea of 'planning' in India dates back to much earlier times.

As noted in Chapter 2, there were indications of India opting for planned development even in the 1930's. (See pp. 2.2). Nehru was deeply impressed by the great strides that the Soviet Union was making with 'planned development' under Lenin's communist regime, and had set his mind on developing India on similar lines once India gained independence.

As Chairman of the National Planning Committee set up by the Congress, Nehru had prepared a memorandum in 1939 which stated that State had to control, or at least regulate, in the interest of all, public utilities, large-scale industries, and industries which were likely to become monopolistic in nature. Market forces would be controlled and 'planning' would serve as the guiding force to bring about economic and social transformation.

Sir M. Visvesaraya (1861-1962), the renowned engineer-stateman of the then Mysore state, had authored a book in 1934, 'Planned Economy for India'.

Role of Planning Commission

The primary functions of the Planning Commission were as follows:

- To prepare a blueprint for socio-economic development, over every five-year period, keeping in view the perspective of long-term interests of the country.
- Assess the physical and financial resources available, find ways of augmenting deficient resources.
- Draw up priority to be accorded to various sectors and set targets to be achieved.
- Allocate the financial resources balancing the needs of both the Centre and the States.
- The Commission would also carry out mid-term review of the Plans to assess the progress made under various programmes and, if required, revise the targets to be achieved.

The Transition

With the passage of time, the functions of Planning Commission also evolved to keep in tune with the changed circumstances.

- From a highly centralized planning system, the Indian economy had gradually moved towards indicative planning where Planning Commission concerned itself with formulating a long term strategic vision of the future and decide on priorities of the nation.
- It worked out sectoral targets and provided promotional stimulus to the economy to grow in the desired direction.
- The Commission played an integrative role in the development of a holistic approach to the policy formulation in critical areas of human and economic development.

Relevance of Planning Commission

While India implemented eleven Five Year Plans and some Annual Plans between 1951 and 2012, over a time-span of sixty years, and achieved considerable progress, the relevance of the role of the Commission and the way it functioned, in the changed circumstances, came to be questioned. Some of the issues raised during the UPA government regime were:

- Were tools and approaches which were designed for a different era still being used.
- Have new functions and layers been added in the Commission without any restructuring in its more traditional activities.
- What additional roles should the Commission play and what capacities does it need to ensure that it continues to be relevant to the growth process.
- Governance issues being integral to economic growth, are these areas for the Commission to delve into.

Need for Reform and Restructuring

A study carried out on the role and relevance of the Commission came to the conclusion that the reform of the Commission was long overdue and that the Commission's role and functioning should be changed on the following lines:

- The Commission should be a 'Systems Reform Commission' and not a budget-making body. Another suggestion was that the Commission should be converted into a Reforms and Solutions Commission (RSC).
- It was felt that the methods of communication adopted by the Commission needed to be changed. Instead of voluminous Plan documents that hardly anyone, save some scholars and researchers, read, it should adopt more coherent and persuasive forms of communication that all stakeholders could easily comprehend and assimilate.
- However, some did express reservations on these suggestions saying that the challenges faced by the country cannot be resolved by a few persons with sectoral expertise limited to the narrow confines of a discipline.
- Without disparaging the constructive work done by the now defunct body, it may be stated that there was a need for a set-up having a wider perspective and adopting multi-disciplinary approach to find systemic solutions cutting across ministries and sectors.
- The restructured body would have persons who will bring to bear fresh thinking and systemic approach keeping in view the liberalized economic regime, challenges that a globalized and interdependent world poses, environmental concerns, social compulsions, etc.

Rationale for Setting up NITI Aayog

After the NDA government took office in 2014, the whole issue was considered and it was decided to disband the Planning Commission and set up what was called "National Institution for Transforming India' (NITI) Aayog" – NITI Aayog in brief. The rationale advanced by the new government for this change was: the rationale for the change was that India has undergone a major transformation in the past sixty years-politically, economically, socially, technologically, and demographically. The role of government in the development process has also seen many changes.

The need was felt for an institution that will play a catalytic role and serve as a Think Tank of the government-a directional and policy dynamo. It would provide governments at the central and state levels with relevant strategic and technical advice across the spectrum of key elements of policy. This includes matters of national and international importance on the economic front, dissemination of best practices from within the country as well as from other nations, the infusion of new policy ideas, and specific issue-based support. The institution has to be able to respond to the changing and more integrated world that India is a part of.

Structure and Functions of NITI Aayog

With the Prime Minister as its Chairman and a well-known economist as Vice-chairman, the NITI Aayog has a CEO, five full-time members, and up to two part-time members from leading universities and research organizations, apart from four ex-officio members from the Union Council of Ministers nominated by the Prime Minister.

The staff of the institution has been formed into two large hubs-the Knowledge and Innovation hub and the Team India hub. The former has the responsibility to create, accumulate, and disseminate knowledge, while the latter serves as the link between the States and the ministries at the Centre.

The Knowledge and Innovation hub will have 12-14 verticals and they would develop expertise in different sectors such as macroeconomy and trade, health, agriculture, rural development, education, and skill development.

Functions: NITI Aayog's functions include the following:

- ***Cooperative Federalism:*** Be the primary platform for enabling States to have active participation in the formulation of national policy, as well as achieving time-bound implementation of quantitative and qualitative targets through the combined authority of the Prime Minister and Chief Ministers.

  The above mandate is sought to be achieved by means of systematic and structured interactions between the Union and State Governments, to better understand developmental issues, as well as forge a consensus on strategies and implementation mechanisms. The above would mark the replacement of the one-way flow of policy from centre-to-state, with a genuine and continuing Centre-State partnership.
- ***Shared National Agenda:*** Evolve a shared vision of national development priorities and strategies, with the active involvement of States. This will provide the framework 'national agenda' for the Prime Minister and Chief Ministers to implement.
- ***Decentralized Planning:*** Restructure the planning process into a bottom-up model, empowering States, and guiding them to further empower local governments. Develop mechanisms to formulate credible plans at the village level, which are progressively aggregated up to the higher levels of government.
- ***Think Tank:*** As a dedicated Think Tank of the Government, NITI Aayog will carry out this 'directional' role, strategically charting the future of the nation. It will provide specialised inputs–strategic, functional, and technical–to the Prime Minister and the Government (Centre as well as States), on matters critical to the fulfilment of the national development agenda.
- ***Vision and Scenario Planning:*** Design medium and long-term strategic frameworks of the big picture and vision of India's future–across schemes, sectors, regions, and time, factoring in all possible alternative assumptions and counterfactuals. These would be the drivers of the national reforms agenda, especially focussed on identifying critical gaps and harnessing untapped potentialities. The same would need to be intrinsically dynamic with their progress and efficacy constantly monitored for necessary mid-course recalibration; and the overall environment, domestic and global, continuously scanned for incorporating evolving trends and addressing emerging challenges.

Divergent Views

Some sceptics have criticized the move to disband the Planning Commission saying that with all its deficiencies, it was a positive and dynamic platform for steering the economy. Whereas some experts while agreeing with the need for reforming the institution, and even replacing it with a new body, have put forth ideas for giving it a new role and redefined functions.

Those who find merit in the new set-up are of the view that as the country moves to a market-oriented economy, it may not be possible to have Five Year Plans the way it was being done in the past. Under a regime of controlled and licensed investment and foreign trade, administered pricing, and distribution which India had been practising, such planning and allocation of resources by the planning body had relevance. But when entrepreneurs, investors, and consumers are sought to be empowered to take decisions, such an approach may be incongruous.

However, in view of the wide disparitites in the economic status of, and distribution of income and wealth between, various strata of society, the government and NITI Aaoyog have to keep a watch on the trends in the economy so as to ensure that the fruits of development are distributed equitably and reach all sections of the people, particularly the vulnerable sections. NITI Aayog will have to guide the government and give proper direction to the policy in this regard. The real test of the functioning of the new body will be seen as things pan out in the future.

Box 19.4: NITI Aayog's Working: A Critical Assessment

- **Serves as Think Tank:** The NITI Aayog serves as a think tank where new and innovative ideas come from diverse sources — industry, academia, civil society or foreign specialists — and flow into the government system for implementation.

  It holds regular brainstorming sessions with stakeholders from various industries and sectors. Initiatives like Ayushmaan Bharat, the approach towards Artificial Intelligence (AI), water conservation measures, and the draft bill to establish the National Medical Commission to replace the Medical Council of India were all conceptualised in NITI Aayog, and taken forward by the respective Ministries.
- **Action-oriented approach:** It also functions as an action-oriented body. Collecting and collating fresh ideas, it shares them with the Central and State governments to make them act as agents of change to improve governance and implement innovative measures for better delivery of public services.

  Convergence of Action: While dealing with major issues, NITI Aayog cuts across the silos within the government. For example, on the issue of malnourished children, of which India has the largest number in the world and is trying to bring down the number vastly, it calls for a high degree of convergence across a number of Ministries, and between Central and State governments. NITI Aayog is well placed to achieve this convergence and push the agenda forward.
- **Accountability:** NITI Aayog is also bringing about a greater level of accountability in the system. In the case of Five-Year Plans, the Planning Commission would mostly evaluate long after the Plan period had ended. NITI Aayog has a Development Monitoring and Evaluation Office (DMEO) which collects data on the performance of various Ministries on real-time basis. The data are then analysed and used at the highest policymaking levels to establish accountability and improve performance. This performance- and outcome-based real-time monitoring and evaluation of government work has significant impact on improving the efficiency of governance.
- **Promoting innovation:** Spurring innovation to impart dynamism to the economy and respond to changing environment and needs forms an important part of NITI Aayog's mandate. For instance, the Atal Innovation Mission (AIM), which was established on NITI Aayog's initiative for encouraging young innovators and start-ups, has done significant work in improving the innovation ecosystem in India as will be seen from the following facts:

- Over 8,700 Atal Tinkering Labs (ATL) set up in 34 States and Union Territories spanning 722 districts.
- More than 5000 Mentors of Change are engaged for mentoring 70 lakh students actively engaged in ATLs.

- 70 per cent of ATLs are set up in Govt./ Govt. Aided schools, Girls/Co-Ed Schools.
- 1.8 Lakh Innovation Projects have been created.

➢ **Lacunae of the new Structure:** While protagonists of the new structure put up in place of Planning Commission laud its objectives and working, some experts have articulated the lacunae in the mandate and method of working of NITI Aayog.

Basically, they question how far NITI Aayog could tackle fundamental problems afflicting a large economy as that of India without a planned approach for directing public and private investments in a focussed manner. These problems include poverty and gross inequality, a dominant unorganised, informal sector without proper social security system, persisting pressure of population on the farm sector, fairly high degree of unemployment and plethora of issues in the social sector of health and education.

➢ **Assessment of Performance:** NITI Aayog critically assesses the performance of various schemes initiated by the Union Ministries and the States and focusses attention on achieving outcomes. As the nodal agency responsible for charting India's quest for attaining the commitments under the Sustainable Development Goals (SDGs), it is necessary to devise a mechanism for measuring outcomes particularly in the critical social sectors – such as Health and Education, where India's record has been less than stellar. It comes up with performance-based rankings of States across various verticals to foster a spirit of competitive federalism which is another major mandate of NITI Aayog. Such an approach provides feedback to all stakeholders as to whether we are on course to achieve set objectives, and deviations, if any, are observed in time to carry out mid-course correction. It has come up with Health Index and School Education Quality Index on the performance of States and Union Territories. This helps to identify the best practices in different States in various sectors and try to replicate them in other States.

The NITI Aayog, with its current mandate, result-oriented approach and outreach across a range of sectors and activities and combined with its unique work culture, remains an integral and relevant component of the government's plans to put in place an efficient, transparent, innovative and accountable governance system in the country.

Also with the abolition of the Planning Commission, the States have greater autonomy vis-à-vis the Centre. While under the former set up, the Centre decided how much grant was to be given to each state and for what purpose, states now get resources as part of statutory transfers with discretion over how to utilize it.

Box 19.5: India's Growth Pattern

Contrary to the usual pattern of development, why India leapfrogged from agriculture to services bypassing manufacturing?

India's growth pattern has not followed the traditional theory of development which held good for two centuries since the Industrial Revolution. According to this theory and conventional wisdom, nations transition from a traditional agrarian economy to manufacturing industry and then to wider growth in the services sector. The assumption was that there could be explosive growth only in manufacturing which would absorb the growing population and the surplus labour force in agriculture. This was the path followed by the developed nations in the west as also East Asian economies when they registered rapid growth. The growth path of China which witnessed astounding growth since the 1980s also conforms to this trend.

However, India's growth did not follow this path. Though India did embark on industrialisation from the Second Plan (1956-61) and tried to follow it through subsequent plans, India could not become a manufacturing powerhouse. The policy of 'import substitution' and self-sufficiency adopted in the first three decades after independence hampered industrial growth. The predominant role assigned to the public sector, relegation of private sector and highly restrictive industrial policies further impaired the process. India also did not make efforts to adopt advanced technology and to produce high quality products with a view to promote exports to capture a share of world markets.

All this while, the services sector, especially transport, construction and banking segments, kept growing at steady pace to meet the needs of a growing population. The onset of computer revolution in the 1980s and the '90s further accentuated the growth of the tertiary sector. India's predominance in the IT-BPO business in the global arena led to explosive growth of the sector (as already seen in chapter 12). The share of services (tertiary sector) in GDP rose from 36.0 per cent in 1980-81 to 59.6 per cent in 2012-13. Whereas the share of agriculture (primary sector) came down from 38.1 per cent to15.6 per cent and that of industry (secondary sector) declined from 25.9 per cent to 24.8 per cent during the same period (see Table 19.5). And the share of manufacturing in the secondary sector is a low 15 per cent only. In contrast, out of 32.0 per cent share of Industry in China's GDP, the share of Manufacturing was as high as 27.9 per cent in 2019 (see Table 19.3 (b) and Table 8.5 (b) in chapter 8).

In view of the above, there is dire need for India to step up the share of manufacturing which is the primary goal of 'Make in India' programme. Investments in physical and human infrastructure is crucial for attracting new enterprises in both manufacturing and service sectors to drive growth and job creation.

There is need for a word of caution here. While promoting domestic production, India should not revert to the policy of 'import substitution' followed in the initial years of planned development by raising barriers against imports or subsidising our products which will only undermine the gains from international trade. International trade enables a country to export products that it produces at the lowest cost and import those that the trading partners produce at the lowest cost which will be more beneficial for both countries. However, limited tariffs on certain products to promote domestic industry and ensure job creation can be justified provided productivity levels and quality of products are not compromised. India is following this policy in regard to electronic industry.

Sustainability of Services-led Growth

There is rapid growth in global trade in services in contrast to trade in goods. Services account for over 70 per cent of global output. A host of services which can be digitized are transportable, tradable and scalable. Globalization, digital revolution and expanding internet usage has helped to boost the growth of services across countries. But some of the countries are unwilling to allow free flow of services and manpower as found by India in negotiations under RCEP (see chapter 20 under 'Regional Comprehensive Economic Partnership' on this). The restrictions placed by the US on offshoring of services by Indian IT companies are also a pointer to this trend. India will have to overcome these challenges.

Box 19.6: Contribution of Dr V.K.R.V. Rao on India's National Income Accounts – An Evaluation –

➢ **Pre-Independence Era:** Amid the impoverishment of the masses during the colonial rule, the need for an estimation of per capita income was first recognized by Dadabhai Naoroji who presented his estimate of per capita income in 1867-68. His attempt was followed other scholars of the time, viz., Willium Digby (1899) and later by Findlay Shirras (1911, 1922 and 1934), Shah and Khambatta (1921), V.K.R.V. Rao (1925-29 and 1931-32) and R.C. Desai (1931-40).

❖ **Naoroji's work:** Dadabhai Naoroji, who was a bitter critic of Britain for draining away India's wealth, had made pioneering studies about poverty in India and made some estimations of per capita income (PCI). Naoroji calculated PCI in Bombay Presidency for 1867-70 to be ₹20 whereas the income needed for bare subsistence then was ₹34. He observed that while the upper classes had much higher income, the poor masses could barely make both ends meet and were poverty-stricken.

Though Naoroji's study lacked some details and had flaws in the methodology, Dr. V.K.R.V. Rao who had examined the study later defended him and stated that the results obtained by Naoroji were based on data used by a government commission and hence it was to be accepted as authoritative.

The national income estimates prepared during the colonial era became a subject of debate. F. J. Atkinson, Accountant General of British India, tried to reply to William Digby and Dadabhai Naoroji's allegation that India had become impoverished under British rule by attempting to show that agricultural productivity and per capita income had increased over the period 1875-1895. Another estimate by Alan Heston in *The Cambridge Economic History of India* claimed that per capita income had increased by 0.62 per cent per year between 1868 and 1920.

Economists have argued that Atkinson's estimate of increase in per capita income from ₹30.5 in 1875 to ₹41.7 in 1895 (in 1875 prices) could not be accepted because Atkinson assumed, without any supporting evidence, that agricultural productivity had increased all round over the period. This was the period that witnessed the devastating famine of 1876, which affected most of southern and western India, as well as famines in Punjab and elsewhere which officially designated as "scarcity". Later studies have shown that many of the official claims about increases in productivity per acre cannot stand careful scrutiny.

Among all these pre-independence estimates of national income in India, the estimates of Naoroji, Findlay Shirras and Shaw and Khambatta computed the value of the output raised by the agricultural sector and then added some portion of the income earned by the non-agricultural sector. But these estimates had no scientific basis of their own.

- **V K R V Rao, an Academic Colossus:** It would be instructive to know Prof. Rao's academic background in his early years while assessing his contribution in this field. Even while doing MA degree in Economics at Bombay School under another stalwart, Prof. C.N. Vakil, Rao wrote a thesis on Taxation which was published as a book in 1931, in a series on *Studies in Indian Economics*, edited by Prof. Vakil. After two to three years' teaching experience at Wilson College, Bombay, Rao proceeded as a Tata scholar in 1932 to Cambridge where he delivered a series of memorial lectures in the presence of top ministers.

At Cambridge, Rao came into close contact with two eminent economists, John M. Keynes and Maurice Dobb. According to Rao's own admission, M. Dobb, who was a card-holding member of the Communist Party, "made me build up care, precision and objectivity in my thinking........but I must say that during the many hours I spent with him he never made the least attempt to convert me to his creed".

❖ **Doctoral thesis on National Income:** After completing the Economics Tripos in 1934, Rao took up doctoral work under the guidance of Colin Clark, a British-Australian economist, who was a lecturer in Statistics in Cambridge from 1931 to 1938 and a pioneer in studies on National Income. As a faculty, Clark completed three books: *The National Income 1924–31* (1932), *The Economic Position of Great Britain* (jointly with A. C. Pigou) (1936) and *National Income and Outlay* (1937).

Having come under the fold of Colin Clark, Rao, for his dissertation for doctorate, chose study of estimating India's national income. That Rao chose this theme for research shows the abiding interest he had in exploring a less trodden and intractable path. The thesis finally appeared as a book, **"The National Income of British India, 1931- 32"** in 1940, published by Macmillan in London, and became a classic which served as a benchmark for all future works aimed at estimating national income.

Rao had also written a prize essay titled ***Essay on India's National Income (1925-29)***, at the invitation of Dadabhai Naoroji Memorial Prize Essay Fund.

❖ **Paucity of Data:** In the first half of the 20th century, lack of precise and reliable data was a major handicap in working out national accounts. A major part of the economy was not monetized. Data on large scale industries only was available and so the incomes of remaining industries had to be assessed indirectly. Hence estimation was partly conjectural. Rao departed from the then prevalent trend of excluding services from national income accounting. He presented a practical application of Alfred Marshall and A.C. Pigou's synthesis that advocated reckoning everything that has money value, including services, into account.

❖ **Rao's study:** Dr. Rao examined the national income estimates made by Naoroji, Digby, Shah and Khambhata and framed the following principles for basing his calculation of national income:

- Special attention to non-agricultural sources of income.
- Income from livestock.
- Method of average value per acre to the area for which reliable estimates of crop yields and prices were not available.
- Calculations of deductions in the form of seeds, wastage, imported raw materials, depreciation, etc.
- Estimate national income for a period instead of a year.

With these guiding principles, Rao reckoned the various sources of national income. He applied a combination of output and income methods. While dividing the whole economy into two separate categories, he included agriculture, pastures, forests, fishing, hunting and mines in the first category and applied output method to derive the value of output of these sectors.

The other activities like industry, trade, transport, administrative and public services, professions, liberal arts and domestic services were included in second category and applied income method to derive the amount of income raised from all these sources.

He also added income from house property and other internal incomes along with the total income earned from abroad to the two sub-totals mentioned above. Just to derive the net aggregate income, he excluded those values of goods and services which were consumed in the process of production thus avoiding double counting.

With these, he arrived at the gross income and after making necessary deductions, he calculated the per capita income for the period 1925-29.

- **Post-Independence period:** Once India became independent and had decided to launch Five Year Plans, the need for credible data on national and per capita income became imperative to assess the extent of economic growth and how the fruits of development were getting distributed among the people.

National Income Committee (1949)

In 1949, the Government of India appointed the National Income Committee with Prof. P.C. Mahalanobis as its chairman and Prof. D.R. Gadgil and Dr. V.K.R.V. Rao as its two members to compile a national income estimates rationally on scientific basis. The first report of this committee was prepared in 1951.

In its report, the total national income of the year 1948-49 was estimated at ₹8,830 crore and the per capita income of the year was calculated at ₹265 per annum. The committee continued its estimation works for another three years and the final report was published in 1954.

The report of this Committee provided complete statistics on the national income of the whole country.

- **Main features of the Report**: The following were the main features of the National Income Committee report:
- Agriculture including forestry, animal husbandry and fishery contributed about one half of the national income of the country during 1950-51.
- Mining, manufacturing and hand trades contributed nearly one-sixth of the national income India.
- Commerce, transport and communication also contributed a little more than one-sixth of the total national income of the country.
- Income earned from other services such as professions and liberal arts, house property, administrative and domestic services contributed nearly 15 per cent of the total national income of the country.
- Commodity production constituted nearly two-thirds share of the national income whereas services contributed the remaining one-third of the national income of India.
- In 1950-51, the share of the Government sector contributed about 7.6 per cent of net domestic product.
- In the computation of national income estimates, the margin of error was estimated at about 10 per cent.

❖ The Mahalanobis Committee (1960)

The significance of the studies of indices of growth like National and per capita incomes by Prof. Rao and others can be gauged from the fact that even in the early stages of planning, India was conscious of increase in these indices and its impact on the welfare of people. At the end of the first two Five Year Plans (1951-60), when Prime Minister Nehru was informed that there was a certain rise in real per capita incomes, he raised a question in the Lok Sabha in August 1960 as to how this increase was shared and how far the poor sections benefited from the increase. The Government of India then set up a committee in 1960, headed by Prof. P.C. Mahalanobis and consisting of prominent economists, Prof. V.K.R.V. Rao, Dr. P.S. Lokanathan and Prof. B.N. Madan to review:

- Changes in the levels of income,
- Distribution of income and wealth, and
- Concentration of wealth and means of production, following the implementation of the first two Plans.

The Committee, which submitted its report in two parts in 1964 and 1969, had examined a wide range of evidence but failed to come to any definitive conclusion on the changes in income distribution during the two Plans. It also came to the conclusion that planned development had led to the rise of big companies in the economy.

➢ **Central Statistical Organization (CSO):** The CSO was formed as a part of the Cabinet Secretariat with co-ordination and advisory functions. It was established in 1951 as the Central Statistical Institute which was later merged with CSO in 1954.

CSO's functions: The main functions of the CSO are:

- Compilation of National Accounts Statistics (NAS) and its publication.
- Coordinate with State Directorates of Statistics which compile state domestic products and other aggregates.
- Conduct the Annual Survey of Industries (ASI) and publish survey result.
- Play advisory role in statistical matters
- Provide national statistics to the United Nations.
- Attend to statistical work and collaboration with the erstwhile Planning Commission and now NITI Aayog.

➢ **Contribution of Rao to National Income Methodology:** Dr. Rao was the first to adopt scientific approach in the estimation of India's National Income. It was his unique achievement during a phase when data was scanty and it posed severe limitations. His relentless efforts and the refinements he introduced gained credibility over the years and paved the way for building a robust system in the field of national income accounting.

Dr. Rao's work has been recognized internationally too. Along with Professor D.R. Gadgil, Dr. Rao was closely associated with the processes of estimation of the official development assistance (ODA) that the developed countries, at one per cent of their national income, were required to transfer to developing countries. Of this one per cent, 0.7 per cent was to constitute the ODA.

➤ **Rao, an institution builder:** Prof. V K R V Rao has made monumental contribution to the development of the study of Economics in India, primarily at the University of Delhi in the 1940s-50s, where he founded the Delhi School of Economics and the Institute of Economic Growth, on both of which he bestowed tender care to transform them into institutions of international repute. This helped him to nurture a huge crop of prominent, young scholars who went on to occupy prominent positions in the government and in academia in India and abroad. Rao who served in various capacities in the government, including as Union Minister of Education, on retirement, founded the Institute for Social and Economic Change (ISEC), a reputed research institute in Bengaluru, which stands as a monument to his phenomenal work of decades.

➤ Impact of Covid-19 on Indian Economy

The pandemic, Covid-19, which broke out in China in early 2020 and spread all over the world has turned out to be a humanitarian crisis, something like which has not been seen in a century. A comparable episode is the Spanish flu which occurred in 1918, affected an estimated 500 million people the world over and took a heavy toll of some 50 million deaths. Covid-19 has infected about 22.75 crore people globally between January 2020 and September 2021 and has taken a toll of 4.6 million deaths.

Though India has had a history of epidemics of cholera, malaria, etc., they were more localised in nature and could be brought under control in shorter spells. Whereas Covid-19 affected 3.34 crore people nationwide between January 2020 and September 2021, causing 4.4 lakh deaths. Still there was no sign of its ending though vaccines have been developed and population has been getting vaccinated in a phased manner.

The pandemic has had untold economic and social consequences for the people and families. Faced with this major health crisis and uncertainty, India focused on saving lives and livelihoods by taking both short- and long-term measures. An initial stringent, nationwide lockdown was imposed to contain its spread and further lockdowns were imposed in phases and in a localized manner by various states. No sector was spared and due to virtual cessation of all economic activity for some months, millions of people sustained not only loss of incomes but even their jobs.

- **Impact on the Economy: The** impact was compounded by the fact that even prior to the outbreak of Covid-19, Indian economy was already on a downward trend since 2015-16 and the annual GDP growth had declined to 4.2 per cent in 2019-20. While the agricultural sector and rural economy could, relatively speaking, withstand the impact better, the industrial and services sectors suffered the most. And among them, the segments which were virtually devastated were the self-employed (shops, small businesses, etc.), building and construction, hotels, hospitality and tourism, the entire transport spectrum (road, rail, shipping and air) and MSMEs to name only a few. This apart, all large industrial establishments and factories had to be shut for about five months bringing production processes to a grinding halt.

- **Migrant labour issues:** One of the most disastrous outcomes of the pandemic was the untold hardship which the vast numbers of migrant labour had to go through. There are about 50 million "seasonal" migrant workers in India (though the total number of migrants as per Census is much more). The migrant labour, who hail from distant rural areas, is engaged in the construction of buildings, and roads, civic works, factories and in diverse service activities, mostly in large cities and towns.

Deprived of jobs and income and unable to sustain themselves at their places of work hundreds of thousands of migrant workers had to return to their villages. Back in the villages, the Central and State governments activated the MNREG scheme on a wide scale to provide temporary work and source of income to these distressed labour force. But as the economy gradually opened, part of this labour force returned to cities to resume work. However, it would still take some time for the economy to bounce back to pre-Covid-19 levels and absorb all the displaced labour.

The problem is compounded as out of the total workforce of about 465 million, over 80 per cent of the workers are in informal employment in the unorganized sector. And with loss of jobs and an uncertain future, they are at risk of falling into poverty. As a long term measure, India must ensure more balanced development of all regions to stem inter-state migration of labour on large scale. **(See Box 19.2: Regional Balance in Development in this chapter and chapter 4, p. 4.6 on this).**

- **Relief measures:** The government, both at the Centre and State levels did take a series of relief measures. Apart from providing part-time employment in rural areas, people in the BPL/APL categories were provided with free rations of food for a prolonged period. Besides, some cash was also provided under the DBT scheme to vulnerable sections and farmers in their bank accounts.

Both the Union government and Reserve Bank of India took several steps to ease liquidity in the economy to enable various sectors to access loans on easy terms with moratorium periods for loan repayment. But economic recovery is constrained and gradual due to demand constraints. By the middle of FY 2021, the economy is on a recovery path.

- **Recovery path:** Much will depend on the pace and coverage of the entire eligible population with vaccination and economy opening in full measure all over the country so that labour force is fully in place and production and supply chains are totally uninterrupted. Normalcy need to return in other countries also so that international travel could become normal as before, world trade revives fully and it could boost exports to pre-Covid levels.

- **Need to Strengthen Health Infrastructure:** The pandemic has exposed the weaknesses of India's health infrastructure. Instances of avoidable deaths of children and adults, which have occurred not only during the pandemic but even in normal times, especially in government hospitals in some states, point to serious deficiencies. Though in regard to indicators like infant and maternal mortality rates and life expectancy, India has made steady progress over the years, more concerted action is required to fulfil the UN's Sustainable Development Goals (SDGs).

These problems are more pronounced in the health centres in rural areas. India's expenditure on health, as a percentage of GDP, has been stagnant at 1.3 per cent which is far below that in other emerging economies like Thailand and Brazil which devote more funds for public health. Efforts need to be made to raise the public outlay in the health sector to 2.5 per cent of GDP as envisaged in the National Health Policy, 2017. The 15th Finance Commission, in its report submitted in November 2020, has observed that the allocation for the health sector is woefully inadequate and also that the geographical spread of the health infrastructure is skewed with some states faring better than others. **(For more on this, see chapter 26 on Social Sector).**

Ensuring Inclusive Growth

Even as India traverses on high growth trajectory, it should ensure that the growth is inclusive, just and equitable. Reducing poverty further, improving the quality of life, and ensuring that all parts of the society benefit from the economic growth should be the primary focus of an inclusive growth plan. India's policies at macro and micro levels should be attuned to achieve this.

The macro level measures include:

- Transparency and accountability in governance.
- Reducing income and wealth inequality through monetary and fiscal policies.
- Better financial regulations and financial inclusion of all sections.
- Openness to foreign investment and trade liberalization.
- Benign and predictable tax regime.
- Adequate social safety schemes for the vulnerable sections.
- Legal and judicial reforms.

The micro level steps include the following:

- Upgrade education and healthcare infrastructure and its standards with special focus on smaller towns and villages.
- Promoting industries, especially MSMEs in Tier II and III towns to stem labour migration.
- Strengthening Self-help Groups (SHGs) for women's empowerment through income-generating activities.
- Improving governance and accountability of municipal bodies and panchayats to ensure better civic services at local levels.
- Ensuring more accountability on the part of elected representatives at all levels in monitoring implementation of policies and schemes.

In this Chapter we discussed.....

- Planning in China and reforms effected
- Objective of, and factors influencing development.
- Historical trends: development in India and western countries following the Industrial Revolution.
- Distinction between 'economic growth' and 'development'; growth must lead to improving the 'quality of life' of people; modern development economics has laid stress on this aspect; UNDP's Human Development Reports highlight this issue.
- International comparisons between growth in Gross National Income (GNI) and improvements in social parameters.
- Comparison between Indian states on growth in Net State Domestic Product (NSDP) and progress on social indices.
- Development theories: Rostow's 'Stages of economic growth', Lewis' and Nurkse's theory of 'Surplus labour and capital formation', Vakil-Brahmananda model, the 'Big push theory', 'Harrod-Domar model', and Hirschman's 'Unbalanced growth theory'.

- Contrast between developed and developing nations in development process; problems faced by developing economies.
- Structural changes in economy following development; changes in sectoral shares in GDP and employment in selected countries.
- Regional balance in development: need for balanced growth of various regions.
- Development goals–Millennium Development Goals (MDGs) and Sustainable Development Goals (SDGs); India and Millennium Development Goals (MDGs); UN Task Force findings on India's performance.
- Sustainable Development and SDGs; Brundtland Commission; steps taken by India on sustainable development.
- Planning Commission and NITI Aayog; role and relevance of Planning Commission; need for reform and restructuring.
- Rationale for setting up NITI Aayog.
- Structure and Functions of NITI Aayog; divergent views on planning body. NITI Aayog: A Critical Assessment.
- Ensuring inclusive growth.
- Contribution of Dr V.K.R.V. Rao on India's National Income Accounts - An Evaluation.
- Impact of Covid-19 on Indian economy.

Important Terms to Note in this Chapter

Economic growth; Development; Human development; Gross national income; Life expectancy; Infant mortality rate (IMR); Net state domestic product (NSDP); Capital formation; Lewisian turning point; Disguised unemployment; Big push theory; Sustainable development; Climate change; Covid-19 pandemic.

Practice Questions

1. Economists argue that mere increase in Gross Domestic Product (GDP) or Per Capita Income (PCI) does not constitute economic development and progress. Do you agree? Comment on this with your reasoning.
2. What structural changes have taken place in Indian economy since independence? In this context, bring out the relative shares of Primary, Secondary and Tertiary sectors in Gross Domestic Product (GDP) and employment.

3. While the share of agriculture in India's GDP has come down over the years, there has not been a corresponding reduction of its share in employment. What are the reasons for this and how can it be remedied?

4. The share of industry and manufacturing in India's GDP is still relatively low compared to that in the advanced economies. What are the reasons for it and how can the share be increased?

5. What are various stages identified in Walt Rostow's theory of development? Has India passed through these stages and where does India stand now?

6. Some economists have argued that India should have laid greater stress on agriculture, irrigation, etc. rather than developing basic and heavy industries in the initial years of planning. Do you agree or disagree with this assessment? Discuss it with cogent reasoning.

7. The economic growth registered by India in the initial decades of development has been referred to as 'the Hindu rate of growth". What were the reasons for this and how far this statement is justified? Discuss with supporting data.

8. Compare the role played by the erstwhile Planning Commission and the NITI Aayog which has been set up in place of the former. What are the broad differences in their set-up, functioning and objectives?

9. Normally countries shift from agriculture to industry and then later to services, but India shifted directly from agriculture to services. What are the reasons for the huge growth of services vis-a¬vis industry in the country? Can India become a developed country without a strong industrial base? *[UPSC Main 2014 (General Studies Paper)]*

10. Capitalism has guided the world economy to unprecedented prosperity. However, it often encourages short-sightedness and contributes to wide disparities between the rich and the poor. In this light, would it be correct to believe and adopt capitalism for bringing inclusive growth in India? Discuss. *[UPSC Main 2014 (Economics Optional Paper)]*

11. Why socialist model of development could not bring about equitable distribution of income in India and the country remained on a slow growth ' trajectory of 3 to 3.5 per cent for a long time? Discuss. *[UPSC Main 2014 (Economics Optional Paper)]*

12. Do you think Gandhian vision of development is still relevant in India? Explain: with reasons. *[UPSC Main 2014 (Economics Optional Paper)]*

13. Highlight the structural changes in Indian economy before 1991. *[UPSC Main 2014 (Economics Optional Paper)]*

14. In Indian economy, dichotomy of development emerged during the pre-reform period despite efforts of holistic development. Delineate the factors responsible for it. *[UPSC Main 2014 (Economics Optional Paper)]*

15. While Indian economic growth in recent years is services-led growth and Chinese model is manu-facturing-led growth, show the implications of the two models for long-term sustainable development. *[UPSC Main 2014 (Economics Optional Paper)]*

16. 'Elitist bias' and 'crony capitalism' have eclipsed the issues of efficiency and distributive justice in India. Elaborate. *[UPSC Main 2014 (Economics Optional Paper)]*

17. Vitalization of rural economy is key to 'inclusive growth' which is possible through 'strategic management' and technological upgradation. Explain.

[UPSC Main 2014 (Economics Optional Paper)]

18. Why did the socialist order fail and the country had to resort to the market economy system? Give reasons. *[UPSC Main 2015 (Economics Optional Paper)]*

19. Explain the major factors that affected the growth rate of the economy in post- independence India till 1991. *[UPSC Main 2015 (Economics Optional Paper)]*

20. The 'dichotomy of development' in India emerged owing to 'governance deficit' and crony capitalism'. Examine. *[UPSC Main 2015 (Economics Optional Paper)]*

21. Market economy excludes poor from the consumer as well as employment market. Discuss how one can safeguard the interests of population below poverty line.

[UPSC Main 2015 (Economics Optional Paper)]

22. Discuss the changes in the sectoral composition of GDP in recent years.

[UPSC Main 2016 (Economics Optional Paper)]

23. Manufacturing sector needs to be strengthened and developed but the role of the service sector cannot be ignored. Discuss. *[Indian Economic Service/Indian Statistical Service 2015]*

24. "In the changing economic environment, the goal of self-reliance is a myth." Do you agree?

[Indian Economic Service/Indian Statistical Service 2015]

25. India's human development record continues to be gloomy. Can you suggest measures to improve it? *[Indian Economic Service/Indian Statistical Service 2015]*

26. Critically evaluate inclusiveness and sustainability of growth as the development strategy in India in recent times. *[Indian Economic Service/Indian Statistical Service 2017]*

27. How will you explain the paradox of high economic growth and low human development in India in recent times? *[Indian Economic Service/Indian Statistical Service 2017]*

28. Why do the basic objectives of planning remain unfulfilled in India? Can India achieve these objectives in the post-liberalisation period?

[Indian Economic Service/Indian Statistical Service 2017]

29. Explain intra-generational and inter-generational issues of equity from the perspective of inclusive growth and sustainable development. *[UPSC Main 2020 (General Studies Paper)]*

30. Define potential GDP and explain its determinants. What are the factors that have been inhibiting India from realizing its potential GDP? *[UPSC Main 2020 (General Studies Paper)]*

31. Differentiate between plan and non-plan expenditure as used in the government budget. Is this distinction relevant for government finances in India today?

[UPSC Main 2019 (Economics Optional Paper)]

32. Do you agree with the view that steady GDP growth and low inflation have left the Indian economy in good shape? Give reasons in support of your arguments.

[UPSC Main 2019 (General Studies Paper)]

33. Define the concept of carrying capacity of an ecosystem as relevant to an environment. Explain how understanding this concept is vital while planning for sustainable development of a region.

[UPSC Main 2019 (General Studies Paper)]

34. 'In the context of neo-liberal paradigm of development planning, multi-level planning is expected to make operations cost-effective and remove many implementation blockages.' — Discuss.

[UPSC Main 2019 (General Studies Paper)]

35. Despite Consistent experience of high growth, India still goes with the lowest indicators of human development. Examine the issues that make balanced and inclusive development elusive.

[UPSC Main 2019 (General Studies Paper)]

36. The need for cooperation among various service sectors has been an inherent component of development discourse. Partnership bridges the gap among the sectors. It also sets in motion a culture of 'collaboration' and 'team spirit'. In the light of statements above examine India's development process. *[UPSC Main 2019 (General Studies Paper)]*

37. How are the principles followed by the NITI Aayog different from those followed by the erstwhile Planning Commission in India? *[UPSC Main 2018 (General Studies Paper)]*

38. Do you think that planning has a role in the context of market-based development of India? Answer with arguments. *[UPSC Main 2019 (Economics Optional Paper)]*

39. Discuss whether formation of new states in recent times is beneficial or not for the economy of India. *[UPSC Main 2018 (General Studies Paper)]*

40. Mention core strategies for the transformation of aspirational districts in India and explain the nature of convergence, collaboration and competition for its success.

[UPSC Main 2018 (General Studies Paper)]

41. Evaluate the contributions of V.K.R.V. Rao in the National Income Accounting of India.

[UPSC Main 2020 (Economics Optional Paper)]

42. Discuss the changes in sectoral composition of GDP with the changes in the sectoral components of employment in India since Independence.

[UPSC Main 2020 (Economics Optional Paper)]

43. Discuss the relevance of decentralised planning after the implementation of the 74th Constitutional Amendment Act, 1992. *[UPSC Main 2020 (Economics Optional Paper)]*

44. Examine the causes and consequences of the recent slowdown in the Indian Economy. What are the initiatives undertaken by the Government to overcome it? Give your suggestions.

[Indian Economic Service/Indian Statistical Service 2020]

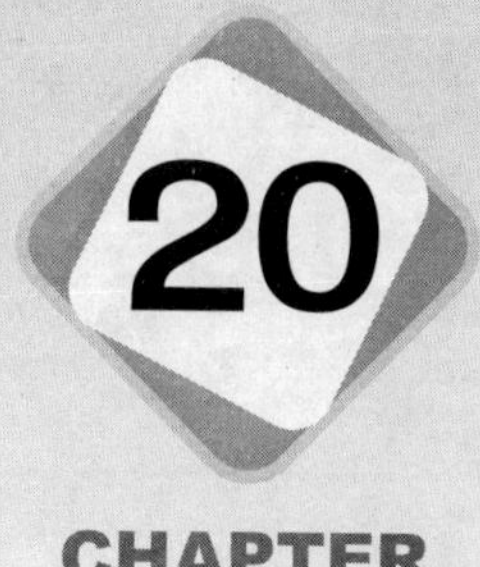

CHAPTER

INTERNATIONAL ECONOMIC ISSUES

- Globalisation and its Benefits
- Challenges and Limits to Globalisation
- Free Trade and Crime
- Globalisation and Inclusivity
- Resistance to Globalisation
- Is there Trend Towards Deglobalisation
- Britain's Exit from EU: Causes and Consequences
- How Globalisation has impacted Indian Economy
- Trends in World Trade
- China's Economic Slowdown and Reforms
- China's One Belt, One Road (OBOR) Initiative
- International Institutions: The World Bank, IMF, etc.
- India and International Institutions
- International Economic Groupings: EU, ASEAN, SAARC, etc.
- Trans-Pacific Partnership (TPP) and CPTPP
- Regional Comprehensive Economic Partnership (RCEP)
- India's Experience with Trade Agreements
- WTO Issues and Food Subsidy Regime
- Geopolitics and Economic Development
- Indo-US Ties
- Bilateralism vs. Multilateralism
- Transfer of Technology and UNCTAD
- Europe's Migrants Problem
- Climate Change

- 21st Conference of Parties (COP 21), 2015
- The Path Ahead on Climate Change
- Climate Change Target and India
- International Solar Alliance (ISA)
- Limitations of Solar and Wind Energy
- Externalities from Pollution
- El Niño and La Niña and Asian Economies

❑ INTRODUCTION

International relations in general, and international economic issues in particular, have assumed great importance in present times as the world has become more globalized and nations more interdependent on one another than ever before. Events in one region could have serious impact on other regions. Shrinking space, shrinking time, and disappearing borders are linking people's lives more deeply, intimately, and intensely than ever before.

There is growing evidence that economic growth calls for policies oriented towards integration into the global economy. Nations withdrawing into a shell and unwilling to engage with other nations may get marginalized and lag behind other countries in terms of growth and human development.

❑ GLOBALISATION

Globalization is not a new phenomenon. It has existed in different forms, and in varying degrees, through the centuries. Nations have been trading with one another for ages, people have been travelling form one country to another, and large scale economic and cultural migrations have been taking place. But as nations progressed, with industrialization and technological advances, particularly in transport and communications, the process gained momentum.

Main Features of Globalisation

- In simple terms, globalization implies integration of a nation's economy with the global economy.
- It results in much freer movement of goods, services, capital, technology, and people between countries, across national boundaries.
- Capital, which is surplus in one country, will tend to move to other countries which offer more attractive returns.
- Also, skilled labour and manpower with highly professional expertise will also be in demand in other countries where such labour and manpower may be in short supply. Such movement is possible and becomes easier when economies are more open in a globalized and liberalized environment.
- The integration happens not only in the economic sphere but political, social, and cultural arenas too.
- International and regional political and economic groupings are indications of such integration. These trends help to speed up development by sharing one another's strengths, exchange of ideas, and expertise.
- The world today is like a 'global village', connected by modern transport, communications, and media, and networked international markets and institutions.

Benefits of Globalisation

The present era of globalization is opening many opportunities for millions of people around the world.

- With cooperation among nations, sharing of knowledge, and optimizing the use of scarce world resources.
- It provides immense opportunities for the international community to jointly promote human welfare, solving problems like poverty, combating climate change challenges, and facing natural disasters.
- Increasing trade, booming international travel, new technologies, foreign investments, expanding media, and Internet connections are all fuelling economic growth and human progress.
- It has also led to greater exchange of ideas and information, and people now engage in collaborative ventures that transcend national borders.
- It offers enormous potential to eradicate poverty in the 21st century, to build on the unprecedented progress achieved in the 20th century. There is more wealth and technology now to be harnessed and more commitment to a global community than before.
- Global markets, global technology, global ideas, and global solidarity helps to enrich people's lives everywhere, greatly expanding their choices.
- The growing interdependence of people and nations promotes shared values and gives rise to shared commitment to advance human development of all and thus sharing the fruits of development in a more just and equitable manner.

Challenges and Limits to Globalisation

Even as globalization confers many benefits, it also brings in its train some major challenges as mentioned below.

- **Compromise on Sovereignty:** Globalization may involve making some compromises in a country's absolute sovereignty. To gain some advantage, a country may have to make some sacrifices in dealing with other nations.
- **Hard Bargaining:** It may involve hard bargaining between nations or groups of nations as witnessed in the various negotiations under the aegis of the World Trade Organization (WTO).
- **Conflicting interests:** There is often friction due to conflicting interests in such negotiations and rigid and hard positions taken by some countries. A glaring instance of this can be seen in the irony of developed countries which extend farm subsidies or support to their farmers, demanding and insisting on developing countries to give up similar practice followed in their countries in support of farmers.
- **Cascading fall-out of events:** Events in a country or one region could impact other countries or regions, and if the events are of adverse economic nature, they are bound to have cascading effect with adverse consequences for other countries, as some events in the last few years have shown. Two such instances are:
- The southeast and east Asian financial crisis of 1997 which started in Thailand spread to other countries in the region, viz., Indonesia and South Korea and, to some extent, Malaysia, Philippines, and Japan causing slump in those economies.
- The subprime crisis that surfaced in the US around August 2007 and the collapse of the Lehman

Brothers in mid-September 2008 disrupted financial institutions there including the shadow banking system, leading to a crisis of confidence in the financial markets. The resulting heightened uncertainty cascaded into a full-blown financial crisis of global dimensions that stymied prospects of an early recovery. The economies of US and Europe took long to fully recover from its devastating effects and it impacted all other regions too due to fall in exports to the US and European markets. (On this, see chapter 15, pp. 15.9-10).

❑ FREE TRADE AND CRIME

A new dimension which has emerged in the context of free trade is the spawning of crime. A globalized and interconnected world is fertile ground for crime and violence unless adequate counter measures are taken. The UN Office on Drugs and Crime (UNODC), which operates in over 80 countries around the world through its network of 115 field offices, works closely with Governments and civil society towards combating drug trafficking and other criminal activities and building security and justice for all as mentioned below.

- **Drugs and crime:** Increasing, and liberalized, trade ties between countries, especially in Asia and Africa, has increased the potential for criminal activities taking advantage of the relaxed customs and trade controls. In the face of such integration, the UN Office on Drugs and Crime (UNODC) has cautioned about the danger posed by criminal activities such as drug and human trafficking and maritime piracy, if adequate security precautions are not taken. The extent of drug menace can be seen from the following facts put out by UNODC:
- Opium poppy cultivation is a major source of drugs. The total area under opium poppy cultivation worldwide increased to about 420,000 hectares in 2017 and more than 75 per cent of that area is in Afghanistan which accounts for well over 80 per cent of opiate production.
- Although there has been decline in opium poppy cultivation Afghanistan, it is still high. Heroin, morphine and opium produced from the 2017 and 2018 Afghan opium crops had begun to enter international markets, having significant impact on global health.
- In 2018, UNODC designed and implemented small-scale and community-based Alternative Development interventions in Counter Narcotics in priority districts. UNODC was implementing projects to give over 26,000 farmers agriculture inputs and support.
- An estimated 35-40 per cent of all Afghan produced opiates are trafficked to Iran. A large haul of drugs clandestinely shipped from Iran to India in September 2021, which was confiscated in Gujarat, is a case in point. Iran is also investing heavily in addressing the challenges of drug users. UNODC works closely in Iran and Pakistan in fighting this menace.
- 204,013 individual drug seizure cases had been registered by the end of 2018.
- The drugs trade finances organized crime and terrorism, harms development and deepens the vulnerability of Member States. 585,000 people died as a result of drug use in 2017. Only 1 in 7 of those people receive treatment and services are often of poor quality.
- **Arms and threat to peace:** Illegal and underground funds from drug trafficking are used by crime syndicates to acquire armaments and deadly weapons to cause unrest and violence in various regions disturbing peace and security.
- **Illegal trading and Revenue loss:** Illicit wealth flowing in the region due to trade in drugs, wildlife, and fake products could be used for funding destabilizing the region. The loss in tax revenues reduces the benefits of trade liberalization and hurts law abiding businesses.

- **Lack of surveillance:** Some countries which throw open their borders to earn foreign exchange are unprepared to do adequate surveillance of goods and people passing through their frontiers giving scope for criminal activities.
- **Surge in Travel and Tourism:** There is a surge in tourist travel in the Asia-Pacific region and trade worth about $5 trillion pass through the south-east Asian waters which makes the task of enhanced security more imperative and challenging. The UNODC has called for countries to share real time intelligence using modern tools and technology.
- **Maritime piracy:** This is another issue impacting world trade. Instances of pirates attacking merchant ships have occurred off and on in the Arabian sea between Africa and India. To counter this, governments arrange Navy ships to escort merchant vessels.
- **Economic costs:** Apart from the dark side of crime, the world is also paying a heavy price on account of terrorism since the 9/11 attack in New York. According to the annual Global Terrorism Index, put out by the Institute for Economics and Peace (IEP), the acts of terror cost the world $52.9 billion in 2014 which compares with $51.5 billion cost in the aftermath of 9/11. The loss includes the value of properties damaged or destroyed, cost of death and injury including medical care costs, and lost earnings. (See also problems due to terror-related migration in a later section in this chapter).

International cooperation

Various steps are taken at the global level to overcome these challenges. The 14th UN Crime Congress, held in March 2021 in Kyoto, Japan on the theme "Advancing crime prevention, criminal justice and the rule of law: towards the achievement of the 2030 (SDG) Agenda", brought together more than 5,000 participants from all over the world. A record 152 Member States were represented at the Congress along with 114 non-governmental organizations, 37 intergovernmental organizations, 600 individual experts and several UN entities and institutes.

Such Congresses have been held every five years since 1955 in different parts of the world, dealing with a vast array of topics. They have made considerable impact in the field of crime prevention and criminal justice and influenced national and international policies and professional practices.

❑ GLOBALISATION AND INCLUSIVITY

While globalization involving exchange of ideas and resources are generally beneficial, the benefits of it do not always percolate to all sections of the population. Its impact is usually confined to the upper and middle segments of society, leaving the lower and vulnerable sections behind. For instance, if the movement of goods, ideas, and technology helps in generating jobs on a substantial scale and its benefits touches the working class, and helps them in upgrading their skills and productivity, it will have very beneficial impact and meet with less resistance.

Globalization has certain other ramifications as well. It could result in:

- **Economic exclusion:** Tariff or non-tariff barriers may keep markets of developed countries closed to poor countries' exports. If in the face of competition, less developed economies are pushed to the margin, the process of globalization is bound to meet with resistance.
- **Political exclusion:** The views and opinions of developing countries in trade negotiations may not receive adequate consideration. For example, as mentioned earlier, the discussions at the WTO on food security issues of developing countries, which is a matter of serious concern for the millions of poor and highly vulnerable sections in those countries, has so far bordered on confrontation and met with intransigence from the developed countries' lobby. Such an attitude on the part of developed nations bodes ill for the success of international cooperation and its impact may be felt even in other domains.

- **Cultural exclusion:** Global flows of goods, ideas, people, and capital may pose a threat to national culture in many ways. They can lead to the abandonment of traditional values and practices and may affect the very survival of indigenous cultures, traditions, and knowledge. The exclusion of traditional knowledge from global regimes for intellectual property is an issue which should receive attention. Traditional knowledge in developing countries in the field of medicine, agriculture, etc. should be recognized and brought within the body of organized knowledge and given intellectual property rights.

❑ RESISTANCE TO GLOBALISATION

- That globalization is not seen as a panacea for problems the world faces is evident from the various protest movements staged against it by civil society activists in different parts of the world—Seattle, Davos, Prague, Washington, etc.
- The opposition is engendered primarily due to the asymmetry and inequality existing between the developed and less developed countries. Though the developed countries do their bit by extending financial and technical aid to the latter bilaterally or through multilateral aid agencies, the persisting differences in the levels of development and gross inequalities stand in the way of mutual trust and confidence.
- The political and economic dominance of a small group of countries (read G8 nations) at world fora and in institutions like the UN, the IMF, and the World Bank, which may have been justified when they were created several decades ago, only exacerbates the hiatus.
- Though the world's balance of power has undergone significant change and many emerging nations have appeared on the world stage in their own right and there is strident clamor for rearranging the architecture of the international bodies, the few advanced nations are unwilling to concede it or let go of their vice grip on them for their own narrow interests. Unless such issues are resolved by mutual consultations and consensus, irritants in international relations will continue harming the cause of global cooperation.
- When the Trans-Pacific Partnership (TPP) was being negotiated in 2015, there were protests not only in some of the emerging countries, but demonstrations took place even in some of the advanced countries like New Zealand, the US, and Japan who were signatories to the pact.
- For instance, there were fears that big pharmaceutical companies would demand long 12-year patents that would give them a monopoly over the next-generation medicines. As a result, the period of exclusivity was cut to five years. Also, a country providing subsidized medicines to its citizens might be challenged by pharmaceutical giants who want to sell drugs at a price they want. There were also concerns that 'corporate rights' could come into conflict with 'sovereign rights' due to agreements like TPP. (For more on TPP see pp.20.21-2)

❑ IS GLOBALISATION IN RETREAT? IS THERE A TREND TOWARDS 'DEGLOBALISATION'?

Introduction

The serious financial crisis which broke out in the US in 2007 and impacted other countries resulting in serious, world-wide economic meltdown, dubbed the 'Great Recession, has already been referred to. (See p. 20.3-4). (The term 'economic recession' signifies a slowdown in economic activity, slump in the production of, and demand for, goods and services and downturn in the business cycle.). Considered to be the most devastating economic crisis since the 'Great Depression' of the 1930's, the world took much time to fully recover from it.

The protracted slump is undermining the case for open markets and free trade on which globalisation rests. The world has been witnessing decline in world trade, steep fall in exports due to sluggish demand in the advanced economies and creeping protectionist measures to insulate domestic industry.

Criticism and Fragility of Globalisation

The charges that anti-globalists make against the international market economy spawned by globalisation are that it widens the inequality and asymmetry between the rich and the poor nations, that it hurts the poor and accentuates poverty, extends or entrenches the use of child labour, worsens the plight of women in the developing countries, erodes democracy, imperils local cultures and ravages the environment by reckless plunder.

There are many factors at work, as mentioned below, which have exposed the fragility of the process of globalisation which seemed like an irreversible economic force bringing prosperity to the rich and the poor alike until the 2007 crisis threw the world economy into turmoil.

- There are signs that negative sentiment towards trade and globalization is on the rise. The perception that the costs of globalization exceed its benefits and that globalization raises inequality figures prominently among the reasons for this apparent change in attitude.
- The turbulence that followed the financial crisis made many governments and companies realize that there are risks to too much exposure to the ebbs and flows of the international system.
- Developing countries have to be cautious about so-called 'financial deepening' – expanding their banking sectors and opening up their capital markets - without proper regulation as it can be too risky. Inflows of speculative 'hot money' can boost asset prices and lead to a borrowing spree by consumers and businesses - which may get disrupted when global investors pull their money out. ('Hot money' refers to funds that move regularly and quickly, between financial markets so that investors get the highest short-term interest rates available. Hot money continuously shifts from countries with low interest rates to those with higher rates). The impact of Federal Reserve raising the interest rates in the US will depend on how foreign institutional investors (FIIS) react to the Fed hike.
- The US administration under President Trump had mooted the idea of 'reshoring' of factories and 'outsourced' work back to the United States to revitalise the US economy and boost employment. Besides, Trump pulled the US out of the Trans-Pacific Partnership (TPP), a multilateral trade agreement comprising 12 nations.
- Terrorism and political instability could slow the process further, adding another layer of cost to global production networks. Mass migration of people from war-torn nations like Syria, Iraq, Libya, Yemen and Afghanistan to European and other countries is creating a backlash against globalisation.
- Trends like Britain's decision to exit from the European Union and US President Donald Trump's rhetoric against free trade and in favour of policies to protect US economy do not augur well for an open international economy.
- Just about everywhere, political establishments are being blamed for tepid economic growth, for too few jobs being created and for favouring global financial markets over the common people. Asian Development Bank has highlighted the dangers of protectionism to the Asian region and urged for strengthening trade linkages and attracting foreign direct investment (FDI) to boost growth in Asia-Pacific region.
- The pushback against globalisation and increasing political pressures against trade openness, in

the face of sluggish economies and rising unemployment, could create more hurdles to the trade environment, potentially retarding the progress of regional and inter-regional integration.

- The prolonged US – China trade dispute has struck another blow to multilateralism and stability of world trade. The trade disputes in WTO between the advanced and developing nations over food subsidy regime are also impacting world trade.
- Globalisation is under attack. It was meant to be the unstoppable economic force bringing prosperity to rich and poor alike, but that was before the financial crisis ripped up the rulebook. Now countries are resorting to tariffs and protectionism fearing setback to their development plans.

❑ BRITAIN'S EXIT FROM THE EUROPEAN UNION: ITS CAUSES AND CONSEQUENCES

Introduction

The European Economic Community (EEC) was founded in 1957 but Britain could join it only in 1973 after her earlier applications were twice vetoed by France. Britain joined the European Community as it thought it would help to arrest its relative economic decline. While in 1950 UK's per capita GDP was almost one third higher than the average of the six founding members of the EEC, viz., Belgium, France, Italy, Luxembourg, the Netherlands and West Germany, by 1973 it had declined to about 10 per cent less. Britain then realized that joining the European bloc would help her to have better access to the markets of the advanced countries in Europe and bolster the economy. Since it joined, Britain's economy has been comparatively stable.

With the adoption of the Maastricht Treaty in November 1993, the European Union (EU), an economic and political partnership, came into being. EU had 28 European countries, including the UK, as members. As a member of the EU, Britain was able to punch above its weight owing to its size, imperial history and financial clout. Due to various factors discussed later in this section, Britain faced a dilemma as to whether she should remain in the EU or exit from the bloc. Following former Prime Minister, David Cameron's decision to hold a referendum on the issue, Britain held protracted renegotiation of the extant conditions of Britain's membership at a summit in Brussels, the EU headquarters.

The Referendum on Brexit

Brexit is an abbreviated expression for UK leaving the EU, by merging the words Britain and exit. In the referendum held in June 2016 to decide whether the UK should leave or remain in the EU, those in favour of exiting from the EU won by 52 per cent to 48 per cent who voted against leaving the EU.

On leaving EU, Britain faced two key issues:

- How British firms would do business in the EU and,
- What curbs would be put in place on the rights of EU nationals to live and work in the UK.

Following the vote, UK had two years to exit from EU completely, as per the provisions of Article 50 of the Lisbon Treaty. Once Article 50 was invoked, UK had a two-year deadline to negotiate trade agreements with the remaining 27 countries in the EU. Significantly, the EU accounted for as much as 48 per cent of UK's exports and 51 per cent of its imports.

Britain finally leaves the European Union

Britain officially left the EU on January 31, 2020, after three and a half years of negotiations and hard bargaining. It heralded the start of a new, uncertain phase in the U.K.'s national life. Britain's lawmakers gave up their seats in the European Parliament, its trade officials became free to start negotiating with other countries.

With this the U.K. entered a "transition period" which was to end in December 2020. Till then, most E.U. laws continued to apply in Britain, including the rights of E.U. citizens to live and work in the country. Although new immigration rules were announced Feb. 19, they were to come into force only in 2021.

Factors behind Brexit

Immigration and Impact on Jobs

Immigration from EU member states into UK was one of the major factors. Between 2004 and 2007, EU admitted 12 countries, formerly communist, from Central and Eastern Europe most of which were far poorer than the West European nations. Though Britain had the option of restricting the entry of people from these new member-countries for the first 7 years as per a Treaty, the government under Tony Blair opened its borders for all newcomers from Eastern Europe while Germany and France kept their immigration controls on East Europeans.

Britain was already home to a large chunk of immigrants, including from outside the EU, having admitted more than five million foreigners as permanent residents over the past two decades. One of the reasons for this move was that, on an average, East European migrants were 10 per cent more productive to the British economy than local citizens.

This influx of migrants had serious impact on Jobs for millions of Britons stuck in the decaying old industrial towns of the north of England. While in the past, the locals had to compete for jobs in a domestic market of about 64 million people, as a member of the EU, they had to compete in a labour market almost 10 times bigger – the population in the EU being 508.5 million in 2015.

Regulatory Regime

Pro-Brexit lobby were of the view that Britain was being held back by the EU, which imposed too many petty regulations on business and charged billions of pounds a year in membership fees for little in return.

They also cited issues of sovereignty and democracy. EU, with its regulations, deprives member-countries of the control over their own affairs and so people wanted Britain to take back full control of its borders and reduce the number of people coming to live and/or work.

Issues of Free Movement

One of the main principles of EU membership is 'free movement', which means one doesn't need to get a visa to go and live in another EU country. The 'Exit' group also objected to the idea of 'ever closer union' between EU member states which they saw as moves towards the creation of a "United States of Europe".

Consequences for Britain

There are many issues confronting Britain on leaving the EU grouping as discussed below. It is to be seen how these will play out in times to come.

Immigration rules

Ending Britain's obligation to allow any E.U. citizen to travel, settle and work in the country was one of the driving factors behind the 2016 Brexit vote. Accordingly, setting out new stricter immigration rules has been a priority for Britain under PM Boris Johnson. Britain has announced a new "points-based" immigration system under which foreign workers must pass an English test and hold a job offer at an "appropriate skill level" from an "approved sponsor." While this would fetch 50 "points" in the new system, a foreign worker to be eligible to enter U.K., must hold 70 points. More points are awarded, in bands, for higher salaries, higher educational qualifications, or if an applicant is seeking a "shortage" job, like nursing, where workers are in demand.

Trade

For UK, trade with EU countries was of much consequence as the EU accounted for as much as 48 per cent of UK's exports and 51 per cent of its imports. The EU and UK signed the Trade and Cooperation Agreement on 30 December 2020 which came into force on 1 May 2021.

The agreement covers not only trade in goods and services, but also a broad range of other areas such as investment, competition, State aid, tax transparency, air and road transport, energy and sustainability, fisheries, data protection, and social security coordination.

- It provides for zero tariffs and zero quotas on all goods that comply with the appropriate rules of origin.
- Both parties have committed to a robust level playing field by maintaining high levels of protection in areas such as environmental protection, the fight against climate change and carbon pricing, social and labour rights, tax transparency and binding dispute settlement mechanism.
- The EU and the UK agreed on joint management of fishing in EU and UK waters. The UK will be able to further develop British fishing activities, while the activities and livelihoods of European fishing communities will be safeguarded, and natural resources preserved.
- On transport, the agreement provides for continued and sustainable air, road, rail and maritime connectivity, with provisions for competition between EU and UK operators on a level playing field, so that passenger rights, workers' rights and transport safety are not undermined.
- On energy, the agreement provides a new model for trading and interconnectivity, with guarantees for open and fair competition, including on safety standards for offshore, and production of renewable energy.
- On social security, the agreement protects number of rights of EU citizens and UK nationals. This concerns EU citizens working in, travelling or moving to the UK, and to UK nationals working in, travelling or moving to the EU from January 2021.
- Finally, the agreement enables the UK's continued participation in a number of flagship EU programmes for the period 2021-2027 subject to a financial contribution by the UK to the EU budget.

Other Trade deals

Britain hopes to have a Free Trade Agreement (FTA) with the US. While President Trump was quite enthusiastic about it, President Biden has not shown keenness for it though talks would continue. Supporters of Brexit hope to explore the possibility of Britain joining the USMCA, the new NAFTA trade agreement between the US, Canada and Mexico, or join the Trans Pacific Partnership (TPP), now refashioned as the Comprehensive and Progressive Agreement for Trans-Pacific Partnership (CPTPP). UK has already sought admission to CPTPP which is pending. Joining one of these major trading blocs would be beneficial for Britain.

Energy supplies

Quitting the EU's internal energy market means that Britain is no longer part of a network that allowed it to buy cheaper power in times of need – like when renewable energy sources are impacted by low amounts of sun and wind. It also means higher prices for the UK gas that comes from the EU from France, Belgium, the Netherlands. There is further concern that if the crisis deepens, those countries might prioritise EU supplies under a 'solidarity principle', leaving Britain literally out in the cold.

Travel and Tourism

Brexit means European travel rules change for the British. It puts an end to free movement of people and goods and services between the UK and the EU. This means significant differences to, and restrictions on, how people live, work and travel. Tourists from the U.K. will not need visas for trips of less than 90 days to the E.U., Iceland, Liechtenstein, Norway or Switzerland. But people wanting to work, study, or travel for business will need more documentation.

Conclusion

The dominant view among foreign policy analysts around the world is that Britain's exit from the EU would diminish the country's standing and influence rather than enhance it. Although the UK's economy appears to have weathered the initial shock of the Brexit vote, opinion is sharply divided over the long-term effects of the country quitting the Union.

❑ HOW GLOBALISATION HAS IMPACTED INDIAN ECONOMY

The impact of globalization on the Indian economy has been increasingly visible particularly after the 1991 reforms and liberalization when the country opened up the economy. The structure of the Indian economy has seen perceptible changes since then, such as increasing importance of external trade and external capital flows. The services sector has become a major part of the economy with over 50 per cent share in the GDP and the country becoming an important hub for exporting IT services.

The reforms process and rapid growth of the economy has made India an attractive destination for foreign capital inflows. Foreign portfolio investment has added buoyancy to the Indian capital markets and Indian corporates have been on aggressive acquisition spree overseas, as seen in the high volume of outbound direct investment flows.

Another crucial factor is the continued high degree of dependence on imported energy sources, especially crude oil, with the share of imported crude being about 75 per cent. The sharp fall in international crude prices has had a benign effect on the economy helping India face the adverse effect of fall in exports due to the persisting recession in the advanced economies.

India could not insulate itself from the adverse developments in the international financial markets following the financial crisis of 2008, despite India's banking and financial system having had little to do with the US subprime mortgage debacle, which culminated in the global crisis. The initial effect of the subprime crisis on India was positive, as the country received accelerated Foreign Institutional Investment (FII) flows during September 2007 to January 2008. This led to a belief that the emerging economies could remain largely insulated from the crisis and provide an alternative engine of growth to the world economy. But it was soon disproved as the global crisis intensified and spread to the emerging economies through capital and current account of the Balance of Payments (BoP). The net portfolio flows to India soon turned negative as Foreign Institutional Investors (FIIs) rushed to sell equity stakes in a bid to replenish overseas cash balances. This had a knock-on effect on the stock market and the exchange rates by creating the supply–demand imbalance in the foreign exchange market. The current account was impacted after September 2008 through slowdown in exports. Despite setbacks, however, the BoP situation of the country continued to remain resilient. The global crisis resulted in the economy experiencing extreme volatility in terms of fluctuations in stock market prices, exchange rates, and inflation.

However, it is widely held that trade liberalization during the 1980s and the 1990s have had a positive impact on productivity growth. Growth of labour productivity is crucial in the context of the current emphasis on manufacturing. Productivity is affected by many factors, one of the most important being technological progress. Increased application of information and communication technology (ICT) in manufacturing, accompanied with commensurate upgradation of labour skills and knowledge, would have multidimensional effects on productivity growth. With more transfer of technology through international cooperation and greater skilling of the labour force, India should be able to upgrade systems and improve overall productivity in industry.

❑ TRENDS IN WORLD TRADE

World trade is an important means towards greater integration between nations. It not only ensures optimum use of scarce resources in production based on the principle of 'comparative advantage', but also helps developing and least developed countries participate in trade and thereby, promote development in those countries. Increasing trends in world trade in the last few decades show how closely interlinked nations are and how important foreign trade is in the scheme of things. Despite the financial crisis the world has been going through, the share of world trade in GDP is much higher today than it was 20 years ago. The average share of exports and imports of goods and commercial services in world GDP increased significantly from 20 per cent in 1995 to 30 per cent in 2014 (in value terms) proving that, in present times, GDP is highly influenced by international trade.

However, the economic crisis of 2008, triggered by the subprime lending crisis in the United States and subsequent developments in the European economies, affected exports and imports in 2009. (See Table 20.1). It led to a global recession between 2008 and 2011. Between the fall of 2008 and the spring of 2009, global trade collapsed by 20 per cent in volume. Having initially rebounded sharply in mid-2009, growth in international merchandize trade slowed again in the course of 2010. Though it recovered in that year, the global crisis appears to have left a marked impact on the dynamism of global trade. World trade has further recovered between 2014 and 2019.

Table 20.1: World Trade—Exports and Imports (in US$ billion)

Year	World Exports	World Imports	Year	World Exports	World Imports
1990	1,378	1,347	2009	13,775	12,350
1995	4,683	4,738	2010	16,688	14,987
2000	7,057	6,480	2012	19,649	17,609
2005	11,495	10,467	2013	20,291	17,919
2007	15,279	13,905	2014	15,864	16,362
2008	17,555	16,074	2019	20,538	18,449

Source: World Bank, WITS-World Integrated Trade Solution.

Various crises have had an impact on trade between 1995 and 2001. These included Mexico's monetary crisis (1995–2001), the east Asian financial crisis of 1997, and the bursting of the dotcom bubble in 2001.

China's accession to the WTO in December 2001 paved the way for its economic rise and contributed significantly to increasing world trade from 2002 to 2008. But the recent slump in Chinese growth and its nascent economic transition was the key factor in a sharp slowdown in global trade in 2014. The decline in trade, one of the key drivers of economic growth in recent years, was mostly due to cyclical shifts, especially the downturn in demand growth for commodities in China and emerging countries in Asia, besides the slump in exports to the US and Europe.

But behind that slowdown is the beginning of China's transition from an export-driven economy to one more rooted in domestic consumption. Trade flows may continue to be volatile over the coming years, depending on the pace of China's transformation and on the recovery in the US and European economies.

❑ CHINA'S ECONOMIC SLOWDOWN AND REFORMS

The economic slowdown in China since 2015 has had far-reaching consequences for countries in Asia and beyond. After decades of double-digit growth, the weakened performance of the world's second largest economy is a matter of concern for the world economy, which is already rattled by the recession in the US and European economies. The unexpected devaluation of 'yuan', the Chinese currency in August 2015, responding to signals from investors that the currency was overvalued, threw not only the Chinese economy out of gear, but has had a chilling effect on the world economy. Some observers have said that the Chinese move on the currency was intended to give unfair advantage to its exporters.

The industrial slowdown in China, which is one of the biggest buyers and consumers of commodities and oil, means considerable slump in demand for these items and it is impacting the economies in Central Asia, Africa, and Latin America, which were suppliers of these products. The fall in demand for oil from China and the production of shale gas in the US has already caused steep fall in international oil prices and seriously affected the oil-producing economies in the Gulf. Japan which supplies intermediate manufactured parts and electronic components to China has also been impacted.

But China's slowdown could also have some positive consequences for other countries like Vietnam and Taiwan who could ramp up production of electronic goods and other consumer products for export, partly replacing China's share in the world markets.

Rebalancing the Economy

China has started rebalancing its economy from an export-led one to one driven by domestic consumption to reduce its over dependence on exports. As the slowdown of Chinese economy could be a long-term phenomenon, countries like India and Indonesia could also take advantage by improving their capacity for export of quality products. Rising labour costs in China could benefit countries like India, Bangladesh, Vietnam, and Myanmar where labour costs are relatively less to boost export of textiles and apparels and other products. For this, these countries have to further modernize their infrastructure and logistics systems, and reform financial and banking sectors and regulatory regimes, which will help to attract more foreign direct investment (FDI).

Reforming State-owned Enterprises

China has begun a process of reforming its state-owned enterprises with new ownership structures with a view to upgrade domestic industry and dominate overseas markets. Despite major achievements, the state enterprises suffer from imbalances and structural flaws and needed to create management systems and market mechanisms better suited to China's needs in the changing global environment. The government has chosen more state-owned firms to participate in mixed ownership structure aimed at injecting private capital into the state sector. This measure is designed to infuse market discipline into China's debt-ridden industrial giants in the state sector and pump more finances into them. It will also help to attract new investors, boost corporate governance and set up new internal incentive mechanisms.

China's Economic Growth

Chinese economy was expected to grow at an average rate of 6.5 per cent during 2017-21. Its per capita GDP in 2020 is US$ 10,500 as compared to per capita GDP of US$ 63,543 of USA. In total GDP terms, China's economy has grown from $11 trillion in 2017 to US$ 14.7 trillion in 2020, which is still below that of United States' GDP of US$ 20.9 trillion in 2020. Even by 2035, China would still not be an affluent society like the US and its per capita GDP by then will only be half that of US.

US – China trade dispute

The prolonged trade dispute between US and China has added a new dimension to China's problems and it has also disrupted world trade and has had a ripple effect on the economies of many countries.

This conflict has been made worse following the outbreak of Covid-19 pandemic which originated in China in early 2020, spread worldwide and has taken a toll of millions of lives in different countries. This has led to mistrust between China and many other nations and virtually thrown the global economy out of gear.

China's One Belt, One Road (OBOR) Initiative

This is an ambitious strategic initiative – an adaptation of the historical Silk Road – conceived and driven by China's President Xi Jinping which marks the beginning of a new geopolitical era that will impact Asia, Africa and Europe. At the heart of the project lies the creation of an economic land belt that includes countries on the original Silk Road through Central Asia, West Asia, the Middle East and Europe, as well as a maritime route that links China with Africa through the Arabian Sea and passing through the Suez Canal into the Mediterranean.

The plan involves more than 60 countries, representing a third of the world's total economy and more than half the global population. The project aims to reorient the country's domestic over-capacity and capital towards regional infrastructure development and to improve trade relations with Asean, Central Asian and European countries.

A new economic paradigm

In just about thirty years, China has developed from a poor inward-looking agrarian economy to a global manufacturing powerhouse. Its model of investing and producing at home and exporting to developed markets has elevated it to the world's second-largest economy after the USA. Now faced with a slowing economy at home, China's leadership is looking for new channels to sustain its appetite for growth at a time when other developing countries are experiencing rapidly rising demand and require vast infrastructural development which China hopes to cater to with its vast financial resources. China realizes that its future growth is linked to Asia and beyond and is banking on responding to its neighbours' huge infrastructure needs via the One Belt, One Road initiative.

There are also compelling geopolitical reasons, such as energy security, for China to push forward with the OBOR plan at a time when its trading partners are potentially excluding it from strategic agreements. While China is a member of the mega trade pact, Regional Comprehensive Economic Partnership (RCEP), an economic grouping of 15 major economies in Asia Pacific region, China's application for admission to the Comprehensive and Progressive Agreement for Trans-Pacific Partnership (CPTPP), which is another major trade group, is yet to be decided.

Silk Road Infrastructure Fund

Launched in February 2014, the China-led US$40 billion Silk Road Infrastructure Fund is to invest in OBOR infrastructure projects. The fund is capitalised mainly by China's forex reserves and is intended to be managed like China's sovereign wealth fund.

But even China's deep pockets have limits, with the country's total debt to GDP at 250 per cent. Three financial institutions have been set up to support its development, which have met with some resistance in the West, given that they serve as alternatives to the World Bank, IMF and ADB.

Challenges before OBOR

The initiative is not without its challenges. It calls for cooperation and coordination with partner countries over the long term for it to be a lasting legacy.

To allay the fears of countries participating in the project, China has put forth three conditions it will observe, namely:

- No interference in the internal affairs of other nations;
- Does not seek to increase the so called 'sphere of influence'; and
- Does not strive for hegemony or dominance.

However, some countries view the project with scepticism knowing China's various actions in the global arena, such as not only its forceful occupation but militarisation of territories in the South China sea over which Philippines, Vietnam, Brunei, Indonesia, Malaysia and Taiwan have legitimate rights under international laws. And despite an International Court of Justice (ICJ) ruling against China's illegal occupation of these areas, China has decided to reject the ICJ verdict. Similar is the situation in the East China sea where there are unresolved disputes between Japan and China. All these point to hegemonistic tendencies on the part of China which casts a shadow over projects like the OBOR.

One Belt, One Road could have as much impact on China's internal economy as it will have internationally. China's top priority is to stimulate the domestic economy via exports from industries with major overcapacity such as steel, cement and aluminum.

India and OBOR

India decided to stay away from the One Belt One Road (OBOR) or the Belt Road Initiative (BRI) of China due to sovereignty concerns over the China-Pakistan Economic Corridor, which is a part of OBOR, as it passes through Pakistan-occupied Kashmir which India considers, is an integral part of India.

The Quad Initiative

India, Japan, Australia and the US, who form the Quadrilateral (Quad in short) strategic grouping, are also considering developing an Asia-Africa Growth Corridor which is expected to propel growth and investment in Africa and Asia. It will also create a free and open Indo-Pacific region through new sea corridors that will link the African continent with India and countries in South Asia and South-East Asia. It will help to build institutional, industrial and transport infrastructure in growth poles among countries in Asia and Africa.

(See also section "Geopolitics and Economic Development: The Emerging World Order" later in this chapter).

❑ INTERNATIONAL INSTITUTIONS

The Second World War (1939–45) had taken a heavy toll on Europe and ravaged its economies, especially Germany, which along with Italy and Japan formed the Axis powers fighting against the European countries and the US, known as the Allied powers. Both Germany and Japan and many other countries had been devastated by the costly war.

Marshall Plan

A programme for the recovery of Europe was mooted by George Marshall, the then US Secretary of State which came to be known as Marshall Plan. About $13 billion was provided by the US under this Plan between 1948 and 1951 for the economic recovery of Europe. It largely achieved the objective of restoring confidence in the people of Europe about their economic future. The Plan also promoted a sense of unity, bond, and spirit of federalism among the west European countries which augured well for their future.

Bretton Woods Institutions: The World Bank and IMF

An important development towards the close of the war was an international conference organized at Bretton Woods in the US in 1944 to work out the financial arrangements which will be needed to achieve stability once the war ended. It led to the creation of two institutions, viz., the International Bank for Reconstruction and Development (IBRD) and the International Monetary Fund, both based in Washington D.C., USA. It may be recalled here that J.M. Keynes, by then a celebrated economist, had played a crucial role in the negotiations contributing his ideas at this conference.

The World Bank the Organization and its Role

The World Bank has evolved from the International Bank for Reconstruction and Development (IBRD) and its mandate is the alleviation of poverty worldwide. The World Bank is a vital source of financial and technical assistance to developing countries around the world. It works in a unique way partnering with member countries to reduce poverty and support development.

The Bank provides low-interest loans, zero to low-interest credits, and grants to developing countries. The aid supports investments in diverse areas such as education, health, public administration, infrastructure, financial and private sector development, agriculture, and environmental and natural resource management. Some of the projects are co-financed with governments, other multilateral institutions, commercial banks, export credit agencies, and private sector investors.

The World Bank Group consists of five institutions:

- International Bank for Reconstruction and Development;
- International Development Association;
- International Finance Corporation;
- Multilateral Guarantee Agency, and
- International Centre for the Settlement of Investment Disputes.

The Bank has set the following targets to be achieved:

- End extreme poverty by decreasing the percentage of people living on less than $1.90 a day to no more than 3 per cent; and
- Promote shared prosperity by fostering the income growth of the bottom 40 per cent in every country.

International Bank for Reconstruction and Development (IBRD)

IBRD which is the original World Bank institution and is the lending arm of the World Bank works closely with the rest of the World Bank Group to help developing countries reduce poverty, promote economic growth, and build prosperity.

International Development Association (IDA)

Set up in 1960, the International Development Association (IDA), which is part of the World Bank, complements the World Bank's original lending wing—the IBRD—and functions as a self-sustaining organization providing loans and advice to middle-income and credit-worthy poor countries. IDA is one of the largest sources of assistance for basic social services for the world's 77 poorest countries, 39 of which are in Africa.

Aid from IDA brings about positive change to the 1.3 billion people who live in countries served by IDA. It has supported development programmes in 112 countries. IDA aims to reduce poverty by providing loans (called "credits") and grants for programs that boost economic growth, reduce inequalities, and improve people's living conditions.

IDA lends money on concessional terms. Thus, IDA loans have a zero or very low interest charge and repayments are spread over 25 to 38 years, including a 5- to 10-year grace period. IDA also provides grants to countries at risk of debt distress.

International Finance Corporation (IFC)

The International Finance Corporation, which is also part of the World Bank Group, is the largest global development institution focused exclusively on the private sector. It helps developing countries achieve sustainable growth by financing investment, mobilizing capital in international financial markets, and providing advisory services to businesses and governments. Its investment and advice is tailored to the client's specific needs and helps to attract other investors who could provide the client with new sources of capital and better ways of doing business.

IFCs aid helps private sector to develop entrepreneurship and build sustainable businesses with advice on a wide range of issues, including environmental, social, and governance standards. It provides access to critical finance for individuals and micro, small, and medium enterprises by working with financial intermediaries. In 2015, long-term investments by IFC in developing countries totalled $17.7 billion, a 17 per cent increase over the previous year. More than a third of that amount—over $7 billion—was mobilized from other investors.

International Monetary Fund (IMF): Its Role

The fundamental mandate of IMF is to ensure the stability of the international monetary system. It performs this function by keeping track of the global economy and the economies of member countries, lending to countries which face balance of payments problems and providing practical help and advice to members.

In 1969, the IMF created an instrument, Special Drawing Rights (SDR), to serve as an international reserve asset. The SDR is not a currency but a potential claim on the freely usable currencies of IMF members. Holders of SDRs can obtain the freely usable currencies in exchange for their SDRs. Though reliance on the SDR as a global reserve asset declined in course of time, SDR allocations in 2009 totalling SDR 182.6 billion played a critical role in providing liquidity to the global economic system and supplementing member countries' official reserves following the global financial crisis.

The IMF oversees the international monetary system and monitors the economic and financial policies of member countries. As part of this process, which takes place both at the international level and with individual countries, the IMF highlights possible risks to stability and advises on any policy adjustments required. The IMF helps member countries to prepare economic policies and manage their financial affairs more effectively by strengthening their human and institutional capacity through technical assistance and training.

The IMF derives its resources from the member countries, primarily through their payment of 'Quotas' which it utilizes for providing loans to countries needing assistance. Quotas which are subscriptions from member countries form an important source of IMF's financial resources. Each member country of the IMF is assigned a Quota, based broadly on its relative position in the world economy. India's 'Quota' in IMF, as on March 2016, stood at 13,114.4 million SDRs, which is 2.80 per cent of the total. The Quota and voting shares of members change as members' pay up increases in their Quota. (See also 'Special Drawing Rights' in Glossary).

❑ OTHER INTERNATIONAL INSTITUTIONS

There are many other specialized organizations in the economic sphere in the UN system which play an important part in promoting global development and cooperation among the member countries. These include the Food and Agricultural Organization (FAO), the International Labour Organization (ILO), and UN Conference on Trade and Development (UNCTAD).

Asian Development Bank (ADB)

Conceived as a financial institution to promote economic cooperation and growth in the Asian region, the Asian Development Bank was set up in 1966 headquartered at Manila. It has played an important role in developing various spheres in the region such as food production and rural development, improving infrastructure, job creation, and poverty reduction. It has also provided assistance at times of unprecedented natural disasters such as the tsunami in 2004 which devastated parts of India, Indonesia, Maldives, and Sri Lanka.

It is estimated that to ensure continued economic growth, job creation, and poverty reduction, the region requires $60 billion in annual investments for road, rail, power, water, and other critical infrastructure. Members of ASEAN, one of the fastest growing regions in the world, possess over $700 billion in foreign exchange reserves, but these funds are being largely invested outside the region. The ASEAN Infrastructure Fund (AIF) is an innovative ASEAN initiative to mobilize the region's resources for its infrastructure development needs.

Asian Infrastructure Investment Bank (AIIB)

AIIB, launched in December 2015 in Beijing, is an international financial institution and development bank set up at the initiative of China to support infrastructure building in the Asia-Pacific countries. Perceived as an alternative to the World Bank and the ADB, which are already functioning and helping countries catered to by AIIB, it will serve as an additional source for funding the massive infrastructure building requirements in the region. The United Nations has hailed the launch of AIIB as having potential for "scaling up financing for sustainable development" in the region. AIIB has authorized capital of $100 billion with China, India, and Russia as the largest shareholders. The bank will invest in sectors including energy, transportation, urban construction, and logistics as well as education and healthcare. The establishment of the AIIB marks a milestone in the reform of global economic governance system. It also signals the growing clout of emerging nations like China and India in the changing global economic order.

New Development Bank (NDB)

NDB, also referred to as BRICS Development Bank, is a multilateral development bank established by the BRICS group of countries—Brazil, Russia, India, China, and South Africa. Based in Shanghai, China, it started functioning in 2015 and has an initial authorized capital of $100 billion. The Bank will support public or private projects through loans, guarantees, equity participation, and other financial instruments. Its resources will be used for infrastructure and sustainable development projects in BRICS and other emerging and developing countries. It will also cooperate with other international organizations.

The establishment of both AIIB and NDB heralds a new chapter in meeting global development challenges and will complement the efforts of institutions like the World Bank and ADB.

❑ INDIA AND INTERNATIONAL INSTITUTIONS

India has been one of the largest recipients of financial assistance from the World Bank. The aid has been to fund a variety of projects of economic and social nature such as improving infrastructure, industrial development, agricuture, education and heath services, etc. The aid has been channelled to many specific projects in various Indian states.

In 2014, projects worth $24.12 billion of World Bank aid were under execution. This included $12.86 billion aid from the IBRD and $11.16 billion in active projects from the IDA. India also has the largest single portfolio exposure from the IFC, the private sector arm of the World Bank Group, with commitments of over $4.5 billion. Between July 2013 and June 2014, the World Bank Group offered financial assistance worth $6.4 billion to India.

From the IMF, India borrowed SDR 3.9 billion in 1981-82, under an Extended Fund Facility, the largest arrangement in IMF history at the time. In 1991-93, India borrowed a total of SDR 2.2 billion under two standby arrangements, and in 1991 it borrowed SDR 1.4 billion under the Compensatory Financing Facility. The Fund has also provided India with technical assistance in developing the government securities market, reforming the foreign exchange market, public expenditure management, tax and customs administration, and strengthening statistical systems.

India is an important and founding member in both the Asian Infrastructure Investment Bank (AIIB) and the New Development Bank (NDB) referred to earlier.

❑ INTERNATIONAL ECONOMIC GROUPINGS

Realizing the importance of international economic cooperation, various countries have joined together to form economic groupings—regional and international—for enhanced trade and aid cooperation. It is a trend towards globalization and should be seen as positive development rather than as a threat to the global trading system so long as no nation or group of nations try to exploit or harm the interests of any other nation. Free trade agreement is a legally binding document committing two or more countries to reducing or eliminating trade barriers. It helps smooth flow of goods and services between nations.

While liberalization and free trade act as a check against protectionism, it should lead to greater prosperity among the participating nations. As there are likely to be domestic pressures against such pacts, such groupings must act in a transparent manner to convince people at home that trade benefits all and sheltering the nation from competition may only hamper progress. And the benefits of free trade and cooperation must show visible results on the ground by enhancing prosperity and well-being of the people. There are many international and regional groupings. Some of them are discussed below.

G8 and G20

The G8 and G20 are two important groups. G8, founded in 1975, consists of the world's richest economies—the US, UK, France, Germany, Italy, Japan, Canada, and Russia. The European Union is also represented in this group. In due course, the group was expanded to form G20 in 1999 with the addition of emerging nations which include China, India, Brazil, Mexico, S.Korea, Turkey, Indonesia, and few other countries.

The G20 group meets at the level of Heads of State or the Government and the Finance Ministers periodically to discuss issues relating to international financial stability and economic cooperation. The G20 member-countries account for about 80 per cent of world's gross product and world trade and two-thirds of world population which highlights its importance. The G20 group has dealt with such crucial issues as the economic slowdown, recession, fragile recovery, and the need for stimulus since the 2008 crisis broke out and which has persisted for eight years. Adding to the crisis is the setback to China's economy which has compounded the problem.

G77

The Group of 77 is another coalition of developing countries formed to promote the members' collective economic interests and boost their joint negotiating capacity in the United Nations. There were 77 founding members in the organization, but by November 2013, the organization expanded to 134 member countries.

European Union

The EU is a unique economic and political partnership between 28 European countries that together cover much of the continent. The first steps were to foster economic cooperation so that countries who trade with one another become economically interdependent and so more likely to avoid conflict.

The result was the creation of European Economic Community (EEC) in 1958, and initially increasing economic cooperation between six countries: Belgium, Germany, France, Italy, Luxembourg, and the Netherlands. Since then, a vast single market has been created and continues to develop towards its full potential.

What began as a purely economic union evolved into an organization spanning many areas, from development aid to environment. The change of name from the EEC to the European Union (EU) in 1993 signifies this.

The EU has delivered half a century of peace, stability, and prosperity and helped to raise the living standards. The Union also launched a single European currency, the 'Euro', which is now the common currency in 19 out of 27 EU countries and used by some 338.6 million people every day. The benefits of the common currency are seen while travelling abroad or shopping online on websites based in another EU country. The abolition of border controls between EU countries has helped people to travel freely throughout most of the continent. The single or 'internal' market is the EU's main economic engine, enabling hassle free movement of most goods, services, money, and people.

APEC and ASEAN

Asia-Pacific Economic Cooperation (APEC), set up in 1989 initially with 12 countries and now having 21 member-countries, is an important grouping and, as its name suggests, consists of countries from the Asian and Pacific region. These include Australia, New Zealand, US, Japan, China, S. Korea, Malaysia, Singapore, Indonesia, Thailand, Vietnam, and some other Asian countries. Its primary goal is to support sustainable economic growth and prosperity in the Asia-Pacific region. The terms 'economic' and 'cooperation' in its title indicate the emphasis the group places on a cooperative approach focussed on economic and trade issues. APEC is committed to move towards greater regional economic integration by endorsing a roadmap to translate the vision of the Free Trade Area of the Asia-Pacific (FTAAP) into a reality.

Association of South East Asian Nations (ASEAN) is another important grouping of south-east Asian countries founded in 1967. Started with 5 countries–Indonesia, Malaysia, the Philippines, Singapore, and Thailand–it now has 10 members including also Brunei, Vietnam, Laos, Myanmar, and Cambodia. ASEAN aims to accelerate economic growth, social progress, and cultural development in the region through joint endeavours, promote regional peace and stability, and foster collaboration and mutual assistance in the economic, social, cultural, technical, and scientific fields. China has a full Dialogue Partner status in ASEAN.

ASEAN and India

India has a Dialogue partnership with ASEAN which has been elevated to ASEAN-India summit since 2002 and it is being held annually. At the 2012 summit held in New Delhi, an ASEAN-India Vision Statement was issued according to which the ASEAN-India Partnership was elevated to Strategic Partnership. India's collaboration with ASEAN transcends the realm of functional cooperation and covers political and security domains. India participates in a series of consultative meetings with ASEAN which includes the East Asia Summit (EAS), Mekong-Ganga Cooperation, and Bengal Initiative for Multisectoral Technical and Economic Cooperation (BIMSTEC), which help to broaden the dialogue and accelerate regional integration.

ASEAN and China–The South China sea dispute

Of late, the relationship between some of the ASEAN countries and China has been fraught with tension due to developments in the South China sea. China is claiming most of the South China sea, parts of which overlap areas claimed by some of the ASEAN states—Philippines, Vietnam, Malaysia, and Brunei.

China has been building artificial islands, an airstrip, placed a large oil rig in the disputed waters, and is even constructing military facilities much to the chagrin of the other claimant states. Apart from the unilateral actions by China, contrary to international law, in areas over which other south-east Asian states have legal rights, China's actions could also affect vital global trade routes through which about $5 trillion worth of goods pass a year. US, Japan, Australia, etc. have raised objections over China's provocative actions and US has carried out freedom-of-navigation patrols in the area.

Such incidents only reinforce the fact that peace and political stability are essential for economic progress.

South Asian Association for Regional Cooperation (SAARC)

Set up in 1985, South Asian Association for Regional Cooperation is an economic and geopolitical organization comprising eight South Asian countries, viz., Afghanistan, Bangladesh, Bhutan, India, Maldives, Nepal, Pakistan, and Sri Lanka besides Observer members.

SAARC aims at promoting economic and social development and welfare, and cultural relations between member countries. Agreements among SAARC members include energy (electricity) cooperation, avoidance of double taxation, customs matters, establishment of South Asia Free Trade Area (SAFTA), a food bank, and a Regional Standards Organization. The areas on which member countries cooperate include agriculture and rural development, biotechnology, trade, environment, education, culture, etc. A Visa Exemption scheme also exists under which certain categories of persons are issued Special Travel document, which exempt them from visas within the region.

SAARC symbolizes the affinity that prevails between the south Asian nations and their desire to promote not only development but cordial relations between the countries and their peoples.

Trans-Pacific Partnership (TPP)

Yet another development in the area of 'free trade' is the Trans-Pacific Partnership (TPP) which brings together a group of developed and emerging countries in the Asia-Pacific region. It includes US, Canada, Japan, Australia, New Zealand, Mexico, Malaysia, Singapore, Vietnam, Peru, and Chile. The TPP promises to advance economic growth, support high-paying jobs, and raise living standards across the region. Though a framework agreement has been arrived at and it is a significant development, it is not yet final as the member countries have to overcome the challenge of domestic resistance and ratification by lawmakers in the respective countries.

As stated earlier, there has been opposition to TPP also in the member countries on the ground that negotiations were conducted in secrecy and the text of the pact was released only after the agreement was arrived at. Liberalizing the farm sector could be an issue in some countries. In Japan, rice farmers stand to lose their long-standing protection as the country may allow 78,000 tonnes of tariff-free rice to be imported which is about one per cent of its total production. There is opposition to TPP in the US too on the ground that it is not very beneficial to the country.

The pact is said to be anything but equally beneficial to all. There were other rumblings too. New Zealand failed to get substantial market access for its dairy products in Canada, US, and Japan. Besides, before the TPP can come into effect, economies accounting for at least 85 per cent of the total gross domestic product of the 12 signatories should have ratified it. And without the US, other nations do not make up the 85 per cent target, which shows that US can call the shots.

But TPP also has some positives to offer. It may mark a shift from US hegemony to a more multilateral approach to liberalizing trade and ensuring international stability. With uniform rules put in place, it could boost investments in less developed member countries like Chile, Peru, and Vietnam as overseas companies find it easier to do business. The coalition will also help Asian countries involved in dispute over the South China sea to counter China's increasing economic and military dominance.

CPTPP

A major setback to this trade pact is the decision of the US, under President Trump, to withdraw from it on the plea that it is inimical to the economic interests of the US. After withdrawal of the US, the trade deal has been resurrected due to the initiative of Japan involving the 11 remaining members in the form of Comprehensive and Progressive Agreement for TPP. However, it is doubtful how far TPP will be meaningful without US participation. Some experts argue that this limitation can be largely remedied if the two Asian giants, China and India, also join the grouping. It would then cover countries with total population of about 3 billion instead of 500 million and a combined GDP of $25 trillion instead of $ 13 trillion. Also, being excluded, China and India stand to lose out from TPP. They will face higher tariffs in TPP member economies than would the TPP members when they trade with each other. China and India also stand to lose in the area of services and inward foreign investment as TPP members will be more committed to protecting the rights of investors. TPP members too face the prospect of high tariffs on some goods, including farm products, when they sell to the huge markets of China and India.

China's response to exclusion from TPP has been to accelerate other trade agreements to which it is a party, notably the 16-country Regional Comprehensive Economic Partnership (RCEP). China has sought admission to CPTPP pact which is pending. But as Taiwan has also submitted application to the CPTPP, the members of the 11-nation trade bloc are in a fix. If China is admitted, she is sure to object to Taiwan's admission. India is yet to join the RCEP pact. (See section on RCEP below).

Regional Comprehensive Economic Partnership (RCEP)

Regional Comprehensive Economic Partnership (RCEP) is a mega trade deal which was to include 10-member ASEAN group + 6 countries -- Australia, China, India, Japan, South Korea and New Zealand. The grouping envisages regional economic integration, leading to the creation of the largest regional trading bloc in the world accounting for nearly 45 per cent of the world's population with a combined gross domestic product of $21.3 trillion, 30 per cent of global trade and 26 per cent of FDI flows. Initiated in 2012, its conclusion has been repeatedly delayed due to protracted negotiations. If concluded, the pact could provide the size and scale to unleash new growth potentials and write new rules of international trade order.

While the group has discussed issues regarding goods, services, investment and rules and prepared a draft of joint assessment report, progress has been held up due to the sensitivities and political constraints of each country. One of the sticking points is India's insistence on greater liberalization in services sectors, especially in easier movement of its professionals to RCEP member countries. However, most countries are resisting any ambitious deal in services under RCEP.

India is also concerned as it has trade deficit with ASEAN and partner countries of RCEP. The deficit with the bloc has risen from $9 billion in FY 05 to $83 billion in FY 17 of which China alone accounts for 60 per cent of the deficit. While India had offered complete liberalization on almost 75 per cent of tariff lines, the group demands to liberalize over 90 per cent of total tariff lines.

One of the most comprehensive trade deals so far signed by India is with the ten ASEAN countries -- AIFTA (ASEAN-India Free Trade Area) under which tariffs were reduced for two-way trade. While India's strength lies in services trade, India did not get a fair deal under AIFTA services pact. Greater market access in services and investment would have helped to offset the loss in goods trade. Overall, India has not benefited from this deal. This holds a lesson for India while negotiating under RCEP. (See India's FTA with ASEAN countries below).

After 8 years of protracted negotiations, the RCEP grouping of 15 nations finally formalized and concluded the trade pact, without India, in November 2020. They have also said that as and when India decides and is ready to join the pact later, India would be welcomed into it.

India's Experience with Trade Agreements

India has preferential access, economic cooperation and Free Trade Agreements (FTA) with about 54 individual countries. India has signed bilateral trade deals in the form of Comprehensive Economic Partnership Agreement (CEPA)/Comprehensive Economic Cooperation Agreement (CECA)/FTA and Preferential Trade Agreements (PTAs) with some 18 groups/countries. India is a late, and cautious, starter in concluding comprehensive preferential tariff agreements covering substantially all trade with some of its trading partners.

India engages in regional and bilateral trade negotiations to diversify and expand in export markets while ensuring access to the raw materials, intermediates, and capital goods needed to stimulate value-added domestic manufacturing. The following are some of the major regional and bilateral trade agreements India has entered into, while there are several other smaller agreements too.

India's FTAs

- Asia Pacific Trade Agreement (APTA) - India, Bangladesh, China, Lao PDR, South Korea, Sri Lanka,
- India-ASEAN Trade in Goods Agreement (India ASEAN TIG) – India, Brunei, Cambodia, Indonesia, Laos,
- Malaysia, Myanmar, Philippines, Singapore, Thailand and Vietnam.
- South Asia Free Trade Agreement (SAFTA) - India, Pakistan, Nepal, Sri Lanka, Bangladesh, Bhutan and the
- Maldives
- BIMSTEC: India, Bangladesh, Sri Lanka, Myanmar, Thailand.
- India-Sri Lanka FTA (ISLFTA).
- India has bilateral Comprehensive Economic Partnership Agreement (CEPA) with Japan (JICEPA) and South Korea (IKCEPA), and Comprehensive Economic Cooperation Agreement (CECA) with Malaysia (IMCECA), Singapore (ISCECA), and some more countries.

Shortfall in outcomes

India had signed a series of FTAs with Asian countries that came into force in the 2000s. Industry and policy makers have found that these FTAs have brought little tangible benefit to India while it has helped the partner countries. Further, they have adversely impacted India's manufacturing which the government has been trying to boost through 'Make in India' scheme.

India-ASEAN FTA:

A look at the pact India signed in 2010 with the Asean 10-member group and trends in trade would reveal how it has not been beneficial to India. This is a major trade pact since taken up for review. The group includes Indonesia, Malaysia, Thailand, Philippines, Singapore, Vietnam, Myanmar, Laos, Cambodia and Brunei.

Widening trade deficit

The data below shows the persisting trade deficit with imports from ASEAN nations outstripping India's exports to them.

Table 20.2: India's Trade with ASEAN Group

(In $ billion)

	2014-15	2015-16	2017-18	2018-19	2019-20
Exports	31.81	25.13	34.20	37.40	31.54
Imports	44.71	39.90	47.13	59.32	55.36
Deficit	–12.90	–14.77	–12.93	–21.92	–23.82
Total Trade with bloc	76.52	65.03	81.33	96.72	86.90

Source: Dept. of Commerce, Govt. of India.

Factors behind trade imbalance

The following factors have contributed to the imbalance in trade.

- Imports have been higher in several product segments as domestic producers in India have been uncompetitive compared to foreign entities.
- Products from 'third country' are found to be routed to India via India's FTA partners in the group. Particularly, products such as set-top boxes from China, which is outside the group, are sent to Asean countries where they are repackaged without value addition and exported to India. This benefits Chinese producers by enjoying the tariff concessions under the agreement.
- Industries in India have also not been able to make full use of the lower duty benefits and step up exports to Asean nations.

Anomalies in the pact

There have been other anomalies too in the working of the pact as mentioned below.

- Indian exporters have not been able to get a level playing field. Indonesia had lowered duties only on 50 per cent of the items while it was getting customs duty benefit on about 75 per cent of its products in India.
- Against 35 per cent duty on rice for trade among Asean members, Indian rice faced a 50 per cent levy.
- Japanese automobiles can be imported into Thailand and Indonesia at 5 per cent duty, while Indian cars faced 35 per cent tariff.
- The services component in which India has advantage was signed only in 2019 and it is yet to be ratified.

Impact on Electronic sector

For instance, under the India-Asean FTA, for TV sets of screen sizes up to 105 cm., the basic customs duty is nil, as against 10 per cent duty levied when imported from elsewhere. When they can be imported at reduced or even zero duty, no one would want to manufacture the same product in India.

So also, the FTAs with Asean, South Korea, Japan and other countries hamper India's plans to emerge as a manufacturing powerhouse for electronic items. The problem has arisen because the agreements India has signed are with some of the economies who are major competitive producers of these items resulting in finished products being imported into India at a lower cost than could have been manufactured in India.

Misuse FTA

A third country, outside the trade pact, could take advantage of tariff concessions provided in the FTA by routing its products through one of the partners in the pact. Such misuse of the concessions has been observed in India's FTA with Asean nations where products from China have been routed to India through some of the Asean countries thereby Chinese exporters getting the benefit of tariff concessions. It is not only a violation of the agreement but also places the domestic producers in India, whose products may be less competitive, at a disadvantage. It will also distort India's trade balance.

Rule of origin

One of the main issues in FTA with Asean countries is the "Rule of Origin' clause. India has been demanding enforcing the rules of origin criterion as it apprehends that in its absence, third countries could circumvent the rules and dump goods into India through Asean countries thereby enjoying tariff concessions. As stated above, there have been instances of China routing goods into Indian market via India's FTA partner countries in ASEAN. India has since decided that the benefit of concessional customs duties, including zero duty, would be available to Indian importers only if they can prove that products have undergone "value addition" of at least 35 per cent in the country of origin. With this stipulation, a mere exporters' certificate for "country of origin" which was sufficient earlier will not be enough.

Review of Pact with ASEAN

India is reviewing FTA strategy to ensure that the treaties provide economic and strategic benefit. Asean has agreed to India's long-pending demand to review the pact. Earlier, Asean members were linking the review to India agreeing to join the Regional Comprehensive Economic Partnership (RCEP).

Successful sectors

On the other hand, India has performed well in manufacture and on export front in some sectors like automobiles, pharmaceuticals, garments and apparels, mobile handsets, etc.

- **Digital India:** Under the Digital India initiative, India has been able to step up production of mobile phones with major producers like Apple, Samsung, LG, Nokia, and Motorola setting up production facilities in India, apart from the presence of many domestic firms, which will boost the export of mobile phones from India. India is the world's second largest mobile phone manufacturer after China. There are over 100 firms engaged in mobile phone industry in India.

It points to the need for India to create benign investment climate to attract major international forms to invest in India and set up manufacturing units and also for Indian industry to become improve productivity and become more competitive.

- **Automotive sector:** The performance of India in the automobile, two-wheeler and automotive components industry is a success story where there are many well established firms catering to not only domestic market but exporting on a substantial scale.

Trade Deals under Negotiation

India - United States trade

- India currently has no trade agreement with the United States of America.
- In April 2018, the United States launched an eligibility review of India's compliance with the General System of Preferences (GSP) market access criterion.
- In March 2019, it was decided that India no longer meets the GSP eligibility criteria and revoked India's GSP status.
- Termination of GSP benefits removed special duty treatment for $5.6 billion of exports to the United States, particularly affecting India's export-oriented sectors, such as pharmaceuticals, textiles, agricultural products, and automotive parts.

- The United States and India continue holding discussions to address trade issues and to prepare a limited trade deal.

India - EU trade position

- India still does not have a trade pact with European Union which is the second largest importer of goods in the world with a share of 28% in world imports, after Asia's 38 per cent share.
- The EU is India's third largest trading partner, accounting for €62.8 billion worth of trade in goods in 2020 or 11.1% of total Indian trade, after China (12%) and the US (11.7%). The EU is the second-largest destination for Indian exports (14% of the total) after the USA.
- India is the EU's 10th largest trading partner, accounting for 1.8% of EU total trade in goods in 2020, well behind China (16.1%), the USA (15.2%), and the UK (12.2%).
- Trade in goods between the EU and India increased by 12.5% in the last decade.
- India-EU trade deal
- In 2007, India and the EU began negotiations on a broad-based Bilateral Trade and Investment Agreement (BTIA).
- A key EU objective in its trade relations with India is to work towards a sound, transparent, open, non-discriminatory and predictable regulatory and business environment for European companies trading with or investing in India, including the protection of their investments and intellectual property. The aim is to contribute to unlocking the untapped potential of two-way trade between the EU and India.
- Currently, India's trade regime and regulatory environment remains relatively restrictive.

India-UAE Trade pact

- India and the United Arab Emirates (UAE) have begun official discussions on a Comprehensive Economic Partnership Agreement (CEPA), which aims to boost bilateral trade and investment and hope to sign trade pact by Mar 2022.
- In 2019, India was the UAE's second-largest trading partner.
- The UAE is also India's eighth-largest investor, having invested US$ 11 billion between April 2000 and March 2021, while Indian firms have invested over US$ 85 billion in the UAE.

Conclusion

Free trade agreements are useful for expanding a country's trade basket. But if it results in a surge in imports without corresponding expansion of exports, it would hurt domestic industry. The success of an FTA is to be judged on the criterion of enhancing trade and fairness of the deal. If the proportion, and not just the absolute level, of both imports and exports between the countries concerned has grown, then the FTA is successful for both parties. It achieves the objective of moving trade in the direction of the FTA country relative to others. If only either imports or exports have grown, then the benefits would be one-sided.

At the same time, it is important that domestic producers should not take shelter behind protective tariff barriers. They must improve their production techniques, step up productivity and become competitive in global markets. It would be relevant to recall here India's inward-looking, import-substitution (IS) policy of the 1950s, in contrast to the forward-looking export-promotion (EP) strategy of East Asian economies, during the same period, which held back India's competitiveness and progress for the next three decades until she opened up and integrated with the global economy in the 1990s.

Box 20.1: Note on Trade Agreements

Free Trade Agreement (FTA)

Free Trade Agreements (FTAs) are arrangements between two or more countries or trading blocs that primarily agree to reduce or eliminate customs tariff and non tariff barriers on substantial trade between them.

Features of FTAs:

- In FTAs, tariffs on items covering substantial bilateral trade are eliminated between the partner countries. However, each maintains individual tariff structure for non-members. India - Sri Lanka FTA is an example.
- FTAs normally cover trade in goods (such as agricultural or industrial products) or trade in services (such as banking, construction, trading etc.).
- FTAs can also cover other areas such as intellectual property rights (IPRs), investment, government procurement and competition policy, etc.

❖ **Types of Trade Agreements:** There are different types of trade agreements such as:

- **Preferential Trade Agreement (PTA):** In a PTA, two or more partners agree to reduce tariffs on agreed number of tariff lines. The list of products on which the partners agree to reduce duty is called positive list. India MERCOSUR PTA is such an example. However, in general PTAs do not cover substantially all trade.

Difference between FTA and PTA: The difference between an FTA and a PTA is that while in a PTA, there is a positive list of products on which duty is to be reduced whereas in an FTA, there is a negative list on which duty is not reduced or eliminated. Thus, compared to a PTA, FTAs are generally more ambitious in coverage of tariff lines (products) on which duty is to be reduced.

- **Regional Trade Agreement (RTA):** RTA is a treaty between two or more governments that define the rules of trade for all signatories. Examples of RTAs include the North American Free Trade Agreement (NAFTA), the European Union (EU) and Asia-Pacific Economic Cooperation (APEC).

RTAs are increasing in number and changing their nature. While there were fifty trade agreements in force in 1990, there were more than 280 in 2017. In many trade agreements today, negotiations go beyond tariffs to cover multiple policy areas that affect trade and investment in goods and services, including behind-the-border regulations such as competition policy, government procurement rules, and intellectual property rights.

- **Comprehensive Economic Cooperation Agreement (CECA) and Comprehensive Economic Partnership Agreement (CEPA):** These terms describe agreements which consist of an integrated package on goods, services and investment along with other areas including IPR, competition etc. The India Korea CEPA is one such example and it covers a broad range of other areas like trade facilitation and customs cooperation, investment, competition, IPR etc.
- **Customs Union:** A customs union is an agreement between two or more neighboring countries to remove trade barriers, reduce or abolish customs duty, and eliminate quotas. Such unions were defined by the General Agreement on Tariffs and Trade (GATT) and is a form of economic integration.

Unlike in FTAs, a common external tariff is imposed on non-members of the union. When countries outside the union trade with countries in the customs union, they need to make a single payment (duty fee) for the goods that have crossed the border. Once inside the union, they can trade freely with no added tariffs.

- **Economic Union:** An economic union is one of the different types of trade blocs. It refers to an agreement between countries that allows products, services, and workers to cross borders freely. The union is aimed at eliminating internal trade barriers between the member countries, with the goal of economically benefitting all the member countries.

The union requires the integration of monetary and fiscal policies, so that member countries coordinate policies, taxation, and government spending related to the agreement. They also use a common currency that comes with fixed exchange rates.

European Union (EU) is an example of Economic Union. The EU is the world's largest trade bloc. Importing goods and services from more than 100 countries, it is the biggest import market, as well as the biggest exporter in the world. The EU's common currency is the euro, which is used by its member states:

Other Groupings

There are other international groups such as the African Union, Organization for Economic Cooperation and Development (OECD), Organization of Petroleum Exporting Countries (OPEC), Gulf Cooperation Council (GCC), etc. all of which play important role in their respective spheres of operation.

❑ WTO ISSUES AND FOOD SUBSIDY REGIME

Some of the issues discussed above in the context of TPP are equally relevant in trade negotiations at WTO. As stated in Chapter 15, there is considerable disagreement between the stand taken by developed nations and what the developing countries are seeking. (See pp.15.24-6). The main issue relates to food subsidies and protection of farmers in developing countries to which the developed nations object as they want greater access to markets in developing and emerging countries like India, China, Brazil, Vietnam, etc. The US has been dragging its feet on an agreement on Doha Development Agenda (DDA). The US blames India, China, and Brazil for non-conclusion of Doha talks and has now called for scrapping it. At the same time, the US and its allies have managed to get a trade facilitation agreement though it was not part of the core Doha agenda. Not only that, while objecting to farm subsidies and subsidized PDS in India, the US has adopted a trade distorting Farm bill exposing their hypocritical stance. India wants a permanent settlement of the core issue of public stockholding programme for food security before taking up any new issues at WTO. Such actions by developed nations reveal their real intentions in imposing their agenda on less developed countries which have a large proportion of poor people and poor farmers who deserve protection.

The issue came up again in the 11th Ministerial conference of WTO held in Buenos Aires in December 2017 when India aggressively pursued solving the question of public procurement and stockholding of food grains and ensuring food security for the vulnerable sections and farmers. But the US refused to agree to a permanent solution to the issue, as committed at the Nairobi ministerial meet in 2015. This has cast a pall over the sanctity of pledges made at WTO and the very functioning of the world body. However, India is protected by a 'peace clause' secured in 2013 in Bali meet and which received permanent status in 2014. The peace clause implies that even if a developing country gave subsidy for food procurement exceeding 10 percent of the value of production, which is the provision under WTO's

Agreement on Agriculture (AOA), no other country could challenge it at WTO till 2017. In 2014, the WTO General Council approved extension of peace clause till such time a permanent solution is agreed to by the members. Thus India has protection but yet it is seeking a permanent solution over and above the existing 'peace clause' to give stronger legal basis to its programme to procure, stock and distribute food. (For more on this see Chapter 15, p. 15.24 under INDIA AND WTO).

G33 Developing Nations Reiterate stand in WTO

Ahead of WTO meet due towards the end of 2021, G33 nations, of which India is a part has floated a proposal as per which WTO members will not challenge through Dispute Settlement Mechanism the support that developing countries provide for foodstuff under public stockholding programmes. A developing member country will also endeavour not to export from the procured stocks unless requested by an importing member.

India has urged that as part of trust building exercise, G33 must strive for positive outcomes on permanent solution to public stockholding for food security purposes which is of utmost importance, early finalization of a special safeguard mechanism and a balanced outcome of domestic support.

Distortion in Subsidies:

India has pointed out that seven members – the European Union, Japan, the US, Russia, Switzerland, Canada and Norway – have more than 96 per cent of the global entitlement of the trade distorting farm subsidies (called Final Bound Total Aggregate Measurement of Support) while the remaining members have less than 4 per cent share.

As per the proposal, all members with such entitlements between $1-10 billion will be required to reduce their support for each agricultural product and cap it at their de minimis levels, through equal annual instalments, within a period of five years from the date to be decided by the members. De minimis, or the threshold, caps the domestic support at 10 per cent of the value of production but many developed countries have entitlements to provide domestic support well over 10 per cent of the value of production.

- **India's submission:** India has pointed out in its submission, "It is a supreme irony that developed members, with relatively fewer farmers, have significant flexibility to provide trade-distorting support to their farmers. On the other hand, most developing Members, w ith a very large number of farmers, do not have the policy space for providing support to their farmers".

Quoting studies, India said that the de minimis entitlement and the amount of trade distorting subsidy per person employed in agriculture in Switzerland was $37,952, in the US was $24,714) and in the EU was $12,361 compared to China's $1,208, India's $451 and Kenya's $206.

- **African Group submission:** The African Group has highlighted the damage caused by the European Union, the United States, Japan, Switzerland, and Canada among others through their billions of dollars of high trade-distorting domestic farm subsidies.

In a comprehensive paper titled, "Domestic support: disciplines on final bound AMS entitlements", the African Group has called for sharp reductions in the Aggregate Measurement of Support (AMS) that indicates the volume of the most trade-distorting domestic support as well as the product-specific support.

Need to Reform India's Food Subsidy Regime

Public procurement of foodgrains at remunerative prices is needed to protect the farmers and, equally, food security through the Public Distribution System (PDS) is vital for a country like India with a sizeable poor population. But there is no reason why India should persist with the expensive manner in which it pursues food security and there is imperative need to reform them. Foodgrains are procured far in excess of requirements and the buffer stocking norms under the PDS. This takes away grains from the market pushing up prices and adds to the government's costs of procurement, storage and carryover. The inability and inefficiency of the public sector agency, viz., the Food Corporation of India (FCI), which has a monopoly, results, year after year, in spoilage and pilferage of millions of tonnes of foodgrains meant for public distribution. There is scope to decentralize the stockholding by involving private trade, limit the role of FCI to holding minimum physical stocks and play an active role in the forward markets in grains to stabilise prices. The use of cash subsidies in urban areas through the Direct Benefit Transfer (DBT) scheme, on the lines of LPG subsidy, could also help to streamline the PDS by preventing leakages and save valuable public funds.

❑ GEOPOLITICS AND ECONOMIC DEVELOPMENT : THE EMERGING WORLD ORDER

There is increasingly close linkage between geopolitics and economic development as seen from the emerging world order. With the emergence, and rising economic and political influence, of nations like China, India, Brazil, South Africa, Mexico, Indonesia, Vietnam, etc., the global balance of power is undergoing change.

While under President Trump the US was retreating from global institutions, the new US administration under President Joe Biden is enlarging US participation and role in global affairs keeping in view also the strategic interests of the US as well as domestic concerns. The firmness in dealing with the hegemonic and expansionist actions of China adopted by Trump is being continued by Biden also.

As noted earlier, the increasing assertiveness of China – both economic and political – as evidenced by ambitious projects like One Belt, One Road (OBOR) running through a host of countries linking Asia with Africa and Europe, China's claim to virtually the whole of South China sea, its dispute with Japan in East China sea, China's century-old dispute with Japan over 'Senkaku' islands which the Chinese call 'Diaoyu', etc. are signs of its growing economic clout. China has become the second largest economy and one of the biggest traders in the world and is aiming to limit the global influence of Western powers. China joined the WTO in 2001 committing to open its markets to foreign goods and investment in return for better access to foreign markets for its exports. While China benefited from the manufacturing boom and exports, it failed to keep the other side of the bargain, viz., to open up its markets. Foreign investors and companies still face many barriers and conditions such as having to tie up with local partners and firms, on transfer of technology, intellectual property rights, etc. The mounting trade deficit of the US with China has become a contentious issue between the two countries. The belligerence and threatening postures of North Korea, whose close ally and prop is China, has only compounded matters.

In the Asia-Pacific region, US, Japan, Australia and India are forging close defence and economic cooperation as a counterbalance to the dominance of China. These countries hold regular joint military exercises in the Indo-Pacific region to forge close alliance. They are also asserting their rights of navigation and ensuring security of sea-borne trade valued over $5 trillion which passes through the Straits of Malacca and the Indian Ocean.

The Quad Group and China: The quadrilateral grouping between the US, India, Japan and Australia, referred to as the 'Quad', is another important move, in response to the ambitions of rising China.

The primary objective of the Quad is to ensure that the Indo-Pacific region stretching from the eastern part of Africa all the way up to the Pacific Ocean remains open, free, rooted in rule-based order and in consonance with international law as this is vital for smooth and unhindered flow of a major chunk of international trade.

China's assertive actions in claiming the entire South China sea and militarizing many islands therein, despite persistent objections from some of the Asean states who have legitimate claims over parts of it, are clearly violative of the UN Convention on the Law of the Sea (UNCLOS). China has even refused to honour the verdict of the International Court of Justice (ICJ) in favour of Philippine's claims over its exclusive economic zone in South China sea.

South-east Asia and China: China's strident claim and belligerence over Taiwan, which it claims to be an inalienable part of China and Taiwan's firm refusal to accept this clam, adds to the tensions in this region. These have serious implications for peace and stability in the South-east Asia region which is home to the 10-member ASEAN group with a population of over 620 million. The criticality of this region for the global economy can be gauged from the fact that if ASEAN were a country, it would be the seventh-largest economy in the world, with a combined GDP of US$ 2.6 trillion. By 2050, it is projected to rank as the fourth-largest economy. It has a larger population than the European Union or North America and has the third-largest labour force in the world, behind China and India.

Other Challenges: The world is now confronted with many other challenges such as terrorism, armed conflicts, drug trafficking, etc. The latest problems in Afghanistan, following the withdrawal of US forces from there after two decades, has added a new dimension to threats in South Asia and neighbouring countries. This will have not only political ramifications but will impact world trade since Afghanistan, which is landlocked, could serve as a gateway and a land route from Iran to Central Asian states and beyond to Russia and Europe. It will also impact India's plans to access Central Asian states through Chabahar port in Iran which India built in collaboration with Iran. Further, China is trying to forge strategic links with Afghanistan which is rich in mineral resources and could serve China's vital industrial needs. These developments could mean political instability in this critical part of Asia, and it remains to be seen how things will play out in the years to come.

Indo-US Ties

The push for maritime security is also a shared concern of India and the US, especially in the backdrop of Chinese warships and submarines making regular forays into the Indian Ocean Region. India and the US, along with Japan, engage in major joint maritime security exercises in the Bay of Bengal.

The Quad grouping of US, Japan, India and Australia, referred to above, is countering China's aggressive actions in the Indo-Pacific region. Against this background, India has been building strong strategic partnership with these countries which plan to build "Resilient Supply Chain Initiative" (RSCI) to avoid over-dependence on China which is now having virtual monopoly over many critical ingredients and intermediate products. The fragility of this situation was starkly exposed during the pandemic, Covid-19, when many countries faced problems in production, including of vital pharmaceutical products, due to disruptions in supplies from China. (See more on this under "Perceptible change" in the section on Transfer of Technology and UNCTAD below).

Bilateralism vs. Multilateralism

As economies are getting more interconnected and with trade playing an important role in growth, trade pacts between countries have come into sharp focus. Trade pacts have strategic and security implications when it involves foreign investments in critical sectors like energy and defence and due to issues like access to, and transfer of, advanced technologies. Nations are also guarding against unfair trade deals which give advantage to one side while adversely impacting others. The withdrawal of the US from the Trans-Pacific Partnership (TPP), comprising some of the major economies in the Asia-Pacific region, representing a substantial part of world trade, is an example.

❑ TRANSFER OF TECHNOLOGY AND UNCTAD

In the early 1960s, there were growing concerns about the place of developing countries in international trade which led many of those countries to call for the convening of a full-fledged conference specifically devoted to tackling these problems and identifying appropriate international actions. The first United Nations Conference on Trade and Development (UNCTAD) was held in Geneva in 1964. Given the magnitude of the problems at stake and the need to address them, the conference was institutionalized to meet every four years, with inter-governmental bodies meeting between sessions and a permanent secretariat providing the necessary substantive and logistical support. Simultaneously, the developing countries established the Group of 77 to voice their concerns. The Group now has 134 members. UNCTAD has also played an important role in facilitating transfer of technology between countries.

UNCTAD became a forum for North-South dialogue and negotiations on issues of interest to developing countries, including debates on the 'New International Economic Order'.

Some of the important Agreements launched by UNCTAD include:

- The Generalized System of Preferences (1968), by which developed economies granted improved market access to exports from developing countries.
- A number of International Commodities Agreements aimed at stabilizing the prices of export products crucial for developing countries.

Transfer of Technology and UNCTAD

The 1979 UNCTAD conference held at Vienna adopted a 'Programme of Action on Science and Technology for Development'. It rested on two basic ideas—strengthening of science and technology (S & T) capacities of the developing countries and restructuring of the then existing pattern of international S & T relations which included transfer of technology. The issue was rather complex as for the acquiring country to make full use of a technology, it may have to expand its capacity to generate, absorb, adapt, and apply the S & T know-how. The country will also have to create or expand institutions capable of advising the government or industry on the suitability and adoption of the technology.

Transfer of technology, especially advanced technology, helps developing countries to strengthen their creative and innovative capacities. Such transfers take place at the level of governments or through transnational corporations. However, undue dependence on foreign technology may hamper development of technology in the recipient country and care has also to be taken to ensure that the technology transferred is one most appropriate to it. Such transfers are beneficial to the transferring entity as it often helps to export and thus create market for their products and services in the form of capital equipments and technical personnel provided.

Another issue for caution is that advanced countries may not, in most cases, provide the latest technology for fear of losing their monopoly over it and transfer only an outdated, if not obsolete, one. It may create further problems in future for the receiving country as it would be difficult to get spares for the systems in use and the final product also may become totally outdated by the time it comes into the market. Such issues have cropped up particularly in niche areas such as advanced armaments required for defence and frontier areas like nuclear plants, space technology, advanced aircraft, etc. where advanced nations are reticent to effect transfers.

Lately, there are signs of some change in the attitudes of advanced countries due to compelling need for international cooperation. Such a need may arise out of increasing production and labour costs in those countries or on considerations of security or simply to expand markets for their products. This is evident from the willingness of countries like France, US, UK, Germany, etc. to start production of high-tech items in countries like China, India, Brazil, etc. The shifting of R & D units involving advanced technology and processes by some of the multinationals in the IT sector and starting of automotive manufacture and proposals to manufacture fighter aircraft and airplane components in India which are under consideration are examples of this. Such transfer of high-tech industries is beneficial to the developing countries which are able to absorb advanced technology and develop highly skilled manpower.

Perceptible change:

There are, of late, indications of change in the attitude of some of the advanced countries in sharing technology and collaborating with developing countries to co-produce certain items, particularly defence-related hi-tech products. This is due to a variety of compelling factors like need for markets for the products of advanced countries, higher labour-wage costs in those countries and geopolitical issues arising from the dominance and aggressive moves on the part of China which has been a "factory to the world" for nearly three decades. This has led to the need for the advanced countries to rely increasingly on other emerging economies like India, Brazil, Mexico, South Korea and countries in south-east Asia to forge strategic and security partnerships.

The US under President Biden has pledged unwavering commitment to India as a "Major Defense Partner" including strengthening cooperation in advanced military technologies. The Defense Technology and Trade Initiative between US and India calls upon government and private stakeholders to use the existing ecosystems of innovation and entrepreneurship in defence industries for co-development, co-production and expanding mutual defence trade. This mechanism would not only enable India to circumvent outright purchase, but also get around any hurdles n US legislature.

Evidence of such cooperation can be seen from recent projects approved, between US and India such as to co-develop air-launched unmanned aerial vehicles (UAVs or Drones). Another important deal giving a boost to the "Make in India" initiative is the joint project between Airbus Defence and Tata advanced systems, valued ₹20,000 crore to build the C-295 medium transport aircraft which will replace Avro-748 planes of the Indian Air Force. The contract signed between India's Ministry of Defence and Airbus Defence & Space, Spain was cleared by the Cabinet Committee on Security of Govt. of India. Under the deal, 16 aircraft will be delivered in a flyaway condition by the Airbus Defence and Space within 48 months of signing the contract. The remaining 40 planes will be manufactured in India by a consortium of the Airbus Defence and Space and Tata Advanced Systems Limited (TASL) within 10 years of signing the contract. All 56 aircraft will be installed with indigenous electronic warfare suite and a large array of parts, sub-assemblies and major component assemblies of aerostructure are scheduled to be manufactured in India.

The above ventures will eventually enlarge the role of the firms not only on the operational aspects but also on industrial and technological development. These contracts will support further development of India's aerospace ecosystem bringing additional jobs and developing high-tech skills in the coming years.

❑ EUROPE'S MIGRANTS PROBLEM

The problem of the surge of migrants coming to Europe as refugees from West Asia and northern Africa poses a serious socio-economic problem. It is a multi-dimensional issue with strong political under currents. The immediate provocation for such large-scale movement of people is the escalation of war and terror in Iraq-Syria region and Libya. Millions were fleeing turmoil at home and seeking safe havens in Europe. Migrants coming to Europe is not a new phenomenon but what was worrying is not just the scale of the arrivals, but the sheer number and variety of places they were coming from. A majority of them undertake the hazardous journey across the Mediterranean in overcrowded, unsafe, and illegal boats resulting in the tragic death of many, including women, children, and elderly people in mid-sea. Many migrants are from countries where the West tried to intervene militarily and failed—Iraq, Libya, and Afghanistan in particular, and Gaza, sub-Saharan Africa, and even Haiti.

These refugees enter Europe through various points – Greece, Italy, Turkey, Hungary, Slovenia, and even Norway going through Russia. It is estimated that there are more displaced people and refugees now than at any other time in recorded history – some 60 million, numbers not seen since World War II.

Economic and Social Consequences

- This massive inflow of migrants has huge economic and social consequences and costs for Europe. Most of the European nations are unwilling to accept refugees in such large numbers, fearing it may create social instability and disharmony.
- The crisis has evoked a backlash among Europe's right-wing nationalist parties. It also involves heavy economic costs as these people will have to be provided homes and jobs, besides the increased pressure of population on the cost and standard of living for the native citizens.
- Though many European nations are facing declining population and could afford to absorb reasonable additions to the population, it raises many other questions. The refugees may not be having the requisite qualifications for the jobs on offer.
- Rise of IT-based Jobs and Businesses: The information technology revolution resulted in socio-economic transition which changed the attitude of the liberal West European states and aggravated the immigration problems. The labour market that hitherto depended largely on physical labour like manufacture, mining, and heavy industry transitioned to an information and service economy that relied on high skill labour in offices. As traditional jobs became redundant, the immigrants were forced into low-tech workshops, construction jobs, agriculture, or unskilled work in hospitals, hotels, and restaurants, etc. This has led to widening disparities with resultant dissatisfaction and social tensions.
- Another worry has been that many suspected terrorists and criminals may sneak in along with the refugees causing serious security issues.

Schism within Europe

Another consequence is the disparate views held by European states on the migrants issue. While most of the states were unwilling to accommodate migrants and refugees in large numbers, the stance of Germany has been an exception. Germany took 800,000 migrants in 2015, four times as many as in 2014. Germany has appealed to other nations to take a reasonable view of the humanitarian problem. German Chancellor Angela Merkel was criticized for the way she managed the dominance of her country's economy and her liberal attitude toward immigration. Most of this criticism came from countries like Greece and Italy that were burdened by heavy public debt.

Meanwhile, the European Union had approved a €1.8 billion action plan to try and stem the unprecedented and politically explosive flow of migrants from Africa across the Mediterranean. Though people are still trying to reach Europe, the number of refugees has come down from the peak in 2015-16 following a 2016 EU deal with Turkey and stricter border controls. By the end of 2019, of all the world's refugees, only a fraction of internally displace persons were living in the EU. The share of refugees in the EU is 0.6 per cent compared to its total population.

❑ CLIMATE CHANGE

Climate change, pollution, and environmental degradation are two of the most grim challenges facing humanity. Life on planet earth faces global warming catastrophe. The World Bank has warned that global warming could elevate levels of disease, ravage crops, and push 100 million people more into poverty by 2030. This is over and above the 900 million people expected to be living in extreme poverty, if development progresses slowly.

The World Bank has highlighted the devastating effects of global warming on the poor who are more vulnerable to climate-related shocks than wealthier people because they are more exposed, lose more in relative terms, and lack the financial systems and social safety nets that would allow them to better prepare and cope.

Climate change, which has now been universally recognized as a serious threat to the present and future generations, is an issue that has been engaging the attention of international community since long. Though the problem is the outcome of the actions of almost all countries, particularly the advanced nations which had embarked on large-scale industrialization ever since the Industrial Revolution, the problem came to the fore only some three decades back when the world started witnessing cataclysmic events causing untold misery such as heavy floods, hurricanes and typhoons, tsunami, erratic monsoon, monsoon failure and recurrent droughts, excessive heat, earthquakes, and above all mysterious and hitherto unseen changes in weather cycles. Much of these changes in nature has been attributed to greenhouse gas emissions, burning of coal, indiscriminate use of fossil fuels, deforestation, relentless urbanization, vehicular pollution, and so on.

The First World Climate Conference was held in February 1979 in Geneva and sponsored by the World Meteorological Organization (WMO). Some of the important timelines of action taken under the aegis of the UN bodies to tackle the problem are mentioned below:

- **November 1988:** World Meteorological Organization (WMO) and UN Environment Programme (UNEP) set up the Intergovernmental Panel on Climate Change (IPCC)
- **November 1990:** The IPCC releases the first assessment report saying "emissions resulting from human activities are substantially increasing the atmospheric concentrations of greenhouse gases" leading to calls by the IPCC and the second World Climate Conference for a global treaty.
- **June 1992:** The UN Framework Convention on Climate Change (UNFCCC) brought the world together in Rio to curb greenhouse gas emissions and adapt to climate change. Two Conventions were also agreed upon in Rio, viz., the UN Convention on Biological Diversity and the Convention to Combat Desertification.
- **December 1997:** A historical milestone was reached when the Third Conference of the Parties (COP3) adopted the Kyoto Protocol, the world's first greenhouse gas emissions reduction treaty.
- **June 2001:** A major breakthrough was achieved at the Sixth Conference of the Parties (COP6) in Bonn, when governments reached broad political agreement on the operational rulebook for the 1997 Kyoto Protocol.
- **December 2012:** At COP18 in Doha, governments agreed to speedily work toward a universal climate change agreement by 2015 and find ways to scale up efforts, before 2020, beyond the existing pledges to curb emissions.

- **September 2014:** UN Secretary-General hosted a Climate Summit in New York, with Heads of State and Government, business, finance, civil society, and local leaders to mobilize action on climate change ahead of the crucial COP 21 in Paris in 2015.

❑ 21ST CONFERENCE OF PARTIES (COP21), PARIS

At the conference in Paris in Nov–Dec. 2015, after intense negotiations, 195 nations reached a historic agreement which emphasized the following plan of action:

- to reduce greenhouse gas emissions blamed for global warming and cut dependence on fossil fuels;
- to make provisions to enable the shift to clean energy sources;
- to increase the ability to adapt to adverse impacts of climate change without jeopardizing food production;
- to recognize that all countries do not have the wherewithal to undertake these efforts;
- to realize that industrialized countries must continue to take the lead with developing countries chipping in;
- to agree to embed the principle of common but differentiated responsibilities; and
- to acknowledge the difference in the level of obligation and responsibility of the rich industrialized countries and those of the developing countries.

The Paris Agreement

The Paris Agreement, the world's response to hotter temperatures, rising seas and other impacts of climate change was a major breakthrough in UN climate negotiations after years of wrangling and after years of dispute, as to who should do what and how much. Failure to act could be catastrophic in some places, wiping out crops, flooding coastal areas and melting Arctic sea ice, some of which are already visible and the planet has been experiencing. The melting of the Greenland ice sheet is happening at an unprecedented rate while closer home, India is experiencing hottest summer ever and millions of Indians are facing the consequences of a severe drought. The first three months of 2016 were the warmest on record as temperatures were a staggering 1.35 degrees Celsius above the long term average.

The effort will require titanic shifts in the ways countries generate electricity, fuel vehicles and run factories, largely by forsaking coal, oil and natural gas and opting for renewable sources.

A Historic Step

In a significant development on 'Climate change' issue, 171 countries formally signed the Paris climate accord at the U.N. headquarters in 2016 on April 22 which is observed as the Earth Day. This is a record of most number of states endorsing an international agreement on a single day, which is reflective of the concerns which nations have on this portentous issue and the importance they attach to it. This historic step should inspire and spur many nations to act on the commitments given on steps to curb rapid global warming. As U.N. Secretary-General said on the occasion, "This is a moment in history".

The Paris accord will not immediately solve the problem of climate change but it commits about 200 nations to progressively bring down greenhouse gas emissions and to limit global warming to below 2 degrees Celsius compared with pre-industrial times, and to strive for 1.5 degrees Celsius. It will enter into force 30 days after at least 55 countries, accounting for 55 per cent of global greenhouse gas emissions, deposit their instruments of ratification. After signing, countries must formally approve the Agreement through their domestic procedures.

❑ THE PATH AHEAD ON CLIMATE CHANGE

China is the world's top emitter of greenhouse gas, followed by the US and India. Australia is the largest emitter per capita. The formal target is to limit global warming to 2 degrees C above the pre-industrial levels. Most countries have pledged to achieve cuts by 2030. But scientists say that this is not attainable with the pledges made so far. Temperatures will rise by anything between 2.7 to 3.6 degrees C by 2100.

There has been considerable divergence of views between the developed and developing nations on the responsibility of both on achieving the targets. The latter group attributes the present predicament on global warming and climate change to the profligate manner in which the advanced nations conducted themselves over the last two centuries while industrializing and the excessive and reckless use of natural resources. They further contend that with the problems of poverty and lack of development they are faced with, they are not on equal footing with the advanced countries who must bear greater share of the burden of reducing emissions. It is also a moot point that rich countries are less vulnerable to future climate change as their wealth would help them to adapt to the change.

Financing Climate Action Plan

A sticking point at COP negotiations has been the extent of compensatory finance that rich nations will provide to developing countries for emission reductions. This is because any such reduction by developing nations will retard their development process and it may mean that more people may remain trapped in poverty. Rich nations had pledged at a UN summit in Copenhagen in 2009 to muster \$100 billion (94 billion euros) annually in financial support to poor countries starting in 2020. Some leaders from developing nations have urged that developed countries should honour their commitment of mobilizing \$100 billion each year from 2020 and provide stronger financial support to developing countries afterwards.

A Setback and Stalemate

The ambitious climate pact has, however, received a serious setback with then President Trump deciding to pull the US, one of the largest polluter, out of it. This has met with much criticism from other nations and experts. However, the US stance has changed since president Biden has taken over and has pledged full support to climate change action programme.

There was continued divergence of views between the developed and developing countries in the climate talks held in Bonn, Germany in November 2017. While the Paris Agreement requires all countries to take measures to tackle climate change from 2020, in the pre-2020 period, the onus is on developed countries. But developed countries were not agreeable to this. Developing nations also contend that the rich nations are not keeping up the commitment to provide \$100 billion a year by 2020 - from public and private sources alike -- to help developing countries switch from fossil fuels to greener energy sources and adapt to the effects of climate change. French President Macron has urged wealthy nations and global companies to commit more funds to combating global warming and help poorer nations deal with the impact of climate change.

Since then, concerted efforts have been made by UN agencies and member countries to mobilise more funds as will be seen from data below:

- According to aggregate estimates from OECD data, public climate finance from developed to developing countries increased by 44 percent from US\$ 37.9 billion in 2013 to USD 54.5 billion in 2017, and US\$ 56.7 billion including climate-related officially supported export credits.

- US President Biden has pledged to double funds to US$ 11.4 billion per year by 2024 to support developing nations shift from polluting energy sources like coal in support of climate change action for vulnerable countries.
- Green Climate Fund (GCF) financing committed (USD): US$ 8.8 billion. Of this, climate action projects worth US$ 6.1 billion are under implementation.
- World Bank Green Bond Program launched in 2008 has raised USD 12.6 Billion over a 10-year period upto 2018.

Climate Change Target and India

According to estimates, the US and member countries of the EU contributed 21.2 per cent and 18.4 per cent of the total cumulative CO_2 emissions. Russia, Japan, and Canada together accounted for 12.9 per cent of the emissions. Therefore, the rich countries are jointly responsible for more than half of the emissions. In comparison, India's share is just 2.8 per cent. As per current emission levels, US, Europe, Russia, Japan, and Canada jointly contributed 40.6 per cent of the emissions in 2012. As against this, the contribution of India in 2012 stood at 5.7 per cent.

India is the fastest growing economy now with its GDP growth around 7 per cent and it is expected to go up. It is also one of the largest emitters of carbon. India still has some 250 million people below the World Bank poverty line of $1.90 per capita per day at the PPP 2011 prices. These people have little access to energy including electricity.

A major challenge India faces in living up to commitments made on Climate change is in regard to thermal power plants. In India, coal based power accounts for around 60 per cent of installed capacity. In various States, there are thermal power plants which are more than 25 years old. According to international standards, which have been endorsed by the Central Electricity Authority (CEA) also, the life of coal-based units is only 25 years. After 25 years, the plants consume more fuel, produce less power and emit more of polluting gases and hence have to be scrapped. India has committed to achieve about 40 per cent cumulative electric power installed capacity from non-fossil fuel-based energy resources by 2030 with the help of transfer of technology and low cost international finance including from the Green Climate Fund (GCF). Hence, going forward, India has to lay emphasis on greening coal technology and improve energy efficiency of thermal plants with newer technology apart from increasing the share of renewable energy sources.

- **Role of NTPC:** In this context, the National Thermal Power Corporation (NTPC), which is the largest thermal power generating company in the country, has a major role to play in India living up to the target. It has total installed capacity of 62.9 GW, of which 45.4 GW is coal-based thermal power. NTPC is now adopting environmentally sustainable power generation.

Adoption of clean coal technologies such as ultra-super critical thermal power technology could help reduce emissions. Experts are of the view that such technologies are available and techno-economically feasible to bring down emissions. NTPC has to adopt such technology in its thermal plants.

In a positive development, NTPC is adding renewable energy (RE) in its portfolio and, by 2032, it plans to have a 32 GW (32,000 MW) capacity through renewable sources which will be nearly 25 per cent of its overall power generation capacity. The initiative of NTPC, the major state-run thermal producing undertaking, to take up RE projects will be an added boost.

- **India's Commitment:** But despite its extremely low contribution to emission and need to bring electricity to all households, India has embarked upon a huge renewable programme to make its commitment under the 'Intended Nationally Determined Contributions' (INDCs) to combat climate change credible. India has proposed to cut emissions by 35 per cent by 2030 which will require at least $2.5 trillion with 40 per cent of power coming from non-fossil fuels.
- **Renewable Energy:** India launched the National Solar Mission (NSM) in 2010 under the National Action Plan on Climate Change (NAPCC). The initial target of installing 20 GW grid-connected "solar power" plants by 2022 was first enhanced to 100 GW. Solar power capacity increased by more than 14 times in five years from 2.6 GW in 2014 to 37.5 GW in 2019. (1 Gigawatt = 1,000 Megawatt)

In 2015, the Govt. of India revised the target to 175 GW of cumulative "renewable power" installed capacity by the year 2022. Against this, capacity of 85.90 GW of renewable power has been set up by December 2019, which constituted more than 23 percent of the total installed power generation capacity of 368.78 GW in the country.

- The share of Renewables (non-fossil fuels) including hydro, nuclear, solar, wind, biomass, etc. in total installed capacity which stood at 29 per cent in 2019-20 has risen to 39.6 per cent by August 2021. The share of fossil fuels (coal, lignite, gas and diesel) has come down from 73 per cent to 60.9 per cent. (See Table 20.3).
- **Global ranking:** India is one of the leading generators of solar and wind power and holds the 5th and 4th global positions in solar and wind power deployment respectively.
- **Other sources:** India is also utilizing small hydro power and biomass for power generation as part of the renewable energy programme.
- **Job potential:** Since 2013-14 till December 2019, the renewable power deployment has more than doubled and annually more than 10 million man-days of employment is being created in the sector.

Table 20.3: Electricity: Installed capacity
(Percentage share)

Category	2019-20	As on 31 August 2021
Fossil fuels	73.0	60.9
Wind, Solar, others →	4.0	25.9
Hydro →	21.5	12.0
Nuclear →	3.5	1.7
Total Non-Fossil fuels	29.0	39.6

The PM has also stated that India will not shy away from doing her bit to solve the problem. Thus, any positive commitments made by India to regulate its emissions without compensation itself is a generous gesture. (On this, see also chapter 11, pp. 11.9-10 under RENEWABLE ENERGY).

International Solar Alliance (ISA)

Meanwhile, India and France have launched a programme with $1 trillion potential to help developing countries harness fully their solar resources for a clean energy future to meet the 'biggest challenge humanity has ever faced'.

India and France announced the solar finance programme that aims to lower the cost of finance and facilitate the flow of more than $1 trillion investment to members of the International Solar Alliance (ISA).

The programme launched at the ISA meeting held during the signing ceremonies for the Paris Climate Change Agreement at the UN aims to make available solar technology for farmers. The meeting was attended by representatives of over 25 countries including the US, Brazil, Bangladesh and Nigeria. Beyond providing clean energy and dealing with climate change, the harnessing of solar energy was also about energy security. (On solar energy, see chapter 11, p. 11.10 and chapter 24, p.24.20-2)

ISA has set a target to install 1,000 GW of solar energy by 2030 across various sunshine-abundant countries and to mobilise US$ 1,000 billion to achieve the target.

Since its launch, in four years 101 nations have joined the alliance with the US being the latest to join in November 2021. The Alliance would help member countries, mostly developing economies, with solar power solutions and thus help reduce the global carbon footprint.

Limitations of Solar and Wind Energy

According to International Energy Agency (IEA), only about 0.4 per cent of global energy now comes from solar and wind. Even in 2040, with all governments implementing all of their green promises, solar and wind will make up only 2.2 per cent of global energy. This is partly because wind and solar help to reduce greenhouse gas emissions only from electricity generation—which account for 42 per cent of the total—but not from the energy used in industry, transport, buildings, and agriculture. So, much wider application for solar and wind energy in other areas will have to found if it is to make a meaningful impact on the problem.

While globally wind farms have grown over fivefold in the last decade and plunging costs have made them a key way of reducing carbon emissions from fossil fuel burning, a word of caution is due. Recent research suggests that global warming will significantly reduce the power of wind across northern mid-altitudes, including the US, the UK and the Mediterranean region. However, some places, including eastern Australia, will see winds pick up. As climate change might cause wind resources to decline across the Northern Hemisphere, it is to be seen how far it will impact India which has set ambitious targets for this energy source.

Box 20.2: Carbon Sink and Forest Cover

An important area of action on climate change and safeguarding environment is expanding forest and tree cover, which are important reservoirs of "carbon sink". ("Carbon sink" is any reservoir, natural or otherwise, that absorbs more carbon than it releases, and thereby lowers the CO2 in the atmosphere). India plans to increase its forest cover which will absorb 2.5 to 3 billion tonnes of carbon dioxide (CO2, the main gas responsible for global warming) by 2030.

Forest Survey of India (FSI), under the Ministry of Environment, Forest and Climate Change, conducts nationwide survey of forest and tree cover and related biodiversity aspects keeping in view the above-mentioned targets to be met by India.

- **Forest cover:** The total forest and tree cover (FTC) of the country, as per the India State of Forest Report (ISFR) which stood at 7,89,164 sq. km. in 2013 has increased to 8,07,276 sq. km. in 2019. As percentage of total geographical area of India, the forest cover rose from 24.01 per cent in 2013 to 24.56 per cent in 2019.

- **Forest development schemes:** For development and conservation of the forest cover in the country, Ministry has been taking several initiatives. These include ongoing Centrally Sponsored Schemes such as National Afforestation Programme, National Mission for a Green India and Development of Wildlife Habitats. Compensatory Afforestation Fund Rules, 2018 also contain provisions for taking up assisted natural regeneration, artificial regeneration and silvi-cultural operations in forests which contribute to increase in forest cover.

The challenges:

- There is concern over forest degradation that could mar India's prospect of creating an additional 2.5 to 3 billion tonnes of carbon sink through forestation by 2030.
- Though the forest cover has shown increase from 2013 to 2019, it still falls short of the required target. The total forest and tree cover percentage of 24.56 of geographical area reached, as per 2019 report, falls very much short of the target of 33 per cent to be reached to fulfil commitment under Climate change action.
- The quality of forests has also to be improved. Open forests, degraded forest and moderate forests should be converted to dense and very dense forests to reach the goals.
- The shortage of firewood and fodder, the poverty among forest-dependent communities, the declining water table and the frequent occurrences of forest fire are also cause for concern as they would have adverse impact on the forestry sector.

Externalities from Pollution

In this context, it may be mentioned that there are other relevant aspects related to environmental degradation or pollution which, in economic parlance, are known as 'externalities'. Externalities mean the benefits or harm accruing to a person or any entity resulting from the actions of another person or entity in the course of an economic activity. For example, an industry causing pollution to the water source used by the population in the neighbourhood is causing harm which is an externailty. The smoke emanating from thermal plants, the untreated effluents discharged by industries into nearby rivers or lakes, and pollution caused by vehicles on roads are all common instances of externalities causing harm to others. But no payment or compensation is usually paid for such objectionable actions unless the principle of 'polluter pay' is enforced. Enormous pollution caused to the Ganga and Yamuna rivers by various sources are other examples.

Such instances can occur at an international level also where the actions of one country harm another country. An example of this is the 'hazy thick smog' from raging fires caused by farmers in Indonesia by burning forests which not only affects the people in parts of Indonesia but spreads to neighbouring countries like Malaysia, Singapore, Brunei, Thailand, and Philippines and covers the sky for days together. It is a source of health hazard causing even schools to remain closed for children's safety. This issue has been taken up by these countries with Indonesia and they are jointly trying to tackle the menace. Objections raised by some islanders in the Pacific area for fear of radiation due to nuclear tests conducted near their islands by nuclear powers is another example.

Carbon emissions caused by industries like thermal plants, chemical industries, etc. affecting climatic factors and causing environmental pollution also fall in this category. They cause much harm to the health of the people.

Box 20.3: El Nino and La Nina and Asian Economies

During 2014 and 2015, India faced acute drought conditions with serious impact on agriculture and the economy, and untold distress to the farming community resulting even in the suicide of many farmers in drought-hit areas in Vidarbha, Marathawada, Telengana, etc. About 330 million people have been affected by water scarcity and crop damage, with blazing temperatures leading to heat-stroke deaths and dead livestock.

This was attributed to the occurrence of El Niño, an ocean-warming phenomenon that erupts in the Pacific region. Not only India, but virtually the whole of Asia – Malaysia, Thailand, Vietnam, Philippines which form the rice bowl of Asia – has been affected by the withering drought and sizzling temperatures from El Niño. It has ravaged farming across Asia and led to food and water shortages.

The 2015 El Niño, said to be one of the strongest ever, has left the Mekong River at its lowest level in decades, and caused food-related unrest in the Philippines, and smothered vast regions with a heat wave which often topped 40 degrees Celsius or more. According to some estimates, the economic losses to Southeast Asia caused by this unrelenting weather could be in the range of $10 billion, apart from the human misery resulting from it.

Experts are of the view that El Niño could be followed by its stormy sister, La Niña, a cooling of the central Pacific area, which could bring heavy rains to flood-prone regions of Asia with possible flooding which could be a double-whammy for the Asian economies.

While conditions looked good for La Niña in April 2016, cooling weakened after a while and temperature did not go down as expected. As a result, the monsoon too was not as strong as was predicted.

The Indian monsoon is also influenced by certain other phenomena. These include Indian Ocean Dipole, an oscillation of temperatures between the western and eastern parts of Indian Ocean, Equinoo which results in varying cloudiness between western and eastern parts of Indian Ocean. According to another view, the temperature and the wind conditions over the Atlantic Ocean also influence the course of Indian monsoon – the warming of the Atlantic Ocean reduce rains over Central India while cooling over there increase the rainfall. However, the extent of the effect of some of these phenomena on Indian monsoon is yet to be firmly established and meteorologists are continuing to study and unravel them.

These events point to dramatic changes in climatic conditions and a forewarning of things to come in the not too distant future.

In this Chapter we discussed.....

- Globalization and its benefits.
- Challenges, limits and risks of globalization.
- Resistance to globalization. Rise of protectionism; Is globalization in retreat?
- Britain and the European Union; Britain's decision to exit the Union– its causes and consequences.
- Free trade and crime; need for greater security measures; socio-economic costs of terrorism.
- China's economic slowdown and its impact; its positive effect on other economies; China's transition from export-led economy to one driven by domestic consumption.
- Globalization and inclusivity; need to guard against economic, political, and cultural exclusion of countries owing to globalization.
- Resistance to globalization; need to avoid dominance by few countries.
- Globalization and Indian economy; impact of 2008 financial crisis on India; positive effects of trade liberalization.
- Trends in world trade; impact of 2008 crisis on world trade; China's accession to the WTO and its outcome.
- International institutions—Bretton Woods conference and founding of the World Bank (IBRD) and IMF; institutions in the World Bank group; roles of World Bank and IMF; other UN agencies.
- Asian Development Bank (ADB), Asian Infrastructure Investment Bank (AIIB); New Development Bank (NDB).
- India and international institutions.
- International economic groupings—G8; G20; G77; European Union; APEC; ASEAN; ASEAN and India; ASEAN and China: the South China sea dispute; South Asian Association for Regional Cooperation (SAARC); Trans-Pacific Partnership (TPP).
- WTO issues and Food subsidy regime; Developing countries' stand on food subsidy.
- Transfer of technology and UNCTAD; aspects to be kept in view in technology transfer; transfer of advanced technology. Perceptible change in attitude of advanced nations.
- Europe's migrants' problem; its social and economic implications for European countries.
- Climate change and its consequences; steps taken under the aegis of UN to combat the problem; decisions taken at the 21st Conference of Parties (COP21), Paris; position taken by developed and developing countries;

- 171 countries formally signed the Paris climate accord at the U.N. headquarters in 2016, on April 22, observed as the Earth Day.
- Climate change target and India; limitations of India in adhering to target; plans for solar and wind energy in India. Increasing the share of Renewables. India heavily dependent on thermal plants which will have to be phased out over time.
- Financing of climate change programme; role of developed countries.
- India and France have launched a programme under International Solar Alliance (ISA),with $1 trillion potential, to help developing countries harness fully their solar resources for a clean energy future, lower the cost of finance and facilitate the flow of more funds to members of the Alliance.
- Limitations of solar and wind energy. Forest cover and Carbon sink.
- Externalities from pollution; instances of externalities—environmental pollution.

Important Terms to Note in this Chapter

Globalization; Free trade; Foreign direct investment (FDI); Foreign institutional investment (FII); Intellectual property right (IPR); Current account; Capital account; Balance of payments (BoP); IMF Quotas; Technology transfer; Climate change; Greenhouse gas; Carbon emission; Solar energy; Wind energy; Renewables; Forest cover; Carbon sink; Externalities

Practice Questions

1. What is meant by 'globalisation'? Is globalisation beneficial to poor and developing countries, if so, in what way?
2. There have been protest movements in some countries against the trend of globalisation. What are the reasons for such protests? Do you think they are justified? Explain with cogent reasons.
3. Some have opined that in the light of some recent developments, the process of globalisation may be slowed down, if not reversed. Do you agree with this view? Justify your answer.
4. Britain has decided to exit from the European Union (EU). What were the factors which led Britain to take this decision and what will be its consequences for both Britain and the EU?
5. What were the factors which led to the global financial crisis of 2007-08? Has the world economy recovered from it? Substantiate your answer.

6. In what way the financial crisis of 2007-08 and the consequent global economic slowdown affected India? Has India been able to withstand it? Give justification for your answer.

7. What is meant by 'free trade' and what are its features? Mention at least two Free Trade pacts and their importance.

8. What is the role of World Trade Organization (WTO)? In what way it has helped to promote world trade and economic development?

9. What is the role played by The World Bank in alleviating poverty and ensuring development in the poorer countries? How far they have been successful?

10. What is India's stand at the WTO on subsidy given to her farmers and public stockholding of foodgrains under the Public Distribution System (PDS)? Why are the developed countries like the US objecting to India's stand? Do you think their stand is justified? Explain with cogent reasons.

11. Do you think India's food security scheme under the Public Distribution System (PDS) and food subsidy regime for farmers need overhaul and reform? What are the deficiencies in them and how can they be improved?

12. Describe the role played by the U.N. Conference on Trade and Development (UNCTAD). How far it has helped to promote world trade and transfer of technology between nations?

13. What are the limitations in transfer of technology from the advanced nations to developing countries? Suggest steps to overcome them.

14. In what way geopolitics and strategic interests affect economic development? Cite some instances where geopolitical interests in the emerging global order have impacted development of countries.

15. Environmental degradation and climate change are two of the most critical problems facing humanity. Do you agree? What are its causes and implications and what steps are to be taken to overcome them?

16. What are the implications of the decisions taken in the 21st Conference of Parties (COP21), PARIS on climate change for India? What are the major steps to be taken by India to fulfill them?

17. The United States has pulled out of the Climate Change pact agreed upon under the aegis of the UN. What were the reasons for this decision by the US and how will it impact global economy in the long run?

18. In what way will the steps to be taken by India on 'Climate Change', in accordance with 21st Conference of Parties (COP21), PARIS, affect India's development prospects? Explain with cogent reasons.

19. What are the steps taken by the government of India to promote renewable energy sources like Solar and Wind energy? To what extent it will help India to fulfill the commitments given under

the UN Climate Change pact?

20. Subsidy is a contentious issue and roadblock in the WTO. Examine India's stand for protecting its farmers' interests.

[UPSC Main 2014 (Economics Optional Paper)]

21. Write on the Look East Policy of India. *[UPSC Main 2014 (Economics Optional Paper)]*

22. Critically discuss India's 'Food Security Act, 2013' and point out its incongruity with the WTO norms as recently proclaimed at recently concluded Bali Summit.

[Indian Economic Service/Indian Statistical Service 2014]

23. Do you agree with the view that the process of globalization in India has led to 'unequal competition'? *[Indian Economic Service/Indian Statistical Service 2016]*

24. Examine the status of forest resources of India and its resultant impact on climate change.

[UPSC Main 2020 (General Studies Paper)]

25. Critically examine the role of WTO on agricultural exports in India.

[UPSC Main 2019 (Economics Optional Paper)]

26. What are the key areas of reform if the WTO has to survive in the present context of Trade War, especially keeping in mind the interest of India?

[UPSC Main 2018 (General Studies Paper)]

PART-III

Policies and Reforms from 2014

Chapter 21 *Make in India Programme*

Chapter 22 *Ease of Doing Business*

Chapter 23 *Start-up Mission and Venture Capital*

Chapter 24 *Infrastructure*

Chapter 25 *Financial Sector and Tax Reforms*

Chapter 26 *Social Sector and CSR*

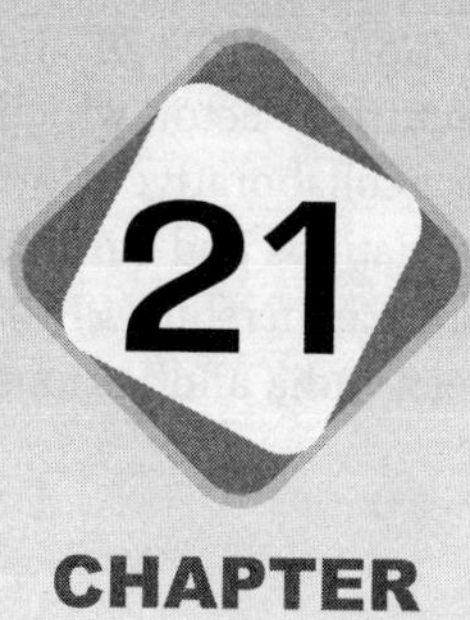

MAKE IN INDIA PROGRAMME

CHAPTER

- India's strengths
- Measures taken to boost Make in India
- New Labour Laws passed
- Main Features of Labour laws
- One District One Product (ODOP) scheme
- Skill Development
- Outcomes of Make in India initiative
- Role for MSMEs:
- Challenges and Limitations of Make in India
- Production Linked Incentive (PLI) scheme
- Conclusion

❑ INTRODUCTION

The 'Make in India' programme was launched in September 2014 as part of a wider spectrum of nation-building initiatives and is one of the main planks of the NDA government's plans for re-energising the economy. It aims to give fillip to the industrial and manufacturing sector and transform India into a global design and manufacturing hub. By 2013, the economy seemed paralysed and stagnant and India's growth rate had fallen to a new low. That the world economy had also remained battered by a stubborn and persisting slowdown added to the problems. A sense of despair prevailed over the performance and state of the economy. It was against this backdrop that this initiative to revive the economy was set in motion.

It must be stated, in this context, that the previous UPA government had set up in 2004 a National Manufacturing Competitiveness Council (NMCC) to energise and sustain the growth of manufacturing industries in India. The present initiative is a step forward in this direction.

The 'Make in India' initiative is crucial and has come none too soon, not only from the viewpoint of economic growth and modernising and diversifying the economy, but due to the imperative need to create jobs for the millions of youth who are joining the labour force each year, at an average rate of one million per month, a trend predicted to continue for the next decade and a half or even longer. The agriculture sector in India is overburdened with excess and redundant labour which needs to be redeployed in other sectors in more productive occupations.

Conceived and piloted by the Department of Industrial Policy and Promotion (DIPP) of the Government of India, the initiative aims at raising the contribution of the manufacturing sector, which is now around 16 per cent, to 25 per cent of the GDP by 2020. The programme is a collaborative effort involving the Central and State governments, industry leaders, chambers and associations and various knowledge partners. It seeks to leverage the transformational power of public-private partnership (PPP), including India's global partners, as evidenced by the in-depth interactions between India and various other countries and transnational corporations at the highest levels.

The Strengths

India, already the world's fourth largest economy, is on the cusp of major changes and far-reaching reforms, and is poised to become the third largest economy of the world by 2030. Endowed with the advantages of being a democratic polity, with a burgeoning young population who can be skilled and with a huge internal market creating massive demand, the country could well draw on these strengths to forge ahead if proper policies are put in place and implemented with rigour. These strengths are further reinforced with India having an English-speaking, highly qualified technical and engineering work force and a sound legal and IPR regime. The government has also embarked on removing some of the weaknesses in the business environment such as the absence of a bankruptcy law and exit policy, and deficiencies in the banking and financial sector with a better regulatory regime.

The Indian economy has passed through different phases during the last six decades:

- Beginning with the early phase of industrialisation backed by a rigid licence and control regime, India moved to a phase of halting liberalisation in the 1980s.
- This phase was followed by radical reforms in the 1990s and opening up of the economy.
- Since then, the economy has been moving on a high trajectory with greater inflow of foreign capital and Indian corporates targeting global markets with acquisition of foreign business entities.
- All this has helped to place India on the global industrial map and make our companies globally competitive.
- The stage is thus set for the Indian industry to expand further and become a manufacturing hub in the world economy.

Measures Taken

The new government which assumed office in May 2014 has initiated several measures to translate the ***Make in India*** programme into reality. Some of the reform measures taken may appear small but cumulatively they will have substantial positive impact on reviving growth, generating productive livelihoods and making a dent on poverty. The government does not view different strands of reforms in isolation but has tried to form them into a total package, and apply them to various schemes and programs so as to make a greater impact and create an atmosphere of trust among the various stakeholders to achieve the desired outcomes. The most important aspect of these measures is that the government has assiduously tried to bring in transparency in all its dealings which is reassuring. It has helped to enhance India's credibility globally and drive investment, foster innovation, develop skills, protect Intellectual Property (IP) and build world class manufacturing infrastructure. A significant aspect of the programme is the opening up of key sectors – including railways, defence, insurance and medical devices – to higher levels of Foreign Direct Investment (FDI).

However, it must be stated, with a degree of pragmatism, that the new reform measures are a work in progress and much more ground has to be covered for them to produce results on the ground. For one thing, many of these steps taken have a long gestation period to produce outcomes, and secondly, the global economy is much more competitive today with many new, aspiring and emerging economies vying to achieve the same objectives.

The measures taken by the government include:

- **Make doing business easier:** Launching a business venture entails many initial steps which could be complex and time-consuming such as land acquisition with proper land titles, registration and raising capital, and getting infrastructural facilities, some of which involve interface with the State or Central government. Both the Central and some of the State governments and their concerned agencies have introduced single-window clearance facility for approvals with fixed time-lines to make the procedure hassle-free.
- **Infrastructure improvement:** Having world class infrastructure –roads and highways, rail transport, ports, power and communication facilities – *is sine qua non* for nurturing and supporting a globally competitive industrial and manufacturing sector. Without it, it would be well-nigh impossible to attract foreign capital and investors. China's phenomenal rise and success in the last few decades was primarily due to the vast and sprawling infrastructural facilities she built and provided at very economical rates, apart from the cheap labour that she had to offer. The Indian government has since taken steps to revive and speed up stalled highway projects, further modernise and upgrade railways and airports and expand port facilities. Of course, these are time-consuming and their full impact will take time to show.
- **Reforming labour laws:** Making labour laws flexible, even while protecting the interests of workers, is found necessary to generate jobs. The government has linked reforming labour laws as part of its 'Ease of doing business' programme to encourage investments. The initiatives taken by the Rajasthan government in this regard are a pointer to this.

Under the constitutional provisions, labour is a subject in the Concurrent List. Individual States can amend labour laws, send them to the Union government which forwards them to the President for assent. Once the President gives the assent, the States are free to implement the amended laws.

New Labour Laws Passed

Four codes passed: The Parliament passed in September 2020 three labour codes. A code on minimum wages was already passed in 2019. A total of 44 extant labour laws have now been subsumed into four codes. The laws merged with these codes include the Factories Act, the Trade Union Act, the Mining Act, the Industrial Disputes Act, the ESI Act, the EPF Act and the Maternity Benefit Act. The four codes approved are:

- Industrial Relations Code Bill, 2020.
- Code on Social Security Bill, 2020.
- Occupational Safety, Health and Working Conditions Code Bill, 2020.
- Minimum wages code (passed in 2019).

The labour ministry is to frame the rules and guidelines under these laws which will clarify many of the new provisions and the laws will be implemented after that. (For details on the new Labour Laws, see Box 16.4 in chapter 16, pp. 16.15-8)

Main Features of Labour laws

While making certain provisions stringent for labour like changing the threshold for layoffs and retrenchment, making flash strikes illegal, new provisions for recognition of Trade Unions and dispute resolution mechanism, the new laws provide many positive and worker-friendly features. These include:

- **Social security benefits:** It provides for universal social security for both organised and informal workers as well as gig and platform workers.
- **Social Security Board:** A National Social Security Board will be set up for formulating suitable schemes for unorganized workers, gig workers and platform workers. It also brings these sections of workers under the ambit of social security schemes that include life and disability insurance, PF, health and maternity benefits and skill upgradation.
- **Gender equality:** To promote gender equality, employment of women has been allowed in all establishments for all types of works and in the night shift, subject to their consent and subject to provisions of safety, holidays, working hours or any other condition being in place. The Codes also ensure their pay parity with their male counterparts.
- **Occupational Safety and health:** The Central Government shall declare, by notification, standards on occupational safety and health for work places relating to factories, mines, dock work, building and other construction work and other establishments.
- **Working environment:** The employer shall ensure cleanliness and hygiene, proper ventilation, temperature and humidity, environment free from dust, noxious gas, fumes and other impurities, cooling in work rooms, potable drinking water and hygienic sanitation facilities.
- **Migrant workers:** It has special provisions to take care of the interests of migrant workers. To ensure ease of living at affordable rent, the Central Government has announced a scheme of housing for migrant workers, as being done for urban poor. The Ration (Family) Card will be portable so that any member of a family included in a card could draw ration anywhere in the country thus facilitating migrant workers to draw ration at the place they work.
- **Database on Unorganised labour:** In the backdrop of a massive reverse migration of migrant labour due to outbreak of Covid-19 in early 2020, the Centre and the State governments are working together to build a comprehensive database of labour in the unorganized sector, who constitute about 85 per cent of total workforce. This will include mapping the skills of the workers, occupations they are engaged in and details of their nativity and place where they are employed, etc. The government seeks to ensure that the benefits of social welfare schemes reach vulnerable people by enlisting unorganized sector workers on the database.

  Launched in August 2021, the database has added 17 million informal workers, including gig workers, within a month. About half of them are women. Workers from Bihar, Uttar Pradesh, Madhya Pradesh, Odisha, West Bengal and Andhra Pradesh made up most of those registered on the database. Around 78 per cent of registrations were facilitated by the government-run Common Service Centres (CSCs), while individual workers did the rest directly. The government's target is to enrol more than 380 million workers in the unorganized sector.
- **Objective of Database** The primary objective of the database is to capture the details of workers who have migrated for jobs, map their skills and to provide, in the medium and long term, jobs near their native place, or within their state, so that the need for migration to distant place is avoided. Bihar and UP from where large scale out-migration takes place have initiated schemes to develop industries locally to absorb local labour. The "One District One Product" (ODOP) scheme is also working towards this objective. **(See Box 21.1 on this below).**

Box No. 21.1 One District One Product (ODOP)

To generate more local employment in various states and arrest the migration of labour to distant places and increase exports of products, the Centre and the States are adopting a scheme known as "One District One Product (ODOP).

- **Objectives:** Piloted by the Ministry of Food Processing Industries (MoFPI), the scheme aims to reap the benefit of scale in terms of procurement of inputs, availing common services and marketing of products. ODOP for the scheme will provide the framework for value chain development and alignment of support infrastructure. There may be more than one cluster of ODOP products in one district. There may also be a cluster of ODOP products consisting of more than one adjacent district in a State.
- **The Scheme:** In January 2021, the government has approved ODOP products for 707 districts in 35 States and Union territories. The main features of the scheme are:
- The ODOP product could be a perishable agri produce, cereal-based product, or a food product widely produced in a district and their allied sectors.
- The States would carry out baseline study and identify the food product for a district, keeping in perspective the focus of the scheme on perishables.
- Support for agricultural products would be for their processing along with efforts to reduce wastage, proper assaying, and storage and marketing.
- New units, whether of individuals or groups, would only be supported for ODOP products.
- Support to groups processing other products in such districts would only be for those already processing those products and with adequate technical, financial, and entrepreneurial strength.
- In providing support for capital investment to existing individual micro-units, preference would be given to those producing ODOP products. However, existing units producing other products would also be supported. In the case of capital investment by groups, predominately those involved in ODOP products would be supported.
- **Export Promotion:** The Department of Commerce is focusing on agriculture crops on a cluster approach for support for exports under the Agriculture Export Policy. The Ministry of Agriculture is also focusing on a cluster approach for the development of specific agriproducts in districts having a comparative advantage. The ODOP approach of the scheme would facilitate provision of common facilities and other support services.

This is a transformational and progressive step towards realizing the true potential of a district, fuel economic growth and generate employment and rural entrepreneurship, taking us to the goal of AtmaNirbhar Bharat.

- **Export promotion:** The following promotional measures are being taken up to give fillip to the scheme: and promote exports:
- Exporter conclaves/meets in over 700 districts, organized by the Directorate General of Foreign Trade (DGFT) along with Export and Market Development Assistance (E&MDA) and respective State Governments.
- District Export Promotion Committees (DEPCs), chaired by the District Commissioners /Collectors will be key stakeholders in organizing these conclaves. It will include handholding sessions for local exporters/entrepreneurs on foreign trade issues involving stakeholders such as the Lead Bank, local export chambers/ associations and Export Promotion Councils (EPCs).
- Export Promotion events/exhibitions by EPCs with at least one event in each State/UT showcasing India as a Rising Economic Force.
- The EPCs will mobilize the local exporters, manufacturers and industrial units to make Export Promotion a Jan Andolan with Union Ministers and Chief Ministers/Ministers of States participating.
- Department for Promotion of Industry and Internal Trade (DPIIT) is organising launch of two events, namely National Single Window System and Industrial Park Rating System. The digital platform will allow investors to identify and apply for various pre-operations approvals required for commencing a business in India.

Examples of ODOP products with Districts identified:

- **Andhra Pradesh:** Chittoor: Tomato; East Godavari: Coconut Products; Guntur: Spices (Chilli and Turmeric).
- **Assam:** Baksa: Honey; Barpeta: Milk Products; Bongaigaon: Turmeric.
- **Bihar:** Arwal: Mango; Aurangabad: Strawberry; Banka: Rice; Begusarai: Chilly; Bhagalpur: Jardalu Mango; Bhojpur: Pea; East Champaran: Litchi; Gaya: Mushroom.
- **Gujarat:** Ahmedabad: Wheat based Products; Amreli: Groundnut based Products; Aravalli: Potato based Products; Banaskantha: Pomegranate based products.
- **Punjab:** Amritsar: Pickle & Murabba; Barnala: Meat/ Chicken/ Poultry Products; Fatehgarh Sahib: Jaggery; Faridkot & Mansa: Milk and Milk Products; Ferozpur: Chillies; Jalandhar & Moga: Potato; Kapurthala: Tomato.
- **Uttar Pradesh:** Agra: Petha; Aligarh & Auraiya: Milk Products, Ghee; Ambedkar Nagar: Chilli;. Amroha: Mango; Etawah: Mustard; Farrukhabad & Firozabad: Potato.

Skill Development

The issue of improving the skills of workers has assumed importance in the light of the drive to boost the manufacturing sector. Even the UPA government had initiated several steps in this direction in the Eleventh (2007-12) and the Twelfth (2012-17) Plans. The constant refrain of industry and their chambers and associations has been that the labour available are mostly unskilled and not suited for the jobs on offer and training them costs both time and money. As discussed in chapter 16, rapid advances in technology result in obsolescence of workers unless they upgrade their skills and keep themselves abreast of the changes. This is even more vital when India is trying to become a manufacturing centre globally. (For more on this, see chapter 16, pp. 16.32-7).

❑ OUTCOMES OF 'MAKE IN INDIA' INITIATIVE

The Make in India initiative has resulted in many positive outcomes for the country. With the second generation liberalisation process set in motion, India is turning out to be an attractive investment destination for foreign capital. This is especially so when the global economy has been sluggish and India is touted by the IMF as a bright spot with growth hovering around 7 per cent and which is likely to go up further. According to observers, India has all the ingredients required to transform its economy into a manufacturing hub – a demographic dividend, a booming internal market and a stable currency. To the world, India is an area of focus and holds much potential across diverse sectors such as defence production, electronics, automotives, aircraft industry, insurance, healthcare, real estate, tourism and hospitality.

Some of the major policy decisions and initiatives taken to boost "Make in India" and their outcomes and are mentioned below.

- **Defence spending:** India accounts for 3.7 per cent of global military spending, making it the third highest military spender in the world. The defence expenditure constituted 2.9 per cent of India's total GDP with approximately US$ 72.9 billion spent on defence in 2020. Hence indigenization of defence production is a priority and steps have been taken under the "Make in India" initiative as explained below.
- **Defence Sector Indigenisation**: The Defence Industry, which was hitherto reserved for the public sector, was opened up to 100 per cent for Indian private sector participation in May, 2001. Ministry of Defence has notified a 'Positive Indigenisation list' of 209 items for which there would be an embargo on import beyond the timeline prescribed. This offers great opportunity to the Indian defence industry to manufacture items using their own design and development capabilities and meet the requirements of the Armed Forces in the coming years.
- India's defence exports in the last seven years crossed the mark of ₹38,000 crore, and notably, with more than 10,000 small businesses joining the defence sector due to affirmative action taken by the government. This shows not only a boost to exports but an important role assigned to the MSME sector. Further, rapid changes are expected to take place in the global security scenario which would increase demand for military equipment, and hence Indian industry must focus on boosting production.
- **Major Defence products:** As a result of these policies, many vital defence equipments such as 155mm Artillery Gun system 'Dhanush', Bridge Laying Tank, Thermal Imaging Sight Mark-II for T-72 tank, Light Combat Aircraft 'Tejas', 'Akash' Surface to Air Missile system, Submarine 'INS Kalvari', 'INS Chennai', Anti-Submarine Warfare Corvette (ASWC), Arjun Armoured Repair and Recovery Vehicle, Landing craft utility, etc. have been produced in the country under 'Make in India' initiative in the last few years.

- **Defence Industrial Corridors (DICs):** Government has established two DICs, one each in Uttar Pradesh and Tamil Nadu with a targeted investment of ₹20,000 crore by the year 2024. In July 2021, investment of ₹3,342 crore has been made in both the corridors by public and private sector companies. Besides, the two State Governments have also announced their Aerospace and Defence Policies to attract private players as well as foreign companies including Original Equipment Manufacturers (OEMs) in these two corridors.

It is noteworthy that Aerospace Engineers, an MSME unit located in Salem, Tamil Nadu has won a long-term contract from Boeing to manufacture and supply critical aviation components. This firm proposes to set up an additional civil aerospace production unit at Hosur in Tamil Nadu. These steps will generate additional employment and help to upgrade skills of workers in the region.

- **R & D and Innovation:** An innovation ecosystem for Defence titled "Innovations for Defence Excellence" (iDEX) has been launched in April 2018. iDEX is aimed at creation of an ecosystem to foster innovation and technology development in Defence and Aerospace by engaging industries including MSMEs, Start-ups, Individual Innovators, R&D institutes and Academia, and provide them grants/funding and other support to carry out R&D which has potential for future adoption for Indian defence and aerospace needs. It may also be noted that the Space agency, ISRO, is also now partnering with the private sector and procuring equipments needed for space activities.
- **Technology Transfer and Offsets:** Reforms in "Offset policy" have been included in Defence Acquisition Procedure (DAP)-2020 (DAP 2020), with thrust on attracting investment and Transfer of Technology for defence manufacturing. Government has notified the 'Strategic Partnership (SP)' model in May 2017, under which Indian entities would tie up long-term strategic partnerships with global Original Equipment Manufacturers (OEMs), through a transparent and competitive process, to seek technology transfers and set up domestic manufacturing infrastructure and supply chains.
- **Aerospace Industry:** US and India are to co-develop air-launched unmanned aerial vehicles (UAVs or Drones). An important deal giving boost to the "Make in India" is the joint project between Airbus Defence and Space (ADS) and Tata Advanced Systems Limited (TASL), valued ₹20,000 crore, to build the C-295 medium transport aircraft which will replace Avro-748 planes of the Indian Air Force. Under the deal, 16 aircraft will be delivered in a flyaway condition by ADS while the remaining 40 planes will be manufactured in India by a consortium of the ADS and TASL All 56 aircraft will be installed with indigenous electronic warfare suite and a large array of parts, sub-assemblies and major component assemblies of aerostructure are scheduled to be manufactured in India.

Many major industrial houses like the Tatas, L& T, Mahindras, ADAG, Bharat Forge, etc. have committed to invest in the defence sector and some of them have entered into partnership with foreign firms to get the latest technology which augurs well for the indigenisation programme. While the broader idea of strategic partnership (SP) model to identify and encourage private sector players for manufacturing in defence is a welcome move, care has to be taken to see that it does not lead to a situation of monopoly control by any one company or a group of companies. This is especially important considering the strategic value and the security aspects of items to be developed and manufactured for defence purposes.

Role for MSMEs: A core issue in Make in India programme is the role to be assigned to MSME units which generates employment on a substantial scale. The MSME sector in India has been playing a crucial role in manufacturing and exports and is a supplier of 'niche' hardware and software items for the defence sector. However, they are handicapped for lack of capital and surplus funds to invest in innovation, R&D and upgradation. Government could develop a defence industry ecosystem for a robust supply chain in which the small and medium enterprises would be an important link.

❑ CHALLENGES AND LIMITATIONS TO 'MAKE IN INDIA'

Introduction

Historically, all developed countries – UK, US, Germany, Japan or S. Korea – have scaled the economic ladder and attained prosperity driven by the growth of manufacturing. The growth and expansion of factories helped them to shift labour from agriculture to industry which provided more productive occupations and through value-addition contributed to the prosperity of the nation and its people.

With wages of labour rising and excess capacity built up in China, which has been world's manufacturing hub for about three decades, India with her abundant skilled labour has sensed an opportunity in taking on a similar role replacing China and providing jobs to millions. Could this become a reality and with problems in China, could India ipso facto turn into a manufacturing power? In the light of various transformational changes taking place in the world of manufacturing, India need to bear in mind the pitfalls she may encounter on the road ahead.

India faces a difficult task in replicating the experience of South-east and East Asian countries which experienced rapid growth in the 1970s and China in later years through industrialization. It is now more difficult for newcomers to break into world markets due to intense competition and other factors like protectionist tendencies, tariff barriers and reluctance on the part of advanced nations to part with high technology.

In the early stages of industrialisation, manufacturing became a powerful engine of economic development due to following factors:

- Manufacturing jobs didn't require much skill. Farmers could become industrial workers in factories with little additional training.
- It was easier to procure and absorb technology from other countries and generate high productivity jobs.
- Demand for manufactured goods was not constrained by low level of domestic incomes or domestic market. The manufactured goods could be exported to foreign markets.

These conditions no longer exist. Manufacturing has become highly skill-intensive and largely based on high level technology. With globalization, competition has also become more intense with many emerging countries vying for global markets. Therefore, much will depend on India's ability to procure advanced technology, rapidly upgrading the skills of labour and providing a competitive environment for corporations to invest and set up industries in India. The slow pace of progress in 'Make-in-India' programme is a pointer to the challenges ahead. (See also chapter 8, pp. 8.12-4 under 'Constraints faced by Indian Industry' and chapter 19, Box 19.5. 'Why India Leapfrogged from Agriculture to Services bypassing Manufacturing'?).

Automation

A major factor which may disrupt India's plans is the emergence of new, radical technologies in production such as 3D printing, smart robotics and artificial intelligence which would replace labour. These changes herald the new phase of transformative changes which should alter the very landscape of manufacturing.

According to the World Economic Forum in its *Global Competitiveness Report 2015-16*, the world is passing through the Fourth Industrial Revolution. The First Industrial Revolution used water and steam power to mechanize production, the Second used electric power to create mass production and the Third used electronics and information technology to automate production. Now a Fourth Industrial Revolution is building on the Third, the digital revolution that has been occurring since the middle of the last century. It is characterized by a fusion of technologies that is blurring the lines between the physical, digital, and biological spheres.

Automation also holds promise of reduction in costs of production which makes adopting the above-mentioned methods in place of labour, both cost effective and beneficial. Especially, in countries like US and western Europe which are faced with declining population, automation would be the ideal mode of production.

It is also relevant to note in this context that though the Indian economy registered impressive growth after the 1991 reforms and liberalisation, it was not accompanied by commensurate growth in employment. Again, much of the growth in employment was in the informal sector and the jobs were of informal and casual nature rather than quality jobs.(For more details on this, see chapter 16, pp. 16.11-3).

India has to factor in these potential changes while going ahead with programmes like Make in India lest she be caught unawares later with far-reaching consequences. (See also Box 16.6 Automation and Employment in chapter 16, pp. 16.34-6).

Competition from Rivals

A factor to be reckoned is the competition from other emerging economies. This is already in evidence in sectors like textiles, garments and apparels where India is facing intense competition in exports from China, Bangladesh, Pakistan, Vietnam, etc. Even in the IT-BPO sector, where India holds much edge over other countries due to the superior intellectual and technological capabilities of her youth, apart from command over English language, India is facing competition from China, Malaysia, Philippines, etc. which may intensify in the years to come. That apart, the recent moves by the new US administration to hike visa fee and restrict entry of foreign workforce in IT sector is bound to Impact India. India needs to have countervailing plans to overcome these challenges.

A major initiative to give fillip to Make in India is the Production Linked Incentive (PLI) Scheme launched in April 2020.

❑ PRODUCTION LINKED INCENTIVE (PLI) SCHEME

The salient features of this scheme and its outcome are discussed below.

Salient features

To begin with, it was introduced to provide financial incentives to boost domestic mobile and electronics manufacturing and attract large scale investments. Later it was expanded to cover diverse sectors such as pharma for bulk drugs and Active Pharmaceutical Ingredients (API) and medical devices, automotive and auto components, textiles, air conditioners, batteries, LED lights, solar PV modules, battery storage, food processing and specialty steel.

The scheme

- Companies registered in India and involved in manufacturing products covered under the target segments are eligible under the PLI scheme.
- The government will pay a certain percentage of the value of additional production that companies make after fulfilling incremental investment and production criteria.

- The companies could earn as direct payments, on an average, 4 to 6 per cent more than what they would otherwise get.
- The scheme is not location-specific and companies can operate existing or new manufacturing unit(s) at one or more locations in the country.
- The scheme, though supported by incentives provided by the State, is compliant with WTO regulations.

Rationale for the scheme

- The scheme would significantly boost investment, production and creation of jobs. For instance, the electronics sector could create 2 lakh direct and 6 lakh indirect jobs over five years.
- It would offset higher costs incurred by industry due to high taxes, power tariffs, logistics costs, land prices, etc. and thus help manufacturing sector achieve scale and become globally competitive.
- This is especially opportune when MNCs are planning to relocate from China to other countries due to cost considerations and many geopolitical factors and security issues.
- To promote exports and reduce dependence on imports for many critical items. Of an estimated production of ₹10.5 lakh crore, around 60 per cent would be exported.

Outcomes of the scheme

Mobiles and Electronics

The scheme has given an initial fillip especially for the manufacture of mobiles and the electronics sector. Major foreign companies like Apple and Samsung and domestic companies are setting up additional production capacities with potential investment of ₹11,000 crore over five years. This could result in foreign firms producing ₹9 lakh crore worth of mobile phones (of unit price of ₹15,000 or more) and the domestic firms making additional ₹1.24 lakh crore worth of feature and smart phones. It would fetch the government about ₹36,000 crore in tax revenue against payment of about ₹40,000 crore worth of payments as incentives.

IT Hardware

Next to mobiles, IT hardware would see much expansion. The thrust is on desktops, laptops, tablets and servers which are currently mostly or wholly imported. The proposed incentive outlay is about ₹7,000 crore and with this the domestic value addition in IT hardware will go up by about 25 per cent by 2025. The incentive of ₹2,000 crore for telecom equipment would cover 4G/5G network, switches, routers and transmission systems.

Pharma sector

The scheme relating to the pharma sector would cover 41 critical, mostly imported, drug ingredients or intermediaries. It may be recalled that when the pandemic Covid-19 struck in 2020, India and much of the world struggled to get Active Pharma Ingredients (API) from China which was the major source for them and it led to serious disruption in the production of many drugs in many countries. This exposed the weakness of over-dependence for such vital inputs on one country.

The scheme would also help in developing high-tech items used in emerging therapies and medical devices currently not made in India. The sector has already received, in the initial phase, committed investment of over ₹5,000 crore.

Automotive sector

The Indian automobile industry, employing 35 million people, is the fifth largest producer of cars and seventh largest producer of commercial vehicles in the world. India, now the world's fourth largest vehicles market, is expected to become the third largest market by volume by 2026. The sector, including auto components manufacturing, is expected to be valued ₹16 to 18 trillion (about US$ 250 to 280 billion) by 2026. The electric vehicle (EV) segment itself, driven by two- and three-wheelers, is estimated to be valued ₹50,000 crore by 2025. Recognizing the potential of this sector, a major PLI scheme with an incentive of over ₹57,000 crore is proposed for it, spread over the period 2022-23 to 2026-27. Besides, ₹18,000 crore is envisaged for promoting batteries for E-mobility which would also help electronics and renewable energy sectors.

Textiles

India is the sixth largest exporter of textiles and apparels but has only 5 per cent of global market share. The PLI scheme of ₹10,683 crore is timely as the sector, which is one of the most labour intensive, has been adversely hit by the Covid-19 pandemic. The scheme aims to develop the manmade fibre segment with fabric, design and product development and setting up mega textile parks.

The government has reiterated that only manufacturing companies registered in India will be eligible to participate under the PLI scheme approved for the textiles sector.

Other sectors

Other important sectors, covered under the scheme, include food processing industry and speciality steel.

The food processing industry will have an outlay of ₹10,900 crore to promote cooked items, processed fruits and vegetables and marine products. This is a vital sector, not only from the viewpoint of employment generation potential, but also to reduce spoilage of fruits and vegetables as their wastage is as high as 30 to 40 per cent. With reduced wastage, it will also help farmers and growers of fruits and vegetables to realize better prices for their produce. Promoting marine products would go a long way to help fisheries sector and improve the lot of fishermen who face many problems due to seasonal factors, diminishing potential of marine produce due to excessive exploitation and pollution of seas, etc. **(On this, see also Box 21.1 on "One District One Product" (ODOP) in this chapter, and** for **more on the potential of Food Processing Industry, see chapter 7, pp. 7.14-6).**

Production of speciality and high-end steel has assumed importance with metro and high-speed rail systems under construction and increase in demand both domestically and for exports.

❑ CONCLUSION

While India has made some progress under the Make in India and other initiatives, there is still a long way to go to achieve the stated goals to increase the share of the manufacturing sector from the present level of 15 per cent to 25 per cent of GDP and to create millions of additional jobs in the manufacturing sector. Apart from the challenges faced by India discussed earlier, there are still some roadblocks which stand in the way of India realizing the goals set. Some of these are:

- **Market access:** Now Indian companies invest in substantial measure as FDI in other countries, and India is now one of the top 20 origin countries for global FDI. Despite the risk that corporates face in venturing into foreign shores, they value the access to coveted markets, the potential they offer on global markets and investment friendly regime. Thus, Tata Steel bought Corus and acquired JLR automobiles, for instance. In the Services sector, many of the Indian IT companies have bought over or invested in foreign entities to enlarge their presence and widen their business prospects.

- **Technology:** Another factor is the scope to acquire high-end technology. Tata Steel wanted technology for special steels, Tata Motors bought Jaguar Land Rover for its world class technology and design capability.
- **Talent acquisition:** The third factor is the opportunity to acquire talent especially in high-tech areas. In the IT sector, for instance, availability of higher managerial skills, tightened visa rules, and restrictions limiting access from offshore, particularly for government orders, have led to Indian IT behemoths like TCS, Infosys, etc. creating more capacity in the US where there are huge vacancies to be filled.
- **Need for Natural resources:** Indian companies in manufacturing and oil sector need natural resources like coal, oil, natural gas, etc. For instance, oil companies like ONGC acquire oil and gas fields for exploration to augment oil supplies which India needs. The Adani and Tata Group have bid and bought coal mines and minerals abroad.

India has to reckon with these factors while going ahead with programmes like Make in India lest she be caught unawares. Measures like ease of doing business, manufacturing competitiveness, world class infrastructure, assured power supply and transport and communication network, smooth land acquisition process, skilled labour and congenial labour market, simplified tax structure and robust legal framework to settle business issues and macro-economic stability will form the backbone of a successful 'Make in India' programme.

In this Chapter we discussed.....

- The 'Make in India' programme was launched in September 2014 as part of a wider spectrum of nation-building initiatives; aims to transform India into a global design and manufacturing hub; this initiative was taken against the backdrop of India's stagnant and low growth rate.
- A National Manufacturing Competitiveness Council (NMCC) had been set up in 2004 to energise the growth of manufacturing in India; the present initiative is a step forward in this direction.
- This is in the context of the imperative need to create jobs for the millions of youth who are joining the labour force each year, at an average rate of one million per month.
- It aims to raise the contribution of the manufacturing sector to the GDP, currently around 16 per cent, to 25 per cent by 2020.
- India has advantage of being ademocratic polity, qualified technical and engineering work force, with a burgeoningyoung population who can be skilled, a sound legal and IPR regime and with a huge internal market creating massive demand; need to remove weaknesses like the absence of a bankruptcy law and exit policy, and deficiencies in the banking and financial sector with a better regulatory regime.

- Measures taken to promote 'Make in India' programme: transparency in all actions; making doing business easier; single-window clearance facility for approvals with fixed time-lines; improving infrastructure; reforming labour laws; skill development.
- The government has passed bills reforming the Labour laws which have been approved by the Parliament; the new laws contain labour-friendly proposals and social security measures for unorganized labour, gig workers, hawkers and women workers. Stricter provisions for strikes, recognition of trade unions and for retrenchments and layoffs are rather contentious issues.
- Major steps taken to liberalise and strengthen and give a boost to the defence, aviation and space sector; emphasis on indigenisation of manufacture; vital role of MSME sector.
- Smart cities programme will give boost to engineering industries, power sector and other infrastructure providers and create vast employment opportunities in Tier-II and Tier-III towns and their hinterland areas.
- Defence Procurement Procedure (DPP) cleared by Defence Ministry in March 2016; preference for Indigenously Designed, Developed and Manufactured (IDDM) category of weapons; 'fast-track' route to acquire weapons.
- Transfer of technology and adoption of 'Offsets' policy.
- Challenges and limitations: Can India replace China as a manufacturing hub? competition from other emerging economics is a factor to be resource likely challenges due to automation—3D printing, robotics, artificial intelligence, etc. in manufacturing; competition from other emerging economies; on-shoring of businesses by US.
- Protectionist trends in the advanced economics on sharing of business and manufacturing by US and European nation to impact emerging economics.
- Comprehensive action on many fronts needed: doing business, manufacturing competitiveness, world class infrastructure, assured power supply and transport and communication network, smooth land acquisition process, skilled labour and implementation of new labour laws, simplified tax structure and robust legal framework to settle business issues and ensuring macro-economic stability.

Important Terms to Note in this Chapter

Bankruptcy law; Exit policy; Intellectual property rights (IPR); Foreign direct investment (FDI); Automation; 3D printing; Robotics; Artificial intelligence; Skill development; Protectionism; Onshoring; Offshoring; Technology transfer; Offsets; Productivity Linked Initiative.

Practice Questions

1. What are the main features on Make in India programme initiated by the Government of India?
2. How far the Make in India programme has been successful in achieving The objectives set out for it?
3. What are the challenges faced by the Make in India programme? Suggest Measures to overcome them.
4. Why is India finding it difficult to expand its manufacturing sector in the same way that China has been able to achieve? What steps can be taken to overcome this handicap?
5. To what extent the process of automation will impact India's Make in India programme and potential to create jobs?
6. It is said that the Make in India programme should not result in 'import substitution' policy which India adopted in the early years of planning and which impeded India's economic growth. Critically analyse this statement.
7. Mention the salient features and objectives of the Productivity Linked Initiative (PLI) introduced by the Government of India. Examine how far it will help to boost India's manufacturing sector and make India a manufacturing hub? Justify your reasoning.
8. Explain the rationale for the One District One Product (ODOP) scheme introduced by the government. How far it would help to promote industries in States and Union Territories and provide jobs locally to the labour. Cite some examples of products being promoted under the scheme.
9. What are the main pillars of the "Make in India' programme? Discuss the impact of it on (a) manufacturing and (b) automobile sector.

[Indian Economic Service/Indian Statistical Service 2020]

CHAPTER 22 EASE OF DOING BUSINESS

- Changing Global scenario
- World Ranking on Ease of Doing Business
- New Generation Reforms
- WEF Survey
- Revamp and Simplification of Procedures:
- Centre's Initiatives
- State Government Initiatives
- States Reforms: An Assessment
- FDI Policy
- Insolvency and Bankruptcy Law
- Ease of Doing Business: India and Other Countries

❑ INTRODUCTION

If the development of industries and services sector is to be speeded up, the process of starting industries and business has to be made smooth and hassle-free. One of the main constraints of industrial development in India has been the labyrinth of complex procedures infamously referred to as 'red tape'. As brought out in earlier chapters, the initial decades were notorious for rigid government controls and 'licence raj' in granting approvals to start industries which also bred corruption in many forms. Though the then governments came out with Industrial Policies in 1956, 1977 and 1980 (see chapter 4, pp. 4.1-6), it did little to promote industrial growth in a big way. With the public sector continuing to dominate many crucial sectors, it left little room for the private sector to operate, much less flourish, and contribute to any significant extent to the growth of the economy. The major turning point came when following the reforms of 1991, the government unshackled the industrial and services sectors from many of these controls and restrictions, assigned a major role to the private sector, opened up the economy and liberalised imports and exports. It brought a breath of fresh air to what for long had been a stifling atmosphere.

Changing Global Scenario

The world and global economy has seen a sea-change since the 1990s. Globalisation has made countries even more interdependent than ever before, many emerging economies have come up, countries are entering into bilateral or multilateral free trade agreements and there are many critical, and often conflicting, trade issues which are under discussion and dispute needing resolution at WTO. The structure, architecture and role of the Bretton Woods institutions – the IMF and the World Bank – also need a relook in view of many new, emerging economies, the rise of China and India and the changing balance of economic power. Both advanced and emerging economies have to grow and move forward in unison. This is especially important for while the monetary policies followed by the Central banks of developed countries may serve their domestic interests, it could result in disrupting and creating instability elsewhere and even affecting stability of the global economy.

❑ WORLD BANK RANKINGS ON EASE OF DOING BUSINESS

The World Bank has been ranking countries on 'Ease of Doing Business' based on 11 criteria such as ease of starting a business, getting construction permits, getting electricity, registering property, getting credit, paying taxes, protecting minority investors, trading across borders, enforcing contracts, resolving insolvency and labour market regulation. According to the Bank, "a high ease of doing business ranking means the regulatory environment is more conducive to the starting and operation of a local firm".

India has been steadily improving her rank over the years. While India was ranked 134 out of 189 countries in 2014, she was ranked 100 in 2018 and 77 out of 190 countries as per Doing Business Report (DBR) 2019. And as per Doing Business Report (DBR) 2020, India improved her position by 14 places to be ranked at 63 riding on the Government's 'Make in India' scheme and other reforms attracting foreign investment.

These improvements are as a result of the regulatory reforms launched to make it easier to do business in India. The program represents a great deal of effort to create a more business-friendly environment. The World Bank Doing Business report is based on surveys only on Delhi and Mumbai.

- **Criteria adopted**: The DBR covers 10 indicators which span the lifecycle of a business.
- Among the indicators, India has ranked high on Protecting Minority Investors (rank 7), Getting Credit (22), Getting Electricity (24) and Dealing with Construction Permits (52).
- But on certain other crucial parameters, India ranks low, viz., Trading Across Borders (80), Resolving Insolvency (108), Paying Taxes (121), Starting a Business (137), Enforcing Contracts (163) and Registering Property (166).
- While the 2019 report acknowledges that India is one of the top 10 improvers, second time in a row, with an improvement of 53 ranks in two years, the highest jump by any large country since 2011, India has a long way to go on other important parameters like Registering Property, Enforcing Contracts, Resolving Insolvency and Starting a Business.

The rankings of economies with populations over 100 million as of 2013 (Bangladesh, Brazil, China, India, Indonesia, Japan, Mexico, Nigeria, Pakistan, the Russian Federation and the United States) were based on data for 2 cities. In the case of India, it was based on Mumbai and Delhi.

❑ NEW GENERATION REFORMS

Referring to the NDA government's initiative to enhance the ease of doing business since it assumed office in May 2014, the World Bank's *Doing Business Report 2016* said: "Spanning a range of areas measured by Doing Business, the program represents a great deal of effort to create a more business-friendly environment, particularly in Delhi and Mumbai." Citing the area of 'Starting a Business' as the biggest improvement, the World Bank said: "In the past year, India eliminated the paid-in minimum capital requirement and streamlined the process for starting a business. More reforms are ongoing—in starting a business and other areas measured by Doing Business—though the full effects have yet to be felt."

While the NDA government and various State governments have taken a series of measures to ease and improve business environment (see next section), India has been able to improve her rank with the passing of the Bankruptcy and Insolvency Law, providing for easy exit in case of genuine business failures. India has also set up Courts to expeditiously deal with commercial disputes and contractual agreements.

India, which was ranked 130 in 2017 by the World Bank, registered significant improvement and leapfrogged by 30 places to be placed at 100 out of 190 countries for 2018. On two of the parameters in World Bank's survey, India has forged ahead. On 'paying taxes', India has moved up from 172 in 2017 to 119 and on 'resolving insolvency' from 136 to 103. But on certain other parameters, India is still way below -- on 'construction permits' at 181, 'enforcing contracts' at 164, on 'starting a business' at 156 and on 'registering property' at 154. India, which aims to be within rank 50, has to make concerted efforts to improve on these criteria.

❑ WEF SURVEY

In another survey of 140 countries done by the World Economic Forum (WEF) published in the *Global Competitiveness Report 2015-16*, India's rank improved by 16 places to 55 from 71 the previous year. It is indicative of the improvement in business sentiment and the positive way in which the current government is viewed by investors. The WEF report stated that improvement is largely attributable to the momentum initiated by the PM, "whose pro-business, pro-growth, and anti-corruption stance has improved the business community's sentiment toward the government".

In the 2017-18 report of World Economic Forum on Global Competitiveness Index (GCI), India improved its rank to 40 following its big leap forward of the previous two years. WEF has observed that the score improved "across most pillars of competitiveness, particularly infrastructure (66th, up two), higher education and training (75th, up six), and technological readiness (107th, up three), reflecting recent public investments in these areas. Performance also improved in ICT indicators, particularly Internet bandwidth per user, mobile phone and broadband subscriptions, and Internet access in schools. The quality of institutions has increased further, especially in terms of efficiency of public spending (20th), but the private sector still considers corruption to be the most problematic factor for doing business in India."

In another study by the World Economic Forum, The Global Competitiveness Report 2020, certain transformational criteria relating to institutional governance, infrastructure upgrade, progressive taxation, updating education curricula to suit skills needed for tomorrow's jobs, labour laws to protect new economy and meet needs of the workforce and healthcare infrastructure have been examined and assessed for major economies. The performance of countries is marked on a scale ranging from 0 to 100 using a min-max transformation score. The results for India, Indonesia and Brazil from the study is shown in Table 22.1 below.

Table 22.1 Transformation Readiness framework

Performance on Economic Transformation Priorities, by 2020 score (0–100 scale)

Item No.	Criteria	India	Indonesia	Brazil
1	Ensure public institutions embed strong governance principles and a longterm vision and build trust by serving their citizens	49.4	58.8	45.3
2	Upgrade infrastructure to accelerate the energy transition and broaden access to electricity and ICT	72.6	62.7	79.4
3	Shift to more progressive taxation, rethinking how corporations, wealth and labour are taxed, nationally and in an international cooperative framework	55.8	53.7	44.0
4	Update education curricula and expand investment in the skills needed for jobs and "markets of tomorrow"	43.5	49.0	39.5
5	Rethink labour laws and social protection for the new economy and the new needs of the workforce	44.4	n/a	51.0
6	Expand eldercare, childcare and healthcare infrastructure, access and innovation for the benefit of people and the economy	n/a	n/a	n/a

Source: Table 5.1, Performance on Economic Transformation Priorities, The Global Competitiveness Report 2020, World Economic Forum.

It will be seen that all the three countries have scored high on infrastructure upgrade. On other parameters, India has above 50 only on progressive taxation and below 50 on other criteria. Indonesia has fared better on two other criteria and Brazil in one other scoring over 50.

❑ REVAMP AND SIMPLIFICATION OF PROCEDURES

Centre's Initiatives

Some of the concrete steps taken to simplify procedures and create a business friendly environment are mentioned below:

- Unified online portal for registration of Labour Identification Number (LIN); submitting combined returns under labour laws and grievance redressal;
- Online portals for Employees State Insurance Corporation (ESIC) and Employees Provident Fund Organization (EPFO) which facilitates real-time registration, payments through accredited banks;
- Online application process for environmental and forest clearances, 14 government services delivered via eBiz, a single-window online portal and an Investor Facilitation Cell set up;
- No objection certificate not required for new electricity connections, documents for exports and imports reduced, forms simplified for Industrial Licence;
- Licence not required for any defence sector dual-use products and validity of security clearance from Ministry of Home Affairs extended to 3 years.

Further measures proposed include removal of requirement of minimum paid-up capital, integrated processes for obtaining PAN, TAN, ESIC and EPFO registration with incorporation of company and single-window clearance for import and export.

e-Biz Project: eBiz project is one of Mission Mode Projects (MMPs) under the Digital India program of Government of India. The project envisages setting up a G2B portal to serve as a one-stop shop for delivery of services to the investors and addresses the need of business and industry from inception through the entire life-cycle. The eBiz project is being implemented on a Public Private Partnership (PPP) model, with M/s Infosys Technologies Ltd selected as the concessionaire for designing, developing, maintaining and expanding the eBiz solution & services for 10 years.

❑ STATE GOVERNMENT INITIATIVES

As stated earlier, the survey by the World Bank covers only the two cities of Mumbai and Delhi and India has to proactively improve ease of doing business nationally covering many other cities. Many State governments have also taken steps to ease procedures to create a business friendly climate and attract investments. Many of them have held International Investor Meets and Global Business Summits where they have signed MOU with prominent companies for starting business ventures. This is an indication of healthy 'competitive federalism' which augurs well for the country as a whole.

Some of the initiatives taken by States to improve and ease the business environment are mentioned below:

* GIS-based land identification system (Gujarat).
* Online consent system for environmental clearances; Extended validity of consent under environmental provisions (Chhattisgarh).
* Unified process with single ID for VAT and Professional Tax registration; Number of procedures and time for getting an electricity connection reduced; Commercial benches established in Mumbai High Court (Maharashtra).
* Creation of Invest Punjab, as a one-stop clearance system for investment projects; 131 industries exempted from consent requirement by Pollution Control Board (Punjab).
* Real-time allotment of TIN - Taxpayer Identification Number; Online application portal for residential and industrial building permits; Commercial benches established in High Court; Online portal for construction permits for institutional and commercial buildings (Delhi).
* Static check posts replaced by mobile squads (Uttarakhand)
* Green industries exempted from inspection by Pollution Control Committee (Puducherry).
* Checklist for 86 government services and delivery timelines across 23 departments/organizations made available on Karnataka UdyogMitra, an online portal (Karnataka).

❑ ASSESSMENT OF STATE IMPLEMENTATION OF BUSINESS REFORMS 2016

The Department of Industrial Policy and Promotion (DIPP) had drawn up a 340-point Business Reform Action Plan (BRAP) for States/UTs, covering the period July 2015 to June 2016. The BRAP includes recommendations for reforms on 58 regulatory processes, policies, practices or procedures spread across 10 reform areas spanning the lifecycle of a typical business. The reforms covered areas such as single-window systems for various regulatory approvals, automated construction permit approval, environment and labour reforms and user-friendly inspection procedures. Data collected on this from State Governments showed that 32 State and UT Governments submitted evidence of implementation of

7,124 reforms. These submissions were reviewed by the World Bank team and validated by DIPP's team to study whether they met the objectives of the BRAP.

The results of the assessment demonstrate that States have increasingly risen to address the challenge of making it easier to do business. The national implementation average stood at 48.93 per cent, significantly higher than previous year's national average of 32 per cent. This demonstrates the significant progress made by States.

According to the ranking of the States done as on October 2016, Andhra Pradesh and Telangana tied for the first rank, followed by Gujarat, Chhattisgarh, Madhya Pradesh and Haryana. The ranks are dynamic and will keep changing depending on the range and pace of reforms undertaken by the states.

- **Action by States:** The Department for Promotion of Industry & Internal Trade (DPIIT) has initiated similar reform exercise in all States and UTs since setting up businesses concerns them also. States and UTs are being ranked based on implementation of reforms by them to create a conducive business environment by streamlining regulatory structures and creating an investor-friendly business climate.
- **World Bank's role:** The World Bank has also partnered with DPIIT in this reform plan and 18 joint workshops were conducted along with World Bank specialists to help Departments in the States and UTs understand the essence of the reforms better and to give the exercise momentum.
- **Progress in States/UTs:** The assessment of Business Reform Action Plan, 2017-18, released jointly by DPIIT and the World Bank in July 2018, showed the progress achieved by states/UTs States as follows:
- 9 states had achieved over 95 per cent of targets and were ranked "Top achievers". This included Andhra Pradesh, Telangana, Haryana, Jharkhand, Gujarat, Chhattisgarh, MP, Karnataka and Rajasthan.
- 6 states had achieved 90-95 per cent of targets and were ranked "Achievers". These were West Bengal, Uttarakhand, UP, Maharashtra, Odisha and Tamil Nadu.
- Himachal Pradesh, Assam and Bihar had achieved 80-90 per cent of targets and were ranked "Fast movers".
- Remaining 18 states/UTs had achieved less than 80 per cent of targets and were ranked "Aspirers". This included Punjab, Goa, Kerala, J&K, Delhi and other states and all UTs.
- **NITI Aayog study and findings:** NITI Aayog has also done a study, "***An Enterprise Survey of Indian States***" in association with IDFC Institute, a Mumbai-based think tank in 2017. It is a survey of manufacturing firms across Indian states and union territories with a view to assess the business regulations and enabling environment across India from the viewpoint of firms. This survey included in-depth interviews with lawyers, chartered accountants, and company secretaries in several states and is, therefore, a comprehensive study.

The Survey which covered over 3,200 manufacturing enterprises, including 141 early stage firms, across 23 manufacturing sectors, have revealed some positive aspects but also areas needing further action and improvement. The crucial findings were as follows:

- The awareness among enterprises about single window systems, instituted by states, is low. Even among experts, only 41 per cent have any knowledge of the existence of these facilities. There is, therefore, a clear need for creating greater awareness.
- On average, only about 20 per cent of start-ups, which are of recent origin, report using single window facilities introduced by state governments for setting up a business.

- Enterprises in high-growth states are significantly less likely to report major or very severe obstacles in land and construction related approvals, environmental approvals and water and sanitation availability as compared to enterprises located in low-growth states.
- Enterprises in high-growth states take less time on average for nearly all aspects of doing business.
- Specific areas where high-growth states do very well are in getting construction permits, labour renewals, and access to electricity and water connections.
- Firms in high-growth states also report 25 per cent less power shortage in a typical month, compared to firms in low-growth states.
- Comparison of young firms with old ones showed that newer and younger firms report a more favourable business environment in that they take less time in obtaining approvals. And they don't find regulatory processes a major obstacle to doing business which is a positive sign.
- Labour-intensive sectors have a special place as they can create proportionately more jobs per unit of capital investment. The survey found that these sectors felt more constrained by labour related regulations. For them, finding skilled workers, hiring contract labour, and terminating employees, is a major obstacle. It points to the centrality of labour law reforms for expansion of labour-intensive sectors and job creation.

❑ FDI POLICY

A liberalised foreign direct investment (FDI) regime is also necessary to promote investment, trade and economic growth. As seen in chapter 6, as part of the 1991 reforms, India had taken some significant steps towards liberalising trade and investment. The present NDA government has further liberalised foreign investment policy. *The major changes are mentioned below.*

- The government has already relaxed the FDI policy in over a dozen sectors, including defence, railway, medical devices and civil aviation.
- FDI ceiling in the defence sector has been hiked to 49 per cent under the automatic route. FDI beyond 49 per cent to be granted with the approval of FIPB in case of induction of modern and state-of-the-art technology.
- The government had earlier increased the foreign Investment cap in insurance and pension from 26 per cent to 49 per cent subject to the condition that ownership and control remains with the Indian promoter at all times. Further liberalizing FDI in the insurance and pension sectors, the government announced in Union budget for 2016-17 that overseas investment up to 49 per cent will be allowed in these sectors under the automatic route which means investors will not have to approach the Foreign Investment Promotion Board (FIPB) for increasing their stakes. However, the guidelines on Indian management and control will have to be verified by the respective regulators, the Insurance Regulatory and Development Authority of India (IRDA) and the Pension Fund Regulatory and Development Authority (PFRDA).
- The 2016-17 budget announced 100 per cent FDI in asset reconstruction companies through the automatic route. Also, the existing 24 per cent limit for investment by foreign portfolio investors (FPIs) in central public sector enterprises, other than banks, listed in stock exchanges, would be increased to 49 per cent to obviate the need for prior government approval.
- A lot of fruits and vegetables grown by farmers do not fetch right prices or reach the markets. To benefit farmers and give fillip to food processing industry, it was announced in the budget for 2016-17 that 100 per cent FDI will be allowed through FIPB route in marketing of food products produced and manufactured in India. If implemented and foreign investment flows in, this will help

to expand cold storage facilities, reduce the enormous wastage of farm products now occurring due to spoilage, contain inflation and create vast employment opportunities particularly in rural and semi-urban areas.

- In 2015, the government decided that non-repatriable investments by Non-resident Indians (NRIs) will be treated as domestic investments and will not be subject to FDI caps. For the purposes of FDI policy, investment by NRIs under FEMA regulations will be deemed to be domestic investment at par with the investment made by residents. This measure is expected to speed up the approval process for large FDI projects and encourage foreign investment by NRIs in India. The Finance Minister has announced in the 2017-18 budget that further liberalisation of FDI policy is under consideration.

❑ INSOLVENCY AND BANKRUPTCY LAW

The absence of a proper bankruptcy law has been a major drawback in India's business ecosystem. The glaring gap in efficiency in dealing with insolvency issues can be seen from the time taken to settle them in India and some of the other countries according to the World Bank's *Doing Business 2016 report*. While it takes in some of the advanced countries less than a year to 1½ years, it takes as long as 4.3 years in India. (See Table 22.1). India's overall rank in the report is 130 out of 189 countries whereas in resolving insolvency, her rank is 136. This has been one of the main reasons for projects in building national highways and in the power sector getting stalled in India. A robust legal framework on this will promote investments and reassure investors and venture capitalists of a sound system of winding up a company or business.

Two Acts enacted a century ago – the Presidency Towns Insolvency Act and the Provincial Insolvency Act–were never operationalized. Though defaults in bank debts have been dealt with under the Sick Industrial Companies Act (SICA) and provisions under the Board for Industrial and Financial Reconstruction (BIFR), these provisions have been often misused by debtors to get stay and dodge settlement. The Securitisation and Reconstruction of Financial Assets and Enforcement of Security Interest Act (SARFAESI), 2002 was enacted to address this problem.

New Legislation

Insolvency and Bankruptcy Code, 2016 (IBC)

The Insolvency and Bankruptcy Code, 2016, the new bankruptcy law of India, has created a single law for insolvency and bankruptcy. The Insolvency and Bankruptcy Code, 2015 was passed by the Parliament and received the assent of the President of India in 2016. The bankruptcy code is a one stop solution for resolving insolvencies which earlier entailed a long process and was not an economically viable arrangement. A strong insolvency framework where the cost, time, incurred is minimised in attaining liquidation was long overdue in India. The code will be able to protect the interests of small investors and make the process of doing business a less cumbersome process

The Code has significantly improved the time taken for resolving insolvency issues. While the time taken prior to the passing of the code was as high as 4.3 years, it has come down to 1.6 years. (See Table 22.2).

Table 22.2 Time taken for Resolving Insolvency (in years) -Data for 2019

Country	Resolving Insolvency (yrs)	Country	Resolving Insolvency (yrs)
Australia	1.0	Japan	0.6
China	1.7	Singapore	0.8
France	1.9	South Korea	1.5
Germany	1.2	UK	1.0
India	1.6	USA	1.0

Source: World Bank Data for 2019.

The Code supersedes the earlier laws and in addition, seeks to amend 11 laws, including the Companies Act, 2013, Recovery of Debts Due to Banks and Financial Institutions Act, 1993 and Sick Industrial Companies (Special Provisions) Repeal Act, 2003, among others. The Code will apply to companies, partnerships, limited liability partnerships (LLPs), individuals and any other body specified by the Central government. The insolvency resolution process (IRP) for individuals varies from that of companies. These processes may be initiated by either the debtor or the creditors.

Considering the shortcomings found in the operation of IBC, the government amended certain provisions in it in 2019 to make it more effective. It is hoped that with all these new measures in place and more action to follow, India's business environment will vastly improve and her rank in regard to ease of doing business will go up significantly. (For details on the new Insolvency and Bankruptcy Code, see Chapter 13, pp. 13.9-10).

It is not only India which is striving to improve its 'Ease of Doing Business' record. All countries are striving to improve their position and attract investments. The ranking in Doing Business Report 2020 throws up some ranks on expected lines while some are surprising as seen from the following Table:

Table 22.3 Ease of Doing Business – Ranks in 2020

Country	Rank	Country	Rank
New Zealand	1	Vietnam	70
Singapore	2	Indonesia	73
South Korea	5	Bhutan	89
Malaysia	12	Nepal	94
Thailand	21	Sri Lanka	99
China	31	Pakistan	108
India	63	Bangladesh	168

Source: Doing Business Report 2020, World Bank.

- **Conclusion:** To sum up, India has made significant strides in creating a more investment-friendly and hassle-free environment for businesses and enterprises, both at the centre and state levels. This has helped India to improve her rank in the World Bank surveys. But, as pointed out earlier, in some areas like Resolving Insolvency, Tax Payment, Enforcing Contracts and Registering Property, India still has to show much improvement if she is to break into the top 50 rank in all these parameters.

The World Bank to discontinue *Doing Business Report*

The World Bank Group has since stated that it will discontinue "Doing Business Report " (DBR) after certain data irregularities were reported internally in June 2020 in DBR 2018 and 2020. The Group issued a statement: "Trust in the research of the World Bank Group is vital. World Bank Group research informs the actions of policymakers, helps countries make better-informed decisions, and allows stakeholders to measure economic and social improvements more accurately. Such research has also been a valuable tool for the private sector, civil society, academia, journalists, and others, broadening understanding of global issues."

However, "The World Bank Group remains firmly committed to advancing the role of the private sector in development and providing support to governments to design the regulatory environment that supports this. Going forward, we will be working on a new approach to assessing the business and investment climate. We are deeply grateful to the efforts of the many staff members who have worked diligently to advance the business climate agenda, and we look forward to harnessing their energies and abilities in new ways."

Box No. 22.1 Ease of Doing Business

It is not only India which is striving to improve its 'Ease of doing business' record. Indonesia, another emerging economy in Asia, where setting up a business is now complicated is trying to scrap many procedures to save time and money and incentivise starting enterprises. Already, deregulation measures initiated have seen 94 procedures cut down by almost half to 49, and the time taken on fulfilling procedures brought down significantly. This is especially crucial for small and medium enterprises who are the most impacted by a labyrinth of complex procedures and regulations.

Indonesia, ranked 120 in 2015 and 109 in 2016 among 189 economies surveyed in the World Bank's Doing Business Report, 2017 aims to improve its rank to 40. This is necessary to make the economy competitive with other Asian economies which are ahead in ranking – Singapore at No. 1 position, Malaysia at 18, Thailand at 49 and Vietnam at 90.

In this Chapter we discussed.....

- The process of starting industries and business has to be made smooth and hassle-free to promote investments and business.
- India's policy of rigid government controls and 'licence raj' in granting approvals to start industries in the initial decades had stalled investments and bred corruption; dominance of public sector had a stifling effect on the private sector.
- The reforms of 1991 assigned a major role to the private sector, opened up the economy and liberalised imports and exports.
- There has been a sea-change in global scenario since the 1990s and countries are entering into bilateral or multilateral free trade agreements.
- In view of the changed conditions, there is need for a relook at the structure, architecture and role of the Bretton Woods institutions – the IMF and the World Bank.
- The monetary policies followed by the Central banks of developed countries to be such as not to cause disruption in developing countries or even in global economy.
- In the World Bank's rankings on Ease of Doing Business, India was ranked 134 out of 189 countries in 2014 and 130 in 2015.
- The NDA government has taken various initiatives to enhance the ease of doing business since it assumed office in May 2014 which has been acknowledged by the World Bank in its Doing Business Report 2016 but their full effects have yet to be felt.
- The passing of the Bankruptcy and Insolvency Code in 2016 has helped India to improve her rank in 'Ease of Doing Business'. The code has provisions for exit in case of genuine business failures. Courts have been set up to deal with commercial disputes, contractual agreements are streamlined and labour laws are reformed.
- As per the World Economic Forum (WEF)'s Global Competitiveness Report 2017-18, India's rank improved to 40 from 55 in 2015-16 which is indicative of the improvement in business sentiment and the positive way the current government is viewed by investors.
- To revamp and simplify business procedures both the Centre and the States have taken various initiatives which would promote investments.
- While multilateralism is still in vogue, countries are now turning more towards bilateral and regional free trade agreements (FTAs) such as TPP and RCEP are still under negotiation; thus India's efforts to have FTAs with European Union and Asean assume importance.

- Poor outcomes from the Bay of Bengal Initiative for Multisectoral Technical and Economic Cooperation (BIMSTEC) which came into being in 1 997 and involves 5 south Asian and 2 south-east Asian nations show that apart from breaking down tariff barriers, regional pacts require proper infrastructure and connectivity for their success.
- India and the US are working on 'Ease of Doing Business' as part of the first US-India Strategic and Commercial Dialogue to increase bilateral trade five-fold to $ 500 billion.
- Liberalisation effected in Foreign direct investment (FDI) in over a dozen sectors, including defence, railway, medical devices and civil aviation; 100 per cent FDI allowed in asset reconstruction companies through the automatic route; FDI will be allowed through FIPB route in marketing of food products produced and manufactured in India; investments by NRI's also liberalised.
- The absence of a proper bankruptcy law has been a major drawback in India's business ecosystem; India's insolvency laws were archaic; there was wide gulf between developed countries and India in the time taken for resolving insolvency; the government prepared a new Insolvency and Bankruptcy Code, 2016 which was passed by Parliament in May 2016. It has helped to reduce the time taken for resolving insolvency and bankruptcy cases.
- The World Bank to discontinue Doing Business Report

Important Terms to Note in this Chapter

Free trade agreement (FTA); Monetary policy; Competitive federalism; Bilateralism; Multilateralism; Foreign portfolio investment; Foreign direct investment (FDI); Bankruptcy, Insolvency.

Practice Questions

1. Enumerate the various steps taken by the government of India to improve the business environment in India.
2. What is India's position in the ranking done by the World Bank on 'Ease of Doing Business' in the last few years. What steps were taken by India improve her rank?
3. What are the various factors considered by the World Bank while assessing the 'Ease of Doing Business' in a country?

4. What are the various steps on which the government of India is pursuing the States and Union Territories (UTs) to improve the business environment and ease of doing business? Mention some of the steps taken by the States and UTs in this regard.
5. India has passed the Bankruptcy and Insolvency Code. What are its features and how will it help businesses which face financial crisis and seek insolvency?
6. How is the Bankruptcy and Insolvency Code passed by India an improvement over the earlier laws to deal with bankruptcy problems faced by businesses?
7. What steps have been taken by the government of India to liberalise and promote foreign direct investment (FDI) in the last few years?

CHAPTER

STARTUP MISSION AND VENTURE CAPITAL

- Startup Mission
- Steps taken to nurture the Startup ecosystem
- Atal Innovation Mission (AIM)
- Atal Incubation Centers (AICs)
- Atal Tinkering Lab (ATL)
- India – A Leading Startup Nation
- Rapid Growth and Employment Potential
- Hiring by Startups
- Role of Startups
- Union Budget 2018-19 and Startups
- Changing Manufacturing and Trade Landscape
- Funding for Startups
- Limitations and Challenges to Startups

❑ STARTUP MISSION

Introduction

After the Prime Minister had flagged off the 'Startup India, Stand up India' mission during his Independence day address on August 15, 2015, the government formally launched the initiative in January 2016. Its primary objective is to tap the entrepreneurial potential and talent, particularly among the youth. Inaugurating the mission, the Prime Minister mentioned that successful Startups are usually created by those who are driven by an idea or an urge to solve a problem faced by the people. More than earning money, which would be a by-product and not the main objective , the PM said that Startup innovators are often driven by a sense of compassion to help others. The PM also appealed to the youth of India to become job-creators rather than job-seekers. Even if a Startup could provide employment to five people, it will a big service to the nation.

During the inauguration of the event, there was a virtual exhibition and the PM interacted with ten outstanding Startup innovators who shared their thoughts and experiences with the audience. There was also a day-long workshop on various aspects of entrepreneurship.

Some of the steps the government announced while launching the programme to promote and incentivize Startups were as follows:

- A Startup India hub to provide a single point of contact for the entire Startup ecosystem and enable exchange of knowledge and access to funding;
- Exemption from paying income tax on their profit for the first three years;
- Exemption from capital gains tax if the investor invests capital gains in a registered fund of funds;
- Startup fests at national and international venues to provide visibility and encourage collaboration;
- A dedicated Startup fund worth ₹ 10,000 crore (with annual corpus of ₹ 2,500 per year for four years) will be created for funding of Startups;
- Patent applications of Startups would be fast-tracked. A Startup Intellectual Property Protection (SIPP) scheme will facilitate filing of patents, trademarks, and designs by innovative Startups;
- An 80 per cent exemption in patent fee for Startup businesses;
- A self-certification based compliance system for Startups would be introduced for nine labour and environment laws to reduce regulatory burden;
- An insolvency expert to be appointed to wind up the Startup within 90 days for faster exit in case of failure;
- The government to launch 'Atal Innovation Mission' (AIM) and 'Self-Employment and Talent Utilization' (SETU) to serve as platforms for innovation hubs;
- A National Initiative for Developing and Harnessing Innovations (NIDHI) scheme to award ₹ 10 lakh each to 20 students to promote a culture of innovation among students;
- Ten Incubators, selected through a grand challenge to be given ₹ 10 crore each to encourage the mentoring of Startups; and
- Public-private partnership for setting up 70 incubators across the country.

The scheme is being implemented by the Department for Promotion of Industry and Internal Trade (DPIIT) under the Ministry of Commerce.

Steps taken by government to nurture the startup ecosystem

1. Fund of Funds For providing fund support for Startups

Government has created a 'Fund of Funds for Startups' (FFS) at Small Industries Development Bank of India (SIDBI) with a corpus of ₹10,000 crore. The FFS shall contribute to the corpus of Alternate Investment funds (AIFs) for investing in equity and equity linked instruments of various Startups. The FFS is managed by Small Industries Bank of India (SIDBI).

As of 1st December 2020, SIDBI has committed ₹4,326.95 crore to 60 SEBI registered Alternative Investment Funds (AIFs). These funds have raised a corpus fund of ₹31,598 crore. ₹1,270.46 crore have been drawn from the FFS and ₹4509.16 crore have been invested into 384 startups.

2. Credit Guarantee Fund for Startups

Since debt funding for Startups is perceived as high risk activity, action has been initiated to set up a Credit Guarantee Fund for Startups with a budgetary corpus of ₹500 crore per year, over the next four years, to provide credit guarantee cover to banks and lending institutions providing loans to Startups. The scheme, on the lines of credit guarantee scheme for MSME, will provide impetus for flow of much needed credit to the Startups running into thousands of crores.

3. Relaxed Norms in Public Procurement for Startups

Provision has been introduced in the procurement policy of Ministry of Micro, Small and Medium Enterprises (MSMEs) to relax norms pertaining to prior experience / turnover for Micro and Small Enterprises. Department of Expenditure has issued a notification for relaxing public procurement norms in respect of all Startups (including medium enterprises) by all central Ministries/Departments.

4. Tax Incentives

3 Year Tax Exemption: The Finance Act, 2016 has provision for Startups (Companies and LLPs) to get income tax exemption for 3 years in a block of 5 years, if they are incorporated between 1st April 2016 and 31st March 2019. To avail these benefits, a Startup must get a Certificate of Eligibility from the Inter-Ministerial Board.

Removal of Angel Tax

Tax exemption on investments made in excess of face value in the shares of a Startup company has been introduced on 14 June 2016. So far 319 startups have been granted income tax exemptions till November-2020.

5. Tax Exemption on Capital Gains

A section has been introduced in the Finance Act, 2016 providing for exemption of capital gain (not exceeding ₹50 lakh in a financial year) arising out of transfer of long term capital asset invested in a fund notified by Central Government. Income Tax Act, 1961 has also been amended to provide for exemption from tax on capital gains arising out of sale of residential house or a residential plot of land if the net consideration is invested in equity shares of eligible Startups.

6. Legal Support and Fast-tracking Patent Examination at Lower Costs

DIPP is entrusted with the responsibility of formulation of policy on Intellectual Property Rights (IPRs), i.e. Patents, Designs, Trade Marks and Geographical Indications of Goods. The department administers IPR legislations, namely, the Patents Act, 1970, the Designs Act, 2000, the Trade Marks Act, 1999 and the Geographical Indications of Goods (Registration & Protection) Act, 1999.

A scheme for Startups IPR Protection (SIPP) for facilitating fast track filing of Patents, Trademarks and Designs by Startups has been introduced. The scheme provides for speedy examination of patents filed by Startups. The fee for filing of patents for Startups has also been reduced up to 80 per cent.

Panels of facilitators for Patents and Trademark applications have been formed to facilitate the process of patent filing and acquisition. The facilitators would provide legal guidance and handholding through the entire patent acquisition process free of cost.

As of June-2020, 510 patent facilitators and 392 trademark facilitators have been empanelled to provide free-of-charge services to Startups.

7. Self-Certification based Compliance Regime

Compliance norms relating to Environmental and Labour laws have been eased in order to reduce the regulatory burden on Startups thereby allowing them to focus on their core business and keep compliance costs low.

Ministry of Environment and Forests (MoEF) has published a list of 36 white category industries. Startups falling under the "White category" would be able to self-certify compliance in respect of 3 Environment Acts -

- The Water (Prevention & Control of Pollution) Act, 1974

- The Water (Prevention & Control of Pollution) Cess (Amendment) Act, 2003
- The Air (Prevention & Control of Pollution) Act, 1981)

Further, Ministry of Labour and Employment (MoLE) has issued guidelines to State Governments whereby Startups shall be allowed to self-certify compliance in respect of 6 Labour laws. These shall be effective after concurrence of States/UT.

8. Setting up Incubators

Atal Incubation Centers: Under Atal Innovation Mission (AIM), NITI Ayog will set up Atal Incubation Centers (AICs) in public and private sector. NITI Aayog has received over 3,600 applications from academic and non-academic institutions from both Public and Private sector organizations for setting up AICs.

Under the Mission, a grant-in-aid of ₹10 crore would be provided to scale up an existing incubator for a maximum of 5 years to cover the capital and operational costs in running the centre. NITI Aayog has received over 200 applications for providing scale up support for established incubation centres.

NITI Aayog has approved 22 institutes to establish new incubators with a total grant of ₹54 crore. A grant-in-aid of INR 10 Crore would be provided to each Established Incubator Centre (EIC) for a maximum of 5 years to cover the capital and operational costs in running a centre. 8 established incubators have received a total scale-up grant of ₹34 crore. (On AIM, see Box 23.1 at the end of this chapter).

Atal Tinkering Lab: Over the last 4 years, AIM has launched the Atal Tinkering Lab (ATL) program. ATL is a state-of-the-art space established in a school with a goal to foster curiosity and innovation in young minds, between grade 6th to 12th across the country through 21st century tools and technologies such as Internet of Things, 3D printing, rapid prototyping tools, robotics, miniaturized electronics, do-it-yourself kits and many more. The aim is to stimulate a problem-solving innovative mindset within the children of the ATL and nearby communities. Till date, AIM has selected 10,000 schools in 680+ districts of the country for the establishment of ATLs. More than 7,000 schools are funded till now and over 2 million students have access to ATLs.

9. Setting up of Startup Centers and Technology Business Incubators (TBIs)

14 Startup Centres and 15 Technology Business Incubators are being setup collaboratively by Ministry of Human Resource Development (MHRD) and the Department of Science and Technology (DST). Out of the 14 Startup Centers, 10 have been approved. Once MHRD releases its share of ₹25 lakh each for the Startup centers, the Startup centers would be supported by DST. Against the target of sanctioning 15 TBIs, 9 TBIs have been approved and other 6 TBIs are under process.

10. Research Parks

The objective of setting up Research Parks is to propel successful innovation through incubation and joint Research and Development (R&D) efforts between academia and industry. 8 Research Parks are being setup under Startup India initiative. Research Park at IIT Kharagpur is under construction and ₹100 crore has been released. The Research Park at IIT Gandhinagar is being set up by DST which has sanctioned ₹90 crore and disbursed an initial instalment of ₹40 crore. The remaining 5 are being set up by Ministry of Human Resource Development (MHRD) at IIT Guwahati, IIT Hyderabad, IIT Kanpur, IIT Delhi and IISC Bangalore with a budget of ₹375 crore. In addition, another Research Park at IIT Bombay is under construction and ₹34 crore has been released.

11. StartupYatra

StartupYatra (an initiative that travels to Tier 2 and Tier 3 cities of India to search for entrepreneurial talent by conducting day long bootcamps) has been conducted across 23 States in 207 districts impacting 78346 aspiring entrepreneurs. A total of 1,424 incubation offers have been given to the startups as a result of this initiative.

Further to boost innovation in the sector and encourage the youths to secure their rights on technology and the product developed by them, startup have been provided 80 per cent rebate in patent filing fees and 50 per cent rebate on trademark filing fees. Additionally, facility of expedited examination of patent applications to reduce the time taken in granting patents is also available to the startups. As of June-2020, 3618 patent applications were granted 80 per cent rebate on the filing fee and 6832 trademark applications were granted a 50 per cent rebate on filing fee.

❑ INDIA—A LEADING STARTUP NATION

Rapid Growth and Employment potential

India continues to be one of the fastest growing startup landscape in the world with every major accelerator, investor and angel group participating in its growth. While more than 1,400 new startups emerged in 2016, over 1,000 tech startups were registered in 2017.

The rapid growth in start-up ecosystem has been driven by government's efforts of boosting entrepreneurship. According to Economic Survey of the Ministry of Finance for 2020-21, as of December 23, 2020, the government has recognized a total of 41,061 startups and 4,70,000 jobs have been reported by more than 39,000 startups. As per information given in Parliament in March 2021, the number of recognized Startups stood at 44,766. (Question No. 2780 answered in Rajya Sabha on 19.03.2021).

With over 50 unicorns ("unicorns" are startups valued over $ 1 billion), and a beeline of IPO-bound companies, the Indian start-up ecosystem has witnessed exponential growth in the past few years and is hailed as the third largest ecosystem in the world after the US and UK. Sometimes India rivals UK by securing the second spot.

Drivers of Growth

With support from Government and Corporates, there is significant increase in the number of active incubators and accelerators which are aiding entrepreneurs experiment with new ideas and providing them with functional expertise and resources. While Bengaluru, NCR, Hyderabad and Mumbai continue to be the major Startup hubs, a positive development is that with increased interest in entrepreneurship, 20 per cent of startups have emerged from Tier-II/III cities.

Undeterred by the risk of failure or downturns, young entrepreneurs are driving a wave of Startup movement in the country. There is increased interest from student entrepreneurs and in 2016, over 350 Startups were founded by young students.

India has the advantage of talent, technology and market. Indian Startups are able to provide critical services and solutions for large multinationals on the back of digital revolution which is sweeping the world. Due to growing need for scaling up capabilities and operations, Indian entrepreneurs will continue to attract global attention for funding.

The Changing Scene

The mix of categories of startups is undergoing change in response to technological changes and need to cater to changing requirements of industry and society.

- While B2C category of startups is dominant in India, those in B2B segment is also growing. Between 2014 and 2018, the number of B2B startups in India more than tripled from 900 to 3,200. In 2018, overall investment in India's B2B startups stood at $ 3.7 billion.
- Number of advanced tech startups estimated to be over 700 is growing at 25 to 30 per cent. This growth is driven mainly by need for expertise in areas like artificial intelligence and machine learning.
- Indian Startups catering to domains like education, healthcare, fintech, etc. are mushrooming to meet the changing societal needs. They are disrupting way ahead of the industry, seizing upon opportunities and disrupting the status quo, and are innovating across sectors, be it health, manufacturing, education, financial inclusion, transport and logistics, sustainability or agriculture.

Hiring by Startups

The Startup rush to recruit talent has reached IITs, NITs, IIMs, engineering colleges, and some of the leading undergraduate colleges in Economics and Commerce and Design schools. Annual salaries offered by startups at Engineering colleges and Business schools have increased substantially.

Startups are hiring students for diverse roles which include software development engineers, data scientists, analytics, core management, product and graphic designers, operations and marketing, merchant acquisition, and human resource management.

Startups are keen to tap fresh talent to work on cutting-edge technology and delivery models. Most Startups are tech-based and growing at a fast pace. Many Startups prefer campus-fresh talent who may bring in fresh ideas, rather than experienced hands, for innovative projects which involve applying new generation technology and systems.

❑ ROLE OF STARTUPS

India has a plethora of socio-economic problems which call for innovative and cost-effective solutions which can reach a wider section of the society. Startups are entering new, uncharted areas and leveraging technology to solve myriad problems the country is facing with innovative products and unique solutions. *Some of these are*:

- **Traffic:** Traffic congestion is estimated to cost the nation $10 billion. Intelligent traffic planning and monitoring provide real time information and solutions;
- **Agriculture productivity and prices:** Web and mobile based ICT help farmers to enhance their efficiency and improve yields and fetch better prices for produce through real time information;
- **Skilling and employment:** A two-way recruitment platform to link industry and firms with candidates seeking jobs and help aspiring candidates find suitable jobs;
- **Web based and mobile platform to connect patients with doctors:** IT based healthcare solutions and diagnostic procedures which can help, particularly those in rural areas lacking healthcare facilities;
- **Educational platforms:** These platforms impart learning and connect teachers with students seeking assistance in education;
- **Developing financial platforms:** These platforms facilitate banking services and partnering with banks to promote schemes like financial inclusion, especially in rural areas; providing information to people needing credit on sources of finance.

- **Other Potential Domains for Startups:** The Startup scene has been continuously evolving with fast-paced changes happening across the spectrum. Apart from domains like online retailing, food-tech, education and healthcare, startups are venturing into areas like biotech, logistics, fintech, B2B commerce, machine learning, data analytics, artificial intelligence, and Blockchain which offer great potential for growth of startups.

❑ UNION BUDGET 2018-19 AND START UPS

The Union budget for 2018-19 refers to many of these areas, as mentioned below, which will also open up many vistas for startups to work on and find solutions suited to India's needs.

- Global economy is transforming into a digital economy thanks to development of cutting edge technologies in digital space – machine learning, artificial intelligence, internet of things, 3D printing and the like. Initiatives such as Digital India, Start Up India, Make in India would help India establish itself as a knowledge and digital society. NITI Aayog will initiate a national program to direct efforts in the area of artificial intelligence, including research and development of its applications.
- Combining cyber and physical systems have great potential to transform not only innovation ecosystem but also our economies and the way we live. To invest in research, training and skilling in robotics, artificial intelligence, digital manufacturing, big data analysis, quantum communication and internet of things, Department of Science & Technology will launch a Mission on Cyber Physical Systems to support establishment of Centres of Excellence. The budget has doubled the allocation on Digital India programme to ₹3,073 crore in 2018-19.
- The task of connecting one lakh Gram Panchayats through high speed optical fiber network has been completed under Phase I of the Bharatnet project. This has enabled broadband access to over 20 crore rural Indians in about 2,50,000 villages. The Government also proposes to set up five lakh Wi-Fi hotspots which will provide broadband access to five crore rural citizens. The budget has provided ₹10,000 crore in 2018-19 for creation and augmentation of telecom infrastructure.
- Distributed ledger system or the Blockchain technology allows organization of any chain of records or transactions without the need of intermediaries. The Government will explore use of Blockchain technology proactively for ushering in digital economy.

❑ CHANGING MANUFACTURING AND TRADE LANDSCAPE

Digital technologies are transforming the pattern and mode of manufacturing and global trade. Automation of industry is taking manufacturing back to the West, a trend which, if it continues on a large scale, will shrink global trade in physical form and will open up opportunities for nations well-grounded in digital technology to develop platforms for the age of digital trade. This is an area which startups can potentially exploit in future. With reshoring of manufacturing to the West, East-West physical trade flows will decline.

For instance, Adidas, the giant sports-goods firm, a $80 billion-a-year industry, which had outsourced production largely to China, Vietnam and Indonesia is setting up factories in Germany and the US to start production there. Many factors are behind this move. Apart from rising labour costs in production facilities in Asian countries where the work is done mostly manually, these offshore centres are unable to keep pace with changes in fashions and designs which consumers in western markets are looking for, and problems in supply chain and shipping costs. The new factories will be highly automated and driven by software with robots, knitting machines and 3D printers taking instructions directly from the computer-design program. This will enable them to switch from one design and one product to another quickly, without having to send samples back and forth, stop production for several days in order to retool conventional machines and instructing manual workers.

The new functions will also be more highly skilled. For now, Adidas wants the new plants to complement the Asian operations, not to compete with them. But as advanced manufacturing expands, the need for armies of manual workers in Asian factories will surely diminish which will have adverse impact on jobs in these countries.

At the same time, small and medium enterprise (SME) trade will rise globally and within the country, driven by growth of e-commerce and digital platforms like Amazon, Flipkart, etc. All these changes in global trade will provide scope for startups to come up with innovative solutions.

The current environment for manufacturing and international trade is conducive and presents India with an unprecedented opportunity to chart a labour-intensive, export-driven growth and thereby create job opportunities on a large-scale for our burgeoning youth. Continual upgrading the skills of India's workforce will be crucial in this plan.

By integrating 'Assemble in India for the world' into 'Make in India', India can create an estimated 4 crore well-paid jobs by 2025 and 8 crore jobs by 2030. Exports of network products, which is expected to equal $ 7 trillion worldwide in 2025, can contribute a quarter of the increase in value-added towards India's target of $5 trillion economy.

India should reap gains from participation in "global value chains" (GVCs) by promoting strong linkages among domestic industries and engaging in GVCs wherein linkages are globally dispersed. This has become critical with many MNCs trying to quit China following Covid-19 and disruptions in supplies from China which had virtual monopoly in many areas.

❑ FUNDING FOR STARTUPs

There has been no dearth of funds for Startups in India though the sector is at a nascent stage. Venture capital (VC) firms and Angel investors are two prime sources which provide seed capital and funds for Startups. A Startup goes through different stages in its growth, such as the seed stage, the early stage, and the growth stage and the extent of funding depends upon the stage and success potential of the business model.

Venture Capital

Venture capital is fund provided by investors to Startup firms and small businesses which are perceived to have growth potential over the long term. They invest at an early stage of a Startup and are an important source of funding for Startups which do not have access to capital markets. It entails risk for the investor, but it has the potential for fetching better returns. Where the investment amount is high, the venture capital firm may choose to take a minority stake in the Startup. Venture capital firms are likely to help Startups in garnering funds in subsequent rounds also. Where there is certainty of the scalability of the venture and the promoter is not obsessive about retaining independent control, there are better chances of securing private funding.

Angel Investors

Angel investors are high net worth individuals or serial entrepreneurs or leading business executives who invest in a Startup. They may also be a group of individuals who pool in funds to invest. One needs to have the right contacts or professional network to land such funding, besides having the right credentials and a passable business proposition.

Some of the most sought-after sectors are biotech, IT and IT-enabled services, education, healthcare, mobile value-added services, E-commerce, and green technology ventures.

Funding Position in India

As stated earlier, the government has created a 'Fund of Funds for Startups' (FFS) at Small Industries Development Bank of India (SIDBI) with a corpus of ₹10,000 crore. The FFS shall contribute to the corpus of Alternate Investment funds (AIFs) for investing in equity and equity linked instruments of various Startups.

Venture capital firms and Angel investors have helped to drive innovation and provide momentum for the growth of the Startup segment in India. In 2014, an E-commerce firm could raise $1 billion. Following that, other smaller Internet companies could also raise substantial funds giving a fillip to the sector.

After a phase of slow but mature growth, the ecosystem has come a long way and witnessed rising trends in funding from 2015. While 2020 was buffeted by the pandemic Covid-19, the adoption of internet-based solutions in the country has had a positive impact and this will improve the investor confidence in 2021 and perhaps beyond.

For long the Indian startup ecosystem has banked on ecommerce giants and other vertical platforms. But over the past six years, the average annual growth rate of capital inflow in fintech startups is higher as compared to ecommerce. Other major segments of the Indian tech startups, education and health tech which also get sizeable portion of funding.

India has become a preferred investment destination due to expanding online consumer base, stock market listing of startups and China's crackdown on tech companies. Indian internet startups have raised over $20 billion from global investors in 2021, breaking previous record.

Startup India Seed Fund Scheme (SISFS)

Easy availability of capital is essential for entrepreneurs at the early stages of growth of an enterprise. Funding from angel investors and venture capital firms becomes available to startups only after the proof of concept has been provided. Similarly, banks provide loans only to asset-backed applicants. It is essential to provide seed funding to startups with an innovative idea to conduct proof of concept trials.

The Startup India initiative of the Government of India envisages building a robust Start-up ecosystem in the country for nurturing innovation and providing opportunities to budding entrepreneurs. Many activities have been undertaken to encourage Startups. One such scheme is Startup India Seed Fund Scheme (SISFS) which provides financial assistance to early-stage startups.

DPIIT has created SISFS with an outlay of ₹945 Crore to provide financial assistance to startups for Proof of Concept, prototype development, product trials, market entry, and commercialization. It would support an estimated 3,600 entrepreneurs through 300 incubators over 4 years.

❑ LIMITATIONS AND CHALLENGES TO STARTUPS

While the environment for Startups has been conducive with the economy on a high growth trajectory, the risks associated with Startups remain. Some Startups may not take off and fail within the first five years. In the early stages, a Startup may need handholding by a mentor or incubator to figure out and develop a suitable business model.

Unless an entrepreneur is very experienced, he would not be able to deal with the challenges posed by a Startup single-handedly. The entrepreneur's credentials, integrity, sustainability, and capital efficiency of the business model are crucial and should not become limiting factors. That is why many IT Startups, which are both capital-efficient and easily scalable, find favour with investors. The investors may also be chary of one-man enterprises where everything depends on one person and the risk factor is more.

There is also the need for an exit strategy. The basic aim of a venture capital investor will be to sell his stake for a profit after 4 to 5 years. So the need for options for the next round of investment, from a private equity player or the possibility of an IPO or a potential buyer, becomes necessary.

In the ultimate analysis, the Startup movement is critical for India for promoting entrepreneurship and generation of much needed jobs for youth and hence, both the government and the industry should work hand in hand for its success.

As stated earlier, the government has taken steps to promote innovation and entrepreneurship among the youth through Atal Innovation Mission (AIM) launched by NITI Aayog. (See Box 23.1).

Box 23.1 Atal Innovation Mission (AIM)

Atal Innovation Mission (AIM) which aims at Self-Employment and Talent Utilization (SETU) is Government of India's endeavour to promote a culture of innovation and entrepreneurship. Its objective is to serve as a platform for promotion of world-class Innovation Hubs, Grand Challenges, Startup businesses and other self-employment activities, particularly in technology driven areas.

The Mission has two core objectives:

- Entrepreneurship promotion through Self-Employment and Talent Utilization, wherein innovators would be supported and mentored to become successful entrepreneurs;
- Innovation promotion: to provide a platform where innovative ideas are generated.

The scheme has three components:

- Atal Tinkering Labs;
- Atal Incubation Centres; and
- Scale-up support to established incubators.

Atal Tinkering Labs (ATL): Atal Tinkering Lab is a work space where young minds can give shape to their ideas through hands on do-it-yourself mode; and learn innovation skills. Young children will get a chance to work with tools and equipment to understand the concepts of STEM (Science, Technology, Engineering and Math). The mission will provide grant-in-aid that includes a one-time establishment cost of ₹10 lakh and operational expenses of ₹10 lakh for a maximum period of 5 years to each ATL. Schools (having Grades VI - X) managed by Government, local body or private trusts/ society are eligible to set up ATL.

Atal Incubation Centres (AICs): The mission aims to create AICs that would nurture innovative Startup businesses in their pursuit to become scalable and sustainable enterprises. The AICs would create world class incubation facilities in various parts of India with suitable physical infrastructure in terms of capital equipment and operating facilities, with sectoral experts for mentoring the Startups, business planning support, access to seed capital, industry partners, training and other support needed for encouraging innovative Startups. AICs would be established in subject specific areas such as manufacturing, transport, energy, health, education, agriculture, water and sanitation etc. Higher educational institutions, R&D institutes, corporate sector, alternative investment funds registered with SEBI, business accelerators, group of individuals, and individuals are eligible to set up AICs. They have to provide ready-to-use, built-up space, for the exclusive use of the AIC. They will be given a grant-in-aid of up to ₹10 crore for a maximum period of 5 years to cover the capital and operational expenditures to establish the AIC.

Scale-up support to Established Incubation Centres (EICs): This aims to augment capacity of established incubators the in the country and radically transform the Startup ecosystem by upgrading the EICs to world-class standards.

EIC should be registered in India as public, private or public-private partnership and must have been in operation for a minimum of three years as of 1st August 2017. NITI Aayog has selected six EICs for scale-up support.

In this Chapter we discussed.....

- 'Startup India, Stand up India' mission launched to tap the entrepreneurial potential and talent, particularly among the youth.
- Launching the initiative, the PM pointed out that successful Startups are driven by an idea or an urge to solve a problem and a sense of compassion to help others.
- The government announced a series of measures to promote and incentivize Startups including tax exemption for sometime, financial support, the government has followed up on these and taken various steps to foster the startup ecosystem.

- The scheme is handled by the Department for Promotion of Industry and Internal Trade (DPIIT) under the Ministry of Commerce which has held consultations with IITs, IIMs, some existing Startups, as also mentors and incubators.
- India is a leading Startup nation behind only the US and UK; number of startups reached 44,766 by March 2021. A sizeable section of the founders are of less than 35 years of age; incubators and accelerators which help the startups are drivers of growth.
- Startups recruit talent from IITs, NITs, IIMs, engineering colleges, and leading undergraduate colleges in Economics and Commerce and Design schools.
- Startups can play an important role in solving socio-economic problems which call for innovative and cost-effective solutions such as traffic problems, agricultural productivity, skilling and employment, education, and healthcare.
- Startups are also engaged in diverse domains such as product design and architecture, mobile technology and IT services, software development, semiconductor technology, online ticketing services, home delivery services, etc.
- Many other domains like biotech, logistics, fintech, B2B commerce, machine learning, data analytics, artificial intelligence, and Blockchain have emerged which offer great potential for growth of startups.
- The Union budget for 2018-19 has referred to many of the above-mentioned domains and for which funding has also been increased.
- Changing landscape of manufacturing and global trade holds potential for tech startups well grounded in digital technology to develop digital platforms for various services.
- Venture capital (VC) firms and Angel investors are two prime sources of funds for Startups; Startups having growth potential over the long term and having scope for scalability of the venture have better chances of securing private funding; Angel investors are high net worth individuals or serial entrepreneurs or leading business executives who invest in a Startup; funding position for startups in the last few years presents a mixed picture.
- India has become a preferred investment destination. India internet startups have raised over $20 billion from global investors in 2021, breaking previous record.
- Some of the most sought-after sectors are biotech, IT and IT-enabled services, education, healthcare, mobile value-added services, E-commerce, and green technology ventures.
- Startup India Seed Fund Scheme (SISFS) has been set up for nurturing innovation and providing opportunities to budding entrepreneurs.
- Insolvency and Bankruptcy Board of India has been constituted. Startups shall be able to wind up their business on fast track basis.

- While the environment for Startups has been conducive, the risks associated with Startups remain and the sector faces some limitations and challenges; the entrepreneur's credentials, integrity, sustainability, and capital efficiency of the business model are crucial and should not become limiting factors; investors also expect good returns; a business with low scope for growth and scalability may not find favour with investors.
- With larger, young workforce technically skilled and managerial aspersion and a vast domestic market, India offers an ideal ground for startups to promote at entrepreneurship and creation of jobs.
- Atal Innovation Mission (AIM) which aims at Self-Employment and Talent Utilization (SETU) is being implemented by NITI Aayog to promote a culture of innovation and entrepreneurship.

Important Terms to Note in this Chapter

Startup; Ecosystem; Incubator; Accelerators; Tinkering lab; Patent; Intellectual property right; Venture capital; Angel investor; Private equity; E-commerce; Scalability; Unicorn; Cyber Securities; Fintech; Drones; Robotics.

Practice Questions

1. What are the main features of the 'Start Up India' mission launched by the Government of India? Critically examine how successful the programme has been.
2. Enumerate the various steps taken by Government of India to promote the Startup ecosystem?
3. In what way the Indian economy will be benefited by the Startup ecosystem?
4. How effective has been venture capital financing for Startups in India?
5. What is meant by the terms 'Venture Capital' and 'Angel Investment'? What is their role in the growth of startups?
6. Enumerate the steps Indian startups need to take to attract more funds for their operations and scaling up.
7. In the Indian and global context, identify the domains and emerging areas which hold potential for startups to develop and grow.
8. In what way startups can contribute to the socio-economic development of the country.
9. What are the challenges faced by Startups in India and how can they be overcome?
10. Explain the objectives and salient features of Atal Innovation Mission. In what way it would help to develop and expand the Startup ecosystem in India?

INFRASTRUCTURE

- Infrastructure in Union Budget
- Road sector – National Highways
- National Highway Projects: Funding and Execution
- Bharatmala Project
- Pradhan Mantri Gram Sadak Yojana (PMGSY)
- Status of Electric Vehicles (EVs) in India
- Setu Bharatam Project
- Railways: Growth and Modernisation
- Aviation Sector and UDAN Scheme
- Ports and Shipping
- Maritime Summit and Sagarmala Project
- Power Sector Reforms
- UJALA: Affordable and Health-Safe LED Lighting Scheme
- Saubhagya Yojana: Household Electrification
- Renewable Energy: Solar and Wind Power
- Telecommunications
- Digital India: BharatNet Project
- National Investment & Infrastructure Fund
- National Monetisation Pipeline (NMP)
- Economic Growth and Employment: Role of Infrastructure

❑ INTRODUCTION

The importance of infrastructure—various modes of transport and means of communications—has been brought out in Chapter 10. The railways and roadways which carry a major part of both freight and passenger traffic are particularly crucial. While India has developed a good network of highways in the last decade and a half, in the last few years many projects got stalled due to various reasons—land acquisition delays, want of environment clearances, budget constraints, unfavourable market conditions,

* *For more on the topics in this chapter, see also chapter 10*

or lack of promoter interest in the case of private sector or PPP projects. As a result, large quantum of loans advanced to the sector by the banks had come under stress and turned bad, adding to the problem of loan defaults faced by banks. Since taking over office in May 2014, the government has taken several steps to revive the projects and put them on track.

❑ INFRASTRUCTURE IN UNION BUDGET

Given the importance of infrastructure in a vast country of sub-continental size like India, it is accorded high priority in Union budgets. India needs massive investments, estimated to be in excess of ₹50 lakh crore, in infrastructure to increase the growth of GDP, connect and integrate the nation with a network of roads, railways, airports, ports and inland waterways and to provide good quality services to people. Estimated expenditure on infrastructure in Union budget for 2018-19 is pegged at ₹5.97 lakh crore as against ₹4.94 lakh crore provided in 2017-18 budget, a 20 per cent increase.

❑ ROAD SECTOR—NATIONAL HIGHWAYS

The National and State highways are of vital importance. The length of National highways which was 70,934 kms. in 2011 has risen to 1,14,158 kms. in 2017 and to 1,36,440 km in 2020 but they constitute just a little over 2 per cent of the total road network but carry as much as 40 per cent of the total road traffic. National and State highways together constitute 4.98 per cent of total road network in the country. (See chapter 10, Table 10.3 on p. 10.5).

The National Highways & Infrastructure Development Corporation Limited (NHIDCL) has been entrusted by the Govt. of India with the task of developing and improving road connectivity in length of about 13,000 km including the international trade corridor in the North-Eastern region of India. Special attention has been paid to building road network in the border states of Assam, Arunachal Pradesh, Manipur, Meghalaya, Mizoran, Nagaland, J & K and other areas.

Apart from the highways, the road network consists of PWD roads, Panchayati Raj roads, PMGSY roads and other rural and urban roads. In course of time, more of the PWD (district) roads will get upgraded to State highways and State highways to National highways. Such upgradation of both urban and rural roads is essential to cater to the needs of the expanding economy.

Reviving Highway Projects: Earlier, many of the National highway projects had got stalled due to various reasons including land acquisition, utility shifting, delay in obtaining statutory clearances, litigations and financial problems of the concessionaires and frequent ban in mining nearby the project area and insufficient availability of raw material for construction etc. While some of them could not be resolved and had to be terminated, others were revived after the government took various remedial measures. These included:

- One-time fund infusion to revive and physically complete those projects under Public-Private Partnership (PPP) mode.
- Providing rationalised compensation to concessionaires where delays were not attributable to them and by increased flow of funds into the highway sector.
- Adopting Hybrid Annuity model for construction.
- Monetization of public funded highways.
- Exit policy permitting 100 per cent divestment. (See chapter 10, p. 10.6-7 on this).

The Toll-Operate-Transfer (TOT) aimed at monetizing public funded highways has found positive response from investors. The National Highway Authority plans to award toll roads to private sector entities for operations and maintenance for a fixed period in lieu of an upfront fee under the TOT model. This would help to mobilise additional resources for constructing new highways. (See Box 24.1)

Box 24.1 National Highway Projects: Funding and Execution

In India, highway road projects are awarded via one of the three models: Build-Operate-Transfer (BOT)-Annuity, BOT-Toll, and EPC (Engineering, Procurement and Construction) contract. After the BOT model of Public Private Partnership (PPP), an advanced version of the Model Concession Agreement (MCA), presently called as Hybrid Annuity Model (HAM), is seen to be a more viable model for road projects. The hybrid model is supposed to be a win-win situation for the government and developers.

Reforms in Funding and Execution of Highway Projects

To ensure Ease of Doing Business and the financing and execution of National Highway projects, the Government has taken several steps as detailed below.

- **InvIT:** To improve NHAI's resource mobilization, the government has authorized NHAI to set up Infrastructure Investment Trust (InvIT) to monetize completed National Highways that have a toll collection track record of at least one year. NHAI reserves the right to levy toll on the identified highway and incorporate Special Purpose Vehicles (SPVs), which are an essential part of the InvIT structure.

Toll Operate Transfer (TOT)

With a view to expanding the project base available with NHAI for monetization under TOT mode and for raising finance against toll receipts from identified Public Funded/Hybrid Annuity Model (HAM) projects,

NHAI has been allowed to raise long-term finance from banks by securitizing the user fee receipts from fee plazas as alternate mode of asset monetization.

NHAI has been authorized by the Ministry in August 2020 to form Special Purpose Vehicle (SPV), wholly owned by NHAI, for financing, construction and operation of Delhi-Mumbai Greenfield Expressway under Companies Act 2013, which will work on raising low interest capital through securitization of user fee receipts.

Changes in Model Concession Agreement (MCA) of BOT (Toll) Project

Considering the key challenges in Build-Operate-Transfer (BOT) - (Toll) model faced by stakeholders, changes have been brought about in this framework in regard to Project Preparation, Dispute Resolution limitation of liability, policy for resolution of stuck projects, etc. Besides, other reforms such as use of latest technology for traffic and road condition monitoring, Additional Performance Security, etc. have also been introduced.

Changes in MCA of HAM model

To address the issues under Hybrid Annuity Mode (HAM) raised by stakeholders, changes in the provisions relating to Change in Ownership (Exit Option), Shifting of Utilities, Maintenance during Construction Period, Financial Close, Payment during Construction Period, applicable Bank Rate, Termination Payment and Dispute Resolution, etc. in the Model Concession Agreement (MCA) of HAM have been made.

Conditions for works under HAM and EPC Models

Conditions for these works being executed by different agencies have been reformed as mentioned below to facilitate smooth execution of works taking into account unforeseen contingencies which may be faced.

- Condition in Contracts has been relaxed to enable payments at monthly interval for the work completed as per specifications.
- Extension of time allowed to contractors under Force Majeure Clause due to COVID pandemic.
- Direct payments to approved subcontractors by the Departmental authority towards works done by them wherever competent authority is satisfied that it is required for early completion of work in accordance with contract.
- Expeditious approval of change of scope of work if required, and payment to the extent of work executed as per specification.
- Waiver of penalty for delay in submission of Performance Security/ Bank Guarantee for new contracts entered into during March - September 2020 period.
- Performance Security provided by contractor/supplier to be returned by the Contractee (Government Department/Agency) in proportion to the supplies made/contract work completed.

Bharatmala Project

The government has approved the ambitious 'Bharatmala Pariyojana' to develop about 35,000 kms. in the first phase for providing seamless connectivity of interior and backward regions and border areas of the country. The expanded border road projects such as the completed all-weather proof Rohtang tunnel linking Ladakh region and the Zojila Pass and Sela Pass tunnels will provide enhanced security to our borders.

Bharatmala Pariyojana (Phase-1) approved in October 2017 involved construction/up-gradation of National Highways of 34,800 kms length over a period of 5 years from 2017 to 2022. Estimated to cost ₹ 5,35,000 crore, the project consists of Border Roads, International Connectivity Roads, Economic Corridor and Feeder Route-Inland Waterways and is being executed by NHIDCL.

Under this, 35 locations have been identified for development of Multimodal Logistics Parks to reduce congestion on proposed Corridors, enhance logistic efficiency and reduce logistics costs of freight movements. It is estimated that more than 35 crore man-days of employment shall be generated under Phase-I of the programme.

Pradhan Mantri Gram Sadak Yojana (PMGSY)

The Rural Roads programme, known as the Pradhan Mantri Gram Sadak Yojana (PMGSY) was launched in December, 2000. It is an infrastructure critical to social, economic and agricultural growth and for poverty alleviation in the country. Since inception, it has made substantial progress as can be seen from Table 24.1.

Table 24.1 PMGSY Programme (2000 - 2017)

Habitations eligible for PMGSY roads	1,71,184
Habitations sanctioned for PMGSY roads	1,57,443 (91.9 %)
Habitations covered by PMGSY roads	1,53,918 (97.8 %)
Road length built under PMGSY since inception	6,41,650 kms.

Source: Ministry of Rural Development, Govt. of India

Since inception, 6,41,650 all-weather roads have been constructed under PMGSY improving connectivity of villages with nearby towns and urban areas. Further construction and upgradation of existing village roads is also in progress. Special focus is given on consolidation of existing Through Routes and Major Rural Links that connect habitations to Gramin Agricultural Markets (GrAMs), Higher Secondary Schools and Hospitals.

This is significant considering that contrary to the common perception about predominance of agriculture in rural economy, about two-third of rural income is now generated in non-agricultural activities and more than half of the value added in manufacturing sector in India is contributed by rural areas as observed in a NITI Aayog paper on "Changing Structure of Rural Economy of India: Implications for Employment and Growth".

❑ Electric Vehicles

There is a growing realisation in India and elsewhere that hybrid and electric cars are needed in view of the growing threat of environmental pollution which also poses serious health hazard. The need is felt even more as thousands of air polluting petrol and diesel vehicles are coming on the road day after day. More and more automobile and bike companies have evinced interest in manufacturing electric vehicles and are entering this niche segment.

An electric vehicle (EV) can be powered by electricity from off-vehicle sources or with a battery, solar panels. EVs include road and rail vehicles, surface and underwater vessels, electric aircraft, and electric spacecraft. The biggest challenge with electric vehicles so far was storing enough power, so that it can go long distances with few batteries in the vehicle. But lately there have been major breakthroughs in battery technology opening up more prospects for their introduction on larger scale.

Benefits of Electric Vehicles

- **Cost-effective:** As electric engines are more efficient, they are inherently more cost-effective.
- **Less pollution:** Petrol-driven vehicles contribute to pollution in many ways right from the extraction of petrol to its burning. These include air and noise pollution, and release of harmful gases in the environment. Electric Vehicles, on the other hand, can use renewable energy.
- **Low maintenance:** With less complex mechanisms, electric vehicles require considerably less maintenance over the course of their lifetime.

- **Energy efficient:** Electric Vehicles are more energy efficient as they do not consume electricity while stationary, unlike internal combustion engines which consume fuel while idling. The efficiency of conventional vehicles is mostly 30 to 40 per cent, while electric vehicles can be up to 90 to 95 per cent efficient.

Status of Electric Vehicles (EVs) in India

There is an imperative case for introducing Electric Vehicles (EVs) in India. India imports more than 80 per cent of the petroleum it uses. The shift towards electric vehicles will have a positive and far-reaching impact on the economy as well as the environment. While the future of EVs – cars and bikes – is inevitable, it is to be seen how soon India will be able to adapt to it. The explosion of mobile phones in India is an indication that people will adapt and accept change if it eases their lives and prices and running costs are at affordable levels.

If well implemented, the shift towards EVs will enhance India's energy security, reduce dependence on oil imports, save valuable foreign exchange and help India in fulfilling its commitments in Paris Climate Change Agreement.

India has unveiled in 2013 the **'National Electric Mobility Mission Plan 2020'**, an ambitious initiative by the Government of India which has the potential to bring about a transformational, paradigm shift in the automotive and transportation sector in the country. This is the result of a comprehensive and collaborative planning for promotion of hybrid and electric mobility in India through policies aimed at gradually ensuring a vehicle population of about 6 to 7 million electric / hybrid vehicles in India by 2020. It also envisages a certain level of indigenisation of technology to ensure India's leadership in vehicle segments.

In 2015, the Union government came up with the FAME scheme (Faster Adoption and Manufacturing of Electrical Vehicles) in India. It aims to provide subsidy for EVs to boost its adoption in the country. Some of the automobile and bike manufacturers in India have already taken the initiative to produce electric vehicles and are planning to expand production facilities. Electric two-wheelers which need lighter batteries for charging are relatively more viable for adoption than electric cars. Firms are also planning to make lithium-ion (Li-on) batteries, which are much lighter and have longer life than the earlier lead-acid batteries, for use in EVs.

Status of EV Mobility in India

There is an imperative case for introducing Electric Vehicles (EVs) in India. India imports more than 80 per cent of the petroleum it uses. The shift towards electric vehicles will have a positive and far-reaching impact on the economy as well as the environment. While the future of EVs - cars and bikes - is inevitable, it is to be seen how soon India will be able to adapt to it. The explosion of mobile phones in India is an indication that people will adapt and accept change if it eases their lives and prices and running costs are at affordable levels. The fairly enthusiastic response to electric Two-wheeler vehicles is a pointer to this.

A look at the overall size of India's automobile market and the extent of sales of electric vehicles shown below will give an idea of the imperative need for India to switch to EVs to improve environmental standards, meet commitments made in Paris Climate Agreement and the long way India has to go.

Box 24.2 India's Automobile Market: Salient Facts

- In 2020, India was the fifth largest automobile market.
- It was the seventh largest manufacturer of commercial vehicles in 2019.
- In FY 2020-21, the total passenger vehicles production reached 22,652,108 (22.65 million).
- In FY 2019-20, two wheelers and passenger cars accounted for 80.8 per cent and 12.9 per cent market share, respectively, accounting for a combined sale of over 20.1 million vehicles.
- Overall, automobile export reached 4.77 million vehicles in 2019-20, growing at a CAGR of 6.94% during 2016-20. Two wheelers made up 73.9% of the vehicles exported, followed by passenger vehicles at 14.2%, three wheelers at 10.5% and commercial vehicles at 1.3%.
- The two wheelers segment dominate the market in terms of volume owing to a growing middle class and a young population. Passenger car sales are dominated by small and mid-sized cars.
- The growing interest of auto companies in exploring the rural markets has aided the growth of the sector.

Table 24.2 Sales of Electric Vehicles in FY 2020 and FY 2021

Category	FY 2021 (units)	FY 2020 (units)	Growth (%)
Two-wheelers	1,43,837	1,52,000	-- 5.37
Three-wheelers	88,378	1,40,683	-- 37.18
Cars	5,905	2,814	109.84
Total	2,38,120	2,95,497	-- 19.42

Source: Society of Manufacturers of Electric Vehicles (SMEV).

India is obliged to reduce its global emissions, owing to the Paris Climate Agreement it signed in 2016. Backing the government's e-mobility targets set for 2030, the NITI Aayog has proposed that only electric vehicles (EVs) should be sold in India by 2030. It has asked the Ministry of Road Transport and Highways to prepare a framework to stop sale of Internal Combustion Engine (ICE) vehicles as such a move will expand India's clean fuel vision.

NEMM Plan 2020

India unveiled in 2013 **he National Electric Mobility Mission Plan 2020 (NEMMP 2020)**, one of the most important and ambitious initiatives undertaken by the Government of India, that has the potential to bring about a transformational paradigm shift in the automotive and transportation industry in the country. This is a culmination of a comprehensive collaborative planning for promotion of hybrid and electric mobility in India through a combination of policies aimed at gradually ensuring a vehicle population of about 6-7 million electric/hybrid vehicles in India by the year 2020 along with a certain level of indigenisation of technology ensuring India's global leadership in some vehicle segments.

Though India had set ambitious target for EV's, by July 2021, only 5.20 lakh electrical automobiles had been registered within the nation. The government of India has undertaken multiple initiatives to promote manufacturing and adoption of electric vehicles in India. With support of the government, electric vehicles have started penetrating in the Indian market.

NITI Aayog on E-Mobility

The government think-tank NITI Aayog has recommended providing incentives to manufacturers of EVs to facilitate the growth of the EV industry. NITI Aayog has estimated that electric cars, buses, and metros could help India save $60 billion by 2030.

It will also require a nationwide revamp of the existing infrastructure in urban and rural areas. The challenge is to build infrastructure for battery charging across the country. If the government allocates enough resources to a designated authority and align it with the Smart City scheme under execution and housing and electrification schemes, the switch over could be that much smoother.

Box 24.3 Promoting Electric Vehicles in India

The Indian Electric Vehicle (EV) Market is segmented by Vehicle Type (Passenger Cars, Commercial Vehicles, Two- and Three-wheelers), and Power Source Type (Battery Electric Vehicle, Plug-in Electric Vehicle, and Hybrid Electric Vehicle).

The Indian Electric Vehicle Market was valued at US$ 5 billion in 2020, and it is expected to reach US$ 47 billion by 2026, registering a CAGR of above 44 per cent during 2021-2026 period.

With the growing need for controlling GHG (Greenhouse gases) emissions from vehicles, the government is encouraging the use of electric-powered vehicles across various states, including electric buses in India. The market is driven by factors such as the rising costs of oil bulk of which is imported, increase in domestic manufacturing, rapid urbanization, and increasing environmental awareness.

The EV market in India has gained significant momentum after the implementation of FAME India scheme. The total EV sales in 2018 hit 365,920 Units and expected to grow at a CAGR of 36% till 2026. The EV battery market in India is estimated to be US$ 520 Million in 2018 and forecasted to grow at a CAGR of 30% till 2026.

Emission Standards

As a result of the surging pollution, the national government has launched stringent policies to curb vehicular emissions. The industry is to transition from Bharat Stage V (BSV) to BSVI emission standards. From 1st April 2020 onward, automakers are only allowed to sell BSVI-compliant vehicles in the nation, driving the push toward electric variants.

Electric Two-wheeler Vehicles Poised for Healthy Growth

With transportation still being a challenge in India, a lot of people look forward to the two-wheeler industry in India. In particular, the jump from Bharat Stage V (BSV) to BSVI emission standards is expected to benefit the Indian electric scooter and motorcycle market, by raising the prices of petrol-driven two-wheelers by 7–15%. From 1st April 2020 onward, automakers are only allowed to sell BSVI-compliant vehicles in the nation, driving the push toward electric variants.

For extracting the maximum revenue from the rapidly growing Indian electric scooter and motorcycle market, original equipment manufacturers (OEMs) are expanding their facilities.

Public Transport

India is experimenting with e-Mobility for public transport, and the country has deployed electric inter-city buses across some major cities. In addition, state governments are also playing an active role in the deployment of policies encouraging the usage of EVs.

Many local bus manufacturers are trying to cater to the rising demand for electric buses in India.

In February 2020, India's first inter-city electric bus service, with indigenously manufactured electric bus with a range of 300 km on a full charge was launched.

A major positive is the growing demand for EVs from the booming e-commerce sector in India. E-commerce companies are launching initiatives to use e-Mobility for last-mile deliveries to reduce carbon footprint. The need for last-mile mobility and cost-efficient logistics means e-commerce firms see EVs being cheaper to maintain compared to ICE vehicles. Recent moves in this direction from Amazon India and Flipkart confirm plans to use EVs in their fleet of delivery vehicles.

Positive Factors

EV Policy Implementation at State Level

The early implementation of state-level policy could assist in creating a larger ecosystem in the country that would help the industry to grow at a much faster pace. Additionally, the state government policy should be focused on demand generation for the initial period that would help in getting more volumes on the road.

What augurs well for the long-term future of e-mobility in the country is that a number of states, including Delhi, Maharashtra, Andhra Pradesh, Bihar, Chandigarh, Haryana, Karnataka, Kerala, Madhya Pradesh, Odisha, Meghalaya Punjab, Tamil Nadu, Telangana, Uttar Pradesh and Uttarakhand have rolled out their EV policies. However, some states are yet to implement the policy.

EV charging infrastructure

Yet another positive factor is the fast-growing EV charging infrastructure in India. At present, around 1,300 charging stations have been set up and a number of leading players like Tata Power have announced rapid expansion plans. Other companies have also begun installing charging stations across the country. It is expected that by 2026, India should have a robust charging infrastructure in place.

In January 2020, the Department of Heavy Industries (DHI) of India approved 2,636 electric vehicle charging stations in 62 cities across 24 Indian states and union territories (UTs) under the second phase of the FAME program to promote e-mobility.

Challenges to greater EV adoption

A strong bank finance mechanism for EVs is still missing in the country. Only few banks offer loans on selected models. The government should urge banks to offer loans on EVs, which will augment sales.

There also needs to be greater awareness about green vehicles. The Central and state governments can play a crucial role in motivating and encouraging citizens to adopt e-vehicles.

International Action: UNEP's Electric Mobility Programme

The programme supports developing and transitional countries shift from fossil fuel to electric vehicles. Today's transport sector is almost completely dependent on fossil fuels but this doesn't have to be the case. Leading by example, countries like Norway and China have put in place policies to support the use of electric vehicles with measurable success. Such practices need to be scaled up and replicated around the world.

Electric Mobility for Reducing GHG emissions and Air Pollution

UN Environment's Electric Mobility Programme (UNEP) supports countries, with a special focus on emerging economies, in introducing electric mobility. The Programme will be a major contribution to UN Environment's work on air quality, the UN Environment Assembly's Air Quality Resolution and the implementation of the Paris Climate Agreement.

Setu Bharatam Project

This is an ambitious project which envisages construction of bridges to make National highways free from railway level crossings across the country by 2019. Estmated to cost ₹ 50,800, it involves construction of 208 bridges at ₹ 20,800 crore and reconstruction of 1,500 old bridges at ₹ 30,000 crore.

This major step, as also all other measures to improve roads, will greatly enhance road safety which is critical considering India's horrifying road accidents record. One serious road accident occurs every minute in the country and 16 people die on Indian roads every hour. An estimated 1214 road crashes occur every day in India. Two wheelers account for 25 per cent of total road crash deaths.

Inaugurating the project in February 2016, the Prime Minister said the government aims to take a quantum leap, and not incremental steps in infrastructural development, to meet the aspirations of people and adopt a comprehensive and integrated approach.

The government has also set up an Indian Bridge Management System which will carry out a survey of the condition of all bridges by using mobile inspection units.

❑ RAILWAYS : GROWTH AND MODERNISATION

Railway transport is far more energy efficient as compared to road transport. Railways are six times more energy efficient as compared to road, four times more economical in land use and six times more cost effective vis-à-vis road in construction costs for comparable levels of traffic.

An important lifeline of the nation, the railways is overburdened by demands of traffic and has been facing a resource crunch. While there has been considerable expansion, standards of service and safety records have been below par calling for drastic action. Several committees have gone into these aspects and suggested remedies for improvement. On assuming office in 2014, the new railway dispensation has taken the bull by the horns and tackle some of the serious issues which were discussed in Chapter 10.

Strengthening the railway network and enhancing Railways' carrying capacity has been a major focus of the Government. A large part of the capital expenditure is devoted to capacity creation, by doubling the lines, building third and fourth lines and gauge conversion which would eliminate capacity constraints and transform almost entire network into Broad Gauge.

Indian Railways, an over 160 years old behemoth, has been taking several steps over the years to modernize the system. It has been facing many hurdles in its attempts to upgrade the infrastructure, improve operations and shore up its finances. While budgetary support has been on the increase, railways require more funds to be raised through other sources like multilateral funding, FDI and private capital through joint ventures to fund its expansion plans, enhance safety measures and meet rising customer expectations.

A major thrust in the recent past has been to modernize it through advanced technology particularly with a view to ensure safety in operations. Railways is planning a complete overhaul of the signaling system which is regarded as one of the root causes of rail accidents. It will be adopting cutting-edge technology of world class standard in signaling system. It will also help to enhance the capacity of the tracks as the interval between the running of trains can be reduced allowing more trains to pass through within a specified time. With more sidings and loop lines put in place, slow moving trains could be diverted to them to give way to faster trains so that track capacity is utilized more optimally instead of keeping tracks idle for long stretches of time.

Some of the important developments in Railways are mentioned here:

- **Dedicated Freight Corridor (DFC):** An important project of economic benefit, work on the Eastern and Western dedicated Freight Corridors is in progress.
- **High speed rail projects:** The railways is pursuing the ambitious plan to have a Diamond Quadrilateral Network of High Speed Rail, connecting major metros and growth centres of the country. The High Speed Rail Corporation of India Limited (HSRC) has been formed for development and implementation of high speed rail projects. While bullet trains would require completely new infrastructure, higher speed for existing trains will be achieved by upgrading the present network. Hence, efforts are being taken to increase the speed of trains to 160–200 kmph in selected sectors so as to significantly reduce travel time between major cities.
- **Railway stations redevelopment:** Redevelopment of 600 major railway stations is being taken up by Indian Railway Station Development Co. Ltd. All stations with more than 25,000 footfalls will

have escalators. All railway stations and trains will be progressively provided with Wi-Fi. CCTVs will be provided at all stations and on trains to enhance security of passengers. Other essential facilities like catering, ATM, pharmacy, Internet, etc. will be provided at the concourse.

- **Modern train-sets** with state-of-the-art amenities and features are being designed at Integrated Coach Factory, Chennai. First such train-set is to be commissioned during 2018-19.
- **To enhance safety**, track renewal is carried out on a continual basis and over 4,200 unmanned level crossings in the broad gauge network will be eliminated over 2018-20 period. Other measures include use of technology like 'Fog Safe' and 'Train Protection and Warning System'.
- Railways plans ₹10 lakh crore **high-speed train corridors** to connect all major cities in the country, covering almost 10,000 kms. along the lines of the government's Bharatmala highways development programme. Trains would be able to run at 200 km per hour on the new rail lines that would come elevated atop the existing or upcoming national highways or on rail land that runs parallel to existing rail routes.
- **MOU:** MOU signed by Railways with the Ministry of Skill Development and Entrepreneurship to make available Railway infrastructure for setting up of Skill training centres.
- **Fund generation:** Railways plan for new ways to generate funding, including through offshore rupee bonds, to meet its ambitious capital expenditure plan. It is also looking at forming joint ventures with States, signing new agreements, and engaging multilateral and bilateral agencies to mop up investments.

Railway Electrification

By March'2020, electrification on Indian Railways has been extended to 39,329 route kms out of the total rail network of 67,956 route kms. This constitutes 57.87 per cent of the total Railway Network. On this electrified route, 67.3 per cent of freight traffic & 59.6% of Passenger traffic is hauled with fuel cost on electric traction being merely 38.4 per cent of the total traction fuel cost on Indian Railways. Further, Indian Railways has planned to electrify balance BG rail routes by 2021-22 to achieve 100% electrification of BG rail routes except some spur routes. By phasing out diesel locomotives, the national transporter will save around ₹ 11,500 crore annually.

The General Electric (GE) company is setting up a diesel locomotive factory at Marhowra in Bihar, after approval by the Govt. of India, at an estimated cost of over ₹2,000 crore with limited equity contribution by the Ministry of Railways. Though the railways have said this project would go on, the plan to convert all trains to electric traction is bound to impact this manufacturing facility. This factory is to deliver 100 diesel locomotives per year on an average and 1,000 locomotives to Indian Railways over 11 years.

The Madhepura electric locomotive factory, set up in collaboration with French major Alstom for supply of 800 high-power engines, to the Railways is going ahead in full steam and electric locos have started rolling out of the factory since 2018. These heavy-haul freight service locos would be utilised for transportation of coal on Dedicated Freight Corridors.

Advantages of Railway Electrification

- **Energy Conservation: Among the modes of rail transport, electric traction is the most energy efficient. Every 100 route kilometers electrified results in saving of consumption of more than four million litres of diesel oil in a year, which will save ₹2500 crore worth of foreign exchange annually.**

- **Role of Electric Traction in Suburban Transport:** Electric Multiple Units (EMUs) are ideal for suburban services with higher acceleration and braking features required for frequent starts and stops. EMU services form the backbone of suburban transportation in the metropolitan cities of Mumbai, Kolkata and Chennai which carry millions of passengers daily. It may be mentioned in this context that the Metro systems in cities also operate on electricity.
- **Haulage of Heavier Freight Trains and Longer Passenger Trains:** Electric traction makes possible running of heavier freight trains compared to diesel locomotives, haul more number of passenger coaches in a rake and navigate difficult gradients.
- **Benefits of clearer environment:** One of the major advantages of electric traction is it causes less pollution not only for the passengers but also to the surrounding environment. Electric traction is proven to be less polluting than the existing diesel mode and thus could be more eco-friendly to areas with delicate flora and fauna. It also reduces noise and air pollution and result in lesser disturbance to wild life habitats in the vicinity.
- **Technology Upgradation:** A spin off of the process of electrification in railways in India is that it has led to major impetus to upgrading technology. Some of these are listed below:

(i) Modernization of equipment: State-for-the-art power supply equipment and modern telecommunication and signaling systems help to improve reliability and savings in maintenance costs. It also results in enhanced safety in operations and speedier movement of traffic. Underground cables provided along with electrification results in more reliable and better quality of communication.

(ii) Supervisory Remote Control & Data Acquisition System: The power supply network for electrification extending along the track length of about 200-300 kms. is centrally controlled through remote control mode to ensure un-interrupted power supply to the track. Presently, in electrification projects, state-of-the-art microprocessor-based control and data acquisition system is being employed as against the earlier electro-mechanical system. It helps to control power factor on a real-time basis and thus economise the power consumption charges. In addition, this system provides for automatic trouble shooting and isolation of faulty section.

(iii) Optical Fibre Communication: Indian Railways has also taken a policy decision that going forward along with electrification, they will lay Fibre Optic cable for a modern system of communication. Railways have also initiated steps for commercial exploitation of its communication infrastructure and claim its 'right of way' along the tracks with private parties laying their Optical Fibre Cables.

(iv) Reduction in Staff and Inventories: Even as the work of railway electrification is going on apace, it has given scope for continuous reduction of staff in the organization. There is also reduction in inventories and material costs following electrification.

(On Reforms in Railways, see chapter 10, pp. 10.12-3).

❑ AVIATION SECTOR

The aviation sector has been expanding at rapid pace in the last decade and a half even as the economy was on a high growth trajectory. In the last three years, domestic air passenger traffic grew at 18 per cent per annum and Indian airline companies have placed orders for more than 900 aircraft. The air traffic figure has crossed 250 million mark in 2016-17 and touched nearly 350 million by 2019-20 as shown in data below.

Table 24.3 Total Number of Airline Passengers (Domestic & International) (Including Departures and Arrivals)

2015-16	2016-17	2019-20
220 million	262 million	347 million

Source: Director-General of Civil Aviation and Airport Authority of India.

Note: See also Table 10.6 in chapter 10, p. 10.16 for more details.

The airport capacity which had been a bottleneck in the past has also eased considerably with the modernization and expansion of all the Metro cities airports where there is concentration of both domestic and international traffic. Further expansion of airports in Tier II and III cities has also been going on.

However, the air traffic is expected to grow further exponentially and this calls for further expansion or additional airports in Metro cities in the coming few years. IATA, the International Air Transport Association, has said that its projection of India becoming the world's third largest aviation market is contingent upon the growth of its airport infrastructure and other related facilities.

The Airport Authority of India (AAI) manages 124 airports. It is proposed to expand the airport capacity more than five times to handle a billion trips a year under a new initiative -- NABH Nirman. AAI will be enabled to leverage more resources to fund this expansion.

UDAN Scheme

The regional air connectivity scheme, UDAN (Ude Desh ka Aam Nagrik) has been initiated by the government in 2017 under the Regional Connectivity Scheme (RCS) of the National Civil Aviation Policy (NCAP), 2016. The UDAN scheme essentially aims at promoting safe and affordable flying for the masses. UDAN will propel aviation activity and start commercial flying at un-served and under-served airports in India. It will link 56 unserved airports and 31 unserved helipads across the country. Operations have already begun at some of these airports. This scheme is expected to spur further growth of the sector, increase tourism and economic activity and open up more employment opportunities.

Considering the growth in air passenger traffic India is poised to have, India needs to have a Perspective Plan for the aviation sector with a long-range view spanning 20-25 years.

❑ PORTS AND SHIPPING

The importance of shipping and coastal development to India's economy cannot be over-emphasized as brought out below:

- India's coastline is 7,500km long spanning 13 maritime States and Union Territories;
- 20 per cent of India's population live in coastal areas;
- The contribution of maritime States to India's GDP is 60 per cent (as of 2012-13);
- India has 12 major and about 200 non-major (minor) ports;
- 95 per cent of India's trade by volume and 70 per cent by value take place through maritime transport.

India's maritime sector has been handicapped by the following factors:

- Lack of cohesive institutional arrangement;
- Presence of a dual institutional structure leading to development of major and non-major ports as separate, unconnected entities which restricts their potential;
- Involvement of multiple agencies in the development of its infrastructure resulting in tardy development of ports;
- Limited mechanization, lack of scale, deep draft and other facilities at various ports;
- Inadequate development of hinterland areas around ports resulting in slow cargo movement and increase in transportation costs;
- Sub-optimal transport modal mix for shipment and evacuation at major and non-major ports;
- Limited affirmative action on skill development and benefits to peripheral trades like fisheries.

The above-mentioned deficiencies mean that ports and the maritime sector, as a whole, are not exploited to the fullest extent which results in limited economic benefit to the nation and the community.

A comparison of India's shipping sector with China's, given below, brings out starkly how far India has lagged behind:

Table 24.4 Shipping Sector – India & China

Shipping Sector	India	China
Container traffic (Mn TEU)	10	155
Number of ports in Global top 20	0	9
Number of shipyards	7	70
Contribution of waterways in domestic transportation	2%	25%
Average Turn-around time (Days)	4,5	1

Note: TEU stands for 'Twenty foot Equivalent Unit'. It is a common international standard of container dimension which determines the number of containers that a ship can load.

Maritime Summit

A Maritime India Summit was held for the first time in Mumbai in April 2016 with Republic of Korea, which is a leading maritime nation with considerable strengths and expertise in ship building, maritime technology, financing and security and port-led development, as Partner country. The summit which was attended by large number of delegates from 42 countries resulted in business agreements worth ₹ 82,905 crore investments. The objective of the summit was to highlight the role of port based development for faster and sustainable economic growth. The country's 7,500 km long coastline and 14,000 km of navigable inland waterwayscan be ideal engines of growth providing vast potential for developing ports, coastline and international shipping and generating employment.Plans are also afoot for developing 40 coastal Special Economic Zones (SEZs) which would create one lakh jobs.

The National Perspective Plan of Sagarmala project, which was released by the Prime Minister during the summit underlined Government's seriousness in boosting port led infrastructure development.

The Summit showcased around 240 projects which present investment opportunities for the next five years. The investment potential of these projects is around $ 66 billion (₹ 4.34 lakh crores). The Ministry of Shipping has established an Investment Facilitation Cell in Indian Ports Association to follow up on these opportunities with potential investors and ensure that the announcements and intent expressed during the summit materialize into actual projects and investments.

Sagarmala Project

The Sagarmala is a series of projects to leverage the country's coastline and inland waterways to drive industrial development. *Its objectives are:*

Port-led Development

- Undertake development of Coastal economic zones with projects like port-based industrialization, coastal tourism, Logistics parks, warehousing, fisheries etc.

Port Infrastructure Enhancement

- Action points on transforming existing ports into world class ports by developing deep drafts, mechanization of existing berths, creation of new capacity and greenfield ports.

Efficient Evacuation

- Expansion of rail / road network / inland waterways connected to ports and identification of congested routes;
- Find optimized transport solution for bulk and container cargo.

To implement the project, the government has set up Sagarmala Development Company (SDC).

Coastal Berthing scheme

The government has taken up projects worth ₹2,302 crore for financial assistance under the Coastal Berth Scheme of the Sagarmala programme. The scheme provides financial support to ports or State governments for creation of infrastructure for movement of cargo and passenger by sea or national waterways. Once completed, the projects will help promote coastal shipping and increase its share in domestic cargo movement.

The projects are distributed over eight states viz., Maharashtra, Andhra Pradesh & Goa, Karnataka, Kerala and Tamil Nadu, Gujarat and West Bengal. Out of the 47 projects, 23 projects worth ₹1,075.61 crore have been sanctioned and ₹230.01 crore has been released to major ports, State Maritime Boards and State governments. The remaining 24 projects are under various stages of development and approval. (See also chapter 10., pp. 10.13-5 on this).

Coastal shipping

In November 2017, a consignment of 2.3 lakh tonnes of steel cargo from Visakhapatnam Port destined to Ahmedabad, Mumbai and Kochi was sent by coastal transport opening a new era of coastal shipping. This mode of transport will bring down logistics costs, encourage industrial growth, give boost to the economy and create more employment in coastal regions.

Indigenisation of Technology

As part of the Sagarmala project, the Shipping Ministry has set up the National Technology Centre for Ports, Waterways and Coasts (NTCPWC) to help increase India's operational ability to handle complex port projects and reducing costs arising from foreign consultations. It is a joint initiative with IIT, Chennai to boost development of indigenous technology for the port and maritime sector in India. This serves as a model template of collaboration for applied research between the government, academia and industry. The institution will work on futuristic projects with thrust on domains like modeling and software products and testing facilities.

❑ POWER SECTOR REFORMS

Power is another sector which has been a drag on the economy for long. The Power Ministry has embarked upon game-changing reforms which will change the entire scenario in a few years.

- A path-breaking scheme is UDAY (Ujwal Discom Assurance Yojana) which will turn around highly debt-ridden State power distribution companies (Discoms), the weakest link in the entire power value chain. Discoms across the country have accumulated mounting debts. UDAY will bring down the cost of power, coal, and renewable energy by about ` 1.8 trillion every year by 2019. This will make Discoms financially much better without burdening the consumer with tariff increases. As the cost of power comes down, Discoms will be incentivized to buy more power and provide reliable services to consumers. The savings will also enable distributors to invest in smart meters and other infrastructure and upgrade the systems. It is, however, to be ensured that in this process, the debt position of State governments is not adversely affected as the Discoms will be allowed to convert their debt into State bonds (See Chapter 11, pp. 11.11-3 and Box 11.1, p. 11.19-21).
- 18,452 villages remained unelectrified as of April 2015. By the end of April 018, all the remaining unelectrified villages were provided with electricity. This was a challenging task given that many of these villages were in remote, far-flung areas with inhospitable terrain and some of them were disturbed areas being affected by violence.

  In this context, it is pertinent to note that the criterion for considering a village as 'electrified' had been changed. As per changed norm, at least 10 percent of homes need to have electric connection for the village to be treated as electrified. Additionally, electricity is to be provided to public places like schools, health centre, panchayat office and community centre. However, a parliamentary panel has recommended that a village should be declared electrified only after providing power connections to all households there or, in any case, only when at least 80 per cent of households in the village is covered.

❑ UJALA: AFFORDABLE AND HEALTH-SAFE LED LIGHTING SCHEME

Unnat Jyoti by Affordable LEDs for ALL (UJALA) scheme was launched by the Prime Minister in January 2015. Under the scheme, LED bulbs, LED Tube lights and Energy efficient fans are being provided to domestic consumers for replacement of conventional and inefficient lighting.

All-UJALA, the world's largest zero-subsidy LED bulb programme, set a target of replacing 770 million incandescent lamps with LED bulbs. In addition, the Street Lighting National Programme (SLNP) which aimed to replace conventional streetlights with smart and energy-efficient LED streetlights, was also launched.

Minamata Convention on Mercury

The LED lighting programme is a sequel to the Minamata Convention on Mercury, which is a multilateral environmental agreement, which India joined in 2014. The Convention addresses problems due to specific human activities which contribute to widespread mercury pollution. (The Convention is named after the city of Minamata in Japan, which experienced a severe, decades-long incidence of mercury poisoning after industrial wastewater from a chemical factory was discharged into Minamata Bay).

LED lighting can help rid the world of a large source of mercury pollution — a toxic pollutant that can lead to long-term neurological deficiencies and other health hazards.

In 2018, India exercised a provision in the Convention and extended the phase-out date for several mercury-based fluorescent lighting products through 2025. However, India has achieved far more since then, revolutionising the promotion and adoption of LED and emerging as the second largest producer of LED in the world.

Compact Fluorescent Lamps (CFLs) and Fluorescent Tube Lights (FTLs) accounted for 2% and 9% respectively of the 1.4 billion lamps produced in 2018-2019.

- **LED Lights and Energy, Costs Saved:** Till September 2021, 36.78 crore LED bulbs, 72.02 lakh LED Tube lights and 23.35 lakh Energy efficient fans have been distributed by Energy Efficiency Services Limited (EESL), a public sector unit, across India. This has resulted in estimated energy savings of 48.08 billion kWh per year with avoided peak demand of 9,724 MW, GHG emission reduction of 39 million tonnes of CO_2 per year and estimated annual monetary savings of ₹19,200 crore in consumer electricity bills.
- **Street Lighting:** SNLP is the largest LED street-lighting programme in the world. Under SLNP, 1508 Urban Local Bodies (ULBs) have been enrolled, out of which work has been completed in 972 ULBs.

Till 2021, EESL has installed over 12 million LED streetlights in ULBs and Gram Panchayats across India with a target for another 30 million by 2024.

This has resulted in estimated energy savings of 7.35 billion kWh per year with avoided peak demand of 1,224 MW, GHG emission reduction of 5.05 million tonnes of CO_2 per year and estimated annual monetary savings of ₹ 5,142 crore in electricity bills of municipalities.

- **LEDs in Villages:** EESL is also implementing LED Street lighting projects in Gram Panchayats, on the same service model as the SLNP for municipalities, with the objective to promote the use of efficient lighting in rural areas. So far, EESL has installed 29.5 lakh LED streetlights in rural areas of Andhra Pradesh, Andaman & Nicobar Islands, Jharkhand, Goa and Telangana.

LED Market

Expansion of LED Market: The domestic LED market has expanded exponentially since the start of the programmes. Over 1.15 billion LEDs, far more than UJALA's target of 700 million, have been sold. The share of LED in the lighting market registered a 135% increase, and by 2018-2019, accounted for approximately 80 per cent of the total value. Domestic production increased exponentially from 4.8 million in 2014-2015 to 661 million in 2018-19.

EESL pools all the procurement prices and passes on this price advantage to the consumers. The procured price reduced by almost 90% between 2014 and 2017, from ₹310 to ₹38 and this took UJALA to the stage where LEDs were priced at ₹70 each and consumers, knowing the benefits of energy and costs savings and with the prices becoming lower than CFLS, started to buy LEDs paying upfront instead of EMIs. The sale of bulbs increased and EESL ramped up the selling outlets in the country and was achieving sale of 6 lakh bulbs every day as compared to 6 lakh sale in 4 months.

Business Model: UJALA

EESL has evolved a service model where it works with electricity distribution companies (DISCOMs) through a benefit sharing approach. The Unnat Jyoti by Affordable LED for All (UJALA) obviates the need for DISCOMs to invest in the upfront cost of LED bulbs. EESL procures the LEDs bulbs and provides to consumers at affordable rates against their market price. The upfront investment made by EESL is paid back in different ways as indicated under:

- **Upfront Model**-Under this model, consumers purchase the energy efficient appliances at upfront cost and gets benefited by savings in their electricity bill.
- **DISCOM Cost Recovery Model:** Under this model consumer pays only a small part of the cost of bulbs to EESL and balance amount is paid by the DISCOMs to EESL. The investments of EESL is recovered from the DISCOMs as annuity over a period of 3-10 years by monetizing the energy savings that accrue as a result of replacement of incandescent lamps with LEDs. Each replacement leads to a reduction of connected load by 53W. The energy savings are monetized based on the peak procurement cost of DISCOM and is used to pay back the investment made by EESL under approval by the State Electricity Regulatory Commission. This was implemented in Puducherry and A.P.
- **On Bill Financing (OBF) Model:** Under this Model, the entire cost is recovered from the consumers by deduction of easy instalments of every month for 8-12 months. The entire cost of the LED bulbs, including the distribution and cost of capital is recovered from the consumers' Electricity bills. This was implemented all over the country.

Saubhagya Yojana

Keeping in view the role of electricity in human and socio-economic development, the government of India formulated a scheme to ensure last mile connectivity and electricity connections to all remaining un-electrified households in the country. In September 2017, the Pradhan Mantri Sahaj Bijli Har Ghar Yojana (Saubhagya Yojana) was launched. The objective of the scheme is to achieve universal household electrification by providing electricity connections to all households in rural and urban areas through financial assistance to the DISCOMs / Power departments from the Union government.

Under the Saubhagya scheme, about 4 crore poor households are to be provided with electricity connection free of charge. Non poor households will have to pay ten installments of ₹50 each, along with the bill each month, totaling ₹500. The scheme is estimated to cost off about ₹16,320 crore as a means of sourcing funds for the scheme, instead of subsidizing the under recovery for kerosene by oil companies, the same money could be progressively re allocated for Saubhagya.

In April 2017, out of a total of about 17.96 crore rural households, 13.36 crore households were electrified and remaining 4.60 crore households were yet to be electrified. And about 50 lakh urban households were also estimated to be un-electrified. Since the launch of the scheme, over 5 million households have been connected under the scheme. Further, another 1.3 million households are being provided connection under 'Gram Swaraj Abhiyan' across 20,000 villages.

Progress since October 2017: Under the Saubhagya scheme, about 2.63 crore rural households had been electrified since October 2017. With this the total number of households electrified works out to 15.99 crore. That leaves another 1.97 crore households still to be electrified.

By 2021, by connecting more households, the total consumer base has expanded to touch 28.2 million new consumers. With this expansion and growing needs of the economy, the country's power demand is expected to cross 200 GW. Peak power demand in a day stood at 180.74 GW in September 2021 as against 176.56 GW in the same month in 2020 and 173.14 GW in 2019.

- **Challenges ahead:** But providing connection to the remaining, especially remote, households in the surrounding areas can be expensive and pose a challenge.

Some people may also forgo accessing electricity by choice because of the monthly bills that come with it, especially if power supply is not reliable and blackouts are frequent. The ability of some households to pay the charges could be a hindrance.

A major challenge will be to provide quality service, ideally 24x7 supply to all households.

Mandating the provision of a meter is a welcome step to ensure that consumers pay notified tariffs even if the tariff is low and subsidized. This creates the mindset and culture of paying and instils the habit of economising in usage and consumption of power.

A positive aspect is that most villages are now connected to the grid, and locations far from the grid are slated for generation of mostly renewable power. A major challenge will be to provide quality service, ideally 24x7 supply. Another is about payment of usage charges and the ability of some households to pay the charges. Mandating the provision of a meter is a welcome step to ensure that consumers pay notified tariffs even if the tariff is low and subsidized. This creates the mindset and culture of paying and instills the habit of economising in usage and consumption of power.

Renewable Energy

The government of India has set an ambitious target to have 175 GW of total renewable capacity by the end of 2022. This includes 60 GW from wind power, 100 GW from solar power, 10 GW from biomass power and 5 GW from small hydro power.

The government has ambitious plans for tapping renewable energy sources. It has revised the earlier target of achieving 20,000 MW of solar energy capacity by 2022 to 100,000 MW which will be the world's most ambitious solar power generation programme. India is ideally suited for solar power generation as the country receives solar radiation of 5 to 7 kWh per sq. m. for over 300 days in a year.

Earlier companies have bid for projects to sell solar power in the range of ₹4.63 per unit to ₹5.17 per unit. With the price of solar modules and solar inverters falling, the bids for solar power units has further come down. The cost of solar power has been steadily coming down and, if sustained, it will provide electricity cheaper. The per unit cost of solar power had come down to as low as ₹ 2,36. But some experts are of the view that the true cost of renewable energy has to be higher if it is to be sustained over the long term. Also, evacuation of solar power requires investment in grids by the public sector. Transmission infrastructure needs to be strengthened and it may involve land acquisition processes.

Out of the 100 GW solar power, 40 GW is to be achieved from grid connected solar rooftops in residential, social, institutional and government sectors in the country. The Standing Committee on Energy (2016-17) of the Ministry of New and Renewable Energy had said in its report tabled in Parliament in 2017 that the rooftop solar target of 40 GW by 2022 may not be fulfilled and needs to be reconsidered.

The share of Fossil fuels and Non-Fossil fuels (Renewables) as on August 2021 can be seen in Table 24.5. While fossil fuels account for 60.4 per cent, the share of Renewables is 39.6 per cent.

Table 24.5 Installed Generation Capacity (Fuel-wise) As on 31.08.2021

Category	Installed Generation Capacity (MW)	% Share in Total
Fossil Fuel		
Coal	2,02,805	52.6 %
Lignite	6,620	7 %
Gas	24,924	6.5 %
Diesel	510	0.1 %
Total Fossil Fuel	2,34,258	60.4 %
Non-Fossil Fuel		
RES (Incl. Hydro)	1,47,096	37.9 %
Hydro	46,412	12.0 %
Wind, Solar & Other Renewables	1,00,683	25.9 %
Nuclear	6,780	1.7%
Total Non-Fossil Fuel	1,53,876	39.6%
Total Installed Capacity (Fossil & Non-Fossil Fuel)	3,88,134	100%

Source: Power Sector at a Glance: All India - Ministry of Power, Govt. of India.

Another challenge for India in this domain has been that, following a dispute with the US, the World Trade Organization (WTO) had ruled against India's stipulation on domestic content requirements for manufacturing solar cells and modules. The ruling held that India violated global trade rules such as national treatment obligations which required India to treat imported solar cells and modules on par with domestically produced products without any discrimination.

However, despite various challenges, there are encouraging signs which should spur India to push along the path of renewable energy. India has been ranked in the top 10 for the second year in a row in global Climate Change Performance Index (CCPI) for 2021, which was released in Germany in December 2020, for reducing greenhouse gas (GHG) emissions by opting to transform its electricity sector towards green technology. The Climate Change Performance Index (CCPI) is prepared after assessing the performances of 57 countries and the European Union (as a whole) in four categories. These 57 countries and the European Union collectively are responsible for about 90 percent of the global GHG emissions.

Solar power at Airports: Ministry of Civil Aviation has since asked all airports in the country to install solar energy plants. While Kochi International airport was the first to adopt it, Delhi and Hyderabad have also followed suit. In all, 38 airports in India have so far adopted solar energy for power supply.

Solar power in Railways: The Railways has set the target of 100 per cent electrification of railway routes by the year 2023. Besides, 960 railways stations have solar installations in place to meet their power requirements. Also, 198 MW of rooftop solar capacity for 550 stations, are under execution. Some of the stations that were solarized are Varanasi, New Delhi, Old Delhi, Jaipur, Secunderabad, Kolkata, Guwahati, Hyderabad, and Howrah, among others.

The Railways also want to utilize solar energy for meeting its traction power requirement and become a complete 'green mode of transportation.' This is in line with the directive of the Prime Minister to solarize railway stations and utilize vacant railway lands for renewable energy projects. These steps are part of the Railways' endeavour to expand the usage of renewable energy.

If these efforts are scaled up gradually, it can make a significant contribution to the nation's power generation programme, mitigate power shortages, and accelerate economic growth.

Power produced from solar and wind projects will become more viable and attractive for Discoms as the government has now waived off inter-state transmission charges for solar and wind projects commissioned till March 2022 with a view to encourage the use of power generated through these sources. This move will take away the future possibilities of additional cost to Discoms and encourage them to purchase power produced from these projects.

World Bank Aid for Solar Programme: The World Bank Group (WBG) is helping India deliver on its plans with more than $1 billion in lending. This is the Bank's largest-ever support for solar power in any country.

The Bank's aid covers from installing solar panels on rooftops to setting up massive solar parks which will catapult India to the forefront of the global effort to bring electricity to all, mitigate the effects of climate change, and set the country on a path to become the 'India of the future'.

The WBG is also backing the India-led International Solar Alliance which aims to promote solar use globally by mobilizing $1 trillion in investments by 2030.

Box 24.4 India's Renewable Energy Scenario

India's commitment on Renewables

- India has committed to reduce greenhouse gas (GHG) emissions intensity by 33-35 per cent below 2005 levels and achieve 40 per cent of installed electric capacity from non-fossil sources by 2030.
- India has set ambitious target to install 175 gigawatts (GW) of renewable power (RE) capacity by 2022. The installed RE capacity in August 2021 was 153.9 GW which formed 39.6 per cent of total installed capacity. As against this, the share of thermal power was around 60 per cent.
- More RE projects are under various stages of implementation. The government has estimated an investment of about ₹ 4 lakh crore during 2019-22 period to meet the country's 175 GW renewable energy target by 2022.
- Most of the grid connected RE projects are being implemented by private sector developers selected through transparent bidding process.

Promotion of Renewables

- India is endowed with abundant natural and renewable resources of energy viz., sun, wind, and biomass.

- India holds 5th Global position for overall installed renewable energy capacity, 4th position for wind power and 5th position for solar power.
- In the infrastructure sector, renewable energy projects are giving good returns and hence have been attracting significant foreign capital. This is supported by robust government policy.
- The initiative of NTPC, the major state-run thermal producing undertaking, to take up RE projects will be an added boost. NTPC is adding significant capacities of RE and by 2032, the company plans to have a minimum of 32,000 MW (32 GW) capacity through RE sources constituting nearly 25 per cent of its overall power generation capacity.
- The cost of solar power has been steadily coming down and, if sustained, it will provide electricity cheaper. The per unit cost of solar power had come down to as low as ₹ 2.36. But some experts are of the view that the true cost of renewable energy has to be higher if it is to be sustained over the long term.
- The reduction of cost of power for industries will help in promoting local manufacturing and make exports competitive.
- Under the Solar Park Scheme, the target was to develop at least 50 solar parks with aggregate installed capacity of 40,000 MW of solar power by 2021-22. As of December 2019, 39 solar parks of aggregate capacity 22,879 MW (22.8 GW) have been approved and these solar parks are at different stage of development.

Challenges

While India is making concerted efforts to promote renewable energy and meet the targets set, there are some challenges in the way. These can be overcome by suitable policy changes even if it takes some time to fructify. These challenges are:

- **Supply of equipments:** China has been a major supplier of equipments for solar power. India is trying to reduce imports from China and encourage domestic manufacturing by levying customs duty on cells, modules and inverters. But as the local manufacturing capacity is able to meet only part of the demand and ramping up production will take time, India will have to source them from other countries and prices will go up which could impact power tariffs.
- **Land Scarcity**: Land is a scarce resource in India and per capita land available is very low. Having dedicated land area near substations for exclusive installation of solar cells have to compete with other demands for land.

- **Solar parks:** The scheme for development of Solar Parks and Ultra Mega Solar Power projects and grid connected Solar Power plants face problems of land acquisition and right of way and challenges in evacuating the power generated in these parks.
- **Energy Storage:** Off-grid PV systems typically use batteries for storing energy, and the use of batteries could increase the size, cost and complexity of the system.
- **Lead-acid batteries:** Where grid connections are not possible or reliable, as may be the case in rural areas, lead-acid batteries are used for storage in rooftop solar installations. They pose risks of health and environmental problems from contamination, if recycling of these batteries is not adequately regulated and done properly.

International Solar Alliance (ISA)

Apart from the initiatives to promote generation of solar power in India, India has also taken steps for its adoption across countries as part of efforts to combat climate change. Towards this, the International Solar Alliance (ISA) was jointly launched in 2015 at the UN Climate Change conference (COP 21) in Paris by PM Narendra Modi and French President Francois Hollande. The goal of ISA is to install 1,000 GW of solar energy by 2030 and mobilise US$ 1,000 billion to achieve the target.

- Since its founding, 83 nations located between the Tropic of Cancer and Tropic of Capricorn have joined the alliance in just four years. ISA has launched five programmes to boost different sectors where solar technologies can be applied.
- **Global drive:** India has called upon sunshine-abundant nations to join the International Solar Alliance in larger numbers to hasten the global energy transition from fossil fuels.

This move by India also has geopolitical implications. As an emerging power on the global arena, it helps India to collaborate with many developing countries in the Asia-Pacific, Africa and Latin America regions. Once India starts manufacturing solar equipments and scales it up, she can also supply them and technical support to those countries and collaborate with projects there.

- **Conclusion:** On the one hand, India will have to continue to rely on coal-based thermal power considering India's rising energy needs and abundant coal reserves she has. But India adopt clean-coal technology in power generation, so that its ill-effects can be largely contained. At the same time, India has to pursue vigorously sourcing power from renewable sources. Considering the measures so far taken by the government and if this momentum is maintained, India will be on course to achieve an affordable, secure, inclusive and environmentally friendly energy ecosystem.

❑ TELECOMMUNICATIONS

The problems faced by the Telecom sector before the reforms and liberalization in 1990s and the impressive growth registered by it since then have been discussed in chapter 10. This sector has further forged ahead with expansion and played a significant part in the development of the economy.

Box 24.5 Status of the Telecommunications Sector (as of May 2021)

- Indian telecom network is the second largest in the world after China, in terms of the number of telephone connections
- The country has 1198.43 million telephone connections, including 1176.77 million wireless telephone connections.
- Overall tele-density (i.e., per 100 population) in the country is 87.83, urban tele-density is 140.30 and rural tele-density is 60.14.
- The share of wireless telephones in total telephones is 97.19 percent
- The share of private sector in total telephones is 89.14 per cent.
- Total No. of Internet Subscribers (in March 2021): 825.30 million.

Source: Monthly Telecom Scenario, May 2021 - Department of Telecommunications, Ministry of Communications, Govt. of India,

While India is one of the largest countries connected by fixed lines and mobile, it remains largely poorly connected by Internet and Broadband. Less than 30 per cent of Indians and just 15 per cent in rural areas have access to Internet and Broadband. Of the total number of Internet Subscribers of 825.30 million in March 2021, 322.77 million were rural subscribers and 502.53 million were urban subscribers.

For more inclusive growth, to improve governance and make a success of the Digital India, Smart Cities and such other ambitious programmes, net connectivity and access has to be substantially increased and the government has been moving in this direction. (See 'Digital India' section later below).

Since 1990s when major economic reforms were initiated, India has had three national telecom policies – NTP-1994, NTP-1999 and NTP-2012. While NTP-1994 ushered in telecom reforms and paved the way for private participation, NTP-1999 brought about structural changes leading to healthy competition among the service providers bringing down the costs and exponential growth in mobile subscriptions.

As per estimates, the mobile industry in India currently contributes 6.5 per cent ($140 billion) to country's GDP, and employs over 4 million people (direct and indirect). India, with 275 million smart-phone subscribers, has the second largest smart-phone subscriber base in the world. Since September 2015, 38 new mobile manufacturing units have been set up, which has ramped up the manufacturing of mobile phone units.

The Department of Telecom has taken following measures to develop the network and improve the sector and services:

Full Mobile Number Portability (MNP): As a consumer empowerment measure, the government has allowed 'One Nation-Full Mobile Number Portability' (MNP). MNP allows subscribers to retain their existing mobile number when they shift from place to place or switch from one service provider to another irrespective of technology or service area limitation. This helps in using the mobile numbers as an identity of individuals for providing various government services and welfare programmes and implement the Jan Dhan-Aadhaar-Mobile (JAM) Trinity scheme.

Rationalisation of Spectrum: As spectrum is a scarce and finite resource and there is chronic shortage of it, its efficient utilisation is critical to the success of the telecom industry. Keeping this in view and the industry requirements, the government has taken the following steps for its optimal use:

- Since 2016, spectrum sharing was allowed when operators could pool their respective spectrum holdings and use as whole spectrum block. Spectrum efficiency increases exponentially with the size of the spectrum block.
- Trading of spectrum was permitted by allowing a service provider to transfer spectrum usage rights to another service provider.
- Mega auction of spectrum of various bands was held in 2016.
- Harmonisation of spectrum in different bands and rationalisation of spectrum holdings of telecom service providers.

These measures have helped to increase spectrum efficiency, reduce call drops, improve the quality of service and generate additional revenue for the Government.

Challenges facing the Telecom Sector: Yet the sector is still dogged by problems like call drops and slow internet impacting the quality of service, predatory tariffs and intense competition affecting the viability of some of the service providers. It has even led to a service provider which had substantial foreign investment having to shut down and file for bankruptcy.

Also, for all the expansion which has taken place, India's broadband average speed is abysmal at 6.5 Mbps compared to many countries – for example, South Korea (28.6), Norway (23.5), Hong Kong (21.9).

There is need for a new, revamped Telecom policy taking into account the changed scenario and rising demands of a fast expanding economy and customer expectations.

❑ DIGITAL INDIA: BHARATNET PROJECT

Digital India is an umbrella programme that covers multiple Government Ministries and Departments to transform India into a digitally empowered society and knowledge economy. Though India took e-Governance initiatives from 1990s, both at Central and State levels, for providing citizen-centric services, it did not have the desired impact especially since rural areas were not covered under them. Hence the need was felt for a comprehensive scheme to promote inclusive growth that provides electronic services and job opportunities to a wider section of the population.

The Phase -I target of covering 1 lakh GPs under Phase-1 was completed by Dec 2017. Additional 25,000 GPs was covered under Phase-1. More than 1,21,000 GPs have been made service ready. Phase- II would connect remaining 1,25,000 GPs by a mix of different modes like underground optical fibre cable (OFC), Aerial OFC, Radio and Satellite. The project also includes setting up last mile infrastructure using Wi-Fi hotspots in PPP model to cover all the GPs and providing connectivity to government institution at GP level.

The task of connecting one lakh GPs through high speed OFC under Phase I has been completed. This has enabled broadband access to over 20 crore rural Indians in about two lakh fifty thousand villages. As proposed in the Union budget 2018-19, the government propose to set up five lakh Wi-Fi hotspots which will provide broadband access to five crore rural citizens. Department of Electronics and IT has developed a model of "Wi-Fi Choupal" to build rural Wi-Fi infrastructure and create an empowered 'Smart Village'.

Benefits of Digital India

- It will give thrust to Broadband highways, Universal Access to mobile connectivity and Public Internet Access.
- It will widen the scope of e-Governance through electronic delivery of services in rural areas and bring in transparency, effective service delivery and good governance in the country; A wide range of e-services will be provided through a single-window technology platform.
- Disseminate information for rural population through Community Service Centres (CSCs) which will serve as multi-functional end-points for service delivery.
- CSCs are to be managed by Village-Level Entrepreneurs (VLEs) which will foster a culture of entrepreneurship in villages. Preference is given to women thus empowering rural women.
- Digital Literacy and training program on a mass scale will bridge the digital divide. The Pradhanmantri Grameen Digital Saksharata Abhiyan (PMGDISHA), which is now underway, is targeted at promoting digital literacy among the rural population.

Technology will be deployed for the following which will have a multiplier effect:

- **Education:** Schools connected with broadband; Free WiFi in about 2,50,000 schools.
- **Farmers:** Real time information on prices; Online ordering of inputs; Online cash, loan, relief payments with mobile banking.
- **Health:** e-Healthcare; Online medical consultation, medical records and medicine supply; Facility for pan-India exchange of patient information.
- **Financial Inclusion:** Through mobile banking; Micro-ATM facility at CSCs / Post Offices.
- **Digital Payments:** The spread of digital networks would promote digital payments mode and cashless transactions and help convert India into a less-cash society with its attendant benefits of a cleaner economy.
- **Boost IT Sector:** Promote electronics manufacturing and develop IT sector as a whole.
- **Job Creation:** Create jobs on large scale in IT, Telecom and Electronics domains; Direct and indirect jobs will be created.

The Digital India programme involves community participation and collective action leading to transformational societal changes, sustainable socio-economic development and long-term rural prosperity. (On this project, see also chapter 10 (pp. 10.24-5) and chapter 12 (pp. 12.11-2).

❑ NATIONAL INVESTMENT AND INFRASTRUCTURE FUND (NIIF)

In the Budget for 2015-16, the Finance Minister had announced the setting up of a National Investment and Infrastructure Fund (NIIF) which would have an annual flow of ₹ 20,000 crore. This will enable it to raise debt and invest as equity in infrastructure finance companies such as the Indian Railway Finance Corporation (IRFC), which is a dedicated financing arm of the Ministry of Railways to raise money from the market to part finance the plan outlay of Indian Railways, and National Housing Bank (NHB), which provides a viable and cost effective housing finance system to cater to all segments of the population. The infrastructure finance companies could leverage this extra equity.

The Budget also permitted tax-free infrastructure bonds for projects in the rail, road, and irrigation sectors. The Budget referred to the problem faced in the PPP mode of infrastructure development and the need to balance the risks and stated that the sovereign would have to bear a major part of the risk without absorbing it entirely.

Box 24.6 National Monetisation Pipeline (NMP)

Creation of National Monetisation Pipeline (NMP) is a pioneering initiative of Government of India to establish a medium-term pipeline along with a roadmap to monetise select ready assets. Developed in the backdrop of the unprecedented Covid-induced economic and fiscal shocks, NMP lists out assets and asset classes, under various infrastructure ministries, which will be monetised over a period of time. NMP would also serve as a medium – term roadmap for financing opportunities and enlist public sponsor as well as private sector/ institutional investors towards financing the infrastructure gap.

The pipeline has been developed by NITI Aayog, in consultation with infrastructure-line ministries, based on the mandate for 'Asset Monetisation' proposed in the Union Budget 2021-22. NMP estimates aggregate monetisation potential of ₹ 6.0 lakh crore through core assets of the Central Government, over a four-year period, from FY 2022 to FY 2025.

NMP provides visibility on the volume of assets to be monetised and the potential value that can be realized. It reflects the Government's commitment to scale up infrastructure investments despite the fiscal pressures, the critical role of infrastructure in overall economic growth and potential multiplier effect.

Objectives and Rationale

Key Objectives of NMP are:

- Serve as a medium-term roadmap for the line ministries and agencies.
- Provide medium-term visibility to investors on infrastructure assets pipeline.
- Provide a platform for ministries to track asset performance.
- Bring in greater efficiency and transparency in public assets management.

Availability of a sustained and robust asset pipeline has been cited as a key concern by investors to the Government at various forums. A well laid out pipeline hence gives a comprehensive view to investors and developers of brown-field investment avenues in Infrastructure.

It presents an immense opportunity for public asset owners to deleverage the balance sheets and easing of fiscal space to take up more greenfield infrastructure creation. In terms of other longer-term benefits, it creates an enabling environment for participation of long-term institutional investors in infrastructure asset management.

Asset monetisation is critical to attract the required quantum of capital into infrastructure sector. However, it is not to be viewed just as a funding mechanism but is an overall strategy for bringing about a paradigm shift in expanding and upgrading infrastructure, service delivery and maintenance. It helps to harness the resource and capital efficiencies and potential of private sector along with the ability to adapt to the evolving global and economic scenario.

Scope and Coverage

This is a major venture as it includes assets like 25 airports, 400 railway stations, 90 trains, four hill railways, more than 26,000 kilometres of highways, around 28,000 circuit kilometres of power lines, more than 8,000 kilometres of natural gas lines, around three lakh kilometres of optical fibre cables, cell phone tower assets numbering around 15,000, hotels owned by the Indian Tourism Development Corporation, ports, coal projects and stadiums under the Sports Authority of India.

As much as 81 per cent of the aggregate value of the monetisation pipeline comes from five sectors—roads (27 per cent), railways (25), power (15), oil and gas (8) and telecom (6).

Besides these conventional infrastructure sectors, assets from mining and housing redevelopment sectors have also been included in the NMP owing to the potential of these sectors to spur private sector investment and to enable tracking of transactions as part of the Monetisation pipeline.

But monetization through disinvestment and monetization of non-core assets (such as land, building, and pure real estate assets) have ***not*** been included in the NMP.

Sectoral Break-up

As stated above, the aggregate asset pipeline over FY 2022-25 under NMP is indicatively valued at ₹ 6.0 lakh crore. The top 5 sectors (by estimated value) account for 83% of the aggregate pipeline value. These top 5 sectors include: Roads (27%), followed by Railways (25%), Power (15%), oil & gas pipelines (8%) and Telecom (6%). Roads and Railways together contribute 52% of the total NMP value.

Assessment of Value

The potential for monetisation of asset classes has been assessed based on multiple factors varying across sectors. It has factored in visible revenue streams, commercial potential, utilisation levels, investor appetite, ability to tap private sector efficiencies in operations and maintenance, with focus to tap institutional investment in the sector.

The monetisation value that is expected to be realised by the public asset owner through the monetisation process, either in form of upfront accruals or by way of private sector investment, has been taken as the Indicative Monetisation Value. Several brownfield asset classes are proposed to be monetised through Operate Maintain and Develop (OMD) based models or assets where significant capital expenditure (Capex) may be involved over transaction life towards augmentation or rehabilitation of assets. In such cases, estimated capex to be funded through private sector investment has been taken as indicative monetisation value.

Asset base to remain with, and revert, to the Government

The scale of monetisation under NMP has been envisaged based on multiple factors. Crucially, bulk of the asset base, will remain with the government. Further, under the framework for core asset monetisation, the assets monetised will be handed back at the end of transaction life. The property or asset does not change hands, but the investor can invest in it to generate revenue while discharging his duty to maintain the asset. It stops short of the stigmatised avenues of privatisation and disinvestment, both of which involve selling assets, and focuses instead on ensuring "private participation" in managing assets in a more efficient and profitable manner.

As for the criticism voiced in many quarters, it is not a case of "selling government silver", but of getting regular income while keeping the title. The government need innovative ideas to generate resources.

Implementation is Key

Experts have given the scheme a cautious welcome. According to them, implementation and timely execution, will be key. That the government's disinvestment plans for Air India, Bharat Petroleum and other proposals have been caught in red tape and such delays, should they occur, may dampen the enthusiasm of the private sector for the monetisation project.

Box 24.7 Economic Growth and Employment: Role of Infrastructure

An issue that has been causing concern and much debated in the last few years is the paradoxical phenomenon of "jobless growth". Even as the economy has been growing and expanding, it has not only not led to commensurate growth in employment but even shown decline in some years. A question posed, in the Indian context, is how the economy could grow, even if at a slower pace, without generating jobs. A related issue is the quality of jobs created and the share of employment in the Formal and Informal sectors. One plausible explanation put forth is the way in which employment data is collected in India which results in not covering the full range of the economy and capturing the total number of people employed in its entirety.

To resolve this dilemma, some analysts have tried to examine employment figures from various angles, apart from the data from the conventional sources like NSSO and Labour Department surveys.

These include data from Employees' Provident Funds Organisation (EPFO) and Employees State Insurance Corporation (ESIC) and enterprises paying taxes (GST, etc.) as the Economic Survey 2017-18 has also attempted. These have led to not only higher figures but conclusion that the number of people in formal employment is more than estimated hitherto.

Only companies with 20 and more employees are registered under the EPF, while the ESIC covers those with a minimum of 10 employees. The Labour Ministry estimates that if the coverage of EPFO is extended to smaller firms with 10 to 20 workers, there could be an addition of 30 million to its existing subscriber base of 60 million. More than 10 million people are likely to be added to job data if ESIC coverage is extended to firms with less than 10 workers. Currently, the formal workforce count under the two social security programmes is pegged at 75 million by the Labour Ministry. The ministry is considering including all enterprises with less than 20 workers while computing employment data.

Features of Indian Labour Scene

Some of the features of the Indian labour scene have been already detailed in chapter 16. It may also be added that:

- The rate of employment generation declined, across both rural and urban areas, during the 1990s following reforms and liberalisation though it revived later between 1999-2000 and 2004-05. There has been decline again in subsequent years.
- While regular employment had been declining as a share of total employment, there was increase in the share of wage employment due to increase in employment on casual and contract basis.
- While there has been a significant decline in the share of agriculture in rural employment, employment of rural workers in manufacturing did not go up commensurately but there was shift of rural workers to construction, and to some extent to trade, hotels and restaurants.
- There has been significant increase in self-employment among both rural and urban workers in India. This is a positive trend as it reduces the number of people seeking employment and the pressure of labourforce on jobs. But the flip side of it is that the conditions of work and the level of earnings of many of the self-employed may not be up to the desired level nor do they enjoy security in their occupation due to severe competition in the market. This calls for social security measures that cover not just informal workers in the unorganised and organized sectors, but also such self-employed who need protection.

Employment Generation

The economy has to tap those sectors which have high potential for creation of jobs. Infrastructure comprising roads, railways, ports, aviation and communications have considerable scope in this regard. Schemes like 'Housing for All' and PM's Gram Sadak Yojana are labour-intensive. It is unclear as to how despite heavy public investment in the last few years, there has not been visible pick up in job creation. Sluggishness in private investment due to varied reasons – rising corporate debt, high interest rates, excess capacity in industry, etc.– has compounded the problem.

Another area which can propel job creation in a big way is social infrastructure – education and health – as rightly emphasized in the

Finance Ministry's Economic Survey for 2017-18. Apart from improving human capital and health outcomes, investment in these sectors require manpower on a massive scale and creation of physical infrastructure all of which have much potential for job creation.

As noted in the Survey, expenditure on education as a proportion of GDP has been around 3 per cent and that on health has been stagnant at less than 2 per cent during 2008-09 to 2014-15. During 2013-14, out of the total expenditure on social services, 11.6 per cent was spent on education and just 4.6 per cent was spent on health. Shortfalls in expenditure on these two sectors result not only in shortage of manpower like teachers, doctors and paramedical staff but affects human capabilities and retards development. While secondary education plays a transformative role in the lives of adolescents, a significant proportion of children in the 14-plus age group drop out of school after elementary education. Lack of education and skills appropriate for employment also affects the employability of the youth entering the labour market resulting in wastage of precious resources. Absence of skilled labour and the slow pace at which skilling ecosystem is progressing makes the task of job creation that much more difficult.

The private sector could play a complementary role in building social infrastructure through schemes like Corporate Social Responsibility.

In this Chapter we discussed.....

- Problems due to stalled infrastructure; projects got stalled due to various reasons; has also led to loan defaults, a problem faced by banks.
- Stalled road projects, national highway projects, and efforts to revive them.
- Infrastructure in Union budget
- Roads; National highways; Bharatmala project; Pradhan Mantri Gram Sadak Yojana (PMGSY).
- Sethu Bharatam project.
- Railways network; major developments; railway electrification and its advantages.

- Aviation sector; UDAN scheme.
- Ports and shipping; Maritime summit; Sagarmala project.
- Power sector reforms; UDAY (Ujwal Discom Assurance Yojana) to turn around highly debt-ridden State power distribution companies (Discoms); electrification of all remaining unelectrified villages; national LED programme launched for providing efficient lighting at affordable rates in households and public places which would save considerable energy; electrification of remaining unelectrified villages; Saubhagya scheme – electricity for all households.
- Solar power and challenges faced.
- Telecommunications sector; reforms effected; challenges facing the sector.
- Digital India: Bharatnet project to connect 2,50,000 Gram Panchayats—a transformational project.; benefits of Digital India programme.
- National Investment and Infrastructure Fund (NIIF) set up.
- Economic Growth and Employment: role of infrastructure; importance of developing social infrastructure.

Important Terms to Note in this Chapter

Gross budgetary support; Bharatmala; Setu Bharatam; Climate change; Electric vehicles; BS-emission norms; Dedicated Freight Corridor (DFC); Sagarmala; LED lighting; Digital India; Bharatnet

Practice Questions

1. What are the major steps taken by the government in recent years to improve and upgrade infrastructural sectors such as roads, rail and ports?
2. Describe the steps taken to develop and modernise India's national highways. What are the obstacles faced in executing highway projects and mention the steps taken by the government to overcome them.
3. Describe the salient features of Prime Minister's Gram Sadak Yojana (PMGSY) programme. Discuss its impact and role in uplifting the rural economy.

4. Despite significant expansion and attempts at modernization, the Indian Railways still suffer from many deficiencies and face many challenges. Identify the deficiencies and challenges faced by it and steps that need to be taken to overcome them.
5. In what way the electrification of railways will help to improve the rail system?
6. Explain the features of Sagarmala project initiated by the government of India. What are its benefits for the Indian economy?
7. The inland waterways and coastal shipping can play a major role in the development of the economy in a country like India which has large river systems and long sea coastline. Do you agree? What measures have been taken by the government to tap this potential and what more needs to be done?
8. Enumerate the recent trends in the expansion of the aviation sector, both airlines and airports, in India and bring out the importance of its role in the economy.
9. In view of the burgeoning growth in air traffic, India needs a 'Perspective Plan' with long-term vision for the aviation sector. Do you agree? Justify your answer.
10. Compare the position of India's telecommunication sector before and after its liberalisation in 1980's and 1990's. How far the liberalisation has helped to reform and expand the sector?
11. Despite remarkable growth, the telecom sector in India has, of late, come under much stress and it has even affected the quality of services provided by them. What are the reasons for this and what steps need to be taken to resolve them?
12. The telecommunications sector in India is facing many challenges. Identify the challenges and steps to be taken to resolve them.
13. Explain the salient features of Digital India programme. In what way it would give a boost to rural economy?
14. What are the various benefits the Digital India programme will have for Indian economy?
15. Infrastructure has much potential for job creation. Do you agree with this statement? Justify your answer with cogent reasoning.
16. Explain the paradox of India making substantial investments and economic progress and yet it is said to be "jobless growth". Is this statement justified? What are the reasons for this view and the pitfalls of such an assertion?
17. India's 'Social infrastructure' comprising education and health sectors has not been developed to its full potential. Explain how developing them to the fullest extent can contribute to India's human development.

18. What are 'Smart Cities'? Examine their relevance for urban development in India. Will it increase rural-urban differences? Give arguments for 'Smart Villages' in the light of PURA and RURBAN Mission. [UPSC Main 2016 (Economics Optional Paper)]

19. What are the main features and objectives of UJALA- LED lighting scheme launched by the government? Explain the ways in which it is beneficial to consumers of electricity and the economy.

20. Critically examine the "National Monetisation Pipeline" (NMP) scheme launched the government of India. What are its main objectives and see how far it would benefit the economy?

21. Explain the meaning of investment in an economy in terms of capital formation. Discuss the factors to be considered while designing a concession agreement between a public entity and a private entity. *[UPSC Main 2020 (General Studies Paper)]*

22. India has immense potential of solar energy though there are regional variations in its developments. Elaborate. *[UPSC Main 2020 (General Studies Paper)]*

FINANCIAL SECTOR AND TAX REFORMS

- Financial Inclusion (PMJDY)
- Financial Literacy
- JAM and Aadhaar
- Expansion of Banking Facilities: Payments Banks and SFBs
- MUDRA Yojana: Funding the Unfunded
- Banks: NPAs and Recapitalisation of Banks
- Need for Banking Reforms
- Amalgamation of Public Sector Banks (PSBs)
- Merits of Public Sector Bank Mergers
- Black Money
- Double Tax Avoidance Agreement: Features
- Petition on Black Money and Black Money Law
- Black Money in India: Steps to Curb Black Money
- Demonetisation: Its Objectives and Impact Assessment
- Low Level of Tax base and Tax Compliance in India
- Towards Digital and Less Cash Economy
- India's Thriving Fintech Industry
- Electoral Funding and Electoral Bonds
- Black Money Problem in the US and European Countries
- International Tax Reform
- Gold Monetisation Scheme
- Tax Reforms: Corporate Tax: Phased Reduction
- Goods and Services Tax (GST): Its Merits and Demerits
- GST and Transport & Logistics sector in India

❑ INTRODUCTION

Soon after assuming office in May 2014, the NDA government took a number of steps to rejuvenate the economy which was in a sluggish mode due to a variety of factors, both internal and external. Some of these developments and schemes have been covered in the preceding chapters.

❑ FINANCIAL INCLUSION (PMJDY)

A major flagship programme implemented is Pradhan Mantri Jan Dhan Yojana (PMJDY) with a view to expand the reach of banking facilities and bring millions of those who had no access to banking within its fold. The scheme was announced by the Prime Minister in his Independence Day address on 15th August, 2014 and was launched across the country on 28th August, 2014.

It is a 'National Mission on Financial Inclusion' encompassing an integrated approach to bring about, in a comprehensive way, financial inclusion of all the households in the country. The plan envisages universal access to banking facilities with at least one basic banking account for every household, financial literacy, access to credit, insurance, and pension facility. It seeks to provide financial services, namely, Savings and Deposit Accounts, Remittance and Credit facility, Insurance, and Pension to every account holder in an affordable manner under the scheme.

In addition, the beneficiaries would get RuPay Debit card having inbuilt accident insurance cover of ₹ 1 lakh. The plan also envisages channelizing all Government benefits and payouts from the Centre, States, and Local bodies directly to the beneficiaries' accounts, thus implementing and widening the Direct Benefits Transfer (DBT) scheme of the Union and State Governments. The related technological issues such as poor telecom and Net connectivity required for online transactions would be resolved. Mobile transactions through telecom operators and their established centres as Cash Out Points are planned to be used for financial inclusion under the scheme. Also, an effort is being made to reach out and involve the youth of the country in this Mission Mode Programme.

The PMJDY Scheme and Its Benefits

The account can be opened in any bank branch or at Business Correspondent (Bank Mitras) outlet. PMJDY accounts are being opened with Zero balance. However, if the account holder wishes to get a cheque book, he or she will have to fulfil the minimum balance criteria.

The Special Benefits under PMJDY Scheme include:

- Interest on deposit.
- Accidental insurance cover of Rs. 1.00 lac
- No minimum balance required.
- Life insurance cover of Rs. 30,000/-
- Easy transfer of money across India
- Beneficiaries of Government Schemes will get Direct Benefit Transfer in these accounts.
- After satisfactory operation of the account for 6 months, an overdraft facility will be permitted
- Access to Pension and insurance products.
- Accidental Insurance Cover (RuPay Debit Card must be used at least once in 45 days)
- Overdraft facility upto Rs. 5000/- is available in only one account per household, preferably lady of the household.

Progress of PM Jan Dhan Yojana

- As will be seen from Table 25.1, the number of JDY accounts has gone up from 14.72 crore in March 2015 to 41.60 crore in January 2021.
- Of this, 23.04 crore accounts, forming 55.38 per cent, are held by women, and about 27.36 crore accounts (forming 65.77 per cent) are opened in rural and semi-urban areas.
- And deposits in JDY accounts have risen from ₹ 14,641 crore in March 2015 to ₹ 1,35,740 crore in January 2021.
- The average deposit balance is approx. ₹ 3263 per PMJDY account.
- Out of total operative accounts opened under PMJDY, 84.10 per cent have been seeded with Aadhaar number of the account holder on user consent basis, which has enabled interoperable and immediate Aadhaar based transactions, including for Direct Benefit transfer (DBT) through Aadhaar Payment Bridge.
- About 30.60 crore RuPay cards with an inbuilt accidental insurance of ₹ 1 lakh (₹ 2 lakh for accounts opened after 28.8.2018) coverage have also been provided to PMJDY account holders.
- As on January 2021, 31.71 crore beneficiaries have been enrolled under PM Suraksha Bima Yojana (PMSBY) and PM Jeevan Jyoti Bima Yojana (PMJJBY). Taking into account the premium of ₹ 12 per annum and ₹ 330 per annum for PMSBY and PMJJBY respectively, eligible beneficiaries under these 2 schemes can get accidental and life insurance cover of ₹ 4 lakh at an average premium of less than Rs.1 per day.

Table 25.1 Pradhan Mantri Jan Dhan Yojana

(Accounts Opened from 2016 to 2021)

As on	PMJDY Accounts (in crore)	Breakup by Gender No. of PMJDY Accounts		Breakup by Geography No. of PMJDY Accounts		Deposits In PMJDY Accounts
		Male	Female	Male	Female	
				Rural / Semi Urban	Urban / Metro	Deposits In PMJDY Accounts (In ₹ Crore)
March'15	14.72	7.15	7.39	8.68	5.86	14,641
March'16	21.43	10.37	11.05	13.17	8.26	35,672
March'17	28.17	13.67	14.49	16.87	11.3	62,972
March'18	31.44	14.85	16.60	18.52	12.92	78,494
March'19	35.27	16.53	18.74	20.90	14.37	96,107
March'20	38.33	17.85	20.48	22.63	15.70	1,18,434
06.01.2021	41.60	18.56	23.04	30.60	14.24	1,35,740

Source: Annual Report, 2020-21, Department of Financial Services, Ministry of Finance, Govt. of India,

BCAs and Bank Mitras

In the Urban and Rural areas where opening of a brick-and-mortar branch or ATM is not viable, banks have engaged Business Correspondent Agents/Bank Mitras (BCAs/BMs) for providing the banking services. The Business Correspondent Agents/Bank Mitras represent the concerned banks and offer banking services. They work online, on real time mode, using various types of telecom connectivity. Around 1.26 lakh BCAs/BMs have been deployed by the banks for attaining the goal under the PMJDY program.

According to the RBI Annual Report 2019-20, there are 5, 41,175 Business Correspondents in villages, and 6,35,046 urban locations covered by agents. Presumably, this number includes the 1.26 lakh Bank Mitras operating under PMJDY.

The outlets of BCAs/Bank Mitras, in both rural and urban areas, are fully equipped with the infrastructure required for delivery of banking services like opening account, cash deposit, withdrawal, and fund transfer (remittances). They also provide the insurance and pension related services. These services are delivered through biometric authentication and by using RuPay ATM/ Debit cards swiping with PINs.

Role of IT and Intermediaries in Financial inclusion: The use of information technology (IT) and intermediaries in the form of Information and Communication Technology (ICT) based models including BCs, ATMs and mobile vans has increased outreach, scale and depth of banking services at an affordable cost. Payments Banks have also been included under the Lead Bank Scheme (LBS). As on September 30, 2019 (as reported by SLBCs across the country), 4,87,496 (99.2 per cent) out of 4,91,490 identified villages across the country with population less than 2,000, have been provided with banking services. Out of the 8,687 identified villages with population more than 5,000, 8,200 (94.4 per cent) have been provided with banking services.

Financial Literacy and FLCs

Educating those who are new to using the banking system and ensuring 'financial literacy' for them is an important part of the programme. Reserve Bank of India (RBI) has issued operational guidelines for conducting financial literacy camps by Financial Literacy Centres (FLCs) and rural branches of banks. As at the end of March 2020, 1,467 Financial Literacy Centres (FLCs) were operational in the country. During 2019-20, 1,48,444 financial literacy related activities were conducted by the FLCs, up from 1,45,427 activities undertaken during the previous year.

Consequent on the efforts to promote financial inclusion by RBI and all banks, considerable ground has been covered. Going forward, the focus will have to be on keeping the accounts open, active, and live with operations.

Financial literacy drive plays an important part in this as it would enable customers to develop the habit of thrift and saving, learn the benefits of various financial products, and to make choices according to their needs. FLCs and rural branches of banks could adopt a tailored approach for different target groups, viz., farmers, artisans, micro and small entrepreneurs, women and SHGs, senior citizens, school children, etc. There should also be coordinated action at the ground level between the different stakeholders, viz., NABARD, representatives of RBI and banks, cooperatives, district and local administration, block and village level officials, panchayats, NGOs, SHGs, BCs, Farmers' groups, etc. during the conduct of financial literacy camps.

❑ JAM AND AADHAAR

Building on the momentum generated by PMJDY, the government is further consolidating it through 'JAM' which stands for Jan Dhan Yojana, Aadhaar, and Mobile. The Unique Identity number–**Aadhaar**– which has been assigned to nearly 125 crore people becomes a useful and effective tool for identifying every citizen and will thus help in linking bank accounts and various transactions especially for Direct Benefit Transfer (DBT) under welfare schemes and subsidies, flawlessly.

Some concerns have been expressed about the privacy of citizens being compromised and also the fear of exclusion, especially of the most vulnerable sections, in getting social security benefits for not being registered under the scheme. Yet, the benefits of the scheme far outweigh the issues of concern being put forth. Like what they say, lengthen the bed instead of cutting the leg because the bed is short, what is necessary is to track those not yet registered and get them included in the scheme and legally enforce safeguards to ensure that citizens' details are not divulged under any circumstances.

A digital pipeline of Jan-Dhan Aadhaar Mobile (JAM) has been laid by linking of Jan-Dhan account with mobile number and Aadhaar. This infrastructure pipeline is providing the necessary backbone for and easing DBT flows, adoption of social security/pension schemes, facilitating credit flows, promoting digital payments, etc. As it is done without any intervention, it becomes a fool-proof arrangement. And Mobile, being ubiquitous and held by almost every adult citizen, serves as a useful platform for transfer of money from banks to beneficiary accounts. It is particularly useful in rural areas where bank penetration may be low and there are last-mile problems in reaching beneficiaries and their accounts.

Thus, JAM will serve as the bedrock of many initiatives to come. It helps to provide maximum value for every rupee spent, maximum empowerment for our poor, and maximum technology penetration among the masses providing various facilities.

❑ EXPANSION OF BANKING FACILITIES AND PAYMENTS BANKS AND SFBs

In the Budget speech of the Union Finance Minister for the year 2010-11, it was announced, *inter alia*, that there was a need to extend the geographic coverage of banks and improve access to banking services and that RBI was considering giving some additional banking licences to private sector players.

Based on the recommendations of a High Level Committee set up by the RBI in October, 2013, headed by former RBI Governor, Dr. Bimal Jalan, the RBI granted 'in-principle' approval in 2014 to two applicants viz., IDFC Limited and Bandhan Financial Services Pvt. Ltd., to set up banks in the private sector.

Payments Banks and Small Finance Banks

Further, in the Union Budget for 2014-15, the Finance Minister announced that "*RBI will create a framework for licensing small banks and other differentiated banks. Differentiated banks serving niche interests, local area banks, payment banks, etc. are contemplated to meet credit and remittance needs of small businesses, unorganized sector, low income households, farmers and migrant workforce*".

Accordingly, based on the report submitted in January 2014 by a 'Committee on Comprehensive Financial Services for Small Businesses and Low Income Households', headed by Dr. Nachiket Mor, the RBI granted 'in-principle' approval to 11 applicants in August 2015 to set up Payments Banks under the 'Guidelines for Licensing of Payments Banks' issued in November, 2014.

According to the RBI Notification, the 'in-principle' approval granted will be valid for a period of 18 months, during which time the applicants have to comply with the requirements under the Guidelines and fulfil other conditions as may be stipulated by the Reserve Bank. On being satisfied that the applicants have complied with the requisite conditions laid down, RBI would consider granting them a licence for commencement of banking business.

There are 11 Small Finance Banks (SFBs) and 6 Payments Banks operational.

The primary objective of setting up of Payments Banks is to further financial inclusion by providing:

(i) Small savings accounts, and

(ii) Payments/ remittance services to migrant labour workforce, low income households, small businesses, other unorganized sector entities, and other users. It would result in high volume–low value transactions in deposits and payments/remittance services in a secured technology-driven environment.

Payments Banks can undertake the following activities and functions:

(a) Acceptance of demand deposits. Payments bank will initially be restricted to holding a maximum balance of ₹1,00,000 per individual customer.

(b) Issuance of ATM/debit cards. Payments banks cannot issue credit cards.

(c) Payments and remittance services through various channels.

(d) Business Correspondent (BC) of another bank, subject to the Reserve Bank guidelines on BCs.

(e) Distribution of non-risk sharing simple financial products like mutual fund units and insurance products, etc.

Payments banks have to follow the following conditions in deploying the funds:

(i) The payments bank cannot undertake lending activities.

(ii) Apart from amounts maintained as Cash Reserve Ratio (CRR) with the Reserve Bank, they have to invest minimum 75 per cent of its "demand deposit balances" in Statutory Liquidity Ratio (SLR) eligible Government securities / treasury bills with maturity up to one year and hold maximum 25 per cent in current and time/fixed deposits with other scheduled commercial banks for operational purposes and liquidity management.

Payments banks can give an impetus to the financial inclusion initiative and to widening the digital payment system. It could also encourage the spread of FinTech culture in the Indian banking landscape. Yet, they face some challenges in their working.

- As their deposits are capped at ₹1 lakh, they have to operate with low account balances and rely on high volume-low margin transactions which may affect their profitability.
- Selling insurance and mutual fund products is closely regulated by sectoral regulators (IRDA) and (SEBI). The distribution and sales commissions are capped, and there are strict requirements to prevent miss-selling. Both these require certified and trained manpower to sell the products, which implies hiring better quality manpower, training expense and longer gestation before getting returns. In other words, it involves higher costs and limited earnings.
- With existing Scheduled banks intensifying their focus, multiple payments banks and Small Finance banks (see next section below) vying for the customer base and even the FinTech startups disrupting the existing models, the segment becomes too crowded and competitive. While some of the players like Telecom companies and India Post who have entered with their existing wide network and large customer base have an advantage, for others, it's a long haul to acquire critical mass. They also have to invest in creating the infrastructure.

Small Finance Banks (SFBs)

The RBI has also issued licences for second set of differentiated Small Finance Banks with a view to further financial inclusion with the following objectives:

(i) Provision of savings instruments; and

(ii) Supply of credit to small business units, small and marginal farmers, micro and small industries, and other unorganised sector entities, through high technology-low cost operations

The following are eligible to set up SFBs:

- Resident individuals/professionals with 10 years of experience in banking and finance;
- Companies and societies owned and controlled by residents
- Existing Non-Banking Finance Companies (NBFCs), Micro Finance Institutions (MFIs), and Local Area Banks (LABs) that are owned and controlled by residents can opt for conversion into SFBs.
- Promoter/promoter groups should be 'fit and proper' with a sound track record of professional experience or of running their businesses for at least a period of five years in order to be eligible to promote SFBs.

Among those granted licence for SFBs, Micro Finance Institutions (MFIs) are dominant. It indicates that the RBI clearly wants micro-lenders to play a bigger role in taking banking to the rural poor, who are not yet covered by the existing full-service banks. By having small banks, India now will have a network of small, focused lenders, specifically targeting the low-income segment and furthering financial inclusion and credit expansion drive.

Small finance banks can undertake:

- Almost all operations of a normal commercial bank, albeit on a smaller scale.
- They shall primarily undertake basic banking activities of acceptance of deposits and lending to unserved and underserved sections.
- The RBI clearly restricts these banks to operate in low-income segment, by stipulating that 75 per cent of the total credit extended by these banks should be given to borrowers who qualify to be in the Priority sector as defined by the central bank.
- There will not be any restriction in the area of operations of small finance banks.

By paving the way for Payments and Small banks, the central bank has radically transformed the country's banking landscape and taken reforms to a new level. These steps enhance the reach of banking services to larger sections of the population and help to revitalize the economy.

❑ MUDRA YOJANA—FUNDING THE UNFUNDED

Yet another initiative of the government was the launch of the MUDRA Bank (Micro Units Development and Refinance Agency Bank) in April 2015. Announced in the Union Budget for 2015-16, MUDRA Bank is set up for development of micro units and refinancing of Micro Finance Institutions (MFIs) through a Pradhan Mantri Mudra Yojana (PMMY). Aimed at 'funding the unfunded', it will encourage entrepreneurship and reach out to small entrepreneurs who are mostly at the mercy of moneylenders, and support them in their efforts to undertake some productive and income generating activity. While there are a number of facilities provided for the large industries which do play an important role, there is also need to focus on about 5.75 crore small business units which are mostly individual proprietorship.

PMMY credit sanctioned rose from ₹1.37 lakh crore in 2015-16 to ₹ 3.37 lakh crore in 2019-20. More than 27 crore loans were extended of which 88% loans were under SHISHU Category, 68% loans to Women and 51% loans to SC/ST/OBC. Since the inception of the scheme, 27.28 crore loans have been sanctioned amounting to ₹14,02,436 crore.

It has also been seen that while some borrowers in large industries are not able to repay loans and seek more time, about 90 per cent of small borrowers, including women SHGs, repay loans on time. By extending credit to micro enterprises, Mudra will create a sound ecosystem which will pave the way for major banks also to give credit to aspiring entrepreneurs. Honesty and integrity shown by borrowers in the small sector is commendable.

❑ BANKS: NPAs AND RECAPITALISATION

Non-Performing Assets (NPAs) and their Recoveries

The problem of mounting bad loans and stressed assets in public sector banks (PSBs), discussed in Chapter 13 (see pages 13.7-8) continue to haunt banks. Gross non-performing assets (NPAs) of many banks have climbed to nearly 10 per cent after RBI's asset quality review and banks had to set aside large sums to cover bad loans.

- According to Reserve Bank data, the gross non-performing assets (GNPAs) of banks rose from 9.3 per cent in 2016-17 to 11.2 per cent amounting to ₹10.39 trillion in 2017-18. Of this, the share of public sector banks (PSBs) stood at ₹8.95 trillion (14.6 per cent).
- In contrast, the GNPA ratio of private sector banks stood at a much lower level of 4.7 per cent in 2017-18. Concerted efforts through higher write-offs and better recoveries helped private sector banks to maintain lower GNPA ratio. (On this, see Table 5.5 in chapter 5, p.5.14).
- The GNPAs of many banks rose to nearly 10 per cent following asset quality review (AQR) by the RBI. This was also due to due to restructured advances slipping into NPAs and better recognition of advances as NPAs. Due to this, the banks had to set aside large sums to cover bad loans which reflected on their balance sheets.
- Power, infrastructure and steel sectors together account for half of the stressed assets.

Though the RBI and the government have been making concerted efforts to bring down the level of NPAs in the banks, it has not made much headway. To mitigate the problem, the government has addressed structural issues in various sectors like steel, power, coal, highways, and sugar. The banks are also trying to effect recoveries of loans and focus on revival of stalled projects. The Finance Ministry has set in motion a revamp plan for PSBs called 'Indradhanush'. As part of the revamp of PSBs and to bolster the system, the government has taken various measures as shown in this section.

- Separation of the post of Chairman and MD & CEO of PSBs. Chairman will be non-Executive Chairman.
- The selection process for both these positions will be on transparent and meritocratic basis.
- A Bank Board Bureau (BBB) is set up, consisting of three eminent professionals and three officials, replacing the Appointments Board for appointment of whole-time Directors as well as non-Executive Chairman of PSBs.
- To de-stress banks' position on loan defaults due to delay of projects, meetings are held with banks and concerned sectors in default and measures taken to speed up clearances which were holding up projects.
- For better risk control and to keep close watch on NPAs, RBI has issued guidelines for 'Early Recognition of Financial Distress, Prompt Steps for Resolution and Fair Recovery for Lenders: Framework for Revitalizing Distressed Assets in the Economy'.

Steps to Improve Recoveries

After the Insolvency and Bankruptcy Code (IBC) was enacted, the Banking Regulation Act, 1949 was amended empowering the Reserve Bank to issue directions to any bank to initiate action for insolvency in respect of a default under the IBC. It also empowers the RBI to specify authorities or committees with members appointed or approved by it to advise bank(s) on resolution of stressed assets. And under the Banking Regulation (Amendment) Act, 2017, the RBI has taken several steps to hasten the process of resolution of large value stressed accounts.

The RBI's internal advisory committee identified, in the first instance, 12 large stressed assets for proceedings under the IBC. Subsequently, RBI advised banks to set aside 50 per cent provisioning (setting apart funds) against secured exposure and 100 per cent against unsecured exposure in all cases referred for bankruptcy. The RBI in a second list of big defaulters of loans asked banks to resolve 28 large accounts failing which to refer them to National Company Law Tribunal (NCLT) for insolvency proceedings. These 28 accounts together account for 40 per cent of bad loans of about ₹4 lakh crore.

Box 25.1 Setting up of Bad bank: The Objectives and Implications

In the backdrop of high level of unpaid loans which corporates owe to banks and banks faced with mounting NPAs (Non-Performing Assets, i.e., assets in default), the Government of India has set up in September 2021a "Bad Bank". A bad bank takes over the unpaid loans, usually below the book value, manages them and tries to recover the money over some years.

According to Reserve Bank data, the gross non-performing assets (GNPAs) of banks rose from 9.3 per cent in 2016-17 to 11.2 per cent in 2017-18. Of this, the share of public sector banks (PSBs) stood at 14.6 per cent. Further, the Scheduled Commercial Banks' (SCBs') GNPA ratio declined to 7.48 per cent in March 2021 but may rise to 9.8 per cent by March 2022 and to 11.22 per cent under a severe stress scenario.

Setting up of ARC: In the budget speech for FY 2021-22, Finance Minister, Nirmala Sitharaman, had mentioned the government's intention to set up asset management and reconstruction companies that would "take over the existing stressed debt and then manage and dispose of the assets to Alternate Investment Funds and other potential investors for eventual value realization".

Provided with a capital base of ₹ 36,000 crore, the National Asset Reconstruction Company Ltd (NARCL), as it is officially called, will help banks clear their balance sheet and focus on core business and lending activities. It entails moving the bad loans of the public sector banks to a newly created entity which will then try to recover the defaulted loans by selling the assets offered as a collateral against such loans.

NARCL has been set up by banks to aggregate and consolidate stressed assets for their subsequent resolution. PSBs will maintain 51 per cent ownership in NARCL while FIs or debt management companies will hold 49 per cent.

IDRCL: Along with NARCL, the government has set up the India Debt Resolution Company Ltd (IDRCL). It is a service company/operational entity which will manage the asset and engage market professionals and turnaround experts. Public Sector Banks (PSBs) and Public FIs will hold a maximum of 49 per cent stake and the rest will be with private sector lenders.

Role of NARCL and IDRCL

A question is why NARCL-IDRCL is needed when there are 28 existing ARCs. The existing ARCs have been helpful in resolution of stressed assets, especially for smaller value loans. But most of them do not have much capital to buy bad loans. Unlike them, the bad bank is owned and funded by the Indian government and some public sector banks.

Many public sector banks have in the past been reluctant to transfer their non-performing assets (bad loans) to private ARCs, not trusting their capitalisation or fearing investigations. But in the case of an entity run by the government, banks may participate more readily, with a sense of security.

Various available resolution mechanisms, including IBC have proved to be useful. However, considering the large stock of legacy NPAs, additional options/alternatives are needed and hence the initiative to set up NARCL and IRDCL.

- NARCL proposes to resolve stressed loan assets above ₹ 500 crore each amounting to about ₹ 2 lakh crore **in** phases within the extant regulations of RBI. It will acquire these through 15 per cent Cash and 85 per cent in Security Receipts (SRs).
- In phase I, fully provisioned assets of about ₹ 90,000 crore are expected to be transferred to NARCL, while the remaining assets with lower provisions would be transferred in phase II.
- The NARCL will pick up bad loans above a certain threshold from banks and would aim to sell them to prospective buyers of distressed debt.
- The NARCL will acquire assets by making an offer to the lead bank. Once NARCL's offer is accepted, then, IDRCL will be engaged for management and value addition.
- It will also be responsible for valuing bad loans to determine at what price they would be sold.
- It would provide government receipts to banks as it takes on non-performing assets from their books.

Need for Government Guarantee

Resolution mechanisms of this nature which deal with a backlog of NPAs typically require a backstop from Government. This imparts credibility and provides for contingency buffers. Hence, Govt of India Guarantee of up to ₹ 30,600 crore will back Security Receipts (SRs) issued by NARCL. The guarantee will be valid for 5 years. The guarantee shall cover the shortfall between the face value of the SR and the actual realisation. Government's guarantee will also enhance liquidity of SRs as such SRs are tradable.

Benefits and Outcome of Bad Bank

There are divided opinions among experts on the move to set up such an entity to deal with the problem of NPAs faced by banks.

Benefits

- The main advantage of setting up a bad Bank is argued, it can help to consolidate all the bad loans of banks under a single exclusive entity. And let banks concentrate on core banking activity.

- A Bad Bank to achieve effective resolution of the problem will require highly skilled and professional experts to create a legal framework and commercial ecosystem to make it successful.
- Besides, it needs good governance for tailor-made accounting and governance rules and ensure independence and effectiveness in functioning.
- In addition, it will have to make a homogenous portfolio so that it can easily manage and sell the assets in question.

The Flip side

This set up should not be a permanent structure and should wind up after it resolves the existing cases. It cannot be open ended because then it will be a moral hazard

Many of the experts believe that Bad Bank backed by the government will merely shift bad assets.

And some argue that it may end up in mere transfer of assets from one pocket of the government (the PSBs) to another agency of the government (NARCL).

In the light of this move, structural reforms in banking sector must not be neglected. These include better governance and greater diligence in the lending process, and stringent monitoring of loans for early detection of distress signs.

Recapitalisation of Banks

Recapitalisation of banks has been an affirmative policy response the world over to strengthen banks' balance sheets and potentially increase their ability to expand their credit, including in periods of stress. If credit growth helps the economy to pick up, support through capital infusion by government provides a lifeline for potentially viable banks to survive the pangs of balance sheet distress.

Capital adequacy of public sector banks (PSBs) and the need for recapitalising them has been a major issue. The Government of India wants to adequately capitalise all the banks to keep a safe buffer over and above the minimum norms of Basel III. (On Basel norms, see chapter 13, p. **13.6**)

This problem is not new and the government has recapitalised PSBs in the past. To ensure that banks maintain Tier I capital adequacy, the Government started capital infusion programme from 2007-08 onwards. A cumulative amount of ₹131 billion was injected in PSBs during 2007-08 to 2009-10. Capital infusion by the government continued in subsequent years as well, wherein an attempt was made to link it with bank performance. A total amount of ₹666 billion was injected in PSBs during 2010-11 to 2014-15.

The banks which got a recap of ₹25,000 crore in the Budget for 2016–17 got a further relief of ₹35,000 crore as the RBI revised norms allowing banks to assign higher value to hidden assets in the balance sheet. The assets include undervalued real estate, taxes paid but not reckoned, and forex reserves. Until now, banks could revalue assets and recognize half of the gains as part of Tier II capital. Now RBI has allowed banks to recognize 45 per cent of the valuation gains as Tier I capital, which will reduce their burden of capital requirement.

In October 2017, the government announced infusion of an unprecedented ₹2.11 lakh crore capital over two years in public sector banks. (PSBs). Of this, ₹1.35 lakh crore would be infused through recapitalisation bonds and ₹76,000 crore through budgetary support and bank equity sales.

In 2018-19, the bank recapitalisation program was launched with bonds of ₹ 800 billion being issued that year. The programme was integrated with a reform agenda, under the template of an "Enhanced Access and Service Excellence" (EASE) programme. This recapitalisation paved the way for the public sector banks to lend additional credit of ₹ 5 trillion. Further recapitalization done was ₹ 70,000 crore in 2019-20, ₹ 20,000 crore each in 2020-21 and 2021-22.

Need for Reforms

Though recapitalisation of banks is a significant step in strengthening the balance sheet of banks, as it enables banks to scale up credit to productive sectors, it is not a panacea for the ills of banking sector. It has to be backed by a string of reforms to improve the resilience of banks, both the public sector banks and private banks. Reforms are needed so that genuine borrowers do not suffer and get hassle-free, need-based credit. Some of the reforms required are: (On this, see also "Way forward for Banking Reforms: P J Nayak Committee report" on p. 5.13 in Box 5.1 in chapter 5).

- The release of capital by the Government to be subject to the performance of banks. Public sector banks need to undertake certain performance obligations and commitments in respect of parameters such as changes in operational policies and in organisational structure, and use of upgraded technology to ensure an improvement in productivity, viability and profitability.
- While infusing fresh capital, priority to be given to those banks which have shown improved performance, efficiency and profitability. This will send the message that government will reward those banks with more capital which show better results.
- Banks should chalk out plans to ensure excellence in customer service and maintenance of a high level of efficiency in providing various services.
- To ensure that genuine borrowers do not suffer and get hassle-free, need based credit. Special focus to be given to micro, small and medium enterprises (MSMEs), and on financial inclusion and job creation.
- Exercise due diligence in lending improve credit appraisal and monitoring and ensure additional securities and documentation.
- Strengthening of Bank Boards, and resolving HR issues.
- Ensuring full autonomy of banks and freeing them of political and other interference and influences in their functioning particularly in the sanctioning of loans.
- **Consolidation and amalgamation of public sector banks (PSBs):** A panel of ministers under the chairmanship of then Finance and Corporate Affairs Minister, Arun Jaitley, was set up to examine proposals from banks for in-principle approval for amalgamation of PSBs. The panel's proposals were placed before the Cabinet and proposals of merger of certain PSBs were approved by the government. **(See next section on the merger of PSBs).**
- Even if banks are well-capitalized, are ready and able to lend, there may not be demand for credit. Unless excess productive capacities are exhausted, industries will not take up expansion and there will be limited demand for bank credit from businesses regardless of government plans. Uptick in the economy, robust domestic demand and steady growth are pre-requisites for demand for bank credit. India's recent experience of investment slump in the private sector and sluggish demand for bank credit from the private sector is a pointer to this. As the saying goes, 'one can take the horse to the water but cannot make him drink unless he is thirsty'.

(On Nationalisation of Banks, NPAs and reforming PSBs, see chapter 5, pp. 5.7-10 and Box 5.1 on pp. 5.10-4).

Amalgamation of Public Sector Banks (PSBs)

Merger of State Bank of India with its Subsidiaries: The reform measures initiated and institution of robust systems across PSBs strengthened the banks. This helped to harness the potential for inter-bank synergy and scale benefits through merger.

The State Bank of India (SBI), India's largest bank, was merged with its five commercial banking subsidiaries on April 1, 2017. The five subsidiaries are the State Bank of Bikaner & Jaipur, State Bank of Hyderabad, State Bank of Mysore, State Bank of Patiala and State Bank of Travancore. The Bharatiya Mahila Bank was also merged with SBI on the same date. This was the first ever major consolidation in the Indian banking industry and the move is in consonance with the government's stated intention of encouraging consolidation among state-owned banks.

The SBI originally had seven associates, of which two – State Bank of Saurashtra and State Bank of Indore – were merged with it earlier.

This merger makes the combined entity's balance sheet a whopping ₹ 37 trillion, making it one of the top 50 banks in the world. The company is on the Fortune Global 500 list of the world's biggest corporations and it will now have more visibility at global level.

With the merger, the bank has on its rolls 278,000 employees, 420 million customers, and more than 24,000 branches and 59,000 ATMs. It has 198 offices in 37 countries and 301 correspondents in 72 countries. While the network of SBI expands and its reach widens, it can reap efficiencies from rationalization of branches, common treasury pooling and proper deployment of a large skilled resource base. Cost savings on account of treasury operations, audit, technology, etc., would lower cost-to-income ratio in the long term. But a negative impact in the near term would be from pension liability provisions due to different employee benefit structures and harmonization of accounting policies and provisioning for non-performing assets (NPA).

Strengthening and Merger of more PSBs

Over the last few years, PSBs have not only cleaned up legacy stress and addressed underlying systemic weaknesses but have emerged stronger as a result of comprehensive and institutionalised EASE (Enhanced Access and Service Excellence) reforms. To further leverage the positive impacts brought about though reforms and with the aim of creating strong and efficient banks, more PSBs were amalgamated which is expected to significantly improve the operating efficiency of the consolidated banks. The mergers effected are:

- Dena Bank and Vijaya Bank were merged with Bank of Baroda.
- Punjab National Bank, Oriental Bank of Commerce and United Bank was merged to become the second largest PSB in India after State Bank of India.
- Canara Bank and Syndicate Bank were merged into one entity.
- Andhra Bank, and Corporation Bank have been amalgamated with Union Bank of India.
- Allahabad Bank was merged with Indian Bank.

These mergers have brought down the number of PSBs from 27 to 12. This was expected to scale up investments in technology, ensure better customer reach, offer wider array of products and services, enhanced lending capacity and improve operating efficiency.

Merits of Public Sector Bank Mergers

- Leverage economies of scale and synergies for operational efficiencies and improve banks' service delivery.

- Greater financial capacity to support economic growth.
- Mergers enable a large capital base that will aid to offer a bigger loan amount.
- Customers of the bank will have a much wider range of products they can choose from in mutual funds, insurance products, loans and deposits.
- The need for recapitalisation from the government will reduce after a merger.
- The bank will have an opportunity to establish technological advancements in their processes.

Challenges in Merger

- The merger and consolidation has come even as the government is grappling with issues of rising bad debts in the banking system.
- The need to ensure efficient utilization of capital.
- To make the combined entity stronger and more competitive through prudent policies and operations.

❑ BLACK MONEY

The 'Black money' issue has been in public domain and discussed for long in India but no effective steps were taken by successive governments. Undisclosed wealth had also apparently spawned a huge parallel economy in the country causing disruptions in the economic policies of the government. In 1997, a tax amnesty scheme, known as the Voluntary Disclosure of Income Scheme (VDIS), was announced by the Union Government. Against the money disclosed, the government then collected taxes to the tune of about ₹ 10,000 crore. (See Income Declaration Scheme, 2016 on p. 25.17 & 25.21).

The Central Government took the following steps in regard to black money during the 2010-11 period and thereafter.

- Three government institutes were asked in March 2011 to conduct separate studies on black money:
  1. National Institute of Public Finance and Policy (NIPFP)
  2. National Institute of Financial Management (NIFM); and
  3. National Council of Applied Economic Research (NCAER).

  The government then took further action on curbing black money. These included:
- India joined as the 34th member of Financial Action Task Force (FATF) in June 2010. FATF membership would help India to build the capacity to fight terrorism and trace terror funds and to successfully investigate and prosecute money laundering and terrorist financing offences.
- India has joined the Asia Pacific Group (APG) against money laundering.
- India has gained Membership of the Eurasian Group (EAG) in December 2010.
- India has joined the Egmont Group which is an international network fostering improved communication and interaction among Financial Intelligence Units (FIU).

Double Tax Avoidance Agreement: Features

- India has one of the largest networks of tax treaties for the avoidance of double taxation and prevention of tax evasion.
- The country has Double Tax Avoidance Agreement (DTAA) with over 85 countries under Section 90 of the Income Tax Act, 1961.

- The purpose of such tax treaties is to ensure a fair and equitable system for allocation of the right to tax different types of income between the 'source' and 'residence' countries.
- The agreement between the negotiating countries provides specific guidelines on how the income generated in one country and transferred to another is to be taxed by the source and resident country.
- This ensures protection to taxpayers against "**double taxation**".
- It prevents any deterrent consequence that double taxation may have in the free flow of international trade, investment, and transfer of technology between the two signatory countries.
- A DTAA between India and other countries covers only residents of India and residents of the negotiating country.
- Any person or a company that is not resident, either in India or in the other country that has entered into an agreement with India, cannot claim benefits under the signed DTAA.
- **Protocol with Switzerland:** Switzerland is especially where Indians are supposed to have stashed income and assets in undisclosed and manner to avoid detection taking advantage the element of secrecy which Swiss laws provided. The protocol amending our tax treaty with Switzerland was signed in August 2010 and was approved by the Swiss Parliament in 2011. India has since started receiving information from the Swiss government on the deposits and assets maintained by India nationals in Swiss banks.

Petition on Black Money

In 2011, on a petition filed by concerned citizens in the Supreme Court (SC), the Court upbraided the Union government for not showing seriousness in bringing back black money stashed abroad, and constituted a Special Investigation Team (SIT) to take steps to bring back unaccounted monies and illegal wealth. However, the then Government prayed for a revision of the SC order, did not take steps to constitute the SIT, or follow up on the SC directive.

When the next NDA government took office in May 2014, it took a decision in the very first Cabinet meeting to constitute the SIT, in compliance with the Supreme Court directive, to pursue the matter, and take action on black money. The SIT is headed by a retired SC judge, Justice M B Shah as Chairman and another former SC judge, Justice Arijit Pasayat as Vice-Chairman. The panel is being assisted by the Revenue Secretary in the Ministry of Finance, directors of CBI, IB, RAW and ED, Chairman of Central Board of Direct Taxes, and a Deputy Governor of the Reserve Bank of India. The SIT has since been pursuing the matter and the progress is being reported periodically by the SIT to the Government, and by the government to the Supreme Court.

Black Money Law

Meanwhile, the Central Government got the Black Money (Undisclosed Foreign Income and Assets) and Imposition of Tax Bill, 2015 passed as an Act by the Parliament (popularly known as the Black Money Act). The Act was passed by both the Houses of Parliament in May 2014 and received the assent of the President of India. It came into effect from July 1, 2015.

The Act aims to curb black money, or undisclosed foreign assets and income, and imposes tax and penalty on such income. The Act gave a one-time, 3-month period for people holding such undisclosed assets to voluntarily declare in which case they would have to pay 30 per cent tax and a 30 per cent penalty on the assets. It was also announced that the names of those who make such voluntary declarations would be kept confidential. If people holding such assets did not declare the assets before September 30, 2015 and if their assets were found out or get reported later, they would have to pay tax and penalty amounting to 120 per cent of the assets and be subject to prosecution and imprisonment which may be up to 10 years.

On the expiry of the 3-month compliance window on September 30, 2015, the government announced that 638 people had declared previously undisclosed foreign assets amounting to a total of ₹ 4,147 crore. While the precise quantum of wealth held abroad by Indians is not known, the amount declared is apparently far less than the amount reportedly stashed abroad, according to different studies and surveys done by various agencies, and is far less than what was expected to be declared. Further, it appears that some of those who have declared have done it out of fear and to avoid any harassment by the IT authorities though the assets held by them may not really be illegal but genuine under the laws. Some others who have moved illegal wealth from one country to another are hoping that it would go undetected and could thus escape any punishment. Such cases could only come to light when all countries are under an international obligation to disclose and exchange information on such cases.

Foreign Countries' Help

Many countries which are considered to be safe havens where wealth is stashed illegally have come on board and agreed to share information on Indians holding such accounts in those countries. They include Switzerland, Germany, France, Mauritius, Seychelles, and British Virgin Islands. From 2017, most countries were to automatically exchange information on tax-evaders. India has signed the Foreign Account Tax Compliance Act (FATCA) with the United States which will help to identify tax evaders who did not come clean during the compliance window period. This will make it easier for India to establish audit trails on complex deals like floating shell companies and creating multiple layers to hide such wealth. The government should take more effective steps and mandate companies to identify their real owners and make the registry public. Also, as the United States has done, India should negotiate with tax havens to secure information relating to past periods, and not just a prospective date, for the practice of stashing illegal wealth dates back to several years. India must leave no stone unturned in tracing and bringing back black money lying abroad in national interest. Such funds repatriated will come handy for the country for developmental purposes.

Action by Overseas Banks

Deterred by India's stringent steps to trace unaccounted and illegal wealth stashed abroad, banks overseas have started asking tough questions of people and entities from India who are seeking to open accounts with them. Banks want to know customers' tax residential status, legal and beneficiary ownership of the accounts, and the use of power of attorney. They also ask for income tax returns, source of funds, and other related information to ensure that the foreign transactions are above board. For instance, it has been reported that those who opened accounts in Swiss banks were opening them in the names of some nominees who act as intermediaries to conceal the identity of the real holders of the accounts.

It is not just those who possess such wealth who will get punished but also those who help them to move that money will face harsh action under the laws. India has signed global agreements and tax treaties with many countries in pursuit of tracking black money. Given the reduced global tolerance of tax evasion, banks will be under close scrutiny. Overseas financial institutions are also seeking the help of local experts to vet prospective customers.

❑ BLACK MONEY IN INDIA

The issue of black money has both an external and internal dimension. In fact, according to some reports and studies, the undisclosed, illegal wealth circulating within India is much more than what may be stashed abroad by Indians. Not only that, part of the undisclosed wealth abroad has been, and is being, routed back to India through illegal means, variously known as 'round-tripping', 'money laundering', 'hawala', etc., and is being invested in various companies and sectors in India without being detected.

Such undisclosed assets have virtually created what is called a 'parallel economy', causing much havoc to the economy. Hence, the government has proposed various steps to curb such black money within India—such as strictly enforcing Know Your Customer (KYC) norm, mandating the mention of PAN number for all transactions above a certain threshold, inter-linking of Aadhaar, bank accounts, PAN, property registration, and Income Tax returns, encouraging and even enforcing 'Cashless transactions' in certain cases, regulating the Real Estate and other sectors where undisclosed wealth from abroad could be invested without being detected and converted as legitimate funds.

The action on black money is showing signs of impact in different ways. In July 2014, India's stock markets were jolted by the Supreme Court-appointed Special Investigation Team's report on black money. This report called for identification of the owners of Participatory Notes (P-Notes), the instruments used for a good part of foreign investment in the stock market. The history of P-note investment goes back to the early 1990s since when they have served as conduits for converting illegitimate money as legitimate and have defied half-hearted attempts at control and dismantling.

Unless one is an NRI, all income earned, including what is earned outside India, whether taxed outside India or not, is to be reported in tax return. If tax has been already deducted on foreign income, one is allowed to take credit of such taxes under the DTAA treaty as permissible.

Provision in Budget to Declare Undisclosed Income

In the Union Budget presented for 2016-17, another opportunity has been afforded for declaring undisclosed income or income in the form of any asset and clear past transgressions by paying tax at 30 per cent and surcharge at 7.5 per cent and penalty of 7.5 per cent which works out to 45 per cent of the undisclosed income. It is a small compliance window which will be open from June 1 to September 30, 2016 with an option to pay amount due within two months of declaration. There will be no scrutiny or enquiry on this declaration under the Income Tax or Wealth Tax Act and the declarants will have immunity from prosecution. Immunity under the Benami Transaction (Prohibition) Act, 1988 will also be there subject to certain conditions. For more on this, see *Pradhan Mantri Garib Kalyan Yojana*, 2016 on p.25.21.

The surcharge of 7.5 per cent levied is called Krishi Kalyan surcharge which will be used for agriculture and rural economy.

Steps to Curb Black Money

Many suggestions have been put forth by various committees and enlightened citizens to curb the menace of black money and hidden, undisclosed wealth. Transparency in funding political parties for election purposes or otherwise and in all works, contractual or otherwise, awarded by any governmental or public bodies using State funds are two of the most important measures which can have a perceptible and profound impact in this regard. The very reason for political parties being unwilling to be brought under the RTI Act is precisely not to be subjected to any checks or transparency regarding funds being collected by, or gifted to them. It is another matter that corporate houses and individuals donating money to political parties also would not want any such openness for then their political affiliations as well as their donations will be fully exposed.

Real estate is another sector where such undisclosed money is generated and keeps circulating as it involves land deals and there is considerable scope for undervaluing assets and materials used. Various governmental approvals required in all constructions, both in the governmental and private sector, breeds corruption as graft is involved in many such approvals, which is reminiscent of the 'Licence Raj' that flourished in the industrial sector in the early decades after independence. All such approvals have to be made strictly online, to the maximum extent possible, so as to minimize any human intervention.

Banks' Role and Responsibility

Instances where officials in some banks in India have abused the system to aid money laundering have raised alarm bells. In 2013, a news portal had, through a sting operation at some of the country's largest banks, exposed violations of basic banking rules like the KYC norms, Anti-Money Laundering rules, and the Foreign Exchange Management (FEMA) Act, 1999. Considering the laxity found on the part of big banks, RBI carried out a thematic study of the cases which confirmed the transgressions. The RBI then took serious note of the issue and imposed a ₹ 50 crore penalty on a number of banks.

In 2015, another major fraud occurred in a nationalized bank where some bank officials in some of its branches allegedly colluded with traders to remit overseas over ₹ 6,000 crore illegally. The *modus operandi* involved opening multiple accounts over a period of time, without adhering to the KYC norms, and misusing provisions such as pre-payment for imports. Most of the funds were transferred electronically and not deposited in cash. The remittances done for some export and import houses were done on the basis of forged import documents. This may indicate the possible involvement of some other banks which was also under scrutiny. The Enforcement Directorate initiated probe into the case.

This apart, instances of abuse of powers and corruption on the part of bank officials have also come to notice in the recent past. There was a case of a loan-for-bribe scam involving the chief of a nationalized bank where he was alleged to have taken a big sum as bribe for sanctioning loans to a company. Also, huge loans issued by some banks to loss-making enterprises, which were sure to turn bad loans, pointed to questionable lending practices, adversely impacting an already stressed banking sector, weighed down by non-performing assets (NPAs).

Globally also, bank frauds and malpractices have increased and some of the world's largest banks have had to pay billions of dollars in fine over the past few years for breach of financial regulations. All these point to systemic failures and lack of integrity and probity in the functioning of some banks.

Money laundering and other banking frauds are serious crimes which undo the government's efforts to curb black money. Both the RBI and the government have expressed concern over this trend and directed all banks to tighten surveillance over the functioning of branches and adherence to all norms and regulations.

❑ DEMONETISATION

Introduction

In a further drive to unearth and flush out unaccounted 'black' money from the economy, the government came up with a surprise announcement of demonetising high value currencies of ₹500 and ₹1,000 denomination from the midnight of November 8, 2016. The announcement was made by the Prime Minister, Narendra Modi over the media on the evening of November 8, 2016. The move came by surprise and with many restrictions and riders with a view to prevent laundering of illegal and unaccounted money held in the form of these high value currencies.

Demonetisation in the Past

This was not the first time demonetisation was resorted to in India. During pre-independence period, in January 1946, the government passed the High Denomination Bank Notes (Demonetisation) Ordinance. It was soon after the World War II ended when businessmen in India were supposed to have made huge fortune by making supplies to the Allied forces for the requirements of the war but concealed the profits and evaded taxes. But the leaders of the Indian nationalist movement, while expressing no sympathy for dealers in black market and profiteers, criticised the move as it hurt the interests of, and caused inconvenience to, the honest and those in the lower and middle classes.

Again, when the Janata government headed by Morarji Desai was in power during 1977-80, in January 1978, the government withdrew currency notes of ₹1,000, ₹5,000 and ₹10,000 denomination from circulation with a view to reduce illegal transactions and curb black money.

Objectives of Demonetisation

Justifying the move taken in 2016, the government contended that unaccounted black money, which virtually works as a parallel, underground and shadow economy, was roiling and disrupting the mainstream economy and negating, to a great extent, the strenuous efforts at social and economic development. It was also being used, or rather misused, by terrorists, drug cartels and anti-social elements posing serious threat to the security of the country. The measure was taken to combat corruption, tax evasion, smuggling and counterfeiting of notes.

As already noted earlier, since 2014 the government had taken several steps to unearth unaccounted, black money. These were :

- On the orders of the Supreme Court, set up a 3-member Special Investigation Team (SIT) under Justice M. B. Shah in 2014 and the progress on this is monitored by the Supreme Court;
- The Black Money (Undisclosed Foreign Income and Assets) and Imposition of Tax Act 2015 came into effect;
- India and US signed agreement for information sharing under the Foreign Account Tax Compliance Act (FATCA) to increase transparency on tax matters and identify tax evaders;
- India has amended Double Tax Avoidance Agreement (DTAA) with Mauritius, Cyprus and Singapore to allow tax department to impose capital gains tax on investments routed through those countries and check round-tripping of funds into the country and plug possible misuse of benefits;
- Under the Income Declaration Scheme 2016, ₹65,250 crore of hitherto undeclared income and assets was unearthed;

Implications of Demonetisation

The total value of currencies circulated by Reserve Bank of India till March 2016 amounted to ₹16,415 billion of which ₹500 currency accounted for ₹7,854 billion (47.8 %) and ₹1,000 for ₹6,326 billion (38.5%). Thus, these two denominations together added up to 86.3 per cent of the total value of all notes in circulation. The other lower denominations amounted to ₹2,235 billion which works out to only about 13.62 per cent of the total value of currencies in circulation.

The position remained almost the same in November 2016 when the demonetisation was implemented.

According to information given in Parliament, the total value of currency in circulation as on November 11, 2016 was ₹17645 billion of which the value of ₹500 and ₹1,000 notes was ₹15,441 billion. Thus, as much as 87.5 per cent of all notes (in value) in circulation was scrapped at one stroke which was bound to cause a major jolt to the economy and shock to the people at large. (see Table 25.2).

Table 25.2: Number and Value of Currencies in Circulation

	Number (Million Pieces)		Value (₹ Billion)		Total value of ₹500 & ₹1,000 in Circulation (₹ Billion)	Total Value of All Notes in Circulation (₹ Billion)
	₹500	₹1,000	₹500	₹1,000		
March 2016	15,707	6,326	7854 (47.8)	6326 (38.5)	14,180 (86.3)	16415
November 2016	17,165	6,858	8583 (48.6)	6858 (38.8)	15,441 (87.4)	17,645 (as on Nov. 4,2016)

Note: Figures in brackets refer to percentage of value of scrapped notes to total value of notes in circulation.

Source: Information given in Parliament and Reserve Bank of India Statistical Supplement.

With a view to make the demonetisation move effective and achieve its objectives, the government imposed various temporary restrictions. These included:

- Banks and post offices were closed for public transactions on November 9, 2016, the day after demonetisation was announced and ATMs did not function for two days from the midnight of November 8.
- Those holding ₹500 and ₹1000 notes were allowed to exchange or deposit in banks or post offices from November 10 till December 30, 2016 on proper identification;
- Initially, the government and the RBI imposed limits for withdrawals from accounts and ATMs; the limits were gradually relaxed and raised later;
- During this period, transactions with cheques, debit cards, e-transactions were allowed to continue. All electronic transactions on account of business firms, companies and individuals were also allowed;
- The use of scrapped notes was also allowed for extended period for payments at petrol bunks, toll booths, pharmacies and government hospitals.

According to the government, these measures were necessary to maintain economic integrity of the nation. While in the near and short-term the move caused much disruption and pain to people at large, it was contended that in the medium and long-term, it would have a positive impact on the economy and will spur its growth. The government emphasized that while honest people would not face any trouble following this radical measure, those holding unaccounted money and do not come clean would face strict penal consequences. The government also said that once this action ended, further action against those holding black money was not ruled out.

Challenges and Impact of the Scheme

The demonetization scheme was implemented in the face of many challenges and its implementation left much to be desired as outlined below.

- Firstly, the process had to be done in utmost secrecy lest those holding illicit and unaccounted wealth would find ways to convert black money into white defeating the very purpose of the scheme. This meant that detailed advance preparation – printing and supply of new currencies -- could not be done which led to many of the problems mentioned below.
- As 87.4 per cent of currency in value was declared to be not legal tender at one stroke, it caused much disruption in the economy and inconvenience to public in conducting day to day transactions.

Also, as initially the new ₹2,000 note was released in large quantity and release of new ₹500 note was delayed, it caused much problem as it was not practical to use ₹2000 note for small transactions at retail outlets.

- Depositing and exchanging the invalidated notes at banks posed many problems due to the long queues, massive rush at banks and ATMs, as also lack of adequate stock of lower denomination notes in banks.
- The new ₹2,000 note was not compatible with ATM machines which necessitated recalibrating some two lakh machines across the country which was another lapse in implementation. Due to this and shortage of currency in ATMs, people could not withdraw money from ATMs for a number of days.
- Being a massive, nationwide operation which had wide ramifications and affected every individual in the country and involved printing newly designed currency notes in billions, it was a daunting task leading to much delay in normalising the situation.
- Yet, as the operation was conceived with good intent of rooting out illicit wealth and rampant corruption which was causing havoc in the economy and was a laudable objective, it had popular support from common people notwithstanding the hardships caused.
- Yet, it was not without its critics as it struck at the very root of hordes of illegal money stashed and used stealthily by unscrupulous sections of society. These vested interests were against such radical measures for obvious reasons.
- Besides, political parties of different hues also came out vehemently against it for fear that such a radical measure – welcomed by the masses and not attempted by previous administrations, despite being aware of the cancer of illicit wealth eating into the vitals of the nation and the economy – would boost the popularity of the incumbent government.
- Those at the lower rungs of society were the most adversely affected as a majority of them were outside the pale of banking system – despite the Jan Dhan Yojana scheme implemented earlier. They did not have the facility of Credit, Debit or ATM cards to be used for purchases.
- The scheme adversely impacted both the urban and rural sector, the latter even more as villages were widely dispersed and far removed causing logistical issues in reaching currencies to rural branches of banks.

Pradhan Mantri Garib Kalyan Yojana, 2016

Following the demonetisation, the government announced yet another income declaration scheme, viz., 'Taxation and Investment Regime for Pradhan Mantri Garib Kalyan Yojana, 2016' (PMGKY). The scheme provided another opportunity to persons having undisclosed income in the form of cash to declare such income and pay tax, surcharge and penalty, totalling in all to 49.9 per cent of income declared. Further they had to make a mandatory deposit of 25 per cent of such income in a non-interest bearing deposit for four years under the Pradhan Mantri Garib Kalyan Deposit Scheme, 2016. This amount would be utilised for schemes like irrigation, housing, provision of toilets, infrastructure, primary education, primary health, livelihood mission, etc., to promote welfare and larger social good. The Scheme started on 17.12.2016 and was to remain open for declarations / deposit up to 31.03.2017.

Other Follow-up Action on Black Money

While implementing demonetisation, the government had said that further measures would be taken to weed out the menace of black money. One of the main priorities of the Government is to eliminate black money component from the economy while, at the same time, keeping taxation rates more reasonable, tax administration more fair and expand the tax base. This approach will, in course of time, change the complexion of money and transform the economy into a more transparent and cleaner one. The following steps were taken to eliminate black money.

- **High value deposits:** Following demonetisation, suspicious deposits of high value have been made by a large number of people in bank accounts. Preliminary analysis of data of deposits made by people in old currency showed that between November 8 and December 30, 2016, deposits ranging from ₹2 lakh and ₹80 lakh were made in about 1.09 crore accounts, the average deposit being ₹5.03 lakh. Deposits of over ₹80 lakh were made in 1.48 lakh accounts with average deposit being ₹3.31 crore. This data will help in widening the tax net and garnering more revenues.

IT Department has been analysing such deposits as part of its 'Swachh Dhan Abhiyan' (Operation Clean Money) drive using Big Data analytics and matching with the tax profile of those depositors and their tax returns of preceding years. The IT department has issued notices to depositors, whose large deposits are not in conformity with their tax returns, to seek information on the source of such funds. Those who do not come clean on their sources of income will face penal action.

- **Interlinking of Data:** The government has taken action to interlink various sources of information such as PAN number, Aadhaar, bank accounts, income tax returns, property records, etc. of individuals, which enables it to track their financial profiles and dealings and detect attempts at concealing wealth, tax evasion, dubious transactions, etc. Banks are also reporting information on high value deposits to tax authorities. Banks are enforcing the 'Know Your Customer' (KYC) norm to get all relevant information about depositors which ensures more transparency and act as a check on false information.
- **Deposits in Cooperative banks:** Heavy deposits with scrapped notes of ₹500 and ₹1000 were found to have been made in Cooperative Banks in various States giving rise to suspicion that many people have made irregular deposits to launder unaccounted money. Due to this, Reserve Bank of India directed those banks to monitor such deposits.
- **Shell Companies:** The government initiated crackdown on 'Shell companies' that were apparently used to launder money after high valus notes were invalidated. Bank accounts of such companies would be frozen and action initiated under the Benami Transactions (Prohibition) Amendment Act, 2016 which gives powers to confiscate assets held in the name of another person or under a fictitious name to avoid tax and conceal unaccounted wealth. Many of these shell companies operate with fictitious addresses in India or abroad and engage in money laundering.

Low Level of Tax base and Tax Compliance in India

The Union budget for 2017-18 had observed that "India's tax to GDP ratio is very low, and the proportion of direct tax to indirect tax is not optimal from the view point of social justice." The budget put out the following data to indicate that our direct tax collection is not commensurate with the income and consumption pattern of Indian economy.

- As against estimated 4.2 crore persons engaged in organised sector employment, the number of individuals filing return for salary income are only 1.74 crore.
- As against 5.6 crore informal sector individual enterprises and firms doing small business in India, the number of returns filed by this category are only 1.81 crore.
- Out of the 13.94 lakh companies registered in India up to 31st March, 2014, 5.97 lakh companies had filed their returns for Assessment Year 2016 -17. Of these 5.97 lakh companies which have filed their returns for Assessment Year 2016-17 (at the time of the budget presentation), as many as 2.76

lakh companies had shown losses or zero income. 2.85 lakh companies had shown profit before tax of less than ₹1 crore. 28,667companies had shown profit between ₹1 crore to ₹10 crore, and only 7,781companies had profit before tax of more than ₹10 crore.

- Data presented in the budget for 2017-18 in respect of income tax paid by 3.7 crore individuals who had filed tax returns in 2015-16 revealed position as below:

Income declared	No. of Persons
Below ₹2.5 lakh (Exemption limit)	99 lakh
₹2.5 to ₹5 lakh	1.95 crore
₹5 to ₹10 lakh	52 lakh
Above ₹10 lakh	24 lakh
Above ₹50 lakh	1.72 lakh

The budget further contrasted the above position with the fact that in the preceding five years, more than 1.25 crore cars had been sold, and number of Indian citizens who flew abroad, either for business or tourism in the year 2015 was 2 crore. The budget added that "From all these figures, we can conclude that we are largely a tax non-compliant society. The predominance of cash in the economy makes it possible for the people to evade their taxes. When too many people evade taxes, the burden of their share falls on those who are honest and compliant". It shows there is scope to widen the tax base and bring more people into tax net.

On the positive side, there has been significant increase in the number of returns filed by taxpayers. In the financial year 2016-17, 85.51 lakhs new taxpayers filed their returns of income.

As against 3.7 crore individuals who filed income tax returns in 2015-16, the total number of people who file income tax returns in 2017-18 rose to 5.87 crore. Of them, those who filed Zero income return was 10.60 lakh and those who had income between Zero and ₹ 1.5 lakh was 32.78 lakh.

❑ ASSESSMENT OF DEMONETISATION

As has been already brought out, there have been divergent views on the process of demonetisation, the manner in which it was implemented and the undue hardship it caused to common people. While its objective and the need to root out corruption and black money is not contested, many have opined that it was not the right means or solution to the problem. The critics contend that black or unaccounted money stashed away in cash within the country is minuscule and that bulk of it is in the form of assets like jewellery, real estate and other forms of investments and caused by factors like political and election funding (discussed in a later section here). Hence the pain inflicted on people through demonetisation was not worth it as it does not go to the root of the problem.

Another criticism was that a major part of the invalidated currency was deposited in banks and thus found its way back into the economy, indicating that hoarders of illegal wealth were able to adopt dubious means and game the system. Demonetisation also caused much disruption in the economy adversely impacting all sectors which was bound to affect growth in the near term. All sections of people were adversely affected but, to a large extent, people put up with the hardship with equanimity as the avowed objective was to root out black money.

However, it must be conceded that demonetisation did, to some extent, unearth large sums of unaccounted cash hoarded by unscrupulous persons. As stated earlier, high value deposits made in banks are under scrutiny by Income Tax authorities and those who are unable to explain the source of such funds are liable to be penalised. The government is also earning more revenue through penal taxes levied on illicit funds detected.

The larger purpose of this bold and decisive measure was to punish tax evaders and send a strong message to hoarders of illicit wealth. Tax evasion compromises public interest, results in unjust enrichment of tax evaders to the detriment of the poor and deprived sections. Demonetisation helps to transfer resources from the tax evaders to the State which can then be used for the welfare of the poor. It will also lead to a cleaner and more transparent economy and result in more robust growth in the long term.

❑ TOWARDS DIGITAL AND LESS CASH ECONOMY

A logical sequence to the efforts to cleanse the economy and rid it of the scourge of black money was the suggestion that India should move towards a digital economy where the use of cash will be substantially reduced. Evidently, it is the use of cash that breeds the culture of corruption and unaccounted money, and creates the black, parallel economy. Digital modes of payments like cheques, credit and debit cards, electronic payments and fund transfer create a trail which ensures transparency of transactions carried out.

Cash has been the most common and preferred mode of payment in India. With only about 2 per cent of consumer transactions in India being cashless, India has a long way to go.

Promotion of digital economy can have a transformative impact leading to greater formalisation of the economy and directing financial savings into the banking system. This will energise private investment through lower cost of credit. The government has initiated several measures to popularise digital payments as discussed below.

- **CMs' Panel:** A panel of Chief Ministers on digital transactions, headed by N. Chandrababu Naidu, then Chief Minister of Andhra Pradesh, had suggested measures to reduce the country's dependency on cash and promote digital transactions. They include putting a cap on use of cash in all types of large transactions and levying a banking cash transaction tax (BCTT) on cash withdrawals ₹50,000 and above.
- **Limit on Transactions in Cash:** The Special Investigation Team (SIT), set up by the Government to look into the issue of black money, has suggested that no transaction above ₹3 lakh should be permitted in cash. The Government has decided to accept this proposal. Suitable amendment to the Income-tax Act is proposed in the Finance Bill for 2017-18 for enforcing this decision.
- **Structural reforms in Payments:** A Committee on Digital Payments set up by the Department of Economic Affairs has recommended structural reforms in the payment eco system, including amendments to the Payment and Settlement Systems Act, 2007. Government will undertake a comprehensive review of this Act and bring about appropriate amendments. It is proposed to create a Payments Regulatory Board in the Reserve Bank of India by replacing the existing Board for Regulation and Supervision of Payment and Settlement Systems. Necessary amendments have been proposed on this in the Finance Bill 2017.
- **Digital Payments App:** With the launch of a new digital payments app named BHIM (Bharat Interface for Money). there is evidence of increased digital transactions. It is an app based on the Unified Payments Interface (UPI) from the National Payments Corporation of India (NPCI), the umbrella organisation for all retail payments systems in India. If one signs up for UPI-based payments on one's bank account, which is also linked to his mobile phone number, he will be able to use the BHIM app to carry out digital transactions. It will unleash the power of mobile phones for digital payments and financial inclusion. 12.5 million people had adopted this facility by January 2017. The Government propose to launch two new schemes to incentivise the usage of BHIM; viz., a Referral Bonus Scheme for individuals and a Cashback Scheme for merchants.

Total number of digital transactions done via UPI from July 2016 till September 2021 amounted to 10.66 crore which shows the wide usage of the facility.

- **Government Purchases:** As part of digital drive, the government has plans to move all government purchases to an online marketplace. It will cut bureaucratic delays, avert corruption, ensure competitiveness and transparency by leaving a digital trail and also result in savings on every transaction. Necessary training of staff for this is underway.
- **JAM Trinity:** The government's efforts to promote financial inclusion of common people already implemented through JAM trinity – Jan Dhan Yojana, Aadhaar and Mobile – will help to popularise digital transactions on a large scale. With a high percentage of mobile phone users, India has considerable scope to promote digital mode for financial transactions.
- **Direct Benefit Transfer (DBT):** The government's move to route all payments to beneficiaries of various social welfare schemes and subsidy payments by direct transfer to the bank accounts of beneficiaries is a major step in reducing use of cash. Already, 84 schemes are on DBT platform and more schemes will be brought into this fold.The total payout and transfer of funds to beneficiaries under DBT since 2014-15 amounted to ₹1891.6 billion. This has also helped to ensure timely payments and avoid intermediaries and leakages of money in payments to actual beneficiaries.

Challenges in Digitisation

However, there are some limitations which India has to overcome in her drive towards a digital economy.

- **PoS devices:** Getting more merchant outlets to use digital mode for transactions and procuring more Point of Sale (PoS) devices pose a challenge. To promote the use of PoS machines, the government proposed exemption from duty on imports of these machines in 2017-18 budget. Besides, the budget also proposed to exempt parts and components for manufacture of such devices, so as to encourage domestic manufacturing of these devices.
- **Reimbursement of Debit card charges:** In a bid to encourage digital transactions following the demonetisation, the Union government has decided to reimburse banks Merchant Discount Rate (MDR) charges on debit cards. The Reserve Bank of India would start reimbursing MDR charges to banks for payments made through debit cards from January 1, 2017.
- **Technology limitation:** While India has 250 million 'smartphone' users, about 350 million have only 'feature' phones and another 350 million do not have a phone at all. Hence there is need to find ways to meet the requirements of those many of whom are economically challenged and have limited or no access to technology. Apps which can work on feature phones have also been developed.
- **Rural areas lack Digital Infrastructure:** To overcome this, there are plans to draw those enrolled in Aadhaar and enlist the remaining towards micro ATMs promoted by big lenders and startups which already have a presence in 130,000 village retail outlets or kirana stores. With Digital India project also covering 2,50,000 gram panchayats, there is scope to widen the digital coverage.
- Task of connecting one lakh gram panchayat through high speed optical fiber network has been completed under phase I of the Bharatnet project. Additional 25,000 GPs was covered under Phase-1. More than 1,21,000 GPs have been made service ready. This has enabled broadband access to over 20 crore rural Indians in about two lakh fifty thousand villages. The Government also proposes to setup five lakh wi-fi hotspots which will provide broadband access to five crore rural citizens. As mentioned in 2018-19 budget, ₹10000 crore has been provided for creation and augmentation of telecom infrastructure.

India's Thriving Fintech Industry

Despite all the challenges of vast geographical spread, digital payments and the Fintech industry in India is thriving. At 87 per cent, India's financial technological (Fintech) adoption rate is much higher than the global average of 64 per cent. By May 2021, India's United Payments Interface (UPI) platform saw participation of 224 banks and recorded 2.6 billion transactions. And in August 2021, it touched 3.6 billion transactions worth over $ 68 billion to create a record. India's fintech industry came to the rescue of the people at the critical time of Covid-19 pandemic, enabling them to carry out crucial activities from the safety of their homes.

The JAM (Jan Dhan-Aadhaar-Mobile) trinity, besides Direct Benefit Transfer (DBT), not only brought in transparency, integrity and timely delivery of financial benefits and services to the vast population in rural and urban areas, but enabled India to leverage its technical capabilities for developing the fintech sector. In 2020, over two trillion transactions were processed using the Aadhar-enabled payment system (AePS).

❑ ELECTORAL FUNDING AND ELECTORAL BONDS

Presenting the 2017-18 Union budget, the Finance Minister observed "Political parties are an essential ingredient of a multi-party Parliamentary democracy. Even 70 years after Independence, the country has not been able to evolve a transparent method of funding political parties which is vital to the system of free and fair elections."

Drawbacks of the Present System

That corrupt practices in Indian elections are a major source of generation of black, unaccounted money is well known. This issue has been in public domain and debated for years in various fora and by various Commissions and expert bodies and social activists. But due to deeply entrenched vested interests of political parties and politicians, no effective corrective action was taken over the years. Some of the major ills afflicting the electoral system are:

- Expenditure incurred by parties and candidates far beyond the limits prescribed under rules by the Election Commission; this flow of money power not only disrupts level playing field among candidates but voters are unduly influenced and prevented from making informed choice while casting votes;
- Under reporting of election expenditure by candidates;
- Secrecy and opacity of contributions and donations to political parties and candidates; candidates rely almost completely on unaccounted cash from undisclosed donors. This also negates the transparency initiatives of the Election Commission;
- Donations made by cash instead of more transparent means like cheques, through bank transfers, etc;
- Corrupt practice of candidates bribing voters during election times with cash and gifts all of which involves money;
- These unethical practices eventually result in outside pressure being exerted over government policies and functioning of the State and the bureaucracy by vested interests distorting larger public good;

Many suggestions have been put forth and efforts made by the Election Commission and social activists to reform the system but these have met with resistance from parties and politicians for obvious reasons. Some of the major reform measures suggested are:

- **State Funding of Elections:** Government to fund elections including financial assistance – in cash or kind – to political parties for contesting elections. This will prevent parties and candidates spending money and influencing voters. It will also help in controlling the flow of unaccounted money and muscle power during elections and bring down the levels of corruption in public life.
- **Financial and expenditure limits:** Limits on how much will be spent on candidates and parties in an election even if State funding is introduced.
- **Ban on Fund collections:** Neither candidates nor parties could raise any funds for election purposes. There will be need for this once state funding is introduced.
- **Bringing Political Party under RTI Act:** The Central Information Commission (CIC) has ruled that National Political Parties are public authorities within the meaning of Sec 2(h) of Right to Information (RTI) Act and directed them to appoint public information officer to provide necessary information as required by the citizens. But all the national parties have contested this on the ground that they are not 'public authorities' within the meaning of RTI Act. This would have brought about much transparency in the functioning of political parties and cleansed the system.

Past efforts at Electoral reform

An attempt was made in the past by amending the provisions of the Representation of Peoples Act, the Companies Act and the Income Tax Act to incentivise donations by individuals, partnership firms, HUFs and companies to political parties. Both the donor and the donee were granted exemption from payment of tax if the accounts were transparently maintained and returns were filed with the competent authorities. Additionally, a list of donors who contributed more than ₹20,000/- to any party in cash or cheque is required to be maintained. The situation only marginally improved since these provisions were brought into force. Political parties continued to receive most of their funds through anonymous donations which are shown in cash.

As part of the 2017-18 Union budget, the following further steps were taken in an attempt effort to cleanse the system of funding of political parties:

- In accordance with the suggestion made by the Election Commission, the maximum amount of cash donation that a political party can receive was fixed at ₹2000/- from one person.
- Political parties will be entitled to receive donations by cheque or digital mode from their donors.
- Every political party would have to file its return within the time prescribed in accordance with the provision of the Income-tax Act.
- An amendment was proposed to the Reserve Bank of India Act to enable the issuance of Electoral Bonds as per a scheme the Government of India would frame in this regard.
- The existing exemption to the political parties from payment of income-tax would be available only subject to the fulfilment of these conditions. This reform will bring about greater transparency and accountability in political funding, while preventing future generation of black money.

Electoral Bonds

Taking forward the steps to make political funding more transparent, the government announced in January 2018 in the Parliament that an Electoral Bonds scheme has been prepared. The broad contours of the scheme are:

- Those interested in donating money to a political party can buy these bonds. The party can convert these bonds back into money via their bank accounts.

- A citizen of India or a body incorporated in India will be eligible to purchase the bond.
- The electoral bonds will be available at specified branches of State Bank of India (SBI) for 10 days each in months of January, April, July and October.
- The electoral bonds would be valid for 15 days and will not carry any interest.
- The electoral bonds can be bought for any value, in multiples of ₹1,000, ₹10,000, ₹1 lakh, ₹10 lakh or ₹1 crore.
- The lender will remain the custodian of the donor's funds until the political parties are paid. The scheme allows donors to pay political parties using banks as an intermediary.
- The issuing bank will remain the custodian of the donor's funds until the political party redeems the bond.
- Every party that is registered under section 29A of the Representation of the People Act, 1951 and has secured at least 1 per cent of the votes polled in the most recent Lok Sabha or Assembly election will be allotted a verified account by the Election Commission. Electoral bond transactions can be made only via that account.
- The bonds will not carry the donor's name even though the purchaser would have to fulfil KYC norms at the bank.

Flip side of the Scheme

The Chief Election Commissioner has opined that while the electoral bond scheme is a step in the right direction, it will not solve all problems pertaining to transparency in political funding. The Election Commission, in a written submission to the Parliamentary Standing Committee on Law and Personnel, had said that changes made in the election laws after the introduction of the bonds would compromise transparency in political funding. The amendment in Section 29 C of the Representation of the People Act, 1951 making it no longer necessary to report details of donations received through electoral bonds will be a retrograde step as transparency of political funding would be compromised as a result of the change.

One of the main criticisms of this scheme is that the name of the donor is not revealed and remains unknown. As to the name of the donor not being disclosed, it is said that past experience has shown that once the names are disclosed, there is a tendency to shift to cash donations. The present system operates largely on unclean money while the bond scheme ensures the use of clean money and a substantial, if not total, degree of transparency. In the case of corporates and other organisations, the bonds would get reflected in the balance sheet of the donors.

A political party had filed a petition in the Supreme Court against the bond scheme on the ground that the no disclosure clause in electoral bonds will create opacity in funding and bodes ill for democracy. This party has demanded that the move to float electoral bonds be scrapped. As an alternative, it has suggested that the government designate an institution like the Election Commission of India, to which corporates can donate funds, and which can be monitored by the EC. Under the proposed bond scheme, only the corporates and the government will know about the funds transferred and thus it lacks transparency.

The Supreme Court which heard the petition has made the following observations:

- One of the contentions of the petitioners was that though the first purchase of bond may be through banking channels paid for in white money, someone may repurchase the bonds from the first buyer using black money and hand it over to a politicalparty. But this contention arises out of ignorance of the scheme.

- Under Clause 14 of the Scheme, the bonds are not tradable. Moreover, the first buyer will not stand will not stand to gain anything out of such sale except losing white money for the black.
- The apprehension that foreign corporate houses may buy the bonds and attempt to influence the electoral process in the country is also misconceived. Under Clause 3 of the Scheme, the Bonds may be purchased only by a person who is a citizen of India or incorporated or established in India.
- The Scheme was introduced in January 2018. The bonds are released at periodical intervals in January, April, July and October of every year. They had been so released in the years 2018, 2019 and 2020 without any impediments. And certain safeguards have already been provided by the Supreme Court in its interim order of April 2019, Hence the Court did not find any justification to grant "stay" and dismissed the petition in March 2021.

❑ BLACK MONEY PROBLEM IN THE US AND EUROPEAN COUNTRIES

Black money problem is not confined to India alone. The United States and European countries too face the problem as some citizens in these countries also have hidden wealth elsewhere to evade taxes. In fact, it is estimated that some of the largest American companies collectively hold trillions of dollars in accumulated profits offshore to avoid US taxes. According to a study, several firms on the Fortune 500 list of the biggest American companies operate subsidiaries in countries like Luxembourg, Ireland, Netherlands, and Bermuda.

The escalation in money laundering has led the European Union (EU) also to create heightened awareness of the potential effects of this dubious practice. The European Union enacted its First Directive to combat money laundering in 1991. The European Union Anti-Money Laundering and Financing of Terrorism Directives aim to protect the financial system and other vulnerable professions from being misused for money laundering. The Directive mandates that due diligence and checks must be carried out by all credit and financial institutions before entering into any business relationship or before conducting any transaction over a certain threshold. The EU has issued further directives to tighten its anti-money laundering regime.

International Tax Reform

The OECD/G20 group of countries has proposed international tax reform, the "OECD/G20 Inclusive Framework Tax Deal". This deal was previously proposed at the G7 meeting in June 2021, but the OECD tax plan has added special rules for some sectors and companies. The main aspects of the new tax proposal are:

- It calls for the redistribution of profits generated by the largest companies to the domicile markets where they actually make their sales instead of simply where they are headquartered.
- It establishes a global minimum effective tax rate of 15 per cent determined on a country-by-country basis.
- **Need for Change:** The rationale for this move is that the century-old international tax system is no longer fit in the current scenario of a globalised and digitalised 21st century economy.

130 countries and jurisdictions, representing more than 90 per cent of global GDP have joined the Statement establishing the new framework for international tax reform. A small group of the Inclusive Framework's 139 members were yet to join.

The Group of 20 (G20) countries, whose membership includes the world's 19 biggest economies and the European Union (EU), would attempt to forge a political agreement on the global tax deal. This is bound to get contentious, as these reforms could adversely impact the post-pandemic economic recovery plans of several tax-friendly states.

- **Two-pillar Package:** The two-pillar package which has been under negotiations, coordinated by the OECD for a good part of the last decade, aims to ensure that large Multinational Enterprises (MNEs) pay tax where they operate and earn profits, while adding much-needed certainty and stability to the international tax system.
- Pillar One will ensure a fairer distribution of profits and taxing rights among countries with respect to the largest MNEs, including digital companies. It would re-allocate some taxing rights over MNEs from their home countries to the markets where they have business activities and earn profits, regardless of whether firms have a physical presence there.
- Pillar Two seeks to put a minimum ceiling (level) on corporate income tax, through the introduction of a global minimum corporate tax rate that countries can use to protect their tax bases.

These proposals are to be further discussed and finalized by OECD and other countries.

Implications for India and Emerging Economies

India has joined OECD members in endorsing the global tax reform in principle and has committed to working towards the deal's final approval.

- In India's view, some significant issues including share of profit allocation and scope of the tax rules remain to be addressed. Further, the technical details of the proposal are to be worked out and a consensus arrived at among the participating countries.
- The principles underlying the new framework vindicates India's stand for a greater share of profits for the markets, consideration of demand side factors in profit allocation and the need to seriously address the issue of cross border shifting of profit.
- While most of the G20, including India, backed the global tax plan at the OECD meeting on July 2021, smaller, low-tax EU-member countries like Hungary, Estonia, and Ireland declined to support the 15 per cent minimum corporate tax rate. The EU needs complete consensus among its members to implement the tax reform as EU law.

❑ GOLD MONETISATION

Objectives

- The gold monetisation scheme was launched in 2015 to mobilise gold held by individuals, institutions, and rich temples for recycling and to reduce imports.
- Gold lying in the locker appreciates in value when gold price goes up but it does not fetch interest or dividend. On the contrary, one incurs carrying costs on it, the bank locker charges. It provides the customers an opportunity to earn interest income on their idle gold holdings.
- The gold mobilized could be put to productive use.

Features of the Scheme

- The monetisation scheme will allow the owner to earn some regular interest on gold and save the carrying costs as well.
- The scheme envisages a gold savings account which will earn interest for the gold that is deposited.
- The gold can be deposited in any physical form - jewellery, coins, or bars and it will earn interest based on the weight of gold and also the appreciation of the metal value.

- The depositor can get back the gold in appropriate quality or the value in Indian rupees as preferred, the option being exercised at the time of deposit. The gold will be securely maintained by the bank.
- The designated banks may sell or lend the gold accepted under the short-term bank deposit to MMTC for minting India Gold Coins and to jewellers, or sell to other designated banks participating in the scheme.
- India is the world's second biggest consumer of gold after China and imports account for a good part of India's trade deficit. The scheme garnered about 3 tonnes of gold in in the initial four months out of a national hoard estimated to be in thousands of tonnes.

Eligibilty of Depositor

- Resident Indians (Individuals, HUF, and Trusts including Mutual Funds/Exchange Traded Funds registered under SEBI (Mutual Fund) Regulations, Companies, Charitable institutions, Central and State governments can make deposits under the scheme.
- The opening of gold deposit accounts will be subject to the same rules with regard to customer identification as applicable to any other deposit account.
- Those depositing gold will be given a certificate mentioning the amount and purity of the deposited gold. Banks will open a 'Gold Savings Account' on the basis of such certificates. The rate at which interest will be paid is left for the bank to decide.
- The Tirumala Tirupati Devasthanam (TTD), which is in charge of the Sri Venkateswara Swamy Temple in Tirupati, one of the world's richest temples, has deposited gold for long-term deposits with banks under the gold monetization scheme.
- The Travancore Devaswom Board (TDB) plans to deposit about 500kg of gold under the scheme. The board has catalogued the stock lying at various temples and strongrooms. It expects an approximate annual return of ₹ 5 crore from the deposit.
- Participation of TTD and other religious institutions in the gold scheme is crucial to its success since many of them hold large stock of the metal. However, temples may be reluctant to part with the gold forever because of its religious and emotional significance.

❑ TAX REFORMS

The tax reforms implemented have been discussed in Chapter 14 (see pp. 14.9-14). Tax reforms and rationalization of taxes is an ongoing process spread over a period of time. The direct tax rates were rationalized in the Union Budget of 1997-98 by Finance Minister (FM) P. Chidambaram when personal income tax slabs with rates of 15, 30, and 40 per cent were replaced by new rates of 10, 20, and 30 per cent. As for indirect taxes, in the Budget for 2000-01, FM Yashwant Sinha introduced three excise duty rates of 8, 16, and 24 per cent keeping the rate for raw materials and intermediates at 16 per cent CENVAT rate.

The VAT

Next came the Value Added Tax (VAT) which had been recommended by the Chelliah Committee on Tax Reforms set up in 1991. As stated in Chapter 14, presenting the Budget for 2005-06, Finance Minister P. Chidambaram mentioned that this was the most important tax reform ever attempted in this country, viz., to introduce the value added tax (VAT) with effect from April 1, 2005. He stated that "VAT is a modern, simple and transparent tax system that will replace the existing sales tax and eliminate the cascading effect of sales tax. It is in force in more than 130 countries ranging from Sri Lanka to China. India too has a VAT at the Central level (CENVAT), but only for goods." He also added that the long-term goal was to cover the entire production-distribution by a national VAT or still better by a Goods and Services Tax (GST) encompassing both the Centre and the States.

Corporate Tax: Phased Reduction

The government has been rationalizing Corporate tax to give fillip to companies. It was observed in the Budget for 2015-16 that the basic rate of Corporate tax in India at 30 per cent was higher than the rates in other major Asian economies, making our domestic industry less competitive. It was then proposed to reduce the rate from 30 to 25 per cent over a period, accompanied by rationalization and removal of various tax exemptions.

In the Union Budget, 2016-17, corporate tax rate was reduced to 25 per cent for companies whose turnover was less than ₹ 50 crore in financial year 2015-16. This benefitted 96 per cent of the total number of companies filing tax returns. In the budget for 2018-19, the benefit of this reduced rate of 25 per cent was extended to companies who have reported turnover up to ₹ 250 crore in the financial year 2016-¬17. This will benefit the entire class of micro, small and medium enterprises (MSMEs) which account for almost 99 per cent of companies filing their tax returns.

In a significant move to boost industries and manufacturing, the Government of India announced reduction in corporate tax rates for domestic companies in India with effect from FY 2019-20. The key proposals are as follows.

- Domestic companies have the option to avail lower tax rate of 22 per cent – i.e. 25.17 per cent inclusive of surcharge at 10 per cent and cess at 4 per cent. No exemption/incentive shall be claimed by such companies. Further, no minimum alternate tax (MAT) will be levied on such companies.
- To give boost to 'Make-in-India' initiative, fresh investment in a Company set up after October 1, 2019 in manufacturing sector shall have an option to pay tax at the rate of 15 per cent – i.e. 17.16 per cent including surcharge of 10 per cent and cess of 4 per cent – provided such company starts manufacturing on or before 31 March 2023. No exemption/incentive shall be claimed by such companies. Also, no MAT will be levied on such companies.
- A company which does not opt for the concessional tax regime and avails the tax exemptions/ incentives, shall continue to pay tax at the pre-amended rate (i.e. currently approx. 34.94%). However, these companies can opt for the concessional tax regime after the expiry of their tax holiday/exemption period; MAT rate for such companies to be reduced from 18.5% to 15%; Option once exercised cannot be withdrawn subsequently.

FURTHER TAX REFORMS

Justice (Retd.) R.V. Easwar Committee set up by the government in 2015 to look into simplifying the Income Tax Act had made important recommendations to make the tax system more taxpayer-friendly and to improve the ease of doing business. The recommendations included:

Simplifying provisions relating to tax deducted at source (TDS), to raise the threshold for TDS, not to adjust tax demand of a taxpayer against legitimate refunds due, reduce delays in paying refund due to a taxpayer and pay higher interest for delays in refunds.

Importantly, the panel suggested to move towards electronic tax processes to minimize human interface which will empower the taxpayer to follow his or her tax processes in a more convenient manner. This facility has since been introduced marking a major departure in dealings between the tax payer and the tax authorities.

❑ GOODS AND SERVICES TAX (GST)

Introduction

The genesis of having a Goods and Services Tax (GST) regime dates back to 2004 when a Task Force headed by Vijay Kelkar recommended to have a fully integrated 'GST' on national basis. Later, while presenting the Central Budget for 2007-2008, the then Union Finance Minister, Shri P. Chidambaram, announced that GST would be introduced from April 1, 2010. But due to various issues and differences of opinion, the proposal got stalled. It was revived and gained momentum in 2014 when the NDA Government tabled the Constitution (122nd Amendment) Bill, 2014 for the introduction of GST in the Parliament in December, 2014.

This landmark legislation, the biggest indirect tax reform since Independence, sought to replace a slew of central and state levies with a uniform GST rate to convert the country into a single territory and single market. The major central and state taxes were to be subsumed into GST which reduces the multiplicity of taxes and brings down the compliance cost. The introduction of GST is expected to boost economic growth.

The Divergence on GST

This major transformational tax reform passed through many vicissitudes. Some States had reservations about it for fear of loss of revenue or giving up their extant rights or autonomy to levy taxes on some lucrative items. It took several sittings of a Committee of State Finance Ministers and debates in the Parliament to narrow down the differences and thrash out an agreeable solution.

The sticking points and the divergent views which held up the passage of the Constitution amendment bill related to capping the GST rate at 18 per cent and the mode of enforcing the cap. The government did not want to fix the cap in the Constitution amendment bill, as contended by some political parties, for then if the rate is to be changed in any emergency, a Constitutional amendment will be necessary which will be a complex and protracted process. Instead, the government proposed that the rates could be fixed by the GST Council which has representatives of the Centre and States at the ministerial level.

Passing of GST Bill, States on Board: A Historic Step

In a historic development, the Lok Sabha passed the Bill in May 2015 and Rajya Sabha in August 2016 paving the way for adoption of the Goods and Services Tax (GST). The Bill was passed with the amendments proposed by the government, including a dispute-settlement mechanism, firm assurance to States on compensation for loss of revenue and dropping a 1 per cent tax on inter-state sales. Being a constitutional amendment, the legislation had also to be ratified by at least 50 per cent of State Assemblies.

Many States were keen to have the legislation approved quickly as the GST scheme was to the advantage of States also. After the Parliament passed the bill on August 8, 2016 as many as 16 states, starting with Assam, ratified the bill by September 1, 2016. The other States which passed the legislation during this period included Bihar, Jharkhand, Chhattisgarh, Himachal Pradesh, Gujarat, Madhya Pradesh, Delhi, Nagaland, Maharashtra, Haryana, Sikkim, Mizoram, Telangana, Goa and Odisha.

Following this, the President gave assent to the GST Constitution Amendment Bill on September 8, 2016 when it became the GST Constitution (101st Amendment) Act, 2016. This Act empowered the Central government to levy excise duty on manufacturing and service tax on the supply of services till September 16, 2017. Similarly, the Act empowered the State governments to levy sales tax or Value Added Tax (VAT) on the sale of goods till September 16, 2017. This step was to provide time to roll out the GST regime after passing the relevant tax laws.

In March, 2017, the Central GST legislations – Central Goods and Services Tax (CGST) Bill, 2017, Integrated Goods and Services Tax (IGST) Bill, 2017, Union Territory Goods and Services Tax (UTGST)

Bill, 2017 and Goods and Services Tax (Compensation to States) Bill, 2017 were introduced in Lok Sabha. The Lok Sabha passed these bills on 29th March, 2017 and with the receipt of the President's assent on 12th April, 2017, the Bills were enacted. The enactment of the Central Acts was followed by the enactment of the State GST laws by various State Legislatures.

The GST regime finally became operational from July 1, 2017. With the GST, the nation has executed one of the most ambitious and remarkable tax reforms in its independent history. Encompassing both goods and services, it is implemented by the Centre, 29 States and 2 Union Territories. It impacts potentially some 8 million tax entities, and by marshalling the latest technology it vastly improves tax implementation.

Committee on Possible Tax rates under GST

A committee headed by the Chief Economic Adviser in the Ministry of Finance, Arvind Subramanian, had been tasked to go into all aspects of the structure and implications of this tax legislation and make recommendations. Its recommendations are summed up below.

- The GST should aim at tax rates that protect revenue, simplify administration, encourage compliance, avoid adding to inflationary pressures, and keep India in the range of countries with reasonable levels of indirect taxes.
- The term revenue neutral rate (RNR) refers to a single rate which preserves revenue at desired (current) levels. It gets converted into a range of rates, depending on exemptions, what commodities to charge at a lower rate and what to charge at a very high rate. On the RNR, the Committee's suggested the range should be between 15 percent and 15.5 percent (Centre and states combined) but with a preference for the lower end of that range.
- While India should strive toward a one-rate structure as the medium-term goal, the Committee recommended a two-rate structure. The Committee recommended that lower rates be kept around 12 per cent (Centre plus states) with standard rates varying between 17 and 18 per cent. (The 'standard' rate in a GST regime being the rate which is applied to all goods and services whose taxation is not explicitly specified).
- It is a growing international practice to levy sin/demerit rates—in the form of excises outside the scope of the GST--on goods and services that create negative externalities for the economy. Accordingly, the Committee recommended that this sin/demerit rate be fixed at about 40 percent (Centre plus States) and apply to luxury cars, aerated beverages, paan masala, and tobacco and tobacco products (for the States).
- The Committee did not favour having a "band" of rates which will make tax administration complex, especially since States will preserve considerable flexibility and autonomy under the GST (including the ability to tax petroleum, alcohol, and other goods and services).

The preparatory work for this path-breaking reform was a top priority for the Government. Several teams of officers both from the States and Central Board of Excise and Customs had worked tirelessly to give final shape to the Model GST law and rules and other details. Government also promptly gave effect to various provisions of the Constitutional Amendment Act, including constituting the GST Council.

GST Council

Under the provisions of the GST Act, the government set up the all-powerful GST Council (GSTC) which consists of the Union Finance Minister as Chairman, the Union Minister of State of Finance and the Finance Minister of each state as members.

The constitution of the Council is such that neither the Centre nor the States will be able to take a decision without the other's concurrence – a move that will necessitate consensual approach and promote cooperative federalism. It also gives the States a major say in the way indirect taxes will be administered across the country. In case voting becomes necessary for a decision, it will require at least a three-fourths vote in favour. The Centre has one-third vote in the Council while States have a two-thirds vote.

Terms of Reference of the GST Council

Under the GST Act, the GST Council shall make recommendations to the Union and the States on:

(a) The taxes, cesses and surcharges levied by the Union, the States and the local bodies which may be subsumed in the goods and services tax;

(b) The goods and services that may be subjected to, or exempted from, the goods and services tax;

(c) Model Goods and Services Tax Laws, principles of levy, apportionment of Integrated Goods and Services Tax and the principles that govern the place of supply;

(d) The threshold limit of turnover below which goods and services may be exempted from goods and services tax;

(e) The rates including floor rates with bands of goods and services tax;

(f) Special provision with respect to the States of Arunachal Pradesh, Assam, Jammu and Kashmir, Manipur, Meghalaya, Mizoram, Nagaland, Sikkim, Tripura, Himachal Pradesh and Uttarakhand;

(g) Any special rate or rates for a specified period, to raise additional resources during any natural calamity or disaster; and,

(h) Any other matter relating to the goods and services tax, as the Council may decide.

Approval of GST Laws

By March 16, 2017, the GST Council cleared the legislations pertaining to GST, viz., the Central GST bill, the State GST bill, the Union Territory (UT) GST bill, the Integrated GST bill and the Compensation bill. The government moved further swiftly and on March 20, 2017, the Union Cabinet approved four laws coming within Centre's purview, viz., CGST, UTGST, IGST and the bill to compensate States for revenue losses arising from transition to GST. Simultaneously, the State GST bill was sent to States for approval by the respective State legislatures.

These bills were passed by the Parliament and State Assemblies paving the way for roll out of GST from July 1, 2017 after giving time for industry and business establishments to prepare and adopt it.

Salient Features of GST

The following are the salient features of the pan-India Goods and Services Tax regime:

1. GST will unite the country into a common, unified market and remove barriers across states.
2. GST is a destination-based tax that will subsume various Central indirect taxes like excise duty, countervailing duty and service tax, and the State levies such as value-added tax, octroi and entry tax, entertainment tax and luxury tax.
3. It will remove the cascading impact of taxes, bring in efficiency, check tax evasion, ensure better compliance, expand the tax payer base and thereby increase tax revenues.
4. It is estimated that implementation of GST will add up to 2 per cent to the country's gross domestic product (GDP) and ensure revenue buoyancy.

5. The final consumer will bear only the GST charged by the last dealer in the supply chain, with set-off benefits at all the previous stages.
6. As a measure of support for the states, petroleum products, alcohol for human consumption and tobacco have been kept out of the purview of the GST.
7. It will have two components – Central GST levied by the Centre and State GST levied by the States. Besides, for inter-State transactions, Integrated GST will be adopted by appropriately aligning and integrating CGST and IGST. The Centre will levy and collect GST on supplies in the course of inter-state trade or commerce.
8. The tax collected would be divided between the Centre and the States in a manner approved by Parliament, on the recommendations of the GST Council.

Some of these features and important aspects of GST regime such as the Composition Scheme, GST rates and their rationalisation, E-Permit and offences under GST laws are discussed later in this chapter. (See also Positives of GST regime in Box 25.1 later in this chapter).

Shift from Originating Point to Destination

As against the previous system where the taxes like Excise and Central sales tax were levied on manufacturing at the factory gate or on inter-state movement of goods, the GST involves taxation at the destination point. This could result in gains for the consuming state and loss for the manufacturing state. This is why states with good manufacturing base like Tamil Nadu was opposed to the GST while consuming states like Bihar, West Bengal and Odisha favoured it. But, the GST Bill provides for fully compensating the losses sustained by the States for five years. An earlier proposal to have an additional one per cent levy to compensate losing states was done away with.

GST Council Meetings

As the government was keen to introduce the GST regime, meetings of the Council were convened in quick succession. A series of crucial meetings of the Council were held from September 2016 to discuss various issues relating to GST, including broad contours of the GST rate structure, threshold for exemption, parameters for Composition scheme, compensation to States due to implementation of GST, examination of draft models of GST laws, the Compensation Law and administrative mechanism for GST.

Most of the decisions were taken by the Council by consensus among the representatives of both the Centre and States. But due to the complexity of the issues involved, the deliberations in the Council continued to have them resolved in subsequent meetings.

The important decisions taken by the Council are:

- No GST shall be levied on turnover up to ₹10 lakh in the case of North-east, hill and Special category states and ₹20 lakh in all other states.
- The jurisdiction of an assessee having turnover below ₹1.5 crore shall vest with State tax officials and above ₹1.5 crore with either the Centre or the State depending on the tax profile.
- Service providers registered with the Centre will be assessed by Centre's tax officials and the Centre will have exclusive administration on service providers till the time states become competent to administer the regime.
- All cesses will be subsumed in GST.
- As regards the crucial question of GST rate structure, the Council proposed to have 4 rates ranging from 5 per cent to 28 per cent. These rates are 5 per cent, 12 per cent, 18 per cent and 28 per cent.

The GST regime consists of:

- Central GST (CGST) collected by the Central Govt.;
- State GST (SGST) collected by the State Govt.;
- Union Territory GST (UTGST) collected by the Union Territories; and
- Integrated GST (IGST) collected by the Central Govt.

For sale within a state, CGST and SGST will be levied. The collection goes equally to the Central government and the State government. In the case of inter-state sales, the whole of IGST goes to the Central government.

Jurisdiction

The question of jurisdiction and dual control between Centre and the States which was a contentious issue was settled by a compromise formula put forth by the Finance Minister which was accepted by all the States. Under this, 90 per cent of the assessees below the turnover of ₹1.5 crore and 50 per cent of the assessees above the turnover of ₹1.5 crore shall be under control of the State authorities for the purpose of audit, inspection and assessment, while the rest shall be under the control of the Centre.

GST Rates and their Rationalisation

A Technical Committee comprising of Central and State government officials worked out the allocation of various items into different tax slabs for consideration by the GST Council.

As stated earlier, there are 4 tax slabs under the GST viz., 5 per cent, 12 per cent, 18 per cent and 28 per cent. The primary concern of the Council in fixing the rates was to protect the common man from spiraling prices of essential goods and keep the incidence of indirect tax on people to the minimum. The broad decisions on rates are:

- About 50 per cent of items that make up the Consumer Price Index (CPI) basket, including foodgrains, are not taxed; in other words, they are exempted from GST.
- Mass consumption items like spices, tea, mustard oil, etc. are taxed at the lowest rate of 5 per cent.
- There are two standard rates of 12 per cent and 18 per cent at which majority of items used by the common man are taxed.
- Certain demerit, sin and luxury goods have been placed in the top 28 percent bracket.

After the implementation of GST, there was considerable criticism and feedback from industry and traders that many of the items have been placed in the higher tax slabs and that it has hit hard many sectors and businesses. Following this and after a review of the working of the GST system, the GST Council has tweaked the rates and moved a large number of items into lower slabs. Similar review of rates may take place after seeing the full impact of the tax in the long run. (See also 'Downside of GST' in Box 25.1 on this).

Composition scheme

The Composition scheme covers small traders, dealers and manufacturers with lower turnover who pay a fixed low rate of tax. This helps to ensure lesser compliance burden, provide a seamless supply chain, make the scheme more attractive and check tax evasion. The threshold for availing the Composition scheme was initially fixed at annual turnover of ₹50 lakh but later the GST Council raised the threshold allowing those having annual turnover of up to ₹1.5 crore to opt for the Composition scheme.

It was expected that the move to raise the threshold would not result in significant revenue loss to the Government, as the dealers opting for the Composition scheme would have to forgo the input tax credit (ITC) facility. (See section later below on Input Tax Credit).

Under the Composition scheme, tax rate is 1 per cent for traders, 2 per cent for manufacturers and 5 per cent for restaurants. A Composition Dealer is not allowed to recover the GST from the customers or avail the benefit of input tax credit. Further, they are also not allowed to raise GST invoice which would help those who buy from them to avail input tax credit. This meant that large registered dealers were wary of purchasing from such entities registered under the scheme. But as per the decision of the Council, large registered dealers can pay the tax equivalent to the composition rate on purchases made from small unregistered dealers.

The Composition Scheme is available only for dealers doing intra-state supplies. If a dealer is involved in inter-State supplies, then they have to opt out of the scheme.

Input Tax Credit

Input Tax Credit (ITC) means that at the time of paying tax on output, one can reduce the tax(es) already paid on inputs and pay the balance amount. One of the fundamental features of GST is the seamless flow of input credit across the production chain (from the manufacture of goods till it is consumed) and across the country. It thus averts the cascading impact of taxes.

As stated earlier, those registered under the Composition scheme in GST cannot avail the benefit of input tax credit.

Compensation

The Centre will compensate States for any loss of revenue due to implementation of GST during the first 5 years. To arrive at the compensation, the base year for the revenue of the State to be reckoned would be 2015-16 and a fixed growth rate of 14 per cent will be applied to it.

Commodities basket and Rate Structure

An ideal GST regime should have few exempted commodities and a single rate for all commodities. Of over 150 countries which have adopted VAT/GST, 69 have single rate with some exemptions, and 83 countries have multiple rates but less than four rates which India has proposed.

The advantage of a single rate is that tax evasion can be easily tracked, especially as we move towards electronic payments systems. Multiple rates give scope for misdeclaration of items so as to take advantage of lower rate slab.

Exempting too many items from GST also necessitates taxing other items at higher rates to maintain revenue neutrality. There is need to bring down the number of items exempted. Also keeping petroleum products, real estate and electricity out of the ambit of GST is not a sound proposition. Real estate which attracts large investments and is prone to generation of black money also need to be under GST.

GST Network

Under GST, the entire dealer registration, tax payment, tax return filing and refund will be in Online mode and administered by the GST Network (GSTN). The GSTN was set up in 2013 as a not-for-profit firm and was envisaged as the technology backbone for GST. As part of its revenue model and to sustain its operations, GSTN will recover these costs by levying a fee for transactions undertaken on the network. GSTN initiated the process of registering tax payers in November 2016. An estimated 8 million taxpayers were to be given a GST ID number – a 15-digit number based on their income tax PAN – to operate under the GST regime. GSTN is prepared to handle 3 billion invoices a month. Entities that generate a large volume of invoices would be encouraged to upload them daily to lessen the burden on the system. One of the main difficulties faced by the assessees under the GST is that many of the smaller traders and businesses are not familiar with the technical process involved in filing the returns. The government has taken steps to ease the process of filing returns.

E-way bill

An E-way bill system will be in force to ensure seamless movement of goods across state borders. If any document checking is enforced at state borders, it will be a retrograde step and archaic. It defeats the very purpose of GST and the free market it purports to be. It would significantly dilute the fundamental principles of GST relating to seamless movement of goods across states. The law provides for ample monitoring through the credit matching and compliance requirements under GST. It is to be seen if this will be enforced or diluted in any way due to opposition to it.

Offences

The GST regime has identified some 21 offences and breach of rules which may occur for which penalty has also been prescribed. Some of these offences are:

- Not registering under GST, even though required by law.
- Supply of any goods/services without any invoice or issuing a false invoice.
- The issue of invoices by a taxable person using the GSTIN of another bona fide taxpayer.
- Submission of false information while registering under GST.
- Submission of fake financial records/documents or files, or fake returns to evade tax.
- Deliberate suppression of sales to evade tax.
- Opting for composition scheme even though a taxpayer is ineligible.

GST data given below will indicate that despite some teething troubles faced, the system has been stabilizing with the cooperation between the Centre and State governments and the spirit of consensus displayed in GST Council meetings.

Box 25.2 GST Statistics (as on October 3, 2021)

- Total Return Filed: 74.43 crore
- Registered Tax Payers: 1.32 crore
- E-way Bill: 216.00 crore
- Total Invoice Upload: 1371 crore
- Payment Through the Portal (Excluding IGST on Imports): ₹ 37.34 lakh crore
- Total No. of Payment Transactions: 20.56 crore
- Highest Returns Transactions in a day: 23.86 lakh
- Highest Payment Transactions in a day: 9.55 lakh

Total GST collected till September 2021: ₹ 78,681.50 billion

Conclusion

GST is a historic, game-changing tax reform which was long overdue. India has now joined a group of over 150 nations where VAT/GST is in force. The manner in which GST Council held deliberations over several crucial meetings and arrived at decisions by consensus, rather than voting, despite occasional differences which were smoothly ironed out, is ample proof of the way in which cooperative federalism, involving the Centre and the States/UT's, on critical issues can function in practice.

Domestically, it will help improve governance, strengthen tax institutions, facilitate 'Make in India by Making One India', impart buoyancy to the tax base and tax collections and boost economic growth. GST has been envisaged as an efficient tax system, neutral in its application and distributionally beneficial. It will also set the global standard for a value-added tax (VAT).

To recapitulate, GST paves the way for :

- Elimination of multiplicity of taxes and their cascading effects;
- Rationalization of tax structure and simplification of compliance procedures;
- Harmonization of Central and State tax administrations which would reduce duplication and compliance costs;
- Widening tax base and eliminating classification disputes; and

- Automation of compliance procedures to reduce errors and increase efficiency in tax administration.
- Implementing e-invoicing and new returns.
- Reducing litigations related to transitional credits.
- Centralising advance ruling authority.
- Having a single jurisdiction for audits and investigations.
- Strengthening the GSTN system would be the key areas to watch out for in the near future.

Box 25.3 In what way is the Goods and Taxes (GST) regime more beneficial for the economy than the previous system of indirect taxes? Bring out the relative merits and demerits of the two systems of indirect taxation.

Goods and Services Tax (GST), introduced in India from July 1, 2017, is a path-breaking indirect tax reform which creates a common national market by dismantling inter-State trade barriers. GST has subsumed multiple indirect taxes like excise duty, service tax, VAT, CST, luxury tax, entertainment tax, entry tax, etc. which existed at Central and State levels. GST is a value added tax levied on manufacture, sale and consumption of goods and services.

GST offers comprehensive and continuous chain of tax credits from the producer's point/service provider's point up to the retailer's/consumer's level, thereby taxing only the value added at each stage of supply chain. The supplier at each stage is permitted to avail credit of GST paid on the purchase of goods and/or services and can set off this credit against the GST payable on the supply of goods and services to be made by him. Thus, the final consumer bears only the GST charged by the last supplier in the supply chain, with set-off benefits at all the previous stages. Thus, there is no tax on tax or cascading of taxes under GST system. GST does not differentiate between goods and services and thus, the two are taxed at a single rate.

In the previous indirect tax regime, a manufacturer of goods liable for excise charged excise duty and value added tax (VAT) on intra-State sale of goods. And the next dealer on subsequent intra-State sale of goods charged VAT (as per VAT rate prevalent in the state) on value which included basic value of the item + excise duty charged by manufacturer + profit by dealer). This duplication of taxes added to the cost and final price of the product or service to the ultimate consumer/user.
The earlier indirect tax framework in India suffered from various shortcomings.

Under that the various indirect taxes being levied were not necessarily mutually exclusive. For instance, when the goods were manufactured and sold, both the central excise duty (CENVAT) and State-Level VAT were levied. Though CENVAT and State-Level VAT are essentially value added taxes, set off of one against the credit of another was not possible as CENVAT was a Central levy while the State-Level VAT was a State levy. Moreover, CENVAT was applicable only at manufacturing level and not at distribution levels.

The previous sales tax regime was a combination of origin-based Central Sales Tax (CST) and destination-based multi-point system of taxation (State-Level VAT). Despite the adoption of the principle of taxation of value added in India – at the Central level in the form of CENVAT and at the State level in the form of State VAT – its application had remained piecemeal and fragmented on account of the following reasons:

- Non-inclusion of several local levies in State VAT such as luxury tax, entertainment tax, etc.
- Cascading effect of taxes on account of inclusion of CENVAT in the value while levying VAT.
- Non-integration of VAT & service tax.
- Double taxation of a transaction as both goods and services.

Positive Aspects

The GST has many other positive aspects as compared to the previous indirect tax system.

- It helps to create a common, unified market across States.
- It plugs the loopholes in the earlier regime and ensures better tax compliance as GST creates a continuous trail of transactions at every stage. The electronic mode used in GST greatly aids in this process.
- GST will be a simpler and more transparent system. The simplicity and transparency of the system will induce more people to pay taxes rather than evade them which will help to boost revenue.
- GST is beneficial from the viewpoint of both consumers and industry. As credit of input tax is available against output tax, it will reduce the tax burden on producers. The reduction in production cost will benefit consumers within India and also make exports more competitive.
- Simplified and cost-effective system as procedural cost will be less due to uniform accounting for all types of taxes.
- Only three accounts, viz., Central GST, State/UT GST and Integrated GST have to be maintained.
- GST with an E-permit system in place will ensure seamless movement of goods across State borders. (See portion below on GST to Improve Transport and Logistics).
- With resort to electronic processing under GST, the need for physical interface between tax authorities and assessees will be considerably reduced thus averting scope for harassment and corruption in dealings.
- In the long term, it could lead to a higher output, more employment opportunities, and economic boom.

GST will transform the Transport & Logistics sector in India

While at a basic level, most industries are likely to benefit from GST as it makes the entire process of taxation simpler, less bureaucratic and more efficient, the one industry that will benefit the most is transport and logistics. For decades, the transport and logistics sector was designed and structured based on the state taxation system which made it inefficient and cumbersome. With GST, the scenario will undergo much change and the entire transport and logistics infrastructure in India will become more competitive and optimal in terms of its structure.

For this sector, the concern was not so much about the rates of taxation or mode of collection of taxes but speedy movement of goods across the length and breadth of the country traversing thousands of miles. The delays and hazards faced by personnel manning containers, trucks and lorries in covering long distances due to the condition of roads and highways, traffic bottlenecks, toll gates, etc. were exacerbated by delays and harassment caused at border check points and octroi posts. Often, such delays at each state border ranged from one to three or more days resulting in substantial wastage of time, labour and money and consequent delays in turnaround of vehicles and productivity losses for both manpower and vehicles.

According to industry estimates of 2013, the logistics and transportation sector is worth $130 billion annually, but this industry is largely scattered and unorganized due to the nature of state level of taxation. The inter-state taxation system required companies to set up and maintain warehouses in each state, which makes the supply chain longer and inefficient. With such a complex structure and convoluted tax system, the logistics industry spent nearly 50 to 60 per its of its time in tax compliance, interstate check points manoeuvring, scrutiny and tracking of inter-state sales tax. This has created a paradoxical situation for the logistics and transportation industry which functions as vital support to make the core operations of the business and other sectors more efficient, but instead gets caught in a tangle of regulations and compliances vastly eroding its efficiency.

With GST in place, there could be regional warehouse hubs. Unlike in the earlier regime, the manufacturer or supplier will not require a warehouse in each state, tranship goods at multiple warehouses for supply to the distributors at final destinations. This will lead to consolidation and economies of scale in logistical operations.

With GST, this will change as the entire transport and logistics infrastructure and India will become more competitive in global markets also.

Downside of GST

While the GST system has many positives and advantages as explained above, it also poses some challenges in implementation. Some of these are:

- A GST regime must have few tax slabs – ideally, one rate or at the most two and with no or very few items in exempted category. Multiplicity of slabs and rates makes the system less beneficial and more complex in operation. But in a country like India, with a large part of the population in lower and middle income groups, not to speak of those even below the poverty line, a one-slab GST or no exempted items will mean taxing essential commodities which will have inflationary impact and make many items unaffordable to large sections. And higher rates have been kept with a view to raise revenue from items consumed by the affluent sections. India has opted for four slabs, apart from zero tax items, which leaves scope for reducing the number of slabs and rationalising rates on more items in due course. Already, the GST Council has moved several items from higher to lower slabs. And the need now is to reduce the number of slabs after seeing revenue realisation.
- The advantage of a single rate is that tax evasion can be easily tracked, especially as we move towards electronic payments systems. Multiple rates give scope for misdeclaration of items so as to take advantage of lower rate slab.
- As GST is a destination-based tax, while manufacturing states like Maharashtra, Tamil Nadu, Gujarat, etc. stand to lose, other consumption-based states like UP, Bihar, Odisha, etc. may get more revenue from GST. This was a contentious issue in the GST Council and it was resolved by the Centre agreeing to make up the losses sustained by any state for a period of five years. The revenue accruing to the Centre and various states has to be watched to see how this revenue-sharing arrangement will pan out in future.
- Certain critical items like petroleum and alcohol and the real estate sector have been kept out the purview of GST due to the insistence by states. These need to be brought under the regime to make it more effective from the economy's point of view.

Conclusion

According to estimates, the implementation of GST is likely to add nearly 2 per cent to India's annual GDP growth. Already at 7 to 7.5 per cent growth, India is one of the fastest growing major economies in the world. The benign impact of an additional 2 per cent on a base annual GDP of $2 trillion will have a substantial trickle-down effect.

Group of Ministers on GST

The Government has set up in September 2021 a seven-member Group of Ministers (GoM), headed by Karnataka Chief Minister (CM), Basavaraj S. Bommai and Maharashtra Deputy CM, Ajit Pawar as Convenor, to suggest changes, as well as a roadmap, for short- and medium-term changes to the GST rate structure. The Committee which is to give its report in two months consists of Finance Ministers from other States.

According to the terms of reference for the GoM, it shall review the current tax slab rates and recommend changes in the same as may be needed to garner required resources, review the current rate slab structure of GST and special rates, and recommend rationalisation measures, including merger of tax rate slabs, required for a simpler rate structure in GST.

In this Chapter we discussed.....

- Financial inclusion programme: Jan Dhan Yojana and its significance; the scheme and its benefits; progress of the scheme; importance of financial literacy of customers.
- JAM (Jan Dhan Yojana, Aadhaar, and Mobile) scheme to reach out to people; importance of 'Aadhaar'; usefulness of Aadhaar for remitting subsidies and direct benefit transfers.
- Expansion of Banking facilities and Payments banks and Small Finance banks given licence by RBI; they will service small savings account holders, remittances of migrant labour, low income households, small businesses and other unorganised sector entities.
- Payments banks will service small savings account holders, remittances of migrant labour, low income households, small businesses, and other unorganized sector entities.
- PM Mudra Yojana (PMMY) started for development of micro units and refinancing of Micro Finance Institutions (MFIs) and 'funding the unfunded', will encourage entrepreneurship and reach out to small entrepreneurs.
- Problem of non-paying assets (NPAs) and recpitalization; revamp plan for PSBs called 'Indradhanush' set in motion; Bank Board Bureau set up; government to infuse capital into banks; RBI also steps in to ease the capital position of banks; the FM has hinted that after strengthening banks, the question of consolidation of banks could be considered subject to the government's shareholding being maintained. a major infusion of capital in PSBs announced.

- Setting up of Bad Bank (Asset Reconstruction Company): The Objectives and Implications
- Black money and a parallel economy of undisclosed wealth has been a major problem disrupting the economy; though various steps have been taken and a Supreme Court-appointed SIT has been pursuing the matter, they have not been very effective.
- Demonetisation effected; high value currencies invalidated in November 2016 and replaced with new notes; much disruption in the economy in the near term but it will cleanse the economy and spur growth in the medium and long term.
- Further Income Declaration scheme announced following demonetisation which have unearthed unaccounted money; tax authorities examining large deposits made in banks and cooperative societies during demonetisation; notices issued to those who have failed to declare unaccounted money and penal action may be taken where deposits made do not match with their tax returns.
- Measures to make the economy more digital-oriented and less cash-based to prevent corruption and disrupt the parallel, underground economy.
- Steps to reform funding of political parties and elections, a long-pending issue, initiated to make the system more transparent and clean; an Electoral Bond scheme announced; the scheme is still not foolproof.
- Even after a stringent Black Money law was passed by the Parliament and a limited time-window provided for disclosure of illegal wealth kept in India or stashed abroad, only a very modest amount could be garnered; more foreign countries and OECD are cooperating to help to track such illegal wealth and banks overseas have also tightened checks on Indians; another opportunity has been given in Union Budget for 2016–17 for people to declare undisclosed income.
- More steps like making funding of political parties transparent, transparency in all governmental contracts, and control of sectors like real estate are needed to curb black money within the country.
- Illegal transfers of money to foreign countries through banks and loans- for-bribe scams have also taken place in some banks which calls for closer monitoring of banks; RBI has initiated corrective steps on these issues.

- Black money problem exists in the u.s. and other developed economies; the European Union has enacted its First Directive to combat money laundering in 1991 and later issued the Anti-Money Laundering and Financing of Terrorism Directives to protect the financial system and other vulnerable professions from being misused for money laundering.
- OECD has prepared a 15-point plan to prevent firms from exploiting different countries' tax rules and issued Base Erosion and Profit Shifting (BEPS) plan; India has welcomed it and taken action on it.
- A goldnmonetization scheme has been launched to mobilize gold held by individuals, institutions, and rich temples for recycling and to reduce imports; resident Indians (Individuals, HUF, and Trusts including Mutual Funds/Exchange Traded Funds registered under SEBI (Mutual Fund) Regulations and Companies) can make deposits under the scheme.
- Major indirect tax reforms – the VAT and GST; GST legislation passed and GST Council set up; GST rates fixed; periodic review of GST rates on commodities; it replaces the existing Central and State indirect taxes and eliminate the cascading effect of various duties and taxes; move to make the tax system modern, simple and transparent; GST will promote business and industry and spur economic growth.
- More tax reforms effected based on Justice Easwar Committee report; changes proposed in Corporate income tax; income tax for companies with annual turnover up to ₹250 crore reduced to 25 per cent; this will help MSMEs in particular.

Important Terms to Note in this Chapter

Direct Benefits Transfer (DBT); Business Correspondent; Bank Mitras; JAM scheme; Aadhaar; Payments Bank; Small Finance Bank; Non¬performing assets (NPAs); Bad Bank; Asst Reconstruction; Recapitalization (of banks); Black economy; Parallel economy; Round-tripping; Money laundering; Demonetisation; Participatory Notes (P-notes); Gold monetization; Value Added Tax; Goods and Services Tax (GST); Corporate income tax

Practice Questions

1. What is meant by 'Financial inclusion' and what is its significance in the Indian context? What steps have been taken by successive governments to promote it and how effective they have been?
2. Explain the main features of the Pradhan Mantri Jan Dhan Yojana (PMJDY). How far it has helped to provide banking facilities to those who were outside the fold of banking in India?

3. What are the new trends in banking and the steps taken to modernise banking in India? How have these measures benefited the customers and the economy?
4. The banking sector has, of late, come under severe stress due to bad loans and non-performing assets. Discuss the reasons which led to this and the steps taken by the government and the Reserve Bank of India to contain the problem.
5. Mere capitalization of banks will not solve the problem faced by banks but reforms in banking sector are also required. Do you agree with this statement? Justify your answer.
6. Discuss the pros and cons of merging the State Bank of India with its subsidiaries.
7. What is meant by "Payments bank' and 'Small Finance bank' and what is their role in the economy? How far do you think they will be beneficial to the economy and the people at large?
8. In November 2016, the government of India resorted to 'Demonetisation'. What were its features, objectives and consequences?
9. Black money, unaccounted wealth and 'parallel economy' are the sources of major problems in Indian economy. Do you agree? What are the effective steps which can be taken to tackle them?
10. It is said that 'Demonetisation' process attempted in November 2016 did not achieve its main objectives. Do you agree? Justify your answer with cogent reasons.
11. Why is it said that 'Demonetisation' alone cannot root out the menace of black money and illicit wealth in India? What other measures need to be taken to solve the problem?
12. The government has initiated a scheme of 'Electoral Bonds' to tackle the problem of undisclosed money in funding political parties in India. What are the main features of the scheme and why is it said that this scheme is still not perfect and would not solve the problem? What additional measures need to be taken to make the scheme foolproof?
13. It is argued that India needs to move to a 'Digital economy' and reduce the use of cash. Do you agree? Give reasons for your views and suggest measures to achieve these objectives.
14. Explain the main features of Goods and Services Tax (GST) regime introduced in India. What are its advantages over the previous indirect tax system?
15. What were the challenges in implementing the Goods and Services Tax (GST) regime in India? What steps were taken by the government to overcome them?
16. It is said that an ideal Goods and Services Tax (GST) regime should have only a single rate of tax whereas India has multiple rates. Explain why India has adopted multiple rates and whether India can have a single rate, if not, why?
17. Describe the composition and the Terms of Reference of the GST Council and the role played by it in introducing the Goods and Services Tax (GST) system in India.
18. In what way the Goods and Services Tax (GST) regime can give a boost to the Indian economy? Give some specific instances and examples to justify your answer.
19. Craze for gold in Indians has led to a surge in import of gold in recent years and put pressure on balance of payments and external value of rupee. In view of this, examine the merits of the Gold Monetization Scheme. *[UPSC Main 2015 (Economics Optional Paper)]*

20. Pradhan Mantri Jan-Dhan Yojana (PMJDY) is necessary for bringing unbanked to the institutional finance fold. Do you agree with this for financial inclusion of the poorer section of the Indian society? Give arguments to justify your opinion.

[UPSC Main 2016(Economics Optional Paper)]

21. Financial inclusion is a must for healthy growth of the Indian economy. In this context, what measures would you suggest to promote household savings in India?

[Indian Economic Service/Indian Statistical Service 2015]

22. 'Financial inclusion is one of the most essential components of inclusive growth.' Comment.

[UPSC Main 2015 (Economics Optional Paper)]

23. What constitutes Black Economy of India? Enumerate its dimensions.

[Indian Economic Service/Indian Statistical Service 2014]

24. What are the consequences of black money in India?

[Indian Economic Service/Indian Statistical Service 2017]

25. What are the broad features of the proposed GST Model?

[UPSC Main 2015 (Economics Optional Paper)]

26. Mention the major hurdles in implementing the proposed Goods and Services Tax (GST) in the country. *[Indian Economic Service/Indian Statistical Service 2014]*

27. Examine the process of introducing and passing GST Bill in Parliament. How it helps in Fiscal Consolidation in the country? *[UPSC Main 2016 (Economics Optional Paper)]*

28. Do you think the imposition of GST will lead to enhanced tax collection for the Centre and the States? Will it reduce the incidence of taxation on the common people?

[Indian Economic Service/Indian Statistical Service 2017]

29. Point out the problems of Indian capital market. In this context, evaluate the role of SEBI in strengthening capital market.

[Indian Economic Service/Indian Statistical Service 2016]

30. Give an account of the progress and expansion of banking network and Pradhan Mantri Jan Dhan Yojana in the context of financial inclusion in rural India.

[Indian Economic Service/Indian Statistical Service 2020]

31. Explain the rationale behind the Goods and Services Tax (Compensation to States) Act of 2017. How has COVID-19 impacted the GST compensation fund and created new federal tensions?

[UPSC Main 2020 (General Studies Paper)]

32. Enumerate the indirect taxes which have been subsumed in the Goods and Services Tax (GST) in India. Also, comment on the revenue implications of the GST introduced in India since July 2017.

[UPSC Main 2019 (General Studies Paper)]

33. Comment on the important changes introduced in respect of the Long-term Capital Gains Tax (LCGT| and Dividend Distribution Tax (DDT) in the Union Budget for 2018-2019,

[UPSC Main 2018 (General Studies Paper)]

34. Critically examine the role of the RBI in maintaining financial stability under the new regime of monetary system. *[UPSC Main 2020 (Economics Optional Paper)]*

35. Explain the objectives of the Government of India setting up Asset Reconstruction and Management companies for the banking sector and their working.

CHAPTER

SOCIAL SECTOR AND CSR

- Education – A Visible Change
- Critical Role of Female Teachers
- National Education Policy (NEP) 2020
- Health Sector: Health Facilities
- National Rural Health Mission (NRHM) (2005-12)
- Health Manpower
- Expenditure on Health
- Need to Upgrade Health Facilities
- National Health Policy, 2017 and Ayushman Bharat
- Challenges for Health Schemes
- Housing for Weaker Sections: IAY and PMAY
- Household Water supply: Jal Jeevan Mission
- Swachh Bharat Mission
- Total Sanitation Campaign
- Smart Cities Programme
- Waste Management
- Corporate Social Responsibility (CSR)

❑ INTRODUCTION

Considering the wide disparities and inequities in Indian society, development in the social sector assumes great importance. Apart from education and health, housing and other basic facilities like safe drinking water and sanitation are of equal importance. Large sections of people, both in urban and rural areas, do not have decent houses and, even after six decades of development, continue to live in ramshackle dwellings in the midst of squalor. This is especially so, and strikingly visible, in the metros and larger towns where due to the density of population and limited land area, people are forced to live in overcrowded slums. According to estimates, nearly 50 per cent of Mumbai city's population live in such forbidding and loathsome conditions. As a result, members of the families of these most vulnerable sections, especially children in their formative years, are exposed to unhealthy and unhygienic conditions and are deprived of access to proper healthcare and the children are denied of proper education.

Despite the government's earnest efforts in successive Plans and investment in the social sector, the benefits have not trickled down to the poorer sections in adequate measure.

❑ EDUCATION

Educational attainment is an important prerequisite for improving a person's quality of life. It enhances the person's capabilities, gives greater freedom of choice, helps improve productivity, widens access to, and acquire, more knowledge, and helps to move up further in life. And deprived of a reasonably good education, the person is denied much of these. This has been the fate of large sections of our population in the disadvantaged sections both in urban and rural areas.

Neglect of school education, for whatever reason it may have been, in the early phase of planning has been referred to in Chapter 2 (See p-2.7.8). As will be seen from Table 26.2, it is not that in the initial Plans, adequate attention or allocation was not made for the education sector. Percentage wise, the sector did receive reasonable allocation, considering the total financial resources available then.It was that the magnitude of the problem and the expansion of educational facilities that was called for was huge while the resources available were grossly inadequate for the task on hand. And there were other pressing and competing demands such as in agriculture, irrigation, industry, and small and village industries which were all critical for the economy. The question is whether within the allocation made for education, more could have been set apart for elementary education in the initial three or four Plans so as to build a strong base upon which more could have been achieved in subsequent Plans.

Educational facilities have since expanded phenonmenally and school dropout rates have come down over the years. For instance, as observed by the Planning Commission, interventions through Sarva Shiksha Abhiyan (SSA) brought down the number of out-of-school children from 32 million in 2001–02 to 7.0 million in 2006–07 (Eleventh Plan, Vol. III). The Right to Education (RTE) Act is also a significant step to bring about equity in the sector. Yet, there are several other issues which need to be addressed to achieve the universal education goal and improve the quality and standard of education, especially for the weaker sections, as outlined below.

- A study done of rural India places the proportion of children not enrolled in schools at 3.5 per cent. However, in a few States like Rajasthan and UP, the percentage of girls in the age group of 11–14 years, not in school, is as high as 8.9 per cent and 9.7 per cent respectively.
- While children can be enrolled in schools at an early age, retaining them, especially disadvantaged children, through up to the high school level, is a far more challenging task. As the Eleventh Plan (2007–12) document has observed, around 22 per cent children dropped out in classes I and II.
- Several factors, apart from their adverse socioeconomic conditions are responsible for this. The opportunity cost of sending a girl-child to school is high, especially in the rural set-up. With both parents, who may themselves not have had the benefit of education and hence do not realize the value of education, out on work, the girl child may neither be in school nor figure in the labour force but will be engaged at home doing domestic chores.
- The number of schools also decrease sharply beyond the upper primary level. In 2015-16, for every 100 elementary schools (classes I to VIII) in rural India, there were only 14 schools offering secondary (classes IX to X) and six offering higher secondary (classes XI –XII). Even if private secondary schools are there, it may not help due to higher fees, distances involved, etc.

A Visible Change

However, with the new generation coming up, there are encouraging signs of change. Even parents in the lower rungs of society, particularly in the urban areas, are keen to send their children, boy or girl, to a school and continue their education without break. And what's more, many of them are keen on their children receiving English-medium education and labour hard to send them, not to government run schools which pale in comparison to private and convent-run schools, but to the latter, even if it means incurring more expenses. This is not to cast any aspersion on government schools, many of which will be having teachers with equal commitment and dedication as in private schools, and one cannot generalize or make any sweeping conclusions. But it is well known that many of the government run schools suffer from lack of good infrastructure (building, toilets, etc.), lower teaching standards, untrained or inadequately trained teachers, and frequent absence of teachers, not to speak of facilities like a good lab and library. This only points to the dire need to improve the state of government-run schools in all respects. This is an area where CSR can play a significant role. (For more on this, see under CSR later in this chapter).

Facilities like adequate separate toilet for girls, an issue which has come to the fore lately, is another crucial factor. For lack of this facility, particularly in rural schools, girls have refrained from attending school or discontinued education midstream.

In a pioneering effort to prevent drop-out of girls and to retain them in schools and continue their education, Kerala government has started a scheme to supply free sanitary pads to girls in higher standards. The scheme is also aimed at creating greater awareness about health and hygiene. Such measures could be replicated in other states to improve the attendance of girls in schools.

Critical Role of Female Teachers

Two factors that profoundly impinge on girls' education are environment and security, and facilities in schools. It is well established that the presence of female teachers plays a critical role in reducing the gender gap in schools at primary and secondary education levels. Girls learn better and stay in school longer when their teachers are women. Female teachers also serve as a role model for girls and their presence gives them a sense of security and assurance, and acts positively on girl children's enrolment and attendance. Facilities like adequate separate toilet for girls, an issue which has come to the fore lately, is another crucial factor. For lack of this facility, particularly in rural schools, girls have refrained from attending school or discontinued education midstream. (See section below on Toilet facility in Schools).

As for the number of female teachers, the educationally backward States have a poor record as will be seen from Table 26.1 (a) below. While the number of Female teachers per 100 Male teachers in the three levels of Primary, Upper Primary and High school is quite high in the educationally progressive States, the numbers are quite low in the backward States. Thus, there is a need to increase the proportion of female teachers in the educationally weaker States which will go a long way in retaining girl students in schools.

Table 26.1 (a): Number of Female Teachers per 100 Male Teachers (2011-12)

State	Primary	Upper Primary	High School	State	Primary	Upper Primary	High School
Goa	1013	271	167	Bihar	68	64	22
Kerala	313	235	321	Chhattisgarh	59	57	65
Puducherry	399	168	199	MP	45	44	78
Tamil Nadu	288	200	130	Rajasthan	47	47	40
Delhi	255	525	226	UP	60	47	26
Punjab	176	173	219	Odisha	74	51	34

Source: Statistics of School Education 2011-12, Ministry of Human Resource Development, Govt. of India.

Table 26.1 (b) shows a comparative position of India vis-à-vis some selected countries as to the number of Female teachers per 100 Male teachers in 2014 (2008 in case of Argentina). In the case of Primary and Secondary levels, India compares quite adversely with other countries shown, save South Africa which too has quite low percentage of Female teachers. As for Tertiary level (of Higher education), the percentages are low for all these countries, including UK.

Table 26.1 (b): Percentage of Teachers who are Female (%)- India & Selected Countries

Country	Percentage of Teachers who are Female (%)					
	Primary		Secondary		Tertiary	
	Year	%	Year	%	Year	%
India	2014	49.49	2014	43.21	2014	39.03
Argentina	2008	87.42	2008	68.32	2009	48.56
Brazil	2014	89.64	2014	65.16	2014	45.41
Russian Federation	2014	98.81	2012	82.08	2013	58.16
South Africa	2014	48.56	2009	54.76	--	--
United Kingdom	2014	86.98	2014	61.4	2014	44.34

Source: United Nations & UNESCO Institute for Statistics, cited in Educational Statistics at A Glance, 2018, Department of School Education & Literacy, Ministry of Education, Govt. of India.

Toilet facility in Schools: Adequacy and Maintenance issues

Infrastructure in schools -- libraries, labs, toilets, etc. – is an important aspect of school education which is a formative period in children's lives. Toilet facility is a critical factor impacting children's education, especially of girls, and is one of the factors for drop out of girls in schools. For want of separate toilet for girls, many drop out of education midstream as they go up to higher standards.

Table 26.2 : Percentage of Schools with Girls' Toilet (2015-16)

State	Primary	Upper Primary	High School	State	Pri-mary	Upper Primary	High School
Karnataka	99.78	99.97	99.96	**Bihar**	89.85	96.43	94.98
Tamil Nadu	99.88	99.99	100	**Jharkhand**	96.86	97.68	97.3
Maharashtra	99.31	99.76	99.84	**MP**	96.9	97.55	97.49
Gujarat	99.97	99.97	99.93	**Rajasthan**	99.69	99.86	99.79
Punjab	99.82	99.84	99.92	**UP**	99.8	99.84	99.66
Haryana	99.62	99.85	99.82	**Odisha**	97.82	96.79	95.49

Source: Table 49- National Institute of Educational Planning & Administration, New Delhi, cited in Educational Statistics at A Glance, 2018, Department of School Education & Literacy, Ministry of Education, Govt. of India.

The data in Table 26.2 shows that most states have achieved a high percentage of coverage, ranging from 95 to 99 per cent. But related critical issues, important from the health point of view, are:

- Adequate number of separate toilets for Girls and Boys considering the number of boys and girls.
- Proper maintenance of toilets in hygienic condition.
- Availability of adequate and assured water supply.

There have been reports of some schools having just one or two separate toilets even where there are over 100 to 150 boys and girls. The problem may be more pronounced in government schools and schools in rural areas.

An Audit report on toilets constructed in schools by CPSEs under the Swachh Vidyalaya Abhiyan is quite revealing on the deficiencies noticed. (See Box 26.1).

Box 26.1: School Toilets Constructed under Swachh Vidyalaya Abhiyan by CPSEs: An Audit Report

The Norms for schools under the Right of Children to Free and Compulsory Education Act 2009 (RTE Act) prescribe separate toilets for boys and girls. There have been gaps in achieving this objective mainly due to poor maintenance of toilets, lack of dedicated funds and poor water availability inside toilets. To achieve the objective of separate toilets for boys and girls within a year, HRD Ministry launched in September 2014, Swachh Vidyalaya Abhiyan (SVA) and sought co-operation of other Ministries to ask Central Public Sector Enterprises (CPSEs) to participate in a project for construction of toilets in government schools.

53 CPSEs, under the Ministries of Power, Coal and Petroleum & Natural Gas, executed a project and constructed 1,40,997 toilets for schools at the instance of HRD Ministry. Seven CPSEs constructed about 5,000 toilets each and 1,30,703 toilets in all, at a cost of ₹2,162.60 crore.

Comptroller and Auditor General (C & AG) examined this project and also conducted physical survey of a sample of 2,695 toilets across 2,048 schools in 15 States. Main Audit findings are as under:

- **Non-existing and Partially Constructed Toilets**: Out of 2,695 toilets in the audit sample, the CPSEs did not construct 83 toilets though they were identified for construction. Of the remaining 2,612 toilets reported to have been constructed, 200 toilets were not found constructed in the respective schools and 86 toilets were found to be only partially constructed. The non-existing and partially constructed toilets constituted 11 per cent of toilets surveyed.

Out of 1,967 co-educational schools surveyed by Audit, 99 schools had no functional toilets while 436 schools had ***only one functional toilet. The objective of providing separate toilets for boys and girls was not fulfilled in these 535 schools (27 per cent of 1967 Schools).***

- **Toilets constructed, but not in use**: Out of 2,326 constructed toilets surveyed, 691 (30 per cent) were found not in use mainly due to lack of running water, lack of cleaning arrangements, damages to the toilets and other reasons like use of toilets for other purposes, toilets locked up, etc.
- **Lack of running water and other facilities**: As per the SVA norms, the toilets are to have running water, hand washing facilities and proper/regular maintenance, so as to effectively change the behaviour of users. The survey showed that 1,679 (72 per cent) out of 2,326 constructed toilets were without running water facility inside toilets. Further, hand washing facility was not available in 1,279 (55 per cent) out of 2,326 constructed toilets. Audit also noticed cases of defective construction of toilets, non-provision of foundation/ramp/staircase and damaged/overflowed leach pit, which led to ineffective use of toilets.
- **Maintenance arrangements for toilets:** The Ministries had directed the CPSEs to maintain the toilets constructed by them for three to five years and book the annual expenses to their CSR budget. During the survey, Audit noticed that proper maintenance/ sanitation was not available in 1,812 out of 2,326 toilets. 715 out of 1,812 toilets were not being cleaned. 1,097 toilets were being cleaned twice in a week to once in a month whereas, the norm was for daily cleaning at least once. Thus, 75 per cent of selected toilets were not maintained hygienically. Cases of non-provision of soap, bucket, cleaning agents and disinfectants in toilets and inadequate cleanliness of pathway were also noticed.

(**Source**: CAG's Audit Report on Construction of toilets in schools by CPSEs presented in Parliament in September 2020).

UNICEF which works with the government and partners to ensure that every child in India has access to clean water, basic toilets and practices good hygiene behaviour has observed that surveys done few years back in India's schools have found that 22 per cent did not have appropriate toilets for girls, 58 per cent of pre-schools had no toilet at all and 56 per cent of pre-schools had no water on the premises.

All this calls for periodic, regular inspection and checks of these facilities by education authorities at district, tehsil and village levels. Parent-Teacher Committees and Gram Sabhas in villages could also be empowered to look into these aspects. School authorities too should be asked to report any deficiencies found in the provision and maintenance of toilet facilities to authorities concerned for remedial action.

Quality and Standards of Education

While enrolment at the lower primary level has improved considerably, the focus now has to be on improving learning outcomes attained by children who complete five years of primary schooling. Independent surveys have pointed to very low levels of learning among children at this level. Some findings show that a good proportion of children in class V are unable to read class II level books.

In a 'Programme for International Student Assessment' (PISA) study conducted in 2009 by OECD of 15-year old students in 73 countries, who were tested on their reading, math, and science abilities, India was placed at the tail-end in international comparisons rating. The test was conducted in two states in India that year: Tamil Nadu and Himachal Pradesh. India was placed at 72nd position (rank) among 73 participating countries.

Asian education systems have come to dominate the upper rankings in PISA over the years. The top spots for mathematics in the PISA 2015 results were all occupied by Asian countries – Singapore followed by Hong Kong, Macau, Taiwan, Japan, China and South Korea.

This is despite India being seen as an education powerhouse – based not only on the reputation of islands of academic excellence such as the IITs, but several high-grade Universities and colleges and a vast chain of public and international schools. While these institutions are at one end of the spectrum, there is, indeed, much work to be done to improve quality in institutions at the other end, pointing once again to the wide disparities in educational facilities in the country.

The methodology adopted by PISA has been questioned by many experts. After the 2009 survey, the then government decided not to participate in future surveys. However, the government has since reviewed the position and is of the view that "if 80 countries can participate in PISA, including China and Vietnam, then there is no reason why children in India cannot appear for it." India decided to take part in the 2021 PISA test but the test has been postponed to 2022 due to the pandemic situation. Kendriya Vidyalayas, Navodaya Vidyalayas, and all schools, private and government, in Chandigarh are to take part in the forthcoming test.

In an effort to revamp the education system, the Government of India has come up with a New Education Policy in 2020. (See Box 26.2 on this).

Box 26.2: National Education Policy (NEP) 2020

Education in India is poised at an interesting inflection point. On the one hand, it is set to shed an outdated model for a revamped system under the new National Education Policy 2020.The new digital platforms of learning and innovative techniques of teaching would propel it to global standards to create new benchmarks.

The National Education Policy (NEP) 2020, prepared by a Committee of experts and educationists, was released by the HRD Ministry after wide public consultations with all stakeholders in the field. It replaces the National Policy on Education 1986.

Objectives of NEP 2020

The new policy has provisions for revamping the curriculum structure, assessment criteria and regulations, promises a new approach to teaching and learning. The broad objectives of NEP are:

Strong learning foundation and robust academic growth

Research suggests that most of the development of brain in a child happens by the age of six. The new 5+3+3+4 education pattern proposed provides for the first five years dedicated to foundational learning, followed by a regularly assessed academic growth through the preparatory, middle and secondary stages.

Holistic development for students of all grades

NEP will inspire a shift from rote learning to in-depth understanding. The curriculum content will be reduced to core essentials and create more space for critical thinking, discussions, and analysis. Teaching and learning will be more interactive, exploratory, collaborative, and experiential.

Flexibility in choice of subjects

Students will enjoy far greater flexibility in choice of subjects, with no hard separation between the streams of arts, humanities, commerce and sciences.

Better student assessment

NEP 2020 proposes Standardized state school exams for grades 3, 5 and 8. Board exams for 10 and 12. Exams to test literacy, numeracy, and foundational skills will be very important.

Skill development

The proposal of a yearlong course in grade 6-8 in carpentry, electric work, gardening, pottery, metal work etc. will help in skill development.

- ICT in Education: The integration of information technology (IT) with the education sector is inadequate despite Computer Literacy and Studies in Schools. IT is to be taken up for teacher training, adult literacy, remedial education and as a learning tool in higher education. This would also include developing online skill-based courses.

New platforms and techniques of teaching-learning

Digital revolution and pedagogical innovations are perpetually creating new platforms of learning and techniques for teaching. NEP 2020 will further open the field for creativity. The educational institutions will have to overhaul their infrastructure to accommodate new facilities.

NEP mandates all teachers and principals to take at least 50 hours of Continuous Professional Development workshops each year. This will refine teaching skills and techniques.

Fundamental Principles

Besides, the NEP 2020 recognizes and emphasizes the following fundamental principles that will guide and enrich both the education system at large, as well as the institutions within it.

- **Full equity and inclusivity** are the cornerstone of all educational decisions to ensure that all students are able to thrive in the education system.
- **Synergy in curriculum across all levels of education** from early childhood care and education to school education to higher education. Multi-disciplinarity and a holistic education across the sciences, social sciences, arts, humanities, and sports for a multidisciplinary world in order to ensure the unity and integrity of all knowledge.

- **Emphasis on conceptual understanding** rather than rote learning and learning-for-exams. Creativity and critical thinking in students to encourage logical decision-making, research and innovation.
- **Teachers and faculty as the heart of the learning process** – their recruitment process, continuous professional development, positive working environment and service conditions are crucial.
- **Ethics and human and Constitutional values** like empathy, respect for others, cleanliness, courtesy, democratic spirit, spirit of service, respect for public property, scientific temper, liberty, responsibility, pluralism, equality, and justice.
- **Promoting multilingualism and the power of language** in teaching and learning.
- **Life skills** such as communication, cooperation, teamwork, and resilience.

Implementation of NEP

Finances and proper and timely implementation at the Centre and State levels will be key to the success of the new forward-looking policy and ensure that it keeps pace with the fast changing development and technology landscape.

Financing: Affordable and Quality Education for All

The Policy commits to significantly raising educational investment, as there is no better investment towards a society 's future than the high-quality education of young people. Unfortunately, public expenditure on education in India has not come close to the recommended level of 6 per cent of GDP, as envisaged by the 1968 Policy, reiterated in the Policy of 1986, and which was further reaffirmed in the 1992 review of the Policy.

The current public (Centre and States) expenditure on education in India has been around 4.43 per cent of GDP and only around 10 per cent of the total Government spending towards education (as noted in Economic Survey 2017-18). These numbers are far smaller than in the most developed and even developing countries.

To attain the education goals envisaged in the new policy, with corresponding benefits to the Nation and the economy, it calls for substantial increase in public investment in education by both the Central government and all State Governments which will need to work together to increase investment in Education sector and reach the target of 6 per cent of GDP at the earliest. This is considered extremely critical for achieving the high-quality and equitable public education system that is truly needed for India's future economic, social, cultural, intellectual, and technological progress and growth.

Plan Outlays on Education and Health

Plan Outlays on Education and Health: Table 26.3 gives the outlays on Education and Health in the eleven Five Year Plans from 1951 to 2012.

Table 26.3: Plan Outlays on Education and Health

Plan	Total outlay (Centre, States, & UTs) (in ₹ crore)		Total Plan Outlay in Public Sector
	Education	Health & Family Welfare	(In ₹ crore)
First Plan (1951–56)	164.00 (8.37)	140.00 (7.14)	1960
Second Plan (1956–61)	208.00 (4.45)	274.00 (5.86)	4672
Third Plan (1961–66)	497.00 (5.79)	225.86 (2.63)	8577
Fourth Plan (1969–74)	822.66 (5.21)	433.53 (2.75)	15779
Fifth Plan (1974–79)	1284.29 (3.26)	na	39426
Sixth Plan (1980–85)	2976.00 (2.69)	3412.02 (3.09)	110467
Seventh Plan (1985–90)	7685.50 (3.51)	6809.40 (3.11)	218730
Eighth Plan (1992–97)	19599.70 (4.04)	14075.90 (2.90)	485457
Ninth Plan (1997–2002)	52173.30 (6.41)	34386.60 (4.22)	813998
Tenth Plan (2002–07)	62461.00 (4.97)	45771.00 (3.64)	1255784
Eleventh Plan (2007–12)	274228.00 (7.65)	123900.00 (3.46)	3582768

Source: Sector outlays from Plan documents, Planning Commission; Total outlay from NITI Aayog, cited in Indian Public Finance Statistics, 2014-2015, Ministry of Finance, Dept. of Economic Affairs.

Note: The figures in brackets under total outlay represent percentages to total plan outlay.

❑ HEALTH SECTOR

As already seen in Chapter 18, following the concerted action taken by the government under health and family welfare programmes over the years, India registered significant progress on containing birth and death rates and also bringing down the infant mortality rate (IMR) and maternal mortality rate (MMR). (See Chapter 18, pp. 18.7-9). However, on population control, there was not as much success in the 1970s and 1980s as the rate of growth of population remained steady. But since 1991, there is decline in the growth rate of population which is a positive sign. (See Table 18.1 on p. 18.7).

But it must be noted that even in regard to IMR and MMR, some of the other comparable countries are far ahead of India and even Bangladesh is ahead of India on IMR as will be seen from Table 26.4.

Table 26.4: Infant Mortality Rates and Maternal Mortality Ratios in India and Selected Countries

Country	* IMR			Infant Under 5 #			$ MMR	
	1970	2002	2019	1970	2002	2019	1985–2002	2012-18
India	127	67	28.3	202	93	34.3	540	143 (2017)
China	85	31	6.8	120	39	7.9	53	27 (2013)
Brazil	95	30	12.4	135	36	13.9	160	59 (2018)
Mexico	79	24	12.2	110	29	14.2	79	36 (2016)
Sri Lanka	65	17	6.1	100	19	7.1	92	43 (2018)
Bangladesh	145	51	25.6	239	77	30.8	380	215 (2017)
Indonesia	104	33	20.2	172	45	23.9	380	282(2012)

Source: Data for 2019 for IMR and Under 5 Mortality Rate and MMR for 2012-18 from World Bank Data site. Other data from UNDP, Human Development Reports, 2004, 2013.

Note: * IMR is probability of infant dying between birth and exactly age 1, expressed per 1,000 live births; # Under 5 years mortality rate is probability of infant dying between birth and age 5, expressed per 1,000 live births;

$ MMR, maternal mortality ratio, is deaths per 100,000 live births.

By 2013, Bangladesh has been able to achieve both infant and under-5 years mortality rate lower than that of India and that position continues to be so even in 2019. According to the UNDP report, this is attributable to three factors:

- Economic empowerment of women through employment in the garment industry and access to microcredit which transformed their lives;
- Social and political empowerment of women through regular meetings of women's groups organized by non-governmental organizations; and,
- Higher participation of girls in formal education has been enhanced by non-governmental organizations. Informal schools run by a non-governmental organization offer four years of accelerated primary schooling to adolescents who have never attended school, and the schools have retention rates over 94 per cent. After graduation, students can join the formal schooling system, which most do.

The above factors highlight the importance of education of girls and employment for women which lead to their empowerment. India too can achieve similar outcomes as the Panchayati Raj system has empowered Gram Sabhas and women have greater representation and voice in decision-making on socio-economic issues in the villages. Many women's self-help groups, set up under the rural development programmes, have taken up income-generating activities. India also has a strong NGO movement which can be leveraged to advocate women's causes and ensure their greater empowerment. Education of girls and employment for women are two critical factors which will play a catalytic role in attaining these social objectives and improve the welfare of the family as a whole.

On Maternal Mortality Ratio (MMR), as seen from Table 26.4, India's position is better than that of Bangladesh and Indonesia but is far behind other countries shown in the Table.

Wide Inter-State Variations

While India made progress over the years in controlling population growth and on other parameters like death rate, TFR, IMR and MMR, there are large inter-State variations in these outcomes.

- Life expectancy ranges from 65 years in Uttar Pradesh to 75.2 years in Kerala.
- TFR in Tamil Nadu and Kerala is 1.59 and 1.79 respectively, similar to that in advanced countries, but States like Bihar and Uttar Pradesh have TFR well above the Replacement rate of 2.1.
- IMR in Nagaland is 4 compared to 48 in Madhya Pradesh. Many other States like Arunachal Pradesh, Assam, Bihar, Chhattisgarh, Meghalaya, Odisha, Rajasthan and Uttar Pradesh have high IMR.
- The rate of institutional deliveries in Kerala is 99.8 per cent, while it is only 32.8 per cent in Nagaland. States like Arunachal Pradesh, Assam, Bihar, Jharkhand, Manipur, Meghalaya, Nagaland, Uttar Pradesh and Uttarakhand have a very poor rate of institutional deliveries.
- This disparity is also present in nutritional outcomes. Bihar, Chhattisgarh, Gujarat, Jharkhand, Madhya Pradesh, Rajasthan and Uttar Pradesh have very high proportion of children who are underweight and stunted.
- States like Haryana, Jharkhand, Madhya Pradesh and Uttar Pradesh have a very high rate of children with anaemia. As a result, on Hunger Index, India ranks quite low among countries.

(For more on these, see Chapters 18 and 19).

Health Facilities and Outcomes

While in regard to vital statistics issues, India has made considerable progress as mentioned above, the problems in the health sector relate more to health facilities available, their quality and standards, and accessibility for the people, especially in the rural areas. The public health infrastructure available at the district level are the district and municipal hospitals and dispensaries, and at lower levels–talukas (tehsils) and villages–there are Primary health centres (PHCs), Sub-Centres, and Community health centers (CHCs). Their numbers have grown over the years to cater to the growing population, as will be seen from Table 26.5 (b).

Rural health set-up:

The healthcare infrastructure in rural areas has been developed as a three tier system and is based on the following population norms as shown in Table 26.5 (a):

Table 26.5 (a): Three Tier System of Rural Healthcare Infrastructure

	Centre	Population Norms	
		Plain Area	Hilly/Tribal/Difficult Area
1.	Sub-Centre	5000	3000
2.	Primary Health Centre	30,000	20,000
3.	Community Health Centre	1,20,000	80,000

Table 26.5 (b): Number of PHCs, SCs, and CHCs

	1968	1985	1997	2008	2012	2019
No. of PHCs	4840	9115	22457	23458	24049	24855
No. of CHCs	na	761	1910	4276	4833	5335
No. of SCs	na	na	na	146036	148366	157411

Source: Data for 1968, 1985, and 1997, Health Information of India, DG, HS; Data for 2008, 2012 and 2019 Rural Health Statistics, M/o H&FW.

The Sub-Centre is the most peripheral and first contact point between the primary health care system and the community. It is manned by at least one Auxiliary Nurse Midwife (ANM)/Female Health Worker and one Male Health Worker. PHC is the first contact point between village community and the Medical Officer. The PHCs are to provide integrated curative and preventive healthcare to the rural population. It is a referral unit for 6 Sub-centres, with 4-6 beds, with a Medical Officer supported by 14 paramedical staff.

CHCs are being established and maintained by the State Government. As per minimum norms, a CHC is required to be manned by four Medical Specialists, i.e., Surgeon, Physician, Gynaecologist, and Pediatrician, supported by 21 paramedical and other staff. It has 30 indoor beds with one OT, X-ray, Labour Room, and Laboratory facilities.

As on March 2019, there are a total 1,60,713 Sub Centres (SCs) (157411 rural + 3302 urban) and 30,045 PHCs (24855 rural + 5190 urban) functioning. Further, there are 5,685 Community Health Centres (CHCs) (5335 rural + 350 urban)

Tables 26.6 (a) and (b) show the position in respect of rural health infrastructure in selected states.

Some states like Kerala, Tamil Nadu, Karnataka and Gujarat have rural health facilities in excess of the norms. It is noteworthy that among the weaker states, Rajasthan has exceeded the norms in all the three categories while Odisha has only marginal shortfall in SC and PHC. Note that even among Group II states in Table 26 (b), which are considered relatively advanced, Maharashtra and Karnataka have shortfalls of facilities. Bihar, UP and MP have heavy shortfall in all the three categories – SCs & HWSCs, PHCs & HWPHCs and Community Health Centres. This would mean that people in rural areas in these states grossly suffer from inadequacy of health facilities. It is a sign of poor governance despite funds being available.

It is also worth recollecting that both Bihar and UP have had instances of serial deaths of newborn infants for lack of proper medical facilities and attention. Apart from this, the overcrowding and the unhygienic and filthy state of many of the government hospitals is well documented, crying for drastic improvements.

Table 26.6 (a): Health Infrastructure in Rural Areas: Group I States

State	Sub-Centres & HWC-SCs			PHCs & HWC-PHCs			CHCs		
	Norm	Available	Shortfall	Norm	Available	Shortfall	Norm	Available	Shortfall
Bihar	21337	9949	11388 (53%)	3548	1899	1649 (46%)	887	150	737 (83%)
UP	34726	20782	13944 (40%)	5781	2936	2845 (49%)	1445	679	766 (53%)
MP	13935	10226	3709 (27%)	2233	1199	1034 (46%)	558	309	249 (45%)
Raj	12761	13512	--	2073	2082	--	518	571	--
Odisha	8382	6688	1694 (20%)	1345	1288	57 (4%)	336	377	--

Table 26.6 (b): Health facilities in Rural Areas: Group II States

State	Sub-Centres & HWC-SCs			PHCs & HWC-PHCs			CHCs		
	Norm	Available	Shortfall	Norm	Available	Shortfall	Norm	Available	Shortfall
Kerala	2340	5380	--	388	848	--	97	227	--
Tamil Nadu	7355	8713	--	1222	1422	--	305	385	--
Maharashtra	14112	10668	3444 (24%)	2299	1828	471 (20%)	574	364	210 (37%)
Karnatka	8028	9758	--	1318	2127	--	329	198	131 (40%)
Gujarat	8055	9166	--	1308	1476	--	327	362	--

Source: Rural Health Statistics, 2018-19, Ministry of Health and Family Welfare, Govt. of India.

Note: HWC: Health & Wellness Centre; Raj: Rajasthan. Figures in brackets indicate percentage of shortfall.

National Rural Health Mission (NRHM) (2005–12):

NRHM was initiated to provide effective healthcare to the rural population throughout the country with special focus on 18 states, which have weak public health indicators and/or weak infrastructure. The Mission was part of the commitment of the Government to raise public (state) spending on Health from 0.9 per cent of GDP to 2-3 per cent of GDP.

NRHM aimed to enhance the capacity of Panchayati Raj Institutions (PRIs) to own, control, and manage public health services through the following:

- Promote access to improved healthcare at household level through the female health activist (ASHA).
- Prepare health Plan for each village through Village Health Committee of the Panchayat.
- Strengthen Sub-centre through an untied fund to enable local planning and action and more Multi-Purpose Workers (MPWs).
- Strengthen the existing PHCs and CHCs, and provision of 30–50 bedded CHC per lakh population for improved curative care.

❑ HEALTH INFRASTRUCTURE AND MANPOWER

Health infrastructure and manpower are for important indicators gauging the healthcare policy and status, and the welfare system of a country. One of the major problems in the health sector in India is the wide gap that exists between hospital and medical facilities available in the public health sector and the private sector. The public healthcare facilities fall far short of the demand which results in overcrowding in hospitals, inadequacy of beds for patients, and non-availability of drugs. A government hospital serves, on an average, around 61,000 people, with one bed catering to about 1800 patients. All this impacts most adversely the lower segments of the society who have to depend on these hospitals as the private facilities are beyond their reach due to high costs involved. As is well known, the costs of treatment are exorbitant in the well-equipped private hospitals which only the affluent are able to afford and access.

Health Manpower

The doctor-patient ratio in India is less than the WHO-prescribed limit of 1:1000. According to data put out by the World Bank, the ratio in 2018 is 1.98 in China, 2.1 in Brazil, 0.8 in Thailand, 0.4 in Indonesia, and 0.58 in Bangladesh, 3.3 in France, 2.8 in UK, 2.6 in USA, while it is 0.85 in India. To enhance accessibility of quality medical education and health care, the government has been setting up more institutions and increasing the intake of students over the years to enhance qualified medical personnel available. Health infrastructure is also being expanded. (See Tables 26.7 (a) and 26.7 (b).

Besides allopathic doctors and dental surgeons, India has Ayush practitioners practising Indian systems of medicine, viz., Ayurveda, Unani, Siddha, Naturopathy and Homeopathy.

Table 26.7 (a): Human Resources for Health

Category	2010	2015	2019-20
Doctors	8,16,629	9,60,233	12,34,205
Dental Surgeons	1,04,603	1,56,391	2,77,428
Ayush Doctors *	7,52,254	7,44,563	7,99,879
Nurses/ Midwives	10,73,638	17,93,337	21,17,649
Auxiliary Nurse Midwives	5,76,542	7,89,796	8,79,508
Lady Health Visitors	52,375	56,096	56,644

Note: * Ayush doctors include Indian systems of Medicine: Ayurveda, Unani, Siddha, Naturopathy and Homeopathy

Table 26.7 (b): Health Infrastructure

Category	2010	2015	2019
Medical Colleges	300	412	542
Dental Colleges	290	308	313
Ayush Institutes	492	544	702
Hospitals (Rural & Urban)	12760	19653	40,883
Hospital Beds (Govt.)	576793	7,54,724	8,18,396
Population Served Per Govt. Hospital	90972	64425	--
Population Served Per Govt. Hospital Bed	2012	1678	--

Skewed distribution

Apart from shortage, the skewed and uneven distribution of both doctors and hospitals is a major issue. There are wide disparities in their distribution between various States as well as between urban and rural areas.

It is found that 52 per cent of these doctors are practising in just five States – Maharashtra (15%), Tamil Nadu (12%), Karnataka (10%), Andhra Pradesh (8%) and Uttar Pradesh (7%).

Delhi, Assam and Odisha have 2 per cent of the total Allopathic doctors while Haryana, Chhattisgarh, Uttarakhand, Telangana and Jharkhand have 1 per cent.

As for doctor-population ratio (considering number of doctors per 1,000 population) among States, Karnataka (1.76), Kerala (1.71), Tamil Nadu (1.67), Punjab (1.59), Maharashtra (1.39) and Jammu & Kashmir (1.03) are relatively better placed as will be seen from the figures shown in brackets against them.

As against this, the doctor-population ratio for other states with large population are less than 1.0 as shown here: Bihar (0.33), Uttar Pradesh (0.35) Madhya Pradesh (0.46), Rajasthan (0.52), Odisha (0.49) and Jharkhand (0.17).

According to Dr. Devi Shetty, a renowned specialist and domain expert, 600 district hospitals in the country should be converted as medical nursing and paramedical schools to train 5 million doctors, nurses and paramedics which can meet not only India's requirements but also global needs. According to the World Bank, there will be demand for over 80 million health workers across the world in just 13 years. Evidently, there is need for a more ambitious plan to develop trained personnel in this sector which will lead to job creation on a massive scale as also help improve health standards of the population and usher in a virtual a medical and health revolution.

On the positive side, India has had a very successful immunization and polio vaccine administering programme for infants which has shown remarkable results. India has also shown improvement in controlling mortality from various communicable diseases such as malaria, kala azar, and dengue whereas non-communicable diseases such as cardiovascular diseases, chronic respiratory diseases, cancer, and diabetes are on the rise and pose a serious challenge.

Need to Upgrade Facilities

Considering the vast difference between the private and public health facilities, there is need to upgrade the facilities in government hospitals which is mainly accessed by the disadvantaged sections who cannot afford to go to private hospitals. While many of the government and medical college-attached hospitals have specialists of high calibre comparable to those in the high-end private hospitals, there is heavy demand and pressure on the personnel and services available in public hospitals, so much so there is overcrowding in OPDs, acute shortage of in-patient beds, lack of medicines, unhygienic conditions, etc. The only solution to these endemic problems is to step up investment in public healthcare and expand the network and capacity of hospitals and manpower. Needless to say, the levels of cleanliness and hygiene need to be improved by educating both the personnel manning the hospitals and the users through sustained campaigns.

The Swachh Bharat mission and the CSR concept discussed later could be leveraged to cover the massive task of upgrading public health sector.

National Health Mission (NHM)

Various initiatives taken up under the National Health Mission (NHM) for providing free health care through a network of CHCs, PHCs and Sub-Centres (SCs), in both rural and urban areas, have brought about significant improvement in creation of new facilities and infrastructure and improved availability of drugs. It has facilitated comprehensive health care and improved quality of life of children through early detection. Initiatives such as Rashtriya Bal Swasthya Karyakram (RBSK) and Rashtriya Kishor

Swasthya Karyakram (RKSK) were also launched in 2013 and 2014 respectively under the NHM to provide comprehensive healthcare for children. Yet, India still faces an uphill task in providing quality healthcare and making it accessible to large segments of the population.

Since drugs constitute the bulk of out-of-pocket expenditure, the Government of India has intensified efforts for provision of free essential drugs in public health facilities under the NHM Free Drugs Initiative. 'Jan Aushadhi Scheme' for providing quality generic medicines at affordable prices in collaboration with the State Governments has been launched.

❑ NATIONAL HEALTH POLICY, 2017 AND AYUSHMAN BHARAT

In view of the persisting deficiencies and limitations of India's healthcare system, the new National Health Policy, 2017 and Ayushman Bharat announced in the Union budget for 2018-19 assume importance. These ambitious schemes aim to step up and upgrade the health facilities in the country -- at primary, secondary and tertiary levels – covering both prevention and health promotion to a new higher level. These steps will help the 'New India 2022' initiative and ensure enhanced productivity, well-being and avert wage loss and impoverishment. It will address long persisting inequities and development lag in districts and has the potential to generate lakhs of jobs, particularly in rural areas and for women. The main components of these initiatives are as follows:-

(i) Setting up 1.5 lakh Health and Wellness Centres;

(ii) National Health Protection Insurance Scheme.

(i) Health and Wellness Centres

The National Health Policy, 2017 has envisioned setting up 1,50,000 Health and Wellness Centres to serve as the foundation of India's health system. These centres will bring health care system closer to the homes of people. They will be the main points of contact for communities with the public health system and will be improved versions of the existing health Sub-centres (SCs) and primary health centres (PHCs). The Budget has allocated ₹1200 crore for this flagship programme and has envisaged that private sector, through CSR, and philanthropic institutions will come forward to contribute and adopt these centres.

Main Features of Health and Wellness Centres

- A Health and Wellness Centre will provide comprehensive healthcare including for non-communicable diseases and maternal and child health services.
- Doctor at the centre will not only provide diagnosis and treatment service but also ensure medication for chronic illness and follow up care.
- Under 'Free Diagnostics Service Initiative', funding is provided to States to provide free essential diagnostic services at public health facilities. The free diagnostic services, either in-house or in PPP mode, has been rolled out in 29 states/UTs.
- Under 'NHM-Free Drug Service initiative', funds are being provided to states/UTs for provision of free drugs in public health facilities and setting up IT-backed systems for drug procurement and quality assurance. All 36 states/UTs have notified policy to provide essential drugs free of cost in public health facilities.

This revamp of the primary healthcare system is much overdue as the existing system has not been able to provide satisfactory services to bulk of the urban and rural population in lower income groups who have had to suffer neglect or depend on expensive private healthcare facilities which they could ill afford.

(ii) Ayushman Bharat - PM Jan Arogya Yojana (PMJAY)

An important programme is Ayushman Bharat - Pradhan Mantri Jan Arogya Yojana (PMJAY), launched in September.2018, is one of the largest fully Government-financed health protection schemes of the world.

Its key features are:

- Health cover: Provides health cover of up to ₹5 lakh per family per year, for secondary and tertiary care hospitalization through a network of Empanelled Health Care Providers (EHCP).
- Population covered: Around 10.74 crore vulnerable families (approximately 50 crore beneficiaries)
- Cashless service: Facility of cashless and paperless access to services for the beneficiary at the point of service.
- No cap: There is no cap on family size, age or gender.
- Improve affordability – Enables the bottom 40 per cent of the population to afford and access secondary and tertiary care including pre-hospitalisation and post-hospitalisation expenses.
- The Pradhan Mantri Suraksha Bima Yojana, an Accident Insurance policy, was launched in 2015. 24.57 crore persons have enrolled in this scheme.
- 2.27 crore cases of free treatment have been done under PMJAY till October 2021.

Challenges for the Health Sector

Low Public Health Spending: The public expenditure (Union and State combined) on health as percentage of GDP in India has been around 1 per cent (see Table 26.8). Though the Eleventh Plan (2007-2012) targeted to increase the total expenditure at the Centre and the States to at least 2 per cent of GDP, it was not achieved. The National Health Policy 2017 (NHP 2017) recommended the ramping up of public health expenditure to 2.5 per cent of GDP by 2025.

An international comparison of Health expenditure and Per capita expenditure on health can be seen in Table 26.9. It shows how India compares with some other countries, both Advanced and Emerging.

Table 26.8 : Trends in India's Public Expenditure on Health

Year	Public expenditure on Health (in ₹crore)	Per capita Public Expenditure on Health (in₹)	Public expenditure as % of GDP
2009-10	72,536	621	1.12
2013-14	1,12,270	913	1.00
2014-15	1,21,600.23	973	0.98
2016-17 (RE)	1,78,875.63	1397	1.17
2017-18 (BE)	2,13,719.58	1657	1.28

Source: Public expenditure on Health from "Health Sector Financing by Centre and States/UTs in India 2015-16 to 2017-18", National Health Accounts Cell, Ministry of Health & Family Welfare.

Role of Centre and States in Health Sector

In India, while both the Centre and States spend on health, the primary responsibility for delivery of healthcare services is that of state governments. Under the Constitution, public health and sanitation, hospitals and dispensaries fall under the purview of State governments while population control and family planning, medical profession and medical education are in the Concurrent list for which both the Centre and the States have a role.

Public expenditure on health is incurred by three tiers of the Government: the Central Government, the State Governments and the local bodies. The Central Government spends directly on health and also provides grants-in-aid to State Governments for incurring health expenditure. The State Governments, in addition to spending out of the grants-in-aid received from the Centre, incur health expenditure directly out of the resources available with them. Their health expenditure also includes transfers to rural and urban local bodies for health spending.

Table 26.9 : Health Expenditure (as % of GDP) and Per capita expenditure on Health - 2017

International comparison

Group I Countries			Group II Countries		
Country	Health expenditure as % of GDP	Per capita Expenditure (international $)	Country	Health expenditure as % of GDP	Per capita Expenditure (international $)
USA	17.06	10,246.14	Brazil	9.47	1,472.23
Germany	11.25	5,922.64	South Africa	8.11	1,097.82
France	11.31	5,011.20	Russia	5.34	1,404.22
Japan	10.94	4,563.46	China	5.15	841.11
UK	9.63	4,338.37	Thailand	3.75	670.88
Australia	9.21	4,816.15	**India**	**3.53**	**253.32**

Source: World Bank data: Current Health Expenditure as Percentage of GDP (2017). World Health Organization - Global Health Expenditure database.

15th Finance Commission on Health Sector

Presently 35 per cent of the public health expenditure is borne by the Centre and 65 per cent by the state governments. In the presentation before the 15th Finance Commission, the Union Health Ministry, in the context of the pandemic Covid-19, stressed the importance of the need to strengthen the public health sector, surveillance and public health management, preventive and promotive health care with special focus on urban health. The Commission agreed that there was a need to increase public sector health outlay and also to develop a professional cadre of health workers.

Further, the Commission has pointed out the deficiencies in the health sector which impairs the level and quality of service rendered to the public. These include governance and other issues mentioned below.

- Critical gaps in health infrastructure like sub centres, PHCs, CHCs and human resource for health like doctors, nurses and paramedics.
- Insufficient focus on core public health functions such as disease surveillance and testing.
- Shortcomings in the quality of care (apart from a select few facilities) despite improvement in access.
- Inadequate attention to urban health systems and the role of municipalities, which have a key role to play in public health, including air and water pollution, road traffic injuries and pandemic-related vulnerabilities.
- Government service delivery system which has traditionally focused more on reproductive health and infectious diseases and lesser on non-communicable diseases, which are now the dominant share of the disease burden.
- Fragmentation and lack of coordination between different levels and sectors, including a weakly

regulated private sector which dominates service provision.

- Weak local governance, especially at the sub-district level, where government capacity to deliver is poor and a lack of accountability in the service delivery model.
- Demand-side factors, including gender and social norms, compounded by low levels of educational attainment, serve as a major barrier to improving access and quality in health care facility.

The outbreak of Covid-19 pandemic in the early part of 2020 and its aftermath exposed the frailties of India's healthcare system and the challenges it faced. It has reinforced the need for strengthening the public healthcare facilities on which a large section of the population, especially the poor and vulnerable, depends.

❑ HOUSING FOR WEAKER SECTIONS

Housing, a basic necessity for every family, has been a major problem for the poor and vulnerable sections, both in the urban and rural areas. For the rural areas, a formal village housing scheme was launched as early as 1957 as part of the Community Development programme. Later, in 1980, the programme was enlarged and construction of houses was taken up as a major activity under the National Rural Employment Guarantee Programme (NREGP) and in 1983 under the Rural Landless Employment Guarantee Programme (RLEGP).

Indira Awas Yojana (IAY)

Main Features of the Scheme

- In 1985-86, Indira Awas Yojana (IAY) was started and continued as a sub-scheme under other rural development programmes. In January 1996, IAY was made an independent scheme.
- IAY was a cash subsidy-based programme, under which assistance was provided to rural BPL families for constructing dwelling units on their own, using their own design and technology. Emphasis was also laid on use of cost effective, disaster resistant, and environment friendly technologies in rural housing.
- Selection of IAY beneficiaries was done by Gram Sabhas.
- 60 per cent of the funds under IAY was meant for SC and ST beneficiaries and the subsidy is sanctioned either in the name of the female member of the household or jointly in the names of both spouses.
- The per unit assistance for construction of house was ₹25,000 in plain areas and ₹27,500 in hilly and difficult areas which was raised during the Eleventh Plan (2007-12) to ₹45,000 and ₹48,500 respectively. For upgradation of unserviceable houses, ₹15,000 was given.
- An important aspect was that a sanitary latrine and smokeless chullah were required to be constructed along with each IAY house. For construction of the sanitary latrine, financial assistance was made available from the Total Sanitation Campaign (TSC) funds, in addition to IAY assistance.
- **Funding:** Funding under IAY was provided by the Centre and the State in the ratio of 75:25.

  Apart from Plan funds, National Housing Bank (NHB), National Bank for Agriculture and Rural Development (NABARD), and Housing and Urban Development Corporation (HUDCO) also provided support for rural housing. The NHB is the apex financial institution for housing in the country.
- **Progress under IAY:** Under the Indira Awas Yojana (IAY), since inception, 303.83 lakh houses were constructed incurring an expenditure of about ₹94,086.61 crore upto December 2012 (as per Annual

Report, Ministry of Rural Development, 2012-13).

Pradhan Mantri Awas Yojana (PMAY)

Main Features of the Scheme

- In June 2015, the NDA government approved a new ₹3 trillion programme, Pradhan Mantri Awas Yojana (PMAY), to build 20 million houses for low-income group and economically weaker sections in urban areas.
- And in March 2016, another programme to build 10 million houses for the rural poor was approved as part of PMAY. It is an ambitious 'Housing for All' programme which the government planned to complete in three phases by 2022.
- Under the Mission, a house is deemed completed when it has the basic amenities like electricity, water supply, kitchen and toilet. A PMAY(U) house ensures dignified living along with sense of security and pride of ownership to the beneficiaries.
- The Mission also promotes women empowerment by providing the ownership of houses in name of female member or in joint name. Preference is also given to persons with disabilities, ST/ SC/OBCs/ Minorities and Transgenders.
- Beneficiaries would be chosen from the Socio-Economic Caste Census, 2011. Those eligible include persons in economically sections (EWS) and in low and middle income groups (LIG and MIG).
- The subsidy amount to be given for construction of houses will be ₹1.2 lakh in rural areas and ₹2.4 lakh in urban areas. Funds will be transferred electronically directly to the beneficiary's account.
- The services of those working under MGNREGS can be availed for the construction. To create synergy between PMAY and MGNREGS, manufacture of bricks would be taken up under MGNREGS.
- Given the multiplier effect of construction activity, the schemes have the potential to generate jobs in a substantial way in both rural and urban areas and thus give fillip to the economy.
- Apart from being an asset for the family, a house confers intangible benefits such as security, comfort, health benefit, sanitation facility, and improved living. It is also a symbol of upward social mobility for the family members.

Box 26.3: Progress of PMAY – Urban and Grameen Housing Scheme

PMAY – Urban: Progress till March 2021	PMAY-Grameen: Progress till October 2021
No. of Houses sanctioned: 1.09 crore	Total target: 2.01 crore
No. of Houses grounded for construction: 70.20 lakh	Total Beneficiaries Registered: 2.17 crore
No. of Houses completed: 40.44 lakh	Total Geo-tagged: 2.12 crore
No. of Houses occupied: 37.47 lakh	Total Houses sanctioned: 2.05 crore
	Total Houses completed: 1.59 crore

Source: PMAY website and Ministry of Housing & Urban Affairs and Ministry of Rural development.

Box 26.4: Jal Jeevan Mission for Water Supply

Access to Safe Drinking Water

As per Census of India, if a household has access to drinking water supplied from a tap or a hand pump/tube well situated within or outside the premises, it is considered as having access to safe drinking water. Millions of people in the country suffer from water borne diseases on account of lack of access to safe drinking water. It is the poor who suffer from higher prevalence of disease as compared to the rich.

The **India-National Human Development Report, 2001** had observed thus: "In 1991, the Census reported nearly 62 per cent of households in India as having access to safe drinking water as compared to about 38 per cent in 1981. Over 81 per cent of urban households and around 56 per cent of rural households had access to safe drinking water in 1991. The corresponding figures for 1981 were 75 per cent and 27 per cent, respectively. There are widespread inter-State differences, though these differences have declined in the eighties, both in rural and urban areas."

But providing piped tap water connection to every household, especially in rural areas, has been a challenge. The problem has been compounded by the steady increase in population. The **Jal Jeevan Mission** initiated in 2019 has to be viewed against this background.

Water Supply: Jal Jeevan Mission (JJM) - Har Ghar Jal

Functional Household Tap Connection (FHTC) in every rural home

The Scheme

- On August 15, 2019, Jal Jeevan Mission was announced by Prime Minister Narendra Modi from the ramparts of the Red Fort with an aim to provide **Functional Household Tap Connection (FHTC)** to every rural household and public institution, viz., GP building, School, Anganwadi centre, Health centre, wellness centres, etc. by 2024.
- A massive program, Jal Jeevan Mission is under implementation since August 2019 in partnership with the State governments with the aim to provide potable water in adequate quantity and of prescribed quality on regular and long-term basis.
- Under this campaign, potable tap water will not only be available for drinking and cooking mid-day meals, but also for hand washing and running tap water in toilets.
- A '100-Day campaign' under the Jal Jeevan Mission was launched on October 2, 2020 to provide piped water supply to every school, Anganwadi centre (AWC) and Ashramshala (that is residential schools for children from tribal communities).
- Every State/ UT is doing extensive planning, following 'bottom-up approach' and have firmed up their plan to provide tap water connection to every home.
- States are giving priority to water quality-affected areas, Scheduled Caste/ Scheduled Tribe majority villages, aspirational districts, village in drought prone and desert areas and quality-affected habitations. States are working to ensure that piped water supply reaches the regions affected by Fluoride and Arsenic at the earliest as well.

Components of the Scheme

- Development of in-village piped water supply infrastructure, to provide **Functional Household Tap Connection (FHTC)** to every rural household and public institutions in the village mentioned above.

- To prioritize provision of FHTCs in quality affected areas, villages in drought prone and desert areas, Sansad Adarsh Gram Yojana (SAGY) villages, etc.
- To monitor functionality of tap connections and technological interventions for removal of contaminants where water quality is an issue.
- To promote and ensure voluntary ownership among local community by way of contribution in cash, kind and/ or labour and voluntary labour (shramdaan).
- Support activities, i.e., IEC (Information, Education and Communication), HRD, training, development of utilities, water quality laboratories, water quality testing & surveillance, R&D, knowledge centre, capacity building of communities, etc.
- To assist in ensuring sustainability of water supply system, i.e., water source, water supply infrastructure, and funds for regular O&M.
- To empower and develop human resource in the sector such that the demands of construction, plumbing, electrical, water quality management, water treatment, catchment protection, O&M, etc. are taken care of in short and long term.
- To bring awareness on various aspects and significance of safe drinking water and involvement of stakeholders in manner that make water everyone's business.
- Manage any unforeseen challenges/ issues emerging due to natural disasters/ calamities which affect the goal of FHTC to every household by 2024, as per guidelines of Ministry of Finance on Flexi Funds.

Box 26.5: JJM: Factsheet on the Scheme and Progress (as of October 2021)

- As on August 15, 2019, out of 18.93 crore rural households, 3.23 crore (17 per cent) had tap water connections.
- The untiring efforts of States/ UTs have helped Jal Jeevan Mission provide 3 crore tap water connections since August, 2019.
- Goa has become the first state in the country to provide 100 per cent FHTCs and became 'Har Ghar Jal' State.
- Punjab and Tamil Nadu have become the first States to provide every school with tap water supply. Also, every AWC in Tamil Nadu is provided with tap water.
- So far more than 4.4 lakh rural schools and about 3.73 lakh AWCs have started getting potable tap water.
- 26 districts, 457 Blocks, 34,919 Panchayats and 65,627 villages have become 'Har Ghar Jal' meaning every family living in these rural areas is getting assured tap water supply in their homes and 'no one is left behind'.
- States are competing with each other and focusing on the set target to ensure that every household in the country gets safe drinking water adhering to the core principle of 'equity and inclusiveness'.
- The Mission has met with challenges and disruptions due to COVID-19 pandemic from March 2020.

Table 26.10 below shows that there is much ground to cover if the target is to be achieved by 2024.

Table 26. 10 Progress of Jal Jeevan Mission (as on Oct 13, 2021)

Total No. of Rural Households	Households with Tap water connections on Aug 15, 2019	Households with Tap Water connections on Oct 15,2021	Total No. of Connections Provided since launch of the Mission
19,22,49,980 (19.22 crore)	3,23,62,838 (16.83%)	8,33,04,936 (43.33%)	5,09,42,098 (26.50%)

Source: Jal Jeevan Mission, **Department of Drinking Water & Sanitation, Ministry of Jal Shakti**, Govt. of India.

❑ SWACHH BHARAT MISSION

Swachh Bharat Mission (Abhiyan) is a 'Clean India' campaign, an initiative of the Government of India to create mass awareness of the importance of cleanliness and hygiene and make India cleaner by the year 2019, which was to coincide with the 150th birth anniversary of Mahatma Gandhi who was a staunch advocate of cleanliness. Prime Minister Narendra Modi launched "Swachh Bharat Mission (Abhiyan)" from Red Fort on the Independence Day in 2014.

The mission to be successful, has to have a multi-pronged approach with several components, including the construction of toilets in households not having them and in all schools, removal of garbage, and scientific handling and disposal of solid waste, particularly of non-biodegradable, hospital, electronic and other hazardous materials, non-dumping of construction materials in a haphazard manner, etc. This calls for involvement and active cooperation of all citizens, every household, institutions, industry, and the corporate sector.

Swachh Bharat Mission (SBM)

The Swachh Bharat Mission covers both urban and rural areas. The Urban mission has two primary components of implementation: To achieve,

- 100 per cent open defecation free (ODF) status, and
- 100 per cent scientific processing of solid waste – in all statutory towns in the country.

❑ TOTAL SANITATION CAMPAIGN (RURAL)

A Total Sanitation Campaign (TSC) had been launched in 1999 as a community-led programme as part of 'Rural development' programmes. The TSC was able to accelerate sanitation coverage from 22 per cent as per the 2001 Census to 31 per cent in 2011, with over 28,000 panchayats becoming 'Open Defecation Free' (ODF). TSC received a major boost during the latter half of the decade, with the introduction of the Nirmal Gram Puraskar (NGP) in 2005, an innovative incentive scheme for Gram Panchayats, blocks, and districts, that have attained 100 per cent sanitation coverage.

The programme in rural areas got further fillip with the launch of Swachh Bharat Mission (Abhiyan) in 2014.

Progress

According to the Ministry of Housing & Urban Affairs (MoH & UA):

- 66.72 lakh units of Individual Household Toilets (IHHL) have been constructed and/or under construction (i.e., 113 per centr progress against target of 58.99 lakhs) by December 2020.
- Further, 3 lakh IHHL units were to be constructed between January - March 2021.
- 6.28 lakh seats of Community and Public Toilet seats (CT/PT) have been constructed and/or under construction (i.e., 124 per cent progress against target of 5.07 lakhs) by December 2020.

- Further, 25000 CT/PT Seats were to be constructed between January and March 2021.

Financing: For this SBM (Urban) scheme, during 2020-21, a total of ₹988.09 crore has been released by the Centre to States under various components of the Mission, up to December 2020. Cumulatively, ₹10,915 crore (against Mission allocation of ₹14,013 crore from Centre), has been released.

Swachh Bharat Mission (Rural)

This programme was launched on October 2, 2014 with the aim to achieve Open Defecation Free (ODF) status by October 2, 2019. Coming under the Dept. of Drinking Water & Sanitation, Ministry of Jal Shakti, the programme has seen sustained progress. A total of 10.71 crore toilets have been built in rural areas from October 2014 till 2021 resulting in 61 per cent increase in the number of households having toilet.

- **Outcomes:** The construction of toilets on such a massive scale has been a stupendous achievement. Total number of 11.30 crore household toilets have been built from 2014 to 2021.

As per MoH & UA, a total of 4,340 cities (out of 4,372) have declared themselves ODF marking 99 per cent progress. Of these, 4,258 cities/ ULBs have been certified as ODF after third party certification by December 2020. From January to March 2021, 4270 Urban Local Bodies (ULBs) were estimated to be certified as ODF.

And under the SBM (Rural) scheme, 6.03 lakh villages in 711 districts have self-declared Open Defecation Free (ODF) by 2021.

The Flip side

While the ODF declaration by urban centres and rural areas is impressive, it cannot perhaps be said that in practice all the toilets provided are being used and serving the purpose. While a good percentage of people have changed the practice, certain surveys and studies have shown that there are people who are still not using the toilet due to various reasons.

This requires attitudinal and behavioral changes on the part of the people who are resisting the use of toilet facility. Hopefully, this would come about over time and with new generations coming up and adopting it. There are signs of such changes coming even in rural areas.

Positives from the Programme

Increased use of toilets has brought about benefits to the people. These include:

- Safety and personal dignity, especially for women and girls, in having and using toilet at home.
- Children are not weakened by frequent incidence of diarrhoea nor do they become more susceptible to malnutrition, stunting, and infections such as pneumonia.
- Improved health conditions will have a positive effect on school going children improving their learning abilities.
- Better hygiene at home and improved environment in the neighbourhood and surrounding areas.

Adverse effects of Open Defecation

- This practice of open defecation results in tonnes of faeces being introduced daily into the open spaces which contaminates the environment and have adverse impact on the health of adults, and even more so of children, through direct exposure.
- Open defecation and lack of regular handwashing poses the risk of spreading diarrheal and waterborne diseases and microbial contamination of water used in the homes and by the community.
- Such a situation has contributed to high infant mortality and diarrhoeal deaths of children under five years.

- Poor sanitation can also have a ripple effect as it hinders national development because workers suffer from illnesses and shorter lives.
- Ill health impacts the earning capacity of households and their incomes which could have adverse effect on the education and future of children.

(On this, see also Box 26.1: School Toilets Constructed under Swachh Vidyalaya Abhiyan by CPSEs: An Audit Report earlier in this chapter).

❑ SMART CITIES PROGRAMME

With increasing and rapid urbanization, the challenges related to urban infrastructure are also on the rise. It is in response to this that the Government of India launched an ambitious flagship programme for urban development and build 'Smart Cities', in collaboration with States and Union Territories. The smart cities will drive economic growth and improve the quality of life of people by enabling local area development and harnessing technology.

The programme aims at providing core infrastructure and a decent quality of life to its citizens and a clean and sustainable environment. The focus is on inclusive development to create a replicable model which can be replicated in other aspiring cities. The core infrastructure in a smart city includes:

- Adequate water supply.
- Assured electricity supply.
- Sanitation, including solid waste management.
- Efficient urban mobility and public transport.
- Affordable housing, especially for the poor.
- Robust IT connectivity and digitalization.
- Good governance, especially e-Governance and citizen participation.
- Sustainable and inclusive environment.
- Safety and security of citizens, particularly women, children, and the elderly; and
- Health and education facilities.

Development Strategy for Smart Cities

The strategic components of Smart Cities' initiative are Area-Based Development (ABD) involving city improvement (retrofitting), city renewal (redevelopment) and city extension (Greenfield development) and a Pan-city development in which Smart Solutions are applied covering larger parts of the city.

- **Retrofitting** will introduce planning in an existing built-up area to achieve Smart City objectives, along with other objectives, to make the existing area more efficient and liveable. In retrofitting, an area consisting of more than 500 acres will be identified by the city in consultation with citizens.
- **Redevelopment** will effect a replacement of the existing built-up environment and enable co-creation of a new layout with enhanced infrastructure using mixed land use and increased density. Redevelopment envisages an area of more than 50 acres, identified by Urban Local Bodies (ULBs) in consultation with citizens.
- **Greenfield** development will introduce most of the Smart Solutions in a previously vacant area (more than 250 acres) using innovative planning, plan financing and plan implementation tools (e.g. land pooling/ land reconstitution) with provision for affordable housing, especially for the poor.

Greenfield developments are required around cities in order to address the needs of the expanding population.

One well known example is the GIFT City in Gujarat. Unlike retrofitting and redevelopment, greenfield developments could be located either within the limits of the ULB or within the limits of the local Urban Development Authority (UDA).

Selection and Financing

100 smart cities, as targeted, were selected in various Rounds under the Mission. The 100 cities have proposed to execute 5,151 projects worth ₹2,05,018 crore in 5 years from their respective dates of selection. Innovative financing is built into the design of capital investment plans.

The distribution of funding envisaged from different sources is as follows:

- Central and State Government: ₹93,552 crore (45%).
- Convergence funding from other missions, programs of the Central/State Governments and/or ULBs: ₹42,028 crore (21%).
- Funds from PPP: ₹41,022 crore (21%), Loans/Debt: ₹9,843 crore (4%).
- Own Sources: ₹2,644 crore (1%), and
- Other sources: ₹15,930 crore (8%).

Significant progress has been made with respect to implementation of projects pertaining to Integrated Command and Control Centres, Smart Roads, Smart Water, Solar Rooftops, and Vibrant Public Spaces. Works completed are as follows:

- Smart Command and Control Centres: 53 cities: ₹7,428 crore.
- Vibrant public spaces: 63 projects: ₹986 crore.
- Public Private Partnership (PPP): 110 projects: ₹4,082 crore.
- Smart water supply: 84 projects: ₹4,161, crore.
- Smart roads: 263 projects: ₹4,272 crore.
- Smart solar: : 47 projects: ₹482 crore.

Assessment of Mission

In order to assess the impact of the schemes, a framework on Ease of Living Index (EoLI) and Municipal Performance Index (MPI) for cities was launched in June 2017. The index enables a shift to data driven approach in urban planning and management and promote healthy competition among cities.

Ease of Living Index (EoLI)

- The first Liveability Report was published in August 2018 while the EoL Index 2019-20, which is an improved version, is more focused on outcomes.
- The EoL Index, 2019 aims to assess the ease of living of citizens across three pillars: Quality of Life, Economic Ability and Sustainability which are further divided into 14 categories across 50 indicators.
- Citizen Participation was included in the EOL 2019 exercise that will contribute 30 per cent towards the scoring for the Ease of Living Index.
- The EOL 2019-20 was expanded to 114 cities in the country and more than 32 lakh citizens participated in the Citizen survey which was carried out during February - March 2020.

Municipal Performance Index (MPI)

The 2019 is a first of its kind initiative which examines the sectoral performance of Municipalities across a set of 5 verticals, viz., Service, Finance, Planning, Technology and Governance.

These 5 verticals have been further divided into 20 sectors which will be evaluated across 100 indicators.

These indices will help build a mature data ecosystem with a common baseline data that can be leveraged by States and cities as an instrument for urban planning and management. It will facilitate a competitive environment among cities and enhance avenues of investment.

The Ease of Living indicators are strongly linked to United Nations' Sustainable Development Goals (SDGs) and this exercise will help India to track and achieve SDGs.

Climate Smart Cities

An important initiative in the context of current efforts to tackle Climate Change is "Climate SMART Cities Assessment Framework" launched for the 100 Smart cities. It aims to incentivize a holistic, climate responsive development and creating a green mind-set in cities while they plan and undertake various developmental projects.

The Framework includes various air and climate relevant parameters that shall guide the cities and help them to assess their own preparedness to tackle the menace of climate change and degrading air quality. The Urban Affairs Ministry has announced the individual city readiness report of the first cycle of Climate Smart Cities Assessment Framework during the 3rd Smart City CEO Conference held at Vishakhapatnam in January2020.

The cities can view their scores, performance report and recommendation for further improvement on the SmartNet portal. The assessment did not intend to rank the cities but to help them understand their status regarding climate mitigation and adaptation.

AMRUT Mission

A related scheme is AMRUT – The Atal Mission for Rejuvenation and Urban Transformation (AMRUT) launched in June 2015 and covering 500 cities selected across the country. All Urban Local Bodies (ULBs with a population of one lakh or more as per Census 2011, all other capital cities of States/ Union Territories (UTs), all HRIDAY cities, identified cities on the stem of the main rivers, from hill states, islands and tourist destinations were included as Mission cities. Approximately 60 per cent of urban population in the country is covered under AMRUT.

AMRUT is a Centrally Sponsored Scheme with a total Central outlay of ₹50,000 crore spread over 5 years from 2015-2016 to 2019-20 which was extended up to March 2021 to complete the grounded projects.

The purpose of this mission is to:

Ensure that every household has access to a tap with assured supply of water and a sewerage connection.

Increase the amenity value of cities by developing greenery and well-maintained open spaces (e.g., parks).

Reduce pollution by switching to public transport or constructing facilities for non-motorized transport (e.g, walking and cycling).

Accordingly, the Mission focuses on the following Thrust Areas:

- Water supply.
- Sewerage facilities and septage management.
- Storm water drains to reduce flooding.
- Pedestrian, non-motorized and public transport facilities, parking spaces; and

- Enhancing amenity value of cities by creating and upgrading green spaces, parks and recreation centres, especially for children.

Solid Waste Management

Solid Waste Management (SWM) is another critical issue concerning both urban and rural areas in India.

It is especially a major problem for many urban local bodies (ULBs), where urbanization, industrialization and economic growth have resulted in increased municipal solid waste (MSW) generation. The problem is compounded in cities with high population density.

India generates an estimated 133,760 tonnes of MSW per day, of which approximately 91,152 tonnes is collected and approximately 25,884 tonnes is treated. The waste is composed of wide range of items such as plastics, paper, glass, metals and textiles and hazardous wastes such as pesticides, paints, used medicine and batteries. Biomedical and healthcare waste contains disposable syringes, sanitary materials and blood containing textiles. Besides, there is compostable organics which include fruits, vegetables and food waste.

SWM Mission: Action Taken

Several measures have been taken to tackle the problem of waste collection and proper disposal.

- According to Ministry of Housing & Urban Affairs, 83,500 wards (out of the total 86,284 wards), i.e., 97 per cent of wards are covered by 100 per cent door-to-door collection of waste. 78 per cent wards are practicing source segregation and 68 per cent of the total waste generated is being processed, and by 31.12.20. More wards are to be covered under door-to-door collection.
- There are 1311 functional waste-to-compost plants with capacity to process 0.612 lakh tonnes of waste per day, and another 408 plants are under construction, with input capacity of about 0.14 lakhs tonnes per day (TPD).
- 90 waste-to-energy (waste-to-electricity/biogas/bio-methanation) plants are functioning with input capacity of 4 lakh TPD, and another 44 plants under construction with capacity to process 0.12 lakh TPD of waste. Additionally, 3 functional plants, with input capacity of 7,378 tonnes per day, and another 5 plants are under construction with combined input capacity of 2050 tonnes per day.
- **Mission monitoring:** The Ministry of H & UA is monitoring implementation of schemes and ranking cities which has given rise to a spirit of healthy competition between cities in their urge to become the 'cleanest' city. The monitoring involves getting citizen feedback also about cleanliness status in their cities. This data becomes an integral input for cities' rankings.
- **Challenges:** Despite several steps taken to tackle waste management, India faces many challenges as mentioned below.
- **Waste collection:** The informal sector, comprising small-scale, labour-intensive and unorganised units which lack technical skills for proper waste disposal, plays an important role in this sector in India. Large number of waste pickers, who depend on waste for an income and livelihood, collect household or commercial/industrial waste, with associated social issues and health risks for them.
- **Waste disposal:** Though many cities have introduced the concept of segregation of dry and wet waste at source, i.e., households and commercial establishments, the system does not work efficiently due to various reasons. Where segregation is done and handed over in separate bins, they again get mixed up in handling by waste handling agencies defeating the very purpose. In-house composting of wet waste by large apartments, which could help reduce waste sent to landfills or to waste disposal plants, also does not happen in an organized manner.

Waste-to-energy

The problems due to improper waste disposal could be significantly mitigated by material recovery. Separation at source of inert and high moisture content items would maximize the potential for thermal recovery and other treatment options. Waste-to-energy technologies produce energy, recover materials and free land that would otherwise be used for dumping. Adopting maximum recycling with waste-to-energy in an integrated waste management system would significantly reduce dumping. Waste-to-energy technologies are available that can process unsegregated low-calorific value waste, and industry is keen to exploit these technologies in India.

- **Skilling staff:** While all sections of society have to undertake proper segregation of waste at the source of generation, the personnel engaged in clearing the garbage and other waste also need to be trained. Experience so far has shown that even after handing over the segregated waste, it is not being handled properly, defeating the very purpose of segregation at source.
- **Protection for staff:** The people handling the waste are also not given due health protection in many cities and towns as they handle the waste with bare hands, do not wear masks and shoes, are not given tools to pick the waste so as to avoid handling them by hand, etc., as is the practice in advanced countries. Thus, the whole system is hazardous and injurious for the health of these staff. A national campaign and plan of action is to be drawn up, and all necessary kits and tools must be given to the workers who should use them as a matter of course.

❑ CONCLUSION

Schemes such as Swachh Bharat Mission and Waste Management require cooperation of people with the local bodies if they are to be a success. Local bodies also should involve representatives from amongst citizens who are activists in the field with domain knowledge of scientific practices in drawing up plans and in the process of implementation. It is generally the experience that local bodies and authorities do not involve citizens and are not transparent in the implementation of plans, funding, expenditure incurred, etc. The whole system must be uploaded on a digital platform which is open and accessible to all.

❑ CORPORATE SOCIAL RESPONSIBILITY (CSR)

The Corporate Social Responsibility (CSR) regime was introduced under Section 135 of the Companies Act, 2013. Under the CSR norms, companies with an annual turnover of ₹ 1,000 crore and more, or a net worth of ₹ 500 crore and more, or a net profit of ₹ five crore and more, need to spend at least 2 per cent of their average net profit in the previous three years on CSR activities, in each financial year starting from 2014-15.

Successful companies have a social responsibility to make the world a better place and not just take from it. The rationale of CSR is not just Corporate Philanthropy but goes beyond. It aims to involve proactively the corporate sector in the country's developmental endeavours and partner with the government in integrating social, environmental and human development concerns in the entire value chain of corporate business. It is a collective responsibility to build a society, which supplements Government's efforts, to achieve inclusive growth which includes broad-based benefits and ensures equity, justice and equal opportunities for all.

The National Voluntary Guidelines (NVGs) on Social, Environmental and Economic Responsibilities of Business released by the Ministry of Corporate Affairs (MCA) in July 2011, is essentially a set of nine principles that offer Indian businesses an understanding and approach to inculcate responsible business conduct. These nine principles are:

1. Conduct and govern themselves with ethics, transparency and accountability.
2. Provide goods and services that are safe and that contribute to sustainability throughout their life cycle.
3. Promote the well-being of all employees.
4. Respect the interests of, and be responsive towards all stakeholders, especially those who are disadvantaged, vulnerable and marginalized.
5. Respect and promote human rights.
6. Protect and make efforts to restore the environment.
7. When engaged in influencing public and regulatory policy, they should do so in a responsible manner.
8. Support inclusive growth and equitable development.
9. Engage with, and provide value to, their customers and consumers in a responsible manner.

Activities and sectors on which companies may spend the CSR funds are:

(i) eradicating extreme hunger and poverty;
(ii) promotion of education;
(iii) promoting gender equality and empowering women;
(iv) reducing child mortality and improving maternal health;
(v) combating human immuno-deficiency virus, acquired immune deficiency syndrome, malaria, and other diseases;
(vi) ensuring environmental sustainability;
(vii) employment-enhancing vocational skills;
(viii) social business projects;
(ix) contribution to the Prime Minister's National Relief Fund or any other fund set up by the Central Government or the State Governments for socio-economic development and relief and funds for the welfare of the Scheduled Castes, the Scheduled Tribes, other backward classes, minorities, and women; and
(x) such other matters as may be prescribed.

Even prior to the introduction of CSR, many Indian corporates and other social foundations were already engaged in the kind of activities envisaged under the CSR. Some of them had set up specific foundations with funds set apart for this purpose. Foundations like that of Tatas, Mahindra and Mahindra, Reliance, Infosys, Azim Premji, ITC and Shiv Nadar have been rendering yeoman service by sponsoring social causes like education, healthcare, skill development, women's welfare, etc. Besides, organizations like ISKCON which runs 'Akshaya Patra' programme for midday meals in schools are also doing much service. These are all shining examples of philanthropy and service in the spirit of CSR.

The provision made in the Companies Act has now formalized, mandated, and institutionalized the regime. Many of the corporate houses have their industries located in the rural and semi-urban areas, besides in the periphery of large cities, and thus, they have a connect with the local populace around their production units. Often, many of the workers in the factories are also drawn from the local population. There are also large PSU and private units with their own townships where they set up schools, hospitals, and other facilities.

Tables 26.11 and 26.12 show that the corporates have responded well and extended much support to the well-intentioned scheme.

Table 26.11 Performance under CSR between 2014-15 and 2019-20

	2014-15	2016-17	2017-18	2019-20
Total No. of Companies	16,548	19,552	21,515	22,155
Total Amount Spent on CSR (₹crore)	10,066	14,344	17,079	24,063
Total No. of CSR Projects	9,365	23,076	26,830	34,291
Development Sectors entered by Companies	29	29	29	29
States & UTs Covered	36	36	36	36

Table 26.12 Amount Spent under CSR – Development Sector-wise

(Figures in Rs. crore)

	2014-15	2015-16	2016-17	2017-18	2018-19	2019-20
Clean Ganga Fund	5.47	32.82	24.37	33.96	8.11	5.72
Conserving Natural Resources	44.60	49.85	119.09	228.14	172.68	156.02
Environmental Sustainability	773.99	796.69	1,076.46	1,299.18	1,356.67	1,432.53
Education	2,589.42	4,057.45	4,504.91	5,756.15	6,071.06	7,030.22
Health Care	1,847.74	2,569.43	2,491.52	2,770.23	3,593.90	4,573.34
Livelihood Enhancement	280.17	393.38	515.47	833.14	906.64	1,004.58
Poverty, Eradicating Hunger, Malnutrition	274.70	1,252.08	606.55	811.18	1,189.22	1,111.02
Rural Development Projects	1,059.35	1,376.16	1,554.78	1,722.78	2,426.32	2,251.34
Safe Drinking Water	103.95	180.16	149.69	220.87	225.15	243.36
Sanitation	299.54	631.80	421.71	459.70	506.00	507.39
Swachh Bharat Kosh	113.86	325.52	184.06	272.07	95.50	52.38
Vocational Skills	277.07	344.40	373.46	545.77	785.51	1,158.91
Women Empowerment	72.87	122.79	141.62	251.25	236.06	245.69
Slum Area Development	101.14	14.10	51.49	39.16	51.06	42.08

Note: Data only for Selected sectors/Activities.

Source: Source: Ministry of Corporate Affairs website: https://www.csr.gov.in/static_report.php

The CSR widens the scope and responsibility of corporate houses to engage in a more profound way and bring about perceptible change in the environment where they may undertake any of the activities prescribed, listed above. It is a unique opportunity to give back to society which forms part of their vast clientele.

As stated in the earlier sections in this chapter, there is a dire need to step up investment in sectors like education and health, particularly in the rural areas. For instance, the various corporate houses can adopt rural schools and equip them with better infrastructure–build toilets, provide labs, and library. As for the hospital sector, they can help the State governments to improve the primary and community health centres, provide them with more medical equipments, and even expand them with more in-patient facilities. Such measures will have an immediate visible and salutary impact on people and society.

A positive trend is that the landscape of philanthropy is changing in India with younger generation in affluent families who inherit wealth taking up social causes. Many groups of dedicated young people driven by passion to help are also resorting to 'crowd funding' with the proceeds to be used to improve government schools in rural and urban areas.

It is heartening to note that many of the enlightened industrialists have pledged to give and do more in this direction. Many of the companies have also taken up 'volunteerism' by which their employees are asked to devote a certain part of their time and effort to do socially beneficial activity—like working at orphanages, old age homes, hospitals, etc. These types of activities and the empathy it symbolizes will not only benefit specific sections of society who receive help and aid but will go a long way in bringing about fraternal feelings in society and social harmony.

In this Chapter we discussed.....

- Importance of development in Social sector–education and health, housing, and other basic facilities like safe drinking water and sanitation–in India.
- Plight of disadvantaged and vulnerable sections in regard to housing.
- Benefits of development have not trickled down to the poorer sections in adequate measure.
- Importance of education in improving a person's quality of life; how India could not devote more for school education in the early Plans.
- Educational facilities have expanded quantitatively but need to improve quality and standards; 'missing' girl-child in school education; visible change in the attitude towards education even among the lower segments of society in present times.
- Public schools and government-run schools–the contrast; need to improve the government-run schools; the role of CSR in this context.
- Critical role of female teachers in promoting education of girl children; enrolment at the lower primary level has improved considerably, the focus now has to be on improving learning outcomes.
- Plan outlays on Education and Health in the eleven Five Year Plans.

- Health sector has registered significant progress; birth and death rates, contained and the infant mortality rate (IMR) and maternal mortality rate (MMR) brought down; but other comparable countries are far ahead of India and even Bangladesh is ahead of India on IMR.
- Economic, social, and political empowerment of women and higher participation of girls in formal education responsible for Bangladesh's creditable performance.
- India has set targets to bring down IMR and MMR further.
- The public health infrastructure available at the district level and at lower levels–talukas (tehsils) and villages; problems in the health sector and health facilities available; three-tier rural health set-up; increase in the number of Sub-centres, Primary health centres (PHCs), Community health centers and their role in providing rural health service.
- National Rural Health Mission (NRHM) (2005-12) initiated to provide effective healthcare to rural population throughout the country; NRHM, part of the Government's commitment to raise public (state) spending on health from 0.9 per cent of GDP to 2-3 per cent of GDP.
- NRHM aims to enhance the capacity of Panchayati Raj Institutions (PRIs) to own, control, and manage public health services.
- Health infrastructure, an important indicator for gauging the healthcare policy and the welfare system of a country; inadequacy of public healthcare facilities in India and low doctor-patient ratio judged by WHO norm and compared to other countries.
- Ayushman Bharat - PM Jan Arogya Yojana (PMJAY) launched in September 2018. 2.27 crore cases of free treatment have been done under PMJAY till October 2021.
- The Pradhan Mantri Suraksha Bima Yojana, an Accident Insurance policy, was launched in 2015. 24.57 crore persons have enrolled in this scheme.
- India's successful immunization and polio vaccine administering programme for infants with remarkable results; and improvement in controlling mortality from various communicable diseases.
- The total spending on healthcare in the country in 2011 was about 4.1 per cent of GDP; as per global evidence, a country needs to spend at least 5–6 per cent of its GDP on health and major part of it is to be done by the Government for effective healthcare system; National Health Policy, 2002 and the NRHM devised to increase health expenditure by the State to 2 to 3 per cent of the GDP.
- The National Health Policy 2017 (NHP 2017) recommended the ramping up of public health expenditure to 2.5 per cent of GDP by 2025.

- Fifteenth Finance Common on the Health Sector.
- Vast difference between the private and public health facilities, and need to upgrade the facilities in government hospitals.
- Housing for weaker sections; Indira Awas Yojana (IAY); Under the Indira Awas Yojana (IAY), since inception, 303.83 lakh houses were constructed incurring an expenditure of about ₹94,086.61 crore upto December 2012.
- Pradhan Mantri Awas Yojana (PMAY) launched; ambitious 'Housing for All' programme to build 20 million houses, at a cost of ₹ 3 trillion, for low income and economically weaker sections in urban areas; and another programme to build 10 million houses for the rural poor approved by the NDA government; construction to be completed by 2022; amount for construction of houses will be ₹ 1.2 lakh in plain areas and ₹ 2.4 lakh in urban areas.
- A total of 1.99 crore houses have been built under PMAY in urban and rural areas from June 2015 till October 2021.
- Water Supply: Jal Jeevan Mission (JJM) - Har Ghar Jal Functional Household Tap Connection (FHTC) in every rural home and public institutions in villages. Since launch of the Mission in August 2019, 5.09 crore tap connections have been given till October 2021.
- Swachh Bharat Mission (Abhiyan) is a 'Clean India' campaign, an initiative of the Government of India to create mass awareness of the importance of cleanliness and hygiene; Total Sanitation Campaign (TSC) was launched in 1999; SBM programme launched in 2014 to include construction of toilets in households and in all schools; Total number of 11.30 crore household toilets have been built from 2014 to 2021.
- Removal of garbage and scientific waste management; need for involvement and active cooperation of all citizens, every household, institutions, industry, and the corporate sector.
- Smart Cities programme for urban renewal. 100 cities being covered under this scheme with 5,151 projects worth ₹2,05,018 crore being executed in 5 years.
- Corporate Social Responsibility (CSR) regime introduced under the Companies Act, 2013. Under this, companies with certain annual turnover, net worth, and net profit need to spend at least 2 per cent of their average net profit in the previous three years on CSR activities; activities include programmes to eradicate hunger and poverty, promotion of education, empowering women, reducing child mortality and improving maternal health, skill development, etc.
- Many Indian corporates and other social foundations were already engaged in the kind of activities envisaged under the CSR. Some of them had set up specific foundations with funds set apart for this purpose.

- Under CSR, corporates can contribute in a profound way to improve government-run schools and hospitals so as to benefit the disadvantaged sections in the society.

Important Terms to Note in this Chapter

Birth rate; Death rate; Infant mortality rate (IMR); Maternal mortality rate (MMR); Primary health centres (PHCs); Sub-Centres; Community health centers (CHCs); Doctor-Patient ratio; Communicable diseases; Non-communicable diseases; Total Sanitation Campaign (TSC); ;Swachh Bharat Mission; Solid waste management; Biogas; Bio-methanation plant; Smart Cities; Corporate Social Responsibility (CSR)

Practice Questions

1. What are the major domains in the Social sector and how well has India performed in these areas?
2. While India has done relatively well to promote higher education, she has lagged behind in regard to school education at primary and secondary levels. Do you agree? Give your views with cogent reasoning and suggest measures to remedy this.
3. What are the challenges faced by India in the education sector? What steps need to be taken to overcome them?
4. While India has made much progress in quantitative terms in the field of education, there is much to be desired in regard to qualitative improvement. Do you agree? Give your views with cogent reasoning.
5. The industrial sector and associations connected with it complain that those coming out of schools, colleges and technical institutions are not readily employable and need to be further trained involving heavy costs and time-lag. What are the reasons for this situation and what steps need to be taken to remedy it?
6. Give an outline of the 'Skill Development' mission initiated by the government. Why is such a programme needed and what are the steps required to make it a success?
7. The health sector in India is plagued by a plethora of problems. Identify the major problems which are adversely affecting people in urban and rural areas and suggest radical steps to tackle them.
8. The private and well-equipped hospitals in India are beyond the reach of the vast majority of the people who have to depend on government hospitals which have less facilities. Do you agree? If so, what steps need to be taken to remedy this position?
9. The Union government has announced a National Health Policy in 2017 and Ayushman Bharat scheme. What are the main features of the scheme? Identify the challenges in implementing it.

10. The health sector in India cannot be improved without improving the infrastructure and increasing manpower in hospitals and rural health centres. Do you agree? Suggest measures to overcome these deficiencies.
11. India's expenditure on health sector is very low compared to that in many other countries. Suggest measures to increase the spending on health and bring out the role that the government and the private sector can play in this.
12. Explain the importance of housing programmes for rural and urban areas launched by the government. How far they will help to overcome shortage of housing for the low income and weaker sections?
13. Bring out the importance of Swachh Bharat mission .for India. Its success will depend on people's active participation and cooperation and the role of non-governmental agencies. Comment.
14. What is meant by 'Corporate Social Responsibility' (CSR). Mention the main features of CSR obligations devolving on the.

    Corporate sector as per the legislation incorporated in the Companies Act 2013?
15. Describe the role of NGO's in India. What are the factors behind the controversies surrounding the operations of some of the NGO's? Do you agree that some restrictions placed on NGO's to make them more accountable are in order, and the NGO's also need to act in a more responsible way by being transparent in regard to their funding and activities?
16. "Second generation economic reforms should be accompanied with human capital formation for sustained development in India." Discuss.

    [Indian Economic Service/Indian Statistical Service 2015]
17. It is not the population but the poverty and unemployment are the two most chronic problems of the Indian economy. What policy measures would you suggest to solve these problems?

    [Indian Economic Service/Indian Statistical Service 2015]
18. Why is India's human development record still poor in spite of higher GDP growth rate?

    [Indian Economic Service/Indian Statistical Service 2016]
19. Appropriate local community-level health cam intervention is a prerequisite to achieve 'Health for All' in India. Explain. *[UPSC Main 2018 (General Studies Paper)]*
20. Bring out the factors responsible for rapid urbanization in India. What are the policy measures taken to prevent the undesirable effects of rapid urbanization?

    [Indian Economic Service/Indian Statistical Service 2020]
21. What are the objectives and features of Smart Cities Mission in India?

    [Indian Economic Service/Indian Statistical Service 2020]
22. Explain the features of 'Smart Cities' programme and bring out the challenges in implementing the scheme.
23. What are 'Smart Cities'? Examine their relevance for urban development in India. Will it increase rural-urban difference? Give arguments for 'Smart Villages' in the light of PURA and RURBAN Mission.

    [UPSC Main 2016 (Economic Optional Paper)]

GLOSSARY

❑ AGRICULTURAL SEASONS

There are two main cropping seasons, in northern India, viz., 'Kharif' and 'Rabi. The 'kharif' season coincides with the June- September south-west monsoon when rice, bajra, jowar, tur, cotton and jute are grown. The 'rabi' season is during winter, beginning in October- November and ending in March-April, when the temperatures are low and wheat and gram are grown. In southern India, where temperatures are high, kharif crops can be grown during any part of the year when there is soil moisture.

❑ BALANCE OF PAYMENTS

It covers all aspects of a country's transactions with the rest of the world such as exports, imports, remittances, interest payments, aid receipts and foreign loans from IMF and other international aid agencies.

Balance of payments consists of ***'Current account*** and ***'Capital account.***

The '**current account**' refers to trade in goods (also called merchandise or visible trade) and services plus profits and interest earned from overseas assets, net of those paid abroad. Items in the current account which are not visible goods are called '**invisibles**'. Invisibles are mainly services like financial services such as banking and insurance, tourism, shipping and air transport services. Gifts sent abroad and received from abroad, interests, profit and dividends and private transfer of funds also form part of invisibles.

The '**capital account** 'is made up of inward and outward flow of money for investment and international loans and grants.

❑ BIRTH RATE

It is the number of live births per thousand populations in a given year. It is also referred to as Crude birth rate.

❑ BUSINESS CYCLE (ALSO CALLED TRADE CYCLE)

Business or trade cycle refer to periodic fluctuations in macroeconomic variables like GDP, agricultural output, industrial production, price levels, employment, incomes, consumer demand, international trade, etc. These changes result in upward (peaks) and downward (troughs) trends in economic activity. Upward trends cause boost to economic activity while downward trends lead to recession in the economy. Business cycles are seen to be inherent feature of free-market capitalist system which occur in a cyclical, sometimes alternating, pattern and lasting for varying periods. The "Great Depression" of 1930s was a serious economic crisis that affected the US economy the most and lasted from 1929 to late 1930s. It led to stock market crash and steep fall in production, employment and incomes of people and required intervention major intervention by the US government under President Franklin D. Roosevelt. In more recent times was the 2007-08 "Great Recession" which broke out in the US and adversely affected global economy and many countries for a prolonged period.

❑ CAPITAL ACCOUNT

See under 'Balance of Payments'

❑ CAPITAL EXPENDITURE

It refers to expenditure incurred by the government which leads to creation of physical or financial assets or reduction of financial liabilities. Expenditure on acquiring land, buildings, machinery, etc. fall in this category.

❑ CAPITAL FORMATION

Additions to fixed assets or capital stock, i.e., capital goods, in the economy is known as capital formation or investment in economic parlance. Fixed assets or capital goods consist of machinery, buildings, infrastructure like roads, bridges, rail, ports, airports, etc. Investment or capital formation is categorized as 'gross' or 'net' as explained below.

Gross fixed capital formation (GCFC) or gross investment consists of value of capital goods added to during a year. It includes 'depreciation', i.e., capital goods which have worn out and need to be replaced. Net investment excludes depreciation; in other words, it is the net addition to the capital stock.

❑ CAPITAL GOODS

These are goods of a durable character like tools, equipments and machinery which are used for the production of other commodities. They are not final goods to be ultimately consumed and they are not transformed in the process of production.

❑ CAPITAL-OUTPUT RATIO

COR is the ratio of capital required to produce a unit of output over a period of time. Incremental capital-output ratio (ICOR) refers to the additional capital required to generate additional output.

❑ CAPITAL RECEIPTS

Capital receipts include loans raised by the government from the public which are called market borrowings, borrowings from the Reserve Bank of India, commercial banks and other financial institutions through sale of Treasury bills, loans from foreign governments and aid agencies, recoveries of loans granted by the Central government to States, funds raised from small savings through post offices and proceeds from disinvestment of government shares in public enterprises.

❑ CARBON CREDITS

These are credits earned by enterprises which shift to cleaner technologies in their operations and productive activities, thus saving on energy consumption and thereby reducing greenhouse gas (GHG) emissions. For a certain quantum of carbon dioxide (the major GHG) emissions avoided, the entity can get a carbon emission certificate which they can sell either immediately or through a futures market, just like any other commodity. The credits can be exchanged between businesses or bought and sold in the international markets at the prevailing market price. Credits can be used to finance carbon reduction schemes between trading partners. The scheme is aimed at mitigating global warming and issues arising out of climate change.

❑ CARBON SINK

Carbon sink is a forest, ocean or other natural environment which has the ability to absorb carbon dioxide (CO2) from the atmosphere. Vegetation and the ocean are the most important carbon sinks. It is any reservoir, natural or otherwise, that absorbs more carbon than it releases and thus lowers the concentration of CO2 from the atmosphere. In climate negotiations, this temporary reduction of CO2 in the atmosphere is known as "negative emissions".

❑ CARBON TAX

It is a tax imposed on firms and units that cause emissions or pollution and is based on the polluter-pay principle. The tax will be based on the extent of damage or suffering caused by the pollution and the revenue earned from it can be used to compensate those who were adversely affected by it.

❑ CASH RESERVE RATIO (CRR)

CRR is the proportion of the deposits which the commercial banks are required to keep with the Central Bank, in India, the Reserve Bank of India.

❑ CLOSED ECONOMY

Closed economy is one that does not interact with other countries. It does not indulge in imports or exports of goods or services or any economic or trade transactions with the rest of the world.

❑ CONSUMER GOODS

These are goods which are consumed when purchased by the ultimate consumers. Food, clothing and services like recreation are consumer goods.

❑ CURRENT ACCOUNT

See under '**Balance of Payments**'.

❑ DEATH RATE

It is the number of deaths per thousand population in a given year. It is also referred to as Crude death rate

❑ DEFICIT FINANCING

This is resorted to by the government to cover the excess of government's expenditure over the revenue from taxes, earnings from state enterprises, borrowing from public and other sources. Fiscal deficits are covered by borrowing from the central bank (the RBI in India) which is as good as printing money, or by borrowing from other domestic and foreign sources. These measures if carried on beyond a limit, increases the financial burden of the government. It leads to a debt trap and would also lead to inflationary pressures in the economy.

❑ DEFLATION

Deflation refers to a sustained reduction in the general price level. Deflation is often, though not necessarily, accompanied by decline in output and employment.

Deflation is to be distinguished from '**disinflation**' which refers to a reduction in the rate of inflation. In other words, prices are still rising but the rate of increase has come down.

❑ DEMOGRAPHY

It is the study of the characteristics of human populations, such as size, rate of growth, density, gender ratio, distribution between urban and rural areas and vital statistics. (See also Vital statistics).

❑ DEMOGRAPHIC DIVIDEND

Demographic dividend occurs when the proportion of working population in the total population is high which indicates that more people have the potential to be productive and contribute to growth of the economy. Countries with large working age population relative to the overall population stand to benefit from greater economic dynamism. Younger populations are more entrepreneurial, add to productivity growth, tend to save more which could boost the economy and have a larger fiscal base because of economic growth and with fewer dependents (children and elderly) for the economy and government to support.

There is, however, no guarantee that demographic dividend will automatically translate to economic growth. Countries need to put in place appropriate social and economic policies and institutions to promote growth and absorb the rapidly growing labour force.

While India enjoys the benefit of 'demographic dividend' by having a large young, working age population, it has to create employment opportunities and skill manpower on a large scale. Reforms in the health and education sector, financial inclusion and adequate employment opportunities are essential pre-requisites to take advantage of India's young population.

❑ DEPENDENCY RATIO

Dependency ratio is the ratio of total number of children (0-14 years of age) and or pensioners and non-working people to the working population; in other words, the number of non-working people in an economy relative to those who are of working age.

The ratio of non-working age to working age groups, multiplied by 100, gives the percentage.

The inverse is the 'Support ratio'.

❑ DEPRECIATION

Depreciation refers to the reduction in the value of an asset through wear and tear. In other words, it is the result of consumption of fixed assets. Depreciation is taken into account and allowance made for it while calculating the profit of an enterprise.

❑ DEVALUATION

It means decreasing or lowering the exchange value of domestic currency against other (foreign) currencies under pegged exchange rate through official action. A pegged or fixed exchange rate implies a regime where the exchange rate is set or maintained by government decisions or actions.

Devaluation helps to promote the exports of a country as foreigners importing the items will have to pay less in their currency due to devaluation of the currency of the exporting country. Conversely, the imports into the country which has devalued its currency will become more expensive as now the importers will have to pay more of their currency per a unit of the foreign currency.

❑ DISGUISED UNEMPLOYMENT

(see under **Unemployment**).

❑ ECOSYSTEM

Eco system, in the strict sense, refers to an ecological community together with its physical environment, considered as a unit. The term when applied to any sector or activity encompasses all aspects, internal and external, which influence it, and the complex set of relationships and inter-action between them, and the likely future trajectories and behaviour of the activity.

❑ EXCHANGE CONTROL

It implies controls that a government may impose to ban or restrict the amount of foreign currency or local currency that is allowed to be traded or purchased. Common exchange controls include banning the use of foreign currency and restricting the amount of domestic currency that can be exchanged within the country. Article XIV of the Articles of Agreement of the IMF provides for a country to impose exchange controls. It is economies in transition or the weaker economies that resort to exchange controls. With globalization, free trade and the trend towards economic liberalization, the tendency or need to impose such controls has come down.

❑ EXTERNALITIES

Externalities mean the benefits or harm accruing to a person or any entity resulting from the actions of another person or entity in the course of an economic activity. No payment is made for the benefit received nor is any compensation given for the harm caused to the other party. For example, an industry causing pollution to the water source used by the population in the neighbourhood is causing harm which is an externality. Other examples are smoke emanating from thermal plants, the untreated effluents discharged by industries into nearby rivers or lakes, pollution caused by vehicles on roads, all of which cause harm to others.

(See 'Carbon tax').

❑ FERTILITY RATE

It is the annual number of births per woman expressed per 1,000 women.

Age-specific fertility rate is the annual number of births per woman, in a particular age-group, expressed per 1,000 women in that age-group.

❑ TOTAL FERTILITY RATE (TFR)

TFR is the average number of children that would be born to a woman during her entire child-bearing years in accordance with the prevailing age-specific fertility rates. A TFR level of 2.1 children per woman is **'Replacement level'** fertility which ensures that each generation will exactly replace itself in the absence of migration.

❑ FISCAL DEFICIT

Fiscal deficit is the difference between the government's total expenditure and its total receipts excluding borrowing. Total receipts include revenue receipts and capital receipts which are not borrowings and are not debt - e.g., it includes recovery of loans and proceeds from sale of public sector undertakings. Fiscal deficit is financed through borrowing.

❑ FISCAL POLICY

The planned actions of a government to mobilise financial resources such as taxes for meeting its expenditure and regulating the economic activities of a country.

❑ FOREIGN EXCHANGE

Refers to foreign currency and all currencies other than the domestic currency of a country.

Foreign exchange (also briefly known as Forex) reserves: It means the foreign assets mainly foreign currencies, foreign treasury bills and foreign government securities, held by the Central Bank of a country. In a broad sense, it also includes gold reserves and Special Drawing Rights (SDRs) held by the Central Bank with the International Monetary Fund (IMF).

❑ FREE TRADE AGREEMENTS

Free trade is the condition which ensures free flow of goods and services through foreign trade without being restricted or encouraged by direct government intervention. It involves removal of import and export barriers. Economists view international free trade policy as helping to optimise world output and income levels in the long run. FTAs may be bilateral between two nations, or multilateral involving many nations, like the Regional Comprehensive Economic Partnership (RCEP) negotiated between Asia-Pacific nations.

❑ GIG ECONOMY

In a gig economy, workers take freelance work or short-term contracts for the gigs (informal jobs) they do. There is no formal contract signed with the employee. The main companies driving this economy are food delivery companies, fast service food joints, logistics and e- commerce firms and transportation network companies. These employees get few benefits that regular employees get such as graded wages with increments, bonus, health and insurance benefits. There is no security of job though they may earn reasonably good salaries when they work.

❑ GINI COEFFICIENT

This concept was developed by an Italian statistician, Corrado Gini (1884-1965). It shows the inequality in a Frequency Distribution, say distribution of personal income. Its value ranges from 0 to 1, Gini coefficient of zero indicating complete equality while the maximum value 1 represents complete inequality. As in the Lorenz curve in a graph, a 45 degree line represents complete equality while the curvature below it will show the degree of inequality. (See under Lorenz curve).

❑ GLOBALISATION

Globalization implies integration of a nation's economy with the global economy and it results in much freer movement of goods, services, capital, technology and people between countries, across national boundaries. It involves geographic dispersion of industrial and service activities across national borders.

❑ GLOCALISATION

While countries, especially the developing nations, are integrating with the world economy, they are also devolving more power to local governments and communities. This combination of globalisation and localisation is called 'glocalisation'. In this process, the centralised nation state is giving space to both supra-national and sub-national institutions.

❑ GROSS DOMESTIC PRODUCT

GDP is the sum total of the value of final goods and services created within the geographical boundary of a country in a particular year. To put it differently, GDP measures the aggregate production of final goods and services taking place within the domestic economy during a year.

GDP includes incomes earned by foreigners within the domestic economy and excludes incomes earned by the citizens in a foreign country.

GDP growth rate is one of the important indicators of the economic performance of a country.

❑ NOMINAL AND REAL GDP

GDP can be assessed in two ways. The value of GDP at the current prevailing prices is known as Nominal GDP. Whereas GDP evaluated at some constant prices or constant set of prices is called **Real GDP**. If the real GDP goes up or down, it indicates that the volume of production has changed since in this case the prices remain fixed or constant.

Gross National Product (GNP): GNP = GDP + Factor income earned abroad by the domestic factors of production - Factor income earned by the factors of production of the rest of the world in the domestic economy.

In other words, GNP = GDP + Net factor income from abroad (NFIA).

Net factor Income from Abroad (NFIA): Factor income earned by domestic factors of production employed abroad - Factor income earned by factors of production of other countries employed in the domestic economy.

GNP includes depreciation on fixed assets whereas Net National Product (NNP) excludes it. In other words, NNP = GNP -Depreciation.

❑ GROSS VALUE ADDED

See under **'Value added'.**

❑ HUMAN DEVELOPMENT

It is a process of improving people's choices and standard of living with better access to education and health, better housing, means of livelihood and higher per capita income. It implies higher longevity of life, higher literacy and education, food security and nutrition. In short, it should lead to a person's well-being and better quality of life.

While earlier, when the GDP or the per capita income of a country increased, it was considered to be a sign of development. But later, economists argued that mere increase in incomes alone does not signify human development but that there should be improvement in the various attributes, referred to above, reflecting in better 'quality of life for the people. One of the reasons for adopting this approach is that even if incomes rise, it may not be distributed fairly, resulting in wide disparities in the living conditions of people. Hence the need for a better measure.

❑ UNDP'S HDR

United Nations Development Programme (UNDP), has been studying human development (HD) across countries since 1990, using various socio-economic parameters such as longevity of life, education as per school enrolment ratio, mean years of schooling, adult literacy, and per capita GDP and per capita Gross National Income (GNI) to assess the progress made by each country. Based on these, UNDP assigns a HD Index and ranks the countries according to it. It also collects and publishes in the Human Development Report (HDR) updated statistical data on a wide range of issues like literacy and education, health conditions, availability of, and people's access to, water and sanitation, gender inequality and bias, empowerment of women, income inequality, political freedom, etc. Each year, the HDR issued by the UNDP focusses on a specific socio-economic theme which is of international concern and will impact future generations and relate to sustainable development.

❑ IMPERFECT AND MONOPOLISTIC COMPETITION

By the early part of the 20th century, economists began to challenge the notion of perfect competition, advocated by the Classicists, in which there are a large number of firms – both buyers and sellers who cannot make any impact on market price individually. But economists pointed out there are other types of market and industrial structure like imperfect and monopolistic competition.

It was no longer the case that no producer could influence or control the price. In the extreme case of monopoly, a single producer could set the price in a way to maximize his profits. In between this and a perfect competition, there exist a range of possibilities. There could be monopolistic and imperfect markets which are dominated by a few large firms – a case of oligopoly – in which each produce products which are similar but not perfect substitutes. The products have slight differentiation and consumers prefer the product of one firm to that of its competitors, even if its price slightly goes up, exhibiting a degree of loyalty to the brand. In this regard, the firm has some degree of power over the market and price-setting.

Also, under monopolistic competition, a producer could advertise the unique features of a product and brand, its superior qualities and establish a limited monopoly. Major industries like automobiles, steel, oil, chemicals, etc. are examples of such market structure.

Though oligopoly and monopolistic competition with few firms dominating the market have their pitfalls and the risk of concentration of economic power, they have come to be accepted in the modern corporate world. Economist Joseph Schumpeter defended monopoly due to the potential for innovations that a monopolist entrepreneur could bring to the enterprise which was free from the threat of competition and imitation. The few large firms constituting oligopoly, though socially iniquitous, held the potential of innovation and product improvement with the sizeable financial resources they command. In the IT sector, firms like Microsoft, Google, Apple, Dell, HP, tec. Wield much control over their respective market.

❑ INFANT MORTALITY RATE

(See under 'Mortality rate').

❑ INFLATION

Inflation is a sustained increase in the general price level of goods and services in an economy over a period of time. As the price level rises, each unit of currency will buy fewer goods and services. In other words, inflation results in a reduction in the purchasing power of money.

❑ INFORMAL ECONOMY

Informal economy or informal sector is the part of an economy that is neither subjected to government regulations or taxation nor monitored by any form of government. In under-developed and developing countries, the informal sector may form a significant part of the economy and, though it may not provide many of the benefits enjoyed by labour in the formal sector, it provides critical economic and employment opportunities.

It may also refer to the underground, parallel economy which carries on economic activity in an unauthorised manner, avoiding payment of taxes and operates outside government regulations. It operates on, and generates, black money or illicit wealth. This causes much harm to, and distorts, the normal functioning of an economy.

❑ INVISIBLES

See under **'Balance of Payments'**).

❑ INTELLECTUAL PROPERTY RIGHT (IPR)

Intellectual property (IP) is a monopoly conferred by the government under law on an inventor for an innovation of a product or process. Inventors could hold the right for an assigned period exclusively or could license its use to others for a consideration or royalty payment.

❑ INVESTMENT

See under **'Capital formation'**.

❑ KHARIF SEASON

See under **'Agricultural seasons'**.

❑ LABOUR FORCE

All persons who are working and those not working but seeking and/or are available for work are deemed to constitute the labour force. As a corollary, all those who are not working or are neither seeking nor available for work are considered to be outside the labour force.

Work force

A distinction is made between labour force and work force. Work force refers to the number of persons actually working and does not account for those who are willing or are offering themselves to work.

❑ LAISSEZ-FAIRE

Laissez-faire was a term originally used by the Physiocrats, a school of French classical thinkers. (A French term, it literally means let or allow (them) to do). The Physiocrats argued that only soil and agriculture were the source of all wealth. Believing in "natural order", they advocated maximum economic freedom and were against any interference by the State in economic matters which was the opposite of mercantilist approach (See under, Mercantilism). This principle of non-interference by the government in economic affairs was also fully supported by Classical economists, down from Adam Smith. In more recent times, laissez-faire thinking has been associated with the Chicago school of economists led by economist Milton Friedman.

❑ LIBERALISATION

Liberalization implies relaxation or removal of government restrictions and controls, especially in economic and social spheres. Under this policy, trade barriers are lifted, free enterprise is allowed with greater role assigned to private entities and private sector and there is labour market flexibility.

❑ LIFE EXPECTANCY AT BIRTH

It denotes the number of years a new-born infant would live if prevailing patterns of age-specific mortality rates continue to be the same throughout the child's life.

❑ LIQUIDITY

In economic parlance, liquidity denotes the degree to which an asset can be quickly and cheaply turned into money.

❑ LIQUIDITY PREFERENCE

It refers to the desire to hold money rather than other forms of wealth, e.g. stocks and bonds. This preference can arise from transaction motive, speculative motive or precautionary motive.

❑ LITERACY RATE

Percentage of literates to the population of a country, usually in the age group 7 years and above. Literacy rate can be assessed for different age-groups also like 'adult literacy rate' of those of 15 years of age and above.

❑ LORENZ CURVE

This is a concept developed by Marx O. Lorenz (1880- 1962), an American economist. Lorenz curve is a graphical representation which shows the degree of inequality in a Frequency Distribution in which the cumulative percentages of a population are plotted against the cumulative percentages of a variable, say, the percentage of population having certain levels of income, or paying income tax.

A straight line at an angle of 45 degrees from the start of the graph indicates perfect equality - say, top 10% of population account for 10% of total income, top 30% of population account for 30% of income and so on. Where a small number of people earn bulk of the income and large number of people account for much less of the income, the distribution will be unequal and highly skewed. When this is plotted on a graph, a curve will be formed below the 45 degree line and the degree of the curvature will be greater the greater the inequality.

A related concept is Gini coefficient. (See Gini co-efficient)

❑ MARKET, INDUSTRY STRUCTURES

Economic theory recognizes different types of market structures and industrial systems. These are markets with Perfect competition, Imperfect and Monopolistic competition, Monopoly, Oligopoly, Monopsony and Duopoly. For these types of markets and their characteristic features, see under respective alphabetical order.

❑ MATERNAL MORTALITY RATIO (MMR)

(**See under** 'Mortality rate).

❑ MERCANTILISM

Mercantilism was a policy and practice that prevailed in England, France, Germany and Spain between the mid-16th and late 18th centuries. Mercantilists argued for achieving favourable balance in international trade, i.e., exports exceeding imports, and thereby the country amassing wealth in the form of gold and silver. They advocated regulation and intervention by the State in every sphere to promote general well-being. It was the very antithesis of *laissez faire* policy that governments should not intervene in economic affairs. This policy came under attack from Classical economists who stood for maximum economic freedom and non-interference by the State in economic affairs of a country.

❑ MERCHANT DISCOUNT RATE

Merchant Discount Rate (MDR) is a charge to a merchant by a bank for accepting payments from their customers in credit and debit cards every time a card is used for payments (like swiping) in their stores. The merchant discount rate is expressed in percentage of the transaction amount.

The rationale for levying MDR is that to facilitate digital transactions, the merchants have to set up payment infrastructure like 'Point of Sale' (PoS) machines and they have to start a unique account called 'Merchant Account' with a bank to avail payments from the customers. As the banks provide payment services, the merchants have to give a payment to the bank for using the payment infrastructure set up by the bank. This payment is MDR.

To encourage cashless transactions, the Reserve Bank of India has set an upper limit for MDR to be levied by banks for debit cards.

❑ MERIT GOODS

Merit goods are commodities or services, the provision and consumption of which is considered to be socially desirable, irrespective of consumers' preferences, for example, education and healthcare. Governments would subsidize such goods or services for their beneficent effects and larger good of the society.

❑ MIXED ECONOMY

An economy in which both the capitalist and the socialist system operates. It is also one where the public sector and the private sector operate. They compete for the same limited resources in development but the government, as the sovereign authority, regulates the functioning of the economy.

❑ MONETARY POLICY

It is a government's policy, managed by the Central Bank of a country, on regulating the quantity of money in the economy, the rate of interest and the exchange rate of the currency. It has a predominant role in the control of aggregate demand, price levels and inflation.

❑ MONOPOLY

This is a market in which there is only one supplier. In a monopoly market, the firm is motivated by profits, stands alone and prevent new firms from entering the industry. The monopolist, by its own actions, is able to affect the market price of its output. It will make profits in excess of those necessary to just stay in business, and no pressure exists for the price to fall. According to theory, under monopoly, prices are higher and output lower than they would be under "perfect competition". Given these characteristics, most nations choose to control monopolies. (See 'Oligopoly').

❑ MONOPSONY

This is a market in which there is only one buyer for the item sold. In this condition, being the sole buyer and because of his unique position, he is able to wield a lot of power and control the market. A monopsonist buyer, which is a large firm, could use its size to its advantage and bargain to obtain low prices because rival sellers would vie for its business. The single buyer has greater leverage to negotiate prices and terms with their suppliers and is in a controlling position to drive price levels down. For example, a winery which is the sole producer of a particular and popular brand of wine could negotiate with grape growers from a position of strength and obtain the best terms of price and sale.

❑ MORTALITY RATE

Mortality rate (or, death rate) is the number of deaths during a particular period of time among a particular type or age-group of people.

❑ INFANT MORTALITY RATE

The probability of dying between birth and exactly one year of age, expressed per 1,000 live births.

❑ UNDER-FIVE MORTALITY RATE

The probability of dying between birth and exactly five years of age, expressed per 1,000 live births.

Maternal mortality ratio (MMR): The annual number of female deaths from pregnancy-related causes per 100,000 live births.

❑ MOST FAVOURED NATION (MFN) POLICY

Under this policy in international trade, one country grants to another country favourable trading terms and specific trade benefits, such as reduced tariffs on imported goods, in foreign exchange allocations, facility for setting up enterprises of the other country's nationals in its territory, etc. MFN status is critically important for smaller and developing countries as it gives them access to the larger market. It lowers the cost of their exports in view of reduced trade barriers which makes their products more competitive.

❑ NATIONAL INCOME

National income (also known as Net National Product at Factor cost or NNP at FC) is Gross National Product (GNP) minus the value of depreciation on fixed assets.

GNP includes depreciation on fixed assets whereas NNP excludes it. NNP at FC (National Income) = GNP - Depreciation.

❑ NET VALUE ADDED

See under '**Value added**'.

❑ OLIGOPOLY

Oligopoly is a market structure in which there are a few firms none of which can prevent the others from having significant influence. These small number of firms collude, either explicitly or tacitly, and act like a cartel to restrict output and/or fix prices, in order to achieve above normal market returns. Firms in oligopolistic markets recognize their inter-dependence and that they are affected by the actions and behaviour of their rivals. One among them may be a leader setting the price that others follow. All firms benefit from the stability and predictability of the industry. There is no precise upper limit to the number of firms in an oligopoly, but the number must be low enough that the actions of one firm significantly influence the others.

The firms resort to product differentiation through advertising and other marketing strategies like gifts and free offers to win over customers. The economic and legal concern is that an oligopolistic industry can block new entrants, slow innovation, and increase prices, all of which harm consumers.

❑ OPEN ECONOMY

An open economy is one that trades with other nations in goods and services and also in financial assets. It involves imports and exports with other countries. Total foreign trade (imports + exports) as a proportion of the GDP is a measure of the degree of openness of an economy.

❑ OPEN MARKET OPERATIONS (OMO)

Open market operations is a mechanism of credit control employed by the Central Bank (RBI in India) under which it sells or purchases securities. The sale of securities results in contraction of credit which helps to contain inflation, while the purchase of securities leads to expansion of credit which helps to stimulate the economy.

❑ PERFECT COMPETITION

Perfect competition signifies a perfectly competitive industry in which there are many buyers and sellers. All firms sell an identical, homogenous product or commodity, and none of them can influence the market price of their product which is determined by supply and demand. The large population of both buyers and sellers ensures that forces of supply and demand remain constant in the market. As such, buyers can easily substitute products made by one firm for another. Buyers have complete or "perfect" information about the product being sold and the prices charged by each firm.

Firms can enter or exit the market freely and there is perfect mobility of labour. Firms earn just enough profit to stay in business and no more. If they were to earn excess profits, other companies would enter the market and drive profits down.

A market where perfect competition exists is a theoretical construct and it does not exist in real world scenario.

❑ PRIMARY SECTOR

Agriculture and allied activities such as fisheries, forestry, horticulture constitute the primary sector.

❑ PRIVATE SECTOR

It refers to all establishments, industries, etc. which are owned and operated by individuals or group of individuals.

❑ PUBLIC DEBT

Public debt, also known as National debt, is the total out- standing borrowings of the government. The public debt of India includes the internal and external debt of the Government of India. A more comprehensive definition of Indian public debt would include the debt of all the three levels of government - Centre, States and Local - and all public enterprises, to the domestic private sector and the external sector.

❑ PUBLIC GOOD

These are goods and services which are consumed collectively and which do not exclude any one from enjoying its benefits. They are non-rivalrous in nature and non-excludable, and consumption by one does not deprive others from using or consuming them.

❑ PUBLIC SECTOR

It refers to all establishments and enterprises which are owned and operated by the government. They include those run by the Central, State or Local governments independently or jointly.

❑ PURCHASING POWER PARITY (PPP)

PPP denotes the number of units of a country's currency required to buy in the domestic market the same basket of goods or services as one US dollar would fetch in the US. For example, if for the same basket of items, It costs \$1 in the US and ⊠ 20 in India, then the exchange rate between the Indian Rupee and the US dollar as per the PPP concept will be \$1= ⊠ 20. The PPP concept helps to determine the purchasing power of each currency and also compare the cost of living vis-a-vis the income levels in different countries.

❑ QUANTITATIVE EASING

It is a monetary policy stance under which the Central bank of a country (RBI in India) buys government securities or bonds from commercial banks or other financial institutions to increase money supply (liquidity) in the economy. This method is adopted when an economy is going through a low growth phase when investor confidence is low and there is little incentive to spend and to prevent the economy going into a deeper depression.

This has been resorted to on a large scale by the Central bank of UK, USA (the Federal Reserve System), Japan, etc. following the financial and banking crisis of 2007-08 to stimulate the economy.

But when the economy shows signs of recovery or inflationary trends show up and concerns arise out of too much money feeding into the system, the Central Bank may start winding down the purchase of assets and selling the assets it purchased. This gradual withdrawal or reversal of 'quantitative easing' is called '**Tapering**' in economic parlance.

❑ QUATERNARY SECTOR

This sector involves:

Collection, production and dissemination of information.

Activities like research and development and services involving specialized knowledge and technical skill fall in this category.

Persons working in offices, schools and universities, hospitals, accounting firms and theatres all fall in this category.

Quaternary Sector has become an important part of economies and it offers much scope for employment. There has been high demand for, and consumption of, information-based services like Tax Consultants, Software Developers and Statisticians. Over half of all workers in developed economies are in "Knowledge sector". Like some of tertiary functions, quaternary activities can also be outsourced (i.e., can be got performed by other agencies). They are not tied to resources, affected by environment or localised by market.

Rabi season

See under '**Agricultural seasons**'.

❑ REPLACEMENT RATE (OF POPULATION)

See **TOTAL FERTILITY RATE (TFR)** under FERTILITY RATE.

Repo (Repurchase) rate

It is the rate at which the Reserve Bank of India lends shot-term money to commercial banks against securities. When the repo rate increases, borrowing from RBI becomes more expensive for banks. Similarly, when the RBI reduces the repo rate, it becomes cheaper for banks to borrow money.

(See **Reverse Repo rate**).

❑ REVENUE DEFICIT

Revenue deficit is the excess of government's revenue expenditure over revenue receipts. Revenue deficit results in government using up the savings or resources meant for capital or welfare expenditure to finance part of its consumption expenditure. It not only adds up to debt and interest liabilities, but will also adversely affect the development and welfare programmes of government.

❑ REVENUE EXPENDITURE

It is the expenditure incurred by the government for purposes other than the creation of physical or financial assets. It includes expenditure incurred for normal functioning of the government, interest to be paid on debt incurred by the government and grants given to State governments for purposes other than creation of assets.

❑ REVERSE REPO RATE

It is the rate which the Reserve Bank of India (RBI) pays banks when they park their short-term excess liquidity with the RBI. Reverse repo rate signifies the rate at which the Central Bank absorbs surplus liquidity from the banks. (See also Repo rate).

❑ SCALABILITY

Scalability is the capability of a system, network, or process to handle a growing amount of work, or its potential to be enlarged in order to accommodate that growth. For example, it can refer to the capability of a system to increase its total output under an increased load when resources (typically hardware) are added. In the context of a company or business model, it implies the potential for growth of the business.

❑ SECONDARY SECTOR

Mining and quarrying, industry and manufacturing, electricity, water, etc. and construction constitute the secondary sector in an economy.

SECTORS IN AN ECONOMY

See under terms Primary, Secondary and Tertiary.

❑ SHARE CROPPING

Also known as 'tithe' cultivation. A system under which a tenant cultivator keeps a portion of the farm produce while the landowner gets the rest. This system is quite common in many of the developing countries.

❑ SOCIAL OVERHEAD CAPITAL

Also known as infrastructure, social overhead capital consists of public utilities such as roads, railways, airports, telecommunications, water supply and sewage systems. Development of infrastructure is *sine qua non* for the progress of any economy.

SPECIAL DRAWING RIGHTS (SDR's)

SDRs is an international reserve asset, created by the International Monetary Fund (IMF) to supplement the existing official reserves of member countries. SDR is neither a currency but a potential claim on the freely usable currencies of IMF members. Member countries of IMF holding SDRs can obtain these currencies in exchange for their SDRs in two ways: either through the arrangement of voluntary exchanges between members or by the IMF designating members with strong external positions to purchase SDRs from members with weak external positions. Besides its role as a supplementary reserve asset, the SDR also serves as the unit of account of the IMF and some other international organizations.

Until recently there were four freely usable reserve currencies that constituted the SDR. They were the US dollar, the euro, UK's pound sterling and the Japanese yen. From October 1, 2016, China's 'yuan' gained a new status as a member of the IMF's SDR basket. That makes it a part of one of the global economy's exclusive clubs.

❑ STAGFLATION

A condition in an economy of slow economic growth and relatively high unemployment and inflation. It is a state of economic stagnation accompanied by rising inflation rates.

❑ STATUTORY LIQUIDITY RATIO (SLR)

SLR is the fraction of the total demand and time deposits, with the commercial banks, which they are required by the Reserve Bank of India to invest in specified liquid assets - gold, cash or other approved securities.

❑ STERLING BALANCES

Sterling balances was the foreign exchange asset India had accumulated by the end of the World War II (1939-45). This was on account of purchases made by Britain in India for her requirements for the war. This asset came quite handy after independence to pay for imports and for developmental purposes.

❑ SWISS CHALLENGE METHOD

It is a new process of giving contracts. Any person with credentials can submit a proposal to the government for a notified project. That proposal will be thrown open and other persons can give suggestions to improve and better that proposal. The best proposal will be selected, and the original proposer will get a chance to accept it if it is an improvement on his proposal. In case the original proposer is not able to match the more attractive and competing counter proposal, the project will be awarded to the counter-proposal. This is a transparent method of approving and granting contract.

❑ TAPERING

See under **'Quantitative easing'**.

❑ TERMS OF TRADE

Terms of trade is the value of a country's exports relative to that of its imports or the ratio of the index of export prices to the index of import prices. There will be improvement in terms of trade if export prices rise more quickly than import prices or fall more slowly than import prices. The concept could also apply to the relationship between the prices of the products of one sector and the prices of products of another sector, say, between the products of agriculture and those of industry in an economy.

❑ TERTIARY SECTOR

Trade, hotels and restaurants, transport and communication, storage and ware housing, and other services like banking and insurance, IT sector, etc. constitute the Tertiary sector. It is also referred to as the Services sector.

❑ TOTAL FERTILITY RATE (TFR)

(**See under** 'Fertility Rate').

❑ UNDP's HDR:

See under **HUMAN DEVELOPMENT.**

❑ UNEMPLOYMENT

Unemployment refers to those who are not working but are willing and seeking to work but cannot find employment. It also includes those who are not seeking work but when asked whether they are available for work reply in the affirmative.

❑ VOLUNTARY AND INVOLUNTARY UNEMPLOYMENT

Economists make a distinction between these two types of unemployment. Voluntary unemployment occurs when a person in the labour force choose not to take up a job for reasons such as not willing to work at the going wage rate or for any other reason of his own volition.

Whereas involuntary unemployment occurs when a person is willing to work at the prevailing wage rate, yet he cannot find a job and remain unemployed. In an economy with involuntary unemployment, there is a surplus of labour at the current wage rates.

❑ DISGUISED UNEMPLOYMENT

Disguised unemployment exists where part of the labour force is either left without work or is working in a redundant manner where worker productivity is virtually zero. An economy or a sec- tor demonstrates disguised unemployment when productivity is low, and where too many workers are there when the need is for a much lesser number of persons. In such a situation, the total output will not be affected even if the surplus labour is withdrawn. Disguised unemployment exists in the agricultural sector in India which has surplus labour due to the pressure of population on the limited land available and dearth of non-farm jobs in rural areas.

❑ VALUE ADDED

Value added is the net contribution made by firms in an economy. It is the value of the production of the firm minus the value of intermediate goods (like raw materials or other inputs) used by the firm in production. In this method of calculating the aggregate value of goods and services, there will be no double counting of items used in production.

GROSS VALUE ADDED (GVA) will include depreciation or consumption of fixed capital, i.e., wear and tear of machinery, etc.

NET VALUE ADDED (NVA) will not include depreciation.

❑ VITAL STATISTICS

Refers to data that record significant events and changes in human life, such as the rate of births, deaths, fertility and longevity of life (life expectancy at birth).

❑ WAGE GOODS

Wage goods include food items, clothing and other basic items of daily personal consumption.

❑ WORK FORCE

See under **Labour force.**

STATISTICAL TABLES

INDIA DATA

TABLE 1: INDIA: DEMOGRAPHIC DATA AT A GLANCE

Table 1.1: Population

(In Million)

Pre-Independence		Post-Independence			
Year	**Population**	**Year**	**Population**	**Year**	**Population**
1901	238.3	**1951**	361.0	**1991**	846.3
1911	252.0	**1961**	439.1	**2001**	1028.7
1921	251.2	**1971**	548.2	**2011**	1210.6
1931	278.9	**1981**	685.2	**2018***	1349.8
1941	318.5				

* 2018 Population: Estimated.

Table 1.2: Decadal Growth of Population

(Increase in Million & Percentage)

Decade	In Million	Percentage	Decade	In Million	Percentage
1951-61	78.14	21.64	**1981-91**	162.97	23.85
1961-71	108.93	24.80	**1991-2001**	180.71	21.35
1971-81	135.17	24.66	**2001-11**	181.83	17.68

Table 1.3: Density of Population

(Population per square kilometre)

Year	Density	Year	Density
1951	117	**1991**	267
1961	142	**2001**	325
1971	177	**2011**	382
1981	216		

Table 1.4: Rural & Urban Population

(In Percentage)

Year	Rural	Urban	Year	Rural	Urban
1961	82.03	17.97	**1991**	74.29	25.71
1971	80.09	19.91	**2001**	72.19	27.81
1981	76.62	23.38	**2011**	68.84	31.16

Table 1.5: Male & Female Population

(In Million & Percentage)

Year	Female	Male	Year	Female	Male
1951	175.56 (48.62)	185.53 (51.38)	**1991**	407.07 (48.10)	439.2 (51.90)
1961	212.94 (48.49)	226.29 (51.53)	**2001**	495.74 (48.26)	531.2 (51.74)
1971	264.11 (48.18)	284.05 (51.82)	**2011**	586.47 (48.46)	623.7 (51.54)
1981	329.96 (48.29)	353.37 (51.71)			

Note: Figures in brackets are percentages to Total Population.

Table 1.6: Sex Ratio

(Number of Females per 1,000 Males)

Year	Sex Ratio	Year	Sex Ratio
1951	946	**1991**	927
1961	941	**2001**	933
1971	930	**2011**	943
1981	934		

Source: Tables 1.1 to 1.6: Census of India reports, Registrar General of India.

TABLE 2: VITAL STATISTICS

(The source for Vital statistics data is Census of India – Sample Registration System (SRS)

Table 2.1: Birth Rate (Number of live births per 1,000 of the population per year)

Year	Birth Rate	Year	Birth Rate
1971	36.9	**2000**	25.8
1976	34.4	**2010**	22.1
1986	32.6	**2015**	20.8
1990	30.2	**2018**	20.0

Table 2.2: Death Rate(Number of deaths per 1,000 of the population per year)

Year	Death Rate	Year	Death Rate
1971	14.9	**2000**	8.5
1976	15.0	**2005**	7.6
1986	11.1	**2010**	7.2
	9.7	**2018**	6.2

Table 2.3: Infant Mortality Rate (IMR)

(The probability of dying between birth and exactly one year of age per 1,000)

Year	IMR	Year	IMR
1971	129	**2000**	68
1986	96	**2010**	47
1990	80	**2018**	32

Table 2.4 Life Expectancy at Birth

(The number of years a newborn infant would live if prevailing patterns of mortality at the time of birth were to stay the same throughout the child's life.)

Year	Life Expectancy	Year	Life Expectancy
1970-75	49.7	**2002**	63.7
1976-80	52.3	**2010**	67.9
1990-94	60.0	**2018**	69.4

Table 2.5: Family Planning: Couple Protection Rate (CPR)

(Percentage of couples effectively protected by all methods of family planning)

Year	CPR (In percentage)	Year	CPR (In percentage)
1971	12.7	1990	43.3
1980	22.3	1993	43.5
1985	32.1	1999	48.6

Table 2.6: Total Fertility Rate (TFR), India

(Total fertility rate is the average number of children that would be born alive to a woman during her lifetime if she were to bear children at each age in accordance with prevailing age-specific fertility rates.)

Year	Total Fertility Rate (TFR)
1980-82	4.5 (Rural & Urban combined)
1985	4.3
1990-92	3.7 (Rural & Urban combined)
1995-97	3.4
2005	2.9
2018	2.2

Note: 2.1 is the Replacement rate to be achieved by India and all States/UTs.
Source: Tables 2.1 to 2.6: SRS (Sample Registration Systems) Bulletins, Registrar General of India.

Table 2.7 (a): Total Fertility Rates: 1998 & 2016 – States & UTs

State	1998	2016	State	1998	2016
Maharashtra	2.7	1.8	Himachal Pradesh	2.1	1.7
Kerala	1.8	1.8	Bihar	4.3	3.3
Tamil Nadu	2.0	1.6	Madhya Pradesh	3.9	2.8
Karnataka	2.4	1.8	Odisha	2.9	2.0
Haryana	3.3	2.3	Rajasthan	4.1	2.7
West Bengal	2.4	1.6	Uttarakhand	--	1.9
Telangana	--	1.7	Uttar Pradesh	4.6	3.1
Jammu & Kashmir	2.7	1.7	Chhattisgarh	--	2.5
Andhra Pradesh	2.4	1.7	Jharkhand	--	2.6
Gujarat	3.0	2.2	Assam	3.2	2.3

Table 2.7 (b): Total Fertility Rates: 1998 & 2016

State	1998	2016
Meghalaya	4.57	2.7
Tripura	--	1.3
Manipur	3.04	1.5
Mizoram	2.89	1.5
Nagaland	3.77	1.6
Arunachal Pradesh	2.52	--
Puducherry	--	1.7
Goa	1.77	1.4

Note: On TFR, see also Chapter 18, Table 18.3 on P. 18.9.

Source:

1. 1998 data for States, UTs and India: Draft Tenth Five Year Plan (2002-07), Vol. III, State Plans, Trends Concerns and Strategies, p.46, Planning Commission, Govt. of India.
2. 2016 data for Group I & II States: SRS Statistical Report, Registrar General of India cited in Table 1.2.12, Total Fertility Rate (TFR) of Major States, National Health Profile 2018, Central Bureau of Health Intelligence DGHS, Ministry of Health & Family Welfare, Government of India
3. Data for Group III states/UTs is for 2013 from Sample Registration System cited by NITI Aayog on its website: https://niti.gov.in/content/total-fertility-rate-tfr-birthwoman

Table 3: Growth Performance in the Five Year Plans

Plan Period	Target	Achieved	Plan Period	Target	Achieved
1 First Plan (1951-56)	2.1	3.5	7. Sixth Plan (1980-84)	5.2	5.5
2. Second Plan (1956-61)	4.5	4.2	8. Seventh Plan (1985-90)	5.0	5.6
3. Third Plan (1961-66)	5.6	2.8	9. Annual Plans (1990-92)	--	3.4
4. Annual Plans (1966-69)	--	3.9	10. Eighth Plan (1992-97)	5.6	6.5
5. Fourth Plan (1969-74)	5.7	3.2	11 Ninth Plan (1997-2002)	6.5	5.5
6. Fifth Plan (1974-78)	4.4	4.7	12. Tenth Plan (2002-07)	7.9	7.7

Source: Eleventh Five Year Plan (2007-12), Vol I, Planning Commission.

Note: The growth targets for the first three Plans were set with respect to National Income. In the Fourth Plan, it was Net Domestic Product. The actual growth rates are in terms of GDP at factor cost. Average growth rates over a short period can be misleading because of fluctuations in agricultural output due to variable monsoon.

TABLE 4 : Number And Percentage of Population Below the Poverty Line (Major states)

S.No	State	1993 – 94	2004 – 05	2011 – 12	
				Number of Persons (lakhs)	Percentage
1.	Andhra Pradesh	44.6	29.9	78.78	9.20
2.	Assam	51.8	34.4	101.27	31.98
3.	Bihar	60.5	54.4	358.15	33.74
4.	Gujarat	37.8	31.8	102.23	16.63
5.	Haryana	35.9	24.1	28.83	11.16
6.	Himachal Pradesh	34.6	22.9	5.59	8.06
7.	Jammu & Kashmir	26.3	13.2	13.27	10.35
8.	Karnataka	49.5	33.4	129.76	20.91
9.	Kerala	31.3	19.7	23.95	7.05
10.	Madhya Pradesh	44.6	48.6	234.06	31.65
11.	Maharashtra	47.9	38.1	197.92	17.35
12.	Odisha	59.1	57.2	138.53	32.59
13.	Punjab	22.4	20.9	23.18	8.26
14.	Rajasthan	38.3	34.4	102.92	14.71
15.	Tamil Nadu	44.6	28.9	82.63	11.28
16.	Uttar Pradesh	48.4	40.9	598.19	29.43
17.	West Bengal	39.4	34.3	184.98	19.98
18.	**All India**	**45.3**	**37.2**	**2697.83**	**21.92**

Note: Data based on Tendulkar Methodology,

Source: Data for 1993-94 and 2004-05: Databook December 2014: Planning Commission and for 2011-12, Press note on poverty estimates, 2011-12, Planning Commission, July 2013.

Table 5: India's rank in UNDP's Human Development Reports (for select years)

Year	Rank	HDI Value	Year	Rank	HDI Value
1990	130	0.427	2010	130	0.586
1995	127	0.548	2014	130	0.618
2000	126	0.577	2016	130	0.636
2004	126	0.611	2017	130	0.640

Note: HDI stands for Human Development Index value.

Source: UNDP's Human Development Reports for various years.

NAME INDEX

A

Aquinas, St. Thomas xii
Ahluwalia, Montek S. 17.20
Alkire, Sabina 17.8
Ambedkar, Bhimrao Ramji 1.12
Aristotle, xii, xv
Arkwright, Richard 1.4
Arrow, Kenneth xviii
Atkinson, Anthony B. 17.6
Atkinson, F.J. 19.23

B

Babur 1.12
Bardhan, P.K. 17.20, 17.46
Bell, Graham 1.11
Bentham, Jeremy xvi, 17.12-3
Bhagwati, Jagdish 17.16-7
Bhave, Acharya Vinobha 3.3
Biden, Joe 20.30, 20.33, 20.38
Birla, G.D. 2.2
Bommai, Basavaraj 25.44
Borlaug, Norman 3.7-8
Bose, Netaji Subhas Chandra 1.12
Brahmananda, P.R. 2.5, 19.7
Brundtland, Gro Harlem 19.14

C

Cameron, David 20.8
Cantillon, Richard 18.3-4
Chancel, Lucas 6.12
Chelliah, Raja J. 14.11-2
Chidambaram, P. 14.13, 25.31
Chola, Karikala 1.6
Confucius xii
Cornwallis, Lord 1.6
Clark, Colin 19.24
Condorcet, Marquis de 18.3
Confucius xii, xv
Cornwallis, Lord 1.6
Cotton, Sir Arthur 1.7
Crompton, Samuel 1.4

D

Dalwai, Ashok 7.41, 7.44
Dandekar, V.M. 17.20
Deaton, Angus 17.21-2
Desai, Morarji 2.6, 25.19
Desai, R.C. 19.22
Digby, William 19.22-3
Dobb, Maurice 19.23
Domar, Evsey 19.5, 19.7-8
Drèze, Jean xviii, 17.16
Dutt, Ramesh Chandra xiv, 1.12

E

Easwar, Justice R.V. 25.32
Engels, Friedrich xiii

F

Foster, James 17.8
Friedman, Milton 16.4

G

Gadgil, D.R. 17.20
Gama, Vasco da 1.3
Gandhi, Indira 2.6
Gandhi, Rajiv 6.4
Gandhi(ji), Mahatma 1.12, 2.9, 3.3, 26.24
Ganguli, B.N. 17.20
Ghatak, Maitreesh 17.46
Gini, Corrado xvii
Godwin, William 18.3
Gokhale, Gopal Krishna 1.12
Gorwala, A.D. 5.6
Greer, Joel 17.6
Gupta, S.P. 9.11

H

Hall, Charles 17.16
Haq, Mahbub ul 17.6
Hargreaves, James 1.4
Harrod, Sir Roy 19.5, 19.7-8
Heckscher, Eli, 15.3
Heston, Alan 19.23
Hicks, John 17.14
Hirschman, Albert 19.5, 19.8
Hobson, John 17.14
Haq, Mahbub ul xviii, 17.6
Hussain, Abid 4.5, 9.11

J

Jaitley, Arun 14.20
Jalan, Bimal 13.22, 25.5
Jha, L.K. 14.10
Jinping, Xi, xii, 20.14
Johansson, Sten xviii
Johnson, Boris 20.9
Johnson, Lyndon B. 3.5
Joshi, Vijay 17.46

K

Kakodkar, Anil 10.11
Kaldor, Nicholas 17.14
Kale, Vaman Govind 1.12
Karve, D.G. 9.3
Kautilya xi, xv
Kelkar, Vijay 14.22, 25.33
Keynes, John Maynard xiii, xiv, 14.4, 19.23, 20.16
Khambatta, K.G. 19.22
Krishna, Raj, 15.4
Kuznets, Simon 17.51

L

Laffer, Arthur 14.6
Lagarde, Christine 17.35
Lakdawala, D.T. 17.22
Lenin, Vladimir 2.2, 19.15
Lewis, Arthur 19.4, 19.6-7, 19.8
Lokanathan, Dr. P.S. 14.2, 17.20, 19.26
Lorenz, Max xvii

M

Macaulay, Thomas 1.5
Madan, B.N. 14.2, 19.26
Malthus, Thomas Robert 18.2-4
Mahalanobis, P.C. 2.4, 12.3, 14.2, 19.25-6
Mao Zedong (see under Z)
Marshall, Alfred xiii, xvi, 19.24
Marshall, George 20.15
Marx, Karl xii, 16.2
Masani, M.R. 2.9, 17.20
Mathew P.C. 14.2
Mehta, Ashok 17.20
Mercantilists xii
Merkel, Angela 20.34
Mill, James, 15.2
Mill, John Stuart xiii, xvi, 18.3
Minhas, B.S. 17.20
Mirabeau, Marquis de xii
Mitchell, Wesley 17.14
Modi, Narendra 26.22, 26.24
Mor, Nachiket 13.12
Morse, Samuel 1.11
Myrdal, Gunnar xviii

N

Naoroji, Dadabhai xiv, 1.9, 1.12, 17.19, 19.22-3
Narasimhmam, M. 13.3, 13.5
Nayak, P.J. 5.13, 8.18
Nayak, P.R. 9.8

Nehru, Jawaharlal (Pandit) 1.12, 2.2-3, 14.2, 19.15-6, 19.26
Nemours, Pierre de xii
Nurkse, Ragnar 19.4, 19.6-7, 19.8
Nussbaum, Martha xviii

O

Ohlin, Bertil, 15.3
Oresme, Nicholas xii
Owen, Robert 17.16

P

Padmanabhan, S. 13.4
Panagariya, Arvind 17.16
Pant, Pitambar 17.20
Pareto, Vilfredo xvi, 17.13
Pasayat, Justice Arijit 25.15
Patel, H.M. 2.9
Patel, Sardar Vallabhbhai 1.12
Patel, Urjit 13.15
Pawar, Ajit 25.44
Petty, William 18.4
Phillips, William 16.4
Physiocrats xii, 16.2
Pigou, A.C. xvi, 17.14, 19.24
Piketty, Thomas 6.12
Pillai, V.O. Chidambaram 1.8
Piquet, Henri 10.15
Pitroda, Sam 10.22
Plato xii, xv
Prabhu, Lobo 2.9
Proudhon, Pierre 17.16

Q

Quesnay, François xii, 18.3

R

Rai, Balwant 17.33
Raj, K.N. 2.3, 14.27
Rajagopalachari, C. (Rajaji) 2.9
Ranade, Mahadev Govind xiv, 1.12
Ranga, N.G. 2.9
Rangarajan, C. 14.22, 17.23-4
Ravallion, Martin 17.6
Rao, P.V. Narasimha 6.5, 6.13, 14.11
Rao, V.K.R.V. 14.2, 17.19-20, 19.22-7
Rath, N. 17.20
Ravallion, Martin 17.6
Rawls, John 17.12, 17.14
Ray, Debraj 17.46
Reagan, Ronald 14.6
Reddy, Y.V. 14.22
Ricardo, David xiii, 15.2, 16.2, 17.15-6
Rodan, Paul Rosenstein 19.5, 19.7
Roosevelt, Franklin xiii, 14.4
Rostow, W.W. 19.4-6
Rousseau, Jean J. 17.16

S

Samuelson, Paul 17.14
Sen, Amartya xviii, 17.5, 17.6-7, 17.13-4, 17.16-7, 18.14
Sengupta, Arjun 4.5, 8.11, 16.12
Shah, Justice, A.P. 14.14
Shah, Justice M.B. 25.15
Shah, K.T. 19.22-3
Shenoy, B.R. 2.9
Shetty, Devi 26.16
Shirras, Findlay 19.22-3
Simon, Saint 17.16
Singh, Jaswant 12.5
Singh, Manmohan 6.5, 6.14, 14.11
Singh N.K. 14.18, 14.23-4
Sinha, U.K. 9.15
Sinha, Yashwant 25.31
Sismondi, Jean 17.16
Smith, Adam iii, xii-xiii, 15.2, 16.2, 17.12, 18.3
Standing, Guy 17.46
Stephenson, George 1.5, 1.11
Subramanian, Arvind 25.34
Swaminathan M.S. 3.8, 7.10-1, 7.25, 7.41

T

Tagore, Rabindranath 1.12
Tarapore, S.S. 13.5
Tata, Jamshedji 1.8, 4.7
Tata, J.R.D. 2.2, 10.15

Tendulkar, Suresh 17.23
Thakurdas, Purushothamdas 2.2
Thompson, William 17.16
Thorbecke, Erik 17.6
Thungon, P.K. 17.33
Tilak, Bal Gangadhar 1.12
Tiruvalluvar xii
Todaro, Michel 19.8
Torrens, Col. Robert 15.2
Trump, Donald 20.7, 20.22, 20.30, 20.37
Turgot, Anne xii

V

Vakil, C.N. 2.5, 19.7, 19.23
Veblen, Thorstein 16.2
Visvesaraya, Sir M. 1.7, 19.16
Vivekananda, Swami 1.12
Voltaire 17.16
Vyas, V.S. 13.11

W

Wacha, Dinshaw Edulji xiv, 1.12
Walras, Léon xvi, 17.13
Wanchoo, Justice K.N. 14.10
Watt, James 1.5

X

Xiaoping, Deng 18.13

Z

Zedong, Mao 2.9

SUBJECT INDEX

A

Aadhaar 25.4-5
  and direct benefit transfer 7.18, 25.5
  (*see also* direct benefit transfer)
Afghanistan 20.21, 20.34
  and opium cultivation 20.4
  India's access to 10.33
Africa xv, 19.2, 20.4, 20.5, 20.30, 20.33
  India's exports to 15.21-2
  Quad initiative and 20.15
agrarian scene (*see under* colonial rule, land tenure)
agriculture
  and food processing 7.13-6
  and environmental concerns 18.5
  as priority sector 5.6-7, 7.21-3
  capital formation, subsidies in 7.31-2
  challenges facing 7.4-8, 7.36
  commercialisation of 1.7
  contract farming 7.29-31
  cooperative and group farming 7.26-9
  credit for 7.21-3, 5.6-7
  Dalwai Committee on 'Doubling Farmers' Income' 7.41, 7.44-5
  debt relief for farmers 7.24-6
  de-dieselising (Kusum scheme) 11.16-7
  diversification of crops, nutrition 7.11-2
  e-NAM 7.18-9
  Farmer Producer Organisations 7.19-21
  factors behind success in 3.4-7, 7.2-3
  food processing industry 7.14-6
  integrated farming and secondary agriculture 7.43-5
  limitations of technology in 3.8, 7.8
  marketing in 7.17-21 (*see also* APMCs)
  measures to promote 3.4-7, 7.9-11
  new approaches to 3.6, 7.10-1, 7.27
   PM Fasal Bima Yojana 7.26
  problems in 3.8-9, 7.4-8
  processing in 7.12-3
  research, role of scientists in 1.6, 3.8
  reforms and repeal of farm laws xvii, 7.36-43
  soil fertility and productivity in 7.5-6
  Parliament Standing Committee on agriculture marketing 7.41-2
  trends during 1950-2020 in 7.2-3
  vis- à-vis industry 7.1-2
  (*see also* farmers, farming, farm laws, food security and nutrition, green revolution)
Agriculture Produce Market Committee (APMC) 7.17-8, 7.37-43
  Parliament Committee on 7.41-2
air transport 10.15-6 (*see also* aviation)
Alkire-Foster (AF) Multidimensional Index of Poverty 17.6-8
AMRUT Mission 26.28-9

Angel investors (*see under* Start-Up India mission)
An Uncertain Glory: India and Its Contradictions 17.16
Arabian sea and piracy 20.5
Arabs 1.3
Arthaśāstra xi
ASEAN 16.35, 20.5, 20.31
  and India 20.20
  and South China dispute 20.15, 20.20-1, 20.30-1
  India's trade with 15.17, 15.21, 20.22-5
ASEAN group +3 15.21
ASEAN group + 6 20.22
Asia xv, 1.5, 2.9, 15.2, 19.2, 20.4, 20.30
Asia Minor 1.3
Asia-Pacific Economic Cooperation (APEC) 20.20, 25.14
Asia-Pacific region, trade with 15.21
Asian Development Bank (ADB) vii, ix, 2.11, 17.17, 18.23, 20.14, 20.18
  on inequality in Asian countries 17.18-9
  on protectionism 20.7
Asian Development Outlook 2012-Confronting Rising Inequality in Asia, (ADB) 17.17-8
Asian economies, demographic and economic data 2.11
Asian Infrastructure Investment Bank 20.18-9
Asian Tigers 2.10, 15.18
Astrakhan (Russia) 10.32
Atal Innovation Mission 23.10-1
Australia 19.10, 20.21, 22.9
automation
  impact on employment 16.34-7
  in India 16.37, 21.11-2
Avarice and Profusion, Of 18.3
aviation sector
  airports, modernisation of 10.16-8, 24.13-4

B
Babylon xi
Bad Bank (*see under* banks)
Bandar Abbas (Iran) 10.32-3
Bangladesh 19.3, 20.21, 20.40, 21.12, 22.9
  better than India on death rate, IMR 18.16, 26.10-1
  liberation war of 1971 15.4
banking
  at independence 5.1-2
  correspondents 17.49, 25.3-4
  expansion of 25.5-7
  (*see also* Payments Banks, Small Finance Banks)
banking reforms
  factors behind 13.2-3
  Narasimham I Committee, 1991 on 13.3-4
  Narasimham IICommittee,1998 13.5-6
  on cash reserve ratio 13.3, 13.16
  on statutory liquidity ratio 13.3, 13.16
P J Nayak Committee on 5.13-4, 25.12
Bankruptcy law
  Insolvency and Bankruptcy Code 2015 13.9-10, 22.3, 22.8-9
banks
  amalgamation and consolidation of 5.2, 13.10, 25.13-4
  and financial inclusion 13.23-4 25.2-4
  as agents of change 5.5-6
  autonomy of 13.6
  Bad Bank, setting up of 25.9-11
  Basel norms for 13.6, 25.7
  computerisation of 13.6-7
  Debt Recovery Tribunals 13.8
  expansion and penetration of 5.5
  limitations of nationalisation of 5.9
  modernisation and computerisation of 13.6-7
  nationalisation of 5.7-9, 5.10-14
  non-performing assets of 13.2, 13.3-4, 13.7

recapitalisation of 13.6, 25.8-9, 25.11-2
debt and stressed assets of 13.7
restructuring of debt of 13.8
SARFAESI Act 13.7, 22.8
barter system xi
Basel norms for banks (*see under* banks)
Bear Stearns 15.9
Belgium 20.8, 20.10, 20.20
Bengal famine, the Great 1.17, 18.6
Bengal Iron Works 1.8
Bangalore 23.4
below poverty line (BPL) 6.10-1, 17.19-24 (*see also* poverty and poverty line)
Bhagawati-Sen debate 17.16-7
Bhoodan movement 3.3
Bhutan 20.21, 22.9
and Gross Happiness Index 17.8
HDI rank higher than India 17.6
Biblical times, literature xi, xv
Bihar 1.6
bilateralism vs multilateralism 20.31
BIMSTEC 20.20, 20.23
birth rate (*see under* vital statistics)
black money
action by overseas banks on 25.16
banks' responsibility on 25.18
European Union on 25.29-30
foreign countries on 25.14-6
law on 25.15-6
petition on 25.15
problem in India 25.16-7
problem in US and Europe 25.29-30
steps to curb 25.14-5, 25.17-8
(*sse also* demonetisation, taxation-double tax avoidance)
Bolshevik revolution 2.2
Bombay xiv
Bombay Plan: A Plan for Economic Development of India: 2.2
Bombay Presidency 1.6
bonded labour (*see under* labour)
Brazil 9.18, 15.17, 17.52, 18.15, 19.3, 19.10, 20.28, 20.18-9, 20.40, 22.2-3, 26.6
Bretton Woods xiii, 20.16, 22.2
Brexit (*see under* Britain)
BRICS countries 20.18
Britain (*see also* UK)
and immigration 18.22-3
exits from EU (Brexit) xix, 20.8-11
Brundtland Commission 19.14
Brunei 20.20, 20.41
budget (union)
departure from the past 14.4
(*see also* Union budget)

C

Calcutta xiv
Calicut 1.3
Cambodia 2.9
Cambridge Economic History of India, The 19.23
Canada 20.10, 20.17-8, 20.21, 20.29
capital account convertibility 13.5, 15.14-6
Capital formation in Underdeveloped Countries 19.4-5
carbon sink and forest cover 20.40-1
Cash Reserve Ratio (CRR) and RBI 13.2-3, 13.16
Caspian sea 10.32-3
census of India vi, vii
origin of 18.6
Central Asia 10.32-4
Central India 1.6
Central Statistical Organisation 19.26
Chabahar port (Iran) 10.33
Chicago School 16.4
child labour (*see under* labour)
Chile 20.21
China 2.9, 6.12, 8.16, 9.17, 10.33, 15.11, 15.17, 16.30, 17.52, 18.15-6, 19.1-2, 20.28, 20.18-9, 20.37, 21.11-2, 26.7
accession to WTO 20.12
and Cultural revolution 2.9

and Great Leap Forward 2.9
Quad initiative 20.30-1
and South China sea dispute 20.15, 20.20-1, 20.30-1
decline of poverty in 17.14-5
economic growth, slowdown in 20.13-4
income inequality in 17.19
India's war with 2.6
Japan's war with 2.9
Lewis' turning point in 19.6
One Belt, One Road (OBOR) initiative 10.34, 20.14-5, 20.30
India and OBOR 20.15
one-child and three-child policy 18.12-4
opium export from India to 1.7
planning in 19.2
rise of 19.1-2
State-owned enterprises of 20.13
trade dispute with US xix, 15.22, 20.8, 20.14
climate change v, xix, 19.14
carbon sink and forest cover 20.40-1
challenge India faces and commitments on 11.8-10, 11.18-9, 20.38-40
Conference of Parties (COP21), Paris on 11.10, 20.36-8
divergence between developed and developing nations on 20.37-8
factors behind 20.35
India and 19.15
Inter-Governmental panel on Climate Change (IPCC) 20.35
International Solar Alliance (ISA) 20.39-40
target and India 20.38-9
threats due to 20.35-6
United Nations on 20.35-7
UN Framework Convention (UNFCC) on 19.14, 20.35
Cochin kingdom 1.3
colonial era and underdevelopment xiv-xv, 17.2
colonial rule in India
agrarian scene during 1.5-6, 1.7-8
assessment of 1.10-2
consolidation of 1.5
deindustrialisation during 1.8-11
exploitation under 1.4-5, 1.11-2, 19.2
famines and epidemics 1.16-7
industrial policy during 1.8-10
irrigation in 1.6-7
land tenure during 1.5-6
manufacturing capabilities before xv, 1.3-4, 19.2
per capita income in 17.19
positives and negatives of 1.11-2
price of 1.13-5, 17.2, 19.2
socio- economic impact of xv, 1.17-8
trade policy during 1.10
what if India was not colonized 1.12-3
(*see also* East India Company, poverty)
Committee on Distribution of Income and Levels of Living 14.2
comparative advantage, theory of,
Adam Smith on 15.2
and international trade 15.2-3
David Ricardo on 15.2-3
Comprehensive Agreement for Trans-Pacific Partnership 20.10, 20.22
communications
postal and courier services 10.18-20
revolution in 10.18
computer
evolution and impact of 12.1-2
growth in usage of 12.2-3
impact of 12.1-2, 16.30
(*see also* information technology)
Confronting Rising Inequality in Asia, Asian Development Bank *17.17*
Constitution of India 2.2, 14.20-1, 17.33
and gender equality and justice 17.2, 17.35
and Union budget 14.4

Directive Principles of State Policy 2.2, 17.2
  on bonded labour 16.29
consumer price index (*see under* price indexes)
Cornell University 17.6
corporate social responsibility xvii, 16.3, 26.30-3
  and education sector 26.3
  areas covered by CSR 26.31
  importance of 26.33
  performance under 26.32
Covid-19 v, 15.10-1, 16.13, 17.28, 20.14, 23.9, 26.19
  and child labour 16.27
  and employment 16.9
  and poverty 17.15
  role of women SHGs during 17.26
  impact on economy 19.27-8

D

Das Capital 16.2
Davos 20.6
death rate (*see under* vital statistics)
debt (*see under* public debt)
Debt Recovery Tribunals (*see under* banks)
Deccan Development Society 7.27
Delhi xiv, 22.2
demographic dividend
  age structure and 16.13, 16.32, 18.9-11
  divergence in 18.11
  India's 18.10-1
  need for nuanced policies 18.11-2
  (*see also* population)
demography
  India's 18.6-8
  transition phase in 18.5-6
  (*see also* population)
demonetisation 25.18-20
  assessment of 25.23-4
  challenges of the scheme 25.20-1
  low tax compliance 25.22-3
  PM Garib Kalyan Yojana 25.21
  (*see also* digital economy)
devaluation of rupee 6.5, 6.14, 15.5, 15.7
developing nations and developed nations 19.2-3
  contrast 19.8-10
development 19.1-2
  and structural changes in economy 19.9-11
  concept and indicators of 17.3-7
  economists on 19.2-3
  factors influencing19.1
  India's growth pattern 19.21-2
  international comparison in 19.3
  Lewis' turning point 19.6
  MDGs and SDGs 19.13-5
  North-South divide in 19.2
  regional balance in 4.6-11, 8.4-5, 19.11-2
  social and political consciousness and 17.12
  socialist model of 2.2-3
  theories of 19.4-8
  to be inclusive 19.29
  versus growth 19.2-3 (*see also* growth)
development, theories of
  Harrod-Domar model 19.5, 19.7-8
  Hirschman's Unbalanced growth theory 19.5, 19.8
  Lewis growth model 19.4, 19.6-7
  Lewisian turning point 19.6
  Nurkse's Balanced growth theory 19.6-7
  Rostow's 'Stages of Economic Growth' 19.4-6
  Rosenstein-Rodan's Big Push Theory 19.7
  Vakil-Brahmananda Model 2.5, 19.7
Development with unlimited supplies of labour 19.4, 19.6
digital, cashless economy 25.24-6
Digital India programme 12.11-2, 16.14, 17.49, 22.5, 23.7, 24.26-7
direct benefit transfer (DBT)14.25
  benefits of 7.22, 7.36, 20.30, 25.2, 25.5, 25.25

disinvestment 8.11-2, 8.18-9
division of labour xi
Adam Smith on xiii, 16.2
Doing Business Report
and The World Bank 22.2, 22.10
domestic workers, ILO on 16.10-1
drugs and crime 20.4-5
Dutch 1.4
E
Ease of Doing Business 8.16, 22.1
changing global scenario and 22.2
DIPP's Action Plan on 22.5-7
India's rank on 22.3
new reforms and 22.2-4
NITI Aayog study on 22.6-7
simplification of procedures by Centre, States for 22.4-7
WEF survey on 22.3
World Bank rankings on 22.2
Ease of Living Index 26.27
East Asia financial crisis xix, 15.8, 20.3
East Asia summit and India 20.20
East Asian miracle 2.9-11, 6.6, 15.2, 17.51
East China sea dispute 20.15, 20.30
East Europe, India's trade with 15.20
East India Company 1.4, 1.5, 10.19
e-Biz project 22.5
economic crisis of 1991 6.4-5
economic crisis of 2007-08 15.9-10
economic growth, development (*see under* development)
Economic Inequality, On, 17.13
Economic Position of Great Britain, The 19.24
Economic Possibilities for Our Grandchildren xiv
economic reforms of 1991
and impact on poverty 6.10-1
and inequality 6.12
and new industrial policy 6.7-9, 6.15-6
and new trade policy 6.6-7, 6.14-5, 15.7-9, 15.18
crisis of 1985-91and 6.3-5, 6.13
impact of 6.9-10, 10.8, 20.11
India before and after 2.12-5, 6.3-5
new reform measures 6.6-9
of 1991 and turnaround 6.5, 15.7-8
salient features of 6.13-6
Economic science, theory xii-xiv
Economic Table (*see under Tableau Economique*)
Economics of Welfare, The xvi
education
and development 26.1-2
challenges in 26.2-3, 26.4-6
changing attitudes towards 26.2-3
expansion of 26.2
importance of girls' 26.2-3
mid-day meals in schools and 17.33
National Education Policy 26.7-9
neglect of school 2.7-8, 17-11-2, 18.2, 26.2
Plan outlays on 26.10
quality and standard of 26.6-7
Right to Education Act (RTE) 26.2
role of female teachers in 26.3-4
Sarva Shiksha Abhiyan (SSA) 26.2
toilet facility in schools 26.4-6
Ecuador15.21
Egypt xi, 20.21
Nile valley in xi
El Niño, La Niña, impact of 20.42
electoral funding 25.26-7
reform of 25.27-9
electric vehicles 24.5-6
National Electric Mobility Mission 24.7-8
promoting EVs in India 24.8-10
Elements of Political Economy, 15.2
employment
automation and 16.34-7, 21.12-4
challenge of generating 16.13-4
Commission on unorganized sector 16.12-3

female participation rate in 16.7-9, 17.40-1
impact of computers on 16.30, 16.34-7
importance of creation of 16.1-2
in infrastructure 10.30-2
in organized and unorganized sectors 16.11-3
labour force and 16.3-4, 16.5-7
measuring 16.4-5
programmes 17.25-30
technology versus 16.34-7
trends in unemployment and 16.7-8
(*see also* sector-wise share in employment, labour, skill development)
energy
coal production, sector reforms 11.9
commercial and non-commercial 11.2-5
DD Upadhyaya Gram Jyoti Yojana for 11.16
efficiency and use of LEDs (*see* UJALA LED lighting scheme below)
generation and distribution of 11.10-1
importance of LPG supply 11.3
installed capacity, generation of 11.5-7
oil and natural gas as source of 11.9
power sector reforms 11.11-2, 11.16-7, 11.19-21, 24.17
renewables- solar, wind energy 11.7, 11.9-10, 20.38-40, 24.20-4
rural electrification 11.13-6
scenario in India 11.1-2
Saubhagya Yojana 24.19-20
SEBs' debt problems 11.11
sources of energy and power 11.8-9
transmission, expansion of 11.10-1
trends in supply and consumption of commercial 11.3-5
UJALA LED lighting scheme 11.17-8, 24.17-9 (*see also* solar energy)
England 1.5
industrial revolution and 1.4-5
protection policy of 1.10
Enquiry Concerning the Principles of Political Justice and its Influence on General Virtue and Happiness, An 18.3
environmental issues xix, 18.5, 20.41
multilateral agreements on 19.14
vehicular pollution control 24.5
Essays in Persuasion xiv
Essay on External Corn Trade, An, 15.2
Essay on Population, An, 18.2-3
Euphrates river xi
Europe 1.3-4, 10.32-4, 15.22, 19.8, 20.30
migration crisis in 18.20-1, 20.33-5
European Common Market, India's trade with 15.20
European Economic Community 20.8, 20.20
European Union (EU) xix, 18.20-2, 20.8-11, 20.19-20, 20.26, 20.29
and Brexit 20.8-11
as Economic Union, trading bloc 20.28
on money laundering 25.29-30
exchange rate policy 15.13
export processing, economic zones 8.4
exports, promotion of 6.6, 6.8, 15.18-9 15.20-3 (*see also* foreign trade)
externalities from pollution 20.41-2
F
factory system
impact on India 1.4-5
family planning (welfare) 18.8-9 26.10-1
(*see also* population, vital statistics)
farmers
debt relief for 7.24-6
distress to 7.3-4, 17.3, 20.28-30
National Commission on 7.25
PM Fasal Bima Yojana 7.25-6
(*see also* agriculture, farm laws, farming)
farm laws and reforms xvii, 7.36-9
Parliament Committee on 7.41
Planning Commission on 7.42

opposition to, repeal of 7.39-41, 7.43
farming
contract farming 7.29-31
cooperative and group farming 7.26-9
integrated farming 7.43-5
(*see also* agriculture, farmers, farm laws)
FDI policy
liberalisation of 6.7-8, 21.4
reform of 15.15-6, 22.7-8
Finance Commission 14.21-3
and Centre-State relations 14.20
awards of 14.22-3
composition and role of 14.21-2
15th Finance Commission 14.23-6
Finance, Ministry of vi, vii, ix
financial crisis 2007-8 xix, 15.9, 20.3-4, 20.6-7, 20.11-2
and impact on world trade 15.10
impact on India 15.10
(*see also* East Asia financial crisis)
financial inclusion (*see under* Jan Dhan Yojana)
fintech industry in India 25.26
fiscal deficit 6.4, 14.15, 14.19
and GDP 14.10-1, 14.15, 14.18-9
crisis of 1990-91 14.11
fiscal management
and FRBM Act 14.17-9
fiscal policy
and inequality 14.3
role of 14.4
Five Year Plans 1.9, 1.11, 15.4, 16.2, 19.12
and distributive justice 14.2
assessment of early Plans 2.6-8
dissenting voices on 2.5, 2.9
early plans 2.3-6
on poverty and inequality 17.9-11
Vakil-Brahmananda plan 2.5, 19.7
Food and Agriculture Organization (FAO) vii, ix, 7.27, 20.17
food processing industry (*see under* agriculture)
food security and nutrition 7.10-2
challenges to 18.4-5
National Food Security Mission 7.10
(*see also* WTO and India's food security)
Foreign Exchange Management Act (FEMA) 15.12-4, 15.16, 25.18
foreign exchange reserves
management of 6.14-5, 15.11-4
remittances from Gulf 15.5
foreign trade
after 1991 reforms 6.6-9, 15.7-9
composition of India's 15.17-9
direction of India's 15.20-1
importance of 15.1-2
leading sectors in 15.21-2
of India in 1950s, 1960s 15.4-5
in 1970s, 1980s 15.5-6
policy 2015-20 15.22-3
since 1991 reforms 15.7-8
trade-GDP ratio 15.6-7, 15.9
Foster-Greer-Thorbecke measure of Poverty 17.6
France 14.9, 19.10, 20.8, 20.9, 20.19-20, 22.9
free trade 20.10
agreement(s) 20.21-2, 20.27-8
agreements of India 8.14, 15.28-30, 20.23-6
and crime 20.4-5
policy 2015-20 15.22-3
French 1.4, 1.11
French revolution 17.16
G
G-8, G-20, G-77 groups 10.34, 19.13, 20.6, 20.19, 25.29
G33 nations and WTO 20.29
Gambhira Coop. Farming Society 7.28
Gangetic plains 1.6
Gaza 20.34
gender bias and inequality 17.34-41
gender budgeting 17.41-3

General Agreement on Tariffs and Trade (GATT) 15.24
General Theory of Employment, Interest and Money, The xiii
geopolitics and economic development xix, 20.30-1
Germany 14.9, 17.51, 19.13, 20.8, 20.19-20, 21.11, 22.9
Gini coefficient xviii
  and inequality 6.12, 17.18-9
Global Competitiveness Report, 2015-16, 21.12, 22.3
Global Hunger Index 7.12
Global Multidimensional Poverty Index (MPI) 17.6-8
Global Terrorism Index 20.5
globalisation 20.2-3, 22.2
  and inclusivity 20.5-6
  and Indian economy 20.11
  and interdependence xix, 20.1-4
  challenges to 20.3-4
  in retreat? 20.6-8
  resistance and protests against 20.6
Godavari delta 1.7
Gold monetisation scheme 25.30-1
goods and Services tax (GST) (*see under* taxes)
Grand Anicut 1.6
Grand Trunk Road 10.19
Great Depression xiii, 1.9, 15.9
  and New Deal xiii, 14.4
Great Recession 20.6 (*see also* financial crisis 2007-08)
Greece 20.34
Green revolution 2.5, 3.1, 7.38, 15.5
  early phase of 3.6-7
  HYV seeds 3.6
  later phase of 3.7
  phase preceding 3.4-6
gross domestic product (GDP) xviii, 6.1, 6.9-10, 14.11, 14.18, 17.5, 19.10-1, 20.12
gross national happiness
  of Bhutan 17.8
gross national income (GNI)
  international comparison of 19.3
growth and inequality
  Asian experience 17.18-9
  versus inequality 17.16-7
  versus poverty 2.7
  (*see also* development, inequality, poverty)
Gulf Cooperation Council (GCC) 15.21, 20.28
Gulf war 1990 14.11

H

Haiti 20.34
Han Chinese xi
Handbook of National Committee 2.2
Harappan civilization xi
Harrod-Domar model growth 19.7-8
Hebrew thought xv
health
  15th Finance Commission on 26.19-20
  and Five Year Plans 18.6-9, 26.10
  Ayushman Bharat 19.19, 26.17-8
  challenges for the sector 26.18-9
  decline in birth and death rates 18.6-9, 26.10-1
  doctor-patient ratio 26.15-6
  expenditure on 19.28, 26.18-19
  facilities 26.12-6
  improvements in 26.10, 26.12
  IMR and MMR - of India (*see under* vital statistics)
  inter-state variations in 26.12, 26.16
  life expectancy (*see under* vital statistics)
  National (Rural) Health Mission (NHM, NRHM) 26.14, 26.16
  need to upgrade facilities 26.16-7
  rural health set-up 26.12-4
Heckscher-Ohlin model
  international trade 15.3
Hindu rate of growth 6.3, 15.4

Hirschman's unbalanced growth
theory 19.8
Hong Kong 2.10, 9.17, 15.21, 17.51, 26.7
housing
for weaker sections - IAY, PMAY
17.30, 17.32, 26.20-1
PMAY and MNREGS synergy 26.21
human development index xviii, 17.6
Human Development Reports (HDRs)
of UNDP vi, vii, ix, xviii, 12.2, 17.6, 19.3
India's rank in 17.6
HDR surveys in India 17.8
Hungary 20.34
I
ICRISAT on millets 7.11
India 1.3-4, 15.10, 17.52, 20.18,
access to Afghanistan 10.33
access to Central Asia 10.32
aid from World Bank and IMF 20.18-9
adopts socialist pattern of
development 2.2-4
and China, the difference 6.12
and international institutions 20.18-9
and economic crisis of 1991 6.4-5, 15.7
and MDGs and SDGs 19.13-5
and WTO 15.24-6, 20.28-9
at independence, 1.10, 2.1
backwardness of xiv-xv, 1.11-2, 17.2, 19.2
birth rates in (*see under* vital statistics)
death rates in (*see under* vital statistics)
defence manufacturing in 21.9-10
dispersal of industries in 4.6-10
employment in 3.1, 4.11, 6.10, 8.14,
16.11-2
famines and epidemics in 1.16-7
financial institutions in 5.9
financial system of 13.2
foreign trade of (*see under* foreign trade)
forex reserves of 15.11-4
growth pattern of 19.21-2
impact of Covid-19 on 15.10-1, 19.27-8
impact of globalisation on 20.11
import substitution policy of 15.2, 15.4
income inequality in 6.12-3, 17.18-9
industrial policies of 4.1-3, 6.7-9,
8.2-3, 22.1
industrial, trade policy in colonial 1.8-10
industrial development in 4.1-5, 8.2-3
industrial licensing, control 4.5, 22.1
industrialisation in colonial 1.8-10
inward-looking approach of xix, 2.8, 6.11
large scale industries in 4.6-11
liberalisation process in 8.2-3
life expectancy in (*see under* vital
statistics)
literacy rates in (*see under* literacy)
location, dispersal of industries 4.6-11,
8.4-5, 19.11-2
manufacturing capabilities in pre-
colonial era in xv, 1.3, 1.5, 19.2
measures to alleviate poverty in
17.24-33
neglect of school education in
2.7-8, 26.2
on liberalisation of 4.5
Operation Flood project 7.27
planning in 2.2, 19.15-7
population, age structure of 16.13,
18.11
population below poverty line in
6.10-1, 17.20-4
population control in 18.8-9
public sector in 4.3-4, 8.11-2
reform of capital market of 13.4
role of SHGs in 17.25-7
sectoral share in economy (GDP)
(*see under* sectoral share)
sectoral share in employment
(*see under* sectoral share)
share in world trade 15.16-7
small and village industries in 4.11-3
9.2-3
sterling balances of 1.10, 2.5
(*see also* colonial rule, demography,

five year plans, foreign trade, free trade, planning, population, poverty, vital statistics)
India-EU trade 20.26
India-UAE trade 20.26
India's trade (*see under* foreign trade)
Indian Agricultural District Programme 3.5
Indian Agriculture Research Institute 1.6
Indian Council of Agricultural Research 3.8
Indian Fiscal Commission 1.10
Indian Income Inequality 1922-2014 6.12
Indian Institute of Science (Centre for Contemporary Studies) viii, x
Indian Labour Conference 17.20
Indian National Congress
Avadi (Madras) session of 2.4
Indian Ocean 10.32, 20.42
Indian Ocean Dipole 20.42
Indian states
comparative profile of 19.4
on population control 18.8-9
Indian Statistical Institute 12.3
Indira Awas Yojana (IAY) (*see under* housing)
Indo-China wars 2.9
Indo-Pakistan conflict 2.6
Indo-US trade, ties 20.25, 20.31
Indonesia xix, 2.9, 15.8, 17.51, 18.15, 20.3, 20.18, 20.23, 22.3, 26.11, 26.15
Ease of doing business in 22.9-10
Indus Valley xi
industrial cooperatives, estates (*see under* small and medium scale industries)
industrial development
controls and licensing hampers 2.8-9, 4.5
delicensing and 6.6-9
Expert Committees on 4.5
impact of MRTP Act on 6.8
industrial policies (*see under* India)
Industrial Revolution xiii, xv, 17.2, 20.35
and Britain 1.4-5, 19.2
impact of 1.4-5, 1.11-2, 19.2
in later periods 21.12
industrial sector in India
an overview 8.1-3, 8.6-9
constraints faced by 8.12-4
measures to promote 8.14-7
(*see also* Make in India, Production Linked Incentive (PLI) scheme)
inequality xix, 17.44-5, 19.3
and fiscal policy 14.3
and growth–Asian experience 17.18-9
and growth: Sen-Bhagwati on 17.16-7
economists on 17.15-6
five year plans on 17.8-11
in India and China 17.18-9
income distribution and xvii-xviii 14.2-3
liberalisation and 6.12
manifestation of 17.3
Piketty-Chancel study on 6.12
versus growth 14.2, 17.16-7, 19.2-3
(*see also* poverty, growth)
infant mortality rate (IMR) (*see under* vital statistics)
inflation and unemployment (Phillip's curve)16.4
Information technology (IT) sector
BharatNet project 10.24-5, 12.11-2, 24.26
challenges faced in 12.13-4, 21.11-2
digital divide in 10.25, 12.2
Digital India programme and e-governance 12.11-2, 24.25-7
employment in 12.10
exports from India 12.9-10
genesis of computers and 12.3
genesis of IT sector in India 12.3
impact of global slowdown on 12.14
India's strategic advantage in 12.12-3
Internet penetration in India,

other countries 10.24, 12.9, 24.25
NIC and spread of 12.3-4
National Optical Fibre Network (NOFN) project 10.24-5, 12.11-2
PC and Internet penetration 10.24, 12.2-3, 12.9
role of Indians in 12.12-4
software parks 12.7-8
Task force on 12.5-6
(*see also* computer)
infrastructure
and employment 10.30-2, 24.31-3
importance of 10.2, 24.1-2
in Union budget 24.2
National Investment Infrastructure Fund 24.27-8
National Monetisation Pipeline 24.28-30
plan allocations for 10.3
Sagarmala project 24.16
Setu Bharatam project 24.10-1
(*see also* aviation, communications, inland waterways, logistics, media, ports, railways, roadways, shipping, telecom sector)
inland water transport and national waterways 10.14-5
Inquiry into the Nature and Causes of the Wealth of Nations, An iii, xii-xiii, 15.2, 16.2, 17.12
Insolvency and bankruptcy code (*see* under Bankruptcy law)
Institute for Economics and Peace (IEP) 20.5
Integrated Child Development Services (ICDS) 17.32-3
integrated farming and secondary agriculture 7.43-5
Integrated Rural Development Programme (IRDP) 17.25
International Bank for Reconstruction and Development (IBRD) xiii, 20.16
aid to India 20.18
International Development Association 20.16
International economic groupings 20.19-22
International Finance Corporation 20.17
International Labour Organization (ILO) 20.17
on automation and jobs 16.36
on bonded, forced labour 16.29-30
on child labour 16.25-7
on domestic workers 16.10-1
International Monetary Fund (IMF) xiii, 6.5, 15.14, 17.35, 20.6, 20.14, 20.16, 22.2
role of 20.17
Special drawing Rights (SDRs) and Quota system in 20.17
SDRs for India 20.19
International Multi-modal Transport (INSTC) 10.32-4
International Solar Alliance 20.39-40 24.24
international tax reform 25.29-30
International Telecommunications Union (ITU) 12.2-3, 12.9
international trade, theory of 15.2-3, 20.1-2 (*see also* comparative advantage, foreign trade, world trade, WTO)
Iran 10.32-3, 15.20, 20.4
Iraq 20.34
irrigation 7.5
in colonial era 1.6-7
Israel 17.52
IT sector (*see under* information technology)
Italy 20.15, 20.19
J
Jal Jeevan Mission 26.22-4
JAM (Jhan Dhan Yojana, Aadhaar, Mobile) 7.23, 24.25, 25.5, 25.25
Jan DhanYojana, PM 7.23, 13.7

and financial inclusion 25.2-4
Japan 8.16, 9.17, 15.9, 17.51-2, 20.5, 20.18-9, 20.29, 21.11, 22.9, 26.7
rise of 2.9
India's trade with 15.20-1
JNNURM (J Nehru National Urban Renewal Mission) 17.31, 19.15

K

Kaveri (Cauvery) river 1.6, 1.7
Keynesian economics xiii, 14.4
Khmers Rouges 2.9
Korea, Republic of
maritime cooperation with 24.15
Korean war 2.9
Krishna delta 1.7
Krishnaraja Sagar dam 1.7
Kudumbasree scheme (Kerala) 7.28
Kuznet's hypothesis 6.12, 17.51-2

L

La Niña, impact of 20.42
labour
bonded labour 16.28-30
child labour in India 16.24-7
computers and aftermath on 16.30
data on 16.3
deficiencies in new laws 16.22-3
domestic workers and ILO 16.10-1
economists on 16.2-3
fall in FLPR 16.6-9, 17.40-1
labour force, jobs mismatch 16.31-2
labour force and workforce 16.5-7
migrant labour issues 16.18-24
scene in India 16.7-9
unorganised workers 16.11-3
(*see also* employment, labour reforms)
labour reforms xvi-xvii, 16.15-8, 21.5-6
Laffer curve (on taxes) 14.6
laissez-faire policy xii
land reforms 3.2-3
land tenure 1.5
mahalwari system 1.6
rvotwari system 1.6
zamindari system 1.5-6
(*see also* Permanent Settlement Act)
Laos 20.20
Latin America xv, 19.2
India's trade with 15.22
Lehman Brothers, collapse of xix, 15.9-10, 20.3-4
Lewis' growth model 19.6-7, 19.8
Lewis' turning point 19.6
liberalisation
and inequality 6.12
of telecom sector 10.22-4
of trade 6.6-8
(*see also* economic reforms)
Libya 20.34
life expectancy (*see under* vital statistics)
Lisbon Treaty, 20.8
literacy rates
of India 1.13-4, 2.1, 18.7
of some Indian states 18.9
logistics industry, services
in India 10.20-1, 25.42-3
Planning Commission on 10.21
Lorenz curve xvii
LPG supply (*see under* energy)
Luxembourg 20.8, 20.20

M

Maastricht Treaty 20.8
Macau 26.7
Madras Presidency 1.6
Maharashtra 15.28
Make in India programme 10.13, 23.7-8
challenges to 21.11-2, 21.14-5
India's strengths for 21.4
outcomes of 21.9-10
role of MSME sector in 21.9-10
steps taken to promote 21.4-6
(*see also* Production Linked Incentive scheme, One District One Product (ODOP) scheme)

Malabar coast 1.3
Malaysia 2.10, 8.13, 15.21, 17.51, 18.15-7, 19.3, 20.3, 20.20-1, 20.42, 21.12, 22.9-10
Maldives 20.21
Manchester 1.12
Manifesto of the Communist Party 16.2
Maratha(s) empire 1.3-4
Marathawada 7.8, 20.42
Marshall Plan 20.15
Masulipatam 1.4
maternal mortality ratio (MMR) (*see under* vital statistics)
Mauritius 25.19
media services
  ISRO and satellites 10.30
  radio, TV and others 10.30
Mediterranean sea 10.33, 20.34
Mekong river 20.42
Mercantilists x
Merrill Lynch 15.11
Mesopotamia ix
Mexico 3.7, 15.14, 19.3, 18.17, 20.10, 20.19, 20.21, 26.6
midday meal scheme 17.33
Middle East 15.17, 20.21
migrant labour (worker) 16.17
  housing for 16.17
  problems faced by 16.13, 16.21
  remedial measures 16.21-2
migration
  factors behind 16.20, 18.20-3
  international 16.23-4
  level and pattern of internal 16.19-20
  problem in Europe 20.33-5
Migration and Remittances Factbook, 2016: World Bank 15.11
Millennium Development Goals (MDGs) vi, 17.14, 19.13-4, 19.18
  India and 19.13-15
Minimum Wages Act 17.20
mixed economy 2.5
Monetary Policy Committee 13.16-7
MNREGS (*see under* National Rural Employment Guarantee scheme)
mortality (death) rate (*see under* vital statistics)
MSME sector (*see under* small and medium industries)
Mudra Yojana 25.7
Mughal empire (period) 1.3, 1.5
Mughals 1.3, 1.12
Multidimensional Poverty (*see under* poverty)
multimodal transport (INSTC) 10.32-4
multinational corporations 15.26-8
Mumbai 10.32, 22.2, 23.3, 24.5, 26.1
Municipal Performance Index 26.27-8
Myanmar 20.5, 20.13, 22.5
Mysore kings 1.4

N

National Accounts Statistics 17.16, 17.18 (see also national income)
National Bank for Agriculture and Rural Development (NABARD) 7.7, 7.28, 26.12
  and credit for rural sector 5.7, 7.22
  and Farmer Producer Organisation (FPOs) 7.19-21, 7.39
National Capital region (NCR) 23.3
National Commission on Farmers 7.25-6, 7.41
National Council of Applied Economic Research (NCAER) 17.8
National Education Policy 26.7-9
National Food Security Act 7.10 (*see also* food security and nutrition)
national income
  contribution of VKRV Rao on 19.22-7
  distribution of 14.2 (*see also* gross domestic product and national accounts statistics)
National Income, The 1924–31 19.24
National Income and Outlay 19.24

National Income of British India, The
1931-32 19.24
National Rural Employment Guarantee scheme (NREGS) 16.14, 17.26, 19.13, 26.20-1
an assessment of 17.27-30
National Rural Livelihood Mission (NRLM) 7.28, 17.25-6
National Sample Survey (NSSO) 6.10, 16.5, 17.21-2, 17.31, 17.41
on agricultural households 7.40
Nepal 20.21, 22.9
Netherlands 20.8, 20.10, 20.20
New Deal xiii, 14.4
New Development Bank 20.18-9
New Zealand 20.21
Nigeria 15.20, 18.4, 18.19, 20.40
Nile valley xi
NITI Aayog
critical assessment of 19.19-20
divergent views on 19.18-9
rationale for setting up 19.17
structure and functions of 19.17-8
(*see also* Planning Commission)
Non-Banking Finance Companies (NBFCs) 13.11-2
Shah Committee on 13.12
Nordic countries 17.52
North Korea 20.30
North-South divide xv, 19.2, 20.32
Norway 19.14, 20.11, 20.34
NTPC and thermal power 20.38-9
Nurkse's theory of balanced growth 19.4, 19.6-7

O

One Belt, One Road (OBOR) 20.14-5
and India 20.15
(*see also under* China)
One District, One Product (ODOP) scheme 21.7-8
Operation Flood project 7.27
opportunity cost 15.3, 26.2
Organization for Economic Cooperation and Development (OECD) 14.9, 17.19,17.52, 26.6
India's trade with 15.21
inequality in 17.52
to check black money, tax evasion 25.29-30
Organization for Petroleum Exporting Countries (OPEC) 20.28
India's trade with 15.20
Orissa 1.6

P

Pakistan xviii, 17.6, 20.4, 21.12, 22.9
1965 war with 15.4
influx of refugees from 18.6
Panchayati Raj and Rural Rejuvenation 17.33-4
Gram Sabhas: features of 17.34
Pareto optimal, efficiency concept of xvi, 17.13
Amartya Sen on xvi, 17.13-4
Payments Banks 13.24, 17.49, 25.5-6
per capita income xviii, 14.2-3, 17.5, 19.2-4
Permanent Settlement Act 1.6
Peru 20.21
Philippines 15.11-2, 20.3, 20.20, 20.42, 21.12
and South China sea dispute 20.15
Phillip's curve (*see under* inflation)
Physiocrats xii, 16.2
planning
in China 19.2
in India (*see under* Five Year Plans)
PL 480 programme 3.5
Planning Commission vii, ix, xiv, 1.7, 1.9, 4.8, 6.10, 15.4, 17.20, 19.19
and Five Year Plans 17.9-11
genesis of 2.3, 19.15-6
on reforms in agriculture 7.42
on public sector units 4.4
on role of Reserve Bank of India 5.4
role and relevance of 19.16
restructuring of 19.17

(*see also* NITI Aayog)
Planning for an Expanding Economy 2.5
PM's Gram Sadak Yojana (PMGSY)
(*see under* roadways)
PM Awas Yojana (*see under* housing)
PMJDY (*see under* Jan Dhan Yojana)
PM Krishi Sinchai Yojana 7.5
Pondicherry (Puducherry) 1.4
Poona xiv
population
age structure of Indian 16.31, 18.9-10
and dependency ratio 18.10
and food supply and security 18.4-5
challenges due to 18.12
changes in US and Europe 18.20-3
China's one-child and three-child policy 18.12-4
control in Indian states of 18.8-9
decline in global v, 18.18-20
economists on 18.2-4
global scenario of 18.2, 18.4
growth in India's 18.6-8
growth rate in India and China 18.13-4
impact on migration 18.20, 18.22-3
Malthus on 18.2-4
compared with other countries 18.15-7
rural and urban 1.15-6
(*see also* demographic dividend, demography, migration, vital statistics)
Population. An Enquiry Concerning the Power of Increase in the Numbers of Mankind, Of, 18.3
ports 10.14
and shipping 10.13-4, 24.14-5
Maritime India summit 24.15-6
Sagarmala project 24.16
Portuguese 1.3-4, 1.11
postal, courier system (*see under* communications)
poverty xix, 17.2, 19.3
absolute, relative and extreme 17.3-4
Adam Smith on 17.12
Alkire-Foster method on 17.8
and inequality 6.12, 14.2-3, 17.3, 17.8-9
Angus Deaton on 17.21-2
CSR and 17.50
colonialism and xiv-xv, 1.13-8, 19.2
early studies on 17.20-1
estimation of 17.19-24
Expert Groups on 17.22-4
five year plans and 17.9-11
global scene of 17.14-5
impact of reforms on 6.10-2
manifestation of 17.3
measures to alleviate 17.24-33
Multidimensional Index of 17.6-8, 17.15
NSS estimates of 6.10-1,17.21-2
trap 17.4, 19.2
(*see also* colonial era, rule, growth, inequality, Universal Basic Income)
poverty line
identification of 17.19-20
international 17.4
people below 6.10-1, 17.20-4
Sen's poverty index 17.5
World Bank norms on 17.14-5
(*see also under* poverty)
Poverty and Un-British Rule in India 1.12
power (*see under* energy)
Pradhan Mantri Awas Yojana (PMAY)
(*see under* housing)
Prague 20.6
price indexes, WPI and CPI 13.13-5
Principles of Political Economy and Taxation, The 15.2, 17.15
privatisation 8.18-9 (*see also* disinvestment)
Production Linked Incentive scheme 21.12-4 (*see also* Make in India)
protectionism xii, 1.10
public debt 6.4-5, 14.14-5
public distribution system (PDS) 7.32-4, 14.16-7, 15.24-6, 17.24

and WTO 7.34-5, 20.28-30
Committee on reforming 7.34
need to reform 7.35-6
One Nation, One Card 7.34, 16.22
public private partnership (PPP) 10.6, 22.5
public sector
and disinvestment 8.11-2, 8.18-9
role of 2.8-9, 4.3-4
strengthening of 6.8-9
Punjab 1.7
depletion of water sources in 7.12
purchasing power parity (PPP) 2.12, 17.4, 17.14

Q

Quad initiative, The 20.15
and China 20.30-1
quality of life xviii, 6.11, 17.3, 17.6, 18.1-2, 19.29
factors behind 19.1-2, 26.2

R

radio 10.30
railways
electrification of 24.12-3
growth and expansion of 10.9-10
growth and modernisation 24.11-2
improvements and new initiatives in 10.10-2
in colonial era 1.11
reforms in 10.12-3
Red Sea 1.3
reforms, (*see under* economic reforms)
regional balance in development (*see under* development)
Regional Comprehensive Economic Partnership (RCEP) 19.22, 20.22
Regional rural banks 5.7, 13.10-1
recapitalisation of 13.11
Vyas Committee on reforming 13.11
renewable energy (*see under* energy)
Republic (Plato's) xii
Reserve Bank of India (RBI) vi, vii, ix, 5.2 25.27
All India Rural Credit Survey by 5.6
and agricultural credit 5.6
and bank rate 13.16-7
and inflation control 13.16
and monetary policy 13.16-8
and NPAs of banks 13.7-8
and repo and reverse repo rates 13.16
and resolution of bank debts 13.8
functions of 5.4
Planning Commission on RBI's role 5.3-4
setting up and role of 5.2-3
transfer of reserves to government 13.22-3 (*see also* CRR and SLR *under* banking reforms)
Right to Education Act (*see under* education)
roadways
Bharatmala project 24.4
challenges facing road sector 10.4-6, 10.8-9
growth of 10.3-6
highway projects 10.6-7, 24.2
funding and execution of 24.3-4
PM Gram Sadak Yojana (PMGSY) 10.6, 10.7, 17.30-1, 24.5
and motor vehicles 10.5
Setu Bharatam project 24.10-1
(*see also* electric vehicles)
Rosenstein-Rodan's 'Big Push' theory 19.7
Rostow's stages of growth 19.4-5
critical assessment of 19.5-6
rural development programmes 17.25-31
MaNREGA scheme 17.26-30
rural livelihoods mission 17.25-6
rural electrification (*see under* energy)
rural health set-up (*see under* health)
rural housing (see under housing)
rural roads: PMGSY (*see under* roadways)
Rupee, devaluation of (*see under* devaluation)

Russia 16.30, 20.18, 20.34
multi-modal transport to 10.32-4
S
sanitation
toilet facility in schools 26.4-6
Total Sanitation Campaign (TSC) 26.24-5
SARFAESI Act 13.7, 22.8
Sarva Shiksha Abhiyan (*see under* education)
Saudi Arabia 15.20
Seattle 20.6
sectoral share in employment in India 4.11, 6.10, 7.1, 10.31, 16.12, 19.11
at independence 2.3, 3.1
at start of First Plan 1.9-10
in other countries 19.10
sectoral shares in GDP, economy 1.9, 4.11, 6.9-10, 7.1, 8.9, 8.11, 19.11
at independence 2.3, 3.1
compared with other countries 8.9-11, 19.9-10
Self-help groups (SHGs) 17.25-7, 26.11
Setu Bharatam project 24.11-2
sex ratio (*see under* vital statistics)
shipping (*see under* ports)
Sikhs 1.4
Singapore 2.10, 15.17, 17.51, 20.21, 22.9-10, 25.19, 26.7
skill development 21.9
importance and challenge of 16.31
labour-jobs mismatch and need for 16.31-2
mission on 16.32-3
Slovenia 20.34
small and medium scale industries
and employment 9.7
and exports 9.8
constraints faced by 2.4, 9.13-7
credit, marketing support for 9.8-10
defined, new criteria 9.2-3
expert committees on 9.11-3
growth, progress of 4.11-3, 9.6-7
in other countries 9.17-8
industrial cooperatives, estates 9.4-5
Karve Committee on 4.12, 9.3
National Small Industries Corp. 9.3-4
Plan allocations for 4.13, 9.5
reservation for 6.7-8
role in Make in India programme 21.9-10
role of village and 4.11-3, 9.1, 9.18-9
Tiruppur – a success story of 9.10-1
Small Finance Banks 25.6-7
Smart Cities programme 26.26-9
social and political consciousness
importance of 17.12
social justice
Constitution of India and 17.2
five year plans and 17.9-11
social sector
and CSR 26.30-3
criticality of 26.1
Plan outlays for 26.10
(*see also* education, health, housing)
socialist pattern of society in India 2.3-4, 2.8, 2.12
socialist system in Soviet Union 2.2-3
solar energy 11.10, 11.9-10, 20.39-40, 24.20-4
limits to solar and wind energy 20.40
(*see also* climate change, energy, International Solar Alliance)
Solid waste management (SWM)
Mission 26.29
waste to energy 26.30
South Africa 18.15, 19.3, 20.18
South Asia 17.15
South Asia Free Trade Area (SAFTA) 20.21
South Asian Association for Regional Cooperation (SAARC) 20.21
South China sea dispute (see under ASEAN, China)

South-East Asia 2.12, 15.17, 20.31
financial crisis of xix, 20.3
(*see also* ASEAN)
South Korea xix, 2.10, 8.16, 9.18, 15.8, 15.17, 16.31, 17.51, 18.17, 19.3, 20.3, 21.11, 22.9, 26.7
Soviet Union 2.2
disintegration of 6.4
New Economic Policy in 2.2
Special economic zones (SEZ) 8.4
specialisation xi, xiii,
Sri Lanka 17.6, 18.19, 19.3, 20.18, 26.11
Stages of Economic Growth 19.4
standard of living xviii
working group on 17.20
(*see also* quality of life)
Startups
Atal Innovation Mission 23.10-1
funding for: angel investors and venture capital 23.8-9
hiring by 23.6
India mission 23.1
India, leading nation on on 23.6
India Seed Fund scheme 23.8-9
limitations and challenges to 23.9
role of 23.6
steps taken to promote 23.1-5
Union budget 2017-18 on 23.7
State Bank of India
setting up of 5.5
Statutory liquidity ratio (SLR)
and RBI 13.2-3, 13.16
Sterling balances 1.10, 2.5
Studies in Indian Economics 19.23
Subprime crisis, in USA, 2007-08
impact of 15.9-10, 20.3-4
subsidies 14.16
and WTO 20.28-30
distortion in 14.3
and leakages in PDS 14.16-7
Sub-Saharan Africa 17.15, 18.19, 20.34
Suez Canal 10.33
Surat 1.4
sustainable development
Brundtland Commission on 19.14
goals (SDGs), agenda vi, 19.14, 20.5
India and 19.13-5
Swachh Bharat mission 26.24-6
Sweden 17.51
Swedish *Level of Living* survey xviii
Switzerland 20.11
Syria 20.7, 20.34
T
Tableau Economique **xii**
Taiwan 2.9, 9.17, 15.17, 17.51, 26.7
Tamil literature xii
tax and non-tax revenue 14.7
tax-GDP ratio 14.8-9
taxing agriculture sector 14.27-9
tax reforms 25.31-2
Chelliah Committee on 14.11-3
Justice Easwar Committee on 25.32
Justice Wanchoo Committee on 14.10
L.K. Jha Committee on 14.10
tax system and budget 14.4
taxation
Direct Tax Code bill 14.19-20
double tax avoidance 25.14-5
Laffer curve principle in 14.6
principle of equity in 14.7-8
features of sound 14.5-6
retrospective: its consequences 14.26-7
(*see also* demonetisation, international tax reform)
taxes
CENVAT 14.12, 25.31
corporate tax reduction 25.32
direct and indirect 6.4, 14.6-8
goods and services tax (GST) 14.13, 25.33-44
minimum alternate tax (MAT) 14.13-4
service tax 14.13
value added tax 14.10, 14.12-3, 25.31
Telangana 7.8, 20.42

telecom sector
5G services in rural India 10.25-7
advances in and expansion of 10.21-2, 24.25
broadband policy 10.24
Centre for Development of Telematics (C-DOT) and 10.22
challenges and rise of 10.25-7
Digital India, Bharatnet project 10.24-5, 12.11-2, 17.12, 23.7, 24.26-7
financial state of 10.27-9
National Optical Fibre Network Project (*see above* Digital India)
National Telecom Policy 10.22-4
Radio access network (RAN) 10.29
spectrum
allocation and pricing 10.28-9
rationalisation of 24.26
telegraphy
introduction in India 1.11, 10.19
telephone
introduction in India 1.11, 10.19
television 10.30
textile industry, 4.7-9
industrial revolution and 1.4-5, 1.8
Thailand xix, 2.10, 9.18, 15.8, 15.17, 15.21, 17.38, 17.51, 18.17-8, 19.3, 20.3, 20.20, 20.42, 22.9-10, 26.15
Theory of Economic Growth, The 19.6
Theory of Moral Sentiments, The, xiii, 17.12
Tigris river xi
Tirukkural xii
Tiruppur 9.10-1
Total Sanitation Campaign (*see under* sanitation)
Tract on Monetary Reform, A xiii
trade (*see under* world trade, foreign trade)
Trans-Pacific Partnership (TPP) 20.10, 20.6-7, 20.21-2, 20.31
transfer of technology
and Offsets 21.10 (*see also* UNCTAD)
Treatise on Money, A xiii
Turkey 20.34

U

U.A.E. 15.21
Ujwal Discom Assurance Yojana (UDAY) 13.8, 24.17
unemployment (*see under* employment)
Union budget 24.2, 25.32
and Startups 23.7
change in presentation date 14.4
UK 14.9, 15.20, 16.31, 17.51, 20.8-11, 21.11, 22.9
(*see also* Britain)
United Nations (UN) vi, vii, ix, 18.23, 19.14, 20.5-6, 20.35-7
and MDGs, SDGs viii, x, 19.13-5
(*see also* Climate Change)
UN Conference on Trade and Development (UNCTAD) 20.17
and transfer of technology 20.32-3
United Nations Development Programme (UNDP) vi, vii, ix, xviii, 2.11, 12.2, 17.6, 19.3
(*see also Human Development Reports*)
UN International Children's Emergency Fund xviii, 18.23, 26.6
and ICDS 17.32-3
UN Office on Drugs and Crime (UNODC) 20.4-5
UN Population Division data vi, vii, 2.11, 18.4, 18.18
United States (USA) xiii, 9.18, 15.9, 15.20-2, 16.31, 17.51,18.4, 20.3, 20.7, 20.10, 20.13, 20.16, 20.40, 21.11, 22.9
and the Quad initiative 20.15
demographic changes in 18.20-2
ties with India 20.25, 20.31
trade dispute with China xix, 20.8, 20.14
vis-à-vis China's economic growth 20.13
Universal Basic Income (UBI) 17.43-50
Utilitarianism xv-xvi

USSR 15.20 (*see also* Soviet Union)
Uttar Pradesh (UP) 1.7, 7.7

V

Vakil-Brahmananda model of development 2.5, 19.7
Venezuela 15.25
venture capital (*see under* Start-Up India mission)
Vidarbha 7.8, 20.42
Vienna 20.32
Vietnam 2.9, 17.52, 20.13, 20.15, 20.20-1, 20.23, 21.12, 22.9-10, 26.7
village industries (*see under* small and medium scale industries)
vital statistics
  birth rate of India 1.14, 2.7, 18.6-8
  birth rate of Indian states 18.9
  death rate of India 1.14, 2.7, 18.6-8
  infant mortality (rate) (IMR) 17.3, 17.37, 18.8, 19.2-4, 26.10-1
  life expectancy 1.14-5, 17.38-9, 18.7, 19.2-3
  maternal mortality (rate) 17.3, 26.10-1
  India compared with other countries 18.15-7, 26.10-1
  sex (female-male) ratio 1.16, 17.36
  total fertility rate (TFR) of India,18.9
  total fertility rate (TFR) of some Indian States 18.9

W

wages, nominal and real 17.30
Washington 20.6
waste management 26.29-30
water (Jal Jeevan Mission) 26.22-4
Wealth of Nations, The (see under Inquiry into the Nature)
welfare economics xv-xvi, xviii
  economists and xvi, xviii, 17.12-4
wholesale price index (*see under* price indexes)
Why Growth Matters: How Economic Growth in India Reduced Poverty and the Lessons for Other developing Countries 17.16
wind energy 11.9, 20.40, 24.20-1, 24.23 (*see also* solar energy)
World Bank, The vi, vii, ix, xiii, xviii, 6.5, 7.27, 7.45, 15.5, 15.8, 18.23, 20.6, 22.6, 20.16, 22.6
  and MDGs, SDGs 17.14, 19.13-4
  discontinues Ease of Doing Business report 22.10
  on climate change 20.35
  on global poverty (line) 17.4, 17.6, 17.14-5
  organisation, role of 20.16-7
  ranking on 'Ease of Doing Business' 22.2
  Support for India's solar programme 24.22
World Economic Forum (WEF) 21.12, 22.3
World Integrated Trade Solution (WITS) vii, ix, 15.8, 20.12
World Meteorological Organization (WMO) 20.35
world trade, trends in 20.12
  India's share in 15.16-22
World Trade Organization (WTO) vii, ix 15.21, 20.3, 20.5, 20.12, 22.2, 24.21
  and Declaration at Bali 15.24
  and Doha Development Agenda 15.24, 20.28
  and food subsidy regime 15.24-6, 20.8, 20.28-9
  and G33 nations 20.29
  and India's food security 15.24-6, 20.29-30
  on India's PDS 7.34-5
  and Uruguay round, on world trade 15.24
World War I (First) 1.8, 1.10
World War II (Second) xiii, 1.10, 2.1, 2.5, 2.9, 12.2, 19.3, 20.15, 20.15, 25.18

Y

Yemen 20.7